Inside the Fed Boxes

FYI Boxes

THE ECONOMICS OF MONEY, BANKING, AND FINANCIAL MARKETS

BUSINESS SCHOOL EDITION

The Pearson Series in Economics

Abel/Bernanke/Croushore
*Macroeconomics**

Bade/Parkin
*Foundations of Economics**

Berck/Helfand
The Economics of the Environment

Bierman/Fernandez
Game Theory with Economic Applications

Blanchard
*Macroeconomics**

Blau/Ferber/Winkler
The Economics of Women, Men and Work

Boardman/Greenberg/Vining/Weimer
Cost-Benefit Analysis

Boyer
Principles of Transportation Economics

Branson
Macroeconomic Theory and Policy

Brock/Adams
The Structure of American Industry

Bruce
Public Finance and the American Economy

Carlton/Perloff
Modern Industrial Organization

Case/Fair/Oster
*Principles of Economics**

Caves/Frankel/Jones
World Trade and Payments: An Introduction

Chapman
Environmental Economics: Theory, Application, and Policy

Cooter/Ulen
Law & Economics

Downs
An Economic Theory of Democracy

Ehrenberg/Smith
Modern Labor Economics

Ekelund/Ressler/Tollison
*Economics**

Farnham
Economics for Managers

Folland/Goodman/Stano
The Economics of Health and Health Care

Fort
Sports Economics

Froyen
Macroeconomics

Fusfeld
The Age of the Economist

Gerber
*International Economics**

Gordon
*Macroeconomics**

Greene
Econometric Analysis

Gregory
Essentials of Economics

Gregory/Stuart
Russian and Soviet Economic Performance and Structure

Hartwick/Olewiler
The Economics of Natural Resource Use

Heilbroner/Milberg
The Making of the Economic Society

Heyne/Boettke/Prychitko
The Economic Way of Thinking

Hoffman/Averett
Women and the Economy: Family, Work, and Pay

Holt
Markets, Games and Strategic Behavior

Hubbard/O'Brien
*Economics**

*Money, Banking, and the Financial System**

Hubbard/O'Brien/Rafferty
*Macroeconomics**

Hughes/Cain
American Economic History

Husted/Melvin
International Economics

Jehle/Reny
Advanced Microeconomic Theory

Johnson-Lans
A Health Economics Primer

Keat/Young
Managerial Economics

Klein
Mathematical Methods for Economics

Krugman/Obstfeld/Melitz
*International Economics: Theory & Policy**

Laidler
The Demand for Money

Leeds/von Allmen
The Economics of Sports

Leeds/von Allmen/Schiming
*Economics**

Lipsey/Ragan/Storer
*Economics**

Lynn
Economic Development: Theory and Practice for a Divided World

Miller
*Economics Today**

Understanding Modern Economics

Miller/Benjamin
The Economics of Macro Issues

Miller/Benjamin/North
The Economics of Public Issues

Mills/Hamilton
Urban Economics

Mishkin
*The Economics of Money, Banking, and Financial Markets**

*The Economics of Money, Banking, and Financial Markets, Business School Edition**

*Macroeconomics: Policy and Practice**

Murray
Econometrics: A Modern Introduction

Nafziger
The Economics of Developing Countries

O'Sullivan/Sheffrin/Perez
*Economics: Principles, Applications and Tools**

Parkin
*Economics**

Perloff
*Microeconomics**

*Microeconomics: Theory and Applications with Calculus**

Perman/Common/McGilvray/Ma
Natural Resources and Environmental Economics

Phelps
Health Economics

Pindyck/Rubinfeld
*Microeconomics**

Riddell/Shackelford/Stamos/Schneider
Economics: A Tool for Critically Understanding Society

Ritter/Silber/Udell
*Principles of Money, Banking & Financial Markets**

Roberts
The Choice: A Fable of Free Trade and Protection

Rohlf
Introduction to Economic Reasoning

Ruffin/Gregory
Principles of Economics

Sargent
Rational Expectations and Inflation

Sawyer/Sprinkle
International Economics

Scherer
Industry Structure, Strategy, and Public Policy

Schiller
The Economics of Poverty and Discrimination

Sherman
Market Regulation

Silberberg
Principles of Microeconomics

Stock/Watson
Introduction to Econometrics

Introduction to Econometrics, Brief Edition

Studenmund
Using Econometrics: A Practical Guide

Tietenberg/Lewis
Environmental and Natural Resource Economics

Environmental Economics and Policy

Todaro/Smith
Economic Development

Waldman
Microeconomics

Waldman/Jensen
Industrial Organization: Theory and Practice

Weil
Economic Growth

Williamson
Macroeconomics

*denotes MyEconLab titles

THE ECONOMICS OF MONEY, BANKING, AND FINANCIAL MARKETS

BUSINESS SCHOOL EDITION

Third Edition

Frederic S. Mishkin
Columbia University

PEARSON

Boston Columbus Indianapolis New York San Francisco Upper Saddle River
Amsterdam Cape Town Dubai London Madrid Milan Munich Paris Montreal Toronto
Delhi Mexico City São Paulo Sydney Hong Kong Seoul Singapore Taipei Tokyo

Editorial Director: Sally Yagan
Editor in Chief: Donna Battista
Acquisitions Editor: Noel Kamm Seibert
Editorial Project Manager: Carolyn Terbush
Editorial Assistant: Emily Brodeur
VP/Director of Marketing: Patrice Jones
Director of Marketing: Maggie Moylan
Executive Marketing Manager: Lori DeShazo
Marketing Assistant: Kim Lovato
Senior Managing Editor: Nancy H. Fenton
Senior Production Project Manager: Kathryn Dinovo
Permissions Project Supervisor: Michael Joyce
Senior Manufacturing Buyer: Carol Melville
Cover Designer: Jonathan Boylan
Text Designer: Cenveo Publisher Services/Nesbitt Graphics, Inc.
Media Director: Susan Schoenberg
Senior Media Producer: Melissa Honig
Content Lead, MyEconLab: Noel Lotz
Supplements Editors: Alison Eusden and Kathryn Dinovo
Full-Service Project Management/Composition: Cenveo Publisher Services/Nesbitt Graphics, Inc.
Printer/Binder: R. R. Donnelley/Willard
Cover Printer: Lehigh-Phoenix Color/Hagerstown
Text Font: ITC Berkeley Oldstyle Std
Cover Art: Federal Reserve Seal, Nomad_Soul/Shutterstock; Wall Street Bull, © emin kuliyev/Shutterstock.com; Euro Banknotes, © vinz89/Shutterstock.com; Rubik's Cube, © Icefields/Dreamstime.com

Credits and acknowledgments borrowed from other sources and reproduced, with permission, in this textbook appear on the appropriate page within text or on page C-1.

Library of Congress Cataloging-in-Publication Data

Mishkin, Frederic S.
The economics of money, banking & financial markets / Frederic S. Mishkin. –
10th ed.(and the 3rd ed. of the business ed.)
p. cm.
Includes bibliographical references and index.
ISBN 13: 978-0-13-277024-8 (main ed : alk. paper)
ISBN 10: 0-13-277024-5 (main ed : alk. paper)
ISBN 13: 978-0-13-274137-8 (business ed : alk. paper)
ISBN 10: 0-13-274137-7 (business ed : alk. paper)
1. Finance. 2. Money. 3. Banks and banking. I. Title. II. Title: The economics of money, banking, and financial markets.
HG173.M632 2013
332–dc23

2011045340

10 9 8 7 6 5 4 3 2 1

PEARSON

www.pearsonhighered.com

ISBN 10: 0-13-274137-7
ISBN 13: 978-0-13-274137-8

To Sally

Brief Contents

Contents

CHAPTER 7
The Stock Market, the Theory of Rational Expectations, and the Efficient Market Hypothesis 141

PART 3 FINANCIAL INSTITUTIONS 161

CHAPTER 8
An Economic Analysis of Financial Structure 162

CHAPTER 11
Economic Analysis of Financial Regulation 242

CHAPTER 12
Banking Industry: Structure and Competition 269

CHAPTER 17
The Money Supply Process 395

CHAPTER 18
Tools of Monetary Policy 425

APPENDIX TO CHAPTER 23
The Phillips Curve and the Short-Run Aggregate Supply Curve 601

CHAPTER 24
Monetary Policy Theory 609

CHAPTER 25
Transmission Mechanisms of Monetary Policy 628

CONTENTS ON THE WEB

The following updated appendices are available on our Companion Website at www.pearsonhighered.com/mishkin.

Preface

HALLMARKS

Although this text has undergone a major revision, it retains the basic hallmarks that have made it the best-selling textbook on money and banking over the past nine editions:

- A unifying, analytic framework that uses a few basic economic principles to organize students' thinking about the structure of financial markets, the foreign exchange markets, financial institution management, and the role of monetary policy in the economy
- A careful, step-by-step development of models (an approach found in the best principles of economics textbooks), which makes it easier for students to learn
- The complete integration of an international perspective throughout the text
- A thoroughly up-to-date treatment of the latest developments in monetary theory
- A special feature called "Following the Financial News" to encourage reading of a financial newspaper
- An applications-oriented perspective with numerous applications and special-topic boxes that increase students' interest by showing them how to apply theory to real-world examples

WHAT'S NEW IN THE THIRD EDITION

In addition to the expected updating of all data through 2011 whenever possible, there is major new material in every part of the text.

The Business School Edition

I am pleased to continue providing two versions of *The Economics of Money, Banking, and Financial Markets*. While both versions contain the core chapters that all professors want to cover, *The Economics of Money, Banking, and Financial Markets*, Business School Edition, is designed for those professors who prefer to focus more on finance, or who simply do not cover as much monetary theory. The Business School Edition includes not only chapters on nonbank finance and financial derivatives, but also an entire chapter on the conflicts of interest in the financial industry. The Business School Edition omits the chapters on the *IS* curve and on the monetary policy and aggregate demand curves as well as the chapter on the role of expectations in monetary policy. For those professors whose courses have less of an emphasis on monetary theory, *The Economics of Money, Banking, and Financial Markets*, Business School Edition, will more closely fit your needs.

For those professors who want a comprehensive discussion of monetary theory and monetary policy, *The Economics of Money, Banking, and Financial Markets*, Tenth Edition, contains all of the chapters on monetary theory. Professors who do want this coverage are often hard-pressed to cover all the finance and institutions chapters. To that end, the Tenth Edition omits the chapters on nonbank finance, financial derivatives, and conflicts of interest. The Companion Website, which can be found at www.pearsonhighered.com/mishkin for each edition provides the omitted chapters, making them readily available for those who do wish to utilize them in their courses.

Revised Chapter 9: Financial Crises

The previous edition of this textbook contained a new chapter on financial crises, including the most recent one. It was written, however, before the global financial crisis was over. Now with the perspective of a couple of years after the crisis, I have been able to improve this chapter substantially, first, by completely reorganizing the chapter to tell a more coherent story and second, by adding new sections, such as the run on the shadow banking system. In addition, I have added new boxes on collateralized debt obligations (CDOs), Ireland and the financial crisis, and whether the Federal Reserve was to blame for the housing bubble. The material in this chapter continues to be very exciting for students. Indeed, students continue to be more engaged with this material than with anything else I have taught in my entire teaching career of over 30 years.

Compelling New Material on the Global Financial Crisis Throughout the Text

The aftermath of the global financial crisis of 2007–2009 has led to ongoing changes in the structure of the financial system and the way central banks operate. This has required the addition of many timely new sections, applications, and boxes throughout the rest of the book.

- A new box on Ireland and the 2007–2009 financial crisis (Chapter 9)
- A new Inside the Fed box on whether the Fed was to blame for the housing price bubble (Chapter 9)
- A new section on the Dodd-Frank bill and future regulation (Chapter 11)
- A new box on where the Basel Accord is heading after the global financial crisis (Chapter 11)
- A new box on the money supply during the 2007–2009 financial crisis (Chapter 17)
- A new section on nonconventional monetary policy tools (Chapter 18)
- A new section on quantitative versus credit easing (Chapter 18)
- A new Inside the Fed box on Federal Reserve lending facilities during the global financial crisis (Chapter 18)
- A new section on lessons for monetary policy strategy from the global financial crisis (Chapter 19)
- A new application on negative supply and demand shocks and the 2007–2009 financial crisis (Chapter 23)
- A new application on the United Kingdom and the 2007–2009 financial crisis (Chapter 23)
- A new application on China and the 2007–2009 financial crisis (Chapter 23)
- A new application on quantitative (credit) easing in response to the global financial crisis (Chapter 24)
- A new box on the activist/nonactivist debate over the Obama fiscal stimulus package (Chapter 24)

Additional New Material on Financial Markets and Institutions and Monetary Policy

There have also been changes in financial markets and institutions in recent years that have not been directly related to the global subprime financial crisis, and I have added the following new material to keep the text current:

- A new section on why the efficient markets hypothesis does not imply that financial markets are efficient (Chapter 7)
- A new box on collateralized debt obligations (CDOs) (Chapter 9)
- A new section on the Dodd-Frank bill and conflicts of interest (Chapter 15)
- A new section on the new monetary policy tool of paying interest on reserves (Chapter 18)
- An update on the Inside the Fed box on Chairman Bernanke and inflation targeting (Chapter 19)
- A new section on the policy trilemma (Chapter 21)
- A new application on the Zimbabwean hyperinflation (Chapter 22)
- A new application on the "Great Inflation" (Chapter 24)

A Dynamic Approach to Monetary Theory

In past editions, I have used static aggregate demand and supply (AD/AS) framework, in which the price level is on the vertical axis in AD/AS diagrams to discuss monetary theory. Over the years, I have found it more and more difficult to teach with this framework because it does not emphasize the dynamic interaction of inflation with economic activity, which is what modern monetary theory is all about. In this edition, I have completely rewritten chapters 23 and 24 to develop a powerful, dynamic aggregate demand and supply model that highlights the interaction of inflation and economic activity by putting inflation on the vertical axis in the AD/AS diagram.

- Chapter 23 derives the short- and long-run aggregate supply curves and then puts all of them together with the aggregate demand curve to develop the dynamic aggregate demand and supply model. This model is then put to use with numerous applications analyzing business cycle fluctuations in the United States and in foreign countries.

- Chapter 24 makes use of the dynamic AD/AS model to examine the theory of monetary policy and enables students to understand how monetary policymakers can respond to shocks to the economy in order to stabilize both inflation and economic activity.

In addition, I have revised Chapter 22 to make it more dynamic by emphasizing the link between the demand for money, quantity theory and inflation.

The Interaction of Finance and Monetary Theory

In the aftermath of the global financial crisis, monetary theory has been challenged by critics as being inadequate because in the past it has not given a prominent role to finance in economic fluctuations. In response, economists are now focusing on the link from finance to economic fluctuations in recent research, but this has not yet been reflected in textbooks. This book is the first textbook that I know of that responds to the challenges raised by critics of monetary theory by bringing finance directly into the aggregate demand and supply model at the outset. Barriers to the efficient functioning of financial markets from asymmetric information problems, known as financial frictions, are treated as one of the key factors affecting aggregate demand when this concept is first discussed. Then the impact of increases in financial frictions, as occurred during the global financial crisis, are easy to analyze using the aggregate demand and supply model. By emphasizing the interaction of finance and monetary theory, this book greatly enhances the realism of the aggregate demand and supply model, increasing the relevance of the analysis in the monetary theory part of the book.

End of Chapter Questions and Applied Problems

Because students best learn by doing, in this edition, we have substantially expanded the number of end-of-chapter questions and problems for each chapter. We have also added a new type of problem under the heading of "Applied Problems." These problems, written by Aaron Jackson of Bentley University, are more analytical and applied and so give the student more hands-on practice applying the economic concepts in the text.

Chapters and Appendices on the Web

The Companion Website for the book, www.pearsonhighered.com/mishkin, is an essential resource for additional content.

The Web chapters for the Third Edition of *The Economics of Money, Banking, and Financial Markets, Business School Edition,* include the unique chapters from the Tenth Edition. These chapters are:

Web Chapter 1: The *IS* Curve
Web Chapter 2: The Monetary Policy and Aggregate Demand Curves
Web Chapter 3: The Role of Expectations in Monetary Policy
Web Chapter 4: The *ISLM* Model

The Web appendices include:

Chapter 4: Measuring Interest-Rate Risk: Duration
Chapter 5: Models of Asset Pricing
Chapter 5: Applying the Asset Market Approach to a Commodity Market: The Case of Gold
Chapter 5: Loanable Funds Framework
Chapter 7: Evidence on the Efficient Market Hypothesis
Chapter 10: Duration Gap Analysis
Chapter 10: Measuring Bank Performance
Chapter 11: The Savings and Loan Crisis and Its Aftermath
Chapter 11: Banking Crises Throughout the World
Chapter 17: The Fed's Balance Sheet and the Monetary Base
Chapter 17: The M2 Money Multiplier
Chapter 17: Explaining the Behavior of the Currency Ratio
Chapter 19: Monetary Targeting
Chapter 22: The Baumol-Tobin and Tobin Mean Variance Model
Chapter 22: Empirical Evidence on the Demand for Money
Chapter 23: The Effects of Macroeconomic Shocks on Asset Prices
Chapter 23: The Algebra of the Aggregate Demand and Supply Model
Chapter 23: Aggregate Demand and Supply: A Numerical Example
Chapter 23: The Taylor Principle and Inflation Stability
Chapter 25: Evaluating Empirical Evidence: The Debate Over the Importance of Money in Economic Fluctuations

Instructors can either use these Web chapters or appendices in class to supplement the material in the textbook or recommend them to students who want to expand their knowledge of the money and banking field.

FLEXIBILITY AND MODULARITY

In using previous editions, adopters, reviewers, and survey respondents have continually praised this text's flexibility and modularity, that is, the ability to pick and choose which chapters to cover and in what order to cover them. Flexibility and modularity are especially important in the money and banking course because there are as many ways to teach this course as there are instructors. To satisfy the diverse needs of instructors, the text achieves flexibility as follows:

- Core chapters provide the basic analysis used throughout the book, and other chapters or sections of chapters can be used or omitted according to instructor preferences. For example, Chapter 2 introduces the financial system and basic concepts such as transaction costs, adverse selection, and moral hazard. After covering Chapter 2, the instructor may decide to give more detailed coverage of financial structure by assigning Chapter 8, or may choose to skip Chapter 8 and take any of a number of different paths through the book.
- Part 6 on monetary theory can easily be taught before Part 4 of the book in order to give students a deeper understanding of the rationale for monetary policy.
- Chapter 25 on the transmission mechanisms of monetary policy can be taught at many different points in the course—either with Part 4 of the book when monetary policy is discussed or with Chapter 23 when the concept of aggregate demand is developed. It could also be taught at the end of the book as a special topic.
- The internationalization of the text through marked international sections within chapters, as well as through complete separate chapters on the foreign exchange market and the international monetary system, is comprehensive yet flexible. Although many instructors will teach all the international material, others will not. Instructors who want less emphasis on international topics can easily skip Chapter 20 on the foreign exchange market and Chapter 21 on the international financial system and monetary policy. The international sections within chapters are self-contained and can be omitted with little loss of continuity.

To illustrate how this book can be used for courses with varying emphases, several course outlines are suggested for a semester teaching schedule. More detailed information about how the text can be used flexibly in your course is available in the Instructor's Manual.

- *General Money and Banking Course:* Chapters 1–5, 10-12, 16, 18, 19, 23–24, with a choice of 6 of the remaining 12 chapters.
- *General Money and Banking Course with an International Emphasis:* Chapters 1–5, 10–12, 16, 18–21, 23–24, with a choice of 4 of the remaining 10 chapters.
- *Financial Markets and Institutions Course:* Chapters 1–12, with a choice of 7 of the remaining 13 chapters.

PEDAGOGICAL AIDS

In teaching theory or its applications, a textbook must be a solid motivational tool. To this end, I have incorporated a wide variety of pedagogical features to make the material easy to learn:

1. **Previews** at the beginning of each chapter tell students where the chapter is heading, why specific topics are important, and how they relate to other topics in the book.

2. **Applications**, numbering around 50, demonstrate how the analysis in the book can be used to explain many important real-world situations.
3. **Following the Financial News boxes** introduce students to relevant news articles and data that are reported daily in the press and explain how to read them.
4. **Inside the Fed boxes** give students a feel for what is important in the operation and structure of the Federal Reserve System.
5. **Global boxes** include interesting material with an international focus.
6. **FYI boxes** highlight dramatic historical episodes, interesting ideas, and intriguing facts related to the subject matter.
7. **Summary tables** provide a useful study aid in reviewing material.
8. **Key statements** are important points set in boldface italic type so that students can easily find them for later reference.
9. **Graphs** with captions, numbering more than 150, help students clearly understand the interrelationship of the variables plotted and the principles of analysis.
10. **Summary** at the end of each chapter lists the main points covered.
11. **Key terms** are important words or phrases, boldface when they are defined for the first time and listed by page number at the end of the chapter.
12. **End-of-chapter questions and applied problems**, numbering more than 600, help students learn the subject matter by applying economic concepts.
13. **Web Exercises** encourage students to collect information from online sources or use online resources to enhance their learning experience.
14. **Web Sources** report the Web URL source of the data used to create the many tables and charts.
15. **Web References** point the student to Web sites that provide information or data that supplement the text material.
16. **Glossary** at the back of the book provides definitions of all the key terms.

AN EASIER WAY TO TEACH: SUPPLEMENTS TO ACCOMPANY THE THIRD EDITION

The Economics of Money, Banking, and Financial Markets, Business School Edition, includes the most comprehensive program of supplements of any money, banking, and financial markets textbook.

MyEconLab

MyEconLab has been designed and refined with a single purpose in mind: to create those moments of understanding that transform the difficult into the clear and obvious. With comprehensive homework, quiz, test, and tutorial options, instructors can manage all their assessment needs in one program.

MyEconLab for *The Economics of Money, Banking, and Financial Markets* offers the following resources for students and instructors:

- **All end-of-chapter questions and applied problems** from the text are available in MyEconLab.
- **Applications** from the text are also available with assignable questions.

- **Mishkin Interview Video Clips** discuss the financial crisis with the author, complete with assignable questions.
- **Personal Study Plans** are created for each individual student based on their performance on assigned and sample exercises.
- **Instant tutorial feedback** on a student's problem and graphing responses to questions.
- **Interactive Learning Aids**, such as *Help Me Solve This* (a step-by-step tutorial), help the student right when they need it. Key figures from the text are also presented in step-by-step animations with audio explanations of the action.
- **News articles** are available for classroom and assignment use. Up-to-date news articles and complimentary discussion questions are posted weekly to bring today's news into the classroom and course.
- **Real-Time Data Analysis Exercises** allow instructors to assign problems which use up-to-the-minute data. Each RTDA exercise loads the appropriate and most currently available data from FRED, a comprehensive and up-to-date data set maintained by the Federal Reserve Bank of St. Louis. Exercises are graded based on that instance of data, and feedback is provided.
- **An Enhanced Pearson eText** available within the online course materials and offline via an iPad app, the enhanced eText allows instructors and students to highlight, bookmark, and take notes.
- **Prebuilt courses** offer a turn-key way for instructors to create a course that includes prebuilt assignments distributed by chapter.
- **Auto Graded Problems and Graphs** for assignments.
- **A powerful Gradebook** flexible and rich with information, including student and class data on assignment performance and time on task.
- **Advanced Communication Tools** provides students and instructors the capability to communicate through email, discussion board, chat, and ClassLive.
- **Customization Options** provide new and enhanced ways to share documents, add content, and rename menu items.
- **Temporary Access** for students who are awaiting financial aid, a seventeen-day grace period of temporary access
- **One Place for students to access all of their MyLab courses**. Students and instructors can register, create, and access all of their MyLab courses, regardless of discipline, from one convenient online location: www.pearsonmylab.com.

For more information, please visit www.myeconlab.com.

Additional Instructor Resources

1. **Instructor's Resource Manual**. This online supplement, prepared by me, offers conventional elements such as sample course outlines, chapter outlines, and answers to questions and problems in the text.
2. **PowerPoint® Presentation**. This online supplement provides not only all the tables and graphs in the text, but very detailed lecture notes for all the material in the course. The basis of the lecture notes is, in fact, the notes I use in class—and they should help other instructors prepare their lectures as they have helped me. In this edition, Michael Carew of Baruch College has enhanced the presentation by adding additional lecture notes. Some instructors might use these PowerPoint slides as their own class notes and prefer to teach with a blackboard. But for those who prefer to teach with visual aids, the PowerPoint slides, which are fully customizable, afford the flexibility to take this approach.

3. **Test Item File**. This online supplement, updated and revised by James Hueng of Western Michigan University and Kathy Kelly of the University of Texas at Arlington, is comprised of more than 2,500 multiple-choice and essay test items, many with graphs. The authors of the test item file have connected questions to the general knowledge and skill guidelines found in The Association to Advance Collegiate Schools of Business (AACSB) assurance of learning standards. AACSB is a not-for-profit corporation of educational institutions, corporations, and other organizations devoted to the promotion and improvement of higher education in business administration and accounting. One of the criteria for AACSB accreditation is quality of the curricula. Although no specific courses are required, the AACSB expects a curriculum to include learning experiences in the following areas—Communication, Ethical Reasoning, Analytic Skills, Use of Information Technology, Multiculturalism and Diversity, and Reflective Thinking. Questions that test skills relevant to these guidelines are appropriately tagged for easy identification and assessment of student mastery.
4. **TestGen**. This online supplement allows the instructor to produce exams efficiently. This product consists of the multiple-choice and essay questions in the online Test Item File and offers editing capabilities. It is available in Windows and Macintosh versions.
5. **Mishkin Companion Website,** located at www.pearsonhighered.com/mishkin, features appendices on a wide variety of topics (see "Appendices on the Web"), omitted chapters, and links to the URLs that appear at the end of the chapters.

Additional Student Resources

1. **Study Guide**, fully revised and updated by Aaron Jackson of Bentley University, includes chapter synopses and completions, exercises, self-tests, and answers to the exercises and self-tests.
2. **Readings on Money, Banking, and Financial Markets**, edited by James W. Eaton of Bridgewater College and me, is updated annually, with over half the articles new each year to enable instructors to keep the content of their course current throughout the life of an edition of the text. The readings are available within MyEconLab.

ACKNOWLEDGMENTS

As always in so large a project, there are many people to thank. My gratitude goes especially to Donna Battista, economics and finance editor-in-chief at Pearson and Noel Seibert, my editor. I would also like to thank Laura Town, Kathryn Dinovo, Carolyn Terbush, and Kathy Smith for their contributions as well. I also have been assisted by comments from my colleagues at Columbia and from my students.

In addition, I have been guided by the thoughtful commentary of outside reviewers and correspondents, especially Jim Eaton and Aaron Jackson. Their feedback has made this a better book. In particular, I thank the following professors who reviewed the text in preparation of this edition:

Mohammed Akacem, Metropolitan State College of Denver
Stefania Albanesi, Columbia University
Nancy Anderson, Mississippi College
Bob Barnes, Northern Illinois University
Larry Belcher, Stetson University
Michael Carew, Baruch College
Matthew S. Chambers, Towson University
Chi-Young Choi, University of Texas, Arlington
Julie Dahlquist, University of Texas, San Antonio
Marc Fusaro, Arkansas Tech University
Edgar Ghossoub, University of Texas, San Antonio
Mark Gibson, Washington State University
James Hueng, Western Michigan University
Aaron Jackson, Bentley University
Kathy Kelly, University of Texas, Arlington
Michael Kelsay, University of Missouri, Kansas City
Paul Kubik, DePaul University
Sungkyu Kwak, Washburn University
W. Douglas McMillin, Louisiana State University
Carrie Meyer, George Mason University
George Monokroussos, University of Albany
Andy Prevost, Ohio University
Richard Stahl, Louisiana State University
Rubina Vohra, New Jersey City University
Yongsheng Wang, Washington and Jefferson College
David Zalewski, Providence College

My special thanks go to the following individuals who analyzed the manuscript in previous editions:

Burt Abrams, University of Delaware
Francis W. Ahking, University of Connecticut
Mohammed Akacem, Metropolitan State College of Denver
Stefania Albanesi, Columbia University
Muhammad Anwar, University of Massachusetts
Harjit K. Arora, Le Moyne College
Stacie Beck, University of Delaware
Gerry Bialka, University of North Florida
Daniel K. Biederman, University of North Dakota

John Bishop, East Carolina University
Daniel Blake, California State University, Northridge
Robert Boatler, Texas Christian University
Henning Bohn, University of California, Santa Barbara
Michael W. Brandl, University of Texas at Austin
Oscar T. Brookins, Northeastern University
William Walter Brown, California State University, Northridge
James L. Butkiewicz, University of Delaware
Colleen M. Callahan, Lehigh University
Ray Canterbery, Florida State University
Mike Carew, Barauch University
Tina Carter, University of Florida
Sergio Castello, University of Mobile
Jen-Chi Cheng, Wichita State University
Patrick Crowley, Middlebury College
Sarah E. Culver, University of Alabama, Birmingham
Maria Davis, San Antonio College
Ranjit S. Dighe, State University of New York, Oswego
Richard Douglas, Bowling Green University
Donald H. Dutkowsky, Syracuse University
Richard Eichhorn, Colorado State University
Paul Emberton, Southwest Texas State University
Erick Eschker, Humboldt State University
Robert Eyler, Sonoma State University
L. S. Fan, Colorado State University
Imran Farooqi, University of Iowa
Sasan Fayazmanesh, California State University, Fresno
Dennis Fixler, George Washington University
Gary Fleming, Roanoke College
Grant D. Forsyth, Eastern Washington University
Timothy Fuerst, Bowling Green State University
James Gale, Michigan Technological University
Shirley Gedeon, University of Vermont
Lance Girton, University of Utah
Stuart M. Glosser, University of Wisconsin, Whitewater
Fred C. Graham, American University
Jo Anna Gray, University of Oregon
David Gulley, Bentley College
Ralph Gunderson, University of Wisconsin
Daniel Haak, Stanford University
Larbi Hammami, McGill University
Bassan Harik, Western Michigan University
J. C. Hartline, Rutgers University
Scott Hein, Texas Tech
Robert Stanley Herren, North Dakota State University
Jane Himarios, University of Texas, Arlington
Chad Hogan, University of Michigan
Linda Hooks, Washington and Lee University
James Hueng, Western Michigan

Dar-Yeh Hwang, National Taiwan University
Jayvanth Ishwaran, Stephen F. Austin State University
Jonatan Jelen, Queens College and City College of CUNY
U Jin Jhun, State University of New York, Oswego
Frederick L. Joutz, George Washington University
Ahmed Kalifa, Colorado State University
Bryce Kanago, University of Northern Iowa
Magda Kandil, International Monetary Fund
Theodore Kariotis, Towson University
George G. Kaufman, Loyola University Chicago
Richard H. Keehn, University of Wisconsin, Parkside
Elizabeth Sawyer Kelly, University of Wisconsin, Madison
Fritz Laux, Northeastern State University
Jim Lee, Fort Hays State University
Robert Leeson, University of Western Ontario
Tony Lima, California State University, Hayward
Fiona Maclachlan, Manhattan College
Elham Mafi-Kreft, Indiana University
Bernard Malamud, University of Nevada, Las Vegas
James Maloy, University of Pittsburgh
James Marchand, Mercer University
Marvin Margolis, Millersville University
Elaine McBeth, College of William and Mary
Stephen McCafferty, Ohio State University
James McCown, Ohio State University
Cheryl McGaughey, Angelo State University
W. Douglas McMillin, Louisiana State University
William Merrill, Iowa State University
Carrie Meyer, George Mason University
Stephen M. Miller, University of Connecticut
Masoud Moghaddam, Saint Cloud State University
Thomas S. Mondschean, DePaul University
Clair Morris, U.S. Naval Academy
Jon Nadenichek, California State University, Northridge
John Nader, Grand Valley State University
Leonce Ndikumana, University of Massachusetts, Amherst
Ray Nelson, Brigham Young University
Inder P. Nijhawan, Fayetteville State University
Nick Noble, Miami University of Ohio
Dennis O'Toole, Virginia Commonwealth University
Mark J. Perry, University of Michigan, Flint
Chung Pham, University of New Mexico
Marvin M. Phaup, George Washington University
Ganga P. Ramdas, Lincoln University
Ronald A. Ratti, University of Missouri, Columbia
Hans Rau, Ball State University
Prosper Raynold, Miami University
Javier Reyes, Texas A&M University
Jack Russ, San Diego State University

Steve Russell, IUPUI
Robert S. Rycroft, Mary Washington College
Joe Santos, South Dakota State University
Lynn Schneider, Auburn University, Montgomery
Walter Schwarm, Colorado State University
John Shea, University of Maryland
Harinder Singh, Grand Valley State University
Rajesh Singh, Iowa State University
Larry Taylor, Lehigh University
Leigh Tesfatsion, Iowa State University
Aditi Thapar, New York University
Frederick D. Thum, University of Texas, Austin
Robert Tokle, Idaho State University
C. Van Marrewijk, Erasmus University
Christopher J. Waller, Indiana University
Chao Wei, George Washington University
Maurice Weinrobe, Clark University
James R. Wible, University of New Hampshire
Philip R. Wiest, George Mason University
William Wilkes, Athens State University
Thomas Williams, William Paterson University
Elliot Willman, New Mexico State University
Donald Wills, University of Washington, Tacoma
Laura Wolff, Southern Illinois University, Edwardsville
JaeJoon Woo, DePaul University
Robert Wright, University of Virginia
Ben T. Yu, California State University, Northridge
Ky H. Yuhn, Florida Atlantic University
Ed Zajicek, Winston-Salem State University
Jeffrey Zimmerman, Methodist College

Finally, I want to thank my wife, Sally; my son, Matthew; and my daughter, Laura, who provide me with a warm and happy environment that enables me to do my work, and my father, Sidney, now deceased, who a long time ago put me on the path that led to this book.

Frederic S. Mishkin

About The Author

Frederic S. Mishkin is the Alfred Lerner Professor of Banking and Financial Institutions at the Graduate School of Business, Columbia University. He is also a Research Associate at the National Bureau of Economic Research, co-director of the U.S. Monetary Policy Forum, a member of the Squam Lake Working Group on Financial Reform, and past president of the Eastern Economics Association. Since receiving his Ph.D. from the Massachusetts Institute of Technology in 1976, he has taught at the University of Chicago, Northwestern University, Princeton University, and Columbia. He has also received an honorary professorship from the People's (Renmin) University of China. From 1994 to 1997, he was Executive Vice President and Director of Research at the Federal Reserve Bank of New York and an associate economist of the Federal Open Market Committee of the Federal Reserve System. From September 2006 to August 2008, he was a member (governor) of the Board of Governors of the Federal Reserve System.

Professor Mishkin's research focuses on monetary policy and its impact on financial markets and the aggregate economy. He is the author of more than twenty books including *Macroeconomics: Policy and Practice* (Addison-Wesley, 2012); *Financial Markets and Institutions*, Seventh Edition (Prentice Hall, 2012); *Monetary Policy Strategy,* (MIT Press, 2007); *The Next Great Globalization: How Disadvantaged Nations Can Harness Their Financial Systems to Get Rich* (Princeton University Press, 2006); *Inflation Targeting: Lessons from the International Experience* (Princeton University Press, 1999); *Money, Interest Rates, and Inflation* (Edward Elgar, 1993); and *A Rational Expectations Approach to Macroeconometrics: Testing Policy Ineffectiveness and Efficient Markets Models* (University of Chicago Press, 1983). In addition, he has published more than 200 articles in such journals as *American Economic Review*, *Journal of Political Economy*, *Econometrica*, *Quarterly Journal of Economics*, *Journal of Finance*, and *Journal of Monetary Economics*.

Professor Mishkin has served on the editorial board of *American Economic Review* and has been an associate editor at *Journal of Business and Economic Statistics*, the *Journal of Applied Econometrics*, *Journal of Economic Perspectives*, and *Journal of Money, Credit and Banking*; he also served as the editor of the Federal Reserve Bank of New York's *Economic Policy Review*. He is currently an associate editor (member of the editorial board) at five academic journals, including *Journal of International Money and Finance*; *International Finance*; *Finance India*; *Review of Development Finance*, and *Emerging Markets, Finance and Trade*. He has been a consultant to the Board of Governors of the Federal Reserve System, the World Bank, and the International Monetary Fund, as well as to many central banks throughout the world. He was also a member of the International Advisory Board to the Financial Supervisory Service of South Korea and an advisor to the Institute for Monetary and Economic Research at the Bank of Korea. Professor Mishkin was a Senior Fellow at the Federal Deposit Insurance Corporation's Center for Banking Research and was an academic consultant to and serves on the Economic Advisory Panel of the Federal Reserve Bank of New York.

Part 1

Introduction

Crisis and Response: Global Financial Crisis and Its Aftermath

In August 2007, financial markets began to seize up, and over the next two years the world economy experienced a global financial crisis that was the most severe since the Great Depression years of the 1930s. Housing prices plummeted, the stock market crashed, unemployment skyrocketed, and both businesses and households found they couldn't get credit. Not only did the central bank in the United States, the Federal Reserve, respond by sharply lowering interest rates and intervening in credit markets to provide them with massive amounts of liquidity, but also the federal government entered the act with a $700 billion bailout of weakened financial institutions and huge fiscal stimulus packages totaling over $1 trillion. However, even with these aggressive actions to stabilize the financial system and boost the economy, four years after the crisis the U.S. economy was still experiencing an unemployment rate above 9%, with many households losing their homes, and the finances of many governments throughout the world were in tatters.

The global financial crisis and its aftermath demonstrate the importance of banks and the financial system to economic well-being and the major role of money in the economy. Part I of this book provides an introduction to the study of money, banking, and financial markets. Chapter 1 outlines a road map of the book and discusses why it is so worthwhile to study money, banking, and financial markets. Chapter 2 provides a general overview of the financial system. Chapter 3 then explains what money is and how it is measured.

1 Why Study Money, Banking, and Financial Markets?

Preview

On the evening news you have just heard that the Federal Reserve is raising the federal funds rate by $\frac{1}{2}$ of a percentage point. What effect might this have on the interest rate of an automobile loan when you finance your purchase of a sleek new sports car? Does it mean that a house will be more or less affordable in the future? Will it make it easier or harder for you to get a job next year?

This book provides answers to these and other questions by examining how financial markets (such as those for bonds, stocks, and foreign exchange) and financial institutions (banks, insurance companies, mutual funds, and other institutions) work and by exploring the role of money in the economy. Financial markets and institutions not only affect your everyday life but also involve flows of trillions of dollars of funds throughout our economy, which in turn affect business profits, the production of goods and services, and even the economic well-being of countries other than the United States. What happens to financial markets, financial institutions, and money is of great concern to politicians and can even have a major impact on elections. The study of money, banking, and financial markets will reward you with an understanding of many exciting issues. In this chapter, we provide a road map of the book by outlining these issues and exploring why they are worth studying.

WHY STUDY FINANCIAL MARKETS?

Part 2 of this book focuses on **financial markets**, markets in which funds are transferred from people who have an excess of available funds to people who have a shortage. Financial markets such as bond and stock markets are crucial to promoting greater economic efficiency by channeling funds from people who do not have a productive use for them to those who do. Indeed, well-functioning financial markets are a key factor in producing high economic growth, and poorly performing financial markets are one reason that many countries in the world remain desperately poor. Activities in financial markets also have direct effects on personal wealth, the behavior of businesses and consumers, and the cyclical performance of the economy.

The Bond Market and Interest Rates

A **security** (also called a *financial instrument*) is a claim on the issuer's future income or **assets** (any financial claim or piece of property that is subject to ownership). A **bond** is a debt security that promises to make payments periodically for a specified period of

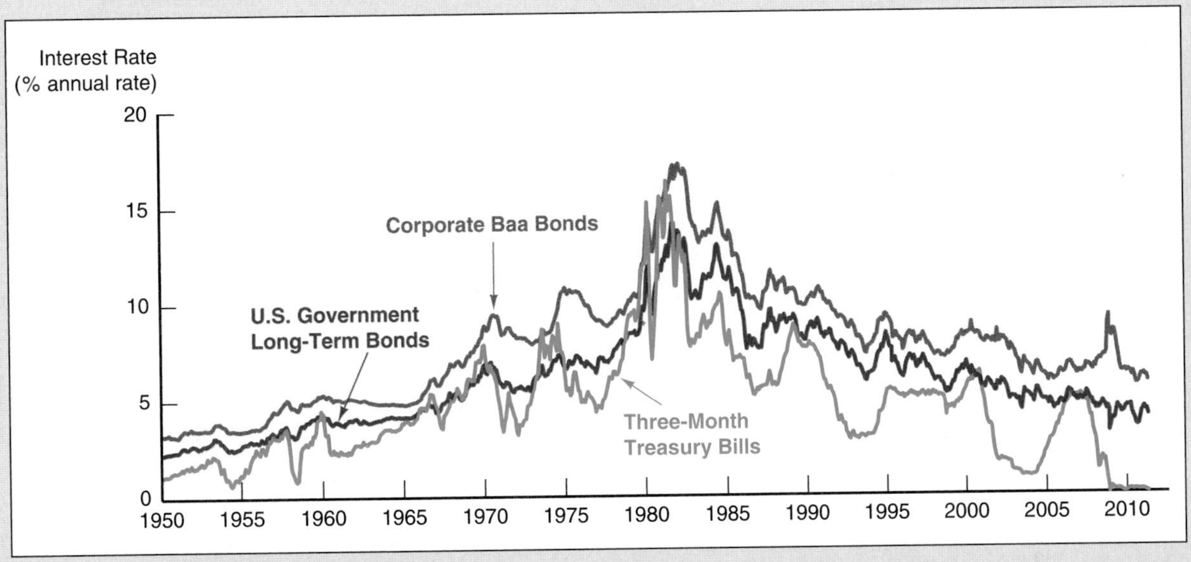

FIGURE 1 Interest Rates on Selected Bonds, 1950–2011

Although different interest rates have a tendency to move in unison, they do often differ substantially and the spreads between them fluctuate.

Sources: Based on **Federal Reserve Bulletin;** www.federalreserve.gov/releases/H15/data.htm.

time.[1] The bond market is especially important to economic activity because it enables corporations and governments to borrow to finance their activities and because it is where interest rates are determined. An **interest rate** is the cost of borrowing or the price paid for the rental of funds (usually expressed as a percentage of the rental of $100 per year). Many types of interest rates are found in the economy—mortgage interest rates, car loan rates, and interest rates on many different types of bonds.

Interest rates are important on a number of levels. On a personal level, high interest rates could deter you from buying a house or a car because the cost of financing it would be high. Conversely, high interest rates could encourage you to save because you can earn more interest income by putting aside some of your earnings as savings. On a more general level, interest rates have an impact on the overall health of the economy because they affect not only consumers' willingness to spend or save but also businesses' investment decisions. High interest rates, for example, might cause a corporation to postpone building a new plant that would provide more jobs.

Because changes in interest rates have important effects on individuals, financial institutions, businesses, and the overall economy, it is important to explain fluctuations in interest rates that have been substantial over the past 30 years. For example, the interest rate on three-month Treasury bills peaked at over 16% in 1981. This interest rate fell to 3% in late 1992 and 1993, rose to above 5% in the mid- to late 1990s, fell to below 1% in 2004, rose to 5% by 2007, only to fall close to zero from 2008 to 2011.

Because different interest rates have a tendency to move in unison, economists frequently lump interest rates together and refer to "the" interest rate. As Figure 1 shows,

[1]The definition of *bond* used throughout this book is the broad one in common use by academics, which covers both short- and long-term debt instruments. However, some practitioners in financial markets use the word *bond* to describe only specific long-term debt instruments such as corporate bonds or U.S. Treasury bonds.

however, interest rates on several types of bonds can differ substantially. The interest rate on three-month Treasury bills, for example, fluctuates more than the other interest rates and is lower, on average. The interest rate on Baa (medium-quality) corporate bonds is higher, on average, than the other interest rates, and the spread between it and the other rates became larger in the 1970s, narrowed in the 1990s, rose briefly in the early 2000s, narrowed again and rose sharply starting in the summer of 2007, and then only began to decline toward the end of 2009.

In Chapter 2 we study the role of bond markets in the economy, and in Chapters 4 through 6 we examine what an interest rate is, how the common movements in interest rates come about, and why the interest rates on different bonds vary.

The Stock Market

A **common stock** (typically just called a **stock**) represents a share of ownership in a corporation. It is a security that is a claim on the earnings and assets of the corporation. Issuing stock and selling it to the public is a way for corporations to raise funds to finance their activities. The stock market, in which claims on the earnings of corporations (shares of stock) are traded, is the most widely followed financial market in almost every country that has one; that's why it is often called simply "the market." A big swing in the prices of shares in the stock market is always a major story on the evening news. People often speculate on where the market is heading and get very excited when they can brag about their latest "big killing," but they become depressed when they suffer a big loss. The attention the market receives can probably be best explained by one simple fact: It is a place where people can get rich—or poor—quickly.

As Figure 2 indicates, stock prices are extremely volatile. After the market rose in the 1980s, on "Black Monday"—October 19, 1987—it experienced the worst one-day drop in its entire history, with the Dow Jones Industrial Average (DJIA) falling by 22%. From then until 2000, the stock market experienced one of the greatest bull markets in its history, with the Dow climbing to a peak of over 11,000. With the collapse of the high-tech bubble in 2000, the stock market fell sharply, dropping by over 30% by late 2002. It then rose to an all-time high above the 14,000 level in 2007, only to fall below 8,000 early in 2009, but recovered to over 12,000 by 2011. These considerable fluctuations in stock prices affect the size of people's wealth and as a result may affect their willingness to spend.

The stock market is also an important factor in business investment decisions, because the price of shares affects the amount of funds that can be raised by selling newly issued stock to finance investment spending. A higher price for a firm's shares means that it can raise a larger amount of funds, which it can use to buy production facilities and equipment.

In Chapter 2 we examine the role that the stock market plays in the financial system, and we return to the issue of how stock prices behave and respond to information in the marketplace in Chapter 7.

WHY STUDY FINANCIAL INSTITUTIONS AND BANKING?

Part 3 of this book focuses on financial institutions and the business of banking. Banks and other financial institutions are what make financial markets work. Without them, financial markets would not be able to move funds from people who save to people who have productive investment opportunities. Thus they play a crucial role in the economy.

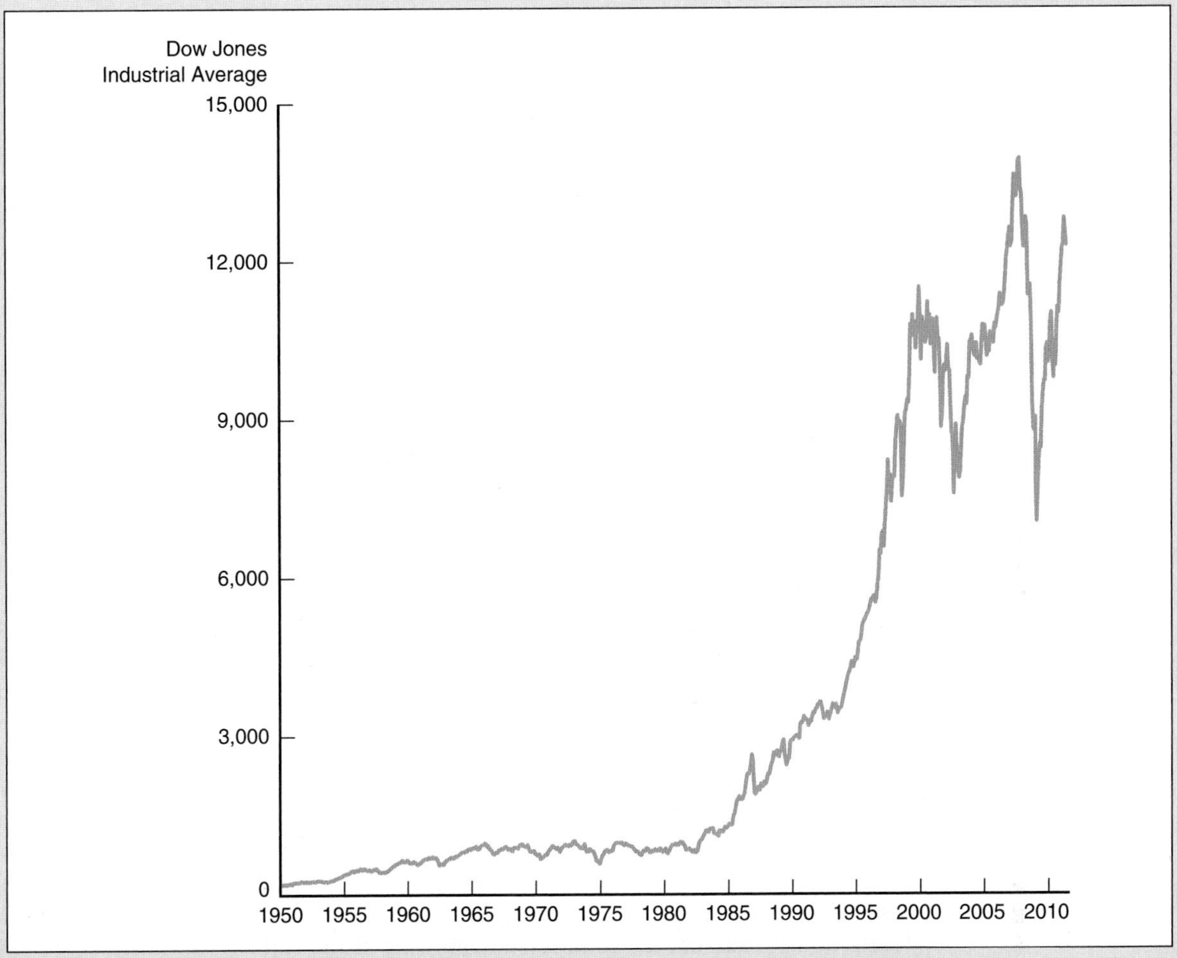

FIGURE 2 Stock Prices as Measured by the Dow Jones Industrial Average, 1950–2011
Stock prices are extremely volatile.
Source: Based on Dow Jones Indexes: http://nance.yahoo.com/?u.

Structure of the Financial System

The financial system is complex, comprising many different types of private sector financial institutions, including banks, insurance companies, mutual funds, finance companies, and investment banks, all of which are heavily regulated by the government. If an individual wanted to make a loan to IBM or General Motors, for example, he or she would not go directly to the president of the company and offer a loan. Instead, he or she would lend to such companies indirectly through **financial intermediaries**, institutions that borrow funds from people who have saved and in turn make loans to others.

Why are financial intermediaries so crucial to well-functioning financial markets? Why do they extend credit to one party but not to another? Why do they usually write complicated legal documents when they extend loans? Why are they the most heavily regulated businesses in the economy?

We answer these questions in Chapter 8 by developing a coherent framework for analyzing financial structure in the United States and in the rest of the world.

Financial Crises

At times, the financial system seizes up and produces **financial crises**, major disruptions in financial markets that are characterized by sharp declines in asset prices and the failures of many financial and nonfinancial firms. Financial crises have been a feature of capitalist economies for hundreds of years and are typically followed by the most severe business cycle downturns. Starting in August 2007, the U.S. economy was hit by the worst financial crisis since the Great Depression. Defaults in subprime residential mortgages led to major losses in financial institutions, producing not only numerous bank failures but also the demise of Bear Stearns and Lehman Brothers, two of the largest investment banks in the United States. The result of the crisis was the worst recession since World War II, and as a result, it is now referred to as the "Great Recession."

Why these crises occur and do so much damage to the economy is discussed in Chapter 9.

Banks and Other Financial Institutions

Banks are financial institutions that accept deposits and make loans. Included under the term *banks* are firms such as commercial banks, savings and loan associations, mutual savings banks, and credit unions. Banks are the financial intermediaries that the average person interacts with most frequently. A person who needs a loan to buy a house or a car usually obtains it from a local bank. Most Americans keep a large proportion of their financial wealth in banks in the form of checking accounts, savings accounts, or other types of bank deposits. Because banks are the largest financial intermediaries in our economy, they deserve the most careful study. However, banks are not the only important financial institutions. Indeed, in recent years, other financial institutions such as insurance companies, finance companies, pension funds, mutual funds, and investment banks have been growing at the expense of banks, so we need to study them as well.

In Chapter 10, we examine how banks and other financial institutions manage their assets and liabilities to make profits. In Chapter 11, we extend the economic analysis in Chapter 8 to understand why financial regulation takes the form it does and what can go wrong in the regulatory process. In Chapter 12, we look at the banking industry; we examine how the competitive environment has changed in this industry and learn why some financial institutions have been growing at the expense of others.

Financial Innovation

Financial innovation, the development of new financial products and services, can be an important force for good by making the financial system more efficient. Unfortunately, as we will see In Chapter 9, financial innovation can have a dark side: It can lead to devastating financial crises, such as the one we have recently experienced. In Chapter 12 we study why and how financial innovation takes place, with particular emphasis on how the dramatic improvements in information technology have led to new financial products and the ability to deliver financial services electronically, in what has become known as **e-finance**. We also study financial innovation, because it shows us how creative thinking on the part of financial institutions can lead to higher profits but can sometimes result in financial disasters. By seeing how and why financial institutions have been creative in the past, we obtain a better grasp of how they may be creative in the future. This knowledge provides us with useful clues about how the financial system may change over time and will help keep our knowledge about banks and other financial institutions from becoming obsolete.

WHY STUDY MONEY AND MONETARY POLICY?

Money, also referred to as the **money supply**, is defined as anything that is generally accepted in payment for goods or services or in the repayment of debts. Money is linked to changes in economic variables that affect all of us and are important to the health of the economy. The final two parts of the book examine the role of money in the economy.

Money and Business Cycles

In 1981–1982, total production of goods and services (called **aggregate output**) in the U.S. economy fell and the **unemployment rate** (the percentage of the available labor force unemployed) rose to over 10%. After 1982, the economy began to expand rapidly, and by 1989 the unemployment rate had declined to 5%. In 1990, the eight-year expansion came to an end, with the unemployment rate rising above 7%. The economy bottomed out in 1991, and the subsequent recovery was the longest in U.S. history, with the unemployment rate falling to around 4%. A mild economic downturn began in March 2001, with unemployment rising to 6%; the economy began to recover in November 2001, with unemployment eventually declining to a low of 4.4%. Starting in December 2007, the economy went into recession and unemployment rose to over 10% before the economy slowly began to recover in June 2009.

Why did the economy undergo such pronounced fluctuations? Evidence suggests that money plays an important role in generating **business cycles**, the upward and downward movement of aggregate output produced in the economy. Business cycles affect all of us in immediate and important ways. When output is rising, for example, it is easier to find a good job; when output is falling, finding a good job might be difficult. Figure 3 shows the movements of the rate of money growth over the 1950–2011 period, with the shaded areas representing **recessions**, periods of declining aggregate output. What we see is that the rate of money growth has declined before almost every recession, indicating that changes in money might be a driving force behind business cycle fluctuations. However, not every decline in the rate of money growth is followed by a recession.

We explore how money and monetary policy might affect aggregate output in Chapters 22 through 25 in Part 6 of this book, where we study **monetary theory**, the theory that relates the quantity of money and monetary policy to changes in aggregate economic activity and inflation.

Money and Inflation

Thirty years ago, the movie you might have paid $10 to see last week would have set you back only a dollar or two. In fact, for $10 you could probably have had dinner, seen the movie, and bought yourself a big bucket of hot buttered popcorn.

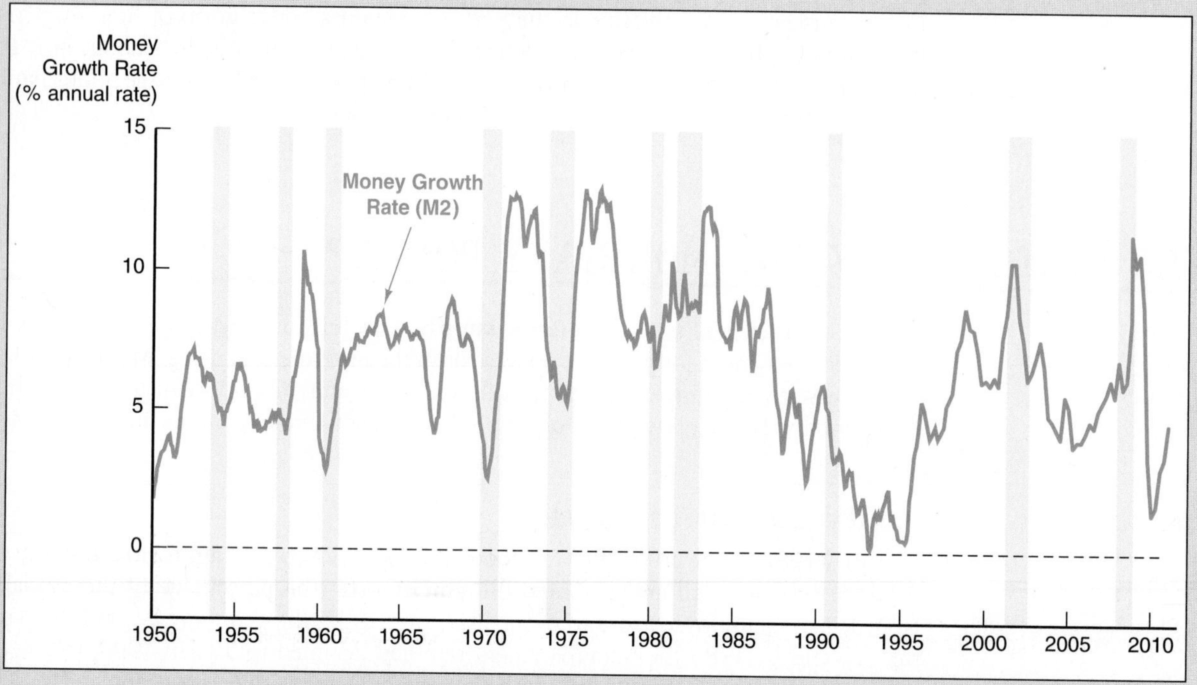

FIGURE 3 Money Growth (M2 Annual Rate) and the Business Cycle in the United States, 1950–2011
Although money growth has declined before every recession, not every decline in the rate of money growth is followed by a recession. Shaded areas represent recessions.
Source: Based on **Federal Reserve Bulletin**, p. A4, Table 1.10; www.federalreserve.gov/releases/h6/hist/h6hist1.txt.

As shown in Figure 4, which illustrates the movement of average prices in the U.S. economy from 1950 to 2011, the prices of most items are quite a bit higher now than they were then. The average price of goods and services in an economy is called the **aggregate price level**, or, more simply, the *price level* (a more precise definition is found in the appendix to this chapter). From 1950 to 2011, the price level has increased more than sixfold. **Inflation**, a continual increase in the price level, affects individuals, businesses, and the government. It is generally regarded as an important problem to be solved and is often at the top of political and policymaking agendas. To solve the inflation problem, we need to know something about its causes.

What explains inflation? One clue to answering this question is found in Figure 4, which plots the money supply and the price level. As we can see, the price level and the money supply generally rise together. These data seem to indicate that a continuing increase in the money supply might be an important factor in causing the continuing increase in the price level that we call inflation.

Further evidence that inflation may be tied to continuing increases in the money supply is found in Figure 5. For a number of countries, it plots the average **inflation rate** (the rate of change of the price level, usually measured as a percentage change per year) over the ten-year period 2000–2010 against the average rate of money growth

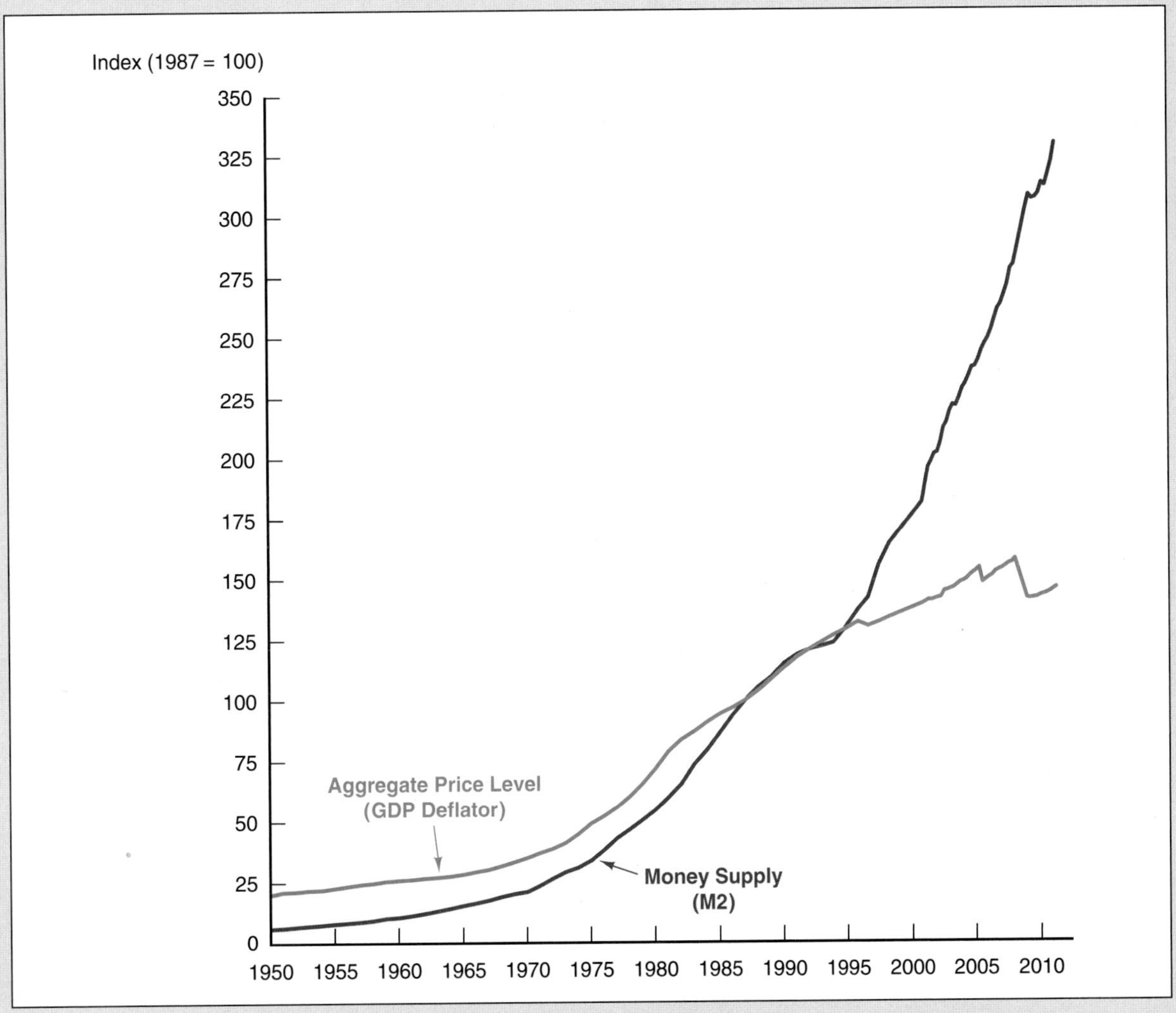

FIGURE 4 Aggregate Price Level and the Money Supply in the United States, 1950–2011
From 1950 to 2011, the price level has increased more than sixfold.
Sources: Based on www.stls.frb.org/fred/data/gdp/gdpdef; www.federalreserve.gov/releases/h6/hist/h6hist10.txt.

over the same period. As you can see, a positive association exists between inflation and the growth rate of the money supply: The countries with the highest inflation rates are also the ones with the highest money growth rates. Turkey, Ukraine and Zambia, for example, experienced high inflation during this period, and their rates of money growth were high. By contrast, Sweden and the United States had low inflation rates over the same period, and their rates of money growth have been low. Such evidence led Milton Friedman, a Nobel laureate in economics, to make the famous statement, "Inflation is always and everywhere a monetary phenomenon."[2] We look at the quantity of money and monetary policy's role in creating inflation in Chapters 22 and 24.

[2]Milton Friedman, *Dollars and Deficits* (Upper Saddle River, NJ: Prentice Hall, 1968), p. 39.

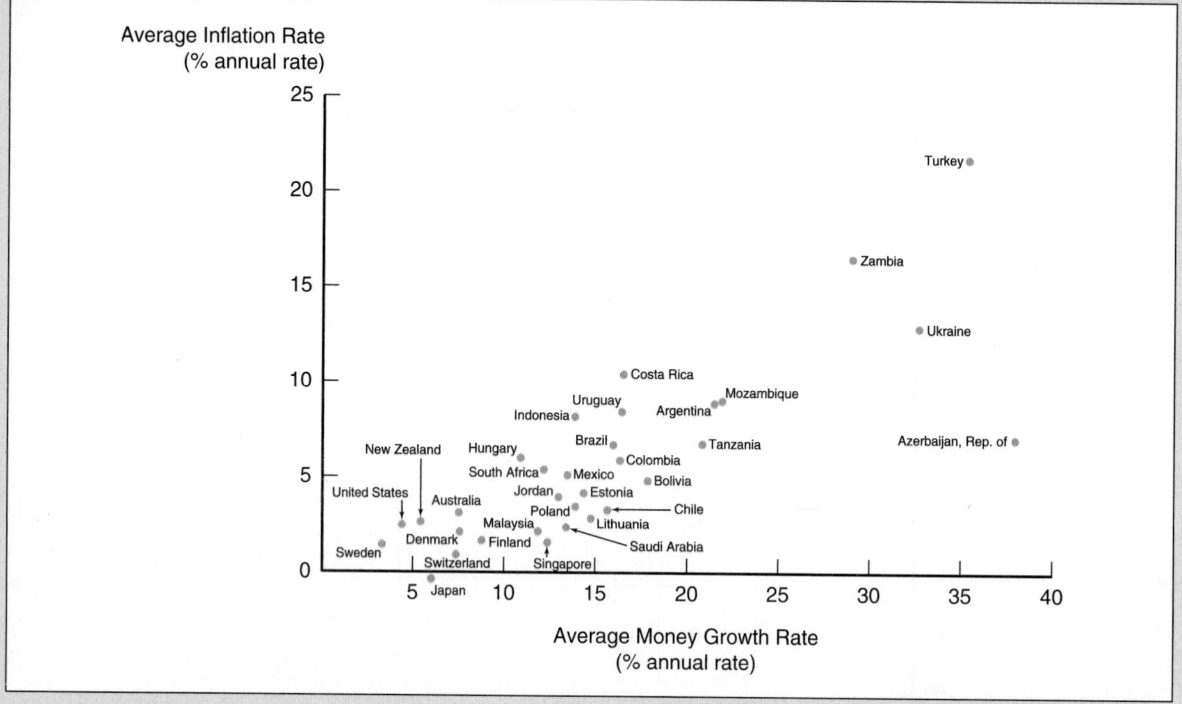

FIGURE 5 Average Inflation Rate Versus Average Rate of Money Growth for Selected Countries, 2000–2010

A positive association can be seen between the ten-year averages of inflation and the growth rate of the money supply: The countries with the highest inflation rates are also the ones with the highest money growth rates.

Source: Based on International Financial Statistics. www.imfstatistics.org/imf.

Money and Interest Rates

In addition to other factors, money plays an important role in interest-rate fluctuations, which are of great concern to businesses and consumers. Figure 6 shows the changes in the interest rate on long-term Treasury bonds and the rate of money growth. As the money growth rate rose in the 1960s and 1970s, the long-term bond rate rose with it. However, the relationship between money growth and interest rates has been less clear-cut since 1980. We analyze the relationship between money and interest rates when we examine the behavior of interest rates in Chapter 5.

Conduct of Monetary Policy

Because money can affect many economic variables that are important to the well-being of our economy, politicians and policymakers throughout the world care about the conduct of **monetary policy**, the management of money and interest rates. The organization responsible for the conduct of a nation's monetary policy is the **central bank**. The United States' central bank is the **Federal Reserve System** (also called simply **the Fed**). In Chapters 16 through 19 (Part 4), we study how central banks like the Federal Reserve

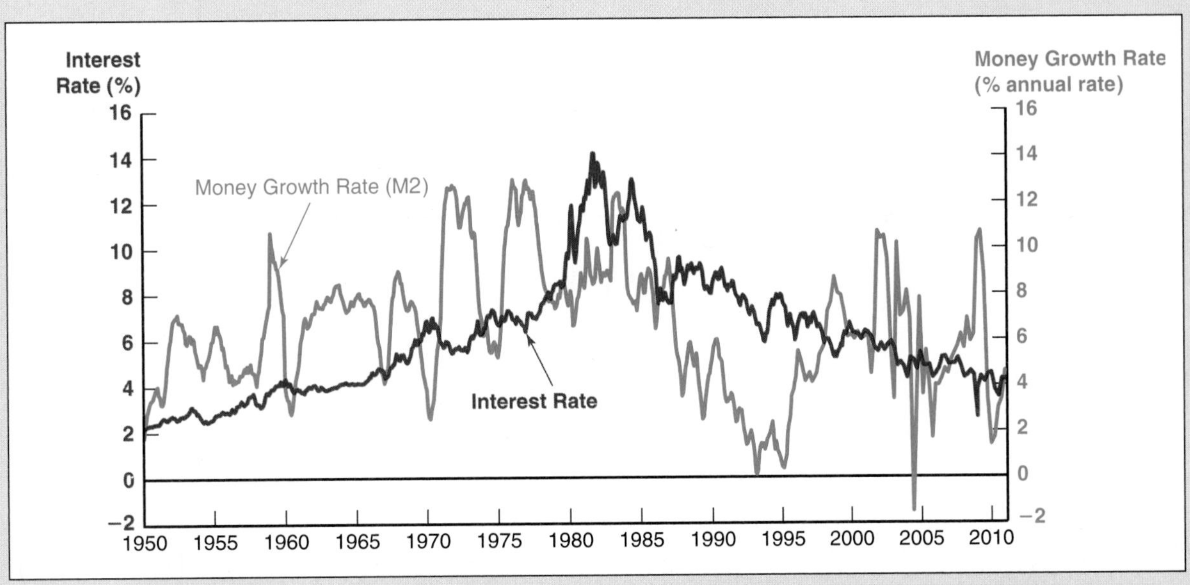

FIGURE 6 Money Growth (M2 Annual Rate) and Interest Rates (Long-Term U.S. Treasury Bonds), 1950–2011

As the money growth rate rose in the 1960s and 1970s, the long-term bond rate rose with it. However, the relationship between money growth and interest rates has been less clear-cut since 1980.

Sources: Based on **Federal Reserve Bulletin, p. A4, Table 1.10;** www.federalreserve.gov/releases/h6/hist/h6hist1.txt.

System can affect the quantity of money and interest rates in the economy and then we look at how monetary policy is actually conducted in the United States and elsewhere.

Fiscal Policy and Monetary Policy

Fiscal policy involves decisions about government spending and taxation. A **budget deficit** is the excess of government expenditures over tax revenues for a particular time period, typically a year, while a **budget surplus** arises when tax revenues exceed government expenditures. The government must finance any deficit by borrowing, while a budget surplus leads to a lower government debt burden. As Figure 7 shows, the budget deficit, relative to the size of the U.S. economy, peaked in 1983 at 6% of national output (as calculated by the **gross domestic product**, or *GDP*, a measure of aggregate output described in the appendix to this chapter). Since then, the budget deficit at first declined to less than 3% of GDP, rose again to 5% by the early 1990s, and fell subsequently, leading to budget surpluses from 1999 to 2001. In the aftermath of the terrorist attacks of September 11, 2001, the war in Iraq that began in March 2003, and the 2007–2009 financial crisis, the budget has swung back again into deficit, with recent deficits exceeding 10% of GDP. What to do about budget deficits has been the subject of legislation and bitter battles between the president and Congress in recent years.

You may have heard statements in newspapers or on TV that budget surpluses are a good thing while deficits are undesirable. We explore the accuracy of such claims in Chapters 9 and 21 by seeing how budget deficits might lead to a financial crisis, as they did in Argentina in 2001. In Chapter 22, we examine why deficits might result in a higher rate of money growth, a higher rate of inflation, and higher interest rates.

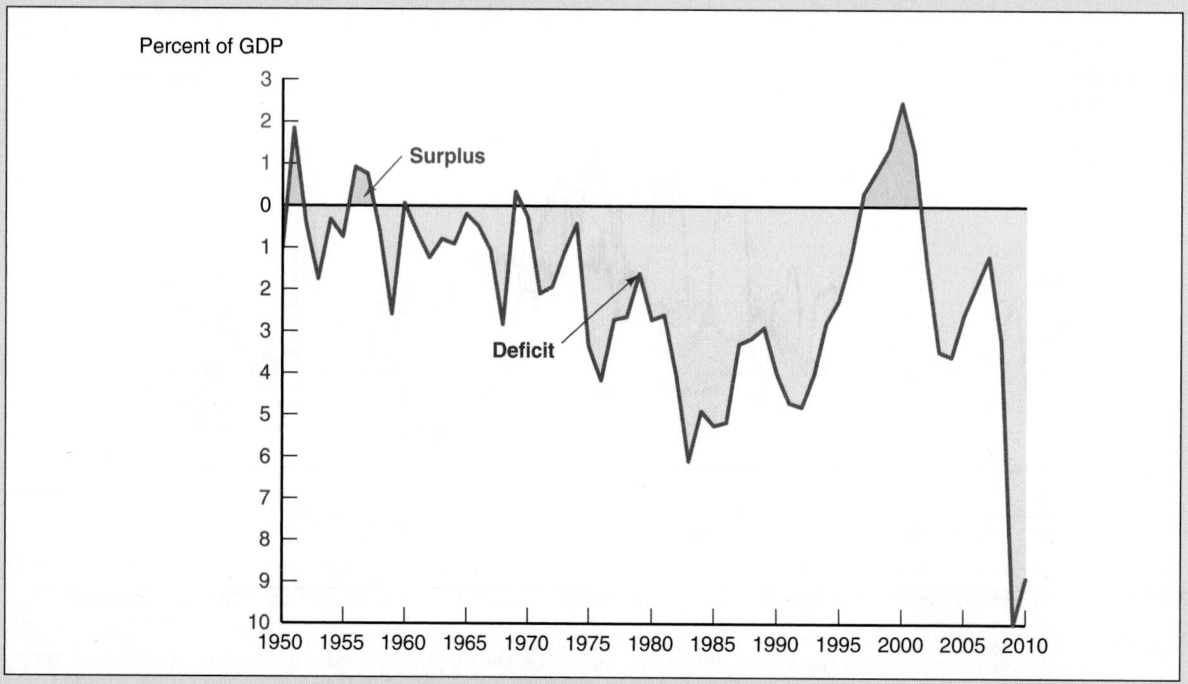

FIGURE 7 Government Budget Surplus or Deficit as a Percentage of Gross Domestic Product, 1950–2010

The budget deficit, relative to the size of the U.S. economy, has fluctuated a lot over the years, rising to 6% of GDP in 1983, falling subsequently so there were budgeted surpluses from 1999 to 2001, only to rise subsequently, with budget deficits climbing to 10% of GDP in 2009.

Source: www.gpoaccess.gov/usbudget/fy06/sheets/hist01z2.xls.

WHY STUDY INTERNATIONAL FINANCE?

The globalization of financial markets has accelerated at a rapid pace in recent years. Financial markets have become increasingly integrated throughout the world. American companies often borrow in foreign financial markets, and foreign companies borrow in U.S. financial markets. Banks and other financial institutions, such as JP Morgan Chase, Citigroup, UBS, and Deutschebank, have become increasingly international, with operations in many countries throughout the world. Part 5 of this book explores the foreign exchange market and the international financial system.

The Foreign Exchange Market

For funds to be transferred from one country to another, they have to be converted from the currency in the country of origin (say, dollars) into the currency of the country they are going to (say, euros). The **foreign exchange market** is where this conversion takes place, so it is instrumental in moving funds between countries. It is also important because it is where the **foreign exchange rate**, the price of one country's currency in terms of another's, is determined.

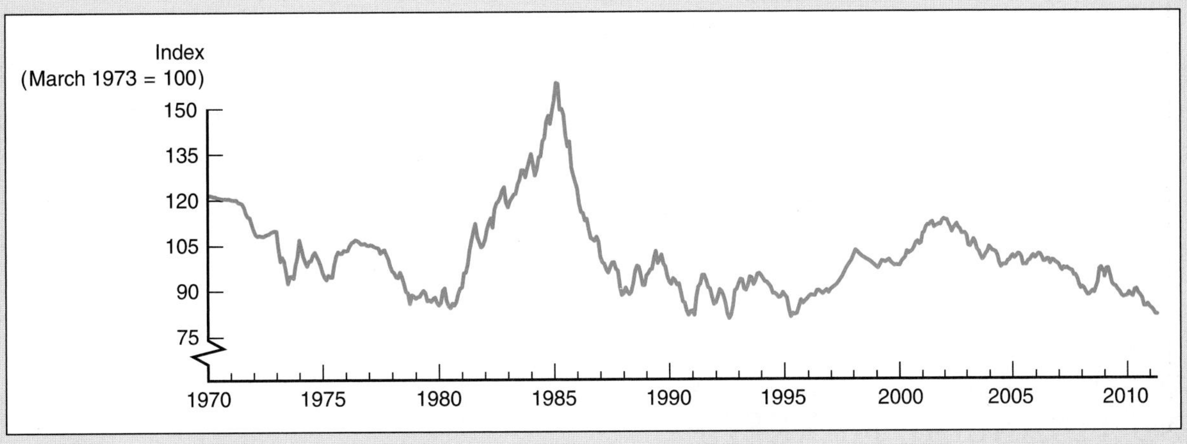

FIGURE 8 Exchange Rate of the U.S. Dollar, 1970–2011
The value of the U.S. dollar relative to other currencies has fluctuated substantially over the years.
Source: **Federal Reserve;** www.federalreserve.gov/releases/H10/summary/indexbc_m.txt/.

Figure 8 shows the exchange rate for the U.S. dollar from 1970 to 2011 (measured as the value of the U.S. dollar in terms of a basket of major foreign currencies). The fluctuations in prices in this market have been substantial: The dollar's value weakened considerably from 1971 to 1973, rose slightly until 1976, and then reached a low point in the 1978–1980 period. From 1980 to early 1985, the dollar's value appreciated dramatically, and then declined again, reaching another low in 1995. The dollar appreciated from 1995 to 2000, only to depreciate thereafter.

What have these fluctuations in the exchange rate meant to the American public and businesses? A change in the exchange rate has a direct effect on American consumers because it affects the cost of imports. In 2001 when the euro was worth around 85 cents, 100 euros of European goods (say, French wine) cost $85. When the dollar subsequently weakened, raising the cost of a euro near $1.50, the same 100 euros of wine now cost $150. Thus a weaker dollar leads to more expensive foreign goods, makes vacationing abroad more expensive, and raises the cost of indulging your desire for imported delicacies. When the value of the dollar drops, Americans decrease their purchases of foreign goods and increase their consumption of domestic goods (such as travel in the United States or American-made wine).

Conversely, a strong dollar means that U.S. goods exported abroad will cost more in foreign countries, and hence foreigners will buy fewer of them. Exports of steel, for example, declined sharply when the dollar strengthened in the 1980–1985 and 1995–2001 periods. A strong dollar benefited American consumers by making foreign goods cheaper but hurt American businesses and eliminated some jobs by cutting both domestic and foreign sales of their products. The decline in the value of the dollar from 1985 to 1995 and 2001 to 2011 had the opposite effect: It made foreign goods more expensive but made American businesses more competitive. Fluctuations in the foreign exchange markets have major consequences for the American economy.

In Chapter 20 we study how exchange rates are determined in the foreign exchange market, in which dollars are bought and sold for foreign currencies.

The International Financial System

The tremendous increase in capital flows among countries heightens the international financial system's impact on domestic economies. Issues we will explore in Chapter 21 include:

- How does a country's decision to fix its exchange rate to that of another nation shape the conduct of monetary policy?
- What is the impact of capital controls that restrict mobility of capital across national borders on domestic financial systems and the performance of the economy?
- What role should international financial institutions such as the International Monetary Fund play in the international financial system?

HOW WE WILL STUDY MONEY, BANKING, AND FINANCIAL MARKETS

This textbook stresses the economic way of thinking by developing a unifying framework to study money, banking, and financial markets. This analytic framework uses a few basic economic concepts to organize your thinking about the determination of asset prices, the structure of financial markets, bank management, and the role of money in the economy. It encompasses the following basic concepts:

- A simplified approach to the demand for assets
- The concept of equilibrium
- Basic supply and demand to explain behavior in financial markets
- The search for profits
- An approach to financial structure based on transaction costs and asymmetric information
- Aggregate supply and demand analysis

The unifying framework used in this book will keep your knowledge from becoming obsolete and make the material more interesting. It will enable you to learn what *really* matters without having to memorize a mass of dull facts that you will forget soon after the final exam. This framework will also provide you with the tools you need to understand trends in the financial marketplace and in variables such as interest rates, exchange rates, inflation, and aggregate output.

To help you understand and apply the unifying analytic framework, simple models are constructed in which the variables held constant are carefully delineated, each step in the derivation of the model is clearly and carefully laid out, and the models are then used to explain various phenomena by focusing on changes in one variable at a time, holding all other variables constant.

To reinforce the models' usefulness, this text uses case studies, applications, and special-interest boxes to present evidence that supports or casts doubts on the theories being discussed. This exposure to real-life events and empirical data should dissuade you from thinking that all economists make abstract assumptions and develop theories that have little to do with actual behavior.

To function better in the real world outside the classroom, you must have the tools to follow the financial news that appears in leading financial publications and on the Web. To help and encourage you to read the financial news, this book contains a set of special boxed inserts, titled Following the Financial News, that provide detailed information and definitions to help you evaluate data that are discussed frequently in the media. This book also contains over 500 end-of-chapter problems that ask you to apply the analytic concepts you have learned to other real-world issues.

Exploring the Web

The World Wide Web has become an extremely valuable and convenient resource for financial research. We emphasize the importance of this tool in several ways. First, wherever we utilize the Web to find information to build the charts and tables that appear throughout the text, we include the source site's URL. These sites often contain additional information and are updated frequently. Second, we have added Web exercises to the end of each chapter. These exercises prompt you to visit sites related to the chapter and to work with real-time data and information. We also have supplied Web references to the end of each chapter; these list the URLs of sites related to the material being discussed. Visit these sites to further explore a topic you find of particular interest. Website URLs are subject to frequent change. We have tried to select stable sites, but we realize that even government URLs change. The publisher's website (www.myeconlab.com) will maintain an updated list of current URLs for your reference.

Collecting and Graphing Data

The following Web exercise is especially important because it demonstrates how to export data from a website into Microsoft® Excel for further analysis. We suggest you work through this problem on your own so that you will be able to perform this activity when prompted in subsequent Web exercises.

WEB EXERCISES

You have been hired by Risky Ventures, Inc., as a consultant to help the company analyze interest-rate trends. Your employers are initially interested in determining the historical relationship between long- and short-term interest rates. The biggest task you must immediately undertake is collecting market interest-rate data. You know the best source of this information is the Web.

1. You decide that your best indicator of long-term interest rates is the ten-year U.S. Treasury note. Your first task is to gather historical data. Go to www.federalreserve.gov/releases/H15. The site should look like Figure 9. At the top, click on Historical data. Now scroll down to Treasury constant maturities and click on the Annual tag to the right of the 10-year category.
2. Now that you have located an accurate source of historical interest-rate data, the next step is getting it onto a spreadsheet. The Federal Reserve data will open and download into Excel, however, it will not be formatted to let you manipulate the data. To convert the data into a format you can easily use, select and copy the data you want, open a new sheet and click past/past special/values and number format. Repaste the converted series on top of the old data (see Figure 10).

   Repeat the preceding steps to collect the one-year interest rate series. Put it in the column next to the ten-year series. Be sure to line up the years correctly and delete any years that are not included in both series and label your columns.

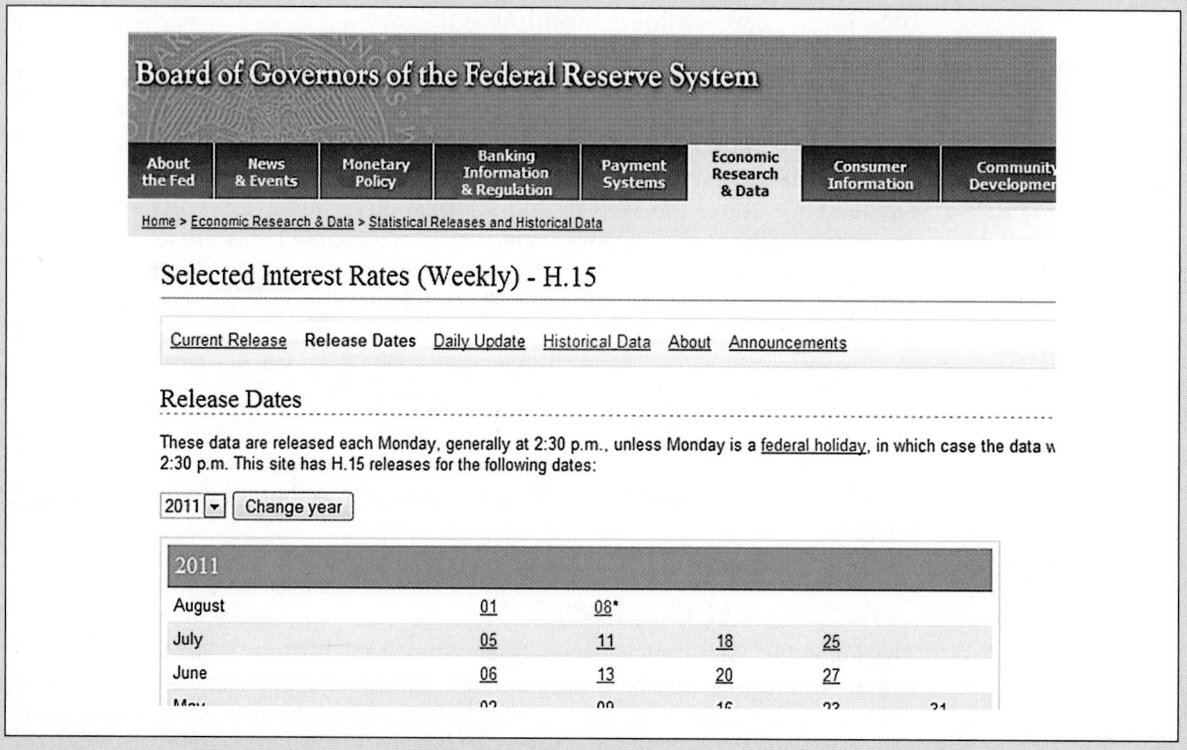

FIGURE 9 Federal Reserve Board Website

The Federal Reserve provides interest rate data on this website.

Source: www.federalreserve.gov/releases/H15.

3. You now want to analyze the interest rates by graphing them. Again highlight the two columns of data you just created in Excel along with the year. Click on the charts icon on the toolbar (or INSERT/CHART). Select scatter diagram and choose any type of scatter diagram that connects the dots. Let the Excel wizard take you through the steps of completing the graph (see Figure 11).

CONCLUDING REMARKS

The topic of money, banking, and financial markets is an exciting field that directly affects your life—interest rates influence earnings on your savings and the payments on loans you may seek on a car or a house, and monetary policy may affect your job prospects and the prices of goods in the future. Your study of money, banking, and financial markets will introduce you to many of the controversies about the conduct of economic policy that are hotly debated in the political arena and will help you gain a clearer understanding of economic phenomena you hear about in the news media. The knowledge gained will stay with you and benefit you long after the course is over.

FIGURE 10
Excel Spreadsheet with Interest-Rate Data
This spreadsheet contains the interest rate data downloaded from the Federal Reserve website.

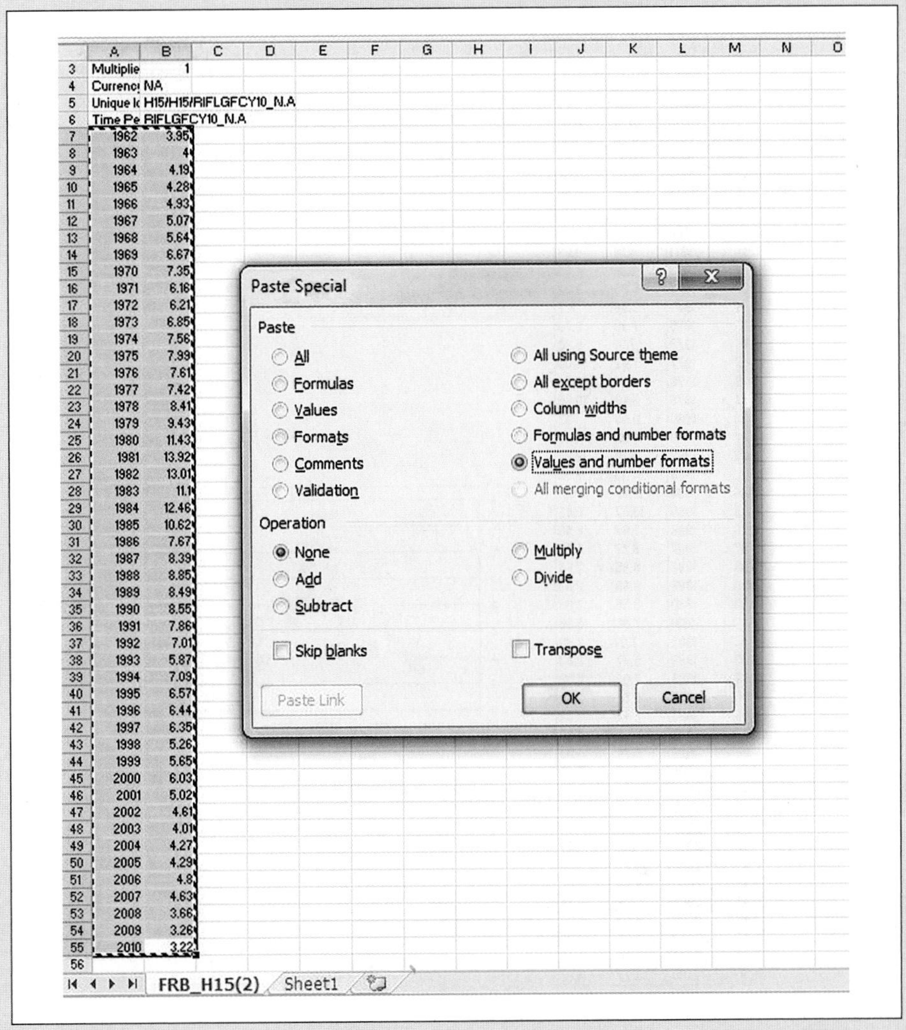

Summary

1. Activities in financial markets have direct effects on individuals' wealth, the behavior of businesses, and the efficiency of our economy. Three financial markets deserve particular attention: the bond market (where interest rates are determined), the stock market (which has a major effect on people's wealth and on firms' investment decisions), and the foreign exchange market (because fluctuations in the foreign exchange rate have major consequences for the U.S. economy).
2. Banks and other financial institutions channel funds from people who might not put them to productive use to people who can do so and thus play a crucial role in improving the efficiency of the economy. When the financial system seizes up and produces a financial crisis, financial firms fail, which causes severe damage to the economy.
3. Money and monetary policy appear to be major influences on inflation, business cycles, and interest rates. Because these economic variables are so important to the health of the economy, we need to understand how monetary policy is and should be conducted. We also need to study government fiscal policy because

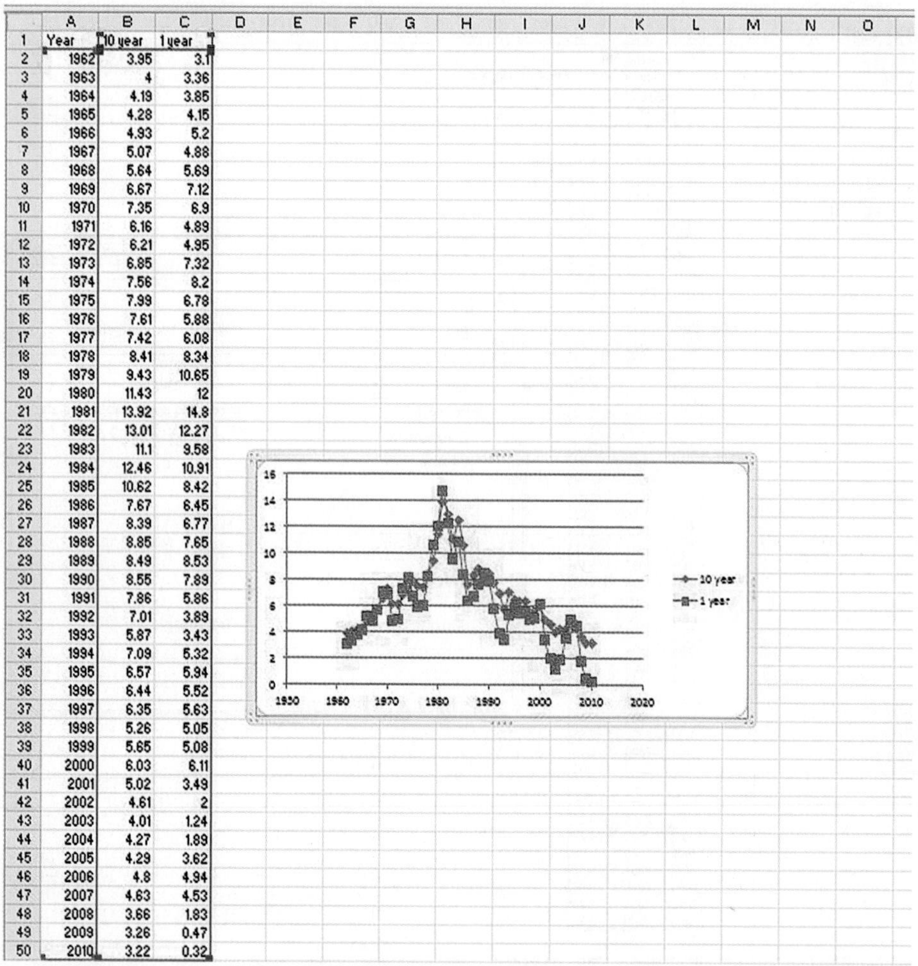

	A	B	C
1	Year	10 year	1 year
2	1962	3.95	3.1
3	1963	4	3.36
4	1964	4.19	3.85
5	1965	4.28	4.15
6	1966	4.93	5.2
7	1967	5.07	4.88
8	1968	5.64	5.69
9	1969	6.67	7.12
10	1970	7.35	6.9
11	1971	6.16	4.89
12	1972	6.21	4.95
13	1973	6.85	7.32
14	1974	7.56	8.2
15	1975	7.99	6.78
16	1976	7.61	5.88
17	1977	7.42	6.08
18	1978	8.41	8.34
19	1979	9.43	10.65
20	1980	11.43	12
21	1981	13.92	14.8
22	1982	13.01	12.27
23	1983	11.1	9.58
24	1984	12.46	10.91
25	1985	10.62	8.42
26	1986	7.67	6.45
27	1987	8.39	6.77
28	1988	8.85	7.65
29	1989	8.49	8.53
30	1990	8.55	7.89
31	1991	7.86	5.86
32	1992	7.01	3.89
33	1993	5.87	3.43
34	1994	7.09	5.32
35	1995	6.57	5.94
36	1996	6.44	5.52
37	1997	6.35	5.63
38	1998	5.26	5.05
39	1999	5.65	5.08
40	2000	6.03	6.11
41	2001	5.02	3.49
42	2002	4.61	2
43	2003	4.01	1.24
44	2004	4.27	1.89
45	2005	4.29	3.62
46	2006	4.8	4.94
47	2007	4.63	4.53
48	2008	3.66	1.83
49	2009	3.26	0.47
50	2010	3.22	0.32

FIGURE 11 Excel Graph of Interest-Rate Data
This spreadsheet shows the graph of the interest rate data.

it can be an influential factor in the conduct of monetary policy.

4. This textbook stresses the economic way of thinking by developing a unifying analytic framework for the study of money, banking, and financial markets, using a few basic economic principles. This textbook also emphasizes the interaction of theoretical analysis and empirical data.

Key Terms

aggregate income, p. 22
aggregate output, p. 7
aggregate price level, p. 8
asset, p. 2
banks, p. 6
bond, p. 2
budget deficit, p. 11
budget surplus, p. 11
business cycles, p. 7

central bank, p. 10
common stock, p. 4
e-finance, p. 6
Federal Reserve System (the Fed), p. 10
financial crises, p. 6
financial innovation, p. 6
financial intermediaries, p. 5
financial markets, p. 2
fiscal policy, p. 11
foreign exchange market, p. 12
foreign exchange rate, p. 12
gross domestic product, p. 11
inflation, p. 8
inflation rate, p. 8
interest rate, p. 3
monetary policy, p. 10
monetary theory, p. 7
money (money supply), p. 7
recession, p. 7
security, p. 2
stock, p. 4
unemployment rate, p. 7

Questions

All questions are available in MyEconLab *at* www.myeconlab.com.

1. What is the typical relationship between interest rates on three-month Treasury bills, long-term Treasury bonds, and Baa corporate bonds?

2. What effect might a fall in stock prices have on business investment?

3. What effect might a rise in stock prices have on consumers' decisions to spend?

4. Why are financial markets important to the health of the economy?

5. What was the main cause of the recession that began in 2007?

6. What is the basic activity of banks?

7. What are the other important financial intermediaries in the economy besides banks?

8. Can you think of any financial innovation in the past ten years that has affected you personally? Has it made you better off or worse off? Why?

9. Has the inflation rate in the United States increased or decreased in the past few years? What about interest rates?

10. If history repeats itself and we see a decline in the rate of money growth, what might you expect to happen to

a. real output?

b. the inflation rate?

c. interest rates?

11. When interest rates decrease, how might businesses and consumers change their economic behavior?

12. Is everybody worse off when interest rates rise?

13. Why do managers of financial institutions care so much about the activities of the Federal Reserve System?

14. How does the current size of the U.S. budget deficit compare to the time period since 1950?

15. How does a fall in the value of the pound sterling affect British consumers?

16. How does an increase in the value of the pound sterling affect American businesses?

17. How can changes in foreign exchange rates affect the profitability of financial institutions?

18. According to Figure 8, in which years would you have chosen to visit the Grand Canyon in Arizona rather than the Tower of London?

19. When the dollar is worth more in relation to currencies of other countries, are you more likely to buy American-made or foreign-made jeans? Are U.S. companies that manufacture jeans happier when the dollar is strong or when it is weak? What about an American company that is in the business of importing jeans into the United States?

20. Much of the U.S. government debt is held as treasury bonds and bills by foreign investors. How do fluctuations in the dollar exchange rate affect the value of that debt held by foreigners?

Applied Problems

All applied problems are available in MyEconLab *at* www.myeconlab.com.

21. The following table lists foreign exchange rates between U.S. dollars and British pounds (GBP) during April. Which day would have been the best to convert $200 into British pounds? Which day would have been the worst? What would be the difference in pounds?

Date	U.S. Dollars per GBP
4/1	1.9564
4/4	1.9293
4/5	1.914
4/6	1.9374
4/7	1.961
4/8	1.8925
4/11	1.8822
4/12	1.8558
4/13	1.796
4/14	1.7902
4/15	1.7785
4/18	1.7504
4/19	1.7255
4/20	1.6914
4/21	1.672
4/22	1.6684
4/25	1.6674
4/26	1.6857
4/27	1.6925
4/28	1.7201
4/29	1.7512

Web Exercises

1. In this exercise we will practice collecting data from the Web and graphing it using Excel. Use the example on pages 15–18 as a guide. Go to www.forecasts.org/data/index.htm, click on Stock Index Data at the top of the page, then choose the U.S. Stock Indices—Monthly option. Finally, choose the Dow Jones Industrial Average option.

a. Using the method presented in this chapter, move the data into an Excel spreadsheet.

b. Using the data from part a, prepare a graph. Use the graphing wizard to properly label your axes.

2. In Web Exercise 1 you collected and graphed the Dow Jones Industrial Average (DJIA). This same site reports forecast values of the DJIA. Go to www.forecasts.org/data/index.htm and click on FFC Home at the top of the page. Click on the Dow Jones Industrial link under Forecasts in the far left column.

a. What is the Dow forecast to be in six months?

b. What percentage increase is forecast for the next six months?

Web References

www.federalreserve.gov/releases/

Daily, weekly, monthly, quarterly, and annual releases and historical data for selected interest rates, foreign exchange rates, and so on.

http://stockcharts.com/charts/historical/

Historical charts of various stock indexes over differing time periods.

www.federalreserve.gov

General information, monetary policy, banking system, research, and economic data of the Federal Reserve.

www.bls.gov/data/inflation_calculator.htm

Calculator lets you compute how the dollar's buying power has changed since 1913.

www.kowaldesign.com/budget/

This site reports the current federal budget deficit or surplus and how it has changed since the 1950s. It also reports how the federal budget is spent.

www.brillig.com/debt_clock/

National debt clock. This site reports the exact national debt at each point in time.

APPENDIX TO CHAPTER 1

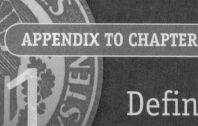

Defining Aggregate Output, Income, the Price Level, and the Inflation Rate

Because these terms are used so frequently throughout the text, we need to have a clear understanding of the definitions of *aggregate output*, *income*, the *price level*, and the *inflation rate*.

AGGREGATE OUTPUT AND INCOME

The most commonly reported measure of aggregate output, the **gross domestic product (GDP)**, is the market value of all final goods and services produced in a country during the course of the year. This measure excludes two sets of items that at first glance you might think it would include. Purchases of goods that have been produced in the past, whether a Rembrandt painting or a house built twenty years ago, are not counted as part of GDP; nor are purchases of stocks or bonds. None of these enters into GDP because they are not goods and services produced during the course of the year. Intermediate goods, which are used up in producing final goods and services, such as the sugar in a candy bar or the energy used to produce steel, are also not counted separately as part of GDP. Because the value of the final goods already includes the value of the intermediate goods, to count them separately would be to count them twice.

Aggregate income, the total income of *factors of production* (land, labor, and capital) from producing goods and services in the economy during the course of the year, is best thought of as being equal to aggregate output. Because the payments for final goods and services must eventually flow back to the owners of the factors of production as income, income payments must equal payments for final goods and services. For example, if the economy has an aggregate output of $10 trillion, total income payments in the economy (aggregate income) are also $10 trillion.

REAL VERSUS NOMINAL MAGNITUDES

When the total value of final goods and services is calculated using current prices, the resulting GDP measure is referred to as *nominal GDP*. The word *nominal* indicates that values are measured using current prices. If all prices doubled but actual production of goods and services remained the same, nominal GDP would double even though people would not enjoy the benefits of twice as many goods and services. As a result, nominal variables can be misleading measures of economic well-being.

A more reliable measure of economic production expresses values in terms of prices for an arbitrary base year, currently 2005. GDP measured with constant prices is referred to as *real GDP*, the word *real* indicating that values are measured in terms of fixed prices. Real variables thus measure the quantities of goods and services and do not change because prices have changed, but rather only if actual quantities have changed.

A brief example will make the distinction clearer. Suppose that you have a nominal income of $30,000 in 2013 and that your nominal income was $15,000 in 2005. If all prices doubled between 2005 and 2013, are you better off? The answer is no: Although your income has doubled, your $30,000 buys you only the same amount of goods because prices have also doubled. A real income measure indicates that your income in terms of the goods it can buy is the same. Measured in 2005 prices, the $30,000 of nominal income in 2013 turns out to be only $15,000 of real income. Because your real income is actually the same in the two years, you are no better or worse off in 2013 than you were in 2005.

Because real variables measure quantities in terms of real goods and services, they are typically of more interest than nominal variables. In this text, discussion of aggregate output or aggregate income always refers to real measures (such as real GDP).

AGGREGATE PRICE LEVEL

In this chapter, we defined the aggregate price level as a measure of average prices in the economy. Three measures of the aggregate price level are commonly encountered in economic data. The first is the *GDP deflator*, which is defined as nominal GDP divided by real GDP. Thus, if 2013 nominal GDP is $10 trillion but 2013 real GDP in 2005 prices is $9 trillion,

$$\text{GDP deflator} = \frac{\$10 \text{ trillion}}{\$9 \text{ trillion}} = 1.11$$

The GDP deflator equation indicates that, on average, prices have risen 11% since 2005. Typically, measures of the price level are presented in the form of a price index, which expresses the price level for the base year (in our example, 2005) as 100. Thus the GDP deflator for 2013 would be 111.

Another popular measure of the aggregate price level (which officials in the Fed frequently focus on) is the *PCE deflator*, which is similar to the GDP deflator and is defined as nominal personal consumption expenditures (PCE) divided by real PCE.

The measure of the aggregate price level that is most frequently reported in the press is the *consumer price index (CPI)*. The CPI is measured by pricing a "basket" of goods and services bought by a typical urban household. If, over the course of the year, the cost of this basket of goods and services rises from $500 to $600, the CPI has risen by 20%. The CPI is also expressed as a price index with the base year equal to 100.

The CPI, the PCE deflator, and the GDP deflator measures of the price level can be used to convert or deflate a nominal magnitude into a real magnitude. This is accomplished by dividing the nominal magnitude by the price index. In our example, in which the GDP deflator for 2013 is 1.11 (expressed as an index value of 111), real GDP for 2013 equals

$$\frac{\$10 \text{ trillion}}{1.11} = \$9 \text{ trillion in 2005 prices}$$

which corresponds to the real GDP figure for 2013 assumed earlier.

GROWTH RATES AND THE INFLATION RATE

The media often talk about the economy's growth rate, and particularly the growth rate of real GDP. A growth rate is defined as the percentage change in a variable, i.e.,

$$\text{growth rate of } x = \frac{x_t - x_{t-1}}{x_{t-1}} \times 100$$

where t indicates today and $t - 1$ a year earlier.

For example, if real GDP grew from \$9 trillion in 2013 to \$9.5 trillion in 2014, then the GDP growth rate for 2014 would be 5.6%:

$$\text{GDP growth rate} = \frac{\$9.5 \text{ trillion} - \$9 \text{ trillion}}{\$9 \text{ trillion}} \times 100 = 5.6\%$$

The inflation rate is defined as the growth rate of the aggregate price level. Thus, if the GDP deflator rose from 111 in 2013 to 113 in 2014, the inflation rate using the GDP deflator would be 1.8%:

$$\text{inflation rate} = \frac{113 - 111}{111} \times 100 = 1.8\%$$

If the growth rate is for a period less than one year, it is usually reported on an annualized basis; that is, it is converted to the growth rate over a year's time, assuming that the growth rate remains constant. For GDP, which is reported quarterly, the annualized growth rate would be approximately four times the percentage change in GDP from the previous quarter. For example, if GDP rose $\frac{1}{2}$% from the first quarter of 2013 to the second quarter of 2013, then the annualized GDP growth rate for the second quarter of 2013 would be reported as 2%($= 4 \times \frac{1}{2}$%). (A more accurate calculation would be 2.02%, because a precise quarterly growth rate should be compounded on a quarterly basis.)

2 An Overview of the Financial System

Preview

Inez the Inventor has designed a low-cost robot that cleans house (even does windows), washes the car, and mows the lawn, but she has no funds to put her wonderful invention into production. Walter the Widower has plenty of savings, which he and his wife accumulated over the years. If Inez and Walter could get together so that Walter could provide funds to Inez, Inez's robot would see the light of day, and the economy would be better off: We would have cleaner houses, shinier cars, and more beautiful lawns.

Financial markets (bond and stock markets) and financial intermediaries (such as banks, insurance companies, and pension funds) have the basic function of getting people like Inez and Walter together so that funds can move from those who have a surplus of funds (Walter) to those who have a shortage of funds (Inez). More realistically, when Apple invents a better iPod, it may need funds to bring its new product to market. Similarly, when a local government needs to build a road or a school, it may require more funds than local property taxes provide. Well-functioning financial markets and financial intermediaries are crucial to economic health.

To study the effects of financial markets and financial intermediaries on the economy, we need to acquire an understanding of their general structure and operation. In this chapter, we learn about the major financial intermediaries and the instruments that are traded in financial markets, as well as how these markets are regulated.

This chapter presents an overview of the fascinating study of financial markets and institutions. We return to a more detailed treatment of the regulation, structure, and evolution of the financial system in Chapters 8 through 12.

FUNCTION OF FINANCIAL MARKETS

Financial markets perform the essential economic function of channeling funds from households, firms, and governments that have saved surplus funds by spending less than their income to those that have a shortage of funds because they wish to spend more than their income. This function is shown schematically in Figure 1. Those who have saved and are lending funds, the lender-savers, are at the left, and those who must borrow funds to finance their spending, the borrower-spenders, are at the right. The principal lender-savers are households, but business enterprises and the government (particularly state and local government), as well as foreigners and their governments, sometimes also find themselves with excess funds and so lend them out. The most important borrower-spenders are businesses and the government (particularly the federal government), but households and foreigners also borrow to finance their purchases of cars, furniture, and houses. The arrows show that funds flow from lender-savers to borrower-spenders via two routes.

In *direct finance* (the route at the bottom of Figure 1), borrowers borrow funds directly from lenders in financial markets by selling them *securities* (also called *financial instruments*), which are claims on the borrower's future income or assets. Securities are assets for the person who buys them but **liabilities** (IOUs or debts) for the individual or firm that sells (issues) them. For example, if Ford needs to borrow funds to pay for a new factory to manufacture electric cars, it might borrow the funds from savers by selling them a *bond*, a debt security, that promises to make payments periodically for a specified period of time, or a *stock*, a security that entitles the owner to a share of the company's profits and assets.

Why is this channeling of funds from savers to spenders so important to the economy? The answer is that the people who save are frequently not the same people who have profitable investment opportunities available to them, the entrepreneurs. Let's first think about this on a personal level. Suppose that you have saved $1,000 this year, but no borrowing or lending is possible because no financial markets are available. If you do not have an investment opportunity that will permit you to earn income with your savings, you will just hold on to the $1,000 and will earn no interest. However, Carl the Carpenter has a productive use for your $1,000: He can use it to purchase a new

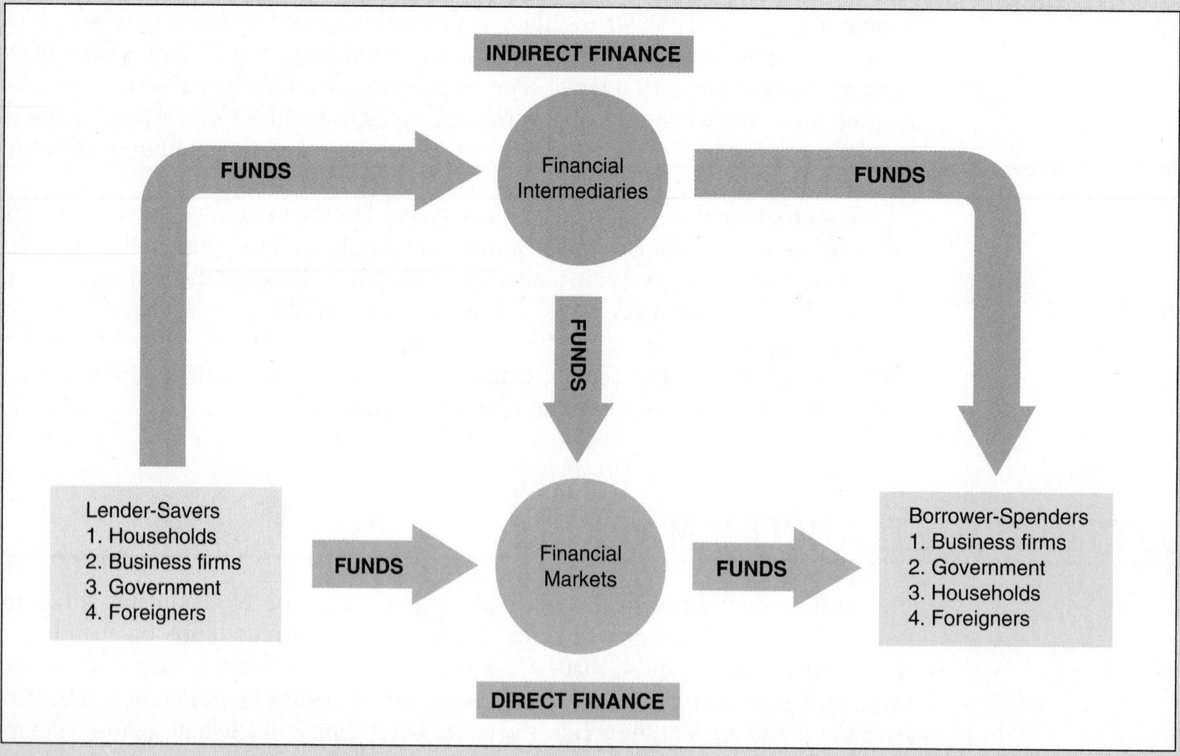

FIGURE 1 Flows of Funds Through the Financial System

The arrows show that funds flow from lender-savers to borrower-spenders via two routes: *direct finance*, in which borrowers borrow funds directly from financial markets by selling securities, and *indirect finance*, in which a financial intermediary borrows funds from lender-savers and then uses these funds to make loans to borrower-spenders.

tool that will shorten the time it takes him to build a house, thereby earning an extra \$200 per year. If you could get in touch with Carl, you could lend him the \$1,000 at a rental fee (interest) of \$100 per year, and both of you would be better off. You would earn \$100 per year on your \$1,000, instead of the zero amount that you would earn otherwise, while Carl would earn \$100 more income per year (the \$200 extra earnings per year minus the \$100 rental fee for the use of the funds).

In the absence of financial markets, you and Carl the Carpenter might never get together. You would both be stuck with the status quo, and both of you would be worse off. Without financial markets, it is hard to transfer funds from a person who has no investment opportunities to one who has them. Financial markets are thus essential to promoting economic efficiency.

The existence of financial markets is beneficial even if someone borrows for a purpose other than increasing production in a business. Say that you are recently married, have a good job, and want to buy a house. You earn a good salary, but because you have just started to work, you have not saved much. Over time, you would have no problem saving enough to buy the house of your dreams, but by then you would be too old to get full enjoyment from it. Without financial markets, you are stuck; you cannot buy the house and must continue to live in your tiny apartment.

If a financial market were set up so that people who had built up savings could lend you the funds to buy the house, you would be more than happy to pay them some interest so that you could own a home while you are still young enough to enjoy it. Then, over time, you would pay back your loan. If this loan could occur, you would be better off, as would the persons who made you the loan. They would now earn some interest, whereas they would not if the financial market did not exist.

Now we can see why financial markets have such an important function in the economy. They allow funds to move from people who lack productive investment opportunities to people who have such opportunities. Financial markets are critical for producing an efficient allocation of **capital** (wealth, either financial or physical, that is employed to produce more wealth), which contributes to higher production and efficiency for the overall economy. Indeed, as we will explore in Chapter 9, when financial markets break down during financial crises, as they did during the recent global financial crisis, severe economic hardship results, which can even lead to dangerous political instability.

Well-functioning financial markets also directly improve the well-being of consumers by allowing them to time their purchases better. They provide funds to young people to buy what they need and can eventually afford without forcing them to wait until they have saved up the entire purchase price. Financial markets that are operating efficiently improve the economic welfare of everyone in the society.

STRUCTURE OF FINANCIAL MARKETS

Now that we understand the basic function of financial markets, let's look at their structure. The following descriptions of several categorizations of financial markets illustrate essential features of these markets.

Debt and Equity Markets

A firm or an individual can obtain funds in a financial market in two ways. The most common method is to issue a debt instrument, such as a bond or a mortgage, which is a contractual agreement by the borrower to pay the holder of the instrument fixed dollar amounts at regular intervals (interest and principal payments) until a specified date (the maturity date), when a final payment is made. The **maturity** of a debt instrument is the number of years (term) until that instrument's expiration date. A debt instrument is **short-term** if its maturity is less than a year and **long-term** if its maturity is ten years or longer. Debt instruments with a maturity between one and ten years are said to be **intermediate-term**.

The second method of raising funds is by issuing **equities**, such as common stock, which are claims to share in the net income (income after expenses and taxes) and the assets of a business. If you own one share of common stock in a company that has issued one million shares, you are entitled to 1 one-millionth of the firm's net income and 1 one-millionth of the firm's assets. Equities often make periodic payments (**dividends**) to their holders and are considered long-term securities because they have no maturity date. In addition, owning stock means that you own a portion of the firm and thus have the right to vote on issues important to the firm and to elect its directors.

The main disadvantage of owning a corporation's equities rather than its debt is that an equity holder is a *residual claimant*; that is, the corporation must pay all its debt holders before it pays its equity holders. The advantage of holding equities is that equity holders benefit directly from any increases in the corporation's profitability or asset value because equities confer ownership rights on the equity holders. Debt holders do not share in this benefit, because their dollar payments are fixed. We examine the pros and cons of debt versus equity instruments in more detail in Chapter 8, which provides an economic analysis of financial structure.

The total value of equities in the United States has typically fluctuated between \$4 and \$20 trillion since the early 1990s, depending on the prices of shares. Although the average person is more aware of the stock market than any other financial market, the size of the debt market is often substantially larger than the size of the equities market: The value of debt instruments was \$43 trillion at the end of 2010, while the value of equities was \$17.2 trillion at the end of 2010.

Primary and Secondary Markets

A **primary market** is a financial market in which new issues of a security, such as a bond or a stock, are sold to initial buyers by the corporation or government agency borrowing the funds. A **secondary market** is a financial market in which securities that have been previously issued can be resold.

The primary markets for securities are not well known to the public because the selling of securities to initial buyers often takes place behind closed doors. An important financial institution that assists in the initial sale of securities in the primary market is the **investment bank**. It does this by **underwriting** securities: It guarantees a price for a corporation's securities and then sells them to the public.

The New York Stock Exchange and NASDAQ (National Association of Securities Dealers Automated Quotation System), in which previously issued stocks are traded, are the best-known examples of secondary markets, although the bond markets, in which previously issued bonds of major corporations and the U.S. government are bought and sold, actually have a larger trading volume. Other examples of secondary markets are foreign exchange markets, futures markets, and options markets. Securities brokers and dealers are crucial to a well-functioning secondary market. **Brokers** are agents of investors who match buyers with sellers of securities; **dealers** link buyers and sellers by buying and selling securities at stated prices.

When an individual buys a security in the secondary market, the person who has sold the security receives money in exchange for the security, but the corporation that issued the security acquires no new funds. A corporation acquires new funds only when its securities are first sold in the primary market. Nonetheless, secondary markets serve two important functions. First, they make it easier and quicker to sell these financial instruments to raise cash; that is, they make the financial instruments more **liquid**. The increased liquidity of these instruments then makes them more desirable and thus easier for the issuing firm to sell in the primary market. Second, they determine the price of the security that the issuing firm sells in the primary market. The investors who buy securities in the primary market will pay the issuing corporation no more than the price they think the secondary market will set for this security. The higher the security's price in the secondary market, the higher the price that the issuing firm will receive for a new security in the primary market, and hence the greater the amount of financial capital it can raise. Conditions in the secondary market are therefore the most relevant to corporations issuing securities. For this reason, books like this one, which deal with financial markets, focus on the behavior of secondary markets rather than primary markets.

Exchanges and Over-the-Counter Markets

Secondary markets can be organized in two ways. One method is to organize **exchanges**, where buyers and sellers of securities (or their agents or brokers) meet in one central location to conduct trades. The New York Stock Exchange for stocks and the Chicago Board of Trade for commodities (wheat, corn, silver, and other raw materials) are examples of organized exchanges.

The other method of organizing a secondary market is to have an **over-the-counter (OTC) market**, in which dealers at different locations who have an inventory of securities stand ready to buy and sell securities "over the counter" to anyone who comes to them and is willing to accept their prices. Because over-the-counter dealers are in contact via computers and know the prices set by one another, the OTC market is very competitive and not very different from a market with an organized exchange.

Many common stocks are traded over-the-counter, although a majority of the largest corporations have their shares traded at organized stock exchanges. The U.S. government bond market, with a larger trading volume than the New York Stock Exchange, by contrast, is set up as an over-the-counter market. Forty or so dealers establish a "market" in these securities by standing ready to buy and sell U.S. government bonds. Other over-the-counter markets include those that trade other types of financial instruments, such as negotiable certificates of deposit, federal funds, and foreign exchange.

Money and Capital Markets

Another way of distinguishing between markets is on the basis of the maturity of the securities traded in each market. The **money market** is a financial market in which only short-term debt instruments (generally those with original maturity of less than one year) are traded; the **capital market** is the market in which longer-term debt (generally those with original maturity of one year or greater) and equity instruments are traded. Money market securities are usually more widely traded than longer-term securities and so tend to be more liquid. In addition, as we will see in Chapter 4, short-term securities have smaller fluctuations in prices than long-term securities, making them safer investments. As a result, corporations and banks actively use the money market to earn interest on surplus funds that they expect to have only temporarily. Capital market securities, such as stocks and long-term bonds, are often held by financial intermediaries such as insurance companies and pension funds, which have little uncertainty about the amount of funds they will have available in the future.

FINANCIAL MARKET INSTRUMENTS

To complete our understanding of how financial markets perform the important role of channeling funds from lender-savers to borrower-spenders, we need to examine the securities (instruments) traded in financial markets. We first focus on the instruments traded in the money market and then turn to those traded in the capital market.

Money Market Instruments

Because of their short terms to maturity, the debt instruments traded in the money market undergo the least price fluctuations and so are the least risky investments. The money market has undergone great changes in the past three decades, with the amount of some financial instruments growing at a far more rapid rate than others.

The principal money market instruments are listed in Table 1 along with the amount outstanding at the end of 1980, 1990, 2000, and 2010. The Following the Financial News box discusses the money market interest rates most frequently reported in the media.

U.S. Treasury Bills These short-term debt instruments of the U.S. government are issued in one-, three-, and six-month maturities to finance the federal government. They pay a set amount at maturity and have no interest payments, but they effectively pay interest by initially selling at a discount, that is, at a price lower than the set amount paid at maturity. For instance, in May 2013 you might buy a six-month Treasury bill for $9,000 that can be redeemed in November 2013 for $10,000.

TABLE 1 Principal Money Market Instruments

	Amount Outstanding ($ billions, end of year)			
Type of Instrument	**1980**	**1990**	**2000**	**2010**
U.S. Treasury bills	216	527	647	1,773
Negotiable bank certificates of deposit (large denominations)	317	543	1,053	1,833
Commercial paper	122	557	1,619	1,057
Federal funds and security repurchase agreements	64	388	768	1,234

Source: Federal Reserve Flow of Funds Accounts; www.federalreserve.gov.

Following the Financial News Money Market Rates

The four interest rates discussed most frequently in the media are these:

Prime rate: The base interest rate on corporate bank loans, an indicator of the cost of business borrowing from banks

Federal funds rate: The interest rate charged on overnight loans in the federal funds market, a sensitive indicator of the cost to banks of borrowing funds from other banks and the stance of monetary policy

Treasury bill rate: The interest rate on U.S. Treasury bills, an indicator of general interest-rate movements

Libor rate: The British Banker's Association average of interbank rates for dollar deposits in the London market

The data for these interest rates are reported daily in newspapers and Internet sites such as www.bankrate.com.

U.S. Treasury bills are the most liquid of all money market instruments because they are the most actively traded. They are also the safest money market instrument because there is almost no possibility of **default**, a situation in which the party issuing the debt instrument (the federal government in this case) is unable to make interest payments or pay off the amount owed when the instrument matures. The federal government is always able to meet its debt obligations because it can raise taxes or issue **currency** (paper money or coins) to pay off its debts. Treasury bills are held mainly by banks, although small amounts are held by households, corporations, and other financial intermediaries.

Negotiable Bank Certificates of Deposit A *certificate of deposit (CD)* is a debt instrument sold by a bank to depositors that pays annual interest of a given amount and at maturity pays back the original purchase price. Negotiable CDs are those sold in secondary markets, with the amount outstanding currently around $1.8 trillion. Negotiable CDs are an extremely important source of funds for commercial banks, from corporations, money market mutual funds, charitable institutions, and government agencies.

Commercial Paper *Commercial paper* is a short-term debt instrument issued by large banks and well-known corporations, such as Microsoft and General Motors. Growth of the commercial paper market has been substantial: The amount of commercial paper outstanding has increased by over 1,200% (from $122 billion to $1,057 billion) in the period 1980–2010. We will discuss why the commercial paper market has had such tremendous growth in Chapter 12.

Repurchase Agreements *Repurchase agreements (repos)* are effectively short-term loans (usually with a maturity of less than two weeks) for which Treasury bills serve as *collateral,* an asset that the lender receives if the borrower does not pay back the loan. Repos are made as follows: A large corporation, such as Microsoft, may have some idle funds in its bank account, say $1 million, which it would like to lend for a week. Microsoft uses this excess $1 million to buy Treasury bills from a bank, which agrees to repurchase them the next week at a price slightly above Microsoft's purchase price. The effect of this agreement is that Microsoft makes a loan of $1 million to the bank and holds $1 million of the bank's Treasury bills until the bank repurchases the bills to pay off the loan. Repurchase agreements are now an important source of bank funds (over $430 billion). The most important lenders in this market are large corporations.

Federal (Fed) Funds These instruments are typically overnight loans between banks of their deposits at the Federal Reserve. The *federal funds* designation is somewhat confusing because these loans are not made by the federal government or by the Federal Reserve but rather by banks to other banks. One reason why a bank might borrow in the federal funds market is that it might find it does not have enough deposits at the Fed to meet the amount required by regulators. It can then borrow these deposits from another bank, which transfers them to the borrowing bank using the Fed's wire transfer system. This market is very sensitive to the credit needs of the banks, so the interest rate on these loans, called the **federal funds rate**, is a closely watched barometer of the tightness of credit market conditions in the banking system and the stance of monetary policy. When high, it indicates that banks are strapped for funds; when the rate is low, banks' credit needs are low.

Capital Market Instruments

Capital market instruments are debt and equity instruments with maturities of greater than one year. They have far wider price fluctuations than money market instruments and are considered to be fairly risky investments. The principal capital market instruments are listed in Table 2, which shows the amount outstanding at the end of 1980, 1990, 2000, and 2010. The Following the Financial News box discusses the capital market interest rates most frequently reported in the media.

TABLE 2

Principal Capital Market Instruments

	Amount Outstanding ($ billions, end of year)			
Type of Instrument	**1980**	**1990**	**2000**	**2010**
Corporate stocks (market value)	1,601	4,146	17,627	17,189
Residential mortgages	1,106	2,886	5,463	9,436
Corporate bonds	366	1,008	2,230	2,983
U.S. government securities (marketable long-term)	407	1,653	2,184	2,803
U.S. government agency securities	193	435	1,616	6,158
State and local government bonds	310	870	1,192	1,807
Bank commercial loans	459	818	1,091	1,031
Consumer loans	355	813	536	710
Commercial and farm mortgages	352	829	1,214	1,919

Source: Federal Reserve Flow of Funds Accounts; www.federalreserve.gov.

Following the Financial News **Capital Market Interest Rates**

The five interest rates on capital market instruments discussed most frequently in the media are:

30-year mortgage: the interest rate on a 30-year fixed-rate residential mortgage that is less than $417,000 ($729,500 in high-cost areas) in amount and is guaranteed by the **Federal Housing Administration (FHA)**.

Jumbo mortgages: the interest rate on a 30-year fixed-rate residential mortgage for prime customers that is in excess of $417,000 (625,000 in high cost areas) in amount.

Five-year adjustable rate mortgages (ARMs): the interest rate for the first five years on a residential mortgage that adjusts after five years for prime customers.

New-car loans: the interest rate on a four-year fixed-rate new-car loan.

10-year Treasury: the interest rate on U.S. Treasury bonds maturing in ten years.

The data for these interest rates are reported daily in newspapers and Internet sites such as www.bankrate.com and www.finance.yahoo.com.

Stocks *Stocks* are equity claims on the net income and assets of a corporation. Their value of $17 trillion at the end of 2010 exceeds that of any other type of security in the capital market. However, the amount of new stock issues in any given year is typically quite small, less than 1% of the total value of shares outstanding. Individuals hold around half of the value of stocks; the rest are held by pension funds, mutual funds, and insurance companies.

Mortgages and Mortgage-Backed Securities ***Mortgages*** are loans to households or firms to purchase land, housing, or other real structures, in which the structure or land itself serves as collateral for the loans. The mortgage market is the largest debt market in the United States, with the amount of residential mortgages (used to purchase residential housing) outstanding more than quadruple the amount of commercial and farm mortgages. Mortgages are provided by financial institutions such as savings and loan associations, mutual savings banks, commercial banks, and insurance companies. However in recent years, a growing amount of the funds for mortgages have been provided by **mortgage-backed securities**, a bond-like debt instrument backed by a bundle of individual mortgages, whose interest and principal payments are collectively paid to the holders of the security. As we will see in Chapter 9, mortgage-backed securities and more complicated variants (CDOs) have become notorious because they played a key role in promoting the recent global financial crisis. The federal government has an active part in the mortgage market via the three government agencies—the Federal National Mortgage Association (FNMA, "Fannie Mae"), the Government National Mortgage Association (GNMA, "Ginnie Mae"), and the Federal Home Loan Mortgage Corporation (FHLMC, "Freddie Mac")—that provide funds to the mortgage market by selling bonds and using the proceeds to buy mortgages.

Corporate Bonds These long-term bonds are issued by corporations with very strong credit ratings. The typical *corporate bond* sends the holder an interest payment twice a year and pays off the face value when the bond matures. Some corporate bonds, called *convertible bonds*, have the additional feature of allowing the holder to convert them into a specified number of shares of stock at any time up to the maturity date. This feature makes these convertible bonds more desirable to prospective purchasers than bonds without it and allows the corporation to reduce its interest payments because these bonds can increase in value if the price of the stock appreciates sufficiently. Because the outstanding amount of both convertible and nonconvertible bonds for any given corporation is small, they are not nearly as liquid as other securities such as U.S. government bonds.

Although the size of the corporate bond market is substantially smaller than that of the stock market, with the amount of corporate bonds outstanding less than one-fifth that of stocks, the volume of new corporate bonds issued each year is substantially greater than the volume of new stock issues. Thus the behavior of the corporate bond market is probably far more important to a firm's financing decisions than is the behavior of the stock market. The principal buyers of corporate bonds are life insurance companies; pension funds and households are other large holders.

U.S. Government Securities These long-term debt instruments are issued by the U.S. Treasury to finance the deficits of the federal government. Because they are the most widely traded bonds in the United States (the volume of transactions on average exceeds $500 billion daily), they are the most liquid security traded in the capital market. They are held by the Federal Reserve, banks, households, and foreigners.

U.S. Government Agency Securities These long-term bonds are issued by various government agencies such as Ginnie Mae, the Federal Farm Credit Bank, and the Tennessee Valley Authority to finance such items as mortgages, farm loans, or power-generating equipment. Many of these securities are guaranteed by the federal government. They function much like U.S. government bonds and are held by similar parties.

State and Local Government Bonds State and local bonds, also called *municipal bonds,* are long-term debt instruments issued by state and local governments to finance expenditures on schools, roads, and other large programs. An important feature of these bonds is that their interest payments are exempt from federal income tax and generally from state taxes in the issuing state. Commercial banks, with their high income tax rate, are the biggest buyers of these securities, owning over half the total amount outstanding. The next biggest group of holders consists of wealthy individuals in high income tax brackets, followed by insurance companies.

Consumer and Bank Commercial Loans These loans to consumers and businesses are made principally by banks but, in the case of consumer loans, also by finance companies.

INTERNATIONALIZATION OF FINANCIAL MARKETS

The growing internationalization of financial markets has become an important trend. Before the 1980s, U.S. financial markets were much larger than those outside the United States, but in recent years the dominance of U.S. markets has been disappearing. (See the Global box "Are U.S. Capital Markets Losing Their Edge?") The extraordinary growth of foreign financial markets has been the result of both large increases in the pool of savings in foreign countries such as Japan and the deregulation of foreign financial markets, which has enabled foreign markets to expand their activities. American corporations and banks are now more likely to tap international capital markets to raise needed funds, and American investors often seek investment opportunities abroad.

Global Are U.S. Capital Markets Losing Their Edge?

Over the past few decades the United States lost its international dominance in a number of manufacturing industries, including automobiles and consumer electronics, as other countries became more competitive in global markets. Recent evidence suggests that financial markets now are undergoing a similar trend: Just as Ford and General Motors have lost global market share to Toyota and Honda, U.S. stock and bond markets recently have seen their share of sales of newly issued corporate securities slip. The London and Hong Kong stock exchanges now handle a larger share of initial public offerings (IPO) of stock than does the New York Stock Exchange, which had been by far the dominant exchange in terms of IPO value before 2000. Furthermore, the number of stocks listed on U.S. exchanges has been falling, while stock listings abroad have been growing rapidly: Listings outside the United States are now about ten times greater than those in the United States. Likewise, the portion of new corporate bonds issued worldwide that are initially sold in U.S. capital markets has fallen below the share sold in European debt markets.

Why do corporations that issue new securities to raise capital now conduct more of this business in financial markets in Europe and Asia? Among the factors contributing to this trend are quicker adoption of technological innovation by foreign financial markets, tighter immigration controls in the United States following the terrorist attacks in 2001, and perceptions that listing on American exchanges will expose foreign securities issuers to greater risks of lawsuits. Many people see burdensome financial regulation as the main cause, however, and point specifically to the Sarbanes-Oxley Act of 2002. Congress passed this act after a number of accounting scandals involving U.S. corporations and the accounting firms that audited them came to light. Sarbanes-Oxley aims to strengthen the integrity of the auditing process and the quality of information provided in corporate financial statements. The costs to corporations of complying with the new rules and procedures are high, especially for smaller firms, but largely avoidable if firms choose to issue their securities in financial markets outside the United States. For this reason, there is much support for revising Sarbanes-Oxley to lessen its alleged harmful effects and induce more securities issuers back to U.S. financial markets. However, evidence is not conclusive to support the view that Sarbanes-Oxley is the main cause of the relative decline of U.S. financial markets and therefore in need of reform.

Discussion of the relative decline of U.S. financial markets and debate about the factors that are contributing to it likely will continue. Chapter 8 provides more detail on the Sarbanes-Oxley Act and its effects on the U.S. financial system.

Similarly, foreign corporations and banks raise funds from Americans, and foreigners have become important investors in the United States. A look at international bond markets and world stock markets will give us a picture of how this globalization of financial markets is taking place.

International Bond Market, Eurobonds, and Eurocurrencies

The traditional instruments in the international bond market are known as **foreign bonds**. Foreign bonds are sold in a foreign country and are denominated in that country's currency. For example, if the German automaker Porsche sells a bond in the United States denominated in U.S. dollars, it is classified as a foreign bond. Foreign bonds have been an important instrument in the international capital market for centuries. In fact, a large percentage of U.S. railroads built in the nineteenth century were financed by sales of foreign bonds in Britain.

A more recent innovation in the international bond market is the **Eurobond**, a bond denominated in a currency other than that of the country in which it is sold—for example, a bond denominated in U.S. dollars sold in London. Currently, over 80% of the new issues in the international bond market are Eurobonds, and the market for these securities has grown very rapidly. As a result, the Eurobond market is now larger than the U.S. corporate bond market.

A variant of the Eurobond is **Eurocurrencies**, which are foreign currencies deposited in banks outside the home country. The most important of the Eurocurrencies are **Eurodollars**, which are U.S. dollars deposited in foreign banks outside the United States or in foreign branches of U.S. banks. Because these short-term deposits earn interest, they are similar to short-term Eurobonds. American banks borrow Eurodollar deposits from other banks or from their own foreign branches, and Eurodollars are now an important source of funds for American banks.

Note that the currency, the euro, can create some confusion about the terms Eurobond, Eurocurrencies, and Eurodollars. A bond denominated in euros is called a Eurobond only *if it is sold outside the countries that have adopted the euro.* In fact, most Eurobonds are not denominated in euros but are instead denominated in U.S. dollars. Similarly, Eurodollars have nothing to do with euros, but are instead U.S. dollars deposited in banks outside the United States.

World Stock Markets

Until recently, the U.S. stock market was by far the largest in the world, but foreign stock markets have been growing in importance, with the United States not always number one. The increased interest in foreign stocks has prompted the development in the United States of mutual funds that specialize in trading in foreign stock markets. As the following the Financial News box indicates, American investors now pay attention not only to the Dow Jones Industrial Average but also to stock price indexes for foreign stock markets, such as the Nikkei 300 Average (Tokyo) and the Financial Times Stock Exchange (FTSE) 100-Share Index (London).

The internationalization of financial markets is having profound effects on the United States. Foreigners, particularly Japanese investors, are not only providing funds to corporations in the United States but are also helping finance the federal government. Without these foreign funds, the U.S. economy would have grown far less rapidly in the past twenty years. The internationalization of financial markets is also leading the way to a more integrated world economy in which flows of goods and technology between countries are more commonplace. In later chapters, we will encounter many examples of the important roles that international factors play in our economy.

FUNCTION OF FINANCIAL INTERMEDIARIES: INDIRECT FINANCE

As shown in Figure 1 (p. 26), funds can move from lenders to borrowers by a second route, called *indirect finance* because it involves a financial intermediary that stands between the lender-savers and the borrower-spenders and helps transfer funds from one to the other. A financial intermediary does this by borrowing funds from the lender-savers and then using these funds to make loans to borrower-spenders. For example, a bank might acquire funds by issuing a liability to the public (an asset for the public) in the form of savings deposits. It might then use the funds to acquire an asset by making a loan to General Motors or by buying a U.S. Treasury bond in the financial market. The ultimate result is that funds have

Following the Financial News — Foreign Stock Market Indexes

Foreign Stock market indexes are published daily in newspapers and Internet sites such as finance.yahoo.com.

The most important of these stock market indices are:

Dow Jones Industrial Average (DJIA): An index of the 30 largest publicly traded corporations in the United States maintained by the Dow Jones Corporation.

S&P 500: An index of 500 of the largest companies traded in the United States maintained by the Standard & Poor's.

Nasdaq Composite: An index for all the stocks that trade on the Nasdaq stock market, where most of the technology stocks in the United States are traded.

FTSE 100: An index the 100 most highly *capitalized* UK companies listed on the London Stock Exchange.

DAX: An index of the 30 largest German companies trading on the Frankfurt Stock Exchange.

CAC 40: An index of the largest 40 French companies traded on Euronext Paris.

Hang Seng: An index of the largest companies traded on the Hong Kong stock markets.

Strait Times: An index of the largest 30 companies traded on the Singapore Exchange.

These indexes are reported daily in newspapers and Internet sites such as www.finance.yahoo.com.

been transferred from the public (the lender-savers) to General Motors or the U.S. Treasury (the borrower-spender) with the help of the financial intermediary (the bank).

The process of indirect finance using financial intermediaries, called **financial intermediation**, is the primary route for moving funds from lenders to borrowers. Indeed, although the media focus much of their attention on securities markets, particularly the stock market, financial intermediaries are a far more important source of financing for corporations than securities markets are. This is true not only for the United States but for other industrialized countries as well (see the Global box). Why are financial intermediaries and indirect finance so important in financial markets? To answer this question, we need to understand the role of transaction costs, risk sharing, and information costs in financial markets.

Transaction Costs

Transaction costs, the time and money spent in carrying out financial transactions, are a major problem for people who have excess funds to lend. As we have seen, Carl the Carpenter needs $1,000 for his new tool, and you know that it is an excellent investment opportunity. You have the cash and would like to lend him the money, but to protect your investment, you have to hire a lawyer to write up the loan contract that specifies how much interest Carl will pay you, when he will make these interest payments, and when he will repay you the $1,000. Obtaining the contract will cost you $500. When you figure in this transaction cost for making the loan, you realize that you can't earn enough from the deal (you spend $500 to make perhaps $100) and reluctantly tell Carl that he will have to look elsewhere.

This example illustrates that small savers like you or potential borrowers like Carl might be frozen out of financial markets and thus be unable to benefit from them. Can anyone come to the rescue? Financial intermediaries can.

Global The Importance of Financial Intermediaries Relative to Securities Markets: An International Comparison

Patterns of financing corporations differ across countries, but one key fact emerges: Studies of the major developed countries, including the United States, Canada, the United Kingdom, Japan, Italy, Germany, and France, show that when businesses go looking for funds to finance their activities, they usually obtain them indirectly through financial intermediaries and not directly from securities markets.* Even in the United States and Canada, which have the most developed securities markets in the world, loans from financial intermediaries are far more important for corporate finance than securities markets are. The countries that have made the least use of securities markets are Germany and Japan; in these two countries, financing from financial intermediaries has been almost ten times greater than that from securities markets. However, after the deregulation of Japanese securities markets in recent years, the share of corporate financing by financial intermediaries has been declining relative to the use of securities markets.

Although the dominance of financial intermediaries over securities markets is clear in all countries, the relative importance of bond versus stock markets differs widely across countries. In the United States, the bond market is far more important as a source of corporate finance: On average, the amount of new financing raised using bonds is ten times the amount raised using stocks. By contrast, countries such as France and Italy make more use of equities markets than of the bond market to raise capital.

*See, for example, Colin Mayer, "Financial Systems, Corporate Finance, and Economic Development," in *Asymmetric Information, Corporate Finance, and Investment*, ed. R. Glenn Hubbard (Chicago: University of Chicago Press, 1990), pp. 307–332.

Financial intermediaries can substantially reduce transaction costs because they have developed expertise in lowering them and because their large size allows them to take advantage of **economies of scale**, the reduction in transaction costs per dollar of transactions as the size (scale) of transactions increases. For example, a bank knows how to find a good lawyer to produce an airtight loan contract, and this contract can be used over and over again in its loan transactions, thus lowering the legal cost per transaction. Instead of a loan contract (which may not be all that well written) costing \$500, a bank can hire a topflight lawyer for \$5,000 to draw up an airtight loan contract that can be used for 2,000 loans at a cost of \$2.50 per loan. At a cost of \$2.50 per loan, it now becomes profitable for the financial intermediary to lend Carl the \$1,000.

Because financial intermediaries are able to reduce transaction costs substantially, they make it possible for you to provide funds indirectly to people like Carl with productive investment opportunities. In addition, a financial intermediary's low transaction costs mean that it can provide its customers with **liquidity services**, services that make it easier for customers to conduct transactions. For example, banks provide depositors with checking accounts that enable them to pay their bills easily. In addition, depositors can earn interest on checking and savings accounts and yet still convert them into goods and services whenever necessary.

Risk Sharing

Another benefit made possible by the low transaction costs of financial institutions is that they can help reduce the exposure of investors to **risk**—that is, uncertainty about the returns investors will earn on assets. Financial intermediaries do this through the process known as **risk sharing**: They create and sell assets with risk characteristics that people are comfortable with, and the intermediaries then use the funds they acquire by selling these assets to purchase other assets that may have far more risk. Low transaction costs allow financial intermediaries to share risk at low cost, enabling them to earn a profit on the spread between the returns they earn on risky assets and the payments they make on the assets they have sold. This process of risk sharing is also sometimes referred to as **asset transformation**, because in a sense, risky assets are turned into safer assets for investors.

Financial intermediaries also promote risk sharing by helping individuals to diversify and thereby lower the amount of risk to which they are exposed. **Diversification** entails investing in a collection (**portfolio**) of assets whose returns do not always move together, with the result that overall risk is lower than for individual assets. (Diversification is just another name for the old adage "You shouldn't put all your eggs in one basket.") Low transaction costs allow financial intermediaries to do this by pooling a collection of assets into a new asset and then selling it to individuals.

Asymmetric Information: Adverse Selection and Moral Hazard

The presence of transaction costs in financial markets explains, in part, why financial intermediaries and indirect finance play such an important role in financial markets. An additional reason is that in financial markets, one party often does not know enough about the other party to make accurate decisions. This inequality is called **asymmetric information**. For example, a borrower who takes out a loan usually has better information about the potential returns and risk associated with the investment projects for which the funds are earmarked than the lender does. Lack of information creates problems in the financial system on two fronts: before the transaction is entered into and after.[1]

Adverse selection is the problem created by asymmetric information *before* the transaction occurs. Adverse selection in financial markets occurs when the potential borrowers who are the most likely to produce an undesirable (*adverse*) outcome—the bad credit risks—are the ones who most actively seek out a loan and are thus most likely to be selected. Because adverse selection makes it more likely that loans might be made to bad credit risks, lenders may decide not to make any loans even though good credit risks exist in the marketplace.

To understand why adverse selection occurs, suppose that you have two aunts to whom you might make a loan—Aunt Louise and Aunt Sheila. Aunt Louise is a conservative type who borrows only when she has an investment she is quite sure will pay off. Aunt Sheila, by contrast, is an inveterate gambler who has just come across a get-rich-quick scheme that will make her a millionaire if she can just borrow $1,000 to invest in it. Unfortunately, as with most get-rich-quick schemes, the probability is high that the investment won't pay off and that Aunt Sheila will lose the $1,000.

Which of your aunts is more likely to call you to ask for a loan? Aunt Sheila, of course, because she has so much to gain if the investment pays off. You, however, would not want to make a loan to her because the probability is high that her investment will turn sour and she will be unable to pay you back.

[1]Asymmetric information and the adverse selection and moral hazard concepts are also crucial problems for the insurance industry.

If you knew both your aunts very well—that is, if your information were not asymmetric—you wouldn't have a problem, because you would know that Aunt Sheila is a bad risk and so you would not lend to her. Suppose, though, that you don't know your aunts well. You are more likely to lend to Aunt Sheila than to Aunt Louise because Aunt Sheila would be hounding you for the loan. Because of the possibility of adverse selection, you might decide not to lend to either of your aunts, even though there are times when Aunt Louise, who is an excellent credit risk, might need a loan for a worthwhile investment.

Moral hazard is the problem created by asymmetric information *after* the transaction occurs. Moral hazard in financial markets is the risk (*hazard*) that the borrower might engage in activities that are undesirable (*immoral*) from the lender's point of view, because they make it less likely that the loan will be paid back. Because moral hazard lowers the probability that the loan will be repaid, lenders may decide that they would rather not make a loan.

As an example of moral hazard, suppose that you made a $1,000 loan to another relative, Uncle Melvin, who needs the money to purchase a computer so that he can set up a business typing students' term papers. Once you have made the loan, however, Uncle Melvin is more likely to slip off to the track and play the horses. If he bets on a 20-to-1 long shot and wins with your money, he is able to pay back your $1,000 and live high off the hog with the remaining $19,000. But if he loses, as is likely, you don't get paid back, and all he has lost is his reputation as a reliable, upstanding uncle. Uncle Melvin therefore has an incentive to go to the track because his gains ($19,000) if he bets correctly are much greater than the cost to him (his reputation) if he bets incorrectly. If you knew what Uncle Melvin was up to, you would prevent him from going to the track, and he would not be able to increase the moral hazard. However, because it is hard for you to keep informed about his whereabouts—that is, because information is asymmetric—there is a good chance that Uncle Melvin will go to the track and you will not get paid back. The risk of moral hazard might therefore discourage you from making the $1,000 loan to Uncle Melvin, even if you were sure that you would be paid back if he used it to set up his business.

The problems created by adverse selection and moral hazard are an important impediment to well-functioning financial markets. Again, financial intermediaries can alleviate these problems.

With financial intermediaries in the economy, small savers can provide their funds to the financial markets by lending these funds to a trustworthy intermediary—say, the Honest John Bank—which in turn lends the funds out either by making loans or by buying securities such as stocks or bonds. Successful financial intermediaries have higher earnings on their investments than do small savers, because they are better equipped than individuals to screen out bad credit risks from good ones, thereby reducing losses due to adverse selection. In addition, financial intermediaries have high earnings because they develop expertise in monitoring the parties they lend to, thus reducing losses due to moral hazard. The result is that financial intermediaries can afford to pay lender-savers interest or provide substantial services and still earn a profit.

As we have seen, financial intermediaries play an important role in the economy because they provide liquidity services, promote risk sharing, and solve information problems, thereby allowing small savers and borrowers to benefit from the existence of financial markets. The success of financial intermediaries in performing this role is evidenced by the fact that most Americans invest their savings with them and obtain loans from them. Financial intermediaries play a key role in improving economic efficiency because they help financial markets channel funds from lender-savers to people with productive investment opportunities. Without a well-functioning set of financial intermediaries, it is very hard for an economy to reach its full potential. We will explore further the role of financial intermediaries in the economy in Part 3.

Economies of Scope and Conflicts of Interest

Another reason why financial intermediaries play such an important part in the economy is that by providing multiple financial services to their customers, such as offering them bank loans or selling their bonds for them, they can also achieve **economies of scope**; that is, they can lower the cost of information production for each service by applying one information resource to many different services. A bank, for example, when making a loan to a corporation, can evaluate how good a credit risk the firm is, which then helps the bank decide whether it would be easy to sell the bonds of this corporation to the public.

Although economies of scope may substantially benefit financial institutions, they also create potential costs in terms of **conflicts of interest**. Conflicts of interest, a type of moral hazard problem, arise when a person or institution has multiple objectives (interests) and, as a result, has conflicts between those objectives. Conflicts of interest are especially likely to occur when a financial institution provides multiple services. The potentially competing interests of those services may lead an individual or firm to conceal information or disseminate misleading information. We care about conflicts of interest because a substantial reduction in the quality of information in financial markets increases asymmetric information problems and prevents financial markets from channeling funds into the most productive investment opportunities. Consequently, the financial markets and the economy become less efficient.

TYPES OF FINANCIAL INTERMEDIARIES

We have seen why financial intermediaries have such an important function in the economy. Now we look at the principal financial intermediaries themselves and how they perform the intermediation function. They fall into three categories: depository institutions (banks), contractual savings institutions, and investment intermediaries. Table 3 provides a guide to the discussion of the financial intermediaries that fit into these three categories by describing their primary liabilities (sources of funds) and assets (uses of funds). The relative size of these intermediaries in the United States is indicated in Table 4, which lists the amount of their assets at the end of 1980, 1990, 2000, and 2010.

Depository Institutions

Depository institutions (for simplicity, we refer to these as *banks* throughout this text) are financial intermediaries that accept deposits from individuals and institutions and make loans. The study of money and banking focuses special attention on this group of financial institutions, because they are involved in the creation of deposits, an important component of the money supply. These institutions include commercial banks and the so-called **thrift institutions (thrifts)**: savings and loan associations, mutual savings banks, and credit unions.

TABLE 3 Primary Assets and Liabilities of Financial Intermediaries

Type of Intermediary	Primary Liabilities (Sources of Funds)	Primary Assets (Uses of Funds)
Depository institutions (banks)		
Commercial banks	Deposits	Business and consumer loans, mortgages, U.S. government securities, and municipal bonds
Savings and loan associations	Deposits	Mortgages
Mutual savings banks	Deposits	Mortgages
Credit unions	Deposits	Consumer loans
Contractual savings institutions		
Life insurance companies	Premiums from policies	Corporate bonds and mortgages
Fire and casualty insurance companies	Premiums from policies	Municipal bonds, corporate bonds and stock, and U.S. government securities
Pension funds, government retirement funds	Employer and employee contributions	Corporate bonds and stock
Investment intermediaries		
Finance companies	Commercial paper, stocks, bonds	Consumer and business loans
Mutual funds	Shares	Stocks, bonds
Money market mutual funds	Shares	Money market instruments

Commercial Banks These financial intermediaries raise funds primarily by issuing checkable deposits (deposits on which checks can be written), savings deposits (deposits that are payable on demand but do not allow their owner to write checks), and time deposits (deposits with fixed terms to maturity). They then use these funds to make commercial, consumer, and mortgage loans and to buy U.S. government securities and municipal bonds. Slightly fewer than 6,500 commercial banks are found in the United States, and, as a group, they are the largest financial intermediary and have the most diversified portfolios (collections) of assets.

Savings and Loan Associations (S&Ls) and Mutual Savings Banks These depository institutions, of which there are approximately 800, obtain funds primarily through savings deposits (often called *shares*) and time and checkable deposits. In the past, these institutions were constrained in their activities and mostly made mortgage loans for residential housing. Over time, these restrictions have been loosened, so the distinction between these depository institutions and commercial banks has blurred. These intermediaries have become more alike and are now more competitive with each other.

TABLE 4

Primary Financial Intermediaries and Value of Their Assets

Type of Intermediary	Value of Assets ($ billions, end of year)			
	1980	1990	2000	2010
Depository institutions (banks)				
Commercial banks	1,481	3,334	6,469	14,336
Savings and loan associations and mutual savings banks	792	1,365	1,218	1,244
Credit unions	67	215	441	912
Contractual savings institutions				
Life insurance companies	464	1,367	3,136	5,176
Fire and casualty insurance companies	182	533	862	1,242
Pension funds (private)	504	1,629	4,355	4,527
State and local government retirement funds	197	737	2,293	2,661
Investment intermediaries				
Finance companies	205	610	1,140	1,439
Mutual funds	70	654	4,435	7,935
Money market mutual funds	76	498	1,812	2,755

Source: Federal Reserve Flow of Funds Accounts; www.federalreserve.gov/releases/Z1/.

Credit Unions These financial institutions, numbering about 7,800, are typically very small cooperative lending institutions organized around a particular group: union members, employees of a particular firm, and so forth. They acquire funds from deposits called *shares* and primarily make consumer loans.

Contractual Savings Institutions

Contractual savings institutions, such as insurance companies and pension funds, are financial intermediaries that acquire funds at periodic intervals on a contractual basis. Because they can predict with reasonable accuracy how much they will have to pay out in benefits in the coming years, they do not have to worry as much as depository institutions about losing funds quickly. As a result, the liquidity of assets is not as important a consideration for them as it is for depository institutions, and they tend to invest their funds primarily in long-term securities such as corporate bonds, stocks, and mortgages.

Life Insurance Companies Life insurance companies insure people against financial hazards following a death and sell annuities (annual income payments upon retirement). They acquire funds from the premiums that people pay to keep their policies in force and use them mainly to buy corporate bonds and mortgages. They also purchase stocks, but are restricted in the amount that they can hold. Currently, with $5.2 trillion in assets, they are among the largest of the contractual savings institutions.

Fire and Casualty Insurance Companies These companies insure their policyholders against loss from theft, fire, and accidents. They are very much like life insurance companies, receiving funds through premiums for their policies, but they have a greater possibility of loss of funds if major disasters occur. For this reason, they use their funds to buy more liquid assets than life insurance companies do. Their largest holding of assets consists of municipal bonds; they also hold corporate bonds and stocks and U.S. government securities.

Pension Funds and Government Retirement Funds Private pension funds and state and local retirement funds provide retirement income in the form of annuities to employees who are covered by a pension plan. Funds are acquired by contributions from employers and from employees, who either have a contribution automatically deducted from their paychecks or contribute voluntarily. The largest asset holdings of pension funds are corporate bonds and stocks. The establishment of pension funds has been actively encouraged by the federal government, both through legislation requiring pension plans and through tax incentives to encourage contributions.

Investment Intermediaries

This category of financial intermediaries includes finance companies, mutual funds, and money market mutual funds.

Finance Companies Finance companies raise funds by selling commercial paper (a short-term debt instrument) and by issuing stocks and bonds. They lend these funds to consumers, who make purchases of such items as furniture, automobiles, and home improvements, and to small businesses. Some finance companies are organized by a parent corporation to help sell its product. For example, Ford Motor Credit Company makes loans to consumers who purchase Ford automobiles.

Mutual Funds These financial intermediaries acquire funds by selling shares to many individuals and use the proceeds to purchase diversified portfolios of stocks and bonds. Mutual funds allow shareholders to pool their resources so that they can take advantage of lower transaction costs when buying large blocks of stocks or bonds. In addition, mutual funds allow shareholders to hold more diversified portfolios than they otherwise would. Shareholders can sell (redeem) shares at any time, but the value of these shares will be determined by the value of the mutual fund's holdings of securities. Because these fluctuate greatly, the value of mutual fund shares will, too; therefore, investments in mutual funds can be risky.

Money Market Mutual Funds These financial institutions have the characteristics of a mutual fund but also function to some extent as a depository institution because they offer deposit-type accounts. Like most mutual funds, they sell shares to acquire funds that are then used to buy money market instruments that are both safe and very liquid. The interest on these assets is paid out to the shareholders.

A key feature of these funds is that shareholders can write checks against the value of their shareholdings. In effect, shares in a money market mutual fund function like checking account deposits that pay interest. Money market mutual funds have experienced extraordinary growth since 1971, when they first appeared. In 2010, their assets had climbed to 2.76 trillion.

Investment Banks Despite its name, an investment bank is not a bank or a financial intermediary in the ordinary sense; that is, it does not take in deposits and then lend them out. Instead, an investment bank is a different type of intermediary that helps a corporation issue securities. First it advises the corporation on which type of securities to issue (stocks or bonds); then it helps sell (**underwrite**) the securities by purchasing them from the corporation at a predetermined price and reselling them in the market. Investment banks also act as deal makers and earn enormous fees by helping corporations acquire other companies through mergers or acquisitions.

REGULATION OF THE FINANCIAL SYSTEM

The financial system is among the most heavily regulated sectors of the American economy. The government regulates financial markets for two main reasons: to increase the information available to investors and to ensure the soundness of the financial system. We will examine how these two reasons have led to the present regulatory environment. As a study aid, the principal regulatory agencies of the U.S. financial system are listed in Table 5.

Increasing Information Available to Investors

Asymmetric information in financial markets means that investors may be subject to adverse selection and moral hazard problems that may hinder the efficient operation of financial markets. Risky firms or outright crooks may be the most eager to sell securities to unwary investors, and the resulting adverse selection problem may keep investors out of financial markets. Furthermore, once an investor has bought a security, thereby lending money to a firm, the borrower may have incentives to engage in risky activities or to commit outright fraud. The presence of this moral hazard problem may also keep investors away from financial markets. Government regulation can reduce adverse selection and moral hazard problems in financial markets and enhance the efficiency of the markets by increasing the amount of information available to investors.

As a result of the stock market crash in 1929 and revelations of widespread fraud in the aftermath, political demands for regulation culminated in the Securities Act of 1933 and the establishment of the Securities and Exchange Commission (SEC) in 1934. The SEC requires corporations issuing securities to disclose certain information about their sales, assets, and earnings to the public and restricts trading by the largest stockholders (known as *insiders*) in the corporation. By requiring disclosure of this information and by discouraging insider trading, which could be used to manipulate security prices, the SEC hopes that investors will be better informed and protected from some of the abuses in financial markets that occurred before 1933. Indeed, in recent years, the SEC has been particularly active in prosecuting people involved in insider trading.

Ensuring the Soundness of Financial Intermediaries

Asymmetric information can lead to the widespread collapse of financial intermediaries, referred to as a **financial panic**. Because providers of funds to financial intermediaries may not be able to assess whether the institutions holding their funds are sound, if they have

TABLE 5

Principal Regulatory Agencies of the U.S. Financial System

Regulatory Agency	Subject of Regulation	Nature of Regulations
Securities and Exchange Commission (SEC)	Organized exchanges and financial markets	Requires disclosure of information, restricts insider trading
Commodities Futures Trading Commission (CFTC)	Futures market exchanges	Regulates procedures for trading in futures markets
Office of the Comptroller of the Currency	Federally chartered commercial banks	Charters and examines the books of federally chartered commercial banks and imposes restrictions on assets they can hold
National Credit Union Administration (NCUA)	Federally chartered credit unions	Charters and examines the books of federally chartered credit unions and imposes restrictions on assets they can hold
State banking and insurance commissions	State-chartered depository institutions	Charter and examine the books of state-chartered banks and insurance companies, impose restrictions on assets they can hold, and impose restrictions on branching
Federal Deposit Insurance Corporation (FDIC)	Commercial banks, mutual savings banks, savings and loan associations	Provides insurance of up to $250,000 for each depositor at a bank, examines the books of insured banks, and imposes restrictions on assets they can hold
Federal Reserve System	All depository institutions	Examines the books of commercial banks that are members of the system, sets reserve requirements for all banks
Office of Thrift Supervision	Savings and loan associations	Examines the books of savings and loan associations, imposes restrictions on assets they can hold

doubts about the overall health of financial intermediaries, they may want to pull their funds out of both sound and unsound institutions. The possible outcome is a financial panic that produces large losses for the public and causes serious damage to the economy. To protect the public and the economy from financial panics, the government has implemented six types of regulations.

Restrictions on Entry State banking and insurance commissions, as well as the Office of the Comptroller of the Currency (an agency of the federal government), have created tight regulations governing who is allowed to set up a financial intermediary. Individuals or groups that want to establish a financial intermediary, such as a bank or an insurance company, must obtain a charter from the state or the federal government.

Only if they are upstanding citizens with impeccable credentials and a large amount of initial funds will they be given a charter.

Disclosure Reporting requirements for financial intermediaries are stringent. Their bookkeeping must follow certain strict principles, their books are subject to periodic inspection, and they must make certain information available to the public.

Restrictions on Assets and Activities Financial intermediaries are restricted in what they are allowed to do and what assets they can hold. Before you put funds into a bank or some other such institution, you would want to know that your funds are safe and that the bank or other financial intermediary will be able to meet its obligations to you. One way of doing this is to restrict the financial intermediary from engaging in certain risky activities. Legislation passed in 1933 (repealed in 1999) separated commercial banking from the securities industry so that banks could not engage in risky ventures associated with this industry. Another way to limit a financial intermediary's risky behavior is to restrict it from holding certain risky assets, or at least from holding a greater quantity of these risky assets than is prudent. For example, commercial banks and other depository institutions are not allowed to hold common stock because stock prices experience substantial fluctuations. Insurance companies are allowed to hold common stock, but their holdings cannot exceed a certain fraction of their total assets.

Deposit Insurance The government can insure people's deposits so that they do not suffer great financial loss if the financial intermediary that holds these deposits should fail. The most important government agency that provides this type of insurance is the Federal Deposit Insurance Corporation (FDIC), which insures each depositor at a commercial bank or mutual savings bank up to a loss of $250,000 per account. Premiums paid by these financial institutions go into the FDIC's Deposit Insurance Fund, which is used to pay off depositors if an institution fails. The FDIC was created in 1934 after the massive bank failures of 1930–1933, in which the savings of many depositors at commercial banks were wiped out. The National Credit Union Share Insurance Fund (NCUSIF) does the same for credit unions.

Limits on Competition Politicians have often declared that unbridled competition among financial intermediaries promotes failures that will harm the public. Although the evidence that competition does indeed have this effect is extremely weak, state and federal governments at times have imposed restrictions on the opening of additional locations (branches). In the past, banks were not allowed to open branches in other states, and, in some states, banks were restricted from opening branches in additional locations.

Restrictions on Interest Rates Competition has also been inhibited by regulations that impose restrictions on interest rates that can be paid on deposits. For decades after 1933, banks were prohibited from paying interest on checking accounts. In addition, until 1986, the Federal Reserve System had the power under *Regulation Q* to set maximum interest rates that banks could pay on savings deposits. These regulations were instituted because of the widespread belief that unrestricted interest-rate competition helped encourage bank failures during the Great Depression. Later evidence does not seem to support this view, and Regulation Q has been abolished (although there are still restrictions on paying interest on checking accounts held by businesses).

In later chapters, we will look more closely at government regulation of financial markets and will see whether it has improved their functioning.

Financial Regulation Abroad

Not surprisingly, given the similarity of the economic systems here and in Japan, Canada, and the nations of Western Europe, financial regulation in these countries is similar to that in the United States. Provision of information is improved by requiring corporations issuing securities to report details about assets and liabilities, earnings, and sales of stock, and by prohibiting insider trading. The soundness of intermediaries is ensured by licensing, periodic inspection of financial intermediaries' books, and provision of deposit insurance (although its coverage is smaller than that in the United States and its existence is often intentionally not advertised).

The major differences between financial regulation in the United States and abroad relate to bank regulation. In the past, the United States was the only industrialized country to subject banks to restrictions on branching, which limited their size and confined them to certain geographic regions. (These restrictions were abolished by legislation in 1994.) U.S. banks are also the most restricted in the range of assets they may hold. Banks abroad frequently hold shares in commercial firms; in Japan and Germany, those stakes can be sizable.

Summary

1. The basic function of financial markets is to channel funds from savers who have an excess of funds to spenders who have a shortage of funds. Financial markets can do this either through direct finance, in which borrowers borrow funds directly from lenders by selling them securities, or through indirect finance, which involves a financial intermediary that stands between the lender-savers and the borrower-spenders and helps transfer funds from one to the other. This channeling of funds improves the economic welfare of everyone in society. Because they allow funds to move from people who have no productive investment opportunities to those who have such opportunities, financial markets contribute to economic efficiency. In addition, channeling of funds directly benefits consumers by allowing them to make purchases when they need them most.
2. Financial markets can be classified as debt and equity markets, primary and secondary markets, exchanges and over-the-counter markets, and money and capital markets.
3. The principal money market instruments (debt instruments with maturities of less than one year) are U.S. Treasury bills, negotiable bank certificates of deposit, commercial paper, repurchase agreements, and federal funds. The principal capital market instruments (debt and equity instruments with maturities greater than one year) are stocks, mortgages, corporate bonds, U.S. government securities, U.S. government agency securities, state and local government bonds, and consumer and bank commercial loans.
4. An important trend in recent years is the growing internationalization of financial markets. Eurobonds, which are denominated in a currency other than that of the country in which they are sold, are now the dominant security in the international bond market and have surpassed U.S. corporate bonds as a source of new funds. Eurodollars, which are U.S. dollars deposited in foreign banks, are an important source of funds for American banks.
5. Financial intermediaries are financial institutions that acquire funds by issuing liabilities and, in turn, use those funds to acquire assets by purchasing securities or making loans. Financial intermediaries play an important role in the financial system because they reduce transaction costs, allow risk sharing, and solve problems created by adverse selection and moral hazard. As a result, financial intermediaries allow small savers and borrowers to benefit from the existence of

financial markets, thereby increasing the efficiency of the economy. However, the economies of scope that help make financial intermediaries successful can lead to conflicts of interest that make the financial system less efficient.

6. The principal financial intermediaries fall into three categories: (a) banks—commercial banks, savings and loan associations, mutual savings banks, and credit unions; (b) contractual savings institutions—life insurance companies, fire and casualty insurance companies, and pension funds; and (c) investment intermediaries—finance companies, mutual funds, and money market mutual funds.

7. The government regulates financial markets and financial intermediaries for two main reasons: to increase the information available to investors and to ensure the soundness of the financial system. Regulations include requiring disclosure of information to the public, restrictions on who can set up a financial intermediary, restrictions on what assets financial intermediaries can hold, the provision of deposit insurance, limits on competition, and restrictions on interest rates.

Key Terms

adverse selection, p. 39
asset transformation, p. 39
asymmetric information, p. 39
brokers, p. 28
capital, p. 27
capital market, p. 29
conflicts of interest, p. 41
currency, p. 31
dealers, p. 28
default, p. 31
diversification, p. 39
dividends, p. 28
economies of scale, p. 38
economies of scope, p. 41
equities, p. 28
Eurobond, p. 36
Eurocurrencies, p. 36
Eurodollars, p. 36
exchanges, p. 29
federal funds rate, p. 32
financial intermediation, p. 37
financial panic, p. 45
foreign bonds, p. 35
intermediate-term, p. 28
investment bank, p. 28
liabilities, p. 26
liquid, p. 29
liquidity services, p. 38
long-term, p. 28
maturity, p. 28
money market, p. 29
moral hazard, p. 40
mortgages, p. 33
mortgage-backed securities, p. 33
over-the-counter (OTC) market, p. 29
portfolio, p. 39
primary market, p. 28
risk, p. 38
risk sharing, p. 39
secondary market, p. 28
short-term, p. 28
thrift institutions (thrifts), p. 41
transaction costs, p. 37
underwrite, p. 45
underwriting, p. 28

Questions

All questions are available in MyEconLab *at* www.myeconlab.com.

1. If I can buy a car today for $5,000 and it is worth $10,000 in extra income next year to me because it enables me to get a job as a traveling salesman, should I take out a loan from Larry the Loan Shark at a 90% interest rate if no one else will give me a loan? Will I be better or worse off as a result of taking out this loan? Can you make a case for legalizing loan sharking?

2. Some economists suspect that one of the reasons that economies in developing countries grow so slowly is that they do not have well-developed financial markets. Does this argument make sense?

3. Why is a share of Microsoft common stock an asset for its owner and a liability for Microsoft?

4. If you suspect that a company will go bankrupt next year, which would you rather hold, bonds issued by the company or equities issued by the company? Why?

5. "Because corporations do not actually raise any funds in secondary markets, they are less important to the economy than primary markets are." Is this statement true, false, or uncertain?
6. For each of the following money market instruments, describe who issues the debt:
   a. Treasury bills
   b. Certificates of deposit
   c. Commercial paper
   d. Repurchase agreement
   e. Fed funds
7. What is the difference between a *mortgage* and a *mortgage-backed security*?
8. The U.S. economy borrowed heavily from the British in the nineteenth century to build a railroad system. Why did this make both countries better off?
9. A significant number of European banks held large amounts of assets as mortgage-backed securities derived from the U.S. housing market, which crashed after 2006. How does this demonstrate both a benefit and a cost to the internationalization of financial markets?
10. How does risk sharing benefit both financial intermediaries and private investors?
11. How can the adverse selection problem explain why you are more likely to make a loan to a family member than to a stranger?
12. One of the factors contributing to the financial crisis of 2007–2009 was the widespread issuance of subprime mortgages. How does this demonstrate adverse selection?
13. Why do loan sharks worry less about moral hazard in connection with their borrowers than some other lenders do?
14. If you are an employer, what kinds of moral hazard problems might you worry about with your employees?
15. If there were no asymmetry in the information that a borrower and a lender had, could a moral hazard problem still exist?
16. "In a world without information costs and transaction costs, financial intermediaries would not exist." Is this statement true, false, or uncertain? Explain your answer.
17. Why might you be willing to make a loan to your neighbor by putting funds in a savings account earning a 5% interest rate at the bank and having the bank lend her the funds at a 10% interest rate rather than lend her the funds yourself?
18. How do conflicts of interest make the asymmetric information problem worse?
19. How can the provision of several types of financial services by one firm be both beneficial and problematic?
20. If you were going to get a loan to purchase a new car, which financial intermediary would you use: a credit union, a pension fund, or an investment bank?
21. Why would a life insurance company be concerned about the financial stability of major corporations or the health of the housing market?
22. In 2008, as a financial crisis began to unfold in the United States, the FDIC raised the limit on insured losses to bank depositors from $100,000 per account to $250,000 per account. How would this help stabilize the financial system?

Applied Problems

All applied problems are available in MyEconLab *at* www.myeconlab.com.

23. Suppose you have just inherited $10,000 and are considering the following options for investing the money to maximize your return:

    Option 1: Put the money in an interest-bearing checking account, which earns 2%. The FDIC insures the account against bank failure.

    Option 2: Invest the money in a corporate bond, with a stated return of 5%, but there is a 10% chance the company could go bankrupt.

    Option 3: Loan the money to one of your friends' roommates, Mike, at an agreed-upon interest rate of 8%, but you believe there is a 7% chance that Mike will leave town without repaying you.

Option 4: Hold the money in cash and earn zero return.

a. If you are risk-neutral (that is, neither seek out nor shy away from risk), which of the four options should you choose to maximize your expected return? (*Hint:* To calculate the *expected return* of an outcome, multiply the probability that an event will occur by the outcome of that event).

b. Suppose Option 3 is your only possibility. If you could pay your friend $100 to find out extra information about Mike that would indicate with certainty whether he will leave town without paying or not, would you pay the $100? What does this say about the value of better information regarding risk?

Web Exercises

1. One of the single best sources of information about financial institutions is the U.S. Flow of Funds report produced by the Federal Reserve. This document contains data on most financial intermediaries. Go to www.federalreserve.gov/releases/Z1/. Go to the most current release. You may have to load Acrobat Reader if your computer does not already have it; the site has a link for a free patch. Go to the Level Tables and answer the following.
   a. What percentage of assets do commercial banks hold in loans? What percentage of assets are held in mortgage loans?
   b. What percentage of assets do savings and loans hold in mortgage loans?
   c. What percentage of assets do credit unions hold in mortgage loans and in consumer loans?
2. The most famous financial market in the world is the New York Stock Exchange. Go to www.nyse.com.
   a. What is the mission of the NYSE?
   b. Firms must pay a fee to list their shares for sale on the NYSE. What would be the fee for a firm with five million common shares outstanding?

Web References

http://stockcharts.com/charts/historical

This page contains historical stock index charts for the Dow Jones Industrial Average, S&P 500, NASDAQ, 30-year Treasury Bond, and Gold prices.

www.nyse.com

New York Stock Exchange. Find listed companies, quotes, company historical data, real-time market indexes, and more.

www.nasdaq.com

Detailed market and security information for the Nasdaq OTC stock exchange.

http://finance.yahoo.com/i

Major world stock indexes, with charts, news, and components.

www.sec.gov

The United States Securities and Exchange Commission home page. It contains vast SEC resources, laws and regulations, investor information, and litigation.

3 What Is Money?

Preview

If you had lived in America before the Revolutionary War, your money might have consisted primarily of Spanish doubloons (silver coins that were also called *pieces of eight*). Before the Civil War, the principal forms of money in the United States were gold and silver coins and paper notes, called *banknotes*, issued by private banks. Today, you use not only coins and dollar bills issued by the government as money, but also checks written on accounts held at banks. Money has been different things at different times, but it has *always* been important to people and to the economy.

To understand the effects of money on the economy, we must understand exactly what money is. In this chapter, we develop precise definitions by exploring the functions of money, looking at why and how it promotes economic efficiency, tracing how its forms have evolved over time, and examining how money is currently measured.

MEANING OF MONEY

As the word *money* is used in everyday conversation, it can mean many things, but to economists, it has a very specific meaning. To avoid confusion, we must clarify how economists' use of the word *money* differs from conventional usage.

Economists define *money* (also referred to as the *money supply*) as anything that is generally accepted in payment for goods or services or in the repayment of debts. Currency, consisting of dollar bills and coins, clearly fits this definition and is one type of money. When most people talk about money, they're talking about **currency** (paper money and coins). If, for example, someone comes up to you and says, "Your money or your life," you should quickly hand over all your currency rather than ask, "What exactly do you mean by 'money'?"

To define money merely as currency is much too narrow for economists. Because checks are also accepted as payment for purchases, checking account deposits are considered money as well. An even broader definition of money is often needed, because other items such as savings deposits can, in effect, function as money if they can be quickly and easily converted into currency or checking account deposits. As you can see, no single, precise definition of money or the money supply is possible, even for economists.

To complicate matters further, the word *money* is frequently used synonymously with *wealth*. When people say, "Joe is rich—he has an awful lot of money," they probably mean that Joe not only has a lot of currency and a high balance in his checking account but also has stocks, bonds, four cars, three houses, and a yacht. Thus, while "currency" is too narrow a definition of money, this other popular usage is much too broad. Economists make a distinction between money in the form of currency, demand deposits, and other items that are used to make purchases and **wealth**, the total collection of pieces of property that serve to store value. Wealth includes not only money but also other assets such as bonds, common stock, art, land, furniture, cars, and houses.

People also use the word *money* to describe what economists call *income*, as in the sentence "Sheila would be a wonderful catch; she has a good job and earns a lot of money." **Income** is a *flow* of earnings per unit of time. Money, by contrast, is a *stock*: It is a certain amount at a given point in time. If someone tells you that he has an income of $1,000, you cannot tell whether he earned a lot or a little without knowing whether this $1,000 is earned per year, per month, or even per day. But if someone tells you that she has $1,000 in her pocket, you know exactly how much this is.

Keep in mind that the money discussed in this book refers to anything that is generally accepted in payment for goods and services or in the repayment of debts and is distinct from income and wealth.

FUNCTIONS OF MONEY

Whether money is shells or rocks or gold or paper, it has three primary functions in any economy: as a medium of exchange, as a unit of account, and as a store of value. Of the three functions, its function as a medium of exchange is what distinguishes money from other assets such as stocks, bonds, and houses.

Medium of Exchange

In almost all market transactions in our economy, money in the form of currency or checks is a **medium of exchange**; it is used to pay for goods and services. The use of money as a medium of exchange promotes economic efficiency by minimizing the time spent in exchanging goods and services. To see why, let's look at a *barter economy*, one without money, in which goods and services are exchanged directly for other goods and services.

Take the case of Ellen the Economics Professor, who can do just one thing well: give brilliant economics lectures. In a barter economy, if Ellen wants to eat, she must find a farmer who not only produces the food she likes but also wants to learn economics. As you might expect, this search will be difficult and time-consuming, and Ellen might spend more time looking for such an economics-hungry farmer than she will teaching. It is even possible that she will have to quit lecturing and go into farming herself. Even so, she may still starve to death.

The time spent trying to exchange goods or services is called a *transaction cost*. In a barter economy, transaction costs are high because people have to satisfy a "double coincidence of wants"—they have to find someone who has a good or service they want and who also wants the good or service they have to offer.

Let's see what happens if we introduce money into Ellen the Economics Professor's world. Ellen can teach anyone who is willing to pay money to hear her lecture. She can then go to any farmer (or his representative at the supermarket) and buy the food she needs with the money she has been paid. The problem of the double coincidence of wants is avoided, and Ellen saves a lot of time, which she may spend doing what she does best: teaching.

As this example shows, money promotes economic efficiency by eliminating much of the time spent exchanging goods and services. It also promotes efficiency by allowing people to specialize in what they do best. Money is therefore essential in an economy: It is a lubricant that allows the economy to run more smoothly by lowering transaction costs, thereby encouraging specialization and division of labor.

The need for money is so strong that almost every society beyond the most primitive invents it. For a commodity to function effectively as money, it has to meet several criteria: (1) It must be easily standardized, making it simple to ascertain its value; (2) it must be widely accepted; (3) it must be divisible, so that it is easy to "make change"; (4) it must be easy to carry; and (5) it must not deteriorate quickly. Objects that have satisfied these criteria have taken many unusual forms throughout human history, ranging from wampum (strings of beads) used by Native Americans; to tobacco and whiskey, used by the early American colonists; to cigarettes, used in prisoner-of-war camps during World War II.[1] The diverse forms of money that have been developed over the years is as much a testament to the inventiveness of the human race as the development of tools and language.

Unit of Account

The second role of money is to provide a **unit of account**; that is, it is used to measure value in the economy. We measure the value of goods and services in terms of money, just as we measure weight in terms of pounds or distance in terms of miles. To see why this function is important, let's look again at a barter economy, in which money does not perform this function. If the economy has only three goods—say, peaches, economics lectures, and movies—then we need to know only three prices to tell us how to exchange one for another: the price of peaches in terms of economics lectures (that is, how many economics lectures you have to pay for a peach), the price of peaches in terms of movies, and the price of economics lectures in terms of movies. If there were 10 goods, we would need to know 45 prices to exchange one good for another; with 100 goods, we would need 4,950 prices; and with 1,000 goods, 499,500 prices.[2]

Imagine how hard it would be in a barter economy to shop at a supermarket with 1,000 different items on its shelves and be faced with deciding whether chicken or fish is a better buy if the price of a pound of chicken were quoted as 4 pounds of butter and the price of a pound of fish as 8 pounds of tomatoes. To make it possible to compare prices, the tag on each item would have to list up to 999 different prices, and the time spent reading them would result in very high transaction costs.

The solution to the problem is to introduce money into the economy and have all prices quoted in terms of units of that money, enabling us to quote the price of economics

[1]An extremely entertaining article on the development of money in a prisoner-of-war camp during World War II is R. A. Radford, "The Economic Organization of a P.O.W. Camp," *Economica* 12 (November 1945): 189–201.

[2]The formula for telling us the number of prices we need when we have N goods is the same formula that tells us the number of pairs when there are N items. It is

$$\frac{N(N-1)}{2}$$

In the case of ten goods, for example, we would need

$$\frac{10(10-1)}{2} = \frac{90}{2} = 45$$

lectures, peaches, and movies in terms of, say, dollars. If there were only three goods in the economy, this would not be a great advantage over the barter system, because we would still need three prices to conduct transactions. But for 10 goods we would need only 10 prices; for 100 goods, 100 prices; and so on. At the 1,000-goods supermarket, now only 1,000 prices need to be looked at, not 499,500!

We can see that using money as a unit of account lowers transaction costs in an economy by reducing the number of prices that need to be considered. The benefits of this function of money grow as the economy becomes more complex.

Store of Value

Money also functions as a **store of value**; it is a repository of purchasing power over time. A store of value is used to save purchasing power from the time income is received until the time it is spent. This function of money is useful, because most of us do not want to spend our income immediately upon receiving it, but rather prefer to wait until we have the time or the desire to shop.

Money is not unique as a store of value; any asset—whether money, stocks, bonds, land, houses, art, or jewelry—can be used to store wealth. Many such assets have advantages over money as a store of value: They often pay the owner a higher interest rate than money, experience price appreciation, and deliver services such as providing a roof over one's head. If these assets are a more desirable store of value than money, why do people hold money at all?

The answer to this question relates to the important economic concept of **liquidity**, the relative ease and speed with which an asset can be converted into a medium of exchange. Liquidity is highly desirable. Money is the most liquid asset of all because it *is* the medium of exchange; it does not have to be converted into anything else to make purchases. Other assets involve transaction costs when they are converted into money. When you sell your house, for example, you have to pay a brokerage commission (usually 4–6% of the sales price), and if you need cash immediately to pay some pressing bills, you might have to settle for a lower price if you want to sell the house quickly. Because money is the most liquid asset, people are willing to hold it even if it is not the most attractive store of value.

How good a store of value money is depends on the price level. A doubling of all prices, for example, means that the value of money has dropped by half; conversely, a halving of all prices means that the value of money has doubled. During inflation, when the price level is increasing rapidly, money loses value rapidly, and people will be more reluctant to hold their wealth in this form. This is especially true during periods of extreme inflation, known as **hyperinflation**, in which the inflation rate exceeds 50% per month.

Hyperinflation occurred in Germany after World War I, with inflation rates sometimes exceeding 1,000% per month. By the end of the hyperinflation in 1923, the price level had risen to more than 30 billion times what it had been just two years before. The quantity of money needed to purchase even the most basic items became excessive. There are stories, for example, that near the end of the hyperinflation, a wheelbarrow of cash would be required to pay for a loaf of bread. Money was losing its value so rapidly that workers were paid and given time off on several occasions during the day to spend their wages before the money became worthless. No one wanted to hold on to money, so the use of money to carry out transactions declined and barter became more and more dominant. Transaction costs skyrocketed, and, as we would expect, output in the economy fell sharply.

EVOLUTION OF THE PAYMENTS SYSTEM

We can obtain a better picture of the functions of money and the forms it has taken over time by looking at the evolution of the **payments system**, the method of conducting transactions in the economy. The payments system has been evolving over centuries, and with it the form of money. At one point, precious metals such as gold were used as the principal means of payment and were the main form of money. Later, paper assets such as checks and currency began to be used in the payments system and viewed as money. Where the payments system is heading has an important bearing on how money will be defined in the future.

Commodity Money

To obtain perspective on where the payments system is heading, it's worth exploring how it has evolved. For any object to function as money, it must be universally acceptable; everyone must be willing to take it in payment for goods and services. An object that clearly has value to everyone is a likely candidate to serve as money, and a natural choice is a precious metal such as gold or silver. Money made up of precious metals or another valuable commodity is called **commodity money**, and from ancient times until several hundred years ago, commodity money functioned as the medium of exchange in all but the most primitive societies. The problem with a payments system based exclusively on precious metals is that such a form of money is very heavy and is hard to transport from one place to another. Imagine the holes you'd wear in your pockets if you had to buy things only with coins! Indeed, for large purchases such as a house, you'd have to rent a truck to transport the money payment.

Fiat Money

The next development in the payments system was *paper currency* (pieces of paper that function as a medium of exchange). Initially, paper currency carried a guarantee that it was convertible into coins or into a fixed quantity of precious metal. However, currency has evolved into **fiat money**, paper currency decreed by governments as legal tender (meaning that legally it must be accepted as payment for debts) but not convertible into coins or precious metal. Paper currency has the advantage of being much lighter than coins or precious metal, but it can be accepted as a medium of exchange only if there is some trust in the authorities who issue it and if printing has reached a sufficiently advanced stage that counterfeiting is extremely difficult. Because paper currency has evolved into a legal arrangement, countries can change the currency they use at will. Indeed, this is what many European countries did when they abandoned their currencies for the euro in 2002.

Major drawbacks of paper currency and coins are that they are easily stolen and can be expensive to transport in large amounts because of their bulk. To combat this problem, another step in the evolution of the payments system occurred with the development of modern banking: the invention of *checks*.

Checks

A check is an instruction from you to your bank to transfer money from your account to someone else's account when she deposits the check. Checks allow transactions to take place without the need to carry around large amounts of currency. The introduction of checks was a major innovation that improved the efficiency of the payments system. Frequently, payments made back and forth cancel each other; without checks, this would involve the movement of a lot of currency. With checks, payments that cancel each other can be settled by canceling the checks, and no currency need be moved. The use of checks thus reduces the transportation costs associated with the payments system and improves economic efficiency. Another advantage of checks is that they can be written for any amount up to the balance in the account, making transactions for large amounts much easier. Checks are also advantageous in that loss from theft is greatly reduced and because they provide convenient receipts for purchases.

Two problems arise, however, with a payments system based on checks. First, it takes time to get checks from one place to another, a particularly serious problem if you are paying someone in a different location who needs to be paid quickly. In addition, if you have a checking account, you know that it often takes several business days before a bank will allow you to make use of the funds from a check you have deposited. If your need for cash is urgent, this feature of paying by check can be frustrating. Second, the paper shuffling required to process checks is costly; currently, the cost of processing all checks written in the United States is estimated at over $10 billion per year.

Electronic Payment

The development of inexpensive computers and the spread of the Internet now make it cheap to pay bills electronically. In the past, you had to pay bills by mailing a check, but now banks provide websites at which you just log on, make a few clicks, and thereby transmit your payment electronically. Not only do you save the cost of the stamp, but paying bills becomes (almost) a pleasure, requiring little effort. Electronic payment systems provided by banks now even spare you the step of logging on to pay the bill. Instead, recurring bills can be automatically deducted from your bank account. Estimated cost savings when a bill is paid electronically rather than by a check exceed one dollar per transaction. Electronic payment is thus becoming far more common in the United States.

E-Money

Electronic payments technology can substitute not only for checks but also for cash, in the form of **electronic money** (or **e-money**)—money that exists only in electronic form. The first form of e-money was the *debit card*. Debit cards, which look like credit cards, enable consumers to purchase goods and services by electronically transferring funds directly from their bank accounts to a merchant's account. Debit cards are used in many of the same places that accept credit cards and are now often becoming faster to use than cash. At most supermarkets, for example, you can swipe your debit card through the card reader at the checkout station, press a button, and the amount of your purchases is deducted from your bank account. Most banks and companies such as Visa and MasterCard issue debit cards, and your ATM card typically can function as a debit card.

A more advanced form of e-money is the *stored-value card*. The simplest form of stored-value card is purchased for a preset dollar amount that the consumer pays up front, like a prepaid phone card. The more sophisticated stored-value card is known as a **smart card**. It contains a computer chip that allows it to be loaded with digital cash from the owner's bank account whenever needed. In Asian countries, such as Japan and Korea, cell phones now have a smart card feature that raises the expression "pay by phone" to a new level. Smart cards can be loaded from ATM machines, personal computers with a smart card reader, or specially equipped telephones.

FYI Are We Headed for a Cashless Society?

Predictions of a cashless society have been around for decades, but they have not come to fruition. For example, *Business Week* predicted in 1975 that electronic means of payment "would soon revolutionize the very concept of money itself," only to reverse its view several years later. Pilot projects in recent years with smart cards to convert consumers to the use of e-money have not been a success. Mondex, one of the widely touted, early stored-value cards that was launched in Great Britain in 1995, is used only on a few British university campuses. In Germany and Belgium, millions of people carry bank cards with computer chips embedded in them that enable them to make use of e-money, but very few use them. Why has the movement to a cashless society been so slow in coming?

Although e-money might be more convenient and efficient than a payments system based on paper, several factors work against the disappearance of the paper system. First, it is very expensive to set up the computer, card reader, and telecommunications networks necessary to make electronic money the dominant form of payment. Second, electronic means of payment raise security and privacy concerns. We often hear media reports that an unauthorized hacker has been able to access a computer database and to alter information stored there. Because this is not an uncommon occurrence, unscrupulous persons might be able to access bank accounts in electronic payments systems and steal funds by moving them from someone else's accounts into their own. The prevention of this type of fraud is no easy task, and a whole new field of computer science has developed to cope with security issues. A further concern is that the use of electronic means of payment leaves an electronic trail that contains a large amount of personal data on buying habits. There are worries that government, employers, and marketers might be able to access these data, thereby encroaching on our privacy.

The conclusion from this discussion is that although the use of e-money will surely increase in the future, to paraphrase Mark Twain, "the reports of cash's death are greatly exaggerated."

A third form of electronic money is often referred to as **e-cash**, which is used on the Internet to purchase goods or services. A consumer gets e-cash by setting up an account with a bank that has links to the Internet and then has the e-cash transferred to her PC. When she wants to buy something with e-cash, she surfs to a store on the Web and clicks the "buy" option for a particular item, whereupon the e-cash is automatically transferred from her computer to the merchant's computer. The merchant can then have the funds transferred from the consumer's bank account to his before the goods are shipped.

Given the convenience of e-money, you might think that we would move quickly to a cashless society in which all payments are made electronically. However, this hasn't happened, as discussed in the FYI box, "Are We Headed for a Cashless Society?"

MEASURING MONEY

The definition of money as anything that is generally accepted in payment for goods and services tells us that money is defined by people's behavior. What makes an asset money is that people believe it will be accepted by others when making payment. As we have seen, many different assets have performed this role over the centuries, ranging from gold to paper currency to checking accounts. For that reason, this behavioral definition does not tell us which assets in our economy should be considered money. To measure money, we need a precise definition that tells us exactly which assets should be included.

The Federal Reserve's Monetary Aggregates

The Federal Reserve System (the Fed), the central banking authority responsible for monetary policy in the United States, has conducted many studies on how to measure money. The problem of measuring money has recently become especially crucial because extensive financial innovation has produced new types of assets that might properly belong in a measure of money. Since 1980, the Fed has modified its measures of money several times and has settled on the following measures of the money supply, which are also referred to as **monetary aggregates** (see Table 1 and the following Financial News box).

The narrowest measure of money that the Fed reports is **M1**, which includes the most liquid assets: currency, checking account deposits, and traveler's checks. The components of M1 are shown in Table 1. The *currency* component of M1 includes only paper money and coins in the hands of the nonbank public and does not include cash held in ATMs or bank vaults. Surprisingly, more than $3,000 cash is in circulation for each person in the United States (see the FYI box). The *traveler's checks* component of M1 includes only traveler's checks not issued by banks. The *demand deposits* component includes business checking accounts that do not pay interest, as well as traveler's checks issued by banks. The *other checkable deposits* item includes all other checkable deposits, particularly interest-bearing checking accounts held by households. These assets are clearly money because they can be used directly as a medium of exchange.

Until the mid-1970s, only commercial banks were permitted to establish checking accounts, and they were not allowed to pay interest on them. With the financial

TABLE 1 Measures of the Monetary Aggregates

	Value as of May 16, 2011 ($ billions)
M1 = Currency	958.8
+ Traveler's checks	4.6
+ Demand deposits	573.1
+ Other checkable deposits	399.0
Total M1	1,935.5
M2 = M1	
+ Small-denomination time deposits	848.3
+ Savings deposits and money market deposit accounts	5,530.4
+ Money market mutual fund shares (retail)	688.4
Total M2	9,002.6

Source: www.federalreserve.gov/releases/h6/hist.

Following the Financial News — The Monetary Aggregates

Every week on Thursday, the Federal Reserve publishes the data for M1 and M2 in its H.6 release and these numbers are often reported on in the media.

The H.6 release can be found at www.federalreserve.gov/releases/h6/current/h6.htm.

innovation that has occurred (discussed more extensively in Chapter 12), regulations have changed so that other types of banks, such as savings and loan associations, mutual savings banks, and credit unions, can also offer checking accounts. In addition, banking institutions can offer other checkable deposits, such as NOW (negotiated order of withdrawal) accounts and ATS (automatic transfer from savings) accounts, which do pay interest on their balances.

The **M2** monetary aggregate adds to M1 other assets that are not quite as liquid as those included in M1: assets that have check-writing features (money market deposit accounts and money market mutual fund shares) and other assets (savings deposits and small-denomination time deposits) that can be turned into cash quickly at very little cost. *Small-denomination time deposits* are certificates of deposit with a denomination of less than $100,000 that can be redeemed only at a fixed maturity date without a penalty. *Savings deposits* are nontransaction deposits that can be added to or taken out at any time. *Money market deposit accounts* are similar to money market mutual funds, but are issued by banks. The *money market mutual fund shares* are retail accounts on which households can write checks.

FYI — Where Are All the U.S. Dollars?

The more than $3,000 of U.S. currency held per person in the United States is a surprisingly large number. U.S. currency is bulky, can be easily stolen, and pays no interest, so it doesn't make sense for most of us to keep a lot of it. Do you know anyone who carries $3,000 in his or her pockets? We have a puzzle: Where are all these dollars and who is holding them?

Criminals are one group who hold a lot of dollars. If you were engaged in illegal activity, you would not conduct your transactions with checks because they are traceable and therefore a potentially powerful piece of evidence against you. That explains why Tony Soprano has so much cash in his backyard. Some businesses also like to retain a lot of cash because if they operate as a cash business that makes their transactions less traceable; thus they can avoid declaring income on which they would have to pay taxes.

Foreigners are the other group who routinely hold U.S. dollars. In many countries, people do not trust their own currency because they often experience high inflation, which erodes the value of that currency; these people hold U.S. dollars as a hedge against this inflation risk. Lack of trust in the ruble, for example, has led Russians to hoard enormous amounts of U.S. dollars. More than half of U.S. dollars are held abroad.

Because economists and policymakers cannot be sure which of the monetary aggregates is the best measure of money, it is logical to wonder if their movements closely parallel one another. If they do, then using one monetary aggregate to predict future economic performance and to conduct policy will be the same as using another, and it does not much matter that we are not sure of the appropriate definition of money for a given policy decision. However, if the monetary aggregates do not move together, then what one monetary aggregate tells us is happening to the money supply might be quite different from what another monetary aggregate would tell us. The conflicting stories might present a confusing picture that would make it hard for policymakers to decide on the right course of action.

Figure 1 plots the growth rates of M1 and M2 from 1960 to 2011. The growth rates of these two monetary aggregates do tend to move together; the timing of their rise and fall is roughly similar until the 1990s, and they both show a higher growth rate, on average, in the 1970s than in the 1960s.

Yet some glaring discrepancies exist in the movements of these aggregates. Contrast M1's high rates of growth from 1992 to 1994 with the much lower growth of M2. Also notice that from 2004 to 2007, M2's growth rate increased slightly, while M1 sharply decelerated and went negative. In 2009, M1 growth surged to over 15% from near zero the year before, while M2 growth rose less dramatically. Thus, the different measures of money tell a very different story about the course of monetary policy in recent years.

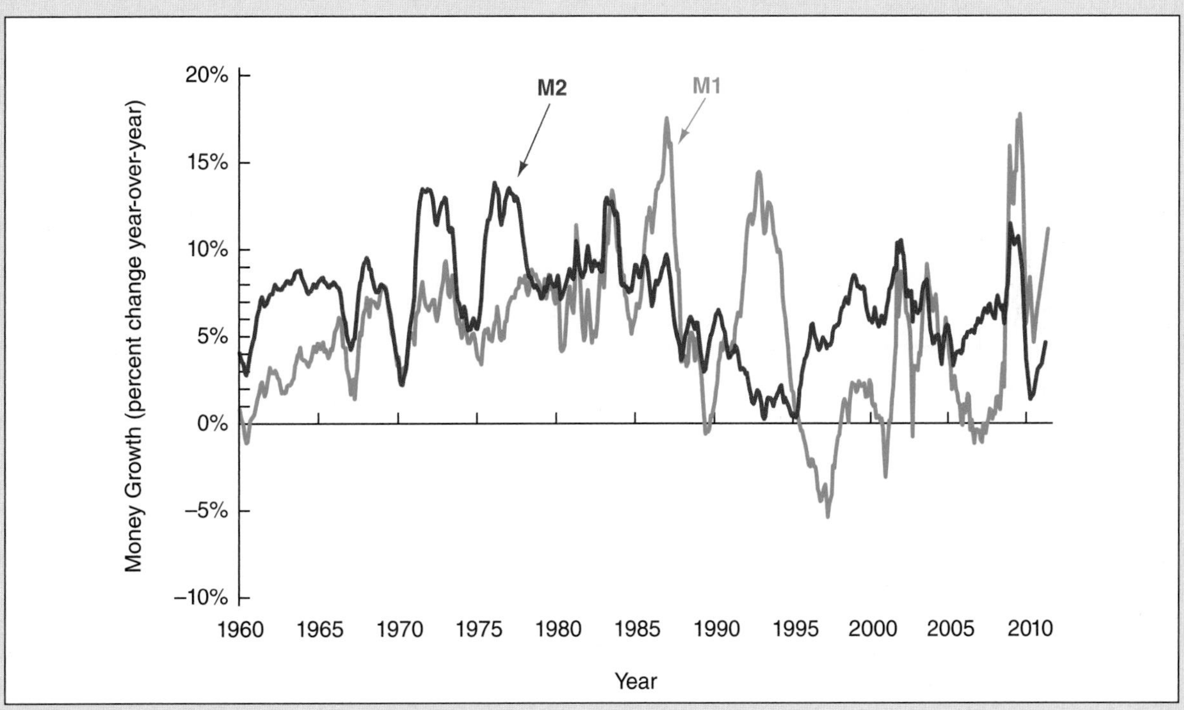

FIGURE 1 Growth Rates of the M1 and M2 Aggregates, 1960–2011

Timing of the rise and fall of growth rates is roughly similar for both M1 and M2. There are, however, periods such as 1992–1994 and 2004–2007, when they move in opposite directions, providing conflicting recommendations about the course of monetary policy.

Sources: **Federal Reserve Economic Database (FRED); Federal Reserve Bank of Saint Louis;** http://research.stlouisfed.org/fred2/categories/25

From the data in Figure 1, you can see that obtaining a single precise, correct measure of money does seem to matter and that it does make a difference which monetary aggregate policymakers and economists choose as the true measure of money.

Summary

1. To economists, the word *money* has a different meaning from *income* or *wealth*. Money is anything that is generally accepted as payment for goods or services or in the repayment of debts.
2. Money serves three primary functions: as a medium of exchange, as a unit of account, and as a store of value. Money as a medium of exchange avoids the problem of double coincidence of wants that arises in a barter economy, and thus lowers transaction costs and encourages specialization and the division of labor. Money as a unit of account reduces the number of prices needed in the economy, which also reduces transaction costs. Money also functions as a store of value, but performs this role poorly if it is rapidly losing value due to inflation.
3. The payments system has evolved over time. Until several hundred years ago, the payments system in all but the most primitive societies was based primarily on precious metals. The introduction of paper currency lowered the cost of transporting money. The next major advance was the introduction of checks, which lowered transaction costs still further. We are currently moving toward an electronic payments system in which paper is eliminated and all transactions are handled by computers. Despite the potential efficiency of such a system, obstacles are slowing the movement to a checkless society and the development of new forms of electronic money.
4. The Federal Reserve System has defined two different measures of the money supply—M1 and M2. These measures are not equivalent and do not always move together, so they cannot be used interchangeably by policymakers. Obtaining the precise, correct measure of money does seem to matter and has implications for the conduct of monetary policy.

Key Terms

Questions

All questions are available in MyEconLab *at* www.myeconlab.com.

1. Why is simply counting currency an inadequate measure of money?
2. In prison, cigarettes are sometimes used among inmates as a form of payment. How is it possible for cigarettes to solve the "double coincidence of wants" problem, even if a prisoner does not smoke?

3. Three goods are produced in an economy by three individuals:

Good	*Producer*
Apples	Orchard owner
Bananas	Banana grower
Chocolate	Chocolatier

If the orchard owner likes only bananas, the banana grower likes only chocolate, and the chocolatier likes only apples, will any trade between these three persons take place in a barter economy? How will introducing money into the economy benefit these three producers?

4. Why did cavemen not need money?

5. Most of the time it is quite difficult to separate the three functions of money. Money performs its three functions at all times, but sometimes we can stress one in particular. For each of the following situations, identify which function of money is emphasized.
   a. Brooke accepts money in exchange for performing her daily tasks at her office, since she knows she can use that money to buy goods and services.
   b. Tim wants to calculate the relative value of oranges and apples, and therefore checks the price per pound of each of these goods quoted in currency units.
   c. Maria is currently pregnant. She expects her expenditures to increase in the future and decides to increase the balance in her savings account.

6. In Brazil, a country that underwent a rapid inflation before 1994, many transactions were conducted in dollars rather than in reals, the domestic currency. Why?

7. Was money a better store of value in the United States in the 1950s than in the 1970s? Why or why not? In which period would you have been more willing to hold money?

8. Why have some economists described money during a hyperinflation as a "hot potato" that is quickly passed from one person to another?

9. Why were people in the United States in the nineteenth century sometimes willing to be paid by check rather than with gold, even though they knew there was a possibility that the check might bounce?

10. In ancient Greece, why was gold a more likely candidate for use as money than wine was?

11. If you use an online payment system such as PayPal to purchase goods or services on the Internet, does this affect the M1 money supply, M2 money supply, both, or neither? Explain.

12. Rank the following assets from most liquid to least liquid:
    a. Checking account deposits
    b. Houses
    c. Currency
    d. Automobile
    e. Savings deposits
    f. Common stock

13. Which of the Federal Reserve's measures of the monetary aggregates—M1 or M2—is composed of the most liquid assets? Which is the larger measure?

14. It is not unusual to find a business that displays a sign saying "no personal checks, please." On the basis of this observation, comment on the relative degree of liquidity of a checking account and currency.

15. For each of the following assets, indicate which of the monetary aggregates (M1 and M2) includes them:
    a. Currency
    b. Money market mutual funds
    c. Small-denomination time deposits
    d. Checkable deposits

16. Assume that you are interested in earning some return on idle balances you usually keep in your checking account and decide to buy some money market mutual funds shares by writing a check. Comment on the effect of your action (with everything else the same) on M1 and M2.

17. In September 2008, the growth rate of the M1 money supply was zero, while the growth rate of the M2 money supply was about 5%. In July 2009, the growth rate of M1 was about 17%, and the growth rate of M2 was about 8%. How should Federal Reserve policymakers interpret these changes in the growth rates of M1 and M2?

18. Suppose that a researcher discovers that a measure of the total amount of debt in the U.S. economy over the past twenty years was a better predictor of inflation and the business cycle than M1 or M2. Does this discovery mean that we should define money as equal to the total amount of debt in the economy?

Applied Problems

All applied problems are available in MyEconLab *at* www.myeconlab.com.

19. The table below shows hypothetical values, in billions of dollars.

a. Use the table to calculate the M1 and M2 money supply for each year, as well as the growth rates of the M1 and M2 money supply from the previous year.

b. Why are the growth rates of M1 and M2 so different? Explain.

		2009	2010	2011	2012
A.	Currency	900	920	925	931
B.	Money market mutual fund shares	680	681	679	688
C.	Saving account deposits	5,500	5,780	5,968	6,105
D.	Money market deposit accounts	1,214	1,245	1,274	1,329
E.	Demand and checkable deposits	1,000	972	980	993
F.	Small denomination time deposits	830	861	1,123	1,566
G.	Traveler's checks	4	4	3	2
H.	3-month treasury bills	1,986	2,374	2,436	2,502

Web Exercises

1. Go to www.federalreserve.gov/releases/h6/Current/.

a. What has been the growth rate in M1 and M2 over the past twelve months?

b. From what you know about the state of the economy, does this seem expansionary or restrictive?

2. Go to www.federalreserve.gov/ and select one topic on which the Federal Reserve has a written policy. Write a one-paragraph summary of this policy.

Web References

www.federalreserve.gov/paymentsystems/default.htm

This site reports on the Federal Reserve's policies regarding payments systems.

www.federalreserve.gov/releases/h6/Current/

The Federal Reserve reports the current levels of M1 and M2 on its website.

Part 2

Financial Markets

Crisis and Response: Credit Market Turmoil and the Stock Market Crash in October 2008

The financial crisis that started during the summer of 2007 began snowballing as the value of mortgage-backed securities on financial institutions' balance sheets plummeted. When the House of Representatives, fearing the wrath of constituents who were angry about bailing out Wall Street, voted down a $700 billion bailout package proposed by the Bush administration on Monday, September 29, 2008, the financial crisis took an even more virulent turn, despite the bailout package that was passed four days later.

A "flight to quality" drove three-month Treasury bill rates down to almost zero, which had last happened during the Great Depression of the 1930s. Credit spreads—an indicator of risk—shot through the roof, with the gap between Eurodollar and Treasury bill rates (the TED spread) going from around 40 basis points (0.40 percentage point) before the financial crisis started to over 450 basis points in mid-October, the highest value in its history. After earlier sharp declines, the stock market crashed further, with the week beginning on October 6, 2008, showing the worst weekly decline in U.S. history.

The recent financial crisis illustrates how volatile financial markets can be. This volatility hit financial consumers directly, with difficulty getting loans, falling home values, declining retirement account values, and jobs in jeopardy. How can policy respond to disruptions in financial markets? We begin addressing this question by examining the inner workings of financial markets, particularly interest rate dynamics. Chapter 4 explains what an interest rate is, as well as the relationship between interest rates, bond prices, and returns. Chapter 5 examines how the overall level of interest rates is determined. In Chapter 6, we extend the analysis of the bond market to explain changes in credit spreads and the relationship of long-term to short-term interest rates. Chapter 7 looks at the role of expectations in the stock market and what drives stock prices.

4 Understanding Interest Rates

Preview

Interest rates are among the most closely watched variables in the economy. Their movements are reported almost daily by the news media, because they directly affect our everyday lives and have important consequences for the health of the economy. They influence personal decisions such as whether to consume or save, whether to buy a house, and whether to purchase bonds or put funds into a savings account. Interest rates also affect the economic decisions of businesses and households, such as whether to use their funds to invest in new equipment for factories or to save their money in a bank.

Before we can go on with the study of money, banking, and financial markets, we must understand exactly what the phrase *interest rates* means. In this chapter, we see that a concept known as the *yield to maturity* is the most accurate measure of interest rates; the yield to maturity is what economists mean when they use the term *interest rate*. We discuss how the yield to maturity is measured. We'll also see that a bond's interest rate does not necessarily indicate how good an investment the bond is because what it earns (its rate of return) does not necessarily equal its interest rate. Finally, we explore the distinction between real interest rates, which are adjusted for inflation, and nominal interest rates, which are not.

Although learning definitions is not always the most exciting of pursuits, it is important to read carefully and understand the concepts presented in this chapter. Not only are they continually used throughout the remainder of this text, but also a firm grasp of these terms will give you a clearer understanding of the role that interest rates play in your life as well as in the general economy.

MEASURING INTEREST RATES

Different debt instruments have very different streams of cash payments to the holder (known as **cash flows**) with very different timing. Thus we first need to understand how we can compare the value of one kind of debt instrument with another before we see how interest rates are measured. To do this, we make use of the concept of *present value*.

Present Value

The concept of **present value** (or **present discounted value**) is based on the commonsense notion that a dollar paid to you one year from now is less valuable than a dollar paid to you today: This notion is true because you can deposit a dollar today in a savings account that earns interest and have more than a dollar in one year. Economists use a more formal definition, as explained in this section.

Let's look at the simplest kind of debt instrument, which we will call a **simple loan.** In this loan, the lender provides the borrower with an amount of funds (called the *principal*) that must be repaid to the lender at the *maturity date*, along with an additional payment for the interest. For example, if you made your friend, Jane, a simple loan of \$100 for one year, you would require her to repay the principal of \$100 in one year's time along with an additional payment for interest—say, \$10. In the case of a simple loan like this one, the interest payment divided by the amount of the loan is a natural and sensible way to measure the interest rate. This measure of the so-called *simple interest rate*, *i*, is

$$i = \frac{\$10}{\$100} = 0.10 = 10\%$$

If you make this \$100 loan, at the end of the year you would have \$110, which can be rewritten as

$$\$100 \times (1 + 0.10) = \$110$$

If you then lent out the \$110, at the end of the second year you would have

$$\$110 \times (1 + 0.10) = \$121$$

or, equivalently,

$$\$100 \times (1 + 0.10) \times (1 + 0.10) = \$100 \times (1 + 0.10)^2 = \$121$$

Continuing with the loan again, you would have at the end of the third year

$$\$121 \times (1 + 0.10) = \$100 \times (1 + 0.10)^3 = \$133$$

Generalizing, we can see that at the end of *n* years, your \$100 would turn into

$$\$100 \times (1 + i)^n$$

The amounts you would have at the end of each year by making the \$100 loan today can be seen in the following timeline:

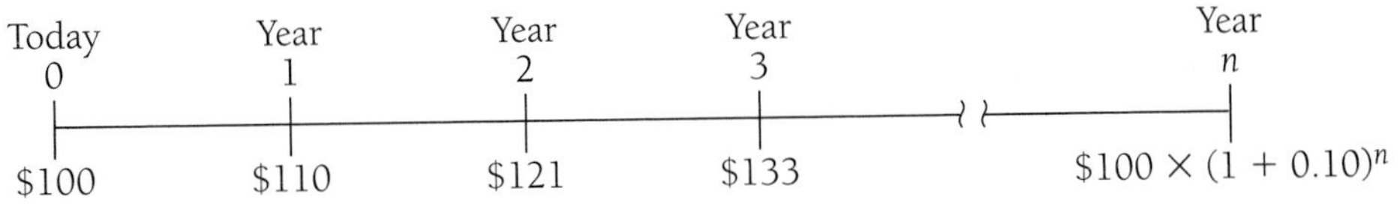

This timeline immediately tells you that you are just as happy having \$100 today as having \$110 a year from now (of course, as long as you are sure that Jane will pay you back). You are also just as happy having \$100 today as having \$121 two years from now, or \$133 three years from now, or $\$100 \times (1 + 0.10)^n$ *n* years from now. The timeline tells us that we can also work backward from future amounts to the present. For example, $\$133 = \$100 \times (1 + 0.10)^3$ three years from now is worth \$100 today, so that

$$\$100 = \frac{\$133}{(1 + 0.10)^3}$$

The process of calculating today's value of dollars received in the future, as we have done above, is called *discounting the future*. We can generalize this process by writing today's (present) value of \$100 as *PV* and the future cash flow (payment) of \$133 as *CF*, and then replacing 0.10 (the 10% interest rate) by *i*. This leads to the following formula:

$$PV = \frac{CF}{(1+i)^n} \tag{1}$$

Intuitively, Equation 1 tells us that if you are promised \$1 of cash flow for certain ten years from now, this dollar would not be as valuable to you as \$1 is today because if you had the \$1 today, you could invest it and end up with more than \$1 in ten years.

The concept of present value is extremely useful, because it allows us to figure out today's value (price) of a credit (debt) market instrument at a given simple interest rate *i* by just adding up the individual present values of all the future payments received. This information enables us to compare the values of two or more instruments with very different timing of their payments.

APPLICATION ◆ Simple Present Value

What is the present value of \$250 to be paid in two years if the interest rate is 15%?

Solution

The present value would be \$189.04. Using Equation 1

$$PV = \frac{CF}{(1+i)^n}$$

where

$$\begin{aligned} CF &= \text{cash flow in two years} &&= \$250 \\ i &= \text{annual interest rate} &&= 0.15 \\ n &= \text{number of years} &&= 2 \end{aligned}$$

Thus

$$PV = \frac{\$250}{(1+0.15)^2} = \frac{\$250}{1.3225} = \$189.04$$

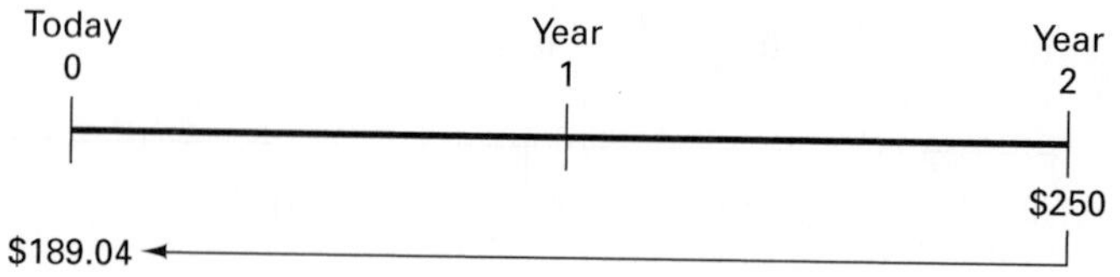

◆

APPLICATION ◆ How Much Is That Jackpot Worth?

Assume that you just hit the \$20 million jackpot in the New York State Lottery, which promises you a payment of \$1 million for the next twenty years. You are clearly excited, but have you really won \$20 million?

Solution

No, not in the present value sense. In today's dollars, that \$20 million is worth a lot less. If we assume an interest rate of 10% as in the earlier examples, the first payment of \$1 million is clearly worth \$1 million today, but the second payment next year is worth only \$1 million/(1 + 0.10) = \$909,090, a lot less than \$1 million. The following year the payment is worth \$1 million/$(1 + 0.10)^2$ = \$826,446 in today's dollars, and so on. When you add all these up, they come to \$9.4 million. You are still pretty excited (who wouldn't be?), but because you understand the concept of present value, you recognize that you are the victim of false advertising. In present value terms, you didn't really win \$20 million, but instead won less than half as much. ◆

Four Types of Credit Market Instruments

In terms of the timing of their cash flow payments, there are four basic types of credit market instruments.

1. A simple loan, which we have already discussed, in which the lender provides the borrower with an amount of funds, which must be repaid to the lender at the maturity date along with an additional payment for the interest. Many money market instruments are of this type—for example, commercial loans to businesses.
2. A **fixed-payment loan** (which is also called a **fully amortized loan**) in which the lender provides the borrower with an amount of funds, which must be repaid by making the same payment every period (such as a month), consisting of part of the principal and interest for a set number of years. For example, if you borrowed \$1,000, a fixed-payment loan might require you to pay \$126 every year for 25 years. Installment loans (such as auto loans) and mortgages are frequently of the fixed-payment type.
3. A **coupon bond** pays the owner of the bond a fixed interest payment (coupon payment) every year until the maturity date, when a specified final amount (**face value** or **par value**) is repaid. (The coupon payment is so named because the bondholder used to obtain payment by clipping a coupon off the bond and sending it to the bond issuer, who then sent the payment to the holder. Today, it is no longer necessary to send in coupons to receive these payments.) A coupon bond with \$1,000 face value, for example, might pay you a coupon payment of \$100 per year for ten years, and at the maturity date repay you the face value amount of \$1,000. (The face value of a bond is usually in \$1,000 increments.)

   A coupon bond is identified by four pieces of information. First, the bond's face value. Second is the corporation or government agency that issues the bond. Third is the maturity date of the bond. Fourth is the bond's **coupon rate**, the dollar amount of the yearly coupon payment expressed as a percentage of the face value of the bond. In our example, the coupon bond has a yearly coupon payment of \$100 and a face value of \$1,000. The coupon rate is then \$100/\$1,000 = 0.10, or 10%. Capital market instruments such as U.S. Treasury bonds and notes and corporate bonds are examples of coupon bonds.
4. A **discount bond** (also called a **zero-coupon bond**) is bought at a price below its face value (at a discount), and the face value is repaid at the maturity date. Unlike a coupon bond, a discount bond does not make any interest payments; it just pays off

the face value. For example, a one-year discount bond with a face value of $1,000 might be bought for $900; in a year's time the owner would be repaid the face value of $1,000. U.S. Treasury bills, U.S. savings bonds, and long-term zero-coupon bonds are examples of discount bonds.

These four types of instruments require payments at different times: Simple loans and discount bonds make payment only at their maturity dates, whereas fixed-payment loans and coupon bonds have payments periodically until maturity. How would you decide which of these instruments provides you with more income? They all seem so different because they make payments at different times. To solve this problem, we use the concept of present value, explained earlier, to provide us with a procedure for measuring interest rates on these different types of instruments.

Yield to Maturity

Of the several common ways of calculating interest rates, the most important is the **yield to maturity**, the interest rate that equates the present value of cash flow payments received from a debt instrument with its value today.[1] Because the concept behind the calculation of the yield to maturity makes good economic sense, economists consider it the most accurate measure of interest rates.

To better understand the yield to maturity, we now look at how it is calculated for the four types of credit market instruments. In all these examples, the key to understanding the calculation of the yield to maturity is equating today's value of the debt instrument with the present value of all of its future cash flow payments.

Simple Loan With the concept of present value, the yield to maturity on a simple loan is easy to calculate. For the one-year loan we discussed, today's value is $100, and the payments in one year's time would be $110 (the repayment of $100 plus the interest payment of $10). We can use this information to solve for the yield to maturity i by recognizing that the present value of the future payments must equal today's value of a loan.

APPLICATION ◆ Yield to Maturity on a Simple Loan

If Pete borrows $100 from his sister and next year she wants $110 back from him, what is the yield to maturity on this loan?

Solution

The yield to maturity on the loan is 10%.

$$PV = \frac{CF}{(1 + i)^n}$$

where

$$\begin{aligned} PV &= \text{amount borrowed} &&= \$100 \\ CF &= \text{cash flow in one year} &&= \$110 \\ n &= \text{number of years} &&= 1 \end{aligned}$$

[1]In other contexts, it is also called the *internal rate of return*.

Thus

$$\$100 = \frac{\$110}{(1 + i)}$$

$$(1 + i)\$100 = \$110$$

$$(1 + i) = \frac{\$110}{\$100}$$

$$i = 1.10 - 1 = 0.10 = 10\%$$

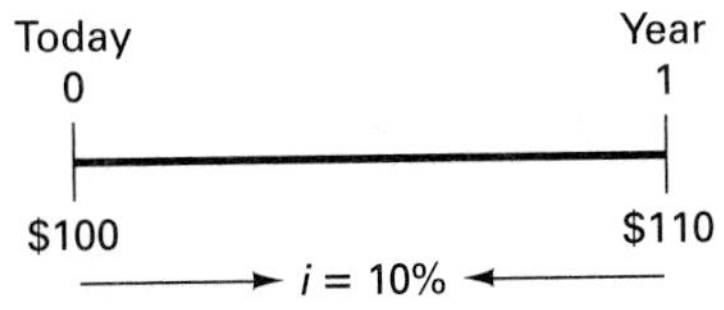

This calculation of the yield to maturity should look familiar, because it equals the interest payment of $10 divided by the loan amount of $100; that is, it equals the simple interest rate on the loan. An important point to recognize is that ***for simple loans, the simple interest rate equals the yield to maturity.*** Hence the same term i is used to denote both the yield to maturity and the simple interest rate.

Fixed-Payment Loan Recall that this type of loan has the same cash flow payment every period throughout the life of the loan. On a fixed-rate mortgage, for example, the borrower makes the same payment to the bank every month until the maturity date, when the loan will be completely paid off. To calculate the yield to maturity for a fixed-payment loan, we follow the same strategy we used for the simple loan—we equate today's value of the loan with its present value. Because the fixed-payment loan involves more than one cash flow payment, the present value of the fixed-payment loan is calculated as the sum of the present values of all cash flow payments (using Equation 1).

In the case of our earlier example, the loan is $1,000 and the yearly payment is $126 for the next 25 years. The present value is calculated as follows: At the end of one year, there is a $126 payment with a *PV* of $\$126/(1 + i)$; at the end of two years, there is another $126 payment with a *PV* of $\$126/(1 + i)^2$; and so on until at the end of the twenty-fifth year, the last payment of $126 with a *PV* of $\$126/(1 + i)^{25}$ is made. Making today's value of the loan ($1,000) equal to the sum of the present values of all the yearly payments gives us

$$\$1{,}000 = \frac{\$126}{1 + i} + \frac{\$126}{(1 + i)^2} + \frac{\$126}{(1 + i)^3} + \ldots + \frac{\$126}{(1 + i)^{25}}$$

More generally, for any fixed-payment loan,

$$LV = \frac{FP}{(1 + i)} + \frac{FP}{(1 + i)^2} + \frac{FP}{(1 + i)^3} + \ldots + \frac{FP}{(1 + i)^n} \tag{2}$$

where LV = loan value
FP = fixed yearly payment
n = number of years until maturity

For a fixed-payment loan, the loan value, the fixed yearly payment and the number of years until maturity are known quantities, and only the yield to maturity is not. So we can solve this equation for the yield to maturity i. Because this calculation is not easy, many financial calculators have programs that allow you to find i given the loan's numbers for LV, FP, and n. For example, in the case of a 25-year loan with yearly payments of \$85.81, the yield to maturity that solves Equation 2 is 7%. Real estate brokers always have a financial calculator that can solve such equations so that they can immediately tell the prospective house buyer exactly what the yearly (or monthly) payments will be if the house purchase is financed by a mortgage.

APPLICATION ◆ Yield to Maturity and the Yearly Payment on a Fixed-Payment Loan

You decide to purchase a new home and need a \$100,000 mortgage. You take out a loan from the bank that has an interest rate of 7%. What is the yearly payment to the bank to pay off the loan in twenty years?

Solution

The yearly payment to the bank is \$9,439.29.

$$LV = \frac{FP}{(1+i)} + \frac{FP}{(1+i)^2} + \frac{FP}{(1+i)^3} + \ldots + \frac{FP}{(1+i)^n}$$

where

$$\begin{aligned} LV &= \text{loan value amount} = 100{,}000 \\ i &= \text{annual interest rate} = 0.07 \\ n &= \text{number of years} = 20 \end{aligned}$$

Thus

$$\$100{,}000 = \frac{FP}{(1+0.07)} + \frac{FP}{(1+0.07)^2} + \frac{FP}{(1+0.07)^3} + \ldots + \frac{FP}{(1+0.07)^{20}}$$

To find the monthly payment for the loan using a financial calculator:

$$\begin{aligned} n &= \text{number of years} &&= 20 \\ PV &= \text{amount of the loan } (LV) &&= -100{,}000 \\ FV &= \text{amount of the loan after 20 years} &&= 0 \\ i &= \text{annual interest rate} &&= .07 \end{aligned}$$

Then push the PMT button = fixed yearly payment (FP) = \$9,439.29. ◆

Coupon Bond To calculate the yield to maturity for a coupon bond, follow the same strategy used for the fixed-payment loan: Equate today's value of the bond with its present value. Because coupon bonds also have more than one cash flow payment, the present value of the bond is calculated as the sum of the present values of all the coupon payments plus the present value of the final payment of the face value of the bond.

The present value of a \$1,000-face-value bond with ten years to maturity and yearly coupon payments of \$100 (a 10% coupon rate) can be calculated as follows: At the end of one year, there is a \$100 coupon payment with a *PV* of $\$100/(1 + i)$; at the end of the second year, there is another \$100 coupon payment with a *PV* of $\$100/(1 + i)^2$; and so on until at maturity, there is a \$100 coupon payment with a *PV* of $\$100/(1 + i)^{10}$ plus the repayment of the \$1,000 face value with a *PV* of $\$1{,}000/(1 + i)^{10}$. Setting today's value of the bond (its current price, denoted by *P*) equal to the sum of the present values of all the cash flow payments for this bond gives

$$P = \frac{\$100}{1+i} + \frac{\$100}{(1+i)^2} + \frac{\$100}{(1+i)^3} + \dots + \frac{\$100}{(1+i)^{10}} + \frac{\$1{,}000}{(1+i)^{10}}$$

More generally, for any coupon bond,[2]

$$P = \frac{C}{1+i} + \frac{C}{(1+i)^2} + \frac{C}{(1+i)^3} + \dots + \frac{C}{(1+i)^n} + \frac{F}{(1+i)^n} \quad (3)$$

where
P = price of coupon bond
C = yearly coupon payment
F = face value of the bond
n = years to maturity date

In Equation 3, the coupon payment, the face value, the years to maturity, and the price of the bond are known quantities, and only the yield to maturity is not. Hence we can solve this equation for the yield to maturity *i*. As in the case of the fixed-payment loan, this calculation is not easy, so business-oriented software and financial calculators have built-in programs that solve this equation for you.

APPLICATION ◆ Yield to Maturity and the Bond Price for a Coupon Bond

Find the price of a 10% coupon bond with a face value of \$1000, a 12.25% yield to maturity, and eight years to maturity.

Solution

The price of the bond is \$889.20. To solve using a financial calculator:

n = years to maturity = 8
FV = face value of the bond (F) = 1,000
i = annual interest rate = 12.25%
PMT = yearly coupon payments (C) = 100

Then push the *PV* button = price of the bond = \$889.20.

Alternatively, you could solve for the yield to maturity given the bond price by putting in \$889.20 for *PV* and pushing the *i* button to get a yield to maturity of 12.25%. ◆

[2]Most coupon bonds actually make coupon payments on a semiannual basis rather than once a year, as assumed here. The effect on the calculations is only very slight and will be ignored here.

TABLE 1

Yields to Maturity on a 10%-Coupon-Rate Bond Maturing in Ten Years (Face Value = $1,000)

Price of Bond ($)	Yield to Maturity (%)
1,200	7.13
1,100	8.48
1,000	10.00
900	11.75
800	13.81

Table 1 shows the yields to maturity calculated for several bond prices. Three interesting facts emerge:

1. When the coupon bond is priced at its face value, the yield to maturity equals the coupon rate.
2. The price of a coupon bond and the yield to maturity are negatively related; that is, as the yield to maturity rises, the price of the bond falls. As the yield to maturity falls, the price of the bond rises.
3. The yield to maturity is greater than the coupon rate when the bond price is below its face value.

These three facts are true for any coupon bond and are really not surprising if you think about the reasoning behind the calculation of the yield to maturity. When you put $1,000 in a bank account with an interest rate of 10%, you can take out $100 every year and you will be left with the $1,000 at the end of ten years. This process is similar to buying the $1,000 bond with a 10% coupon rate analyzed in Table 1, which pays a $100 coupon payment every year and then repays $1,000 at the end of ten years. If the bond is purchased at the par value of $1,000, its yield to maturity must equal 10%, which is also equal to the coupon rate of 10%. The same reasoning applied to any coupon bond demonstrates that if the coupon bond is purchased at its par value, the yield to maturity and the coupon rate must be equal.

It is straightforward to show that the bond price and the yield to maturity are negatively related. As i, the yield to maturity, increases, all denominators in the bond price formula (Equation 3) must necessarily increase, because the rise in i lowers the present value of all future cash flow payments for this bond. Hence a rise in the interest rate, as measured by the yield to maturity, means that the price of the bond must fall. Another way to explain why the bond price falls when the interest rate rises is that a higher interest rate implies that the future coupon payments and final payment are worth less when discounted back to the present; hence the price of the bond must be lower.

The third fact, that the yield to maturity is greater than the coupon rate when the bond price is below its par value, follows directly from facts 1 and 2. When the yield to maturity equals the coupon rate, then the bond price is at the face value; when the yield to maturity rises above the coupon rate, the bond price necessarily falls and so must be below the face value of the bond.

One special case of a coupon bond is worth discussing because its yield to maturity is particularly easy to calculate. This bond is called a **consol** or a **perpetuity**; it is a perpetual bond with no maturity date and no repayment of principal that makes fixed coupon payments of $\$C$ forever. Consols were first sold by the British Treasury during the Napoleonic Wars and are still traded today; they are quite rare, however, in American capital markets. The formula in Equation 3 for the price of the consol P_c simplifies to the following:[3]

$$P_c = \frac{C}{i_c} \tag{4}$$

where P_c = price of the perpetuity (consol)
C = yearly payment
i_c = yield to maturity of the perpetuity (consol)

One nice feature of perpetuities is that you can immediately see that as i_c increases, the price of the bond falls. For example, if a perpetuity pays \$100 per year forever and the interest rate is 10%, its price will be \$1,000 = \$100/0.10. If the interest rate rises to 20%, its price will fall to \$500 = \$100/0.20. We can also rewrite this formula as

$$i_c = \frac{C}{P_c} \tag{5}$$

APPLICATION ◆ Perpetuity

What is the yield to maturity on a bond that has a price of \$2,000 and pays \$100 of interest annually forever?

Solution

The yield to maturity would be 5%.

$$i_c = \frac{C}{P_c}$$

where C = yearly payment = \$100
P_c = price of perpetuity (consol) = \$2,000

Thus

$$i_c = \frac{\$100}{\$2{,}000}$$

$$i_c = 0.05 = 5\%$$ ◆

[3]The bond price formula for a consol is

$$P = \frac{C}{1+i} + \frac{C}{(1+i)^2} + \frac{C}{(1+i)^3} + \ldots$$

which can be written as

$$P = C(x + x^2 + x^3 + \ldots)$$

in which $x = 1/(1+i)$. The formula for an infinite sum is

$$1 + x + x^2 + x^3 + \ldots = \frac{1}{1-x} \text{ for } x < 1$$

and so

$$P = C\left(\frac{1}{1-x} - 1\right) = C\left[\frac{1}{1 - 1/(1+i)} - 1\right]$$

which by suitable algebraic manipulation becomes

$$P = C\left(\frac{1+i}{i} - \frac{i}{i}\right) = \frac{C}{i}$$

The formula in Equation 5, which describes the calculation of the yield to maturity for a perpetuity, also provides a useful approximation for the yield to maturity on coupon bonds. When a coupon bond has a long term to maturity (say, twenty years or more), it is very much like a perpetuity, which pays coupon payments forever. This is because the cash flows more than twenty years in the future have such small present discounted values that the value of a long-term coupon bond is very close to the value of a perpetuity with the same coupon rate. Thus i_c in Equation 5 will be very close to the yield to maturity for any long-term bond. For this reason, i_c, the yearly coupon payment divided by the price of the security, has been given the name **current yield** and is frequently used as an approximation to describe interest rates on long-term bonds.

Discount Bond The yield-to-maturity calculation for a discount bond is similar to that for the simple loan. Let's consider a discount bond such as a one-year U.S. Treasury bill, which pays a face value of $1,000 in one year's time. If the current purchase price of this bill is $900, then equating this price to the present value of the $1,000 received in one year, using Equation 1, gives

$$\$900 = \frac{\$1,000}{1 + i}$$

Solving for i,

$$\begin{aligned}(1 + i) \times \$900 &= \$1,000 \\ \$900 + \$900i &= \$1,000 \\ \$900i &= \$1,000 - \$900 \\ i &= \frac{\$1,000 - \$900}{\$900} = 0.111 = 11.1\%\end{aligned}$$

More generally, for any one-year discount bond, the yield to maturity can be written as

$$i = \frac{F - P}{P} \tag{6}$$

where F = face value of the discount bond
P = current price of the discount bond

In other words, the yield to maturity equals the increase in price over the year $(F - P)$ divided by the initial price (P). In normal circumstances, investors earn positive returns from holding these securities and so they sell at a discount, meaning that the current price of the bond is below the face value. Therefore, $F - P$ should be positive, and the yield to maturity should be positive as well. However, this is not always the case, as recent extraordinary events in Japan indicate (see the Global box).

An important feature of this equation is that it indicates that for a discount bond, the yield to maturity is negatively related to the current bond price. This is the same conclusion that we reached for a coupon bond. For example, Equation 6 shows that a rise in the bond price—say, from $900 to $950—means that the bond will have a smaller increase in its price at maturity, and the yield to maturity falls, from 11.1% to 5.3%. Similarly, a fall in the yield to maturity means that the price of the discount bond has risen.

Global Negative T-Bill Rates? It Can Happen

We normally assume that interest rates must always be positive. Negative interest rates would imply that you are willing to pay more for a bond today than you will receive for it in the future (as our formula for yield to maturity on a discount bond demonstrates). Negative interest rates therefore seem like an impossibility because you would do better by holding cash that has the same value in the future as it does today.

Events in Japan in the late 1990s and in the United States during the global financial crisis have demonstrated that this reasoning is not quite correct. In November 1998, interest rates on Japanese six-month Treasury bills became negative, yielding an interest rate of −0.004%. In September 2008, interest rates on three-month T-bills fell just slightly below zero for a very brief period. Negative interest rates are an extremely unusual event. How could this happen?

As we will see in Chapter 5, the weakness of the economy and a flight to quality during a financial crisis can drive interest rates to low levels, but these two factors can't explain the negative rates. The answer is that large investors found it more convenient to hold these Treasury bills as a store of value rather than holding cash because the bills are denominated in larger amounts and can be stored electronically. For that reason, some investors were willing to hold them, despite their negative rates, even though in monetary terms the investors would be better off holding cash. Clearly, the convenience of T-bills goes only so far, and thus their interest rates can drop only a little bit below zero.

Summary The concept of present value tells you that a dollar in the future is not as valuable to you as a dollar today because you can earn interest on a dollar you have today. Specifically, a dollar received n years from now is worth only $\$1/(1 + i)^n$ today. The present value of a set of future cash flow payments on a debt instrument equals the sum of the present values of each of the future payments. The yield to maturity for an instrument is the interest rate that equates the present value of the future payments on that instrument to its value today. Because the procedure for calculating the yield to maturity is based on sound economic principles, this is the measure that economists think most accurately describes the interest rate.

Our calculations of the yield to maturity for a variety of bonds reveal the important fact that ***current bond prices and interest rates are negatively related: When the interest rate rises, the price of the bond falls, and vice versa***.

THE DISTINCTION BETWEEN INTEREST RATES AND RETURNS

Many people think that the interest rate on a bond tells them all they need to know about how well off they are as a result of owning it. If Irving the Investor thinks he is better off when he owns a long-term bond yielding a 10% interest rate and the interest rate rises to 20%, he will have a rude awakening: As we will shortly see, if he has to sell the bond, Irving has lost his shirt! How well a person does by holding a bond or any other security over a particular time period is accurately measured by the **return**, or, in more precise terminology, the **rate of return**. We will use the concept of *return* continually throughout this book: Understanding it will make the material presented later in the book easier to follow.

For any security, the rate of return is defined as the payments to the owner plus the change in its value, expressed as a fraction of its purchase price. To make this definition clearer, let us see what the return would look like for a $1,000-face-value coupon bond with a coupon rate of 10% that is bought for $1,000, held for one year, and then sold for $1,200. The payments to the owner are the yearly coupon payments of $100, and the change in its value is $1,200 − $1,000 = $200. Adding these together and expressing them as a fraction of the purchase price of $1,000 gives us the one-year holding-period return for this bond:

$$\frac{\$100 + \$200}{\$1{,}000} = \frac{\$300}{\$1{,}000} = 0.30 = 30\%$$

You may have noticed something quite surprising about the return that we have just calculated: It equals 30%, yet as Table 1 indicates, initially the yield to maturity was only 10%. This discrepancy demonstrates that ***the return on a bond will not necessarily equal the yield to maturity on that bond***. We now see that the distinction between interest rate and return can be important, although for many securities the two may be closely related.

More generally, the return on a bond held from time t to time $t + 1$ can be written as

$$R = \frac{C + P_{t+1} - P_t}{P_t} \tag{7}$$

where

R = return from holding the bond from time t to time $t + 1$
P_t = price of the bond at time t
P_{t+1} = price of the bond at time $t + 1$
C = coupon payment

A convenient way to rewrite the return formula in Equation 7 is to recognize that it can be split into two separate terms:

$$R = \frac{C}{P_t} + \frac{P_{t+1} - P_t}{P_t}$$

The first term is the current yield i_c (the coupon payment over the purchase price):

$$\frac{C}{P_t} = i_c$$

The second term is the **rate of capital gain**, or the change in the bond's price relative to the initial purchase price:

$$\frac{P_{t+1} - P_t}{P_t} = g$$

where g is the rate of capital gain. Equation 7 can then be rewritten as

$$R = i_c + g \tag{8}$$

which shows that the return on a bond is the current yield i_c plus the rate of capital gain g. This rewritten formula illustrates the point we just discovered: Even for a bond for which the current yield i_c is an accurate measure of the yield to maturity, the return can differ substantially from the interest rate. Returns will differ from the interest rate, especially if the price of the bond experiences sizable fluctuations that produce substantial capital gains or losses.

TABLE 2

One-Year Returns on Different-Maturity 10%-Coupon-Rate Bonds When Interest Rates Rise from 10% to 20%

(1) Years to Maturity When Bond Is Purchased	(2) Initial Current Yield (%)	(3) Initial Price ($)	(4) Price Next Year* ($)	(5) Rate of Capital Gain (%)	(6) Rate of Return (2 + 5) (%)
30	10	1,000	503	−49.7	−39.7
20	10	1,000	516	−48.4	−38.4
10	10	1,000	597	−40.3	−30.3
5	10	1,000	741	−25.9	−15.9
2	10	1,000	917	−8.3	+1.7
1	10	1,000	1,000	0.0	+10.0

*Calculated with a financial calculator using Equation 3.

To explore this point even further, let's look at what happens to the returns on bonds of different maturities when interest rates rise. Table 2 calculates the one-year return using Equation 8 above on several 10%-coupon-rate bonds all purchased at par when interest rates on all these bonds rise from 10% to 20%. Several key findings in this table are generally true of all bonds:

- The only bond whose return equals the initial yield to maturity is one whose time to maturity is the same as the holding period (see the last bond in Table 2).
- A rise in interest rates is associated with a fall in bond prices, resulting in capital losses on bonds whose terms to maturity are longer than the holding period.
- The more distant a bond's maturity, the greater the size of the percentage price change associated with an interest-rate change.
- The more distant a bond's maturity, the lower the rate of return that occurs as a result of the increase in the interest rate.
- Even though a bond has a substantial initial interest rate, its return can turn out to be negative if interest rates rise.

At first it frequently puzzles students (as it puzzles poor Irving the Investor) that a rise in interest rates can mean that a bond has been a poor investment. The trick to understanding this is to recognize that a rise in the interest rate means that the price of a bond has fallen. A rise in interest rates therefore means that a capital loss has occurred. If this loss is large enough, the bond can be a poor investment indeed. For example, we see in Table 2 that the bond that has 30 years to maturity when purchased has a capital loss of 49.7% when the interest rate rises from 10% to 20%. This loss is so large that it exceeds the current yield of 10%, resulting in a negative return (loss) of –39.7%. If Irving does not sell the bond, his capital loss is often referred to as a "paper loss." This is a loss nonetheless because if he had not bought this bond and had instead put his money in the bank, he would now be able to buy more bonds at their lower price than he presently owns.

Maturity and the Volatility of Bond Returns: Interest-Rate Risk

The finding that the prices of longer-maturity bonds respond more dramatically to changes in interest rates helps explain an important fact about the behavior of bond markets: ***Prices and returns for long-term bonds are more volatile than those for shorter-term bonds***. Price changes of +20% and −20% within a year, with corresponding variations in returns, are common for bonds more than twenty years away from maturity.

We now see that changes in interest rates make investments in long-term bonds quite risky. Indeed, the riskiness of an asset's return that results from interest-rate changes is so important that it has been given a special name, **interest-rate risk**.[4] Dealing with interest-rate risk is a major concern of managers of financial institutions and investors, as we will see in later chapters.

Although long-term debt instruments have substantial interest-rate risk, short-term debt instruments do not. Indeed, bonds with a maturity that is as short as the holding period have no interest-rate risk.[5] We see this for the coupon bond at the bottom of Table 2, which has no uncertainty about the rate of return because it equals the yield to maturity, which is known at the time the bond is purchased. The key to understanding why there is no interest-rate risk for *any* bond whose time to maturity matches the holding period is to recognize that (in this case) the price at the end of the holding period is already fixed at the face value. The change in interest rates can then have no effect on the price at the end of the holding period for these bonds, and the return will therefore be equal to the yield to maturity known at the time the bond is purchased.[6]

[4]Interest-rate risk can be quantitatively measured using the concept of *duration*. This concept and its calculation are discussed in an appendix to this chapter, which can be found on the Companion Website at www.pearsonhighered.com/mishkin.

[5]The statement that there is no interest-rate risk for any bond whose time to maturity matches the holding period is literally true only for discount (zero-coupon) bonds that make no intermediate cash payments before the holding period is over. A coupon bond that makes an intermediate cash payment before the holding period is over requires that this payment be reinvested. Because the interest rate at which this payment can be reinvested is uncertain, some uncertainty exists about the return on this coupon bond even when the time to maturity equals the holding period. However, the riskiness of the return on a coupon bond from reinvesting the coupon payments is typically quite small, so the basic point that a coupon bond with a time to maturity equaling the holding period has very little risk still holds true.

[6]In the text, we are assuming that all holding periods are short and equal to the maturity on short-term bonds and are thus not subject to interest-rate risk. However, if an investor's holding period is longer than the term to maturity of the bond, the investor is exposed to a type of interest-rate risk called *reinvestment risk*. Reinvestment risk occurs because the proceeds from the short-term bond need to be reinvested at a future interest rate that is uncertain.

To understand reinvestment risk, suppose that Irving the Investor has a holding period of two years and decides to purchase a $1,000 one-year bond at face value and then another one at the end of the first year. If the initial interest rate is 10%, Irving will have $1,100 at the end of the year. If the interest rate rises to 20%, as in Table 2, Irving will find that buying $1,100 worth of another one-year bond will leave him at the end of the second year with $\$1{,}100 \times (1 + 0.20) = \$1{,}320$. Thus Irving's two-year return will be $(\$1{,}320 - \${,}1000)/1{,}000 = 0.32 = 32\%$, which equals 14.9% at an annual rate. In this case, Irving has earned more by buying the one-year bonds than if he had initially purchased the two-year bond with an interest rate of 10%. Thus, when Irving has a holding period that is longer than the term to maturity of the bonds he purchases, he benefits from a rise in interest rates. Conversely, if interest rates fall to 5%, Irving will have only $1,155 at the end of two years: $\$1{,}100 \times (1 + 0.05)$. His two-year return will be $(\$1{,}155 - \$1{,}000)/1{,}000 = 0.115 = 15.5\%$, which is 7.2% at an annual rate. With a holding period greater than the term to maturity of the bond, Irving now loses from a decline in interest rates.

We have seen that when the holding period is longer than the term to maturity of a bond, the return is uncertain because the future interest rate when reinvestment occurs is also uncertain—in short, there is reinvestment risk. We also see that if the holding period is longer than the term to maturity of the bond, the investor benefits from a rise in interest rates and is hurt by a fall in interest rates.

Summary

The return on a bond, which tells you how good an investment it has been over the holding period, is equal to the yield to maturity in only one special case—when the holding period and the maturity of the bond are identical. Bonds whose term to maturity is longer than the holding period are subject to interest-rate risk: Changes in interest rates lead to capital gains and losses that produce substantial differences between the return and the yield to maturity known at the time the bond is purchased. Interest-rate risk is especially important for long-term bonds, where the capital gains and losses can be substantial. This is why long-term bonds are not considered safe assets with a sure return over short holding periods.

THE DISTINCTION BETWEEN REAL AND NOMINAL INTEREST RATES

So far in our discussion of interest rates, we have ignored the effects of inflation on the cost of borrowing. What we have up to now been calling the interest rate makes no allowance for inflation, and it is more precisely referred to as the **nominal interest rate**. We distinguish it from the **real interest rate**, the interest rate that is adjusted by subtracting expected changes in the price level (inflation) so that it more accurately reflects the true cost of borrowing. This interest rate is more precisely referred to as the *ex ante real interest rate* because it is adjusted for *expected* changes in the price level. The ex ante real interest rate is most important to economic decisions, and typically it is what economists mean when they make reference to the "real" interest rate. The interest rate that is adjusted for *actual* changes in the price level is called the *ex post real interest rate.* It describes how well a lender has done in real terms *after the fact.*

The real interest rate is more accurately defined from the *Fisher equation*, named for Irving Fisher, one of the great monetary economists of the twentieth century. The Fisher equation states that the nominal interest rate i equals the real interest rate r plus the expected rate of inflation π^e:[7]

$$i = r + \pi^e \tag{9}$$

Rearranging terms, we find that the real interest rate equals the nominal interest rate minus the expected inflation rate:

$$r = i - \pi^e \tag{10}$$

To see why this definition makes sense, let's first consider a situation in which you have made a one-year simple loan with a 5% interest rate $(i = 5\%)$ and you expect the price level to rise by 3% over the course of the year $(\pi^e = 3\%)$. As a result of making

[7]A more precise formulation of the Fisher equation is

$$i = r + \pi^e + (r \times \pi^e)$$

because

$$1 + i = (1 + r)(1 + \pi^e) = 1 + r + \pi^e + (r \times \pi^e)$$

and subtracting 1 from both sides gives us the first equation. For small values of r and π^e, the term $r \times \pi^e$ is so small that we ignore it, as in the text.

the loan, at the end of the year you expect to have 2% more in **real terms**—that is, in terms of real goods and services you can buy. In this case, the interest rate you expect to earn in terms of real goods and services is 2%:

$$r = 5\% - 3\% = 2\%$$

as indicated by the definition in Equation 10.

APPLICATION ◆ Calculating Real Interest Rates

What is the real interest rate if the nominal interest rate is 8% and the expected inflation rate is 10% over the course of a year?

Solution

The real interest rate is −2%. Although you will be receiving 8% more dollars at the end of the year, you will be paying 10% more for goods. The result is that you will be able to buy 2% fewer goods at the end of the year, and you will be 2% worse off in real terms.

$$r = i - \pi^e$$

where

$$i = \text{nominal interest rate} = 0.08$$
$$\pi^e = \text{expected inflation rate} = 0.10$$

Thus

$$r = 0.08 - 0.10 = -0.02 = -2\%$$ ◆

As a lender, you are clearly less eager to make a loan in this case, because in terms of real goods and services you have actually earned a negative interest rate of 2%. By contrast, as the borrower, you fare quite well because at the end of the year, the amounts you will have to pay back will be worth 2% less in terms of goods and services—you as the borrower will be ahead by 2% in real terms. ***When the real interest rate is low, there are greater incentives to borrow and fewer incentives to lend.***

A similar distinction can be made between nominal returns and real returns. Nominal returns, which do not allow for inflation, are what we have been referring to as simply "returns." When inflation is subtracted from a nominal return, we have the real return, which indicates the amount of extra goods and services that we can purchase as a result of holding the security.

The distinction between real and nominal interest rates is important because the real interest rate, which reflects the real cost of borrowing, is likely to be a better indicator of the incentives to borrow and lend. It appears to be a better guide to how people will be affected by what is happening in credit markets. Figure 1, which presents estimates from 1953 to 2011 of the real and nominal interest rates on three-month U.S. Treasury bills, shows us that nominal and real rates often do not move together. (This is also true for nominal and real interest rates in the rest of the world.) In particular, when nominal rates in the United States were high in the 1970s, real rates were actually extremely low—often negative. By the standard of nominal interest rates, you would have thought that credit market conditions were tight in this period,

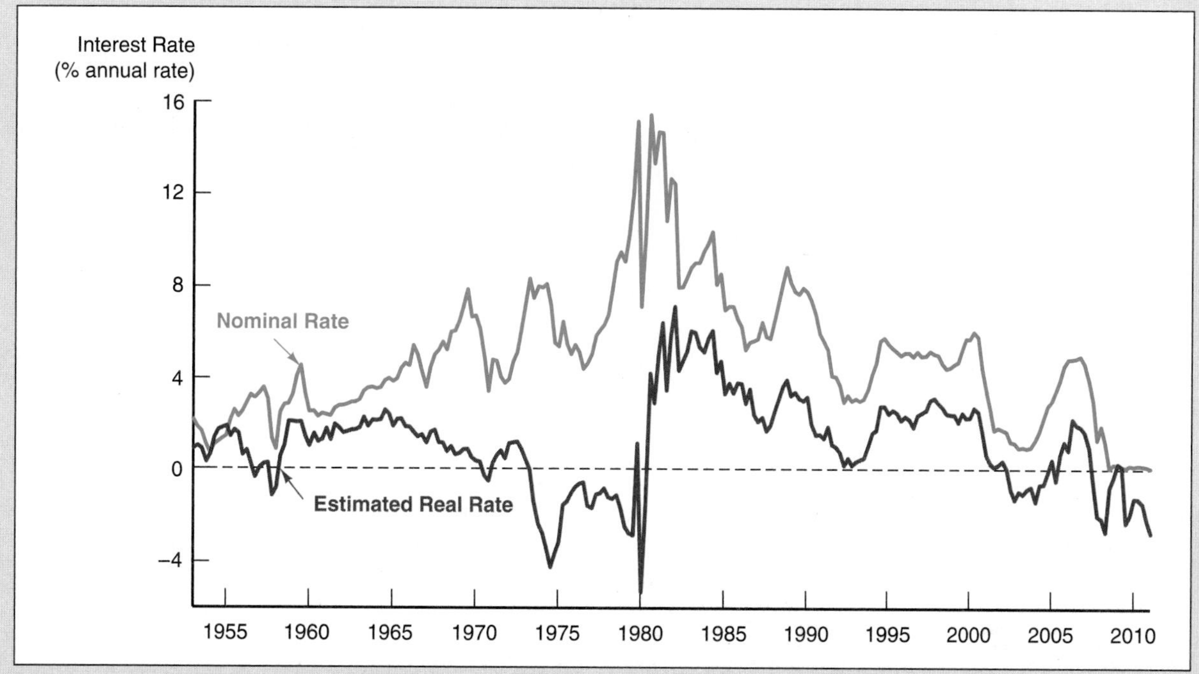

FIGURE 1 Real and Nominal Interest Rates (Three-Month Treasury Bill), 1953–2011
Nominal and real interest rates often do not move together. When U.S. nominal rates were high in the 1970s, real rates were actually extremely low—often negative.

Sources: Nominal rates from www.federalreserve.gov/releases/H15 and inflation from ftp://ftp.bis.gov/special.requests/cpi/cpia.txt. The real rate is constructed using the procedure outlined in Frederic S. Mishkin, "The Real Interest Rate: An Empirical Investigation," *Carnegie-Rochester Conference Series on Public Policy* 15 (1981): 151–200. This procedure involves estimating expected inflation as a function of past interest rates, inflation, and time trends and then subtracting the expected inflation measure from the nominal interest rate.

because it was expensive to borrow. However, the estimates of the real rates indicate that you would have been mistaken. In real terms, the cost of borrowing was actually quite low.[8]

[8]Because most interest income in the United States is subject to federal income taxes, the true earnings in real terms from holding a debt instrument are not reflected by the real interest rate defined by the Fisher equation but rather by the *after-tax real interest rate,* which equals the nominal interest rate *after income tax payments have been subtracted,* minus the expected inflation rate. For a person facing a 30% tax rate, the after-tax interest rate earned on a bond yielding 10% is only 7% because 30% of the interest income must be paid to the Internal Revenue Service. Thus the after-tax real interest rate on this bond when expected inflation is 5% equals $2\% (= 7\% - 5\%)$. More generally, the after-tax real interest rate can be expressed as

$$i(1 - \tau) - \pi^e$$

where $\tau =$ the income tax rate.

This formula for the after-tax real interest rate also provides a better measure of the effective cost of borrowing for many corporations and homeowners in the United States because in calculating income taxes, they can deduct interest payments on loans from their income. Thus, if you face a 30% tax rate and take out a mortgage loan with a 10% interest rate, you are able to deduct the 10% interest payment and lower your taxes by 30% of this amount. Your after-tax nominal cost of borrowing is then 7% (10% minus 30% of the 10% interest payment), and when the expected inflation rate is 5%, the effective cost of borrowing in real terms is again $2\% (= 7\% - 5\%)$.

As the example (and the formula) indicates, after-tax real interest rates are always below the real interest rate defined by the Fisher equation. For a further discussion of measures of after-tax real interest rates, see Frederic S. Mishkin, "The Real Interest Rate: An Empirical Investigation," *Carnegie-Rochester Conference Series on Public Policy* 15 (1981): 151–200.

FYI With TIPS, Real Interest Rates Have Become Observable in the United States

When the U.S. Treasury decided to issue TIPS (Treasury Inflation Protection Securities), a version of indexed Treasury coupon bonds, in January 1997, it was somewhat late in the game. Other countries such as the United Kingdom, Canada, Australia, and Sweden had already beaten the United States to the punch. (In September 1998, the U.S. Treasury also began issuing the Series I savings bond, which provides inflation protection for small investors.)

These indexed securities have successfully carved out a niche in the bond market, enabling governments to raise more funds. In addition, because their interest and principal payments are adjusted for changes in the price level, the interest rate on these bonds provides a direct measure of a real interest rate. These indexed bonds are very useful to policy makers, especially monetary policy makers, because by subtracting their interest rate from a nominal interest rate on a nonindexed bond, they generate more insight into expected inflation, a valuable piece of information. For example, on October 7, 2011, the interest rate on the ten-year Treasury bond was 2.125%, while that on the ten-year TIPS was 0.625%. Thus, the implied expected inflation rate for the next ten years, derived from the difference between these two rates, was 1.50%. The private sector finds the information provided by TIPS very useful: Many commercial and investment banks routinely publish the expected U.S. inflation rates derived from these bonds.

Until recently, real interest rates in the United States were not observable; only nominal rates were reported. This all changed when, in January 1997, the U.S. Treasury began to issue **indexed bonds**, whose interest and principal payments are adjusted for changes in the price level (see the FYI box on TIPS).

Summary

1. The yield to maturity, which is the measure most accurately reflecting the interest rate, is the interest rate that equates the present value of future payments of a debt instrument with its value today. Application of this principle reveals that bond prices and interest rates are negatively related: When the interest rate rises, the price of the bond must fall, and vice versa.
2. The return on a security, which tells you how well you have done by holding this security over a stated period of time, can differ substantially from the interest rate as measured by the yield to maturity. Long-term bond prices have substantial fluctuations when interest rates change and thus bear interest-rate risk. The resulting capital gains and losses can be large, which is why long-term bonds are not considered safe assets with a sure return.
3. The real interest rate is defined as the nominal interest rate minus the expected rate of inflation. It is both a better measure of the incentives to borrow and lend and a more accurate indicator of the tightness of credit market conditions than is the nominal interest rate.

Key Terms

cash flows, p. 66
consol or perpetuity, p. 74
coupon bond, p. 69
coupon rate, p. 69
current yield, p. 76
discount bond (zero-coupon bond), p. 69

face value (par value), p. 69

fixed-payment loan (fully amortized loan), p. 69

indexed bond, p. 84

interest-rate risk, p. 80

nominal interest rate, p. 81

present discounted value, p. 66

present value, p. 66

rate of capital gain, p. 78

real interest rate, p. 81

real terms, p. 82

return (rate of return), p. 77

simple loan, p. 67

yield to maturity, p. 70

Questions

All questions are available in MyEconLab *at* www.myeconlab.com.

1. Would a dollar tomorrow be worth more to you today when the interest rate is 20%, or when it is 10%?
2. Write down the formula that is used to calculate the yield to maturity on a twenty-year 10% coupon bond with $1,000 face value that sells for $2,000.
3. To pay for college, you have just taken out a $1,000 government loan that makes you pay $126 per year for 25 years. However, you don't have to start making these payments until you graduate from college two years from now. Why is the yield to maturity necessarily less than 12% (this is the yield to maturity on a normal $1,000 fixed-payment loan in which you pay $126 per year for 25 years)?
4. Is it better for bondholders when the yield to maturity increases or decreases?
5. A financial adviser has just given you the following advice: "Long-term bonds are a great investment because their interest rate is over 20%." Is the financial adviser necessarily right?
6. If mortgage rates rise from 5% to 10% but the expected rate of increase in housing prices rises from 2% to 9%, are people more or less likely to buy houses?
7. When is the current yield a good approximation to the yield to maturity?
8. Why would a government choose to issue a perpetuity, which requires payments forever, instead of a terminal loan, such as a fixed-payment loan, discount bond, or coupon bond?
9. Under what conditions will a discount bond have a negative nominal interest rate? Is it possible for a coupon bond or a perpetuity to have a negative nominal interest rate?
10. True or False: With a discount bond, the return on a bond is equal to the rate of capital gain.
11. If interest rates decline, which would you rather be holding, long-term bonds or short-term bonds? Why? Which type of bond has the greater interest-rate risk?
12. Interest rates were lower in the mid-1980s than in the late 1970s, yet many economists have commented that real interest rates were actually much higher in the mid-1980s than in the late 1970s. Does this make sense? Do you think that these economists are right?
13. Retired persons often have much of their wealth placed in savings accounts and other interest-bearing investments, and complain whenever interest rates are low. Do they have a valid complaint?

Applied Problems

All applied problems are available in MyEconLab *at* www.myeconlab.com.

14. If the interest rate is 10%, what is the present value of a security that pays you $1,100 next year, $1,210 the year after, and $1,331 the year after that?
15. Calculate the present value of a $1,000 discount bond with five years to maturity if the yield to maturity is 6%.
16. A lottery claims its grand prize is $10 million, payable over 5 years at $2,000,000 per year. If the first payment

is made immediately, what is this grand prize really worth? Use an interest rate of 6%.

17. What is the yield to maturity on a $1,000-face-value discount bond maturing in one year that sells for $800?

18. What is the yield to maturity on a simple loan for $1 million that requires a repayment of $2 million in five years' time?

19. Which $1,000 bond has the higher yield to maturity, a twenty-year bond selling for $800 with a current yield of 15% or a one-year bond selling for $800 with a current yield of 5%?

20. Consider a bond with a 4% annual coupon and a face value of $1,000. Complete the following table. What relationships do you observe between years to maturity, yield to maturity, and the current price?

Years to Maturity	Yield to Maturity	Current Price
2	2%	
2	4%	
3	4%	
5	2%	
5	6%	

21. Consider a coupon bond that has a $1,000 par value and a coupon rate of 10%. The bond is currently selling for $1,044.89 and has two years to maturity. What is the bond's yield to maturity?

22. What is the price of a perpetuity that has a coupon of $50 per year and a yield to maturity of 2.5%? If the yield to maturity doubles, what will happen to its price?

23. Property taxes in a particular district are 4% of the purchase price every year. If you just purchased a $250,000 home, what is the present value of all the future property tax payments? Assume that the house remains worth $250,000 forever, property tax rates never change, and that a 6% interest rate is used for discounting.

24. A $1000-face-value bond has a 10% coupon rate, its current price is $960, and it is expected to increase to $980 next year. Calculate the current yield, the expected rate of capital gain, and the expected rate of return.

25. Assume you just deposited $1,000 into a bank account. The current real interest rate is 2%, and inflation is expected to be 6% over the next year. What nominal rate would you require from the bank over the next year? How much money will you have at the end of one year? If you are saving to buy a fancy bicycle that currently sells for $1,050, will you have enough to buy it?

Web Exercises

1. Investigate the data available from the Federal Reserve at www.federalreserve.gov/releases/. Using current data, answer the following questions:
   a. What is the difference in the interest rates on commercial paper for financial firms when compared to nonfinancial firms?
   b. What is the interest rate on one-month Eurodollar deposits?
   c. What is the interest rate for the 30-year Treasury bond?
2. Figure 1 in the text shows the estimated real and nominal rates for three-month Treasury bills. Go to www.martincapital.com/main/charts.htm and click on Nominal vs. Real Rates, then on Nominal vs. Real Market Rates.
   a. Compare the three-month real rate to the long-term real rate. Which is greater?
   b. Compare the short-term nominal rate to the long-term nominal rate. Which appears most volatile?
3. In this chapter we discussed long-term bonds as if there were only one type, coupon bonds. In fact, there are also long-term discount bonds. A discount bond is sold at a low price and the whole return comes in the form of a price appreciation. You can easily compute the current price of a discount bond using the financial calculator at www.treasurydirect.gov/indiv/tools/tools_savingsbondcalc.htm.

   To compute the values for savings bonds, read the instructions on the page and click on Get Started. Fill in the information (you do not need to fill in the Bond Serial Number field) and click on Calculate.

Web References

www.bloomberg.com/markets/

Under Rates & Bonds, you can access information on key interest rates, U.S. Treasuries, government bonds, and municipal bonds.

www.teachmefinance.com

A review of the key financial concepts: time value of money, annuities, perpetuities, and so on.

www.martincapital.com/main/charts.htm

Go to charts of real versus nominal rates to view 30 years of nominal interest rates compared to real rates for the 30-year T-bond and 90-day T-bill.

Web Appendices

Please visit the Companion Website at www.pearsonhighered.com/mishkin to read the Web appendix to Chapter 4

Appendix 1: **Measuring Interest-Rate Risk: Duration**

5 The Behavior of Interest Rates

Preview

In the early 1950s, nominal interest rates on three-month Treasury bills were about 1% at an annual rate; by 1981, they had reached over 15%; in 2003 they fell below 1%, rose to 5% in 2007, and then fell close to zero starting in 2008. What explains these substantial fluctuations in interest rates? One reason why we study money, banking, and financial markets is to provide some answers to this question.

In this chapter, we examine how the overall level of *nominal* interest rates (which we refer to as simply "interest rates") is determined and which factors influence their behavior. We learned in Chapter 4 that interest rates are negatively related to the price of bonds, so if we can explain why bond prices change, we can also explain why interest rates fluctuate. We make use of supply and demand analysis for bond markets and markets for money to examine how interest rates change.

To derive a demand curve for assets such as money or bonds, the first step in our analysis, we must first understand what determines the demand for these assets. We do this by examining *portfolio theory*, an economic theory that outlines criteria that are important when deciding how much of an asset to buy. Armed with this theory, we can then go on to derive the demand curve for bonds or money. After deriving supply curves for these assets, we develop the concept of *market equilibrium*, the point at which the quantity supplied equals the quantity demanded. Then we use this model to explain changes in equilibrium interest rates.

Because interest rates on different securities tend to move together, in this chapter we will proceed as if there were only one type of security and one interest rate in the entire economy. In the following chapter, we expand our analysis to look at why interest rates on different types of securities differ.

DETERMINANTS OF ASSET DEMAND

Before going on to our supply and demand analysis of the bond market and the market for money, we must first understand what determines the quantity demanded of an asset. Recall that an asset is a piece of property that is a store of value. Items such as money, bonds, stocks, art, land, houses, farm equipment, and manufacturing machinery are all assets. Facing the question of whether to buy and hold an asset or whether to buy one asset rather than another, an individual must consider the following factors:

1. **Wealth**, the total resources owned by the individual, including all assets
2. **Expected return** (the return expected over the next period) on one asset relative to alternative assets

3. **Risk** (the degree of uncertainty associated with the return) on one asset relative to alternative assets
4. **Liquidity** (the ease and speed with which an asset can be turned into cash) relative to alternative assets

Wealth

When we find that our wealth has increased, we have more resources available with which to purchase assets, and so, not surprisingly, the quantity of assets we demand increases. Therefore, the effect of changes in wealth on the quantity demanded of an asset can be summarized as follows: ***Holding everything else constant, an increase in wealth raises the quantity demanded of an asset.***

Expected Returns

In Chapter 4, we saw that the return on an asset (such as a bond) measures how much we gain from holding that asset. When we make a decision to buy an asset, we are influenced by what we expect the return on that asset to be. If an ExxonMobil bond, for example, has a return of 15% half the time and 5% the other half, its expected return (which you can think of as the average return) is 10% $(= 0.5 \times 15\% + 0.5 \times 5\%)$[1] If the expected return on the ExxonMobil bond rises relative to expected returns on alternative assets, holding everything else constant, then it becomes more desirable to purchase it, and the quantity demanded increases. This can occur in either of two ways: (1) when the expected return on the ExxonMobil bond rises while the return on an alternative asset—say, stock in Google—remains unchanged or (2) when the return on the alternative asset, the Google stock, falls while the return on the ExxonMobil bond remains unchanged. To summarize, ***an increase in an asset's expected return relative to that of an alternative asset, holding everything else unchanged, raises the quantity demanded of the asset***.

Risk

The degree of risk or uncertainty of an asset's returns also affects demand for the asset. Consider two assets, stock in Fly-by-Night Airlines and stock in Feet-on-the-Ground Bus Company. Suppose that Fly-by-Night stock has a return of 15% half the time and 5% the other half, making its expected return 10%, while stock in Feet-on-the-Ground has a fixed return of 10%. Fly-by-Night stock has uncertainty associated with its returns and so has greater risk than stock in Feet-on-the-Ground, whose return is a sure thing.

A *risk-averse* person prefers stock in Feet-on-the-Ground (the sure thing) to Fly-by-Night stock (the riskier asset), even though the stocks have the same expected return, 10%. By contrast, a person who prefers risk is a *risk preferrer* or *risk lover*. Most people are risk-averse, especially in their financial decisions: Everything else

[1]If you are interested in finding out more information on how to calculate expected returns, as well as standard deviations of returns that measure risk, you can look at an appendix to this chapter describing models of asset pricing that is on the Companion Website at www.pearsonhighered.com/mishkin. This appendix also describes how diversification lowers the overall risk of a portfolio and has a discussion of systematic risk and basic asset pricing models such as the capital asset pricing model and arbitrage pricing theory.

being equal, they prefer to hold the less risky asset. Hence, ***holding everything else constant, if an asset's risk rises relative to that of alternative assets, its quantity demanded will fall***.

Liquidity

Another factor that affects the demand for an asset is how quickly it can be converted into cash at low costs—its liquidity. An asset is liquid if the market in which it is traded has depth and breadth, that is, if the market has many buyers and sellers. A house is not a very liquid asset, because it may be hard to find a buyer quickly; if a house must be sold to pay off bills, it might have to be sold for a much lower price. And the transaction costs in selling a house (broker's commissions, lawyer's fees, and so on) are substantial. A U.S. Treasury bill, by contrast, is a highly liquid asset. It can be sold in a well-organized market with many buyers, so it can be sold quickly at low cost. ***The more liquid an asset is relative to alternative assets, holding everything else unchanged, the more desirable it is, and the greater will be the quantity demanded.***

Theory of Portfolio Choice

All the determining factors we have just discussed can be assembled into the **theory of portfolio choice**, which tells us how much of an asset people want to hold in their portfolio. It states that, holding all of the other factors constant:

1. The quantity demanded of an asset is positively related to wealth.
2. The quantity demanded of an asset is positively related to its expected return relative to alternative assets.
3. The quantity demanded of an asset is negatively related to the risk of its returns relative to alternative assets.
4. The quantity demanded of an asset is positively related to its liquidity relative to alternative assets.

These results are summarized in Table 1.

SUMMARY TABLE 1

Response of the Quantity of an Asset Demanded to Changes in Wealth, Expected Returns, Risk, and Liquidity

Variable	Change in Variable	Change in Quantity Demanded
Wealth	↑	↑
Expected return relative to other assets	↑	↑
Risk relative to other assets	↑	↓
Liquidity relative to other assets	↑	↑

Note: Only increases in the variables are shown. The effect of decreases in the variables on the change in quantity demanded would be the opposite of those indicated in the rightmost column.

SUPPLY AND DEMAND IN THE BOND MARKET

Our first approach to the analysis of interest-rate determination looks at supply and demand in the bond market to see how the price of bonds is determined. Thanks to our understanding from Chapter 4 of how interest rates are measured, we know that each bond price is associated with a particular level of the interest rate. Specifically, the negative relationship between bond prices and interest rates means that when a bond's price rises, its interest rate falls, and vice versa.

The first step in the analysis is to obtain a bond **demand curve**, which shows the relationship between the quantity demanded and the price when all other economic variables are held constant (that is, values of other variables are taken as given). You may recall from previous economics courses that the assumption that all other economic variables are held constant is called *ceteris paribus*, which means "other things being equal" in Latin.

Demand Curve

To clarify our analysis, let's consider the demand for one-year discount bonds, which make no coupon payments but pay the owner the $1,000 face value in a year. If the holding period is one year, then, as we have seen in Chapter 4, the return on the bonds is known absolutely and is equal to the interest rate as measured by the yield to maturity. This means that the expected return on this bond is equal to the interest rate i, which, using Equation 6 in Chapter 4, is

$$i = R^e = \frac{F - P}{P}$$

where
i = interest rate = yield to maturity
R^e = expected return
F = face value of the discount bond
P = initial purchase price of the discount bond

This formula shows that a particular value of the interest rate corresponds to each bond price. If the bond sells for $950, the interest rate and expected return are

$$\frac{\$1{,}000 - \$950}{\$950} = 0.053 = 5.3\%$$

At this 5.3% interest rate and expected return corresponding to a bond price of $950, let us assume that the quantity of bonds demanded is $100 billion, which is plotted as point A in Figure 1.

At a price of $900, the interest rate and expected return are

$$\frac{\$1{,}000 - \$900}{\$900} = 0.111 = 11.1\%$$

Because the expected return on these bonds is higher, with all other economic variables (such as income, expected returns on other assets, risk, and liquidity) held constant, the quantity demanded of bonds will be higher, as predicted by portfolio theory. Point B in Figure 1 shows that the quantity of bonds demanded at the price of $900 has risen to $200 billion. Continuing with this reasoning, we see that if the bond price is $850 (interest rate and expected return = 17.6%), the quantity of bonds demanded (point C) will be greater than at point B. Similarly, at the lower prices of $800 (interest rate = 25%) and

FIGURE 1

Supply and Demand for Bonds

Equilibrium in the bond market occurs at point C, the intersection of the demand curve B^d and the bond supply curve B^s. The equilibrium price is $P^* =$ \$850, and the equilibrium interest rate is $i^* = 17.6\%$.

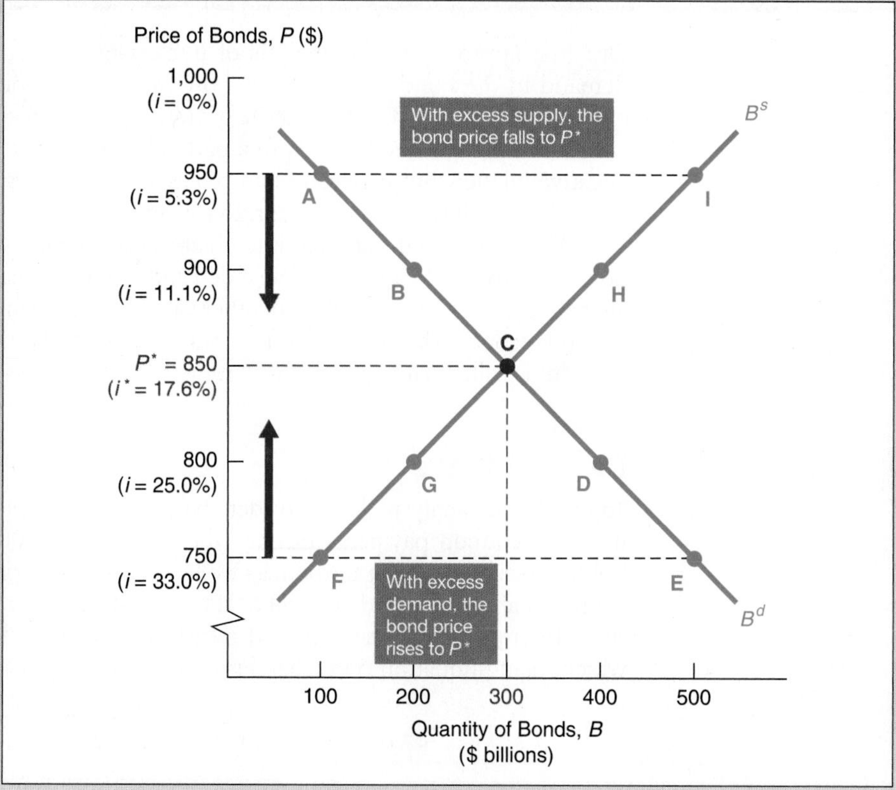

\$750 (interest rate = 33.3%), the quantity of bonds demanded will be even higher (points D and E). The curve B^d, which connects these points, is the demand curve for bonds. It has the usual downward slope, indicating that at lower prices of the bond (everything else being equal), the quantity demanded is higher.[2]

Supply Curve

An important assumption behind the demand curve for bonds in Figure 1 is that all other economic variables besides the bond's price and interest rate are held constant. We use the same assumption in deriving a **supply curve**, which shows the relationship between the quantity supplied and the price when all other economic variables are held constant.

When the price of the bonds is \$750 (interest rate = 33.3%), point F shows that the quantity of bonds supplied is \$100 billion for the example we are considering. If the price is \$800, the interest rate is the lower rate of 25%. Because at this interest rate it is now less costly to borrow by issuing bonds, firms will be willing to borrow more through bond issues, and the quantity of bonds supplied is at the higher level of \$200 billion

[2]Although our analysis indicates that the demand curve is downward-sloping, it does not imply that the curve is a straight line. For ease of exposition, however, we will draw demand curves and supply curves as straight lines.

(point G). An even higher price of \$850, corresponding to a lower interest rate of 17.6%, results in a larger quantity of bonds supplied of \$300 billion (point C). Higher prices of \$900 and \$950 result in even lower interest rates and even greater quantities of bonds supplied (points H and I). The B^s curve, which connects these points, is the supply curve for bonds. It has the usual upward slope found in supply curves, indicating that as the price increases (everything else being equal), the quantity supplied increases.

Market Equilibrium

In economics, **market equilibrium** occurs when the amount that people are willing to buy (*demand*) equals the amount that people are willing to sell (*supply*) at a given price. In the bond market, this is achieved when the quantity of bonds demanded equals the quantity of bonds supplied:

$$B^d = B^s \tag{1}$$

In Figure 1, equilibrium occurs at point C, where the demand and supply curves intersect at a bond price of \$850 (interest rate of 17.6%) and a quantity of bonds of \$300 billion. The price of $P^* = \$850$, where the quantity demanded equals the quantity supplied, is called the *equilibrium* or *market-clearing* price. Similarly, the interest rate of $i^* = 17.6\%$ that corresponds to this price is called the equilibrium or market-clearing interest rate.

The concepts of market equilibrium and equilibrium price or interest rate are useful, because the market tends to head toward them. We can see that it does in Figure 1 by first looking at what happens when we have a bond price that is above the equilibrium price. When the price of bonds is set too high, at, say, \$950, the quantity of bonds supplied at point I is greater than the quantity of bonds demanded at point A. A situation like this, in which the quantity of bonds supplied exceeds the quantity of bonds demanded, is called a condition of **excess supply**. Because people want to sell more bonds than others want to buy, the price of the bonds will fall, which is why the downward arrow is drawn in the figure at the bond price of \$950. As long as the bond price remains above the equilibrium price, an excess supply of bonds will continue to be available, and the price will continue to fall. This decline will stop only when the price has reached the equilibrium price of \$850, where the excess supply of bonds has been eliminated.

Now let's look at what happens when the price of bonds is below the equilibrium price. If the price of the bonds is set too low, at, say, \$750, the quantity demanded at point E is greater than the quantity supplied at point F. This is called a condition of **excess demand**. People now want to buy more bonds than others are willing to sell, so the price of bonds will be driven up, as illustrated by the upward arrow drawn in the figure at the bond price of \$750. Only when the excess demand for bonds is eliminated by the price rising to the equilibrium level of \$850 is there no further tendency for the price to rise.

We can see that the concept of equilibrium price is a useful one because it indicates where the market will settle. Because each price on the vertical axis of Figure 1 corresponds to a particular value of the interest rate, the same diagram also shows that the interest rate will head toward the equilibrium interest rate of 17.6%. When the interest rate is below the equilibrium interest rate, as it is when it is at 5.3%, the price of the bond is above the equilibrium price, and an excess supply of bonds will result. The price of the bond then falls, leading to a rise in the interest rate toward the equilibrium level. Similarly, when the interest rate is above the equilibrium level, as it is when it is at 33.3%, an excess demand for bonds occurs, and the bond price will rise, driving the interest rate back down to the equilibrium level of 17.6%.

Supply and Demand Analysis

Our Figure 1 is a conventional supply and demand diagram with price on the vertical axis and quantity on the horizontal axis. Because the interest rate that corresponds to each bond price is also marked on the vertical axis, this diagram allows us to read the equilibrium interest rate, giving us a model that describes the determination of interest rates. It is important to recognize that a supply and demand diagram like Figure 1 can be drawn for *any* type of bond because the interest rate and price of a bond are *always* negatively related for all kinds of bonds, whether a discount bond or a coupon bond.

An important feature of the analysis here is that supply and demand are always in terms of *stocks* (amounts at a given point in time) of assets, not in terms of *flows*. The **asset market approach** for understanding behavior in financial markets—which emphasizes stocks of assets, rather than flows, in determining asset prices—is the dominant methodology used by economists, because correctly conducting analyses in terms of flows is very tricky, especially when we encounter inflation.[3]

CHANGES IN EQUILIBRIUM INTEREST RATES

We will now use the supply and demand framework for bonds to analyze why interest rates change. To avoid confusion, it is important to make the distinction between *movements along* a demand (or supply) curve and *shifts in* a demand (or supply) curve. When quantity demanded (or supplied) changes as a result of a change in the price of the bond (or, equivalently, a change in the interest rate), we have a *movement along* the demand (or supply) curve. The change in the quantity demanded when we move from point A to B to C in Figure 1, for example, is a movement along a demand curve. A *shift in* the demand (or supply) curve, by contrast, occurs when the quantity demanded (or supplied) changes *at each given price (or interest rate)* of the bond in response to a change in some other factor besides the bond's price or interest rate. When one of these factors changes, causing a shift in the demand or supply curve, there will be a new equilibrium value for the interest rate.

In the following pages, we will look at how the supply and demand curves shift in response to changes in variables, such as expected inflation and wealth, and what effects these changes have on the equilibrium value of interest rates.

Shifts in the Demand for Bonds

The theory of portfolio choice, which we developed at the beginning of the chapter, provides a framework for deciding which factors cause the demand curve for bonds to shift. These factors include changes in four parameters:

1. Wealth
2. Expected returns on bonds relative to alternative assets

[3]The asset market approach developed in the text is useful in understanding not only how interest rates behave but also how any asset price is determined. A second appendix to this chapter, which is on the Companion Website at www.pearsonhighered.com/mishkin, shows how the asset market approach can be applied to understanding the behavior of commodity markets, in particular, the gold market. The analysis of the bond market that we have developed here has another interpretation that uses a different terminology and framework involving the supply and demand for loanable funds. This loanable funds framework is discussed in a third appendix to this chapter, which is also on the book's website.

3. Risk of bonds relative to alternative assets
4. Liquidity of bonds relative to alternative assets

To see how a change in each of these factors (holding all other factors constant) can shift the demand curve, let's look at some examples. (As a study aid, Table 2 summarizes the effects of changes in these factors on the bond demand curve.)

Wealth When the economy is growing rapidly in a business cycle expansion and wealth is increasing, the quantity of bonds demanded at each bond price (or interest rate) increases, as shown in Figure 2. To see how this works, consider point B on the initial demand curve for bonds B_1^d. With higher wealth, the quantity of bonds demanded at the same price must rise, to point B'. Similarly, for point D the higher wealth causes the quantity demanded at the same bond price to rise to point D'. Continuing with this reasoning for every point on the initial demand curve B_1^d, we can see that the demand curve shifts to the right from B_1^d to B_2^d, as indicated by the arrows.

The conclusion we have reached is that ***in a business cycle expansion with growing wealth, the demand for bonds rises and the demand curve for bonds shifts to the right.*** With the same reasoning applied, ***in a recession, when income and wealth are falling, the demand for bonds falls, and the demand curve shifts to the left***.

Another factor that affects wealth is the public's propensity to save. If households save more, wealth increases and, as we have seen, the demand for bonds rises and the demand curve for bonds shifts to the right. Conversely, if people save less, wealth and the demand for bonds will fall and the demand curve shifts to the left.

Expected Returns For a one-year discount bond and a one-year holding period, the expected return and the interest rate are identical, so nothing besides today's interest rate affects the expected return.

FIGURE 2
Shift in the Demand Curve for Bonds
When the demand for bonds increases, the demand curve shifts to the right as shown.

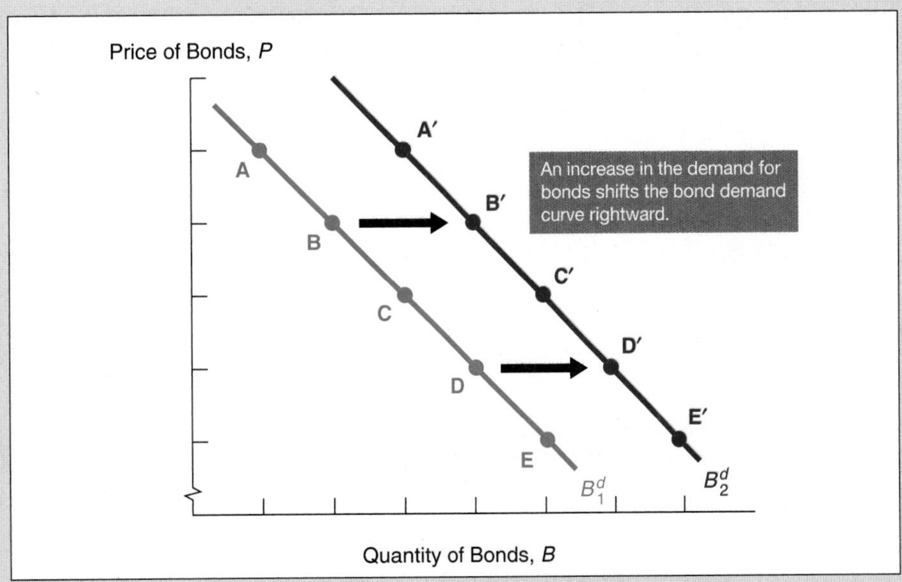

SUMMARY TABLE 2

Factors That Shift the Demand Curve for Bonds

Variable	Change in Variable	Change in Quantity Demanded at Each Bond Price	Shift in Demand Curve
Wealth	↑	↑	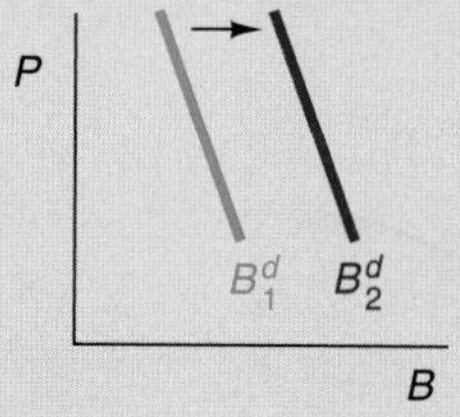
Expected interest rate	↑	↓	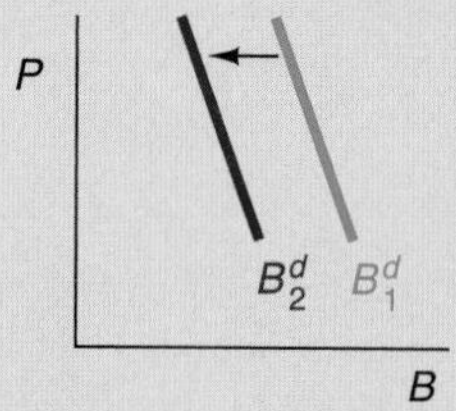
Expected inflation	↑	↓	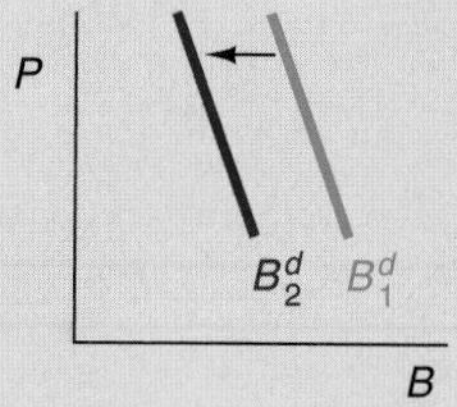
Riskiness of bonds relative to other assets	↑	↓	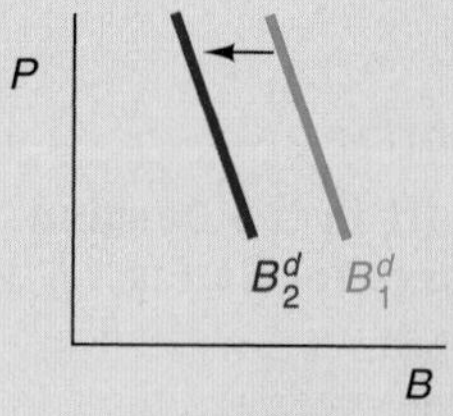
Liquidity of bonds relative to other assets	↑	↑	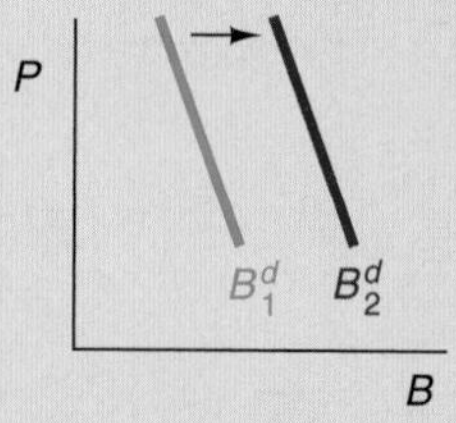

Note: Only increases in the variables are shown. The effect of decreases in the variables on the change in demand would be the opposite of those indicated in the remaining columns.

For bonds with maturities of greater than one year, the expected return may differ from the interest rate. For example, we saw in Chapter 4, Table 2, that a rise in the interest rate on a long-term bond from 10% to 20% would lead to a sharp decline in price and a very large negative return. Hence, if people began to think that interest rates would be higher next year than they had originally anticipated, the expected return today on long-term bonds would fall, and the quantity demanded would fall at each interest rate. ***Higher expected interest rates in the future lower the expected return for long-term bonds, decrease the demand, and shift the demand curve to the left.***

By contrast, a revision downward of expectations of future interest rates would mean that long-term bond prices would be expected to rise more than originally anticipated, and the resulting higher expected return today would raise the quantity demanded at each bond price and interest rate. ***Lower expected interest rates in the future increase the demand for long-term bonds and shift the demand curve to the right*** (as in Figure 2).

Changes in expected returns on other assets can also shift the demand curve for bonds. If people suddenly became more optimistic about the stock market and began to expect higher stock prices in the future, both expected capital gains and expected returns on stocks would rise. With the expected return on bonds held constant, the expected return on bonds today relative to stocks would fall, lowering the demand for bonds and shifting the demand curve to the left.

A change in expected inflation is likely to alter expected returns on physical assets (also called *real assets*) such as automobiles and houses, which affect the demand for bonds. An increase in expected inflation, say, from 5% to 10%, will lead to higher prices on cars and houses in the future and hence higher nominal capital gains. The resulting rise in the expected returns today on these real assets will lead to a fall in the expected return on bonds relative to the expected return on real assets today and thus cause the demand for bonds to fall. Alternatively, we can think of the rise in expected inflation as lowering the real interest rate on bonds, and the resulting decline in the relative expected return on bonds will cause the demand for bonds to fall. ***An increase in the expected rate of inflation lowers the expected return for bonds, causing their demand to decline and the demand curve to shift to the left.***

Risk If prices in the bond market become more volatile, the risk associated with bonds increases, and bonds become a less attractive asset. ***An increase in the riskiness of bonds causes the demand for bonds to fall and the demand curve to shift to the left.***

Conversely, an increase in the volatility of prices in another asset market, such as the stock market, would make bonds more attractive. ***An increase in the riskiness of alternative assets causes the demand for bonds to rise and the demand curve to shift to the right*** (as in Figure 2).

Liquidity If more people started trading in the bond market, and as a result it became easier to sell bonds quickly, the increase in their liquidity would cause the quantity of bonds demanded at each interest rate to rise. ***Increased liquidity of bonds results in an increased demand for bonds, and the demand curve shifts to the right*** (see Figure 2). ***Similarly, increased liquidity of alternative assets lowers the demand for bonds and shifts the demand curve to the left.*** The reduction of brokerage commissions for trading common stocks that occurred when the fixed-rate commission structure was abolished in 1975, for example, increased the liquidity of stocks relative to bonds, and the resulting lower demand for bonds shifted the demand curve to the left.

Shifts in the Supply of Bonds

Certain factors can cause the supply curve for bonds to shift, among them these:

1. Expected profitability of investment opportunities
2. Expected inflation
3. Government budget deficits

We will look at how the supply curve shifts when each of these factors changes (all others remaining constant). (As a study aid, Table 3 summarizes the effects of changes in these factors on the bond supply curve.)

Expected Profitability of Investment Opportunities The more profitable plant and equipment investments that a firm expects it can make, the more willing it will be to borrow for financing these investments. When the economy is growing rapidly, as in

SUMMARY TABLE 3

Factors That Shift the Supply of Bonds

Variable	Change in Variable	Change in Quantity Supplied at Each Bond Price	Shift in Supply Curve
Profitability of investments	↑	↑	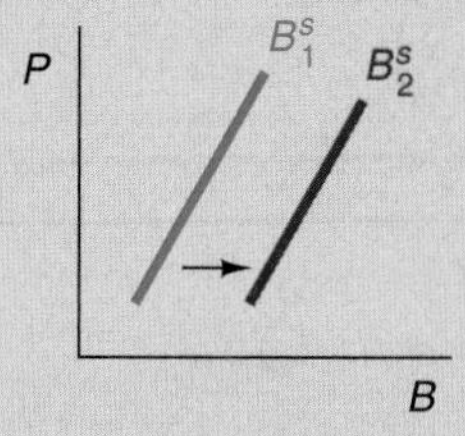
Expected inflation	↑	↑	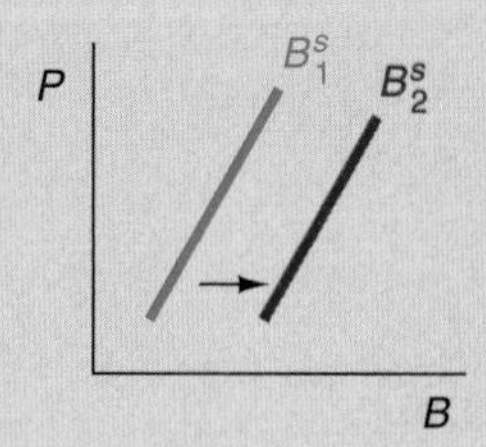
Government deficit	↑	↑	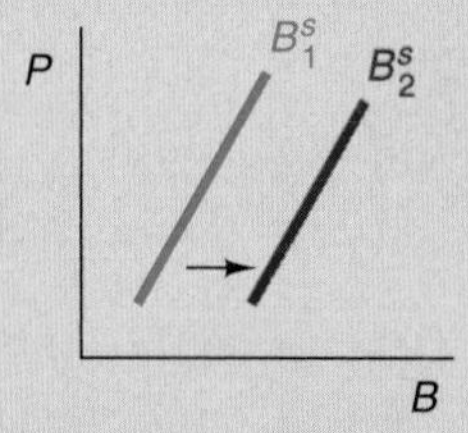

Note: Only increases in the variables are shown. The effect of decreases in the variables on the change in supply would be the opposite of those indicated in the remaining columns.

FIGURE 3
Shift in the Supply Curve for Bonds
When the supply of bonds increases, the supply curve shifts to the right.

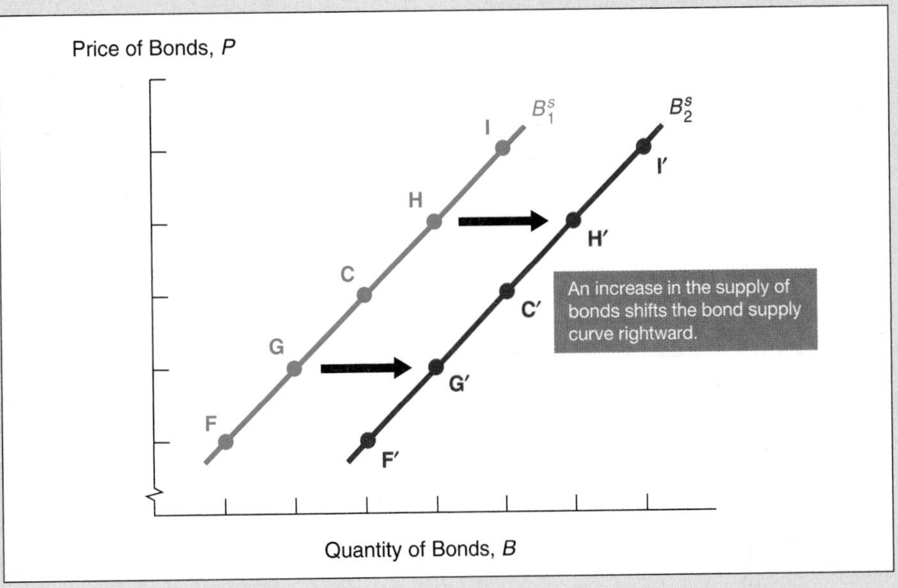

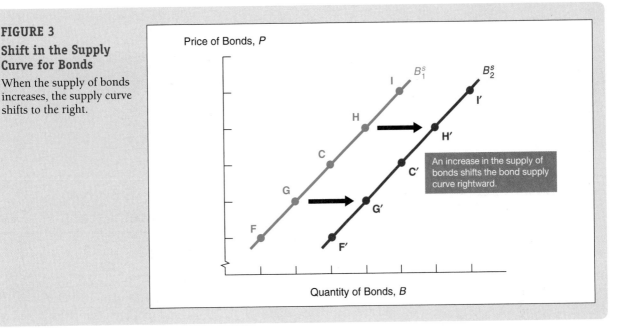

a business cycle expansion, investment opportunities that are expected to be profitable abound, and the quantity of bonds supplied at any given bond price will increase (see Figure 3). ***Therefore, in a business cycle expansion, the supply of bonds increases, and the supply curve shifts to the right. Likewise, in a recession, when far fewer profitable investment opportunities are expected, the supply of bonds falls, and the supply curve shifts to the left.***

Expected Inflation As we saw in Chapter 4, the real cost of borrowing is more accurately measured by the real interest rate, which equals the (nominal) interest rate minus the expected inflation rate. For a given interest rate (and bond price), when expected inflation increases, the real cost of borrowing falls; hence the quantity of bonds supplied increases at any given bond price. ***An increase in expected inflation causes the supply of bonds to increase and the supply curve to shift to the right*** (see Figure 3).

Government Budget Deficits The activities of the government can influence the supply of bonds in several ways. The U.S. Treasury issues bonds to finance government deficits, the gap between the government's expenditures and its revenues. When these deficits are large, the Treasury sells more bonds, and the quantity of bonds supplied at each bond price increases. ***Higher government deficits increase the supply of bonds and shift the supply curve to the right*** (see Figure 3). ***On the other hand, government surpluses, as occurred in the late 1990s, decrease the supply of bonds and shift the supply curve to the left.***

State and local governments and other government agencies also issue bonds to finance their expenditures, and this can affect the supply of bonds, as well. We will see in later chapters that the conduct of monetary policy involves the purchase and sale of bonds, which in turn influences the supply of bonds.

We now can use our knowledge of how supply and demand curves shift to analyze how the equilibrium interest rate can change. The best way to do this is to pursue several applications that are particularly relevant to our understanding of how monetary policy affects interest rates. In going through these applications, keep two things in mind:

1. When you examine the effect of a variable change, remember we are assuming that all other variables are unchanged; that is, we are making use of the *ceteris paribus* assumption.
2. Remember that the interest rate is negatively related to the bond price, so when the equilibrium bond price rises, the equilibrium interest rate falls. Conversely, if the equilibrium bond price moves downward, the equilibrium interest rate rises.

APPLICATION ◆ Changes in the Interest Rate Due to Expected Inflation: The Fisher Effect

We have already done most of the work to evaluate how a change in expected inflation affects the nominal interest rate, in that we have already analyzed how a change in expected inflation shifts the supply and demand curves. Figure 4 shows the effect on the equilibrium interest rate of an increase in expected inflation.

Suppose that expected inflation is initially 5% and the initial supply and demand curves B_1^s and B_1^d intersect at point 1, where the equilibrium bond price is P_1. If expected inflation rises to 10%, the expected return on bonds relative to real assets falls for any given bond price and interest rate. As a result, the demand for bonds falls, and the demand curve shifts to the left from B_1^d to B_2^d. The rise in expected inflation also shifts the supply curve. At any given bond price and interest rate, the real cost of borrowing has declined, causing the quantity of bonds supplied to increase, and the supply curve shifts to the right, from B_1^s to B_2^s.

When the demand and supply curves shift in response to the change in expected inflation, the equilibrium moves from point 1 to point 2, the intersection of B_2^d and B_2^s. The equilibrium bond price has fallen from P_1 to P_2, and because the bond price is negatively related to the interest rate, this means that the interest rate has risen. Note

FIGURE 4

Response to a Change in Expected Inflation

When expected inflation rises, the supply curve shifts from B_1^s to B_2^s, and the demand curve shifts from B_1^d to B_2^d. The equilibrium moves from point 1 to point 2, with the result that the equilibrium bond price falls from P_1 to P_2 and the equilibrium interest rate rises.

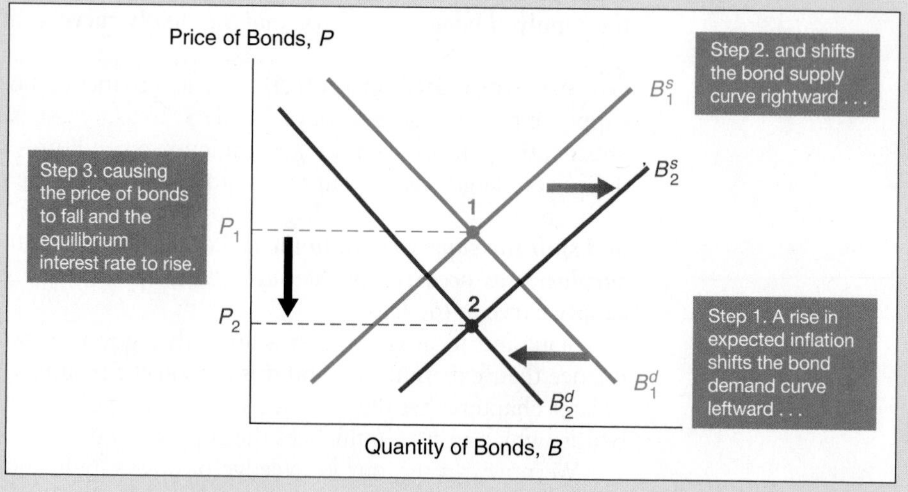
Price of Bonds, P
Step 2. and shifts the bond supply curve rightward . . .
B_1^s
B_2^s
Step 3. causing the price of bonds to fall and the equilibrium interest rate to rise.
P_1
P_2
1
2
Step 1. A rise in expected inflation shifts the bond demand curve leftward . . .
B_1^d
B_2^d
Quantity of Bonds, B

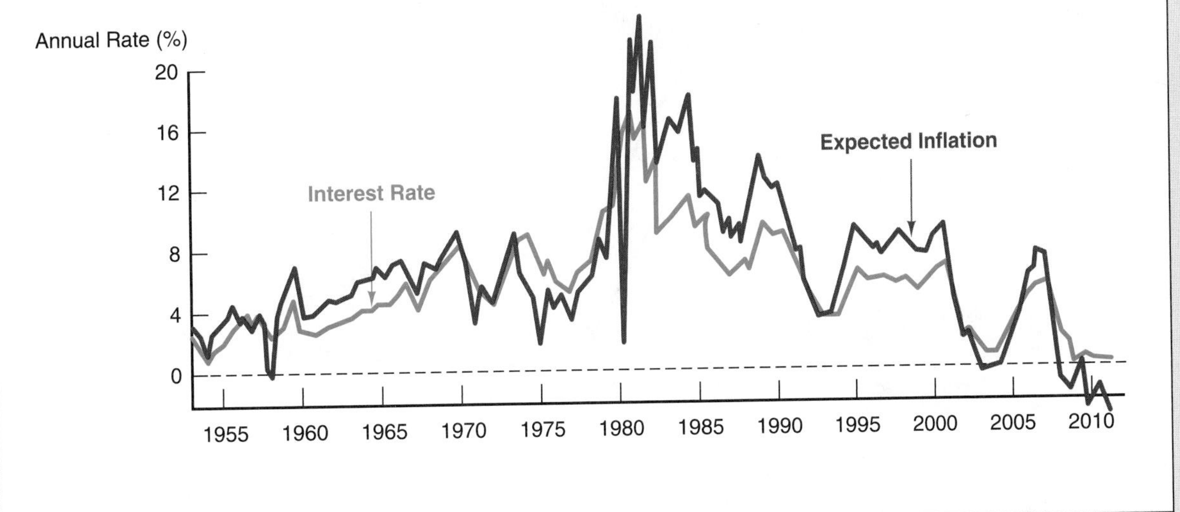

FIGURE 5 Expected Inflation and Interest Rates (Three-Month Treasury Bills), 1953–2011

The interest rate on three-month Treasury bills and the expected inflation rate generally move together, as the Fisher effect predicts.

Source: Expected inflation calculated using procedures outlined in Frederic S. Mishkin, "The Real Interest Rate: An Empirical Investigation," *Carnegie-Rochester Conference Series on Public Policy 15* (1981): 151–200. These procedures involve estimating expected inflation as a function of past interest rates, inflation, and time trends.

that Figure 4 has been drawn so that the equilibrium quantity of bonds remains the same for both point 1 and point 2. However, depending on the size of the shifts in the supply and demand curves, the equilibrium quantity of bonds could either rise or fall when expected inflation rises.

Our supply and demand analysis has led us to an important observation: ***When expected inflation rises, interest rates will rise.*** This result has been named the **Fisher effect**, after Irving Fisher, the economist who first pointed out the relationship of expected inflation to interest rates. The accuracy of this prediction is shown in Figure 5. The interest rate on three-month Treasury bills has usually moved along with the expected inflation rate. Consequently, it is understandable that many economists recommend that inflation must be kept low if we want to keep nominal interest rates low.

APPLICATION ◆ Changes in the Interest Rate Due to a Business Cycle Expansion

Figure 6 analyzes the effects of a business cycle expansion on interest rates. In a business cycle expansion, the amounts of goods and services being produced in the economy increase, so national income rises. When this occurs, businesses will be

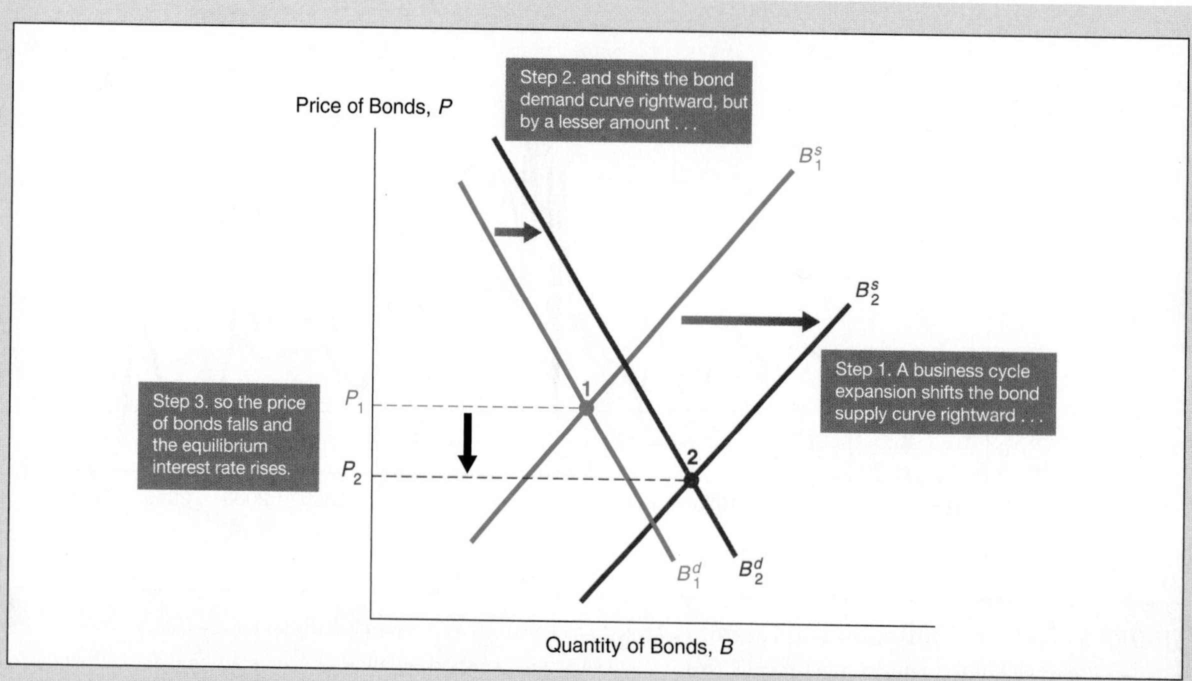
Price of Bonds, P
Step 2. and shifts the bond demand curve rightward, but by a lesser amount . . .
B_1^s
B_2^s
Step 1. A business cycle expansion shifts the bond supply curve rightward . . .
Step 3. so the price of bonds falls and the equilibrium interest rate rises.
P_1
P_2
1
2
B_1^d
B_2^d
Quantity of Bonds, B

FIGURE 6 Response to a Business Cycle Expansion

In a business cycle expansion, when income and wealth are rising, the demand curve shifts rightward from B_1^s to B_2^s. If the supply curve shifts to the right more than the demand curve, as in this figure, the equilibrium bond price moves down from P_1 to P_2, and the equilibrium interest rate rises.

more willing to borrow, because they are likely to have many profitable investment opportunities for which they need financing. Hence at a given bond price, the quantity of bonds that firms want to sell (that is, the supply of bonds) will increase. This means that in a business cycle expansion, the supply curve for bonds shifts to the right (see Figure 6) from B_1^s to B_2^s.

Expansion in the economy will also affect the demand for bonds. As the economy expands, wealth is likely to increase, and the theory of portfolio choice tells us that the demand for bonds will rise as well. We see this in Figure 6, where the demand curve has shifted to the right, from B_1^d to B_2^d.

Given that both the supply and demand curves have shifted to the right, we know that the new equilibrium reached at the intersection of B_2^d and B_2^s must also move to the right. However, depending on whether the supply curve shifts more than the demand curve, or vice versa, the new equilibrium interest rate can either rise or fall.

The supply and demand analysis used here gives us an ambiguous answer to the question of what will happen to interest rates in a business cycle expansion. Figure 6 has been drawn so that the shift in the supply curve is greater than the shift in the demand curve, causing the equilibrium bond price to fall to P_2, leading to a rise in the equilibrium interest rate. The reason the figure has been drawn so that a business cycle expansion and a rise in income lead to a higher interest rate is that this is the outcome we actually see in the data. Figure 7 plots the movement of the interest rate

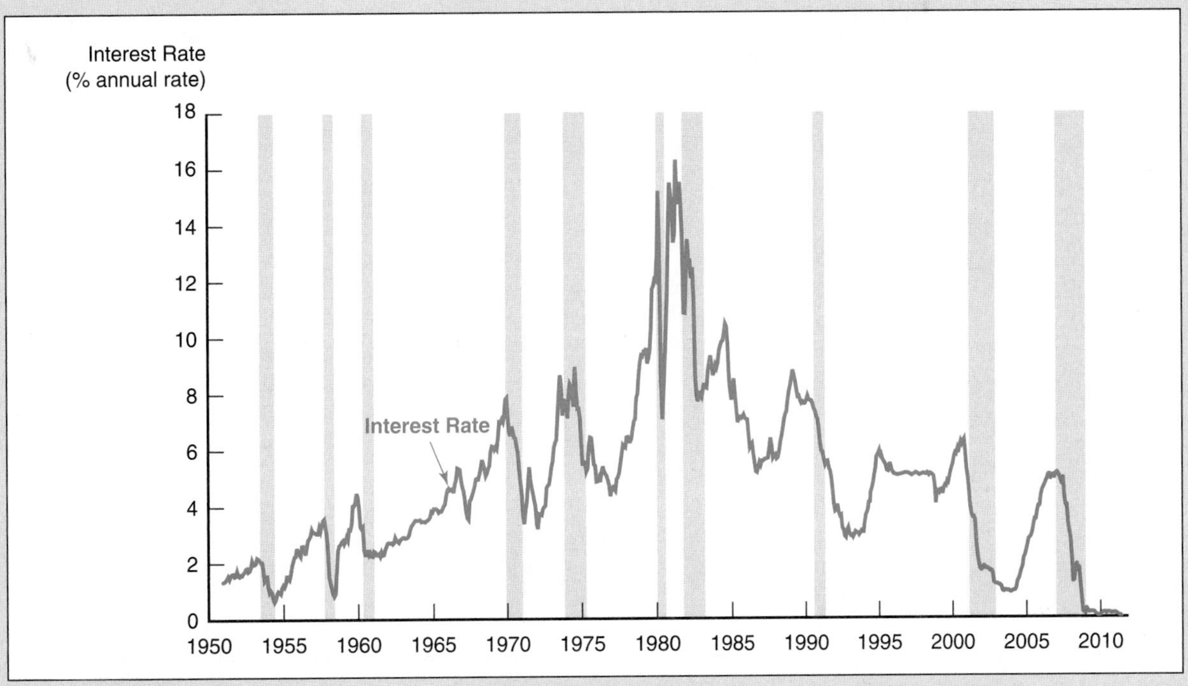

FIGURE 7 Business Cycle and Interest Rates (Three-Month Treasury Bills), 1951–2011

Shaded areas indicate periods of recession. The interest rate tends to rise during business cycle expansions and fall during recessions.

Source: **Federal Reserve:** www.federalreserve.gov/releases/H15/data.htm.

on three-month U.S. Treasury bills from 1951 to 2008 and indicates when the business cycle is undergoing recessions (shaded areas). As you can see, the interest rate tends to rise during business cycle expansions and fall during recessions, which is what the supply and demand diagram in Figure 6 indicates.

APPLICATION ◆ Explaining Low Japanese Interest Rates

In the 1990s and early 2000s, Japanese interest rates became the lowest in the world. Indeed, in November 1998, an extraordinary event occurred: Interest rates on Japanese six-month Treasury bills turned slightly negative (see Chapter 4). Why did Japanese interest rates drop to such low levels?

In the late 1990s and early 2000s, Japan experienced a prolonged recession, which was accompanied by deflation, a negative inflation rate. Using these facts, analysis similar to that used in the preceding applications explains the low Japanese interest rates.

Negative inflation caused the demand for bonds to rise because the expected return on real assets fell, thereby raising the relative expected return on bonds and in turn causing the demand curve to shift to the right. The negative inflation also raised the real interest rate and therefore the real cost of borrowing for any given nominal rate, thereby causing the supply of bonds to contract and the supply curve to shift to the left. The outcome was then exactly the opposite of that graphed in Figure 4: The rightward shift of the demand curve and leftward shift of the supply curve led to a rise in the bond price and a fall in interest rates.

The business cycle contraction and the resulting lack of profitable investment opportunities in Japan also led to lower interest rates, by decreasing the supply of bonds and shifting the supply curve to the left. Although the demand curve also would shift to the left because wealth decreased during the business cycle contraction, we have seen in the preceding application that the demand curve would shift less than the supply curve. Thus, the bond price rose and interest rates fell (the opposite outcome to that in Figure 6).

Usually, we think that low interest rates are a good thing, because they make it cheap to borrow. But the Japanese example shows that just as a fallacy is present in the adage "You can never be too rich or too thin" (maybe you can't be too rich, but you can certainly be too thin and damage your health), a fallacy is present in always thinking that lower interest rates are better. In Japan, the low and even negative interest rates were a sign that the Japanese economy was in real trouble, with falling prices and a contracting economy. Only when the Japanese economy returns to health will interest rates rise back to more normal levels. ◆

SUPPLY AND DEMAND IN THE MARKET FOR MONEY: THE LIQUIDITY PREFERENCE FRAMEWORK

Instead of determining the equilibrium interest rate using the supply of and demand for bonds, an alternative model developed by John Maynard Keynes, known as the **liquidity preference framework**, determines the equilibrium interest rate in terms of the supply of and demand for money. Although the two frameworks look different, the liquidity preference analysis of the market for money is closely related to the supply and demand framework of the bond market.[4]

The starting point of Keynes's analysis is his assumption that people use two main categories of assets to store their wealth: money and bonds. Therefore, total wealth in the economy must equal the total quantity of bonds plus money in the economy, which equals the quantity of bonds supplied (B^s) plus the quantity of money supplied (M^s). The quantity of bonds (B^d) and money (M^d) that people want to hold and thus demand must also equal the total amount of wealth, because people cannot purchase more assets than their available resources allow. The conclusion is that the quantity of bonds and money supplied must equal the quantity of bonds and money demanded:

$$B^s + M^s = B^d + M^d \tag{2}$$

[4]Note that the term *market for money* refers to the market for the medium of exchange, money. This market differs from the *money market* referred to by finance practitioners, which, as discussed in Chapter 2, is the financial market in which short-term debt instruments are traded.

Collecting the bond terms on one side of the equation and the money terms on the other, this equation can be rewritten as

$$B^s - B^d = M^d - M^s \tag{3}$$

The rewritten equation tells us that if the market for money is in equilibrium ($M^s = M^d$), the right-hand side of Equation 3 equals zero, implying that $B^s = B^d$, meaning that the bond market is also in equilibrium.

Thus it is the same to think about determining the equilibrium interest rate by equating the supply and demand for bonds or by equating the supply and demand for money. In this sense, the liquidity preference framework, which analyzes the market for money, is equivalent to a framework analyzing supply and demand in the bond market. In practice, the approaches differ, because by assuming that there are only two kinds of assets, money and bonds, the liquidity preference approach implicitly ignores any effects on interest rates that arise from changes in the expected returns on real assets such as automobiles and houses. In most instances, however, both frameworks yield the same predictions.

The reason that we approach the determination of interest rates with both frameworks is that the bond supply and demand framework is easier to use when analyzing the effects from changes in expected inflation, whereas the liquidity preference framework provides a simpler analysis of the effects from changes in income, the price level, and the supply of money.

Because the definition of money that Keynes used includes currency (which earns no interest) and checking account deposits (which in his time typically earned little or no interest), he assumed that money has a zero rate of return. Bonds, the only alternative asset to money in Keynes's framework, have an expected return equal to the interest rate i.[5] As this interest rate rises (holding everything else unchanged), the expected return on money falls relative to the expected return on bonds, and as the theory of portfolio choice tells us, this causes a fall in the quantity of money demanded.

We can also see that the quantity of money demanded and the interest rate should be negatively related by using the concept of **opportunity cost**, the amount of interest (expected return) sacrificed by not holding the alternative asset—in this case, a bond. As the interest rate on bonds, i, rises, the opportunity cost of holding money rises; thus money is less desirable and the quantity of money demanded must fall.

Figure 8 shows the quantity of money demanded at a number of interest rates, with all other economic variables, such as income and the price level, held constant. At an interest rate of 25%, point A shows that the quantity of money demanded is \$100 billion. If the interest rate is at the lower rate of 20%, the opportunity cost of holding money is lower, and the quantity of money demanded rises to \$200 billion, as indicated by the move from point A to point B. If the interest rate is even lower, the quantity of money demanded is even higher, as is indicated by points C, D, and E. The curve M^d connecting these points is the demand curve for money, and it slopes downward.

At this point in our analysis, we will assume that a central bank controls the amount of money supplied at a fixed quantity of \$300 billion, so the supply curve for money M^s in the figure is a vertical line at \$300 billion. The equilibrium where the quantity of

[5]Keynes did not actually assume that the expected returns on bonds equaled the interest rate but rather argued that they were closely related. This distinction makes no appreciable difference in our analysis.

FIGURE 8

Equilibrium in the Market for Money

Equilibrium in the market for money occurs at point C, the intersection of the money demand curve M^d and the money supply curve M^s. The equilibrium interest is $i^* = 15\%$.

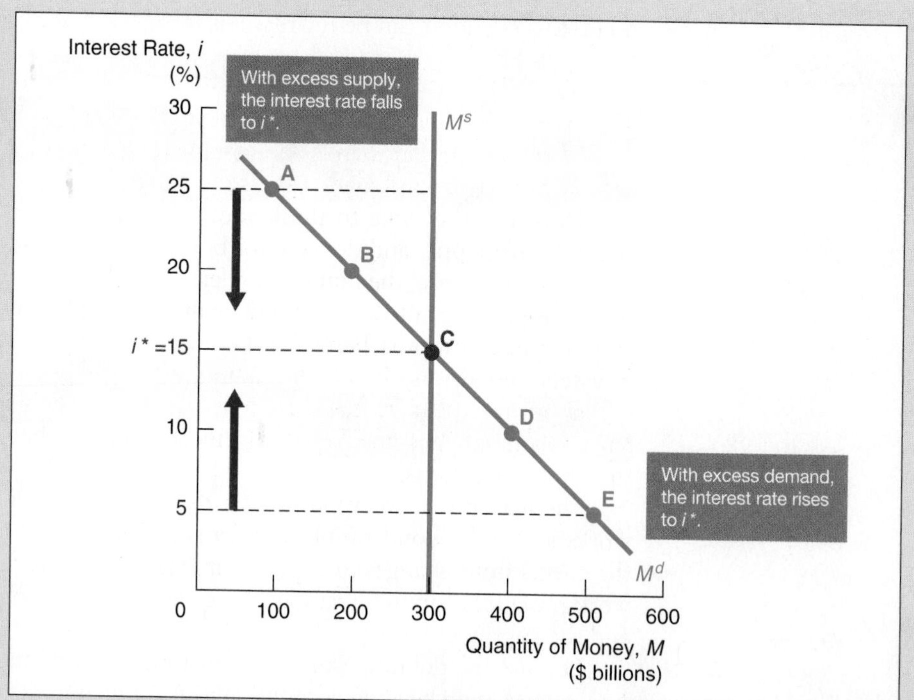

money demanded equals the quantity of money supplied occurs at the intersection of the supply and demand curves at point C, where

$$M^d = M^s \tag{4}$$

The resulting equilibrium interest rate is at $i^* = 15\%$.

We can again see that there is a tendency to approach this equilibrium by first looking at the relationship of money demand and supply when the interest rate is above the equilibrium interest rate. When the interest rate is 25%, the quantity of money demanded at point A is $100 billion, yet the quantity of money supplied is $300 billion. The excess supply of money means that people are holding more money than they desire, so they will try to get rid of their excess money balances by trying to buy bonds. Accordingly, they will bid up the price of bonds. As the bond price rises, the interest rate will fall toward the equilibrium interest rate of 15%. This tendency is shown by the downward arrow drawn at the interest rate of 25%.

Likewise, if the interest rate is 5%, the quantity of money demanded at point E is $500 billion, but the quantity of money supplied is only $300 billion. An excess demand for money now exists because people want to hold more money than they currently have. To try to obtain more money, they will sell their only other asset—bonds—and the price will fall. As the price of bonds falls, the interest rate will rise toward the equilibrium rate of 15%. Only when the interest rate is at its equilibrium value will there be no tendency for it to move further, and the interest rate will settle to its equilibrium value.

CHANGES IN EQUILIBRIUM INTEREST RATES IN THE LIQUIDITY PREFERENCE FRAMEWORK

Analyzing how the equilibrium interest rate changes using the liquidity preference framework requires that we understand what causes the demand and supply curves for money to shift.

Shifts in the Demand for Money

In Keynes's liquidity preference analysis, two factors cause the demand curve for money to shift: income and the price level.

Income Effect In Keynes's view, there were two reasons why income would affect the demand for money. First, as an economy expands and income rises, wealth increases and people will want to hold more money as a store of value. Second, as the economy expands and income rises, people will want to carry out more transactions using money as a medium of exchange, with the result that they will also want to hold more money. The conclusion is that ***a higher level of income causes the demand for money at each interest rate to increase and the demand curve to shift to the right***.

Price-Level Effect Keynes took the view that people care about the amount of money they hold in real terms—that is, in terms of the goods and services it can buy. When the price level rises, the same nominal quantity of money is no longer as valuable; it cannot be used to purchase as many real goods or services. To restore their holdings of money in real terms to the former level, people will want to hold a greater nominal quantity of money, so ***a rise in the price level causes the demand for money at each interest rate to increase and the demand curve to shift to the right***.

Shifts in the Supply of Money

We will assume that the supply of money is completely controlled by the central bank, which in the United States is the Federal Reserve. (Actually, the process that determines the money supply is substantially more complicated, involving banks, depositors, and borrowers from banks. We will study it in more detail later in the book.) For now, all we need to know is that ***an increase in the money supply engineered by the Federal Reserve will shift the supply curve for money to the right***.

APPLICATION ◆ Changes in the Equilibrium Interest Rate Due to Changes in Income, the Price Level, or the Money Supply

To see how we can use the liquidity preference framework to analyze the movement of interest rates, we will again look at several applications that will be useful in evaluating the effect of monetary policy on interest rates. In going through these applications, remember to use the *ceteris paribus* assumption: When examining the effect of a change in one variable, hold all other variables constant. (As a study aid, Table 4 summarizes the shifts in the demand and supply curves for money.)

SUMMARY TABLE 4

Factors That Shift the Demand for and Supply of Money

Variable	Change in Variable	Change in Money Demand (M^d) or Supply (M^s) at Each Interest Rate	Change in Interest Rate	
Income	↑	M^d↑	↑	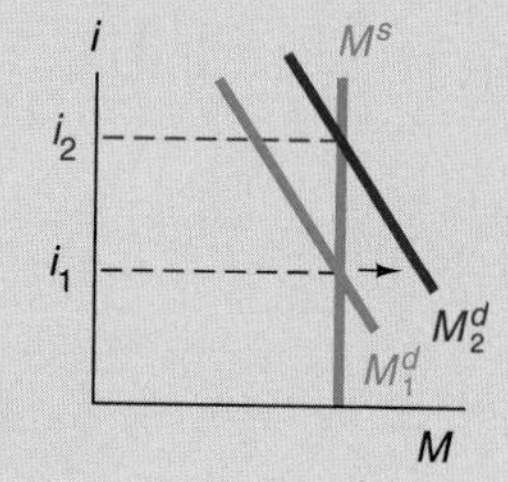
Price level	↑	M^d↑	↑	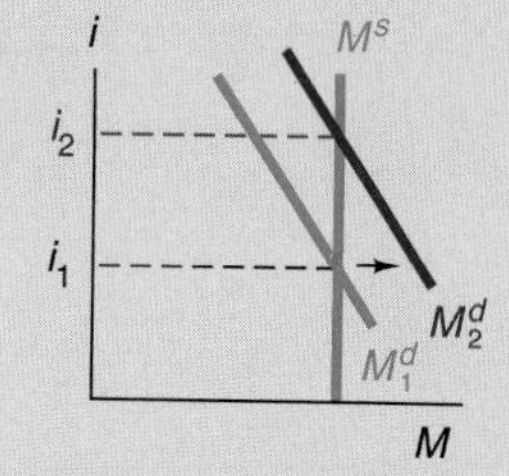
Money supply	↑	M^s↑	↓	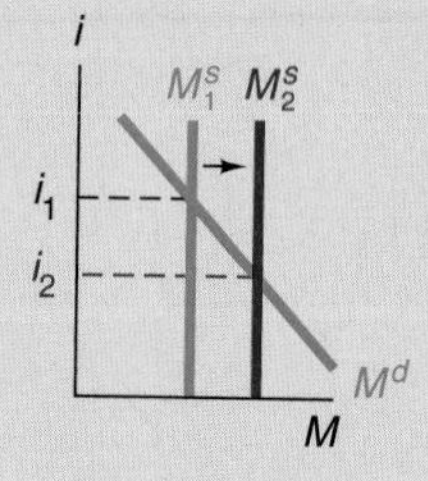

Note: Only increases in the variables are shown. The effect of decreases in the variables on the change in demand would be the opposite of those indicated in the remaining columns.

Changes in Income

When income is rising during a business cycle expansion, we have seen that the demand for money will rise, shown in Figure 9 by the shift rightward in the demand curve from M_1^d to M_2^d. The new equilibrium is reached at point 2 at the intersection of the M_2^d curve with the money supply curve M^s. As you can see, the equilibrium interest rate rises from i_1 to i_2. The liquidity preference framework thus generates the conclusion that ***when income is rising during a business cycle expansion (holding other economic variables constant), interest rates will rise***. This conclusion is unambiguous, unlike

FIGURE 9

Response to a Change in Income or the Price Level

In a business cycle expansion, when income is rising, or when the price level rises, the demand curve shifts from M_1^d to M_2^d. The supply curve is fixed at $M^s = \overline{M}$. The equilibrium interest rate rises from i_1 to i_2.

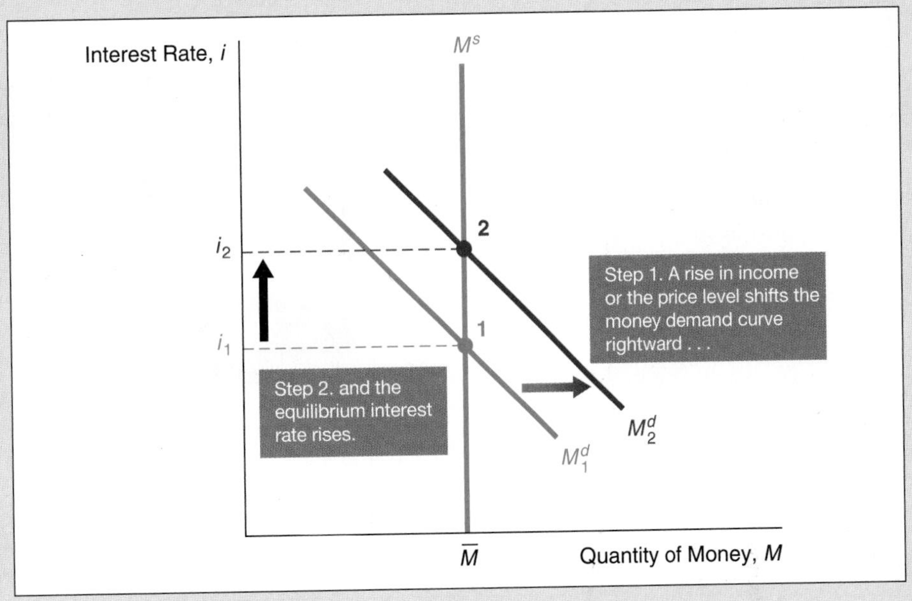

Interest Rate, i
M^s
2
1
i_2
i_1
Step 1. A rise in income or the price level shifts the money demand curve rightward . . .
Step 2. and the equilibrium interest rate rises.
M_1^d
M_2^d
$\overline{M}$
Quantity of Money, M

the conclusion reached about the effects of a business cycle expansion on interest rates using the bond demand and supply framework.

Changes in the Price Level

When the price level rises, the value of money in terms of what it can purchase is lower. To restore their purchasing power in real terms to its former level, people will want to hold a greater nominal quantity of money. A higher price level shifts the demand curve for money to the right from M_1^d to M_2^d (see Figure 9). The equilibrium moves from point 1 to point 2, where the equilibrium interest rate has risen from i_1 to i_2, illustrating that ***when the price level increases, with the supply of money and other economic variables held constant, interest rates will rise***.

Changes in the Money Supply

An increase in the money supply due to expansionary monetary policy by the Federal Reserve implies that the supply curve for money shifts to the right. As shown in Figure 10 by the movement of the supply curve from M_1^s to M_2^s, the equilibrium moves from point 1 down to point 2, where the M_2^s supply curve intersects with the demand curve M^d and the equilibrium interest rate has fallen from i_1 to i_2. ***When the money supply increases (everything else remaining equal), interest rates will decline.***[6]

[6]This same result can be generated using the bond supply and demand framework. As we will see in Chapter 17, the primary way that a central bank increases the money supply is to buy bonds and thereby decrease the supply of bonds to the public. The resulting shift to the left of the supply curve for bonds will lead to an increase in the equilibrium price of bonds and a decline in the equilibrium interest rate.

FIGURE 10

Response to a Change in the Money Supply

When the money supply increases, the supply curve shifts from M_1^s to M_2^s and the equilibrium interest rate falls from i_1 to i_2.

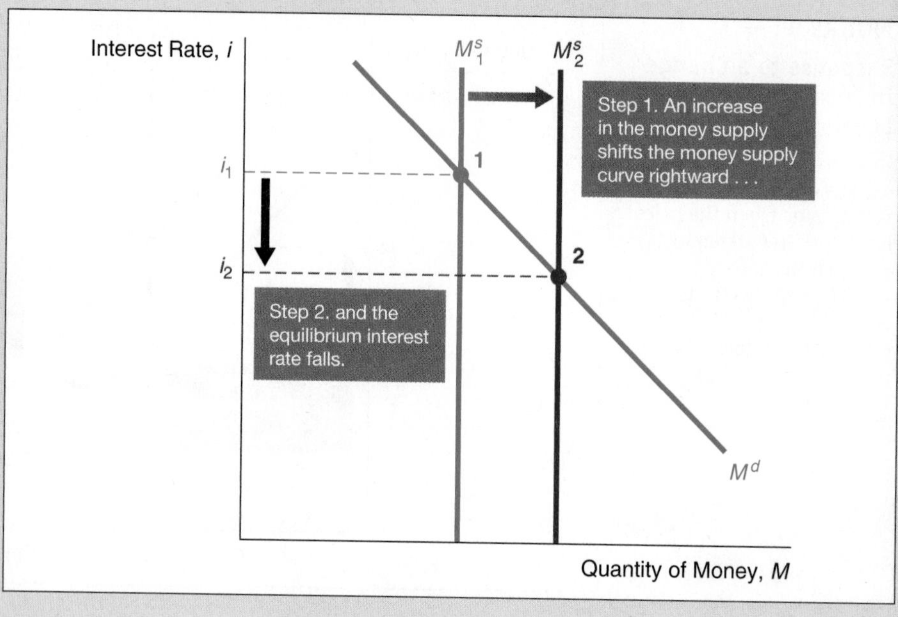
Interest Rate, i
M_1^s
M_2^s
Step 1. An increase in the money supply shifts the money supply curve rightward . . .
i_1
1
i_2
2
Step 2. and the equilibrium interest rate falls.
M^d
Quantity of Money, M

APPLICATION ◆ Money and Interest Rates

The liquidity preference analysis in Figure 10 seems to lead to the conclusion that an increase in the money supply will lower interest rates. This conclusion has important policy implications because it has frequently caused politicians to call for a more rapid growth of the money supply in an effort to drive down interest rates.

But is it correct to conclude that money and interest rates should be negatively related? Might other important factors be left out of the liquidity preference analysis in Figure 10 that would reverse this conclusion? We will provide answers to these questions by applying the supply and demand analysis we have used in this chapter to obtain a deeper understanding of the relationship between money and interest rates.

An important criticism of the idea that an increase in the money supply lowers interest rates was raised by Milton Friedman, a Nobel laureate in economics. He acknowledged that the liquidity preference analysis was correct and called the result—that an increase in the money supply (*everything else remaining equal*) lowers interest rates—the *liquidity effect*. However, he viewed the liquidity effect as merely part of the story: An increase in the money supply might not leave "everything else equal" and will have other effects on the economy that may make interest rates rise. If these effects are substantial, it is entirely possible that when the money supply increases, interest rates may also increase.

We have already laid the groundwork for discussion of these other effects because we have shown how changes in income, the price level, and expected inflation influence the equilibrium interest rate.

1. *Income Effect*. Because an increasing money supply is an expansionary influence on the economy, it should raise national income and wealth. Both the liquidity preference and bond supply and demand frameworks indicate that interest rates will then rise (see Figures 6 and 9). Thus ***the income effect of an increase in the money supply is a rise in interest rates in response to the higher level of income***.

2. *Price-Level Effect*. An increase in the money supply can also cause the overall price level in the economy to rise. The liquidity preference framework predicts that this will lead to a rise in interest rates. Thus ***the price-level effect from an increase in the money supply is a rise in interest rates in response to the rise in price level***.
3. *Expected-Inflation Effect*. The higher inflation rate that results from an increase in the money supply also affects interest rates by influencing the expected inflation rate. Specifically, an increase in the money supply may lead people to expect a higher price level in the future—and hence the expected inflation rate will be higher. The bond supply and demand framework has shown us that this increase in expected inflation will lead to a higher level of interest rates. Therefore, ***the expected-inflation effect of an increase in the money supply is a rise in interest rates in response to the rise in the expected inflation rate***.

At first glance it might appear that the price-level effect and the expected-inflation effect are the same thing. They both indicate that increases in the price level induced by an increase in the money supply will raise interest rates. However, there is a subtle difference between the two, and this is why they are discussed as two separate effects.

Suppose that a one-time increase in the money supply today leads to a rise in prices to a permanently higher level by next year. As the price level rises over the course of this year, the interest rate will rise via the price-level effect. Only at the end of the year, when the price level has risen to its peak, will the price-level effect be at a maximum.

The rising price level will also raise interest rates via the expected-inflation effect, because people will expect that inflation will be higher over the course of the year. However, when the price level stops rising next year, inflation and the expected inflation rate will return to zero. Any rise in interest rates as a result of the earlier rise in expected inflation will then be reversed. We thus see that in contrast to the price-level effect, which reaches its greatest impact next year, the expected-inflation effect will have its smallest impact (zero impact) next year. The basic difference between the two effects, then, is that the price-level effect remains even after prices have stopped rising, whereas the expected-inflation effect disappears.

An important point is that the expected-inflation effect will persist only as long as the price level continues to rise. As we will see in our discussion of monetary theory in subsequent chapters, a one-time increase in the money supply will not produce a continually rising price level; only a higher rate of money supply growth will. Thus a higher rate of money supply growth is needed if the expected-inflation effect is to persist.

DOES A HIGHER RATE OF GROWTH OF THE MONEY SUPPLY LOWER INTEREST RATES?

We can now put together all the effects we have discussed to help us decide whether our analysis supports the politicians who advocate a greater rate of growth of the money supply when they feel that interest rates are too high. Of all the effects, only the liquidity effect indicates that a higher rate of money growth will cause a decline in interest rates. In contrast, the income, price-level, and expected-inflation effects indicate that interest rates will rise when money growth is higher. Which of these effects is largest, and how quickly does each take effect? The answers are critical in determining whether interest rates will rise or fall when money supply growth is increased.

Generally, the liquidity effect from the greater money growth takes effect immediately, because the rising money supply leads to an immediate decline in the equilibrium interest rate. The income and price-level effects take longer to work, because time is needed for the increasing money supply to raise the price level and income, which in turn raise interest rates. The expected-inflation effect, which also raises interest rates, can be slow or fast, depending on whether people adjust their expectations of inflation slowly or quickly when the money growth rate is increased.

Three possibilities are outlined in Figure 11; each shows how interest rates respond over time to an increased rate of money supply growth, starting at time T. Panel (a) shows a case in which the liquidity effect dominates the other effects so that the interest rate falls from i_1 at time T to a final level of i_2. The liquidity effect operates quickly to lower the interest rate, but as time goes by, the other effects start to reverse some of the decline. Because the liquidity effect is larger than the others, however, the interest rate never rises back to its initial level.

Panel (b) has a smaller liquidity effect than the other effects, with the expected-inflation effect operating slowly because expectations of inflation are slow to adjust upward. Initially, the liquidity effect drives down the interest rate. Then the income, price-level, and expected-inflation effects begin to raise it. Because these effects are dominant, the interest rate eventually rises above its initial level to i_2. In the short run, lower interest rates result from increased money growth, but eventually they end up climbing above the initial level.

Panel (c) has the expected-inflation effect dominating as well as operating rapidly because people quickly raise their expectations of inflation when the rate of money growth increases. The expected-inflation effect begins immediately to overpower the liquidity effect, and the interest rate immediately starts to climb. Over time, as the income and price-level effects start to take hold, the interest rate rises even higher, and the eventual outcome is an interest rate that is substantially higher than the initial interest rate. The result shows clearly that increasing money supply growth is not the answer to reducing interest rates; rather, money growth should be reduced to lower interest rates!

An important issue for economic policy makers is which of these three scenarios is closest to reality. If a decline in interest rates is desired, then an increase in money supply growth is called for when the liquidity effect dominates the other effects, as in panel (a). A decrease in money growth is appropriate when the other effects dominate the liquidity effect and expectations of inflation adjust rapidly, as in panel (c). If the other effects dominate the liquidity effect but expectations of inflation adjust only slowly, as in panel (b), then whether you want to increase or decrease money growth depends on whether you care more about what happens in the short run or the long run.

Which scenario is supported by the evidence? The relationship of interest rates and money growth from 1950 to 2011 is plotted in Figure 12. When the rate of money supply growth began to climb in the mid-1960s, interest rates rose, indicating that the liquidity effect was dominated by the price-level, income, and expected-inflation effects. By the 1970s, interest rates reached levels unprecedented in the post–World War II period, as did the rate of money supply growth.

The scenario depicted in panel (a) of Figure 11 seems doubtful, and the case for lowering interest rates by raising the rate of money growth is much weakened. Looking back at Figure 5, which shows the relationship between interest rates and expected inflation, you should not find this too surprising. The rise in the rate of money supply growth in the 1960s and 1970s is matched by a large rise in expected inflation, which would lead us to predict that the expected-inflation effect would be dominant. It is the most plausible explanation for why interest rates rose in the face of higher money

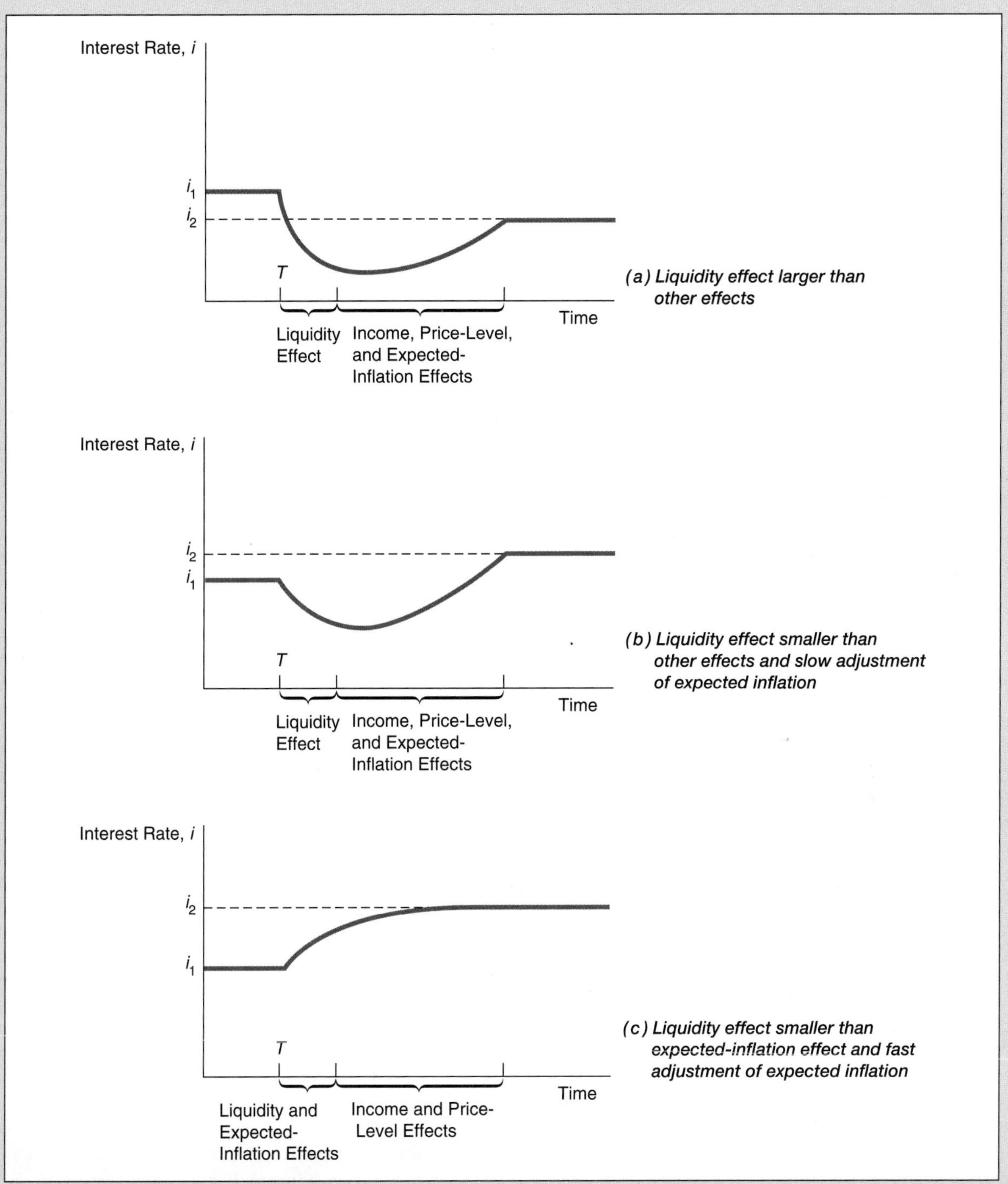

FIGURE 11 Response over Time to an Increase in Money Supply Growth

Each panel shows how interest rates respond over time to an increased rate of money supply growth, starting at time *T*.

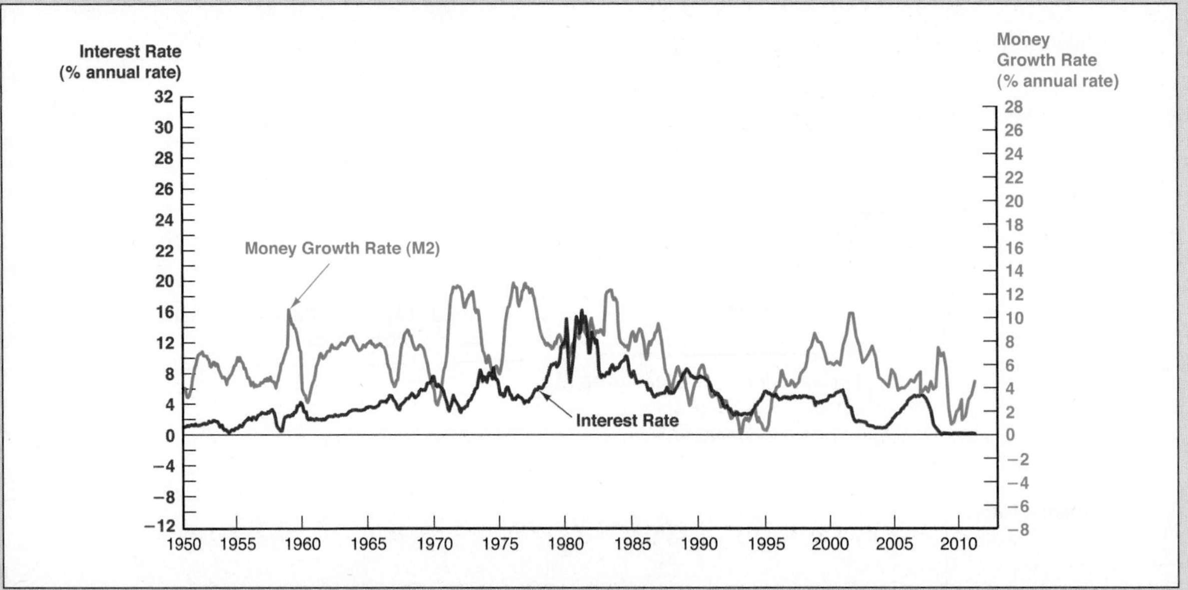

FIGURE 12 Money Growth (M2, Annual Rate) and Interest Rates (Three-Month Treasury Bills), 1950–2011

When the rate of money supply growth began to climb in the mid-1960s, interest rates rose, indicating that the liquidity effect was dominated by the price-level, income, and expected-inflation effects. By the 1970s, both interest rates and money growth reached levels unprecedented in the post–World War II period.

Sources: **Federal Reserve:** www.federalreserve.gov/releases/h6/hist/h6hist1.txt.

growth. However, Figure 12 does not really tell us which one of the two scenarios, panel (b) or panel (c) of Figure 11, is more accurate. It depends critically on how fast people's expectations about inflation adjust. However, research using more sophisticated methods than just looking at a graph like Figure 12 indicates that increased money growth temporarily lowers short-term interest rates. ◆

Summary

1. The theory of portfolio choice tells us that the quantity demanded of an asset is (a) positively related to wealth, (b) positively related to the expected return on the asset relative to alternative assets, (c) negatively related to the riskiness of the asset relative to alternative assets, and (d) positively related to the liquidity of the asset relative to alternative assets.
2. The supply and demand analysis for bonds provides one theory of how interest rates are determined. It predicts that interest rates will change when there is a change in demand because of changes in income (or wealth), expected returns, risk, or liquidity or when there is a change in supply because of changes in the attractiveness of investment opportunities, the real cost of borrowing, or the government budget.
3. An alternative theory of how interest rates are determined is provided by the liquidity preference framework, which analyzes the supply of and demand for

money. It shows that interest rates will change when the demand for money changes because of alterations in income or the price level or when the supply of money changes.

4. There are four possible effects of an increase in the money supply on interest rates: the liquidity effect, the income effect, the price-level effect, and the expected-inflation effect. The liquidity effect indicates that a rise in money supply growth will lead to a decline in interest rates; the other effects work in the opposite direction. The evidence seems to indicate that the income, price-level, and expected-inflation effects dominate the liquidity effect such that an increase in money supply growth leads to higher—rather than lower—interest rates.

Key Terms

asset market approach, p. 94
demand curve, p. 91
excess demand, p. 93
excess supply, p. 93
expected return, p. 88
Fisher effect, p. 101
liquidity, p. 89
liquidity preference framework, p. 104
market equilibrium, p. 93
opportunity cost, p. 105
risk, p. 89
supply curve, p. 92
theory of portfolio choice, p. 90
wealth, p. 88

Questions

All questions are available in MyEconLab *at* www.myeconlab.com.

1. Explain why you would be more or less willing to buy a share of Microsoft stock in the following situations:
   a. Your wealth falls.
   b. You expect the stock to appreciate in value.
   c. The bond market becomes more liquid.
   d. You expect gold to appreciate in value.
   e. Prices in the bond market become more volatile.
2. Explain why you would be more or less willing to buy a house under the following circumstances:
   a. You just inherited $100,000.
   b. Real estate commissions fall from 6% of the sales price to 5% of the sales price.
   c. You expect Microsoft stock to double in value next year.
   d. Prices in the stock market become more volatile.
   e. You expect housing prices to fall.
3. Explain why you would be more or less willing to buy gold under the following circumstances:
   a. Gold again becomes acceptable as a medium of exchange.
   b. Prices in the gold market become more volatile.
   c. You expect inflation to rise, and gold prices tend to move with the aggregate price level.
   d. You expect interest rates to rise.
4. Explain why you would be more or less willing to buy long-term AT&T bonds under the following circumstances:
   a. Trading in these bonds increases, making them easier to sell.
   b. You expect a bear market in stocks (stock prices are expected to decline).
   c. Brokerage commissions on stocks fall.
   d. You expect interest rates to rise.
   e. Brokerage commissions on bonds fall.
5. What would happen to the demand for Rembrandt paintings if the stock market undergoes a boom? Why?
6. "The more risk-averse people are, the more likely they are to diversify." Is this statement true, false, or uncertain? Explain your answer.
7. "No one who is risk-averse will ever buy a security that has a lower expected return, more risk, and less liquidity than another security." Is this statement true, false, or uncertain? Explain your answer.
8. What effect will a sudden increase in the volatility of gold prices have on interest rates?
9. How might a sudden increase in people's expectations of future real estate prices affect interest rates?
10. Explain what effect a large federal deficit should have on interest rates.

11. In the aftermath of the global economic crisis that started to take hold in 2008, U.S. government budget deficits increased dramatically, yet interest rates on U.S. Treasury debt fell sharply and stayed low for quite some time. Does this make sense? Why or why not?
12. Will there be an effect on interest rates if brokerage commissions on stocks fall? Explain your answer.
13. The president of the United States announces in a press conference that he will fight the higher inflation rate with a new anti-inflation program. Predict what will happen to interest rates if the public believes him.
14. Predict what will happen to interest rates if the public suddenly expects a large increase in stock prices.
15. Predict what will happen to interest rates if prices in the bond market become more volatile.
16. Would fiscal policy makers ever have reason to worry about potentially inflationary conditions? Why or why not?
17. Why should a rise in the price level (but not in expected inflation) cause interest rates to rise when the nominal money supply is fixed?
18. If the next chair of the Federal Reserve Board has a reputation for advocating an even slower rate of money growth than the current chair, what will happen to interest rates? Discuss the possible resulting situations.
19. M1 money growth in the U.S. was about 16% in 2008, 7% in 2009, and 9% in 2010. Over the same time period, the yield on 3-month Treasury bills fell from almost 3% to close to 0%. Given these high rates of money growth, why did interest rates fall, rather than increase? What does this say about the income, price-level, and expected-inflation effects?

Applied Problems

All applied problems are available in MyEconLab *at* www.myeconlab.com.

20. Suppose you visit with a financial adviser, and you are considering investing some of your wealth in one of three investment portfolios: stocks, bonds, or commodities. Your financial adviser provides you with the following table, which gives the probabilities of possible returns from each investment:

Stocks		**Bonds**		**Commodities**	
Probability	**Return**	**Probability**	**Return**	**Probability**	**Return**
0.25	12%	0.6	10%	0.2	20%
0.25	10%	0.4	7.50%	0.25	12%
0.25	8%			0.25	6%
0.25	6%			0.25	4%
				0.05	0%

a. Which investment should you choose to maximize your expected return: stocks, bonds, or commodities?
b. If you are risk-averse and had to choose between the stock or the bond investments, which would you choose? Why?

21. An important way in which the Federal Reserve decreases the money supply is by selling bonds to the public. Using a supply and demand analysis for bonds, show what effect this action has on interest rates. Is your answer consistent with what you would expect to find with the liquidity preference framework?

22. Using both the liquidity preference framework and the supply and demand for bonds framework, show why interest rates are procyclical (rising when the economy is expanding and falling during recessions).

23. Using both the supply and demand for bonds and liquidity preference frameworks, show how interest rates are affected when the riskiness of bonds rises. Are the results the same in the two frameworks?

24. The demand curve and supply curve for one-year discount bonds with a face value of $1,000 are represented by the following equations:

B^d: Price = −0.6 Quantity + 1140

B^s: Price = Quantity + 700

a. What is the expected equilibrium price and quantity of bonds in this market?

b. Given your answer to part (a), what is the expected interest rate in this market?

25. The demand curve and supply curve for one-year discount bonds with a face value of $1,000 are represented by the following equations:

B^d: Price = −0.6 Quantity + 1140

B^s: Price = Quantity + 700

Suppose that, as a result of monetary policy actions, the Federal Reserve sells 80 bonds that it holds. Assume that bond demand and money demand are held constant.

a. How does the Federal Reserve policy affect the bond supply equation?

b. Calculate the effect on the equilibrium interest rate in this market, as a result of the Federal Reserve action.

Web Exercises

1. One of the largest single influences on the level of interest rates is inflation. A number of sites report inflation over time. Go to ftp://ftp.bls.gov/pub/special.requests/cpi/cpiai.txt and review the data available. Note that the last columns report various averages. Move these data into a spreadsheet, using the method discussed in the Web exploration at the end of Chapter 1. What has the average rate of inflation been since 1950, 1960, 1970, 1980, and 1990? Which year had the lowest level of inflation? Which year had the highest?

2. Increasing prices erode the purchasing power of the dollar. It is interesting to compute what goods would have cost at some point in the past after adjusting for inflation. Go to http://minneapolisfed.org/index.cfm. What would a car that cost $22,000 today have cost the year that you were born?

3. One of the points made in this chapter is that inflation erodes investment returns. Go to www.moneychimp.com/articles/econ/inflation_calculator.htm and review how changes in inflation alter your real return. What happens to the difference between the adjusted value of an investment and its inflation-adjusted value as
   a. Inflation increases?
   b. The investment horizon lengthens?
   c. Expected returns increase?

Web References

ftp://ftp.bls.gov/pub/special.requests/cpi/cpiai.txt

Contains historical information about inflation.

www.federalreserve.gov/releases/H6/Current

The Federal Reserve reports money supply data at 4:30 p.m. every Thursday.

Web Appendices

Please visit the Companion Website at www.pearsonhighered.com/mishkin to read the Web appendices to Chapter 5.

Appendix 1: **Models of Asset Pricing**

Appendix 2: **Applying the Asset Market Approach to a Commodity Market: The Case of Gold**

Appendix 3: **Loanable Funds Framework**

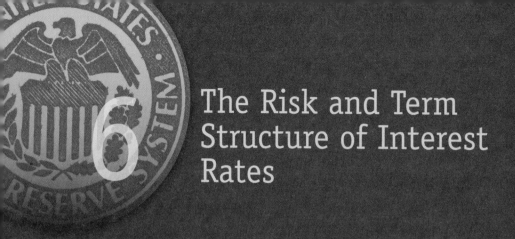

6 The Risk and Term Structure of Interest Rates

Preview

In our supply and demand analysis of interest-rate behavior in Chapter 5, we examined the determination of just one interest rate. Yet we saw earlier that there are enormous numbers of bonds on which the interest rates can and do differ. In this chapter, we complete the interest-rate picture by examining the relationship of the various interest rates to one another. Understanding why they differ from bond to bond can help businesses, banks, insurance companies, and private investors decide which bonds to purchase as investments and which ones to sell.

We first look at why bonds with the same term to maturity have different interest rates. The relationship among these interest rates is called the **risk structure of interest rates**, although risk, liquidity, and income tax rules all play a role in determining the risk structure. A bond's term to maturity also affects its interest rate, and the relationship among interest rates on bonds with different terms to maturity is called the **term structure of interest rates**. In this chapter, we examine the sources and causes of fluctuations in interest rates relative to one another and look at a number of theories that explain these fluctuations.

RISK STRUCTURE OF INTEREST RATES

Figure 1 shows the yields to maturity for several categories of long-term bonds from 1919 to 2011. It shows us two important features of interest-rate behavior for bonds of the same maturity: Interest rates on different categories of bonds differ from one another in any given year, and the spread (or difference) between the interest rates varies over time. The interest rates on municipal bonds, for example, are higher than those on U.S. government (Treasury) bonds in the late 1930s but lower thereafter. In addition, the spread between the interest rates on Baa corporate bonds (riskier than Aaa corporate bonds) and U.S. government bonds is very large during the Great Depression years 1930–1933, is smaller during the 1940s–1960s, and then widens again afterward. Which factors are responsible for these phenomena?

Default Risk

One attribute of a bond that influences its interest rate is its risk of **default**, which occurs when the issuer of the bond is unable or unwilling to make interest payments when promised or pay off the face value when the bond matures. A corporation suffering big losses, such as the major airline companies like United, Delta, US Airways, and Northwest in the

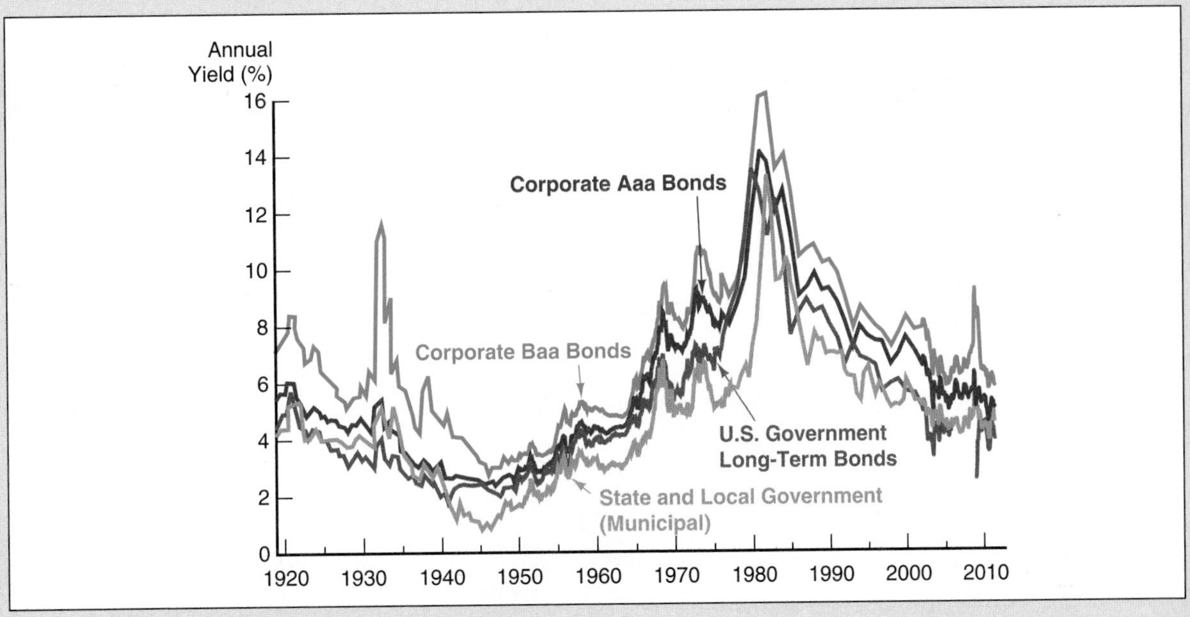

FIGURE 1 Long-Term Bond Yields, 1919–2011

Interest rates on different categories of bonds differ from one another in any given year, and the spread (or difference) between the interest rates varies over time.

Sources: Board of Governors of the Federal Reserve System, *Banking and Monetary Statistics, 1941–1970*; Federal Reserve; www.federalreserve.gov/releases/h15/data.htm.

mid-2000s, might be more likely to suspend interest payments on its bonds. The default risk on its bonds would therefore be quite high. By contrast, U.S. Treasury bonds have usually been considered to have no default risk because the federal government can always increase taxes or print money to pay off its obligations. Bonds like these with no default risk are called **default-free bonds**. (However, during the budget negotiations in Congress in 1995 and 1996, and then again in 2011, the Republicans threatened to let Treasury bonds default, and this had an impact on the bond market.) The spread between the interest rates on bonds with default risk and default-free bonds, both of the same maturity, called the **risk premium**, indicates how much additional interest people must earn to be willing to hold that risky bond. Our supply and demand analysis of the bond market in Chapter 5 can be used to explain why a bond with default risk always has a positive risk premium and why the higher the default risk is, the larger the risk premium will be.

To examine the effect of default risk on interest rates, let's look at the supply and demand diagrams for the default-free (U.S. Treasury) and corporate long-term bond markets in Figure 2. To make the diagrams somewhat easier to read, let's assume that initially corporate bonds have the same default risk as U.S. Treasury bonds. In this case, these two bonds have the same attributes (identical risk and maturity); their equilibrium prices and interest rates will initially be equal $(P_1^c = P_1^T$ and $i_1^c = i_1^T)$, and the risk premium on corporate bonds $(i_1^c - i_1^T)$ will be zero.

If the possibility of a default increases because a corporation begins to suffer large losses, the default risk on corporate bonds will increase, and the expected return on these bonds will decrease. In addition, the corporate bond's return will be more uncertain. The

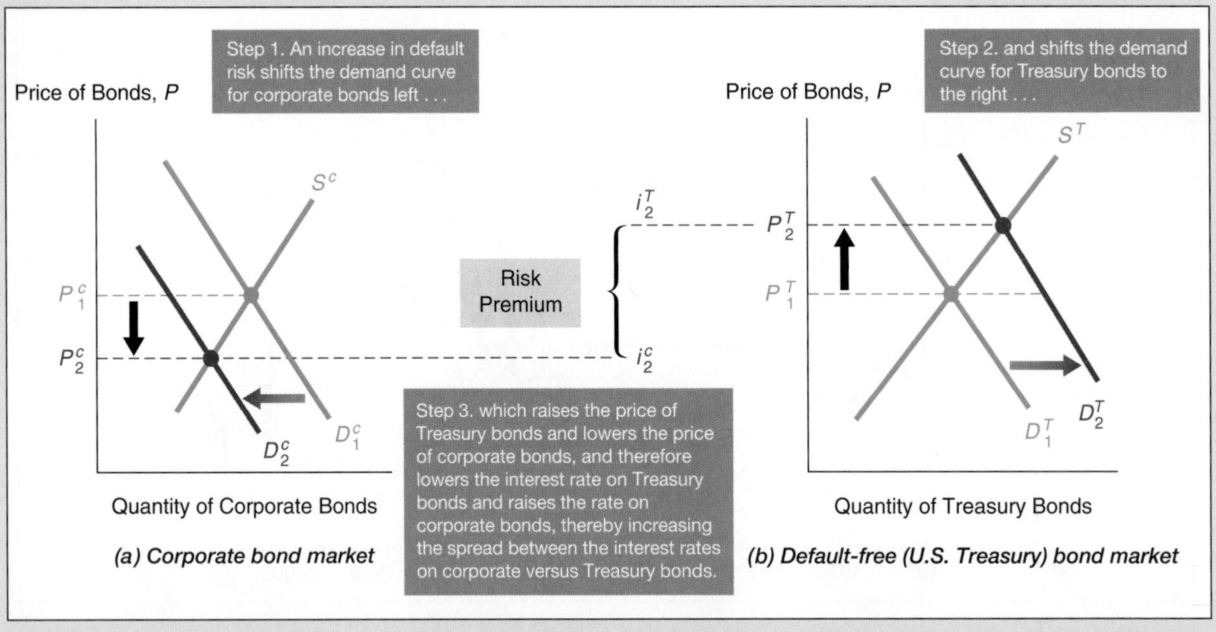

FIGURE 2 Response to an Increase in Default Risk on Corporate Bonds

Initially $P_1^c = P_1^T$ and the risk premium is zero. An increase in default risk on corporate bonds shifts the demand curve from D_1^c to D_2^c. Simultaneously, it shifts the demand curve for Treasury bonds from D_1^T to D_2^T. The equilibrium price for corporate bonds falls from P_1^c to P_2^c, and the equilibrium interest rate on corporate bonds rises to i_2^c. In the Treasury market, the equilibrium bond price rises from P_1^T to P_2^T, and the equilibrium interest rate falls to i_2^T. The brace indicates the difference between i_2^c and i_2^T, the risk premium on corporate bonds. (Note that because P_2^c is lower than P_2^T, i_2^c is greater than i_2^T.)

theory of portfolio choice predicts that because the expected return on the corporate bond falls relative to the expected return on the default-free Treasury bond while its relative riskiness rises, the corporate bond is less desirable (holding everything else equal), and demand for it will fall. Another way of thinking about this is that if you were an investor, you would want to hold (demand) a smaller amount of corporate bonds. The demand curve for corporate bonds in panel (a) of Figure 2 then shifts to the left, from D_1^c to D_2^c.

At the same time, the expected return on default-free Treasury bonds increases relative to the expected return on corporate bonds, while their relative riskiness declines. The Treasury bonds thus become more desirable, and demand rises, as shown in panel (b) by the rightward shift in the demand curve for these bonds from D_1^T to D_2^T.

As we can see in Figure 2, the equilibrium price for corporate bonds falls from P_1^c to P_2^c, and since the bond price is negatively related to the interest rate, the equilibrium interest rate on corporate bonds rises to i_2^c. At the same time, however, the equilibrium price for the Treasury bonds rises from P_1^T to P_2^T and the equilibrium interest rate falls to i_2^T. The spread between the interest rates on corporate and default-free bonds—that is, the risk premium on corporate bonds—has risen from zero to $i_2^c - i_2^T$. We can now conclude that ***a bond with default risk will always have a positive risk premium, and an increase in its default risk will raise the risk premium***.

Because default risk is so important to the size of the risk premium, purchasers of bonds need to know whether a corporation is likely to default on its bonds. This information is provided by **credit-rating agencies**, investment advisory firms that rate

TABLE 1 **Bond Ratings by Moody's, Standard and Poor's, and Fitch**

	Rating		
Moody's	**S&P**	**Fitch**	**Definitions**
Aaa	AAA	AAA	Prime Maximum Safety
Aa1	AA–	AA–	High Grade High Quality
Aa2	AA	AA	
Aa3	AA–	AA–	
A1	A+	A+	Upper Medium Grade
A2	A	A	
A3	A–	A–	
Baa1	BBB+	BBB+	Lower Medium Grade
Baa2	BBB	BBB	
Baa3	BBB–	BBB–	
Ba1	BB+	BB+	Noninvestment Grade
Ba2	BB	BB	Speculative
Ba3	BB–	BB–	
B1	B–	B–	Highly Speculative
B2	B	B	
B3	B–	B–	
Caa1	CCC+	CCC	Substantial Risk
Caa2	CCC	—	In Poor Standing
Caa3	CCC–	—	
Ca	—	—	Extremely Speculative
C	—	—	May Be in Default
—	—	DDD	Default
—	—	DD	—
—	D	D	

the quality of corporate and municipal bonds in terms of the probability of default. Credit-rating agencies have become very controversial in recent years because of the role they played in the global financial crisis of 2007–2009 (see the FYI box, "Conflicts of Interest at Credit-Rating Agencies and the Global Financial Crisis"). Table 1 provides the ratings and their description for the three largest credit-rating agencies, Moody's Investor Service, Standard and Poor's Corporation, and Fitch Ratings. Bonds with relatively low risk of default are called *investment-grade* securities and have a rating of Baa (or BBB) and above. Bonds with ratings below Baa (or BBB) have higher default risk and have been aptly dubbed speculative-grade or **junk bonds**. Because these bonds always have higher interest rates than investment-grade securities, they are also referred to as high-yield bonds.

FYI **Conflicts of Interest at Credit-Rating Agencies and the Global Financial Crisis**

Debt ratings play a major role in the pricing of debt securities and in the regulatory process. Conflicts of interest arose for credit-rating agencies in the years running up to the global financial crisis when they advised clients on how to structure complex financial instruments that paid out cash flows from subprime mortgages. At the same time, they were rating these identical products, leading to the potential for severe conflicts of interest. Specifically, the large fees they earned from advising clients on how to structure products that they were rating meant they did not have sufficient incentives to make sure their ratings were accurate.

When housing prices began to fall and subprime mortgages began to default, it became crystal clear that the ratings agencies had done a terrible job of assessing the risk in the subprime products they had helped to structure. Many AAA-rated products had to be downgraded over and over again until they reached junk status. The resulting massive losses on these assets were one reason why so many financial institutions who were holding them got into trouble. Indeed, some commentators have cited credit-rating agencies as among the chief villains that should be blamed for the global financial crisis.

Next let's look at Figure 1 at the beginning of the chapter and see if we can explain the relationship between interest rates on corporate and U.S. Treasury bonds. Corporate bonds always have higher interest rates than U.S. Treasury bonds because they always have some risk of default, whereas U.S. Treasury bonds do not. Because Baa-rated corporate bonds have a greater default risk than the higher-rated Aaa bonds, their risk premium is greater, and the Baa rate therefore always exceeds the Aaa rate. We can use the same analysis to explain the huge jump in the risk premium on Baa corporate bond rates during the Great Depression years 1930–1933 and the rise in the risk premium after 1970 (see Figure 1). The depression period saw a very high rate of business failures and defaults. As we would expect, these factors led to a substantial increase in the default risk for bonds issued by vulnerable corporations, and the risk premium for Baa bonds reached unprecedentedly high levels. Since 1970, we have again seen higher levels of business failures and defaults, although they have been well below Great Depression levels. Again, as expected, both default risks and risk premiums for corporate bonds rose, widening the spread between interest rates on corporate bonds and those on Treasury bonds.

APPLICATION ◆ The Global Financial Crisis and the Baa-Treasury Spread

Starting in August 2007, the collapse of the subprime mortgage market led to large losses in financial institutions (which we will discuss more extensively in Chapter 9). As a consequence of the subprime collapse, many investors began to doubt the financial health of corporations with low credit ratings such as Baa and even the reliability of the ratings themselves. The perceived increase in default risk for Baa bonds made them less desirable at any given interest rate, decreased the quantity demanded, and shifted the demand curve for Baa bonds to the left. As shown in panel (a) of Figure 2, the interest rate on Baa bonds should have risen, which is indeed what happened. Interest rates on Baa bonds rose by 280 basis points (2.80 percentage points) from 6.63% at the end of July 2007 to 9.43% at the most virulent stage of the global financial crisis in mid-October 2008. But the increase in perceived default risk for Baa bonds in October 2008 made default-free U.S. Treasury bonds relatively more attractive and shifted the demand curve for these securities to the right—an outcome described by some analysts as a "flight to quality." Just as our analysis predicts in Figure 2, interest rates on Treasury bonds fell by 80 basis points, from 4.78% at the end of July 2007 to 3.98% in mid-October 2008. The spread between interest rates on Baa and Treasury bonds rose by 360 basis points, from 1.85% before the crisis to 5.45% afterward. ◆

Liquidity

Another attribute of a bond that influences its interest rate is its liquidity. As we learned in Chapter 4, a liquid asset is one that can be quickly and cheaply converted into cash if the need arises. The more liquid an asset is, the more desirable it is (holding everything else constant). U.S. Treasury bonds are the most liquid of all long-term bonds; because they are so widely traded, they are the easiest to sell quickly and the cost of selling them is low. Corporate bonds are not as liquid, because fewer bonds for any one corporation are traded; thus it can be costly to sell these bonds in an emergency, because it might be hard to find buyers quickly.

How does the reduced liquidity of the corporate bonds affect their interest rates relative to the interest rate on Treasury bonds? We can use supply and demand analysis with the same figure that was used to analyze the effect of default risk, Figure 2, to show that the lower liquidity of corporate bonds relative to Treasury bonds increases the spread between the interest rates on these two bonds. Let's start the analysis by assuming that initially corporate and Treasury bonds are equally liquid and all their other attributes are the same. As shown in Figure 2, their equilibrium prices and interest rates will initially be equal: $P_1^c = P_1^T$ and $i_1^c = i_1^T$. If the corporate bond becomes less liquid than the Treasury bond because it is less widely traded, then (as the theory of portfolio choice indicates) demand for it will fall, shifting its demand curve from D_1^c to D_2^c as in panel (a). The Treasury bond now becomes relatively more liquid in comparison with the corporate bond, so its demand curve shifts rightward from D_1^T to D_2^T as in panel (b). The shifts in the curves in Figure 2 show that the price of the less liquid corporate bond falls and its interest rate rises, while the price of the more liquid Treasury bond rises and its interest rate falls.

The result is that the spread between the interest rates on the two bond types has risen. Therefore, the differences between interest rates on corporate bonds and Treasury bonds (that is, the risk premiums) reflect not only the corporate bond's default risk but also its liquidity. This is why a risk premium is more accurately a "risk and liquidity premium," but convention dictates that it is called a *risk premium*.

Income Tax Considerations

Returning to Figure 1, we are still left with one puzzle—the behavior of municipal bond rates. Municipal bonds are certainly not default-free: State and local governments have defaulted on the municipal bonds they have issued in the past, particularly during the Great Depression and even more recently in the case of Orange County, California, in 1994. Also, municipal bonds are not as liquid as U.S. Treasury bonds.

Why is it, then, that these bonds have had lower interest rates than U.S. Treasury bonds most of the past 70 years, as indicated in Figure 1? The explanation lies in the fact that interest payments on municipal bonds are exempt from federal income taxes, a factor that has the same effect on the demand for municipal bonds as an increase in their expected return.

Let us imagine that you have a high enough income to put you in the 35% income tax bracket, where for every extra dollar of income you have to pay 35 cents to the government. If you own a $1,000-face-value U.S. Treasury bond that sells for $1,000 and has a coupon payment of $100, you get to keep only $65 of the payment after taxes. Although the bond has a 10% interest rate, you actually earn only 6.5% after taxes.

Suppose, however, that you put your savings into a $1,000-face-value municipal bond that sells for $1,000 and pays only $80 in coupon payments. Its interest rate is only 8%, but because it is a tax-exempt security, you pay no taxes on the $80 coupon payment, so you earn 8% after taxes. Clearly, you earn more on the municipal bond after taxes, so you are willing to hold the riskier and less liquid municipal bond even though it has a lower interest rate than the U.S. Treasury bond. (This was not true before World War II, when the tax-exempt status of municipal bonds did not convey much of an advantage because income tax rates were extremely low.)

Another way of understanding why municipal bonds have lower interest rates than Treasury bonds is to use the supply and demand analysis depicted in Figure 3. We initially assume that municipal and Treasury bonds have identical attributes and so have the same bond prices as drawn in the figure: $P_1^m = P_1^T$, and the same interest rates. Once the municipal bonds are given a tax advantage that raises their after-tax expected

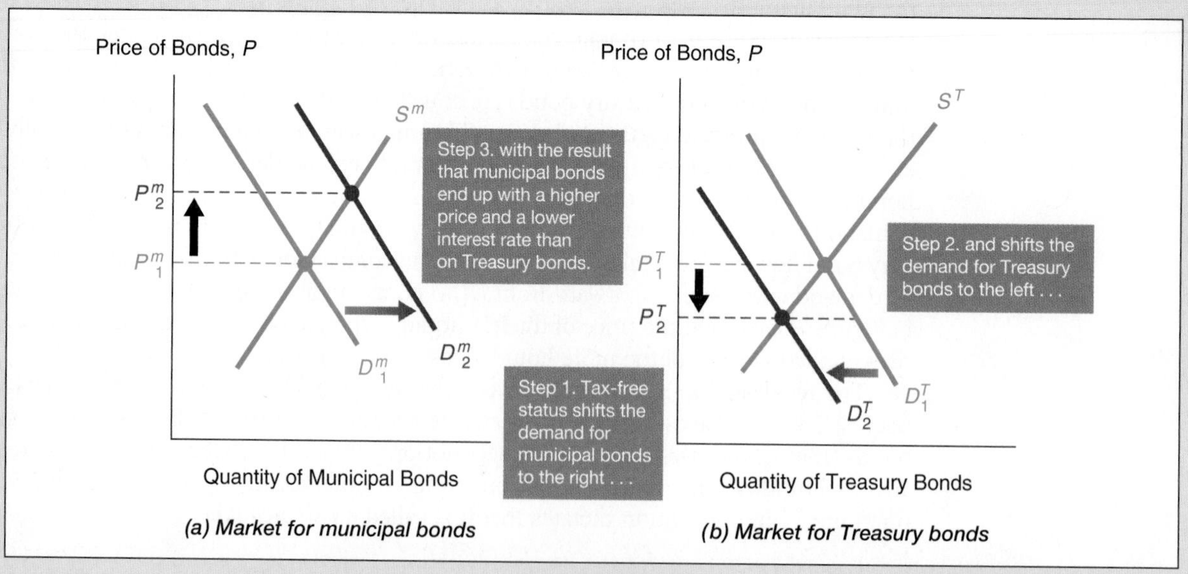

FIGURE 3 Interest Rates on Municipal and Treasury Bonds

When the municipal bond is given tax-free status, demand for the municipal bond shifts rightward from D_1^m to D_2^m and demand for the Treasury bond shifts leftward from D_1^T to D_2^T. The equilibrium price of the municipal bond rises from P_1^m to P_2^m, so its interest rate falls, while the equilibrium price of the Treasury bond falls from P_1^T to P_2^T and its interest rate rises. The result is that municipal bonds end up with lower interest rates than those on Treasury bonds.

return relative to Treasury bonds and makes them more desirable, demand for them rises, and their demand curve shifts to the right, from D_1^m to D_2^m. The result is that their equilibrium bond price rises from P_1^m to P_2^m, and their equilibrium interest rate falls. By contrast, Treasury bonds have now become less desirable relative to municipal bonds; demand for Treasury bonds decreases, and D_1^T shifts to D_2^T. The Treasury bond price falls from P_1^T to P_2^T, and the interest rate rises. The resulting lower interest rates for municipal bonds and higher interest rates for Treasury bonds explain why municipal bonds can have interest rates below those of Treasury bonds.[1]

Summary

The risk structure of interest rates (the relationship among interest rates on bonds with the same maturity) is explained by three factors: default risk, liquidity, and the income tax treatment of a bond's interest payments. As a bond's default risk increases, the risk premium on that bond (the spread between its interest rate and the interest rate on a default-free Treasury bond) rises. The greater liquidity of Treasury bonds also explains why their interest rates are lower than those on less liquid bonds. If a bond has a favorable tax treatment, as do municipal bonds, whose interest payments are exempt from federal income taxes, its interest rate will be lower.

APPLICATION ◆ Effects of the Bush Tax Cut and Its Possible Repeal on Bond Interest Rates

The Bush tax cut passed in 2001 scheduled a reduction of the top income tax bracket from 39% to 35% over a ten-year period. What is the effect of this income tax decrease on interest rates in the municipal bond market relative to those in the Treasury bond market?

Our supply and demand analysis provides the answer. A decreased income tax rate for wealthy people means that the after-tax expected return on tax-free municipal bonds relative to that on Treasury bonds is lower, because the interest on Treasury bonds is now taxed at a lower rate. Because municipal bonds now become less desirable, their demand decreases, shifting the demand curve to the left, which lowers their price and raises their interest rate. Conversely, the lower income tax rate makes Treasury bonds more desirable; this change shifts their demand curve to the right, raises their price, and lowers their interest rates.

Our analysis thus shows that the Bush tax cut raised the interest rates on municipal bonds relative to the interest rate on Treasury bonds.

Although the Bush tax cuts for people with over $250,000 in income were extended in 2010, the Obama administration has supported repeal of these tax cuts. For the possible repeal of the Bush tax cuts for high-income people, the analysis would be reversed. Higher tax rates would raise the after-tax expected return on tax-free municipal bonds relative to Treasurys. Demand for municipal bonds would increase, shifting the demand curve to the right, which raises their price and lowers their interest rate. Conversely, the higher tax rate would make Treasury bonds less desirable, shifting their demand curve to the left,

[1]In contrast to corporate bonds, Treasury bonds are exempt from state and local income taxes. Using the analysis in the text, you should be able to show that this feature of Treasury bonds provides an additional reason why interest rates on corporate bonds are higher than those on Treasury bonds.

lowering their price, and raising their interest rate. Higher tax rates would thus result in lower interest rates on municipal bonds relative to the interest rate on Treasury bonds. ◆

TERM STRUCTURE OF INTEREST RATES

We have seen how risk, liquidity, and tax considerations (collectively embedded in the risk structure) can influence interest rates. Another factor that influences the interest rate on a bond is its term to maturity: Bonds with identical risk, liquidity, and tax characteristics may have different interest rates because their time remaining to maturity is different. A plot of the yields on bonds with differing terms to maturity but the same risk, liquidity, and tax considerations is called a **yield curve**, and it describes the term structure of interest rates for particular types of bonds, such as government bonds. The Following the Financial News box shows a yield curve for Treasury securities. Yield curves can be classified as upward-sloping, flat, and downward-sloping (the last sort is often referred to as an **inverted yield curve**). When yield curves slope upward, the most usual case, the long-term interest rates are above the short-term interest rates; when yield curves are flat, as in the Following the Financial News box, short- and long-term interest rates are the same; and when yield curves are inverted, long-term interest rates are below short-term interest rates. Yield curves can also have more complicated shapes in which they first slope up and then down, or vice versa. Why do we usually see upward slopes of the yield curve but sometimes other shapes?

Following the Financial News Yield Curves

Many newspapers and Internet sites such as www.finance.yahoo.com publish a daily plot of the yield curves for Treasury securities. An example for July 11, 2011 is presented here. The numbers on the vertical axis indicate the interest rate for the Treasury security, with the maturity given on the horizontal axis with "m" denoting month and "y" denoting year.

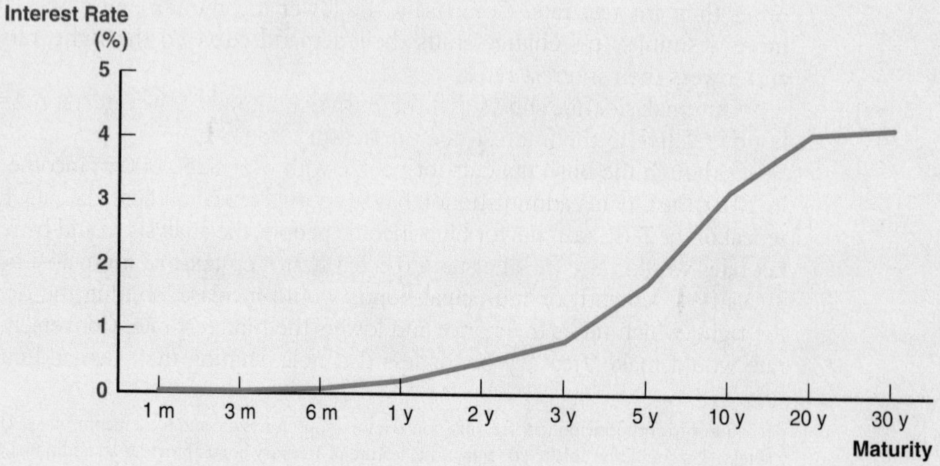

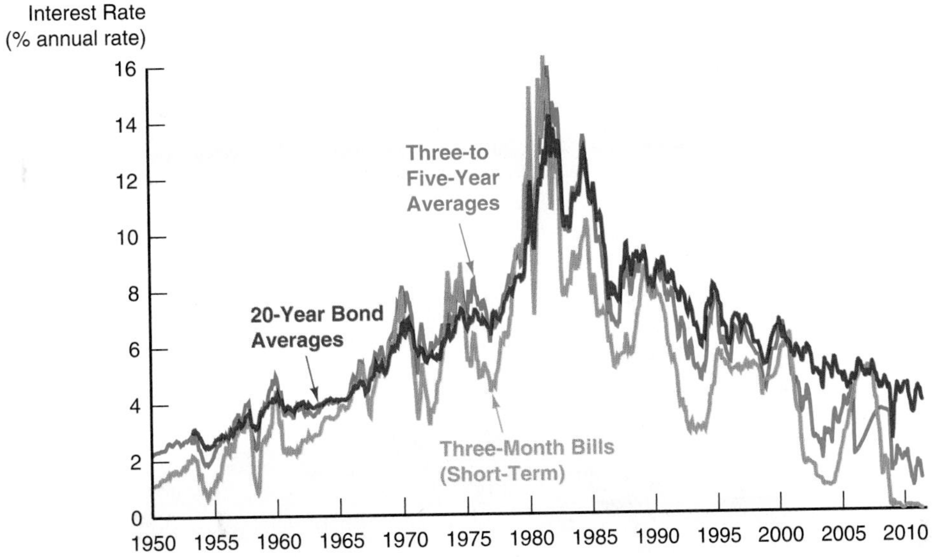

FIGURE 4 Movements over Time of Interest Rates on U.S. Government Bonds with Different Maturities

Interest rates on bonds of different maturities move together over time.

Sources: Federal Reserve; www.federalreserve.gov/releases/h15/data.htm.

Besides explaining why yield curves take on different shapes at different times, a good theory of the term structure of interest rates must explain the following three important empirical facts:

1. As we see in Figure 4, interest rates on bonds of different maturities move together over time.
2. When short-term interest rates are low, yield curves are more likely to have an upward slope; when short-term interest rates are high, yield curves are more likely to slope downward and be inverted.
3. Yield curves almost always slope upward, as in the Following the Financial News box.

Three theories have been put forward to explain the term structure of interest rates—that is, the relationship among interest rates on bonds of different maturities reflected in yield curve patterns: (1) the expectations theory, (2) the segmented markets theory, and (3) the liquidity premium theory, each of which is described in the following sections. The expectations theory does a good job of explaining the first two facts on our list, but not the third. The segmented markets theory can account for fact 3 but not the other two facts, which are well explained by the expectations theory. Because each theory explains facts that the other cannot, a natural way to seek a better understanding of the term structure is to combine features of both theories, which leads us to the liquidity premium theory, which can cover all three facts.

If the liquidity premium theory does a better job of explaining the facts and is hence the most widely accepted theory, why do we spend time discussing the other two theories? There are two reasons. First, the ideas in these two theories lay the groundwork for the liquidity premium theory. Second, it is important to see how economists modify theories to improve them when they find that the predicted results are inconsistent with the empirical evidence.

Expectations Theory

The **expectations theory** of the term structure states the following commonsense proposition: The interest rate on a long-term bond will equal an average of the short-term interest rates that people expect to occur over the life of the long-term bond. For example, if people expect that short-term interest rates will be 10% on average over the coming five years, the expectations theory predicts that the interest rate on bonds with five years to maturity will be 10%, too. If short-term interest rates were expected to rise even higher after this five-year period, so that the average short-term interest rate over the coming 20 years is 11%, then the interest rate on 20-year bonds would equal 11% and would be higher than the interest rate on five-year bonds. We can see that the explanation provided by the expectations theory for why interest rates on bonds of different maturities differ is that short-term interest rates are expected to have different values at future dates.

The key assumption behind this theory is that buyers of bonds do not prefer bonds of one maturity over another, so they will not hold any quantity of a bond if its expected return is less than that of another bond with a different maturity. Bonds that have this characteristic are said to be *perfect substitutes*. What this means in practice is that if bonds with different maturities are perfect substitutes, the expected return on these bonds must be equal.

To see how the assumption that bonds with different maturities are perfect substitutes leads to the expectations theory, let us consider the following two investment strategies:

1. Purchase a one-year bond, and when it matures in one year, purchase another one-year bond.
2. Purchase a two-year bond and hold it until maturity.

Because both strategies must have the same expected return if people are holding both one- and two-year bonds, the interest rate on the two-year bond must equal the average of the two one-year interest rates. For example, let's say that the current interest rate on the one-year bond is 9% and you expect the interest rate on the one-year bond next year to be 11%. If you pursue the first strategy of buying the two one-year bonds, the expected return over the two years will average out to be $(9\% + 11\%)/2 = 10\%$ per year. You will be willing to hold both the one- and two-year bonds only if the expected return per year of the two-year bond equals this return. Therefore, the interest rate on the two-year bond must equal 10%, the average interest rate on the two one-year bonds.

We can make this argument more general. For an investment of $1, consider the choice of holding, for two periods, a two-period bond or two one-period bonds. Using the definitions

$$i_t = \text{today's (time } t\text{) interest rate on a one-period bond}$$

$$i^e_{t+1} = \text{interest rate on a one-period bond expected for next period (time } t+1\text{)}$$

$$i_{2t} = \text{today's (time } t\text{) interest rate on the two-period bond}$$

the expected return over the two periods from investing $1 in the two-period bond and holding it for the two periods can be calculated as

$$(1 + i_{2t})(1 + i_{2t}) - 1 = 1 + 2i_{2t} + (i_{2t})^2 - 1 = 2i_{2t} + (i_{2t})^2$$

After the second period, the $1 investment is worth $(1 + i_{2t})(1 + i_{2t})$. Subtracting the $1 initial investment from this amount and dividing by the initial $1 investment gives the rate of return calculated in the previous equation. Because $(i_{2t})^2$ is extremely small—if $i_{2t} = 10\% = 0.10$, then $(i_{2t})^2 = 0.01$—we can simplify the expected return for holding the two-period bond for the two periods to

$$2i_{2t}$$

With the other strategy, in which one-period bonds are bought, the expected return on the $1 investment over the two periods is

$$(1 + i_t)(1 + i^e_{t+1}) - 1 = 1 + i_t + i^e_{t+1} + i_t(i^e_{t+1}) - 1 = i_t + i^e_{t+1} + i_t(i^e_{t+1})$$

This calculation is derived by recognizing that after the first period, the $1 investment becomes $1 + i_t$. and this is reinvested in the one-period bond for the next period, yielding an amount $(1 + i_t)(1 + i^e_{t+1})$. Then subtracting the $1 initial investment from this amount and dividing by the initial investment of $1 gives the expected return for the strategy of holding one-period bonds for the two periods. Because $i_t(i^e_{t+1})$ is also extremely small—if $i_t = i^e_{t+1} = 0.10$, then $i_t(i^e_{t+1}) = 0.01$—we can simplify this to

$$i_t + i^e_{t+1}$$

Both bonds will be held only if these expected returns are equal—that is, when

$$2i_{2t} = i_t + i^e_{t+1}$$

Solving for i_{2t} in terms of the one-period rates, we have

$$i_{2t} = \frac{i_t + i^e_{t+1}}{2} \tag{1}$$

which tells us that the two-period rate must equal the average of the two one-period rates. Graphically, this can be shown as

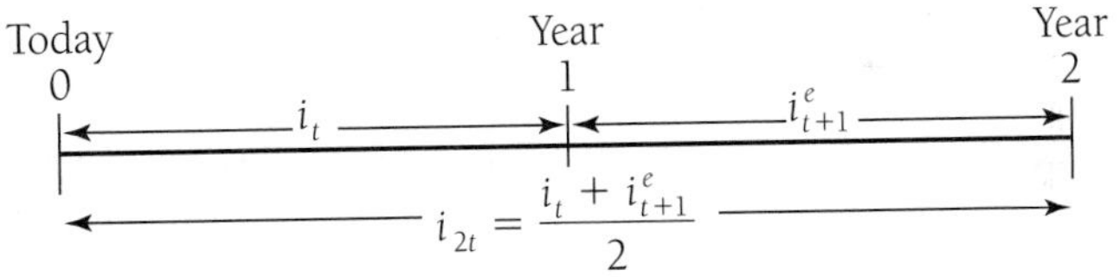

We can conduct the same steps for bonds with a longer maturity so that we can examine the whole term structure of interest rates. Doing so, we will find that the interest rate of i_{nt} on an n-period bond must be

$$i_{nt} = \frac{i_t + i^e_{t+1} + i^e_{t+2} + \ldots + i^e_{t+(n-1)}}{n} \tag{2}$$

Equation 2 states that the n-period interest rate equals the average of the one-period interest rates expected to occur over the n-period life of the bond. This is a restatement of the expectations theory in more precise terms.[2]

A simple numerical example might clarify what the expectations theory in Equation 2 is saying. If the one-year interest rate over the next five years is expected to be 5%, 6%, 7%, 8%, and 9%, Equation 2 indicates that the interest rate on the two-year bond would be

$$\frac{5\% + 6\%}{2} = 5.5\%$$

[2]The analysis here has been conducted for discount bonds. Formulas for interest rates on coupon bonds would differ slightly from those used here, but would convey the same principle.

For the five-year bond it would be

$$\frac{5\% + 6\% + 7\% + 8\% + 9\%}{5} = 7\%$$

Doing a similar calculation for the one-, three-, and four-year interest rates, you should be able to verify that the one- to five-year interest rates are 5.0%, 5.5%, 6.0%, 6.5%, and 7.0%, respectively. Thus we see that the rising trend in expected short-term interest rates produces an upward-sloping yield curve along which interest rates rise as maturity lengthens.

The expectations theory is an elegant theory that explains why the term structure of interest rates (as represented by yield curves) changes at different times. When the yield curve is upward-sloping, the expectations theory suggests that short-term interest rates are expected to rise in the future, as we have seen in our numerical example. In this situation, in which the long-term rate is currently higher than the short-term rate, the average of future short-term rates is expected to be higher than the current short-term rate, which can occur only if short-term interest rates are expected to rise. This result is what we see in our numerical example. When the yield curve is inverted (slopes downward), the average of future short-term interest rates is expected to be lower than the current short-term rate, implying that short-term interest rates are expected to fall, on average, in the future. Only when the yield curve is flat does the expectations theory suggest that short-term interest rates are not expected to change, on average, in the future.

The expectations theory also explains fact 1, which states that interest rates on bonds with different maturities move together over time. Historically, short-term interest rates have had the characteristic that if they increase today, they will tend to be higher in the future. Hence a rise in short-term rates will raise people's expectations of future short-term rates. Because long-term rates are the average of expected future short-term rates, a rise in short-term rates will also raise long-term rates, causing short- and long-term rates to move together.

The expectations theory also explains fact 2, which states that yield curves tend to have an upward slope when short-term interest rates are low and are inverted when short-term rates are high. When short-term rates are low, people generally expect them to rise to some normal level in the future, and the average of future expected short-term rates is high relative to the current short-term rate. Therefore, long-term interest rates will be substantially higher than current short-term rates, and the yield curve would then have an upward slope. Conversely, if short-term rates are high, people usually expect them to come back down. Long-term rates would then drop below short-term rates because the average of expected future short-term rates would be lower than current short-term rates and the yield curve would slope downward and become inverted.[3]

The expectations theory is an attractive theory because it provides a simple explanation of the behavior of the term structure, but unfortunately it has a major shortcoming: It cannot explain fact 3, which says that yield curves usually slope upward. The typical upward slope of yield curves implies that short-term interest rates are usually expected to rise in the future. In practice, short-term interest rates are just as likely to

[3]The expectations theory explains another important fact about the relationship between short-term and long-term interest rates. As you can see in Figure 4, short-term interest rates are more volatile than long-term rates. If interest rates are *mean-reverting*—that is, if they tend to head back down after they are at unusually high levels or go back up when they are at unusually low levels—then an average of these short-term rates must necessarily have less volatility than the short-term rates themselves. Because the expectations theory suggests that the long-term rate will be an average of future short-term rates, it implies that the long-term rate will have less volatility than short-term rates.

fall as they are to rise, and so the expectations theory suggests that the typical yield curve should be flat rather than upward-sloping.

Segmented Markets Theory

As the name suggests, the **segmented markets theory** of the term structure sees markets for different-maturity bonds as completely separate and segmented. The interest rate for each bond with a different maturity is then determined by the supply of and demand for that bond, with no effects from expected returns on other bonds with other maturities.

The key assumption in the segmented markets theory is that bonds of different maturities are not substitutes at all, so the expected return from holding a bond of one maturity has no effect on the demand for a bond of another maturity. This theory of the term structure is at the opposite extreme to the expectations theory, which assumes that bonds of different maturities are perfect substitutes.

The argument for why bonds of different maturities are not substitutes is that investors have very strong preferences for bonds of one maturity but not for another, so they will be concerned with the expected returns only for bonds of the maturity they prefer. This might occur because they have a particular holding period in mind, and if they match the maturity of the bond to the desired holding period, they can obtain a certain return with no risk at all.[4] (We have seen in Chapter 4 that if the term to maturity equals the holding period, the return is known for certain because it equals the yield exactly, and no interest-rate risk exists.) For example, people who have a short holding period would prefer to hold short-term bonds. Conversely, if you were putting funds away for your young child to go to college, your desired holding period might be much longer, and you would want to hold longer-term bonds.

In the segmented markets theory, differing yield curve patterns are accounted for by supply and demand differences associated with bonds of different maturities. If, as seems sensible, risk averse investors have short desired holding periods and generally prefer bonds with shorter maturities that have less interest-rate risk, the segmented markets theory can explain fact 3, which states that yield curves typically slope upward. Because in the typical situation the demand for long-term bonds is relatively lower than that for short-term bonds, long-term bonds will have lower prices and higher interest rates, and hence the yield curve will typically slope upward.

Although the segmented markets theory can explain why yield curves usually tend to slope upward, it has a major flaw in that it cannot explain facts 1 and 2. First, because it views the market for bonds of different maturities as completely segmented, there is no reason for a rise in interest rates on a bond of one maturity to affect the interest rate on a bond of another maturity. Therefore, it cannot explain why interest rates on bonds of different maturities tend to move together (fact 1). Second, because it is not clear how demand and supply for short- versus long-term bonds change with the level of short-term interest rates, the theory cannot explain why yield curves tend to slope upward when short-term interest rates are low and to be inverted when short-term interest rates are high (fact 2).

[4]The statement that there is no uncertainty about the return if the term to maturity equals the holding period is literally true only for a discount bond. For a coupon bond with a long holding period, some risk exists because coupon payments must be reinvested before the bond matures. Our analysis here is thus being conducted for discount bonds. However, the gist of the analysis remains the same for coupon bonds because the amount of this risk from reinvestment is small when coupon bonds have the same term to maturity as the holding period.

Because each of our two theories explains empirical facts that the other cannot, a logical step is to combine the theories, which leads us to the liquidity premium theory.

Liquidity Premium and Preferred Habitat Theories

The **liquidity premium theory** of the term structure states that the interest rate on a long-term bond will equal an average of short-term interest rates expected to occur over the life of the long-term bond plus a liquidity premium (also referred to as a term premium) that responds to supply and demand conditions for that bond.

The liquidity premium theory's key assumption is that bonds of different maturities are substitutes, which means that the expected return on one bond *does* influence the expected return on a bond of a different maturity, but it allows investors to prefer one bond maturity over another. In other words, bonds of different maturities are assumed to be substitutes but not perfect substitutes. Investors tend to prefer shorter-term bonds because these bonds bear less interest-rate risk. For these reasons, investors must be offered a positive liquidity premium to induce them to hold longer-term bonds. Such an outcome would modify the expectations theory by adding a positive liquidity premium to the equation that describes the relationship between long- and short-term interest rates. The liquidity premium theory is thus written as

$$i_{nt} = \frac{i_t + i^e_{t+1} + i^e_{t+2} + \ldots + i^e_{t+(n-1)}}{n} + l_{nt} \qquad (3)$$

where l_{nt} is the liquidity (term) premium for the n-period bond at time t, which is always positive and rises with the term to maturity of the bond, n.

Closely related to the liquidity premium theory is the **preferred habitat theory**, which takes a somewhat less direct approach to modifying the expectations hypothesis but comes to a similar conclusion. It assumes that investors have a preference for bonds of one maturity over another, a particular bond maturity (preferred habitat) in which they prefer to invest. Because they prefer bonds of one maturity over another, they will be willing to buy bonds that do not have the preferred maturity (habitat) only if they earn a somewhat higher expected return. Because investors are likely to prefer the habitat of short-term bonds over that of longer-term bonds, they are willing to hold long-term bonds only if they have higher expected returns. This reasoning leads to the same Equation 3 implied by the liquidity premium theory, with a term premium that typically rises with maturity.

The relationship between the expectations theory and the liquidity premium and preferred habitat theories is shown in Figure 5. There we see that because the liquidity premium is always positive and typically grows as the term to maturity increases, the yield curve implied by the liquidity premium theory is always above the yield curve implied by the expectations theory and generally has a steeper slope. (Note that for simplicity we are assuming that the expectations theory yield curve is flat.)

A simple numerical example similar to the one we used for the expectations hypothesis further clarifies what the liquidity premium and preferred habitat theories in Equation 3 are saying. Again suppose that the one-year interest rate over the next five years is expected to be 5%, 6%, 7%, 8%, and 9%, while investors' preferences for holding short-term bonds means that the liquidity premiums for one- to five-year bonds are 0%, 0.25%, 0.5%, 0.75%, and 1.0%, respectively. Equation 3 then indicates that the interest rate on the two-year bond would be

$$\frac{5\% + 6\%}{2} + 0.25\% = 5.75\%$$

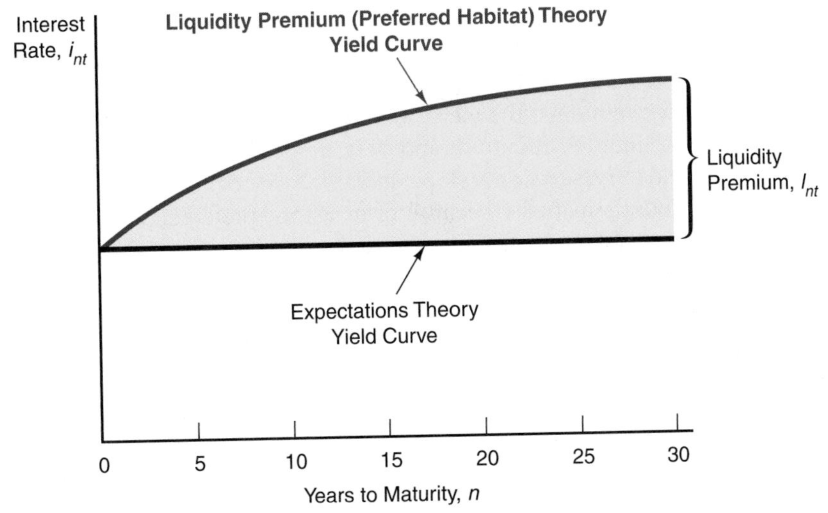

FIGURE 5 The Relationship Between the Liquidity Premium (Preferred Habitat) and Expectations Theory

Because the liquidity premium is always positive and grows as the term to maturity increases, the yield curve implied by the liquidity premium and preferred habitat theories is always above the yield curve implied by the expectations theory and has a steeper slope. For simplicity, the yield curve implied by the expectations theory is drawn under the scenario of unchanging future one-year interest rates.

For the five-year bond it would be

$$\frac{5\% + 6\% + 7\% + 8\% + 9\%}{5} + 1\% = 8\%$$

Doing a similar calculation for the one-, three-, and four-year interest rates, you should be able to verify that the one- to five-year interest rates are 5.0%, 5.75%, 6.5%, 7.25%, and 8.0%, respectively. Comparing these findings with those for the expectations theory, we see that the liquidity premium and preferred habitat theories produce yield curves that slope more steeply upward because of investors' preferences for short-term bonds.

Let's see if the liquidity premium and preferred habitat theories are consistent with all three empirical facts we have discussed. They explain fact 1, which states that interest rates on different-maturity bonds move together over time: A rise in short-term interest rates indicates that short-term interest rates will, on average, be higher in the future, and the first term in Equation 3 then implies that long-term interest rates will rise along with them.

They also explain why yield curves tend to have an especially steep upward slope when short-term interest rates are low and to be inverted when short-term rates are high (fact 2). Because investors generally expect short-term interest rates to rise to some normal level when they are low, the average of future expected short-term rates will be high relative to the current short-term rate. With the additional boost of a positive liquidity premium, long-term interest rates will be substantially higher than current short-term rates, and the yield curve will then have a steep upward slope. Conversely, if short-term rates are high, people usually expect them to come back down. Long-term rates will then drop below short-term rates because the average of expected future short-term rates will be so far below current short-term rates that despite positive liquidity premiums, the yield curve will slope downward.

The liquidity premium and preferred habitat theories explain fact 3, which states that yield curves typically slope upward, by recognizing that the liquidity premium rises with a bond's maturity because of investors' preferences for short-term bonds. Even if short-term interest rates are expected to stay the same on average in the future, long-term interest rates will be above short-term interest rates, and yield curves will typically slope upward.

How can the liquidity premium and preferred habitat theories explain the occasional appearance of inverted yield curves if the liquidity premium is positive? It must be that at times short-term interest rates are expected to fall so much in the future that the average of the expected short-term rates is well below the current short-term rate. Even when the positive liquidity premium is added to this average, the resulting long-term rate will still be lower than the current short-term interest rate.

As our discussion indicates, a particularly attractive feature of the liquidity premium and preferred habitat theories is that they tell you what the market is predicting about future short-term interest rates just from the slope of the yield curve. A steeply rising yield curve, as in panel (a) of Figure 6, indicates that short-term interest rates are expected to rise in the future. A moderately steep yield curve, as in panel (b), indicates that short-term interest rates are not expected to rise or fall much in the future. A flat yield curve, as in panel (c), indicates that short-term rates are expected to fall moderately in the future. Finally, an inverted yield curve, as in panel (d), indicates that short-term interest rates are expected to fall sharply in the future.

Evidence on the Term Structure

In the 1980s, researchers examining the term structure of interest rates questioned whether the slope of the yield curve provides information about movements of future short-term interest rates. They found that the spread between long- and short-term interest rates does not always help predict future short-term interest rates, a finding that may stem from substantial fluctuations in the liquidity (term) premium for long-term bonds. More recent research using more discriminating tests now favors a different view. It shows that the term structure contains quite a bit of information for the very short run (over the next several months) and the long run (over several years) but is unreliable at predicting movements in interest rates over the intermediate term (the time in between). Research also finds that the yield curve helps forecast future inflation and business cycles (see the FYI box).

Summary

The liquidity premium and preferred habitat theories are the most widely accepted theories of the term structure of interest rates because they explain the major empirical facts about the term structure so well. They combine the features of both the expectations theory and the segmented markets theory by asserting that a long-term interest rate will be the sum of a liquidity (term) premium and the average of the short-term interest rates that are expected to occur over the life of the bond.

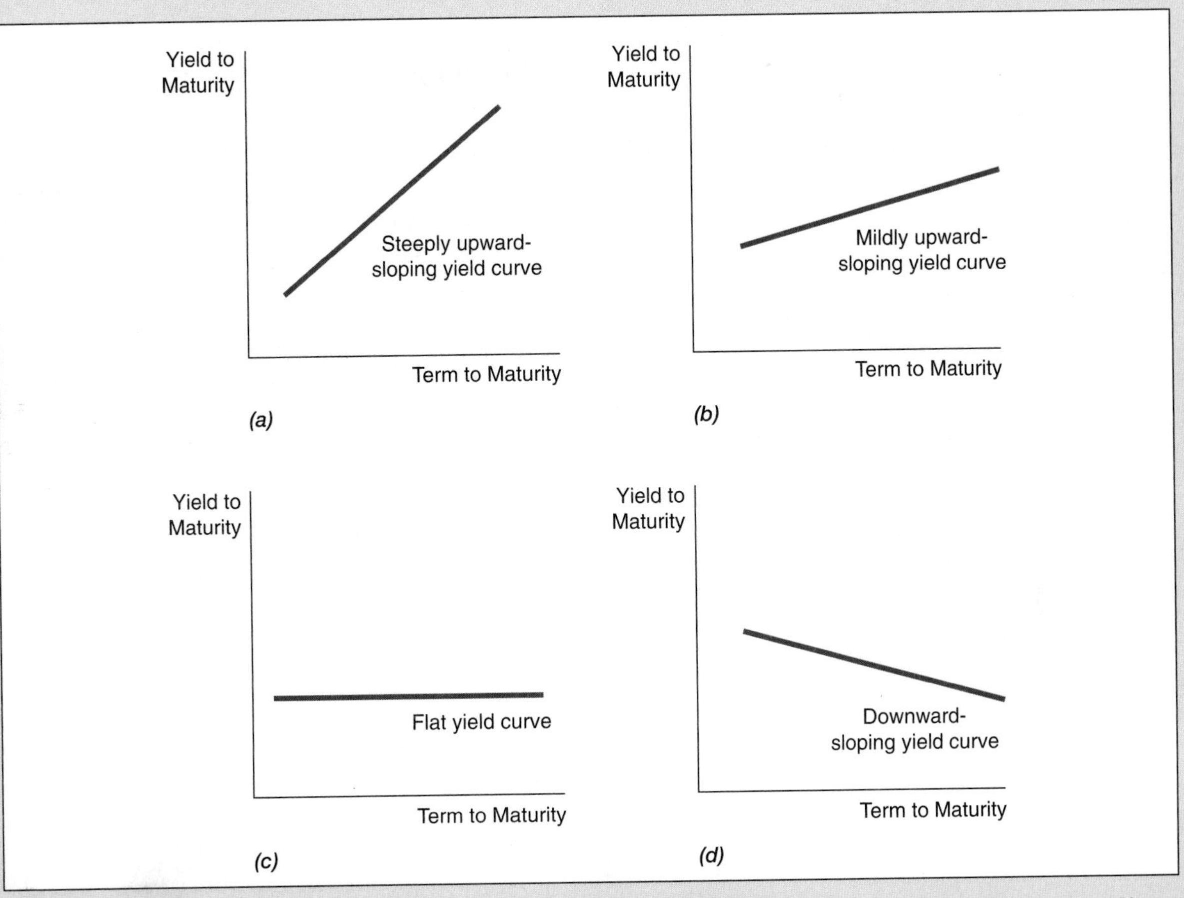

FIGURE 6 Yield Curves and the Market's Expectations of Future Short-Term Interest Rates According to the Liquidity Premium (Preferred Habitat) Theory

A steeply rising yield curve, as in panel (a) of Figure 6, indicates that short-term interest rates are expected to rise in the future. A moderately steep yield curve, as in panel (b), indicates that short-term interest rates are not expected to rise or fall much in the future. A flat yield curve, as in panel (c), indicates that short-term rates are expected to fall moderately in the future. Finally, an inverted yield curve, as in panel (d), indicates that short-term interest rates are expected to fall sharply in the future.

The liquidity premium and preferred habitat theories explain the following facts: (1) Interest rates on bonds of different maturities tend to move together over time; (2) when short-term interest rates are low, yield curves are more likely to have a steep upward slope; (3) yield curves usually slope upward, but when short-term interest rates are high, yield curves are more likely to be inverted.

The theories also help us predict the movement of short-term interest rates in the future. A steep upward slope of the yield curve means that short-term rates are expected to rise, a mild upward slope means that short-term rates are expected to remain the same, a flat slope means that short-term rates are expected to fall moderately, and an inverted yield curve means that short-term rates are expected to fall sharply.

FYI The Yield Curve as a Forecasting Tool for Inflation and the Business Cycle

Because the yield curve contains information about future expected interest rates, it should also have the capacity to help forecast inflation and real output fluctuations. To see why, recall from Chapter 5 that rising interest rates are associated with economic booms and falling interest rates with recessions. When the yield curve is either flat or downward-sloping, it suggests that future short-term interest rates are expected to fall and, therefore, that the economy is more likely to enter a recession. Indeed, the yield curve is found to be an accurate predictor of the business cycle.

In Chapter 4, we also learned that a nominal interest rate is composed of a real interest rate and expected inflation, implying that the yield curve contains information about both the future path of nominal interest rates and future inflation. A steep yield curve predicts a future increase in inflation, while a flat or downward-sloping yield curve forecasts a future decline in inflation.

The ability of the yield curve to forecast business cycles and inflation is one reason why the slope of the yield curve is part of the tool kit of many economic forecasters and is often viewed as a useful indicator of the stance of monetary policy, with a steep yield curve indicating loose policy and a flat or downward-sloping yield curve indicating tight policy.

APPLICATION ◆ Interpreting Yield Curves, 1980–2011

Figure 7 illustrates several yield curves that have appeared for U.S. government bonds in recent years. What do these yield curves tell us about the public's expectations of future movements of short-term interest rates?

The steep inverted yield curve that occurred on January 15, 1981, indicated that short-term interest rates were expected to decline sharply in the future. For longer-term interest rates with their positive liquidity premium to be well below the short-term interest rate, short-term interest rates must be expected to decline so sharply that their average is far below the current short-term rate. Indeed, the public's expectations of sharply lower short-term interest rates evident in the yield curve were realized soon after January 15; by March, three-month Treasury bill rates had declined from the 16% level to 13%.

The steep upward-sloping yield curves on March 28, 1985, and July 11, 2011, indicated that short-term interest rates would climb in the future. The long-term interest rate is higher than the short-term interest rate when short-term interest rates are expected to rise because their average plus the liquidity premium will be higher than the current short-term rate. The moderately upward-sloping yield curves on May 16, 1980, and March 3, 1997, indicated that short-term interest rates were expected neither to rise nor to fall in the near future. In this case, their average remains the same as the current short-term rate, and the positive liquidity premium for longer-term bonds explains the moderate upward slope of the yield curve. The flat yield curve of February 6, 2006, indicated that short-term interest rates were expected to fall slightly. ◆

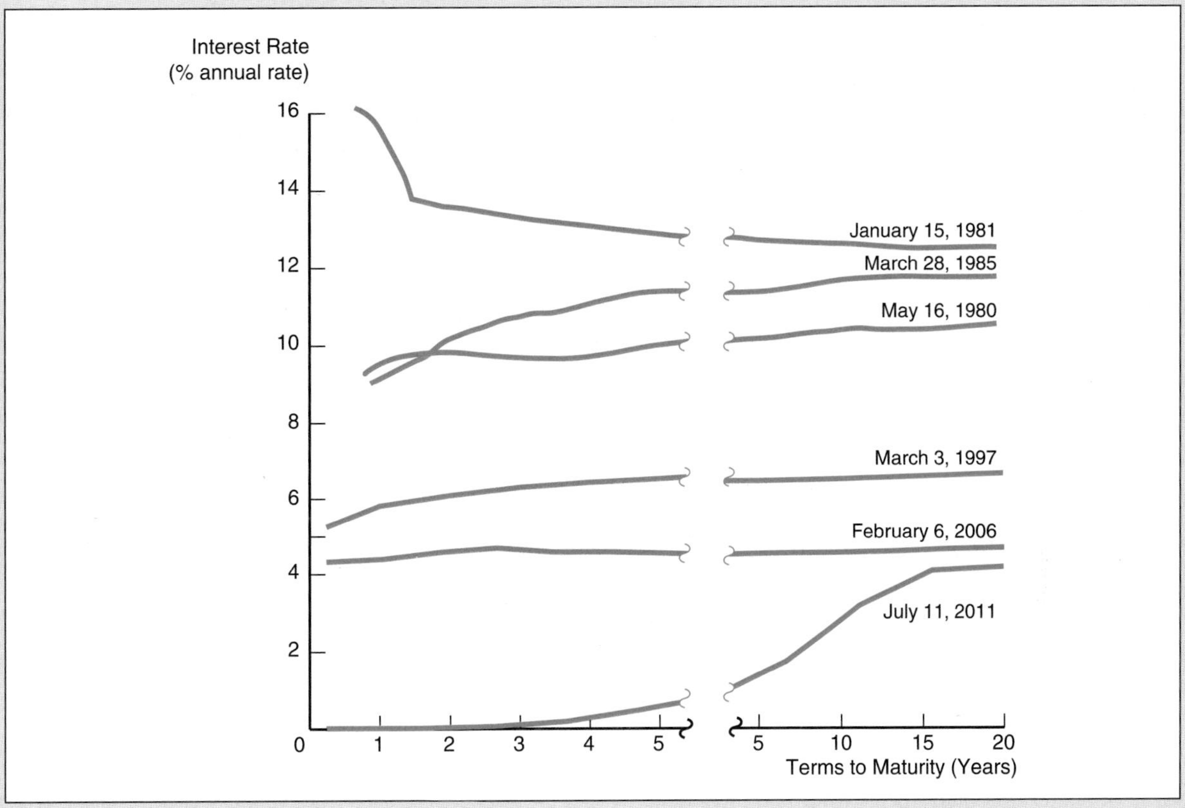

FIGURE 7 Yield Curves for U.S. Government Bonds

Yield curves for U.S. government bonds for different dates from 1981 to 2011.

Sources: Federal Reserve Bank of St. Louis; U.S. Financial Data, various issues; *Wall Street Journal,* various dates.

Summary

1. Bonds with the same maturity will have different interest rates because of three factors: default risk, liquidity, and tax considerations. The greater a bond's default risk, the higher its interest rate relative to other bonds; the greater a bond's liquidity, the lower its interest rate; and bonds with tax-exempt status will have lower interest rates than they otherwise would. The relationship among interest rates on bonds with the same maturity that arises because of these three factors is known as the *risk structure of interest rates.*

2. Four theories of the term structure provide explanations of how interest rates on bonds with different terms to maturity are related. The expectations theory views long-term interest rates as equaling the average of future short-term interest rates expected to occur over the life of the bond. By contrast, the segmented markets theory treats the determination of interest rates for each bond's maturity as the outcome of supply and demand in that market only. Neither of these theories by itself can explain the fact that interest rates on bonds of different maturities move together over time and that yield curves usually slope upward.

3. The liquidity premium (preferred habitat) theory combines the features of the other two theories, and by so doing is able to explain the facts just mentioned. It

views long-term interest rates as equaling the average of future short-term interest rates expected to occur over the life of the bond plus a liquidity premium. This theory allows us to infer the market's expectations about the movement of future short-term interest rates from the yield curve. A steeply upward-sloping curve indicates that future short-term rates are expected to rise; a mildly upward-sloping curve, that short-term rates are expected to stay the same; a flat curve, that short-term rates are expected to decline slightly; and an inverted yield curve, that a substantial decline in short-term rates is expected in the future.

Key Terms

credit-rating agencies, p. 120
default, p. 118
default-free bonds, p. 119
expectations theory, p. 128
inverted yield curve, p. 126
junk bonds, p. 121
liquidity premium theory, p. 132
preferred habitat theory, p. 132
risk premium, p. 119
risk structure of interest rates, p. 118
segmented markets theory, p. 131
term structure of interest rates, p. 118
yield curve, p. 126

Questions

All questions are available in MyEconLab *at* www.myeconlab.com.

1. If junk bonds are "junk," then why would investors buy them?
2. Which should have the higher risk premium on its interest rates, a corporate bond with a Moody's Baa rating or a corporate bond with a C rating? Why?
3. Why do U.S. Treasury bills have lower interest rates than large-denomination negotiable bank CDs?
4. In the fall of 2008, AIG, the largest insurance company in the world at the time, was at risk of defaulting due to the severity of the global financial crisis. As a result, the U.S. government stepped in to support AIG with large capital injections, and an ownership stake. How would this affect, if at all, the yield and risk premium on AIG corporate debt?
5. Risk premiums on corporate bonds are usually *anticyclical*; that is, they decrease during business cycle expansions and increase during recessions. Why is this so?
6. "If bonds of different maturities are close substitutes, their interest rates are more likely to move together." Is this statement true, false, or uncertain? Explain your answer.
7. The U.S. Treasury offers some of its debt as Treasury Inflation Protected Securities, or TIPS, in which the price of bonds is adjusted for inflation over the life of the debt instrument. TIPS bonds are traded on a much smaller scale than nominal U.S. Treasury bonds of equivalent maturity. What can you conclude about the liquidity premium between TIPS and nominal U.S. bonds?
8. Predict what will happen to interest rates on a corporation's bonds if the federal government guarantees today that it will pay creditors if the corporation goes bankrupt in the future. What will happen to the interest rates on Treasury securities?
9. Predict what would happen to the risk premiums on corporate bonds if brokerage commissions were lowered in the corporate bond market.
10. During 2008, the difference in yield (the *yield spread*) between three-month AA-rated financial commercial paper and three-month AA-rated nonfinancial commercial paper steadily increased from its usual level of close to zero, spiking to over a full percentage point at its peak in October 2008. What explains this sudden increase?
11. If the income tax exemption on municipal bonds were abolished, what would happen to the interest rates on these bonds? What effect would the change have on interest rates on U.S. Treasury securities?

12. Prior to 2008, mortgage lenders required a house inspection to assess its value, and often used the same one or two inspection companies in the same geographical market. Following the collapse of the housing market in 2008, mortgage lenders required a house inspection, but this was arranged through a third party. How does this illustrate a conflict of interest similar to the role that credit-rating agencies played in the global financial crisis?

13. "According to the expectations theory of the term structure, it is better to invest in one-year bonds, reinvested over two years, than to invest in a two-year bond, if interest rates on one-year bonds are expected to be the same in both years." Is this statement true, false, or uncertain?

14. If bond investors decide that 30-year bonds are no longer as desirable an investment, predict what will happen to the yield curve, assuming (a) the expectations theory of the term structure holds; and (b) the segmented markets theory of the term structure holds.

15. Suppose the interest rates on one-, five-, and ten-year U.S. Treasury bonds are currently 3%, 6%, and 6%, respectively. Investor A chooses to hold only one-year bonds, and Investor B is indifferent with regard to holding five- and ten-year bonds. How can you explain the behavior of Investors A and B?

16. If a yield curve looks like the one shown in the figure below, what is the market predicting about the movement of future short-term interest rates? What might the yield curve indicate about the market's predictions for the inflation rate in the future?

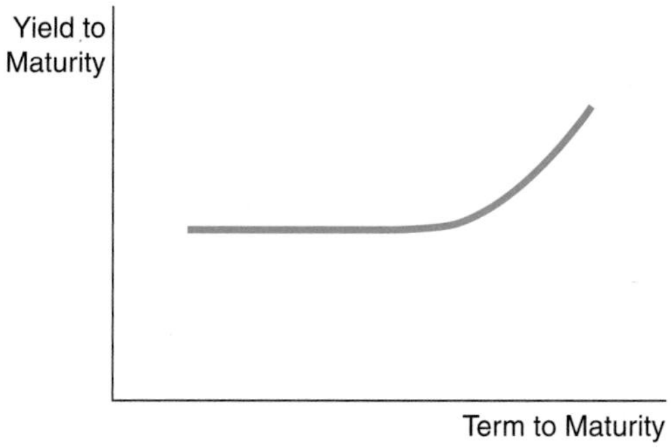

17. If a yield curve looks like the one shown in the figure below, what is the market predicting about the movement of future short-term interest rates? What might the yield curve indicate about the market's predictions for the inflation rate in the future?

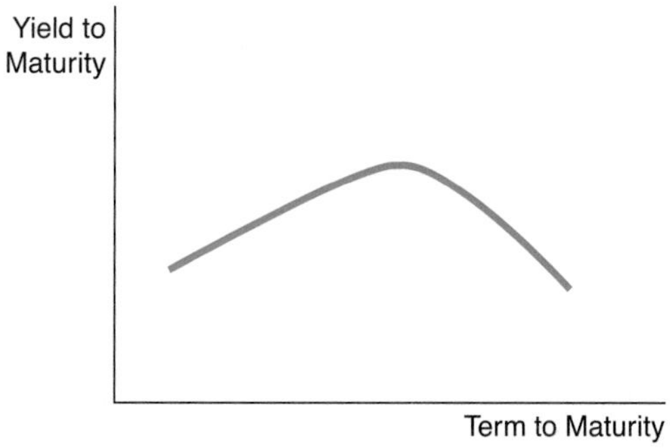

18. If yield curves, on average, were flat, what would this say about the liquidity (term) premiums in the term structure? Would you be more or less willing to accept the expectations theory?

19. If the yield curve suddenly becomes steeper, how would you revise your predictions of interest rates in the future?

20. If expectations of future short-term interest rates suddenly fall, what would happen to the slope of the yield curve?

21. Following a policy meeting on March 19, 2009, the Federal Reserve made an announcement that it would purchase up to $300 billion of longer-term Treasury securities over the following six months. What effect might this policy have on the yield curve?

Applied Problems

All applied problems are available in MyEconLab at www.myeconlab.com.

22. In 2010 and 2011, the government of Greece risked defaulting on its debt due to a severe budget crisis. Using bond market graphs, show the effect on the risk premium between U.S. Treasury debt and comparable maturity Greek debt.

23. Assuming that the expectations theory is the correct theory of the term structure, calculate the interest rates in the term structure for maturities of one to five

years, and plot the resulting yield curves for the following paths of one-year interest rates over the next five years:

a. 5%, 7%, 7%, 7%, 7%
b. 5%, 4%, 4%, 4%, 4%

How would your yield curves change if people preferred shorter-term bonds to longer-term bonds?

24. Assuming that the expectations theory is the correct theory of the term structure, calculate the interest rates in the term structure for maturities of one to five years, and plot the resulting yield curves for the following paths of one-year interest rates over the next five years:

a. 5%, 6%, 7%, 6%, 5%
b. 5%, 4%, 3%, 4%, 5%

How would your yield curves change if people preferred shorter-term bonds over longer-term bonds?

25. The table below shows current and expected future one-year interest rates, as well as current interest rates on multiyear bonds. Use the table to calculate the liquidity premium for each multiyear bond.

Year	One-Year Bond Rate	Multiyear Bond Rate
1	2%	2%
2	3%	3%
3	4%	5%
4	6%	6%
5	7%	8%

Web Exercises

1. The amount of additional interest investors receive due to the various risk premiums changes over time. Sometimes the risk premiums are much larger than at other times. For example, the default risk premium was very small in the late 1990s when the economy was so healthy that business failures were rare. This risk premium increases during recessions.

Go to www.federalreserve.gov/releases/h15 (historical data) and find the interest rate listings for AAA- and Baa-rated bonds at three points in time: the most recent; June 1, 2011; and June 1, 2008. Prepare a graph that shows these three time periods (see Figure 1 for an example). Are the risk premiums stable or do they change over time?

2. Figure 7 shows a number of yield curves at various points in time. Go to www.bloomberg.com/markets/rates/index.html and find the Treasury yield curve. Does the current yield curve fall above or below the most recent one listed in Figure 7? Is the current yield curve flatter or steeper than the most recent one reported in Figure 7?

3. Investment companies attempt to explain to investors the nature of the risk the investor incurs when buying shares in their mutual funds. For example, Vanguard carefully explains interest-rate risk and offers alternative funds with different interest-rate risks. Go to http://personal.vanguard.com/us/funds.

a. Select the bond fund you would recommend to an investor who has a very low tolerance for risk and a short investment horizon. Justify your answer.
b. Select the bond fund you would recommend to an investor who has a very high tolerance for risk and a long investment horizon. Justify your answer.

Web References

www.federalreserve.gov/Releases/h15/update/

The Federal Reserve reports the yields on different-quality bonds. Look at the bottom of the listing of interest rates for AAA- and BBB-rated bonds.

http://stockcharts.com/charts/YieldCurve.html

This site lets you look at the dynamic yield curve at any point in time since 1995.

7 The Stock Market, the Theory of Rational Expectations, and the Efficient Market Hypothesis

Preview

Rarely does a day go by that the stock market isn't a major news item. We have witnessed huge swings in the stock market in recent years. The 1990s were an extraordinary decade for stocks: The Dow Jones and S&P 500 indexes increased more than 400%, while the tech-laden NASDAQ index rose more than 1,000%. By early 2000, all three indexes had reached record highs. Unfortunately, the good times did not last. Starting in early 2000, the stock market began to decline and many investors lost their shirts. The NASDAQ crashed, falling by more than 50%, while the Dow Jones and S&P 500 indexes fell by 30% through January 2003. After subsequently rising over 30%, the stock market crashed again during the global financial crisis, falling by over 50% from its peak in the fall of 2007. Starting in 2009, the stock market recovered quickly, rising by more than 50% by 2011.

Because so many people invest in the stock market and the prices of stocks affect the ability of people to retire comfortably, the market for stocks is undoubtedly the financial market that receives the most attention and scrutiny. In this chapter, we look first at how this important market works.

We begin by discussing the fundamental theories that underlie the valuation of stocks. These theories are critical to understanding the forces that cause the value of stocks to rise and fall minute by minute and day by day. Once we have learned the methods for stock valuation, we need to explore how expectations about the market affect its behavior. We do so by examining the *theory of rational expectations*. When this theory is applied to financial markets, the outcome is the *efficient market hypothesis*, which has some general implications for how markets in other securities besides stocks operate. The theory of rational expectations is also central to debates about the conduct of monetary policy (discussed in Web Chapter 3).

COMPUTING THE PRICE OF COMMON STOCK

Common stock is the principal way that corporations raise equity capital. **Stockholders**—those who hold stock in a corporation—own an interest in the corporation proportional to the percentage of outstanding shares they own. This ownership interest gives them a bundle of rights. The most important are the right to vote and to be the **residual claimant** of all funds flowing into the firm (known as **cash flows**), meaning that the stockholder receives whatever remains after all other claims against the firm's assets have been satisfied. Stockholders may receive dividends from the net earnings of the corporation. **Dividends** are payments made periodically, usually every quarter, to stockholders. The board of directors of the firm sets the level of the dividend, usually based on the recommendation of management. In addition, the stockholder has the right to sell the stock.

One basic principle of finance is that the value of any investment is found by computing the present value of all cash flows the investment will generate over its life. For example, a commercial building will sell for a price that reflects the net cash flows (rents – expenses) it is projected to have over its useful life. Similarly, we value common stock as the value in today's dollars of all future cash flows. The cash flows a stockholder might earn from stock are dividends, the sales price, or both.

To develop the theory of stock valuation, we begin with the simplest possible scenario: You buy the stock, hold it for one period to get a dividend, then sell the stock. We call this the *one-period valuation model*.

The One-Period Valuation Model

Suppose that you have some extra money to invest for one year. After a year, you will need to sell your investment to pay tuition. After watching CNBC or *Nightly Business Report* on TV, you decide that you want to buy Intel Corp. stock. You call your broker and find that Intel is currently selling for \$50 per share and pays \$0.16 per year in dividends. The analyst on CNBC predicts that the stock will be selling for \$60 in one year. Should you buy this stock?

To answer this question, you need to determine whether the current price accurately reflects the analyst's forecast. To value the stock today, you need to find the present discounted value of the expected cash flows (future payments) using the formula in Equation 1 of Chapter 4. In this equation, the discount factor used to discount the cash flows is the required return on investments in equity rather than the interest rate. The cash flows consist of one dividend payment plus a final sales price. When these cash flows are discounted back to the present, the following equation computes the current price of the stock:

$$P_0 = \frac{Div_1}{(1 + k_e)} + \frac{P_1}{(1 + k_e)} \tag{1}$$

where P_0 = the current price of the stock. The zero subscript refers to time period zero, or the present.

Div_1 = the dividend paid at the end of year 1.

k_e = the required return on investments in equity.

P_1 = the price at the end of the first period; the predicted sales price of the stock.

To see how Equation 1 works, let's compute the price of the Intel stock if, after careful consideration, you decide that you would be satisfied to earn a 12% return on the investment. If you have decided that $k_e = 0.12$, are told that Intel pays \$0.16 per year in dividends ($Div_1 = 0.16$), and forecast the share price of \$60 for next year ($P_1 = \$60$), you get the following from Equation 1:

$$P_0 = \frac{0.16}{1 + 0.12} + \frac{\$60}{1 + 0.12} = \$0.14 + \$53.57 = \$53.71$$

On the basis of your analysis, you find that the present value of all cash flows from the stock is \$53.71. Because the stock is currently priced at \$50 per share, you would choose to buy it. However, you should be aware that the stock may be selling for less than \$53.71, because other investors place a different risk on the cash flows or estimate the cash flows to be less than you do.

The Generalized Dividend Valuation Model

Using the present value concept, we can extend the one-period dividend valuation model to any number of periods: The value of a stock today is the present value of all future cash flows. The only cash flows that an investor will receive are dividends and a final sales price when the stock is ultimately sold in period n. The generalized multiperiod formula for stock valuation can be written as

$$P_0 = \frac{D_1}{(1 + k_e)^1} + \frac{D_2}{(1 + k_e)^2} + \dots + \frac{D_n}{(1 + k_e)^n} + \frac{P_n}{(1 + k_e)^n} \tag{2}$$

If you tried to use Equation 2 to find the value of a share of stock, you would soon realize that you must first estimate the value the stock will have at some point in the future before you can estimate its value today. In other words, you must find P_n before you can find P_0. However, if P_n is far in the future, it will not affect P_0. For example, the present value of a share of stock that sells for \$50 seventy-five years from now, using a 12% discount rate, is just one cent $[\$50/(1.12^{75}) = \$0.01]$. This reasoning implies that the current value of a share of stock can be calculated as simply the present value of the future dividend stream. The **generalized dividend model** is rewritten in Equation 3 without the final sales price:

$$P_0 = \sum_{t=1}^{\infty} \frac{D_t}{(1 + k_e)^t} \tag{3}$$

Consider the implications of Equation 3 for a moment. The generalized dividend model says that the price of stock is determined only by the present value of the dividends and that nothing else matters. Many stocks do not pay dividends, so how is it that these stocks have value? *Buyers of the stock expect that the firm will pay dividends someday*. Most of the time a firm institutes dividends as soon as it has completed the rapid growth phase of its life cycle.

The generalized dividend valuation model requires that we compute the present value of an infinite stream of dividends, a process that could be difficult, to say the least. Therefore, simplified models have been developed to make the calculations easier. One such model is the **Gordon growth model**, which assumes constant dividend growth.

The Gordon Growth Model

Many firms strive to increase their dividends at a constant rate each year. Equation 4 rewrites Equation 3 to reflect this constant growth in dividends:

$$P_0 = \frac{D_0 \times (1 + g)^1}{(1 + k_e)^1} + \frac{D_0 \times (1 + g)^2}{(1 + k_e)^2} + \dots + \frac{D_0 \times (1 + g)^{\infty}}{(1 + k_e)^{\infty}} \tag{4}$$

where

D_0 = the most recent dividend paid
g = the expected constant growth rate in dividends
k_e = the required return on an investment in equity

Equation 4 can be simplified to obtain Equation 5:[1]

$$P_0 = \frac{D_0 \times (1 + g)}{(k_e - g)} = \frac{D_1}{(k_e - g)} \tag{5}$$

This model is useful for finding the value of stock, given a few assumptions:

1. *Dividends are assumed to continue growing at a constant rate forever.* Actually, as long as they are expected to grow at a constant rate for an extended period of time, the model should yield reasonable results. This is because errors about distant cash flows become small when discounted to the present.
2. *The growth rate is assumed to be less than the required return on equity, k_e.* Myron Gordon, in his development of the model, demonstrated that this is a reasonable assumption. In theory, if the growth rate were faster than the rate demanded by holders of the firm's equity, in the long run the firm would grow impossibly large.

HOW THE MARKET SETS STOCK PRICES

Suppose you go to an auto auction. The cars are available for inspection before the auction begins, and you find a little Mazda Miata that you like. You test-drive it in the parking lot and notice that it makes a few strange noises, but you decide that you would still like the car. You decide \$5,000 would be a fair price that would allow you to pay some repair bills should the noises turn out to be serious. You see that the auction is ready to begin, so you go in and wait for the Miata to enter.

Suppose another buyer also spots the Miata. He test-drives the car and recognizes that the noises are simply the result of worn brake pads that he can fix himself at a nominal cost. He decides that the car is worth \$7,000. He also goes in and waits for the Miata to come up for auction.

Who will buy the car and for how much? Suppose only the two of you are interested in the Miata. You begin the bidding at \$4,000. Your competitor ups your bid to \$4,500. You bid your top price of \$5,000. He counters with \$5,100. The price is now higher than you are willing to pay, so you stop bidding. The car is sold to the more informed buyer for \$5,100.

[1]To generate Equation 5 from Equation 4, first multiply both sides of Equation 4 by $(1 + k_e)/(1 + g)$ and subtract Equation 4 from the result. This yields

$$\frac{P_0 \times (1 + k_e)}{(1 + g)} - P_0 = D_0 - \frac{D_0 \times (1 + g)^{\infty}}{(1 + k_e)^{\infty}}$$

Assuming that k_e is greater than g, the term on the far right will approach zero and can be dropped. Thus, after factoring P_0 out of the left-hand side,

$$P_0 \times \left[\frac{1 + k_e}{1 + g} - 1\right] = D_0$$

Next, simplify by combining terms:

$$P_0 \times \frac{(1 + k_e) - (1 + g)}{1 + g} = D_0$$

$$P_0 = \frac{D_0 \times (1 + g)}{k_e - g} = \frac{D_1}{k_e - g}$$

This simple example raises a number of points. First, the price is set by the buyer willing to pay the highest price. The price is not necessarily the highest price the asset could fetch, but it is incrementally greater than what any other buyer is willing to pay.

Second, the market price will be set by the buyer who can take best advantage of the asset. The buyer who purchased the car knew that he could fix the noise easily and cheaply. As a consequence, he was willing to pay more for the car than you were. The same concept holds for other assets. For example, a piece of property or a building will sell to the buyer who can put the asset to the most productive use.

Finally, the example shows the role played by information in asset pricing. Superior information about an asset can increase its value by reducing its risk. When you consider buying a stock, the future cash flows have many unknowns. The buyer who has the best information about these cash flows will discount them at a lower interest rate than will a buyer who is very uncertain.

Now let's apply these ideas to stock valuation. Suppose that you are considering the purchase of stock expected to pay a $2 dividend next year. Market analysts expect the firm to grow at 3% indefinitely. You are *uncertain* about both the constancy of the dividend stream and the accuracy of the estimated growth rate. To compensate yourself for this uncertainty (risk), you require a return of 15%.

Now suppose Jennifer, another investor, has spoken with industry insiders and feels more confident about the projected cash flows. Jennifer requires only a 12% return because her perceived risk is lower than yours. Bud, on the other hand, is dating the CEO of the company. He knows with more certainty what the future of the firm actually is, and thus requires only a 10% return.

What are the values each investor will give to the stock? Applying the Gordon growth model yields the following stock prices:

Investor	Discount Rate	Stock Price
You	15%	$16.67
Jennifer	12%	$22.22
Bud	10%	$28.57

You are willing to pay $16.67 for the stock. Jennifer would pay up to $22.22, and Bud would pay $28.57. The investor with the lowest perceived risk is willing to pay the most for the stock. If there were no other traders but these three, the market price would be between $22.22 and $28.57. If you already held the stock, you would sell it to Bud.

We thus see that the players in the market, bidding against one another, establish the market price. When new information is released about a firm, expectations change and with them, prices change. New information can cause changes in expectations about the level of future dividends or the risk of those dividends. Because market participants are constantly receiving new information and revising their expectations, it is reasonable that stock prices are constantly changing as well.

APPLICATION ◆ Monetary Policy and Stock Prices

Stock market analysts tend to hang on every word that the chairman of the Federal Reserve utters because they know that an important determinant of stock prices is monetary policy. But how does monetary policy affect stock prices?

The Gordon growth model in Equation 5 explains this relationship. Monetary policy can affect stock prices in two ways. First, when the Fed lowers interest rates, the return on bonds (an alternative asset to stocks) declines, and investors are likely to accept a lower required rate of return on an investment in equity (k_e). The resulting decline in k_e would lower the denominator in the Gordon growth model (Equation 5), lead to a higher value of P_0, and raise stock prices. Furthermore, a lowering of interest rates is likely to stimulate the economy, so the growth rate in dividends, g, is likely to be somewhat higher. This rise in g also causes the denominator in Equation 5 to decrease, which also leads to a higher P_0 and a rise in stock prices.

As we will see in Chapter 25, the impact of monetary policy on stock prices is one of the key ways in which monetary policy affects the economy.

APPLICATION: ◆ The Global Financial Crisis and the Stock Market

The subprime financial crisis that started in August 2007 led to one of the worst bear markets in the past 50 years. Our analysis of stock price valuation, again using the Gordon growth model, can help us understand how this event affected stock prices.

The subprime financial crisis had a major negative impact on the economy, leading to a downward revision of the growth prospects for U.S. companies, thus lowering the dividend growth rate (g) in the Gordon model. The resulting increase in the denominator in Equation 5 would lead to a decline in P_0 and hence a decline in stock prices.

Increased uncertainty for the U.S. economy and the widening credit spreads resulting from the subprime crisis would also raise the required return on investment in equity. A higher k_e also leads to an increase in the denominator in Equation 5, a decline in P_0, and a general fall in stock prices.

In the early stages of the global financial crisis, the decline in growth prospects and credit spreads were moderate, and so, as the Gordon model predicts, the stock market decline was also moderate. However, when the crisis entered a particularly virulent stage in October 2008, credit spreads shot through the roof, the economy tanked, and as the Gordon model predicts, the stock market crashed. From its peak in October 2007 (high of 14,066 for the DJIA) to the bottom in March 2009 (DJIA low of 6,547) the market lost 53% of its value. ◆

THE THEORY OF RATIONAL EXPECTATIONS

The analysis of stock price evaluation we outlined in the previous section depends on people's expectations—especially of cash flows. Indeed, it is difficult to think of any sector in the economy in which expectations are not crucial; this is why it is important to examine how expectations are formed. We do so by outlining the *theory of rational expectations*, currently the most widely used theory to describe the formation of business and consumer expectations.

In the 1950s and 1960s, economists regularly viewed expectations as formed from past experience only. Expectations of inflation, for example, were typically viewed as being an average of past inflation rates. This view of expectation formation, called **adaptive expectations**, suggests that changes in expectations will occur slowly over time as past data change.[2] So if inflation had formerly been steady at a 5% rate, expectations of future inflation would be 5%, too. If inflation rose to a steady rate of 10%, expectations of future inflation would rise toward 10%, but slowly: In the first year, expected inflation might rise only to 6%; in the second year, to 7%; and so on.

Adaptive expectations have been faulted on the grounds that people use more information than just past data on a single variable to form their expectations of that variable. Their expectations of inflation will almost surely be affected by their predictions of future monetary policy as well as by current and past monetary policy. In addition, people often change their expectations quickly in the light of new information. To meet these objections to adaptive expectations, John Muth developed an alternative theory of expectations, called **rational expectations**, which can be stated as follows: ***Expectations will be identical to optimal forecasts (the best guess of the future) using all available information.***[3]

What exactly does this mean? To explain it more clearly, let's use the theory of rational expectations to examine how expectations are formed in a situation that most of us encounter at some point in our lifetime: our drive to work. Suppose that if Joe Commuter travels when it is not rush hour, it takes an average of 30 minutes for his trip. Sometimes it takes him 35 minutes, other times 25 minutes, but the average non–rush-hour driving time is 30 minutes. If, however, Joe leaves for work during the rush hour, it takes him, on average, an additional 10 minutes to get to work. Given that he leaves for work during the rush hour, the best guess of the driving time—the **optimal forecast**—is 40 minutes.

If the only information available to Joe before he leaves for work that would have a potential effect on his driving time is that he is leaving during the rush hour, what does rational expectations theory allow you to predict about Joe's expectations of his driving time? Since the best guess of his driving time using all available information is 40 minutes, Joe's expectation should also be the same. Clearly, an expectation of 35 minutes would not be rational, because it is not equal to the optimal forecast, the best guess of the driving time.

Suppose that the next day, given the same conditions and expectations, it takes Joe 45 minutes to drive because he hits an abnormally large number of red lights, and the day after that he hits all the lights right and it takes him only 35 minutes. Do these variations mean that Joe's 40-minute expectation is irrational? No, an expectation of 40 minutes' driving time is still a rational expectation. In both cases, the forecast is off by five minutes, so the expectation has not been perfectly accurate. However, the forecast does not have to be perfectly accurate to be rational—it need only be the *best possible* given the available information; that is, it has to be correct *on average,* and the 40-minute expectation meets this requirement. As there is bound to be some randomness in Joe's

[2]More specifically, adaptive expectations—say, of inflation—are written as a weighted average of past inflation rates:

$$\pi_t^e = (1 - \lambda) \sum_{j=0}^{\infty} \lambda^j \pi_{t-j}$$

where π_t^e = adaptive expectation of inflation at time t

π_{t-j} = inflation at time $t - j$

λ = a constant between the values of 0 and 1

[3]John Muth, "Rational Expectations and the Theory of Price Movements," *Econometrica* 29 (1961): 315–335.

driving time regardless of driving conditions, an optimal forecast will never be completely accurate.

The example makes the following important point about rational expectations: ***Even though a rational expectation equals the optimal forecast using all available information, a prediction based on it may not always be perfectly accurate.***

What if an item of information relevant to predicting driving time is unavailable or ignored? Suppose that on Joe's usual route to work an accident occurs and causes a two-hour traffic jam. If Joe has no way of ascertaining this information, his rush-hour expectation of 40 minutes' driving time is still rational, because the accident information is not available to him for incorporation into his optimal forecast. However, if there was a radio or TV traffic report about the accident that Joe did not bother to listen to or heard but ignored, his 40-minute expectation is no longer rational. In light of the availability of this information, Joe's optimal forecast should have been two hours and 40 minutes.

Accordingly, an expectation may fail to be rational for two reasons:

1. People might be aware of all available information but find it takes too much effort to make their expectation the best guess possible.
2. People might be unaware of some available relevant information, so their best guess of the future will not be accurate.

Nonetheless, it is important to recognize that if an additional factor is important but information about it is not available, an expectation that does not take account of it can still be rational.

Formal Statement of the Theory

We can state the theory of rational expectations somewhat more formally. If X stands for the variable that is being forecast (in our example, Joe Commuter's driving time), X^e for the expectation of this variable (Joe's expectation of his driving time), and X^{of} for the optimal forecast of X using all available information (the best guess possible of his driving time), the theory of rational expectations then simply says

$$X^e = X^{of} \qquad (6)$$

That is, the expectation of X equals the optimal forecast using all available information.

Rationale Behind the Theory

Why do people try to make their expectations match their best possible guess of the future, using all available information? The simplest explanation is that it is costly for people not to do so. Joe Commuter has a strong incentive to make his expectation of the time it takes him to drive to work as accurate as possible. If he underpredicts his driving time, he will often be late to work and risk being fired. If he overpredicts, he will, on average, get to work too early and will have given up sleep or leisure time unnecessarily. Accurate expectations are desirable, and the incentives are strong for people to try to make them equal to optimal forecasts by using all available information.

The same principle applies to businesses. Suppose that an appliance manufacturer—say, General Electric—knows that interest-rate movements are important to the sales of appliances. If GE makes poor forecasts of interest rates, it will earn less profit, because it might produce either too many appliances or too few. The incentives are strong for GE to acquire all available information to help it forecast interest rates and use the information to make the best possible guess of future interest-rate movements.

The incentives for equating expectations with optimal forecasts are especially strong in financial markets. In these markets, people with better forecasts of the future get rich. The application of the theory of rational expectations to financial markets (where it is called the **efficient market hypothesis** or the **theory of efficient capital markets**) is thus particularly useful.

Implications of the Theory

Rational expectations theory leads to two commonsense implications for forming expectations that are important in the analysis of both the stock market and the aggregate economy:

1. ***If there is a change in the way a variable moves, the way in which expectations of this variable are formed will change as well.*** This tenet of rational expectations theory can be most easily understood through a concrete example. Suppose that interest rates move in such a way that they tend to return to a "normal" level in the future. If today's interest rate is high relative to the normal level, an optimal forecast of the interest rate in the future is that it will decline to the normal level. Rational expectations theory would imply that when today's interest rate is high, the expectation is that it will fall in the future.

Suppose now that the way in which the interest rate moves changes so that when the interest rate is high, it stays high. In this case, when today's interest rate is high, the optimal forecast of the future interest rate, and hence the rational expectation, is that it will stay high. Expectations of the future interest rate will no longer indicate that the interest rate will fall. The change in the way the interest-rate variable moves has therefore led to a change in the way that expectations of future interest rates are formed. The rational expectations analysis here is generalizable to expectations of any variable. Hence, when a change occurs in the way any variable moves, the way in which expectations of this variable are formed will change, too.

2. ***The forecast errors of expectations will, on average, be zero and cannot be predicted ahead of time.*** The forecast error of an expectation is $X - X^e$, the difference between the realization of a variable X and the expectation of the variable. That is, if Joe Commuter's driving time on a particular day is 45 minutes and his expectation of the driving time is 40 minutes, the forecast error is five minutes.

Suppose that in violation of the rational expectations tenet, Joe's forecast error is not, on average, equal to zero; instead, it equals five minutes. The forecast error is now predictable ahead of time because Joe will soon notice that he is, on average, five minutes late for work and can improve his forecast by increasing it by five minutes. Rational expectations theory implies that this is exactly what Joe will do because he will want his forecast to be the best guess possible. When Joe has revised his forecast upward by five minutes, on average, the forecast error will equal zero so that it cannot be predicted ahead of time. Rational expectations theory implies that forecast errors of expectations cannot be predicted.

THE EFFICIENT MARKET HYPOTHESIS: RATIONAL EXPECTATIONS IN FINANCIAL MARKETS

While monetary economists were developing the theory of rational expectations, financial economists were developing a parallel theory of expectations formation in financial markets. It led them to the same conclusion as that of the rational expectations theorists:

Expectations in financial markets are equal to optimal forecasts using all available information.[4] Although financial economists gave their theory another name, calling it *the efficient market hypothesis,* in fact their theory is just an application of rational expectations to the pricing of stocks and also other securities.

The efficient market hypothesis is based on the assumption that prices of securities in financial markets fully reflect all available information. You may recall from Chapter 4 that the rate of return from holding a security equals the sum of the capital gain on the security (the change in the price), plus any cash payments, divided by the initial purchase price of the security:

$$R = \frac{P_{t+1} - P_t + C}{P_t} \tag{7}$$

where R = rate of return on the security held from time t to $t + 1$ (say, the end of 2012 to the end of 2013)
P_{t+1} = price of the security at time $t + 1$, the end of the holding period
P_t = price of the security at time t, the beginning of the holding period
C = cash payment (coupon or dividend payments) made in the period t to $t + 1$

Let's look at the expectation of this return at time t, the beginning of the holding period. Because the current price P_t and the cash payment C are known at the beginning, the only variable in the definition of the return that is uncertain is the price next period, P_{t+1}.[5] Denoting expectation of the security's price at the end of the holding period as P^e_{t+1}, the expected return R^e is

$$R^e = \frac{P^e_{t+1} - P_t + C}{P_t}$$

The efficient market hypothesis views expectations of future prices as equal to optimal forecasts using all currently available information. In other words, the market's expectations of future securities prices are rational, so that

$$P^e_{t+1} = P^{of}_{t+1}$$

which in turn implies that the expected return on the security will equal the optimal forecast of the return:

$$R^e = R^{of} \tag{8}$$

Unfortunately, we cannot observe either R^e or P^e_{t+1}, so the rational expectations equations by themselves do not tell us much about how the financial market behaves. However, if we can devise some way to measure the value of R^e, these equations will have important implications for how prices of securities change in financial markets.

The supply and demand analysis of the bond market developed in Chapter 5 shows us that the expected return on a security (the interest rate, in the case of the one-year discount bond examined) will have a tendency to head toward the equilibrium return that equates the quantity demanded to the quantity supplied. Supply and demand analysis enables us to determine the expected return on a security with the following equilibrium condition:

[4]The development of the efficient market hypothesis was not wholly independent of the development of rational expectations theory, in that financial economists were aware of Muth's work.

[5]There are cases in which C might not be known at the beginning of the period, but that does not make a substantial difference to the analysis. We would in that case assume that not only price expectations but also the expectations of C are optimal forecasts using all available information.

The expected return on a security R^e equals the equilibrium return R^*, which equates the quantity of the security demanded to the quantity supplied; that is,

$$R^e = R^* \tag{9}$$

The academic field of finance explores the factors (risk and liquidity, for example) that influence the equilibrium returns on securities. For our purposes, it is sufficient to know that we can determine the equilibrium return and thus determine the expected return with the equilibrium condition.

We can derive an equation to describe pricing behavior in an efficient market by using the equilibrium condition to replace R^e with R^* in the rational expectations equation (Equation 8). In this way, we obtain

$$R^{of} = R^* \tag{10}$$

This equation tells us that ***current prices in a financial market will be set so that the optimal forecast of a security's return using all available information equals the security's equilibrium return***. Financial economists state it more simply: In an efficient market, a security's price fully reflects all available information.

Rationale Behind the Hypothesis

To see why the efficient market hypothesis makes sense, we make use of the concept of **arbitrage**, in which market participants (*arbitrageurs*) eliminate **unexploited profit opportunities**, that is, returns on a security that are larger than what is justified by the characteristics of that security. Arbitrage is of two types: *pure arbitrage*, in which the elimination of unexploited profit opportunities involves no risk; and the type of arbitrage we discuss here, in which the arbitrageur takes on some risk when eliminating the unexploited profit opportunities. To see how arbitrage leads to the efficient market hypothesis, suppose that, given its risk characteristics, the normal return on a security, say, ExxonMobil common stock, is 10% at an annual rate, and its current price P_t is lower than the optimal forecast of tomorrow's price P^{of}_{t+1} so that the optimal forecast of the return at an annual rate is 50%, which is greater than the equilibrium return of 10%. We are now able to predict that, on average, ExxonMobil's return would be abnormally high, so there is an unexploited profit opportunity. Knowing that, on average, you can earn such an abnormally high rate of return on ExxonMobil because $R^{of} > R^*$, you would buy more, which would in turn drive up its current price P_t relative to the expected future price P^{of}_{t+1}, thereby lowering R^{of}. When the current price had risen sufficiently so that R^{of} equaled R^* and the efficient market condition (Equation 10) was satisfied, the buying of ExxonMobil would stop, and the unexploited profit opportunity would disappear.

Similarly, a security for which the optimal forecast of the return is −5% and the equilibrium return is 10% ($R^{of} < R^*$) would be a poor investment, because, on average, it earns less than the equilibrium return. In such a case, you would sell the security and drive down its current price relative to the expected future price until R^{of} rose to the level of R^* and the efficient market condition was again satisfied. What we have shown can be summarized as follows:

$$R^{of} > R^* \rightarrow P_t\uparrow \rightarrow R^{of}\downarrow$$

$$R^{of} < R^* \rightarrow P_t\downarrow \rightarrow R^{of}\uparrow$$

until

$$R^{of} = R^*$$

Another way to state the efficient market condition is this: ***In an efficient market, all unexploited profit opportunities will be eliminated.***

An extremely important factor in this reasoning is that ***not everyone in a financial market must be well informed about a security or have rational expectations for its price to be driven to the point at which the efficient market condition holds***. Financial markets are structured so that many participants can play. As long as a few people (often referred to as the "smart money") keep their eyes open for unexploited profit opportunities, they will eliminate the profit opportunities that appear, because in so doing, they make a profit. The efficient market hypothesis makes sense, because it does not require everyone in a market to be cognizant of what is happening to every security.

APPLICATION ◆ Practical Guide to Investing in the Stock Market

The efficient market hypothesis has numerous applications to the real world.[6] It is especially valuable because it can be applied directly to an issue that concerns many of us: how to get rich (or at least not get poor) in the stock market. A practical guide to investing in the stock market, which we develop here, provides a better understanding of the use and implications of the efficient market hypothesis.

How Valuable Are Published Reports by Investment Advisers?

Suppose you have just read in the "Heard on the Street" column of the *Wall Street Journal* that investment advisers are predicting a boom in oil stocks because an oil shortage is developing. Should you proceed to withdraw all your hard-earned savings from the bank and invest it in oil stocks?

The efficient market hypothesis tells us that when purchasing a security, we cannot expect to earn an abnormally high return, a return greater than the equilibrium return.

Information in newspapers and in the published reports of investment advisers is readily available to many market participants and is already reflected in market prices. So acting on this information will not yield abnormally high returns, on average. The empirical evidence for the most part confirms that recommendations from investment advisers cannot help us outperform the general market. Indeed, as the FYI box suggests, human investment advisers in San Francisco do not, on average, even outperform an orangutan!

Probably no other conclusion is met with more skepticism by students than this one when they first hear it. We all know or have heard of someone who has been successful in the stock market for a period of many years. We wonder, "How could

[6]The empirical evidence on the efficient market hypothesis is discussed in an appendix to this chapter, which can be found on the Companion Website at www.pearsonhighered.com/mishkin.

someone be so consistently successful if he or she did not really know how to predict when returns would be abnormally high?" The following story, reported in the press, illustrates why such anecdotal evidence is not reliable.

A get-rich-quick artist invented a clever scam. Every week, he wrote two letters. In letter A, he would pick team A to win a particular football game; in letter B, he would pick the opponent, team B. He would then separate a mailing list into two groups, and he would send letter A to the people in one group and letter B to the people in the other. The following week he would do the same thing but would send these letters only to the group who had received the first letter with the correct prediction. After doing this for ten games, he had a small cluster of people who had received letters predicting the correct winning team for every game. He then mailed a final letter to them, declaring that since he was obviously an expert predictor of the outcome of football games (he had picked winners ten weeks in a row) and since his predictions were profitable for the recipients who bet on the games, he would continue to send his predictions only if he were paid a substantial amount of money. When one of his clients figured out what he was up to, the con man was prosecuted and thrown in jail!

What is the lesson of the story? Even if no forecaster is an accurate predictor of the market, there will always be a group of consistent winners. A person who has done well regularly in the past cannot guarantee that he or she will do well in the future. Note that there will also be a group of persistent losers, but you rarely hear about them because no one brags about a poor forecasting record.

Should You Be Skeptical of Hot Tips?

Suppose your broker phones you with a hot tip to buy stock in the Happy Feet Corporation (HFC) because it has just developed a product that is completely effective in curing athlete's foot. The stock price is sure to go up. Should you follow this advice and buy HFC stock?

The efficient market hypothesis indicates that you should be skeptical of such news. If the stock market is efficient, it has already priced HFC stock so that its expected return will equal the equilibrium return. The hot tip is not particularly valuable and will not enable you to earn an abnormally high return.

You might wonder, though, if the hot tip is based on new information and would give you an edge on the rest of the market. If other market participants have gotten this information before you, the answer is no. As soon as the information hits the street, the unexploited profit opportunity it creates will be quickly eliminated. The stock's price will already reflect the information, and you should expect to realize only the equilibrium return. But if you are one of the first to gain the new information, it can do you some good. Only then can you be one of the lucky ones who, on average, will earn an abnormally high return by helping eliminate the profit opportunity by buying HFC stock.

Do Stock Prices Always Rise When There Is Good News?

If you follow the stock market, you might have noticed a puzzling phenomenon: When good news about a stock, such as a particularly favorable earnings report, is announced, the price of the stock frequently does not rise. The efficient market hypothesis explains this phenomenon.

FYI Should You Hire an Ape as Your Investment Adviser?

The *San Francisco Chronicle* came up with an amusing way of evaluating how successful investment advisers are at picking stocks. They asked eight analysts to pick five stocks at the beginning of the year and then compared the performance of their stock picks to those chosen by Jolyn, an orangutan living at Marine World/Africa USA in Vallejo, California. Consistent with the results found in the "Investment Dartboard" feature of the *Wall Street Journal*, Jolyn beat the investment advisers as often as they beat her. Given this result, you might be just as well off hiring an orangutan as your investment adviser as you would hiring a human being!

Because changes in stock prices are unpredictable, when information is announced that has already been expected by the market, the stock price will remain unchanged. The announcement does not contain any new information that should lead to a change in stock prices. If this were not the case and the announcement led to a change in stock prices, it would mean that the change was predictable. Because that is ruled out in an efficient market, ***stock prices will respond to announcements only when the information being announced is new and unexpected***. If the news is expected, no stock price response will occur. This is exactly what the evidence shows: Stock prices do reflect publicly available information.

Sometimes an individual stock price declines when good news is announced. Although this seems somewhat peculiar, it is completely consistent with the workings of an efficient market. Suppose that although the announced news is good, it is not as good as expected. HFC's earnings may have risen 15%, but if the market expected earnings to rise by 20%, the new information is actually unfavorable, and the stock price declines.

Efficient Market Prescription for the Investor

What does the efficient market hypothesis recommend for investing in the stock market? It tells us that hot tips and investment advisers' published recommendations—all of which make use of publicly available information—cannot help an investor outperform the market. Indeed, it indicates that anyone without better information than other market participants cannot expect to beat the market. So what is an investor to do?

The efficient market hypothesis leads to the conclusion that such an investor (and almost all of us fit into this category) should not try to outguess the market by constantly buying and selling securities. This process does nothing but boost the income of brokers, who earn commissions on each trade.[7] Instead, the investor should pursue a "buy and hold" strategy—purchase stocks and hold them for long periods of time. This

[7]The investor may also have to pay Uncle Sam capital gains taxes on any profits that are realized when a security is sold—an additional reason why continual buying and selling does not make sense.

will lead to the same returns, on average, but the investor's net profits will be higher, because fewer brokerage commissions will have to be paid.

It is frequently a sensible strategy for a small investor, whose costs of managing a portfolio may be high relative to its size, to buy into a mutual fund rather than to buy individual stocks. Because the efficient market hypothesis indicates that no mutual fund can consistently outperform the market, an investor should not buy into one that has high management fees or that pays sales commissions to brokers, but rather should purchase a no-load (commission-free) mutual fund that has low management fees.

The evidence indicates that it will not be easy to beat the prescription suggested here, although some anomalies (discussed in an appendix found on this book's website) to the efficient market hypothesis suggest that an extremely clever investor (which rules out most of us) may be able to outperform a buy-and-hold strategy. ◆

WHY THE EFFICIENT MARKET HYPOTHESIS DOES NOT IMPLY THAT FINANCIAL MARKETS ARE EFFICIENT

Many financial economists take the efficient market hypothesis one step further in their analysis of financial markets. Not only do they believe that expectations in financial markets are rational—that is, equal to optimal forecasts using all available information—but they also add the condition that prices in financial markets reflect the true fundamental (intrinsic) value of the securities. In other words, all prices are always correct and reflect **market fundamentals** (items that have a direct impact on future income streams of the securities) and so financial markets are efficient.

This stronger view of market efficiency has several important implications in the academic field of finance. First, it implies that in an efficient capital market, one investment is as good as any other because the securities' prices are correct. Second, it implies that a security's price reflects all available information about the intrinsic value of the security. Third, it implies that security prices can be used by managers of both financial and nonfinancial firms to assess their cost of capital (cost of financing their investments) accurately and hence that security prices can be used to help them make correct decisions about whether a specific investment is worth making. This stronger version of market efficiency is a basic tenet of much analysis in the finance field.

The efficient market hypothesis may be misnamed, however. It does not imply the stronger view of market efficiency, but rather just that prices in markets like the stock market are unpredictable. Indeed, as the following application suggests, the existence of market crashes and **bubbles**, in which the prices of assets rise well above their fundamental values, casts serious doubt on the stronger view that financial markets are efficient, but provides less of an argument against the basic lessons of the efficient market hypothesis.

APPLICATION ◆ What Do Stock Market Crashes Tell Us About the Efficient Market Hypothesis and the Efficiency of Financial Markets?

On October 19, 1987, dubbed "Black Monday," the Dow Jones Industrial Average declined more than 20%, the largest one-day decline in U.S. history. The collapse of the high-tech companies' share prices from their peaks in March 2000 caused the heavily tech-laden NASDAQ index to fall from about 5,000 in March 2000 to about 1,500 in 2001 and 2002, a decline of well over 60%. These stock market crashes have caused many economists to question the validity of the efficient market hypothesis. They do not believe that a rational marketplace could have produced such a massive swing in share prices. To what degree should these stock market crashes make us doubt the validity of the efficient market hypothesis?

Nothing in efficient markets theory rules out large changes in stock prices. A large change in stock prices can result from new information that produces a dramatic decline in optimal forecasts of the future valuation of firms. However, economists are hard pressed to come up with fundamental changes in the economy that can explain the Black Monday and tech crashes. One lesson from these crashes is that factors other than market fundamentals probably have an effect on asset prices. Indeed, as we will explore in Chapters 8 and 9, there are good reasons to believe that impediments to financial markets working well do exist. Hence these crashes have convinced many economists that the stronger version of market efficiency, which states that asset prices reflect the true fundamental (intrinsic) value of securities, is incorrect. They attribute a large role in determination of stock and other asset prices to market psychology and to the institutional structure of the marketplace. However, nothing in this view contradicts the basic reasoning behind rational expectations or the efficient market hypothesis—that market participants eliminate unexploited profit opportunities. Even though stock market prices may not always solely reflect market fundamentals, as long as market crashes are unpredictable, the basic lessons of efficient markets theory hold.

However, other economists believe that market crashes and bubbles suggest that unexploited profit opportunities may exist and that the efficient market hypothesis might be fundamentally flawed. The controversy over the efficient market hypothesis continues. ◆

BEHAVIORAL FINANCE

Doubts about the efficiency of financial markets, triggered by the stock market crash of 1987, led to the emergence of a new field of study, **behavioral finance**. It applies concepts from other social sciences such as anthropology, sociology, and, particularly, psychology to understand the behavior of securities prices.[8]

[8]Surveys of this field can be found in Hersh Shefrin, *Beyond Greed and Fear: Understanding of Behavioral Finance and the Psychology of Investing* (Boston: Harvard Business School Press, 2000); Andrei Shleifer, *Inefficient Markets* (Oxford, UK: Oxford University Press, 2000); and Robert J. Shiller, "From Efficient Market Theory to Behavioral Finance," Cowles Foundation Discussion Paper No. 1385 (October 2002).

As we have seen, the efficient market hypothesis assumes that unexploited profit opportunities are eliminated by "smart money" market participants. But can smart money dominate ordinary investors so that financial markets are efficient? Specifically, the efficient market hypothesis suggests that smart money participants will sell when a stock price goes up irrationally, with the result that the stock price falls back down to a level that is justified by fundamentals. For this to occur, smart money investors must be able to engage in **short sales**; that is, they must borrow stock from brokers and then sell it in the market, with the aim that they earn a profit by buying the stock back again ("covering the short") after it has fallen in price. Work by psychologists, however, suggests that people are subject to loss aversion: They are more unhappy when they suffer losses than they are happy when they achieve gains. Short sales can result in losses far in excess of an investor's initial investment if the stock price climbs sharply higher than the price at which the short sale is made (and losses have the possibility of being unlimited if the stock price climbs to astronomical heights).

Loss aversion can thus explain an important phenomenon: Very little short selling actually takes place. Short selling may also be constrained by rules restricting it because it seems unsavory for someone to make money from another person's misfortune. The existence of so little short selling can explain why stock prices are sometimes overvalued. That is, the lack of enough short selling means that smart money does not drive stock prices back down to their fundamental value.

Psychologists have also found that people tend to be overconfident in their own judgments. As a result, investors tend to believe that they are smarter than other investors. Because investors are willing to assume that the market typically doesn't get it right, they trade on their beliefs, rather than on pure facts. This theory may explain why securities markets have such a large trading volume—something that the efficient market hypothesis does not predict.

Overconfidence and social contagion (fads) provide an explanation for stock market bubbles. When stock prices go up, investors attribute their profits to their intelligence and talk up the stock market. This word-of-mouth enthusiasm and glowing media reports then can produce an environment in which even more investors think stock prices will rise in the future. The result is a positive feedback loop in which prices continue to rise, producing a speculative bubble, which finally crashes when prices get too far out of line with fundamentals.[9]

The field of behavioral finance is a young one, but it holds out hope that we might be able to explain some features of securities markets' behavior that are not well explained by the efficient market hypothesis.

[9]See Robert J. Shiller, *Irrational Exuberance* (New York: Broadway Books, 2001).

Summary

1. Stocks are valued as the present value of future dividends. Unfortunately, we do not know very precisely what these dividends will be. This uncertainty introduces a great deal of error into the valuation process. The Gordon growth model is a simplified method of computing stock value that depends on the assumption that the dividends are growing at a constant rate forever. Given our uncertainty regarding future dividends, this assumption is often the best we can do.
2. The interaction among traders in the market is what actually sets prices on a day-to-day basis. The trader who values the security the most (either because of less

uncertainty about the cash flows or because of greater estimated cash flows) will be willing to pay the most. As new information is released, investors will revise their estimates of the true value of the security and will either buy or sell it, depending on how the market price compares with their estimated valuation. Because small changes in estimated growth rates or required return result in large changes in price, it is not surprising that the markets are often volatile.

3. The efficient market hypothesis states that current security prices will fully reflect all available information, because in an efficient market, all unexploited profit opportunities are eliminated. The elimination of unexploited profit opportunities necessary for a financial market to be efficient does not require that all market participants be well informed.

4. The efficient market hypothesis indicates that hot tips and investment advisers' published recommendations cannot help an investor outperform the market. The prescription for investors is to pursue a buy-and-hold strategy—purchase stocks and hold them for long periods of time. Empirical evidence generally supports these implications of the efficient market hypothesis in the stock market.

5. The existence of market crashes and bubbles has convinced many economists that the stronger version of market efficiency, which states that asset prices reflect the true fundamental (intrinsic) value of securities, is not correct. It is far less clear that these crashes show that the efficient market hypothesis is wrong. Even if the stock market was driven by factors other than fundamentals, these crashes do not clearly demonstrate that many basic lessons of the efficient market hypothesis are no longer valid, as long as these crashes could not have been predicted.

6. The new field of behavioral finance applies concepts from other social sciences such as anthropology, sociology, and psychology to understand the behavior of securities prices. Loss aversion, overconfidence, and social contagion can explain why trading volume is so high, stock prices become overvalued, and speculative bubbles occur.

Key Terms

adaptive expectations, p. 147
arbitrage, p. 151
behavioral finance, p. 156
bubbles, p. 155
cash flows, p. 141
dividends, p. 141
efficient market hypothesis, p. 149
generalized dividend model, p. 143
Gordon growth model, p. 143
market fundamentals, p. 155
optimal forecast, p. 147
rational expectations, p. 147
residual claimant, p. 141
short sales, p. 157
stockholders, p. 141
theory of efficient capital markets, p. 149
unexploited profit opportunity, p. 151

Questions

All questions are available in MyEconLab *at* www.myeconlab.com.

1. What basic principle of finance can be applied to the valuation of any investment asset?

2. What are the two main sources of cash flows for a stockholder? How reliably can these cash flows be estimated? Compare the problem of estimating stock cash flows to estimating bond cash flows. Which security would you predict to be more volatile?

3. Some economists think that central banks should try to prick bubbles in the stock market before they get out of hand and cause later damage when they burst. How can monetary policy be used to prick a bubble? Explain how it can do this using the Gordon growth model.

4. If monetary policy becomes more transparent about the future course of interest rates, how would that affect stock prices, if at all?

5. "Forecasters' predictions of inflation are notoriously inaccurate, so their expectations of inflation cannot be rational." Is this statement true, false, or uncertain? Explain your answer.

6. "Anytime it is snowing when Joe Commuter gets up in the morning, he misjudges how long it will take him to drive to work. When it is not snowing, his expectations of the driving time are perfectly accurate. Considering that it snows only once every ten years where Joe lives, Joe's expectations are almost always perfectly accurate." Are Joe's expectations rational? Why or why not?

7. If a forecaster spends hours every day studying data to forecast interest rates, but his expectations are not as accurate as predicting that tomorrow's interest rates will be identical to today's interest rate, are his expectations rational?

8. "If stock prices did not follow a random walk, there would be unexploited profit opportunities in the market." Is this statement true, false, or uncertain? Explain your answer.

9. Suppose that increases in the money supply lead to a rise in stock prices. Does this mean that when you see the money supply has sharply increased in the past week, you should go out and buy stocks? Why or why not?

10. If the public expects a corporation to lose $5 per share this quarter and it actually loses $4, which is still the largest loss in the history of the company, what does the efficient market hypothesis say will happen to the price of the stock when the $4 loss is announced?

11. If you read in the *Wall Street Journal* that the "smart money" on Wall Street expects stock prices to fall, should you follow that lead and sell all your stocks?

12. If your broker has been right in her five previous buy and sell recommendations, should you continue listening to her advice?

13. Can a person with rational expectations expect the price of a share of Google to rise by 10% in the next month?

14 "If most participants in the stock market do not follow what is happening to the monetary aggregates, prices of common stocks will not fully reflect information about them." Is this statement true, false, or uncertain? Explain your answer.

15. "An efficient market is one in which no one ever profits from having better information than the rest." Is this statement true, false, or uncertain? Explain your answer.

16. If higher money growth is associated with higher future inflation, and if announced money growth turns out to be extremely high but is still less than the market expected, what do you think would happen to long-term bond prices?

17. "Foreign exchange rates, like stock prices, should follow a random walk." Is this statement true, false, or uncertain? Explain your answer.

18. Can we expect the value of the dollar to rise by 2% next week if our expectations are rational?

19. "Human fear is the source of stock market crashes, so these crashes indicate that expectations in the stock market cannot be rational." Is this statement true, false, or uncertain? Explain your answer.

20. In the late 1990s, as information technology rapidly advanced and the Internet widely developed, U.S. stock markets soared, peaking in early 2001. Later that year, these markets began to unwind, and then crash, with many commentators identifying the previous few years as a "stock market bubble." How might it possible for this episode to be a bubble, but still adhere to the efficient market hypothesis?

21. Why might the efficient market hypothesis be less likely to hold when fundamentals suggest stocks should be at a lower level?

Applied Problems

All applied problems are available in MyEconLab *at* www.myeconlab.com.

22. Compute the price of a share of stock that pays a $1 per year dividend and that you expect to be able to sell in one year for $20, assuming you require a 15% return.

23. After careful analysis, you have determined that a firm's dividends should grow at 7%, on average, in the foreseeable future. The firm's last dividend was $3. Compute the current price of this stock, assuming the required return is 18%.

24. The current price of a stock is $65.88. If dividends are expected to be $1 per share for the next five years, and the required return is 10%, then what should the price of the stock be in 5 years when you plan to sell it? If the dividend and required return remain the same, and

the stock price is expected to increase by $1 five years from now, does the current stock price also increase by $1? Why or why not?

25. A company has just announced a 3-for-1 stock split, effective immediately. Prior to the split, the company had a market value of $5 billion with 100 million shares outstanding. Assuming that the split conveys no new information about the company, what is the value of the company, the number of shares outstanding, and price per share after the split? If the actual market price immediately following the split is $17.00 per share, what does this tell us about market efficiency?

Web Exercises

1. Visit www.forecasts.org/data/index.htm. Click on Stock Index at the very top of the page. Now choose U.S. Stock Indices—monthly. Review the indexes for the DJIA, the S&P 500, and the NASDAQ composite. Which index appears most volatile? In which index would you have rather invested in 1985 if the investment had been allowed to compound until now?

2. The Internet is a great source of information on stock prices and stock price movements. Yahoo Finance is a great source for stock market data. Go to http://finance .yahoo.com and click on the DOW ticker in the Market Summary section to view current data on the Dow Jones Industrial Average. Click on the chart to manipulate the different variables. Change the time range and observe the stock trend over various intervals. Have stock prices been going up or down over the past day, week, three months, and year?

Web References

http://stocks.tradingcharts.com

Access detailed stock quotes, charts, and historical stock data.

www.investorhome.com/emh.htm

Learn more about the efficient market hypothesis.

Web Appendix

Please visit the Companion Website at www.pearsonhighered .com/mishkin to read the Web appendix to Chapter 7:

Appendix : **Evidence on the Efficient Market Hypothesis**

Part 3

Financial Institutions

Crisis and Response: The $700 Billion Bailout Package

After a heated national debate, the U.S. House of Representatives passed the Emergency Economic Stabilization Act on October 3, 2008. This stunning $700 billion bailout package sought to promote recovery from the global financial crisis by authorizing the Treasury to purchase troubled mortgage assets from struggling financial institutions or to inject capital into banking institutions. To calm fears further, the Act raised the federal deposit insurance limit from $100,000 to $250,000.

The initial bill was voted down on September 29, when constituents flooded their representatives with complaints about bailing out the greedy Wall Street executives behind the crisis. The national debate pitted Wall Street against Main Street: Bailing out financial institutions was seen as being in opposition to helping struggling homeowners. How could injecting capital into the financial system help those fearful of losing their job or, worse yet, suddenly without work?

The central role of financial institutions in the working of the economy—the focus of Part 3—was overlooked. Banks and other financial institutions make financial markets work by moving funds from people who save to people who have productive investment opportunities. That bank branch on Main Street was not going to be able to lend freely to a small business owner or recent college graduate looking to fund a new car purchase until capital once again flowed.

The global financial crisis highlights how the financial system changes over time, be it from financial innovations or hard lessons from crises such as the one at hand. Chapter 8 analyzes financial structure in the United States and in the rest of the world. In Chapter 9, we develop a framework to understand the dynamics of financial crises—and focus in particular on the red-hot global crisis of 2007–2009. In Chapter 10, we look at the business and process of banking. In Chapter 11, we extend the economic analysis developed in Chapter 8 to understand the motivations for bank regulation, and we examine the pitfalls in the regulatory process. Chapters 12 and 13 examine how banking and other nonbank financial institutions have evolved over time. Chapter 14 discusses financial derivatives and how they can be used to reduce risk, but can cause serious damage to the economy if used improperly. In Chapter 15, we look at why conflicts of interest in the financial services industry occur and what we should do about them.

8 An Economic Analysis of Financial Structure

Preview

A healthy and vibrant economy requires a financial system that moves funds from people who save to people who have productive investment opportunities. But how does the financial system make sure that your hard-earned savings get channeled to Paula the Productive Investor rather than to Benny the Bum?

This chapter answers that question by providing an economic analysis of how our financial structure is designed to promote economic efficiency. The analysis focuses on a few simple but powerful economic concepts that enable us to explain features of our financial system, such as why financial contracts are written as they are and why financial intermediaries are more important than securities markets for getting funds to borrowers. The analysis also demonstrates the important link between the financial system and the performance of the aggregate economy, which is the subject of Part 5 of the book.

BASIC FACTS ABOUT FINANCIAL STRUCTURE THROUGHOUT THE WORLD

The financial system is complex in structure and function throughout the world. It includes many different types of institutions: banks, insurance companies, mutual funds, stock and bond markets, and so on—all of which are regulated by government. The financial system channels trillions of dollars per year from savers to people with productive investment opportunities. If we take a close look at financial structure all over the world, we find eight basic facts, some of which are quite surprising, that we must explain to understand how the financial system works.

The bar chart in Figure 1 shows how American businesses financed their activities using external funds (those obtained from outside the business itself) in the period 1970–2000 and compares U.S. data with those of Germany, Japan, and Canada. The *Bank Loans* category is made up primarily of loans from depository institutions; *Non-bank Loans* are primarily loans by other financial intermediaries; the *Bonds* category includes marketable debt securities, such as corporate bonds and commercial paper; and *Stock* consists of new issues of new equity (stock market shares).

Now let's explore the eight facts.

1. ***Stocks are not the most important source of external financing for businesses.*** Because so much attention in the media is focused on the stock market, many people have the impression that stocks are the most important source of financing for American corporations. However, as we can see from the bar chart in Figure 1, the stock market

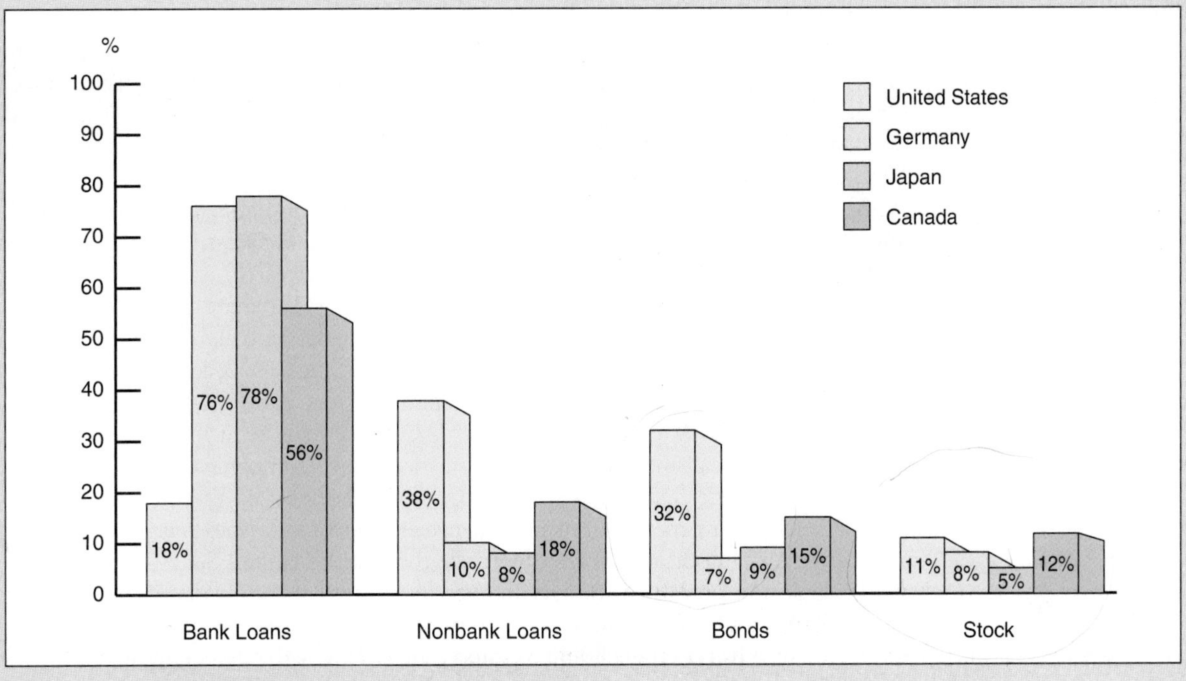

FIGURE 1 Sources of External Funds for Nonfinancial Businesses: A Comparison of the United States with Germany, Japan, and Canada

The *Bank Loans* category is made up primarily of loans from depository institutions; the *Nonbank Loans* are primarily loans by other financial intermediaries; the *Bonds* category includes marketable debt securities, such as corporate bonds and commercial paper; and *Stock* consists of new issues of new equity (stock market shares).

Source: Andreas Hackethal and Reinhard H. Schmidt, "Financing Patterns: Measurement Concepts and Empirical Results," Johann Wolfgang Goethe-Universitat Working Paper No. 125, January 2004. The data are from 1970–2000 and are gross flows as percentage of the total, not including trade and other credit data, which are not available.

accounted for only a small fraction of the external financing of American businesses in the 1970–2000 period: 11%.[1] Similarly small figures apply in the other countries presented in Figure 1 as well. Why is the stock market less important than other sources of financing in the United States and other countries?

2. ***Issuing marketable debt and equity securities is not the primary way in which businesses finance their operations.*** Figure 1 shows that bonds are a far more important source of financing than stocks in the United States (32% versus 11%). However,

[1]The 11% figure for the percentage of external financing provided by stocks is based on the flows of external funds to corporations. However, this flow figure is somewhat misleading, because when a share of stock is issued, it raises funds permanently; whereas when a bond is issued, it raises funds only temporarily until they are paid back at maturity. To see this, suppose that a firm raises $1,000 by selling a share of stock and another $1,000 by selling a $1,000 one-year bond. In the case of the stock issue, the firm can hold on to the $1,000 it raised this way, but to hold on to the $1,000 it raised through debt, it has to issue a new $1,000 bond every year. If we look at the flow of funds to corporations over a 30-year period, as in Figure 1, the firm will have raised $1,000 with a stock issue only once in the 30-year period, while it will have raised $1,000 with debt 30 times, once in each of the 30 years. Thus it will look as though debt is 30 times more important than stocks in raising funds, even though our example indicates that they are actually equally important for the firm.

stocks and bonds combined (43%), which make up the total share of marketable securities, still supply less than one-half of the external funds U.S. corporations need to finance their activities. The fact that issuing marketable securities is not the most important source of financing is true elsewhere in the world as well. Indeed, as we see in Figure 1, other countries have a much smaller share of external financing supplied by marketable securities than does the United States. Why don't businesses use marketable securities more extensively to finance their activities?

3. ***Indirect finance, which involves the activities of financial intermediaries, is many times more important than direct finance, in which businesses raise funds directly from lenders in financial markets.*** Direct finance involves the sale to households of marketable securities, such as stocks and bonds. The 43% share of stocks and bonds as a source of external financing for American businesses actually greatly overstates the importance of direct finance in our financial system. Since 1970, less than 5% of newly issued corporate bonds and commercial paper and less than one-third of stocks have been sold directly to American households. The rest of these securities have been bought primarily by financial intermediaries, such as insurance companies, pension funds, and mutual funds. These figures indicate that direct finance is used in less than 10% of the external funding of American business. Because in most countries marketable securities are an even less important source of finance than in the United States, direct finance is also far less important than indirect finance in the rest of the world. Why are financial intermediaries and indirect finance so important in financial markets? In recent years, indirect finance has been declining in importance. Why is this happening?

4. ***Financial intermediaries, particularly banks, are the most important source of external funds used to finance businesses.*** As we can see in Figure 1, the primary source of external funds for businesses throughout the world comprises loans made by banks and other nonbank financial intermediaries, such as insurance companies, pension funds, and finance companies (56% in the United States, but more than 70% in Germany, Japan, and Canada). In other industrialized countries, bank loans are the largest category of sources of external finance (more than 70% in Germany and Japan and more than 50% in Canada). Thus the data suggest that banks in these countries have the most important role in financing business activities. In developing countries, banks play an even more important role in the financial system than they do in industrialized countries. What makes banks so important to the workings of the financial system? Although banks remain important, their share of external funds for businesses has been declining in recent years. What is driving this decline?

5. ***The financial system is among the most heavily regulated sectors of the economy.*** The financial system is heavily regulated in the United States and all other developed countries. Governments regulate financial markets primarily to promote the provision of information, and to ensure the soundness (stability) of the financial system. Why are financial markets so extensively regulated throughout the world?

6. ***Only large, well-established corporations have easy access to securities markets to finance their activities.*** Individuals and smaller businesses that are not well established are less likely to raise funds by issuing marketable securities. Instead, they most often obtain their financing from banks. Why do only large, well-known corporations find it easier to raise funds in securities markets?

7. ***Collateral is a prevalent feature of debt contracts for both households and businesses.*** **Collateral** is property that is pledged to a lender to guarantee payment in the event that the borrower is unable to make debt payments. Collateralized debt (also known as **secured debt** to contrast it with **unsecured debt**, such as credit card debt, which is not collateralized) is the predominant form of household debt and is widely used in business borrowing as well. The majority of household debt in the United States

consists of collateralized loans: Your automobile is collateral for your auto loan, and your house is collateral for your mortgage. Commercial and farm mortgages, for which property is pledged as collateral, make up one-quarter of borrowing by nonfinancial businesses; corporate bonds and other bank loans also often involve pledges of collateral. Why is collateral such an important feature of debt contracts?

8. ***Debt contracts typically are extremely complicated legal documents that place substantial restrictions on the behavior of the borrower.*** Many students think of a debt contract as a simple IOU that can be written on a single piece of paper. The reality of debt contracts is far different, however. In all countries, bond or loan contracts typically are long legal documents with provisions (called **restrictive covenants**) that restrict and specify certain activities that the borrower can engage in. Restrictive covenants are not just a feature of debt contracts for businesses; for example, personal automobile loan and home mortgage contracts have covenants that require the borrower to maintain sufficient insurance on the automobile or house purchased with the loan. Why are debt contracts so complex and restrictive?

As you may recall from Chapter 2, an important feature of financial markets is that they have substantial transaction and information costs. An economic analysis of how these costs affect financial markets provides us with explanations of the eight facts, which in turn enable a much deeper understanding of how our financial system works. In the next section, we examine the impact of transaction costs on the structure of our financial system. Then we turn to the effect of information costs on financial structure.

TRANSACTION COSTS

Transaction costs are a major problem in financial markets. An example will make this clear.

How Transaction Costs Influence Financial Structure

Say you have $5,000 you would like to invest, and you think about investing in the stock market. Because you have only $5,000, you can buy only a small number of shares. Even if you use online trading, your purchase is so small that the brokerage commission for buying the stock you picked will be a large percentage of the purchase price of the shares. If, instead, you decide to buy a bond, the problem is even worse, because the smallest denomination for some bonds you might want to buy is as much as $10,000, and you do not have that much to invest. You are disappointed and realize that you will not be able to use financial markets to earn a return on your hard-earned savings. You can take some consolation, however, in the fact that you are not alone in being stymied by high transaction costs. This is a fact of life for many of us: Only about one-half of American households own any securities.

You also face another problem related to transaction costs. Because you have only a small amount of funds available, you can make only a restricted number of investments because a large number of small transactions would result in very high transaction costs. That is, you have to put all your eggs in one basket, and your inability to diversify will subject you to a lot of risk.

How Financial Intermediaries Reduce Transaction Costs

This example of the problems posed by transaction costs and the example outlined in Chapter 2 when legal costs kept you from making a loan to Carl the Carpenter, illustrate that small savers like you are frozen out of financial markets and are unable to benefit from them. Fortunately, financial intermediaries, an important part of the financial structure, have evolved to reduce transaction costs and allow small savers and borrowers to benefit from the existence of financial markets.

Economies of Scale One solution to the problem of high transaction costs is to bundle the funds of many investors together so that they can take advantage of *economies of scale*, the reduction in transaction costs per dollar of investment as the size (scale) of transactions increases. Bundling investors' funds together reduces transaction costs for each individual investor. Economies of scale exist because the total cost of carrying out a transaction in financial markets increases only a little as the size of the transaction grows. For example, the cost of arranging a purchase of 10,000 shares of stock is not much greater than the cost of arranging a purchase of 50 shares of stock.

The presence of economies of scale in financial markets helps explain why financial intermediaries developed and have become such an important part of our financial structure. The clearest example of a financial intermediary that arose because of economies of scale is a mutual fund. A *mutual fund* is a financial intermediary that sells shares to individuals and then invests the proceeds in bonds or stocks. Because it buys large blocks of stocks or bonds, a mutual fund can take advantage of lower transaction costs. These cost savings are then passed on to individual investors after the mutual fund has taken its cut in the form of management fees for administering their accounts. An additional benefit for individual investors is that a mutual fund is large enough to purchase a widely diversified portfolio of securities. The increased diversification for individual investors reduces their risk, making them better off.

Economies of scale are also important in lowering the costs of things such as computer technology that financial institutions need to accomplish their tasks. Once a large mutual fund has invested a lot of money in setting up a telecommunications system, for example, the system can be used for a huge number of transactions at a low cost per transaction.

Expertise Financial intermediaries are also better able to develop expertise to lower transaction costs. Their expertise in computer technology enables them to offer customers convenient services like being able to call a toll-free number for information on how well their investments are doing and to write checks on their accounts.

An important outcome of a financial intermediary's low transaction costs is the ability to provide its customers with *liquidity services*, services that make it easier for customers to conduct transactions. Money market mutual funds, for example, not only pay shareholders relatively high interest rates, but also allow them to write checks for convenient bill paying.

ASYMMETRIC INFORMATION: ADVERSE SELECTION AND MORAL HAZARD

The presence of transaction costs in financial markets explains in part why financial intermediaries and indirect finance play such an important role in financial markets (fact 3). To understand financial structure more fully, however, we turn to the role of information in financial markets.

Asymmetric information—a situation that arises when one party's insufficient knowledge about the other party involved in a transaction makes it impossible to make accurate decisions when conducting the transaction—is an important aspect of financial markets. For example, managers of a corporation know whether they are honest or have better information about how well their business is doing than the stockholders do. The presence of asymmetric information leads to adverse selection and moral hazard problems, which were introduced in Chapter 2.

Adverse selection is an asymmetric information problem that occurs *before* the transaction: Potential bad credit risks are the ones who most actively seek out loans. Thus the parties who are most likely to produce an undesirable outcome are the ones most likely to want to engage in the transaction. For example, big risk takers or outright crooks might be the most eager to take out a loan because they know that they are unlikely to pay it back. Because adverse selection increases the chances that a loan might be made to a bad credit risk, lenders might decide not to make any loans, even though good credit risks can be found in the marketplace.

Moral hazard arises *after* the transaction occurs: The lender runs the risk that the borrower will engage in activities that are undesirable from the lender's point of view because they make it less likely that the loan will be paid back. For example, once borrowers have obtained a loan, they may take on big risks (which have possible high returns but also run a greater risk of default) because they are playing with someone else's money. Because moral hazard lowers the probability that the loan will be repaid, lenders may decide that they would rather not make a loan.

The analysis of how asymmetric information problems affect economic behavior is called **agency theory**. We will apply this theory here to explain why financial structure takes the form it does, thereby explaining the facts outlined at the beginning of the chapter.

THE LEMONS PROBLEM: HOW ADVERSE SELECTION INFLUENCES FINANCIAL STRUCTURE

A particular aspect of the way the adverse selection problem interferes with the efficient functioning of a market was outlined in a famous article by Nobel Prize winner George Akerlof. It is called the "lemons problem," because it resembles the problem created by lemons in the used-car market.[2] Potential buyers of used cars are frequently unable to assess the quality of the car; that is, they can't tell whether a particular used car is one that will run well or a lemon that will continually give them grief. The price that a buyer pays must therefore reflect the *average* quality of the cars in the market, somewhere between the low value of a lemon and the high value of a good car.

The owner of a used car, by contrast, is more likely to know whether the car is a peach or a lemon. If the car is a lemon, the owner is more than happy to sell it at the price the buyer is willing to pay, which, being somewhere between the value of a lemon and a good car, is greater than the lemon's value. However, if the car is a peach, the owner knows that the car is undervalued at the price the buyer is willing to pay, and so the owner may not want to sell it. As a result of this adverse selection, few good used cars will come to the market. Because the average quality of a used car available in the

[2]George Akerlof, "The Market for 'Lemons': Quality, Uncertainty and the Market Mechanism," *Quarterly Journal of Economics* 84 (1970): 488–500. Two important papers that have applied the lemons problem analysis to financial markets are Stewart Myers and N. S. Majluf, "Corporate Financing and Investment Decisions When Firms Have Information That Investors Do Not Have," *Journal of Financial Economics* 13 (1984): 187–221; and Bruce Greenwald, Joseph E. Stiglitz, and Andrew Weiss, "Information Imperfections in the Capital Market and Macroeconomic Fluctuations," *American Economic Review* 74 (1984): 194–199.

market will be low and because few people want to buy a lemon, there will be few sales. The used-car market will function poorly, if at all.

Lemons in the Stock and Bond Markets

A similar lemons problem arises in securities markets—that is, the debt (bond) and equity (stock) markets. Suppose that our friend Irving the Investor, a potential buyer of securities such as common stock, can't distinguish between good firms with high expected profits and low risk and bad firms with low expected profits and high risk. In this situation, Irving will be willing to pay only a price that reflects the *average* quality of firms issuing securities—a price that lies between the value of securities from bad firms and the value of those from good firms. If the owners or managers of a good firm have better information than Irving and *know* that they have a good firm, they know that their securities are undervalued and will not want to sell them to Irving at the price he is willing to pay. The only firms willing to sell Irving securities will be bad firms (because his price is higher than the securities are worth). Our friend Irving is not stupid; he does not want to hold securities in bad firms, and hence he will decide not to purchase securities in the market. In an outcome similar to that in the used-car market, this securities market will not work very well because few firms will sell securities in it to raise capital.

The analysis is similar if Irving considers purchasing a corporate debt instrument in the bond market rather than an equity share. Irving will buy a bond only if its interest rate is high enough to compensate him for the average default risk of the good and bad firms trying to sell the debt. The knowledgeable owners of a good firm realize that they will be paying a higher interest rate than they should, so they are unlikely to want to borrow in this market. Only the bad firms will be willing to borrow, and because investors like Irving are not eager to buy bonds issued by bad firms, they will probably not buy any bonds at all. Few bonds are likely to sell in this market, so it will not be a good source of financing.

The analysis we have just conducted explains fact 2—why marketable securities are not the primary source of financing for businesses in any country in the world. It also partly explains fact 1—why stocks are not the most important source of financing for American businesses. The presence of the lemons problem keeps securities markets such as the stock and bond markets from being effective in channeling funds from savers to borrowers.

Tools to Help Solve Adverse Selection Problems

In the absence of asymmetric information, the lemons problem goes away. If buyers know as much about the quality of used cars as sellers, so that all involved can tell a good car from a bad one, buyers will be willing to pay full value for good used cars. Because the owners of good used cars can now get a fair price, they will be willing to sell them in the market. The market will have many transactions and will do its intended job of channeling good cars to people who want them.

Similarly, if purchasers of securities can distinguish good firms from bad, they will pay the full value of securities issued by good firms, and good firms will sell their securities in the market. The securities market will then be able to move funds to the good firms that have the most productive investment opportunities.

Private Production and Sale of Information The solution to the adverse selection problem in financial markets is to reduce asymmetric information by furnishing the people supplying funds with more details about the individuals or firms seeking to finance their investment activities. One way to get this material to saver-lenders is to have private companies collect and produce information that distinguishes good from bad firms and then sell it. In the United States, companies such as Standard and Poor's,

Moody's, and Value Line gather information on firms' balance sheet positions and investment activities, publish these data, and sell them to subscribers (individuals, libraries, and financial intermediaries involved in purchasing securities).

The system of private production and sale of information does not completely solve the adverse selection problem in securities markets, however, because of the **free-rider problem**. The free-rider problem occurs when people who do not pay for information take advantage of the information that other people have paid for. The free-rider problem suggests that the private sale of information will be only a partial solution to the lemons problem. To see why, suppose that you have just purchased information that tells you which firms are good and which are bad. You believe that this purchase is worthwhile because you can make up the cost of acquiring this information, and then some, by purchasing the securities of good firms that are undervalued. However, when our savvy (free-riding) investor Irving sees you buying certain securities, he buys right along with you, even though he has not paid for any information. If many other investors act as Irving does, the increased demand for the undervalued good securities will cause their low price to be bid up immediately to reflect the securities' true value. Because of all these free riders, you can no longer buy the securities for less than their true value. Now because you will not gain any profits from purchasing the information, you realize that you never should have paid for this information in the first place. If other investors come to the same realization, private firms and individuals may not be able to sell enough of this information to make it worth their while to gather and produce it. The weakened ability of private firms to profit from selling information will mean that less information is produced in the marketplace, so adverse selection (the lemons problem) will still interfere with the efficient functioning of securities markets.

Government Regulation to Increase Information The free-rider problem prevents the private market from producing enough information to eliminate all the asymmetric information that leads to adverse selection. Could financial markets benefit from government intervention? The government could, for instance, produce information to help investors distinguish good from bad firms and provide it to the public free of charge. This solution, however, would involve the government in releasing negative information about firms, a practice that might be politically difficult. A second possibility (and one followed by the United States and most governments throughout the world) is for the government to regulate securities markets in a way that encourages firms to reveal honest information about themselves so that investors can determine how good or bad the firms are. In the United States, the Securities and Exchange Commission (SEC) is the government agency that requires firms selling their securities to have independent audits, in which accounting firms certify that the firm is adhering to standard accounting principles and disclosing accurate information about sales, assets, and earnings. Similar regulations are found in other countries. However, disclosure requirements do not always work well, as the collapse of Enron and accounting scandals at other corporations, such as WorldCom and Parmalat (an Italian company), suggest (see the FYI box, "The Enron Implosion").

The asymmetric information problem of adverse selection in financial markets helps explain why financial markets are among the most heavily regulated sectors in the economy (fact 5). Government regulation to increase information for investors is needed to reduce the adverse selection problem, which interferes with the efficient functioning of securities (stock and bond) markets.

Although government regulation lessens the adverse selection problem, it does not eliminate it. Even when firms provide information to the public about their sales, assets, or earnings, they still have more information than investors: A lot more is involved in knowing the quality of a firm than statistics can provide. Furthermore, bad firms have an incentive to make themselves look like good firms, because this would enable them to fetch a higher price for their securities. Bad firms will slant the information they are required to transmit to the public, thus making it harder for investors to sort out the good firms from the bad.

Financial Intermediation So far we have seen that private production of information and government regulation to encourage provision of information lessen, but do not eliminate, the adverse selection problem in financial markets. How, then, can the financial structure help promote the flow of funds to people with productive investment opportunities when asymmetric information exists? A clue is provided by the structure of the used-car market.

An important feature of the used-car market is that most used cars are not sold directly by one individual to another. An individual who considers buying a used car might pay for privately produced information by subscribing to a magazine like *Consumer Reports* to find out if a particular make of car has a good repair record. Nevertheless, reading *Consumer Reports* does not solve the adverse selection problem, because even if a particular make of car has a good reputation, the specific car someone is trying to sell could be a lemon. The prospective buyer might also bring the used car to a mechanic for a once-over. But what if the prospective buyer doesn't know a mechanic who can be trusted or if the mechanic would charge a high fee to evaluate the car?

Because these roadblocks make it hard for individuals to acquire enough information about used cars, most used cars are not sold directly by one individual to another. Instead, they are sold by an intermediary, a used-car dealer who purchases used cars from

FYI The Enron Implosion

Until 2001, Enron Corporation, a firm that specialized in trading in the energy market, appeared to be spectacularly successful. It had a quarter of the energy-trading market and was valued as high as $77 billion in August 2000 (just a little over a year before its collapse), making it the seventh-largest corporation in the United States at that time. However, toward the end of 2001, Enron came crashing down. In October 2001, Enron announced a third-quarter loss of $618 million and disclosed accounting "mistakes." The SEC then engaged in a formal investigation of Enron's financial dealings with partnerships led by its former finance chief. It became clear that Enron was engaged in a complex set of transactions by which it was keeping substantial amounts of debt and financial contracts off its balance sheet. These transactions enabled Enron to hide its financial difficulties. Despite securing as much as $1.5 billion of new financing from J. P. Morgan Chase and Citigroup, the company was forced to declare bankruptcy in December 2001, up to that point the largest bankruptcy in U.S. history.

The Enron collapse illustrates that government regulation can lessen asymmetric information problems, but cannot eliminate them. Managers have tremendous incentives to hide their companies' problems, making it hard for investors to know the true value of the firm.

The Enron bankruptcy not only increased concerns in financial markets about the quality of accounting information supplied by corporations, but also led to hardship for many of the firm's former employees, who found that their pensions had become worthless. Outrage against the duplicity of executives at Enron was high, and several of them were convicted and sent to jail.

individuals and resells them to other individuals. Used-car dealers produce information in the market by becoming experts in determining whether a car is a peach or a lemon. Once they know that a car is good, they can sell it with some form of a guarantee: either a guarantee that is explicit, such as a warranty, or an implicit guarantee, in which they stand by their reputation for honesty. People are more likely to purchase a used car because of a dealer's guarantee, and the dealer is able to make a profit on the production of information about automobile quality by being able to sell the used car at a higher price than the dealer paid for it. If dealers purchase and then resell cars on which they have produced information, they avoid the problem of other people free-riding on the information they produced.

Just as used-car dealers help solve adverse selection problems in the automobile market, financial intermediaries play a similar role in financial markets. A financial intermediary, such as a bank, becomes an expert in producing information about firms so that it can sort out good credit risks from bad ones. Then it can acquire funds from depositors and lend them to the good firms. Because the bank is able to lend mostly to good firms, it is able to earn a higher return on its loans than the interest it has to pay to its depositors. The resulting profit that the bank earns gives it the incentive to engage in this information production activity.

An important element in the bank's ability to profit from the information it produces is that it avoids the free-rider problem by primarily making private loans rather than by purchasing securities that are traded in the open market. Because a private loan is not traded, other investors cannot watch what the bank is doing and bid up the loan's price to the point that the bank receives no compensation for the information it has produced. The bank's role as an intermediary that holds mostly nontraded loans is the key to its success in reducing asymmetric information in financial markets.

Our analysis of adverse selection indicates that financial intermediaries in general—and banks in particular, because they hold a large fraction of nontraded loans—should play a greater role in moving funds to corporations than securities markets do. Our analysis thus explains facts 3 and 4: why indirect finance is so much more important than direct finance and why banks are the most important source of external funds for financing businesses.

Another important fact that is explained by the analysis here is the greater importance of banks in the financial systems of developing countries. As we have seen, when the quality of information about firms is better, asymmetric information problems will be less severe, and it will be easier for firms to issue securities. Information about private firms is harder to collect in developing countries than in industrialized countries; therefore, the smaller role played by securities markets leaves a greater role for financial intermediaries such as banks. A corollary of this analysis is that as information about firms becomes easier to acquire, the role of banks should decline. A major development in the past 30 years in the United States has been huge improvements in information technology. Thus our analysis suggests that the lending role of financial institutions such as banks in the United States should have declined, and this is exactly what has occurred (see Chapter 12).

Our analysis of adverse selection also explains fact 6, which questions why large firms are more likely to obtain funds from securities markets, a direct route, rather than from banks and financial intermediaries, an indirect route. The better known a corporation is, the more information about its activities is available in the marketplace. Thus it is easier for investors to evaluate the quality of the corporation and determine whether it is a good firm or a bad one. Because investors have fewer worries about adverse selection with well-known corporations, they will be willing to invest directly in their securities. Our adverse selection analysis thus suggests that a pecking order for firms that can issue securities should be in place. Hence we have an explanation for fact 6: The larger and more established a corporation is, the more likely it will be to issue securities to raise funds.

Collateral and Net Worth Adverse selection interferes with the functioning of financial markets only if a lender suffers a loss when a borrower is unable to make loan payments and thereby defaults. *Collateral*, property promised to the lender if the borrower defaults, reduces the consequences of adverse selection because it reduces the lender's losses in the event of a default. If a borrower defaults on a loan, the lender can sell the collateral and use the proceeds to make up for the losses on the loan. For example, if you fail to make your mortgage payments, the lender can take the title to your house, auction it off, and use the receipts to pay off the loan. Lenders are thus more willing to make loans secured by collateral, and borrowers are willing to supply collateral because the reduced risk for the lender makes it more likely they will get the loan in the first place and perhaps at a better loan rate. The presence of adverse selection in credit markets thus provides an explanation for why collateral is an important feature of debt contracts (fact 7).

Net worth (also called **equity capital**), the difference between a firm's assets (what it owns or is owed) and its liabilities (what it owes), can perform a similar role to that of collateral. If a firm has a high net worth, then even if it engages in investments that cause it to have negative profits and so defaults on its debt payments, the lender can take title to the firm's net worth, sell it off, and use the proceeds to recoup some of the losses from the loan. In addition, the more net worth a firm has in the first place, the less likely it is to default, because the firm has a cushion of assets that it can use to pay off its loans. Hence, when firms seeking credit have high net worth, the consequences of adverse selection are less important and lenders are more willing to make loans. This analysis lies behind the often-heard lament, "Only the people who don't need money can borrow it!"

Summary So far we have used the concept of adverse selection to explain seven of the eight facts about financial structure introduced earlier: The first four emphasize the importance of financial intermediaries and the relative unimportance of securities markets for the financing of corporations; the fifth, that financial markets are among the most heavily regulated sectors of the economy; the sixth, that only large, well-established corporations have access to securities markets; and the seventh, that collateral is an important feature of debt contracts. In the next section, we will see that the other asymmetric information concept of moral hazard provides additional reasons for the importance of financial intermediaries and the relative unimportance of securities markets for the financing of corporations, the prevalence of government regulation, and the importance of collateral in debt contracts. In addition, the concept of moral hazard can be used to explain our final fact (fact 8): why debt contracts are complicated legal documents that place substantial restrictions on the behavior of the borrower.

HOW MORAL HAZARD AFFECTS THE CHOICE BETWEEN DEBT AND EQUITY CONTRACTS

Moral hazard is the asymmetric information problem that occurs after the financial transaction takes place, when the seller of a security may have incentives to hide information and engage in activities that are undesirable for the purchaser of the security. Moral hazard has important consequences for whether a firm finds it easier to raise funds with debt than with equity contracts.

Moral Hazard in Equity Contracts: The Principal–Agent Problem

Equity contracts, such as common stock, are claims to a share in the profits and assets of a business. Equity contracts are subject to a particular type of moral hazard called the **principal–agent problem**. When managers own only a small fraction of the firm they work for, the stockholders who own most of the firm's equity (called the *principals*) are not the same people as the managers of the firm, who are the *agents* of the owners. This separation of ownership and control involves moral hazard, in that the managers in control (the agents) may act in their own interest rather than in the interest of the stockholder-owners (the principals) because the managers have less incentive to maximize profits than the stockholder-owners do.

To understand the principal–agent problem more fully, suppose that your friend Steve asks you to become a silent partner in his ice-cream store. The store requires an investment of $10,000 to set up and Steve has only $1,000. So you purchase an equity stake (stock shares) for $9,000, which entitles you to 90% of the ownership of the firm, while Steve owns only 10%. If Steve works hard to make tasty ice cream, keeps the store clean, smiles at all the customers, and hustles to wait on tables quickly, after all expenses (including Steve's salary), the store will have $50,000 in profits per year, of which Steve receives 10% ($5,000) and you receive 90% ($45,000).

But if Steve doesn't provide quick and friendly service to his customers, uses the $50,000 in income to buy artwork for his office, and even sneaks off to the beach while he should be at the store, the store will not earn any profit. Steve can earn the additional $5,000 (his 10% share of the profits) over his salary only if he works hard and forgoes unproductive investments (such as art for his office). Steve might decide that the extra $5,000 just isn't enough to make him expend the effort to be a good manager; he might decide that it would be worth his while only if he earned an extra $10,000. If Steve feels this way, he does not have enough incentive to be a good manager and will end up with a beautiful office, a good tan, and a store that doesn't show any profits. Because the store won't show any profits, Steve's decision not to act in your interest will cost you $45,000 (your 90% of the profits if he had chosen to be a good manager instead).

The moral hazard arising from the principal–agent problem might be even worse if Steve were not totally honest. Because his ice-cream store is a cash business, Steve has the incentive to pocket $50,000 in cash and tell you that the profits were zero. He now gets a return of $50,000, and you get nothing.

Further indications that the principal–agent problem created by equity contracts can be severe are provided by past scandals in corporations such as Enron and Tyco International, in which managers were found to have diverted funds for their own personal use. Besides pursuing personal benefits, managers might also pursue corporate strategies (such as the acquisition of other firms) that enhance their personal power but do not increase the corporation's profitability.

The principal–agent problem would not arise if the owners of a firm had complete information about what the managers were up to and could prevent wasteful expenditures or fraud. The principal–agent problem, which is an example of moral hazard, arises only because a manager, such as Steve, has more information about his activities than the stockholder does—that is, information is asymmetric. The principal–agent problem would also not occur if Steve alone owned the store and ownership and control were not separate. If this were the case, Steve's hard work and avoidance of unproductive investments would yield him a profit (and extra income) of $50,000, an amount that would make it worth his while to be a good manager.

Tools to Help Solve the Principal–Agent Problem

Production of Information: Monitoring You have seen that the principal–agent problem arises because managers have more information about their activities and actual profits than stockholders do. One way for stockholders to reduce this moral hazard problem is for them to engage in a particular type of information production, the monitoring of the firm's activities: auditing the firm frequently and checking on what the management is doing. The problem is that the monitoring process can be expensive in terms of time and money, as reflected in the name economists give it, **costly state verification**. Costly state verification makes the equity contract less desirable, and it explains, in part, why equity is not a more important element in our financial structure.

As with adverse selection, the free-rider problem decreases the amount of private information production that would reduce the moral hazard (principal–agent) problem. In this example, the free-rider problem decreases monitoring. If you know that other stockholders are paying to monitor the activities of the company you hold shares in, you can take a free ride on their activities. Then you can use the money you save by not engaging in monitoring to vacation on a Caribbean island. If you can do this, though, so can other stockholders. Perhaps all the stockholders will go to the islands, and no one will spend any resources on monitoring the firm. The moral hazard problem for shares of common stock will then be severe, making it hard for firms to issue them to raise capital (providing an additional explanation for fact 1).

Government Regulation to Increase Information As with adverse selection, the government has an incentive to try to reduce the moral hazard problem created by asymmetric information, which provides another reason why the financial system is so heavily regulated (fact 5). Governments everywhere have laws to force firms to adhere to standard accounting principles that make profit verification easier. They also pass laws to impose stiff criminal penalties on people who commit the fraud of hiding and stealing profits. However, these measures can be only partly effective. Catching this kind of fraud is not easy; fraudulent managers have the incentive to make it very hard for government agencies to find or prove fraud.

Financial Intermediation Financial intermediaries have the ability to avoid the free-rider problem in the face of moral hazard, and this is another reason why indirect finance is so important (fact 3). One financial intermediary that helps reduce the moral hazard arising from the principal–agent problem is the **venture capital firm**. Venture capital firms pool the resources of their partners and use the funds to help budding entrepreneurs start new businesses. In exchange for the use of the venture capital, the firm receives an equity share in the new business. Because verification of earnings and profits is so important in eliminating moral hazard, venture capital firms usually insist on having several of their own people participate as members of the managing body of the firm, the board of directors, so that they can keep a close watch on the firm's activities. When a venture capital firm supplies start-up funds, the equity in the firm is not marketable to anyone *except* the venture capital firm. Thus other investors are unable to take a free ride on the venture capital firm's verification activities. As a result of this arrangement, the venture capital firm is able to garner the full benefits of its verification activities and is given the appropriate incentives to reduce the moral hazard problem. Venture capital firms have been important in the development of the high-tech sector in the United States, which has resulted in job creation, economic growth, and increased international competitiveness.

Debt Contracts Moral hazard arises with an equity contract, which is a claim on profits in all situations, whether the firm is making or losing money. If a contract could be structured so that moral hazard would exist only in certain situations, the need to monitor managers would be reduced, and the contract would be more attractive than the equity contract. The debt contract has exactly these attributes because it is a contractual agreement by the borrower to pay the lender *fixed* dollar amounts at periodic intervals. When the firm has high profits, the lender receives the contractual payments and does not need to know the exact profits of the firm. If the managers are hiding profits or pursuing activities that are personally beneficial but don't increase profitability, the lender doesn't care as long as these activities do not interfere with the ability of the firm to make its debt payments on time. Only when the firm cannot meet its debt payments, thereby being in a state of default, does the lender need to verify the state of the firm's profits. Only in this situation do lenders involved in debt contracts need to act more like equity holders; to get their fair share, now they must know how much income the firm has.

The less frequent need to monitor the firm, and thus the lower cost of state verification, helps explain why debt contracts are used more frequently than equity contracts to raise capital. The concept of moral hazard therefore helps explain fact 1, why stocks are not the most important source of financing for businesses.[3]

HOW MORAL HAZARD INFLUENCES FINANCIAL STRUCTURE IN DEBT MARKETS

Even with the advantages just described, debt contracts are still subject to moral hazard. Because a debt contract requires the borrowers to pay out a fixed amount and lets them keep any profits above this amount, the borrowers have an incentive to take on investment projects that are riskier than the lenders would like.

For example, suppose that because you are concerned about the problem of verifying the profits of Steve's ice-cream store, you decide not to become an equity partner. Instead, you lend Steve the $9,000 he needs to set up his business and have a debt contract that pays you an interest rate of 10%. As far as you are concerned, this is a surefire investment because the demand for ice cream is strong and steady in your neighborhood. However, once you give Steve the funds, he might use them for purposes other than what you intended. Instead of opening up the ice-cream store, Steve might use your $9,000 loan to invest in chemical research equipment because he thinks he has a 1-in-10 chance of inventing a diet ice cream that tastes every bit as good as the premium brands but has no fat or calories.

Obviously, this is a very risky investment, but if Steve is successful, he will become a multimillionaire. He has a strong incentive to undertake the riskier investment with your money, because the gains to him would be so large if he succeeded. You would clearly be very unhappy if Steve used your loan for the riskier investment, because if he were unsuccessful, which is highly likely, you would lose most, if not all, of the money you gave him. And if he were successful, you wouldn't share in his success—you would

[3]Another factor that encourages the use of debt contracts rather than equity contracts in the United States is our tax code. Debt interest payments are a deductible expense for American firms, whereas dividend payments to equity shareholders are not.

still get only a 10% return on the loan because the principal and interest payments are fixed. Because of the potential moral hazard (that Steve might use your money to finance a very risky venture), you would probably not make the loan to Steve, even though an ice-cream store in the neighborhood is a good investment that would provide benefits for everyone.

Tools to Help Solve Moral Hazard in Debt Contracts

Net Worth and Collateral When borrowers have more at stake because their net worth (the difference between their assets and their liabilities) is high or the collateral they have pledged to the lender is valuable, the risk of moral hazard—the temptation to act in a manner that lenders find objectionable—will be greatly reduced because the borrowers themselves have a lot to lose. Another way to say this is that if borrowers have more "skin in the game" because they have higher net worth or pledge collateral, they are likely to take less risk at the lender's expense. Let's return to Steve and his ice-cream business. Suppose that the cost of setting up either the ice-cream store or the research equipment is $100,000 instead of $10,000. So Steve needs to put $91,000 (instead of $1,000) of his own money into the business in addition to the $9,000 supplied by your loan. Now if Steve is unsuccessful in inventing the no-calorie nonfat ice cream, he has a lot to lose—the $91,000 of net worth ($100,000 in assets minus the $9,000 loan from you). He will think twice about undertaking the riskier investment and is more likely to invest in the ice-cream store, which is more of a sure thing. Thus, when Steve has more of his own money (net worth) in the business, and hence more skin in the game, you are more likely to make him the loan. Similarly, if you have pledged your house as collateral, you are less likely to go to Las Vegas and gamble away your earnings that month because you might not be able to make your mortgage payments and might lose your house.

One way of describing the solution that high net worth and collateral provides to the moral hazard problem is to say that it makes the debt contract **incentive-compatible**; that is, it aligns the incentives of the borrower with those of the lender. The greater the borrower's net worth and collateral pledged, then the greater the borrower's incentive to behave in the way that the lender expects and desires, the smaller the moral hazard problem in the debt contract, and the easier it is for the firm or household to borrow. Conversely, when the borrower's net worth and collateral are lower, the moral hazard problem is greater, and it is harder to borrow.

Monitoring and Enforcement of Restrictive Covenants As the example of Steve and his ice-cream store shows, if you could make sure that Steve doesn't invest in anything riskier than the ice-cream store, it would be worth your while to make him the loan. You can ensure that Steve uses your money for the purpose *you* want it to be used for by writing provisions (restrictive covenants) into the debt contract that restrict his firm's activities. By monitoring Steve's activities to see whether he is complying with the restrictive covenants and enforcing the covenants if he is not, you can make sure that he will not take on risks at your expense. Restrictive covenants are directed at reducing moral hazard either by ruling out undesirable behavior or by encouraging desirable behavior. There are four types of restrictive covenants that achieve this objective:

1. ***Covenants to discourage undesirable behavior.*** Covenants can be designed to lower moral hazard by keeping the borrower from engaging in the undesirable behavior of undertaking risky investment projects. Some covenants mandate that a loan can be used only to finance specific activities, such as the purchase of particular equipment or

inventories. Others restrict the borrowing firm from engaging in certain risky business activities, such as purchasing other businesses.

2. ***Covenants to encourage desirable behavior.*** Restrictive covenants can encourage the borrower to engage in desirable activities that make it more likely that the loan will be paid off. One restrictive covenant of this type requires the breadwinner in a household to carry life insurance that pays off the mortgage upon that person's death. Restrictive covenants of this type for businesses focus on encouraging the borrowing firm to keep its net worth high because higher borrower net worth reduces moral hazard and makes it less likely that the lender will suffer losses. These restrictive covenants typically specify that the firm must maintain minimum holdings of certain assets relative to the firm's size.

3. ***Covenants to keep collateral valuable.*** Because collateral is an important protection for the lender, restrictive covenants can encourage the borrower to keep the collateral in good condition and make sure that it stays in the possession of the borrower. This is the type of covenant ordinary people encounter most often. Automobile loan contracts, for example, require the car owner to maintain a minimum amount of collision and theft insurance and prevent the sale of the car unless the loan is paid off. Similarly, the recipient of a home mortgage must have adequate insurance on the home and must pay off the mortgage when the property is sold.

4. ***Covenants to provide information.*** Restrictive covenants also require a borrowing firm to provide information about its activities periodically in the form of quarterly accounting and income reports, thereby making it easier for the lender to monitor the firm and reduce moral hazard. This type of covenant may also stipulate that the lender has the right to audit and inspect the firm's books at any time.

We now see why debt contracts are often complicated legal documents with numerous restrictions on the borrower's behavior (fact 8): Debt contracts require complicated restrictive covenants to lower moral hazard.

Financial Intermediation Although restrictive covenants help reduce the moral hazard problem, they do not eliminate it completely. It is almost impossible to write covenants that rule out *every* risky activity. Furthermore, borrowers may be clever enough to find loopholes in restrictive covenants that make them ineffective.

Another problem with restrictive covenants is that they must be monitored and enforced. A restrictive covenant is meaningless if the borrower can violate it knowing that the lender won't check up or is unwilling to pay for legal recourse. Because monitoring and enforcement of restrictive covenants are costly, the free-rider problem arises in the debt securities (bond) market just as it does in the stock market. If you know that other bondholders are monitoring and enforcing the restrictive covenants, you can free-ride on their monitoring and enforcement. But other bondholders can do the same thing, so the likely outcome is that not enough resources are devoted to monitoring and enforcing the restrictive covenants. Moral hazard therefore continues to be a severe problem for marketable debt.

As we have seen before, financial intermediaries—particularly banks—have the ability to avoid the free-rider problem as long as they make primarily private loans. Private loans are not traded so that no one else can free-ride on the intermediary's monitoring and enforcement of the restrictive covenants. The intermediary making private loans thus receives the benefits of monitoring and enforcement and will work to shrink the moral hazard problem inherent in debt contracts. The concept of moral hazard has provided us with additional reasons why financial intermediaries play a more important role in channeling funds from savers to borrowers than marketable securities do, as described in facts 3 and 4.

Summary

Asymmetric information in financial markets leads to adverse selection and moral hazard problems that interfere with the efficient functioning of those markets. Tools to help solve these problems involve the private production and sale of information, government regulation to increase information in financial markets, the importance of collateral and net worth to debt contracts, and the use of monitoring and restrictive covenants. A key finding from our analysis is that the existence of the free-rider problem for traded securities such as stocks and bonds indicates that financial intermediaries—particularly banks—should play a greater role than securities markets in financing the activities of businesses. Economic analysis of the consequences of adverse selection and moral hazard has helped explain the basic features of our financial system and has provided solutions to the eight facts about our financial structure outlined at the beginning of this chapter.

To help you keep track of all the tools that help solve asymmetric information problems, Table 1 summarizes the asymmetric information problems and tools that help solve them. In addition, it notes how these tools and asymmetric information problems explain the eight facts of financial structure described at the beginning of the chapter.

SUMMARY TABLE 1

Asymmetric Information Problems and Tools to Solve Them

Asymmetric Information Problem	Tools to Solve It	Explains Fact Number
Adverse selection	Private production and sale of information	1, 2
	Government regulation to increase information	5
	Financial intermediation	3, 4, 6
	Collateral and net worth	7
Moral hazard in equity contracts (principal–agent problem)	Production of information: monitoring	1
	Government regulation to increase information	5
	Financial intermediation	3
	Debt contracts	1
Moral hazard in debt contracts	Collateral and net worth	6, 7
	Monitoring and enforcement of restrictive covenants	8
	Financial intermediation	3, 4

Note: List of facts:
1. Stocks are not the most important source of external financing.
2. Marketable securities are not the primary source of finance.
3. Indirect finance is more important than direct finance.
4. Banks are the most important source of external funds.
5. The financial system is heavily regulated.
6. Only large, well-established firms have access to securities markets.
7. Collateral is prevalent in debt contracts.
8. Debt contracts have numerous restrictive covenants.

APPLICATION ◆ Financial Development and Economic Growth

Recent research has found that an important reason why many developing countries or ex-communist countries like Russia (which are referred to as *transition countries*) experience very low rates of growth is that their financial systems are underdeveloped (a situation referred to as *financial repression*).[4] The economic analysis of financial structure helps explain how an underdeveloped financial system leads to a low state of economic development and economic growth.

The financial systems in developing and transition countries face several difficulties that keep them from operating efficiently. As we have seen, two important tools used to help solve adverse selection and moral hazard problems in credit markets are collateral and restrictive covenants. In many developing countries, the system of property rights (the rule of law, constraints on government expropriation, absence of corruption) functions poorly, making it hard to use these two tools effectively. In these countries, bankruptcy procedures are often extremely slow and cumbersome. For example, in many countries, creditors (holders of debt) must first sue the defaulting debtor for payment, which can take several years; then, once a favorable judgment has been obtained, the creditor has to sue again to obtain title to the collateral. The process can take in excess of five years, and by the time the lender acquires the collateral, it may well have been neglected and thus have little value. In addition, governments often block lenders from foreclosing on borrowers in politically powerful sectors such as agriculture. Where the market is unable to use collateral effectively, the adverse selection problem will be worse, because the lender will need even more information about the quality of the borrower so that it can screen out a good loan from a bad one. The result is that it will be harder for lenders to channel funds to borrowers with the most productive investment opportunities. There will be less productive investment, and hence a slower-growing economy. Similarly, a poorly developed or corrupt legal system may make it extremely difficult for lenders to enforce restrictive covenants. Thus they may have a much more limited ability to reduce moral hazard on the part of borrowers and so will be less willing to lend. Again, the outcome will be less productive investment and a lower growth rate for the economy. The importance of an effective legal system in promoting economic growth suggests that lawyers play a more positive role in the economy than we give them credit for (see the FYI box, "Should We Kill *All* the Lawyers?").

Governments in developing and transition countries often use their financial systems to direct credit to themselves or to favored sectors of the economy by setting interest rates at artificially low levels for certain types of loans, by creating development finance institutions to make specific types of loans, or by directing existing institutions to lend to certain entities. As we have seen, private institutions have an incentive to solve adverse selection and moral hazard problems and lend to borrowers with the most productive investment opportunities. Governments have less incentive to do so because they are not driven by the profit motive and thus their directed credit programs may not channel funds to sectors that will produce high growth for the economy. The outcome is again likely to result in less efficient investment and slower growth.

[4]See World Bank, *Finance for Growth: Policy Choices in a Volatile World* (World Bank and Oxford University Press, 2001), and Frederic S. Mishkin, *The Next Great Globalization: How Disadvantaged Nations Can Harness Their Financial Systems to Get Rich* (Princeton University Press, 2006) for a survey of the literature linking economic growth with financial development and a list of additional references.

FYI Should We Kill *All* the Lawyers?

Lawyers are often an easy target for would-be comedians. Countless jokes center on ambulance-chasing and shifty filers of frivolous lawsuits. Hostility to lawyers is not just a recent phenomenon; in Shakespeare's *Henry VI*, written in the late sixteenth century, Dick the Butcher recommends, "The first thing we do, let's kill all the lawyers." Is Shakespeare's Dick the Butcher right?

Most legal work is actually not about ambulance chasing, criminal law, and frivolous lawsuits. Instead, it involves the writing and enforcement of contracts, which is how property rights are established. Property rights are essential to protect investments. A good system of laws, by itself, does not provide incentives to invest, because property rights without enforcement are meaningless. This is where lawyers come in. When someone encroaches on your land or makes use of your property without your permission, a lawyer can stop him or her. Without lawyers, you would be unwilling to invest. With zero or limited investment, there would be little economic growth.

The United States has more lawyers per capita than any other country in the world. It is also among the richest countries in the world, with a financial system that is superb at getting capital to new productive uses such as the technology sector. Is this just a coincidence? Or could the U.S. legal system actually be beneficial to its economy? Research suggests the American legal system, which is based on the Anglo-Saxon legal system, is an advantage of the U.S. economy.*

*See Rafael La Porta, Florencio Lopez-de-Silanes, Andrei Shleifer, and Robert W. Vishny, "Legal Determinants of External Finance," *The Journal of Finance* 52, 3 (July 1997), 1131–1150; and Rafael La Porta, Florencio Lopez-de-Silanes, Andrei Shleifer, and Robert W. Vishny, "Law and Finance," *Journal of Political Economy* 106, 6 (December 1998), 1113-1155.

In addition, banks in many developing and transition countries are owned by their governments. Again, because of the absence of the profit motive, these **state-owned banks** have little incentive to allocate their capital to the most productive uses. Not surprisingly, the primary loan customer of these state-owned banks is often the government itself, which does not always use the funds wisely.

We have seen that government regulation can increase the amount of information in financial markets to make them work more efficiently. Many developing and transition countries have an underdeveloped regulatory apparatus that retards the provision of adequate information to the marketplace. For example, these countries often have weak accounting standards, making it very hard to ascertain the quality of a borrower's balance sheet. As a result, asymmetric information problems are more severe, and the financial system is severely hampered in channeling funds to the most productive uses.

The institutional environment of a poor legal system, weak accounting standards, inadequate government regulation, and government intervention through directed credit programs and state ownership of banks all help explain why many countries stay poor while others grow richer.

APPLICATION ◆ Is China a Counterexample to the Importance of Financial Development?

Although China appears to be on its way to becoming an economic powerhouse, its financial development remains in the early stages. The country's legal system is weak, so that financial contracts are difficult to enforce, while accounting standards are lax, so that high-quality information about creditors is hard to find. Regulation of the banking system is still in its formative stages, and the banking sector is dominated by large state-owned banks. Yet the Chinese economy has enjoyed one of the highest growth rates in the world over the past twenty years. How has China been able to grow so rapidly, given its low level of financial development?

As noted above, China is in an early state of development, with a per capita income that is still less than $10,000, one-fifth of the per capita income in the United States. With an extremely high savings rate, averaging around 40% over the past two decades, the country has been able to rapidly build up its capital stock and shift a massive pool of underutilized labor from the subsistence-agriculture sector into higher-productivity activities that use capital. Even though available savings have not been allocated to their most productive uses, the huge increase in capital, combined with the gains in productivity from moving labor out of low-productivity, subsistence agriculture, have been enough to produce high growth.

As China gets richer, however, this strategy is unlikely to continue to work. The Soviet Union provides a graphic example. In the 1950s and 1960s, the Soviet Union shared many characteristics with modern-day China: high growth fueled by a high savings rate, a massive buildup of capital, and shifts of a large pool of underutilized labor from subsistence agriculture to manufacturing. During this high-growth phase, however, the Soviet Union was unable to develop the institutions needed to allocate capital efficiently. As a result, once the pool of subsistence laborers was used up, the Soviet Union's growth slowed dramatically and it was unable to keep up with the Western economies. Today no one considers the Soviet Union to have been an economic success story, and its inability to develop the institutions necessary to sustain financial development and growth was an important reason for the demise of this superpower.

To move into the next stage of development, China will need to allocate its capital more efficiently, which requires that it improve its financial system. The Chinese leadership is well aware of this challenge; the government has announced that state-owned banks are being put on the path to privatization. In addition, the government is engaged in legal reform to make financial contracts more enforceable. New bankruptcy law is being developed so that lenders have the ability to take over the assets of firms that default on their loan contracts. Whether the Chinese government will succeed in developing a first-rate financial system, thereby enabling China to join the ranks of developed countries, is a big question mark. ◆

Summary

1. There are eight basic facts about U.S. financial structure. The first four emphasize the importance of financial intermediaries and the relative unimportance of securities markets for the financing of corporations; the fifth recognizes that financial markets are among the most heavily regulated sectors of the economy; the sixth states that only large, well-established corporations have access to securities markets; the seventh indicates that collateral is an important feature of debt contracts; and the eighth presents debt contracts as complicated legal documents that place substantial restrictions on the behavior of the borrower.

2. Transaction costs freeze many small savers and borrowers out of direct involvement with financial markets. Financial intermediaries can take advantage of economies of scale and are better able to develop expertise to lower transaction costs, thus enabling their savers and borrowers to benefit from the existence of financial markets.

3. Asymmetric information results in two problems: adverse selection, which occurs before the transaction, and moral hazard, which occurs after the transaction. Adverse selection refers to the fact that bad credit risks are the ones most likely to seek loans, and moral hazard refers to the risk of the borrower's engaging in activities that are undesirable from the lender's point of view.
4. Adverse selection interferes with the efficient functioning of financial markets. Tools to help reduce the adverse selection problem include private production and sale of information, government regulation to increase information, financial intermediation, and collateral and net worth. The free-rider problem occurs when people who do not pay for information take advantage of information that other people have paid for. This problem explains why financial intermediaries, particularly banks, play a more important role in financing the activities of businesses than securities markets do.
5. Moral hazard in equity contracts is known as the principal–agent problem, because managers (the agents) have less incentive to maximize profits than stockholders (the principals). The principal–agent problem explains why debt contracts are so much more prevalent in financial markets than equity contracts. Tools to help reduce the principal–agent problem include monitoring, government regulation to increase information, and financial intermediation.
6. Tools to reduce the moral hazard problem in debt contracts include net worth, monitoring and enforcement of restrictive covenants, and financial intermediaries.

Key Terms

agency theory, p. 167
collateral, p. 164
costly state verification, p. 174
free-rider problem, p. 169
incentive-compatible, p. 176
net worth (equity capital), p. 172
principal–agent problem, p. 173
restrictive covenants, p. 165
secured debt, p. 164
state-owned banks, p. 180
unsecured debt, p. 164
venture capital firm, p. 174

Questions

All questions are available in MyEconLab *at* www.myeconlab.com.

1. For each of the following countries, identify the single most important (largest) and least important (smallest) source of external funding: United States; Germany; Japan; Canada. Comment on the similarities and differences between the countries' funding sources.
2. How can economies of scale help explain the existence of financial intermediaries?
3. Describe two ways in which financial intermediaries help lower transaction costs in the economy.
4. Why are financial intermediaries willing to engage in information collection activities when investors in financial instruments may be unwilling to do so?
5. Suppose you go to a bank, intending to buy a certificate of deposit with your savings. Explain why you would not offer a loan to the next individual who applies for a car loan at your local bank at a higher interest rate than the bank pays on certificates of deposit (but lower than the rate the bank charges for car loans).
6. Wealthy people often worry that others will seek to marry them only for their money. Is this a problem of adverse selection?
7. Do you think the lemons problem would be more severe for stocks traded on the New York Stock Exchange or those traded over-the-counter? Explain.
8. Would you be more willing to lend to a friend if she put all of her life savings into her business than you would if she had not done so? Why?
9. What specific procedures do financial intermediaries use to reduce asymmetric information problems in lending?

10. What steps can the government take to reduce asymmetric information problems and help the financial system function more smoothly and efficiently?

11. How can asymmetric information problems lead to a bank panic?

12. In December 2001, Argentina announced it would not honor its sovereign (government-issued) debt. Many investors were left holding Argentinean bonds priced at a fraction of their previous value. A few years later Argentina announced it would pay back 25% of the face value of its debt. Comment on the effects of information asymmetries on government bond markets. Do you think investors are currently willing to buy bonds issued by the government of Argentina?

13. How does the free-rider problem aggravate adverse selection and moral hazard problems in financial markets?

14. Would moral hazard and adverse selection still arise in financial markets if information were not asymmetric? Explain.

15. How do standardized accounting principles help financial markets work more efficiently?

16. Which firms are most likely to use bank financing rather than to issue bonds or stocks to finance their activities? Why?

17. How can the existence of asymmetric information provide a rationale for government regulation of financial markets?

18. "The more collateral there is backing a loan, the less the lender has to worry about adverse selection." Is this statement true, false, or uncertain? Explain your answer.

19. Explain how the separation of ownership and control in American corporations might lead to poor management.

20. Many policymakers in developing countries have proposed implementing systems of deposit insurance like the one that exists in the United States. Explain why this might create more problems than solutions in the financial system of developing countries.

21. Gustavo is a young doctor who lives in a country with a relatively inefficient legal and financial system. When Gustavo applied for a mortgage, he found that banks usually required collateral for up to 300% of the amount of the loan. Explain why banks might require that much collateral in such a financial system. Comment on the consequences of such a system for economic growth.

Applied Problems

All applied problems are available in MyEconLab *at* www.myeconlab.com.

For Problems 22–25, use the fact that the expected value of an event is a probability weighted average, the sum of each possible outcome multiplied by the probability of the event occurring.

22. You are in the market for a used car. At a used car lot, you know that the blue book value for the cars you are looking at is between $20,000 and $24,000. If you believe the dealer knows *as much* about the car as you, how much are you willing to pay? Why? Assume that you care only about the expected value of the car you buy and that the car values are symmetrically distributed.

23. Refer to Problem 22. Now you believe the dealer knows *more* about the cars than you. How much are you willing to pay? Why? How can this be resolved in a competitive market?

24. You wish to hire Ron to manage your Dallas operations. The profits from the operations depend partially on how hard Ron works, as follows.

	Probabilities	
	Profit = $10,000	Profit = $50,000
Lazy	60%	40%
Hard worker	20%	80%

If Ron is lazy, he will surf the Internet all day, and he views this as a zero cost opportunity. However, Ron would view working hard as a "personal cost" valued at $1,000. What fixed percentage of the profits should you offer Ron? Assume Ron cares only about his expected payment less any "personal cost."

25. You own a house worth $400,000 that is located on a river. If the river floods moderately, the house will be completely destroyed. This happens about once every 50 years. If you build a seawall, the river would have to flood heavily to destroy your house, which happens only about once every 200 years. What would be the annual premium for an insurance policy that offers full insurance? For a policy that pays only 75% of the home value, what are your expected costs with and without a seawall? Do the different policies provide an incentive to be safer (i.e., to build the seawall)?

Web Exercises

1. In this chapter we discuss the lemons problem and its effect on the efficient functioning of a market. This theory was initially developed by George Akerlof. Go to www.nobel.se/economics/laureates/2001/public.html. This site reports that Akerlof, Spence, and Stiglitz were awarded the Nobel Prize in economics in 2001 for their work. Read this report down through the section on George Akerlof. Summarize his research ideas in one page.

Web References

http://nobelprize.org/nobel_prize/economics/laureates/2001/public.html

A complete discussion of the lemons problem on a site dedicated to Nobel Prize winners.

9 Financial Crises

Preview

Financial crises are major disruptions in financial markets characterized by sharp declines in asset prices and firm failures. Beginning in August 2007, defaults in the subprime mortgage market (for borrowers with weak credit records) sent a shudder through the financial markets, leading to the worst financial crisis since the Great Depression. In Congressional testimony, Alan Greenspan, former Chairman of the Fed, described the financial crisis as a "once-in-a-century credit tsunami." Wall Street firms and commercial banks suffered hundreds of billions of dollars of losses. Households and businesses found they had to pay higher rates on their borrowings—and it was much harder to get credit. All over the world, stock markets crashed, with the U.S market falling by 40% from its peak. Many financial firms, including commercial banks, investment banks, and insurance companies, went belly up.

Why did this financial crisis occur? Why have financial crises been so prevalent throughout U.S. history, as well as in so many other countries, and what insights do they provide on the current crisis? Why are financial crises almost always followed by severe contractions in economic activity? We will examine these questions in this chapter by developing a framework to understand the dynamics of financial crises. Building on Chapter 8, we make use of agency theory, the economic analysis of the effects of asymmetric information (adverse selection and moral hazard) on financial markets and the economy, to see why financial crises occur and why they have such devastating effects on the economy. We will then apply the analysis to explain the course of events in a number of past financial crises throughout the world, including the most recent global financial crisis.

WHAT IS A FINANCIAL CRISIS?

In the previous chapter we saw that a well-functioning financial system solves asymmetric information problems (moral hazard and adverse selection) so that capital is allocated to its most productive uses. These asymmetric information problems that act as a barrier to efficient allocation of capital are often described by economists as **financial frictions**. When financial frictions increase, financial markets are less capable of channeling funds efficiently from savers to households and firms with productive investment opportunities, with the result that economic activity declines. A **financial crisis** occurs when information flows in financial markets experience a particularly large disruption, with the result that financial frictions increase sharply and financial markets stop functioning. Then economic activity will collapse.

DYNAMICS OF FINANCIAL CRISES IN ADVANCED ECONOMIES

As earth-shaking and headline-grabbing as the most recent financial crisis was, it was only one of a number of financial crises that have hit industrialized countries like the United States over the years. These experiences have helped economists uncover insights into present-day economic turmoil.

Financial crises in advanced economies have progressed in two and sometimes three stages. To understand how these crises have unfolded, refer to Figure 1, which traces the stages and sequence of financial crises in advanced economies.

Stage One: Initiation of Financial Crisis

Financial crises can begin in several ways: mismanagement of financial liberalization/innovation, asset-price booms and busts, or a general increase in uncertainty caused by failures of major financial institutions.

Mismanagement of Financial Innovation/Liberalization. The seeds of a financial crisis are often sown when an economy introduces new types of loans or other financial products, known as **financial innovation**, or when countries engage in **financial liberalization**, the elimination of restrictions on financial markets and institutions. In the long run, financial liberalization promotes financial development and encourages a well-run financial system that allocates capital efficiently. However, financial liberalization has a dark side: In the short run, it can prompt financial institutions to go on a lending spree, called a **credit boom**. Unfortunately, lenders may not have the expertise, or the incentives, to manage risk appropriately in these new lines of business. Even with proper management, credit booms eventually outstrip the ability of institutions—and government regulators—to screen and monitor credit risks, leading to overly risky lending.

Government safety nets, such as deposit insurance, weaken market discipline and increase the moral hazard incentive for banks to take on greater risk than they otherwise would. Because lender-savers know that government-guaranteed insurance protects them from losses, they will supply even undisciplined banks with funds. Banks and other financial institutions can make risky, high-interest loans to borrower-spenders. They will walk away with nice profits if the loans are repaid, and rely on government deposit insurance, funded by taxpayers, if borrower-spenders default. Without proper monitoring, risk-taking grows unchecked.

Eventually, losses on loans begin to mount, and the value of the loans (on the asset side of the balance sheet) falls relative to liabilities, thereby driving down the net worth (capital) of banks and other financial institutions. With less capital, these financial institutions cut back on their lending to borrower-spenders, a process called **deleveraging**. Furthermore, with less capital, banks and other financial institutions become riskier, causing lender-savers and other potential lenders to these institutions to pull out their funds. Fewer funds mean fewer loans to fund productive investments and a credit freeze: The lending boom turns into a lending crash.

When financial institutions stop collecting information and making loans, financial frictions rise, limiting the financial system's ability to address the asymmetric information problems of adverse selection and moral hazard (as shown in the arrow pointing from the first factor, "Deterioration in Financial Institutions' Balance Sheets," in the top row of Figure 1). As loans become scarce, borrower-spenders are no longer able to fund their productive investment opportunities and they decrease their spending, causing economic activity to contract.

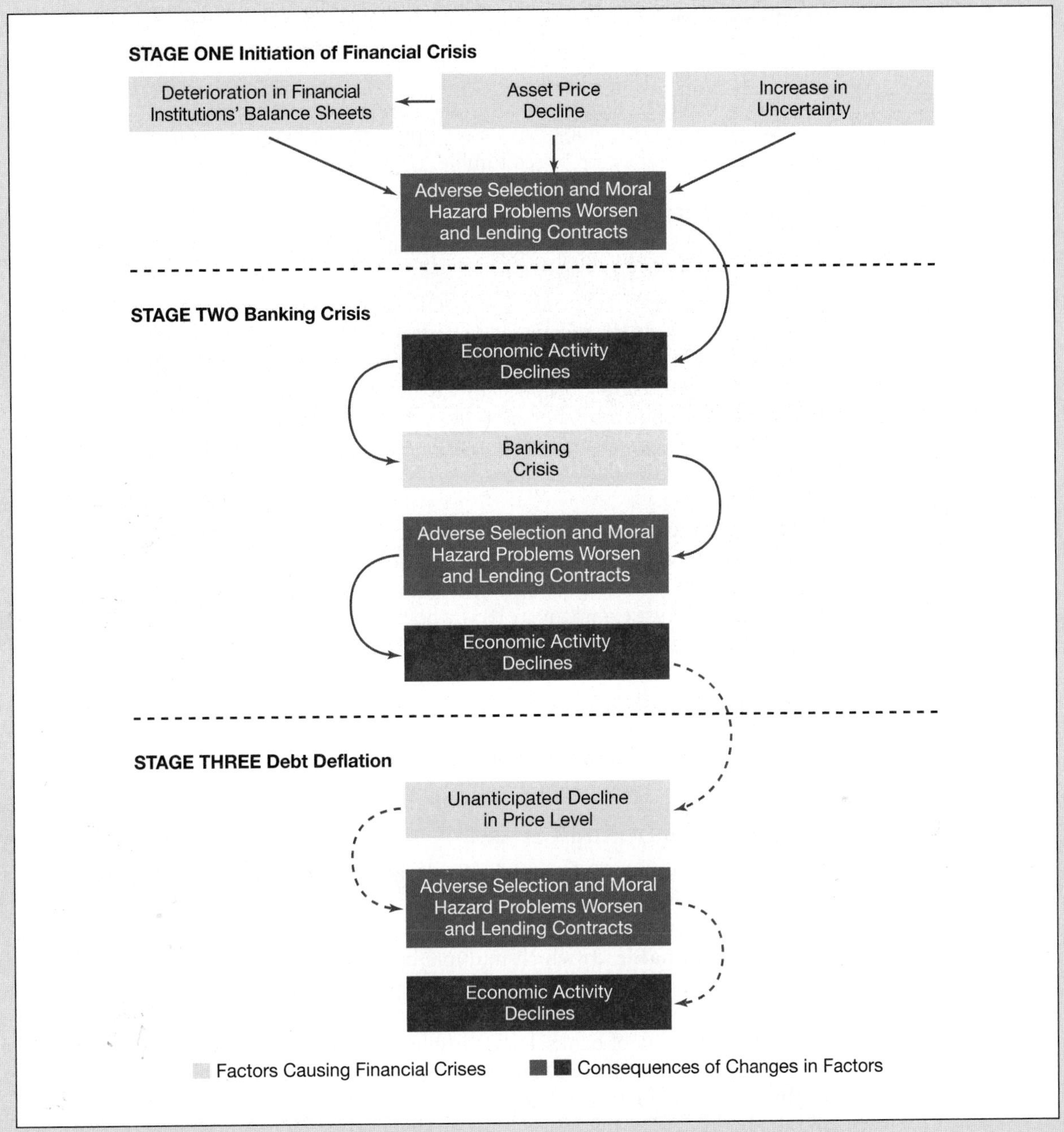

FIGURE 1 Sequence of Events in Financial Crises in Advanced Economies
The solid arrows trace the sequence of events during a typical financial crisis; the dotted arrows show the additional set of events that occur if the crisis develops into a debt deflation. The sections separated by the dashed horizontal lines show the different stages of a financial crisis.

Asset-Price Boom and Bust. Prices of assets such as equity shares and real estate can be driven by investor psychology (dubbed "irrational exuberance" by Alan Greenspan when he was chairman of the Federal Reserve) well above their **fundamental economic values**, that is, their values based on realistic expectations of the assets' future income streams. The rise of asset prices above their fundamental economic values is an **asset-price bubble**. Examples of asset-price bubbles are the tech stock market bubble of the late 1990s and the recent housing price bubble that we will discuss later in this chapter. Asset-price bubbles are often also driven by credit booms, in which the large increase in credit is used to fund purchases of assets, thereby driving up their price.

When the bubble bursts and asset prices realign with fundamental economic values, stock and real estate prices tumble, companies see their net worth (the difference between their assets and their liabilities) decline, and the value of collateral they can pledge drops. Now these companies have less at stake because they have less "skin in the game" and so they are more likely to make risky investments because they have less to lose, the problem of moral hazard. As a result, financial institutions tighten lending standards for borrower-spenders and lending contracts (as shown by the downward arrow pointing from the second factor, "Asset-Price Decline," in the top row of Figure 1).

The asset-price bust also causes a decline in the value of financial institutions' assets, thereby causing a decline in their net worth and hence a deterioration in their balance sheets (shown by the arrow from the second factor to the first factor in the top row of Figure 1), which causes them to deleverage, steepening the decline in economic activity.

Increase in Uncertainty. U.S. financial crises have usually begun in periods of high uncertainty, such as just after the start of a recession, a crash in the stock market, or the failure of a major financial institution. Crises began after the failure of Ohio Life Insurance and Trust Company in 1857; the Jay Cooke and Company in 1873; Grant and Ward in 1884; the Knickerbocker Trust Company in 1907; the Bank of the United States in 1930; and Bear Stearns, Lehman Brothers, and AIG in 2008. With information hard to come by in a period of high uncertainty, financial frictions increase, reducing lending and economic activity (as shown by the arrow pointing from the last factor, "Increase in Uncertainty," in the top row of Figure 1).

Stage Two: Banking Crisis

Deteriorating balance sheets and tougher business conditions lead some financial institutions into insolvency, when net worth becomes negative. Unable to pay off depositors or other creditors, some banks go out of business. If severe enough, these factors can lead to a **bank panic**, in which multiple banks fail simultaneously. The source of the contagion is asymmetric information. In a panic, depositors, fearing for the safety of their deposits (in the absence of or with limited amounts of deposit insurance) and not knowing the quality of banks' loan portfolios, withdraw their deposits to the point that the banks fail. Uncertainty about the health of the banking system in general can lead to runs on banks, both good and bad, which will force banks to sell off assets quickly to raise the necessary funds. These **fire sales** of assets may cause their prices to decline so much that the bank becomes insolvent, even if the resulting contagion can then lead to multiple bank failures and a full-fledged bank panic.

With fewer banks operating, information about the creditworthiness of borrower-spenders disappears. Increasingly severe adverse selection and moral hazard problems in financial markets deepen the financial crisis, causing declines in asset prices and the failure of firms throughout the economy who lack funds for productive investment opportunities. Figure 1 represents this progression in the stage two portion. Bank panics were a feature of all U.S. financial crises during the nineteenth and twentieth centuries, occurring every twenty years or so until World War II—1819, 1837, 1857,

1873, 1884, 1893, 1907, and 1930–1933. (The 1933 establishment of federal deposit insurance, which protects depositors from losses, has prevented subsequent bank panics in the United States.)

Eventually, public and private authorities shut down insolvent firms and sell them off or liquidate them. Uncertainty in financial markets declines, the stock market recovers, and balance sheets improve. Financial frictions diminish and the financial crisis subsides. With the financial markets able to operate well again, the stage is set for an economic recovery.

Stage Three: Debt Deflation

If, however, the economic downturn leads to a sharp decline in the price level, the recovery process can be short-circuited. In stage three in Figure 1, **debt deflation** occurs when a substantial unanticipated decline in the price level sets in, leading to a further deterioration in firms' net worth because of the increased burden of indebtedness.

In economies with moderate inflation, which characterizes most advanced countries, many debt contracts with fixed interest rates are typically of fairly long maturity, ten years or more. Because debt payments are contractually fixed in nominal terms, an unanticipated decline in the price level raises the value of borrowing firms' liabilities in real terms (increases the burden of the debt) but does not raise the real value of borrowing firms' assets. The borrowing firm's net worth in real terms (the difference between assets and liabilities in real terms) thus declines.

To better understand how this decline in net worth occurs, consider what happens if a firm in 2013 has assets of $100 million (in 2013 dollars) and $90 million of long-term liabilities, so that it has $10 million in net worth (the difference between the value of assets and liabilities). If the price level falls by 10% in 2014, the real value of the liabilities would rise to $99 million in 2013 dollars, while the real value of the assets would remain unchanged at $100 million. The result would be that real net worth in 2013 dollars would fall from $10 million to $1 million ($100 million minus $99 million).

The substantial decline in real net worth of borrowers from a sharp drop in the price level causes an increase in adverse selection and moral hazard problems facing lenders. Lending and economic activity decline for a long time. The most significant financial crisis that displayed debt deflation was the Great Depression, the worst economic contraction in U.S. history.

APPLICATION ◆ The Mother of All Financial Crises: The Great Depression

With our framework for understanding financial crises in place, we are prepared to analyze how a financial crisis unfolded during the Great Depression and how it led to the worst economic downturn in U.S. history.

Stock Market Crash

In 1928 and 1929, prices doubled in the U.S. stock market. Federal Reserve officials viewed the stock market boom as excessive speculation. To curb it, they pursued a tightening of monetary policy to raise interest rates to limit the rise in stock prices. The

FIGURE 2
Stock Prices During the Great Depression Period

Stock prices crashed in 1929, falling by 40% by the end of 1929, and then continued to fall to only 10% of their peak value by 1932.

Source: Dow-Jones Industrial Average (DJIA). Global Financial Data; www.globalfinancialdata.com/index_tabs.php?action=detailedinfo&id=1165.

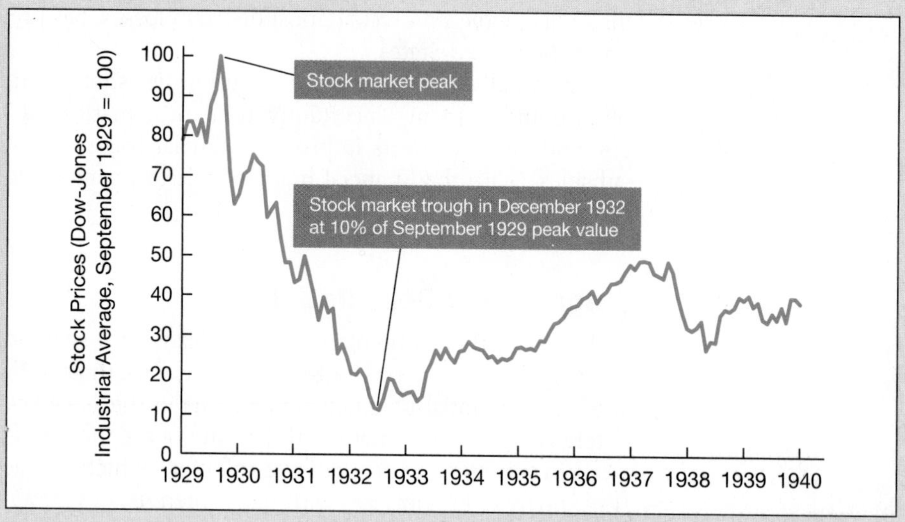

Fed got more than it bargained for when the stock market crashed in October 1929, falling by 40% by the end of 1929, as shown in Figure 2.

Bank Panics

By the middle of 1930, stocks recovered almost half of their losses and credit market conditions stabilized. What might have been a normal recession turned into something far worse, however, when severe droughts in the Midwest led to a sharp decline in agricultural production, with the result that farmers could not pay back their bank loans. The resulting defaults on farm mortgages led to large loan losses on bank balance sheets in agricultural regions. The weakness of the economy and the banks in agricultural regions in particular prompted substantial withdrawals from banks, building to a full-fledged panic in November and December 1930, with the stock market falling sharply. For more than two years, the Fed sat idly by through one bank panic after another, the most severe spate of panics in U.S. history. After what would be the era's final panic in March 1933, President Franklin Delano Roosevelt declared a bank holiday, a temporary closing of all banks. "The only thing we have to fear is fear itself," Roosevelt told the nation. The damage was done, however, and more than one-third of U.S. commercial banks had failed. (These events are described in more detail in Chapter 17.)

Continuing Decline in Stock Prices

Stock prices kept falling. By mid-1932, stocks had declined to 10% of their value at the 1929 peak (as shown in Figure 2), and the increase in uncertainty from the unsettled business conditions created by the economic contraction worsened adverse selection and moral hazard problems in financial markets. With a greatly reduced number of financial intermediaries still in business, adverse selection and moral hazard problems intensified even further. Financial markets struggled to channel funds to borrower-spenders with productive investment opportunities. As our analysis predicts, the

FIGURE 3

Credit Spreads During the Great Depression

Credit spreads (the difference between rates on Baa corporate bonds and U.S. Treasury bonds) rose sharply during the Great Depression.

Source: Federal Reserve Bank of St. Louis FRED database; http://research.stlouisfed.org/fred2/categories/22.

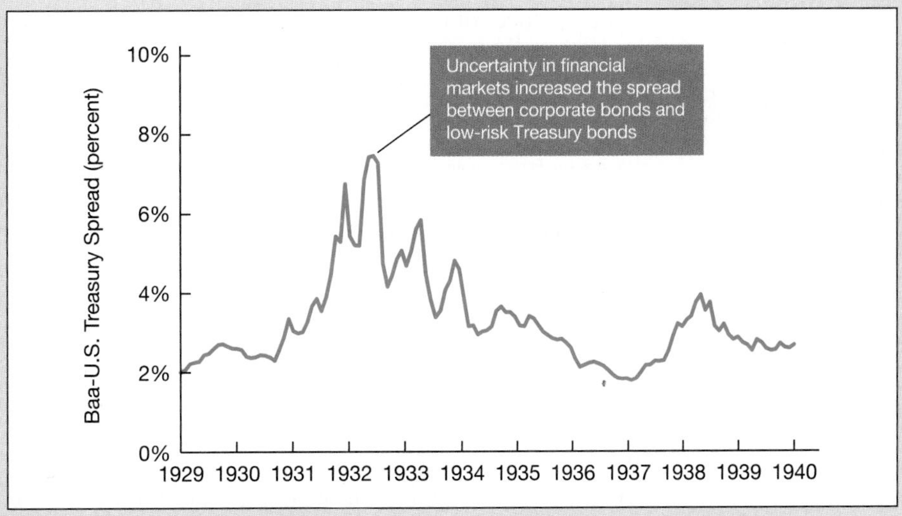

amount of outstanding commercial loans fell by half from 1929 to 1933, and investment spending collapsed, declining by 90% from its 1929 level.

A manifestation of the rise in financial frictions is that lenders began charging businesses much higher interest rates to protect themselves from credit losses. The resulting rise in the **credit spread**—the difference between the interest rate on loans to households and businesses and the interest rate on completely safe assets that are sure to be paid back, such as U.S. Treasury securities—is shown in Figure 3, which displays the difference between interest rates on corporate bonds with a Baa (medium-quality) credit rating and similar-maturity Treasury bonds. (Note the credit spread is closely related to the risk premium discussed in Chapter 5.)

Debt Deflation

The ongoing deflation that started in 1930 eventually led to a 25% decline in the price level. This deflation short-circuited the normal recovery process that occurs in most recessions. The huge decline in prices triggered a debt deflation in which net worth fell because of the increased burden of indebtedness borne by firms and households. The decline in net worth and the resulting increase in adverse selection and moral hazard problems in the credit markets led to a prolonged economic contraction in which unemployment rose to 25% of the labor force. The financial crisis in the Great Depression was the worst ever experienced in the United States, which explains why the economic contraction was also the most severe ever experienced by the nation.

International Dimensions

Although the Great Depression started in the United States, it was not just a U.S. phenomenon. Bank panics in the United States also spread to the rest of the world, and the contraction of the U.S. economy sharply decreased the demand for foreign goods. The worldwide depression caused great hardship, with millions upon millions of people out of work, and the resulting discontent led to the rise of fascism and World War II. The consequences of the Great Depression financial crisis were disastrous.

APPLICATION ◆ The Global Financial Crisis of 2007–2009

Most economists thought that financial crises of the type experienced during the Great Depression were a thing of the past for advanced countries like the United States. Unfortunately, the financial crisis that engulfed the world in 2007–2009 proved them wrong.

Causes of the 2007–2009 Financial Crisis

We begin our look at the 2007–2009 financial crisis by examining three central factors: financial innovation in mortgage markets, agency problems in mortgage markets, and the role of asymmetric information in the credit-rating process.

Financial Innovation in The Mortgage Markets. Before 2000, only the most credit-worthy (prime) borrowers could obtain residential mortgages. Advances in computer technology and new statistical techniques, known as data mining, however, led to enhanced, quantitative evaluation of the credit risk for a new class of risky residential mortgages. Households with credit records could now be assigned a numerical credit score, known as a FICO score (named after the Fair Isaac Corporation, which developed it), that would predict how likely they would be to default on their loan payments. In addition, by lowering transactions costs, computer technology enabled the bundling together of smaller loans (like mortgages) into standard debt securities, a process known as **securitization**. These factors made it possible for banks to offer **subprime mortgages** to borrowers with less-than-stellar credit records.

The ability to cheaply quantify the default risk of the underlying high-risk mortgages and bundle them in a standardized debt security called **mortgage-backed securities** provided a new source of financing for these mortgages. Financial innovation didn't stop there. **Financial engineering**, the development of new, sophisticated financial instruments, led to **structured credit products** that pay out income streams from a collection of underlying assets, designed to have particular risk characteristics that appeal to investors with differing preferences. The most notorious of these products were collateralized debt obligations (CDOs) (discussed in the FYI box, "Collateralized Debt Obligations).

Agency Problems in The Mortgage Markets. The mortgage brokers that originated the loans often did not make a strong effort to evaluate whether the borrower could pay off the loan, since they would quickly sell (distribute) the loans to investors in the form of mortgage-backed securities. Indeed, in some cases mortgage brokers would even extend loans that they knew were beyond the capability of the borrower to pay back. This **originate-to-distribute** business model was exposed to **principal–agent (agency) problems** of the type discussed in Chapter 8, in which the mortgage brokers acted as agents for investors (the principals) but did not have the investors' best interests at heart. Once the mortgage broker earns his or her fee, why should the broker care if the borrower makes good on his or her payment? The more volume the broker originates, the more he or she makes.

FYI Collateralized Debt Obligations (CDOs)

The creation of a collateralized debt obligation involves a corporate entity called a *special purpose vehicle (SPV)* which buys a collection of assets such as corporate bonds and loans, commercial real estate bonds, and mortgage-backed securities. The SPV then separates the payment streams (cash flows) from these assets into a number of buckets that are referred to as tranches. The highest rated tranches, called super senior tranches, are the ones that are paid off first and so have the least risk. The super senior CDO is a bond that pays out these cash flows to investors, and because it has the least risk, it also has the lowest interest rate. The next bucket of cash flows, known as the senior tranche, is paid out next; the senior CDO has a little more risk and pays a higher interest rate. The next tranche of payment streams, the mezzanine tranche of the CDO, is paid out after the super senior and senior tranches and so it bears more risk and has an even higher interest rate. The lowest tranche of the CDO is the equity tranche; this is the first set of cash flows that are not paid out if the underlying assets go into default and stop making payments. This tranche has the highest risk and is often not traded.

If all of this sounds complicated, it is. There were even CDO^2s and CDO^3s that sliced and diced risk even further, paying out the cash flows from CDOs to CDO^2s and from CDO^2s to CDO^3s. Although financial engineering has the potential benefit of creating products and services that match investors' risk appetites, it also has a dark side. Structured products like CDOs, CDO^2s, and CDO^3s can get so complicated that it can be hard to value cash flows of the underlying assets for a security or to determine who actually owns these assets. Indeed, at a speech given in October 2007, Ben Bernanke, the chairman of the Federal Reserve, joked that he "would like to know what those damn things are worth." In other words, the increased complexity of structured products can actually reduce the amount of information in financial markets, thereby worsening asymmetric information in the financial system and increasing the severity of adverse selection and moral hazard problems.

Not surprisingly, adverse selection became a major problem. Risk-loving investors lined up to obtain loans to acquire houses that would be very profitable if housing prices went up, knowing they could "walk away" if housing prices went down. The principal–agent problem also created incentives for mortgage brokers to encourage households to take on mortgages they could not afford, or to commit fraud by falsifying information on a borrower's mortgage applications in order to qualify them for mortgages. Compounding this problem was lax regulation of originators, who were not required to disclose information to borrowers that would have helped them assess whether they could afford the loans.

The agency problems went even deeper. Commercial and investment banks, which were earning large fees by underwriting mortgage-backed securities and structured credit products like CDOs, also had weak incentives to make sure that the ultimate holders of the securities would be paid off. Large fees from writing financial insurance contracts called **credit default swaps**, which provide payments to holders of bonds if they default, also drove units of insurance companies like AIG to write hundreds of billions of dollars' worth of these risky contracts.

Asymmetric Information and Credit-Rating Agencies. Credit-rating agencies, who rate the quality of debt securities in terms of the probability of default, were another contributor to asymmetric information in financial markets. The rating agencies advised clients on how to structure complex financial instruments, like CDOs, at the same time they were rating these identical products. The rating agencies were thus subject to conflicts of interest because the large fees they earned from advising clients on how to structure products they were rating meant that they did not have sufficient incentives to make sure their ratings were accurate. The result was wildly inflated ratings that enabled the sale of complex financial products that were far riskier than investors recognized.

Effects of the 2007–2009 Financial Crisis

Consumers and businesses alike suffered as a result of the 2007–2009 financial crisis. The impact of the crisis was most evident in five key areas: the U.S. residential housing market, financial institutions' balance sheets, the shadow banking system, global financial markets, and the headline-grabbing failures of major firms in the financial industry.

Residential Housing Prices: Boom and Bust Aided by liquidity from huge cash inflows into the United States from countries like China and India, and low interest rates on residential mortgages, the subprime mortgage market took off after the recession ended in 2001. By 2007, it had become over a trillion-dollar market. The development of the subprime mortgage market was lauded by economists and politicians alike because it led to a "democratization of credit" and helped raise U.S. homeownership rates to the highest levels in history. The asset-price boom in housing (see Figure 4), which took off after the 2000–2001 recession was over, also helped stimulate the growth of the subprime mortgage market. High housing prices meant that subprime borrowers could refinance their houses with even larger loans when their homes appreciated in value. With housing prices rising, subprime borrowers were also unlikely to default because they could always sell their house to pay off the loan, making investors happy because the securities backed by cash flows from subprime mortgages had high returns. The growth of the subprime mortgage market,

FIGURE 4

Housing Prices and the Financial Crisis of 2007–2009

Housing prices boomed from 2002 to 2006, fueling the market for subprime mortgages and forming an asset-price bubble. Housing prices began declining in 2006, falling by more than 30% subsequently, which led to defaults by subprime mortgage holders.

Source: Case-Shiller U.S. National Composite House Price Index; www.macromarkets.com/csi_housing/index.asp.

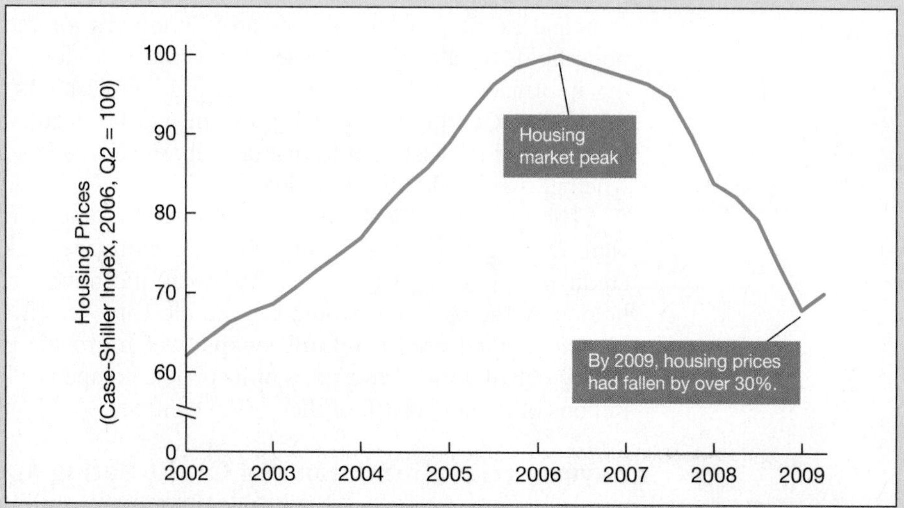

in turn, increased the demand for houses and so fueled the boom in housing prices, resulting in a housing price bubble. (A highly controversial issue is whether the Federal Reserve was to blame for the housing price bubble, and this is discussed in the Inside the Fed box.)

As housing prices rose and profitability for mortgage originators and lenders was high, the underwriting standards for subprime mortgages fell to lower and lower standards. High-risk borrowers were able to obtain mortgages, and the amount of the mortgage relative to the value of the house, the loan-to-value ratio (LTV), rose. Borrowers were often able to get piggyback, second, and third mortgages on top of their original 80% loan-to-value mortgage, so that they had to put almost no money down. When asset prices rise too far out of line with fundamentals—in the case of housing, how much housing costs if purchased relative to the cost of renting it, or the cost of houses relative to households' median income—they must come down. Eventually, the housing price bubble burst. With housing prices falling after their peak in 2006 (see Figure 4), the rot in the financial system began to be revealed. The decline in housing prices led to many subprime borrowers finding that their mortgages were "underwater"—that is, the value of the house fell below the amount of the mortgage. When this happened, struggling homeowners had tremendous incentives to walk away from their homes and just send the keys back to the lender. Defaults on mortgages shot up sharply, eventually leading to millions of mortgages in foreclosure.

Deterioration of Financial Institutions' Balance Sheets. The decline in U.S. housing prices led to rising defaults on mortgages. As a result, the value of mortgage-backed securities and CDOs collapsed, leaving banks and other financial institutions

Inside the Fed — Was the Fed to Blame for the Housing Price Bubble?

Some economists—most prominently, John Taylor of Stanford University—have argued that the low interest rate policy of the Federal Reserve in the 2003–2006 period caused the housing price bubble.* During this period, the Federal Reserve relied on easing of monetary policy to set the federal funds rate well below the level that the Taylor rule, discussed in Chapter 19, suggested was appropriate. Taylor argues that the low federal funds rate led to low mortgage rates that stimulated housing demand and encouraged the issuance of subprime mortgages, both of which led to rising housing prices and a bubble.

In a speech given in January 2010, Federal Reserve Chairman Ben Bernanke countered this argument.† He concluded that monetary policy was not to blame for the housing price bubble. First, he said, it is not at all clear that the federal funds rate was below what the Taylor rule suggested would be appropriate. Rates seemed low only when current values, not forecasts, were used in the output and inflation calculations for the Taylor rule. Rather, the culprits were the proliferation of new mortgage products that lowered mortgage payments, a relaxation of lending standards that brought more buyers into the housing market, and capital inflows from countries such as China and India. Bernanke's speech was very controversial, and the debate over whether monetary policy was to blame for the housing price bubble continues to this day.

*John Taylor, "Housing and Monetary Policy," in Federal Reserve Bank of Kansas City, *Housing, Housing Finance and Monetary Policy* (Kansas City: Federal Reserve Bank of Kansas City, 2007), 463–476.

†Ben S. Bernanke, "Monetary Policy and the Housing Bubble," speech given at the annual meeting of the American Economic Association, Atlanta Georgia, January 3, 2010; www.federalreserve.gov/newsevents/speech/bernanke20100103a.htm.

with a lower value of assets and thus a decline in net worth. With weakened balance sheets, these banks and other financial institutions began to deleverage, selling off assets and restricting the availability of credit to both households and businesses. With no one else able to step in to collect information and make loans, the reduction in bank lending meant that financial frictions increased in financial markets.

Run on the Shadow Banking System. The sharp decline in the value of mortgages and other financial assets triggered a run on the **shadow banking system**, composed of hedge funds, investment banks, and other nondepository financial firms, which are not as tightly regulated as banks. Funds from shadow banks flowed through the financial system and for many years supported the issuance of low interest-rate mortgages and auto loans.

These securities were funded primarily by **repurchase agreements (repos)**, short-term borrowing that, in effect, uses assets like mortgage-backed securities as collateral. Rising concern about the quality of a financial institution's balance sheet led lenders to require larger amounts of collateral, known as **haircuts**. For example, if a borrower took out a \$100 million loan in a repo agreement, it might have to post \$105 million of mortgage-backed securities as collateral, and the haircut is then 5%.

With rising defaults on mortgages, the value of mortgage-backed securities fell, which then led to a rise in haircuts. At the start of the crisis, haircuts were close to zero, but eventually rose to nearly 50%.[1] The result was that the same amount of collateral would allow financial institutions to borrow only half as much. Thus, to raise funds, financial institutions had to engage in fire sales and sell off their assets very rapidly. Because selling assets quickly requires lowering their price, the fire sales led to a further decline in financial institutions' asset values. This decline lowered the value of collateral further, raising haircuts and thereby forcing financial institutions to scramble even more for liquidity. The result was similar to the run on the banking system that occurred during the Great Depression, causing massive deleveraging that resulted in a restriction of lending and a decline in economic activity.

The decline in asset prices in the stock market (which fell by over 50% from October 2007 to March 2009, as shown in Figure 5) and the more than 30% drop in residential house prices (shown in Figure 4), along with the fire sales resulting from the run on the shadow banking system, weakened both firms' and households' balance sheets. This worsening of financial frictions manifested itself in widening credit spreads, causing higher costs of credit for households and businesses and tighter lending standards. The resulting decline in lending meant that both consumption expenditure and investment fell, causing the economy to contract.[2]

Global Financial Markets. Although the problem originated in the United States, the wake-up call for the financial crisis came from Europe, a sign of how extensive the globalization of financial markets had become. After Fitch and Standard & Poor's announced ratings downgrades on mortgage-backed securities and CDOs totaling more than \$10 billion, on August 7, 2007, a French investment house, BNP Paribas,

[1]See Gary Gorton and Andrew Metrick, "Securitized Banking and the Run on Repo," National Bureau of Economic Research Working Paper No. 15223 (August 2009).

[2]During this period there was also a substantial supply shock because oil and other commodity prices rose sharply until the summer of 2008, but then fell precipitously thereafter. We discuss the aggregate demand and supply analysis of the impact of this supply shock in Chapter 23.

FIGURE 5

Stock Prices and the Financial Crisis of 2007–2009

Stock prices fell by 50% from October 2007 to March 2009.

Source: Dow-Jones Industrial Average (DJIA). Global Financial Data; www.globalfinancialdata.com/index_tabs.php?action=detailedinfo&id=1165.

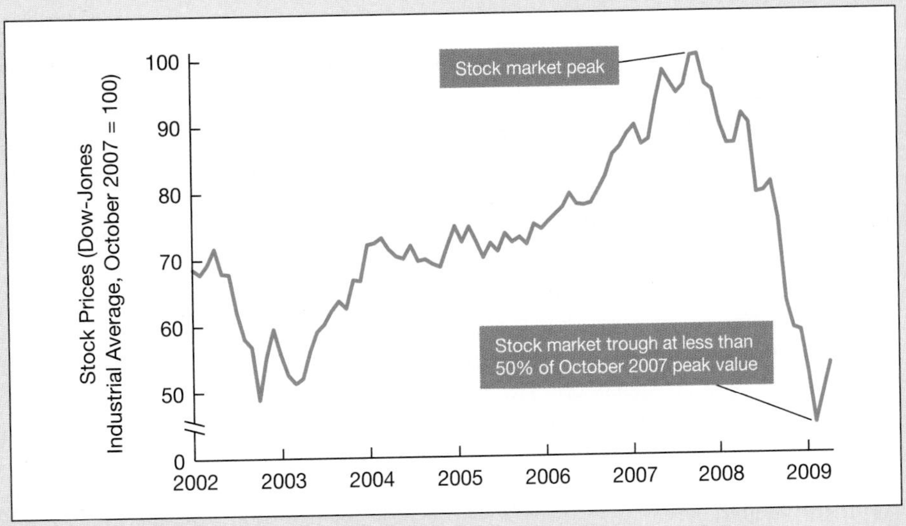

suspended redemption of shares held in some of its money market funds, which had sustained large losses. The run on the shadow banking system began, only to become worse and worse over time. Despite huge injections of liquidity into the financial system by the European Central Bank and the Federal Reserve, discussed later in this chapter, banks began to horde cash and were unwilling to lend to each other. The drying up of credit led to the first major bank failure in the United Kingdom in over 100 years, when Northern Rock, which had relied on short-term borrowing in the repo market rather than deposits for its funding, collapsed in September 2007. A string of other European financial institutions then failed as well. Particularly hard hit were countries like Ireland, which up until this crisis was seen as one of the most successful countries in Europe with a very high rate of economic growth (see the Global box, "Ireland and the 2007–2009 Financial Crisis"). European countries actually experienced a more severe economic downturn than did the United States.

Failure of High-Profile Firms. The impact of the financial crisis on firm balance sheets forced major players in the financial markets to take drastic action. In March 2008, Bear Stearns, the fifth-largest investment bank in the United States, which had invested heavily in subprime-related securities, had a run on its repo funding and was forced to sell itself to J.P. Morgan for less than 5% of what it was worth just a year earlier. To broker the deal, the Federal Reserve had to take over $30 billion of Bear Stearns's hard-to-value assets. In July, Fannie Mae and Freddie Mac, the two privately owned government-sponsored enterprises that together insured over $5 trillion of mortgages or mortgage-backed assets, were propped up by the U.S. Treasury and the Federal Reserve after suffering substantial losses from their holdings of subprime securities. In early September 2008, they were then put into conservatorship (in effect run by the government).

On Monday, September 15, 2008, after suffering losses in the subprime market, Lehman Brothers, the fourth-largest investment bank by asset size with over $600 billion in assets and 25,000 employees, filed for bankruptcy, making it the largest bankruptcy filing in U.S. history. The day before, Merrill Lynch, the third-largest investment

Global Ireland and the 2007–2009 Financial Crisis

From 1995 to 2007, Ireland had one of the highest economic growth rates in the world, with real GDP growing at an average annual rate of 6.3%. As a result, Ireland earned the title the "Celtic Tiger," and it became one of Europe's wealthiest nations, with more Mercedes owners per capita than even Germany. But behind the scenes, soaring real estate prices and a boom in mortgage lending were laying the groundwork for a major financial crisis that hit in 2008, sending the Irish economy into a severe recession.

Irish banks eased loan standards, offering to cover a greater share of housing costs and at longer terms. As in the United States, a housing price bubble got underway, with Irish home values rising even more rapidly, doubling once between 1995 and 2000, and then again from 2000 to 2007. By 2007, residential construction reached 13% of GDP, twice the average of other wealthy nations, with Irish banks increasing their mortgage loans by 25% a year.

With the onset of the financial crisis in late 2007, home prices collapsed—falling nearly 20%, among the steepest housing price declines in the world. Irish banks were particularly vulnerable because of their exposure to mortgage markets and because they had funded their balance sheet expansions through short-term borrowing in the repo market. The combination of tighter funding and falling asset prices led to large losses, and in October 2008, the Irish government guaranteed all deposits. By early 2009, the government had nationalized one of the three largest banks and injected capital into the other two. Banks remained weak, with the government announcing a plan to shift "toxic" bank assets into a government-funding vehicle.

The financial crisis in Ireland triggered a painful recession, among the worst in modern Irish history. Unemployment rose from 4.5% before the crisis to 12.5%, while GDP levels tumbled by more than 10%. Tax rolls thinned, and losses in the banking sector continued to escalate, leading to an astronomical government budget deficit of over 30% of GDP in 2010. In dire straights, Ireland suffered the humiliation of having to be bailed out by the European Union and the IMF.

bank, who also suffered large losses on its holding of subprime securities, announced its sale to Bank of America for a price 60% below its value a year earlier. On Tuesday, September 16, AIG, an insurance giant with assets of over $1 trillion, suffered an extreme liquidity crisis when its credit rating was downgraded. It had written over $400 billion of insurance contracts (credit default swaps) that had to make payouts on possible losses from subprime mortgage securities. The Federal Reserve then stepped in with an $85 billion loan to keep AIG afloat (with total government loans later increased to $173 billion).

Height of the 2007–2009 Financial Crisis

The financial crisis reached its peak in September 2008 after the House of Representatives, fearing the wrath of constituents who were angry about bailing out Wall Street, voted down a $700 billion dollar bailout package proposed by the Bush administration. The Emergency Economic Stabilization Act finally passed nearly a week later. The stock market crash accelerated, with the week beginning October 6, 2008, showing the worst weekly decline in U.S. history. Credit spreads went through the roof over the next three weeks, with the spread between Baa corporate bonds (just above investment grade) and U.S. Treasury bonds going to over 5.5 percentage points (550 basis points), as illustrated by Figure 6.

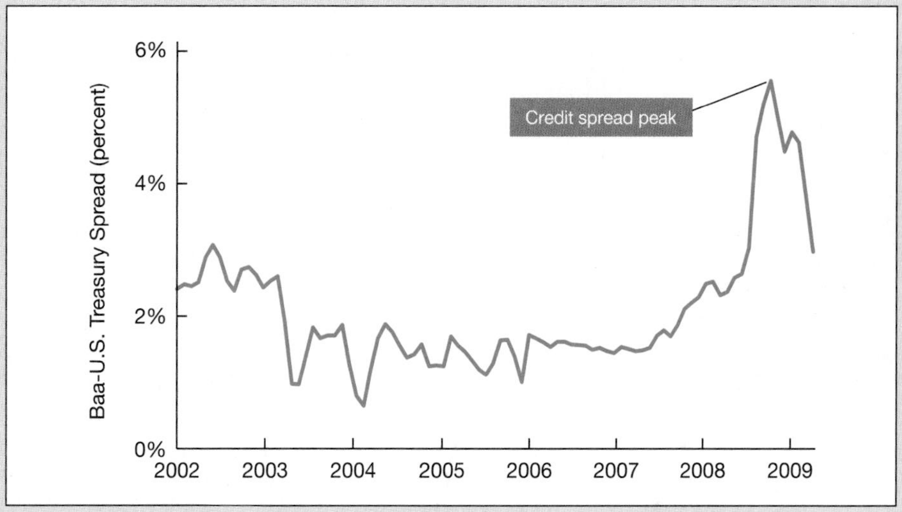

FIGURE 6

Credit Spreads and the 2007–2009 Financial Crisis

Credit spreads (the difference between rates on Baa corporate bonds and U.S. Treasury bonds) rose by more than 4 percentage points (400 basis points) during the crisis. Debate over the bailout package and the stock market crash caused credit spreads to peak in December 2008.

Source: Federal Reserve Bank of St. Louis FRED database; http://research.stlouisfed.org/fred2/categories/22.

The impaired financial markets and surging interest rates faced by borrower-spenders led to sharp declines in consumer spending and investment. Real GDP declined sharply, falling at a −1.3% annual rate in the third quarter of 2008 and then at a −5.4% and −6.4% annual rate in the next two quarters. The unemployment rate shot up, going over the 10% level in late 2009. The recession that started in December 2007 became the worst economic contraction in the United States since World War II and as a result is now referred to as the "Great Recession."

Government Intervention and the Recovery

Although the recession produced by the global financial crisis was very severe, the economic contraction was far smaller in magnitude than during the Great Depression because of massive interventions by governments to prop up financial markets and stimulate the economy.

As we will see in Chapter 18, the Federal Reserve took extraordinary actions to contain the crisis involving both monetary policy to stimulate the economy and liquidity provision to support orderly functioning of financial markets. In addition, the U.S. government engaged in massive bailouts with over \$150 billion of loans to AIG and the **Troubled Asset Relief Plan (TARP)**, the most important provision of the Bush administration's Economic Recovery Act passed in October 2008, which authorized the Treasury to spend \$700 billion purchasing subprime mortgage assets from troubled financial institutions or to inject capital into these institutions—the route actually followed. In addition, the Act raised the federal deposit insurance limit temporarily from \$100,000 to \$250,000 in order to limit withdrawals from banks. Shortly thereafter, the FDIC put in place a guarantee for certain debt newly issued by banks, and the Treasury guaranteed for a year money market mutual fund shares at par value. Similarly European governments conducted massive bailouts, which were in excess of \$10 trillion, in order to prop up their banking systems (see the Global box, "Worldwide Government Bailouts During the 2007–2009 Financial Crisis").

Fiscal stimulus to stimulate the economy was another key piece of the U.S. government's response to the crisis. In February 2008, Congress passed the Bush administration's

Global Worldwide Government Bailouts During the 2007–2009 Financial Crisis

The spreading bank failures in Europe in the fall of 2008 led to massive bailouts of financial institutions: the Netherlands, Belgium, and Luxembourg injected $16 billion to prop up Fortis, a major European bank; the Netherlands injected $13 billion into ING, a banking and insurance giant; Germany provided a $50 billion rescue package for Hypo Real Estate Holdings; and Iceland took over its three largest banks after its banking system collapsed. Ireland's government guaranteed all the deposits of its commercial banks as well as interbank lending, as did Greece. Spain implemented a bailout package similar to the United States' to buy up to 50 billion euros ($70 billion) of assets in its banks in order to encourage them to lend. The U.K. Treasury set up a bailout plan with a similar price tag to that of the U.S. Treasury's plan of 400 billion pounds ($699 billion). It guaranteed 250 billion pounds of bank liabilities, added 100 billion pounds to a facility that swaps these assets for government bonds, and allowed the U.K. government to buy up to 50 billion pounds of equity stakes in British banks. Bailout plans to the tune of over $100 billion in South Korea, $200 billion in Sweden, $400 billion in France, and $500 billion in Germany, all of which guaranteed the debt of their banks as well as injecting capital into them, then followed. Both the scale of these bailout packages and the degree of international coordination was unprecedented.

Economic Stimulus Act of 2008, which gave one-time tax rebates of $78 billion by sending $600 checks to individual taxpayers. Shortly after coming to office the Obama administration proposed and got passed the American Recovery and Reinvestment Act of 2009, a much bigger $787 billion fiscal stimulus package which, to this day, is highly controversial and is discussed more extensively in Part 6 of the book.

With the government bailouts, the Fed's extraordinary actions and fiscal stimulus, starting in March 2009 a bull market in stocks got under way, (see Figure 5), and credit spreads began to fall (Figure 6).[3] With the recovery in financial markets, the economy started to recover, but unfortunately, the pace of recovery has been slow. ◆

DYNAMICS OF FINANCIAL CRISES IN EMERGING MARKET ECONOMIES

Before the financial crisis of 2007–2009, economists looked abroad for recent examples of financial crises. **Emerging market economies**, economies in an earlier stage of market development that have recently opened up to the flow of goods, services, and

[3]The financial market recovery was aided by U.S. Treasury's requirement announced in February 2009 that the nineteen largest banking institutions undergo what became known as the *bank stress tests* (the Supervisory Capital Assessment Program or SCAP). The stress tests were a supervisory assessment, led by the Federal Reserve in cooperation with the Office of the Comptroller of the Currency and the FDIC, of the balance sheet position of these banks to ensure that they had sufficient capital to withstand bad macroeconomic outcomes. The Treasury announced the results in early May and they were well received by market participants, allowing these banks to raise substantial amounts of capital from private capital markets. The stress tests were a key factor that helped increase the amount of information in the marketplace, thereby reducing asymmetric information and adverse selection and moral hazard problems.

capital from the rest of the world, are particularly vulnerable. With the opening up of their economies to markets, emerging market countries have been no stranger to devastating financial crises in recent years. The dynamics of financial crises in emerging market economies have many of the same elements as those found in the United States, but with some important differences. Figure 7 outlines the key stages and sequence of events in financial crises in these economies that we will address in this section.

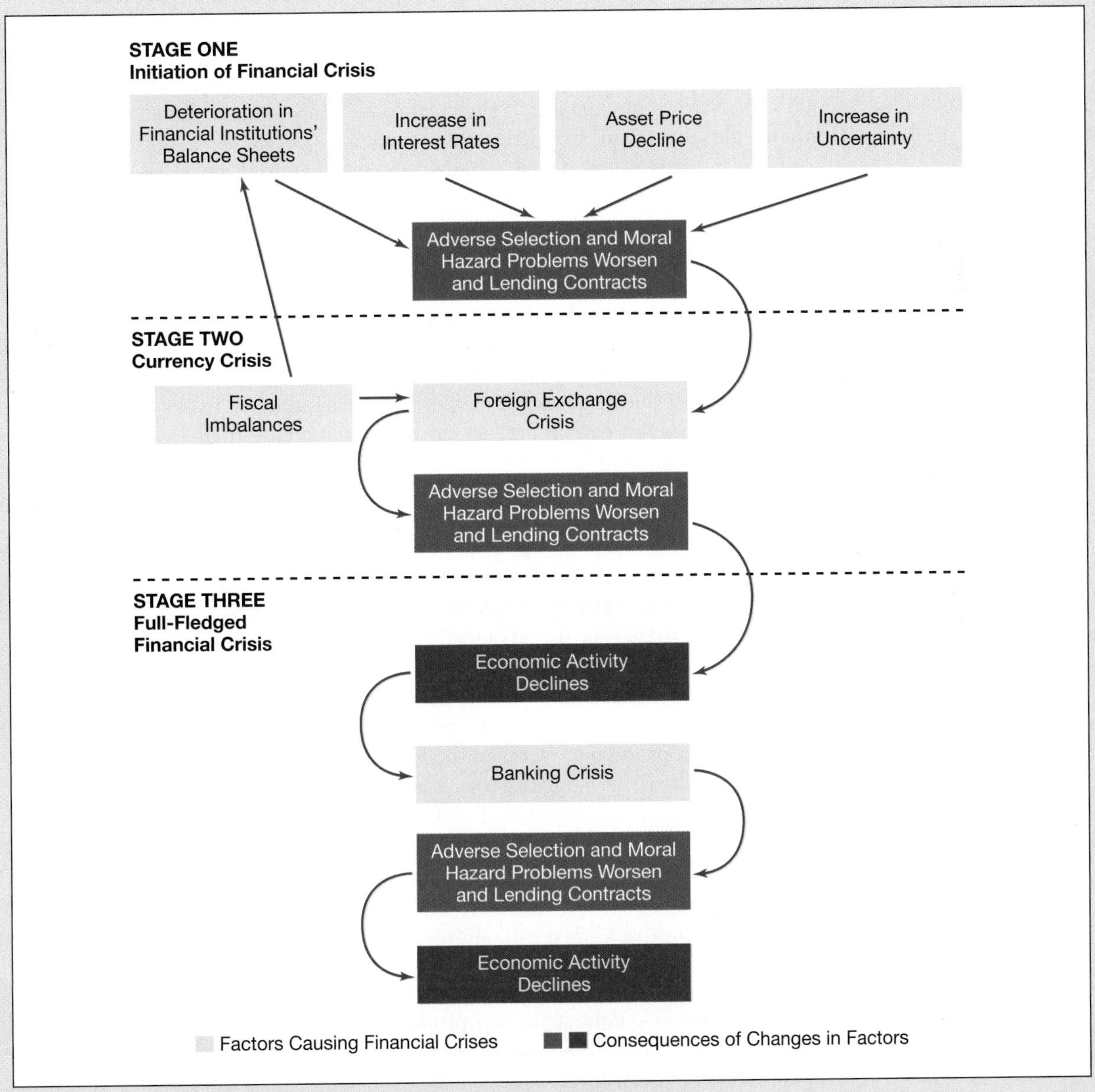

FIGURE 7 Sequence of Events in Emerging Market Financial Crises

The arrows trace the sequence of events during a financial crisis. The sections separated by the dashed horizontal lines show the different stages of a financial crisis.

Stage One: Initiation of Financial Crisis

Crises in advanced economies can be triggered by a number of different factors. But in emerging market countries, financial crises develop along two basic paths: either the mismanagement of financial liberalization and globalization or severe fiscal imbalances. The first path of mismanagement of financial liberalization/globalization is the most common culprit, precipitating the crises in Mexico in 1994 and many East Asian crises in 1997.

Path A: Mismanagement of Financial Liberalization/Globalization. As in the United States, the seeds of a financial crisis in emerging market countries are often sown when countries liberalize their financial systems. Countries liberalize by eliminating restrictions on financial institutions and markets domestically and opening up their economies to flows of capital and financial firms from other nations, a process called **financial globalization**. Countries often begin the process with solid fiscal policy. In the run-up to crisis, Mexico had a budget deficit of only 0.7% of GDP, a number to which most advanced countries would aspire. The countries in East Asia even ran budget surpluses before their crises struck.

It is often said that emerging market financial systems have a weak "credit culture," with ineffective screening and monitoring of borrowers and lax government supervision of banks. Lending booms that accompany financial liberalization in emerging market nations are typically marked by especially risky lending practices, sowing the seeds for enormous loan losses down the road. The financial globalization process adds fuel to the fire because it allows domestic banks to borrow abroad. Banks pay high interest rates to attract foreign capital and so can rapidly increase their lending. The capital inflow is further stimulated by government policies that fix the value of the domestic currency to the U.S. dollar, which provides foreign investors a sense of comfort.

Just as in advanced countries like the United States, the lending boom ends in a lending crash. Significant loan losses emerge from long periods of risky lending, weakening bank balance sheets and prompting banks to cut back on lending. The deterioration in bank balance sheets has an even greater negative impact on lending and economic activity than in advanced countries, which tend to have sophisticated securities markets and large nonbank financial sectors that can pick up the slack when banks falter. So as banks stop lending, no other players are available to solve adverse selection and moral hazard problems, and financial frictions increase (as shown by the arrow pointing from the first factor in the top row of Figure 7).

The story told so far suggests that a lending boom and crash are inevitable outcomes of financial liberalization and globalization in emerging market countries, but this is not the case. They occur only when an institutional weakness prevents the nation from successfully navigating the liberalization/globalization process. More specifically, if prudential regulation and supervision to limit excessive risk taking were strong, the lending boom and bust would not happen. Why are regulation and supervision typically weak? The answer is the principal–agent problem, discussed in the previous chapter, which encourages powerful domestic business interests to pervert the financial liberalization process. Politicians and prudential supervisors are ultimately agents for voters-taxpayers (principals)—that is, the goal of politicians and prudential supervisors is, or should be, to protect the taxpayers' interest. Taxpayers almost always bear the cost of bailing out the banking sector if losses occur.

Once financial markets have been liberalized, however, powerful business interests that own banks will want to prevent the supervisors from doing their job properly, and so prudential supervisors may not act in the public interest. Powerful business interests who contribute heavily to politicians' campaigns are often able to persuade politicians to weaken regulations that restrict their banks from engaging in high-risk/high-payoff strategies. After all, if bank owners achieve growth and expand bank lending rapidly, they stand to make a fortune. If the bank gets in trouble, though, the government is likely to bail it out and the taxpayer foots the bill. In addition, these business interests can also make sure that the supervisory agencies, even in the presence of tough regulations, lack the resources to effectively monitor banking institutions or to close them down.

Powerful business interests also have acted to prevent supervisors from doing their job properly in advanced countries like the United States. The weak institutional environment in emerging market countries adds to the perversion of the financial liberalization process. In emerging market economies, business interests are far more powerful than they are in advanced economies, where a better-educated public and a free press monitor (and punish) politicians and bureaucrats who are not acting in the public interest. Not surprisingly, then, the cost to society of the principal–agent problem we have been describing here is particularly high in emerging market economies.

Path B: Severe Fiscal Imbalances. The financing of government spending can also place emerging market economies on a path toward financial crisis. The financial crisis in Argentina in 2001–2002 is of this type; other crises—for example, in Russia in 1998, Ecuador in 1999, and Turkey in 2001—have some elements of this type of crisis, as well.

When Willie Sutton, a famous bank robber, was asked why he robbed banks, he answered, "Because that's where the money is." Governments in emerging market countries sometimes have the same attitude. When they face large fiscal imbalances and cannot finance their debt, they often cajole or force banks to purchase government debt. Investors who lose confidence in the ability of the government to repay this debt unload the bonds, which causes their prices to plummet. Banks that hold this debt then face a big hole on the asset side of their balance sheets, with a huge decline in their net worth. With less capital, these institutions will have fewer resources to lend and lending will decline. The situation can even be worse if the decline in bank capital leads to a bank panic, in which many banks fail at the same time. The result of severe fiscal imbalances is therefore a weakening of the banking system, which leads to a worsening of adverse selection and moral hazard problems (as shown by the arrow from the first factor in Stage Two of Figure 7).

Additional Factors. Other factors also often play a role in the first stage in crises. For example, another precipitating factor in some crises (e.g., the Mexican crisis) was a rise in interest rates from events abroad, such as a tightening of U.S. monetary policy. As we saw in Chapter 8, individuals and firms with the riskiest investment projects are those who are willing to pay the highest interest rates. Hence, when interest rates rise, good credit risks are less likely to want to borrow, whereas bad credit risks are still willing to borrow. Because of the resulting increase in adverse selection, lenders will no longer want to make loans.

Increases in interest rates can also have a part in promoting a financial crisis through their effect on **cash flow**, the difference between cash receipts and expenditures. A firm with sufficient cash flow can finance its projects internally, and no asymmetric information is present because it knows how good its own projects are. (Indeed, most businesses fund their investments with internal funds.) An increase in interest rates, and therefore in household and firm interest payments, decreases their cash flow. With less cash flow, the firm has fewer internal funds and must raise funds from an external source, say, a bank, which does not know the firm as well as its owners or managers. How can the bank be sure that the firm will invest in safe projects and not take on big risks and then be unlikely to pay back the loan? Because of this increased adverse selection and moral hazard, the bank may choose not to lend firms, even those with good risks, the money to undertake potentially profitable investments. Thus, increases in interest rates abroad that raise domestic interest rates increase financial frictions (as shown by the arrow from the second factor in the top row of Figure 7).

Because asset markets are not as large in emerging market countries as they are in advanced countries, they play a less prominent role in financial crises. Asset-price declines in the stock market do, nevertheless, decrease the net worth of firms and so increase adverse selection problems. Less collateral is available for lenders to seize and moral hazard problems are increased because, given their decreased net worth, the owners of the firm have less to lose if they engage in riskier activities than they did before the crisis. Asset-price declines can therefore worsen adverse selection and moral hazard problems directly and also indirectly by causing a deterioration in banks' balance sheets from asset write-downs (as shown by the arrow pointing from the third factor in the first row of Figure 7).

As in advanced countries, when an emerging market economy is in a recession or a prominent firm fails, people become more uncertain about the returns on investment projects. In emerging market countries, notoriously unstable political systems are another source of uncertainty. When uncertainty increases, it becomes hard for lenders to screen out good credit risks from bad and to monitor the activities of firms to whom they have loaned money, again worsening adverse selection and moral hazard problems (as shown by the arrow pointing from the last factor in the first row of Figure 7).

Stage Two: Currency Crisis

As the effects of any or all of the factors at the top of the diagram in Figure 7 build on each other, participants in the foreign exchange market sense an opportunity: They can make huge profits if they bet on a depreciation of the currency. A currency that is fixed against the U.S. dollar now becomes subject to a **speculative attack**, in which speculators engage in massive sales of the currency. As currency sales flood the market, supply far outstrips demand, the value of the currency collapses, and a currency crisis ensues (see the stage two section of Figure 7). High interest rates abroad, increases in uncertainty, and falling asset prices all play a role. The deterioration in bank balance sheets and severe fiscal imbalances, however, are the two key factors that trigger speculative attacks and plunge the economies into a full-scale, vicious downward spiral of currency crisis, financial crisis, and meltdown.

Deterioration of Bank Balance Sheets Triggers Currency Crises. When banks and other financial institutions are in trouble, governments have a limited number of options. Defending their currencies by raising interest rates should encourage capital inflows. If the government raises interest rates, banks must pay more to obtain funds. This increase in costs decreases bank profitability, which may lead them to insolvency. Thus when the banking system is in trouble, the government and central bank are now between a rock and a hard place: If they raise interest rates too much, they will destroy their already weakened banks and further cripple their economy. It they don't, they can't maintain the value of their currency.

Speculators in the market for foreign currency recognize the troubles in a country's financial sector and realize that when the government's ability to raise interest rates and defend the currency is so costly the government is likely to give up and allow the currency to depreciate. They will seize an almost sure-thing bet because the currency can only go downward in value. Speculators engage in a feeding frenzy and sell the currency in anticipation of its decline, which will provide them with huge profits. These sales rapidly use up the country's holdings of reserves of foreign currency because the country has to sell its reserves to buy the domestic currency and keep it from falling in value. Once the country's central bank has exhausted its holdings of foreign currency reserves, the cycle ends. It no longer has the resources to intervene in the foreign exchange market and must let the value of the domestic currency fall: That is, the government must allow a devaluation.

Severe Fiscal Imbalances Trigger Currency Crises. We have seen that severe fiscal imbalances can lead to a deterioration of bank balance sheets, and so can help produce a currency crisis along the lines described immediately above. Fiscal imbalances can also directly trigger a currency crisis. When government budget deficits spin out of control, foreign and domestic investors begin to suspect that the country may not be able to pay back its government debt and so will start pulling money out of the country and selling the domestic currency. Recognition that the fiscal situation is out of control thus results in a speculative attack against the currency, which eventually results in its collapse.

Stage Three: Full-Fledged Financial Crisis

In contrast to most advanced economies that typically denominate debt in domestic currency, emerging market economies denominate many debt contracts in foreign currency (dollars), while their assets are denominated in domestic currency, leading to what is known as **currency mismatch**. An unanticipated depreciation or devaluation of the domestic currency (for example, pesos) in emerging market countries increases the debt burden of domestic firms in terms of domestic currency. That is, it takes more pesos to pay back the dollarized debt. Because most firms price the goods and services they produce in domestic currency, the firms' assets do not rise in value in terms of pesos, while the debt does. Depreciation of the domestic currency increases the value of debt relative to assets, and the firm's net worth declines. The decline in net worth then increases the adverse selection and moral hazard problems described earlier. The rise in financial frictions, in turn, leads to a decline in investment and economic activity (as shown by the stage three section of Figure 7).

We now see how the institutional structure of debt markets in emerging market countries interacts with currency devaluations to propel the economies into full-fledged financial crises. A currency crisis, with its resulting depreciation of the currency, leads to a deterioration of firms' balance sheets, which sharply increases financial frictions. Economists often call a concurrent currency crisis and financial crisis the "twin crises."

The collapse of a currency also can result in higher inflation. The central banks in most emerging market countries, in contrast to those in advanced countries, have little credibility as inflation fighters. Thus, a sharp depreciation of the currency after a currency crisis leads to immediate upward pressure on import prices. A dramatic rise in both actual and expected inflation will likely follow. The resulting increase in interest payments causes reductions in firms' cash flow, which lead to increased adverse selection and moral hazard problems because firms are now more dependent on external funds to finance their investment. This asymmetric information analysis suggests that the resulting increase in financial frictions leads to a reduction in investment and economic activity.

As shown in Figure 7, further deterioration in the economy occurs. The collapse in economic activity and the deterioration of cash flow and of firm and household balance sheets mean that many debtors are no longer able to pay off their debts, resulting in substantial losses for banks. Sharp rises in interest rates also have a negative effect on banks' profitability and balance sheets. Even more problematic for the banks is the sharp increase in the value of their foreign currency–denominated liabilities after the devaluation. Thus, bank balance sheets are squeezed from both sides—the value of their assets falls as the value of their liabilities rises.

Under these circumstances, the banking system will often suffer a banking crisis in which many banks are likely to fail (as in the United States during the Great Depression). The banking crisis and the contributing factors in the credit markets explain a further worsening of adverse selection and moral hazard problems and a further collapse of lending and economic activity in the aftermath of the crisis.

APPLICATION ◆ Financial Crises in Mexico, 1994–1995; East Asia, 1997–1998; and Argentina, 2001–2002

When emerging market countries opened up their markets to the outside world in the 1990s, they had high hopes that globalization would stimulate economic growth and eventually make them rich. Instead of leading to high economic growth and reduced poverty, however, many of them experienced financial crises that were every bit as devastating as the Great Depression was in the United States.

The most dramatic of these crises were the Mexican crisis, which started in 1994; the East Asian crisis, which started in July 1997; and the Argentine crisis, which started in 2001. We now apply the asymmetric information analysis of the dynamics of financial crises to explain why a developing country can shift dramatically from a path of high growth before a financial crisis—as was true in Mexico and particularly the East Asian countries of Thailand, Malaysia, Indonesia, the Philippines, and South Korea—to a sharp decline in economic activity.[4]

Before their crises, Mexico and the East Asian countries had achieved a sound fiscal policy. The East Asian countries ran budget surpluses, and Mexico ran a budget deficit of less than 1% of GDP, a number that most advanced countries, including the United States, would be thrilled to have today. The key precipitating factor driving these crises was the deterioration in banks' balance sheets because of increasing loan losses. When financial markets in these countries were liberalized and opened to foreign capital markets in the early 1990s, a lending boom ensued. Bank credit to the private nonfinancial business sector accelerated sharply, with lending expanding at 15–30% per year. Because of weak supervision by bank regulators, aided and abetted by powerful business interests (see the Global box on "Perversion of the Financial Liberalization/Globalization Process: Chaebols and the South Korean Crisis") and a lack of expertise in screening and monitoring borrowers at banking institutions, losses on loans began to mount, causing an erosion of banks' net worth (capital). As a result of this erosion,

[4]This application does not examine four other crises, those in Russia, Brazil, Ecuador, and Turkey. Russia's financial crisis in August 1998 can also be explained with the asymmetric information story here, but it is more appropriate to view it as a symptom of a wider breakdown in the economy. The Brazilian crisis in January 1999 has features of a more traditional balance-of-payments crisis (see Chapter 21) rather than a financial crisis. Ecuador's crisis of 1999 and the Turkish crisis of 2001 have features of both types of emerging market financial crises discussed in the application, with mismanagement of financial liberalization/globalization and severe fiscal imbalances playing prominent roles..

Global The Perversion of the Financial Liberalization/Globalization Process: Chaebols and the South Korean Crisis

Although there are similarities with the perversion of the financial liberalization/globalization process that occurred in many emerging market economies, South Korea exhibited some particularly extraordinary elements because of the unique role of the chaebols, which are large, family-owned conglomerates. Because of their massive size—sales of the top five chaebols were nearly 50% of GDP right before the crisis—the chaebols were politically very powerful. The chaebols' influence extended the government safety net far beyond the financial system because the government had a long-standing policy of viewing the chaebols as being "too big to fail." With this policy in place, the chaebols would receive direct government assistance or directed credit if they got into trouble. Not surprisingly, given this guarantee, chaebols borrowed like crazy and were highly leveraged.

In the 1990s, the chaebols were in trouble: They weren't making any money. From 1993 to 1996, the return on assets for the top 30 chaebols was never much more than 3% (a comparable figure for U.S. corporations is 15–20%). In 1996 right before the crisis hit, the rate of return on assets had fallen to 0.2%. Furthermore, only the top five chaebols had any profits; the sixth to thirtieth chaebols never had a rate of return on assets much above 1% and in many years had negative rates of returns. With this poor profitability and the already high leverage, any banker would pull back on lending to these conglomerates if no government safety net existed. Because the banks knew the government would make good on the chaebols' loans if they were in default, the opposite occurred: Banks continued to lend to the chaebols and, in effect, threw good money after bad.

Even though the chaebols were getting substantial financing from commercial banks, it was not enough to feed their insatiable appetite for more credit. The chaebols decided that the way out of their troubles was to pursue growth, and they needed massive amounts of funds to do it. Even with the vaunted Korean national savings rate of over 30%, there just were not enough loanable funds to finance the chaebols' planned expansion. Where could they get it? The answer was in the international capital markets.

The chaebols encouraged the Korean government to accelerate the process of opening up Korean financial markets to foreign capital as part of the liberalization process. In 1993, the government expanded the ability of domestic banks to make loans denominated in foreign currency by expanding the types of loans for which this was possible. At the same time, the Korean government effectively allowed unlimited short-term foreign borrowing by financial institutions, but maintained quantity restrictions on long-term borrowing as a means of managing capital flows into the country. Opening up short-term but not long-term to foreign capital flows made no economic sense, as short-term capital flows make an emerging market economy financially fragile: *Short-term* capital can fly out of the country extremely rapidly if any whiff of a crisis is present.

Opening up primarily to short-term capital, however, made complete political sense. The chaebols needed the money, and it is much easier to borrow short-term funds at lower interest rates in the international market because long-term lending is much riskier for foreign creditors. Keeping restrictions on long-term international borrowing, however, allowed the government to say that it was still restricting foreign capital inflows and to claim that it was opening up to foreign capital in a prudent manner. In the aftermath of these changes, Korean banks opened 28 branches in foreign countries that gave them access to foreign funds.

Although Korean financial institutions now had access to foreign capital, the chaebols still had a problem. They were not allowed to own commercial banks, and so the chaebols might not obtain all of the bank loans that they needed. What was the answer? The chaebols needed to get their hands on financial institutions that they could own, that were allowed to borrow abroad, and that were subject to very little regulation. The financial institution could

(continued)

The Perversion of the Financial Liberalization/Globalization Process (continued)

then engage in connected lending by borrowing foreign funds and then lending them to the chaebols who owned the institution.

An existing type of financial institution specific to South Korea perfectly met the chaebols' requirements: the merchant bank. Merchant banking corporations were wholesale financial institutions that engaged in underwriting securities, leasing, and short-term lending to the corporate sector. They obtained funds for these loans by issuing bonds and commercial paper and by borrowing from interbank and foreign markets.

At the time of the Korean crisis, merchant banks were allowed to borrow abroad and were virtually unregulated. The chaebols saw their opportunity. Government officials, often lured with bribery and kickbacks, allowed many finance companies (some already owned by the chaebols) that were not allowed to borrow abroad to be converted into merchant banks, which could. In 1990 only six merchant banks existed and all of them were foreign affiliated. By 1997, after the chaebols had exercised their political influence, merchant banks numbered 30, 16 of which were owned by chaebols; 2 of which were foreign owned but in which chaebols were major stockholders; and 12 of which were independent of the chaebols, but Korean owned. The chaebols were now able to exploit connected lending with a vengeance. The merchant banks channeled massive amounts of funds to their chaebol owners, where they flowed into unproductive investments in steel, automobile production, and chemicals. When the loans went sour, the stage was set for a disastrous financial crisis.

banks had fewer resources to lend. This lack of lending led to a contraction of economic activity along the lines outlined in the previous section.

In contrast to Mexico and the East Asian countries, Argentina had a well-supervised banking system, and a lending boom did not occur before the crisis. The banks were in surprisingly good shape before the crisis, even though a severe recession had begun in 1998. This recession led to declining tax revenues and a widening gap between expenditures and taxes. The subsequent severe fiscal imbalances were so large that the government had trouble getting both citizens and foreigners to buy enough of its bonds, so it coerced banks into absorbing large amounts of government debt. Investors soon lost confidence in the ability of the Argentine government to repay this debt. The price of the debt plummeted, leaving big holes in banks' balance sheets. This weakening helped lead to a decline in lending and a contraction of economic activity, as in Mexico and East Asia.

Another precipitating factor in the Mexican and Argentine (but not East Asian) financial crises was a rise in interest rates abroad. Before the Mexican crisis, in February 1994, and before the Argentine crisis, in mid-1999, the Federal Reserve began a cycle of raising the federal funds rate to head off inflationary pressures. Although the Fed's monetary policy actions were successful in keeping U.S. inflation in check, they put upward pressure on interest rates in both Mexico and Argentina. The rise in interest rates in Mexico and Argentina directly added to increased adverse selection and moral hazard problems in their financial markets. As discussed earlier, it was more likely that the parties willing to take on the most risk would seek loans, and the higher interest payments led to a decline in firms' cash flow.

Also consistent with the U.S. experience, stock market declines and increases in uncertainty initiated and contributed to full-blown financial crises in Mexico, Thailand, South Korea, and Argentina. (The stock market declines in Malaysia, Indonesia, and the

Philippines, on the other hand, occurred simultaneously with the onset of these crises.) The Mexican economy was hit by political shocks in 1994 (specifically, the assassination of the ruling party's presidential candidate, Luis Colosio, and an uprising in the southern state of Chiapas) that created uncertainty, whereas the ongoing recession increased uncertainty in Argentina. Right before their crises, Thailand and South Korea experienced major failures of financial and nonfinancial firms that increased general uncertainty in financial markets.

As we have seen, an increase in uncertainty and a decrease in net worth as a result of a stock market decline promotes financial frictions. It becomes harder to screen out good from bad borrowers. The decline in net worth decreases the value of firms' collateral and increases their incentives to make risky investments because there is less equity to lose if the investments are unsuccessful. The increase in uncertainty and stock market declines that occurred before the crises, along with the deterioration in banks' balance sheets, worsened adverse selection and moral hazard problems and made the economies ripe for a serious financial emergency.

At this point, full-blown speculative attacks developed in the foreign exchange market, plunging these countries into a full-scale crisis. With the Colosio assassination, the Chiapas uprising, and the growing weakness in the banking sector, the Mexican peso came under attack. Even though the Mexican central bank intervened in the foreign exchange market and raised interest rates sharply, it was unable to stem the attacks and was forced to devalue the peso on December 20, 1994. In the case of Thailand, concerns about the large current account deficit and weakness in the Thai financial system—culminating with the failure of a major finance company, Finance One—led to a successful speculative attack. The Thai central bank was forced to allow the baht to depreciate in July 1997. Soon thereafter, speculative attacks developed against the other countries in the region, leading to the collapse of the Philippine peso, the Indonesian rupiah, the Malaysian ringgit, and the South Korean won. In Argentina, a full-scale banking panic began in October–November 2001. This, along with realization that the government was going to default on its debt, also led to a speculative attack on the Argentine peso, resulting in its collapse on January 6, 2002.

The institutional structure of debt markets in Mexico and East Asia now interacted with currency devaluations to propel the economies into full-fledged financial crises. Because so many firms in these countries had debt denominated in foreign currencies like the dollar and the yen, depreciation of their currencies resulted in increases in their indebtedness in domestic currency terms, even though the value of their assets remained unchanged. When the peso lost half its value by March 1995 and the Thai, Philippine, Malaysian, and South Korean currencies lost between one-third and one-half of their value by the beginning of 1998, firms' balance sheets took a big negative hit, causing a dramatic increase in adverse selection and moral hazard problems. This negative shock was especially severe for Indonesia and Argentina, which saw the value of their currencies fall by more than 70%, resulting in insolvency for firms with substantial amounts of debt denominated in foreign currencies.

The collapse of currencies also led to a rise in actual and expected inflation in these countries. Market interest rates rose sky-high (to around 100% in Mexico and Argentina). The resulting increase in interest payments caused reductions in household and firm cash flows. A feature of debt markets in emerging market countries, like those in Mexico, East Asia, and Argentina, is that debt contracts have very short durations, typically less than one month. Thus the rise in short-term interest rates in these countries made the effect on cash flow and hence on balance sheets substantial. As our asymmetric information analysis suggests, this deterioration in households' and firms' balance sheets increased financial frictions, making domestic and foreign lenders even less willing to lend.

Consistent with the theory of financial crises outlined in this chapter, the sharp decline in lending helped lead to a collapse of economic activity, with real GDP growth falling sharply. Further deterioration in the economy occurred because the collapse in economic activity and the deterioration in the cash flow and balance sheets of both firms and households worsened banking crises. Many firms and households were no longer able to pay off their debts, resulting in substantial losses for the banks. Even more problematic for the banks were their many short-term liabilities denominated in foreign currencies. The sharp increase in the value of these liabilities after the devaluation led to a further deterioration in the banks' balance sheets. Under these circumstances, the banking system would have collapsed in the absence of a government safety net—as it did in the United States during the Great Depression. With the assistance of the International Monetary Fund, these countries were in some cases able to protect depositors and avoid a bank panic. However, given the loss of bank capital and the need for the government to intervene to prop up the banks, the banks' ability to lend was nevertheless sharply curtailed. As we have seen, a banking crisis of this type hinders the ability of the banks to lend and also makes adverse selection and moral hazard problems worse in financial markets, because banks are less capable of playing their traditional financial intermediation role. The banking crisis, along with other factors that increased adverse selection and moral hazard problems in the credit markets of Mexico, East Asia, and Argentina, explains the collapse of lending and hence economic activity in the aftermath of the crisis.

Following their crises, Mexico began to recover in 1996, whereas the crisis countries in East Asia tentatively began their recovery in 1999, with a stronger recovery later. Argentina was still in a severe depression in 2003, but subsequently the economy bounced back. In all these countries, the economic hardship caused by financial crises was tremendous. Unemployment rose sharply, poverty increased substantially, and even the social fabric of the society was stretched thin. For example, after the financial crises, Mexico City and Buenos Aires became crime-ridden, and Indonesia experienced waves of ethnic violence. ◆

Summary

1. A financial crisis occurs when a particularly large disruption to information flows occurs in financial markets, with the result that financial frictions increase sharply, thereby rendering financial markets incapable of channeling funds to households and firms with productive investment opportunities, and causing a sharp contraction in economic activity.
2. Financial crises can start in advanced countries like the United States in several possible ways: mismanagement of financial liberalization/innovation, asset-price booms and busts, or a general increase in uncertainty when major financial institutions fail. The result is a substantial increase in adverse selection and moral hazard problems that lead to a contraction of lending and a decline in economic activity. The worsening business conditions and deterioration in bank balance sheets then triggers the second stage of the crisis, the simultaneous failure of many banking institutions, a banking crisis. The resulting decrease in the number of banks causes a loss of their information capital, leading to a further decline of lending and a spiraling down of the economy. In some instances, the resulting economic downturn leads to a sharp slide in prices, which increases the real liabilities of firms and households and therefore lowers their net worth, leading to a debt deflation. The further decline in borrowers' net worth worsens adverse selection and moral hazard problems, so that lending, investment spending, and aggregate economic activity remain depressed for a long time.

3. The most significant financial crisis in U.S. history, that which led to the Great Depression, involved several stages: a stock market crash, bank panics, worsening of asymmetric information problems, and finally a debt deflation.
4. The global financial crisis of 2007–2009 was triggered by mismanagement of financial innovations involving subprime residential mortgages and the bursting of a housing price bubble. The crisis spread globally, with substantial deterioration in banks' and other financial institutions' balance sheets, a run on the shadow banking system, and the failure of many high-profile firms.
5. The 2007–2009 financial crisis did not lead to a depression because of aggressive Federal Reserve actions and worldwide government intervention through bailouts of financial institutions.
6. Financial crises in emerging market countries develop along two basic paths: one involving the mismanagement of financial liberalization/globalization, which weakens bank balance sheets, and the other involving severe fiscal imbalances. Both lead to a speculative attack on the currency, and eventually to a currency crisis in which the value of domestic currency sharply declines. This decline causes a sharp rise in the debt burden of domestic firms, which leads to a decrease in firms' net worth, as well as increases in inflation and interest rates. Adverse selection and moral hazard problems then worsen, leading to a collapse of lending and economic activity. The worsening economic conditions and increases in interest rates result in substantial losses for banks, leading to a banking crisis, which further depresses lending and aggregate economic activity.
7. The financial crises in Mexico in 1994–1995, East Asia in 1997–1998, and Argentina in 2001–2002 led to great economic hardship and weakened the social fabric of these countries.

Key Terms

asset-price bubble, p. 188
bank panic, p. 188
cash flow, p. 203
credit boom, p. 186
credit default swaps, p. 193
credit spread, p. 191
currency mismatch, p. 205
debt deflation, p. 189
deleveraging, p. 186
emerging market economies, p. 200
financial crisis, p 185
financial engineering, p. 192
financial frictions, p. 185
financial globalization, p. 202
financial innovation, p. 186
financial liberalization, p. 186
fire sales, p. 188
fundamental economic values, p. 187
haircuts, p. 196
mortgage-backed securities, p. 192
originate-to-distribute, p. 192
repurchase agreements (repos), p. 196
securitization, p. 192
shadow banking system, p. 196
speculative attack, p. 204
structured credit products, p. 192
subprime mortgages, p. 192
Troubled Asset Relief Program (TARP), p. 199

Questions

All questions are available in MyEconLab *at* www.myeconlab.com.

1. How does the concept of asymmetric information help to define a financial crisis?
2. How can a bursting of an asset-price bubble in the stock market help trigger a financial crisis?
3. How does an unanticipated decline in the price level cause a drop in lending?
4. How can a decline in real estate prices cause deleveraging and a decline in lending?
5. How does a deterioration in balance sheets of financial institutions and the simultaneous failures of these institutions cause a decline in economic activity?
6. How does a general increase in uncertainty as a result of a failure of a major financial institution lead to an increase in adverse selection and moral hazard problems?

7. Why do credit spreads rise significantly during a financial crisis?
8. How can government fiscal imbalances lead to a financial crisis?
9. How can financial liberalizations lead to financial crises?
10. What role does weak financial regulation and supervision play in causing financial crises?
11. Describe two similarities and two differences between the United States' experiences during the Great Depression and the financial crisis of 2007–2009.
12. What do you think prevented the financial crisis of 2007–2009 from becoming a depression?
13. What technological innovations led to the development of the subprime mortgage market?
14. Why is the originate-to-distribute business model subject to the principal–agent problem?
15. "Financial engineering always leads to a more efficient financial system." Is this statement true, false, or uncertain?
16. How did a decline in housing prices help trigger the subprime financial crisis starting in 2007?
17. What is the *shadow banking system,* and why is it an important part of the 2007–2009 financial crisis?
18. Why would haircuts on collateral increase sharply during a financial crisis? How would this lead to fire sales on assets?
19. What similarities exist between experiences in the United States and in Ireland during the 2007–2009 financial crisis?
20. When can a decline in the value of a country's currency exacerbate adverse selection and moral hazard problems? Why?
21. Why do debt deflations occur in advanced countries, but not in emerging market countries?
22. How can opening up to capital flows from abroad lead to a financial crisis?
23. Why does the "twin crises" phenomenon of currency and banking crises occur in emerging market countries?
24. How can a currency crisis lead to higher interest rates?
25. How can a deterioration in bank balance sheets lead to a currency crisis?

Web Exercises

1. This chapter discusses how an understanding of adverse selection and moral hazard can help us better understand financial crises. The greatest financial crisis faced by the United States was the Great Depression of 1929–1933. Go to www.amatecon.com/greatdepression.html. This site contains a brief discussion of the factors that led to the Great Depression. Write a one-page summary explaining how adverse selection and moral hazard contributed to the Great Depression.
2. Go to the International Monetary Fund's Financial Crisis page at www.imf.org/external/np/exr/key/finstab.htm. Report on the most recent three countries that the IMF has given emergency loans in response to a financial crisis. According to the IMF, what caused the crisis in each country?
3. One of the countries hardest hit by the global financial crisis of 2008 was Iceland. Go to http://assets.opencrs.com/ rpts/RS22988_20081120.pdf and summarize the causes and events that led to the crisis in Iceland.

Web References

www.amatecon.com/gd/gdtimeline.html

A time line of the Great Depression.

www.imf.org

The International Monetary Fund is an organization of 185 countries that works on global policy coordination (both monetary and trade), stable and sustainable economic prosperity, and the reduction of poverty.

assets.opencrs.com/rpts/RS22988_20081120.pdf

The Congressional Research Service (CRS) report to Congress about Iceland's financial crisis of 2008.

10 Banking and the Management of Financial Institutions

Preview

Because banking plays such a major role in channeling funds to borrowers with productive investment opportunities, this financial activity is important in ensuring that the financial system and the economy run smoothly and efficiently. In the United States, banks (depository institutions) supply on the order of $10 trillion in credit annually. They provide loans to businesses, help us finance our college educations or the purchase of a new car or home, and provide us with services such as checking and savings accounts, debit cards, and ATMs.

In this chapter, we examine how banking is conducted to earn the highest profits possible: how and why banks make loans, how they acquire funds and manage their assets and liabilities (debts), and how they earn income. Although we focus on commercial banking, because this is the most important financial intermediary activity, many of the same principles are applicable to other types of financial intermediation.

THE BANK BALANCE SHEET

To understand how banking works, we start by looking at the bank **balance sheet**, a list of the bank's assets and liabilities. As the name implies, this list balances; that is, it has the characteristic that

$$\text{total assets} = \text{total liabilities} + \text{capital}$$

A bank's balance sheet is also a list of its *sources* of bank funds (liabilities) and *uses* to which the funds are put (assets). Banks obtain funds by borrowing and by issuing other liabilities, such as deposits. They then use these funds to acquire assets such as securities and loans. Banks make profits by earning interest on their asset holdings of securities and loans that is higher than the interest and other expenses on their liabilities. The balance sheet of all commercial banks as of June 2011 appears in Table 1.

Liabilities

A bank acquires funds by issuing (selling) liabilities, such as deposits, which are the *sources of funds* the bank uses. The funds obtained from issuing liabilities are used to purchase income-earning assets.

Checkable Deposits Checkable deposits are bank accounts that allow the owner of the account to write checks to third parties. Checkable deposits include all accounts

TABLE 1

Balance Sheet of All Commercial Banks (items as a percentage of the total, June 2011

Assets (Uses of Funds)*		Liabilities (Sources of Funds)	
Reserves and cash items	15%	Checkable deposits	10%
Securities		Nontransaction deposits	
U.S. government and agency	13	Small-denomination time deposits (< $100,000) + savings deposits	41
State and local government and other securities	6	Large-denomination time deposits	14
Loans		Borrowings	23
Commercial and industrial	10	Bank capital	12
Real estate	28		
Consumer	9		
Interbank	1		
Other	8		
Other assets (for example, physical capital)	9		
Total	100	Total	100

*In order of decreasing liquidity.

Source: www.federalreserve.gov/releases/h8/current/.

on which checks can be drawn: non–interest-bearing checking accounts (demand deposits), interest-bearing NOW (negotiable order of withdrawal) accounts, and money market deposit accounts (MMDAs). Introduced with the Depository Institutions Act in 1982, MMDAs have features similar to those of money market mutual funds and are included in the checkable deposits category. However, MMDAs are not subject to reserve requirements (discussed later in the chapter), as checkable deposits are, and are not included in the M1 definition of money. Table 1 shows that the category of checkable deposits are 10% of bank liabilities. Once checkable deposits were the most important source of bank funds (more than 60% of bank liabilities in 1960), but with the appearance of new, more attractive financial instruments, such as money market deposit accounts, the share of checkable deposits in total bank liabilities has shrunk over time.

Checkable deposits and money market deposit accounts are payable on demand; that is, if a depositor shows up at the bank and requests payment by making a withdrawal, the bank must pay the depositor immediately. Similarly, if a person who receives a check written on an account from a bank presents that check at the bank, it must pay the funds out immediately (or credit them to that person's account).

A checkable deposit is an asset for the depositor because it is part of his or her wealth. Because the depositor can withdraw funds and the bank is obligated to pay, checkable deposits are a liability for the bank. They are usually the lowest-cost source of bank funds because depositors are willing to forgo some interest to have access to a liquid asset that they can use to make purchases. The bank's costs of maintaining checkable deposits include interest payments and the costs incurred in servicing these accounts—processing, preparing, and sending out monthly statements; providing efficient tellers (human or otherwise); maintaining an impressive building and conveniently located branches; and advertising and marketing to entice customers to deposit their funds with a given bank. In recent years, interest paid on deposits (checkable and nontransaction) has accounted for around 25% of total bank operating expenses, whereas the costs involved in servicing accounts (employee salaries, building rent, and so on) have been approximately 50% of operating expenses.

Nontransaction Deposits Nontransaction deposits are the primary source of bank funds (55% of bank liabilities in Table 1). Owners cannot write checks on nontransaction deposits, but the interest rates paid on these deposits are usually higher than those on checkable deposits. There are two basic types of nontransaction deposits: savings accounts and time deposits (also called certificates of deposit, or CDs).

Savings accounts were once the most common type of nontransaction deposit. In these accounts, to which funds can be added or from which funds can be withdrawn at any time, transactions and interest payments are recorded in a monthly statement or in a passbook held by the owner of the account.

Time deposits have a fixed maturity length, ranging from several months to over five years, and assess substantial penalties for early withdrawal (the forfeiture of several months' interest). Small-denomination time deposits (deposits of less than $100,000) are less liquid for the depositor than passbook savings, earn higher interest rates, and are a more costly source of funds for the banks.

Large-denomination time deposits (CDs) are available in denominations of $100,000 or more and are typically bought by corporations or other banks. Large-denomination CDs are negotiable; like bonds, they can be resold in a secondary market before they mature. For this reason, negotiable CDs are held by corporations, money market mutual funds, and other financial institutions as alternative assets to Treasury bills and other short-term bonds. Since 1961, when they first appeared, negotiable CDs have become an important source of bank funds (14% in Table 1).

Borrowings Banks also obtain funds by borrowing from the Federal Reserve System, the Federal Home Loan banks, other banks, and corporations. Borrowings from the Fed are called **discount loans** (also known as *advances*). Banks also borrow reserves overnight in the federal (fed) funds market from other U.S. banks and financial institutions. Banks borrow funds overnight to have enough deposits at the Federal Reserve to meet the amount required by the Fed. (The *federal funds* designation is somewhat confusing, because these loans are not made by the federal government or by the Federal Reserve, but rather by banks to other banks.) Other sources of borrowed funds are loans made to banks by their parent companies (bank holding companies), loan arrangements with corporations (such as repurchase agreements), and borrowings of Eurodollars (deposits denominated in U.S. dollars residing in foreign banks or foreign branches of U.S. banks). Borrowings have become a more important source of bank funds over time: In 1960, they made up only 2% of bank liabilities; currently, they are 23% of bank liabilities.

Bank Capital The final category on the liabilities side of the balance sheet is bank capital, the bank's net worth, which equals the difference between total assets and liabilities (12% of total bank assets in Table 1). Bank capital is raised by selling new equity (stock) or from retained earnings. A bank's capital is a cushion against a drop in the value of its assets, which could force the bank into insolvency (having liabilities in excess of assets, meaning that the bank can be forced into liquidation).

Assets

A bank uses the funds that it has acquired by issuing liabilities to purchase income-earning assets. Bank assets are thus naturally referred to as *uses of funds*, and the interest payments earned on them are what enable banks to make profits.

Reserves All banks hold some of the funds they acquire as deposits in an account at the Fed. **Reserves** are these deposits plus currency that is physically held by banks (called **vault cash** because it is stored in bank vaults overnight). Although reserves earn a low interest rate, banks hold them for two reasons. First, some reserves, called **required reserves**, are held because of **reserve requirements**, the regulation that for every dollar of checkable deposits at a bank, a certain fraction (10 cents, for example) must be kept as reserves. This fraction (10% in the example) is called the **required reserve ratio**. Banks hold additional reserves, called **excess reserves**, because they are the most liquid of all bank assets and a bank can use them to meet its obligations when funds are withdrawn, either directly by a depositor or indirectly when a check is written on an account.

Cash Items in Process of Collection Suppose that a check written on an account at another bank is deposited in your bank and the funds for this check have not yet been received (collected) from the other bank. The check is classified as a cash item in process of collection, and it is an asset for your bank because it is a claim on another bank for funds that will be paid within a few days.

Deposits at Other Banks Many small banks hold deposits in larger banks in exchange for a variety of services, including check collection, foreign exchange transactions, and help with securities purchases. This is an aspect of a system called *correspondent banking*.

Collectively, reserves, cash items in process of collection, and deposits at other banks are referred to as *cash items*. As can be seen in Table 1, in June 2011, they made up 15% of total assets.

Securities A bank's holdings of securities are an important income-earning asset: Securities (made up entirely of debt instruments for commercial banks, because banks are not allowed to hold stock) account for 19% of bank assets in Table 1, and they provide commercial banks with about 10% of their revenue. These securities can be classified into three categories: U.S. government and agency securities, state and local government securities, and other securities. The U.S. government and agency securities are the most liquid because they can be easily traded and converted into cash with low transaction costs. Because of their high liquidity, short-term U.S. government securities are called **secondary reserves**.

Banks hold state and local government securities because state and local governments are more likely to do business with banks that hold their securities. State and local government and other securities are both less marketable (less liquid) and riskier than U.S. government securities, primarily because of default risk: Some possibility exists that the issuer of the securities may not be able to make its interest payments or pay back the face value of the securities when they mature.

Loans Banks make their profits primarily by issuing loans. In Table 1, some 56% of bank assets are in the form of loans, and in recent years they have generally produced more than half of bank revenues. A loan is a liability for the individual or corporation receiving it, but an asset for a bank, because it provides income to the bank. Loans are typically less liquid than other assets, because they cannot be turned into cash until the loan matures. If the bank makes a one-year loan, for example, it cannot get its funds back until the loan comes due in one year. Loans also have a higher probability of default than other assets. Because of the lack of liquidity and higher default risk, the bank earns its highest return on loans.

As you saw in Table 1, the largest categories of loans for commercial banks are commercial and industrial loans made to businesses and real estate loans. Commercial banks also make consumer loans and lend to each other. The bulk of these interbank loans are overnight loans lent in the federal funds market. The major difference in the balance sheets of the various categories of depository institutions is primarily in the type of loan in which they specialize. Savings and loans and mutual savings banks, for example, specialize in residential mortgages, while credit unions tend to make consumer loans.

Other Assets The physical capital (bank buildings, computers, and other equipment) owned by banks is included in this category.

BASIC BANKING

Before proceeding to a more detailed study of how a bank manages its assets and liabilities to make the highest profit, you should understand the basic operation of a bank.

In general terms, banks make profits by selling liabilities with one set of characteristics (a particular combination of liquidity, risk, size, and return) and using the proceeds to buy assets with a different set of characteristics. This process is often referred to as *asset transformation*. For example, a savings deposit held by one person can provide the funds that enable the bank to make a mortgage loan to another person. The bank has, in effect, transformed the savings deposit (an asset held by the depositor) into a mortgage loan (an asset held by the bank). Another way to describe this process of asset transformation is to say that the bank "borrows short and lends long" because it makes long-term loans and funds them by issuing short-dated deposits.

The process of transforming assets and providing a set of services (check clearing, record keeping, credit analysis, and so forth) is like any other production process in a firm. If the bank produces desirable services at low cost and earns substantial income on its assets, it earns profits; if not, the bank suffers losses.

To make our analysis of the operation of a bank more concrete, we use a tool called a **T-account**. A T-account is a simplified balance sheet, with lines in the form of a T, that lists only the changes that occur in balance sheet items starting from some initial balance sheet position. Let's say that Jane Brown has heard that the First National Bank provides excellent service, so she opens a checking account with a $100 bill. She now has a $100 checkable deposit at the bank, which shows up as a $100 liability on the bank's balance sheet. The bank now puts her $100 bill into its vault so that the bank's assets rise by the $100 increase in vault cash. The T-account for the bank looks like this:

First National Bank			
Assets		**Liabilities**	
Vault cash	+$100	Checkable deposits	+$100

Because vault cash is also part of the bank's reserves, we can rewrite the T-account as follows:

Assets		**Liabilities**	
Reserves	+$100	Checkable deposits	+$100

Note that Jane Brown's opening of a checking account leads to ***an increase in the bank's reserves equal to the increase in checkable deposits***.

If Jane had opened her account with a $100 check written on an account at another bank, say, the Second National Bank, we would get the same result. The initial effect on the T-account of the First National Bank is as follows:

Assets		**Liabilities**	
Cash items in process of collection	+$100	Checkable deposits	+$100

Checkable deposits increase by $100 as before, but now the First National Bank is owed $100 by the Second National Bank. This asset for the First National Bank is entered in the T-account as $100 of cash items in process of collection because the First National Bank will now try to collect the funds that it is owed. It could go directly to the Second National Bank and ask for payment of the funds, but if the two banks are in separate states, that would be a time-consuming and costly process. Instead, the First National Bank deposits the check in its account at the Fed, and the Fed collects the funds from the Second National Bank. The result is that the Fed transfers $100 of reserves from the Second National Bank to the First National Bank, and the final balance sheet positions of the two banks are as follows:

First National Bank				Second National Bank			
Assets		**Liabilities**		**Assets**		**Liabilities**	
Reserves	+$100	Checkable deposits	+$100	Reserves	−$100	Checkable deposits	−$100

The process initiated by Jane Brown can be summarized as follows: When a check written on an account at one bank is deposited in another, the bank receiving the deposit gains reserves equal to the amount of the check, while the bank on which the check is written sees its reserves fall by the same amount. Therefore, ***when a bank receives additional deposits, it gains an equal amount of reserves; when it loses deposits, it loses an equal amount of reserves.***

Now that you understand how banks gain and lose reserves, we can examine how a bank rearranges its balance sheet to make a profit when it experiences a change in its deposits. Let's return to the situation when the First National Bank has just received the extra $100 of checkable deposits. As you know, the bank is obliged to keep a certain fraction of its checkable deposits as required reserves. If the fraction (the required reserve ratio) is 10%, the First National Bank's required reserves have increased by $10, and we can rewrite its T-account as follows:

First National Bank

Assets		Liabilities	
Required reserves	+$10	Checkable deposits	+$100
Excess reserves	+$90		

Let's see how well the bank is doing as a result of the additional checkable deposits. Servicing the extra $100 of checkable deposits is costly, because the bank must keep records, pay tellers, pay for check clearing, and so forth. Because reserves earn little interest, the bank is taking a loss! The situation is even worse if the bank makes interest payments on the deposits, as with NOW accounts. To make a profit, the bank must put to productive use all or part of the $90 of excess reserves it has available. One way to do this is to invest in securities. The other is to make loans; as we have seen, loans account for approximately 60% of the total value of bank assets (uses of funds). Because lenders are subject to the asymmetric information problems of adverse selection and moral hazard (discussed in Chapter 8), banks take steps to reduce the incidence and severity of these problems. Bank loan officers evaluate potential borrowers using what are called the "five C's": character, capacity (ability to repay), collateral, conditions (in the local and national economies), and capital (net worth) before they agree to lend. (Later in this chapter is a more detailed discussion of the methods banks use to reduce the risk involved in lending.)

Let's assume that the bank chooses not to hold any excess reserves but to make loans instead. The T-account then looks like this:

Assets		Liabilities	
Required reserves	+$10	Checkable deposits	+$100
Loans	+$90		

The bank is now making a profit because it holds short-term liabilities, such as checkable deposits, and uses the proceeds to fund longer-term assets, such as loans with higher interest rates. As mentioned earlier, this process of asset transformation is frequently described by saying that banks are in the business of "borrowing short and lending long." For example, if the loans have an interest rate of 10% per year, the bank earns $9 in income from its loans over the year. If the $100 of checkable deposits is in a NOW account with a 5% interest rate and it costs another $3 per year to service the account, the cost per year of these deposits is $8. The bank's profit on the new deposits is then $1 per year, plus any interest that is paid on required reserves.

GENERAL PRINCIPLES OF BANK MANAGEMENT

Now that you have some idea of how a bank operates, let's look at how a bank manages its assets and liabilities to earn the highest possible profit. The bank manager has four primary concerns. The first is to make sure that the bank has enough ready cash to pay its depositors when there are **deposit outflows**—that is, when deposits are lost because depositors make withdrawals and demand payment. To keep enough cash on hand, the bank must engage in **liquidity management**, the acquisition of sufficiently liquid assets to meet the bank's obligations to depositors. Second, the bank manager must pursue an acceptably low level of risk by acquiring assets that have a low rate of default and by diversifying asset holdings (**asset management**). The third concern is to acquire funds at low cost (**liability management**). Finally, the manager must decide the amount of capital the bank should maintain and then acquire the needed capital (**capital adequacy management**).

To understand bank and other financial institution management fully, we must go beyond the general principles of bank asset and liability management described next and look in more detail at how a financial institution manages its assets. The two sections following this one provide an in-depth discussion of how a financial institution manages **credit risk**, the risk arising because borrowers may default, and how it manages **interest-rate risk**, the riskiness of earnings and returns on bank assets that results from interest-rate changes.

Liquidity Management and the Role of Reserves

Let's see how a typical bank, the First National Bank, can deal with deposit outflows that occur when its depositors withdraw cash from checking or savings accounts or write checks that are deposited in other banks. In the example that follows, we assume that the bank has ample excess reserves and that all deposits have the same required reserve ratio of 10% (the bank is required to keep 10% of deposits as reserves). Suppose that the First National Bank's initial balance sheet is as follows:

Assets		**Liabilities**	
Reserves	$20 million	Deposits	$100 million
Loans	$80 million	Bank capital	$ 10 million
Securities	$10 million		

The bank's required reserves are 10% of $100 million, or $10 million. Given that it holds $20 million of reserves, the First National Bank has excess reserves of $10 million.

If a deposit outflow of $10 million occurs, the bank's balance sheet becomes

Assets		Liabilities	
Reserves	$10 million	Deposits	$90 million
Loans	$80 million	Bank capital	$10 million
Securities	$10 million		

The bank loses $10 million of deposits ***and*** $10 million of reserves, but because its required reserves are now 10% of only $90 million ($9 million), its reserves still exceed this amount by $1 million. In short, ***if a bank has ample excess reserves, a deposit outflow does not necessitate changes in other parts of its balance sheet.***

The situation is quite different when a bank holds insufficient excess reserves. Let's assume that instead of initially holding $10 million in excess reserves, the First National Bank makes additional loans of $10 million, so that it holds no excess reserves. Its initial balance sheet would then be

Assets		Liabilities	
Reserves	$10 million	Deposits	$100 million
Loans	$90 million	Bank capital	$ 10 million
Securities	$10 million		

When it suffers the $10 million deposit outflow, its balance sheet becomes

Assets		Liabilities	
Reserves	$ 0	Deposits	$90 million
Loans	$90 million	Bank capital	$10 million
Securities	$10 million		

After $10 million has been withdrawn from deposits and hence reserves, the bank has a problem: It has a reserve requirement of 10% of $90 million, or $9 million, but it has no reserves! To eliminate this shortfall, the bank has four basic options. One is to acquire reserves to meet a deposit outflow by borrowing them from other banks in the federal funds market or by borrowing from corporations.[1] If the First National

[1]One way that the First National Bank can borrow from other banks and corporations is by selling negotiable certificates of deposit. This method for obtaining funds is discussed in the section on liability management.

Bank acquires the $9 million shortfall in reserves by borrowing it from other banks or corporations, its balance sheet becomes

Assets		Liabilities	
Reserves	$ 9 million	Deposits	$90 million
Loans	$90 million	Borrowings from other banks or corporations	$ 9 million
Securities	$10 million	Bank capital	$10 million

The cost of this activity is the interest rate on these borrowings, such as the federal funds rate.

A second alternative is for the bank to sell some of its securities to help cover the deposit outflow. For example, it might sell $9 million of its securities and deposit the proceeds with the Fed, resulting in the following balance sheet:

Assets		Liabilities	
Reserves	$ 9 million	Deposits	$90 million
Loans	$90 million	Bank capital	$10 million
Securities	$ 1 million		

The bank incurs some brokerage and other transaction costs when it sells these securities. The U.S. government securities that are classified as secondary reserves are very liquid, so the transaction costs of selling them are quite modest. However, the other securities the bank holds are less liquid, and the transaction cost can be appreciably higher.

A third way that the bank can meet a deposit outflow is to acquire reserves by borrowing from the Fed. In our example, the First National Bank could leave its security and loan holdings the same and borrow $9 million in discount loans from the Fed. Its balance sheet would then be

Assets		Liabilities	
Reserves	$ 9 million	Deposits	$90 million
Loans	$90 million	Borrowings from the Fed	$ 9 million
Securities	$10 million	Bank capital	$10 million

The cost associated with discount loans is the interest rate that must be paid to the Fed (called the **discount rate**).

Finally, a bank can acquire the $9 million of reserves to meet the deposit outflow by reducing its loans by this amount and depositing the $9 million it then receives with the Fed, thereby increasing its reserves by $9 million. This transaction changes the balance sheet as follows:

Assets		Liabilities	
Reserves	$ 9 million	Deposits	$90 million
Loans	$81 million	Bank capital	$10 million
Securities	$10 million		

The First National Bank is once again in good shape because its $9 million of reserves satisfies the reserve requirement.

However, this process of reducing its loans is the bank's costliest way of acquiring reserves when a deposit outflow exists. If the First National Bank has numerous short-term loans renewed at fairly short intervals, it can reduce its total amount of loans outstanding fairly quickly by *calling in* loans—that is, by not renewing some loans when they come due. Unfortunately for the bank, this is likely to antagonize the customers whose loans are not being renewed because they have not done anything to deserve such treatment. Indeed, they are likely to take their business elsewhere in the future, a very costly consequence for the bank.

A second method for reducing its loans is for the bank to sell them off to other banks. Again, this is very costly because other banks do not personally know the customers who have taken out the loans and so may not be willing to buy the loans at their full value (This is just the lemons adverse selection problem described in Chapter 8.)

The foregoing discussion explains why banks hold excess reserves even though loans or securities earn a higher return. When a deposit outflow occurs, holding excess reserves allows the bank to escape the costs of (1) borrowing from other banks or corporations, (2) selling securities, (3) borrowing from the Fed, or (4) calling in or selling off loans. ***Excess reserves are insurance against the costs associated with deposit outflows. The higher the costs associated with deposit outflows, the more excess reserves banks will want to hold.***

Just as you and I would be willing to pay an insurance company to insure us against a casualty loss such as the theft of a car, a bank is willing to pay the cost of holding excess reserves (the opportunity cost, that is, the earnings forgone by not holding income-earning assets, such as loans or securities) to insure against losses due to deposit outflows. Because excess reserves, like insurance, have a cost, banks also take other steps to protect themselves; for example, they might shift their holdings of assets to more liquid securities (secondary reserves).

Asset Management

Now that you understand why a bank has a need for liquidity, we can examine the basic strategy a bank pursues in managing its assets. To maximize its profits, a bank must simultaneously seek the highest returns possible on loans and securities, reduce risk, and make adequate provisions for liquidity by holding liquid assets. Banks try to accomplish these three goals in four basic ways.

First, banks try to find borrowers who will pay high interest rates and are unlikely to default on their loans. They seek out loan business by advertising their borrowing rates and by approaching corporations directly to solicit loans. It is up to the bank's loan officer to decide if potential borrowers are good credit risks who will make interest and principal payments on time (i.e., engage in screening to reduce the adverse selection problem). Typically, banks are conservative in their loan policies; the default rate is usually less than 1%. It is important, however, that banks not be so conservative that they miss out on attractive lending opportunities that earn high interest rates.

Second, banks try to purchase securities with high returns and low risk. Third, in managing their assets, banks must attempt to lower risk by diversifying. They accomplish this by purchasing many different types of assets (short- and long-term, U.S. Treasury, and municipal bonds) and approving many types of loans to a number of customers. Banks that have not sufficiently sought the benefits of diversification often come to regret it later. For example, banks that had overspecialized in making loans to energy companies, real estate developers, or farmers suffered huge losses in the 1980s, with the slump in energy, property, and farm prices. Indeed, many of these banks went broke because they had "put too many eggs in one basket."

Finally, the bank must manage the liquidity of its assets so that it can meet deposit outflows and still satisfy its reserve requirements without bearing huge costs. This means that it will hold liquid securities even if they earn a somewhat lower return than other assets. The bank must decide, for example, how much in excess reserves must be held to avoid costs from a deposit outflow. In addition, it will want to hold U.S. government securities as secondary reserves so that even if a deposit outflow forces some costs on the bank, these will not be terribly high. Again, it is not wise for a bank to be too conservative. If it avoids all costs associated with deposit outflows by holding only excess reserves, the bank suffers losses because reserves earn low interest, while the bank's liabilities are costly to maintain. The bank must balance its desire for liquidity against the increased earnings that can be obtained from less liquid assets, such as loans.

Liability Management

Before the 1960s, liability management was a staid affair: For the most part, banks took their liabilities as fixed and spent their time trying to achieve an optimal mix of assets. There were two main reasons for the emphasis on asset management. First, more than 60% of bank funds were obtained through checkable (demand) deposits that by law could not pay any interest. Thus banks could not actively compete with one another for these deposits by paying interest on them, and so their amount was effectively a given for an individual bank. Second, because the markets for making overnight loans between banks were not well developed, banks rarely borrowed from other banks to meet their reserve needs.

Starting in the 1960s, however, large banks (called **money center banks**) in key financial centers, such as New York, Chicago, and San Francisco, began to explore ways in which the liabilities on their balance sheets could provide them with reserves and liquidity. This move led to an expansion of overnight loan markets, such as the federal funds market, and the development of new financial instruments, such as negotiable CDs (first developed in 1961), which enabled money center banks to acquire funds quickly.[2]

[2]Because small banks are not as well known as money center banks and so might be a higher credit risk, they find it harder to raise funds in the negotiable CD market. Hence they do not engage nearly as actively in liability management.

This new flexibility in liability management meant that banks could take a different approach to bank management. They no longer needed to depend on checkable deposits as the primary source of bank funds and as a result no longer treated their sources of funds (liabilities) as given. Instead, they aggressively set target goals for their asset growth and tried to acquire funds (by issuing liabilities) as they were needed.

For example, today, when a money center bank finds an attractive loan opportunity, it can acquire funds by selling a negotiable CD. Or, if it has a reserve shortfall, it can borrow funds from another bank in the federal funds market without incurring high transaction costs. The federal funds market can also be used to finance loans. Because of the increased importance of liability management, most banks now manage both sides of the balance sheet together in an *asset–liability management (ALM) committee*.

The greater emphasis on liability management explains some of the important changes over the past three decades in the composition of banks' balance sheets. While negotiable CDs and bank borrowings have greatly increased in importance as a source of bank funds in recent years (rising from 2% of bank liabilities in 1960 to 34% by mid-2011), checkable deposits have decreased in importance (from 61% of bank liabilities in 1960 to 10% by mid-2011). Newfound flexibility in liability management and the search for higher profits have also stimulated banks to increase the proportion of their assets held in loans, which earn higher income (from 46% of bank assets in 1960 to 56% by mid-2011).

Capital Adequacy Management

Banks have to make decisions about the amount of capital they need to hold for three reasons. First, bank capital helps prevent *bank failure*, a situation in which the bank cannot satisfy its obligations to pay its depositors and other creditors and so goes out of business. Second, the amount of capital affects returns for the owners (equity holders) of the bank. Third, a minimum amount of bank capital (bank capital requirements) is required by regulatory authorities.

How Bank Capital Helps Prevent Bank Failure Let's consider two banks with identical balance sheets, except that High Capital Bank has a ratio of capital to assets of 10% while Low Capital Bank has a ratio of 4%.

High Capital Bank				Low Capital Bank			
Assets		**Liabilities**		**Assets**		**Liabilities**	
Reserves	$10 million	Deposits	$90 million	Reserves	$10 million	Deposits	$96 million
Loans	$90 million	Bank capital	$10 million	Loans	$90 million	Bank capital	$ 4 million

Suppose both banks got caught up in the euphoria of the housing market, only to find that $5 million of their housing loans became worthless later. When these bad loans are written off (valued at zero), the total value of assets declines by $5 million. As a consequence, bank capital, which equals total assets minus liabilities, also declines by $5 million. The balance sheets of the two banks now look like this:

High Capital Bank				Low Capital Bank			
Assets		**Liabilities**		**Assets**		**Liabilities**	
Reserves	$10 million	Deposits	$90 million	Reserves	$10 million	Deposits	$96 million
Loans	$85 million	Bank capital	$ 5 million	Loans	$85 million	Bank capital	−$ 1 million

High Capital Bank takes the $5 million loss in stride because its initial cushion of $10 million in capital means that it still has a positive net worth (bank capital) of $5 million after the loss. Low Capital Bank, however, is in big trouble. The value of its assets has fallen below its liabilities, and its net worth is now −$1 million. Because the bank has a negative net worth, it is insolvent: It does not have sufficient assets to pay off all holders of its liabilities. When a bank becomes insolvent, government regulators close the bank, its assets are sold off, and its managers are fired. Because the owners of Low Capital Bank will find their investment wiped out, they would clearly have preferred the bank to have had a large enough cushion of bank capital to absorb the losses, as was the case for High Capital Bank. We therefore see an important rationale for a bank to maintain a sufficient level of capital: ***A bank maintains bank capital to lessen the chance that it will become insolvent.***

How the Amount of Bank Capital Affects Returns to Equity Holders

Because owners of a bank must know whether their bank is being managed well, they need good measures of bank profitability. A basic measure of bank profitability is the **return on assets (ROA)**, the net profit after taxes per dollar of assets:

$$\text{ROA} = \frac{\text{net profit after taxes}}{\text{assets}}$$

The return on assets provides information on how efficiently a bank is being run, because it indicates how much profit is generated, on average, by each dollar of assets.

However, what the bank's owners (equity holders) care about most is how much the bank is earning on their equity investment. This information is provided by the other basic measure of bank profitability, the **return on equity (ROE)**, the net profit after taxes per dollar of equity (bank) capital:

$$\text{ROE} = \frac{\text{net profit after taxes}}{\text{equity capital}}$$

There is a direct relationship between the return on assets (which measures how efficiently the bank is run) and the return on equity (which measures how well the owners are doing on their investment). This relationship is determined by the **equity multiplier (EM)**, the amount of assets per dollar of equity capital:

$$\text{EM} = \frac{\text{assets}}{\text{equity capital}}$$

To see this, we note that

$$\frac{\text{net profit after taxes}}{\text{equity capital}} = \frac{\text{net profit after taxes}}{\text{assets}} \times \frac{\text{assets}}{\text{equity capital}}$$

which, using our definitions, yields

$$\text{ROE} = \text{ROA} \times \text{EM} \qquad (1)$$

The formula in Equation 1 tells us what happens to the return on equity when a bank holds a smaller amount of capital (equity) for a given amount of assets. As we have seen, High Capital Bank initially has $100 million of assets and $10 million of equity, which gives it an equity multiplier of 10(= $100 million/$10 million). Low Capital Bank, by contrast, has only $4 million of equity, so its equity multiplier is higher, equaling 25(= $100 million/$4 million). Suppose that these banks have been equally well run so that they both have the same return on assets, 1%. The return on equity for High Capital Bank equals 1% × 10 = 10%, whereas the return on equity for Low Capital Bank equals 1% × 25 = 25%. The equity holders in Low Capital Bank are clearly a lot happier than the equity holders in High Capital Bank because they are earning more than twice as high a return. We now see why owners of a bank may not want it to hold too much capital. ***Given the return on assets, the lower the bank capital, the higher the return for the owners of the bank.***

Trade-off Between Safety and Returns to Equity Holders We now see that bank capital has both benefits and costs. Bank capital benefits the owners of a bank in that it makes their investment safer by reducing the likelihood of bankruptcy. But bank capital is costly because the higher it is, the lower will be the return on equity for a given return on assets. In determining the amount of bank capital, managers must decide how much of the increased safety that comes with higher capital (the benefit) they are willing to trade off against the lower return on equity that comes with higher capital (the cost).

In more uncertain times, when the possibility of large losses on loans increases, bank managers might want to hold more capital to protect the equity holders. Conversely, if they have confidence that loan losses won't occur, they might want to reduce the amount of bank capital, have a high equity multiplier, and thereby increase the return on equity.

Bank Capital Requirements Banks also hold capital because they are required to do so by regulatory authorities. Because of the high costs of holding capital for the reasons just described, bank managers often want to hold less bank capital relative to assets than is required by the regulatory authorities. In this case, the amount of bank capital is determined by the bank capital requirements. We discuss the details of bank capital requirements and their important role in bank regulation in Chapter 11.

APPLICATION ◆ Strategies for Managing Bank Capital

Suppose that as the manager of the First National Bank, you have to make decisions about the appropriate amount of bank capital. Looking at the balance sheet of the bank, which like High Capital Bank, has a ratio of bank capital to assets of 10% ($10 million of capital and $100 million of assets), you are concerned that the large amount of bank capital is causing the return on equity to be too low. You conclude that the bank has a capital surplus and should increase the equity multiplier to raise the return on equity. What should you do?

To lower the amount of capital relative to assets and raise the equity multiplier, you can do any of three things: (1) You can reduce the amount of bank capital by buying back some of the bank's stock. (2) You can reduce the bank's capital by paying out higher dividends to its stockholders, thereby reducing the bank's retained earnings. (3) You can keep bank capital constant but increase the bank's assets by acquiring new funds—say, by issuing CDs—and then seeking out loan business or purchasing more securities with these new funds. Because you think that it would enhance your position with the stockholders, you decide to pursue the second alternative and raise the dividend on the First National Bank stock.

Now suppose that the First National Bank is in a situation similar to that of Low Capital Bank and has a ratio of bank capital to assets of 4%. You now worry that the bank is short on capital relative to assets because it does not have a sufficient cushion to prevent bank failure. To raise the amount of capital relative to assets, you now have the following three choices: (1) You can raise capital for the bank by having it issue equity (common stock). (2) You can raise capital by reducing the bank's dividends to shareholders, thereby increasing retained earnings that it can put into its capital account. (3) You can keep capital at the same level but reduce the bank's assets by making fewer loans or by selling off securities and then using the proceeds to reduce its liabilities. Suppose that raising bank capital is not easy to do at the current time because capital markets are tight or because shareholders will protest if their dividends are cut. Then you might have to choose the third alternative and decide to shrink the size of the bank.

Our discussion of strategies for managing bank capital for the First National Bank leads to the following conclusion that deserves some emphasis: ***A shortfall of bank capital is likely to lead to a bank reducing its assets and therefore a contraction in lending.*** In past years, many banks experienced capital shortfalls and had to restrict asset and lending growth. The important consequences of this for the credit markets are illustrated by the application that follows.

APPLICATION ◆ How a Capital Crunch Caused a Credit Crunch During the Global Financial Crisis

The dramatic slowdown in the growth of credit in the wake of the financial crisis starting in 2007 triggered a "credit crunch" in which credit was hard to get. As a result, the performance of the economy in 2008 and 2009 was very poor. What caused the credit crunch?

Our analysis of how a bank manages its capital indicates that the 2008–2009 credit crunch was caused, at least in part, by the capital crunch, in which shortfalls of bank capital led to slower credit growth.

As we discussed in the previous chapter, a major boom and bust in the housing market led to huge losses for banks from their holdings of securities backed by residential mortgages. In addition, banks had to take back onto their balance sheets many of the structured investment vehicles (SIVs) they had sponsored. The losses that reduced bank capital, along with the need for more capital to support the assets coming back onto their balance sheets, led to capital shortfalls: Banks had to either raise new capital or restrict asset growth by cutting back on lending. Banks did raise some capital, but with the growing weakness of the economy, raising new capital was extremely difficult, so banks also chose to tighten their lending standards and reduce lending. Both of these helped produce a weak economy in 2008 and 2009. ◆

MANAGING CREDIT RISK

As seen in the earlier discussion of general principles of asset management, banks and other financial institutions must make successful loans that are paid back in full (and so subject the institution to little credit risk) if they are to earn high profits. The economic concepts of adverse selection and moral hazard (discussed in Chapters 2 and 8) provide a framework for understanding the principles that financial institutions have to follow to reduce credit risk and make successful loans.[3]

Adverse selection in loan markets occurs because bad credit risks (those most likely to default on their loans) are the ones who usually line up for loans; in other words, those who are most likely to produce an *adverse* outcome are the most likely to be *selected*. Borrowers with very risky investment projects have much to gain if their projects are successful, so they are the most eager to obtain loans. Clearly, however, they are the least desirable borrowers because of the greater possibility that they will be unable to pay back their loans.

Moral hazard exists in loan markets because borrowers may have incentives to engage in activities that are undesirable from the lender's point of view. In such situations, it is more likely that the lender will be subjected to the *hazard* of default. Once borrowers have obtained a loan, they are more likely to invest in high-risk investment projects—projects that pay high returns to the borrowers if successful. The high risk, however, makes it less likely that they will be able to pay the loan back.

To be profitable, financial institutions must overcome the adverse selection and moral hazard problems that make loan defaults more likely. The attempts of financial institutions to solve these problems help explain a number of principles for managing credit risk: screening and monitoring, establishment of long-term customer relationships, loan commitments, collateral and compensating balance requirements, and credit rationing.

Screening and Monitoring

Asymmetric information is present in loan markets because lenders have less information about the investment opportunities and activities of borrowers than borrowers do. This situation leads to two information-producing activities by banks and other financial institutions—screening and monitoring. Indeed, Walter Wriston, a former head of Citicorp, the largest bank corporation in the United States, was often quoted as stating that the business of banking is the production of information.

Screening Adverse selection in loan markets requires that lenders screen out the bad credit risks from the good ones so that loans are profitable to them. To accomplish

[3]Other financial intermediaries, such as insurance companies, pension funds, and finance companies, also make private loans, and the credit risk management principles we outline here apply to them as well.

effective screening, lenders must collect reliable information from prospective borrowers. Effective screening and information collection together form an important principle of credit risk management.

When you apply for a consumer loan (such as a car loan or a mortgage to purchase a house), the first thing you are asked to do is fill out forms that elicit a great deal of information about your personal finances. You are asked about your salary, your bank accounts and other assets (such as cars, insurance policies, and furnishings), and your outstanding loans; your record of loan, credit card, and charge account repayments; the number of years you've worked and who your employers have been. You also are asked personal questions such as your age, marital status, and number of children. The lender uses this information to evaluate how good a credit risk you are by calculating your credit score, a statistical measure derived from your answers that predicts whether you are likely to have trouble making your loan payments. Deciding on how good a risk you are cannot be entirely scientific, so the lender must also use judgment. The loan officer, whose job is to decide whether you should be given the loan, might call your employer or talk to some of the personal references you supplied. The officer might even make a judgment based on your demeanor or your appearance. (This is why most people dress neatly and conservatively when they go to a bank to apply for a loan.)

The process of screening and collecting information is similar when a financial institution makes a business loan. It collects information about the company's profits and losses (income) and about its assets and liabilities. The lender also has to evaluate the likely future success of the business. So, in addition to obtaining information on such items as sales figures, a loan officer might ask questions about the company's future plans, the purpose of the loan, and the competition in the industry. The officer may even visit the company to obtain a firsthand look at its operations. The bottom line is that, whether for personal or business loans, bankers and other financial institutions need to be nosy.

Specialization in Lending One puzzling feature of bank lending is that a bank often specializes in lending to local firms or to firms in particular industries, such as energy. In one sense, this behavior seems surprising, because it means that the bank is not diversifying its portfolio of loans and thus is exposing itself to more risk. But from another perspective, such specialization makes perfect sense. The adverse selection problem requires that the bank screen out bad credit risks. It is easier for the bank to collect information about local firms and determine their creditworthiness than to collect comparable information on firms that are far away. Similarly, by concentrating its lending on firms in specific industries, the bank becomes more knowledgeable about these industries and is therefore better able to predict which firms will be able to make timely payments on their debt.

Monitoring and Enforcement of Restrictive Covenants Once a loan has been made, the borrower has an incentive to engage in risky activities that make it less likely for the loan to be paid off. To reduce this moral hazard, financial institutions must adhere to the principle for managing credit risk that a lender should write provisions (restrictive covenants) into loan contracts that restrict borrowers from engaging in risky activities. By monitoring borrowers' activities to see whether they are complying with the restrictive covenants and by enforcing the covenants if they are not, lenders can make sure that borrowers are not taking on risks at their expense. The need for banks and other financial institutions to engage in screening and monitoring explains why they spend so much money on auditing and information-collecting activities.

Long-Term Customer Relationships

An additional way for banks and other financial institutions to obtain information about their borrowers is through long-term customer relationships, another important principle of credit risk management.

If a prospective borrower has had a checking or savings account or other loans with a bank over a long period of time, a loan officer can look at past activity on the accounts and learn quite a bit about the borrower. The balances in the checking and savings accounts tell the banker how liquid the potential borrower is and at what time of year the borrower has a strong need for cash. A review of the checks the borrower has written reveals the borrower's suppliers. If the borrower has borrowed previously from the bank, the bank has a record of the loan payments. Thus long-term customer relationships reduce the costs of information collection and make it easier to screen out bad credit risks.

The need for monitoring by lenders adds to the importance of long-term customer relationships. If the borrower has borrowed from the bank before, the bank has already established procedures for monitoring that customer. Therefore, the costs of monitoring long-term customers are lower than those for new customers.

Long-term relationships benefit the customers as well as the bank. A firm with a previous relationship will find it easier to obtain a loan at a low interest rate because the bank has an easier time determining if the prospective borrower is a good credit risk and incurs fewer costs in monitoring the borrower.

A long-term customer relationship has another advantage for the bank. No bank can think of every contingency when it writes a restrictive covenant into a loan contract; there will always be risky borrower activities that are not ruled out. However, what if a borrower wants to preserve a long-term relationship with a bank because it will be easier to get future loans at low interest rates? The borrower then has the incentive to avoid risky activities that would upset the bank, even if restrictions on these risky activities are not specified in the loan contract. Indeed, if a bank doesn't like what a borrower is doing even when the borrower isn't violating any restrictive covenants, it has some power to discourage the borrower from such activity: The bank can threaten not to let the borrower have new loans in the future. Long-term customer relationships therefore enable banks to deal with even unanticipated moral hazard contingencies.

Loan Commitments

Banks also create long-term relationships and gather information by issuing **loan commitments** to commercial customers. A loan commitment is a bank's commitment (for a specified future period of time) to provide a firm with loans up to a given amount at an interest rate that is tied to some market interest rate. The majority of commercial and industrial loans are made under the loan commitment arrangement. The advantage for the firm is that it has a source of credit when it needs it. The advantage for the bank is that the loan commitment promotes a long-term relationship, which in turn facilitates information collection. In addition, provisions in the loan commitment agreement require that the firm continually supply the bank with information about the firm's income, asset and liability position, business activities, and so on. A loan commitment arrangement is a powerful method for reducing the bank's costs for screening and information collection.

Collateral and Compensating Balances

Collateral requirements for loans are important credit risk management tools. Collateral, which is property promised to the lender as compensation if the borrower defaults, lessens the consequences of adverse selection because it reduces the lender's losses in the case of a loan default. It also reduces moral hazard because the borrower has more to lose from a default. If a borrower defaults on a loan, the lender can sell the collateral and use the proceeds to make up for its losses on the loan. One particular form of collateral required when a bank makes commercial loans is called **compensating balances**: A firm receiving a loan must keep a required minimum amount of funds in a checking account at the bank. For example, a business getting a $10 million loan may be required to keep compensating balances of at least $1 million in its checking account at the bank. This $1 million in compensating balances can then be taken by the bank to make up some of the losses on the loan if the borrower defaults.

Besides serving as collateral, compensating balances help increase the likelihood that a loan will be paid off. They do this by helping the bank monitor the borrower and consequently reduce moral hazard. Specifically, by requiring the borrower to use a checking account at the bank, the bank can observe the firm's check payment practices, which may yield a great deal of information about the borrower's financial condition. For example, a sustained drop in the borrower's checking account balance may signal that the borrower is having financial trouble, or account activity may suggest that the borrower is engaging in risky activities; perhaps a change in suppliers means that the borrower is pursuing new lines of business. Any significant change in the borrower's payment procedures is a signal to the bank that it should make inquiries. Compensating balances therefore make it easier for banks to monitor borrowers more effectively and are another important credit risk management tool.

Credit Rationing

Another way in which financial institutions deal with adverse selection and moral hazard is through **credit rationing**: refusing to make loans even though borrowers are willing to pay the stated interest rate or even a higher rate. Credit rationing takes two forms. The first occurs when a lender refuses to make a loan *of any amount* to a borrower, even if the borrower is willing to pay a higher interest rate. The second occurs when a lender is willing to make a loan but restricts the size of the loan to less than the borrower would like.

At first you might be puzzled by the first type of credit rationing. After all, even if the potential borrower is a credit risk, why doesn't the lender just extend the loan but at a higher interest rate? The answer is that adverse selection prevents this solution. Individuals and firms with the riskiest investment projects are exactly those that are willing to pay the highest interest rates. If a borrower took on a high-risk investment and succeeded, the borrower would become extremely rich. But a lender wouldn't want to make such a loan precisely because the credit risk is high; the likely outcome is that the borrower will *not* succeed and the lender will not be paid back. Charging a higher interest rate just makes adverse selection worse for the lender; that is, it increases the likelihood that the lender is lending to a bad credit risk. The lender would therefore rather not make any loans at a higher interest rate; instead, it would engage in the first type of credit rationing and would turn down loans.

Financial institutions engage in the second type of credit rationing to guard against moral hazard: They grant loans to borrowers, but not loans as large as the borrowers want. Such credit rationing is necessary because the larger the loan, the greater the benefits from moral hazard. If a bank gives you a $1,000 loan, for example, you are likely to take actions that enable you to pay it back because you don't want to hurt your credit rating for the future. However, if the bank lends you $10 million, you are more likely to fly down to Rio to celebrate. The larger your loan, the greater your incentives to engage in activities that make it less likely that you will repay the loan. Because more borrowers repay their loans if the loan amounts are small, financial institutions ration credit by providing borrowers with smaller loans than they seek.

MANAGING INTEREST-RATE RISK

With the increased volatility of interest rates that occurred in the 1980s, banks and other financial institutions became more concerned about their exposure to interest-rate risk, the riskiness of earnings and returns that is associated with changes in interest rates. To see what interest-rate risk is all about, let's again take a look at the First National Bank, which has the following balance sheet:

First National Bank

Assets		**Liabilities**	
Rate-sensitive assets	$20 million	Rate-sensitive liabilities	$50 million
Variable-rate and short-term loans		Variable-rate CDs	
Short-term securities		Money market deposit accounts	
Fixed-rate assets	$80 million	Fixed-rate liabilities	$50 million
Reserves		Checkable deposits	
Long-term loans		Savings deposits	
Long-term securities		Long-term CDs	
		Equity capital	

A total of $20 million of its assets are rate-sensitive, with interest rates that change frequently (at least once a year), and $80 million of its assets are fixed-rate, with interest rates that remain unchanged for a long period (over a year). On the liabilities side, the First National Bank has $50 million of rate-sensitive liabilities and $50 million of fixed-rate liabilities. Suppose that interest rates rise by 5 percentage points on average, from 10% to 15%. The income on the assets increases by $1 million (= 5% × $20 million of rate-sensitive assets), while the payments on the liabilities increase by $2.5 million (= 5% × $50 million of rate-sensitive liabilities). The First National Bank's profits now decline by $1.5 million (= $1 million − $2.5 million). Conversely, if interest rates fall by 5 percentage points, similar reasoning tells us that the First National Bank's profits increase by $1.5 million. This example illustrates the following point: ***If a bank has more rate-sensitive liabilities than assets, a rise in interest rates will reduce bank profits and a decline in interest rates will raise bank profits.***

Gap and Duration Analysis

The sensitivity of bank profits to changes in interest rates can be measured more directly using **gap analysis**, in which the amount of rate-sensitive liabilities is subtracted from the amount of rate-sensitive assets. In our example, this calculation (called the "gap") is $-\$30$ million ($= \$20$ million $- \$50$ million). By multiplying the gap times the change in the interest rate, we can immediately obtain the effect on bank profits. For example, when interest rates rise by 5 percentage points, the change in profits is $5\% \times -\$30$ million, which equals $-\$1.5$ million, as we saw.

The analysis we just conducted is known as *basic gap analysis*, and it can be refined in two ways. Clearly, not all assets and liabilities in the fixed-rate category have the same maturity. One refinement, the *maturity bucket approach*, is to measure the gap for several maturity subintervals, called *maturity buckets*, so that effects of interest-rate changes over a multiyear period can be calculated. The second refinement, called *standardized gap analysis*, accounts for the differing degrees of rate sensitivity for different rate-sensitive assets and liabilities.

An alternative method for measuring interest-rate risk, called **duration analysis**, examines the sensitivity of the market value of the bank's total assets and liabilities to changes in interest rates. Duration analysis is based on what is known as Macaulay's concept of *duration*, which measures the average lifetime of a security's stream of payments.[4] Duration is a useful concept because it provides a good approximation of the sensitivity of a security's market value to a change in its interest rate:

$$\text{percent change in market value of security} \approx -\text{percentage-point change in interest rate} \times \text{duration in years}$$

where $\approx$ denotes "approximately equals."

Duration analysis involves using the average (weighted) duration of a financial institution's assets and of its liabilities to see how its net worth responds to a change in interest rates. Going back to our example of the First National Bank, suppose that the average duration of its assets is three years (that is, the average lifetime of the stream of payments is three years), whereas the average duration of its liabilities is two years. In addition, the First National Bank has \$100 million of assets and, say, \$90 million of liabilities, so its bank capital is 10% of assets. With a 5-percentage-point increase in interest rates, the market value of the bank's assets falls by $15\% \,(= -5\% \times 3 \text{ years})$, a decline of \$15 million on the \$100 million of assets. However, the market value of the liabilities falls by $10\% \,(= -5\% \times 2 \text{ years})$, a decline of \$9 million on the \$90 million of liabilities. The net result is that the net worth (the market value of the assets minus the liabilities) has declined by \$6 million, or 6% of the total original asset value. Similarly, a 5-percentage-point decline in interest rates increases the net worth of the First National Bank by 6% of the total asset value.

As our example makes clear, both duration analysis and gap analysis indicate that the First National Bank will suffer if interest rates rise but will gain if they fall. Duration analysis and gap analysis are thus useful tools for telling a manager of a financial institution its degree of exposure to interest-rate risk.

[4]Algebraically, Macaulay's duration, D, is defined as

$$D = \sum_{\tau=1}^{N} \tau \frac{CP_\tau}{(1+i)^\tau} \Big/ \sum_{\tau=1}^{N} \frac{CP_\tau}{(1+i)^\tau}$$

where τ = time until cash payment is made
CP_τ = cash payment (interest plus principal) at time τ
i = interest rate
N = time to maturity of the security

For a more detailed discussion of duration gap analysis using the concept of Macaulay's duration, you can look at an appendix to this chapter that is on this book's website at www.myeconlab.com.

APPLICATION ◆ Strategies for Managing Interest-Rate Risk

Suppose that as manager of the First National Bank, you have done a duration and gap analysis for the bank, as discussed in the text. Now you need to decide which alternative strategies you should pursue to manage the interest-rate risk.

If you firmly believe that interest rates will fall in the future, you may be willing to take no action because you know that the bank has more rate-sensitive liabilities than rate-sensitive assets and so will benefit from the expected interest-rate decline. However, you also realize that the First National Bank is subject to substantial interest-rate risk because there is always a possibility that interest rates will rise rather than fall. What should you do to eliminate this interest-rate risk? One thing you could do is to shorten the duration of the bank's assets to increase their rate sensitivity. Alternatively, you could lengthen the duration of the liabilities. By this adjustment of the bank's assets and liabilities, the bank's income will be less affected by interest-rate swings.

One problem with eliminating the First National Bank's interest-rate risk by altering the balance sheet is that doing so might be very costly in the short run. The bank may be locked into assets and liabilities of particular durations because of where its expertise lies. Fortunately, recently developed financial instruments known as financial derivatives—financial forwards and futures, options, and swaps—can help the bank reduce its interest-rate risk exposure but do not require that the bank rearrange its balance sheet. ◆

OFF-BALANCE-SHEET ACTIVITIES

Although asset and liability management has traditionally been the major concern of banks, in the more competitive environment of recent years banks have been aggressively seeking out profits by engaging in off-balance-sheet activities.[5] **Off-balance-sheet activities** involve trading financial instruments and generating income from fees and loan sales, activities that affect bank profits but do not appear on bank balance sheets. Indeed, off-balance-sheet activities have been growing in importance for banks: The income from these activities as a percentage of assets has nearly doubled since 1980.

Loan Sales

One type of off-balance-sheet activity that has grown in importance in recent years involves income generated by loan sales. A **loan sale**, also called a *secondary loan participation*, involves a contract that sells all or part of the cash stream from a specific loan and thereby removes the loan so that it no longer is an asset on the bank's balance sheet. Banks earn profits by selling loans for an amount slightly greater than that of the original loan. Because the high interest rate on these loans makes them attractive, institutions are willing to buy them, even though the higher price means that they earn

[5]Managers of financial institutions also need to know how well their banks are doing at any point in time. A second appendix to this chapter discusses how bank performance is measured; it can be found on the book's website at www.myeconlab.com.

a slightly lower interest rate than the original interest rate on the loan, usually on the order of 0.15 percentage point.

Generation of Fee Income

Another type of off-balance-sheet activity involves the generation of income from fees that banks receive for providing specialized services to their customers, such as making foreign exchange trades on a customer's behalf, servicing a mortgage-backed security by collecting interest and principal payments and then paying them out, guaranteeing debt securities such as banker's acceptances (by which the bank promises to make interest and principal payments if the party issuing the security cannot), and providing backup lines of credit. There are several types of backup lines of credit. We have already mentioned the most important, the loan commitment, under which, for a fee, the bank agrees to provide a loan at the customer's request, up to a given dollar amount, over a specified period of time. Credit lines are also now available to bank depositors with "overdraft privileges"—these bank customers can write checks in excess of their deposit balances and, in effect, write themselves a loan. Other lines of credit for which banks get fees include standby letters of credit to back up issues of commercial paper and other securities and credit lines (called *note issuance facilities*, NIFs, and *revolving underwriting facilities*, RUFs) for underwriting Euronotes, which are medium-term Eurobonds.

Off-balance-sheet activities involving guarantees of securities and backup credit lines increase the risk a bank faces. Even though a guaranteed security does not appear on a bank's balance sheet, it still exposes the bank to default risk: If the issuer of the security defaults, the bank is left holding the bag and must pay off the security's owner. Backup credit lines also expose the bank to risk because the bank may be forced to provide loans when it does not have sufficient liquidity or when the borrower is a very poor credit risk.

Banks also earn fees by creating financial instruments like the structured investment vehicles (SIVs) mentioned in the previous chapter and selling them to investors. However, as became clear during the global financial crisis, when they decline in value, many of these financial instruments have to be taken back onto the balance sheet of the bank (like Citigroup) sponsoring them, because to do otherwise would severely damage the reputation of the bank. Even though these financial instruments at first appear to be off-balance-sheet, in reality they are back on the balance sheet if they are subjected to large losses. To their regret, banks such as Citigroup ended up taking large losses on these financial instruments during the global financial crisis, indicating that these off-balance-sheet vehicles exposed banks to just as much risk as if they had been part of their balance sheets from the outset.

Trading Activities and Risk Management Techniques

We have already mentioned that banks' attempts to manage interest-rate risk led them to trading in financial futures, options for debt instruments, and interest-rate swaps. Banks engaged in international banking also conduct transactions in the foreign exchange market. All transactions in these markets are off-balance-sheet activities because they do not have a direct effect on the bank's balance sheet. Although bank trading in these markets is often directed toward reducing risk or facilitating other bank business, banks also try to outguess the markets and engage in speculation. This speculation can be a very risky business and indeed has led to bank insolvencies, the most dramatic being the failure of Barings, a British bank, in 1995.

Global Barings, Daiwa, Sumitomo, and Société Générale: Rogue Traders and the Principal–Agent Problem

The demise of Barings, a venerable British bank more than a century old, is a sad morality tale of how the principal–agent problem operating through a rogue trader can take a financial institution that has a healthy balance sheet one month and turn it into an insolvent tragedy the next.

In July 1992, Nick Leeson, Barings's new head clerk at its Singapore branch, began to speculate on the Nikkei, the Japanese version of the Dow Jones stock index. By late 1992, Leeson had suffered losses of $3 million, which he hid from his superiors by stashing the losses in a secret account. He even fooled his superiors into thinking he was generating large profits, thanks to a failure of internal controls at his firm, which allowed him to execute trades on the Singapore exchange *and* oversee the bookkeeping of those trades. (As anyone who runs a cash business, such as a bar, knows, there is always a lower likelihood of fraud if more than one person handles the cash. Similarly, for trading operations, you never mix management of the back room with management of the front room; this principle was grossly violated by Barings management.)

Things didn't get better for Leeson, who by late 1994 had losses exceeding $250 million. In January and February 1995, he bet the bank. On January 17, 1995, the day of the earthquake in Kobe, Japan, he lost $75 million, and by the end of the week had lost more than $150 million. When the stock market declined on February 23, leaving him with a further loss of $250 million, he called it quits and fled Singapore. Three days later, he turned himself in at the Frankfurt airport. By the end of his wild ride, Leeson's losses, $1.3 billion in all, ate up Barings's capital and caused the bank to fail. Leeson was subsequently convicted and sent to jail in Singapore for his activities. He was released in 1999 and apologized for his actions.

Our asymmetric information analysis of the principal–agent problem explains Leeson's behavior and the danger of Barings's management lapse. Letting Leeson control both his own trades and the back room increased asymmetric information, because it reduced the principal's (Barings's) knowledge about Leeson's trading activities. This lapse increased the moral hazard incentive for him to take risks at the bank's expense, as he was now less likely to be caught. Furthermore, once he had experienced large losses, he had even greater incentives to take on even higher risk because if his bets worked out, he could reverse his losses and keep in good standing with the company, whereas if his bets soured, he had little to lose because he was out of a job anyway. Indeed, the bigger his losses, the more he had to gain by bigger bets, which explains the escalation of the amount of his trades as his losses mounted. If Barings's managers had understood the principal–agent problem, they would have been more vigilant at finding out what Leeson was up to, and the bank might still be here today.

Unfortunately, Nick Leeson is no longer a rarity in the rogue traders' billionaire club, those who have lost more than $1 billion. Over eleven years, Toshihide Iguchi, an officer in the New York branch of Daiwa Bank, also had control of both the bond trading operation and the back room, and he racked up $1.1 billion in losses over the period. In July 1995, Iguchi disclosed his losses to his superiors, but the management of the bank did not disclose them to its regulators. The result was that Daiwa was slapped with a $340 million fine and the bank was thrown out of the country by U.S. bank regulators.

Yasuo Hamanaka is another member of the billionaire club. In July 1996, he topped Leeson's and Iguchi's record, losing $2.6 billion for his employer, the Sumitomo Corporation, one of Japan's top trading companies. Jerome Kerviel's loss for his bank, Société Générale, in January 2008 set the all-time record for a rogue trader: His unauthorized trades cost the French bank $7.2 billion.

The moral of these stories is that management of firms engaged in trading activities must reduce the principal–agent problem by closely monitoring their traders' activities, or the rogues' gallery will continue to grow.

Trading activities, although often highly profitable, are dangerous because they make it easy for financial institutions and their employees to make huge bets quickly. A particular problem for management of trading activities is that the principal–agent problem, discussed in Chapter 8, is especially severe. Given the ability to place large bets, a trader (the agent), whether she trades in bond markets, in foreign exchange markets, or in financial derivatives, has an incentive to take on excessive risks: If her trading strategy leads to large profits, she is likely to receive a high salary and bonuses, but if she takes large losses, the financial institution (the principal) will have to cover them. As the Barings Bank failure in 1995 so forcefully demonstrated, a trader subject to the principal–agent problem can take an institution that is quite healthy and drive it into insolvency very rapidly (see the Global box).

To reduce the principal–agent problem, managers of financial institutions must set up internal controls to prevent debacles like the one at Barings. Such controls include the complete separation of the people in charge of trading activities from those in charge of the bookkeeping for trades. In addition, managers must set limits on the total amount of traders' transactions and on the institution's risk exposure. Managers must also scrutinize risk assessment procedures using the latest computer technology. One such method involves the value-at-risk approach. In this approach, the institution develops a statistical model with which it can calculate the maximum loss that its portfolio is likely to sustain over a given time interval, dubbed the value at risk, or VaR. For example, a bank might estimate that the maximum loss it would be likely to sustain over one day with a probability of 1 in 100 is \$1 million; the \$1 million figure is the bank's calculated value at risk. Another approach is called "stress testing." In this approach, a manager asks models what would happen if a doomsday scenario occurs; that is, she looks at the losses the institution would sustain if an unusual combination of bad events occurred. With the value-at-risk approach and stress testing, a financial institution can assess its risk exposure and take steps to reduce it.

U.S. bank regulators have become concerned about the increased risk that banks are facing from their off-balance-sheet activities, and, as we will see in Chapter 11, are encouraging banks to pay increased attention to risk management. In addition, the Bank for International Settlements is developing additional bank capital requirements based on value-at-risk calculations for a bank's trading activities.

Summary

1. The balance sheet of commercial banks can be thought of as a list of the sources and uses of bank funds. A bank's liabilities are its sources of funds, which include checkable deposits, time deposits, discount loans from the Fed, borrowings from other banks and corporations, and bank capital. A bank's assets are its uses of funds, which include reserves, cash items in process of collection, deposits at other banks, securities, loans, and other assets (mostly physical capital).
2. Banks make profits through the process of asset transformation: They borrow short (accept short-term deposits) and lend long (make long-term loans). When a bank takes in additional deposits, it gains an equal amount of reserves; when it pays out deposits, it loses an equal amount of reserves.
3. Although more-liquid assets tend to earn lower returns, banks still desire to hold them. Specifically, banks hold excess and secondary reserves because they provide insurance against the costs of a deposit outflow. Banks manage their assets to maximize profits by seeking the highest returns possible on loans and securities while at the same time trying to lower risk and making adequate provisions for liquidity. Although liability management was once a staid affair, large (money center) banks now actively seek out sources of funds by issuing liabilities such as negotiable CDs or by actively borrowing

from other banks and corporations. Banks manage the amount of capital they hold to prevent bank failure and to meet bank capital requirements set by the regulatory authorities. However, they do not want to hold too much capital because by so doing they will lower the returns to equity holders.

4. The concepts of adverse selection and moral hazard explain many credit risk management principles involving loan activities: screening and monitoring, establishment of long-term customer relationships and loan commitments, collateral and compensating balances, and credit rationing.
5. With the increased volatility of interest rates that occurred in the 1980s, financial institutions became more concerned about their exposure to interest-rate risk. Gap and duration analyses tell a financial institution if it has more rate-sensitive liabilities than assets (in which case a rise in interest rates will reduce profits and a fall in interest rates will raise profits). Financial institutions manage their interest-rate risk by modifying their balance sheets but can also use strategies involving financial derivatives.
6. Off-balance-sheet activities consist of trading financial instruments and generating income from fees and loan sales, all of which affect bank profits but are not visible on bank balance sheets. Because these off-balance-sheet activities expose banks to increased risk, bank management must pay particular attention to risk assessment procedures and internal controls to restrict employees from taking on too much risk.

Key Terms

asset management, p. 220
balance sheet, p. 213
capital adequacy management, p. 220
compensating balances, p. 232
credit rationing, p. 232
credit risk, p. 220
deposit outflows, p. 220
discount loans, p. 215
discount rate, p. 222
duration analysis, p. 234
equity multiplier (EM), p. 226
excess reserves, p. 216
gap analysis, p. 233
interest-rate risk, p. 220
liability management, p. 220
liquidity management, p. 220
loan commitment, p. 231
loan sale, p. 235
money center banks, p. 224
off-balance-sheet activities, p. 235
required reserve ratio, p. 216
required reserves, p. 216
reserve requirements, p. 216
reserves, p. 216
return on assets (ROA), p. 226
return on equity (ROE), p. 226
secondary reserves, p. 216
T-account, p. 217
vault cash, p. 216

Questions

All questions are available in MyEconLab *at* www.myeconlab.com.

1. Why might a bank be willing to borrow funds from other banks at a higher rate than it can borrow from the Fed?
2. Rank the following bank assets from most to least liquid:
   a. Commercial loans
   b. Securities
   c. Reserves
   d. Physical capital
3. The bank you own has the following balance sheet:

Assets		Liabilities	
Reserves	\$ 75 million	Deposits	\$500 million
Loans	\$525 million	Bank capital	\$100 million

   If the bank suffers a deposit outflow of \$50 million with a required reserve ratio on deposits of 10%, what actions should you take?

4. If a deposit outflow of $50 million occurs, which balance sheet would a bank rather have initially, the balance sheet in Question 3 or the following balance sheet? Why?

Assets		Liabilities	
Reserves	$100 million	Deposits	$500 million
Loans	$500 million	Bank capital	$100 million

5. Why has the development of overnight loan markets made it more likely that banks will hold fewer excess reserves?
6. If the bank you own has no excess reserves and a sound customer comes in asking for a loan, should you automatically turn the customer down, explaining that you don't have any excess reserves to lend out? Why or why not? What options are available for you to provide the funds your customer needs?
7. If a bank finds that its ROE is too low because it has too much bank capital, what can it do to raise its ROE?
8. If a bank is falling short of meeting its capital requirements by $1 million, what three things can it do to rectify the situation?
9. Why do equity holders care more about ROE than about ROA?
10. If a bank doubles the amount of its capital and ROA stays constant, what will happen to ROE?
11. What are the benefits and costs for a bank when it decides to increase the amount of its bank capital?
12. Why is being nosy a desirable trait for a banker?
13. A bank almost always insists that the firms it lends to keep compensating balances at the bank. Why?
14. If the president of a bank told you that the bank was so well run that it has never had to call in loans, sell securities, or borrow as a result of a deposit outflow, would you be willing to buy stock in that bank? Why or why not?
15. "Because diversification is a desirable strategy for avoiding risk, it never makes sense for a bank to specialize in making specific types of loans." Is this statement true, false, or uncertain? Explain your answer.
16. If you are a banker and expect interest rates to rise in the future, would you want to make short-term or long-term loans?
17. "Bank managers should always seek the highest return possible on their assets." Is this statement true, false, or uncertain? Explain your answer.
18. Why has noninterest income been growing as a source of bank operating income?

Applied Problems

All applied problems are available in MyEconLab *at* www.myeconlab.com.

19. Using the T-accounts of the First National Bank and the Second National Bank, describe what happens when Jane Brown writes a $50 check on her account at the First National Bank to pay her friend Joe Green, who in turn deposits the check in his account at the Second National Bank.
20. What happens to reserves at the First National Bank if one person withdraws $1,000 of cash and another person deposits $500 of cash? Use T-accounts to explain your answer.

Questions 21 and 22 relate to the first month's operations of NewBank.

21. NewBank started its first day of operations with $6 million in capital. A total of $100 million in checkable deposits is received. The bank makes a $25 million commercial loan and another $25 million in mortgage loans. If required reserves are 8%, what does the bank balance sheet look like?
22. NewBank decides to invest $45 million in 30-day T-bills. The T-bills are currently trading at $4,986.70 (including commissions) for a $5,000 face value instrument. How many do they purchase? What does the balance sheet look like?
23. X-Bank reported an ROE of 15% and an ROA of 1%. How well capitalized is this bank?
24. Suppose that you are the manager of a bank whose $100 billion of assets have an average duration of four years and whose $90 billion of liabilities have an average duration of six years. Conduct a duration analysis for the bank, and show what will happen to the net

worth of the bank if interest rates rise by 2 percentage points. What actions could you take to reduce the bank's interest-rate risk?

25. Suppose that you are the manager of a bank that has $15 million of fixed-rate assets, $30 million of rate-sensitive assets, $25 million of fixed-rate liabilities, and $20 million of rate-sensitive liabilities. Conduct a gap analysis for the bank, and show what will happen to bank profits if interest rates rise by 5 percentage points. What actions could you take to reduce the bank's interest-rate risk?

Web Exercises

1. Table 1 reports the balance sheet of all commercial banks based on aggregate data found in the Federal Reserve *Bulletin*. Compare this table to the most recent balance sheet reported by Bank of America. Go to www.bankofamerica.com/investor.index.cfm?section=700 and click on Annual Reports to view the balance sheet. Does Bank of America have more or less of its portfolio in loans than the average bank? Which type of loan is most common?

2. It is relatively easy to find up-to-date information on banks because of their extensive reporting requirements. Go to www2.fdic.gov/qbp/. This site is sponsored by the Federal Deposit Insurance Corporation. You will find summary data on financial institutions. Go to the most recent Quarterly Banking Profile. Scroll to the bottom and open Table 1-A.

a. Have banks' return on assets been increasing or decreasing over the past few years?

b. Has the core capital been increasing, and how does it compare to the capital ratio reported in Table 1 in the text?

c. How many institutions are currently reporting to the FDIC?

Web References

www.bankofamerica.com/investor/index.cfm?section=700

Click on Annual Reports to view the balance sheet.

www.federalreserve.gov/boarddocs/SupManual/default.htm#trading

The Federal Reserve Bank Trading and Capital Market Activities Manual offers an in-depth discussion of a wide range of risk management issues encountered in trading operations.

Web Appendices

Please visit our Web site at www.pearsonhighered.com/mishkin to read the Web appendices to Chapter 10.

Appendix 1: **Duration Gap Analysis**

Appendix 2: **Measuring Bank Performance**

11 Economic Analysis of Financial Regulation

Preview

As we have seen in previous chapters, the financial system is among the most heavily regulated sectors of the economy, and banks are among the most heavily regulated of financial institutions. In this chapter, we develop an economic analysis of why regulation of the financial system takes the form it does.

Unfortunately, the regulatory process may not always work very well, as evidenced by the recent global financial crisis. Here we also use our economic analysis of financial regulation to explain the worldwide crises in banking and to consider how the regulatory system can be reformed to prevent future disasters.

ASYMMETRIC INFORMATION AND FINANCIAL REGULATION

In earlier chapters, we have seen how asymmetric information—the fact that different parties in a financial contract do not have the same information—leads to adverse selection and moral hazard problems that have an important impact on our financial system. The concepts of asymmetric information, adverse selection, and moral hazard are especially useful in understanding why government has chosen the form of financial regulation we see in the United States and in other countries. There are ten basic categories of financial regulation: the government safety net, restrictions on asset holdings, capital requirements, prompt corrective action, chartering and examination, assessment of risk management, disclosure requirements, consumer protection, restrictions on competition, and macroprudential supervision.

Government Safety Net

As we saw in Chapter 8, financial intermediaries, like banks, are particularly well suited to solving adverse selection and moral hazard problems because they make private loans that help avoid the free-rider problem. However, this solution to the free-rider problem creates another asymmetric information problem, because depositors lack information about the quality of these private loans. This asymmetric information problem leads to several reasons why the financial system might not function well.

Bank Panics and the Need for Deposit Insurance Before the FDIC started operations in 1934, a **bank failure** (in which a bank is unable to meet its obligations to pay its depositors and other creditors and so must go out of business) meant that depositors would have to wait to get their deposit funds until the bank was liquidated (until its assets had been turned into cash); at that time, they would be paid only a fraction of the value of their deposits. Unable to learn if bank managers were taking on too much risk or were outright crooks, depositors would be reluctant to put money in banks, thus making banking institutions less viable. Second, depositors' lack of information about the quality of bank assets can lead to bank panics, which, as we saw in Chapter 9, can have serious harmful consequences for the economy. To understand this, consider the following situation. Deposit insurance does not exist, and an adverse shock hits the economy. As a result of the shock, 5% of banks have such large losses on loans that they become insolvent (have a negative net worth and so are bankrupt). Because of asymmetric information, depositors are unable to tell whether their bank is a good bank or one of the 5% that are insolvent. Depositors at bad *and* good banks recognize that they may not get back 100 cents on the dollar for their deposits and will want to withdraw them. Indeed, because banks operate on a "sequential service constraint" (a first-come, first-served basis), depositors have a very strong incentive to show up at the bank first, because if they are last in line, the bank may run out of funds and they will get nothing. Uncertainty about the health of the banking system in general can lead to runs on banks both good and bad, and the failure of one bank can hasten the failure of others (referred to as the *contagion effect*). If nothing is done to restore the public's confidence, a bank panic can ensue.

Indeed, bank panics were a fact of American life in the nineteenth and early twentieth centuries, with major ones occurring every 20 years or so, in 1819, 1837, 1857, 1873, 1884, 1893, 1907, and 1930–1933. Bank failures were a serious problem even during the boom years of the 1920s, when the number of bank failures averaged around 600 per year.

A government safety net for depositors can short-circuit runs on banks and bank panics, and by providing protection for the depositor, it can overcome reluctance to put funds in the banking system. One form of the safety net is deposit insurance, a guarantee such as that provided by the Federal Deposit Insurance Corporation (FDIC) in the United States, in which currently depositors are paid off in full on the first $250,000 they have deposited in a bank if the bank fails. With fully insured deposits, depositors don't need to run to the bank to make withdrawals—even if they are worried about the bank's health—because their deposits will be worth 100 cents on the dollar no matter what. From 1930 to 1933, the years immediately preceding the creation of the FDIC, the number of bank failures averaged more than 2,000 per year. After the establishment of the FDIC in 1934, bank failures averaged fewer than 15 per year until 1981.

The FDIC uses two primary methods to handle a failed bank. In the first, called the *payoff method*, the FDIC allows the bank to fail and pays off deposits up to the $250,000 insurance limit (with funds acquired from the insurance premiums paid by the banks who have bought FDIC insurance). After the bank has been liquidated, the FDIC lines up with other creditors of the bank and is paid its share of the proceeds from the liquidated assets. Typically, when the payoff method is used, account holders with deposits in excess of the $250,000 limit get back more than 90 cents on the dollar, although the process can take several years to complete.

In the second method, called the *purchase and assumption method*, the FDIC reorganizes the bank, typically by finding a willing merger partner who assumes (takes over) all of the failed bank's liabilities so that no depositor or other creditor loses a penny. The FDIC often sweetens the pot for the merger partner by providing it with subsidized loans or by buying some of the failed bank's weaker loans. The net effect of the purchase and assumption method is that the FDIC has guaranteed *all* liabilities and deposits, not just deposits under the $250,000 limit. The purchase and assumption method is typically more costly for the FDIC than the payoff method, but nevertheless was the FDIC's more common procedure for dealing with a failed bank before new banking legislation in 1991.

In recent years, government deposit insurance has been growing in popularity and has spread to many countries throughout the world. Whether this trend is desirable is discussed in the Global box, "The Spread of Government Deposit Insurance Throughout the World: Is This a Good Thing?"

Other Forms of the Government Safety Net Deposit insurance is not the only form of government safety net. In other countries, governments have often stood ready to provide support to domestic banks facing runs even in the absence of explicit deposit insurance. Furthermore, banks are not the only financial intermediaries that can pose a systemic threat to the financial system, as our discussion of financial crises in Chapter 9 has illustrated. When financial institutions are very large or highly interconnected with other financial institutions or markets, their failure has the potential to bring down the entire financial system. Indeed, as we saw in Chapter 9, this is exactly what happened with Bear Stearns and Lehman Brothers, two investment banks, and AIG, an insurance company, during the global financial crisis in 2008.

One way governments provide support is through lending from the central bank to troubled institutions, as the Federal Reserve did during the global financial crisis (more on this in Chapter 18). This form of support is often referred to as the "lender of last

Global The Spread of Government Deposit Insurance Throughout the World: Is This a Good Thing?

For the first 30 years after federal deposit insurance was established in the United States, only six countries emulated the United States and adopted deposit insurance. However, this began to change in the late 1960s, with the trend accelerating in the 1990s, when the number of countries adopting deposit insurance topped 70. Government deposit insurance has taken off throughout the world because of growing concern about the health of banking systems, particularly after the increasing number of banking crises in recent years (documented at the end of this chapter). Has this spread of deposit insurance been a good thing? Has it helped improve the performance of the financial system and prevent banking crises?

The answer seems to be no under many circumstances. Research at the World Bank has found that, on average, the adoption of explicit government deposit insurance is associated with less banking sector stability and a higher incidence of banking crises.* Furthermore, on average, it seems to retard financial development. However, the negative effects of deposit insurance appear only in countries with weak institutional environments: an absence of rule of law, ineffective regulation and supervision of the financial sector, and high corruption. This situation is exactly what might be expected because, as we will see later in this chapter, a strong institutional environment is needed to limit the moral hazard incentives for banks to engage in the excessively risky behavior encouraged by deposit insurance. The problem is that developing a strong institutional environment may be very difficult to achieve in many emerging market countries. We are left with the following conclusion: Adoption of deposit insurance may be exactly the wrong medicine for promoting stability and efficiency of banking systems in emerging market countries.

*See World Bank, *Finance for Growth: Policy Choices in a Volatile World* (Oxford: World Bank and Oxford University Press, 2001).

resort" role of the central bank. In other cases, funds are provided directly to troubled institutions, as was done by the U.S. Treasury and by other governments in 2008 during a particularly virulent phase of the subprime financial crisis. Governments can also take over (nationalize) troubled institutions and guarantee that all creditors will be repaid their loans in full.

Moral Hazard and the Government Safety Net Although a government safety net can help protect depositors and other creditors and prevent, or ameliorate, financial crises, it is a mixed blessing. The most serious drawback of the government safety net stems from moral hazard, the incentives of one party to a transaction to engage in activities detrimental to the other party. Moral hazard is an important concern in insurance arrangements in general because the existence of insurance provides increased incentives for taking risks that might result in an insurance payoff. For example, some drivers with automobile collision insurance that has a low deductible might be more likely to drive recklessly, because if they get into an accident, the insurance company pays most of the costs for damage and repairs.

Moral hazard is a prominent concern in government arrangements to provide a safety net. With a safety net, depositors and creditors know they will not suffer losses if a financial institution fails, so they do not impose the discipline of the marketplace on these institutions by withdrawing funds when they suspect that the financial institution is taking on too much risk. Consequently, financial institutions with a government safety net have an incentive to take on greater risks than they otherwise would, with taxpayers paying the bill if the bank subsequently goes belly up. Financial institutions have been given the following bet: "Heads I win, tails the taxpayer loses."

Adverse Selection and the Government Safety Net A further problem with a government safety net like deposit insurance arises because of adverse selection, the fact that the people who are most likely to produce the adverse outcome insured against (bank failure) are those who most want to take advantage of the insurance. For example, bad drivers are more likely than good drivers to take out automobile collision insurance with a low deductible. Because depositors and creditors protected by a government safety net have little reason to impose discipline on financial institutions, risk-loving entrepreneurs might find the financial industry a particularly attractive one to enter—they know that they will be able to engage in highly risky activities. Even worse, because protected depositors and creditors have so little reason to monitor the financial institution's activities, without government intervention outright crooks might also find finance an attractive industry for their activities because it is easy for them to get away with fraud and embezzlement.

"Too Big to Fail" The moral hazard created by a government safety net and the desire to prevent financial institution failures have presented financial regulators with a particular quandary. Because the failure of a very large financial institution makes it more likely that a major financial disruption will occur, financial regulators are naturally reluctant to allow a big institution to fail and cause losses to its depositors and creditors. Indeed, consider Continental Illinois, one of the ten largest banks in the United States when it became insolvent in May 1984. Not only did the FDIC guarantee depositors up to the $100,000 insurance limit (the maximum at that time), but it also guaranteed accounts exceeding $100,000 and even prevented losses for Continental Illinois bondholders. Shortly thereafter, the Comptroller of the Currency (the regulator of national banks) testified to Congress that eleven of the largest banks would receive a similar treatment to that of Continental Illinois. Although the comptroller did not use the term "too big to fail" (it was actually used by Congressman Stewart McKinney in those hearings), this term is now applied to a policy in which the government provides guarantees of repayment of large uninsured creditors of the largest banks, so that no depositor or creditor suffers a loss, even when they are not automatically entitled to this guarantee. The FDIC would do this by using the purchase and assumption method, giving the insolvent bank a large infusion of capital and then finding a willing merger partner to take over the bank and its deposits. The too-big-to-fail policy was extended to big banks that were not even among the eleven largest. (Note that "too big to fail" is somewhat misleading because when a financial institution is closed or merged into another financial institution, the managers are usually fired and the stockholders in the financial institution lose their investment.)

One problem with the too-big-to-fail policy is that it increases the moral hazard incentives for big banks. If the FDIC were willing to close a bank using the payoff method, paying depositors only up to the current $250,000 limit, large depositors with more than $250,000 would suffer losses if the bank failed. Thus they would have an incentive to monitor the bank by examining the bank's activities closely and pulling their money out if the bank was taking on too much risk. To prevent such a loss of deposits, the bank would be more likely to engage in less risky activities. However, once large depositors know that a bank is too big to fail, they have no incentive to monitor the bank and pull out their deposits when it takes on too much risk: No matter what the bank does, large depositors will not suffer any losses. The result of the too-big-to-fail policy is that big banks might take on even greater risks, thereby making bank failures more likely.

Similarly, the too-big-to-fail policy increases the moral hazard incentives for nonbank financial institutions that are extended a government safety net. Knowing that the financial institution will get bailed out, creditors have little incentive to monitor the institution and pull their money out when the institution is taking on excessive risk. As a result, large or interconnected financial institutions will be more likely to engage in highly risky activities, making it more likely that a financial crisis will occur.

Financial Consolidation and the Government Safety Net With financial innovation and the passage of the Riegle-Neal Interstate Banking and Branching Efficiency Act of 1994 and the Gramm-Leach-Bliley Financial Services Modernization Act in 1999, financial consolidation has been proceeding at a rapid pace, leading to both larger and more complex financial organizations. Financial consolidation poses two challenges to financial regulation because of the existence of the government safety net. First, the increased size of financial institutions as a result of financial consolidation increases the too-big-to-fail problem, because there will now be more large institutions whose failure would expose the financial system to systemic (system-wide) risk. Thus more financial institutions are likely to be treated as too big to fail, and the increased moral hazard incentives for these large institutions to take on greater risk can then increase the fragility of the financial system. Second, financial consolidation of banks with other financial services firms means that the government safety net may be extended to new activities, such as securities underwriting, insurance, or real estate activities, as has occurred during the global financial crisis. This situation increases incentives for greater risk taking in these activities, which can also weaken the fabric of the financial system. Limiting the moral hazard incentives for the larger, more complex financial organizations that have arisen as a result of recent changes in legislation will be one of the key issues facing banking regulators in the aftermath of the recent global financial crisis.

Restrictions on Asset Holdings

As we have seen, the moral hazard associated with a government safety net encourages too much risk taking on the part of financial institutions. Bank regulations that restrict asset holdings are directed at minimizing this moral hazard, which can cost the taxpayers dearly.

Even in the absence of a government safety net, financial institutions still have the incentive to take on too much risk. Risky assets may provide the financial institution with higher earnings when they pay off; but if they do not pay off and the institution fails, depositors and creditors are left holding the bag. If depositors and creditors were able to monitor the bank easily by acquiring information on its risk-taking activities, they would immediately withdraw their funds if the institution was taking on too much risk. To prevent such a loss of funds, the institution would be more likely to reduce its risk-taking activities. Unfortunately, acquiring information on an institution's activities to learn how much risk it is taking can be a difficult task. Hence most depositors and many creditors are incapable of imposing discipline that might prevent financial institutions from engaging in risky activities. A strong rationale for government regulation to reduce risk taking on the part of financial institutions therefore existed even before the establishment of government safety nets like federal deposit insurance.

Because banks are most prone to panics, they are subjected to strict regulations to restrict their holding of risky assets, such as common stocks. Bank regulations also promote diversification, which reduces risk by limiting the dollar amount of loans in particular categories or to individual borrowers. With the extension of the government safety net during the global financial crisis, and the calls for regulatory reform in its aftermath, it is likely that nonbank financial institutions may face greater restrictions on their holdings of risky assets. The danger exists, however, that these restrictions may become so onerous that the efficiency of the financial system will be impaired.

Capital Requirements

Government-imposed capital requirements are another way of minimizing moral hazard at financial institutions. When a financial institution is forced to hold a large amount of equity capital, the institution has more to lose if it fails and is thus more likely to pursue less risky activities. In addition, as was illustrated in Chapter 10, capital functions as a cushion when bad shocks occur, making it less likely that the financial institution will fail, thereby directly adding to the safety and soundness of financial institutions.

Capital requirements for banks take two forms. The first type is based on the **leverage ratio**, the amount of capital divided by the bank's total assets. To be classified as well capitalized, a bank's leverage ratio must exceed 5%; a lower leverage ratio, especially one below 3%, triggers increased regulatory restrictions on the bank. Through most of the 1980s, minimum bank capital in the United States was set solely by specifying a minimum leverage ratio.

In the wake of the Continental Illinois and savings and loans bailouts in the 1980s, regulators in the United States and the rest of the world have become increasingly worried about banks' holdings of risky assets and about the increase in banks' **off-balance-sheet activities**, activities that involve trading financial instruments and generating income from fees, which do not appear on bank balance sheets but nevertheless expose banks to risk. An agreement among banking officials from industrialized nations set up the **Basel Committee on Banking Supervision** (because it meets under the auspices of the Bank for International Settlements in Basel, Switzerland), which has implemented the **Basel Accord**, which deals with a second type of capital requirements, risk-based capital requirements. The Basel Accord, which required that banks hold as capital at least 8% of their risk-weighted assets, has been adopted by more than 100 countries, including the United States. Assets and off-balance-sheet activities were allocated into four categories, each with a different weight to reflect the degree of credit risk. The first category carries a zero weight and includes items that have little default risk, such as reserves and government securities issued by the Organization for Economic Cooperation and Development (OECD—industrialized) countries. The second category has a 20% weight and includes claims on banks in OECD countries. The third category has a weight of 50% and includes municipal bonds and residential mortgages. The fourth category has the maximum weight of 100% and includes loans to consumers and corporations. Off-balance-sheet activities are treated in a similar manner by assigning a credit-equivalent percentage that converts them to on-balance-sheet items to which the appropriate risk weight applies, and there are minimum capital requirements for risks in banks' trading accounts.

Over time, limitations of the Basel Accord have become apparent, because the regulatory measure of bank risk, as stipulated by the risk weights, can differ substantially from the actual risk the bank faces. This has resulted in regulatory arbitrage, a practice in which banks keep on their books assets that have the same risk-based capital requirement but are relatively risky, such as a loan to a company with a very low credit rating, while taking off their books low-risk assets, such as a loan to a company with a very high credit rating. The Basel Accord could thus lead to increased risk taking, the opposite of its intent. To address these limitations, the Basel Committee on Bank Supervision came up with a new capital accord, often referred to as Basel 2, but in the aftermath of the global financial crisis, it developed an even newer accord, which the media has dubbed "Basel 3." These accords are described in the Global box, "Where Is the Basel Accord Heading After the Global Financial Crisis?"

Prompt Corrective Action

If the amount of a financial institution's capital falls to low levels, two serious problems result. First, the bank is more likely to fail because it has a smaller capital cushion if it suffers loan losses or other asset write-downs. Second, with less capital, a financial institution has less "skin in the game" and is therefore more likely to take on excessive risks. In other words, the moral hazard problem becomes more severe, making it more likely that the institution will fail and the taxpayer will be left holding the bag. To prevent this, the Federal Deposit Insurance Corporation Improvement Act of 1991 adopted prompt corrective action provisions that require the FDIC to intervene earlier and more vigorously when a bank gets into trouble.

Banks are now classified into five groups based on bank capital. Group 1, classified as "well capitalized," comprises banks that significantly exceed minimum capital requirements and are allowed privileges such as the ability to do some securities underwriting. Banks in group 2, classified as "adequately capitalized," meet minimum capital requirements and are not subject to corrective actions but are not allowed the privileges of the well-capitalized banks. Banks in group 3, "undercapitalized," fail to meet capital requirements. Banks in groups 4 and 5 are "significantly undercapitalized" and "critically undercapitalized," respectively, and are not allowed to pay interest on their deposits at rates that are higher than average. In addition, for group 4 and 5 banks, the FDIC is required to take prompt corrective actions, such as requiring them to submit a capital restoration plan, restrict their asset growth, and seek regulatory approval to open

Global — Where Is the Basel Accord Heading After the Global Financial Crisis?

Starting in June 1999, the Basel Committee on Banking Supervision released several proposals to reform the original 1988 Basel Accord. These efforts have culminated in what bank supervisors refer to as Basel 2, which is based on three pillars.

1. Pillar 1 links capital requirements for large, internationally active banks more closely to actual risk of three types: market risk, credit risk, and operational risk. It does so by specifying many more categories of assets with different risk weights in its standardized approach. Alternatively, it allows sophisticated banks to pursue an internal ratings-based approach that permits banks to use their own models of credit risk.
2. Pillar 2 focuses on strengthening the supervisory process, particularly in assessing the quality of risk management in banking institutions and evaluating whether these institutions have adequate procedures to determine how much capital they need.
3. Pillar 3 focuses on improving market discipline through increased disclosure of details about a bank's credit exposures, its amount of reserves and capital, the officials who control the bank, and the effectiveness of its internal rating system.

Although Basel 2 made great strides toward limiting excessive risk taking by internationally active banking institutions, it greatly increased the complexity of the accord. The document describing the original Basel Accord was 26 pages, whereas the final draft of Basel 2 exceeded 500 pages. The original timetable called for the completion of the final round of consultation by the end of 2001, with the new rules taking effect by 2004. However, criticism from banks, trade associations, and national regulators led to several postponements. The final draft was not published until June 2004, and Basel 2 began to be implemented at the start of 2008 by European banks. U.S. banks submitted plans for compliance with Basel 2 in 2008, but full implementation did not occur until 2009. Only the dozen or so largest U.S. banks are subject to Basel 2: All others will be allowed to use a simplified version of the standards it imposes.

The global financial crisis, however, revealed many limitations of the new accord. First, Basel 2 did not require banks to have sufficient capital to weather the financial disruption during this period. Second, risk weights in the standardized approach are heavily reliant on credit ratings, which proved to be so unreliable in the run-up to the financial crisis. Third, Basel 2 is very procyclical. That is, it demands that banks hold less capital when times are good, but more when times are bad, thereby exacerbating credit cycles. Because the probability of default and expected losses for different classes of assets rises during bad times, Basel 2 may require more capital at exactly the time when capital is most short. This has been a particularly serious concern in the aftermath of the global financial crisis. As a result of this crisis, banks' capital balances eroded, leading to a cutback on lending that was a big drag on the economy. Basel 2 made this cutback in lending even worse, doing yet more harm to the economy. Fourth, Basel 2 did not focus sufficiently on the dangers of a possible drying up of liquidity, which brought financial institutions down during the financial crisis.

As a result of these limitations, in 2010 the Basel Committee developed a new accord, Basel 3. It beefs up capital standards by not only raising them substantially but also improving the quality of the capital, makes them less procyclical by raising capital requirements in good times and lowering them in bad, makes new rules on the use of credit ratings, and requires financial institutions to have more stable funding so that they are better able to withstand liquidity shocks. Measures to achieve these objectives are highly controversial because of concerns that tightening up capital standards might cause banks to restrict their lending, which would make it harder for economies throughout the world to recover from the recent deep recession. Basel 3 is being implemented slowly over time, with the target for full implementation extending out to the end of 2019. Whether Basel 3 will be fully in place by that date and be successful in restraining risk taking is highly uncertain.

new branches or develop new lines of business. Banks that are so undercapitalized as to have equity capital that amounts to less than 2% of assets fall into group 5, and the FDIC must take steps to close them down.

Financial Supervision: Chartering and Examination

Overseeing who operates financial institutions and how they are operated, referred to as **financial supervision** or prudential supervision, is an important method for reducing adverse selection and moral hazard in the financial industry. Because financial institutions can be used by crooks or overambitious entrepreneurs to engage in highly speculative activities, such undesirable people would be eager to run a financial institution. Chartering financial institutions is one method for preventing this adverse selection problem; through chartering, proposals for new institutions are screened to prevent undesirable people from controlling them.

Regular on-site examinations, which allow regulators to monitor whether the institution is complying with capital requirements and restrictions on asset holdings, also function to limit moral hazard. Bank examiners give banks a *CAMELS rating*. The acronym is based on the six areas assessed: capital adequacy, asset quality, management, earnings, liquidity, and sensitivity to market risk. With this information about a bank's activities, regulators can enforce regulations by taking such formal actions as *cease and desist orders* to alter the bank's behavior or even close a bank if its CAMELS rating is sufficiently low. Actions taken to reduce moral hazard by restricting banks from taking on too much risk help reduce the adverse selection problem further, because with less opportunity for risk taking, risk-loving entrepreneurs will be less likely to be attracted to the banking industry. Note that the methods regulators use to cope with adverse selection and moral hazard have their counterparts in private financial markets (see Chapters 8 and 10). Chartering is similar to the screening of potential borrowers, regulations restricting risky asset holdings are similar to restrictive covenants that prevent borrowing firms from engaging in risky investment activities, capital requirements act like restrictive covenants that require minimum amounts of net worth for borrowing firms, and regular examinations are similar to the monitoring of borrowers by lending institutions.

A commercial bank obtains a charter either from the Comptroller of the Currency (in the case of a national bank) or from a state banking authority (in the case of a state bank). To obtain a charter, the people planning to organize the bank must submit an application that shows how they plan to operate the bank. In evaluating the application, the regulatory authority looks at whether the bank is likely to be sound by examining the quality of the bank's intended management, the likely earnings of the bank, and the amount of the bank's initial capital. Before 1980, the chartering agency typically explored the issue of whether the community needed a new bank. Often a new bank charter would not be granted if existing banks in a community would be hurt by its presence. Today this anticompetitive stance (justified by the desire to prevent failures of existing banks) is no longer as strong in the chartering agencies.

Once a bank has been chartered, it is required to file periodic (usually quarterly) *call reports* that reveal the bank's assets and liabilities, income and dividends, ownership, foreign exchange operations, and other details. The bank is also subject to examination by the bank regulatory agencies to ascertain its financial condition at least once a year. To avoid duplication of effort, the three federal agencies work together and usually accept each other's examinations. This means that, typically, national banks are examined by the Office of the Comptroller of the Currency, state banks that are members of the Federal Reserve System are examined by the Fed, and insured nonmember state banks are examined by the FDIC.

Bank examinations are conducted by bank examiners, who sometimes make unannounced visits to the bank (so that nothing can be "swept under the rug" in anticipation of their examination). The examiners study a bank's books to see whether it is complying with the rules and regulations that apply to its holdings of assets. If a bank is holding securities or loans that are too risky, the bank examiner can force the bank to get rid of them. If a bank examiner decides that a loan is unlikely to be repaid, the examiner can force the bank to declare the loan worthless (to write off the loan, which reduces the bank's capital). If, after examining the bank, the examiner feels that it does not have sufficient capital or has engaged in dishonest practices, the bank can be declared a "problem bank" and will be subject to more frequent examinations.

Assessment of Risk Management

Traditionally, on-site examinations have focused primarily on assessment of the quality of a financial institution's balance sheet at a point in time and whether it complies with capital requirements and restrictions on asset holdings. Although the traditional focus is important for reducing excessive risk taking by financial institutions, it is no longer thought to be adequate in today's world, in which financial innovation has produced new markets and instruments that make it easy for financial institutions and their employees to make huge bets easily and quickly. In this new financial environment, a financial institution that is healthy at a particular point in time can be driven into insolvency extremely rapidly from trading losses, as forcefully demonstrated by the failure of Barings in 1995 (discussed in Chapter 10). Thus an examination that focuses only on a financial institution's position at a point in time may not be effective in indicating whether it will, in fact, be taking on excessive risk in the near future.

This change in the environment for financial institutions has resulted in a major shift in thinking about the prudential supervisory process throughout the world. Bank examiners, for example, are now placing far greater emphasis on evaluating the soundness of a bank's management processes with regard to controlling risk. This shift in thinking was reflected in a new focus on risk management by the Federal Reserve System, starting with 1993 guidelines to examiners on trading and derivatives activities. The focus was expanded and formalized in the Trading Activities Manual issued early in 1994, which provided bank examiners with tools to evaluate risk management systems. In late 1995, the Federal Reserve and the Comptroller of the Currency announced that they would be assessing risk management processes at the banks they supervise. Now bank examiners give a separate risk management rating from 1 to 5 that feeds into the overall management rating as part of the CAMELS system. Four elements of sound risk management are assessed to arrive at the risk management rating: (1) the quality of oversight provided by the board of directors and senior management, (2) the adequacy of policies and limits for all activities that present significant risks, (3) the quality of the risk measurement and monitoring systems, and (4) the adequacy of internal controls to prevent fraud or unauthorized activities on the part of employees.

This shift toward focusing on management processes is also reflected in recent guidelines adopted by the U.S. bank regulatory authorities to deal with interest-rate risk. These guidelines require the bank's board of directors to establish interest-rate risk limits, appoint officials of the bank to manage this risk, and monitor the bank's risk exposure. The guidelines also require that senior management of a bank develop formal risk management policies and procedures to ensure that the board of directors' risk limits are not violated and to implement internal controls to monitor interest-rate risk and compliance with the board's directives. Particularly important is the implementation of **stress tests**, which calculate losses under dire scenarios and the need for more capital, or **value-at-risk (VaR)** calculations, which measure the size of the loss on a trading portfolio—say, over a two-week period—that might happen 1% of the time. In addition to these guidelines, bank examiners will continue to consider interest-rate risk in deciding the bank's capital requirements.

Disclosure Requirements

The free-rider problem described in Chapter 8 indicates that individual depositors and creditors will not have enough incentive to produce private information about the quality of a financial institution's assets. To ensure better information is available in the marketplace, regulators can require that financial institutions adhere to certain standard accounting principles and disclose a wide range of information that helps the market assess the quality of an institution's portfolio and the amount of its exposure to risk. More public information about the risks incurred by financial institutions and the quality of their portfolios can better enable stockholders, creditors, and depositors to evaluate and monitor financial institutions and so act as a deterrent to excessive risk taking.

Disclosure requirements are a key element of financial regulation. Basel 2 puts a particular emphasis on disclosure requirements, with one of its three pillars focusing on increasing market discipline by mandating increased disclosure by banking institutions of their credit exposure, amount of reserves, and capital. The Securities Act of 1933 and the Securities and Exchange Commission (SEC), which was established in 1934, also impose disclosure requirements on any corporation, including financial institutions, that issues publicly traded securities. In addition, it has required financial institutions to provide additional disclosure regarding their off-balance-sheet positions and more information about how they value their portfolios.

Regulation to increase disclosure is needed to limit incentives to take on excessive risk and to upgrade the quality of information in the marketplace so that investors can make informed decisions, thereby improving the ability of financial markets to allocate capital to its most productive uses. The efficiency of markets is assisted by the SEC's disclosure requirements mentioned above, as well as its regulation of brokerage firms, mutual funds, exchanges, and credit-rating agencies to ensure that they produce reliable information and protect investors. The Sarbanes-Oxley Act of 2002 took disclosure of information even further by increasing the incentives to produce accurate audits of corporate income statements and balance sheets, establishing the Public Company Accounting Oversight Board (PCAOB) to oversee the audit industry, and putting in place regulations to limit conflicts of interest in the financial services industry.

Particularly controversial in the wake of the global financial crisis is the move to so-called **mark-to-market accounting**, also called **fair-value accounting**, in which assets are valued in the balance sheet at what they could sell for in the market (see the FYI box, "Mark-to-Market Accounting and the Global Financial Crisis").

Consumer Protection

The existence of asymmetric information also suggests that consumers may not have enough information to protect themselves fully. Consumer protection regulation has

FYI Mark-to-Market Accounting and the Global Financial Crisis

The controversy over mark-to-market accounting has made accounting a hot topic. Mark-to-market accounting was made standard practice in the U.S. accounting industry in 1993. The rationale behind mark-to-market accounting is that market prices provide the best basis for estimating the true value of assets, and hence capital, in the firm. Before mark-to-market accounting, firms relied on the traditional historical-cost (book value) basis in which the value of an asset was set at its initial purchase price. The problem with historical-cost accounting is that fluctuations in the value of assets and liabilities because of changes in interest rates or default risk are not reflected in the calculation of the firm's equity capital. Yet changes in the market value of assets and liabilities—and hence changes in the market value of equity capital—are what indicates if a firm is in good shape, or alternatively, if it is getting into trouble and may therefore be more susceptible to moral hazard.

Mark-to-market accounting, however, is subject to a major flaw. At times markets stop working, as occurred during the global financial crisis. The price of an asset sold at a time of financial distress does not reflect its fundamental value. That is, the fire-sale liquidation value of an asset can at times be well below the present value of its expected future cash flows. Many people, particularly bankers, have criticized mark-to-market accounting during the recent global financial crisis episode, claiming that it has been an important factor driving the crisis. They claim that the seizing up of financial markets has led to market prices being well below fundamental values. Mark-to-market accounting requires that the financial firms' assets be marked down in value. This markdown creates a shortfall in capital that leads to a cutback in lending, which causes a further deterioration in asset prices, which in turn causes a further cutback in lending. The resulting adverse feedback loop can then make the financial crisis even worse. Although the criticisms of mark-to-market accounting have some validity, some of the criticism by bankers is self-serving. The criticism was made only when asset values were falling, when mark-to-market accounting was painting a bleaker picture of banks' balance sheets, as opposed to when asset prices were booming, when it made banks' balance sheets look very good.

The criticisms of mark-to-market accounting led to a Congressional focus on mark-to-market accounting that resulted in a provision in the Emergency Economic Stabilization Act of 2008, discussed in Chapter 9, that required the SEC, in consultation with the Federal Reserve and the U.S. Treasury, to submit a study of mark-to-market accounting applicable to financial institutions. Who knew that accounting could get even politicians worked up!

taken several forms. The Consumer Protection Act of 1969 (more commonly referred to as the Truth in Lending Act) requires all lenders, not just banks, to provide information to consumers about the cost of borrowing, including a standardized interest rate (called the *annual percentage rate*, or *APR*), and the total finance charges on the loan. The Fair Credit Billing Act of 1974 requires creditors, especially credit card issuers, to provide information on the method of assessing finance charges and requires that billing complaints be handled quickly. Both of these acts are administered by the Federal Reserve System under Regulation Z.

Congress has also passed legislation to reduce discrimination in credit markets. The Equal Credit Opportunity Act of 1974 and its extension in 1976 forbid discrimination by lenders based on race, gender, marital status, age, or national origin. It is administered by the Federal Reserve under Regulation B. The Community Reinvestment

Act (CRA) of 1977 was enacted to prevent "redlining," a lender's refusal to lend in a particular area (marked off by a hypothetical red line on a map). The Community Reinvestment Act requires that banks show that they lend in all areas in which they take deposits, and if banks are found to be in noncompliance with the act, regulators can reject their applications for mergers, branching, or other new activities.

FYI The Subprime Mortgage Crisis and Consumer Protection Regulation

Because of the principal–agent problem inherent in the originate-to-distribute model for subprime mortgages discussed in Chapter 9, incentives were weak for mortgage originators, typically mortgage brokers who were virtually unregulated, to ensure that subprime borrowers had an ability to pay back their loans. After all, mortgage brokers keep their large fees from mortgage originations even if sometime down the road the borrowers default on their loans and lose their houses. With these incentives, mortgage brokers weakened their underwriting standards, leading to subprime mortgage products such as "no-doc loans," more pejoratively referred to as "liar loans," in which borrowers did not have to produce documentation about their assets or income. A particular infamous variant of the no-doc loan was dubbed the NINJA loan because it was issued to borrowers with No Income, No Job, and No Assets. Mortgage brokers also had incentives to saddle households with very complicated mortgage products borrowers could not understand and which they couldn't afford to pay. In some cases, mortgage brokers even engaged in fraud by falsifying information on borrowers' mortgage applications in order to qualify them for mortgage loans.

Lax consumer protection regulation was an important factor in producing the subprime mortgage crisis. Mortgage originators were not required to disclose information to borrowers that would have helped them better understand complicated mortgage products and whether they could afford to repay them. Outrage over the surge of foreclosures has been an important stimulus for new regulation to provide better information to mortgage borrowers and to ban so-called "unfair and deceptive" practices. Under Regulation Z of the Truth in Lending Act, in July 2008, the Federal Reserve issued a final rule for subprime mortgage loans with the following four elements: (1) a ban on lenders making loans without regard to borrowers' ability to repay the loan from income and assets other than the home's value; (2) a ban on no-doc loans; (3) a ban on prepayment penalties (i.e., a penalty for paying back the loan early) if the interest payment can change in the first four years of the loan; and (4) a requirement that lenders establish an escrow account for property taxes and homeowner's insurance to be paid into on a monthly basis. In addition, the rule stipulated the following new regulations for all mortgage loans, not just subprime mortgages: (1) a prohibition on mortgage brokers coercing a real estate appraiser to misstate a home's value; (2) a prohibition on putting one late fee on top of another and a requirement to credit consumers' loan payments as of the date of receipt; (3) a requirement for lenders to provide a good-faith estimate of the loan costs within three days after a household applies for a loan; and (4) a ban on a number of misleading advertising practices, including representing that a rate or payment is "fixed" when the payment can change.

Because the view was held that more needed to be done, the Obama administration and Congress have stepped in by creating a new consumer protection agency as part of the financial reform legislation of 2010; this is discussed later in the chapter. The mandate of this agency is to further strengthen consumer protection regulation on subprime mortgages and other financial products.

The subprime mortgage crisis has illustrated the need for greater consumer protection because so many borrowers took out loans with terms they did not understand and that were well beyond their means to repay. The result was millions of foreclosures, with many households losing their homes. Because weak consumer protection regulation played a prominent role in this crisis, demands to strengthen this regulation have been increasing, as discussed in the FYI box, "The Subprime Mortgage Crisis and Consumer Protection Regulation."

Restrictions on Competition

Increased competition can also increase moral hazard incentives for financial institutions to take on more risk. Declining profitability as a result of increased competition could tip the incentives of financial institutions toward assuming greater risk in an effort to maintain former profit levels. Thus governments in many countries have instituted regulations to protect financial institutions from competition. These regulations have taken two forms in the United States in the past. First were restrictions on branching, described in Chapter 12, which reduced competition between banks, but these were eliminated in 1994. The second form involved preventing nonbank institutions from competing with banks by engaging in banking business, as embodied in the Glass-Steagall Act, which was repealed in 1999.

Although restrictions on competition propped up the health of banks, they also had serious disadvantages: They led to higher charges to consumers and decreased the efficiency of banking institutions, which did not have to compete as vigorously. Thus, although the existence of asymmetric information provided a rationale for anticompetitive regulations, it did not mean they would be beneficial. Indeed, in recent years, the impulse of governments in industrialized countries to restrict competition has been waning.

Macroprudential Versus Microprudential Supervision

Before the global financial crisis, the regulatory authorities engaged in **microprudential supervision**, which focuses on the safety and soundness of *individual* financial institutions. Microprudential supervision looks at each individual institution separately and assesses the riskiness of its activities and whether it complies with disclosure requirements. Most importantly, it checks whether that institution satisfies capital *ratios* and, if not, either it engages in prompt corrective action to force the institution to raise its capital ratios or the supervisor closes it down, along the lines we have discussed above.

Discussion of the global financial crisis in Chapter 9 reveals that a focus on microprudential supervision is not enough to prevent financial crises. The run on the shadow banking system illustrates how the problems of one financial institution can harm other financial institutions that are otherwise healthy. When the troubled financial institution is forced to engage in fire sales and sell off assets to meet target capital ratios or haircut requirements, this leads to a decline in asset values. This decline in asset values then causes other institutions to engage in fire sales, leading to a rapid deleveraging process and a systemic crisis. In situations like this, even institutions that would normally be healthy and have high capital ratios may find themselves in trouble.

The global financial crisis has therefore made it clear that there is a need for **macroprudential supervision**, which focuses on the safety and soundness of the financial system *in the aggregate*. Rather than focus on the safety and soundness of individual institutions, macroprudential supervision seeks to mitigate system-wide fire sales and deleveraging by assessing the overall capacity of the financial system to avoid them. In addition, because many institutions that were well capitalized faced liquidity shortages and found that their access to short-term funding was cut off, macroprudential supervision focuses not only on capital adequacy as a whole but also on whether the financial system has sufficient liquidity.

Macroprudential policies can take several forms. The run-up to the global financial crisis included a so-called **leverage cycle**, in which there was a feedback loop from a boom in issuing credit, which led to higher asset prices, which resulted in higher capital buffers at financial institutions, which supported further lending

Global International Financial Regulation

Because asymmetric information problems in the banking industry are a fact of life throughout the world, financial regulation in other countries is similar to that in the United States. Financial institutions are chartered and supervised by government regulators, just as they are in the United States. Disclosure requirements for financial institutions and corporations issuing securities are similar in other developed countries. Deposit insurance is also a feature of the regulatory systems in most other countries, although its coverage is often smaller than that in the United States and is intentionally not advertised. We have also seen that capital requirements are in the process of being standardized across countries in compliance with agreements like the Basel Accord.

Particular problems in financial regulation occur when financial institutions operate in many countries and thus can readily shift their business from one country to another. Financial regulators closely examine the domestic operations of financial institutions in their country, but they often do not have the knowledge or ability to keep a close watch on operations in other countries, either by domestic institutions' foreign affiliates or by foreign institutions with domestic branches. In addition, when a financial institution operates in many countries, it is not always clear which national regulatory authority should have primary responsibility for keeping the institution from engaging in overly risky activities.

The difficulties inherent in international financial regulation were highlighted by the collapse of the Bank of Credit and Commerce International (BCCI). BCCI, which, although operating in more than 70 countries, including the United States and the United Kingdom, was supervised by Luxembourg, a tiny country unlikely to be up to the task. When massive fraud was discovered, the Bank of England closed BCCI down, but not before depositors and stockholders were exposed to huge losses. Cooperation among regulators in different countries and standardization of regulatory requirements provide potential solutions to the problems of international financial regulation. The world has moved in this direction through agreements like the Basel Accord and oversight procedures announced by the Basel Committee in July 1992, which require a bank's worldwide operations to be under the scrutiny of a single home-country regulator with enhanced powers to acquire information on the bank's activities. The Basel Committee also ruled that regulators in other countries can restrict the operations of a foreign bank if they believe it lacks effective oversight. Whether agreements of this type will solve the problem of international financial regulation in the future is an open question.

in the context of unchanging capital requirements, which then raised asset prices further, and so on; in the bust, the value of the capital dropped precipitously, leading to a cut in lending. To short-circuit this leverage cycle, macroprudential policies would make capital requirements countercyclical; that is, they would be adjusted upward during a boom and downward during a bust. In addition, during the upward swing in the leverage cycle, macroprudential policies might involve forcing financial institutions to tighten credit standards or even direct limits on the growth of credit. In the downward swing, macroprudential supervision might be needed to force the banking system as a whole to raise an aggregate amount of new capital so that banks would not curtail lending in order to reduce the level of their assets and raise capital ratios. To ensure that financial institutions have enough liquidity, macroprudential policies could require that financial institutions have a sufficiently low *net stable funding ratio* (NSFR), which is the percentage of the institution's short-term funding in relation to total funding. Macroprudential policies of the type discussed here are being considered as part of the Basel 3 framework, but have not yet been completely worked out.

Summary

Asymmetric information analysis explains what types of financial regulations are needed to reduce moral hazard and adverse selection problems in the financial system. However, understanding the theory behind regulation does not mean that regulation and supervision of the financial system are easy in practice. Getting regulators and supervisors to do their job properly is difficult for several reasons. First, as we will see in the discussion of financial innovation in Chapter 12, in their search for profits, financial institutions have strong incentives to avoid existing regulations by loophole mining. Thus regulation applies to a moving target: Regulators are continually playing cat-and-mouse with financial institutions—financial institutions think up clever ways to avoid regulations, which then lead regulators to modify their regulation activities. Regulators continually face new challenges in a dynamically changing financial system, and unless they can respond rapidly to change, they may not be able to keep financial institutions from taking on excessive risk. This problem can be exacerbated if regulators and supervisors do not have the resources or expertise to keep up with clever people in financial institutions seeking to circumvent the existing regulations.

Financial regulation and supervision are difficult for two other reasons. In the regulation and supervision game, the devil is in the details. Subtle differences in the details may have unintended consequences; unless regulators get the regulation and supervision just right, they may be unable to prevent excessive risk taking. In addition, regulated firms may lobby politicians to lean on regulators and supervisors to go easy on them. For all these reasons, there is no guarantee that regulators and supervisors will be successful in promoting a healthy financial system. These same problems bedevil financial regulators in other countries besides the United States, as the Global box, "International Financial Regulation," indicates. Indeed, as we will see, financial regulation and supervision have not always worked well, leading to banking crises in the United States and throughout the world.

Because so many laws regulating the financial system have been passed in the United States, it is hard to keep track of them all. As a study aid, Table 1 lists the major financial legislation since the beginning of the twentieth century and its key provisions.

TABLE 1 Major Financial Legislation in the United States

Federal Reserve Act (1913)
Created the Federal Reserve System

McFadden Act of 1927
Effectively prohibited banks from branching across state lines
Put national and state banks on equal footing regarding branching

Banking Acts of 1933 (Glass-Steagall) and 1935
Created the FDIC
Separated commercial banking from the securities industry
Prohibited interest on checkable deposits and restricted such deposits to commercial banks
Put interest-rate ceilings on other deposits

Securities Act of 1933 and Securities Exchange Act of 1934
Required that investors receive financial information on securities offered for public sale
Prohibited misrepresentations and fraud in the sale of securities
Created the Securities and Exchange Commission (SEC)

Investment Company Act of 1940 and Investment Advisers Act of 1940
Regulated investment companies, including mutual funds
Regulated investment advisers

Bank Holding Company Act and Douglas Amendment (1956)
Clarified the status of bank holding companies (BHCs)
Gave the Federal Reserve regulatory responsibility for BHCs

Depository Institutions Deregulation and Monetary Control Act (DIDMCA) of 1980
Gave thrift institutions wider latitude in activities
Approved NOW and sweep accounts nationwide
Phased out interest-rate ceilings on deposits
Imposed uniform reserve requirements on depository institutions
Eliminated usury ceilings on loans
Increased deposit insurance to $100,000 per account

Depository Institutions Act of 1982 (Garn–St. Germain)
Gave the FDIC and the FSLIC emergency powers to merge banks and thrifts across state lines
Allowed depository institutions to offer money market deposit accounts (MMDAs)
Granted thrifts wider latitude in commercial and consumer lending

Competitive Equality in Banking Act (CEBA) of 1987
Provided $10.8 billion to shore up the FSLIC
Made provisions for regulatory forbearance in depressed areas

Financial Institutions Reform, Recovery, and Enforcement Act (FIRREA) of 1989
Provided funds to resolve S&L failures
Eliminated the FSLIC and the Federal Home Loan Bank Board
Created the Office of Thrift Supervision to regulate thrifts
Created the Resolution Trust Corporation to resolve insolvent thrifts
Raised deposit insurance premiums
Reimposed restrictions on S&L activities

TABLE 1 (continued)

Federal Deposit Insurance Corporation Improvement Act (FDICIA) of 1991
Recapitalized the FDIC
Limited brokered deposits and the too-big-to-fail policy
Set provisions for prompt corrective action
Instructed the FDIC to establish risk-based premiums
Increased examinations, capital requirements, and reporting requirements
Included the Foreign Bank Supervision Enhancement Act (FBSEA), which strengthened the Fed's authority to supervise foreign banks

Riegle-Neal Interstate Banking and Branching Efficiency Act of 1994
Overturned prohibition of interstate banking
Allowed branching across state lines

Gramm-Leach-Bliley Financial Services Modernization Act of 1999
Repealed Glass-Steagall and removed the separation of banking and securities industries

Sarbanes-Oxley Act of 2002
Created Public Company Accounting Oversight Board (PCAOB)
Prohibited certain conflicts of interest
Required certification by CEO and CFO of financial statements and independence of audit committee

Federal Deposit Insurance Reform Act of 2005
Merged the Bank Insurance Fund and the Savings Association Insurance Fund
Increased deposit insurance on individual retirement accounts to $250,000 per account

Dodd-Frank Wall Street Reform and Consumer Protection Act of 2010
Creates Consumer Financial Protection Bureau to regulate mortgages and other financial products
Routine derivatives required to be cleared through central clearinghouses and exchanges
New government resolution authority to allow government takeovers of financial holding companies
Creates Financial Stability Oversight Council to regulate systemically important financial institutions
Bans banks from proprietary trading and owning large percentage of hedge funds

THE 1980s SAVINGS AND LOAN AND BANKING CRISIS

Before the 1980s, financial regulation in the United States seemed largely effective in promoting a safe and sound banking system. In contrast to the pre-1934 period, when bank failures were common and depositors frequently suffered losses, the period from 1934 to 1980 was one in which bank failures were a rarity, averaging fifteen per year for commercial banks and fewer than five per year for savings and loan associations (S&Ls). After 1981, this rosy picture changed dramatically. Failures in both commercial banks and S&Ls climbed to levels more than ten times greater than in earlier years, as can be seen in Figure 1. Why did this happen? How did a regulatory system that seemed to be working well for half a century find itself in so much trouble.

The story starts with the burst of financial innovation in the 1960s, 1970s, and early 1980s. As we will see in Chapter 12, financial innovation decreased the profitability of

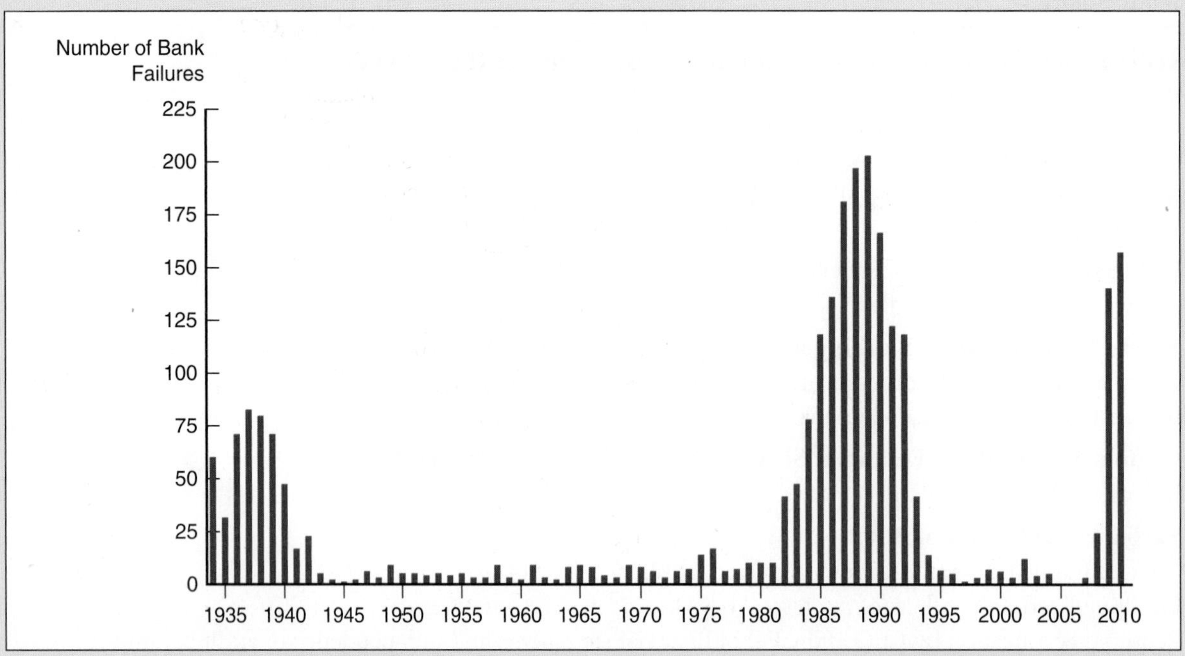

FIGURE 1 Bank Failures in the United States, 1934–2010

Bank failures were a rarity from 1934 to 1980, averaging fewer than fifteen per year, but after 1981 they rose to levels ten times greater.

Source: www.fdic.gov/bank/historical/bank/index.html.

certain traditional lines of business for commercial banks. Banks now faced increased competition for their sources of funds from new financial institutions, such as money market mutual funds, even as they were losing commercial lending business to the commercial paper market and securitization.

With the decreasing profitability of their traditional business, by the mid-1980s commercial banks were forced to seek out new and potentially risky business to keep their profits up. Specifically, they placed a greater percentage of their total loans in real estate and in credit extended to assist corporate takeovers and leveraged buyouts (called highly leveraged transaction loans). The existence of deposit insurance increased moral hazard for banks because insured depositors had little incentive to keep the banks from taking on too much risk. Regardless of how much risk banks were taking, deposit insurance guaranteed that depositors would not suffer any losses.

Adding fuel to the fire, financial innovation produced new financial instruments that widened the scope of risk taking. New markets in financial futures, junk bonds, swaps, and other instruments made it easier for banks to take on extra risk—making the moral hazard problem more severe. New legislation that deregulated the banking industry in the early 1980s, the Depository Institutions Deregulation and Monetary Control Act (DIDMCA) of 1980 and the Depository Institutions (Garn–St. Germain) Act of 1982, gave expanded powers to the S&Ls and mutual savings banks to engage in new risky activities. These thrift institutions, which had been restricted almost entirely to making loans for home mortgages, now were allowed to have up to 40% of their assets in commercial real estate loans, up to 30% in consumer lending, and up to 10%

in commercial loans and leases. In the wake of this legislation, S&L regulators allowed up to 10% of assets to be in junk bonds or in direct investments (common stocks, real estate, service corporations, and operating subsidiaries).

In addition, DIDMCA increased the mandated amount of federal deposit insurance from $40,000 per account to $100,000 and phased out restrictions on the interest rate that could be paid on deposits. Banks and S&Ls that wanted to pursue rapid growth and take on risky projects could now attract the necessary funds by issuing larger-denomination insured certificates of deposit with interest rates much higher than those being offered by their competitors. Without deposit insurance, high interest rates would not have induced depositors to provide the high-rolling banks with funds because of the realistic expectation that they might not get the funds back. But with deposit insurance and the widespread use of the FDIC's purchase and assumption method to handle failed banks, the government was guaranteeing that all deposits were safe, so depositors were more than happy to make deposits in banks with the highest interest rates.

As a result of these forces, commercial banks and savings and loans did take on excessive risks and began to suffer substantial losses. The outcome was that bank failures rose to a level of 200 per year by the late 1980s. The resulting losses for the FDIC meant that it had to be recapitalized. The Financial Institutions Reform, Recovery, and Enforcement Act of 1989, FIRREA, and the Federal Deposit Insurance Corporation and Improvement Act of 1991, FDICIA, provided a bailout of the savings and loan and commercial banking industries and reregulated the banking industry. The cost of the bailout to U.S. taxpayers was on the order of $150 billion, 3% of GDP.[1]

BANKING CRISES THROUGHOUT THE WORLD

Because misery loves company, it may make you feel better to know that the United States was not alone in suffering banking crises even before the global financial crisis of 2007–2009. Indeed, as Figure 2 and Table 2 illustrate, banking crises are very common, and many of them have been substantially worse than the one the United States experienced in the 1980s.

"Déjà vu All Over Again"

In banking crises in different countries, history keeps repeating itself. The parallels between the banking crisis episodes in all these countries are remarkably similar, creating a feeling of déjà vu. They all started with financial liberalization or innovation, with weak bank regulatory systems and a government safety net. Although financial liberalization is generally a good thing because it promotes competition and can make a financial system more efficient, it can lead to an increase in moral hazard, with more risk taking on the part of banks if regulation and supervision are lax; the result can then be banking crises.[2]

[1]The full story of the S&L and banking crisis of the 1980s is a fascinating one, with juicy scandals, even involving Senator John McCain, who was a presidential candidate in 2008. An appendix to this chapter found on this book's website at www.myeconlab.com discusses in more detail why this crisis happened, as well as the legislation in 1989 and 1991 that dealt with it.

[2]An appendix to this chapter can be found on this book's website, www.myeconlab.com, and discusses in detail many of the episodes of banking crises listed in Table 2.

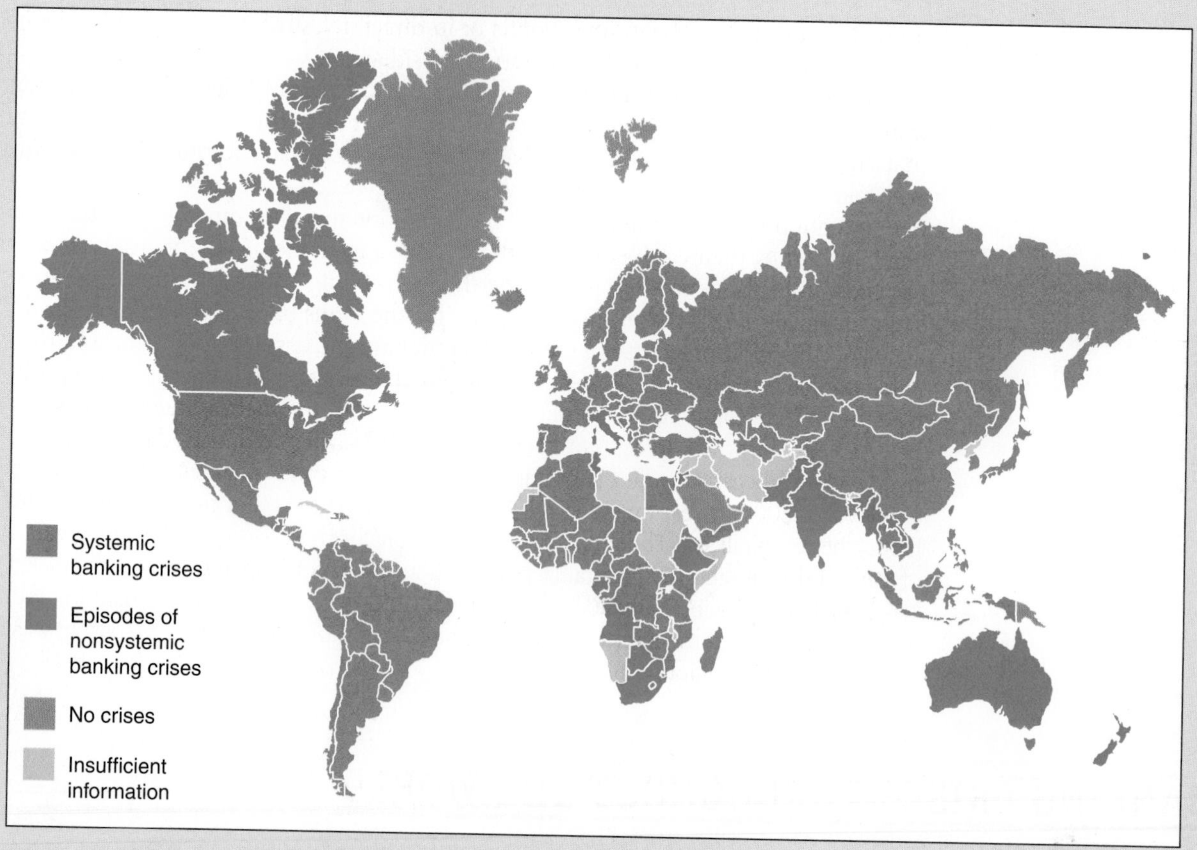

FIGURE 2 Banking Crises Throughout the World Since 1970
Banking crises have been very common throughout the world.
Sources: Data from Gerard Caprio and Daniela Klingebiel, "Episodes of Systemic and Borderline Financial Crises" mimeo., World Bank, October 1999; Luc Laeven and Fabian Valencia, "Resolution of Banking Crises: The Good, the Bad and the Ugly," IMF Working Paper No. WP/10/46 (June 2010) and Luc Laeven, Banking Crisis Database at http://www.luclaeven.com/Data.htm.

However, the banking crisis episodes listed in Table 2 do differ in that deposit insurance has not played an important role in many of the countries experiencing banking crises. For example, the size of the Japanese equivalent of the FDIC, the Deposit Insurance Corporation, was so tiny relative to the FDIC that it did not play a prominent role in the banking system and exhausted its resources almost immediately with the first bank failures. This example indicates that deposit insurance is not to blame for some of these banking crises. However, what is common to all the countries discussed here is the existence of a government safety net, in which the government stands ready to bail out banks whether deposit insurance is an important feature of the regulatory environment or not. It is the existence of a government safety net, and not deposit insurance per se, that increases moral hazard incentives for excessive risk taking on the part of banks.

THE DODD-FRANK BILL AND FUTURE REGULATION

The recent global financial crisis, discussed in detail in Chapter 9, has led to banking crises throughout the world, and it is too soon to tell how large the costs of rescuing the

TABLE 2

The Cost of Rescuing Banks in a Number of Countries

Country	Date 1980–2009	Cost as a Percentage of GDP
Indonesia	1997–2001	57
Argentina	1980–1982	55
Thailand	1997–2000	44
Chile	1981–1985	43
Turkey	2000–2001	32
South Korea	1997–1998	31
Israel	1977	30
Ecuador	1998–2002	22
Mexico	1994–1996	19
China	1998	18
Malaysia	1997–1999	16
Philippines	1997–2001	13
Brazil	1994–1998	13
Finland	1991–1995	13
Argentina	2001–2003	10
Jordan	1989–1991	10
Hungary	1991–1995	10
Czech Republic	1996–2000	7
Sweden	1991–1995	4
United States	1988	4
Norway	1991–1993	3
	2007–2009	
Iceland	2007–2009	13
Ireland	2007–2009	8
Luxembourg	2007–2009	8
Netherlands	2007–2009	7
Belgium	2007–2009	5
United Kingdom	2007–2009	5
United States	2007–2009	4
Germany	2007–2009	1

Sources: Luc Laeven and Fabian Valencia, "Resolution of Banking Crises: The Good, the Bad and the Ugly," IMF Working Paper No. WP/10/46 (June 2010) and Luc Laeven, Banking Crisis Database at http://www.luclaeven.com/Data.htm.

banks will be as a result of this episode (which is why they are not listed in Table 2). Given the size of the bailouts and the nationalization of so many financial institutions, the system of financial regulation is undergoing dramatic changes.

Dodd-Frank Wall Street Reform and Consumer Protection Act of 2010

In July 2010, after more than a year of discussion, the Dodd-Frank bill was passed. It is the most comprehensive financial reform legislation since the Great Depression. It addresses five different categories of regulation that are discussed next.

Consumer Protection This legislation created a new Consumer Financial Protection Bureau that is funded and housed within the Federal Reserve, although it is a completely independent agency. It has the authority to examine and enforce regulations for all businesses engaged in issuing residential mortgage products that have more than $10 billion in assets, as well as for issuers of other financial products marketed to low income people. The legislation requires lenders to make sure there is an ability to repay residential mortgages by requiring verification of income, credit history, and job status. It also bans payments to brokers for pushing borrowers into higher-priced loans. It allows states to impose stricter consumer protection laws on national banks and gives state attorney-generals power to enforce certain rules issued by the new bureau. It also permanently increases the level of federal deposit insurance to $250,000.

Resolution Authority Although before this legislation, the FDIC had the ability to seize failing banks and wind them down, the government did not have such a resolution authority over the largest financial institutions—those structured as holding companies. Indeed, the U.S. Treasury and the Federal Reserve argued that one reason they were unable to rescue Lehman Brothers and instead had to let it go into bankruptcy was that they did not have the legal means to take Lehman over and break it up. The Dodd-Frank bill now provides the U.S. government with this authority for financial firms that are deemed systemic, that is firms who pose a risk to the overall financial system because their failure would cause widespread damage. It also gives regulators the right to levy fees on financial institutions with more than $50 billion in assets to recoup any losses.

Systemic Risk Regulation The bill creates a Financial Stability Oversight Council, chaired by the Treasury secretary, which would monitor markets for asset price bubbles and the buildup of systemic risk. In addition, it would designate which financial firms are systemically important and so received the official designation of **systemically important financial institutions (SIFIs)** These firms would be subject to additional regulation by the Federal Reserve, which would include higher capital standards and stricter liquidity requirements, as well as requirements that they draw up a "living will," that is, a plan for orderly liquidation if the firm gets into financial difficulties.

Volcker Rule Banks would be limited in the extent of their proprietary trading—that is, trading with their own money—and would be allowed to own only a small percentage of hedge and private equity funds. These provisions are named after Paul Volcker, a former Chairman of the Board of Governors of the Federal Reserve, who argued that banks should not be allowed to take large trading risks when they receive the benefits of federal deposit insurance.

Derivatives Financial instruments whose payoffs are linked to (i.e., derived from) previously issued securities are known as **financial derivatives.** As is discussed in Chapter 9, derivatives such as credit default swaps ended up being "weapons of mass destruction" that helped lead to a financial meltdown when AIG had to be rescued after making overly extensive use of them. To prevent this from happening again, the Dodd-Frank bill requires many standardized derivative products to be traded on exchanges and cleared through clearinghouses to reduce the risk of losses if one counterparty in the derivative transaction goes bankrupt. More customized derivative products would be subject to higher capital requirements. Banks would be banned from some of their derivative-dealing operations, such as those involving riskier swaps. In addition, the bill imposes capital and margin requirements on firms dealing in derivatives and forces them to disclose more information about their activities.

Future Regulation

The Dodd-Frank bill leaves out many details of future regulation and does not address some important regulatory issues at all. Here we discuss several areas where regulation may be heading in the future.

Capital Requirements Regulation and supervision of financial institutions to ensure that they have enough capital to cope with the amount of risk they take are likely to be strengthened. Given the risks they were taking before the recent financial crisis, banks and investment banks did not have enough capital relative to their assets and their risky activities. Similarly, the capital at AIG was not sufficient to cover the high risk it was taking by issuing credit insurance. Capital requirements will almost surely be beefed up for all of these institutions. Banks' sponsoring of structured investment vehicles (SIVs), which were supposedly off-balance-sheet but came back on the balance sheet once the SIVs got into trouble, indicate that some off-balance-sheet activities should be treated as though they are on the balance sheet, and this will be a focus of future regulation. In addition, because of the too-big-to-fail problem, systemically important financial institutions are likely to take on more risk, and so the Federal Reserve and the Basel Committee are considering regulations to increase capital requirements for these firms. Capital requirements are also likely to be adjusted to increase in booms and decrease in busts so that they become more countercyclical in order to restrain the boom-and-bust cycle in credit markets.

Compensation As we saw in Chapter 9, the high fees and executive compensation that have so outraged the public created incentives for the financial industry to create securities that turned out to be much riskier than advertised and have proved to be disastrous. Regulators, particularly at the Federal Reserve, are closely studying regulations to modify compensation in the financial services industry to reduce risk taking. For example, regulators are in the process of issuing requirements that bonuses be paid out for a number of years after they have been earned and only if the firm has remained in good health. Such "clawbacks" will encourage employees to reduce the riskiness of their activities so that they are more likely to be paid these bonuses in the future.

Government-Sponsored Enterprises (GSEs) A major gap in the Dodd-Frank bill is that it does not address privately owned government-sponsored enterprises, such as Fannie Mae and Freddie Mac. As we saw in Chapter 8, both of these firms got into serious financial trouble and had to be taken over by the government. The likely result is that taxpayers will be on the hook for several hundred billion dollars. To prevent this from occurring again, the government might take any of four routes:

1. Fully privatize GSEs by taking away their government sponsorship, thereby removing the implicit backing for their debt.
2. Completely nationalize them by taking away their private status and making them government agencies.

3. Leave them as privately owned GSEs, but strengthen regulations to restrict the amount of risk they take and to impose higher capital standards.
4. Leave them as privately owned GSEs, but force them to shrink dramatically so they no longer expose the taxpayer to huge losses or pose a systemic risk to the financial system when they fail.

Credit-Rating Agencies Regulations to restrict conflicts of interest at credit-rating agencies and to give them greater incentives to provide reliable ratings have already been strengthened in the aftermath of the 2007–2009 financial crisis, but even more is likely to be done. The inaccurate ratings provided by credit-rating agencies helped promote risk taking throughout the financial system and led to investors not having the information they needed to make informed choices about their investments. The reliance on credit ratings in the Basel 2 capital requirements may also have to be rethought, given the poor performance of credit-rating agencies in recent years.

The Danger of Overregulation As a result of the 2007–2009 financial crisis, the world of financial regulation will never be the same. Although it is clear that more regulation is needed to prevent such a crisis from ever occurring again, the danger is substantial that too much or poorly designed regulation could hamper the efficiency of the financial system. If new regulations choke off financial innovation that can benefit both households and businesses, economic growth in the future will suffer.

Summary

1. The concepts of asymmetric information, adverse selection, and moral hazard help explain the ten types of financial regulation that we see in the United States and other countries: the government safety net, restrictions on financial institutions' asset holdings, capital requirements, prompt corrective action, financial institution supervision, assessment of risk management, disclosure requirements, consumer protection, restrictions on competition, and macroprudential policies.
2. Financial innovation and deregulation increased adverse selection and moral hazard problems in the 1980s and resulted in huge losses for U.S. S&Ls, banks, and taxpayers. Similar crises occurred in other countries.
3. The parallels between the banking crisis episodes that have occurred in countries throughout the world are striking, indicating that similar forces are at work.
4. The Dodd-Frank Act of 2010 is the most comprehensive financial reform legislation since the Great Depression. It has provisions in five areas: (1) consumer protection, (2) resolution authority, (3) systemic risk regulation, (4) Volcker rule, and (5) derivatives. Future regulation needs to address five areas: (1) capital requirements, (2) compensation, (3) GSEs, (4) credit-rating agencies, and (5) the dangers of overregulation.

Key Terms

bank failure, p. 242
Basel Accord, p. 248
Basel Committee on Banking Supervision, p. 247
fair-value accounting, p. 252
financial derivatives, p. 264
financial supervision (prudential supervision), p. 250
leverage cycle, p. 256
leverage ratio, p. 247
macroprudential supervision, p. 256
mark-to-market accounting, p. 252
microprudential supervision, p. 255
off-balance-sheet activities, p. 247
regulatory arbitrage, p. 248
stress tests, p. 252
systemically important financial institutions (SIFIs), p. 264
value-at-risk (VaR), p. 252

Questions

All questions are available in MyEconLab *at* www.myeconlab.com.

1. Why are deposit insurance and other types of government safety nets important to the health of the economy?
2. If casualty insurance companies provided fire insurance without any restrictions, what kind of adverse selection and moral hazard problems might result?
3. Do you think that eliminating or limiting the amount of deposit insurance would be a good idea? Explain your answer.
4. How could higher deposit insurance premiums for banks with riskier assets benefit the economy?
5. What are the costs and benefits of a too-big-to-fail policy?
6. What types of bank regulations are designed to reduce moral hazard problems? Will they completely eliminate the moral hazard problem?
7. Why does imposing bank capital requirements on banks help limit risk taking?
8. At the height of the global financial crisis in October 2008, the U.S. Treasury forced nine of the largest U.S. banks to accept capital injections, in exchange for nonvoting ownership stock, even though some of the banks did not need the capital and did not want to participate. What could be the rationale for doing this?
9. What special problem do off-balance-sheet activities present to bank regulators, and what have they done about it?
10. What are some of the limitations to the Basel and Basel 2 Accords? How does the Basel 3 Accord attempt to address these limitations?
11. How does bank chartering reduce adverse selection problems? Will it always work?
12. Why has the trend in bank supervision moved away from a focus on capital requirements to a focus on risk management?
13. How do disclosure requirements help limit excessive risk taking by banks?
14. Suppose Universal Bank holds $100 million in assets, which are composed of the following:

Required Reserves:	$10 million
Excess Reserves:	$ 5 million
Mortgage Loans:	$20 million
Corporate Bonds:	$15 million
Stocks:	$25 million
Commodities	$25 million

   a. Do you think it is a good idea for Universal Bank to hold stocks, corporate bonds, and commodities as assets? Why or why not?
   b. If the housing market suddenly crashed, would Universal Bank be better off with a mark-to-market accounting system or the historical-cost system?
   c. If the price of commodities suddenly increased sharply, would Universal Bank be better off with a mark-to-market accounting system or the historical-cost system?
   d. What do your answers to (b) and (c) tell you about the tradeoffs between the two accounting systems?
15. Why might more competition in financial markets be bad? Would restrictions on competition be better? Why or why not?
16. Why is it a good idea for macroprudential policies to require countercyclical capital requirements?
17. How does the process of financial innovation impact the effectiveness of macroprudential regulation?
18. How can the S&L crisis be blamed on the principal–agent problem?
19. Why were consumer protection provisions included in the Dodd-Frank bill, a bill designed to strengthen the financial system?
20. Why is it important for the U.S. government to have resolution authority?

Applied Problems

All applied problems are available in MyEconLab *at* www.myeconlab.com.

21. Consider a failing bank. A deposit of $350,000 is worth how much if the FDIC uses the *payoff method*? The *purchase and assumption method*? Which is more costly to taxpayers?
22. Consider a bank with the following balance sheet:

Assets		Liabilities	
Required reserves	$ 8 million	Checkable deposits	$100 million
Excess reserves	$ 3 million	Bank capital	$ 6 million
T-bills	$45 million		
Commercial loans	$50 million		

The bank makes a loan commitment for $10 million to a commercial customer. Calculate the bank's capital ratio before and after the agreement. Calculate the bank's risk-weighted assets before and after the agreement.

Problems 23–25 relate to a sequence of transactions at Oldhat Financial.

23. Oldhat Financial starts its first day of operations with $9 million in capital. A total of $130 million in checkable deposits are received. The bank makes a $25 million commercial loan and another $50 million in mortgages, with the following terms: 200 standard 30-year, fixed-rate mortgages with a nominal annual rate of 5.25%, each for $250,000.

Assume that required reserves are 8%.

a. What does the bank balance sheet look like?

b. How well capitalized is the bank?

c. Calculate the risk-weighted assets and risk-weighted capital ratio after Oldhat's first day.

24. Early the next day the bank invests $50 million of its excess reserves in commercial loans. Later that day, terrible news hits the mortgage markets, and mortgage rates jump to 13%, implying a present value of its current mortgage holdings of $124,798 per mortgage. Bank regulators force Oldhat to sell its mortgages to recognize the fair market value. What does Oldhat's balance sheet look like? How do these events affect its capital position?

25. To avoid insolvency, regulators decide to provide the bank with $25 million in bank capital. However, the bad news about the mortgages is featured in the local newspaper, causing a bank run. As a result, $30 million in deposits is withdrawn. Show the effects of the capital injection and bank run on the balance sheet. Was the capital injection enough to stabilize the bank? If the bank regulators decide that the bank needs a capital ratio of 10% to prevent further runs on the bank, how much of an additional capital injection is required to reach a 10% capital ratio?

Web Exercises

1. www.fdic.gov/regulations/laws/important/index.html. This site reports on the most significant pieces of legislation affecting banks since the 1800s. Summarize the most recently enacted bank regulation listed on this site.

2. The Office of the Comptroller of the Currency is responsible for many of the regulations affecting bank operations. Go to www.occ.treas.gov/. Click on Legal and Regulatory and then on Law and Regulations. Now click on the 12 CFR Parts 1 to 199. What does Part 1 cover? How many parts are there in 12 CFR? Open Part 18. What topic does it cover? Summarize its purpose.

Web References

www.ny.frb.org/banking/supervisionregulate.html

View bank regulation information.

www.federalreserve.gov/Regulations/default.htm

Access regulatory publications of the Federal Reserve Board.

www.fdic.gov/regulations/laws/important/index.html

Describes the most important laws that have affected the banking industry in the United States.

www.fdic.gov/bank/historical/bank/index.html

Search for data on bank failures in any year.

Web Appendices

Please visit our Web site at www.pearsonhighered.com/mishkin to read the Web appendices to Chapter 11.

Appendix 1: **The Savings and Loan Crisis and Its Aftermath**

Appendix 2: **Banking Crises Throughout the World**

12 Banking Industry: Structure and Competition

Preview

The operations of individual banks (how they acquire, use, and manage funds to make a profit) are roughly similar throughout the world. In all countries, banks are financial intermediaries in the business of earning profits. When you consider the structure and operation of the banking industry as a whole, however, the United States is in a class by itself. In most countries, four or five large banks typically dominate the banking industry, but in the United States there are on the order of 6,500 commercial banks, 1,100 savings and loan associations, 400 mutual savings banks, and 7,500 credit unions.

Is more better? Does this diversity mean that the American banking system is more competitive and therefore more economically efficient and sound than banking systems in other countries? What in the American economic and political system explains this large number of banking institutions? In this chapter, we try to answer these questions by examining the historical trends in the banking industry and its overall structure.

We start by examining the historical development of the banking system and how financial innovation has increased the competitive environment for the banking industry and is causing fundamental changes in it. We go on to look at the commercial banking industry in detail and then discuss the thrift industry, which includes savings and loan associations, mutual savings banks, and credit unions. We spend more time on commercial banks because they are by far the largest depository institutions, accounting for more than two-thirds of the deposits in the banking system. In addition to looking at our domestic banking system, we examine the forces behind the growth in international banking to see how it has affected us in the United States.

HISTORICAL DEVELOPMENT OF THE BANKING SYSTEM

The modern commercial banking industry in the United States began when the Bank of North America was chartered in Philadelphia in 1782. With the success of this bank, other banks opened for business, and the American banking industry was off and running. (As a study aid, Figure 1 provides a time line of the most important dates in the history of American banking before World War II.)

A major controversy involving the industry in its early years was whether the federal government or the states should charter banks. The Federalists, particularly Alexander Hamilton, advocated greater centralized control of banking and federal chartering of banks. Their efforts led to the creation in 1791 of the Bank of the United States, which had elements of both a private bank and a **central bank**, a government

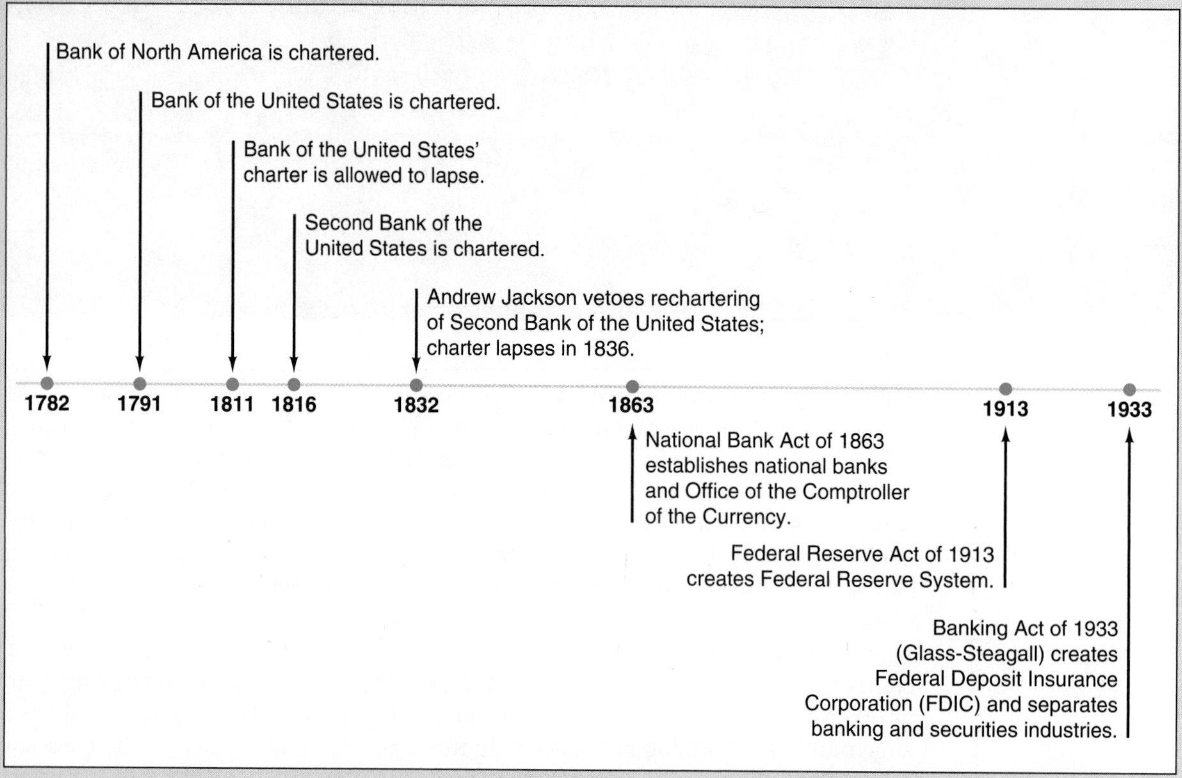

Bank of North America is chartered.
Bank of the United States is chartered.
Bank of the United States' charter is allowed to lapse.
Second Bank of the United States is chartered.
Andrew Jackson vetoes rechartering of Second Bank of the United States; charter lapses in 1836.
1782
1791
1811
1816
1832
1863
1913
1933
National Bank Act of 1863 establishes national banks and Office of the Comptroller of the Currency.
Federal Reserve Act of 1913 creates Federal Reserve System.
Banking Act of 1933 (Glass-Steagall) creates Federal Deposit Insurance Corporation (FDIC) and separates banking and securities industries.

FIGURE 1 Time Line of the Early History of Commercial Banking in the United States
The most important dates in the history of American banking before World War II.

institution that has responsibility for the amount of money and credit supplied in the economy as a whole. Agricultural and other interests, however, were quite suspicious of centralized power and hence advocated chartering by the states. Furthermore, their distrust of moneyed interests in the big cities led to political pressures to eliminate the Bank of the United States, and in 1811 their efforts met with success, when its charter was not renewed. Because of abuses by state banks and the clear need for a central bank to help the federal government raise funds during the War of 1812, Congress was stimulated to create the Second Bank of the United States in 1816. Tensions between advocates and opponents of centralized banking power were a recurrent theme during the operation of this second attempt at central banking in the United States, and with the election of Andrew Jackson, a strong advocate of states' rights, the fate of the Second Bank was sealed. After the election in 1832, Jackson vetoed the rechartering of the Second Bank of the United States as a national bank, and its charter lapsed in 1836.

Until 1863, all commercial banks in the United States were chartered by the banking commission of the state in which each operated. No national currency existed, and banks obtained funds primarily by issuing *banknotes* (currency circulated by the banks that could be redeemed for gold). Because banking regulations were extremely lax in many states, banks regularly failed due to fraud or lack of sufficient bank capital; their banknotes became worthless.

To eliminate the abuses of the state-chartered banks (called **state banks**), the National Bank Act of 1863 (and subsequent amendments to it) created a new banking system of federally chartered banks (called **national banks**), supervised by the Office of the Comptroller of the Currency, a department of the U.S. Treasury. This legislation was originally intended to dry up sources of funds to state banks by imposing a prohibitive tax on their banknotes while leaving the banknotes of the federally chartered banks untaxed. The state banks cleverly escaped extinction by acquiring funds through deposits. As a result, today the United States has a **dual banking system** in which banks supervised by the federal government and banks supervised by the states operate side by side.

Central banking did not reappear in this country until the Federal Reserve System (the Fed) was created in 1913 to promote an even safer banking system. All national banks were required to become members of the Federal Reserve System and became subject to a new set of regulations issued by the Fed. State banks could choose (but were not required) to become members of the system, and most did not because of the high costs of membership stemming from the Fed's regulations.

During the Great Depression years 1930–1933, some 9,000 bank failures wiped out the savings of many depositors at commercial banks. To prevent future depositor losses from such failures, banking legislation in 1933 established the Federal Deposit Insurance Corporation (FDIC), which provided federal insurance on bank deposits. Member banks of the Federal Reserve System were required to purchase FDIC insurance for their depositors, and non–Federal Reserve commercial banks could choose to buy this insurance (almost all of them did). The purchase of FDIC insurance made banks subject to another set of regulations imposed by the FDIC.

Because investment banking activities of the commercial banks were blamed for many bank failures, provisions in the banking legislation in 1933 (also known as the Glass-Steagall Act) prohibited commercial banks from underwriting or dealing in corporate securities (though allowing them to sell new issues of government securities) and limited banks to the purchase of debt securities approved by the bank regulatory agencies. Likewise, it prohibited investment banks from engaging in commercial banking activities. In effect, the Glass-Steagall Act separated the activities of commercial banks from those of the securities industry.

Under the conditions of the Glass-Steagall Act, which was repealed in 1999, commercial banks had to sell off their investment banking operations. The First National Bank of Boston, for example, spun off its investment banking operations into the First Boston Corporation, now part of one of the most important investment banking firms in America, Credit Suisse First Boston. Investment banking firms typically discontinued their deposit business, although J.P. Morgan discontinued its investment banking business and reorganized as a commercial bank; however, some senior officers of J.P. Morgan went on to organize Morgan Stanley, another one of the largest investment banking firms today.

Multiple Regulatory Agencies

Commercial bank regulation in the United States has developed into a crazy quilt of multiple regulatory agencies with overlapping jurisdictions. The Office of the Comptroller of the Currency has the primary supervisory responsibility for national banks that own more than half of the assets in the commercial banking system. The Federal Reserve and the state banking authorities have joint primary responsibility for state banks that are members of the Federal Reserve System. The Fed also has regulatory responsibility over companies that own one or more banks (called **bank holding companies**) and secondary responsibility for the national banks. The FDIC and the state banking authorities jointly supervise state banks that have FDIC insurance but are not members of the Federal Reserve System. The state banking authorities have sole jurisdiction over state banks without FDIC insurance. (Such banks hold less than 0.2% of the deposits in the commercial banking system.)

If you find the U.S. bank regulatory system confusing, imagine how confusing it is for the banks, which have to deal with multiple regulatory agencies. Several proposals have been raised by the U.S. Treasury to rectify this situation by centralizing the regulation of all depository institutions under one independent agency. However, none of these proposals has been successful in Congress, and whether there will be regulatory consolidation in the future is highly uncertain.

FINANCIAL INNOVATION AND THE GROWTH OF THE "SHADOW BANKING SYSTEM"

Although banking institutions are still the most important financial institutions in the U.S. economy, in recent years the traditional banking business of making loans that are funded by deposits has been in decline. Some of this business has been replaced by the **shadow banking system**, in which bank lending has been replaced by lending via the securities markets.

To understand how the banking industry has evolved over time, we must first understand the process of financial innovation, which has transformed the entire financial system. Like other industries, the financial industry is in business to earn profits by selling its products. If a soap company perceives that a need exists in the marketplace for a laundry detergent with fabric softener, it develops a product to fit the need. Similarly, to maximize their profits, financial institutions develop new products to satisfy their own needs as well as those of their customers; in other words, innovation—which can be extremely beneficial to the economy—is driven by the desire to get (or stay) rich. This view of the innovation process leads to the following simple analysis: ***A change in the financial environment will stimulate a search by financial institutions for innovations that are likely to be profitable.***

Starting in the 1960s, individuals and financial institutions operating in financial markets were confronted with drastic changes in the economic environment: Inflation and interest rates climbed sharply and became harder to predict, a situation that changed demand conditions in financial markets. The rapid advance in computer technology changed supply conditions. In addition, financial regulations became more burdensome. Financial institutions found that many of the old ways of doing business were no longer profitable; the financial services and products they had been offering to the public were not selling. Many financial intermediaries found that they were no longer able to acquire funds with their traditional financial instruments, and without these funds they would soon be out of business. To survive in the new economic environment, financial institutions had to research and develop new products and services that would meet customer needs and prove profitable, a process referred to as **financial engineering**. In their case, necessity was the mother of innovation.

Our discussion of why financial innovation occurs suggests that there are three basic types of financial innovation: responses to changes in demand conditions, responses to changes in supply conditions, and avoidance of existing regulations.

These three motivations often interact to produce particular financial innovations. Now that we have a framework for understanding why financial institutions produce innovations, let's look at examples of how financial institutions in their search for profits have produced financial innovations of the three basic types.

Responses to Changes in Demand Conditions: Interest-Rate Volatility

The most significant change in the economic environment that altered the demand for financial products in recent years has been the dramatic increase in the volatility of interest rates. In the 1950s, the interest rate on three-month Treasury bills fluctuated between 1.0% and 3.5%; in the 1970s, it fluctuated between 4.0% and 11.5%; in the 1980s, it ranged from 5% to more than 15%. Large fluctuations in interest rates lead to substantial capital gains or losses and greater uncertainty about returns on investments. Recall that the risk that is related to the uncertainty about interest-rate movements and returns is called *interest-rate risk*, and high volatility of interest rates, such as we saw in the 1970s and 1980s, leads to a higher level of interest-rate risk.

We would expect the increase in interest-rate risk to increase the demand for financial products and services that could reduce that risk. This change in the economic environment would thus stimulate a search for profitable innovations by financial institutions that meet this new demand and would spur the creation of new financial instruments that help lower interest-rate risk. Two examples of financial innovations that appeared in the 1970s confirm this prediction: the development of adjustable-rate mortgages and financial derivatives.

Adjustable-Rate Mortgages Like other investors, financial institutions find that lending is more attractive if interest-rate risk is lower. They would not want to make a mortgage loan at a 10% interest rate and two months later find that they could obtain 12% in interest on the same mortgage. To reduce interest-rate risk, in 1975 savings and loans in California began to issue adjustable-rate mortgages, that is, mortgage loans on which the interest rate changes when a market interest rate (usually the Treasury bill rate) changes. Initially, an adjustable-rate mortgage might have a 5% interest rate. In six months, this interest rate might increase or decrease by the amount of the increase or decrease in, say, the six-month Treasury bill rate, and the mortgage payment would change. Because adjustable-rate mortgages allow mortgage-issuing institutions to earn higher interest rates on existing mortgages when market rates rise, profits remain high during these periods.

This attractive feature of adjustable-rate mortgages has encouraged mortgage-issuing institutions to issue adjustable-rate mortgages with lower initial interest rates than on conventional fixed-rate mortgages, making them popular with many households. However, because the mortgage payment on a variable-rate mortgage can increase, many households continue to prefer fixed-rate mortgages. Hence both types of mortgages are widespread.

Financial Derivatives Given the greater demand for the reduction of interest-rate risk, commodity exchanges such as the Chicago Board of Trade recognized that if they could develop a product that would help investors and financial institutions to protect themselves from, or **hedge**, interest-rate risk, then they could make profits by selling this new instrument. **Futures contracts**, in which the seller agrees to provide a certain standardized commodity to the buyer on a specific future date at an agreed-on price, had been around for a long time. Officials at the Chicago Board of Trade realized that if they created futures contracts in financial instruments, which are called **financial derivatives** because their payoffs are linked to (i.e., derived from) previously issued securities, they could be used to hedge risk. Thus, in 1975, financial derivatives were born.

Responses to Changes in Supply Conditions: Information Technology

The most important source of the changes in supply conditions that stimulate financial innovation has been the improvement in computer and telecommunications technology. This technology, called *information technology,* has had two effects. First, it has lowered the cost of processing financial transactions, making it profitable for financial institutions to create new financial products and services for the public. Second, it has made it easier for investors to acquire information, thereby making it easier for firms to issue securities. The rapid developments in information technology have resulted in many new financial products and services that we examine here.

Bank Credit and Debit Cards Credit cards have been around since well before World War II. Many individual stores (Sears, Macy's, Goldwater's) institutionalized charge accounts by providing customers with credit cards that allowed them to make purchases at these stores without cash. Nationwide credit cards were not established until after World War II, when Diners Club developed one to be used in restaurants all over the country (and abroad). Similar credit card programs were started by American Express and Carte Blanche, but because of the high cost of operating these programs, cards were issued only to selected persons and businesses that could afford expensive purchases.

A firm issuing credit cards earns income from loans it makes to credit card holders and from payments made by stores on credit card purchases (a percentage of the purchase price, say, 5%). A credit card program's costs arise from loan defaults, stolen cards, and the expense involved in processing credit card transactions.

Seeing the success of Diners Club, American Express, and Carte Blanche, bankers wanted to share in the profitable credit card business. Several commercial banks attempted to expand the credit card business to a wider market in the 1950s, but the cost per transaction of running these programs was so high that their early attempts failed.

In the late 1960s, improved computer technology, which lowered the transaction costs for providing credit card services, made it more likely that bank credit card programs would be profitable. The banks tried to enter this business again, and this time their efforts led to the creation of two successful bank credit card programs: BankAmericard (originally started by Bank of America but now an independent organization called Visa) and MasterCharge (now MasterCard, run by the Interbank Card Association). These programs have become phenomenally successful; more than 200 million of their cards are in use. Indeed, bank credit cards have been so profitable that nonfinancial institutions such as Sears (which launched the Discover card), General Motors, and AT&T have also entered the credit card business. Consumers have benefited because credit cards are more widely accepted than checks to pay for purchases (particularly abroad), and they allow consumers to take out loans more easily.

The success of bank credit cards has led these institutions to come up with a new financial innovation, *debit cards*. Debit cards often look just like credit cards and can be used to make purchases in an identical fashion. However, in contrast to credit cards, which extend the purchaser a loan that does not have to be paid off immediately, a debit card purchase is immediately deducted from the card holder's bank account. Debit cards depend even more on low costs of processing transactions, because their profits are generated entirely from the fees paid by merchants on debit card purchases at their stores. Debit cards have grown extremely popular in recent years.

Electronic Banking The wonders of modern computer technology have also enabled banks to lower the cost of bank transactions by having the customer interact with an electronic banking (e-banking) facility rather than with a human being. One important form of an e-banking facility is the **automated teller machine (ATM)**, an electronic machine that allows customers to get cash, make deposits, transfer funds from one account to another, and check balances. The ATM has the advantage that it does not have to be paid overtime and never sleeps, thus being available for use 24 hours a day. Not only does this result in cheaper transactions for the bank, but it also provides more convenience for the customer. Because of their low cost, ATMs can be put at locations other than a bank or its branches, further increasing customer convenience. The low cost of ATMs has meant that they have sprung up everywhere and now number more than 250,000 in the United States alone. Furthermore, it is now as easy to get foreign currency from an ATM when you are traveling in Europe as it is to get cash from your local bank.

With the drop in the cost of telecommunications, banks have developed another financial innovation, *home banking*. It is now cost-effective for banks to set up an electronic banking facility in which the bank's customer is linked up with the bank's computer to carry out transactions by using either a telephone or a personal computer. Now a bank's customers can conduct many of their bank transactions without ever leaving the comfort of home. The advantage for the customer is the convenience of home banking, while banks find that the cost of transactions is substantially less than having the customer come to the bank. The success of ATMs and home banking has led to another innovation, the **automated banking machine (ABM)**, which combines in one location an ATM, an Internet connection to the bank's website, and a telephone link to customer service.

With the decline in the price of personal computers and their increasing presence in the home, we have seen a further innovation in the home banking area, the appearance of a new type of banking institution, the **virtual bank**, a bank that has no physical location but rather exists only in cyberspace. In 1995, Security First Network Bank, based in Atlanta but now owned by Royal Bank of Canada, became the first virtual bank, offering an array of banking services on the Internet—accepting checking account and savings deposits, selling certificates of deposits, issuing ATM cards, providing bill-paying facilities, and so on. The virtual bank thus takes home banking one step further, enabling the customer to have a full set of banking services at home 24 hours a day. In 1996, Bank of America and Wells Fargo entered the virtual banking market, to be followed by many others, with Bank of America now being the largest Internet bank in the United States. Will virtual banking be the predominant form of banking in the future (see the FYI box, "Will 'Clicks' Dominate 'Bricks' in the Banking Industry?")?

Junk Bonds Before the advent of computers and advanced telecommunications, it was difficult to acquire information about the financial situation of firms that might want to sell securities. Because of the difficulty in screening out bad from good credit risks, the only firms that were able to sell bonds were very well-established corporations

FYI Will "Clicks" Dominate "Bricks" in the Banking Industry?

With the advent of virtual banks ("clicks") and the convenience they provide, a key question is whether they will become the primary form in which banks do their business, eliminating the need for physical bank branches ("bricks") as the main delivery mechanism for banking services. Indeed, will stand-alone Internet banks be the wave of the future?

The answer seems to be no. Internet-only banks such as Wingspan (owned by Bank One), First-e (Dublin-based), and Egg (a British Internet-only bank owned by Prudential) have had disappointing revenue growth and profits. The result is that pure online banking has not been the success that proponents had hoped for. Why has Internet banking been a disappointment?

Internet banking has several strikes against it. First, bank depositors want to know that their savings are secure, and so are reluctant to put their money into new institutions without a long track record. Second, customers worry about the security of their online transactions and whether their transactions will truly be kept private. Traditional banks are viewed as being more secure and trustworthy in terms of releasing private information. Third, customers may prefer services provided by physical branches. For example, banking customers seem to prefer purchasing long-term savings products face-to-face. Fourth, Internet banking has run into technical problems—server crashes, slow connections over phone lines, mistakes in conducting transactions—that will probably diminish over time as technology improves.

The wave of the future thus does not appear to be pure Internet banks. Instead, it looks as though "clicks and bricks" will be the predominant form of banking, in which online banking is used to complement the services provided by traditional banks. Nonetheless, the delivery of banking services is undergoing massive changes, with more and more banking services delivered over the Internet and the number of physical bank branches likely to decline in the future.

that had high credit ratings.[1] Before the 1980s, then, only corporations that could issue bonds with ratings of Baa or above could raise funds by selling newly issued bonds. Some firms that had fallen on bad times, known as *fallen angels*, had previously issued long-term corporate bonds with ratings that had now fallen below Baa, bonds that were pejoratively dubbed "junk bonds."

With the improvement in information technology in the 1970s, it became easier for investors to acquire financial information about corporations, making it easier to screen out bad from good credit risks. With easier screening, investors were more willing to buy long-term debt securities from less well-known corporations with lower credit ratings. With this change in supply conditions, we would expect that some smart individual would pioneer the concept of selling new public issues of junk bonds, not for fallen angels but for companies that had not yet achieved investment-grade status. This is exactly what Michael Milken of Drexel Burnham Lambert, an investment banking firm, started to do in 1977. Junk bonds became an important factor in the corporate bond market, with the amount outstanding exceeding $200 billion by the late 1980s. Although there was a sharp slowdown in activity in the junk bond market after Milken was indicted for securities law violations in 1989, it heated up again in the 1990s and 2000s.

[1]The discussion of adverse selection problems in Chapter 8 provides a more detailed analysis of why only well-established firms with high credit ratings were able to sell securities.

Commercial Paper Market *Commercial paper* is a short-term debt security issued by large banks and corporations. The commercial paper market has undergone tremendous growth since 1970, when $33 billion was outstanding, to over $1 trillion outstanding at the end of 2010. Indeed, commercial paper has been one of the fastest-growing money market instruments.

Improvements in information technology also help provide an explanation for the rapid rise of the commercial paper market. We have seen that the improvement in information technology made it easier for investors to screen out bad from good credit risks, thus making it easier for corporations to issue debt securities. Not only did this make it simpler for corporations to issue long-term debt securities, as in the junk bond market, but it also meant they could raise funds by issuing short-term debt securities, such as commercial paper, with greater ease. Many corporations that used to do their short-term borrowing from banks now frequently raise short-term funds in the commercial paper market instead.

The development of money market mutual funds has been another factor in the rapid growth of the commercial paper market. Because money market mutual funds need to hold liquid, high-quality, short-term assets such as commercial paper, the growth of assets in these funds to around $2.3 trillion has created a ready market in commercial paper. The growth of pension and other large funds that invest in commercial paper has also stimulated the growth of this market.

Securitization An important example of a financial innovation arising from improvements in both transaction and information technology is securitization, one of the most important financial innovations in the past two decades, which played an especially prominent role in the development of the subprime mortgage market in the mid-2000s. **Securitization** is the process of transforming otherwise illiquid financial assets (such as residential mortgages, auto loans, and credit card receivables), which have typically been the bread and butter of banking institutions, into marketable capital market securities. As we have seen, improvements in the ability to acquire information have made it easier to sell capital market securities. In addition, with low transaction costs because of improvements in computer technology, financial institutions find that they can cheaply bundle together a portfolio of loans (such as mortgages) with varying small denominations (often less than $100,000), collect the interest and principal payments on the mortgages in the bundle, and then "pass them through" (pay them out) to third parties. By dividing the portfolio of loans into standardized amounts, the financial institution can then sell the claims to these interest and principal payments to third parties as securities. The standardized amounts of these securitized loans make them liquid securities, and the fact that they are made up of a bundle of loans helps diversify risk, making them more desirable. The financial institution selling the securitized loans makes a profit by servicing the loans (collecting the interest and principal payments and paying them out) and charging a fee to the third party for this service.

Avoidance of Existing Regulations

The process of financial innovation we have discussed so far is much like innovation in other areas of the economy: It occurs in response to changes in demand and supply conditions. However, because the financial industry is more heavily regulated than other industries, government regulation is a much greater spur to innovation in this industry. Government regulation leads to financial innovation by creating incentives for firms to skirt regulations that restrict their ability to earn profits. Edward Kane, an economist at

Boston College, describes this process of avoiding regulations as "loophole mining." The economic analysis of innovation suggests that when the economic environment changes such that regulatory constraints are so burdensome that large profits can be made by avoiding them, loophole mining and innovation are more likely to occur.

Because banking is one of the most heavily regulated industries in America, loophole mining is especially likely to occur. The rise in inflation and interest rates from the late 1960s to 1980 made the regulatory constraints imposed on this industry even more burdensome, leading to financial innovation.

Two sets of regulations have seriously restricted the ability of banks to make profits: reserve requirements that force banks to keep a certain fraction of their deposits as reserves (vault cash and deposits in the Federal Reserve System) and restrictions on the interest rates that can be paid on deposits. For the following reasons, these regulations have been major forces behind financial innovation.

1. *Reserve requirements.* The key to understanding why reserve requirements led to financial innovation is to recognize that they act, in effect, as a tax on deposits. Because up until 2008 the Fed did not pay interest on reserves, the opportunity cost of holding them was the interest that a bank could otherwise earn by lending the reserves out. For each dollar of deposits, reserve requirements therefore imposed a cost on the bank equal to the interest rate, i, that could be earned if the reserves could be lent out times the fraction of deposits required as reserves, r. The cost of $i \times r$ imposed on the bank was just like a tax on bank deposits of $i \times r$ per dollar of deposits.

It is a great tradition to avoid taxes if possible, and banks also play this game. Just as taxpayers look for loopholes to lower their tax bills, banks seek to increase their profits by mining loopholes and by producing financial innovations that allow them to escape the tax on deposits imposed by reserve requirements.

2. *Restrictions on interest paid on deposits.* Until 1980, legislation prohibited banks in most states from paying interest on checking account deposits, and through Regulation Q, the Fed set maximum limits on the interest rate that could be paid on time deposits. To this day, banks are not allowed to pay interest on corporate checking accounts. The desire to avoid these **deposit rate ceilings** also led to financial innovations.

If market interest rates rose above the maximum rates that banks paid on time deposits under Regulation Q, depositors withdrew funds from banks to put them into higher-yielding securities. This loss of deposits from the banking system restricted the amount of funds that banks could lend (called **disintermediation**) and thus limited bank profits. Banks had an incentive to get around deposit rate ceilings, because by so doing, they could acquire more funds to make loans and earn higher profits.

We can now look at how the desire to avoid restrictions on interest payments and the tax effect of reserve requirements led to two important financial innovations.

Money Market Mutual Funds Money market mutual funds issue shares that are redeemable at a fixed price (usually $1) by writing checks. For example, if you buy 5,000 shares for $5,000, the money market fund uses these funds to invest in short-term money market securities (Treasury bills, negotiable certificates of deposit, commercial paper) that provide you with interest payments. In addition, you are able to write checks up to the $5,000 held as shares in the money market fund. Although money market fund shares effectively function as checking account deposits that earn interest, they are not legally deposits and so are not subject to reserve requirements or prohibitions on interest payments. For this reason, they can pay higher interest rates than deposits at banks.

The first money market mutual fund was created by two Wall Street mavericks, Bruce Bent and Henry Brown, in 1970. However, the low market interest rates from 1970 to 1977 (which were just slightly above Regulation Q ceilings of 5.25–5.5%) kept them from being particularly advantageous relative to bank deposits. In early 1978, the situation changed rapidly as inflation rose and market interest rates began to climb over 10%, well above the 5.5% maximum interest rates payable on savings accounts and time deposits under Regulation Q. In 1977, money market mutual funds had assets of less than $4 billion; in 1978, their assets climbed to close to $10 billion; in 1979, to more than $40 billion; and in 1982, to $230 billion. Currently, their assets are around $3 trillion. To say the least, money market mutual funds have been a successful financial innovation, which is exactly what we would have predicted to occur in the late 1970s and early 1980s when interest rates soared beyond Regulation Q ceilings.

In a supreme irony, risky investments by a money market mutual fund founded by Bruce Brent almost brought down the money market mutual fund industry during the global financial crisis in 2008 (see the FYI box, "Bruce Bent and the Money Market Mutual Fund Panic of 2008").

Sweep Accounts Another innovation that enables banks to avoid the "tax" from reserve requirements is the **sweep account**. In this arrangement, any balances above

FYI Bruce Bent and the Money Market Mutual Fund Panic of 2008

Bruce Bent, one of the originators of money market mutual funds, almost brought down the industry during the global financial crisis in the fall of 2008. Mr. Bent told his shareholders in a letter written in July 2008 that the fund was managed on a basis of "unwavering discipline focused on protecting your principal." He also wrote the Securities and Exchange Commission in September 2007, "When I first created the money market fund back in 1970, it was designed with the tenets of safety and liquidity." He added that these principles had "fallen by the wayside as portfolio managers chased the highest yield and compromised the integrity of the money fund." Alas, Bent did not follow his own advice, and his fund, the Reserve Primary Fund, bought risky assets so that its yield was higher than the industry average.

When Lehman Brothers went into bankruptcy on September 15, 2008, the Reserve Primary Fund, with assets over $60 billion, was caught holding the bag on $785 million of Lehman's debt, which then had to be marked down to zero. The resulting losses meant that on September 16, Bent's fund could no longer afford to redeem its shares at the par value of $1, a situation known as "breaking the buck." Bent's shareholders began to pull their money out of the fund, causing it to lose 90% of its assets.

The fear that this could happen to other money market mutual funds led to a classic panic in which shareholders began to withdraw their funds at an alarming rate. The whole money market mutual fund industry looked as though it could come crashing down. To prevent this, the Federal Reserve and the U.S. Treasury rode to the rescue on September 19. The Fed set up a facility, discussed in Chapter 18, to make loans to purchase commercial paper from money market mutual funds so they could meet the demands for redemptions from their investors. The Treasury then put in a temporary guarantee for all money market mutual fund redemptions and the panic subsided.

Not surprisingly, given the extension of a government safety net to the money market mutual fund industry, there are calls to regulate this industry more heavily. The money market mutual fund industry will never be the same.

a certain amount in a corporation's checking account at the end of a business day are "swept out" of the account and invested in overnight securities that pay interest. Because the "swept out" funds are no longer classified as checkable deposits, they are not subject to reserve requirements and thus are not "taxed." They also have the advantage that they allow banks in effect to pay interest on these checking accounts, which otherwise is not allowed under existing regulations. Because sweep accounts have become so popular, they have lowered the amount of required reserves to the degree that most banking institutions do not find reserve requirements binding: In other words, they voluntarily hold more reserves than they are required to.

The financial innovations of sweep accounts and money market mutual funds are particularly interesting because they were stimulated not only by the desire to avoid a costly regulation, but also by a change in supply conditions—in this case, information technology. Without low-cost computers to process inexpensively the additional transactions required by these innovations, they would not have been profitable and therefore would not have been developed. Technological factors often combine with other incentives, such as the desire to get around a regulation, to produce innovation.

Financial Innovation and the Decline of Traditional Banking

The traditional financial intermediation role of banking has been to make long-term loans and to fund them by issuing short-term deposits, a process of asset transformation commonly referred to as "borrowing short and lending long." Here we examine how financial innovations have created a more competitive environment for the banking industry, causing the industry to change dramatically, with its traditional banking business going into decline.

In the United States, the importance of commercial banks as a source of funds to nonfinancial borrowers has shrunk dramatically. As we can see in Figure 2, in 1974, commercial banks provided close to 40% of these funds; by 2011, their market share was down to 25%. The decline in market share for thrift institutions has been even more precipitous, from more than 20% in the late 1970s to 3% today. To understand why traditional banking business has declined in size, we need to look at how the financial innovations described earlier have caused banks to suffer declines in their cost advantages in acquiring funds—that is, on the liabilities side of their balance sheet—while at the same time they have lost income advantages on the assets side of their balance sheet. The simultaneous decline of cost and income advantages has resulted in reduced profitability of traditional banking and an effort by banks to leave this business and engage in new and more profitable activities.

Decline in Cost Advantages in Acquiring Funds (Liabilities) Until 1980, banks were subject to deposit rate ceilings that restricted them from paying any interest on checkable deposits and (under Regulation Q) limited them to paying a maximum interest rate of a little more than 5% on time deposits. Until the 1960s, these restrictions worked to the banks' advantage because their major source of funds (in excess of 60%) was checkable deposits, and the zero interest cost on these deposits meant that the banks had a very low cost of funds. Unfortunately, this cost advantage for banks did not last. The rise in inflation beginning in the late 1960s led to higher interest rates, which made investors more sensitive to yield differentials on different assets. The result was the *disintermediation* process, in which people began to take their money out of banks, with their low interest rates on both checkable and time deposits, and began to seek out higher-yielding investments. At the same time, as we have seen, attempts to get around deposit rate ceilings and reserve

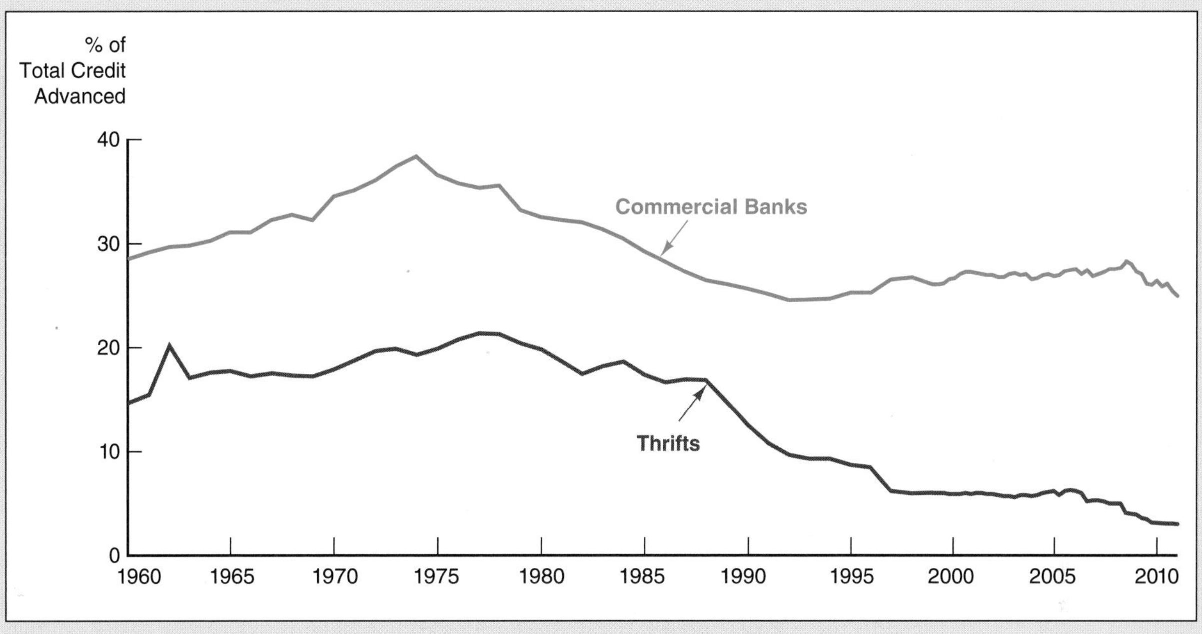

FIGURE 2 Bank Share of Total Nonfinancial Borrowing, 1960–2011

In 1974, commercial banks provided close to 40% of these funds; by 2011, their market share was down to 25%. The decline in market share for thrift institutions has been even more precipitous, from more than 20% in the late 1970s to 3% today.

Source: Federal Reserve *Flow of Funds;* www.federalreserve.gov/releases/z1/Current/z1.pdf. Flow of Funds Accounts; Federal Reserve *Bulletin.*

requirements led to the financial innovation of money market mutual funds, which put the banks at an even further disadvantage because depositors could now obtain checking account–like services while earning high interest on their money market mutual fund accounts. One manifestation of these changes in the financial system was that the low-cost source of funds, checkable deposits, declined dramatically in importance for banks, falling from more than 60% of bank liabilities to 2% today.

The growing difficulty for banks in raising funds led to their supporting legislation in the 1980s that eliminated Regulation Q ceilings on time deposit interest rates and allowed checkable deposit accounts that paid interest. Although these changes in regulation helped make banks more competitive in their quest for funds, it also meant that their cost of acquiring funds had risen substantially, thereby reducing their earlier cost advantage over other financial institutions.

Decline in Income Advantages on Uses of Funds (Assets) The loss of cost advantages on the liabilities side of the balance sheet for American banks is one reason that they have become less competitive, but they have also been hit by a decline in income advantages on the assets side from the financial innovations we discussed earlier—junk bonds, securitization, and the rise of the commercial paper market. The resulting loss of income advantages for banks relative to these innovations has resulted in a loss of market share and has led to the growth of the shadow banking system, which has made use of these innovations to enable borrowers to bypass the traditional banking system.

We have seen that improvements in information technology have made it easier for firms to issue securities directly to the public. This change has meant that instead of going to banks to finance short-term credit needs, many of the banks' best business customers now find it cheaper to go instead to the commercial paper market for funds. In addition, the commercial paper market has allowed finance companies, which depend primarily on commercial paper to acquire funds, to expand their operations at the expense of banks. Finance companies, which lend to many of the same businesses that borrow from banks, have maintained their market share relative to banks: Before 1980, finance company loans to business equaled about 30% of commercial and industrial bank loans; currently, they account for 32%.

The emergence of the junk bond market has also eaten into banks' loan business. Improvements in information technology have made it easier for corporations to sell their bonds to the public directly, thereby bypassing banks. Although *Fortune* 500 companies started taking this route in the 1970s, now lower-quality corporate borrowers are using banks less often because they have access to the junk bond market.

We have also seen that improvements in computer technology have led to securitization, whereby illiquid financial assets such as bank loans and mortgages are transformed into marketable securities. Computers enable other financial institutions to originate loans because they can now accurately evaluate credit risk with statistical methods, while computers also have lowered transaction costs, making it possible to bundle these loans and sell them as securities. When default risk can be easily evaluated with computers, banks no longer have an advantage in making loans. Without their former advantages, banks have lost loan business to other financial institutions even though the banks themselves are involved in the process of securitization. Securitization has been a particular problem for mortgage-issuing institutions such as S&Ls, because most residential mortgages are now securitized.

Banks' Responses In any industry, a decline in profitability usually results in an exit from the industry (often due to widespread bankruptcies) and a shrinkage of market share. This occurred in the banking industry in the United States during the 1980s via consolidations and bank failures (discussed in Chapter 11).

In an attempt to survive and maintain adequate profit levels, many U.S. banks faced two alternatives. First, they could attempt to maintain their traditional lending activity by expanding into new and riskier areas of lending. For example, U.S. banks increased their risk taking by placing a greater percentage of their total funds in commercial real estate loans, traditionally a riskier type of loan. In addition, they increased lending for corporate takeovers and leveraged buyouts, which are highly leveraged transaction loans. The decline in the profitability of banks' traditional business may thus have helped lead to the crisis in banking in the 1980s and early 1990s that we discussed in the last chapter, as well as the global financial crisis from 2007 to 2009.

The second way banks have sought to maintain former profit levels is to pursue new off-balance-sheet activities that are more profitable and in effect embrace the shadow banking system. U.S. commercial banks did this during the early 1980s, more than doubling the share of their income coming from off-balance-sheet, non–interest-income activities. Nontraditional bank activities can be riskier and, therefore, result in excessive risk taking by banks. Indeed, they led to a substantial weakening of bank balance sheets during the global financial crisis, as was discussed in Chapter 9.

The decline of banks' traditional business has thus meant that the banking industry has been driven to seek out new lines of business. This search for business opportunities could be beneficial because, by so doing, banks can keep vibrant and healthy.

Indeed, bank profitability was high up until 2007, and nontraditional, off-balance-sheet activities played an important role in the high bank profits. However, the new directions in banking have led to increased risk taking, and thus the decline in traditional banking has required regulators to be more vigilant. It also poses new challenges for bank regulators, who, as we saw in Chapter 11, must now be far more concerned about banks' off-balance-sheet activities.

Decline of Traditional Banking in Other Industrialized Countries Forces similar to those in the United States have been leading to the decline of traditional banking in other industrialized countries. The loss of banks' monopoly power over depositors has occurred outside the United States as well. Financial innovation and deregulation are occurring worldwide and have created attractive alternatives for both depositors and borrowers. In Japan, for example, deregulation opened a wide array of new financial instruments to the public, causing a disintermediation process similar to that in the United States. In European countries, innovations have steadily eroded the barriers that have traditionally protected banks from competition.

In other countries, banks also faced increased competition from the expansion of securities markets and the growth of the shadow banking system. Both financial deregulation and fundamental economic forces in other countries have improved the availability of information in securities markets, making it easier and less costly for firms to finance their activities by issuing securities rather than going to banks. Further, even in countries where securities markets have not grown, banks have still lost loan business because their best corporate customers have had increasing access to foreign and offshore capital markets, such as the Eurobond market. In smaller economies, like that of Australia, which still do not have as well-developed corporate bond or commercial paper markets, banks have lost loan business to international securities markets. In addition, the same forces that drove the securitization process in the United States have been at work in other countries and have undercut the profitability of traditional banking in these countries as well. The United States has not been unique in seeing its banks face a more difficult competitive environment. Thus, although the decline of traditional banking occurred earlier in the United States than in other countries, the same forces have caused a decline in traditional banking abroad.

STRUCTURE OF THE U.S. COMMERCIAL BANKING INDUSTRY

There are approximately 6,500 commercial banks in the United States, far more than in any other country in the world. As Table 1 indicates, we have an extraordinary number of small banks. Thirty-six percent of the banks have less than $100 million in assets. Far more typical is the size distribution in Canada or the United Kingdom, where five or fewer banks dominate the industry. In contrast, the ten largest commercial banks in the United States (listed in Table 2) together hold just 59% of the assets in their industry.

Most industries in the United States have far fewer firms than the commercial banking industry; typically, large firms tend to dominate these industries to a greater extent than in the commercial banking industry. (Consider the computer software industry, which is dominated by Microsoft, or the automobile industry, which is dominated by General Motors, Ford, Daimler-Chrysler, Toyota, and Honda.) Does the large number of banks in the commercial banking industry and the absence of a few dominant firms suggest that commercial banking is more competitive than other industries?

TABLE 1

Size Distribution of Insured Commercial Banks, March 30, 2011

Assets	Number of Banks	Share of Banks (%)	Share of Assets Held (%)
Less than $100 million	2,328	35.7	1.9
$100 million–$1 billion	3,693	56.6	11.5
$1 billion–$10 billion	423	6.5	12.8
More than $10 billion	86	1.3	73.9
Total	6,530	100.00	100.00

Source: www2.fdic.gov/qbp/2008sep/cb4.html.

Restrictions on Branching

The presence of so many commercial banks in the United States actually reflects past regulations that restricted the ability of these financial institutions to open **branches** (additional offices for the conduct of banking operations). Each state had its own regulations on the type and number of branches that a bank could open. Regulations on both coasts, for example, tended to allow banks to open branches throughout a state; in the middle part of the country, regulations on branching were more restrictive. The McFadden Act of 1927, which was designed to put national banks and state banks on an equal footing (and the Douglas Amendment of 1956,

TABLE 2

Ten Largest U.S. Banks, June 30, 2011

Bank	Assets ($ millions)	Share of All Commercial Bank Assets (%)
1. J.P. Morgan Chase	1,723,460	15.14
2. Bank of America Corp.	1,451,387	13.75
3. Citibank	1,161,359	10.20
4. Wells Fargo	1,093,030	9.60
5. U.S. Bank	305,969	2.69
6. PNC	251,221	2.21
7. Bank of NY Mellon	200,249	1.70
8. HSBC USA	197,545	1.69
9. FIA Card Service	188,639	1.66
10. TD Bank	175,145	1.54
Total	6,743,005	59.25

Source: www.federalreserve.gov/releases/h8/20081229.

which closed a loophole in the McFadden Act), effectively prohibited banks from branching across state lines and forced all national banks to conform to the branching regulations in the state where their headquarters were located.

The McFadden Act and state branching regulations constituted strong anticompetitive forces in the commercial banking industry, allowing many small banks to stay in existence, because larger banks were prevented from opening a branch nearby. If competition is beneficial to society, why have regulations restricting branching arisen in America? The simplest explanation is that the American public has historically been hostile to large banks. States with the most restrictive branching regulations were typically ones in which populist antibank sentiment was strongest in the nineteenth century. (These states usually had large farming populations whose relations with banks periodically became tempestuous when banks would foreclose on farmers who couldn't pay their debts.) The legacy of nineteenth-century politics was a banking system with restrictive branching regulations and hence an inordinate number of small banks. However, as we will see later in this chapter, branching restrictions have been eliminated, and we have moved toward nationwide banking.

Response to Branching Restrictions

An important feature of the U.S. banking industry is that competition can be repressed by regulation but not completely quashed. As we saw earlier in this chapter, the existence of restrictive regulation stimulates financial innovations that get around these regulations in the banks' search for profits. Regulations restricting branching have stimulated similar economic forces and have promoted the development of two financial innovations: bank holding companies and automated teller machines.

Bank Holding Companies A holding company is a corporation that owns several different companies. This form of corporate ownership has important advantages for banks. It has allowed them to circumvent restrictive branching regulations, because the holding company can own a controlling interest in several banks even if branching is not permitted. Furthermore, a bank holding company can engage in other activities related to banking, such as the provision of investment advice, data processing and transmission services, leasing, credit card services, and servicing of loans in other states.

The growth of the bank holding companies has been dramatic over the past three decades. Today bank holding companies own almost all large banks, and more than 90% of all commercial bank deposits are held in banks owned by holding companies.

Automated Teller Machines Another financial innovation that avoided the restrictions on branching is the automated teller machine (ATM). Banks realized that if they did not own or rent the ATM, but instead let it be owned by someone else and paid for each transaction with a fee, the ATM would probably not be considered a branch of the bank and thus would not be subject to branching regulations. This is exactly what the regulatory agencies and courts in most states concluded. Because they enable banks to widen their markets, a number of these shared facilities (such as Cirrus and NYCE) have been established nationwide. Furthermore, even when an ATM is owned by a bank, states typically have special provisions that allow wider establishment of ATMs than is permissible for traditional "brick and mortar" branches.

As we saw earlier in this chapter, avoiding regulation was not the only reason for the development of the ATM. The advent of cheaper computer and telecommunications technology enabled banks to provide ATMs at low cost, making them a profitable innovation. This example further illustrates that technological factors often combine with incentives such as the desire to avoid restrictive regulations like branching restrictions to produce financial innovation.

BANK CONSOLIDATION AND NATIONWIDE BANKING

As we can see in Figure 3, after a remarkable period of stability from 1934 to the mid-1980s, the number of commercial banks began to fall dramatically. Why has this sudden decline taken place?

The banking industry hit some hard times in the 1980s and early 1990s, with bank failures running at a rate of over 100 per year from 1985 to 1992 (more on this later in the chapter; also see Chapter 11). But bank failures are only part of the story. In the years 1985–1992, the number of banks declined by 3,000—more than double the number of failures. And in the period 1992–2007, when the banking industry returned to health, the number of commercial banks decreased by a little over 3,800, less than 5% of which were bank failures, and most of these were of small banks. Thus we see that bank failures played an important, though not predominant, role in reducing the

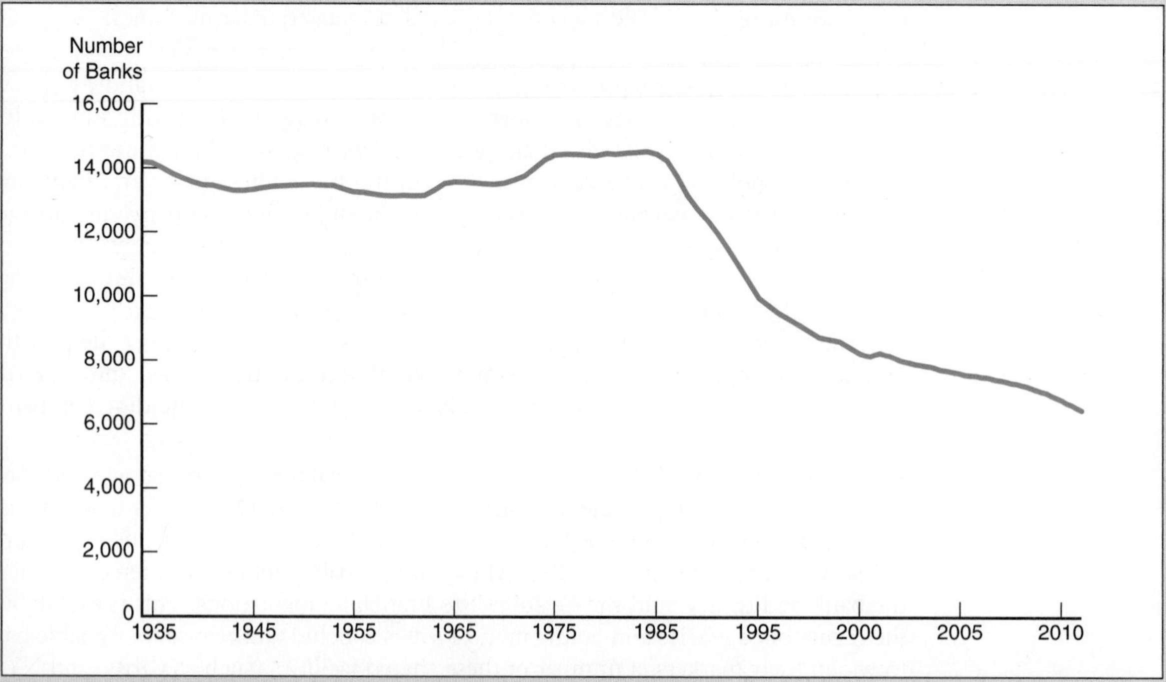

FIGURE 3 Number of Insured Commercial Banks in the United States, 1934–2010 (Third Quarter)
After a period of stability from 1934 to the mid-1980s, the number of commercial banks began to fall dramatically.
Source: www2.fdic.gov/qbp/qbpSelect.asp?menuitem=STAT.

number of banks in the 1985–1992 period and an almost negligible role up through 2007. The financial crisis of 2007–2009 has, however, led to additional declines in the number of banks because of bank failures.

So what explains the rest of the story? The answer is bank consolidation. Banks have been merging to create larger entities or have been buying up other banks. This gives rise to a new question: Why has bank consolidation been taking place in recent years?

As we have seen, loophole mining by banks has reduced the effectiveness of branching restrictions, with the result that many states have recognized that it would be in their best interest if they allowed ownership of banks across state lines. The result has been the formation of reciprocal regional compacts in which banks in one state are allowed to own banks in other states in the region. In 1975, Maine enacted the first interstate banking legislation that allowed out-of-state bank holding companies to purchase banks in that state. In 1982, Massachusetts enacted a regional compact with other New England states to allow interstate banking, and many other regional compacts were adopted thereafter until by the early 1990s, almost all states allowed some form of interstate banking.

With the barriers to interstate banking breaking down in the early 1980s, banks recognized that they could gain the benefits of diversification because they would now be able to make loans in many states rather than just one. This gave them the advantage that if one state's economy was weak, another state in which they operated might have a strong economy, thus decreasing the likelihood that loans in different states would default at the same time. In addition, allowing banks to own banks in other states meant that they could increase their size through out-of-state acquisition of banks or by merging with banks in other states. Mergers and acquisitions explain the first phase of banking consolidation, which has played such an important role in the decline in the number of banks since 1985. Another result of the loosening of restrictions on interstate branching is the development of a new class of banks, the **superregional banks**, bank holding companies that have begun to rival the money center banks in size but whose headquarters are not in one of the money center cities (New York, Chicago, and San Francisco). Examples of these superregional banks are Bank of America of Charlotte, North Carolina, and Banc One of Columbus, Ohio.

Not surprisingly, the advent of the Web and improved computer technology is another factor driving bank consolidation. Economies of scale have increased, because large upfront investments are required to set up many information technology platforms for financial institutions. To take advantage of these economies of scale, banks have needed to get bigger, and this development has led to additional consolidation. Information technology has also been increasing **economies of scope**, the ability to use one resource to provide many different products and services. For example, details about the quality and creditworthiness of firms not only inform decisions about whether to make loans to them, but also can be useful in determining at what price their shares should trade. Similarly, once you have marketed one financial product to an investor, you probably know how to market another. Business people describe economies of scope by saying there are "synergies" between different lines of business, and information technology is making these synergies more likely. The result is that consolidation is taking place not only to make financial institutions bigger, but also to increase the combination of products and services they can provide. This consolidation has had two consequences. First, different types of financial intermediaries are encroaching on each other's territory, making them more alike. Second, consolidation has led to the development of large, complex banking organizations. This development has been facilitated by the repeal of the Glass-Steagall restrictions on combinations of banking and other financial service industries discussed in the next section.

The Riegle-Neal Interstate Banking and Branching Efficiency Act of 1994

Banking consolidation was given further stimulus by the passage in 1994 of the Riegle-Neal Interstate Banking and Branching Efficiency Act. This legislation expanded the regional compacts to the entire nation and overturned the McFadden Act and Douglas Amendment's prohibition of interstate banking. Not only did this act allow bank holding companies to acquire banks in any other state, notwithstanding any state laws to the contrary, but bank holding companies could also merge the banks they own into one bank with branches in different states. States were, however, given the option of opting out of interstate branching, but only Texas did so, although it later reversed its position and now allows it.

The Riegle-Neal Act finally established the basis for a true nationwide banking system. Although interstate banking was accomplished previously by out-of-state purchase of banks by bank holding companies, until 1994 it was virtually nonexistent because very few states had enacted interstate branching legislation. Allowing banks to conduct interstate banking through branching is especially important, because many bankers feel that economies of scale cannot be fully exploited through the bank holding company structure, but only through branching networks in which all of the bank's operations are fully coordinated.

Nationwide banks have now emerged. Starting with the merger in 1998 of Bank of America and NationsBank, which created the first bank with branches on both coasts, consolidation in the banking industry has created some banking organizations with operations in all 50 states.

What Will the Structure of the U.S. Banking Industry Look Like in the Future?

Now that true nationwide banking in the United States is a reality, the benefits of bank consolidation for the banking industry have increased substantially, driving the next phase of mergers and acquisitions and accelerating the decline in the number of commercial banks. With great changes occurring in the structure of this industry, the question naturally arises: What will the industry look like in ten years?

One view is that the industry will become more like that in many other countries (see the Global box, "Comparison of Banking Structure in the United States and Abroad"), and we will end up with only a couple of hundred banks. A more extreme view is that the industry will look like that of Canada or the United Kingdom, with a few large banks dominating the industry. Most experts come up with a different answer. The structure of the U.S. banking industry will still be unique, but not to the degree it once was. The consolidation surge is likely to settle down as the U.S. banking industry approaches several thousand, rather than several hundred, banks.

Banking consolidation will result not only in a smaller number of banks, but as the mergers between Chase Manhattan Bank and Chemical Bank and between Bank of America and NationsBank suggest, a shift in assets from smaller banks to larger banks as well. Within ten years, the share of bank assets in banks with less than $100 million in assets is expected to halve, while the amount at the megabanks, those with more than $100 billion in assets, is expected to more than double. Indeed, the United States now has several trillion-dollar banks (e.g., Citibank, J.P. Morgan Chase, and Bank of America).

Global Comparison of Banking Structure in the United States and Abroad

The structure of the commercial banking industry in the United States is radically different from that in other industrialized nations. The United States is the only country that is just now developing a true national banking system in which banks have branches throughout the country. One result is that many more banks are found in the United States than in other industrialized countries. In contrast to the United States, which has on the order of 6,500 commercial banks, every other industrialized country has far fewer than 1,000. Japan, for example, has fewer than 100 commercial banks—a mere fraction of the number in the United States, even though its economy and population are half the size of those of the United States. Another result of the past restrictions on branching in the United States is that our banks tend to be much smaller than those in other countries.

Are Bank Consolidation and Nationwide Banking Good Things?

Advocates of nationwide banking believe that it will produce more efficient banks and a healthier banking system less prone to bank failures. However, critics of bank consolidation fear that it will eliminate small banks, referred to as **community banks**, and that this will result in less lending to small businesses. In addition, they worry that a few banks will come to dominate the industry, making the banking business less competitive.

Most economists are skeptical of these criticisms of bank consolidation. As we have seen, research indicates that even after bank consolidation is completed, the United States will still have plenty of banks. The banking industry will thus remain highly competitive, probably even more so than now considering that banks that have been protected from competition from out-of-state banks will now have to compete with them vigorously to stay in business.

It also does not look as though community banks will disappear. When New York state liberalized its branching laws in 1962, there were fears that community banks upstate would be driven from the market by the big New York City banks. Not only did this not happen, but some of the big boys found that the small banks were able to run rings around them in the local markets. Similarly, California, which has had unrestricted statewide branching for a long time, continues to have a thriving population of community banks.

Economists see some important benefits from bank consolidation and nationwide banking. The elimination of geographic restrictions on banking will increase competition and drive inefficient banks out of business, increasing the efficiency of the banking sector. The move to larger banking organizations also means that there will be some increase in efficiency because they can take advantage of economies of scale and scope. The increased diversification of banks' loan portfolios may lower the probability of a banking crisis in the future. In the 1980s and early 1990s, bank failures were often concentrated in states with weak economies. For example, after the decline in oil prices in 1986, all of the major commercial banks in Texas, which had been very profitable, found themselves in trouble. At that time, banks in New England were doing fine. However, when the 1990–1991 recession hit New England hard, some

New England banks started failing. With nationwide banking, a bank could make loans in both New England and Texas and would thus be less likely to fail, because when loans go sour in one location, they would probably be doing well in the other. Thus nationwide banking is seen as a major step toward creating a banking system that is less vulnerable to banking crises.

Two concerns remain about the effects of bank consolidation—that it may lead to a reduction in lending to small businesses and that banks rushing to expand into new geographic markets may take increased risks leading to bank failures. The jury is still out on these concerns, but most economists see the benefits of bank consolidation and nationwide banking as outweighing the costs.

SEPARATION OF THE BANKING AND OTHER FINANCIAL SERVICE INDUSTRIES

Another important feature of the structure of the banking industry in the United States until recently was the separation of the banking and other financial services industries—such as securities, insurance, and real estate—mandated by the Glass-Steagall Act of 1933. As pointed out earlier in the chapter, Glass-Steagall allowed commercial banks to sell new offerings of government securities but prohibited them from underwriting corporate securities or from engaging in brokerage activities. It also prevented banks from engaging in insurance and real estate activities. In turn, it prevented investment banks and insurance companies from engaging in commercial banking activities and thus protected banks from competition.

Erosion of Glass-Steagall

Despite the Glass-Steagall prohibitions, the pursuit of profits and financial innovation stimulated both banks and other financial institutions to bypass the intent of the Glass-Steagall Act and encroach on each other's traditional territory. Brokerage firms engaged in the traditional banking business of issuing deposit instruments with the development of money market mutual funds and cash management accounts. After the Federal Reserve used a loophole in Section 20 of the Glass-Steagall Act in 1987 to allow bank holding companies to underwrite previously prohibited classes of securities, banks began to enter this business. The loophole allowed affiliates of approved commercial banks to engage in underwriting activities as long as the revenue didn't exceed a specified amount, which started at 10% but was raised to 25% of the affiliates' total revenue. After the U.S. Supreme Court validated the Fed's action in July 1988, the Federal Reserve allowed J.P. Morgan, a commercial bank holding company, to underwrite corporate debt securities (in January 1989) and to underwrite stocks (in September 1990), with the privilege later extended to other bank holding companies. The regulatory agencies also allowed banks to engage in some real estate and some insurance activities.

The Gramm-Leach-Bliley Financial Services Modernization Act of 1999: Repeal of Glass-Steagall

Because restrictions on commercial banks' securities and insurance activities put American banks at a competitive disadvantage relative to foreign banks, bills to overturn

Glass-Steagall appeared in almost every session of Congress in the 1990s. With the merger in 1998 of Citicorp, the second-largest bank in the United States, and Travelers Group, an insurance company that also owned the third-largest securities firm in the country (Salomon Smith Barney), the pressure to abolish Glass-Steagall became overwhelming. Legislation to eliminate Glass-Steagall finally came to fruition in 1999. This legislation, the Gramm-Leach-Bliley Financial Services Modernization Act of 1999, allows securities firms and insurance companies to purchase banks, and allows banks to underwrite insurance and securities and engage in real estate activities. Under this legislation, states retain regulatory authority over insurance activities, while the Securities and Exchange Commission continues to have oversight of securities activities. The Office of the Comptroller of the Currency has the authority to regulate bank subsidiaries engaged in securities underwriting, but the Federal Reserve continues to have the authority to oversee the bank holding companies under which all real estate and insurance activities and large securities operations will be housed.

Implications for Financial Consolidation

As we have seen, the Riegle-Neal Interstate Banking and Branching Efficiency Act of 1994 has stimulated consolidation of the banking industry. The financial consolidation process has been further hastened by the Gramm-Leach-Bliley Act of 1999, because the way is now open to consolidation in terms not only of the number of banking institutions, but also across financial service activities. Given that information technology is increasing economies of scope, mergers of banks with other financial service firms like that of Citicorp and Travelers have become increasingly common, and more mega-mergers are likely to be on the way. Banking institutions are becoming not only larger, but also increasingly complex organizations, engaging in the full gamut of financial service activities. The trend toward larger and more complex banking organizations has been accelerated by the global financial crisis of 2007–2009 (see the FYI box, "The Global Financial Crisis and the Demise of Large, Free-Standing Investment Banks").

Separation of Banking and Other Financial Services Industries Throughout the World

Not many other countries in the aftermath of the Great Depression followed the lead of the United States in separating the banking and other financial services industries. In fact, in the past this separation was the most prominent difference between banking regulation in the United States and in other countries. Around the world, there are three basic frameworks for the banking and securities industries.

The first framework is *universal banking,* which exists in Germany, the Netherlands, and Switzerland. It provides no separation at all between the banking and securities industries. In a universal banking system, commercial banks provide a full range of banking, securities, real estate, and insurance services, all within a single legal entity. Banks are allowed to own sizable equity shares in commercial firms, and often they do.

The *British-style universal banking system,* the second framework, is found in the United Kingdom and countries with close ties to it, such as Canada and Australia, and now the United States. The British-style universal bank engages in securities underwriting, but it differs from the German-style universal bank in three ways: Separate legal subsidiaries are more common, bank equity holdings of commercial firms are less common, and combinations of banking and insurance firms are less common.

FYI The Global Financial Crisis and the Demise of Large, Free-Standing Investment Banks

Although the move toward bringing financial service activities into larger, complex banking organizations was inevitable after the demise of Glass-Steagall, no one expected it to occur as rapidly as it did in 2008. Over a six-month period from March to September 2008, all five of the largest, free-standing investment banks ceased to exist in their old form. When Bear Stearns, the fifth-largest investment bank, revealed its large losses from investments in subprime mortgage-backed securities, it had to be bailed out by the Fed in March 2008; the price it paid was a forced sale to J.P. Morgan for less than one-tenth what it had been worth only a year or so before. The Bear Stearns bailout made it clear that the government safety net had been extended to investment banks. The tradeoff is that investment banks will be subject to more regulation, along the lines of commercial banks, in the future.

Next to go was Lehman Brothers, the fourth-largest investment bank, which declared bankruptcy on September 15. Only one day before, Merrill Lynch, the third-largest investment bank, which also suffered large losses on its holdings of subprime securities, announced its sale to Bank of America for less than half of its year-earlier price. Within a week Goldman Sachs and Morgan Stanley, the first- and second-largest investment banks, both of whom had smaller exposure to subprime securities, nevertheless saw the writing on the wall. They realized that they would soon become regulated on a similar basis and decided to become bank holding companies so they could access insured deposits, a more stable funding base.

It was the end of an era. Large, free-standing investment banking firms are now a thing of the past.

The third framework features some legal separation of the banking and other financial services industries, as in Japan. A major difference between the U.S. and Japanese banking systems is that Japanese banks are allowed to hold substantial equity stakes in commercial firms, whereas American banks cannot. In addition, most American banks use a bank holding company structure, but bank holding companies are illegal in Japan. Although the banking and securities industries are legally separated in Japan under Section 65 of the Japanese Securities Act, commercial banks are increasingly being allowed to engage in securities activities and, like U.S. banks, are becoming more like British-style universal banks.

THRIFT INDUSTRY: REGULATION AND STRUCTURE

Not surprisingly, the regulation and structure of the thrift industry (savings and loan associations, mutual savings banks, and credit unions) closely parallel the regulation and structure of the commercial banking industry.

Savings and Loan Associations

Just as there is a dual banking system for commercial banks, savings and loan associations (S&Ls) can be chartered either by the federal government or by the states. Most S&Ls, whether state or federally chartered, are members of the Federal Home Loan Bank System (FHLBS). Established in 1932, the FHLBS was styled after the Federal Reserve System. It has twelve district Federal Home Loan banks, which are supervised by the Office of Thrift Supervision.

Federal deposit insurance up to $250,000 per account for S&Ls is provided by the FDIC. The Office of Thrift Supervision regulates federally insured S&Ls by setting minimum capital requirements, requiring periodic reports, and examining the S&Ls. It is also the chartering agency for federally chartered S&Ls, and for these S&Ls it approves mergers and sets the rules for branching.

The branching regulations for S&Ls were more liberal than for commercial banks: In the past, almost all states permitted branching of S&Ls, and since 1980, federally chartered S&Ls were allowed to branch statewide in all states. Since 1981, mergers of financially troubled S&Ls were allowed across state lines, and nationwide branching of S&Ls is now a reality.

The FHLBS, like the Fed, makes loans to the members of the system (obtaining funds for this purpose by issuing bonds). However, in contrast to the Fed's discount loans, which are expected to be repaid quickly, the loans from the FHLBS often need not be repaid for long periods of time. In addition, the rates charged to S&Ls for these loans are often below the rates that the S&Ls must pay when they borrow in the open market. In this way, the FHLBS loan program provides a subsidy to the savings and loan industry (and implicitly to the housing industry, since most of the S&L loans are for residential mortgages).

As we saw in Chapter 11, the savings and loans experienced serious difficulties in the 1980s. Because savings and loans now engage in many of the same activities as commercial banks, many experts view having a separate charter and regulatory apparatus for S&Ls an anachronism that no longer makes sense.

Mutual Savings Banks

Of the 400 or so mutual savings banks, which are similar to S&Ls but are jointly owned by the depositors, approximately half are chartered by states. Although the mutual savings banks are primarily regulated by the states in which they are located, the majority have their deposits insured by the FDIC up to the limit of $250,000 per account; these banks are also subject to many of the FDIC's regulations for state-chartered banks. As a rule, the mutual savings banks whose deposits are not insured by the FDIC have their deposits insured by state insurance funds.

The branching regulations for mutual savings banks are determined by the states in which they operate. Because these regulations are not particularly restrictive, few mutual savings banks have assets of less than $25 million.

Credit Unions

Credit unions are small cooperative lending institutions organized around a particular group of individuals with a common bond (e.g., union members or employees of a particular firm). They are the only depository institutions that are tax-exempt and can be chartered either by the states or by the federal government; more than half are federally chartered. The National Credit Union Administration (NCUA) issues federal charters and regulates federally chartered credit unions by setting minimum capital requirements, requiring periodic reports, and examining the credit unions. Federal deposit insurance (up to the $250,000-per-account limit) is provided to both federally chartered and state-chartered credit unions by a subsidiary of the NCUA, the National Credit Union Share Insurance Fund (NCUSIF). Because the majority of credit union lending is for consumer loans with fairly short terms to maturity, these institutions did not suffer the financial difficulties of the S&Ls and mutual savings banks in the 1980s.

Because their members share a common bond, credit unions are typically quite small; most hold less than $10 million of assets. In addition, their ties to a particular industry or company make them more likely to fail when large numbers of workers in that industry or company are laid off and have trouble making loan payments. Recent regulatory changes allow individual credit unions to cater to a more diverse group of people by interpreting the common bond requirement less strictly, and this has encouraged an expansion in the size of credit unions that may help reduce credit union failures in the future.

Often a credit union's shareholders are dispersed over many states, and sometimes even worldwide, so branching across state lines and into other countries is permitted for federally chartered credit unions. The Navy Federal Credit Union, for example, whose shareholders are members of the U.S. Navy and Marine Corps, has branches throughout the world.

INTERNATIONAL BANKING

In 1960, only eight U.S. banks operated branches in foreign countries, and their total assets were less than $4 billion. Currently, around 100 American banks have branches abroad, with assets totaling more than $2.5 trillion. The spectacular growth in international banking can be explained by three factors.

First is the rapid growth in international trade and multinational corporations that has occurred since 1960. When American firms operate abroad, they need banking services in foreign countries to help finance international trade. For example, they might need a loan in a foreign currency to operate a factory abroad. And when they sell goods abroad, they need to have a bank exchange the foreign currency they have received for their goods into dollars. Although these firms could use foreign banks to provide them with these international banking services, many of them prefer to do business with the U.S. banks with which they have established long-term relationships and which understand American business customs and practices. As international trade has grown, international banking has grown with it.

Second, American banks have been able to earn substantial profits by being very active in global investment banking, in which they underwrite foreign securities. They also sell insurance abroad, and they derive substantial profits from these investment banking and insurance activities.

Third, American banks have wanted to tap into the large pool of dollar-denominated deposits in foreign countries known as Eurodollars. To understand the structure of U.S. banking overseas, let's first look at the Eurodollar market, an important source of growth for international banking.

Eurodollar Market

Eurodollars are created when deposits in accounts in the United States are transferred to a bank outside the country and are kept in the form of dollars. (For a discussion of the birth of the Eurodollar, see the Global box, "Ironic Birth of the Eurodollar Market.") For example, if Rolls-Royce PLC deposits a $1 million check, written on an account at an American bank, in its bank in London—specifying that the deposit is payable in

Global Ironic Birth of the Eurodollar Market

One of capitalism's great ironies is that the Eurodollar market, one of the most important financial markets used by capitalists, was fathered by the Soviet Union. In the early 1950s, during the height of the Cold War, the Soviets had accumulated a substantial amount of dollar balances held by banks in the United States. Because the Russians feared that the U.S. government might freeze these assets in the United States, they wanted to move the deposits to Europe, where they would be safe from expropriation. (This fear was not unjustified—consider the U.S. freeze on Iranian assets in 1979 and Iraqi assets in 1990.) However, they also wanted to keep the deposits in dollars so that they could be used in their international transactions. The solution to the problem was to transfer the deposits to European banks but to keep the deposits denominated in dollars. When the Soviets did this, the Eurodollar was born.

dollars—$1 million in Eurodollars is created.[2] More than 90% of Eurodollar deposits are time deposits, more than half of them certificates of deposit with maturities of 30 days or more. The Eurodollar market is massive, over $5 trillion, making it one of the most important financial markets in the world economy.

Why would companies such as Rolls-Royce want to hold dollar deposits outside the United States? First, the dollar is the most widely used currency in international trade, so Rolls-Royce might want to hold deposits in dollars to conduct its international transactions. Second, Eurodollars are "offshore" deposits—they are held in countries that will not subject them to regulations such as reserve requirements or restrictions (called *capital controls*) on taking the deposits outside the country.[3]

The main center of the Eurodollar market is London, a major international financial center for hundreds of years. Eurodollars are also held outside Europe in locations that provide offshore status to these deposits—for example, Singapore, the Bahamas, and the Cayman Islands.

The minimum transaction in the Eurodollar market is typically $1 million, and approximately 75% of Eurodollar deposits are held by banks. Plainly, you and I are unlikely to come into direct contact with Eurodollars. The Eurodollar market is, however, an important source of funds to U.S. banks. Rather than using an intermediary and borrowing all the deposits from foreign banks, American banks decided that they could earn higher profits by opening their own branches abroad to attract these deposits. Consequently, the Eurodollar market has been an important stimulus to U.S. banking overseas.

Structure of U.S. Banking Overseas

U.S. banks have most of their foreign branches in Latin America, the Far East, the Caribbean, and London. The largest volume of assets is held by branches in London, because

[2]Note that the London bank keeps the $1 million on deposit at the American bank, so the creation of Eurodollars has not caused a reduction in the amount of bank deposits in the United States.

[3]Although most offshore deposits are denominated in dollars, some are denominated in other currencies. Collectively, these offshore deposits are referred to as Eurocurrencies. A Japanese yen-denominated deposit held in London, for example, is called a Euroyen.

it is a major international financial center and the central location for the Eurodollar market. Latin America and the Far East have many branches because of the importance of U.S. trade with these regions. Parts of the Caribbean (especially the Bahamas and the Cayman Islands) have become important as tax havens, with minimal taxation and few restrictive regulations. In actuality, the bank branches in the Bahamas and the Cayman Islands are "shell operations" because they function primarily as bookkeeping centers and do not provide normal banking services.

An alternative corporate structure for U.S. banks that operate overseas is the **Edge Act corporation**, a special subsidiary engaged primarily in international banking. U.S. banks (through their holding companies) can also own a controlling interest in foreign banks and in foreign companies that provide financial services, such as finance companies. The international activities of U.S. banking organizations are governed primarily by the Federal Reserve's Regulation K.

In late 1981, the Federal Reserve approved the creation of **international banking facilities (IBFs)** within the United States that can accept time deposits from foreigners but are not subject to either reserve requirements or restrictions on interest payments. IBFs are also allowed to make loans to foreigners, but they are not allowed to make loans to domestic residents. States have encouraged the establishment of IBFs by exempting them from state and local taxes. In essence, IBFs are treated like foreign branches of U.S. banks and are not subject to domestic regulations and taxes. The purpose of establishing IBFs is to encourage American and foreign banks to do more banking business in the United States rather than abroad. From this point of view, IBFs were a success: Their assets climbed to nearly $200 billion in the first two years, and are in excess of $1 trillion currently.

Foreign Banks in the United States

The growth in international trade has not only encouraged U.S. banks to open offices overseas, but has also encouraged foreign banks to establish offices in the United States. Foreign banks have been extremely successful in the United States. Currently, they hold more than 5% of total U.S. bank assets and do a large portion of all U.S. bank lending, with around a 22% market share for lending to U.S. corporations.

Foreign banks engage in banking activities in the United States by operating an agency office of the foreign bank, a subsidiary U.S. bank, or a branch of the foreign bank. An agency office can lend and transfer funds in the United States, but it cannot accept deposits from domestic residents. Agency offices have the advantage of not being subject to regulations that apply to full-service banking offices (such as requirements for FDIC insurance). A subsidiary U.S. bank is just like any other U.S. bank (it may even have an American-sounding name) and is subject to the same regulations, but it is owned by the foreign bank. A branch of a foreign bank bears the foreign bank's name and is usually a full-service office. Foreign banks may also form Edge Act corporations and IBFs.

Before 1978, foreign banks were not subject to many regulations that applied to domestic banks: They could open branches across state lines and were not expected to meet reserve requirements, for example. The passage of the International Banking Act of 1978, however, put foreign and domestic banks on a more equal footing. The act stipulated that foreign banks could open new full-service branches only in the state they designate as their home state or in states that allow the entry of out-of-state banks. Limited-service branches and agency offices in any other state were permitted, however,

TABLE 3

Ten Largest Banks in the World, 2011

Bank	Assets (U.S. $ millions)
1. BNP Paribas SA, France	2,675,627
2. Deutsche Bank AG, Germany	2,551,727
3. Barclays PLC, UK	2,326,004
4. Credit Agricole SA, France	2,133,810
5. Industrial and Commercial Bank of China, China	2,043,861
6. The Royal Bank of Scotland Group PLC, UK	2,020,790
7. The Bank of Tokyo-Mitsubishi UFJ Ltd, Japan	1,644,768
8. China Construction Bank Corp, China	1,641,683
9. JP Morgan-Chase NA, US	1,621,621
10. Bank Santander, Spain	1,590,560

Source: http://topforeignstocks.com/2008/07/25/the-top-10-banks-in-the-world-2008/.

and foreign banks are allowed to retain any full-service branches opened before the act was ratified.

The internationalization of banking, both by U.S. banks going abroad and by foreign banks entering the United States, has meant that financial markets throughout the world have become more integrated. As a result, there is a growing trend toward international coordination of bank regulation, one example of which is the Basel Accords to standardize minimum bank capital requirements in industrialized countries, discussed in Chapter 11. Financial market integration has also encouraged bank consolidation abroad, culminating in the creation of the first trillion-dollar bank with the merger of the Industrial Bank of Japan, Dai-Ichi Kangyo Bank, and Fuji Bank, in 2002. Another development has been the importance of foreign banks in international banking. As is shown in Table 3, in 2011, nine out of ten of the largest banking groups in the world were foreign. The implications of this financial market integration for the operation of our economy are examined further in Chapter 21 when we discuss the international financial system in more detail.

Summary

1. The history of banking in the United States has left us with a dual banking system, with commercial banks chartered by the states and the federal government. Multiple agencies regulate commercial banks: the Office of the Comptroller, the Federal Reserve, the FDIC, and the state banking authorities.
2. A change in the economic environment will stimulate financial institutions to search for financial innovations. Changes in demand conditions, especially an increase in interest-rate risk; changes in supply conditions, especially improvements in information technology; and the desire to avoid costly regulations have been major driving forces behind financial innovation. Financial innovation has caused banks to suffer declines in cost advantages in acquiring funds and in income advantages on their assets. The resulting squeeze has hurt profitability in banks' traditional lines of business and has led to a decline in traditional banking.

3. Restrictive state branching regulations and the McFadden Act, which prohibited branching across state lines, led to a large number of small commercial banks. The large number of commercial banks in the United States reflected the past *lack* of competition, not the presence of vigorous competition. Bank holding companies and ATMs were important responses to branching restrictions that weakened the restrictions' anticompetitive effect.
4. Since the mid-1980s, bank consolidation has been occurring at a rapid pace. The first phase of bank consolidation was the result of bank failures and the reduced effectiveness of branching restrictions. The second phase has been stimulated by information technology and the Riegle-Neal Interstate Banking and Branching Efficiency Act of 1994, which establishes the basis for a nationwide banking system. Once banking consolidation has settled down, we are likely to be left with a banking system with several thousand banks. Most economists believe that the benefits of bank consolidation and nationwide banking will outweigh the costs.
5. The Glass-Steagall Act separated commercial banking from the securities industry. Legislation in 1999, however, repealed the Glass-Steagall Act, removing the separation of these industries.
6. The regulation and structure of the thrift industry (savings and loan associations, mutual savings banks, and credit unions) parallel closely the regulation and structure of the commercial banking industry. Savings and loans are primarily regulated by the Office of Thrift Supervision, and deposit insurance is administered by the FDIC. Mutual savings banks are regulated by the states, and federal deposit insurance is provided by the FDIC. Credit unions are regulated by the National Credit Union Administration, and deposit insurance is provided by the National Credit Union Share Insurance Fund.
7. With the rapid growth of world trade since 1960, international banking has grown dramatically. United States banks engage in international banking activities by opening branches abroad, owning controlling interests in foreign banks, forming Edge Act corporations, and operating international banking facilities (IBFs) located in the United States. Foreign banks operate in the United States by owning a subsidiary American bank or by operating branches or agency offices in the United States.

Key Terms

automated banking machine (ABM), p. 275
automated teller machine (ATM), p. 275
bank holding companies, p. 272
branches, p. 284
central bank, p. 269
community banks, p. 289
deposit rate ceilings, p. 278
disintermediation, p. 278
dual banking system, p. 271
economies of scope, p. 287
Edge Act corporation, p. 296
financial derivatives, p. 274
financial engineering, p. 272
futures contracts, p. 273
hedge, p. 273
international banking facilities (IBFs), p. 296
national banks, p. 271
securitization, p. 277
shadow banking system, p. 272
state banks, p. 271
superregional banks, p. 287
sweep account, p. 279
virtual bank, p. 275

Questions

All questions are available in MyEconLab *at* www.myeconlab.com.

1. Why was the United States one of the last major industrialized countries to have a central bank?
2. Why does the United States operate under a dual banking system?
3. What were the motivations for the original Glass-Steagall Act in 1933?

4. Which regulatory agency has the primary responsibility for supervising the following categories of commercial banks?
   a. National banks
   b. Bank holding companies
   c. Non–Federal Reserve member state banks
   d. Federal Reserve member state banks
   e. Federally chartered savings and loan associations
   f. Federally chartered credit unions
5. How does the emergence of interest-rate risk help explain financial innovation?
6. Why did new technology make it harder to enforce limitations on bank branching?
7. "The invention of the computer is the major factor behind the decline of the banking industry." Is this statement true, false, or uncertain? Explain your answer.
8. "If inflation had not risen in the 1960s and 1970s, the banking industry might be healthier today." Is this statement true, false, or uncertain? Explain your answer.
9. How do sweep accounts and money market mutual funds allow banks to avoid reserve requirements?
10. If reserve requirements were eliminated in the future, as some economists advocate, what effects would this have on the size of money market mutual funds?
11. Why is loophole mining so prevalent in the banking industry in the United States?
12. Why have banks been losing cost advantages in acquiring funds in recent years?
13. Why have banks been losing income advantages on their assets in recent years?
14. "The commercial banking industry in Canada is less competitive than the commercial banking industry in the United States because in Canada only a few large banks dominate the industry, while in the United States there are around 6.500 commercial banks." Is this statement true, false, or uncertain? Explain your answer.
15. Why is there a higher percentage of banks with less than $25 million of assets among commercial banks than among savings and loans and mutual savings banks?
16. Unlike commercial banks, savings and loans, and mutual savings banks, credit unions did not have restrictions on locating branches in other states. Why, then, are credit unions typically smaller than the other depository institutions?
17. Why has the number of bank holding companies dramatically increased?
18. What are the advantages and disadvantages of interstate banking?
19. How did competitive forces lead to the repeal of the Glass-Steagall Act's separation of the banking and securities industries?
20. What has been the likely effect of the Gramm-Leach-Bliley Act on financial consolidation?
21. What factors explain the rapid growth in international banking?
22. What incentives have regulatory agencies created to encourage international banking? Why have they done this?
23. How could the approval of international banking facilities (IBFs) by the Fed in 1981 have reduced employment in the banking industry in Europe?
24. If the bank at which you keep your checking account is owned by foreigners, should you worry that your deposits are less safe than if the bank were owned by Americans?
25. Why is there only one U.S. bank among the ten largest banks in the world?

Web Exercises

1. Go to www2.fdic.gov/hsob/index.asp. Select Commercial Bank Reports, then Number of Institutions, Branches, and Total Offices. If you look at the trend in bank branches, does the public appear to have more or less access to banking facilities? How many banks were there in 1934 and how many are there now? Does the graph indicate that the trend toward consolidation is continuing?

2. Despite the regulations that protect banks from failure, some do fail. Go to www2.fdic.gov/hsob/index.asp. Select the tab labeled Failures and Assistance Transactions. How many bank failures occurred in the United States during the most recent complete calendar year? What were the total assets held by the banks that failed? How many banks failed in 1937?

Web References

www.fdic.gov/bank/

The FDIC gathers data about individual financial institutions and the banking industry.

www2.fdic.gov/hsob/index.asp

Visit this website to gather statistics on the banking industry.

13

Nonbank Finance

Preview

Banking is not the only type of financial intermediation you are likely to encounter. You might decide to purchase insurance, take out an installment loan from a finance company, or buy a share of stock. In each of these transactions you will be engaged in nonbank finance and will deal with nonbank financial institutions. In our economy, nonbank finance also plays an important role in channeling funds from lender-savers to borrower-spenders. Furthermore, the process of financial innovation we discussed in Chapter 12 has increased the importance of nonbank finance and is blurring the distinction between different kinds of financial institutions. This chapter examines in more detail how institutions engaged in nonbank finance operate, how they are regulated, and what trends in nonbank finance have occurred recently.

INSURANCE

Every day we face the possibility of the occurrence of certain catastrophic events that could lead to large financial losses. A spouse's earnings might disappear due to death or illness; a car accident might result in costly repair bills or payments to an injured party. Because financial losses from crises could be large relative to our financial resources, we protect ourselves against them by purchasing insurance coverage that will pay a sum of money if catastrophic events occur. Life insurance companies sell policies that provide income if a person dies, is incapacitated by illness, or retires. Property and casualty companies specialize in policies that pay for losses incurred as a result of accidents, fire, or theft.

Life Insurance

The first life insurance company in the United States (Presbyterian Ministers' Fund in Philadelphia) was established in 1759 and is still in existence. There are currently about 1,000 life insurance companies, which are organized in two forms: as stock companies or as mutuals. Stock companies are owned by stockholders; mutuals are technically owned by the policyholders. Although more than 90% of life insurance companies are organized as stock companies, some of the largest ones are organized as mutuals.

Unlike commercial banks and other depository institutions, life insurance companies have never experienced widespread failures, so the federal government has not seen the need to regulate the industry. Instead, regulation is left to the states in which a company operates. State regulation is directed at sales practices, the provision of adequate liquid assets to cover losses, and restrictions on the amount of risky assets (such as common stock) that the companies can hold. The regulatory authority is typically a state insurance commissioner.

Because death rates for the population as a whole are predictable with a high degree of certainty, life insurance companies can accurately predict what their payouts to policyholders will be in the future. Consequently, they hold long-term assets that are not particularly liquid—corporate bonds and commercial mortgages as well as some corporate stock.

Life insurance policies are in two principal forms: permanent life insurance (such as whole, universal, and variable life) and temporary insurance (such as term). Permanent life insurance policies have a constant premium throughout the life of the policy. In the early years of the policy, the size of this premium exceeds the amount needed to insure against death because the probability of death is low. Thus the policy builds up a cash value in its early years, but in later years the cash value declines because the constant premium falls below the amount needed to insure against death, the probability of which is now higher. The policyholder can borrow against the cash value of the permanent life policy or can claim it by canceling the policy.

Term insurance, by contrast, has a premium that is matched every year to the amount needed to insure against death during the period of the term (such as one year or five years). As a result, term policies have premiums that rise over time as the probability of death rises (or level premiums with a decline in the amount of death benefits). Term policies have no cash value and thus, in contrast to permanent life policies, provide insurance only, with no savings aspect.

Weak investment returns on permanent life insurance in the 1970s led to slow growth of demand for life insurance products. The result was a shrinkage in the size of the life insurance industry relative to other financial intermediaries, with their share of total financial intermediary assets falling from 15.3% at the end of 1970 to 11.5% at the end of 1980 (see Table 1, which shows the relative shares of financial intermediary assets for each of the financial intermediaries discussed in this chapter).

Beginning in the mid-1970s, life insurance companies began to restructure their business to become managers of assets for pension funds. An important factor behind this restructuring was 1974 legislation that encouraged pension funds to turn fund management over to life insurance companies. Now more than half of the assets managed by life insurance companies are for pension funds, not for life insurance. Insurance companies have also begun to sell investment vehicles for retirement, such as **annuities**, arrangements whereby the customer pays an annual premium in exchange for a future stream of annual payments beginning at a set age, say, 65, and continuing until death. The result of this new business has been that the market share of life insurance companies as a percentage of total financial intermediary assets has held steady since 1980.

Property and Casualty Insurance

Property and casualty insurance companies in the United States number on the order of 2,700, the two largest of which are State Farm and Allstate. Property and casualty companies are organized as both stock and mutual companies and are regulated by the states in which they operate.

Although property and casualty insurance companies had a slight increase in their share of total financial intermediary assets from 1970 to 1990 (see Table 1), in recent years they have not fared well, and insurance premiums have skyrocketed. With the

TABLE 1

Relative Shares of Total Financial Intermediary Assets, 1970–2010 (percent)

	1970	1980	1990	2000	2010
Insurance Companies					
Life insurance	15.3	11.5	12.5	12.0	12.4
Property and casualty	3.8	4.5	4.9	3.3	3.4
Pension Funds					
Private	8.4	12.5	14.9	16.6	14.6
Public (state and local government)	4.6	4.9	6.7	8.8	7.0
Finance Companies	4.9	5.1	5.6	4.4	3.8
Mutual Funds					
Stocks and bonds	3.6	1.7	5.9	17.0	19.0
Money market	0.0	1.9	4.6	6.9	6.6
Depository Institutions (Banks)					
Commercial banks	38.5	36.7	30.4	24.7	24.1
S&Ls and mutual savings banks	19.4	19.6	12.5	4.7	7.0
Credit unions	1.4	1.6	2.0	1.7	2.2
Total	100.0	100.0	100.0	100.0	100.0

Source: Federal Reserve Flow of Funds Accounts; www.federalreserve.gov/releases/z1/Current/z1.pdf.

high interest rates in the 1970s and 1980s, insurance companies had high investment income that enabled them to keep insurance rates low. Since then, however, investment income has fallen with the decline in interest rates, while the growth in lawsuits involving property and casualty insurance and the explosion in amounts awarded in such cases have produced substantial losses for companies.

To return to profitability, insurance companies have raised their rates dramatically—sometimes doubling or even tripling premiums—and have refused to provide coverage for some people. They have also campaigned actively for limits on insurance payouts, particularly for medical malpractice. In the search for profits, insurance companies are also branching out into uncharted territory by insuring the payment of interest on municipal and corporate bonds and on mortgage-backed securities. One worry is that the insurance companies may be taking on excessive risk in an attempt to boost their profits. One result of the concern about the health of the property and casualty insurance industry is that insurance regulators have proposed new rules that would impose risk-based capital requirements on these companies based on the riskiness of their assets and operations.

The investment policies of these companies are affected by two basic facts. First, because they are subject to federal income taxes, the largest share of their assets is held in tax-exempt municipal bonds. Second, because property losses are more uncertain than the death rate in a population, these insurers are less able to predict how much they will have to pay policyholders than life insurance companies are. Natural and unnatural disasters—such as the Los Angeles earthquake in 1994; the September 11,

2001, destruction of the World Trade Center; and Hurricane Katrina, which devastated New Orleans in 2005—exposed the property and casualty insurance companies to billions of dollars of losses. Therefore, property and casualty insurance companies hold more liquid assets than life insurance companies; municipal bonds and U.S. government securities amount to over half their assets, and most of the remainder is held in corporate bonds and corporate stock.

Property and casualty insurance companies will insure against losses from almost any type of event, including fire, theft, negligence, malpractice, earthquakes, and automobile accidents. If a possible loss being insured is too large for any one firm, several firms may join together to write a policy and thus share the risk. Insurance companies may also reduce their risk exposure by obtaining **reinsurance**. Reinsurance allocates a portion of the risk to another company in exchange for a portion of the premium and is particularly important for small insurance companies. You can think of reinsurance as insurance for the insurance company. The most famous risk-sharing operation is Lloyd's of London, an association in which different insurance companies can underwrite a fraction of an insurance policy. Lloyd's of London has claimed that it will insure against any contingency—for a price.

The Competitive Threat from the Banking Industry

Until recently, banks have been restricted in their ability to sell life insurance products. This has been changing rapidly, however. More than two-thirds of the states allow banks to sell life insurance in one form or another. In recent years, the bank regulatory authorities, particularly the Office of the Comptroller of the Currency (OCC), have also encouraged banks to enter the insurance field because getting into insurance would help diversify banks' business, thereby improving their economic health and making bank failures less likely. For example, in 1990, the OCC ruled that selling annuities was a form of investment that was incidental to the banking business and so was a permissible banking activity. As a result, the banks' share of the annuities market has increased to 24%. Most banks also now sell insurance products.

Insurance companies and their agents reacted to this competitive threat with both lawsuits and lobbying actions to block banks from entering the insurance business. Their efforts were set back by several Supreme Court rulings that favored the banks. Particularly important was a ruling in favor of Barnett Bank in March 1996, which held that state laws to prevent banks from selling insurance can be superseded by federal rulings from banking regulators that allow banks to sell insurance. The decision gave banks a green light to further their insurance activities, and with the passage of the Gramm-Leach-Bliley Act of 1999, banking institutions further engaged in the insurance business, thus blurring the distinction between insurance companies and banks.

Credit Insurance

Insurance companies have not taken the encroachment of banks on their territory lying down. They have responded by getting into the business of supplying credit insurance. They have done this in two ways.

Credit Default Swaps One way insurance companies can, in effect, provide credit insurance is by selling a traded derivative called a **credit default swap (CDS)** in which the seller is required to make a payment to the holder of the CDS if there is a *credit event*

FYI The AIG Blowup

American International Group, better known as AIG, was a trillion-dollar insurance giant and before 2008 was one of the twenty largest companies in the world. A small separate unit, AIG's Financial Products division, went into the credit default swap business in a big way, insuring over $400 billion of securities, of which $57 billion were debt securities backed by subprime mortgages. Lehman Brothers' troubles and eventual bankruptcy on September 15, 2008, revealed that subprime securities were worth much less than they were being valued on the books, and investors came to the realization that AIG's losses, which had already been substantial in the first half of the year, could bankrupt the company. Lenders to AIG then pulled back with a vengeance, and AIG could not raise enough capital to stay afloat.

On September 16, the Federal Reserve and the U.S. Treasury decided to rescue AIG because its failure was deemed potentially catastrophic for the financial system. Banks and mutual funds were large holders of AIG's debt, and the bankruptcy of AIG would have rendered worthless all the credit default swaps it had sold, thereby imposing huge losses on financial institutions that had bought them. The Federal Reserve set up an $85 billion credit facility (with the total loan from the Fed and the government eventually reaching $173 billion) to provide liquidity to AIG. The rescue did not come cheap, however: AIG was charged a very high interest rate on the loans from the Fed, and the government was given the rights to an 80% stake in the company if it survived. Maurice Greenberg, former CEO of the company, described the government's actions as a "nationalization" of AIG.

Insurance companies have never been viewed as posing a risk to the financial system as a whole, so their regulation has been left to insurance commissions in each state. Because the problems at AIG nearly brought down the U.S. financial system, this view is no longer tenable. The insurance industry will never be the same.

for that instrument, such as a bankruptcy or downgrading of the firm's credit rating. (Credit derivatives are discussed more extensively in the next chapter.) Issuing a CDS is thus tantamount to providing insurance on the debt instrument because, just like insurance, it makes a payment to the holder of the CDS when a negative credit event occurs. Major insurance companies have entered the CDS market in recent years, sometimes to their great regret (see the FYI box, "The AIG Blowup").

Monoline Insurance Another way of providing credit insurance is to supply it directly, just as with any insurance policy. However, insurance regulations do not allow property and casualty insurance companies, life insurance companies, or insurance companies with multiple lines of business to underwrite credit insurance. **Monoline insurance companies**, which specialize in credit insurance alone, are therefore the only insurance companies allowed to provide insurance that guarantees the timely repayment of bond principal and interest when a debt issuer defaults. These insurance companies, such as Ambac Financial Group and MBIA, have become particularly important in the municipal bond market, where they insure a large percentage of these securities. When a municipal security with a lower credit rating, say, an A rating, has an insurance policy from a monoline insurer, it takes on the credit rating of the monoline insurer, say, AAA. This action lowers the interest cost for the municipality and so makes it worthwhile for the municipality to pay premiums for this insurance policy. Of course, to do this, the

FYI The Global Financial Crisis and the Monoline Insurers

One spillover from the global financial crisis was a hit to the monoline insurers, with knock-on effects on the municipal bond market. Unfortunately for the monoline insurers, they insured not only municipal bonds but also debt securities backed by subprime mortgages. With rising defaults on these mortgages, monoline insurers started to take big losses, resulting in credit downgrades from their AAA status. This downgrading weakened the value of their insurance guarantees, not only on subprime securities but on municipal securities as well. As the global crisis got into full swing, the markets took the view that monoline insurance was not worth much, and so municipal bonds began to trade at lower prices based solely on the municipality's credit rating. The result was that state and local governments now found their interest costs rising. They were hit by a double whammy from the global financial crisis of higher borrowing costs and lower tax revenues because of their weaker economies. The result was weaker state and local finances, as well as cutbacks in spending for roads, schools, and hospitals.

monoline insurers need to have a very high credit rating. When the monoline insurers experienced credit downgrades during the global financial crisis, not only did they suffer, but so did the municipal bond market (see the FYI box, "The Global Financial Crisis and the Monoline Insurers").

APPLICATION ◆ Insurance Management

Insurance, like banking, is in the financial intermediation business of transforming one type of asset into another for the public. Insurance providers use the premiums paid on policies to invest in assets such as bonds, stocks, mortgages, and other loans; the earnings from these assets are then used to pay out claims on the policies. In effect, insurers transform assets such as bonds, stocks, and loans into insurance policies that provide a set of services (for example, claim adjustments, savings plans, and friendly insurance agents). If the insurer's production process of asset transformation efficiently provides its customers with adequate insurance services at low cost and if it can earn high returns on its investments, it will make profits; if not, it will suffer losses.

In Chapter 10 the economic concepts of adverse selection and moral hazard allowed us to understand principles of bank management related to managing credit risk; many of these same principles also apply to the lending activities of insurers. Here again we apply the adverse selection and moral hazard concepts to explain many management practices specific to insurance.

In the case of an insurance policy, moral hazard arises when the existence of insurance encourages the insured party to take risks that increase the likelihood of an insurance payoff. For example, a person covered by burglary insurance might not take as many precautions to prevent a burglary because the insurance company will reimburse most of the losses if a theft occurs. Adverse selection holds that the people most likely to receive large insurance payoffs are the ones who will most want to purchase insurance. For example, a person suffering from a terminal disease would want to take out the biggest life and medical insurance policies possible, thereby exposing the insurance company to potentially large losses. Both adverse selection and moral hazard can result in large losses to insurance companies, because they lead to higher payouts on insurance claims. Lowering adverse selection and moral hazard to reduce these payouts is therefore an extremely important goal for insurance companies, and this goal explains the insurance practices we will discuss here.

Screening

To reduce adverse selection, insurance providers try to screen out good insurance risks from poor ones. Effective information collection procedures are therefore an important principle of insurance management.

When you apply for auto insurance, the first thing your insurance agent does is ask you questions about your driving record (number of speeding tickets and accidents), the type of car you are insuring, and certain personal matters (age, marital status). If you are applying for life insurance, you go through a similar grilling, but you are asked even more personal questions about such things as your health, smoking habits, and drug and alcohol use. The life insurer even orders a medical evaluation (usually done by an independent company) that involves taking blood and urine samples. Just as a bank calculates a credit score to evaluate a potential borrower, the insurers use the information you provide to allocate you to a risk class—a statistical estimate of how likely you are to have an insurance claim. Based on this information, the insurer can decide whether to accept you for the insurance or to turn you down because you pose too high a risk and thus would be an unprofitable customer.

Risk-Based Premiums

Charging insurance premiums on the basis of how much risk a policyholder poses for the insurance provider is a time-honored principle of insurance management. Adverse selection explains why this principle is so important to insurance company profitability.

To understand why an insurance provider finds it necessary to have risk-based premiums, let's examine an example of risk-based insurance premiums that at first glance seems unfair. Harry and Sally, both college students with no accidents or speeding tickets, apply for auto insurance. Normally, Harry will be charged a much higher premium than Sally. Insurance providers do this because young males have a much higher accident rate than young females. Suppose, though, that one insurer did not base its premiums on a risk classification but rather just charged a premium based on the average combined risk for males and females. Then Sally would be charged too much and Harry too little. Sally could go to another insurer and get a lower rate, while Harry would sign up for the insurance. Because Harry's premium isn't high enough to cover the accidents he is likely to have, on average the insurer would lose money on Harry. Only with a premium based on a risk classification, so that Harry is charged more, can the insurance provider make a profit.[1]

[1]Note that the example here is, in fact, the lemons problem described in Chapter 8.

Restrictive Provisions

Restrictive provisions in policies are an insurance management tool for reducing moral hazard. Such provisions discourage policyholders from engaging in risky activities that make an insurance claim more likely. For example, life insurers have provisions in their policies that eliminate death benefits if the insured person commits suicide within the first two years that the policy is in effect. Restrictive provisions may also require certain behavior on the part of the insured. A company renting motor scooters may be required to provide helmets for renters to be covered for any liability associated with the rental. The role of restrictive provisions is not unlike that of restrictive covenants on debt contracts described in Chapter 8: Both serve to reduce moral hazard by ruling out undesirable behavior.

Prevention of Fraud

Insurance providers also face moral hazard because an insured person has an incentive to lie to the insurer and seek a claim even if the claim is not valid. For example, a person who has not complied with the restrictive provisions of an insurance contract may still submit a claim. Even worse, a person may file claims for events that did not actually occur. Thus an important management principle for insurance providers is conducting investigations to prevent fraud so that only policyholders with valid claims receive compensation.

Cancellation of Insurance

Being prepared to cancel policies is another insurance management tool. Insurers can discourage moral hazard by threatening to cancel a policy when the insured person engages in activities that make a claim more likely. If your auto insurance company makes it clear that coverage will be canceled if a driver gets too many speeding tickets, you will be less likely to speed.

Deductibles

The **deductible** is the fixed amount by which the insured's loss is reduced when a claim is paid off. A $500 deductible on an auto policy, for example, means that if you suffer a loss of $1,000 because of an accident, the insurer will pay you only $500. Deductibles are an additional management tool that helps insurance providers reduce moral hazard. With a deductible, you experience a loss along with the insurer when you make a claim. Because you also stand to lose when you have an accident, you have an incentive to drive more carefully. A deductible thus makes a policyholder act more in line with what is profitable for the insurer; moral hazard has been reduced. And because moral hazard has been reduced, the insurance provider can lower the premium by more than enough to compensate the policyholder for the existence of the deductible. Another function of the deductible is to eliminate the administrative costs of handling small claims by forcing the insured to bear these losses.

Coinsurance

When a policyholder shares a percentage of the losses along with the insurer, their arrangement is called **coinsurance**. For example, some medical insurance plans provide coverage for 80% of medical bills, and the insured person pays 20% after a certain deductible has been met. Coinsurance works to reduce moral hazard in exactly the same way that a deductible does. A policyholder who suffers a loss along with the insurer has less incentive to take actions, such as going to the doctor unnecessarily, that involve higher claims. Coinsurance is thus another useful management tool for insurance providers.

Limits on the Amount of Insurance

Another important principle of insurance management is that limits should be placed on the amount of insurance provided, even though a customer is willing to pay for more coverage. The higher the insurance coverage, the more the insured person can gain from risky activities that make an insurance payoff more likely and hence the greater the moral hazard. For example, if Zelda's car were insured for more than its true value, she might not take proper precautions to prevent its theft, such as making sure that the key is always removed or putting in an alarm system. If it were stolen, she would come out ahead because the excessive insurance payment would allow her to buy an even better car. By contrast, when the insurance payments are lower than the value of her car, she will suffer a loss if it is stolen and will thus take precautions to prevent this from happening. Insurance providers must always make sure that their coverage is not so high that moral hazard leads to large losses.

Summary

Effective insurance management requires several practices: information collection and screening of potential policyholders, risk-based premiums, restrictive provisions, prevention of fraud, cancellation of insurance, deductibles, coinsurance, and limits on the amount of insurance. All of these practices reduce moral hazard and adverse selection by making it harder for policyholders to benefit from engaging in activities that increase the amount and likelihood of claims. With smaller benefits available, the poor insurance risks (those who are more likely to engage in the activities in the first place) see less benefit from the insurance and are thus less likely to seek it out. ◆

PENSION FUNDS

In performing the financial intermediation function of asset transformation, pension funds provide the public with another kind of protection: regular income payments during retirement. Employers, unions, or private individuals can set up pension plans, which acquire funds through contributions paid in by the plan's participants. As we can see in Table 1, pension plans both public and private have grown in importance, with their share of total financial intermediary assets rising from 13% at the end of 1970 to 21.6% at the end of 2010. Federal tax policy has been a major factor behind the rapid growth of pension funds because employer contributions to employee pension plans are tax-deductible. Furthermore, tax policy has also encouraged employee contributions to pension funds by making them tax-deductible as well and enabling self-employed individuals to open up their own tax-sheltered pension plans, Keogh plans, and individual retirement accounts (IRAs).

Because the benefits paid out of the pension fund each year are highly predictable, pension funds invest in long-term securities, with the bulk of their asset holdings in bonds, stocks, and long-term mortgages. The key management issues for pension funds revolve around asset management: Pension fund managers try to hold assets with high expected returns and reduce risk through diversification. They also use techniques we discussed in Chapter 10 to manage credit and interest-rate risk. The investment strategies of pension plans have changed radically over time. In the aftermath of World War II, most pension fund assets were held in government bonds, with less than 1% held in stock. However, the strong performance of stocks in the 1950s and 1960s afforded pension plans higher returns, causing them to shift their portfolios into stocks, which currently account for approximately two-thirds of their assets. As a result, pension plans now have a much stronger presence in the stock market: In the early 1950s, they held on the order of 1% of corporate stock outstanding; currently they hold on the order of 10%. Pension funds, along with mutual funds, are now the dominant players in the stock market.

Although the purpose of all pension plans is the same, they can differ in a number of attributes. First is the method by which payments are made: If the benefits are determined by the contributions into the plan and their earnings, the pension is a **defined-contribution plan**; if future income payments (benefits) are set in advance, the pension is a **defined-benefit plan**. In the case of a defined-benefit plan, a further attribute is related to how the plan is funded. A defined-benefit plan is **fully funded** if the contributions into the plan and their earnings over the years are sufficient to pay out the defined benefits when they come due. If the contributions and earnings are not sufficient, the plan is **underfunded**. For example, if Jane Brown contributes $100 per year into her pension plan and the interest rate is 10%, after ten years the contributions and their earnings would be worth $1,753.[2] If the defined benefit on her pension plan pays her $1,753 or less after ten years, the plan is fully funded because her contributions and earnings will fully pay for this payment. But if the defined benefit is $2,000, the plan is underfunded, because her contributions and earnings do not cover this amount.

A second characteristic of pension plans is their *vesting*, the length of time that a person must be enrolled in the pension plan (by being a member of a union or an employee of a company) before being entitled to receive benefits. Typically, firms require that an employee work five years for the company before being vested and qualifying to receive pension benefits; if the employee leaves the firm before the five years are up, either by quitting or being fired, all rights to benefits are lost.

Private Pension Plans

Private pension plans are administered by a bank, a life insurance company, or a pension fund manager. In employer-sponsored pension plans, contributions are usually shared between employer and employee. Many companies' pension plans are underfunded because they plan to meet their pension obligations out of current earnings when the benefits come due. As long as companies have sufficient earnings, underfunding creates no problems, but if not, they may not be able to meet their pension obligations. Because

[2]The $100 contributed in year 1 would become worth $\$100 \times (1+0.10)^{10} = \$259.37$ at the end of ten years; the $100 contributed in year 2 would become worth $\$100 \times (1 + 0.10)^{9} = \$235.79$; and so on until the $100 contributed in year 10 would become worth $\$100 \times (1 + 0.10) = \$110$. Adding these together, we get the total value of these contributions and their earnings at the end of ten years: $259.37 + $235.79 + $214.36 + $194.87 + $177.16 + $161.05 + $146.41 + $133.10 + $121.00 + $110.00 = $1,753.11.

FYI The Perils of Penny Benny: A Repeat of the S&L Bailout?

The current woes of "Penny Benny," the government pension insurance agency, unfortunately display many of the characteristics of the banking crisis discussed in Chapter 11. When an insured company with an underfunded pension plan files for bankruptcy, Penny Benny must pay the company's workers their retirement benefits up to a limit of $54,000 per year per person. Once again we see the moral hazard principle at work: A company is more likely to risk underfunding its pension plan if Penny Benny will foot the pension bill should the firm go bankrupt.

To keep the costs of government insurance programs from getting out of hand, the insurance agency must reduce moral hazard by monitoring the firms to assess the amount of the underfunding in their pension plans and charge higher premiums based on how much more underfunded the plans are. Unfortunately, Penny Benny has not been doing this, and since 2004 the liabilities arising from the responsibility for troubled pension plans have grown at an alarming rate. In 2004, these liabilities exceeded Penny Benny's assets by $23 billion. In 2005, the United Airlines bankruptcy resulted in Penny Benny taking over United's $6.6 billion liability to pay out pension benefits to its workers, even though Penny Benny took in only $1 billion in premiums that year. Congressional estimates suggest that Penny Benny may have to pay out more than $100 billion over the next decade to cover the pension liabilities of bankrupt companies. Taxpayers may be hit with another massive government bailout, the size of which will keep growing unless the government makes a concerted effort to reduce the underfunding of corporate pension plans.

of potential problems caused by corporate underfunding, mismanagement, fraudulent practices, and other abuses of private pension funds (Teamsters' pension funds are notorious in this regard), Congress enacted the Employee Retirement Income Security Act (ERISA) in 1974. This act established minimum standards for the reporting and disclosure of information, set rules for vesting and the degree of underfunding, placed restrictions on investment practices, and assigned the responsibility of regulatory oversight to the Department of Labor.

ERISA also created the Pension Benefit Guarantee Corporation (PBGC, called "Penny Benny"), which performs a role similar to that of the FDIC. It insures pension benefits up to a limit (currently $54,000 per year per person) if a company with an underfunded pension plan goes bankrupt or is unable to meet its pension obligations for other reasons. Penny Benny charges pension plans premiums to pay for this insurance, and it can also borrow up to $100 million from the U.S. Treasury. Unfortunately, the problem of pension plan underfunding has been growing worse in recent years. As a result, Penny Benny, which ensures the pensions of one of every five workers, is encountering severe financial difficulties that may necessitate a federal bailout (see the FYI box, "The Perils of Penny Benny").

Public Pension Plans

The most important public pension plan is Social Security (Old Age and Survivors' Insurance Fund), which covers virtually all individuals employed in the private sector. Funds are obtained from workers through Federal Insurance Contribution Act (FICA) deductions from their paychecks and from employers through payroll taxes. Social Security benefits include retirement income, Medicare payments, and aid to the disabled.

FYI Should Social Security Be Privatized?

In recent years, public confidence in the Social Security system has reached a new low. Some surveys suggest that young people have more confidence in the existence of flying saucers than they do in the government's promise to pay them their Social Security benefits. Without some overhaul of the system, Social Security will not be able to meet its future obligations. The inability of the Social Security system to meet its future obligations is a problem that is not restricted to the United States, however. Indeed, European countries and Japan face an even greater problem because their populations are aging sooner than the U.S. population. What to do about Social Security has become a hotly debated political issue in recent years.

Currently, the assets of the U.S. Social Security system, which reside in a trust fund, are all invested in U.S. Treasury securities. Because stocks and corporate bonds have higher returns than Treasury securities, many proposals to save the Social Security system suggest investing part of the trust fund in corporate securities and thus partially privatizing the system.

Suggestions for privatization take three basic forms:

1. *Government investment of trust fund assets in corporate securities.* This plan has the advantage of possibly improving the trust fund's overall return while minimizing transaction costs because it exploits the economies of scale of the trust fund. Critics warn that government ownership of private assets could lead to increased government intervention in the private sector.
2. *Shift of trust fund assets to individual accounts that can be invested in private assets.* This option, advocated by the Bush administration, has the advantage of possibly increasing the return on investments and does not involve the government in the ownership of private assets. However, critics warn that it might expose individuals to greater risk and to transaction costs on individual accounts that might be very high because of the small size of many of these accounts.
3. *Individual accounts in addition to those in the trust fund.* This option has advantages and disadvantages similar to those of option 2 and may provide more funds to individuals at retirement. However, some increase in taxes would be required to fund these accounts.

Whether some privatization of the Social Security system occurs is an open question. In the short term, Social Security reform is likely to involve an increase in taxes, a reduction in benefits, or both. For example, the age at which benefits begin is already scheduled to increase from 65 to 67, and might be increased further to 70. It is also likely that the cap on wages subject to the Social Security tax will be raised further, thereby increasing taxes paid into the system.

When Social Security was established in 1935, the federal government intended to operate it like a private pension fund. However, unlike a private pension plan, benefits are typically paid out from current contributions, not tied closely to a participant's past contributions. This "pay as you go" system at one point led to a massive underfunding, estimated at more than $1 trillion.

The problems of the Social Security system could become worse in the future because of the growth in the number of retired people relative to the working population. Congress has been grappling with the problems of the Social Security system for years, but the prospect of a huge bulge in new retirees when the 77 million baby boomers born between 1946 and 1964 started to retire in 2011 has resulted in calls for radical surgery on Social Security (see the FYI box, "Should Social Security Be Privatized?").

State and local governments and the federal government, like private employers, have also set up pension plans for their employees. These plans are almost identical in operation to private pension plans and hold similar assets. Underfunding of the plans is also prevalent, and some investors in municipal bonds worry that it may lead to future difficulties in the ability of state and local governments to meet their debt obligations.

FINANCE COMPANIES

Finance companies acquire funds by issuing commercial paper or stocks and bonds or borrowing from banks, and they use the proceeds to make loans (often for small amounts) that are particularly well suited to consumer and business needs. The financial intermediation process of finance companies can be described by saying that they borrow in large amounts but often lend in small amounts—a process quite different from that of banking institutions, which collect deposits in small amounts and then often make large loans.

A key feature of finance companies is that although they lend to many of the same customers that borrow from banks, they are virtually unregulated compared to commercial banks and thrift institutions. States regulate the maximum amount they can loan to individual consumers and the terms of the debt contract, but no restrictions are placed on how they pursue branching, the assets they hold, or how they raise their funds. The lack of restrictions enables finance companies in many cases to tailor their loans to customer needs better than banking institutions can.

Finance companies are of three types: sales, consumer, and business.

1. *Sales finance companies* are owned by a particular retailing or manufacturing company and make loans to consumers to purchase items from that company. Sears Roebuck Acceptance Corporation, for example, finances consumer purchases of goods and services at Sears stores, and General Motors Acceptance Corporation finances purchases of GM cars. Sales finance companies compete directly with banks for consumer loans and are used by consumers because loans can frequently be obtained faster and more conveniently at the location where an item is purchased.

2. *Consumer finance companies* make loans to consumers to buy particular items such as furniture or home appliances, to make home improvements, or to help refinance small debts. Consumer finance companies are separate corporations (like Household Finance Corporation) or are owned by banks (Citigroup owns Person-to-Person Finance Company, which operates offices nationwide). Typically, these companies make loans to consumers who cannot obtain credit from other sources, and they charge higher interest rates.

3. *Business finance companies* provide specialized forms of credit to businesses by making loans and purchasing accounts receivable (bills owed to the firm) at a discount; this provision of credit is called *factoring*. For example, a dressmaking firm might have outstanding bills (accounts receivable) of $100,000 owed by the retail stores that have bought its dresses. If this firm needs cash to buy 100 new sewing machines, it can sell its accounts receivable for, say, $90,000 to a finance company, which is now entitled to collect the $100,000 owed to the firm. Besides factoring, business finance companies also specialize in leasing equipment (such as railroad cars, jet planes, and computers), which they purchase and then lease to businesses for a set number of years.

SECURITIES MARKET OPERATIONS

The smooth functioning of securities markets, in which bonds and stocks are traded, involves several financial institutions, including securities brokers and dealers, investment banks, and organized exchanges. None of these institutions were included in our list of financial intermediaries in Chapter 2, because they do not perform the intermediation function of acquiring funds by issuing liabilities and then using the funds to acquire financial assets. Nonetheless, they are important in the process of channeling funds from savers to spenders and can be thought of as "financial facilitators."

First, however, we must recall the distinction between primary and secondary securities markets discussed in Chapter 2. In a primary market, new issues of a security are sold to buyers by the corporation or government agency borrowing the funds. A secondary market then trades the securities that have been sold in the primary market (and so are secondhand). *Investment banks* assist in the initial sale of securities in the primary market; *securities brokers* and *dealers* assist in the trading of securities in the secondary markets, some of which are organized into exchanges.

Investment Banking

When a corporation wishes to borrow (raise) funds, it normally hires the services of an investment banker to help sell its securities. (Despite its name, an investment bank is not a bank in the ordinary sense; that is, it is not engaged in financial intermediation that takes in deposits and then lends them out.)

Investment bankers assist in the sale of securities as follows. First, they advise the corporation on whether it should issue bonds or stock. If they suggest that the corporation issue bonds, investment bankers give advice on what the maturity and interest payments on the bonds should be. If they suggest that the corporation should sell stock, they give advice on what the price should be. This is fairly easy to do if the firm has prior issues currently selling in the market, called **seasoned issues**. However, when a firm issues stock for the first time in an **initial public offering (IPO)**, it is more difficult to determine what the correct price should be. All the skills and expertise of the investment banking firm then must be brought to bear to determine the most appropriate price. IPOs have become very important in the U.S. economy, because they are a major source of financing for Internet companies, which became all the rage on Wall Street in the late 1990s. Not only have IPOs helped these companies to acquire capital to substantially expand their operations, but they have also made the original owners of these firms very rich. Many a nerdy 20- to 30-year-old became an instant millionaire when his stake in his Internet company was given a high valuation after the initial public offering of shares in the company. However, with the bursting of the tech bubble in 2000, many of them lost much of their wealth when the value of their shares came tumbling down to earth.

When the corporation decides which kind of financial instrument it will issue, it offers the issue to **underwriters**—investment bankers that guarantee the corporation a price on the securities and then sell them to the public. If the issue is small, only one investment banking firm underwrites it (usually the original investment banking firm hired to provide advice on the issue). If the issue is large, several investment banking firms form a syndicate to underwrite the issue jointly, thus limiting the risk that any one investment bank must take. The underwriters sell the securities to the general public by contacting potential buyers, such as banks and insurance companies, directly.

The activities of investment bankers and the operation of primary markets are heavily regulated by the Securities and Exchange Commission (SEC), which was created by the Securities and Exchange Acts of 1933 and 1934 to ensure that adequate information reaches prospective investors. Issuers of new securities to the general public (for amounts greater than $1.5 million in a year, with a maturity longer than 270 days) must file a registration statement with the SEC and must provide to potential investors a prospectus containing all relevant information on the securities. The issuer must then wait 20 days after the registration statement is filed with the SEC before it can sell any of the securities. If the SEC does not object during the 20-day waiting period, the securities can be sold.

Securities Brokers and Dealers

Securities brokers and dealers conduct trading in secondary markets. Brokers act as agents for investors in the purchase or sale of securities. Their function is to match buyers with sellers, a function for which they are paid brokerage commissions. In contrast to brokers, dealers link buyers and sellers by standing ready to buy and sell securities at given prices. Therefore, dealers hold inventories of securities and make their living by selling these securities for a slightly higher price than they paid for them—that is, on the "spread" between the asked price and the bid price. This can be a high-risk business because dealers hold securities that can rise or fall in price; in recent years, several firms specializing in bonds have collapsed. Brokers, by contrast, are not as exposed to risk because they do not own the securities involved in their business dealings.

Brokerage firms engage in all three securities market activities, acting as brokers, dealers, and investment bankers. The SEC not only regulates the investment banking operation of the firms but also restricts brokers and dealers from misrepresenting securities and from trading on *insider information*, nonpublic information known only to the management of a corporation.

The forces of competition led to an important development: Brokerage firms started to engage in activities traditionally conducted by commercial banks. In 1977, Merrill Lynch developed the cash management account (CMA), which provided a package of financial services that includes credit cards, immediate loans, check-writing privileges, automatic investment of proceeds from the sale of securities into a money market mutual fund, and unified record keeping. Similar accounts were adopted by other brokerage firms and spread rapidly. The result is that the distinction between banking activities and those of nonbank financial institutions has become blurred. Another development is the growing importance of the Internet in securities markets.

Organized Exchanges

As discussed in Chapter 2, secondary markets can be organized either as over-the-counter markets, in which trades are conducted using dealers, or as organized exchanges, in which trades are conducted in one central location. The New York Stock Exchange (NYSE), trading thousands of securities, is the largest organized exchange in the world. A number of smaller regional exchanges, which trade only a small number of securities (fewer than 100), exist in places such as Boston and Los Angeles.

Organized stock exchanges actually function as a hybrid of an auction market (in which buyers and sellers trade with each other in a central location) and a dealer market (in which dealers make the market by buying and selling securities at given prices). Securities are traded on the floor of the exchange with the help of a special kind of dealer-broker called a **specialist**. A specialist matches buy and sell orders submitted at the same price and so performs a brokerage function. However, if buy and sell orders do not match up, the specialist buys stocks or sells from a personal inventory of securities, in this manner performing a dealer function. By assuming both functions, the specialist maintains orderly trading of the securities for which he or she is responsible.

Organized exchanges in which securities are traded are also regulated by the SEC. Not only does the SEC have the authority to impose regulations that govern the behavior of brokers and dealers involved with exchanges, but it also has the authority to alter the rules set by exchanges. In 1975, for example, the SEC disallowed rules that set minimum brokerage commission rates. The result was a sharp drop in brokerage commission rates, especially for institutional investors (mutual funds and pension funds), which purchase large blocks of stock. The Securities Amendments Act of 1975 confirmed the SEC's action by outlawing the setting of minimum brokerage commissions.

Furthermore, the Securities Amendments Act directed the SEC to facilitate a national market system that consolidates trading of all securities listed on the national and regional exchanges as well as those traded in the over-the-counter market using the National Association of Securities Dealers' automated quotation system (NASDAQ). Computers and advanced telecommunications, which reduce the costs of linking these markets, have encouraged the expansion of a national market system. We thus see that legislation and modern computer technology are leading the way to a more competitive securities industry.

The growing internationalization of capital markets has encouraged another trend in securities trading. Increasingly, foreign companies are being listed on U.S. stock exchanges, and the markets are moving toward trading stocks internationally, 24 hours a day.

MUTUAL FUNDS

Mutual funds are financial intermediaries that pool the resources of many small investors by selling them shares and using the proceeds to buy securities. Through the asset transformation process of issuing shares in small denominations and buying large blocks of securities, mutual funds can take advantage of volume discounts on brokerage commissions and purchase diversified holdings (portfolios) of securities. Mutual funds allow the small investor to obtain the benefits of lower transaction costs in purchasing securities and to take advantage of the reduction of risk by diversifying the portfolio of securities held. Many mutual funds are run by brokerage firms, but others are run by banks or independent investment advisers such as Fidelity or Vanguard.

Mutual funds have seen a large increase in their market share since 1980 (see Table 1), due primarily to the then-booming stock market. Another source of growth has been mutual funds that specialize in debt instruments, which first appeared in the 1970s. Before 1970, mutual funds invested almost solely in common stocks. Funds that purchase common stocks may specialize even further and invest solely in foreign securities or in specialized industries, such as energy or high technology. Funds that purchase debt instruments may specialize further in corporate, U.S. government, or tax-exempt municipal bonds or in long-term or short-term securities.

Mutual funds are primarily held by households (nearly 90%) with the rest held by other financial institutions and nonfinancial businesses. Mutual funds have become increasingly important in household savings. In 1980, only 6% of households held mutual fund shares; this number has risen to nearly 50% in recent years.

FYI Sovereign Wealth Funds: Are They a Danger?

Sovereign wealth funds have been around a long time: The first, the Kuwait Investment Authority, was established in 1953. When governments accumulate a substantial amount of foreign exchange earnings, as has happened in oil-rich countries, they often recognize that these earnings would be better put into investments in foreign countries rather than kept at home. The largest sovereign wealth funds are the Abu Dhabi Investment Authority, Government Pension Fund of Norway, Government of Singapore Investment Corporation, Kuwait Investment Authority, China Investment Corporation, Singapore's Temasek Holdings, and the Stabilisation Fund of the Russian Federation.

Until recently these funds have been relatively uncontroversial because they were comparatively small and primarily invested in government bonds issued by industrialized countries. In recent years, however, they have grown in size—they now hold over $3 trillion in assets—and, in the search for higher returns, invest in a much broader set of assets. This shift in size and focus has led to serious concerns about them in industrialized countries.

One concern is that as the size of these funds increases, they may play a more important role in asset markets, and since some of them are very large—the Abu Dhabi fund has close to a trillion dollars of assets—the decision of one fund to pull out of a particular asset market could cause market instability. Sovereign wealth funds also raise national security issues because they might use their investments for political purposes. They might buy up strategically important industries or use their clout to get political concessions. This is a particular concern because the governments of Russia, China, and Arab countries control many of the largest of these funds. A third concern is that many of these funds, with the exception of the Norwegian fund, provide very little information about their operations and the assets in which they invest.

Although sovereign wealth funds do pose some dangers, these are probably overplayed. Xenophobia often plays well in politics, and foreign purchase of domestic assets is often prevented under the banner of national security in order to protect domestic companies from unwanted takeovers. The lack of transparency for some of these large funds is a serious problem, however. This is why organizations like the International Monetary Fund (IMF) and the Organisation for Economic Co-operation and Development (OECD) proposed rules to increase the amount of information these funds disclose to the markets.

The growing importance of mutual funds and pension funds, known as *institutional investors*, has resulted in their controlling more than 25% of the outstanding stock in the United States. Increased ownership of stocks has also meant that institutional investors have more clout with corporate boards, often forcing changes in leadership or in corporate policies. Particularly controversial recently has been a type of institutional investor, **sovereign wealth funds**, state-owned investment funds that invest in foreign assets (see the FYI box "Sovereign Wealth Funds: Are They a Danger?").

Mutual funds are structured in two ways. The more common structure is an **open-end fund**, from which shares can be redeemed at any time at a price that is tied to the asset value of the fund. Mutual funds also can be structured as a **closed-end fund**, in which a fixed number of nonredeemable shares are sold at an initial offering and are then traded like a common stock. The market price of these shares fluctuates with the value of the assets held by the fund. In contrast to the open-end fund, however, the price of the shares may be above or below the value of the assets held by the fund, depending on factors such as the liquidity of the shares or the quality of the management. The greater popularity of the open-end funds is explained by the greater liquidity of their redeemable shares relative to the nonredeemable shares of closed-end funds.

Originally, shares of most open-end mutual funds were sold by salespeople (usually brokers) who were paid a commission. Because this commission is paid at the time of purchase and is immediately subtracted from the redemption value of the shares, these funds are called **load funds**. Most mutual funds are currently **no-load funds**; they are sold directly to the public with no sales commissions. In both types of funds, the managers earn their living from management fees paid by the shareholders. These fees amount to approximately 0.5% of the asset value of the fund per year.

Mutual funds are regulated by the Securities and Exchange Commission, which was given the ability to exercise almost complete control over them by the Investment Company Act of 1940. Regulations require periodic disclosure of information on these funds to the public and restrictions on the methods of soliciting business.

Money Market Mutual Funds

An important addition to the family of mutual funds resulting from the financial innovation process described in earlier chapters is the *money market mutual fund*. Recall that this type of mutual fund invests in short-term debt (money market) instruments of very high quality, such as Treasury bills, commercial paper, and bank certificates of deposit. There is some fluctuation in the market value of these securities, but because their maturity is typically less than six months, the change in the market value is small enough that these funds allow their shares to be redeemed at a fixed value. (Changes in the market value of the securities are figured into the interest paid out by the fund.) Because these shares can be redeemed at a fixed value, the funds allow shareholders to redeem shares by writing checks on the fund's account at a commercial bank. In this way, shares in money market mutual funds effectively function as checkable deposits that earn market interest rates on short-term debt securities.

In 1977, the assets in money market mutual funds were less than $4 billion; by 1980, they had climbed to more than $50 billion and now stand at nearly $3 trillion, with a share of financial intermediary assets that has grown to 6.6% (see Table 1). Currently, money market mutual funds account for about one-third of the asset value of all mutual funds.

HEDGE FUNDS

Hedge funds are a special type of investment fund, with estimated assets of more than $2 trillion. Hedge funds have received considerable attention recently due to the shock to the financial system resulting from the near collapse of Long-Term Capital Management, once one of the most important hedge funds (see the FYI box, "The Long-Term Capital Management Debacle"). Well-known hedge funds include Tudor Investment Corporation and the Quantum Group of funds associated with George Soros. Investors in hedge funds, who are limited partners, give money to managing (general) partners to invest on their behalf. Several features distinguish hedge funds from mutual funds. Hedge funds have a minimum investment requirement between $100,000 and $20 million, with the typical minimum investment being $1 million. Long-Term Capital Management required a $10 million minimum investment. Federal law limits hedge funds to have no more than 99 investors (limited partners) who must have steady annual incomes of $200,000 or more or a net worth of $1 million, excluding their homes. These restrictions are aimed at allowing hedge funds to be largely unregulated,

FYI The Long-Term Capital Management Debacle

Long-Term Capital Management (LTCM) was a hedge fund with a star cast of managers, including 25 PhDs, two Nobel Prize winners in economics (Myron Scholes and Robert Merton), a former vice-chairman of the Federal Reserve System (David Mullins), and one of Wall Street's most successful bond traders (John Meriwether). It made headlines in September 1998 because its near-collapse roiled markets and required a private rescue plan organized by the Federal Reserve Bank of New York.

The experience of Long-Term Capital demonstrates that hedge funds are far from risk-free, despite their use of market-neutral strategies. Long-Term Capital got into difficulties when it thought that the spread between prices on long-term Treasury bonds and long-term corporate bonds was too high, and bet that this "anomaly" would disappear and the spread would narrow. In the wake of the collapse of the Russian financial system in August 1998, investors increased their assessment of the riskiness of corporate securities and, as we saw in Chapter 6, the spread between corporates and Treasuries rose rather than narrowed as Long-Term Capital had predicted. The result was that Long-Term Capital took big losses on its positions, eating up much of its equity position.

By mid-September, Long-Term Capital was unable to raise sufficient funds to meet the demands of its creditors. With Long-Term Capital facing the potential need to liquidate its portfolio of $80 billion in securities and more than $1 trillion of notional value in derivatives, the Federal Reserve Bank of New York stepped in on September 23 and organized a rescue plan with Long-Term Capital's creditors. The Fed's rationale for stepping in was that a sudden liquidation of Long-Term Capital's portfolio would create unacceptable systemic risk. Tens of billions of dollars of illiquid securities would be dumped on an already jittery market, causing potentially huge losses to numerous lenders and other institutions. The rescue plan required creditors, banks, and investment banks to supply an additional $3.6 billion of funds to Long-Term Capital in exchange for much tighter management control of funds and a 90% reduction in the managers' equity stake. In the middle of 1999, John Meriwether began to wind down the fund's operations.

on the theory that the rich can look out for themselves. Many of the 5,000 hedge funds are located offshore to escape regulatory restrictions.

Hedge funds also differ from traditional mutual funds in that they usually require that investors commit their money for long periods of time, often several years. The purpose of this requirement is to give managers breathing room to pursue long-run strategies. Hedge funds also typically charge large fees to investors. The typical fund charges a 2% annual fee on the assets it manages plus 20% of profits.

The term *hedge fund* is highly misleading, because the word "hedge" typically indicates strategies to avoid risk. As the near-failure of Long-Term Capital illustrates, despite their name, these funds can and do take big risks. Many hedge funds engage in what are called "market-neutral" strategies where they buy a security, such as a bond, that seems cheap and sell an equivalent amount of a similar security that appears to be overvalued. If interest rates as a whole go up or down, the fund is hedged, because the decline in value of one security is matched by the rise in value of the other. However, the fund is speculating on whether the spread between the price on the two securities moves in the direction predicted by the fund managers. If the fund bets wrong, it can lose a lot of money, particularly if it has leveraged up its positions—that is, has borrowed heavily against these positions so that its equity stake is small relative to the size of its portfolio. When Long-Term Capital was rescued, it had a leverage ratio of 50 to 1; that is, its assets were 50 times larger than its equity, and even before it got into trouble, it was leveraged 20 to 1.

Even though no public funds were expended, the Fed's involvement in organizing the rescue of Long-Term Capital was highly controversial. Some critics argue that the Fed intervention increased moral hazard by weakening discipline imposed by the market on fund managers because future Fed interventions of this type would be expected. Others think that the Fed's action was necessary to prevent a major shock to the financial system that could have provoked a financial crisis. The debate on whether the Fed should have intervened is likely to go on for some time.

In the wake of the near collapse of Long-Term Capital, many U.S. politicians called for regulation of these funds, and the SEC established a new rule that hedge funds will have to register with the agency. However, because many of these funds operate offshore in places like the Cayman Islands and are outside U.S. jurisdiction, they are extremely difficult to regulate. What U.S. regulators can do is ensure that U.S. banks and investment banks have clear guidelines on the amount of lending they can provide to hedge funds and require that these institutions get the appropriate amount of disclosure from hedge funds as to the riskiness of their positions.

PRIVATE EQUITY AND VENTURE CAPITAL FUNDS

Another type of investment fund is the **private equity fund**, which makes long-term investments in companies that are not traded in public markets and has a similar structure to hedge funds. In a private equity fund, investors who are limited partners (e.g., high-wealth individuals, pension funds, financial institutions, and college endowments) place their money with the managing (general) partners who make the private equity investments. Private equity funds are of two types. **Venture capital funds** make investments in new start-up businesses, often in the technology industry. **Capital buyout funds** instead make investments in established businesses, and in many cases, buy publicly traded firms through a so-called **leveraged buyout (LBO)**, in which the publicly traded firm is taken private by buying all of its shares, while financing the purchase by increasing the leverage (debt) of the firm. Among the best-known companies that set up venture capital and capital buyout funds are KKR (Kohlberg, Kravis, Roberts and Co.), Bain Capital, and Blackstone Group.

Private equity has several advantages over investing in publicly traded companies. First, private companies are not subject to the controversial and costly regulations included in the Sarbanes-Oxley Act described in Chapter 15. Second, managers of private companies do not feel pressure to produce immediate profits, as do those at publicly traded companies, and thus can manage their company with their eyes on longer-term profitability. Third, because private equity funds give managers of these companies larger stakes in the firm than is usually the case in publicly traded corporations, they have greater incentives to work hard to maximize the value of the firm. Fourth, private equity overcomes the free-rider problem that we discussed in Chapter 8. In contrast to publicly traded companies, which have a diverse set of owners who are happy to free-ride off of each other, venture capital and capital buyout funds are able to garner almost all the benefits of monitoring the firm and therefore have the incentives to make sure the firm is run properly.

In both venture capital and capital buyout funds, once the start-up or the purchased company is successful, the fund earns its returns by either selling the firm to another company or by selling it off to the public through an initial public offering (IPO). The managing partners of private equity funds are well compensated for their activities: Like hedge funds, they typically earn approximately a 2% fee for management of the equity fund investments and earn 20% of the profits, which is called **carried interest**. Carried interest has been particularly controversial of late because it is taxed at the lower long-term capital gains rate (15%), rather than at a higher income tax rate (35%). This is considered to be patently unfair by many members of Congress, who have proposed raising the tax rate on carried interest to the higher income tax rate. Those in the industry have countered that raising the tax rate on carried interest would stifle investment and therefore hinder economic growth.

Both venture capital and capital buyout funds have been highly profitable. Venture capital firms have been an especially important driver of economic growth in recent years because they have funded so many successful high-tech firms, including Apple Computer, Cisco Systems, Genentech, Microsoft, and Sun Microsystems.

GOVERNMENT FINANCIAL INTERMEDIATION

The government has become involved in financial intermediation in two basic ways: by setting up federal credit agencies that directly engage in financial intermediation and by supplying government guarantees for private loans.

Federal Credit Agencies

To promote residential housing, the government has created a number of government agencies that provide funds, either directly or indirectly, to the mortgage market. Three agencies—the Government National Mortgage Association (GNMA, or "Ginnie Mae"), the Federal National Mortgage Association (FNMA or "Fannie Mae"), and the Federal Home Loan Mortgage Corporation (FHLMC, or "Freddie Mac")—provide funds to the mortgage market by selling bonds and using the proceeds to buy mortgages or mortgage-backed securities. Except for Ginnie Mae, which is a federal agency and thus is an entity of the U.S. government, the other agencies, known as **government-sponsored enterprises (GSEs)**, are federally sponsored agencies that function as private corporations with close ties to the government. Another set of GSEs, the Federal Home Loan Banks, indirectly provide funds to the mortgage markets by selling bonds and then lending the proceeds to banking institutions that make mortgage loans. Although the U.S. government does not explicitly back the debt of the GSEs, as is the case for government-sponsored Treasury bonds, in practice the federal government has not allowed a default on their securities.

Agriculture is another area in which financial intermediation by government agencies plays an important role. The Farm Credit System (composed of Banks for Cooperatives, Farm Credit Banks, and various farm credit associations), as well as the Federal Agricultural Mortgage Corporation ("Farmer Mac"), issues securities and then uses the proceeds to make loans to farmers.

Unfortunately, the implicit government backing of GSE debt leads to the same moral hazard problem that led to the S&L and banking crises in the 1980s and early 1990s, discussed in Chapter 11. Because the government in effect guarantees GSE debt, market discipline to limit excessive risk taking by GSEs is quite weak. The GSEs therefore have incentives to take on excessive risk, and this is exactly what they have done, with the taxpayer left holding the bag. The federal government bailed out the Farm Credit System in 1987, for example, because of the rising tide of farm bankruptcies. The agency was authorized to borrow up to $4 billion to be repaid over a fifteen-year period and received over $1 billion in assistance. All of this pales, however, in comparison to the recent bailout of Fannie Mae and Freddie Mac, which involved $200 billion of government funds (see the FYI box, "The Global Crisis and the Bailout of Fannie Mae and Freddie Mac").

FYI The Global Financial Crisis and the Bailout of Fannie Mae and Freddie Mac

Because it encouraged excessive risk taking, the peculiar structure of Fannie Mae and Freddie Mac—private companies sponsored by the government—was an accident waiting to happen. Earlier editions of this textbook, as well as many economists, predicted exactly what came to pass: a government bailout of both companies, with huge potential losses for American taxpayers.

As we learned in Chapter 11, when a government safety net exists for financial institutions, appropriate government regulation and supervision are needed to make sure these institutions do not take on excessive risk. Fannie and Freddie were given a federal regulator and supervisor, the Office of Federal Housing Enterprise Oversight (OFHEO), as a result of legislation in 1992, but this regulator was quite weak, with only a limited ability to rein them in. This outcome was not surprising. These GSEs had strong incentives to resist effective regulation and supervision because it would cut into their profits. This is exactly what they did: Fannie and Freddie were legendary for their lobbying machine in Congress, and they were not apologetic about it. In 1999, Franklin Raines, at the time Fannie's CEO, said, "We manage our political risk with the same intensity that we manage our credit and interest-rate risks."* Between 1998 and 2008, Fannie and Freddie jointly spent over $170 million on lobbyists, and from 2000 to 2008, they and their employees made over $14 million of political campaign contributions.

Their lobbying efforts paid off: Attempts to strengthen their regulator, OFHEO, in both the Clinton and Bush administrations came to naught, and remarkably this was even true after major accounting scandals at both firms were revealed in 2003 and 2004, in which they cooked the books to smooth out earnings. (It was only in July 2008, after the cat was let out of the bag and Fannie and Freddie were in serious trouble, that legislation was passed to put into place a stronger regulator, the Federal Housing Finance Agency, to supersede OFHEO.)

With a weak regulator and strong incentives to take on risk, Fannie and Freddie grew wildly, and by 2008 had purchased or were guaranteeing over $5 trillion dollars of mortgages or mortgage-backed securities. The accounting scandals might even have pushed them to take on more risk. In the 1992 legislation, Fannie and Freddie had been given a mission to promote affordable housing. What way to better do this than to purchase subprime and Alt-A mortgages or mortgage-backed securities (discussed in Chapter 9)? The accounting scandals made this motivation even stronger because they weakened the political support for Fannie and Freddie, giving them even greater incentives to please Congress and support affordable housing by the purchase of these assets. By the time the global financial crisis hit in force, they had over $1 trillion of subprime and Alt-A assets on their books. Furthermore, they had extremely low ratios of capital relative to their assets. Indeed, their capital ratios were far lower than those for other financial institutions like commercial banks.

By 2008, after many subprime mortgages went into default, Fannie and Freddie had booked large losses.

Their small capital buffer meant that they had little cushion to withstand these losses, and investors started to pull their money out. With Fannie and Freddie playing such a dominant role in mortgage markets, the U.S. government could not afford to have them go out of business because this would have had a disastrous effect on the availability of mortgage credit, which would have had further devastating effects on the housing market. With bankruptcy imminent, the Treasury stepped in with a pledge to provide up to \$200 billion of taxpayer money to the companies if needed. This largess did not come for free. The federal government in effect took over these companies by putting them into conservatorship, requiring that their CEOs step down, and by having their regulator, the Federal Housing Finance Agency, oversee the companies' day-to-day operations. In addition, the government received about \$1 billion of senior preferred stock and the right to purchase 80% of the common stock if the companies recovered. After the bailout, the prices of both companies' common stock was less than 2% of what they had been only a year earlier.

It is not yet clear how much the government bailout of Fannie and Freddie will cost the American taxpayer, but it is expected to be on the order of several hundred billion dollars.

The ultimate fate of these two companies is also unclear. The sad saga of Fannie Mae and Freddie Mac illustrates how dangerous it was for the government to set up GSEs that were exposed to a classic conflict of interest problem because they were supposed to serve two masters: As publicly traded corporations, they were expected to maximize profits for their shareholders, but as government agencies, they were obliged to work in the interests of the public. In the end, neither the public nor the shareholders were well served.

*Quoted in Nile Stephen Campbell, "Fannie Mae Officials Try to Assuage Worried Investors," *Real Estate Finance Today*, May 10, 1999.

Summary

1. Insurance providers, which are regulated by the states, acquire funds by selling policies that pay out benefits if catastrophic events occur. Property and casualty insurance companies hold more liquid assets than life insurance companies because of greater uncertainty regarding the benefits they will have to pay out. All insurers face moral hazard and adverse selection problems that explain the use of insurance management tools, such as information collection and screening of potential policyholders, risk-based premiums, restrictive provisions, prevention of fraud, cancellation of insurance, deductibles, coinsurance, and limits on the amount of insurance.
2. Pension plans provide income payments to people when they retire after contributing to the plans for many years. Pension funds have experienced very rapid growth as a result of encouragement by federal tax policy and now play an important role in the stock market. Many pension plans are underfunded, which means that in future years they will have to pay out higher benefits than the value of their contributions and earnings. The problem of underfunding is especially acute for public pension plans such as Social Security. To prevent abuses, Congress enacted the Employee Retirement Income Security Act (ERISA), which established minimum standards for reporting, vesting, and degree of underfunding of private pension plans. This act also created the Pension Benefit Guarantee Corporation, which insures pension benefits.
3. Finance companies raise funds by issuing commercial paper and stocks and bonds and use the proceeds to make loans that are particularly suited to consumer

and business needs. Virtually unregulated in comparison to commercial banks and thrift institutions, finance companies have been able to tailor their loans to customer needs very quickly and have grown rapidly.

4. Investment bankers assist in the initial sale of securities in primary markets, whereas securities brokers and dealers assist in the trading of securities in the secondary markets, some of which are organized into exchanges. The SEC regulates the financial institutions in the securities markets and ensures that adequate information reaches prospective investors.
5. Mutual funds sell shares and use the proceeds to buy securities. Open-end funds issue shares that can be redeemed at any time at a price tied to the asset value of the firm. Closed-end funds issue nonredeemable shares, which are traded like common stock. They are less popular than open-end funds because their shares are not as liquid. Money market mutual funds hold only short-term, high-quality securities, allowing shares to be redeemed at a fixed value using checks. Shares in these funds effectively function as checkable deposits that earn market interest rates. All mutual funds are regulated by the Securities and Exchange Commission (SEC).
6. Hedge funds are a special type of investment fund. Investors in hedge funds, who are limited partners, give money to managing (general) partners to invest on their behalf. They have large minimum investments and usually require that investors commit their money for long periods of time.
7. Private equity funds make long-term investments in companies that are not traded publicly and are of two types: venture capital funds, which make investments in start-ups, and capital buyout funds, which make investments in established companies, often taking publicly traded firms private.
8. To provide credit to residential housing and agriculture, the U.S. government has created a number of government agencies. Particularly important are government-sponsored enterprises (GSEs), which are federally sponsored agencies that function as private corporations with close ties to the government. Because the government provides an implicit guarantee for GSE debt, market discipline to limit excessive risk taking by GSEs is weak. The resulting moral hazard problem has led to major taxpayer bailouts, especially the recent bailout of Fannie Mae and Freddie Mac, which involved $200 billion of government funds.

Key Terms

annuities, p. 302
brokerage firms, p. 315
capital buyout funds, p. 320
carried interest, p. 321
closed-end fund, p. 317
coinsurance, p. 308
credit default swap (CDS), p. 304
deductible, p. 308
defined-benefit plan, p. 310
defined-contribution plan, p. 310
fully funded, p. 310
government-sponsored enterprises (GSEs), p. 321
hedge fund, p. 318
initial public offering (IPO), p. 314
leveraged buyout (LBO), p. 320
load funds, p. 318
monoline insurance companies, p. 305
no-load funds, p. 318
open-end fund, p. 317
private equity fund, p. 320
reinsurance, p. 304
seasoned issues, p. 314
sovereign wealth funds, p. 317
specialist, p. 316
underfunded, p. 310
underwriters, p. 314
venture capital funds, p. 320

Questions

All questions are available in MyEconLab *at* www.myeconlab.com/mishkin.

1. Why do people choose to buy insurance even if their expected loss is less than the payments they will make to the insurance company?
2. How do insurance companies protect themselves against losses due to adverse selection and moral hazard?
3. What is the difference between term life insurance and whole life insurance?

4. What is the purpose behind reinsurance?
5. Why do property and casualty insurance companies have large holdings of municipal bonds but life insurance companies do not?
6. Why did the Federal Reserve and the government intervene to bail out AIG?
7. "In contrast to private pension plans, government pension plans are rarely underfunded." Is this statement true, false, or uncertain? Explain your answer.
8. Why is Social Security in danger of eventually going bankrupt?
9. What are the three main proposals to privatize Social Security? What are their advantages and disadvantages?
10. What is ERISA and why was it established?
11. If you needed to take out a loan, why might you first go to your local bank rather than a finance company?
12. How are securities brokers/dealers, investment banks, and organized exchanges different from financial intermediaries?
13. What problems or concerns do sovereign wealth funds present? Are they valid?
14. Why can a money market mutual fund allow its shareholders to redeem shares at a fixed price but other mutual funds cannot?
15. What features of mutual funds and the investment environment have led to mutual funds' rapid growth in the last three decades?
16. Is investment banking a good career for someone who is afraid of taking risks? Why or why not?
17. How do hedge funds differ from mutual funds?
18. What lessons can be drawn from the collapse of LTCM?
19. What are the four advantages of private equity funds? How do they help alleviate the free-rider problem?
20. How have GSEs exposed taxpayers to large losses?

Applied Problems

All applied problems are available in MyEconLab *at* www.myeconlab.com/mishkin.

21. Your rich uncle dies, leaving you a life insurance policy worth $100,000. The insurance company also offers you an option to receive $8,225 per year for 20 years, with the first payment due today. Which option should you use?
22. Kio Outfitters estimated the following losses and probabilities from past experience:

Loss	Probability (%)
$30,000	0.25
$15,000	0.75
$10,000	1.50
$5,000	2.50
$1,000	5.00
$250	15.00
$0	75.00

What is the probability Kio will experience a loss of $5,000 or greater? If an insurance company offers a loss policy with a $1,500 deductible, what is the most Kio will pay?

23. Paul's car slid off the icy road, causing $2,500 in damage to his car. He was also treated for minor injuries, costing $1,300. His car insurance has a $500 deductible, after which the full loss is paid. His health insurance has a $100 deductible and covers 75% of medical cost (total). What were Paul's out-of-pocket costs from the incident?
24. An employee contributes $200 a year (at the end of the year) to her pension plan. What would be the total contributions and value of the account after five years? Assume that the plan earns 15% per year over the period.
25. Suppose you contribute $20,000 at the beginning of each year into your defined benefit pension plan, and the interest rate is 10%.
    a. After 8 years, what are the total contributions and value of the account worth?
    b. Suppose that after 8 years you are eligible to receive benefits of $250,000. Is the pension plan underfunded, or fully funded?
    c. Suppose that the pension plan takes a 2% management fee at the time each contribution is made. How does that change your answer to parts (a) and (b), if at all?

Web Exercises

1. In initial public offerings (IPOs), securities are sold to the public for the very first time. Go to http://www.ipohome.com. This site lists various statistics regarding the IPO market.
   a. What is the largest IPO this year ranked by amount raised?
   b. What is the next IPO to be offered to the public?
   c. How many IPOs were priced this year?
2. The Federal Reserve maintains extensive data on finance companies. Go to www.federalreserve.gov/releases and scroll down until you find G.20 Finance Companies. Click on Releases and find the current release.
   a. Review the terms of credit for new car loans. What is the most recent average interest rate and what is the term to maturity? How much is the average new car loan offered by finance companies?
   b. Do finance companies make more consumer loans, real estate loans, or business loans?
   a. Which type of loan has grown most rapidly over the past five years?

Web References

www.iii.org

The Insurance Information Institute publishes facts and statistics about the insurance industry.

www.federalreserve.gov/releases/Z1/

The Flow of Funds Accounts of the United States reports details about the current state of the insurance industry. Scroll down through the table of contents to find the location of data on insurance companies.

www.pbgc.gov/

The website for the Pension Benefit Guarantee Corporation contains information about pensions and the insurance that it provides.

www.ssa.gov/

The website for the Social Security Administration contains information on your benefits available from Social Security.

www.federalreserve.gov/releases/g20/

The Federal Reserve provides information about finance companies.

www.ici.org/about_ici/annuals

The Investment Company Fact Book published by Investment Company Institute includes information about the mutual funds industry's history, regulation, taxation, and shareholders.

http://www.ipoinitialpublicofferings.com/

The site reports initial public offering news and information and includes advanced search tools for IPOs, venture capital research reports, and so on.

www.sec.gov

The Securities and Exchange Commission website contains regulatory actions, concept releases, interpretive releases, and more.

www.nyse.com

At the New York Stock Exchange home page, you will find listed companies, member information, real-time market indices, and current stock quotes.

14 Financial Derivatives

Preview

Starting in the 1970s and increasingly in the 1980s and 1990s, the world became a riskier place for the financial institutions described in this part of the book. Swings in interest rates widened, and the bond and stock markets went through some episodes of increased volatility. As a result of these developments, managers of financial institutions became more concerned with reducing the risk their institutions faced. Given the greater demand for risk reduction, the process of financial innovation described in Chapter 12 came to the rescue by producing new financial instruments that help financial institution managers manage risk better. These instruments, called **financial derivatives**, have payoffs that are linked to previously issued securities and are extremely useful risk reduction tools.

In this chapter, we look at the most important financial derivatives that managers of financial institutions use to reduce risk: forward contracts, financial futures, options, and swaps. We examine not only how markets for each of these financial derivatives work but also how they can be used by financial institutions to manage risk. We also study financial derivatives because they have become an important source of profits for financial institutions, particularly larger banks, which, as we saw in Chapter 12, have found their traditional business declining.

HEDGING

Financial derivatives are so effective in reducing risk because they enable financial institutions to **hedge**—that is, engage in a financial transaction that reduces or eliminates risk. When a financial institution has bought an asset, it is said to have taken a **long position**, and this exposes the institution to risk if the returns on the asset are uncertain. Conversely, if it has sold an asset that it has agreed to deliver to another party at a future date, it is said to have taken a **short position**, and this can also expose the institution to risk. Financial derivatives can be used to reduce risk by invoking the following basic principle of hedging: ***Hedging risk involves engaging in a financial transaction that offsets a long position by taking an additional short position, or offsets a short position by taking an additional long position***. In other words, if a financial institution has *bought* a security and has therefore taken a long position, it conducts a hedge by contracting to *sell* that security (take a short position) at some future date. Alternatively, if it has taken a short position by *selling* a security that it needs to deliver at a future date, then it conducts a hedge by contracting to *buy* that security (take a long position) at a future date. We look at how this principle can be applied using forward and futures contracts.

INTEREST-RATE FORWARD CONTRACTS

Forward contracts are agreements by two parties to engage in a financial transaction at a future (forward) point in time. Here we focus on forward contracts that are linked to debt instruments, called **interest-rate forward contracts**; later in the chapter, we discuss forward contracts for foreign currencies.

Interest-rate forward contracts involve the future sale (or purchase) of a debt instrument and have several dimensions: (1) specification of the actual debt instrument that will be delivered at a future date, (2) amount of the debt instrument to be delivered, (3) price (interest rate) on the debt instrument when it is delivered, and (4) date on which delivery will take place. An example of an interest-rate forward contract might be an agreement for the First National Bank to sell to the Rock Solid Insurance Company, one year from today, $5 million face value of the 6s of 2030 Treasury bonds (that is, coupon bonds with a 6% coupon rate that mature in 2030) at a price that yields the same interest rate on these bonds as today's, say, 6%. Because Rock Solid will buy the securities at a future date, it is said to have taken a long position, whereas the First National Bank, which will sell the securities, has taken a short position.

APPLICATION ◆ Hedging with Interest-Rate Forward Contracts

Why would the First National Bank want to enter into this forward contract with Rock Solid Insurance Company in the first place?

To understand, suppose that you are the manager of the First National Bank and have bought $5 million of the 6s of 2030 Treasury bonds. The bonds are currently selling at par value, so their yield to maturity is 6%. Because these are long-term bonds, you recognize that you are exposed to substantial interest-rate risk: If interest rates rise in the future, the price of these bonds will fall and result in a substantial capital loss that may cost you your job. How do you hedge this risk?

Knowing the basic principle of hedging, you see that your long position in these bonds can be offset by an equal short position for the same bonds with a forward contract. That is, you need to contract to sell these bonds at a future date at the current par value price. As a result, you agree with another party—in this case, Rock Solid Insurance Company—to sell it the $5 million of the 6s of 2030 Treasury bonds at par one year from today. By entering into this forward contract, you have successfully hedged against interest-rate risk. By locking in the future price of the bonds, you have eliminated the price risk you face from interest-rate changes.

Why would Rock Solid Insurance Company want to enter into the futures contract with the First National Bank? Rock Solid expects to receive premiums of $5 million in one year's time that it will want to invest in the 6s of 2030, but worries that interest rates on these bonds will decline between now and next year. By using the forward contract, it is able to lock in the 6% interest rate on the Treasury bonds that will be sold to it by the First National Bank.

Pros and Cons of Forward Contracts

The advantage of forward contracts is that they can be as flexible as the parties involved want them to be. This means that an institution like the First National Bank may be able to hedge completely the interest-rate risk for the exact security it is holding in its portfolio, just as it has in our example.

However, forward contracts suffer from two problems that severely limit their usefulness. The first is that it may be very hard for an institution like the First National Bank to find another party (called a *counterparty*) to make the contract with. There are brokers to facilitate the matching up of parties like the First National Bank with the Rock Solid Insurance Company, but few institutions may want to engage in a forward contract specifically for the 6s of 2030. This means that it may prove impossible to find a counterparty when a financial institution like the First National Bank wants to make a specific type of forward contract. Furthermore, even if the First National Bank finds a counterparty, it may not get as high a price as it wants because there may not be anyone else to make the deal with. A serious problem for the market in interest-rate forward contracts, then, is that it may be difficult to make the financial transaction or that it will have to be made at a disadvantageous price; in the parlance of financial economists, this market suffers from a *lack of liquidity*. (Note that this use of the term *liquidity* when it is applied to a market is somewhat broader than its use when it is applied to an asset. For an asset, liquidity refers to the ease with which the asset can be turned into cash; for a market, liquidity refers to the ease of carrying out financial transactions.)

The second problem with forward contracts is that they are subject to default risk. Suppose that in one year's time, interest rates rise so that the price of the 6s of 2030 falls. The Rock Solid Insurance Company might then decide that it would like to default on the forward contract with the First National Bank, because it can now buy the bonds at the lower price. Or perhaps Rock Solid may not have been rock solid after all, and may have gone bust during the year, and no longer is available to complete the terms of the forward contract. Because no outside organization is guaranteeing the contract, the only recourse is for the First National Bank to go to the courts to sue Rock Solid, but this process will be costly. Furthermore, if Rock Solid is already bankrupt, the First National Bank will suffer a loss; the bank can no longer sell the 6s of 2030 at the price it had agreed on with Rock Solid, but instead will have to sell at a price well below that, because the price of these bonds has fallen.

The presence of default risk in forward contracts means that parties to these contracts must check each other out to be sure that the counterparty is both financially sound and likely to be honest and live up to its contractual obligations. Because this type of investigation is costly and because all the adverse selection and moral hazard problems discussed in earlier chapters apply, default risk is a major barrier to the use of interest-rate forward contracts. When the default risk problem is combined with a lack of liquidity, we see that these contracts may be of limited usefulness to financial institutions. Although a market exists for interest-rate forward contracts, particularly in Treasury and mortgage-backed securities, it is not nearly as large as the financial futures market, to which we turn next. ◆

FINANCIAL FUTURES CONTRACTS AND MARKETS

Given the default risk and liquidity problems in the interest-rate forward market, another solution to hedging interest-rate risk was needed. This solution was provided by the development of financial futures contracts by the Chicago Board of Trade, starting in 1975.

A **financial futures contract** is similar to an interest-rate forward contract, in that it specifies that a financial instrument must be delivered by one party to another on a stated future date. However, it differs from an interest-rate forward contract in several ways that overcome some of the liquidity and default problems of forward markets.

To understand what financial futures contracts are all about, let's look at one of the most widely traded futures contracts—that for Treasury bonds, which are traded on the Chicago Board of Trade. The contract value is for $100,000 face value of bonds. Prices are quoted in points, with each point equal to $1,000, and the smallest change in price is 1/32 of a point ($31.25). This contract specifies that the bonds to be delivered must have at least fifteen years to maturity at the delivery date (and must also not be callable—that is, redeemable by the Treasury at its option—in less than fifteen years). If the Treasury bonds delivered to settle the futures contract have a coupon rate different from the 6% specified in the futures contract, the amount of bonds to be delivered is adjusted to reflect the difference in value between the delivered bonds and the 6% coupon bond. In line with the terminology used for forward contracts, parties who have bought a futures contract and thereby agreed to buy (take delivery of) the bonds are said to have taken a *long position*, and parties who have sold a futures contract and thereby agreed to sell (deliver) the bonds have taken a *short position*.

To make our understanding of this contract more concrete, let's consider what happens when you buy or sell a Treasury bond futures contract. Let's say that on February 1, you sell one $100,000 June contract at a price of 115 (that is, $115,000). By selling this contract, you agree to deliver $100,000 face value of the long-term Treasury bonds to the contract's counterparty at the end of June for $115,000. By buying the contract at a price of 115, the buyer has agreed to pay $115,000 for the $100,000 face value of bonds when you deliver them at the end of June. If interest rates on long-term bonds rise, so that when the contract matures at the end of June, the price of these bonds has fallen to 110 ($110,000 per $100,000 of face value), the buyer of the contract will have lost $5,000, because he or she paid $115,000 for the bonds but can sell them only for the market price of $110,000. But you, the seller of the contract, will have gained $5,000, because you can now sell the bonds to the buyer for $115,000 but have to pay only $110,000 for them in the market.

It is even easier to describe what happens to the parties who have purchased futures contracts and those who have sold futures contracts if we recognize the following fact: ***At the expiration date of a futures contract, the price of the contract converges to the price of the underlying asset to be delivered.*** To see why this is the case, consider what happens on the expiration date of the June contract at the end of June when the price of the underlying $100,000 face value Treasury bond is 110 ($110,000). If the futures contract is selling below 110—say, at 109—a trader can buy the contract for $109,000, take delivery of the bond, and immediately sell it for $110,000, thereby earning a quick profit of $1,000. Because earning this profit involves no risk, it is a great deal that everyone would like to get in on. That means that everyone will try to buy the contract, and as a result, its price will rise. Only when the price rises to 110 will the profit opportunity cease to exist and the buying pressure disappear. Conversely, if the price of the futures contract is above 110—say, at 111—everyone will want to sell the contract. Now the sellers get $111,000 from selling the futures contract but have to pay only $110,000 for the Treasury bonds that they must deliver to the buyer of the contract, and the $1,000 difference is their profit. Because this profit involves no risk, traders will continue to sell the futures contract until its price falls back down to 110, at which price there are no longer any profits to be made. The elimination of riskless profit opportunities in the futures market is referred to as **arbitrage**, and it guarantees that the price of a futures contract at expiration equals the price of the underlying asset to be delivered.[1]

[1]In actuality, futures contracts sometimes set conditions for the timing and delivery of the underlying assets that cause the price of the contract at expiration to differ slightly from the price of the underlying assets. Because the difference in price is extremely small, we ignore it in this chapter.

Armed with the fact that a futures contract at expiration equals the price of the underlying asset makes it even easier to see who profits and who loses from such a contract when interest rates change. When interest rates have risen so that the price of the Treasury bond is 110 on the expiration day at the end of June, the June Treasury bond futures contract will also have a price of 110. Thus, if you bought the contract for 115 in February, you have a loss of 5 points, or $5,000 (5% of $100,000). But if you sold the futures contract at 115 in February, the decline in price to 110 means that you have a profit of 5 points, or $5,000.

APPLICATION ◆ Hedging with Financial Futures

First National Bank can also use financial futures contracts to hedge the interest-rate risk on its holdings of $5 million of the 6s of 2030. To see how, suppose that in March 2013, the 6s of 2030 are the long-term bonds that would be delivered in the Chicago Board of Trade's T-bond futures contract expiring one year in the future, in March 2014. Also suppose that the interest rate on these bonds is expected to remain at 6% over the next year, so that both the 6s of 2030 and the futures contract are selling at par (i.e., the $5 million of bonds is selling for $5 million and the $100,000 futures contract is selling for $100,000). The basic principle of hedging indicates that you, as the manager of First National Bank, need to offset the long position in these bonds with a short position, so you have to sell the futures contract. But how many contracts should you sell? The number of contracts required to hedge the interest-rate risk is found by dividing the amount of the asset to be hedged by the dollar value of each contract, as is shown in Equation 1:

$$NC = VA/VC$$

where NC = number of contracts for the hedge
VA = value of the asset
VC = value of each contract

Given that the 6s of 2030 are the long-term bonds that would be delivered in the CBT T-bond futures contract expiring one year in the future and that the interest rate on these bonds is expected to remain at 6% over the next year, so that both the 6s of 2030 and the futures contract are selling at par, how many contracts must First National sell to remove its interest-rate exposure from its $5 million holdings of the 6s of 2030?[2] Since VA = $5 million and VC = $100,000,

$$NC = \$5 \text{ million}/\$100{,}000 = 50$$

You therefore hedge the interest-rate risk by selling 50 of the Treasury Bond futures contracts.

Now suppose that over the next year, interest rates increase to 8% due to an increased threat of inflation. The value of the 6s of 2030 that the First National Bank is

[2]In the real world, designing a hedge is somewhat more complicated than the example here, because the bond that is most likely to be delivered might not be a 6s of 2030.

holding will then fall to $4,039,640 in March 2014.[3] Thus the loss from the long position in these bonds is $960,360:

Value on March 2014 @ 8% interest rate	$4,039,640
Value on March 2013 @ 6% interest rate	−$5,000,000
Loss	−$ 960,360

However, the short position in the 50 futures contracts that obligate you to deliver $5 million of the 6s of 2030 on March 2010 has a value equal to $4,039,640, the value of the $5 million of bonds after the interest rate has risen to 8%, as we have seen before. Yet when you sold the futures contract, the buyer was obligated to pay you $5 million on the maturity date. Thus the gain from the short position on these contracts is also $960,360:

Amount paid to you on March 2014, agreed upon in March 2013	$5,000,000
Value of bonds delivered on March 2014 @ 8% interest rate	−$4,039,640
Gain	$ 960,360

Therefore the net gain for the First National Bank is zero, indicating that the hedge has been conducted successfully.

The hedge just described is called a **micro hedge** because the financial institution is hedging the interest-rate risk for a specific asset it is holding. A second type of hedge that financial institutions engage in is called a **macro hedge**, in which the hedge is for the institution's entire portfolio. For example, if a bank has more rate-sensitive liabilities than assets, we have seen in Chapter 10 that a rise in interest rates will cause the value of the bank's net worth to decline. By selling interest-rate future contracts that will yield a profit when interest rates rise, the bank can offset the losses on its overall portfolio from an interest-rate rise and thereby hedge its interest-rate risk.

Organization of Trading in Financial Futures Markets

Financial futures contracts are traded in the United States on organized exchanges such as the Chicago Board of Trade and the Chicago Mercantile Exchange. The futures exchanges and all trades in financial futures in the United States are regulated by the Commodity Futures Trading Commission (CFTC), which was created in 1974 to take over the regulatory responsibilities for futures markets from the Department of Agriculture. The CFTC oversees futures trading and the futures exchanges to ensure that prices in the market are not being manipulated, and it also registers and audits the brokers, traders, and exchanges to prevent fraud and to ensure the financial soundness of the

[3]The value of the bonds can be calculated using a financial calculator as follows: *FV* = $5,000,000, *PMT* = $300,000, I = 8%, *N* = 19, *PV* = $4,039,640.

TABLE 1

Widely Traded Financial Futures Contracts in the United States

Type of Contract	Contract Size	Open Interest, May 2011
Interest-Rate Contracts		
Treasury bonds	$100,000	740,953
Treasury notes	$100,000	1,973,136
Five-year Treasury notes	$100,000	1,555,969
Two-year Treasury notes	$200,000	1,046,815
Thirty-day Fed funds rate	$5 million	751,787
Eurodollar	$4 million	10,202,720
Stock Index Contracts		
Standard & Poor's 500 Index	$250 × index	332,153
Standard & Poor's MIDCAP 400	$500 × index	1,721
NASDAQ 100	$100 × index	18,137
Nikkei 225 Stock Average	$5 × index	46,773
Currency Contracts		
Yen	12,500,000 yen	95,929
Euro	125,000 euros	270,101
Canadian dollar	100,000 Canadian $	125,654
British pound	100,000 pounds	108,085
Swiss franc	125,000 francs	67,713
Mexican peso	500,000 new pesos	142,530

Source: CME Goup: www.cmegroup.com/market-data/volume-open-interest/index.html and click on CME Group Open Interest Report.

exchanges. In addition, the CFTC approves proposed futures contracts to make sure that they serve the public interest. Listed in Table 1 are the most widely traded financial futures contracts in the United States, along with their contract size and the number of contracts outstanding, called **open interest**, for May 2011.

Given the globalization of other financial markets in recent years, it is not surprising that increased competition from abroad has been occurring in financial futures markets as well.

The Globalization of Financial Futures Markets

Because American futures exchanges were the first to develop financial futures, they dominated the trading of financial futures in the early 1980s. For example, in 1985, all of the top ten futures contracts were traded on exchanges in the United States. With the rapid growth of financial futures markets and the resulting high profits made by the American exchanges, foreign exchanges saw a profit opportunity and began to enter this business. By the 1990s, Eurodollar contracts traded on the London International Financial Futures

Exchange, Japanese government bond contracts and Euroyen contracts traded on the Tokyo Stock Exchange, French government bond contracts traded on the Marché à Terme International de France (now Euronext), and Nikkei 225 contracts traded on the Osaka Securities Exchange all were among the most widely traded futures contracts in the world.

Foreign competition has also spurred knockoffs of the most popular financial futures contracts initially developed in the United States. These contracts traded on foreign exchanges are virtually identical to those traded in the United States and have the advantage that they can be traded when the American exchanges are closed. The movement to 24-hour-a-day trading in financial futures has been further stimulated by the development of the Globex electronic trading platform, which allows traders throughout the world to trade futures even when the exchanges are not officially open. Financial futures trading has thus become completely internationalized, and competition between U.S. and foreign exchanges is now intense.

Explaining the Success of Futures Markets

The tremendous success of the financial futures market in Treasury bonds alone is evident from the fact that the total open interest of Treasury bond contracts was 740,953 in May 2011, for a total value of \$75 billion (740,953 × \$100,000). Several differences can be noted between financial futures and forward contracts and in the organization of their markets that help explain why financial futures markets such as those for Treasury bonds have been so successful.

Several features of futures contracts were designed to overcome the liquidity problem inherent in forward contracts. The first feature is that, in contrast to forward contracts, the quantities delivered and the delivery dates of futures contracts are standardized, making it more likely that different parties can be matched in the futures market, thereby increasing the liquidity of the market. In the case of the Treasury bond contract, the quantity delivered is \$100,000 face value of bonds, and the delivery dates are set to be the last business day of March, June, September, and December. The second feature is that after the futures contract has been bought or sold, it can be traded (bought or sold) again at any time until the delivery date. In contrast, once a forward contract is agreed on, it typically cannot be traded. The third feature is that in a futures contract, not just one specific type of Treasury bond is deliverable on the delivery date, as in a forward contract. Instead, any Treasury bond that matures in more than fifteen years and is not callable for fifteen years is eligible for delivery. Allowing continuous trading also increases the liquidity of the futures market, as does the ability to deliver a range of Treasury bonds rather than one specific bond.

Another reason why futures contracts specify that more than one bond is eligible for delivery is to limit the possibility that someone might corner the market and "squeeze" traders who have sold contracts. To corner the market, someone buys up all the deliverable securities so that investors with a short position cannot obtain from anyone else the securities that they contractually must deliver on the delivery date. As a result, the person who has cornered the market can set exorbitant prices for the securities that investors with a short position must buy to fulfill their obligations under the futures contract. The person who has cornered the market makes a fortune, but investors with a short position take a terrific loss. Clearly, the possibility that corners might occur in the market will discourage people from taking a short position and might therefore decrease the size of the market. By allowing many different securities to be delivered, the futures contract makes it harder for anyone to corner the market, because a much larger amount of securities would have to be purchased to establish the corner. Corners are a concern to both regulators and the organized exchanges that design futures contracts.

Trading in the futures market has been organized differently from trading in forward markets to overcome the default risk problems arising in forward contracts. In both types, for every contract, there must be a buyer who is taking a long position and a seller who is taking a short position. However, the buyer and seller of a futures contract make their contract not with each other but with the clearinghouse associated with the futures exchange. This setup means that the buyer of the futures contract does not need to worry about the financial health or trustworthiness of the seller, and vice versa, as in the forward market. As long as the clearinghouse is financially solid, buyers and sellers of futures contracts do not have to worry about default risk.

To make sure that the clearinghouse is financially sound and does not run into financial difficulties that might jeopardize its contracts, buyers or sellers of futures contracts must put an initial deposit, called a **margin requirement**, of perhaps \$2,000 per Treasury bond contract into a margin account kept at their brokerage firm. Futures contracts are then **marked to market** every day. What this means is that at the end of every trading day, the change in the value of the futures contract is added to or subtracted from the margin account. Suppose that after you buy the Treasury bond contract at a price of 115 on Wednesday morning, its closing price at the end of the day, the *settlement price*, falls to 114. You now have a loss of 1 point, or \$1,000, on the contract, and the seller who sold you the contract has a gain of 1 point, or \$1,000. The \$1,000 gain is added to the seller's margin account, making a total of \$3,000 in that account, and the \$1,000 loss is subtracted from your account, so you now have only \$1,000 in your account. If the amount in this margin account falls below the maintenance margin requirement (which can be the same as the initial requirement but is usually a little less), the trader is required to add money to the account. For example, if the maintenance margin requirement is also \$2,000, you would have to add \$1,000 to your account to bring it up to \$2,000. Margin requirements and marking to market make it far less likely that a trader will default on a contract, thus protecting the futures exchange from losses.

A final advantage that futures markets have over forward markets is that most futures contracts do not result in delivery of the underlying asset on the expiration date, whereas forward contracts do. A trader who sold a futures contract is allowed to avoid delivery on the expiration date by making an offsetting purchase of a futures contract. Because the simultaneous holding of the long and short positions means that the trader would in effect be delivering the bonds to itself, under the exchange rules the trader is allowed to cancel both contracts. Allowing traders to cancel their contracts in this way lowers the cost of conducting trades in the futures market relative to the forward market in that a futures trader can avoid the costs of physical delivery, which is not so easy with forward contracts.

APPLICATION ◆ Hedging Foreign Exchange Risk

As we discussed in Chapter 1, foreign exchange rates have been highly volatile in recent years. The large fluctuations in exchange rates subject financial institutions and other businesses to significant foreign exchange risk because they generate substantial gains and losses. Luckily for financial institution managers, the financial derivatives discussed in this chapter—forward and financial futures contracts—can be used to hedge foreign exchange risk.

To understand how financial institution managers manage foreign exchange risk, let's suppose that in January, the First National Bank's customer Frivolous Luxuries, Inc., is due a payment of 10 million euros in two months for $10 million worth of goods it has just sold in Germany. Frivolous Luxuries is concerned that if the value of the euro falls substantially from its current value of $1, the company might suffer a large loss because the 10 million euro payment will no longer be worth $10 million. So Sam, the CEO of Frivolous Luxuries, calls his friend Mona, the manager of the First National Bank, and asks her to hedge this foreign exchange risk for his company. Let's see how the bank manager does this using forward and financial futures contracts.

Hedging Foreign Exchange Risk with Forward Contracts

Forward markets in foreign exchange have been highly developed by commercial banks and investment banking operations that engage in extensive foreign exchange trading and are widely used to hedge foreign exchange risk. Mona knows that she can use this market to hedge the foreign exchange risk for Frivolous Luxuries. Such a hedge is quite straightforward for her to execute. Because the payment of euros in two months means that at that time Sam would hold a long position in euros, Mona knows that the basic principle of hedging indicates that she should offset this long position by a short position. Thus she just enters a forward contract that obligates her to sell 10 million euros two months from now in exchange for dollars at the current forward rate of $1 per euro.[4]

In two months, when her customer receives the 10 million euros, the forward contract ensures that it is exchanged for dollars at an exchange rate of $1 per euro, thus yielding $10 million. No matter what happens to future exchange rates, Frivolous Luxuries will be guaranteed $10 million for the goods it sold in Germany. Mona calls her friend Sam to let him know that his company is now protected from any foreign exchange movements, and he thanks her for her help.

Hedging Foreign Exchange Risk with Futures Contracts

As an alternative, Mona could have used the currency futures market to hedge the foreign exchange risk. In this case, she would see that the Chicago Mercantile Exchange has a euro contract with a contract amount of 125,000 euros and a price of $1 per euro. To do the hedge, Mona must sell euros as with the forward contract, to the tune of 10 million euros of the March futures. How many of the Chicago Mercantile Exchange March euro contracts must Mona sell to hedge the 10 million euro payment due in March?

Using Equation 1 with $VA = 10$ million euros and $VC = 125{,}000$ euros,

$$NC = 10 \text{ million}/125{,}000 = 80$$

Thus Mona does the hedge by selling 80 of the CME euro contracts. Given the $1-per-euro price, the sale of the contract yields 80 × 125,000 euros = $10 million.

[4]The forward exchange rate will probably differ slightly from the current spot rate of $1 per euro because the interest rates in Germany and the United States may not be equal. In that case, as we will see from the interest parity condition in the Chapter 20 Appendix, the future expected exchange rate will not equal the current spot rate and neither will the forward rate. However, since interest differentials have typically been less than 6% at an annual rate (1% bimonthly), the expected appreciation or depreciation of the euro over a two-month period has always been less than 1%. Thus the forward rate is always close to the current spot rate, and our assumption in the example that the forward rate and the spot rate are the same is a reasonable one.

This futures hedge enables her to lock in the exchange rate for Frivolous Luxuries so that it gets its payment of $10 million.

One advantage of using the futures market is that the contract size of 125,000 euros, worth $125,000, is quite a bit smaller than the minimum size of a forward contract, which is usually $1 million or more. However, in this case, the bank manager is making a large enough transaction that she can use either the forward or the futures market. Her choice depends on whether the transaction costs are lower in one market than in the other. If the First National Bank is active in the forward market, that market would probably have the lower transaction costs. If First National rarely deals in foreign exchange forward contracts, the bank manager may do better by sticking with the futures market. ◆

OPTIONS

Another vehicle for hedging interest-rate and stock market risk involves the use of options on financial instruments. **Options** are contracts that give the purchaser the option, or *right*, to buy or sell the underlying financial instrument at a specified price, called the **exercise price or strike price**, within a specific period of time (the *term to expiration*). The seller (sometimes called the *writer*) of the option is *obligated* to buy or sell the financial instrument to the purchaser if the owner of the option exercises the right to sell or buy. These option contract features are important enough to be emphasized: The *owner* or buyer of an option does not have to exercise the option; he or she can let the option expire without using it. Hence the owner of an option is not obligated to take any action, but rather has the *right* to exercise the contract if he or she so chooses. The seller of an option, by contrast, has no choice in the matter; he or she *must* buy or sell the financial instrument if the owner exercises the option.

Because the right to buy or sell a financial instrument at a specified price has value, the owner of an option is willing to pay an amount for it called a **premium**. Option contracts are of two types: **American options** can be exercised *at any time up to* the expiration date of the contract, and **European options** can be exercised only *on* the expiration date.

Option contracts are written on a number of financial instruments. Options on individual stocks are called **stock options**, and such options have existed for a long time. Option contracts on financial futures, called **financial futures options** or, more commonly, **futures options**, were developed in 1982 and have become the most widely traded option contracts.

You might wonder why option contracts are more likely to be written on financial futures than on underlying debt instruments such as bonds or certificates of deposit. As you saw earlier in the chapter, at the expiration date, the price of the futures contract and of the deliverable debt instrument will be the same because of arbitrage. So it would seem that investors should be indifferent about having the option written on the debt instrument or on the futures contract. However, financial futures contracts have been so well designed that their markets are often more liquid than the markets in the underlying debt instruments. So investors would rather have the option contract written on the more liquid instrument—in this case, the futures contract. That explains why the most popular futures options are written on many of the same futures contracts listed in Table 1.

The regulation of option markets is split between the Securities and Exchange Commission (SEC), which regulates stock options, and the Commodity Futures Trading Commission (CFTC), which regulates futures options. Regulation focuses on ensuring that writers of options have enough capital to make good on their contractual obligations and on overseeing traders and exchanges to prevent fraud and ensure that the market is not being manipulated.

Option Contracts

A **call option** is a contract that gives the owner the right to buy a financial instrument at the exercise price within a specific period of time. A **put option** is a contract that gives the owner the right to sell a financial instrument at the exercise price within a specific period of time.

Remembering which is a call option and which is a put option is not always easy. To keep them straight, just remember that having a *call* option to buy a financial instrument is the same as having the option to *call* in the instrument for delivery at a specified price. Having a *put* option to sell a financial instrument is the same as having the option to *put* up an instrument for the other party to buy.

Profits and Losses on Option and Futures Contracts

To understand option contracts more fully, let's first examine the option on the same June Treasury bond futures contract that we looked at earlier in the chapter. Recall that if you buy this futures contract at a price of 115 (that is, $115,000), you have agreed to pay $115,000 for $100,000 face value of long-term Treasury bonds when they are delivered to you at the end of June. If you sold this futures contract at a price of 115, you agreed, in exchange for $115,000, to deliver $100,000 face value of the long-term Treasury bonds at the end of June. An option contract on the Treasury bond futures contract has several key features: (1) It has the same expiration date as the underlying futures contract; (2) it is an American option and so can be exercised at any time before the expiration date; and (3) the premium (price) of the option is quoted in points that are the same as in the futures contract, so each point corresponds to $1,000. If, for a premium of $2,000, you buy one call option contract on the June Treasury bond contract with an exercise price of 115, you have purchased the right to buy (call in) the June Treasury bond futures contract for a price of 115 ($115,000 per contract) at any time through the expiration date of this contract at the end of June. Similarly, when for $2,000 you buy a put option on the June Treasury bond contract with an exercise price of 115, you have the right to sell (put up) the June Treasury bond futures contract for a price of 115 ($115,000 per contract) at any time until the end of June.

Futures option contracts are somewhat complicated, so to explore how they work and how they can be used to hedge risk, let's first examine how profits and losses on the call option on the June Treasury bond futures contract occur. In February, our old friend Irving the Investor buys, for a $2,000 premium, a call option on the $100,000 June Treasury bond futures contract with a strike price of 115. (We assume that if Irving exercises the option, it is on the expiration date at the end of June and not before.) On the expiration date at the end of June, suppose that the underlying Treasury bond for the futures contract has a price of 110. Recall that on the expiration date, arbitrage forces the price of the futures contract to be the same as the price of the underlying bond, so it, too, has a price of 110 on the expiration date at the end of June. If Irving exercises the call option and buys the futures contract at an exercise price of 115, he

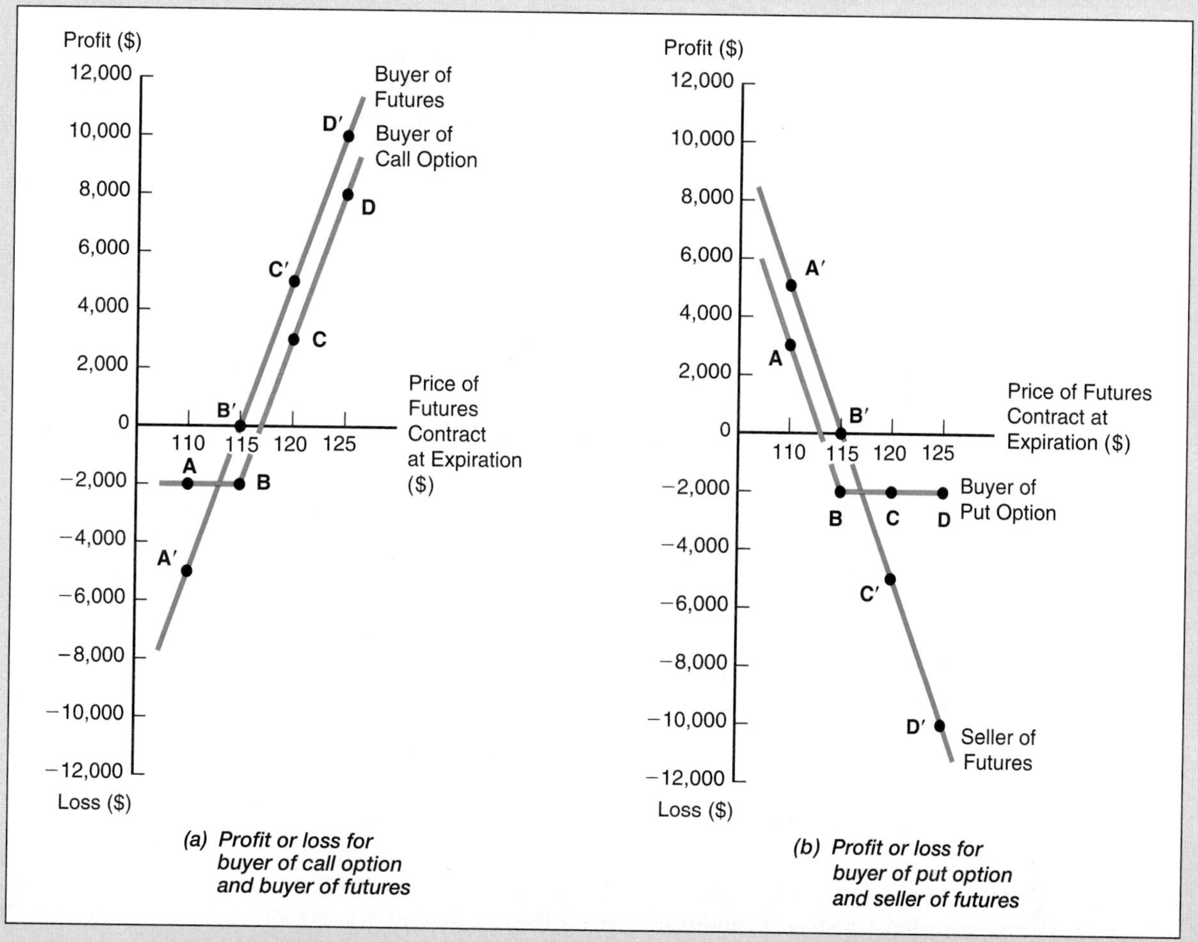

FIGURE 1 Profits and Losses on Options Versus Futures Contracts
The futures contract is the $100,000 June Treasury bond contract, and the option contracts are written on this futures contract with an exercise price of 115. Panel (a) shows the profits and losses for the buyer of the call option and the buyer of the futures contract, and panel (b) shows the profits and losses for the buyer of the put option and the seller of the futures contract.

will lose money by buying at 115 and selling at the lower market price of 110. Because Irving is smart, he will not exercise the option, but he will be out the $2,000 premium he paid. In such a situation, in which the price of the underlying financial instrument is below the exercise price, a call option is said to be "out of the money." At the price of 110 (less than the exercise price), Irving thus suffers a loss on the option contract of the $2,000 premium he paid. This loss is plotted as point A in panel (a) of Figure 1.

On the expiration date, if the price of the futures contract is 115, the call option is "at the money," and Irving is indifferent whether he exercises his option to buy the futures contract, because exercising the option at 115 when the market price is also at 115 produces no gain or loss. Because he has paid the $2,000 premium, at the price of 115 his contract again has a net loss of $2,000, plotted as point B.

If the futures contract instead has a price of 120 on the expiration day, the option is "in the money," and Irving benefits from exercising the option: He would buy the futures contract at the exercise price of 115 and then sell it for 120, thereby earning a 5-point gain ($5,000 profit) on the $100,000 Treasury bond contract. Because Irving paid a $2,000 premium for the option contract, however, his net profit is $3,000 ($5,000 – $2,000). The $3,000 profit at a price of 120 is plotted as point C. Similarly, if the price of the futures contract rose to 125, the option contract would yield a net profit of $8,000 ($10,000 from exercising the option minus the $2,000 premium), plotted as point D. Plotting these points, we get the kinked profit curve for the call option that we see in panel (a).

Suppose that instead of purchasing the futures *option* contract in February, Irving decides instead to buy the $100,000 June Treasury bond *futures* contract at the price of 115. If the price of the bond on the expiration day at the end of June declines to 110, meaning that the price of the futures contract also falls to 110, Irving suffers a loss of 5 points, or $5,000. The loss of $5,000 on the futures contract at a price of 110 is plotted as point A' in panel (a). At a price of 115 on the expiration date, Irving would have a zero profit on the futures contract, plotted as point B'. At a price of 120, Irving would have a profit on the contract of 5 points, or $5,000 (point C'), and at a price of 125, the profit would be 10 percentage points, or $10,000 (point D'). Plotting these points, we get the linear (straight-line) profit curve for the futures contract that appears in panel (a).

Now we can see the major difference between a futures contract and an option contract. As the profit curve for the futures contract in panel (a) indicates, the futures contract has a linear profit function: Profits grow by an equal dollar amount for every point increase in the price of the underlying financial instrument. By contrast, the kinked profit curve for the option contract is nonlinear, meaning that profits do not always grow by the same amount for a given change in the price of the underlying financial instrument. The reason for this nonlinearity is that the call option protects Irving from having losses that are greater than the amount of the $2,000 premium. In contrast, Irving's loss on the futures contract is $5,000 if the price on the expiration day falls to 110, and if the price falls even further, Irving's loss will be even greater. This insurance-like feature of option contracts explains why their purchase price is referred to as a premium. Once the underlying financial instrument's price rises above the exercise price, however, Irving's profits grow linearly. Irving has given up something by buying an option rather than a futures contract. As we see in panel (a), when the price of the underlying financial instrument rises above the exercise price, Irving's profits are always less than that on the futures contract by exactly the $2,000 premium he paid.

Panel (b) plots the results of the same profit calculations if Irving buys not a call but a put option (an option to sell) with an exercise price of 115 for a premium of $2,000 and if he sells the futures contract rather than buying one. In this case, if on the expiration date the Treasury bond futures have a price above the 115 exercise price, the put option is "out of the money." Irving would not want to exercise the put option and then have to sell the futures contract he owns as a result at a price below the market price and lose money. He would not exercise his option, and he would be out only the $2,000 premium he paid. Once the price of the futures contract falls below the 115 exercise price, Irving benefits from exercising the put option because he can sell the futures contract at a price of 115 but can buy it at a price below this. In such a situation, in which the price of the underlying instrument is below the exercise price, the put option is "in the money," and profits rise linearly as the price of the futures contract falls. The profit function for the put option illustrated in panel (b) of Figure 1 is kinked, indicating that Irving is protected from losses greater than the amount of the premium he paid.

The profit curve for the sale of the futures contract is just the negative of the profit for the futures contract in panel (a) and is therefore linear.

Panel (b) of Figure 1 confirms the conclusion from panel (a) that profits on option contracts are nonlinear but profits on futures contracts are linear.

Two other differences between futures and option contracts must be mentioned. The first is that the initial investment on the contracts differs. As we saw earlier in the chapter, when a futures contract is purchased, the investor must put up a fixed amount, the margin requirement, in a margin account. But when an option contract is purchased, the initial investment is the premium that must be paid for the contract. The second important difference between the contracts is that the futures contract requires money to change hands daily when the contract is marked to market, whereas the option contract requires money to change hands only when it is exercised.

APPLICATION ◆ Hedging with Futures Options

Earlier in the chapter, we saw how the First National Bank could hedge the interest-rate risk on its \$5 million holdings of 6s of 2030 by selling \$5 million of T-bond futures. A rise in interest rates and the resulting fall in bond prices and bond futures contracts would lead to profits on the bank's sale of the futures contracts that would exactly offset the losses on the 6s of 2030 the bank is holding.

As panel (b) of Figure 1 suggests, an alternative way for the manager to protect against a rise in interest rates and hence a decline in bond prices is to buy \$5 million of put options written on the same Treasury bond futures. As long as the exercise price is not too far from the current price as in panel (b), the rise in interest rates and decline in bond prices will lead to profits on the futures and the futures put options, profits that will offset any losses on the \$5 million of Treasury bonds.

The one problem with using options rather than futures is that the First National Bank will have to pay premiums on the options contracts, thereby lowering the bank's profits in an effort to hedge the interest-rate risk. Why might the bank manager be willing to use options rather than futures to conduct the hedge? The answer is that the option contract, unlike the futures contract, allows the First National Bank to gain if interest rates decline and bond prices rise. With the hedge using futures contracts, the First National Bank does not gain from increases in bond prices because the profits on the bonds it is holding are offset by the losses from the futures contracts it has sold. However, as panel (b) of Figure 1 indicates, the situation when the hedge is conducted with put options is quite different: Once bond prices rise above the exercise price, the bank does not suffer additional losses on the option contracts. At the same time, the value of the Treasury bonds the bank is holding will increase, thereby leading to a profit for the bank. Thus using options rather than futures to conduct the micro hedge allows the bank to protect itself from rises in interest rates but still allows the bank to benefit from interest-rate declines (although the profit is reduced by the amount of the premium).

Similar reasoning indicates that the bank manager might prefer to use options to conduct the macro hedge to immunize the entire bank portfolio from interest-rate risk. Again, the strategy of using options rather than futures has the disadvantage that the First National Bank has to pay the premiums on these contracts up front. By contrast, using options allows the bank to keep the gains from a decline in interest rates (which will raise the value of the bank's assets relative to its liabilities), because these gains will not be offset by large losses on the option contracts.

In the case of a macro hedge, there is another reason why the bank might prefer option contracts to futures contracts. Profits and losses on futures contracts can cause accounting problems for banks because such profits and losses are not allowed to be offset by unrealized changes in the value of the rest of the bank's portfolio. Consider what happens when interest rates fall. If First National sells futures contracts to conduct the macro hedge, then when interest rates fall and the prices of the Treasury bond futures contracts rise, it will have large losses on these contracts. Of course, these losses are offset by unrealized profits in the rest of the bank's portfolio, but the bank is not allowed to offset these losses in its accounting statements. So even though the macro hedge is serving its intended purpose of immunizing the bank's portfolio from interest-rate risk, the bank would experience large accounting losses when interest rates fall. Indeed, bank managers have lost their jobs when perfectly sound hedges with interest-rate futures have led to large accounting losses. Not surprisingly, bank managers might shrink from using financial futures to conduct macro hedges for this reason.

Futures options, however, can come to the rescue of the managers of banks and other financial institutions. Suppose that First National conducted the macro hedge by buying put options instead of selling Treasury bond futures. Now if interest rates fall and bond prices rise well above the exercise price, the bank will not have large losses on the option contracts, because it will just decide not to exercise its options. The bank will not suffer the accounting problems produced by hedging with financial futures. Because of the accounting advantages of using futures options to conduct macro hedges, option contracts have become important to financial institution managers as tools for hedging interest-rate risk.

Factors Affecting the Option Premiums

Several interesting facts can be noted about how the premiums on option contracts are priced. First, when the strike (exercise) price for a contract is set at a higher level, the premium for the call option is lower and the premium for the put option is higher. For example, in going from a contract with a strike price of 112 to one with 115, the premium for a call option for the month of March might fall from $1\frac{45}{64}$ to $\frac{16}{64}$, and the premium for the March put option might rise from $\frac{19}{64}$ to $1\frac{54}{64}$.

Our understanding of the profit function for option contracts illustrated in Figure 1 helps explain this fact. As we saw in panel (a), a higher price for the underlying financial instrument (in this case, a Treasury bond futures contract) relative to the option's exercise price results in higher profits on the call (buy) option. Thus, the lower the strike price, the higher the profits on the call option contract and the greater the premium that investors like Irving are willing to pay. Similarly, we saw in panel (b) that a higher price for the underlying financial instrument relative to the exercise price lowers profits on the put (sell) option, so that a higher strike price increases profits and thus causes the premium to increase.

Second, as the period of time over which the option can be exercised (the term to expiration) gets longer, the premiums for both call and put options rise. For example, at a strike price of 112, the premium on a call option might increase from $1\frac{45}{64}$ in March to $1\frac{50}{64}$ in April and to $2\frac{28}{64}$ in May. Similarly, the premium on a put option might increase from $\frac{19}{64}$ in March to $1\frac{43}{64}$ in April and to $2\frac{22}{64}$ in May. The fact that premiums increase with the term to expiration is also explained by the nonlinear profit function for option contracts. As the term to expiration lengthens, there is a greater chance that the price of the underlying financial instrument will be very high or very low by the expiration date. If the price becomes very high and goes well above the exercise price, the call (buy) option will yield a high profit; if the price becomes very low and goes well below the exercise price, the losses will be small because the owner of the call option will simply decide not to exercise the option. The possibility of greater variability of the underlying financial instrument as the term to expiration lengthens raises profits, on average, for the call option.

Similar reasoning tells us that the put (sell) option will also become more valuable as the term to expiration increases, because the possibility of greater price variability of the underlying financial instrument increases as the term to expiration increases. The greater chance of a low price increases the chance that profits on the put option will be very high. But the greater chance of a high price does not produce substantial losses for the put option, because the owner will again just decide not to exercise the option.

Another way of thinking about this reasoning is to recognize that option contracts have an element of "heads, I win; tails, I don't lose too badly." The greater variability of where the prices might be by the expiration date increases the value of both kinds of options. Because a longer term to the expiration date leads to greater variability of where the prices might be by the expiration date, a longer term to expiration raises the value of the option contract.

The reasoning that we have just developed also explains another important fact about option premiums. When the volatility of the price of the underlying instrument is great, the premiums for both call and put options will be higher. Higher volatility of prices means that for a given expiration date, there will again be greater variability of where the prices might be by the expiration date. The "heads, I win; tails, I don't lose too badly" property of options then means that the greater variability of possible prices by the expiration date increases average profits for the option and thus increases the premium that investors are willing to pay.

Summary

Our analysis of how profits on options are affected by price movements for the underlying financial instrument leads to the following conclusions about the factors that determine the premium on an option contract:

1. The higher the strike price, everything else being equal, the lower the premium on call (buy) options and the higher the premium on put (sell) options.
2. The greater the term to expiration, everything else being equal, the higher the premiums for both call and put options.
3. The greater the volatility of prices of the underlying financial instrument, everything else being equal, the higher the premiums for both call and put options.

The results we have derived here appear in more formal models, such as the Black-Scholes model, which analyze how the premiums on options are priced. You might study such models in finance courses. ◆

SWAPS

In addition to forwards, futures, and options, financial institutions use one other important financial derivative to manage risk. **Swaps** are financial contracts that obligate each party to the contract to exchange (swap) a set of payments (not assets) it owns for another set of payments owned by another party. Swaps are of two basic kinds. **Currency swaps** involve the exchange of a set of payments in one currency for a set of payments in another currency. **Interest-rate swaps** involve the exchange of one set of interest payments for another set of interest payments, all denominated in the same currency.

Interest-Rate Swap Contracts

Interest-rate swaps are an important tool for managing interest-rate risk, and they first appeared in the United States in 1982, when, as we have seen, demand increased for financial instruments that could be used to reduce interest-rate risk. The most common type of interest-rate swap (called the *plain vanilla swap*) specifies (1) the interest rate on the payments that are being exchanged; (2) the type of interest payments (variable or fixed-rate); (3) the amount of **notional principal**, which is the amount on which the interest is being paid; and (4) the time period over which the exchanges continue to be made. There are many other more complicated versions of swaps, including forward swaps and swap options (called *swaptions*), but here we will look only at the plain vanilla swap. Figure 2 illustrates an interest-rate swap between the Midwest Savings Bank and the Friendly Finance Company. Midwest Savings agrees to pay Friendly Finance a fixed rate of 5% on $1 million of notional principal for the next ten years, and Friendly Finance agrees to pay Midwest Savings the one-year Treasury bill rate plus 1% on $1 million of notional principal for the same period. Thus, as shown in Figure 2, every year the Midwest Savings Bank would be paying the Friendly Finance Company 5% on $1 million, while Friendly Finance would be paying Midwest Savings the one-year T-bill rate plus 1% on $1 million.

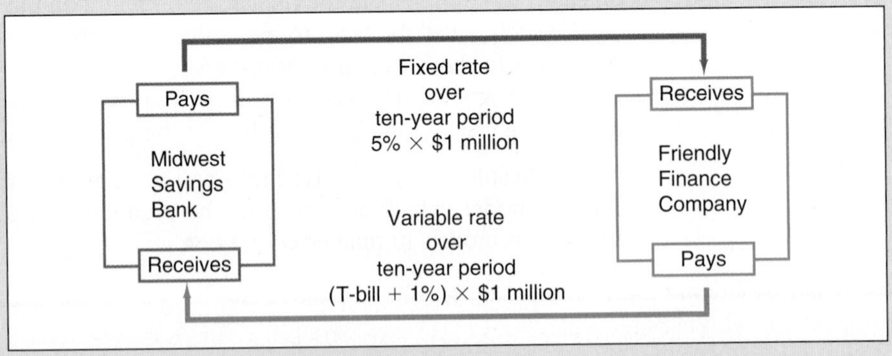

FIGURE 2 Interest-Rate Swap Payments

In this swap arrangement with a notional principal of $1 million and a term of ten years, the Midwest Savings Bank pays a fixed rate of 5% × $1 million to the Friendly Finance Company, which in turn agrees to pay the one-year Treasury bill rate plus 1% × $1 million to the Midwest Savings Bank.

APPLICATION ◆ Hedging with Interest-Rate Swaps

You might wonder why these two parties find it advantageous to enter into this swap agreement. The answer is that it may help both of them hedge interest-rate risk.

Suppose that the Midwest Savings Bank, which tends to borrow short-term and then lend long-term in the mortgage market, has $1 million less of rate-sensitive assets than it has of rate-sensitive liabilities. As we learned in Chapter 10, this situation means that as interest rates rise, the increase in the cost of funds (liabilities) is greater than the increase in interest payments it receives on its assets, many of which are fixed-rate. The result of rising interest rates is thus a shrinking of Midwest Savings' net interest margin and a decline in its profitability. As we saw in Chapter 10, to avoid this interest-rate risk, Midwest Savings would like to convert $1 million of its fixed-rate assets into $1 million of rate-sensitive assets, in effect making rate-sensitive assets equal rate-sensitive liabilities, thereby eliminating the gap. This is exactly what happens when it engages in the interest-rate swap. By taking $1 million of its fixed-rate income and exchanging it for $1 million of rate-sensitive Treasury bill income, it has converted income on $1 million of fixed-rate assets into income on $1 million of rate-sensitive assets. Now when interest rates rise, the increase in rate-sensitive income on its assets exactly matches the increase in the rate-sensitive cost of funds on its liabilities, leaving the net interest margin and bank profitability unchanged.

The Friendly Finance Company, which issues long-term bonds to raise funds and uses them to make short-term loans, finds that it is in exactly the opposite situation to Midwest Savings: It has $1 million more of rate-sensitive assets than of rate-sensitive liabilities. It is therefore concerned that a fall in interest rates, which will result in a larger drop in income from its assets than the decline in the cost of funds on its liabilities, will cause a decline in profits. By doing the interest-rate swap, it eliminates this interest-rate risk because it has converted $1 million of rate-sensitive income into $1 million of fixed-rate income. Now the Friendly Finance Company finds that when interest rates fall, the decline in rate-sensitive income is smaller and so is matched by the decline in the rate-sensitive cost of funds on its liabilities, leaving its profitability unchanged.

Advantages of Interest-Rate Swaps

To eliminate interest-rate risk, both the Midwest Savings Bank and the Friendly Finance Company could have rearranged their balance sheets by converting fixed-rate assets into rate-sensitive assets, and vice versa, instead of engaging in an interest-rate swap. However, this strategy would have been costly for both financial institutions for several reasons. The first is that financial institutions incur substantial transaction costs when they rearrange their balance sheets. Second, different financial institutions have informational advantages in making loans to certain customers who may prefer certain maturities. Thus, adjusting the balance sheet to eliminate interest-rate risk might result in a loss of these informational advantages, which the financial institution is unwilling to give up. Interest-rate swaps solve these problems for financial institutions, because, in effect, they allow the institutions to convert fixed-rate assets into rate-sensitive assets without affecting the balance sheet. Large transaction costs are avoided, and the financial institutions can continue to make loans where they have an informational advantage.

We have seen that financial institutions can also hedge interest-rate risk with other financial derivatives, such as futures contracts and futures options. Interest-rate swaps have one big advantage over hedging with these other derivatives: They can be written for very long horizons, sometimes as long as twenty years, whereas financial futures and futures options typically have much shorter horizons, not much more than a year. If a financial institution needs to hedge interest-rate risk for a long horizon, financial futures and option markets may not do it much good. Instead, it can turn to the swap market.

Disadvantages of Interest-Rate Swaps

Although interest-rate swaps have important advantages that make them very popular with financial institutions, they also have disadvantages that limit their usefulness. Swap markets, like forward markets, can suffer from a lack of liquidity. Let's return to looking at the swap between the Midwest Savings Bank and the Friendly Finance Company. As with a forward contract, it might be difficult for the Midwest Savings Bank to link up with the Friendly Finance Company to arrange the swap. In addition, even if the Midwest Savings Bank could find a counterparty like the Friendly Finance Company, it might not be able to negotiate a good deal because it cannot find any other institution with which to negotiate.

Swap contracts also are subject to the same default risk that we encountered for forward contracts. If interest rates rise, the Friendly Finance Company would love to get out of the swap contract, because the fixed-rate interest payments it receives are less than it could get in the open market. It might then default on the contract, exposing Midwest Savings to a loss. Alternatively, the Friendly Finance Company could go bust, meaning that the terms of the swap contract would not be fulfilled.

Financial Intermediaries in Interest-Rate Swaps

As we have just seen, financial institutions do have to be aware of the possibility of losses from a default on swaps. As with a forward contract, each party to a swap must have a lot of information about the other party to make sure that the contract is likely to be fulfilled. The need for information about counterparties and the liquidity problems in swap markets could limit the usefulness of these markets. However, as we saw in Chapter 8, when informational and liquidity problems crop up in a market, financial intermediaries come to the rescue. That is exactly what happens in swap markets. Intermediaries such as investment banks and especially large commercial banks have the ability to acquire information cheaply about the creditworthiness and reliability of parties to swap contracts and are also able to match parties to a swap. Hence large commercial banks and investment banks have set up swap markets in which they act as intermediaries. ◆

CREDIT DERIVATIVES

In recent years, a new type of derivative has come on the scene to hedge credit risk. Like other derivatives, **credit derivatives** offer payoffs on previously issued securities, but ones that bear credit risk. In the past ten years, the markets in credit derivatives have grown at an astounding pace and the notional amounts of these derivatives now number in the trillions of dollars. These credit derivatives take several forms.

Credit Options

Credit options work just like the options discussed earlier in the chapter: For a fee, the purchaser gains the right to receive profits that are tied either to the price of an underlying security or to an interest rate. Suppose you buy $1 million of General Motors bonds but worry that a potential slowdown in the sale of SUVs might lead a credit-rating agency to *downgrade* (lower the credit rating on) GM bonds. As we saw in Chapter 6, such a downgrade would cause the price of GM bonds to fall. To protect yourself, you could buy an option for, say, $15,000, to sell the $1 million of bonds at a strike price that is the same as the current price. With this strategy, you would not suffer any losses if the value of the GM bonds declined because you could exercise the option and sell them at the price you paid for them. In addition, you would be able to reap any gains that occurred if GM bonds rose in value.

The second type of credit option ties profits to changes in an interest rate, such as a credit spread (the interest rate on the average bond with a particular credit rating minus the interest rate on default-free bonds, such as those issued by the U.S. Treasury). Suppose that your company, which has a Baa credit rating, plans to issue $10 million of one-year bonds in three months and expects to have a credit spread of 1 percentage point (i.e., it will pay an interest rate that is 1 percentage point higher than the one-year Treasury rate). You are concerned that the market might start to think that Baa companies in general will become riskier in the coming months. If this were to happen by the time you are ready to issue your bonds in three months, you would have to pay a higher interest rate than the 1 percentage point in excess of the Treasury rate, and your cost of issuing the bonds would increase. To protect yourself against these higher costs, you could buy for, say, $20,000 a credit option on $10 million of Baa bonds that would pay you the difference between the average Baa credit spread in the market minus the 1 percentage point credit spread on $10 million. If the credit spread jumps to 2 percentage points, you would receive $100,000 from the option (= [2% – 1%] × $10 million), which would exactly offset the $100,000 higher interest costs from the 1 percentage point higher interest rate you would have to pay on your $10 million of bonds.

Credit Swaps

Suppose you manage a bank in Houston called Oil Drillers' Bank (ODB), which specializes in lending to a particular industry in your local area, oil drilling companies. Another bank, Potato Farmers Bank (PFB), specializes in lending to potato farmers in Idaho. Both ODB and PFB have a problem because their loan portfolios are not sufficiently diversified. To protect ODB against a collapse in the oil market, which would result in defaults on most of its loans made to oil drillers, you could reach an agreement to have the loan payments on, say, $100 million worth of your loans to oil drillers paid to the PFB in exchange for PFB paying you the loan payments on $100 million of its loans to potato farmers. Such a transaction, in which risky payments on loans are swapped for each other, is called a **credit swap**. As a result of this swap, ODB and PFB have increased their diversification and lowered the overall risk of their loan portfolios because some of the loan payments to each bank are now coming from a different type of loan.

Another form of credit swap is, for arcane reasons, called a **credit default swap**, although it functions more like insurance. With a credit default swap, one party who wants to hedge credit risk pays a fixed payment on a regular basis, in return for a contingent payment that is triggered by a *credit event,* such as the bankruptcy of a particular firm or the downgrading of the firm's credit rating by a credit-rating agency. For example, you could use a credit default swap to hedge the $1 million of General Motors bonds that you are holding by arranging to pay an annual fee of $1,000 in exchange for a payment of $10,000 if the GM bonds' credit rating is lowered. If a credit event happens and GM's bonds are downgraded so that their price falls, you will receive a payment that will offset some of the loss you suffer if you sell the bonds at this lower price.

Credit-Linked Notes

Another type of credit derivative, the **credit-linked note**, is a combination of a bond and a credit option. Just like any corporate bond, the credit-linked note makes periodic coupon (interest) payments and a final payment of the face value of the bond at maturity. If a key financial variable specified in the note changes, however, the issuer of the note has the right (option) to lower the payments on the note. For example, General Motors could issue a credit-linked note that pays a 5% coupon rate, with the specification that if a national index of SUV sales falls by 10%, then GM has the right to lower the coupon rate by 2 percentage points, to 3%. In this way, GM can lower its risk because when it is losing money as SUV sales fall, it can offset some of these losses by making smaller payments on its credit-linked notes.

APPLICATION ◆ Lessons from the Global Financial Crisis: When Are Financial Derivatives Likely to Be a Worldwide Time Bomb?

Although financial derivatives can be useful in hedging risk, the AIG blowup discussed in the previous chapter illustrates that they can pose a real danger to the financial system. Indeed, Warren Buffet warned about the dangers of financial derivatives by characterizing them as "financial weapons of mass destruction." Particularly scary are the notional amounts of derivatives contracts—more than $500 trillion worldwide. What does the recent global financial crisis tell us about when financial derivatives are likely to be a time bomb that could bring down the world financial system?

Two major concerns surround financial derivatives. The first is that financial derivatives allow financial institutions to increase their leverage; that is, these institutions can, in effect, hold an amount of the underlying asset that is many times greater than the amount of money they have had to put up. Increasing their leverage enables them to take huge bets, which, if they are wrong, can bring down the institution. This is exactly what AIG did, to its great regret, when it plunged into the credit default swap market. Even more of a problem was that AIG's speculation in the credit default swap (CDS) market had the potential to bring down the whole financial system. An important lesson from the global financial crisis is that having one player take huge positions in a derivatives market is highly dangerous.

A second concern is that banks have holdings of huge notional amounts of financial derivatives, particularly interest-rate and currency swaps, that greatly exceed the amount of bank capital, and so these derivatives expose the banks to serious risk of failure. Banks are indeed major players in the financial derivatives markets, particularly in the interest-rate and currency swaps market, where our earlier analysis has shown that they are the natural market makers because they can act as intermediaries between two counterparties who would not make the swap without their involvement. However, looking at the notional amount of interest-rate and currency swaps at banks gives a very misleading picture of their risk exposure. Because banks act as intermediaries in the swap markets, they are typically exposed only to credit risk—a default by one of their counterparties. Furthermore, these swaps, unlike loans, do not involve payments of the notional amount, but rather the much smaller payments that are based on the notional amounts. For example, in the case of a 7% interest rate, the payment is only $70,000 for a $1 million swap. Estimates of the credit exposure from swap contracts indicate that they are on the order of only 1% of the notional value of the contracts and that credit exposure at banks from derivatives is generally less than a quarter of their total credit exposure from loans. Banks' credit exposures from their derivative positions are thus not out of line with other credit exposures they face. Furthermore, an analysis by the GAO indicated that actual credit losses incurred by banks in their derivatives contracts have been very small, on the order of 0.2% of their gross credit exposure. Indeed, during the recent global financial crisis, in which the financial system was put under great stress, derivatives exposure at banks has not been a serious problem.

The conclusion is that recent events indicate that financial derivatives pose serious dangers to the financial system, but some of these dangers have been overplayed. The biggest danger occurs in trading activities of financial institutions, and this is particularly true for credit derivatives, as was illustrated by AIG's activities in the CDS market. As discussed in Chapter 11, regulators have been paying increased attention to this danger and are continuing to develop new disclosure requirements and regulatory guidelines for how derivatives trading should be done. Of particular concern is the need for financial institutions to disclose their exposure in derivatives contracts, so that regulators can make sure that a large institution is not playing too large a role in these markets and does not have too large an exposure to derivatives relative to its capital, as was the case for AIG. Another concern is that derivatives, particularly credit derivatives, need to have a better clearing mechanism so that the failure of one institution does not bring down many others whose net derivatives positions are small, even though they have many offsetting positions. Better clearing could be achieved either by having these derivatives traded in an organized exchange like a futures market or by having one clearing organization net out trades. Regulators such as the Federal Reserve Bank of New York have been active in making proposals along these lines.

The credit risk exposure posed by interest-rate derivatives, by contrast, seems to be manageable with standard methods of dealing with credit risk, both by managers of financial institutions and by the institutions' regulators.

New regulations for derivatives markets are sure to come in the wake of the global financial crisis. The industry has also had a wake-up call as to where the dangers in derivatives products might lie. Now, the hope is that any time bomb arising from derivatives can be defused with appropriate effort on the part of markets and regulators. ◆

Summary

1. Interest-rate forward contracts, which are agreements to sell a debt instrument at a future (forward) point in time, can be used to hedge interest-rate risk. The advantage of forward contracts is that they are flexible, but the disadvantages are that they are subject to default risk and their market is illiquid.
2. A financial futures contract is similar to an interest-rate forward contract, in that it specifies that a debt instrument must be delivered by one party to another on a stated future date. However, it has advantages over a forward contract in that it is not subject to default risk and is more liquid. Forward and futures contracts can be used by financial institutions to hedge (protect) against interest-rate risk.

3. An option contract gives the purchaser the right to buy (call option) or sell (put option) a security at the exercise (strike) price within a specific period of time. The profit function for options is nonlinear—profits do not always grow by the same amount for a given change in the price of the underlying financial instrument. The nonlinear profit function for options explains why their value (as reflected by the premium paid for them) is negatively related to the exercise price for call options; positively related to the exercise price for put options; positively related to the term to expiration for both call and put options; and positively related to the volatility of the prices of the underlying financial instrument for both call and put options. Financial institutions use futures options to hedge interest-rate risk in a similar fashion to the way they use financial futures and forward contracts. Futures options may be preferred for macro hedges because they suffer from fewer accounting problems than financial futures.
4. Interest-rate swaps involve the exchange of one set of interest payments for another set of interest payments and have default risk and liquidity problems similar to those of forward contracts. As a result, interest-rate swaps often involve intermediaries such as large commercial banks and investment banks that make a market in swaps. Financial institutions find that interest-rate swaps are useful ways to hedge interest-rate risk. Interest-rate swaps have one big advantage over financial futures and options: They can be written for very long horizons.
5. Credit derivatives are a new type of derivative that offer payoffs on previously issued securities that have credit risk. These derivatives—credit options, credit swaps, and credit-linked notes—can be used to hedge credit risk.
6. There are two major concerns about the dangers of derivatives: They allow financial institutions to more easily increase their leverage and take big bets (by effectively enabling them to hold a larger amount of the underlying assets than the amount of money put down), and they expose financial institutions to large credit risks because the huge notional amounts of derivative contracts greatly exceed the capital of these institutions. The second danger seems to be overplayed, but the danger from increased leverage using derivatives is very real, as events in the global financial crisis revealed.

Key Terms

American option, p. 337
arbitrage, p. 330
call option, p. 338
credit default swap, p. 347
credit derivatives, p. 346
credit-linked note, p. 348
credit options, p. 347
credit swap, p. 347
currency swaps, p. 344
European option, p. 337
exercise price (strike price), p. 337
financial derivatives, p. 327
financial futures contract, p. 329
financial futures option (futures option), p. 337
forward contracts, p. 337
hedge, p. 327
interest-rate forward contracts, p. 328
interest-rate swaps, p. 344
long position, p. 327
macro hedge, p. 332
margin requirement, p. 335
marked to market, p. 335
micro hedge, p. 332
notional principal, p. 344
open interest, p. 333
option, p. 337
premium, p. 337
put option, p. 338
short position, p. 327
stock option, p. 337
swaps, p. 343

Questions

All questions are available in MyEconLab at www.myeconlab.com.

1. What are the advantages and disadvantages of using forward contracts to hedge?
2. What advantages do futures contracts have over forward contracts?
3. What is the difference between a micro hedge and a macro hedge?

4. What are the advantages and disadvantages of using an options contract rather than a futures contract?

5. Explain why greater volatility or a longer term to maturity leads to a higher premium on both call and put options.

6. Why does a lower strike price imply that a call option will have a higher premium and a put option a lower premium?

7. What are the advantages and disadvantages of using interest-rate swaps?

8. If the finance company you manage has a gap of +$5 million (rate-sensitive assets greater than rate-sensitive liabilities by $5 million), describe an interest-rate swap that would eliminate the company's income gap.

9. If the savings and loan you manage has a gap of −$42 million, describe an interest-rate swap that would eliminate the S&L's income risk from changes in interest rates.

10. How can financial derivatives create excessive risk in the financial system?

Applied Problems

All applied problems are available in MyEconLab *at* www.myeconlab.com.

11. If the pension fund you manage expects to have an inflow of $120 million six months from now, what forward contract would you seek to enter into to lock in current interest rates?

12. If the portfolio you manage is holding $25 million of 6s of 2030 Treasury bonds with a price of 110, what forward contract would you enter into to hedge the interest-rate risk on these bonds over the coming year?

13. If you buy a $100,000 June Treasury bond contract for 108 and the price of the deliverable Treasury bond at the expiration date is 102, what is your profit or loss on the contract?

14. If, at the expiration date, the deliverable Treasury bond is selling for 101 but the Treasury bond futures contract is selling for 102, what will happen to the futures price? Explain your answer.

15. If your company has a payment of 200 million euros due one year from now, how would you hedge the foreign exchange risk in this payment with 125,000-euro futures contracts?

16. If your company has to make a 10 million euro payment to a German company three months from now, how would you hedge the foreign exchange risk in this payment with a 125,000-euro futures contract?

17. Suppose that your company will be receiving 30 million euros six months from now and the euro is currently selling for 1 euro per dollar. If you want to hedge the foreign exchange risk in this payment, what kind of forward contract would you want to enter into?

18. Suppose that the pension fund you are managing is expecting an inflow of funds of $100 million next year and you want to make sure that you will earn the current interest rate of 8% when you invest the incoming funds in long-term bonds. How would you use the futures market to do this?

19. If you buy a put option on a $100,000 Treasury bond futures contract with an exercise price of 95 and the price of the Treasury bond is 120 at expiration, is the contract in the money, out of the money, or at the money? What is your profit or loss on the contract if the premium was $4,000?

20. Suppose that you buy a call option on a $100,000 Treasury bond futures contract with an exercise price of 110 for a premium of $1,500. If, on expiration, the futures contract has a price of 111, what is your profit or loss on the contract?

21. A hedger takes a short position in five T-bill futures contracts at the price of $98\frac{5}{32}$. Each contract is for $100,000 principal. When the position is closed, the price is $95\frac{12}{32}$. What is the gain or loss on this transaction?

22. Futures are available on three-month T-bills with a contract size of $1 million. If you take a long position at 96.22 and later sell the contracts at 96.87, how much would the total net gain or loss be on this transaction?

23. A bank customer will be going to London in June to purchase £100,000 in new inventory. The current spot and futures exchange rates are as follows:

Exchange Rates (dollars/pound)	
Period	**Rate**
Spot	1.5342
March	1.6212
June	1.6901
September	1.7549
December	1.8416

The customer enters into a position in June futures to fully hedge her position. When June arrives, the actual exchange rate is $1.725 per pound. How much did she save?

24. Consider a put contract on a T-bond with an exercise price of 101 $\frac{12}{32}$. The contract represents $100,000 of bond principal and had a premium of $750. The actual T-bond price falls to 98 $\frac{16}{32}$ at the expiration. What is the gain or loss on the position?

25. A swap agreement calls for Durbin Industries to pay interest annually, based on a rate of 1.5% over the one-year T-bill rate, currently 6%. In return, Durbin receives interest at a rate of 6% on a fixed-rate basis. The notional principal for the swap is $50,000. What is Durbin's net interest for the year after the agreement?

Web Exercises

1. The following site can be used to demonstrate how the features of an option affect the option's prices. Go to www.option-price.com/index.php. What happens to the price of an option under each of the following situations?
   a. The strike price increases.
   b. Interest rates increase.
   c. Volatility increases.
   d. The time until the option matures increases.

Web References

www.cmegroup.com

The website of the CME Group reports information on all the contracts traded on their exchanges.

www.rmahq.org

The website of the Risk Management Association reports useful information such as annual statement studies, online publications, and so on.

15

Conflicts of Interest in the Financial Industry

Preview

Since the end of the stock market boom in 2000, financial markets have been jolted by one corporate scandal after another. The cycle began in December 2001 with the spectacular bankruptcy of Enron Corporation (once valued as the seventh-largest corporation in the United States) and the indictment of Enron's auditor, Arthur Andersen, one of the then-"Big Five" accounting firms. Subsequently, revelations of misleading accounting statements at numerous other corporations, including WorldCom, Tyco Industries, and Fannie Mae, have increased investors' doubts about the quality of information coming from the corporate sector. Criminal cases were filed against all of the top investment banks (Morgan Stanley, J. P. Morgan, Merrill Lynch, Lehman Brothers, and Goldman Sachs, among others), who encouraged their stock analysts to hype dubious stocks, which later proved to be disastrous investments.

These scandals have attracted tremendous public attention for several reasons. First, the resulting bankruptcies cost employees of these firms their jobs, their pensions, or both. Second, these activities were likely to have been an important factor in the massive stock market decline that occurred from March 2000 to September 2002; during this downturn, the value of the S&P 500 index declined by 50% and NASDAQ's value declined by 75%. Third, the scandals have created doubts about the ethics of those working in the financial service industry.

Conflicts of interest, a type of moral hazard problem that occurs when a person or institution has multiple objectives (interests) and as a result has conflicts between them, may be responsible for the recent scandals. Conflicts of interest came to the fore again during the global financial crisis of 2007–2009 by compromising the quality of credit ratings. In each case, people who were supposed to act in the investing public's best interests by providing investors with reliable information had incentives to deceive the public and thereby benefit both themselves and their corporate clients. What are these conflicts of interest, and how serious are they? Where do they occur, and why have they been the source of the recent woes in financial markets? What should, and can, we do about them?

This chapter provides a framework for answering these questions. It first explains what conflicts of interest are, why we should care about them, and why they raise ethical issues. It then surveys the different types of conflicts of interest in the financial industry and discusses policies to remedy them.[1]

[1]For a more detailed treatment of the analysis and research discussed in this chapter, see Andrew Crockett, Trevor Harris, Frederic S. Mishkin, and Eugene N. White, *Conflicts of Interest in the Financial Services Industry: What Should We Do About Them?* Geneva Reports on the World Economy 4 (Geneva and London: International Center for Monetary and Banking Studies and Centre for Economic Policy Research, 2003).

WHAT ARE CONFLICTS OF INTEREST, AND WHY ARE THEY IMPORTANT?

In Chapters 2 and 8, we saw how financial institutions play a key role in the financial system. Specifically, their expertise in interpreting signals and collecting information from their customers gives them a cost advantage in the production of information. Furthermore, because they collect, produce, and distribute this information, financial institutions can use the information over and over again in as many ways as they would like, thereby realizing economies of scale. By providing multiple financial services to their customers, they can also realize **economies of scope**—that is, they can lower the costs of information production for each service by applying one information resource to many different services. An investment bank, for example, can evaluate how good a credit risk a corporation is and so arrange to market the corporation's bonds. In addition, by providing multiple financial services to their customers, financial institutions can develop broader and longer-term relationships with firms. These relationships further reduce the cost of producing information and, therefore, enhance economies of scope.

Although economies of scope may substantially benefit financial institutions, they also create potential costs in the form of conflicts of interest. Although conflicts of interest arise in almost all aspects of our lives, we need to be precise about the conflicts of interest that concern us here. Given the crucial role of information in financial markets, we focus on those conflicts of interest that arise when financial service firms or their employees serve one interest at the expense of another, that is, their own interest rather than their customers', or the interest of a firm that wants to sell securities rather than the interest of investors who want to purchase the securities. As a result, the firms or their employees might misuse information, provide false information, or conceal information.

Conflicts of interest may occur within financial institutions that provide a specialized service, but they are most problematic when an institution provides multiple financial services to a given client or to many clients. The competing interests of these services may lead employees or a department of a financial institution to conceal information or disseminate misleading information to financial markets. Combinations of services that bring together any group of depository intermediaries, nondepository intermediaries, and brokers, or that allow any of these groups to invest directly in a business, are most likely to lead to conflicts of interest.

Why Do We Care About Conflicts of Interest?

Conflicts of interest can substantially reduce the quality of information in financial markets, thereby increasing asymmetric information problems. In turn, asymmetric information prevents financial markets from channeling funds into the most productive investment opportunities and causes financial markets and the economy to become less efficient.

ETHICS AND CONFLICTS OF INTEREST

Conflicts of interest raise ethical dilemmas for those engaged in the financial service business by generating incentives for financial service firms or their employees to conceal or provide misleading information, thereby hurting the customers for whom they work. The growing economies of scope in the financial industry that have led financial institutions to offer more services under one roof have increased conflicts of interest and, not surprisingly, led to more unethical behavior. One way to limit unethical behavior is to make those working in the financial industry aware of the ethical issues that arise when they exploit conflicts of interest; with this awareness, employees are less likely to engage in unethical behavior. To address this need to limit unethical behavior, business schools are now bringing the discussion of ethics into the classroom and firms are establishing policies (discussed later in this chapter) that make it harder for individuals to exploit conflicts of interest.

TYPES OF CONFLICTS OF INTEREST

Four areas of financial service activities harbor the greatest potential for generating conflicts of interest that ultimately reduce the amount of information available in financial markets:

- Underwriting and research in investment banking
- Auditing and consulting in accounting firms
- Credit assessment and consulting in credit-rating agencies
- Universal banking

Underwriting and Research in Investment Banking

Investment banks perform two tasks: They *research* corporations issuing securities, and they *underwrite* these securities by selling them to the public on behalf of the issuing corporation. Investment banks often combine research and underwriting because the information synergies created may lead to economies of scope. In other words, information that is produced for one task is also useful for another task. A conflict of interest arises between research and underwriting because the investment bank attempts to serve the needs of two client groups—the firms for which it is issuing the securities and the investors to whom it sells these securities.

These client groups have different information needs: Issuers benefit from optimistic research, whereas investors desire unbiased research. Due to economies of scope, however, both groups will receive the same information. When the potential revenues from underwriting greatly exceed brokerage commissions, the investment bank has a strong incentive to alter the information provided to both types of clients so as to favor the issuing firms' needs. If the information provided is not favorable to the issuing firm, it might take its business to a competitor that is willing to put out more positive information and thereby entice more people to buy the newly issued stock. For example, an internal Morgan Stanley memo excerpted in the *Wall Street Journal* on July 14, 1992, stated: "Our objective . . . is to adopt a policy, fully understood by the entire firm, including the Research Department, that we do not make negative or controversial comments about our clients as a matter of sound business practice."

Because of directives like this one, analysts in investment banks might be persuaded to distort their research to please the underwriting department of their bank and the corporations issuing the securities, and indeed this seems to have happened during the tech boom of the 1990s. Of course, such actions undermine the reliability of the information that investors use to make their financial decisions and, as a result, diminish the efficiency of securities markets.

Another practice that exploits conflicts of interest is **spinning**. Spinning occurs when investment banks allocate hot, but underpriced, **initial public offerings (IPOs)**, shares of newly issued stock, to executives of other companies that may potentially have business with the investment bank (see the FYI box, "Frank Quattrone and Spinning"). Because hot IPOs typically rise immediately in price after they are first purchased by

FYI Frank Quattrone and Spinning

Frank Quattrone of Credit Suisse First Boston was a highly regarded investment banker specializing in technology companies. But his reputation took a big hit in March 2003, when the National Association of Securities Dealers (NASD) filed a complaint against him for improperly pressuring his analysts to provide favorable coverage in an effort to solicit customers for his firm. Allegedly, Quattrone linked his analysts' bonuses to their investment banking work and permitted executives of companies whose stock he handled to make changes in his staff's draft research reports.

NASD also accused Quattrone of spinning because he maintained more than 300 "Friends of Frank" accounts for executives of technology companies that were active or prospective clients of the bank. These "friends" were allocated hot shares at his discretion. Spinning was not isolated to Quattrone's firm; it was actually quite common on Wall Street. Salomon Smith Barney also allocated hard-to-get IPO shares to a number of executives, including Bernard Ebbers of WorldCom, Philip Anshutz and Joe Nacchio of Qwest, Stephen Garfalo of Metromedia, and Clark McLeod of McLeodUSA. The bank claimed that it issued shares to these executives because they were among the firm's best individual customers and not because it wanted to persuade these executives to channel their companies' investment banking business to Salomon Smith Barney. This claim was deemed dubious, at best. Quattrone was convicted in 2004 (the conviction was later overturned) of obstructing the investigation into his activities and was sentenced to eighteen months in prison.

investors, spinning is a form of kickback to other firms' executives, luring them to use that investment bank. When the executive's company plans to issue its own securities, he or she will be more likely to use as an underwriter the investment bank that gave the executive the hot IPO shares, which is not necessarily the investment bank that could get the highest price for the firm's securities. This action may raise the cost of capital for the firm, and therefore hinder the efficiency of the capital market.

Auditing and Consulting in Accounting Firms

Traditionally, an auditor reduces the information asymmetry between a firm's managers and its shareholders by checking the firm's books and monitoring the quality of the information the firm produces. Auditors play an important role in financial markets because they can reduce the inevitable information asymmetry between the firm's managers and its shareholders.

Threats to truthful reporting in an audit arise from several potential conflicts of interest. The conflict of interest that has received the most attention in the media occurs when an accounting firm provides its client with auditing services and nonaudit consulting services—commonly known as **management advisory services**—such as advice on taxes, accounting or management information systems, and business strategies. Accounting firms that provide multiple services enjoy economies of scale and scope, but have two potential sources of conflicts of interest. First, clients may pressure auditors into skewing their judgments and opinions by threatening to take their accounting and management services business to another accounting firm. Second, if auditors are analyzing information systems or examining tax and financial advice put in place by their nonaudit counterparts within the accounting firm, they may be reluctant to criticize the systems or advice. Both types of conflicts may potentially lead to biased audits. With less reliable information available to investors, it becomes more difficult for financial markets to allocate capital efficiently.

FYI The Collapse of Arthur Andersen

In 1913, Arthur Andersen, a young accountant who had denounced the slipshod and deceptive practices that enabled companies to fool the investing public, founded his own firm. Until the early 1980s, auditing was the most important source of profits for this firm. By the late 1980s, however, the consulting part of the business began to experience high revenue growth with high profit margins, even as the audit profits slumped in a more competitive market. Consulting partners began to assume more power within the firm, and the resulting internal conflicts split the firm in two. Arthur Andersen (the auditing service) and Andersen Consulting were established as separate companies in 2000.

During the period of increasing conflict before the split, Andersen's audit partners had faced growing pressure to focus on boosting revenue and profits from audit services. Many of Arthur Andersen's clients that later went bust—Enron, WorldCom, Qwest, and Global Crossing—were also the largest clients in Arthur Andersen's regional offices. The combination of intense pressure to generate revenue and profits from auditing and the fact that some clients dominated the business of regional offices translated into tremendous incentives for regional office managers to provide favorable audit stances for these large clients. The loss of a client such as Enron or WorldCom would have been devastating for a regional office and its partners, even if that client contributed only a small fraction of the overall revenue and profits for Arthur Andersen as a whole.

The Houston office of Arthur Andersen, for example, ignored many problems in Enron's reporting. Arthur Andersen was indicted in March 2002 and then convicted in June 2002 for obstruction of justice for impeding the SEC's investigation of the Enron collapse (the conviction was overturned by the Supreme Court in May 2005). Its conviction—the first ever against a major accounting firm—barred Arthur Andersen from conducting audits of publicly traded firms and so effectively put it out of business.

A third type of conflict of interest arises when an auditor provides an overly favorable audit in an effort to solicit or retain audit business. The unfortunate collapse of Arthur Andersen—once one of the five largest accounting firms in the United States—suggests that this may be the most dangerous conflict of interest (see the FYI box, "The Collapse of Arthur Andersen").

Credit Assessment and Consulting in Credit-Rating Agencies

Investors use credit ratings (e.g., Aaa or Baa) that reflect the probability of default to determine the creditworthiness of particular debt securities. As a consequence, credit ratings provide critical information that is needed to enable credit markets to operate efficiently. Conflicts of interest can arise when multiple users with divergent interests (at least in the short term) depend on the credit ratings. Investors and regulators are seeking a well-researched, impartial assessment of credit quality; the issuer needs a favorable rating. In the credit-rating industry, the issuers of securities pay a rating firm such as Standard and Poor's or Moody's to have their securities rated (see the FYI box, "Why Do Issuers of Securities Pay to Have Their Securities Rated?"). Because the issuers are the parties paying the credit-rating agency, investors and regulators worry that the agency may bias its ratings upward to attract more business from the issuer.

Other conflicts of interest may arise when credit-rating agencies also provide ancillary consulting services. Debt issuers often ask rating agencies to advise them on how to structure their debt issues, usually with the goal of securing a favorable rating. In this

FYI Why Do Issuers of Securities Pay to Have Their Securities Rated?

Prior to the 1970s, credit-rating agencies earned revenues by having subscribers pay to receive information about securities ratings. In the early 1970s, however, the major rating agencies switched to having issuers of securities pay for their ratings. Why would they do this, given that it appears to set up an obvious conflict of interest? The answer is provided by the asymmetric information framework, which was discussed in Chapter 8. By the early 1970s, technological changes, such as the advent of cheap photocopying, made it easier to disseminate information. Market participants were able to readily get information on securities ratings without paying for it. The free-rider problem became more widespread. As a result, the credit-rating agencies were no longer able to earn enough revenues by selling ratings information. The solution was to have the issuers of securities pay for the ratings, and this is the business model that we see currently.

situation, the credit-rating agencies would be auditing their own work and would experience a conflict of interest similar to the one found in accounting firms that provide both auditing and consulting services. Furthermore, credit-rating agencies may deliver favorable ratings to garner new clients for the ancillary consulting business. The possible decline in the quality of credit assessments issued by rating agencies could increase asymmetric information in financial markets, thereby diminishing their ability to allocate credit. As we discussed in Chapter 9, such conflicts of interest were an important factor that helped trigger the global financial crisis of 2007–2009.

Universal Banking

Commercial banks, investment banks, and insurance companies were originally created as distinct financial institutions that offered separate and distinct services. These institutions soon recognized, however, that combining these activities and services would provide economies of scope. In 1933, the Glass-Steagall Act halted the development of universal banking in the United States by banning the consolidation of these services under one organization. When the Glass-Steagall Act was repealed by Congress in 1999, universal banking reappeared. Given that the divisions within universal banks serve multiple clients, many potential conflicts of interest exist. If the potential for revenues in one department increases, employees in that department will have an incentive to distort information (or to pressure employees in another department to distort information) to the advantage of their clients and the profit of their department.

Several types of conflicts of interest can arise in universal banks:

- Securities issuers served by the underwriting department (and the underwriting department itself) will benefit from aggressive sales of the securities issue to customers of the bank, whereas the customers expect unbiased investment advice.
- A bank manager may push the issuing firm's securities to the disadvantage of the customer or may limit losses from a poor IPO by selling the firm's securities to the bank's managed trust accounts.
- A bank with an outstanding loan to a firm whose credit or bankruptcy risk has increased has private knowledge that may encourage the bank to use its underwriting department to sell bonds to the unsuspecting public, thereby paying off the loan and earning a fee.

FYI Banksters

Just as in the aftermath of the collapse of the tech bubble in 2000, the stock market crash of 1929 prompted many investors to question why they had been encouraged to purchase so many securities that declined in value so quickly. The public blamed the universal banks for hyping securities, and bankers were pejoratively referred to as "banksters" to equate them with gangsters. Public pressure led the Senate Banking and Currency Committee to hold hearings to investigate potential abuses by the universal banks. These hearings, which became known as the Pecora hearings after the chief counsel who led them, were as famous in their day as the Watergate hearings that led to President Nixon's resignation in 1974 or the hearings of the 9/11 Commission in 2004.

The Pecora hearings turned up several cases of apparently severe abuses of conflicts of interest in the banking industry. An affiliate of National City Bank (the precursor to Citibank) was accused of selling "unsound and speculative securities" to the bank's customers, particularly bonds from the Republic of Peru that went into default. Chase National Bank and National City Bank were accused of converting bad loans to companies such as General Theaters and Equipment and the General Sugar Company into securities that were sold to the public and investment trusts managed by these banks. The president of National City Bank, Charles E. Mitchell, and the head of Chase National Bank, Albert H. Wiggin, were accused of setting up *pool operations*, in which resources from the banks were used to prop up the bank's stock price for the benefit of these executives and their associates.

The resulting scandals led to passage of the Glass-Steagall Act in 1933, which eliminated the possibility of these conflicts of interest by mandating complete separation of commercial banking from investment banking activities. It was not until 1999 that this act was repealed by Congress to enable banks to be more competitive.

- A bank may make loans to a firm on overly favorable terms to obtain fees from it for performing activities such as underwriting the firm's securities.
- To sell its insurance products, a bank may try to influence or coerce a borrowing or investing customer.

All of these conflicts of interest may decrease the amount of accurate information production by the universal bank, thereby hindering its ability to promote efficient credit allocation. Although there have not been any recent banking scandals involving conflicts of interest, they did surface in the aftermath of the stock market crash of 1929 (see the FYI box, "Banksters").

CAN THE MARKET LIMIT EXPLOITATION OF CONFLICTS OF INTEREST?

Conflicts of interest become a problem for the financial system when they lead to a decrease in the flow of reliable information, either because information is concealed or because misleading information is disseminated. The decline in the flow of reliable information makes it harder for the financial system to solve adverse selection and moral hazard problems, which can slow the flow of credit to parties with productive investment opportunities.

Even though conflicts of interest exist, they do not necessarily reduce the flow of reliable information because the incentives to exploit the conflict of interest may not be very high. When an exploitation of a conflict of interest is visible to the market, it can punish a financial services firm by denying it business. Given the importance of maintaining and enhancing a financial firm's reputation, exploiting any conflicts of interest would decrease the firm's future profitability because it would have greater difficulty selling its services. In this way, the firm has incentives *not* to exploit a conflict of interest. These incentives limit conflicts of interest in the long run, but they may not be effective in the short run, depending on structural factors within the firm, such as a lack of transparency and inappropriate monetary incentives.

One enlightening example of how the market can limit exploitation of conflicts of interest occurs in credit-rating agencies. At first glance, the fact that rating agencies are paid by the firms issuing securities to produce ratings for these securities looks like a serious conflict of interest. Rating agencies would seem to have powerful incentives to gain business by providing security-issuing firms with higher credit ratings than they deserve, making it easier for the firms to sell their securities at higher prices. In reality, little evidence suggests that rating agencies take advantage of this conflict of interest, despite prominent examples such as Enron. Much research has shown that a reasonably close correlation exists between ratings and default probabilities. Ratings agencies do not exploit the conflict of interest because giving higher credit ratings to firms that pay for the ratings would lower the credibility of the ratings, making them less valuable to the market. The market is able to assess the quality of biased ratings because it can observe poorer performance by individual securities. Furthermore, credit-rating agencies themselves provide evidence on the relationship between their ratings and subsequent default history. If a rating agency continually gave high ratings to firms that eventually defaulted, investors in the market would no longer trust its ratings, its reputation would become tarnished, and good, nondefaulting firms would go elsewhere for their ratings. For this reason, the rating agency has an incentive not to exploit this conflict of interest and overrate the bonds of its customers.

Commercial banks that underwrote securities prior to the enactment of the Glass-Steagall Act do not appear to have exploited this conflict of interest. When a commercial bank underwrites securities, the bank may have an incentive to market the securities of financially troubled firms to the public because the firms will then be able to pay back the loans they owe to the bank, while at the same time the bank earns fees from the underwriting services. The evidence suggests that in the 1920s, markets found securities underwritten by bond departments within a commercial bank to be less attractive than securities underwritten in separate affiliates where the conflict of interest was more transparent. To maintain the bank's reputation, commercial banks shifted their underwriting to separate affiliates over time, with the result that securities underwritten by banks became valued as highly as those underwritten by independent investment banks. When affiliates were unable to certify the absence of conflicts, they focused on underwriting securities from well-known firms, for which less of an information asymmetry existed and conflicts of interest were less pronounced. Again, the market provided incentives to control potential conflicts of interest. However, it is important to note that the market solution was not immediate, but took some time to develop.

The responsiveness of the market is also evident in the apparent conflict of interest present in investment banks when underwriters who have incentives to favor issuers over investors pressure research analysts to provide more favorable assessments of issuers' securities. Analysts at an investment bank that is underwriting particular IPOs tend to make more "buy" recommendations for these IPOs than do analysts at other investment banks, and the market takes account of this tendency in pricing these securities. Over a two-year period, the performance of other analysts' recommended securities was

50% better than the performance of securities recommended by analysts at the investment banks that underwrote these IPOs. The market appears to recognize the difference in the quality of information when the potential for a conflict of interest exists.

Fewer empirical studies have examined how the market addresses conflicts of interest that arise in accounting firms, but the limited evidence available does suggest that the market adjusts securities' prices to account for potential conflicts of interest. The evidence indicates that clients, who are concerned about the conflicts of interest that arise from the joint provision of auditing and management advisory services, ascribe less value to audit opinions and limit their nonaudit purchases from the accounting firms that have these conflicts of interest.

Although the market can sometimes ameliorate the effects of conflicts of interest in financial services firms, it cannot always constrain the incentives to exploit conflicts of interest. For the market to prevent this type of exploitation, it needs to have enough information to assess whether an exploitation of conflicts of interest is actually occurring. In some cases, parties who want to take advantage of conflicts of interest will try to hide this information from the market. In other cases, alerting the market to potential conflicts of interest would reveal proprietary information that would help a financial firm's competitors, thus reducing the firm's incentives to reveal its true position.

The recent scandals described in this chapter demonstrate that the exploitation of a conflict of interest often leads to large gains for some members of the financial firm even while it reduces the value of the firm as a whole. Inappropriately designed compensation plans (the result of poor management), for example, may produce conflicts of interest that not only reduce the flow of reliable information to credit markets but also end up destroying the firm. Indeed, the collapse of Arthur Andersen illustrates how the compensation arrangements for one line of business, such as auditing, can create serious conflicts of interest. In the Arthur Andersen case, the partners in regional offices had incentives to please their largest clients even if their actions were detrimental to the firm as a whole. The conflict of interest problem can become even more hazardous when several lines of business are combined and the returns from one of the activities—such as underwriting or consulting—are very high for only a brief amount of time. Also, a compensation scheme that works reasonably well in the short term might become poorly aligned over time.

The extraordinary surge in the stock market created huge temporary rewards, making it possible for well-positioned analysts, underwriters, and audit firm partners to exploit the conflicts before incentives could be realigned. Often, these conflicts of interest were not readily visible to the market, and they may have been invisible even to the top management of a firm. In the most severe cases, opportunistic individuals were able to capture the firm's **reputational rents**, profits that the firm earns because it is trusted by the marketplace. The exploitation of conflicts of interest clearly damaged the reputation of such investment banks as Merrill Lynch, Salomon Smith Barney of Citigroup, and Credit Suisse First Boston—and perhaps the credibility of analysts in general. Audit firms have lost much of their nonaudit business, while Arthur Andersen was destroyed.

WHAT HAS BEEN DONE TO REMEDY CONFLICTS OF INTEREST?

Three major policy initiatives have been implemented to deal with conflicts of interest in financial markets: the Sarbanes-Oxley Act of 2002, the Global Legal Settlement of 2002, and the Dodd-Frank "Wall Street Reform and Consumer Protection Act" of 2010.

Sarbanes-Oxley Act of 2002

In 2002, the public outcry over corporate and accounting scandals led to the passage of the Public Accounting Reform and Investor Protection Act, more commonly referred to as the Sarbanes-Oxley Act after its two principal authors in Congress. This act had four major components.

1. The act increased supervisory oversight to monitor and prevent conflicts of interest:
   - It established a Public Company Accounting Oversight Board (PCAOB), overseen by the SEC, to supervise accounting firms and ensure that audits are independent and controlled for quality.
   - It increased the SEC's budget to supervise securities markets.
2. Sarbanes-Oxley also directly reduced conflicts of interest:
   - The act made it unlawful for a registered public accounting firm to provide any nonaudit service to a client contemporaneously with an impermissible audit (as determined by the PCAOB).
3. Sarbanes-Oxley provided incentives for investment banks not to exploit conflicts of interests:
   - It beefed up criminal charges for white-collar crime and obstruction of official investigations.
4. Sarbanes-Oxley also had measures to improve the quality of information in the financial markets:
   - It required a corporation's chief executive officer (CEO) and chief financial officer (CFO), as well as its auditors, to certify that periodic financial statements and disclosures of the firm (especially regarding off-balance-sheet transactions) are accurate (Section 404).
   - It required members of the audit committee (the subcommittee of the board of directors that oversees the company's audit) to be "independent"—that is, they cannot be managers in the company or receive any consulting or advisory fee from the company.

Global Legal Settlement of 2002

The second policy arose out of a lawsuit brought by New York Attorney General Eliott Spitzer against the ten largest investment banks (Bear Stearns, Credit Suisse First Boston, Deutsche Bank, Goldman Sachs, J. P. Morgan, Lehman Brothers, Merrill Lynch, Morgan Stanley, Salomon Smith Barney, and UBS Warburg). Spitzer alleged that these firms allowed their investment banking departments to have inappropriate influence over their research analysts, thereby creating a conflict of interest. On December 20, 2002, the SEC, the New York Attorney General, NASD, NASAA, NYSE, and state regulators reached a global agreement with these investment banks. The agreement included three key elements:

1. Like Sarbanes-Oxley, the Global Legal Settlement directly reduced conflicts of interest:
   - It required investment banks to sever the links between research and securities underwriting.
   - It banned spinning.

2. The Global Legal Settlement provided incentives for investment banks not to exploit conflicts of interest:
    - It imposed $1.4 billion of fines on the accused investment banks.
3. The Global Legal Settlement had measures to improve the quality of information in financial markets:
    - It required investment banks to make public their analysts' recommendations.
    - It required investment banks, for a five-year period, to contract with no fewer than three independent research firms that would provide research to their brokerage customers.

Dodd-Frank Bill of 2010

Conflicts of interest played a prominent role in the global financial crisis, particularly in credit-rating agencies, with the result that the Dodd-Frank Wall Street Reform and Consumer Protection Act of 2010 included a number of provisions to deal with conflicts of interest in the credit-rating industry.

1. The bill created an Office of Credit Ratings at the SEC with its own staff and the authority to fine credit-rating agencies and to deregister an agency if it produces bad ratings.
2. It forced credit-rating agencies to provide reports to the SEC when their employees go to work for a company that has been rated by them in the past twelve months.
3. It prohibited compliance officers from being involved in producing or selling credit ratings.
4. It required the SEC to prevent issuers of asset-backed securities from choosing the credit-rating agencies that will give them the highest rating and supported earlier initiatives by the SEC to limit conflicts of interest.
5. It authorized investors to bring lawsuits against credit-rating agencies for a reckless failure to get the facts when providing a credit rating.

A FRAMEWORK FOR EVALUATING POLICIES TO REMEDY CONFLICTS OF INTEREST

The information view of conflicts of interest developed in this chapter provides a framework for evaluating whether conflicts of interest require public policy actions to eliminate or reduce them. Some combination of financial services activities may result in incentives for agents to conceal information, but they may also result in synergies that make it easier to produce information. Thus, preventing the combination of activities to eliminate the conflicts of interest may actually make financial markets less efficient. This reasoning suggests that two propositions are critical to evaluating what should be done about conflicts of interest:

1. *The existence of a conflict of interest does not mean that it will have serious adverse consequences*. Even though a conflict of interest exists, the incentives to exploit the conflict of interest may not be very high. An exploitation of a conflict of interest that is visible to the market will typically tarnish the reputation of the financial firm where it takes place. Given the importance of maintaining and enhancing its reputation, exploiting the conflict of interest would decrease the firm's future profitability because the firm would

have greater difficulty selling its services. As a consequence, firms try to structure their salary and reward systems to include incentives to avoid the exploitation of the conflict of interest. Hence, the marketplace may be able to control conflicts of interest because a high value is placed on financial firms' reputations. When evaluating the need for remedies, this proposition raises the issue of whether the market has adequate information and incentives to control conflicts of interest.

2. *Even if incentives to exploit conflicts of interest remain strong, eliminating the economies of scope that create the conflicts of interest may be harmful because it will reduce the flow of reliable information.* Thus, in evaluating possible remedies, we need to examine whether imposing the remedy will do more harm than good by curtailing the flow of reliable information in financial markets.

Approaches to Remedying Conflicts of Interest

In thinking about remedies for specific problematic situations, it is worthwhile to discuss five generic approaches to reconciling conflicts of interest. These approaches are discussed in the order of their intrusiveness, from least intrusive to most intrusive.

Leave It to the Market This approach has a powerful appeal to many economists and may be a sufficient response in many cases. Market forces can work through two mechanisms. First, they can penalize the financial services firm if it exploits a conflict of interest. For example, a penalty may be imposed by the market in the form of higher funding costs or lower demand for the firm's services, in varying degrees, even to the point of forcing the demise of the firm. Second, market forces can promote new institutional means to contain conflicts of interest. For example, they can generate a demand for information from nonconflicted organizations. This is exactly what happened in the United States in the 1920s, when security affiliates took preeminence over in-house bond departments in universal banks.

One advantage of market-driven solutions is that they can hit where it hurts the most, through pecuniary penalties. Moreover, they may help avoid the risk of overreaction. It can be hard to resist the temptation to adopt nonmarket solutions to appease a public outcry that may reduce information production in financial markets. Conversely, market-based solutions may not always work if the market cannot obtain sufficient information to appropriately punish financial firms that are exploiting conflicts of interest. Memories may be short in financial markets, as is suggested by the new field of behavioral finance discussed in Chapter 7. Once a triggering event has faded from memory, conflicts may creep back in unless reforms have been "hard-wired" into the system.

Regulate for Transparency A competitive market structure does not always adequately reduce information asymmetries. The gathering of information is costly, and any individual economic agent will gather information only if the private benefit outweighs the cost. When the information collected becomes available to the market immediately, the free-rider problem may reach serious levels. Information has the attribute of a public good, which will be undersupplied in the absence of some public intervention. To some extent, mandatory information disclosure can alleviate information asymmetries and is a key element of regulation of the financial system.

When mandatory disclosure of information reveals whether a conflict of interest exists, the market is able to discipline the financial firm that fails to ameliorate conflicts of interest. In addition, if a financial institution is required to provide information about potential conflicts of interest, the user of the institution's information services may be able to judge how much weight to place on the information this institution supplies.

At the same time, mandatory disclosure could create problems if it reveals so much proprietary information that the financial institution is unable to profitably engage in the information production business. The result could then be less information production, rather than more. Also, mandatory disclosure may not work if financial firms can successfully avoid the regulation and continue to hide relevant information about potential conflicts of interest. The free-rider problem might likewise result in insufficient monitoring of conflicts of interest because the benefits of monitoring and constraining these conflicts accrue only partially to the monitors. Finally, complying with regulations requiring information disclosure may be costly for financial firms—possibly exceeding the costs due to conflicts of interest.

Supervisory Oversight If mandatory disclosure does not work because firms continue to hide relevant information, because the free-rider problem is severe, or because mandatory disclosure would reveal proprietary information, supervisory oversight can come to the rescue and contain conflicts of interest. Supervisors can observe proprietary information about conflicts of interest without revealing it to a financial firm's competitors so that the firm can continue to profitably engage in information production activities. Armed with this information, the supervisor can take actions to prevent financial firms from exploiting conflicts of interest. As part of this supervisory oversight, standards of practice can be developed, either by the supervisor or by the firms engaged in a specific information production activity. Enforcement of these standards would then be placed in the hands of the supervisor.

As we saw in Chapter 11, supervisory oversight of this type is very common in the banking industry. In recent years, bank supervisors have sharpened their focus on risk management. They now examine banks' risk management procedures to ensure that the appropriate internal controls on risk taking have been established at the bank. In a similar fashion, supervisors can examine banks' internal procedures and controls to restrict conflicts of interest. When they find weak internal controls, they can require the financial institution to modify them so that incentives to exploit conflicts of interest are eliminated.

Although supervisory oversight has proved successful in improving internal controls in financial firms in recent years, if the incentives to exploit conflicts of interest are sufficiently strong, financial institutions may still be able to hide conflicts of interest from the supervisors. Furthermore, supervisors have not always done their job well, as we saw in Chapter 11.

Separation of Functions Where the market cannot obtain sufficient information to constrain conflicts of interest—because there is no satisfactory way of inducing information disclosure by market discipline or supervisory oversight—the incentives to exploit conflicts of interest may be reduced or eliminated by regulations enforcing separation of functions. Several degrees of separation are possible. First, activities may be separated into different in-house departments with firewalls between them. Second, the firm may restrict different activities to separately capitalized affiliates. Third, regulations may prohibit the combination of activities in any organizational form.

The goal of separation of functions is to ensure that agents are not placed in the position of responding to multiple principals. Moving from relaxed to more stringent separation of functions, conflicts of interest are reduced to an increasing degree. Of course, more stringent separation of functions also reduces synergies of information collection, thereby preventing financial firms from taking advantage of economies of scope in information production. The resulting increased cost of producing information could, in turn, lead to a decreased flow of reliable information because it becomes more expensive to produce it. Deciding on the appropriate amount of separation therefore involves a trade-off between the benefits of reducing conflicts of interest and the cost of reducing economies of scope in producing information.

Socialization of Information Production The most radical response to conflicts generated by the existence of asymmetric information is the socialization of the provision or the funding source of the relevant information. For example, much macroeconomic information is provided by publicly funded agencies, because this particular public good is likely to be undersupplied if left to private provision. It is conceivable that other information-providing functions—for example, credit ratings and auditing—could also be publicly supplied. Alternatively, if the information-generating services are left to the private sector, they could be funded by public sources or by a publicly mandated levy to help ensure that information production is not tainted by obligations to fee-paying entities with special interests.

Of course, the problem with this approach is that a government agency or publicly funded entity may not have the same strong incentives as private financial institutions to produce high-quality information. Forcing information production to be conducted by a government or quasi-government entity—although it may diminish conflicts of interest—may reduce the flow of reliable information to financial markets. Furthermore, government agencies may have difficulty paying the market wages required to attract the best people. This problem may become even more serious if economies of scope are affected. For example, analysts in an investment banking firm are likely to receive additional compensation when their research has multiple uses. By contrast, a government agency that is interested in only one use of research may not provide a level of compensation sufficient to produce high-quality information. In addition, the government might not provide sufficient funds for information collection. Indeed, government provision of important series of macroeconomic data has already been discontinued because of a lack of funding.

APPLICATION ◆ Evaluating Sarbanes-Oxley, the Global Legal Settlement, and the Dodd-Frank Bill

Using the analytic framework discussed above, we now can turn to evaluating the Sarbanes-Oxley Act, the Global Legal Settlement, and the Dodd-Frank bill of 2010.

We have seen that policies regulating conflicts of interest can help to increase the amount of information in financial markets. Sarbanes-Oxley did exactly this when it required that the CEO and the CFO certify the periodic financial statements and disclosures of the firm. It increased the likelihood that these statements will provide reliable information. In addition, Sarbanes-Oxley required disclosure of off-balance-sheet transactions and other relationships with special-purpose entities. Again, this step helped increase information in the marketplace because these off-balance-sheet transactions were often used, as in the Enron case, to hide what was going on inside the firm. However, the costs of complying with the new regulations imposed by Sarbanes-Oxley were not cheap. Small firms were hit particularly hard at the time: The estimated costs of complying with Sarbanes-Oxley exceeded $800,000 for smaller firms with revenues of less than $100 million, which amounted to nearly 1.5% of their sales. Sarbanes-Oxley might have severely hurt such companies' profitability and made it harder for them to make productive investments.

We have also seen that the market is often able to constrain conflicts of interest when it has sufficient information to do so. The Global Legal Settlement included a provision that required investment banking firms to make their analysts' recommendations public. This policy helped the market to assess whether the analysts were acting in good faith. The Dodd-Frank bill requires a credit-rating agency to report on employees who go to work for companies that the agency has previously rated, and it supports the SEC's requirements to increase disclosure by investment analysts, credit-rating agencies, and auditors, forcing them to reveal any interests they have in the firms they analyze. Provision of this information makes it more likely that financial institutions will develop internal rules to ensure that conflicts of interest are minimized, so that their reputations remain high and they remain profitable. Importantly, the Dodd-Frank bill did not prohibit companies issuing securities from paying the credit-rating agencies to rate them, thereby accepting the view that the market could successfully constrain this conflict of interest.

The Dodd-Frank bill also prevents activities that increase conflicts of interest, such as having compliance officers work on ratings or allowing issuers of asset-backed securities to shop for the agency that would produce the highest rating. It also enhances the market's ability to reign in conflicts of interest by authorizing investors to sue credit-rating agencies for reckless failure to produce accurate ratings. However, because this measure makes credit-rating agencies liable for the accuracy of their ratings, it may discourage them from allowing companies to use the agencies' ratings in the documents that accompany new bond issues.

Of course, disclosure may not be enough to get markets to control conflicts of interest, because firms still have incentives to hide information so that they can profitably exploit conflicts of interest. Disclosure may also reveal so much proprietary information that the financial institution is unable to profitably engage in the information production business. In addition, some of the most damaging conflicts of interest have resulted from poorly designed internal compensation mechanisms, which are difficult for markets to observe. Supervisory oversight can focus on exactly these issues.

Increased supervisory oversight was a key feature of the Sarbanes-Oxley Act and the Dodd-Frank bill. First, Sarbanes-Oxley established the PCAOB to supervise accounting firms, while Dodd-Frank created the Office of Credit Ratings at the SEC. The PCAOB monitors compensation mechanisms to verify that they are in accord with the best practices to control conflicts of interest. Second, Sarbanes-Oxley and Dodd-Frank provided substantially more resources for the SEC. A supervisory agency cannot do its job properly without adequate resources. Indeed, one reason why the SEC may have failed to provide adequate supervisory oversight during the boom of the 1990s is that it was starved for resources. A similar problem occurred for the supervisors of the savings and loan industry in the 1980s, and it helped lead to scandals and a bailout that cost taxpayers more than $100 billion. By keeping the audit committee independent of management, Sarbanes-Oxley eliminated the conflict of interest that occurs when the management of a firm hires its auditor. The PCAOB will be instrumental in writing the regulations to ensure that auditors will report to, be hired by, and be compensated by an independent audit committee that is supposed to represent shareholders other than management.

The Global Legal Settlement also directly eliminated one Wall Street practice that led to obvious conflicts of interest—spinning, in which executives received hot IPO shares in return for their companies' future business with the investment bank underwriting the new issue. The Global Legal Settlement punished investment banks that exploited conflicts of interest by imposing a fine of more than $1.4 billion. This tough punishment, along with the harsher criminal penalties established by Sarbanes-Oxley, provided incentives for investment banking firms to avoid taking advantage of conflicts of interest in the future.

The more radical parts of Sarbanes-Oxley and the Global Legal Settlement involved separation of functions and socialization of information. Sarbanes-Oxley made it illegal for accounting firms to provide nonaudit consulting services to their audit customers. This law will potentially reduce the economies of scope available to auditing firms that also offer consulting services. It is unlikely that the proscription of nonauditing services in this situation, as envisioned by Sarbanes-Oxley, would have prevented the recent audit failures. However, greater transparency about the nature and role of nonaudit services would be a valuable aid to control a firm's temptation to exploit this conflict of interest. Similarly, the Global Legal Settlement required investment banking firms to sever the link between research and investment banking. This divestiture also has the potential to eliminate economies of scope in information production. After all, analysts may be able to obtain much more information on firms they cover when the investment banking arm of the firm can share information with them.

The Global Legal Settlement required that for a five-year period, brokerage firms contract with independent research firms to provide information to their customers. In addition, part of the $1.4 billion fine paid by the investment banks was required to be used to fund independent research and investor education. This measure has both potentially positive and potentially negative features. Independent research may produce unbiased information. However, by socializing research, firms can no longer compete for customers on the basis of the quality of their research. Because they are being taxed to fund independent research, firms, might have decreased their investment in their own research analysis. Indeed, this is exactly what appears to have happened, with research budgets at the seven largest securities firms cut almost in half after the settlement. If the investment banks do not control the information they are being forced to acquire, the analysis produced may be of a lower quality. ◆

Summary

1. Conflicts of interest arise when financial services firms or their employees are serving multiple interests and develop incentives to misuse or conceal information needed for the effective functioning of financial markets. If taking advantage of conflicts of interest substantially reduces the amount of reliable information in financial markets, asymmetric information increases and prevents financial markets from channeling funds to those firms with the most productive investment opportunities.
2. Four types of financial services activities have the greatest potential for conflicts of interest that reduce reliable information in financial markets: (1) underwriting and research in investment banking, (2) auditing and consulting in accounting firms, (3) credit assessment and consulting in credit-rating agencies, and (4) universal banking.
3. Even though conflicts of interest may exist, they do not necessarily have to reduce the flow of reliable information, because the market provides strong incentives for financial services firms to avoid damaging their reputations. The evidence suggests that the market often succeeds in constraining the incentives to exploit conflicts of interest. However, conflicts of interest still pose a threat to the efficiency of financial markets.
4. Three recent major policy measures deal with conflicts of interest: the Sarbanes-Oxley Act of 2002, the 2002 Global Legal Settlement arising from the lawsuit by the New York Attorney General against the ten largest investment banks, and provisions in the Dodd-Frank Wall Street Reform and Consumer Protection Act of 2010.

5. Two basic propositions are critical to evaluating what should be done about conflicts of interest: (1) The fact that a conflict of interest exists does not mean that the conflict will necessarily have serious adverse consequences; (2) even if incentives to exploit conflicts of interest remain strong, eliminating the conflict of interest may be harmful if it destroys economies of scope, thereby reducing the flow of reliable information. Five approaches to remedying conflicts of interest, going from least intrusive to most intrusive, have been suggested: (1) leave it to the market, (2) regulate for transparency, (3) provide supervisory oversight, (4) mandate separation of functions, and (5) require socialization of information.
6. Sarbanes-Oxley and the Global Legal Settlement help increase the flow of reliable information in financial markets by requiring the CEO and CFO to certify financial statements, corporations to disclose off-balance-sheet transactions and entities, investment banks to make public their analysts' recommendations, and by requiring increased disclosure of potential conflicts of interest. The Dodd-Frank bill also increases the flow of information by requiring a credit-rating agency to report on employees who go to work for companies that the agency has previously rated and by supporting the SEC's requirements to increase disclosure by investment analysts, credit-rating agencies, and auditors, forcing them to reveal any interests they have in the firms they analyze. Sarbanes-Oxley increases supervisory oversight by establishing the Public Company Accounting Oversight Board (PCAOB) and by increasing the resources available to the SEC. Similarly, the Dodd-Frank bill increases regulatory oversight with the creation of the Office of Credit Ratings at the SEC. Sarbanes-Oxley also reduces conflicts of interest in auditing by making the audit committee independent of management. The Global Legal Settlement eliminated the conflict of interest inherent in spinning. The $1.4 billion fine and harsher criminal penalties imposed by Sarbanes-Oxley provide incentives for investment banks not to exploit conflicts of interest in the future. The more radical parts of Sarbanes-Oxley and the Global Legal Settlement, which involve separation of functions (research from underwriting, and auditing from nonaudit consulting) and socialization of research information, may ultimately reduce the information available in financial markets. The Dodd-Frank bill prevents activities that increase conflicts of interest, such as having compliance officers work on ratings or allowing issuers of asset-backed securities to shop for the agency that would produce the highest rating. It also enhances the market's ability to reign in conflicts of interest by authorizing investors to sue credit-rating agencies for reckless failure to produce accurate ratings.

Key Terms

conflicts of interest, p. 353
initial public offerings (IPOs), p. 355
management advisory services, p. 356
economies of scope, p. 354
reputational rents, p. 369
spinning, p. 355

Questions

All questions are available in MyEconLab *at* www.myeconlab.com.

1. Why can the provision of several types of financial services by one firm lead to a lower cost of information production?
2. How does the provision of several types of financial services by one firm lead to conflicts of interest?
3. How can conflicts of interest make financial markets less efficient?
4. How can conflicts of interest lead to unethical behavior?
5. Describe two conflicts of interest that occur when underwriting and research are provided by a single investment banking firm.
6. How does spinning lead to a less efficient financial market?
7. Describe two conflicts of interest that occur in accounting firms.
8. Some commentators have attributed the demise of Arthur Andersen to the combination of auditing and consulting activities in the firm. Is this assessment correct?

9. Describe two conflicts of interest that occur in credit-rating agencies.
10. Describe two conflicts of interest that occur in universal banks.
11. "Conflicts of interest always reduce the flow of reliable information." Is this statement true, false, or uncertain? Explain your answer.
12. Give two examples of conflicts of interest that do not seem to have been exploited and thus did not lead to a reduction of reliable information in the financial markets.
13. When is it more likely that conflicts of interest will be exploited?
14. How can compensation schemes in financial service firms lead to conflicts of interest?
15. What are "reputational rents" and how are they significant?
16. "Sarbanes-Oxley significantly raises compliance costs for firms. Since it dramatically increases market inefficiency, it should be abolished." Do you agree with this statement? Why or why not?
17. Which provisions of the Sarbanes-Oxley Act do you think are beneficial, and which are not?
18. Which provisions of the Global Legal Settlement do you think are beneficial, and which are not?
19. Why might the market be the best mechanism for minimizing conflicts of interest?
20. What are the advantages and disadvantages of mandatory disclosure in dealing with conflicts of interest?
21. How can supervisory oversight help reduce conflicts of interest?
22. What are the disadvantages of separating financial activities into different firms in an effort to avoid conflicts of interest?
23. What are the advantages and disadvantages of government provision of information as a solution to the problems created by conflicts of interest?
24. Why would having compliance officers work on producing credit ratings present a conflict of interest?
25. In what ways is the Dodd-Frank legislation designed to reduce conflicts of interest?

Web Exercises

1. Go to http://www.soxlaw.com/. This site tracks issues and news related to the Sarbanes-Oxley Act.
   a. Summarize in two or three sentences the primary reason for passage of the Sarbanes-Oxley Act.
   b. Summarize one of the articles discussed under the news/current events section. Address how this article relates to conflicts of interest in the financial markets.
2. Go to www.sec.gov/ and click on Press Releases.
   a. Summarize the major types of issues that the SEC addresses in these press releases.
   b. Review the past three months of releases, and count how many appear to be enforcement actions aimed at firms or individuals who have violated SEC regulations. From this review, does the SEC appear to be active in its effort to prevent fraud and misrepresentation in the securities industry?

Web References

http://dodd-frank.com/

A website devoted to discussion and dissemination of information about the Dodd-Frank Act.

www.moodys.com

Moody's is a major rating agency for company debt. To view the Moody's website and learn more about how it evaluates company credit, you must register.

www.sarbanes-oxley.com/

A website devoted to discussion and dissemination of information about the Sarbanes-Oxley Act.

www.sec.gov/

The SEC is primarily responsible for preventing fraud in the securities markets. Click on What We Do to learn what role the SEC envisions for itself in the securities industry.

Part 4

Central Banking and the Conduct of Monetary Policy

Crisis and Response: The Federal Reserve and the Global Financial Crisis

When the Federal Reserve was confronted with what former Chairman Alan Greenspan described as a "once-in-a-century credit tsunami," it resolved to come to the rescue. Starting in September 2007, the Federal Reserve lowered the federal funds rate target, bringing it down to zero by the end of 2008. At the same time, the Fed implemented large liquidity injections into the credit markets to try to get them lending again. In mid-August 2007, the Fed lowered the discount rate at which it lent to banks to just 50 basis points above the federal funds rate target from the normal 100 basis points. Over the course of the crisis, the Fed broadened its provision of liquidity to the financial system well outside its traditional lending to depository institutions. Indeed, after the Fed made loans to assist in the takeover of Bear Stearns by J.P. Morgan in March 2008, Paul Volcker, a former Chairman of the Federal Reserve, described the Fed's actions as going to the "very edge of its lawful and implied powers." The number of new Fed lending programs over the course of the crisis spawned a whole new set of acronyms—the TAF, TSLF, PDCF, AMLF, CPFF, and MMIFF—making the Fed sound like the Pentagon with code-named initiatives and weapons. Like the Pentagon, the Fed was fighting a war, although its weapons were financial rather than guns, tanks, or aircraft.

The recent global financial crisis has demonstrated the importance of central banks like the Federal Reserve to the health of the financial system and the economy. Chapter 16 outlines what central banks are trying to achieve, what motivates them, and how they are set up. Chapter 17 describes how the money supply is determined. In Chapter 18, we look at the tools that central banks like the Fed have at their disposal and how they use them. Chapter 19 extends the discussion of how monetary policy is conducted to focus on the broader picture of central banks' strategies and tactics.

16 Central Banks and the Federal Reserve System

Preview

Among the most important players in financial markets throughout the world are central banks, the government authorities in charge of monetary policy. Central banks' actions affect interest rates, the amount of credit, and the money supply, all of which have direct impacts not only on financial markets, but also on aggregate output and inflation. To understand the role that central banks play in financial markets and the overall economy, we need to understand how these organizations work. Who controls central banks and determines their actions? What motivates their behavior? Who holds the reins of power?

In this chapter, we look at the institutional structure of major central banks, and focus particularly on the Federal Reserve System, one of the most important central banks in the world. We start by examining the elements of the Fed's institutional structure that determine where the true power within the Federal Reserve System lies. By understanding who makes the decisions, we will have a better idea of how they are made. We then examine what explains central bank behavior and whether it is a good idea to make central banks independent by insulating them from politicians. Finally, we look at the structure and independence of other major central banks, particularly the European Central Bank. With this context in place, we will be prepared to comprehend the actual conduct of monetary policy described in the following chapters.

ORIGINS OF THE FEDERAL RESERVE SYSTEM

Of all the central banks in the world, the Federal Reserve System probably has the most unusual structure. To understand why this structure arose, we must go back to before 1913, when the Federal Reserve System was created.

Before the twentieth century, a major characteristic of American politics was the fear of centralized power, as seen in the checks and balances of the Constitution and the preservation of states' rights. This fear of centralized power was one source of American resistance to the establishment of a central bank. Another source was the traditional American distrust of moneyed interests, the most prominent symbol of which was a central bank. The open hostility of the American public to the existence of a central bank resulted in the demise of the first two experiments in central banking, whose function was to police the banking system: The First Bank of the United States was disbanded in 1811, and the national charter of the Second Bank of the United States expired in 1836 after its renewal was vetoed in 1832 by President Andrew Jackson.

Inside the Fed The Political Genius of the Founders of the Federal Reserve System

The history of the United States has been one of public hostility to banks and especially to a central bank. How were the politicians who founded the Federal Reserve able to design a system that has become one of the most prestigious institutions in the United States?

The answer is that the founders recognized that if power was too concentrated in either Washington, DC, or New York, cities that Americans often love to hate, an American central bank might not have enough public support to operate effectively. They thus decided to set up a decentralized system with twelve Federal Reserve banks spread throughout the country to make sure that all regions of the country were represented in monetary policy deliberations. In addition, they made the Federal Reserve banks quasi-private institutions overseen by directors from the private sector living in each district who represent views from their region and are in close contact with the president of their Federal Reserve bank. The unusual structure of the Federal Reserve System has promoted a concern in the Fed with regional issues, as is evident in Federal Reserve bank publications. Without this unusual structure, the Federal Reserve System might have been far less popular with the public, making the institution far less effective.

The termination of the Second Bank's national charter in 1836 created a severe problem for American financial markets, because there was no lender of last resort that could provide reserves to the banking system to avert a bank panic. Hence, in the nineteenth and early twentieth centuries, nationwide bank panics became a regular event, occurring every twenty years or so, culminating in the panic of 1907. The 1907 panic resulted in such widespread bank failures and such substantial losses to depositors that the public was finally convinced that a central bank was needed to prevent future panics.

The hostility of the American public to banks and centralized authority created great opposition to the establishment of a single central bank like the Bank of England. Fear was rampant that the moneyed interests on Wall Street (including the largest corporations and banks) would be able to manipulate such an institution to gain control over the economy and that federal operation of the central bank might result in too much government intervention in the affairs of private banks. Serious disagreements existed over whether the central bank should be a private bank or a government institution. Because of the heated debates on these issues, a compromise was struck. In the great American tradition, Congress wrote an elaborate system of checks and balances into the Federal Reserve Act of 1913, which created the Federal Reserve System with its twelve regional Federal Reserve banks (see the Inside the Fed box, "The Political Genius of the Founders of the Federal Reserve System").

STRUCTURE OF THE FEDERAL RESERVE SYSTEM

The writers of the Federal Reserve Act wanted to diffuse power along regional lines, between the private sector and the government, and among bankers, business people, and the public. This initial diffusion of power has resulted in the evolution of the Federal Reserve System to include the following entities: the **Federal Reserve banks**, the

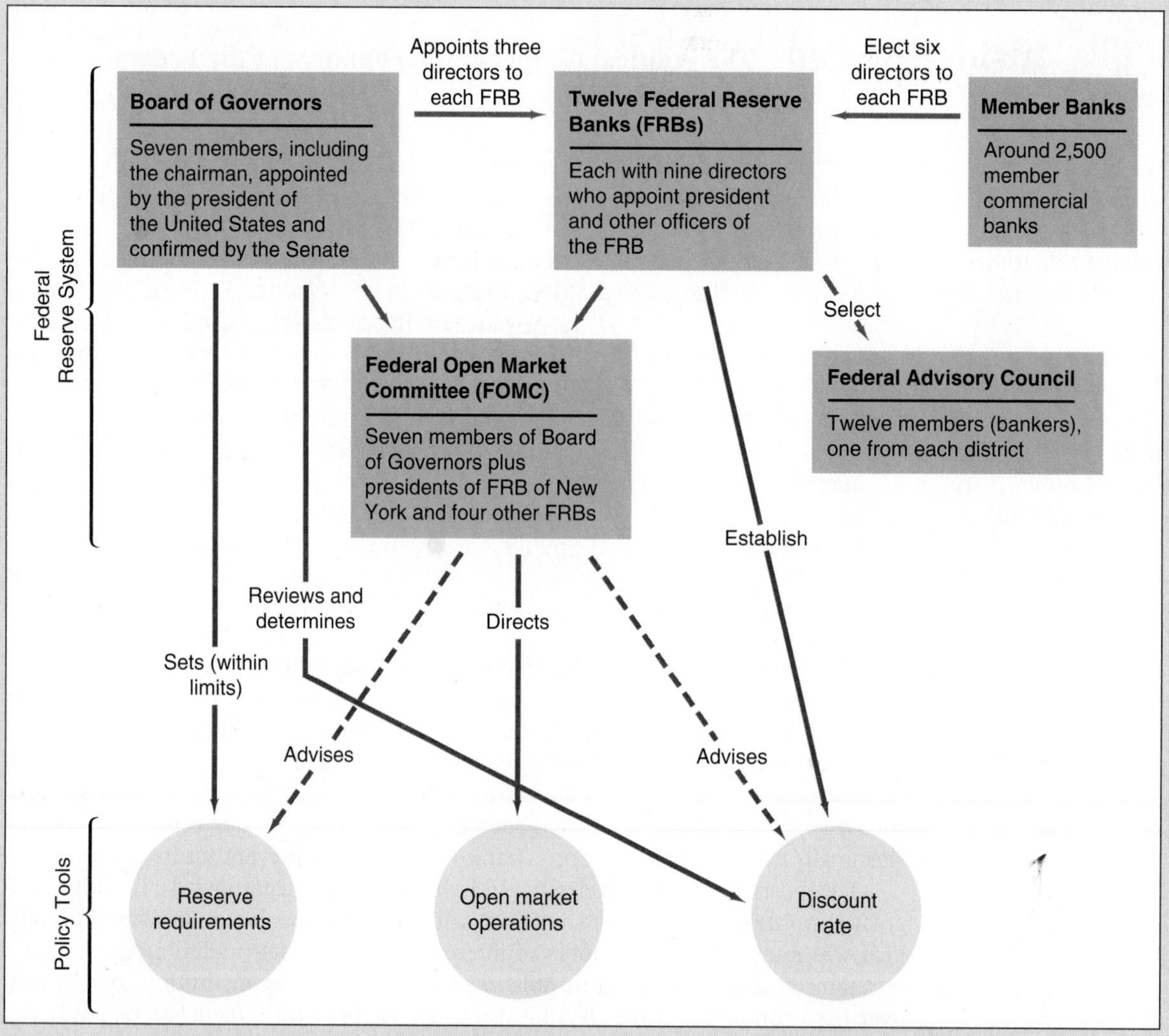

FIGURE 1 Structure and Responsibility for Policy Tools in the Federal Reserve System
The relationships of the Federal Reserve banks, the Board of Governors of the Federal Reserve System, and the FOMC to the three policy tools of the Fed (open market operations, the discount rate, and reserve requirements). Dashed lines indicate that the FOMC "advises" on the setting of reserve requirements and the discount rate.

Board of Governors of the Federal Reserve System, the **Federal Open Market Committee (FOMC)**, the Federal Advisory Council, and around 2,500 member commercial banks. Figure 1 outlines the relationships of these entities to one another and to the three policy tools of the Fed (open market operations, the discount rate, and reserve requirements) discussed in Chapters 17 and 18.

Federal Reserve Banks

Each of the twelve Federal Reserve districts has one main Federal Reserve bank, which may have branches in other cities in the district. The locations of these districts, the Federal

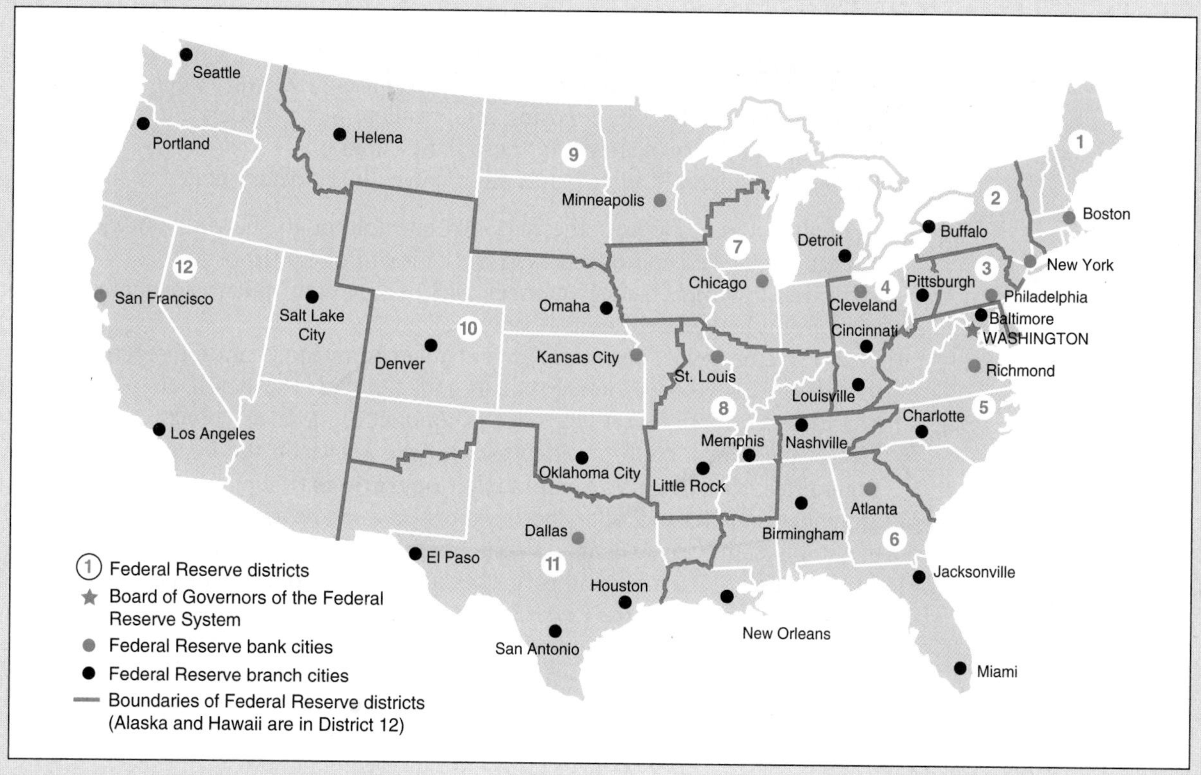

FIGURE 2 Federal Reserve System
The locations of the Federal Reserve districts, the Federal Reserve banks, and their branches.
Source: Federal Reserve *Bulletin.*

Reserve banks, and their branches are shown in Figure 2. The three largest Federal Reserve banks in terms of assets are those of New York, Chicago, and San Francisco—combined they hold more than 50% of the assets (discount loans, securities, and other holdings) of the Federal Reserve System. The New York bank, with around one-quarter of the assets, is the most important of the Federal Reserve banks (see Inside the Fed box, "The Special Role of the Federal Reserve Bank of New York").

Each of the Federal Reserve banks is a quasi-public (part private, part government) institution owned by the private commercial banks in its district that are members of the Federal Reserve System. These member banks have purchased stock in their district Federal Reserve bank (a requirement of membership), and the dividends paid by that stock are limited by law to 6% annually. The member banks elect six directors for each district bank; three more are appointed by the Board of Governors. The directors of a district bank are classified into three categories: A, B, and C. The three A directors (elected by the member banks) are professional bankers, and the three B directors (also elected by the member banks) are prominent leaders from industry, labor, agriculture, or the consumer sector. The three C directors, who are appointed by the Board of Governors to represent the public interest, are not allowed to be officers, employees, or stockholders of banks. The directors oversee the activities of the district bank, but their most important job is to appoint the president of the bank (subject to the approval of the Board of Governors). Up until 2010, all nine directors participated in this decision, but the Dodd-Frank legislation in July 2010 excluded the three class A directors from involvement in choosing the president of the bank. Congress viewed it as inappropriate for bankers to be involved in choosing the president of the Federal Reserve bank that would have supervisory oversight of these same banks.

The twelve Federal Reserve banks are involved in monetary policy in several ways:

- Their directors "establish" the discount rate (although the discount rate in each district is reviewed and determined by the Board of Governors).
- They decide which banks, member and nonmember alike, can obtain discount loans from the Federal Reserve bank.
- Their directors select one commercial banker from each bank's district to serve on the Federal Advisory Council, which consults with the Board of Governors and provides information that helps in the conduct of monetary policy.
- Five of the twelve bank presidents each have a vote on the Federal Open Market Committee, which directs **open market operations** (the purchase and sale of government securities that affect both interest rates and the amount of reserves in the banking system). As explained in the Inside the Fed box, "The Special Role of the Federal Reserve Bank of New York," because the president of the New York Fed is a permanent member of the FOMC, he or she always has a vote on the FOMC, making it the most important of the banks; the other four votes allocated to the district banks rotate annually among the remaining eleven presidents.

The twelve Federal Reserve banks also perform the following functions:

- Clear checks
- Issue new currency and withdraw damaged currency from circulation
- Administer and make discount loans to banks in their districts
- Evaluate proposed mergers and applications for banks to expand their activities
- Act as liaisons between the business community and the Federal Reserve System
- Examine bank holding companies and state-chartered member banks
- Collect data on local business conditions
- Use their staffs of professional economists to research topics related to the conduct of monetary policy

Member Banks

All *national banks* (commercial banks chartered by the Office of the Comptroller of the Currency) are required to be members of the Federal Reserve System. Commercial banks chartered by the states are not required to be members, but they can choose to join. Currently, about a third of the commercial banks in the United States are members of the Federal Reserve System, having declined from a peak figure of 49% in 1947.

Before 1980, only member banks were required to keep reserves as deposits at the Federal Reserve banks. Nonmember banks were subject to reserve requirements determined by their states, which typically allowed them to hold much of their reserves in interest-bearing securities. Because at the time no interest was paid on reserves deposited at the Federal Reserve banks, it was costly to be a member of the system, and as interest rates rose, the relative cost of membership rose, and more and more banks left the system.

This decline in Fed membership was a major concern of the Board of Governors; one reason was that it lessened the Fed's control over the money supply, making it

Inside the Fed The Special Role of the Federal Reserve Bank of New York

The Federal Reserve Bank of New York plays a special role in the Federal Reserve System for several reasons. First, its district contains many of the largest commercial banks in the United States, the safety and soundness of which are paramount to the health of the U.S. financial system. The Federal Reserve Bank of New York conducts examinations of bank holding companies and state-chartered member banks in its district, making it the supervisor of some of the most important financial institutions in our financial system. Not surprisingly, given this responsibility, the bank supervision group is one of the largest units of the New York Fed and is by far the largest bank supervision group in the Federal Reserve System.

The second reason for the New York Fed's special role is its active involvement in the bond and foreign exchange markets. The New York Fed houses the open market desk, which conducts open market operations—the purchase and sale of bonds—that determine the amount of reserves in the banking system. Because of this involvement in the Treasury securities market, as well as its walking-distance location near the New York Stock Exchange, the officials at the Federal Reserve Bank of New York are in constant contact with the major domestic financial markets in the United States. In addition, the Federal Reserve Bank of New York houses the foreign exchange desk, which conducts foreign exchange interventions on behalf of the Federal Reserve System and the U.S. Treasury. Its involvement in these financial markets means that the New York Fed is an important source of information on what is happening in domestic and foreign financial markets, particularly during crisis periods such as the recent subprime meltdown, as well as a liaison between officials in the Federal Reserve System and private participants in the markets.

The third reason for the Federal Reserve Bank of New York's prominence is that it is the only Federal Reserve bank to be a member of the Bank for International Settlements (BIS). Thus the president of the New York Fed, along with the chairman of the Board of Governors, represents the Federal Reserve System in its regular monthly meetings with other major central bankers at the BIS. This close contact with foreign central bankers and interaction with foreign exchange markets means that the New York Fed has a special role in international relations, both with other central bankers and with private market participants. Adding to its prominence in international circles, the New York Fed is the repository for more than $100 billion of the world's gold, an amount greater than the gold at Fort Knox.

Finally, the president of the Federal Reserve Bank of New York is the only permanent voting member of the FOMC among the Federal Reserve bank presidents, serving as the vice-chairman of the committee. Thus he and the chairman and vice-chairman of the Board of Governors are the three most important officials in the Federal Reserve System.

more difficult for the Fed to conduct monetary policy. The chairman of the Board of Governors repeatedly called for new legislation requiring all commercial banks to be members of the Federal Reserve System. One result of the Fed's pressure on Congress was a provision in the Depository Institutions Deregulation and Monetary Control Act of 1980: All depository institutions became subject (by 1987) to the same requirements to keep deposits at the Fed, so member and nonmember banks would be on an equal footing in terms of reserve requirements. In addition, all depository institutions were given access to the Federal Reserve facilities, such as the discount window (discussed in Chapter 18) and Fed check clearing, on an equal basis. These provisions ended the decline in Fed membership and reduced the distinction between member and nonmember banks.

Board of Governors of the Federal Reserve System

At the head of the Federal Reserve System is the seven-member Board of Governors, headquartered in Washington, DC. Each governor is appointed by the president of the United States and confirmed by the Senate. To limit the president's control over the Fed and insulate the Fed from other political pressures, the governors can serve one full nonrenewable fourteen-year term plus part of another term, with one governor's term expiring every other January.[1] The governors (many are professional economists) are required to come from different Federal Reserve districts to prevent the interests of one region of the country from being overrepresented. The chairman of the Board of Governors is chosen from among the seven governors and serves a four-year, renewable term. It is expected that once a new chairman is chosen, the old chairman resigns from the Board of Governors, even if many years are left in his or her term as a governor.

The Board of Governors is actively involved in the conduct of monetary policy in the following ways:

- All seven governors are members of the FOMC and vote on the conduct of open market operations. Because only twelve voting members are on this committee (seven governors and five presidents of the district banks), the Board has the majority of the votes.
- It sets reserve requirements (within limits imposed by legislation).
- It effectively controls the discount rate by the "review and determination" process, whereby it approves or disapproves the discount rate "established" by the Federal Reserve banks.
- The chairman of the Board advises the president of the United States on economic policy, testifies in Congress, and speaks for the Federal Reserve System to the media.

Through legislation, the Board of Governors has often been given duties not directly related to the conduct of monetary policy, which are as follows:

- Sets margin requirements, the fraction of the purchase price of securities that has to be paid for with cash rather than borrowed funds.
- Sets the salary of the president and all officers of each Federal Reserve bank and reviews each bank's budget.
- Approves bank mergers and applications for new activities, specifies the permissible activities of bank holding companies, and supervises the activities of foreign banks in the United States.
- Has a staff of professional economists (larger than those of individual Federal Reserve banks), which provides economic analysis that the Board of Governors uses in making its decisions (see the Inside the Fed box, "The Role of the Research Staff").

Federal Open Market Committee (FOMC)

The FOMC usually meets eight times a year (about every six weeks) and makes decisions regarding the conduct of open market operations and the setting of the policy interest rate, the **federal funds rate**, which is the interest rate on overnight loans from

[1]Although technically the governor's term is nonrenewable, a governor can resign just before the term expires and then be reappointed by the president. This explains how one governor, William McChesney Martin, Jr., served for 28 years. Since Martin, the chairman from 1951 to 1970, retired from the board in 1970, the practice of allowing a governor to in effect serve a second full term has not been done, and this is why Alan Greenspan had to retire from the Board after his fourteen-year term expired in 2006.

Inside the Fed **The Role of the Research Staff**

The Federal Reserve System is the largest employer of economists not just in the United States, but in the world. The system's research staff has approximately 1,000 people, about half of whom are economists. Of these 500 economists, about 250 are at the Board of Governors, 100 are at the Federal Reserve Bank of New York, and the remainder are at the other Federal Reserve banks. What do all these economists do?

The most important task of the Fed's economists is to follow the incoming data from government agencies and private sector organizations on the economy and provide guidance to the policy makers on where the economy may be heading and what the impact of monetary policy actions on the economy might be. Before each FOMC meeting, the research staff at each Federal Reserve bank briefs its president and the senior management of the bank on its forecast for the U.S. economy and the issues that are likely to be discussed at the meeting. The research staff also provides briefing materials or a formal briefing on the economic outlook for the bank's region, something that each president discusses at the FOMC meeting. Meanwhile, at the Board of Governors, economists maintain a large econometric model (a model whose equations are estimated with statistical procedures) that helps them produce their forecasts of the national economy, and they, too, brief the governors on the national economic outlook.

The research staffers at the banks and the board also provide support for the bank supervisory staff, tracking developments in the banking sector and other financial markets and institutions and supplying bank examiners with technical advice they might need in the course of their examinations. Because the Board of Governors has to decide whether to approve bank mergers, the research staffs at both the Board and the bank in whose district the merger is to take place prepare information on what effect the proposed merger might have on the competitive environment. To ensure compliance with the Community Reinvestment Act, economists also analyze a bank's performance in its lending activities in different communities.

Because of the increased influence of developments in foreign countries on the U.S. economy, members of the research staff, particularly those at the New York Fed and the Board, produce reports on the major foreign economies. They also conduct research on developments in the foreign exchange market because of its growing importance in the monetary policy process and to support the activities of the foreign exchange desk. Economists help support the operation of the open market desk by projecting reserve growth and the growth of monetary aggregates.

Staff economists also engage in basic research on the effects of monetary policy on output and inflation, developments in the labor markets, international trade, international capital markets, banking and other financial institutions, financial markets, and the regional economy, among other topics. This research is published widely in academic journals and in Reserve Bank publications. (Federal Reserve bank reviews are a good source of supplemental material for money and banking students.)

Another important activity of the research staff primarily at the Reserve Banks is in the public education area. Staff economists are called on frequently to make presentations to the board of directors at their banks or to make speeches to the public in their district.

one bank to another. (How the FOMC meeting is conducted is discussed in the Inside the Fed box, "The FOMC Meeting," and the documents produced for the meeting are described in the second Inside the Fed box, "Green, Blue, Teal, and Beige: What Do These Colors Mean at the Fed?") Indeed, the FOMC is often referred to as the "Fed" in the press. For example, when the media say that the Fed is meeting, they actually mean that the FOMC is meeting. The committee consists of the seven members of the Board of Governors, the president of the Federal Reserve Bank of New York, and the

Inside the Fed The FOMC Meeting

The FOMC meeting takes place in the boardroom on the second floor of the main building of the Board of Governors in Washington, DC. The seven governors and the twelve Reserve Bank presidents, along with the secretary of the FOMC, the Board's director of the Research and Statistics Division and his or her deputy, and the directors of the Monetary Affairs and International Finance Divisions, sit around a massive conference table. Although only five of the Reserve Bank presidents have voting rights on the FOMC at any given time, all actively participate in the deliberations. Seated around the sides of the room are the directors of research at each of the Reserve Banks and other senior board and Reserve Bank officials, who, by tradition, do not speak at the meeting.

The meeting starts with a quick approval of the minutes of the previous meeting of the FOMC. The first substantive agenda item is the report by the manager of system open market operations on foreign currency and domestic open market operations and other issues related to these topics. After the governors and Reserve Bank presidents finish asking questions and discussing these reports, a vote is taken to ratify them.

The next stage in the meeting is a presentation of the Board staff's national economic forecast by the director of the Research and Statistics Division at the Board. After the governors and Reserve Bank presidents have queried the division director about the forecast, the *go-round* occurs: Each bank president presents an overview of economic conditions in his or her district and the bank's assessment of the national outlook, and each governor, including the chairman, gives a view of the national outlook. By tradition, remarks avoid the topic of monetary policy at this time.

The agenda then turns to current monetary policy and the domestic policy directive. The Board's director of the Monetary Affairs Division leads off the discussion by outlining the different scenarios for monetary policy actions and may describe an issue relating to how monetary policy should be conducted. After a question-and-answer period, each of the FOMC members, as well as the nonvoting bank presidents, expresses his or her views on monetary policy, and on the monetary policy statement. The chairman then summarizes the discussion and proposes specific

presidents of four other Federal Reserve banks. The chairman of the Board of Governors also presides as the chairman of the FOMC. Even though only the presidents of five of the Federal Reserve banks are voting members of the FOMC, the other seven presidents of the district banks attend FOMC meetings and participate in discussions. Hence they have some input into the committee's decisions.

Because open market operations are the most important policy tool the Fed has for controlling the money supply and because it is where decisions about **tightening of monetary policy** (a rise in the federal funds rate) or **easing of monetary policy** (a lowering of the federal funds rate) are made the FOMC is necessarily the focal point for policy making in the Federal Reserve System. Although reserve requirements and the discount rate are not actually set by the FOMC, decisions in regard to these policy tools are effectively made there, and this is why Figure 1 has dashed lines indicating that the FOMC "advises" on the setting of reserve requirements and the discount rate. The FOMC does not actually carry out securities purchases or sales. Instead, it issues directives to the trading desk at the Federal Reserve Bank of New York, where the manager for domestic open market operations supervises a roomful of people who execute the purchases and sales of the government or agency securities. The manager communicates daily with the FOMC members and their staffs concerning the activities of the trading desk.

wording for the monetary policy statement and the directive on the federal funds rate target transmitted to the open market desk, indicating whether the federal funds rate target is to be raised or lowered, say, by 1/4 of a percentage point, or be left unchanged. The secretary of the FOMC formally reads the proposed statement, and the members of the FOMC vote.*

Then there is an informal buffet lunch, and while eating, the participants hear a presentation on the latest developments in Congress on banking legislation and other legislation relevant to the Federal Reserve. At 2:15 p.m. a public announcement is made in regard to the outcome of the meeting: whether the federal funds rate target and discount rate have been raised, lowered, or left unchanged, and an assessment of the "balance of risks" in the future, whether toward higher inflation or toward a weaker economy.†

The postmeeting announcement is an innovation initiated in 1994. Before then, no such announcement was made, and the markets had to guess what policy action was taken. The decision to announce this information was a step in the direction of greater openness by the Fed. A further step in this direction started in April 2011: After the FOMC meetings in April, June, November, and January, the Chairman of the Federal Reserve gives a press conference in which he briefs the press about the FOMC decision.

*The decisions expressed in the directive may not be unanimous, and the dissenting views are made public. However, except in extremely rare cases, the chairman's vote is always on the winning side.

†Half of the meetings have a somewhat different format. Rather than starting Tuesday morning at 9:00 a.m. like the other meetings, they start in the afternoon on Tuesday and go over into Wednesday, with the usual announcement around 2:15 p.m. These longer meetings also consider the longer-term economic outlook and special topics.

Why the Chairman of the Board of Governors Really Runs the Show

At first glance, the chairman of the Board of Governors is just one of twelve voting members of the FOMC and has no legal authority to exercise control over this body. So why does the media pay so much attention to every word the chairman speaks? Does the chairman really call the shots at the Fed? If so, why does the chairman have so much power?

The chairman does indeed run the show. He is the spokesperson for the Fed and negotiates with Congress and the president of the United States. He also exercises control by setting the agenda of Board and FOMC meetings. The chairman also influences

Inside the Fed — Green, Blue, Teal, and Beige: What Do These Colors Mean at the Fed?

Three research documents play an important role in the monetary policy process and at Federal Open Market Committee meetings. Up until 2010, a detailed national forecast for the next three years, generated by the Federal Reserve Board of Governors' Research and Statistics Division, was placed between green covers and was thus known as the "green book." Projections for the monetary aggregates prepared by the Monetary Affairs Division of the Board of Governors, along with typically three alternative scenarios for the stance of monetary policy (labeled A, B, and C), were contained in the "blue book" in blue covers. Both books were distributed to all participants in FOMC meetings. Starting in 2010, the green and blue books were combined into the "teal book" with teal covers: Teal is a combination of green and blue.* The "beige book," with beige covers, is produced by the Reserve Banks and details evidence gleaned either from surveys or from talks with key businesses and financial institutions on the state of the economy in each of the Federal Reserve districts. This is the only one of the three books that is distributed publicly, and it often receives a lot of attention in the press.

*These FOMC documents are made public after five years, and their contents can be found at www.federalreserve.gov/monetarypolicy/fomc_historical.htm.

the Board through the force of stature and personality. Chairmen of the Board of Governors (including Marriner S. Eccles, William McChesney Martin, Jr., Arthur Burns, Paul A. Volcker, Alan Greenspan, and Ben Bernanke) have typically had strong personalities and have wielded great power.

The chairman also exercises power by supervising the Board's staff of professional economists and advisers. Because the staff gathers information for the Board and conducts the analyses the Board uses in its decisions, it has some influence over monetary policy. In addition, in the past, several appointments to the Board itself have come from within the ranks of its professional staff, making the chairman's influence even farther-reaching and longer-lasting than a four-year term. The chairman's style also matters, as the Inside the Fed box, "How Bernanke's Style Differs from Greenspan's," suggests.

HOW INDEPENDENT IS THE FED?

When we look, in the next three chapters, at how the Federal Reserve conducts monetary policy, we will want to know why it decides to take certain policy actions but not others. To understand its actions, we must understand the incentives that motivate the Fed's behavior. How free is the Fed from presidential and congressional pressures? Do economic, bureaucratic, or political considerations guide it? Is the Fed truly independent of outside pressures?

Stanley Fischer, who was a professor at MIT and is now governor of the Bank of Israel, has defined two different types of independence of central banks: **instrument independence**, the ability of the central bank to set monetary policy instruments, and **goal independence**, the ability of the central bank to set the goals of monetary policy. The Federal Reserve has both types of independence and is remarkably free of the political pressures that influence other government agencies. Not only are the members of the Board of Governors appointed for a fourteen-year term (and so cannot be ousted from office), but also the term is technically not renewable, eliminating some of the incentive for the governors to curry favor with the president and Congress.

Probably even more important to its independence from the whims of Congress is the Fed's independent and substantial source of revenue from its holdings of securities and, to a lesser extent, from its loans to banks. In 2010, for example, the Fed had net earnings after expenses of $80 billion—not a bad living if you can find it! Because it returns the bulk of these earnings to the Treasury, it does not get rich from its activities, but this income gives the Fed an important advantage over other government agencies: It is not subject to the appropriations process usually controlled by Congress. Indeed, the General Accounting Office, the auditing agency of the federal government, cannot audit the monetary policy or foreign exchange market functions of the Federal Reserve. Because the power to control the purse strings is usually synonymous with the power of overall control, this feature of the Federal Reserve System contributes to its independence more than any other factor.

Yet the Federal Reserve is still subject to the influence of Congress, because the legislation that structures it is written by Congress and is subject to change at any time. When legislators are upset with the Fed's conduct of monetary policy, they frequently threaten to weaken its independence. A recent example was a bill sponsored by Representative Ron Paul in 2009 to subject the Fed's monetary policy actions to audits by the General Accounting Office (GAO). Threats like this are a powerful club to wield, and they certainly have some effect in keeping the Fed from straying too far from congressional wishes.

Congress has also passed legislation to make the Federal Reserve more accountable for its actions. Under the Humphrey-Hawkins Act of 1978 and later legislation, the Federal Reserve is required to issue a *Monetary Policy Report to the Congress* semiannually, with accompanying testimony by the chairman of the Board of Governors, to explain how the conduct of monetary policy is consistent with the objectives given by the Federal Reserve Act.

The president can also influence the Federal Reserve. Because congressional legislation can affect the Fed directly or affect its ability to conduct monetary policy, the president can be a powerful ally through his influence on Congress. Second, although ostensibly a president might be able to appoint only one or two members to the Board of Governors during each presidential term, in actual practice the president appoints members far more often. One reason is that most governors do not serve out a full fourteen-year term. (Governors' salaries are substantially below what they can earn in the private sector or even at universities, thus providing an incentive for them to return to academia or take private sector jobs before their term expires.) In addition, the president is able to appoint a new chairman of the Board of Governors every four years, and a chairman who is not reappointed is expected to resign from the board so that a new member can be appointed.

The power that the president enjoys through his appointments to the Board of Governors is limited, however. Because the term of the chairman is not necessarily concurrent with that of the president, a president may have to deal with a chairman of the Board of Governors appointed by a previous administration. Alan Greenspan, for example, was appointed chairman in 1987 by President Ronald Reagan and was reappointed to another term by a Republican president, George H. W. Bush, in 1992. When Bill Clinton, a Democrat, became president in 1993, Greenspan had several years left to his term. Clinton was put under tremendous pressure to reappoint Greenspan when his term expired and did so in 1996 and again in 2000, even though Greenspan is a Republican.[2] George W. Bush, a Republican, then reappointed Greenspan in 2004.

You can see that the Federal Reserve has extraordinary independence for a government agency. Nonetheless, the Fed is not free from political pressures. Indeed, to understand the Fed's behavior, we must recognize that public support for the actions of the Federal Reserve plays a very important role.[3]

SHOULD THE FED BE INDEPENDENT?

As we have seen, the Federal Reserve is probably the most independent government agency in the United States; this is also true for central banks in most other countries. Every few years, the question arises in Congress whether the independence given the Fed should be curtailed. Politicians who strongly oppose a Fed policy often want to bring it under their supervision, to impose a policy more to their liking. Should the Fed be independent, or would we be better off with a central bank under the control of the president or Congress?

[2]Similarly, William McChesney Martin, Jr., the chairman from 1951 to 1970, was appointed by President Truman (Dem.) but was reappointed by Presidents Eisenhower (Rep.), Kennedy (Dem.), Johnson (Dem.), and Nixon (Rep.). Also, Paul Volcker, the chairman from 1979 to 1987, was appointed by President Carter (Dem.) but was reappointed by President Reagan (Rep.). Ben Bernanke was appointed by President Bush (Rep.), but was reappointed by President Obama (Dem.).

[3]To get a further inside view of how the Fed has interacted with the public and the politicians, see Bob Woodward, *Maestro: Greenspan's Fed and the American Boom* (New York: Simon and Schuster, 2000) and David Wessel, *In Fed We Trust* (Random House: NY, 2009).

Inside the Fed How Bernanke's Style Differs from Greenspan's

Every Federal Reserve chairman has a different style that affects how policy decisions are made at the Fed. There has been much discussion of how the current chairman of the Fed, Ben Bernanke, differs from Alan Greenspan, who was the chairman of the Federal Reserve Board for nineteen years from 1987 until 2006.

Alan Greenspan dominated the Fed like no other prior Federal Reserve chairman. His background was very different from that of Bernanke, who spent most of his professional life in academia at Princeton University. Greenspan, a disciple of Ayn Rand, is a strong advocate for laissez-faire capitalism and headed a very successful economic consulting firm, Townsend-Greenspan. Greenspan has never been an economic theorist, but is rather famous for immersing himself in the data—literally so, because he is known to have done this in his bath tub at the beginning of the day—and often focused on rather obscure data series to come up with his forecasts. As a result, Greenspan did not rely exclusively on the Federal Reserve Board staff's forecast in making his policy decisions. A prominent example occurred during 1997, when the Board staff was forecasting a surge in inflation, which would have required a tightening of monetary policy. Yet Greenspan believed that inflation would not rise and convinced the FOMC not to tighten monetary policy. Greenspan proved to be right and was dubbed the "maestro" by the media.

Bernanke, on the other hand, before going to Washington as a governor of the Fed in 2002, and then as the chairman of the Council of Economic Advisors in 2005, and finally back to the Fed as chairman in 2006, spent his entire career as a professor, first at Stanford University's Graduate School of Business, and then in the Economics Department at Princeton University, where he became chairman. Because Bernanke did not make his name as an economic forecaster, the Board staff's forecast now plays a much greater role in decision making at the FOMC. In contrast to Greenspan, Bernanke's background as a top academic economist has meant that he focuses on analytics in making his decisions. The result is a much greater use of model simulations in guiding policy discussions.

The style of policy discussions has also changed with the new chairman. Greenspan exercised extensive control of the discussion at the FOMC. During the Greenspan era, the discussion was formal, with each participant speaking after being put on a list by the secretary of the FOMC. Under Bernanke, there is more give and take. Bernanke has encouraged so-called two-handed interventions. When a participant wants to go out of turn to ask a question or make a point about something that one of the other participants has just said, they raise two hands and are then acknowledged by chairman Bernanke and called on to speak.

The order of the discussion at the FOMC has also changed in a very subtle, but extremely important way. Under Greenspan, after the other FOMC participants had expressed their views on the economy, Greenspan would present his views on the state of the economy and then would make a recommendation for what monetary policy action should be taken. This required that the other participants would then just agree or disagree with the chairman's recommendation in the following round of discussion about monetary policy. In contrast, Bernanke usually does not make a recommendation for monetary policy immediately after other FOMC participants have expressed their views on the economy. Instead, he summarizes what he has heard from the other participants, makes some comments of his own, and then waits until after he has heard the views of all the other participants about monetary policy before making his policy recommendation. The process under Greenspan meant that the chairman was pretty much making the decision about policy, whereas Bernanke's procedure is more democratic and enables participants to have greater influence over the chairman's vote.

Another big difference in style is in terms of transparency. Greenspan was famous for being obscure, and even quipped at a Congressional hearing, "I guess I should warn you, if I turn out to be particularly clear, you've probably misunderstood what I've said." Bernanke is known for being a particularly clear speaker. Although advances in transparency were made under Greenspan, he adopted more transparent communication reluctantly. Bernanke has been a much stronger supporter of transparency, having advocated that the Fed announce its inflation objective (see Chapter 19), and having launched a major initiative in 2006 to study Federal Reserve communications that resulted in substantial increases in Fed transparency in November 2007 (as discussed in the Inside the Fed box, "The Evolution of the Fed's Communication Strategy," on page 388).

The Case for Independence

The strongest argument for an independent central bank rests on the view that subjecting it to more political pressures would impart an inflationary bias to monetary policy. In the view of many observers, politicians in a democratic society are shortsighted because they are driven by the need to win their next election. With this as the primary goal, they are unlikely to focus on long-run objectives, such as promoting a stable price level. Instead, they will seek short-run solutions to problems, such as high unemployment and high interest rates, even if the short-run solutions have undesirable long-run consequences. For example, we saw in Chapter 5 that high money growth might lead initially to a drop in interest rates but might cause an increase later as inflation heats up. Would a Federal Reserve under the control of Congress or the president be more likely to pursue a policy of excessive money growth when interest rates are high, even though it would eventually lead to inflation and even higher interest rates in the future? The advocates of an independent Federal Reserve say yes. They believe that a politically insulated Fed is more likely to be concerned with long-run objectives and thus be a defender of a sound dollar and a stable price level.

A variation on the preceding argument is that the political process in America could lead to a **political business cycle**, in which just before an election, expansionary policies are pursued to lower unemployment and interest rates. After the election, the bad effects of these policies—high inflation and high interest rates—come home to roost, requiring contractionary policies that politicians hope the public will forget before the next election. There is some evidence that such a political business cycle exists in the United States, and a Federal Reserve under the control of Congress or the president might make the cycle even more pronounced.

Putting the Fed under the control of the Treasury (making it more subject to influence by the president) is also considered dangerous because the Fed can be used to facilitate Treasury financing of large budget deficits by its purchases of Treasury bonds.[4] Treasury pressure on the Fed to "help out" might lead to more inflation in the economy. An independent Fed is better able to resist this pressure from the Treasury.

Another argument for central bank independence is that control of monetary policy is too important to leave to politicians, a group that has repeatedly demonstrated a lack of expertise at making hard decisions on issues of great economic importance, such as reducing the budget deficit or reforming the banking system. Another way to state this argument is in terms of the principal–agent problem discussed in Chapters 8, 9, and 11. Both the Federal Reserve and politicians are agents of the public (the principals), and both politicians and the Fed have incentives to act in their own interest rather than in the interest of the public. The argument supporting Federal Reserve independence is that the principal–agent problem is worse for politicians than for the Fed because politicians have fewer incentives to act in the public interest.

Indeed, some politicians may prefer to have an independent Fed, which can be used as a public "whipping boy" to take some of the heat off their backs. It is possible that a politician who in private opposes an inflationary monetary policy will be forced to support such a policy in public for fear of not being reelected. An independent Fed can pursue policies that are politically unpopular yet in the public interest.

[4]The Federal Reserve Act prohibited the Fed from buying Treasury bonds directly from the Treasury (except to roll over maturing securities); instead, the Fed buys Treasury bonds on the open market. One possible reason for this prohibition is consistent with the foregoing argument: The Fed would find it harder to facilitate Treasury financing of large budget deficits.

The Case Against Independence

Proponents of a Fed under the control of the president or Congress argue that it is undemocratic to have monetary policy (which affects almost everyone in the economy) controlled by an elite group responsible to no one. The current lack of accountability of the Federal Reserve has serious consequences: If the Fed performs badly, no provision is in place for replacing members (as there is with politicians). True, the Fed needs to pursue long-run objectives, but elected officials of Congress vote on long-run issues also (foreign policy, for example). If we push the argument further that policy is always performed better by elite groups like the Fed, we end up with such conclusions as the Joint Chiefs of Staff should determine military budgets or the IRS should set tax policies with no oversight from the president or Congress. Would you advocate this degree of independence for the Joint Chiefs or the IRS?

The public holds the president and Congress responsible for the economic well-being of the country, yet they lack control over the government agency that may well be the most important factor in determining the health of the economy. In addition, to achieve a cohesive program that will promote economic stability, monetary policy must be coordinated with fiscal policy (management of government spending and taxation). Only by placing monetary policy under the control of the politicians who also control fiscal policy can these two policies be prevented from working at cross-purposes.

Another argument against Federal Reserve independence is that an independent Fed has not always used its freedom successfully. The Fed failed miserably in its stated role as lender of last resort during the Great Depression, and its independence certainly didn't prevent it from pursuing an overly expansionary monetary policy in the 1960s and 1970s that contributed to rapid inflation in this period.

Our earlier discussion also suggests that the Federal Reserve is not immune from political pressures. Its independence may encourage it to pursue a course of narrow self-interest rather than the public interest.

No consensus has yet been reached on whether central bank independence is a good thing, although public support for independence of the central bank seems to have been growing in both the United States and abroad. As you might expect, people who like the Fed's policies are more likely to support its independence, while those who dislike its policies advocate a less independent Fed.

Central Bank Independence and Macroeconomic Performance Throughout the World

We have seen that advocates of an independent central bank believe that macroeconomic performance will be improved by making the central bank more independent. Empirical evidence seems to support this conjecture: When central banks are ranked from least independent to most independent, inflation performance is found to be the best for countries with the most independent central banks. Although a more independent central bank appears to lead to a lower inflation rate, this is not achieved at the expense of poorer real economic performance. Countries with independent central banks are no more likely to have high unemployment or greater output fluctuations than countries with less independent central banks.

EXPLAINING CENTRAL BANK BEHAVIOR

One view of government bureaucratic behavior is that bureaucracies serve the public interest (this is the *public interest view*). Yet some economists have developed a theory of bureaucratic behavior that emphasizes other factors influencing how bureaucracies operate. The *theory of bureaucratic behavior* suggests that the objective of a bureaucracy is to maximize its own welfare, just as a consumer's behavior is motivated by the maximization of personal welfare and a firm's behavior is motivated by the maximization of profits. The welfare of a bureaucracy is related to its power and prestige. Thus this theory suggests that an important factor affecting a central bank's behavior is its attempt to increase its power and prestige.

What predictions does this view of a central bank like the Fed indicate? One is that the Federal Reserve will fight vigorously to preserve its autonomy, a prediction verified time and time again as the Fed has continually counterattacked congressional attempts to control its budget. In fact, it is extraordinary how effectively the Fed has been able to mobilize a lobby of bankers and business people to preserve its independence when threatened.

Another prediction is that the Federal Reserve will try to avoid conflict with powerful groups that might threaten to curtail its power and reduce its autonomy. The Fed's behavior may take several forms. One possible factor explaining why the Fed is sometimes slow to increase interest rates and thus smooth out their fluctuations is that it wishes to avoid a conflict with the president and Congress over increases in interest rates. The desire to avoid conflict with Congress and the president may also explain why in the past the Fed has not embraced transparency (see the Inside the Fed box, "The Evolution of the Fed's Communication Strategy").

The desire of the Fed to hold as much power as possible also explains why it vigorously pursued a campaign to gain control over more banks. The campaign culminated in legislation that expanded jurisdiction of the Fed's reserve requirements to *all* banks (not just the member commercial banks) by 1987.

The theory of bureaucratic behavior seems applicable to the Federal Reserve's actions, but we must recognize that this view of the Fed as being solely concerned with its own self-interest is too extreme. Maximizing one's welfare does not rule out altruism. (You might give generously to a charity because it makes you feel good about yourself, but in the process you are helping a worthy cause.) The Fed is surely concerned that it conduct monetary policy in the public interest. However, much uncertainty and disagreement exist over what monetary policy should be.[5] When it is unclear what is in the public interest, other motives may influence the Fed's behavior. In these situations, the theory of bureaucratic behavior may be a useful guide to predicting what motivates the Fed and other central banks.

[5]One example of the uncertainty over how best to conduct monetary policy was discussed in Chapter 3: Economists are not sure how to measure money. So even if economists agreed that controlling the quantity of money is the appropriate way to conduct monetary policy (a controversial position, as we will see in later chapters), the Fed cannot be sure which monetary aggregate it should control.

Inside the Fed The Evolution of the Fed's Communication Strategy

As the theory of bureaucratic behavior predicts, the Fed has incentives to hide its actions from the public and from politicians to avoid conflicts with them. In the past, this motivation led to a penchant for secrecy in the Fed, about which one former Fed official remarked that "a lot of staffers would concede that [secrecy] is designed to shield the Fed from political oversight."* For example, the Fed pursued an active defense of delaying its release of FOMC directives to Congress and the public. However, as we have seen, in 1994 it began to reveal the FOMC directive immediately after each FOMC meeting. In 1999, it also began to immediately announce the "bias" toward which direction monetary policy was likely to go, later expressed as the balance of risks in the economy. In 2002, the Fed started to report the roll call vote on the federal funds rate target taken at the FOMC meeting. In December 2004, it moved up the release date of the minutes of FOMC meetings to three weeks after the meeting from six weeks, its previous policy.

The Fed has increased its transparency in recent years, but has been slower to do so than many other central banks. One important trend toward greater transparency is the announcement by a central bank of a specific numerical objective for inflation, often referred to as an inflation target, which will be discussed in Chapter 19. Alan Greenspan was strongly opposed to the Fed's moving in this direction, but Chairman Bernanke is much more favorably disposed, having advocated the announcement of a specific numerical inflation objective in his writings and in a speech that he gave as a governor in 2004.†

In November 2007, the Bernanke Fed announced major enhancements to its communication strategy. First, the forecast horizon for the FOMC's projections under "appropriate policy" for inflation, unemployment, and GDP growth, which were mandated by the Humphrey-Hawkins legislation in 1978, was extended from two calendar years to three, with long-run projections added in 2009. Because projections for inflation given appropriate policy should converge to the desired inflation objective eventually, the longer-run projections provide more information about what individual FOMC participants think should be the objective for inflation. This change therefore moves the FOMC closer to specifying a numerical objective for inflation. Second, the Committee now publishes these projections four times a year rather than twice a year. Third, the release of the projections now includes narrative describing FOMC participants' views of the principal forces shaping the outlook and the sources of risks to that outlook. Although these enhancements to Fed communication are major steps forward, there are strong arguments that further increases in transparency could improve the control of inflation by anchoring inflation expectations more firmly, and also help stabilize economic fluctuations.** Indeed in October 2010,‡ Chairman Bernanke proposed moving in this direction, but he was unable to get the FOMC to agree to it. However, in 2011, the Fed announced a further move toward increased transparency: after the FOMC meetings in April, June, November and January, the Chairman of the Federal Reserve will now give a press conference intended to further enhance the clarity and timeliness of the Federal Reserve's monetary policy communication.

*Quoted in "Monetary Zeal: How the Federal Reserve Under Volcker Finally Slowed Down Inflation," *Wall Street Journal*, December 7, 1984, p. 23.

†Ben S. Bernanke, "Inflation Targeting," Federal Reserve Bank of St. Louis *Review* 86, no. 4 (July/August 2004):165–168.

**Frederic S. Mishkin, "Whither Federal Reserve Communications," speech at the Petersen Institute for International Economics, July 28, 2008, http://www.federalreserve.gov/newsevents/speech/mishkin20080728a.htm.

‡Ben S. Bernanke, "Monetary Policy Objectives and Tools in a Low-Inflation Environment," speech at the Revisiting Monetary Policy in a Low-Inflation Environment Conference, Federal Reserve Bank of Boston, Boston, Massachusetts, October 15, 2010, http://www.federalreserve.gov/newsevents/speech/bernanke20101015a.htm.

STRUCTURE AND INDEPENDENCE OF THE EUROPEAN CENTRAL BANK

Until recently, the Federal Reserve had no rivals in terms of its importance in the central banking world. However, this situation changed in January 1999 with the start-up of the

European Central Bank (ECB) and European System of Central Banks (ESCB), which now conduct monetary policy for countries that are members of the European Monetary Union. These countries, taken together, have a population that exceeds that of the United States and a GDP comparable to that of the United States. The Maastricht Treaty, which established the ECB and ESCB, patterned these institutions after the Federal Reserve, in that central banks for each country (referred to as *National Central Banks*, or *NCBs*) have a similar role to that of the Federal Reserve Banks. The European Central Bank, which is housed in Frankfurt, Germany, has an Executive Board that is similar in structure to the Board of Governors of the Federal Reserve; it is made up of the president, the vice president, and four other members, who are appointed to eight-year, nonrenewable terms. The Governing Council, which comprises the Executive Board and the presidents of the National Central Banks, is similar to the FOMC and makes the decisions on monetary policy. While the presidents of the National Central Banks are appointed by their countries' governments, the members of the Executive Board are appointed by a committee consisting of the heads of state of all the countries that are part of the European Monetary Union.

Differences Between the European System of Central Banks and the Federal Reserve System

In the popular press, the European System of Central Banks is usually referred to as the European Central Bank (ECB), even though it would be more accurate to refer to it as the *Eurosystem*, just as it would be more accurate to refer to the Federal Reserve System rather than the Fed. Although the structure of the Eurosystem is similar to that of the Federal Reserve System, some important differences distinguish the two. First, the budgets of the Federal Reserve Banks are controlled by the Board of Governors, whereas the National Central Banks control their own budgets *and* the budget of the ECB in Frankfurt. The ECB in the Eurosystem therefore has less power than does the Board of Governors in the Federal Reserve System. Second, the monetary operations of the Eurosystem are conducted by the National Central Banks in each country, so monetary operations are not centralized as they are in the Federal Reserve System. Third, in contrast to the Federal Reserve, the ECB is not involved in supervision and regulation of financial institutions; these tasks are left to the individual countries in the European Monetary Union.

Governing Council

Just as there is a focus on meetings of the FOMC in the United States, there is a similar focus in Europe on meetings of the Governing Council, which gathers monthly at the ECB in Frankfurt to make decisions on monetary policy. Currently, seventeen countries are members of the European Monetary Union, and the head of each of the seventeen National Central Banks has one vote in the Governing Council; each of the six Executive Board Members also has one vote. In contrast to FOMC meetings, which staff from both the Board of Governors and individual Federal Reserve Banks attend, only the twenty-three members of the Governing Council attend the meetings, with no staff present.

The Governing Council has decided that although its members have the legal right to vote, no formal vote will actually be taken; instead, the Council operates by consensus. One reason the Governing Council has decided not to take votes is because of worries that the casting of individual votes might lead the heads of National Central Banks to support a monetary policy that would be appropriate for their individual countries, but not necessarily for the countries in the European Monetary Union as a whole. This problem is less severe for the Federal Reserve: Although Federal Reserve Bank presidents do live in different regions of the country, all have the same nationality and are more likely to take a national view in monetary policy decisions rather than a regional view.

Just as the Federal Reserve releases the FOMC's decision on the setting of the policy interest rate (the federal funds rate) immediately after the meeting is over, the ECB does the same after the Governing Council meeting concludes (announcing the target for a similar short-term interest rate for interbank loans). However, whereas the Fed simply releases a statement about the setting of the monetary policy instruments, the ECB goes further by having a press conference in which the president and vice president of the ECB take questions from the news media. Holding such a press conference so soon after the meeting is tricky because it requires the president and vice president to be quick on their feet in dealing with the press. The first president of the ECB, Willem F. Duisenberg, put his foot in his mouth at some of these press conferences, and the ECB came under some sharp criticism. His successor, Jean-Claude Trichet, a more successful communicator, has encountered fewer problems in this regard.

Although currently only seventeen countries in the European Monetary Union have representation on the Governing Council, this situation is likely to change in the future. Three countries in the European Community already qualify for entering the European Monetary Union: the United Kingdom, Sweden, and Denmark. Seven other countries in the European Community (the Czech Republic, Hungary, Latvia, Lithuania, Poland, Bulgaria, and Roumania) might enter the European Monetary Union once they qualify, which may not be too far in the distant future. The possible expansion of membership in the Eurosystem presents a particular dilemma. The current size of the Governing Council (twenty-three voting members) is substantially larger than the FOMC (twenty-three members). Many commentators have wondered whether the Governing Council is already too unwieldy—a situation that would get considerably worse as more countries join the European Monetary Union. To deal with this potential problem, the Governing Council decided on a complex system of rotation, somewhat like that for the FOMC, in which National Central Banks from the larger countries will vote more often than National Central Banks from the smaller countries.

How Independent Is the ECB?

Although the Federal Reserve is a highly independent central bank, the Maastricht Treaty, which established the Eurosystem, has made the latter the most independent central bank in the world. Like the Board of Governors, the members of the Executive Board have long terms (eight years), while heads of National Central Banks are required to have terms at least five years long. Like the Fed, the Eurosystem determines its own budget, and the governments of the member countries are not allowed to issue instructions to the ECB. These elements of the Maastricht Treaty make the ECB highly independent.

The Maastricht Treaty specifies that the overriding, long-term goal of the ECB is price stability, which means that the goal for the Eurosystem is more clearly specified than it is for the Federal Reserve System. However, the Maastricht Treaty did not specify exactly what "price stability" means. The Eurosystem has defined the quantitative goal for monetary policy to be an inflation rate slightly less than 2%, so from this perspective, the ECB is slightly less goal-independent than the Fed. The Eurosystem is, however, much more goal-independent than the Federal Reserve System in another way: The Eurosystem's charter cannot be changed by legislation; it can be changed only by revision of the Maastricht Treaty—a difficult process because *all* signatories to the treaty must agree to accept any proposed change.

STRUCTURE AND INDEPENDENCE OF OTHER FOREIGN CENTRAL BANKS

Here we examine the structure and degree of independence of three other important foreign central banks: the Bank of Canada, the Bank of England, and the Bank of Japan.

Bank of Canada

Canada was late in establishing a central bank: The Bank of Canada was founded in 1934. Its directors are appointed by the government to three-year terms, and they appoint the governor, who has a seven-year term. A governing council, consisting of the four deputy governors and the governor, is the policy-making body comparable to the FOMC that makes decisions about monetary policy.

The Bank Act was amended in 1967 to give the ultimate responsibility for monetary policy to the government. So on paper, the Bank of Canada is not as instrument-independent as the Federal Reserve. In practice, however, the Bank of Canada does essentially control monetary policy. In the event of a disagreement between the bank and the government, the minister of finance can issue a directive that the bank must follow. However, because the directive must be in writing and specific and applicable for a specified period, it is unlikely that such a directive would be issued, and none has been to date. The goal for monetary policy, a target for inflation, is set jointly by the Bank of Canada and the government, so the Bank of Canada has less goal independence than the Fed.

Bank of England

Founded in 1694, the Bank of England is one of the oldest central banks. The Bank Act of 1946 gave the government statutory authority over the Bank of England. The Court (equivalent to a board of directors) of the Bank of England is made up of the governor and two deputy governors, who are appointed for five-year terms, and sixteen non-executive directors, who are appointed for three-year terms.

Until 1997, the Bank of England was the least independent of the central banks examined in this chapter because the decision to raise or lower interest rates resided not within the Bank of England but with the Chancellor of the Exchequer (the equivalent of the U.S. Secretary of the Treasury). All of this changed when a new Labour government came to power in May 1997 and the Chancellor of the Exchequer, Gordon Brown, made a surprise announcement that the Bank of England would henceforth have the power to set interest rates. However, the Bank was not granted total instrument independence: The government can overrule the Bank and set rates "in extreme economic circumstances" and "for a limited period." Nonetheless, as in Canada, because overruling the Bank would be so public and is supposed to occur only in highly unusual circumstances and for a limited time, it is likely to be a rare occurrence.

Because the United Kingdom is not a member of the European Monetary Union, the Bank of England makes its monetary policy decisions independently from the European Central Bank. The decision to set interest rates resides in the Monetary Policy Committee, made up of the governor, two deputy governors, two members appointed by the governor after consultation with the chancellor (normally central bank officials), plus four outside economic experts appointed by the chancellor. (Surprisingly, two of the four outside experts initially appointed to this committee were not British citizens—one was Dutch and the other American—and some later appointments have also not been British citizens.) The inflation target for the Bank of England is set by the Chancellor of the Exchequer, so the Bank of England is also less goal-independent than the Fed.

Bank of Japan

The Bank of Japan (Nippon Ginko) was founded in 1882 during the Meiji Restoration. Monetary policy is determined by the Policy Board, which is composed of the governor; two vice-governors; and six outside members appointed by the cabinet and approved by the parliament, all of whom serve for five-year terms.

Until recently, the Bank of Japan was not formally independent of the government, with the ultimate power residing with the Ministry of Finance. However, the Bank of Japan Law, which took effect in April 1998 and was the first major change in the powers of the Bank of Japan in 55 years, changed this situation. In addition to stipulating that the objective of monetary policy is to attain price stability, the law granted greater instrument and goal independence to the Bank of Japan. Before this, the government had two voting members on the Policy Board, one from the Ministry of Finance and the other from the Economic Planning Agency. Now the government may send two representatives from these agencies to board meetings, but they no longer have voting rights, although they do have the ability to request delays in monetary policy decisions. In addition, the Ministry of Finance lost its authority to oversee many operations of the Bank of Japan, particularly the right to dismiss senior officials. However, the Ministry of Finance continues to have control over the part of the Bank's budget that is unrelated to monetary policy, which might limit its independence to some extent.

The Trend Toward Greater Independence

As our survey of the structure and independence of the major central banks indicates, in recent years we have been seeing a remarkable trend toward increasing independence. It used to be that the Federal Reserve was substantially more independent than almost all other central banks, with the exception of those in Germany and Switzerland. Now the newly established European Central Bank is far more independent than the Fed, and greater independence has been granted to central banks like the Bank of England and the Bank of Japan, putting them more on a par with the Fed, as well as to central banks in such diverse countries as New Zealand, Sweden, and the euro nations. Both theory and experience suggest that more independent central banks produce better monetary policy, thus providing an impetus for this trend.

Summary

1. The Federal Reserve System was created in 1913 to lessen the frequency of bank panics. Because of public hostility to central banks and the centralization of power, the Federal Reserve System was created with many checks and balances to diffuse power.
2. The structure of the Federal Reserve System consists of twelve regional Federal Reserve banks, around 2,500 member commercial banks, the Board of Governors of the Federal Reserve System, the Federal Open Market Committee (FOMC), and the Federal Advisory Council. Although on paper the Federal Reserve System appears to be decentralized, in practice it has come to function as a unified central bank controlled by the Board of Governors, especially the board's chairman.
3. The Federal Reserve is more independent than most agencies of the U.S. government, but it is still subject to political pressures because the legislation that structures the Fed is written by Congress and can be changed at any time.
4. The case for an independent Federal Reserve rests on the view that curtailing the Fed's independence and subjecting it to more political pressures would impart

an inflationary bias to monetary policy. An independent Fed can afford to take the long view and not respond to short-run problems that will result in expansionary monetary policy and a political business cycle. The case against an independent Fed holds that it is undemocratic to have monetary policy (so important to the public) controlled by an elite that is not accountable to the public. An independent Fed also makes the coordination of monetary and fiscal policy difficult.

5. The theory of bureaucratic behavior suggests that one factor driving central banks' behavior might be an attempt to increase their power and prestige. This view explains many central bank actions, although central banks may also act in the public interest.
6. The European System of Central Banks has a similar structure to the Federal Reserve System, with each member country having a National Central Bank, and an Executive Board of the European Central Bank being located in Frankfurt, Germany. The Governing Council, which is made up of the six members of the Executive Board (which includes the president of the European Central Bank) and the presidents of the National Central Banks, makes the decisions on monetary policy. The Eurosystem, which was established under the terms of the Maastricht Treaty, is even more independent than the Federal Reserve System because its charter cannot be changed by legislation. Indeed, it is the most independent central bank in the world.
7. There has been a remarkable trend toward increasing independence of central banks throughout the world. Greater independence has been granted to central banks such as the Bank of England and the Bank of Japan in recent years, as well as to other central banks in such diverse countries as New Zealand and Sweden. Both theory and experience suggest that more independent central banks produce better monetary policy.

Key Terms

Board of Governors of the Federal Reserve System, p. 374
easing of monetary policy, p. 380
federal funds rate, p. 378
Federal Open Market Committee (FOMC), p. 374
Federal Reserve banks, p. 373
goal independence, p. 382
instrument independence, p. 382
open market operations, p. 376
political business cycle, p. 385
tightening of monetary policy, p. 380

Questions

All questions are available in MyEconLab *at* www.myeconlab.com.

1. Why was the Federal Reserve System set up with twelve regional Federal Reserve banks rather than one central bank, as in other countries?
2. Why is the Twelfth Federal Reserve district so geographically large, while the Second Federal Reserve district is so small by comparison?
3. Should the Federal Reserve redraw its district boundaries, similar to how congressional districts are periodically realigned? Why or why not?
4. "The Federal Reserve System resembles the U.S. Constitution in that it was designed with many checks and balances." Is this statement true, false, or uncertain? Explain your answer.
5. Which entities in the Federal Reserve System control the discount rate? Reserve requirements? Open market operations?
6. In what ways can the regional Federal Reserve Banks influence the conduct of monetary policy?
7. Why is it important for the regional Federal Reserve bank presidents to attend the FOMC meetings, even if they are nonvoting members?
8. Why is the New York Federal Reserve always a voting member on the FOMC?
9. The presidents of each of the district Federal Reserve banks (including the New York Federal Reserve bank) are currently not required to undergo a formal political appointment and approval process. Do you think this is appropriate? Why or why not?

10. Do you think that the fourteen-year nonrenewable terms for governors effectively insulate the Board of Governors from political pressure?

11. Despite the important role that the Board of Governors has in setting monetary policy, seats to serve on the Board of Governors can sometimes be empty for several years. How could this happen?

12. How is the president of the United States able to exert influence over the Federal Reserve?

13. Why is it unlikely that the policy recommendation put forth by the chairman of the Board of Governors would ever be voted down by the rest of the FOMC?

14. How does the Federal Reserve have a high degree of instrument independence? If it has a specific mandate from Congress to achieve "maximum employment and low, stable prices," then how does the Fed have goal independence?

15. The Fed is the most independent of all U.S. government agencies. What is the main difference between it and other government agencies that explains the Fed's greater independence?

16. What is the primary tool that Congress uses to exercise some control over the Fed?

17. Should the Federal Reserve be subject to periodic auditing of its policies, procedures, and finances? Why or why not?

18. In the 1960s and 1970s, the Federal Reserve System lost member banks at a rapid rate. How can the theory of bureaucratic behavior explain the Fed's campaign for legislation to require all commercial banks to become members? Was the Fed successful in this campaign?

19. "The theory of bureaucratic behavior indicates that the Fed never operates in the public interest." Is this statement true, false, or uncertain? Explain your answer.

20. Why might eliminating the Fed's independence lead to a more pronounced political business cycle?

21. "The independence of the Fed leaves it completely unaccountable for its actions." Is this statement true, false, or uncertain? Explain your answer.

22. "The independence of the Fed has meant that it takes the long view and not the short view." Is this statement true, false, or uncertain? Explain your answer.

23. The Fed promotes secrecy by not releasing the minutes of the FOMC meetings to Congress or the public immediately. Discuss the arguments for and against this policy.

24. Which is more independent, the Federal Reserve or the European Central Bank? Why?

25. Why did the Bank of England up until 1997 have a low degree of independence?

Web Exercises

1. Go to www.federalreserve.gov/ and click on About the Fed. Next click on The Federal Reserve System and then on Structure. According to the Federal Reserve, what is the most important responsibility of the Board of Governors?
2. Go to the previous site and click on Monetary Policy. Then click on Reports and then go on Beige Book. According to the summary of the most recently published book, is the economy weakening or strengthening?

Web References

www.federalreserve.gov/pubs/frseries/frseri.htm

Information on the structure of the Federal Reserve System.

www.federalreserve.gov/otherfrb.htm

Addresses and phone numbers of Federal Reserve Banks, branches, and RCPCs and links to the main pages of the twelve reserve banks and Board of Governors.

www.federalreserve.gov/bios/boardmembership.htm

Lists all the members of the Board of Governors of the Federal Reserve since its inception.

www.federalreserve.gov/fomc

Find general information on the FOMC; its schedule of meetings, statements, minutes, and transcripts; information on its members; and the "beige book."

www.ecb.int

The website for the European Central Bank.

www.bank-banque-canada.ca/

The website for the Bank of Canada.

www.bankofengland.co.uk/index.htm

The website for the Bank of England.

www.boj.or.jp/en/index.htm

The website for the Bank of Japan.

17 The Money Supply Process

Preview

As we saw in Chapter 5 and will see in later chapters on monetary theory, movements in the money supply affect interest rates and inflation and thus affect us all. Because of its far-reaching effects on economic activity, it is important to understand how the money supply is determined. Who controls it? What causes it to change? How might control of it be improved? In this and subsequent chapters, we answer these questions by providing a detailed description of the *money supply process*, the mechanism that determines the level of the money supply.

Because deposits at banks are by far the largest component of the money supply, learning how these deposits are created is the first step in understanding the money supply process. This chapter provides an overview of how the banking system creates deposits, and describes the basic principles of the money supply, needed as a foundation for later chapters.

THREE PLAYERS IN THE MONEY SUPPLY PROCESS

The "cast of characters" in the money supply story is as follows:

1. The *central bank*—the government agency that oversees the banking system and is responsible for the conduct of monetary policy; in the United States, the Federal Reserve System
2. *Banks* (depository institutions)—the financial intermediaries that accept deposits from individuals and institutions and make loans: commercial banks, savings and loan associations, mutual savings banks, and credit unions
3. *Depositors*—individuals and institutions that hold deposits in banks

Of the three players, the central bank—the Federal Reserve System—is the most important. The Fed's conduct of monetary policy involves actions that affect its balance sheet (holdings of assets and liabilities), to which we turn now.

THE FED'S BALANCE SHEET

The operation of the Fed and its monetary policy involve actions that affect its balance sheet, its holdings of assets and liabilities. Here we discuss a simplified balance sheet that includes just four items that are essential to our understanding of the money supply process.[1]

Federal Reserve System	
Assets	**Liabilities**
Securities	Currency in circulation
Loans to financial institutions	Reserves

Liabilities

The two liabilities on the balance sheet, currency in circulation and reserves, are often referred to as the *monetary liabilities* of the Fed. They are an important part of the money supply story, because increases in either or both will lead to an increase in the money supply (everything else being constant). The sum of the Fed's monetary liabilities (currency in circulation and reserves) and the U.S. Treasury's monetary liabilities (Treasury currency in circulation, primarily coins) is called the **monetary base**. When discussing the monetary base, we will focus only on the monetary liabilities of the Fed because those of the Treasury account for less than 10% of the base.[2]

1. *Currency in circulation*. The Fed issues currency (those green-and-gray pieces of paper in your wallet that say "Federal Reserve Note" at the top). Currency in circulation is the amount of currency in the hands of the public. Currency held by depository institutions is also a liability of the Fed, but is counted as part of the reserves.

Federal Reserve notes are IOUs from the Fed to the bearer and are also liabilities, but unlike most, they promise to pay back the bearer solely with Federal Reserve notes; that is, they pay off IOUs with other IOUs. Accordingly, if you bring a $100 bill to the Federal Reserve and demand payment, you will receive either two $50s, five $20s, ten $10s, or one hundred $1 bills.

People are more willing to accept IOUs from the Fed than from you or me because Federal Reserve notes are a recognized medium of exchange; that is, they are accepted as a means of payment and so function as money. Unfortunately, neither you nor I can convince people that our IOUs are worth anything more than the paper they are written on.[3]

[1]A detailed discussion of the Fed's balance sheet and the factors that affect the monetary base can be found in the appendix to this chapter, which you can find on this book's website at www.aw.com/mishkin.

[2]It is also safe to ignore the Treasury's monetary liabilities when discussing the monetary base because the Treasury cannot actively supply its monetary liabilities to the economy due to legal restrictions.

[3]The currency item on our balance sheet refers only to currency *in circulation*—that is, the amount in the hands of the public. Currency that has been printed by the U.S. Bureau of Engraving and Printing is not automatically a liability of the Fed. For example, consider the importance of having $1 million of your own IOUs printed. You give out $100 worth to other people and keep the other $999,900 in your pocket. The $999,900 of IOUs does not make you richer or poorer and does not affect your indebtedness. You care only about the $100 of liabilities from the $100 of circulated IOUs. The same reasoning applies for the Fed in regard to its Federal Reserve notes.

For similar reasons, the currency component of the money supply, no matter how it is defined, includes only currency in circulation. It does not include any additional currency that is not yet in the hands of the public. The fact that currency has been printed but is not circulating means that it is not anyone's asset or liability and thus cannot affect anyone's behavior. Therefore, it makes sense not to include it in the money supply.

2. *Reserves*. All banks have an account at the Fed in which they hold deposits. **Reserves** consist of deposits at the Fed plus currency that is physically held by banks (called *vault cash* because it is stored in bank vaults). Reserves are assets for the banks but liabilities for the Fed, because the banks can demand payment on them at any time and the Fed is required to satisfy its obligation by paying Federal Reserve notes. As you will see, an increase in reserves leads to an increase in the level of deposits and hence in the money supply.

Total reserves can be divided into two categories: reserves that the Fed requires banks to hold (**required reserves**) and any additional reserves the banks choose to hold (**excess reserves**). For example, the Fed might require that for every dollar of deposits at a depository institution, a certain fraction (say, 10 cents) must be held as reserves. This fraction (10%) is called the **required reserve ratio**.

Assets

The two assets on the Fed's balance sheet are important for two reasons. First, changes in the asset items lead to changes in reserves and the monetary base, and consequently to changes in the money supply. Second, because these assets (government securities and Fed loans) earn higher interest rates than the liabilities (currency in circulation, which pays no interest, and reserves), the Fed makes billions of dollars every year—its assets earn income, and its liabilities cost practically nothing. Although it returns most of its earnings to the federal government, the Fed does spend some of it on "worthy causes," such as supporting economic research.

1. *Securities*. This category of assets covers the Fed's holdings of securities issued by the U.S. Treasury and, in unusual circumstances (as discussed in Chapter 18), other securities. As you will see, the primary way the Fed provides reserves to the banking system is by purchasing securities, thereby increasing its holdings of these assets. An increase in government or other securities held by the Fed leads to an increase in the money supply.

2. *Loans to financial institutions*. The second way the Fed can provide reserves to the banking system is by making loans to banks and other financial institutions. For these institutions, the loans they have taken out are referred to as *borrowings from the Fed* or, alternatively, as *borrowed reserves*. These loans appear as a liability on financial institutions' balance sheets. An increase in loans to financial institutions can also be the source of an increase in the money supply. During normal times, the Fed makes loans only to banking institutions and the interest rate charged banks for these loans is called the **discount rate**. (As we will discuss in Chapter 18, during the recent financial crisis, the Fed made loans to other financial institutions.)

CONTROL OF THE MONETARY BASE

The *monetary base* (also called **high-powered money**) equals currency in circulation C plus the total reserves in banking system R.[4] The monetary base MB can be expressed as

$$MB = C + R$$

[4]Here, currency in circulation includes both Federal Reserve currency (Federal Reserve notes) and Treasury currency (primarily coins).

The Federal Reserve exercises control over the monetary base through its purchases or sales of securities in the open market, called **open market operations**, and through its extension of discount loans to banks.

Federal Reserve Open Market Operations

The primary way in which the Fed causes changes in the monetary base is through its open market operations. A purchase of bonds by the Fed is called an **open market purchase**, and a sale of bonds by the Fed is called an **open market sale**.

Open Market Purchase from a Bank Suppose that the Fed purchases $100 million of bonds from banks and pays for them with a check for this amount. To understand what occurs as a result of this transaction, we look at *T-accounts*, which list only the changes that occur in balance sheet items, starting from the initial balance sheet position. The bank will either deposit the check in its account with the Fed or cash it in for currency, which will be counted as vault cash. Either action means that banks will find themselves with $100 million more reserves and a reduction in its holdings of securities of $100 million. The T-account for the banking system, then, is

Banking System

Assets		Liabilities	
Securities	−$100 m		
Reserves	+$100 m		

The Fed, meanwhile, finds that its liabilities have increased by the additional $100 million of reserves, while its assets have increased by the $100 million of additional securities that it now holds. Its T-account is

Federal Reserve System

Assets		Liabilities	
Securities	+$100 m	Reserves	+$100 m

The net result of this open market purchase is that reserves have increased by $100 million, the amount of the open market purchase. Because there has been no change of currency in circulation, the monetary base has also risen by $100 million.

Open Market Purchase from the Nonbank Public To understand what happens when there is an open market purchase from the nonbank public, we must look at two cases. First, let's assume that the people or corporations that sell $100 million of bonds to the Fed deposit the Fed's checks in their local banks. The nonbank public's T-account after this transaction is

Nonbank Public			
Assets		**Liabilities**	
Securities	−$100 m		
Checkable deposits	+$100 m		

When banks receive the checks, they credit depositors' accounts with the $100 million and then deposit the checks in their account with the Fed, thereby adding to their reserves. The banking system's T-account becomes

Banking System			
Assets		**Liabilities**	
Reserves	+$100 m	Checkable deposits	+$100 m

The effect on the Fed's balance sheet is that it has gained $100 million of securities in its assets column, whereas it has an increase of $100 million of reserves in its liabilities column:

Federal Reserve System			
Assets		**Liabilities**	
Securities	+$100 m	Reserves	+$100 m

As you can see in the above T-account, when the Fed's check is deposited in a bank, the net result of the Fed's open market purchase from the nonbank public is identical to the effect of its open market purchase from a bank: Reserves increase by the amount of the open market purchase, and the monetary base increases by the same amount.

If, however, the people or corporations selling the bonds to the Fed cash the Fed's checks either at a local bank or at a Federal Reserve bank for currency, the effect on reserves is different.[5] This sellers will receive currency of $100 million while reducing holdings of securities by $100 million. The nonbank public's seller's T-account will be

Nonbank Public			
Assets		**Liabilities**	
Securities	−$100 m		
Currency	+$100 m		

[5]If bond sellers cash checks at their local banks, the banks' balance sheets will be unaffected, because the $100 million of vault cash that they pay out will be exactly matched by the deposits of the $100 million in checks at the Fed. Thus banks' reserves will remain the same, and their T-accounts will not be affected. That is why a T-account for the banking system does not appear here.

The Fed now finds that it has exchanged $100 million of currency for $100 million of securities, so its T-account is

Federal Reserve System			
Assets		**Liabilities**	
Securities	+$100 m	Currency in circulation	+$100 m

The net effect of the open market purchase in this case is that reserves are unchanged, whereas currency in circulation increases by the $100 million of the open market purchase. Thus the monetary base increases by the $100 million amount of the open market purchase, while reserves do not. This contrasts with the situation in which sellers of the bonds deposit the Fed's checks in banks; in that case, reserves increase by $100 million, and so does the monetary base.

The analysis reveals that ***the effect of an open market purchase on reserves depends on whether the seller of the bonds keeps the proceeds from the sale in currency or in deposits***. If the proceeds are kept in currency, the open market purchase has no effect on reserves; if the proceeds are kept as deposits, reserves increase by the amount of the open market purchase.

The effect of an open market purchase on the monetary base, however, is always the same (the monetary base increases by the amount of the purchase) whether the seller of the bonds keeps the proceeds in deposits or in currency. The impact of an open market purchase on reserves is much more uncertain than its impact on the monetary base.

Open Market Sale If the Fed sells $100 million of bonds to banks or the nonbank public, the monetary base will decrease by $100 million. For example, if the Fed sells bonds to individuals who pay for them with currency, the buyers exchange $100 million of currency for $100 million of bonds, and the resulting T-account is

Nonbank Public			
Assets		**Liabilities**	
Securities	+$100 m		
Currency	−$100 m		

The Fed, for its part, has reduced its holdings of securities by $100 million and has also lowered its monetary liability by accepting the currency as payment for its bonds, thereby reducing the amount of currency in circulation by $100 million:

Federal Reserve System			
Assets		**Liabilities**	
Securities	−$100 m	Currency in circulation	−$100 m

The effect of the open market sale of $100 million of bonds is to reduce the monetary base by an equal amount, although reserves remain unchanged. Manipulations of T-accounts in cases in which buyers of the bonds are banks or buyers pay for the bonds with checks written on a checkable deposit account at a local bank lead to the same $100 million reduction in the monetary base, although the reduction occurs because the level of reserves has fallen by $100 million.

The following conclusion can now be drawn from our analysis of open market purchases and sales: ***The effect of open market operations on the monetary base is much more certain than the effect on reserves.*** Therefore, the Fed can control the monetary base with open market operations more effectively than it can control reserves.

Open market operations can also be done in other assets besides government bonds and have the same effects on the monetary base we have described here.

Shifts from Deposits into Currency

Even if the Fed does not conduct open market operations, a shift from deposits to currency will affect the reserves in the banking system. However, such a shift will have no effect on the monetary base, another reason why the Fed has more control over the monetary base than over reserves.

Let's suppose that during the Christmas season, the public wants to hold more currency to buy gifts and so withdraws $100 million in cash. The effect on the T-account of the nonbank public is

Nonbank Public

Assets		Liabilities	
Checkable deposits	−$100 m		
Currency	+$100 m		

The banking system loses $100 million of deposits and hence $100 million of reserves:

Banking System

Assets		Liabilities	
Reserves	−$100 m	Checkable deposits	−$100 m

For the Fed, the public's action means that $100 million of additional currency is circulating in the hands of the public, while reserves in the banking system have fallen by $100 million. The Fed's T-account is

Federal Reserve System

Assets		Liabilities	
		Currency in circulation	+$100 m
		Reserves	−$100 m

The net effect on the monetary liabilities of the Fed is a wash; the monetary base is unaffected by the public's increased desire for cash. But reserves are affected. Random fluctuations of reserves can occur as a result of random shifts into currency and out of deposits, and vice versa. The same is not true for the monetary base, making it a more stable variable.

Loans to Financial Institutions

In this chapter so far, we have seen how changes in the monetary base occur as a result of open market operations. However, the monetary base is also affected when the Fed makes a loan to a financial institution. When the Fed makes a $100 million loan to the First National Bank, the bank is credited with $100 million of reserves from the proceeds of the loan. The effects on the balance sheets of the banking system and the Fed are illustrated by the following T-accounts:

Banking System				Federal Reserve System			
Assets		Liabilities		Assets		Liabilities	
Reserves	+$100 m	Loans (borrowings from the Fed)	+$100 m	Loans (borrowings from the Fed)	+$100 m	Reserves	+$100 m

The monetary liabilities of the Fed have now increased by $100 million, and the monetary base, too, has increased by this amount. However, if a bank pays off a loan from the Fed, thereby reducing its borrowings from the Fed by $100 million, the T-accounts of the banking system and the Fed are as follows:

Banking System				Federal Reserve System			
Assets		Liabilities		Assets		Liabilities	
Reserves	−$100 m	Loans (borrowings from the Fed)	−$100 m	Loans (borrowings from the Fed)	−$100 m	Reserves	−$100 m

The net effect on the monetary liabilities of the Fed, and hence on the monetary base, is a reduction of $100 million. We see that the monetary base changes one-for-one with the change in the borrowings from the Fed.

Other Factors That Affect the Monetary Base

So far in this chapter, it seems as though the Fed has complete control of the monetary base through its open market operations and loans to financial institutions. However, the world is a little bit more complicated for the Fed. Two important items that affect the monetary base, but are not controlled by the Fed, are *float* and *Treasury deposits at the Fed*. When the Fed clears checks for banks, it often credits the amount of the check to a bank that has deposited it (increases the bank's reserves) before it debits (decreases the reserves of) the bank on which the check is drawn. The resulting temporary net increase in the total amount of reserves in the banking system (and hence in the monetary base) occurring from the Fed's check-clearing process is called **float**. When the U.S. Treasury moves deposits from commercial banks to its account at the Fed, leading to an increase in *Treasury deposits at the Fed*, it causes a deposit outflow at these banks like that shown in Chapter 10 and thus causes reserves in the banking system and the monetary base to decrease. Thus *float* (affected by random events such as the weather, which influences how quickly checks are presented for payment) and *Treasury deposits at the Fed* (determined by the U.S. Treasury's actions) both affect the monetary base but are not controlled by the Fed at all. Decisions by the U.S. Treasury to have the Fed intervene in the foreign exchange market also affect the monetary base.

Overview of the Fed's Ability to Control the Monetary Base

Our discussion above indicates that two primary features determine the monetary base: open market operations and lending to financial institutions. Whereas the amount of open market purchases or sales is completely controlled by the Fed's placing orders with dealers in bond markets, the central bank cannot unilaterally determine, and therefore cannot perfectly predict, the amount of borrowings from the Fed. The Federal Reserve sets the discount rate (interest rate on loans to banks), and then banks make decisions about whether to borrow. The amount of lending, though influenced by the Fed's setting of the discount rate, is not completely controlled by the Fed; banks' decisions play a role, too.

Therefore, we might want to split the monetary base into two components: one that the Fed can control completely and another that is less tightly controlled. The less tightly controlled component is the amount of the base that is created by loans from the Fed. The remainder of the base (called the **nonborrowed monetary base**) is under the Fed's control, because it results primarily from open market operations.[6] The nonborrowed monetary base is formally defined as the monetary base minus borrowings from the Fed, which are referred to as **borrowed reserves**:

$$MB_n = MB - BR$$

where MB_n = nonborrowed monetary base
MB = monetary base
BR = borrowed reserves from the Fed

Factors not controlled at all by the Fed (for example, float and Treasury deposits with the Fed) undergo substantial short-run variations and can be important sources of fluctuations in the monetary base over time periods as short as a week. However, these fluctuations are usually predictable and so can be offset through open market operations. ***Although float and Treasury deposits with the Fed undergo substantial short-run fluctuations, which complicate control of the monetary base, they do not prevent the Fed from accurately controlling it.***

[6]Actually, other items on the Fed's balance sheet (discussed in the appendix on the website) affect the magnitude of the nonborrowed monetary base. Because their effects on the nonborrowed base relative to open market operations are both small and predictable, these other items do not present the Fed with difficulties in controlling the nonborrowed base.

MULTIPLE DEPOSIT CREATION: A SIMPLE MODEL

With our understanding of how the Federal Reserve controls the monetary base and how banks operate (Chapter 10), we now have the tools necessary to explain how deposits are created. When the Fed supplies the banking system with $1 of additional reserves, deposits increase by a multiple of this amount—a process called **multiple deposit creation**.

Deposit Creation: The Single Bank

Suppose that the $100 million open market purchase described earlier was conducted with the First National Bank. After the Fed has bought the $100 million in bonds from the First National Bank, the bank finds that it has an increase in reserves of $100 million. To analyze what the bank will do with these additional reserves, assume that the bank does not want to hold excess reserves because it earns little interest on them. We begin the analysis with the following T-account:

First National Bank

Assets		Liabilities	
Securities	−$100 m		
Reserves	+$100 m		

Because the bank has no increase in its checkable deposits, required reserves remain the same, and the bank finds that its additional $100 million of reserves means that its excess reserves have risen by $100 million. Let's say that the bank decides to make a loan equal in amount to the $100 million rise in excess reserves. When the bank makes the loan, it sets up a checking account for the borrower and puts the proceeds of the loan into this account. In this way, the bank alters its balance sheet by increasing its liabilities with $100 million of checkable deposits and at the same time increasing its assets with the $100 million loan. The resulting T-account looks like this:

First National Bank

Assets		Liabilities	
Securities	−$100 m	Checkable deposits	+$100 m
Reserves	+$100 m		
Loans	+$100 m		

The bank has created checkable deposits by its act of lending. Because checkable deposits are part of the money supply, the bank's act of lending has, in fact, created money.

In its current balance sheet position, the First National Bank still has excess reserves and so might want to make additional loans. However, these reserves will not stay at the bank for very long. The borrowers took out loans not to leave $100 million sitting idle in a checking account at the First National Bank but to purchase goods and services from other individuals and corporations. When the borrowers make these purchases by writing checks, the checks will be deposited at other banks, and the $100 million of reserves will leave the First National Bank. ***As a result, a bank cannot safely make a loan for an amount greater than the excess reserves it has before it makes the loan.***

The final T-account of the First National Bank is

First National Bank			
Assets		**Liabilities**	
Securities	−$100 m		
Loans	+$100 m		

The increase in reserves of $100 million has been converted into additional loans of $100 at the First National Bank, plus an additional $100 million of deposits that have made their way to other banks. (All the checks written on accounts at the First National Bank are deposited in banks rather than converted into cash, because we are assuming that the public does not want to hold any additional currency.) Now let's see what happens to these deposits at the other banks.

Deposit Creation: The Banking System

To simplify the analysis, let's assume that the $100 million of deposits created by First National Bank's loan is deposited at Bank A and that this bank and all other banks hold no excess reserves. Bank A's T-account becomes

Bank A			
Assets		**Liabilities**	
Reserves	+$100 m	Checkable deposits	+$100 m

If the required reserve ratio is 10%, this bank will now find itself with a $10 million increase in required reserves, leaving it $90 million of excess reserves. Because Bank A (like the First National Bank) does not want to hold on to excess reserves, it will make loans for the entire amount. Its loans and checkable deposits will then increase by $90 million, but when the borrowers spend the $90 million of checkable deposits, they and the reserves at Bank A will fall back down by this same amount. The net result is that Bank A's T-account will look like this:

Bank A			
Assets		**Liabilities**	
Reserves	+$10 m	Checkable deposits	+$100 m
Loans	+$90 m		

If the money spent by the borrowers to whom Bank A lent the $90 million is deposited in another bank, such as Bank B, the T-account for Bank B will be

Bank B			
Assets		**Liabilities**	
Reserves	+$90 m	Checkable deposits	+$100 m

The checkable deposits in the banking system have risen by another $90 million, for a total increase of $190 million ($100 million at Bank A plus $90 million at Bank B). In fact, the distinction between Bank A and Bank B is not necessary to obtain the same result on the overall expansion of deposits. If the borrowers from Bank A write checks to someone who deposits them at Bank A, the same change in deposits would occur. The T-accounts for Bank B would just apply to Bank A, and its checkable deposits would increase by the total amount of $190 million.

Bank B will want to modify its balance sheet further. It must keep 10% of $90 million ($9 million) as required reserves and has 90% of $90 million ($81 million) in excess reserves and so can make loans of this amount. Bank B will make loans totaling $81 million to borrowers, who spend the proceeds from the loans. Bank B's T-account will be

Bank B			
Assets		**Liabilities**	
Reserves	+$ 9 m	Checkable deposits	+$90 m
Loans	+$81 m		

The $81 million spent by the borrowers from Bank B will be deposited in another bank (Bank C). Consequently, from the initial $100 million increase of reserves in the banking system, the total increase of checkable deposits in the system so far is $271 million (=$100 m + $90 m + $81 m).

Following the same reasoning, if all banks make loans for the full amount of their excess reserves, further increments in checkable deposits will continue (at Banks C, D, E, and so on), as depicted in Table 1. Therefore, the total increase in deposits from the initial $100 increase in reserves will be $1,000 million: The increase is tenfold, the reciprocal of the 10% (0.10) reserve requirement.

If the banks choose to invest their excess reserves in securities, the result is the same. If Bank A had taken its excess reserves and purchased securities instead of making loans, its T-account would have looked like this:

Bank A			
Assets		**Liabilities**	
Reserves	+$10 m	Checkable deposits	+$100m
Securities	+$90 m		

TABLE 1 **Creation of Deposits (assuming 10% reserve requirement and a $100 million increase in reserves)**

Bank	Increase in Deposits ($)	Increase in Loans ($)	Increase in Reserves ($)
First National	0.00	100.00 m	0.00
A	100.00 m	90.00 m	10.00 m
B	90.00 m	81.00 m	9.00 m
C	81.00 m	72.90 m	8.10 m
D	72.90 m	65.61 m	7.29 m
E	65.61 m	59.05 m	6.56 m
F	59.05 m	53.14 m	5.91 m
.	.	.	.
.	.	.	.
.	.	.	.
Total for all banks	1,000.00 m	1,000.00 m	100.00 m

When the bank buys $90 million of securities, it writes $90 million in checks to the sellers of the securities, who in turn deposit the $90 million at a bank such as Bank B. Bank B's checkable deposits increase by $90 million, and the deposit expansion process is the same as before. ***Whether a bank chooses to use its excess reserves to make loans or to purchase securities, the effect on deposit expansion is the same.***

You can now see the difference in deposit creation for the single bank versus the banking system as a whole. Because a single bank can create deposits equal only to the amount of its excess reserves, it cannot by itself generate multiple deposit expansion. A single bank cannot make loans greater in amount than its excess reserves, because the bank will lose these reserves as the deposits created by the loan find their way to other banks. However, the banking system as a whole can generate a multiple expansion of deposits, because when a bank loses its excess reserves, these reserves do not leave the banking system, even though they are lost to the individual bank. So as each bank makes a loan and creates deposits, the reserves find their way to another bank, which uses them to make additional loans and create additional deposits. As you have seen, this process continues until the initial increase in reserves results in a multiple increase in deposits.

The multiple increase in deposits generated from an increase in the banking system's reserves is called the **simple deposit multiplier**.[7] In our example with a 10% required reserve ratio, the simple deposit multiplier is 10. More generally, the simple deposit multiplier equals the reciprocal of the required reserve ratio, expressed as a fraction (for example, 10 = 1/0.10), so the formula for the multiple expansion of deposits can be written as follows.

$$\Delta D = \frac{1}{rr} \times \Delta R \tag{1}$$

[7]This multiplier should not be confused with the Keynesian multiplier, which is derived through a similar step-by-step analysis. That multiplier relates an increase in income to an increase in investment, whereas the simple deposit multiplier relates an increase in deposits to an increase in reserves.

where ΔD = change in total checkable deposits in the banking system
rr = required reserve ratio (0.10 in the example)
ΔR = change in reserves for the banking system ($100 million in the example)

Deriving the Formula for Multiple Deposit Creation

The formula for the multiple creation of deposits can be derived directly using algebra. We obtain the same answer for the relationship between a change in deposits and a change in reserves.

Our assumption that banks do not hold on to any excess reserves means that the total amount of required reserves for the banking system RR will equal the total reserves in the banking system R:

$$RR = R$$

The total amount of required reserves equals the required reserve ratio rr times the total amount of checkable deposits D:

$$RR = rr \times D$$

Substituting $rr \times D$ for RR in the first equation

$$rr \times D = R$$

and dividing both sides of the preceding equation by rr gives

$$D = \frac{1}{rr} \times R$$

Taking the change in both sides of this equation and using delta to indicate a change gives

$$\Delta D = \frac{1}{rr} \times \Delta R$$

which is the same formula for deposit creation found in Equation 1.[8]

This derivation provides us with another way of looking at the multiple creation of deposits, because it forces us to examine the banking system as a whole rather than one bank at a time. For the banking system as a whole, deposit creation (or contraction) will stop only when excess reserves in the banking system are zero; that is, the banking system will be in equilibrium when the total amount of required reserves equals the total amount of reserves, as seen in the equation $RR = R$. When $rr \times D$ is substituted for RR, the resulting equation $rr \times D = R$ tells us how high checkable deposits will have to be for required reserves to equal total reserves. Accordingly, a given level of reserves in the banking system determines the level of checkable deposits when the banking system is in equilibrium (when $ER = 0$); put another way, the given level of reserves supports a given level of checkable deposits.

[8]A formal derivation of this formula follows. Using the reasoning in the text, the change in checkable deposits is $100($= \Delta R \times 1$) plus $90[$= \Delta R \times (1 - rr)$] plus $81[$= \Delta R \times (1 - rr)^2$], and so on, which can be rewritten as

$$\Delta D = \Delta R \times [1 + (1 - rr) + (1 - rr)^2 + (1 - rr)^3 + \cdots]$$

Using the formula for the sum of an infinite series found in footnote 5 in Chapter 4, this can be rewritten as

$$\Delta D = \Delta R \times \frac{1}{1 - (1 - rr)} = \frac{1}{rr} \times \Delta R$$

In our example, the required reserve ratio is 10%. If reserves increase by $100 million, checkable deposits must rise by $1,000 million for total required reserves also to increase by $100 million. If the increase in checkable deposits is less than this—say, $900 million—then the increase in required reserves of $90 million remains below the $100 million increase in reserves, so excess reserves still exist somewhere in the banking system. The banks with the excess reserves will now make additional loans, creating new deposits; this process will continue until all reserves in the system are used up, which occurs when checkable deposits rise by $1,000 million.

We can also see this by looking at the T-account of the banking system as a whole (including the First National Bank) that results from this process:

Banking System

Assets		Liabilities	
Securities	−$ 100 m	Checkable deposits	+$1,000 m
Reserves	+$ 100 m		
Loans	+$1,000 m		

The procedure of eliminating excess reserves by loaning them out means that the banking system (First National Bank and Banks A, B, C, D, and so on) continues to make loans up to the $1,000 million amount until deposits have reached the $1,000 million level. In this way, $100 million of reserves supports $1,000 million (ten times the quantity) of deposits.

Critique of the Simple Model

Our model of multiple deposit creation seems to indicate that the Federal Reserve is able to exercise complete control over the level of checkable deposits by setting the required reserve ratio and the level of reserves. The actual creation of deposits is much less mechanical than the simple model indicates. If proceeds from Bank A's $90 million loan are not deposited but are kept in currency, nothing is deposited in Bank B and the deposit creation process ceases. The total increase in the money supply is now the $90 million increase in currency plus the initial $100 million of deposits created by First National Bank's loans, which were deposited at Bank A, for a total of only $190 million—considerably less than the $1,000 million we calculated with the simple model above. Another way of saying this is that currency has no multiple deposit expansion, while deposits do. Thus, if some proceeds from loans are not deposited in banks but instead are used to raise the holdings of currency, less multiple expansion occurs overall, and the money supply will not increase by as much as our simple model of multiple deposit creation tells us.

Another situation ignored in our model is one in which banks do not make loans or buy securities in the full amount of their excess reserves. If Bank A decides to hold on to all $90 million of its excess reserves, no deposits would be made in Bank B, and this would also stop the deposit creation process. The total increase in deposits would be only $100 million, not the $1,000 million increase in our example. Hence, if banks choose to hold on to all or some of their excess reserves, the full expansion of deposits predicted by the simple model of multiple deposit creation again does not occur.

Our examples indicate that the Fed is not the only player whose behavior influences the level of deposits and therefore the money supply. Depositors' decisions regarding how much currency to hold and banks' decisions regarding the amount of excess reserves to hold also can cause the money supply to change.

FACTORS THAT DETERMINE THE MONEY SUPPLY

Our critique of the simple model shows how we can expand on it to discuss all the factors that affect the money supply. Let's look at changes in each factor in turn, holding all other factors constant.

Changes in the Nonborrowed Monetary Base, MB_n

As shown earlier in the chapter, the Fed's open market purchases increase the nonborrowed monetary base, and its open market sales decrease it. Holding all other variables constant, an increase in MB_n arising from an open market purchase raises the amount of the monetary base and reserves, so that multiple deposit creation occurs and the money supply increases. Similarly, an open market sale that reduces MB_n shrinks the amount of the monetary base and reserves, thereby causing a multiple contraction of deposits and a decrease in the money supply. We have the following result: ***The money supply is positively related to the nonborrowed monetary base MB_n.***

Changes in Borrowed Reserves, *BR*, from the Fed

An increase in loans from the Fed provides additional borrowed reserves, and thereby increases the amount of the monetary base and reserves, so that multiple deposit creation occurs and the money supply expands. If banks reduce the level of their discount loans, all other variables held constant, the monetary base and amount of reserves would fall, and the money supply would decrease. The result is this: ***The money supply is positively related to the level of borrowed reserves, BR, from the Fed.***

Changes in the Required Reserve Ratio, *rr*

If the required reserve ratio on checkable deposits increases while all other variables, such as the monetary base, stay the same, we have seen that multiple deposit expansion is reduced, and hence the money supply falls. If, on the other hand, the required reserve ratio falls, multiple deposit expansion would be higher and the money supply would rise.

We now have the following result: ***The money supply is negatively related to the required reserve ratio rr.*** In the past, the Fed sometimes used reserve requirements to affect the size of the money supply. In recent years, however, reserve requirements have become a less important factor in the determination of the money multiplier and the money supply, as we shall see in the next chapter.

Changes in Currency Holdings

As shown before, checkable deposits undergo multiple expansion, whereas currency does not. Hence, when checkable deposits are converted into currency, holding the monetary base and other variables constant, a switch is made from a component of the money supply that undergoes multiple expansion to one that does not. The overall level of multiple expansion declines and the money supply falls. On the other hand, if currency holdings fall, a switch is made into checkable deposits that undergo multiple deposit expansion, so the money supply would rise. This analysis suggests the following result: ***The money supply is negatively related to currency holdings.***

Changes in Excess Reserves

When banks increase their holdings of excess reserves, those reserves are no longer being used to make loans, causing multiple deposit creation to stop dead in its tracks, resulting in less expansion of the money supply. If, on the other hand, banks chose to hold fewer excess reserves, loans and multiple deposit creation would increase and the money supply would rise. ***The money supply is negatively related to the amount of excess reserves.***

Recall from Chapter 10 that the primary benefit to a bank of holding excess reserves is that they provide insurance against losses due to deposit outflows; that is, they enable the bank experiencing deposit outflows to escape the costs of calling in loans, selling securities, borrowing from the Fed or other corporations, or bank failure. If banks fear that deposit outflows are likely to increase (that is, if expected deposit outflows increase), they will want more insurance against this possibility and excess reserves will rise.

OVERVIEW OF THE MONEY SUPPLY PROCESS

We now have a model of the money supply process in which all three of the players—the Federal Reserve System, depositors, and banks—directly influence the money supply. As a study aid, Summary Table 1 charts the money supply response to the five factors discussed above and gives a brief synopsis of the reasoning behind them.

SUMMARY TABLE 1

Money Supply Response

Player	Variable	Change in Variable	Money Supply Response	Reason
Federal Reserve System	Nonborrowed monetary base, MB_n	↑	↑	More *MB* for deposit creation
	Required reserve ratio, *rr*	↑	↓	Less multiple deposit expansion
Banks	Borrowed reserves, *BR*	↑	↑	More *MB* for deposit creation
	Excess reserves	↑	↓	Less loans and deposit creation
Depositors	Currency holdings	↑	↓	Less multiple deposit expansion

Note: Only increases (↑) in the variables are shown. The effects of decreases on the money supply would be the opposite of those indicated in the "Money Supply Response" column.

The variables are grouped by the player who is the primary influence behind the variable. The Federal Reserve, for example, influences the money supply by controlling the first two variables. Depositors influence the money supply through their decisions about holdings of currency, while banks influence the money supply with their decisions about borrowings from the Fed and excess reserves.

THE MONEY MULTIPLIER

The intuition in the section above is sufficient for you to understand how the money supply process works. For those of you who are more mathematically inclined, we can derive all of the above results using a concept called the **money multiplier**, denoted by $\boldsymbol{m}$, which tells us how much the money supply changes for a given change in the monetary base. The relationship between the money supply M, the money multiplier, and the monetary base is described by the following equation:

$$M = m \times MB \tag{2}$$

The money multiplier m tells us what multiple of the monetary base is transformed into the money supply. Because the money multiplier is larger than 1, the alternative name for the monetary base, *high-powered money*, is logical: A \$1 change in the monetary base leads to more than a \$1 change in the money supply.

Deriving the Money Multiplier

Let's assume that the desired holdings of currency C and excess reserves ER grows proportionally with checkable deposits D; in other words, we assume that the ratios of these items to checkable deposits are constants in equilibrium, as the braces in the following expressions indicate:

$$c = \{C/D\} = \text{currency ratio}$$
$$e = \{ER/D\} = \text{excess reserves ratio}$$

We will now derive a formula that describes how the currency ratio desired by depositors, the excess reserves ratio desired by banks, and the required reserve ratio set by the Fed affect the multiplier m. We begin the derivation of the model of the money supply with the following equation:

$$R = RR + ER$$

which states that the total amount of reserves in the banking system R equals the sum of required reserves RR and excess reserves ER. (Note that this equation corresponds to the equilibrium condition $RR = R$ earlier in the chapter, where excess reserves were assumed to be zero.)

The total amount of required reserves equals the required reserve ratio rr times the amount of checkable deposits D:

$$RR = rr \times D$$

Substituting $rr \times D$ for RR in the first equation yields an equation that links reserves in the banking system to the amount of checkable deposits and excess reserves they can support:

$$R = (rr \times D) + ER$$

A key point here is that the Fed sets the required reserve ratio rr to less than 1. Thus \$1 of reserves can support more than \$1 of deposits, and the multiple expansion of deposits can occur.

Let's see how this works in practice. If excess reserves are held at zero ($ER = 0$), the required reserve ratio is set at $rr = 0.10$, and the level of checkable deposits in the banking system is \$800 billion, then the amount of reserves needed to support these deposits is \$80 billion ($=0.10 \times$ \$800 billion). The \$80 billion of reserves can support ten times this amount in checkable deposits because multiple deposit creation will occur.

Because the monetary base MB equals currency C plus reserves R, we can generate an equation that links the amount of the monetary base to the levels of checkable deposits and currency by adding currency to both sides of the equation:

$$MB = R + C = (rr \times D) + ER + C$$

Another way of thinking about this equation is to recognize that it reveals the amount of the monetary base needed to support the existing amounts of checkable deposits, currency, and excess reserves.

To derive the money multiplier formula in terms of the currency ratio $c = \{C/D\}$ and the excess reserves ratio $e = \{ER/D\}$, we rewrite the last equation, specifying C as $c \times D$ and ER as $e \times D$:

$$MB = (rr \times D) + (e \times D) + (c \times D) = (rr + e + c) \times D$$

We next divide both sides of the equation by the term inside the parentheses to get an expression linking checkable deposits D to the monetary base MB:

$$D = \frac{1}{rr + e + c} \times MB \qquad (3)$$

Using the M1 definition of the money supply as currency plus checkable deposits ($M = D + C$) and again specifying C as $c \times D$,

$$M = D + (c \times D) = (1 + c) \times D$$

Substituting in this equation the expression for D from Equation 3, we have

$$M = \frac{1 + c}{rr + e + c} \times MB \qquad (4)$$

We have derived an expression in the form of our earlier Equation 2. As you can see, the ratio that multiplies MB is the money multiplier, which tells how much the money supply changes in response to a given change in the monetary base (high-powered money). The money multiplier m is thus

$$m = \frac{1 + c}{rr + e + c} \qquad (5)$$

It is a function of the currency ratio set by depositors c, the excess reserves ratio set by banks e, and the required reserve ratio set by the Fed rr.

Intuition Behind the Money Multiplier

To get a feel for what the money multiplier means, let's construct a numerical example with realistic numbers for the following variables:

$$rr = \text{required reserve ratio} = 0.10$$
$$C = \text{currency in circulation} = \$400 \text{ billion}$$
$$D = \text{checkable deposits} = \$800 \text{ billion}$$
$$ER = \text{excess reserves} = \$0.8 \text{ billion}$$
$$M = \text{money supply (M1)} = C + D = \$1{,}200 \text{ billion}$$

From these numbers we can calculate the values for the currency ratio c and the excess reserves ratio e:

$$c = \frac{\$400 \text{ billion}}{\$800 \text{ billion}} = 0.5$$

$$e = \frac{\$0.8 \text{ billion}}{\$800 \text{ billion}} = 0.001$$

The resulting value of the money multiplier is

$$m = \frac{1 + 0.5}{0.1 + 0.001 + 0.5} = \frac{1.5}{0.601} = 2.5$$

The money multiplier of 2.5 tells us that, given the required reserve ratio of 10% on checkable deposits and the behavior of depositors, as represented by $c = 0.5$, and banks, as represented by $e = 0.001$, a \$1 increase in the monetary base leads to a \$2.50 increase in the money supply (M1).

An important characteristic of the money multiplier is that it is less than the simple deposit multiplier of 10 found earlier in the chapter. The key to understanding this result is to realize that ***although there is multiple expansion of deposits, there is no such expansion for currency***. Thus, if some portion of the increase in high-powered money finds its way into currency, this portion does not undergo multiple deposit expansion. In our simple model earlier in the chapter, we did not allow for this possibility, and so the increase in reserves led to the maximum amount of multiple deposit creation. However, in our current model of the money multiplier, the level of currency does rise when the monetary base MB and checkable deposits D increase because c is greater than zero. As previously stated, any increase in MB that goes into an increase in currency is not multiplied, so only part of the increase in MB is available to support checkable deposits that undergo multiple expansion. The overall level of multiple deposit expansion must be lower, meaning that the increase in M, given an increase in MB, is smaller than the simple model earlier in the chapter indicated.[9]

[9]Another reason the money multiplier is smaller is that e is a constant fraction greater than zero, indicating that an increase in MB and D leads to higher excess reserves. The resulting higher amount of excess reserves means that the amount of reserves used to support checkable deposits will not increase as much as it otherwise would. Hence the increase in checkable deposits and the money supply will be lower, and the money multiplier will be smaller. However, because e is often tiny—about 0.001—the impact of this ratio on the money multiplier can be quite small. But there are periods when e is much larger and so has a more important role in lowering the money multiplier.

Money Supply Response to Changes in the Factors

By recognizing that the monetary base is $MB = MB_n + BR$, we can rewrite Equation 2 as

$$M = m \times (MB_n + BR) \tag{6}$$

Now we can show algebraically all the results in Summary Table 1, which shows the money supply response to the changes in the factors.

As you can see from Equation 6, a rise in MB_n or BR raises the money supply M by a multiple amount because the money multiplier m is greater than one. We can see that a rise in the required reserve ratio lowers the money supply by calculating what happens to the value of the money multiplier using Equation 5 in our numerical example when rr increases from 10% to 15% (leaving all other variables unchanged). The money multiplier then falls from 2.5 to

$$m = \frac{1 + 0.5}{0.15 + 0.001 + 0.5} = \frac{1.5}{0.651} = 2.3$$

which, as we would expect, is less than 2.5.

Similarly, we can see in our numerical example that a rise in currency lowers the money supply by calculating what happens to the money multiplier when c is raised from 0.50 to 0.75. The money multiplier then falls from 2.5 to

$$m = \frac{1 + 0.75}{0.1 + 0.001 + 0.75} = \frac{1.75}{0.851} = 2.06$$

Finally, we can see that a rise in excess reserves lowers the money supply by calculating what happens to the money multiplier when e is raised from 0.001 to 0.005. The money multiplier declines from 2.5 to

$$m = \frac{1 + 0.5}{0.1 + 0.005 + 0.5} = \frac{1.5}{0.605} = 2.48$$

Note that although the excess reserves ratio has risen fivefold, only a small decline has occurred in the money multiplier. This decline is small because in recent years e has usually been extremely small, so changes in it have only a minor impact on the money multiplier. However, there have been times, particularly during the Great Depression period and the recent financial crisis, which we examine in the next two applications, when this ratio was far higher, and its movements had a substantial effect on the money supply and the money multiplier.[10]

[10]All the above results can be derived more generally from the Equation 5 formula for m as follows. When r or e increases, the denominator of the money multiplier increases, and therefore the money multiplier must decrease. As long as $r + e$ is less than 1 (as is the case using the realistic numbers as above), an increase in c raises the denominator of the money multiplier proportionally by more than it raises the numerator. The increase in c causes the multiplier to fall. For more background on the currency ratio c, consult the third Web appendix to this chapter at www.myeconlab.com/mishkin. Recall that the money multiplier in Equation 5 is for the M1 definition of money. A second appendix on the website discusses how the multiplier for M2 is determined.

APPLICATION ◆ The Great Depression Bank Panics, 1930–1933, and the Money Supply

We can also use our money supply model to help us understand major movements in the money supply that have occurred in the past. In this application, we use the model to explain the monetary contraction that occurred during the Great Depression, the worst economic downturn in U.S. history. In Chapter 9, we discussed bank panics and saw that they could harm the economy by making asymmetric information problems more severe in credit markets, as they did during the Great Depression. Here we see that another consequence of bank panics is that they can cause a substantial reduction in the money supply. As we will understand from the chapters on monetary theory later in the book, such reductions can also cause severe damage to the economy.

Figure 1 traces the bank crisis during the Great Depression by showing the volume of deposits at failed commercial banks from 1929 to 1933. In their classic book *A Monetary History of the United States, 1867–1960*, Milton Friedman and Anna Schwartz describe the onset of the first banking crisis in late 1930 as follows:

> Before October 1930, deposits of suspended [failed] commercial banks had been somewhat higher than during most of 1929 but not out of line with experience during the preceding decade. In November 1930, they were more than double the highest value recorded since the start of monthly data in 1921. A crop of bank failures, particularly in Missouri, Indiana, Illinois, Iowa, Arkansas, and North Carolina, led to widespread attempts to convert checkable and time deposits into currency, and also, to a much lesser extent, into postal savings deposits. A contagion of fear spread among depositors, starting from the agricultural areas, which had experienced the heaviest impact of bank failures in the twenties. But failure of 256 banks with \$180 million of deposits in November 1930 was followed by the failure of 532 with over \$370 million of deposits in December (all figures seasonally unadjusted), the most dramatic being the failure on December 11 of the Bank of United States with over \$200 million of deposits. That failure was especially important. The Bank of United States was the largest commercial bank, as measured by volume of deposits, ever to have failed up to that time in U.S. history. Moreover, though it was just an ordinary commercial bank, the Bank of United States's name had led many at home and abroad to regard it somehow as an official bank, hence its failure constituted more of a blow to confidence than would have been administered by the fall of a bank with a less distinctive name.[11]

The first bank panic, from October 1930 to January 1931, is clearly visible in Figure 1 at the end of 1930, when a rise in the amount of deposits at failed banks occurred. Because no deposit insurance was in place at the time (the FDIC wasn't established until 1934), when a bank failed, depositors would receive only partial repayment of their deposits. Therefore, when banks were failing during a bank panic, depositors knew that they would be likely to suffer substantial losses on deposits and thus the expected return on deposits would be negative. The theory of portfolio choice predicts that with the onset of the first bank crisis, depositors would shift their holdings from checkable

[11]Milton Friedman and Anna Jacobson Schwartz, *A Monetary History of the United States, 1867–1960* (Princeton, NJ: Princeton University Press, 1963), pp. 308–311.

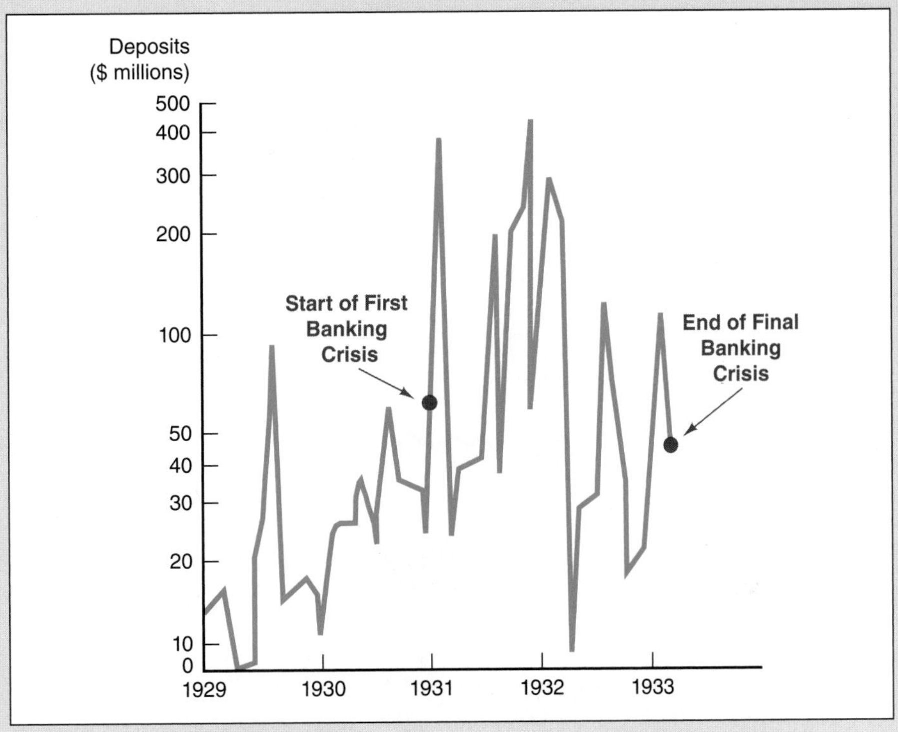

FIGURE 1 Deposits of Failed Commercial Banks, 1929–1933

The volume of deposits at failed commercial banks from 1929 to 1933 traces the bank crisis during the Great Depression.

Source: Milton Friedman and Anna Jacobson Schwartz, *A Monetary History of the United States, 1867–1960* (Princeton, NJ: Princeton University Press, 1963), p. 309.

deposits to currency by withdrawing currency from their bank accounts, and c would rise. Our earlier analysis of the excess reserves ratio suggests that the resulting surge in deposit outflows would cause the banks to protect themselves by substantially increasing their excess reserves ratio e. Both of these predictions are borne out by the data in Figure 2. During the first bank panic (October 1930–January 1931) the currency ratio c began to climb. Even more striking is the behavior of the excess reserves ratio e, which more than doubled from November 1930 to January 1931.

The money supply model predicts that when e and c increase, the money supply will contract. The rise in c results in a decline in the overall level of multiple deposit expansion, leading to a smaller money multiplier and a decline in the money supply, whereas the rise in e reduces the amount of reserves available to support deposits and also causes the money supply to decrease. Thus our model predicts that the rise in e and c after the onset of the first bank crisis would result in a decline in the money supply—a prediction borne out by the evidence in Figure 3.

Banking crises continued to occur from 1931 to 1933, and the pattern predicted by our model persisted: c continued to rise, and so did e. By the end of the crises in March

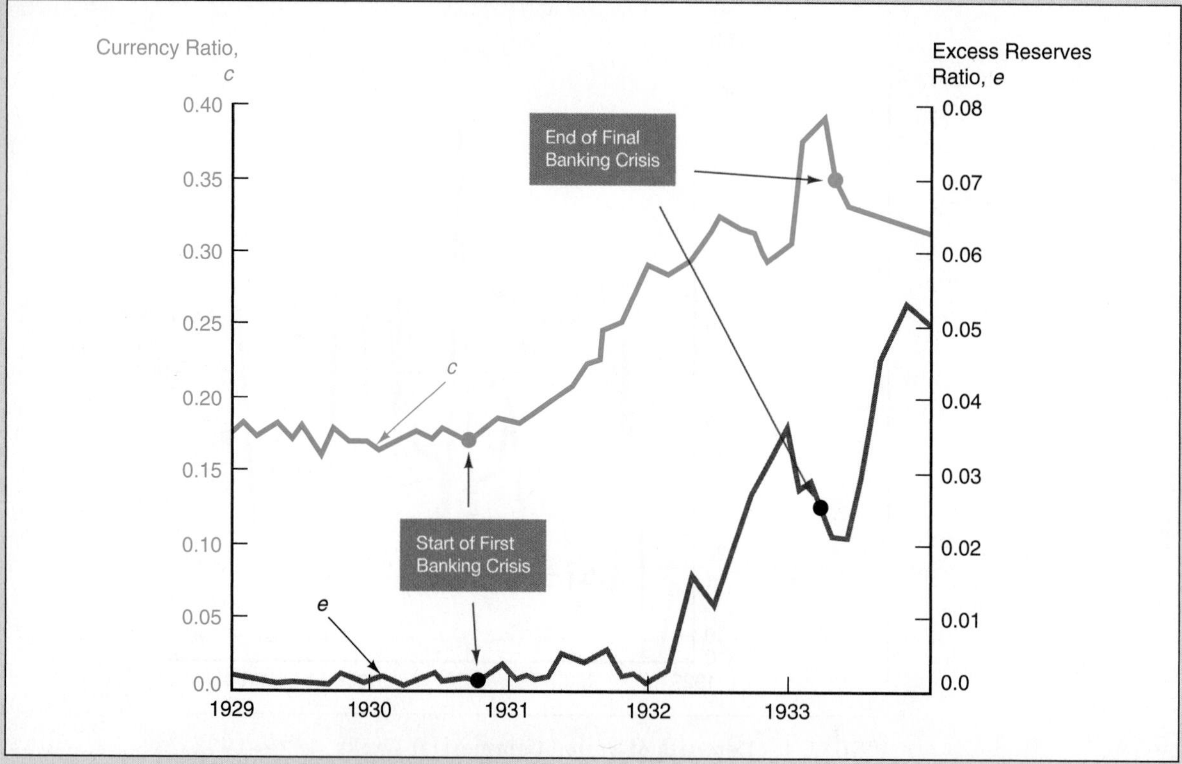

FIGURE 2 Excess Reserves Ratio and Currency Ratio, 1929–1933

During the first bank panic (October 1930–January 1931) *c* began to climb, while *e* more than doubled from November 1930 to January 1931. Subsequently, the ongoing banking crises led to continuing increases in both c and e.

Sources: Federal Reserve *Bulletin;* Milton Friedman and Anna Jacobson Schwartz, *A Monetary History of the United States, 1867–1960* (Princeton, NJ: Princeton University Press, 1963), p. 333.

1933, the money supply (M1) had declined by over 25%—by far the largest decline in all of American history—and it coincided with the nation's worst economic contraction (see Chapter 9). Even more remarkable is that this decline occurred despite a 20% rise in the level of the monetary base—which illustrates how important the changes in *c* and *e* during bank panics can be in the determination of the money supply. It also illustrates that the Fed's job of conducting monetary policy can be complicated by depositor and bank behavior.

APPLICATION ◆ The 2007–2009 Financial Crisis and the Money Supply

The previous application shows that the money supply and the monetary base do not always move in tandem. An even more extraordinary example occurred during the

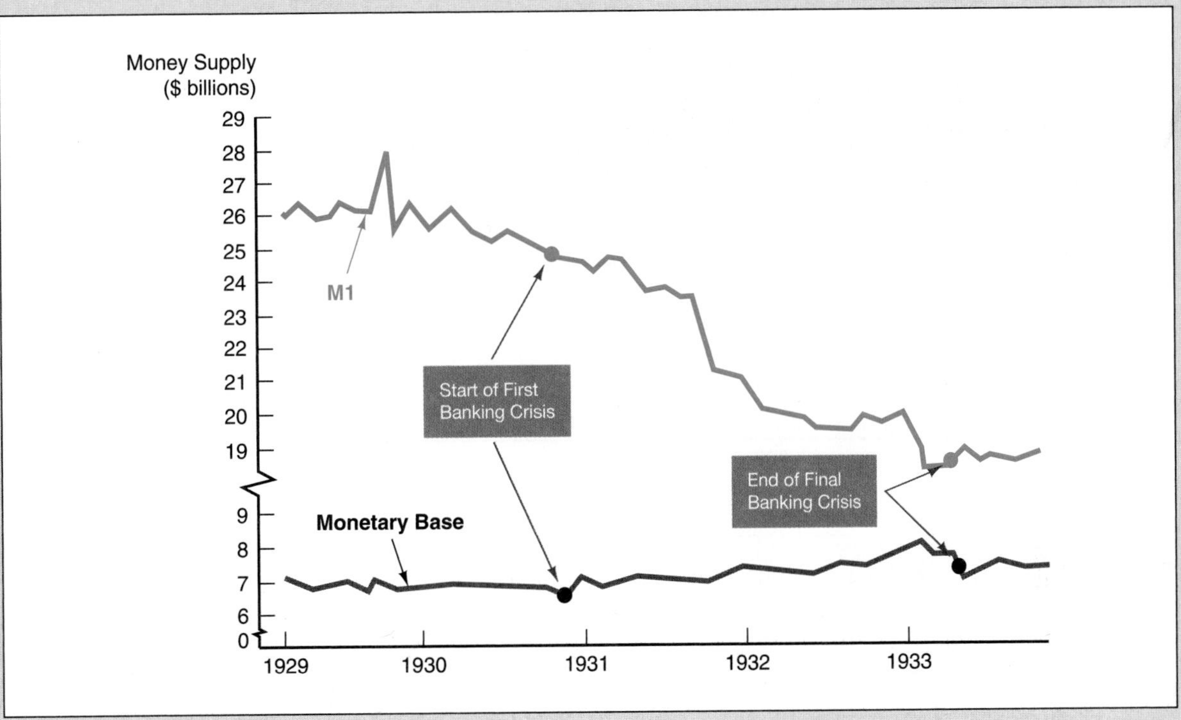

FIGURE 3 M1 and the Monetary Base, 1929–1933

The rise in *e* and *c* after the onset of the first bank crisis led to a decline in the money supply even though the monetary base rose.

Source: Milton Friedman and Anna Jacobson Schwartz, *A Monetary History of the United States, 1867–1960* (Princeton, NJ: Princeton University Press, 1963), p. 333.

recent financial crisis, as shown in Figure 4, when the monetary base increased by more than 200% as a result of the Fed's purchase of assets and creation of new lending facilities to stem the financial crisis (discussed in Chapter 18), while the M1 money supply rose by less than 25%. How does our money supply model explain this?

Figure 5 shows the currency ratio *c* and the excess reserves ratio *e* for the 2007–2009 period. We see that the currency ratio fell somewhat during this period, which our money supply model suggests would raise the money multiplier and the money supply because it would increase the overall level of deposit expansion. However, the effects of the decline in *c* were entirely offset by the extraordinary rise in the excess reserves ratio *e*, which climbed by more than a factor of over 500 during this period. The explanation for this increase in *e* was that banks were willing to hold the huge increase in excess reserves because they had become costless to hold once the Fed began paying interest on these reserves and this interest rate often exceeded the rate at which the banks could lend them out at in the federal funds market. As our money supply model predicts, the huge increase in *e* would lower the money multiplier, and so the money supply would expand only slightly, despite the huge increase in the monetary base.◆

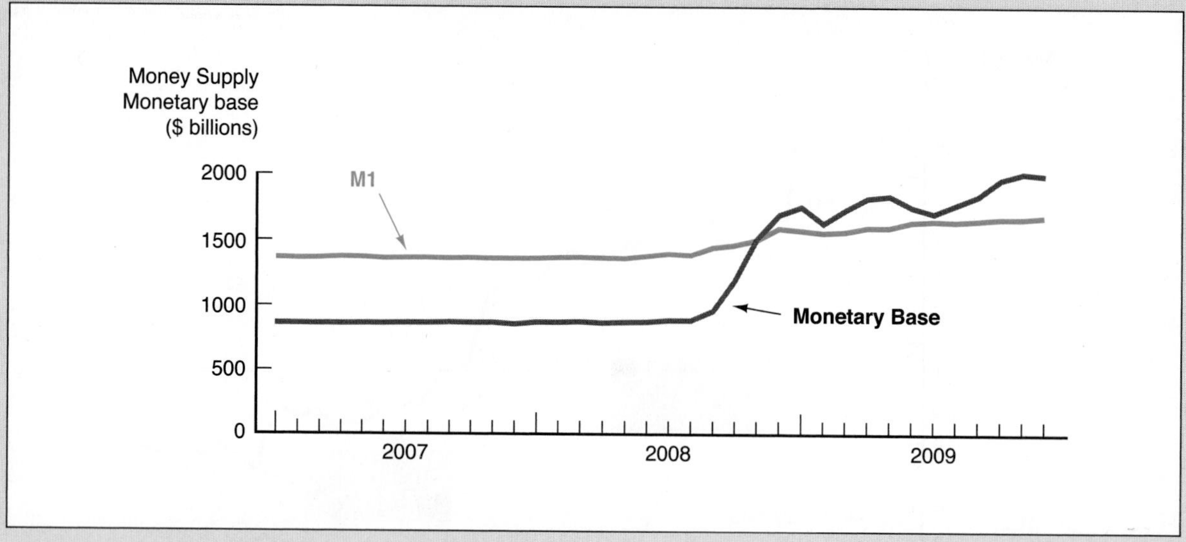

FIGURE 4 M1 and the Monetary Base, 2007–2009
The money supply rose by less than 25% despite the increase in the monetary base by over 200%.
Source: Federal Reserve; www.federalreserve.gov/releases.

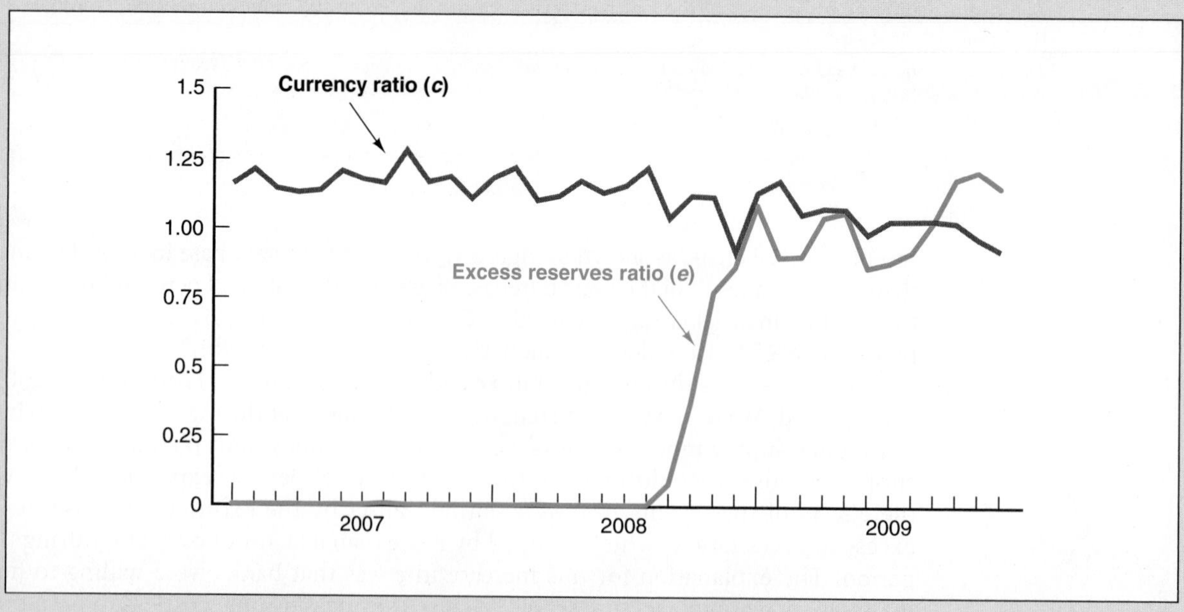

FIGURE 5 Excess Reserves Ratio and Currency Ratio, 2007–2009
The currency ratio c fell during the crisis, whereas the excess reserves ratio e rose by a factor of over 500.
Source: Federal Reserve; www.federalreserve.gov/releases.

Summary

1. The three players in the money supply process are the central bank, banks (depository institutions), and depositors.
2. Four items in the Fed's balance sheet are essential to our understanding of the money supply process: the two liability items, currency in circulation and reserves, which together make up the monetary base, and the two asset items, securities and loans to financial institutions.
3. The Federal Reserve controls the monetary base through open market operations and extension of loans to financial institutions and has better control over the monetary base than over reserves. Although float and Treasury deposits with the Fed undergo substantial short-run fluctuations, which complicate control of the monetary base, they do not prevent the Fed from accurately controlling it.
4. A single bank can make loans up to the amount of its excess reserves, thereby creating an equal amount of deposits. The banking system can create a multiple expansion of deposits, because as each bank makes a loan and creates deposits, the reserves find their way to another bank, which uses them to make loans and create additional deposits. In the simple model of multiple deposit creation in which banks do not hold on to excess reserves and the public holds no currency, the multiple increase in checkable deposits (simple deposit multiplier) equals the reciprocal of the required reserve ratio.
5. The simple model of multiple deposit creation has serious deficiencies. Decisions by depositors to increase their holdings of currency or of banks to hold excess reserves will result in a smaller expansion of deposits than the simple model predicts. All three players—the Fed, banks, and depositors—are important in the determination of the money supply.
6. The money supply is positively related to the nonborrowed monetary base MB_n, which is determined by open market operations, and the level of borrowed reserves (lending) from the Fed, BR. The money supply is negatively related to the required reserve ratio, rr; holdings of currency; and excess reserves. The model of the money supply process takes into account the behavior of all three players in the money supply process: the Fed through open market operations and setting of the required reserve ratio; banks through their decisions to borrow from the Federal Reserve and hold excess reserves; and depositors through their decisions about holding of currency.
7. The monetary base is linked to the money supply using the concept of the money multiplier, which tells us how much the money supply changes when the monetary base changes.

Key Terms

borrowed reserves, p. 403
discount rate, p. 397
excess reserves, p. 397
float, p. 403
high-powered money, p. 397
monetary base, p. 396
money multiplier, p. 412
multiple deposit creation, p. 404
nonborrowed monetary base, p. 403
open market operations, p. 398
open market purchase, p. 398
open market sale, p. 398
required reserve ratio, p. 397
required reserves, p. 397
reserves, p. 397
simple deposit multiplier, p. 407

Questions

All questions are available in MyEconLab *at* www.myeconlab.com. *Unless otherwise noted, the following assumptions are made in all questions: The required reserve ratio on checkable deposits is 10%, banks do not hold any excess reserves, and the public's holdings of currency do not change.*

1. Classify each of these transactions as either an asset, a liability, or neither for each of the "players" in the money supply process—the Federal Reserve, banks, and depositors.

a. You get a $10,000 loan from the bank to buy an automobile.

b. You deposit $400 into your checking account at the local bank.

c. The Fed provides an emergency loan to a bank for $1,000,000.

d. A bank borrows $500,000 in overnight loans from another bank.

e. You use your debit card to purchase a meal at a restaurant for $100.

2. The First National Bank receives an extra $100 of reserves but decides not to lend out any of these reserves. How much deposit creation takes place for the entire banking system?

3. Suppose that the Fed buys $1 million of bonds from the First National Bank. If the First National Bank and all other banks use the resulting increase in reserves to purchase securities only and not to make loans, what will happen to checkable deposits?

4. If a bank depositor withdraws $1,000 of currency from an account, what happens to reserves, checkable deposits, and the monetary base?

5. If a bank sells $10 million of bonds to the Fed to pay back $10 million on the loan it owes, what will be the effect on the level of checkable deposits?

6. If you decide to hold $100 less cash than usual and therefore deposit $100 more cash in the bank, what effect will this have on checkable deposits in the banking system if the rest of the public keeps its holdings of currency constant?

7. "The Fed can perfectly control the amount of reserves in the system." Is this statement true, false, or uncertain? Explain.

8. "The Fed can perfectly control the amount of the monetary base, but has less control over the composition of the monetary base." Is this statement true, false, or uncertain? Explain.

9. The Fed buys $100 million of bonds from the public and also lowers the required reserve ratio. What will happen to the money supply?

10. Describe how each of the following can affect the money supply: (a) the central bank; (b) banks; and (c) depositors.

11. "The money multiplier is necessarily greater than 1." Is this statement true, false, or uncertain? Explain your answer.

12. What effect might a financial panic have on the money multiplier and the money supply? Why?

13. During the Great Depression years from 1930–1933, both the currency ratio c and the excess reserves ratio e rose dramatically. What effect did these factors have on the money multiplier?

14. In October 2008, the Federal Reserve began paying interest on the amount of excess reserves held by banks. How, if at all, might this affect the multiplier process and the money supply?

15. The money multiplier declined significantly during the period 1930–1933 and also during the recent financial crisis of 2008–2010. Yet the M1 money supply decreased by 25% in the Depression period but *increased* by more than 20% during the recent financial crisis. What explains the difference in outcomes?

Applied Problems

All applied problems are available in MyEconLab *at* www.myeconlab.com. *Unless otherwise noted, the following assumptions are made in all the applied problems: The required reserve ratio on checkable deposits is 10%, banks do not hold any excess reserves, and the public's holdings of currency do not change.*

16. If the Fed sells $2 million of bonds to the First National Bank, what happens to reserves and the monetary base? Use T-accounts to explain your answer.

17. If the Fed sells $2 million of bonds to Irving the Investor, who pays for the bonds with a briefcase filled with currency, what happens to reserves and the monetary base? Use T-accounts to explain your answer.

18. If the Fed lends five banks an additional total of $100 million but depositors withdraw $50 million and hold it as currency, what happens to reserves and the monetary base? Use T-accounts to explain your answer.

19. Using T-accounts, show what happens to checkable deposits in the banking system when the Fed lends an additional $1 million to the First National Bank.

20. Using T-accounts, show what happens to checkable deposits in the banking system when the Fed sells $2 million of bonds to the First National Bank.

21. If the Fed buys $1 million of bonds from the First National Bank, but an additional 10% of any deposit is held as excess reserves, what is the total increase in checkable deposits? (*Hint:* Use T-accounts to show what happens at each step of the multiple expansion process.)

22. If reserves in the banking system increase by $1 billion as a result of Fed lending to financial institutions of $1 billion, and checkable deposits increase by $9 billion, why isn't the banking system in equilibrium? What will continue to happen in the banking system until equilibrium is reached? Show the T-account for the banking system in equilibrium.

23. If the Fed reduces reserves by selling $5 million worth of bonds to the banks, what will the T-account of the banking system look like when the banking system is in equilibrium? What will have happened to the level of checkable deposits?

24. If the Fed sells $1 million of bonds and banks reduce their borrowings from the Fed by $1 million, predict what will happen to the money supply.

25. Suppose that currency in circulation is $600 billion, the amount of checkable deposits is $900 billion, and excess reserves are $15 billion.

a. Calculate the money supply, the currency deposit ratio, the excess reserve ratio, and the money multiplier.

b. Suppose the central bank conducts an unusually large open market purchase of bonds held by banks of $1400 billion due to a sharp contraction in the economy. Assuming the ratios you calculated in part a are the same, what do you predict will be the effect on the money supply?

c. Suppose the central bank conducts the same open market purchase as in part b, except that banks choose to hold all of these proceeds as excess reserves rather than loan them out, due to fear of a financial crisis. Assuming that currency and deposits remain the same, what happens to the amount of excess reserves, the excess reserve ratio, the money supply, and the money multiplier?

d. Following the financial crisis in 2008, the Federal Reserve began injecting the banking system with massive amounts of liquidity, and at the same time, very little lending occurred. As a result, the M1 money multiplier was below 1 for most of the time from October 2008 through 2011. How does this relate to your answer to part c?

Web Exercises

1. Go to www.federalreserve.gov/boarddocs/hh/ and find the most recent annual report of the Federal Reserve. Read the first section of the annual report that summarizes Monetary Policy and the Economic Outlook. Write a one-page summary of this section of the report.

2. Go to www.federalreserve.gov/releases/h6/hist/ and find the historical report of M1 and M2. Compute the growth rate in each aggregate over each of the past three years (it will be easier to do if you move the data into Excel, as demonstrated in Chapter 1). Does it appear that the Fed has been increasing or decreasing the rate of growth of the money supply? Is this consistent with what you understand the economy needs? Why?

3. An important aspect of the supply of money is reserve balances. Go to www.federalreserve.gov/Releases/h41/ and locate the most recent release. This site reports changes in factors that affect depository reserve balances.

a. What is the current reserve balance?

b. What is the change in reserve balances since a year ago?

c. Based on parts a and b, does it appear that the money supply should be increasing or decreasing?

Web References

www.federalreserve.gov/boarddocs/rptcongress/annual04/default.htm

See the most recent Federal Reserve financial statement.

http://www.richmondfed.org/about_us/visit_us/tours/money_museum/index.cfm?WT.si_n=Search&WT.si_x=3

A virtual tour of the Federal Reserve Bank of Richmond's money museum.

www.federalreserve.gov/Releases/h3/

The Federal Reserve website reports data about aggregate reserves and the monetary base. This site also reports on the volume of borrowings from the Fed.

www.federalreserve.gov/Releases/h6/

This site reports current and historical levels of M1 and M2, as well as other data on the money supply.

Web Appendices

Please visit the Companion Website at www.pearsonhighered.com/mishkin to read the Web appendices to Chapter 17.

Appendix 1: **The Fed's Balance Sheet and the Monetary Base**

Appendix 2: **The M2 Money Multiplier**

Appendix 3: **Explaining the Behavior of the Currency Ratio**

18 Tools of Monetary Policy

Preview

In this chapter, we examine the tools of monetary policy that the Fed uses to control the money supply and interest rates. Because the Fed's use of these policy tools has such an important impact on interest rates and economic activity, it is vital to understand how the Fed wields them in practice and how relatively useful each tool is.

In recent years, the Federal Reserve has increasingly focused on the **federal funds rate** (the interest rate on overnight loans of reserves from one bank to another) as the primary instrument of monetary policy. Since February 1994, the Fed has announced a federal funds rate target at each Federal Open Market Committee (FOMC) meeting, an announcement that is watched closely by market participants because it affects interest rates throughout the economy. Thus, to fully comprehend how the Fed's tools are used in the conduct of monetary policy, we must understand not only their effect on the money supply, but also their direct effects on the federal funds rate and how they can be used to get the federal funds rate close to the target. The chapter therefore begins with a supply and demand analysis of the market for reserves to explain how the Fed's settings for the four tools of monetary policy—open market operations, discount policy, reserve requirements, and the interest paid on reserves—determine the federal funds rate. We next go on to look in more detail at each of these tools of monetary policy to see how they are used in practice and to gain a sense of their relative advantages. We then examine nonconventional tools of monetary policy that the Federal Reserve used during the recent financial crisis because of the extraordinary circumstances. The chapter ends with a discussion of the tools of monetary policy used by other central banks besides the Federal Reserve.

THE MARKET FOR RESERVES AND THE FEDERAL FUNDS RATE

In Chapter 17, we saw how open market operations (changes in nonborrowed reserves) and Federal Reserve lending (changes in borrowed reserves) affect the balance sheet of the Fed and the amount of reserves. The market for reserves is where the federal funds rate is determined, and this is why we turn to a supply and demand analysis of this market to analyze how the tools of monetary policy affect the federal funds rate.

Demand and Supply in the Market for Reserves

The analysis of the market for reserves proceeds in a similar fashion to the analysis of the bond market we conducted in Chapter 5. We derive a demand and supply curve for reserves. Then the market equilibrium in which the quantity of reserves demanded equals the quantity of reserves supplied determines the level of the federal funds rate, the interest rate charged on the loans of these reserves.

Demand Curve To derive the demand curve for reserves, we need to ask what happens to the quantity of reserves demanded by banks, holding everything else constant, as the federal funds rate changes. Recall from Chapter 17 that the amount of reserves can be split up into two components: (1) required reserves, which equal the required reserve ratio times the amount of deposits on which reserves are required; and (2) excess reserves, the additional reserves banks choose to hold. Therefore, the quantity of reserves demanded by banks equals required reserves plus the quantity of excess reserves demanded. Excess reserves are insurance against deposit outflows, and the cost of holding these excess reserves is their opportunity cost, the interest rate that could have been earned on lending these reserves out, minus the interest rate that is earned on these reserves, i_{or}. Before 2008, the Federal Reserve did not pay interest on reserves, but since the fall of 2008, the Fed has paid interest on reserves at a level that is typically set at a fixed amount below the federal funds rate target and therefore changes when the target changes (see the Inside the Fed box, "Why Does the Fed Need to Pay Interest on Reserves?"). When the federal funds rate is above the rate paid on reserves, i_{or}, as the federal funds rate decreases, the opportunity cost of holding excess reserves falls. Holding everything else constant, including the quantity of required reserves, the quantity of reserves demanded rises. Consequently, the demand curve for reserves, R^d, slopes downward in Figure 1 when the federal funds rate is above i_{or}. If, however, the federal funds rate begins to fall below the interest rate paid on excess reserves i_{or}, banks would not lend in the overnight market at a lower interest rate. Instead, they would just keep on adding to their holdings of excess reserves indefinitely. The result is that the demand curve for reserves, R^d, becomes flat (infinitely elastic) at i_{or} in Figure 1.

FIGURE 1

Equilibrium in the Market for Reserves

Equilibrium occurs at the intersection of the supply curve R^s and the demand curve R^d at point 1 and an interest rate of i^*_{ff}.

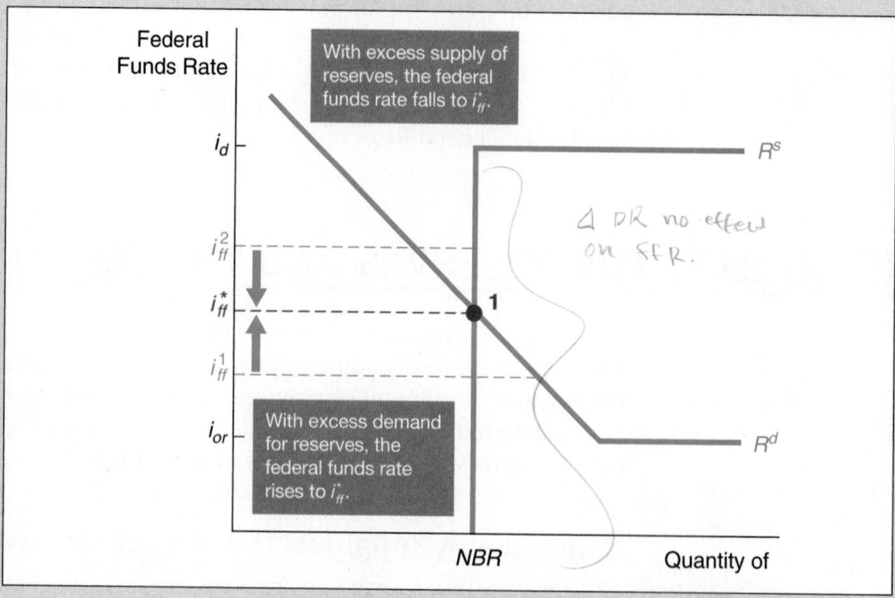

Supply Curve The supply of reserves, R^s, can be broken up into two components: the amount of reserves that are supplied by the Fed's open market operations, called nonborrowed reserves (NBR), and the amount of reserves borrowed from the Fed, called *borrowed reserves* (BR). The primary cost of borrowing from the Fed is the interest rate the Fed charges on these loans, the discount rate (i_d), which is set at a fixed amount above the federal funds target rate and thus changes when the target changes. Because borrowing federal funds from other banks is a substitute for borrowing (taking out discount loans) from the Fed, if the federal funds rate i_{ff} is below the discount rate i_d, then banks will not borrow from the Fed and borrowed reserves will be zero because borrowing in the federal funds market is cheaper. Thus, as long as i_{ff} remains below i_d, the supply of reserves will just equal the amount of nonborrowed reserves supplied by the Fed, NBR, and so the supply curve will be vertical, as shown in Figure 1. However, as the federal funds rate begins to rise above the discount rate, banks would want to keep borrowing more and more at i_d and then lending out the proceeds in the federal funds market at the higher rate, i_{ff}. The result is that the supply curve becomes flat (infinitely elastic) at i_d, as shown in Figure 1.

Market Equilibrium Market equilibrium occurs when the quantity of reserves demanded equals the quantity supplied, $R^s = R^d$. Equilibrium therefore occurs at the intersection of the demand curve R^d and the supply curve R^s at point 1, with an equilibrium federal funds rate of i^*_{ff}. When the federal funds rate is above the equilibrium rate at i^2_{ff}, more reserves are supplied than demanded (excess supply) and so the federal funds rate falls to i^*_{ff}, as shown by the downward arrow. When the federal funds rate is below the equilibrium rate at i^1_{ff}, more reserves are demanded than supplied (excess demand) and so the federal funds rate rises, as shown by the upward arrow. (Note that Figure 1 is drawn so that i_d is above i^*_{ff} because the Federal Reserve now keeps the discount rate substantially above the target for the federal funds rate.)

Inside the Fed Why Does the Fed Need to Pay Interest on Reserves?

For years, the Federal Reserve asked Congress to pass legislation allowing the Fed to pay interest on reserves. In 2006 such legislation was passed, to go into effect in 2011, but the starting date was moved up to October 2008 during the global financial crisis. Why is paying interest on reserves so important to the Fed?

One argument for paying interest on reserves is that it reduces the effective tax on deposits, thereby increasing economic efficiency. As pointed out in Chapter 12, the opportunity cost for a bank of holding reserves is the interest the bank could earn by lending out the reserves minus the interest payment that it receives from the Fed. When no interest was paid on reserves, this opportunity cost of holding them was quite high, and banks went to extraordinary measures to reduce them (for example, sweeping out deposits every night into repurchase agreements in order to reduce their required reserve balances). With the interest rate on reserves set close to the federal funds rate, this opportunity cost is lowered dramatically, sharply reducing the need for banks to engage in unnecessary transactions to avoid this opportunity cost.

The second argument for paying interest on reserves is that it helps improve implementation of monetary policy. The amount of excess reserves fluctuates with changes in the opportunity cost of

(continued)

holding reserves. With the interest rate on reserves set at a fixed amount below the federal funds rate target, the opportunity cost of reserves no longer fluctuates as much. As a result, fluctuations in excess reserves are potentially reduced when interest rates change, which, as we saw in Chapter 17, makes for fewer fluctuations and therefore tighter control of the money supply. In addition, as the supply and demand analysis of the market for reserves outlined in this chapter shows, paying interest on reserves puts a floor under the federal funds rate, and so limits fluctuations of the federal funds rate around its target level.

The third argument for paying interest on reserves became especially relevant during the global financial crisis of 2007–2009. As discussed below, during that period the Fed needed to provide liquidity to particular parts of the financial system, using its lending facilities to limit the damage from the financial crisis. As the discussion of the Fed's balance sheet in Chapter 17 shows, when the Fed provides liquidity through its lending facilities, the monetary base and the amount of reserves will expand, which will raise the money supply and also cause the federal funds rate to decline, as the supply and demand analysis of the market for reserves in this chapter shows. To prevent this, the Fed can conduct offsetting, open market sales of its securities to "sterilize" the liquidity created by its lending and so keep the money supply and the federal funds rate at their prior levels. But doing so leads to a reduction of the holdings of these securities on the Fed's balance sheet. If the Fed were to run out of these securities, it would no longer be able to sterilize the liquidity created by its lending: In other words, it would have used up its balance sheet capacity to channel liquidity to specific sectors of the financial system that needed it, without altering monetary policy. This problem became particularly acute during the global financial crisis when the huge lending operations of the Fed caused a precipitous drop in the Fed's holdings of securities, raising fears that the Fed would not be able to engage in further lending operations.

Having the ability to pay interest on reserves helps solve this balance-sheet-capacity problem. With interest paid on reserves, the Fed can expand its lending facilities as much as it wants, and yet as our supply and demand analysis of the market for reserves demonstrates, the federal funds rate will not fall below the interest rate paid on reserves. If the interest rate paid on reserves is set close to the federal funds rate target, the expansion of the Fed's lending will then not drive down the federal funds rate much below its intended target. The Fed can then do all the lending it wants without having much of an effect on its monetary policy instrument, the federal funds rate.*

Given the huge expansion in the Fed's lending facilities during the global financial crisis, it is no surprise that Chairman Bernanke requested that Congress move up the date when the Fed could pay interest on reserves. This request was granted in the Emergency Economic Stabilization Act passed in October 2008.

*With interest paid on reserves, the expansion of Federal Reserve lending also would not lead to an expansion of the money supply. The supply and demand analysis of the market for reserves shows that once the federal funds rate hits the floor set by the interest rate paid on reserves, increasing the reserves supplied by increasing Fed lending leads to a continuing rise in excess reserves. However, as we saw in Chapter 17, the rise in reserves would not lead to a rise in the money supply: With the increase in reserves going into excess reserves, there would be no multiple deposit expansion and hence no expansion in the money supply.

How Changes in the Tools of Monetary Policy Affect the Federal Funds Rate

Now that we understand how the federal funds rate is determined, we can examine how changes in the four tools of monetary policy—open market operations, discount lending, reserve requirements, and the interest rate paid on reserves—affect the market for reserves and the equilibrium federal funds rate.

Open Market Operations The effect of an open market operation depends on whether the supply curve initially intersects the demand curve in its downward-sloped

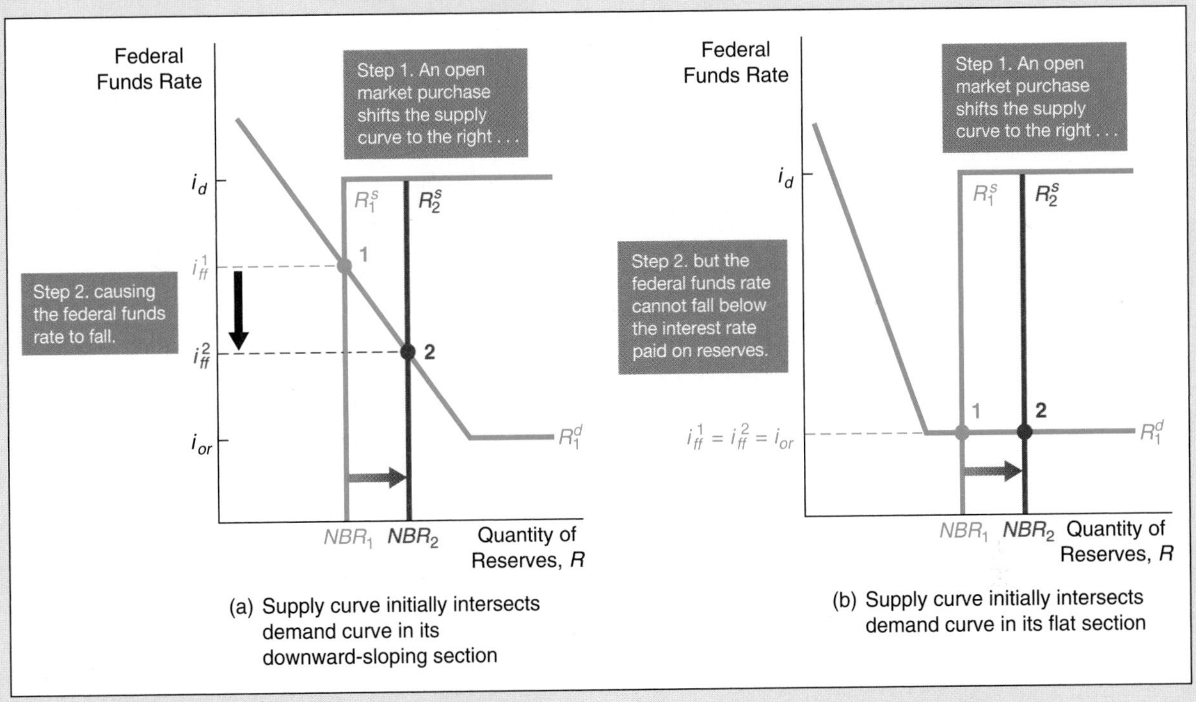

FIGURE 2 Response to an Open Market Operation

An open market purchase increases nonborrowed reserves and hence the reserves supplied, and shifts the supply curve from R_1^s to R_2^s. In panel (a), the equilibrium moves from point 1 to point 2, lowering the federal funds rate from i_{ff}^1 to i_{ff}^2. In panel (b), the equilibrium moves from point 1 to point 2, but the federal funds rate remains unchanged, $i_{ff}^1 = i_{ff}^2 = i_{or}$.

section or its flat section. Panel (a) of Figure 2 shows what happens if the intersection initially occurs on the downward-sloped section of the demand curve. We have already seen that an open market purchase leads to a greater quantity of reserves supplied; this is true at any given federal funds rate because of the higher amount of nonborrowed reserves, which rises from NBR_1 to NBR_2. An open market purchase therefore shifts the supply curve to the right from R_1^s to R_2^s and moves the equilibrium from point 1 to point 2, lowering the federal funds rate from i_{ff}^1 to i_{ff}^2.[1] The same reasoning implies that an open market sale decreases the quantity of nonborrowed reserves supplied, shifts the supply curve to the left, and causes the federal funds rate to rise. Because this is the typical situation—since the Fed usually keeps the federal funds rate target above the interest rate paid on reserves—the conclusion is that ***an open market purchase causes the federal funds rate to fall, whereas an open market sale causes the federal funds rate to rise***.

However, if the supply curve initially intersects the demand curve on its flat section, as in panel (b) of Figure 2, open market operations have no effect on the federal

[1]We come to the same conclusion using the money supply framework in Chapter 17, along with the liquidity preference framework in Chapter 5. An open market purchase raises reserves and the money supply, and then the liquidity preference framework shows that interest rates fall as a result.

funds rate. To see this, let's again look at an open market purchase that raises the quantity of reserves supplied, which shifts the supply curve from R_1^s to R_2^s, but now where initially $i_{ff}^1 = i_{or}$. The shift in the supply curve moves the equilibrium from point 1 to point 2, but the federal funds rate remains unchanged at i_{or} because ***the interest rate paid on reserves, i_{or}, sets a floor for the federal funds rate.***

Discount Lending The effect of a discount rate change depends on whether the demand curve intersects the supply curve in its vertical section or its flat section. Panel (a) of Figure 3 shows what happens if the intersection occurs on the vertical section of the supply curve so there is no discount lending and borrowed reserves, *BR*, are zero. In this case, when the discount rate is lowered by the Fed from i_d^1 to i_d^2, the horizontal section of the supply curve falls, as in R_2^s, but the intersection of the supply and demand curves remains at point 1. Thus, in this case, no change occurs in the equilibrium federal funds rate, which remains at i_{ff}^1. Because this is the typical situation—since the Fed now usually keeps the discount rate above its target for the federal funds rate—the conclusion is that ***most changes in the discount rate have no effect on the federal funds rate.***

However, if the demand curve intersects the supply curve on its flat section, so there is some discount lending (i.e., $BR = 0$), as in panel (b) of Figure 3, changes in the discount rate do affect the federal funds rate. In this case, initially discount lending is

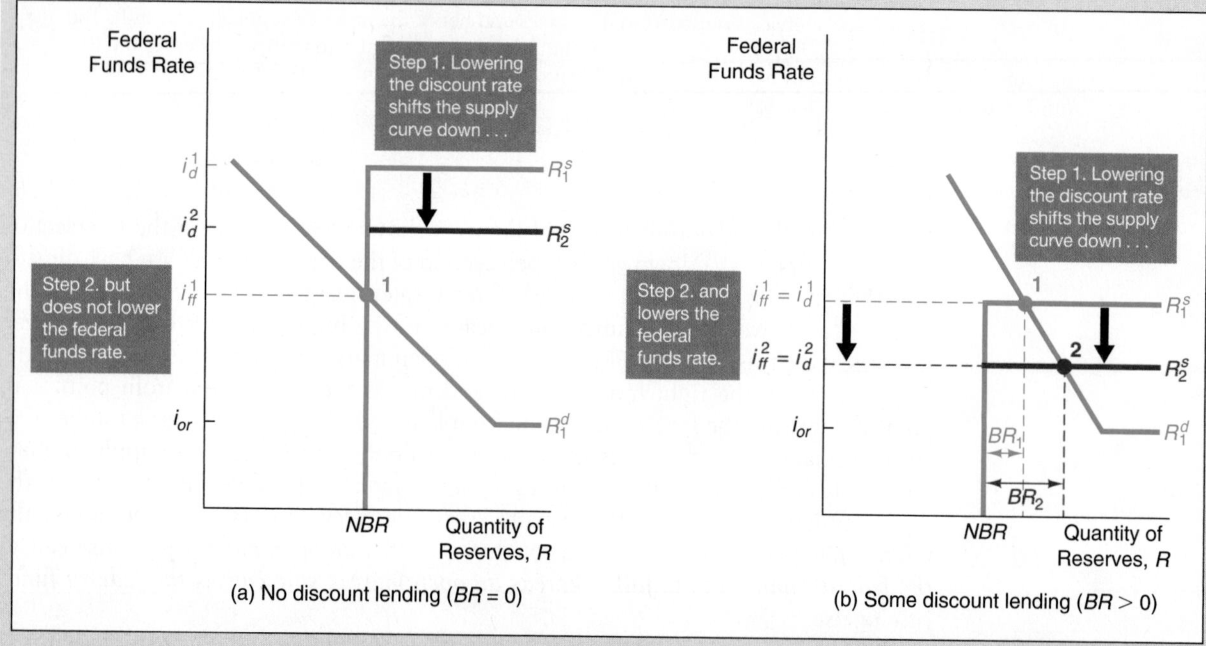

FIGURE 3 Response to a Change in the Discount Rate
In panel (a) when the discount rate is lowered by the Fed from i_d^1 to i_d^2, the horizontal section of the supply curve falls, as in R_2^s, and the equilibrium federal funds rate remains unchanged at i_{ff}^1. In panel (b) when the discount rate is lowered by the Fed from i_d^1 to i_d^2, the horizontal section of the supply curve R_2^s falls, and the equilibrium federal funds rate falls from i_{ff}^1 to i_{ff}^2 as borrowed reserves increase.

FIGURE 4

Response to a Change in Required Reserves

When the Fed raises reserve requirements, required reserves increase, which raises the demand for reserves. The demand curve shifts from R_1^d to R_2^d, the equilibrium moves from point 1 to point 2, and the federal funds rate rises from i_{ff}^1 to i_{ff}^2.

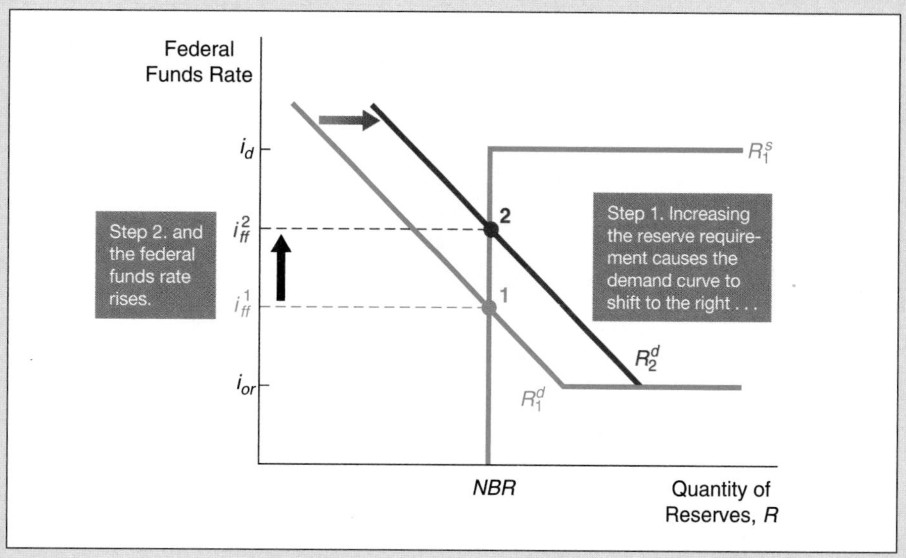

positive and the equilibrium federal funds rate equals the discount rate, $i_{ff}^1 = i_d^1$. When the discount rate is lowered by the Fed from i_d^1 to i_d^2, the horizontal section of the supply curve R_2^s falls, moving the equilibrium from point 1 to point 2, and the equilibrium federal funds rate falls from i_{ff}^1 to i_{ff}^2 $(= i_d^2)$ as shown in panel (b).

Reserve Requirements When the required reserve ratio increases, required reserves increase and hence the quantity of reserves demanded increases for any given interest rate. Thus a rise in the required reserve ratio shifts the demand curve to the right from R_1^d to R_2^d in Figure 4, moves the equilibrium from point 1 to point 2, and in turn raises the federal funds rate from i_{ff}^1 to i_{ff}^2. The result is that ***when the Fed raises reserve requirements, the federal funds rate rises.***[2]

Similarly, a decline in the required reserve ratio lowers the quantity of reserves demanded, shifts the demand curve to the left, and causes the federal funds rate to fall. ***When the Fed decreases reserve requirements, the federal funds rate falls.***

Interest on Reserves The effect of a change in the interest rate the Fed pays on reserves depends on whether the supply curve intersects the demand curve in its downward-sloping or its flat section. Panel (a) of Figure 5 shows what happens if the intersection occurs on the demand curve's downward-sloping section, where the equilibrium federal funds rate is above the interest rate paid on reserves. In this case, when the interest rate on reserves is raised from to i_{or}^1 to i_{or}^2, the horizontal section of the demand curves rises, as in R_2^d, but the intersection of the supply and demand curves

[2]Because an increase in the required reserve ratio means that the same amount of reserves is able to support a smaller amount of deposits, a rise in the required reserve ratio leads to a decline in the money supply. Using the liquidity preference framework, the fall in the money supply results in a rise in interest rates, yielding the same conclusion in the text—that raising reserve requirements leads to higher interest rates.

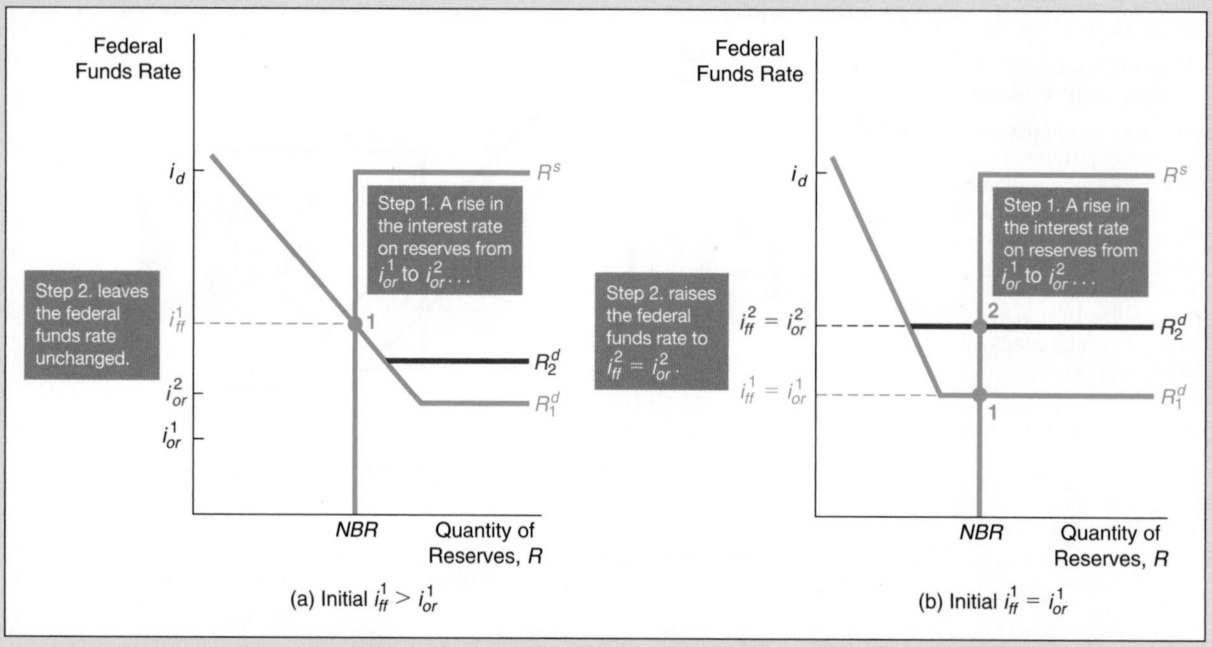

FIGURE 5 Response to a Change in the Interest Rate on Reserves

In panel (a) when the equilibrium federal funds rate is above the interest rate paid on reserves, a rise in the interest rate on reserves from i_{or}^1 to i_{or}^2 raises the horizontal section of the demand curve, as in R_2^d, but the equilibrium federal funds rate remains unchanged at i_{ff}^1. In panel (b) when the equilibrium federal funds rate is at the interest rate paid on reserves, a rise in the interest rate on reserves from i_{or}^1 to i_{or}^2 raises the equilibrium federal funds rate $i_{ff}^1 = i_{or}^1$ to $i_{ff}^1 = i_{or}^1$.

remains at point 1. However, if the supply curve intersects the demand curve on its flat section, where the equilibrium federal funds rate is at the interest rate paid on reserves, as in panel (b) of Figure 5, a rise in the interest rate on reserves from i_{or}^1 to i_{or}^2 moves the equilibrium to point 2, where the equilibrium federal funds rate rises from $i_{ff}^1 = i_{or}^1$ to $i_{ff}^2 = i_{or}^2$. ***When the federal funds rate is at the interest rate paid on reserves, a rise in the interest rate on reserves raises the federal funds rate.***

APPLICATION ◆ How the Federal Reserve's Operating Procedures Limit Fluctuations in the Federal Funds Rate

An important advantage of the Fed's current procedures for operating the discount window and paying interest on reserves is that they limit fluctuations in the federal funds rate. We can use our supply and demand analysis of the market for reserves to see why.

Suppose that initially the equilibrium federal funds rate is at the federal funds rate target of i_{ff}^* in Figure 6. If the demand for reserves has a large unexpected increase, the

FIGURE 6
How the Federal Reserve's Operating Procedures Limit Fluctuations in the Federal Funds Rate

A rightward shift in the demand curve for reserves to $R^{d''}$ will raise the equilibrium federal funds rate to a maximum of $i''_{ff} = i_d$, whereas a leftward shift of the demand curve to $R^{d'}$ will lower the federal funds rate to a minimum of $i'_{ff} = i_{or}$.

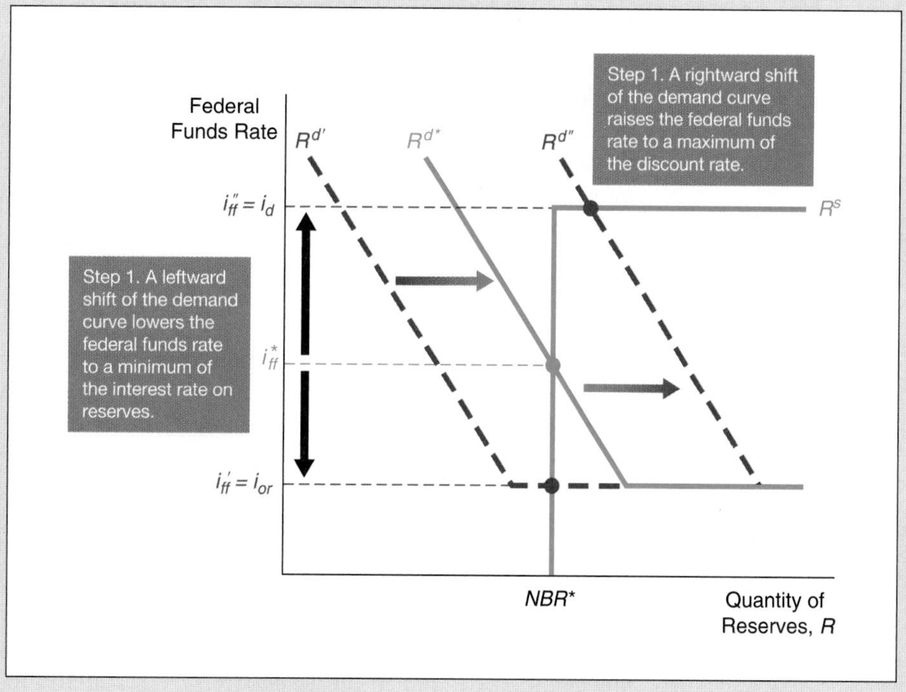

demand curve would shift to the right to $R^{d''}$, where it now intersects the supply curve for reserves on the flat portion, where the equilibrium federal funds rate i''_{ff} equals the discount rate i_d. No matter how far the demand curve shifts to the right, the equilibrium federal funds rate i''_{ff} will stay at i_d because borrowed reserves will just continue to increase, matching the increase in demand. Similarly, if the demand for reserves has a large unexpected decrease, the demand curve would shift to the left to $R^{d'}$, and the supply curve intersects the demand curve on its flat portion, where the equilibrium federal funds rate i'_{ff} equals the interest rate paid on reserves i_{or}. No matter how far the demand curve shifts to the left, the equilibrium federal funds rate i'_{ff} will stay at i_{or} because excess reserves will keep on increasing so that the quantity demanded of reserves equals the quantity of nonborrowed reserves supplied.[3]

Our analysis therefore shows that the ***Federal Reserve's operating procedures limit the fluctuations of the federal funds rate to between i_{er} and i_d.*** If the range between i_{er} and i_d is kept narrow enough, then the fluctuations around the target rate will be small. ◆

[3]There are times when the federal funds rate might fall below the level of the interest rate on reserves. This situation can occur because some participants in the federal funds market, particularly Fannie Mae and Freddie Mac, are not banks and so cannot keep their funds as deposits at the Federal Reserve. When they have excess funds, they may be forced to accept a lower interest rate than that paid on reserves because they don't have access to this higher rate from the Federal Reserve.

CONVENTIONAL MONETARY POLICY TOOLS

During normal times, the Federal Reserve uses three tools of monetary policy—open market operations, discount lending, and reserve requirements—to control the money supply and interest rates, and these are referred to as **conventional monetary policy tools**. We will look at each of them in turn, and an additional possible tool of paying interest on reserves, to see how the Fed wields them in practice and how relatively useful each tool is.

Open Market Operations

Open market operations are the most important conventional monetary policy tool, because they are the primary determinants of changes in interest rates and the monetary base, the main source of fluctuations in the money supply. Open market purchases expand reserves and the monetary base, thereby increasing the money supply and lowering short-term interest rates. Open market sales shrink reserves and the monetary base, decreasing the money supply and raising short-term interest rates. Now that we understand from Chapter 17 the elements in the Fed's balance sheet that influence reserves and the monetary base, we can examine how the Federal Reserve conducts open market operations with the objective of controlling short-term interest rates and the money supply.

Open market operations are of two types: **Dynamic open market operations** are intended to change the level of reserves and the monetary base, and **defensive open market operations** are intended to offset movements in other factors that affect reserves and the monetary base, such as changes in Treasury deposits with the Fed or changes in float. The Fed conducts open market operations in U.S. Treasury and government agency securities, especially U.S. Treasury bills. The Fed conducts most of its open market operations in Treasury securities because the market for these securities is the most liquid and has the largest trading volume. It has the capacity to absorb the Fed's substantial volume of transactions without experiencing excessive price fluctuations that would disrupt the market.

As we saw in Chapter 16, the decision-making authority for open market operations is the Federal Open Market Committee (FOMC), which sets a target for the federal funds rate. The actual execution of these operations, however, is conducted by the trading desk at the Federal Reserve Bank of New York, whose operations are described by the Inside the Fed box, "A Day at the Trading Desk."

Open market operations are conducted electronically with a specific set of dealers in government securities, known as **primary dealers**, by a computer system called TRAPS (Trading Room Automated Processing System), and all open market operations are now performed over this system. A message will be electronically transmitted simultaneously to all the primary dealers over TRAPS, indicating the type and maturity of the operation being arranged. The dealers are given several minutes to respond via TRAPS with their propositions to buy or sell government securities at various prices. The propositions are then assembled and displayed on a computer screen for evaluation. The desk will select all propositions, beginning with the most attractively priced, up to the point where the desired amount of securities is purchased or sold, and it will then notify each dealer via TRAPS which of its propositions have been chosen. The entire selection process is typically completed in a matter of minutes.

These temporary transactions are of two basic types. In a **repurchase agreement** (often called a **repo**), the Fed purchases securities with an agreement that the seller will

Inside the Fed A Day at the Trading Desk

The manager of domestic open market operations supervises the analysts and traders who execute the purchases and sales of securities in the drive to hit the federal funds rate target. To get a grip on what might happen in the federal funds market that day, her workday starts early in the morning, around 7:30 a.m., when her staff begins with a review of developments in the federal funds market the previous day and with an update on the actual amount of reserves in the banking system the day before. Then her staff produces updated reports that contain detailed forecasts of what will be happening to some of the short-term factors affecting the supply and demand of reserves (discussed in Chapter 17). For example, if float is predicted to decrease because good weather throughout the country is speeding up check delivery, the manager of domestic open market operations knows that she will have to conduct a defensive open market operation (in this case, a *purchase* of securities) to offset the expected decline in reserves and the monetary base from the decreased float. However, if Treasury deposits with the Fed are predicted to fall, a defensive open market *sale* would be needed to offset the expected increase in reserves. The report also predicts the change in the public's holding of currency. If currency holdings are expected to rise, then, as we have seen in Chapter 17, reserves fall, and an open market purchase is needed to raise reserves back up again.

This information will help the manager of domestic open market operations and her staff decide how large a change in nonborrowed reserves is needed to reach the federal funds rate target. If the amount of reserves in the banking system is too large, many banks will have excess reserves to lend that other banks may have little desire to hold, and the federal funds rate will fall. If the level of reserves is too low, banks seeking to borrow reserves from the few banks that have excess reserves to lend may push the funds rate higher than the desired level. Also during the morning, the staff will monitor the behavior of the federal funds rate and contact some of the major participants in the market for reserves, which may provide independent information about whether a change in reserves is needed to achieve the desired level of the federal funds rate.

Members of the manager's staff also contact several representatives of the primary dealers that the open market desk trades with. Her staff finds out how the dealers view market conditions to get a feel for what may happen to the prices of the securities they trade in over the course of the day. They also call the Treasury to get updated information on the expected level of Treasury balances at the Fed to refine their estimates of the supply of reserves.

Members of the Monetary Affairs Division at the Board of Governors are then contacted, and the New York Fed's forecasts of reserve supply and demand are compared with the Board's. On the basis of these projections and the observed behavior of the federal funds market, the desk will formulate and propose a course of action to be taken that day, which may involve plans to add reserves to or drain reserves from the banking system through open market operations. If an operation is contemplated, the type, size, and maturity will be discussed.

At about 9 a.m., a daily conference call takes place, linking the desk with the Office of the Director of Monetary Affairs at the Board of Governors and with one of the four voting Reserve Bank presidents outside New York. During the call, a member of the open market operations unit will outline the desk's proposed reserve management strategy for the day. After the plan is approved, it is announced to the markets at 9:30 a.m. and the desk is instructed to execute immediately any temporary open market operations that were planned for that day.

Outright operations, which involve a purchase or sale of securities that is not self-reversing, are traditionally executed later in the day when temporary operations are not being conducted. Even when outright operations are not being conducted, the manager of domestic open market operations and her staff do not stay idle the rest of the day because they are continually monitoring the markets and bank reserves to plan for the next day's operations.

repurchase them in a short period of time, anywhere from one to fifteen days from the original date of purchase. Because the effects on reserves of a repo are reversed on the day the agreement matures, a repo is actually a temporary open market purchase and is an especially desirable way of conducting a defensive open market purchase that will be reversed shortly. When the Fed wants to conduct a temporary open market sale, it engages in a **matched sale–purchase transaction** (sometimes called a **reverse repo**) in which the Fed sells securities and the buyer agrees to sell them back to the Fed in the near future.

At times, the desk may see the need to address a persistent reserve shortage or surplus and wish to arrange an operation that will have a more permanent impact on the supply of reserves. Outright transactions, which involve a purchase or sale of securities that is not self-reversing, are also conducted over TRAPS.

Discount Policy and the Lender of Last Resort

The facility at which banks can borrow reserves from the Federal Reserve is called the **discount window**. The easiest way to understand how the Fed affects the volume of borrowed reserves is by looking at how the discount window operates.

Operation of the Discount Window The Fed's discount loans to banks are of three types: primary credit, secondary credit, and seasonal credit.[4] *Primary credit* is the discount lending that plays the most important role in monetary policy. Healthy banks are allowed to borrow all they want at very short maturities (usually overnight) from the primary credit facility, and it is therefore referred to as a **standing lending facility**.[5] The interest rate on these loans is the discount rate, and as we mentioned before, it is set higher than the federal funds rate target, usually by 100 basis points (one percentage point) because the Fed prefers that banks borrow from each other in the federal funds market so that they continually monitor each other for credit risk. As a result, in most circumstances the amount of discount lending under the primary credit facility is very small. If the amount is so small, why does the Fed have this facility?

The answer is that the facility is intended to be a backup source of liquidity for sound banks so that the federal funds rate never rises too far above the federal funds target set by the FOMC. We have already seen how this works in Figure 6. When the demand for reserves has a large unexpected increase, no matter how far the demand curve shifts to the right, the equilibrium federal funds rate i_{ff}^* will stay at i_d because borrowed reserves will just continue to increase, and the federal funds rate can rise no further. The primary credit facility has thus put a ceiling on the federal funds rate at i_d.

Secondary credit is given to banks that are in financial trouble and are experiencing severe liquidity problems. The interest rate on secondary credit is set at 50 basis points (0.5 percentage point) above the discount rate. The interest rate on these loans is set at a higher, penalty rate to reflect the less-sound condition of these borrowers. *Seasonal*

[4]The procedures for administering the discount window were changed in January 2003. The primary credit facility replaced an adjustment credit facility whose discount rate was typically set below market interest rates, so banks were restricted in their access to this credit. In contrast, now healthy banks can borrow all they want from the primary credit facility. The secondary credit facility replaced the extended credit facility, which focused somewhat more on longer-term credit extensions. The seasonal credit facility remains basically unchanged.

[5]This type of standard lending facility is commonly called a *Lombard facility* in other countries, and the interest rate charged on these loans is often called a *Lombard rate*. (This name comes from Lombardy, a region in northern Italy that was an important center of banking in the Middle Ages.)

credit is given to meet the needs of a limited number of small banks in vacation and agricultural areas that have a seasonal pattern of deposits. The interest rate charged on seasonal credit is tied to the average of the federal funds rate and certificate of deposit rates. The Federal Reserve has questioned the need for the seasonal credit facility because of improvements in credit markets and is thus contemplating eliminating it in the future.

Lender of Last Resort In addition to its use as a tool to influence reserves, the monetary base, and the money supply, discounting is important in preventing and coping with financial panics. When the Federal Reserve System was created, its most important role was intended to be as the **lender of last resort**; to prevent bank failures from spinning out of control, it was to provide reserves to banks when no one else would, thereby preventing bank and financial panics. Discounting is a particularly effective way to provide reserves to the banking system during a banking crisis because reserves are immediately channeled to the banks that need them most.

Using the discount tool to avoid financial panics by performing the role of lender of last resort is an extremely important requirement of successful monetary policy making. As we demonstrated with our money supply analysis in Chapter 17, the bank panics in the 1930–1933 period were the cause of the sharpest decline in the money supply in U.S. history, which many economists see as the driving force behind the collapse of the economy during the Great Depression. Financial panics can also severely damage the economy because they interfere with the ability of financial intermediaries and markets to move funds to people with productive investment opportunities (see Chapter 9).

Unfortunately, the discount tool has not always been used by the Fed to prevent financial panics, as the massive failures during the Great Depression attest. The Fed learned from its mistakes of that period and has performed admirably in its role of lender of last resort in the post–World War II period. The Fed has used its discount lending weapon several times to avoid bank panics by extending loans to troubled banking institutions, thereby preventing further bank failures.

At first glance, it might seem that the presence of the FDIC, which insures depositors up to a limit of $250,000 per account from losses due to a bank's failure, would make the lender-of-last-resort function of the Fed superfluous. There are two reasons why this is not the case. First, it is important to recognize that the FDIC's insurance fund amounts to about 1% of the total amount of deposits banks hold. If a large number of bank failures occurred, the FDIC would not be able to cover all the depositors' losses. Indeed, the large number of bank failures in the 1980s and early 1990s, described in Chapter 11, led to large losses and a shrinkage in the FDIC's insurance fund, which reduced the FDIC's ability to cover depositors' losses. This fact has not weakened the confidence of small depositors in the banking system because the Fed has been ready to stand behind the banks to provide whatever reserves are needed to prevent bank panics. Second, the $1.52 trillion of large-denomination deposits in the banking system are not guaranteed by the FDIC, because they exceed the $250,000 limit. A loss of confidence in the banking system could still lead to runs on banks from the large-denomination depositors, and bank panics could still occur despite the existence of the FDIC. The importance of the Federal Reserve's role as lender of last resort is, if anything, more important today because of the high number of bank failures experienced in the 1980s and early 1990s, and during the global financial crisis from 2007 to 2009.

Not only can the Fed be a lender of last resort to banks, but it can also play the same role for the financial system as a whole. The existence of the Fed's discount window can help prevent and cope with financial panics that are not triggered by bank failures, as was the case, for example, during the Black Monday stock market crash of 1987, and the terrorist destruction of the World Trade Center in September 2001 (discussed in the Inside the Fed box.) Although the Fed's role as the lender of last resort has the benefit of preventing bank and financial panics, it does have a cost. If a bank expects that the Fed will provide it with discount loans when it gets into trouble, it will be willing to take on more risk, knowing that the Fed will come to the rescue. The Fed's lender-of-last-resort role has thus created a moral hazard problem similar to the one created by deposit insurance (discussed in Chapter 11): Banks take on more risk, thus exposing the deposit insurance agency, and hence taxpayers, to greater losses. The moral hazard problem is most severe for large banks, which may believe that the Fed and the FDIC view them as "too big to fail"; that is, they will always receive Fed loans when they are in trouble because their failure would be likely to precipitate a bank panic.

Similarly, Federal Reserve actions to prevent financial panic may encourage financial institutions other than banks to take on greater risk. They, too, expect the Fed to ensure that they could get loans if their failure would cause or worsen a financial panic. When the Fed considers using the discount weapon to prevent panics, it therefore needs to consider the trade-off between the moral hazard cost of its role as lender of last resort and the benefit of preventing financial panics. This trade-off explains why the Fed must be careful not to perform its function as lender of last resort too frequently.

Inside the Fed Using Discount Policy to Prevent a Financial Panic

The Black Monday Stock Market Crash of 1987 and the Terrorist Destruction of the World Trade Center in September 2001. Although October 19, 1987, dubbed "Black Monday," will go down in the history books as the largest one-day percentage decline in stock prices to date (the Dow Jones Industrial Average declined by more than 20%), it was on Tuesday, October 20, 1987, that financial markets almost stopped functioning. Felix Rohatyn, one of the most prominent men on Wall Street, stated flatly: "Tuesday was the most dangerous day we had in 50 years."* Much of the credit for prevention of a market meltdown after Black Monday must be given to the Federal Reserve System and then-Chairman of the Board of Governors, Alan Greenspan.

The stress of keeping markets functioning during the sharp decline in stock prices on Monday, October 19, meant that many brokerage houses and specialists (dealer-brokers who maintain orderly trading on the stock exchanges) were severely in need of additional funds to finance their activities. However, understandably enough, New York banks, as well as foreign and regional U.S. banks, growing very nervous about the financial health of securities firms, began to cut back credit to the securities industry at the very time when it was most needed. Panic was in the air. One chairman of a large specialist firm commented that on Monday, "from 2 p.m. on, there was total despair. The entire investment community fled the market. We were left alone on the field." It was time for the Fed, like the cavalry, to come to the rescue.

Upon learning of the plight of the securities industry, Alan Greenspan and E. Gerald Corrigan, then president of the Federal Reserve Bank of New York and the Fed official most closely in touch with Wall Street, became fearful of a spreading collapse of securities firms. To prevent this from occurring, Greenspan announced before the market opened on Tuesday, October 20, the Federal Reserve System's "readiness to serve as a source of liquidity to support

(continued)

*"Terrible Tuesday: How the Stock Market Almost Disintegrated a Day After the Crash," *Wall Street Journal*, November 20, 1987, p. 1. This article provides a fascinating and more detailed view of the events described here and is the source of all the quotations cited.

the economic and financial system." In addition to this extraordinary announcement, the Fed made it clear that it would provide discount loans to any bank that would make loans to the securities industry, although this did not prove to be necessary. As one New York banker said, the Fed's message was, "We're here. Whatever you need, we'll give you."

The outcome of the Fed's timely action was that a financial panic was averted. The markets kept functioning on Tuesday, and a market rally ensued that day, with the Dow Jones Industrial Average climbing over 100 points.

A similar lender-of-last-resort operation was carried out in the aftermath of the destruction of the World Trade Center in New York City on Tuesday, September 11, 2001—the worst terrorist incident in U.S. history. Because of the disruption to the most important financial center in the world, the liquidity needs of the financial system skyrocketed. To satisfy these needs and to keep the financial system from seizing up, within a few hours of the incident, the Fed made an announcement similar to that made after the crash of 1987: "The Federal Reserve System is open and operating. The discount window is available to meet liquidity needs."† The Fed then proceeded to provide $45 billion to banks through the discount window, a 200-fold increase over the previous week. As a result of this action, along with the injection of as much as $80 billion of reserves into the banking system through open market operations, the financial system kept functioning. When the stock market reopened on Monday, September 17, trading was orderly, although the Dow Jones Average did decline 7%.

The terrorists were able to bring down the twin towers of the World Trade Center, with nearly 3,000 dead. However, they were unable to bring down the U.S. financial system because of the timely actions of the Federal Reserve.

†"Economic Front: How Policy Makers Regrouped to Defend the Financial System," *Wall Street Journal*, September 18, 2001, p. A1, provides more detail on this episode.

Reserve Requirements

As we saw in Chapter 17, changes in reserve requirements affect the money supply by causing the money supply multiplier to change. A rise in reserve requirements reduces the amount of deposits that can be supported by a given level of the monetary base and will lead to a contraction of the money supply. A rise in reserve requirements also increases the demand for reserves and raises the federal funds rate. Conversely, a decline in reserve requirements leads to an expansion of the money supply and a fall in the federal funds rate. The Fed has had the authority to vary reserve requirements since the 1930s; this once was a powerful way of affecting the money supply and interest rates, but is less important now because it is rarely used.

The Depository Institutions Deregulation and Monetary Control Act of 1980 provided a simpler scheme for setting reserve requirements. All depository institutions, including commercial banks, savings and loan associations, mutual savings banks, and credit unions, are subject to the same reserve requirements: Required reserves on all checkable deposits—including non–interest-bearing checking accounts, NOW accounts, super-NOW accounts, and ATS (automatic transfer savings) accounts—are equal to zero for the first $10.7 million of the bank's checkable deposits, 3% on checkable deposits from $10.7 to $58.8 million and10% of the checkable deposits over $58.8 million.[6] The percentage set at 10% can be varied between 8% and 14%, at the Fed's discretion. In extraordinary circumstances, the percentage can be raised as high as 18%.

[6]These figures are for for 2011. Each year, the figures are adjusted upward by 80% of the percentage increase in checkable deposits in the United States.

Interest on Reserves

Because the Fed started paying interest on reserves only in 2008, this tool of monetary policy does not have a long history. For the same reason that the Fed sets the discount rate above the federal funds target—that is, to encourage borrowing and lending in the federal funds market so that banks monitor each other—the Fed to date generally has set the interest rate on reserves below the federal funds target. This means that the Fed has not yet used interest on reserves as a tool of monetary policy, but instead has just used it to help provide a floor under the federal funds rate. However, in the aftermath of the global financial crisis, banks have accumulated huge quantities of excess reserves, and in this situation, to increase the federal funds rate would require massive amounts of open market operations to remove these reserves from the banking system. The interest-on-reserves tool can come to the rescue because raising this interest rate can instead be used to raise the federal funds rate, as is illustrated in panel (b) of Figure 5. Indeed, it is likely that this tool of monetary policy will be extensively used when the Fed wants to raise the federal funds rate and exit from the policy of maintaining it at zero, which started in December 2008.

Relative Advantages of the Different Tools

Open market operations constitute the most important conventional monetary policy tool because they have four basic advantages over the other tools:

1. Open market operations occur at the initiative of the Fed, which has complete control over their volume. This control is not found, for example, in discount operations, in which the Fed can encourage or discourage banks to borrow reserves by altering the discount rate but cannot directly control the volume of borrowed reserves.

2. Open market operations are flexible and precise; they can be used to any extent. No matter how small a change in reserves or the monetary base is desired, open market operations can achieve it with a small purchase or sale of securities. Conversely, if the desired change in reserves or the base is very large, the open market operations tool is strong enough to do the job through a very large purchase or sale of securities.

3. Open market operations are easily reversed. If a mistake is made in conducting an open market operation, the Fed can immediately reverse it. If the trading desk decides that the federal funds rate is too low because it has made too many open market purchases, it can immediately make a correction by conducting open market sales.

4. Open market operations can be implemented quickly; they involve no administrative delays. When the trading desk decides that it wants to change the monetary base or reserves, it just places orders with securities dealers, and the trades are executed immediately. Changes to reserve requirements, on the other hand, take time to implement because banks must be given advance warning so they can adjust their computer systems to calculate required reserves. Also, since it is costly to adjust computer systems, reversing a change in reserve requirements would be burdensome to banks. For these reasons, the policy tool of changing reserve requirements does not have much to recommend it, and it is rarely used.

There are two situations in which the other tools have advantages over open market operations. One is when the Fed wants to raise interest rates after banks have accumulated large amounts of excess reserves. In this case, the federal funds rate can be raised by increasing the interest on reserves, which avoids the need to conduct massive open market operations to raise the federal funds rate by reducing reserves. The second is when discount policy can be used by the Fed to perform its role of lender of last resort.

Experiences with the Black Monday crash, with the terrorist attacks on September 11, 2001, and during the global financial crisis, which we will discuss next, indicate that this role has become more important in the past couple of decades.

NONCONVENTIONAL MONETARY POLICY TOOLS DURING THE GLOBAL FINANCIAL CRISIS

Although in normal times, conventional monetary policy tools, which expand the money supply and lower interest rates, are enough to stabilize the economy, when the economy experiences a full-scale financial crisis like the one we have recently experienced, conventional monetary policy tools cannot do the job for two reasons. First, the financial system seizes up to such an extent that it becomes unable to allocate capital to productive uses, and so investment spending and the economy collapse along the lines we discussed in Chapter 9. Second, the negative shock to the economy can lead to the **zero-lower-bound problem,** in which the central bank is unable to lower short-term interest rates further because they have hit a floor of zero, as occurred at the end of 2008. The zero-lower-bound problem occurs because people can always earn more from holding bonds than holding cash, and therefore nominal interest rates cannot be negative.[7] For both these reasons, central banks need non–interest-rate tools, known as **nonconventional monetary policy tools** to stimulate the economy. These nonconventional monetary policy tools take three forms: (1) liquidity provision, (2) asset purchases, and (3) commitment to future monetary policy actions.

Liquidity Provision

Because conventional monetary policy actions were not sufficient to heal the financial markets and contain the financial crisis, the Federal Reserve implemented unprecedented increases in its lending facilities to provide liquidity to the financial markets.

1. **Discount Window Expansion:** At the outset of the crisis in mid-August 2007, the Fed lowered the discount rate (the interest rate on loans it makes to banks) to 50 basis points (0.50 percentage point) above the federal funds rate target from the normal 100 basis points. It then lowered it further in March 2008 to only 25 basis points above the federal funds rate target. However, since borrowing from the discount window has a "stigma" because it suggests that the borrowing bank may be desperate for funds and thus in trouble, its use was limited during the crisis.
2. **Term Auction Facility:** To encourage additional borrowing, in December 2007 the Fed set up a temporary Term Auction Facility (TAF), in which it made loans at a rate determined through competitive auctions. It was more widely used than the discount window facility because it enabled banks to borrow at a rate lower than the discount rate, and it was determined competitively, rather than being set at a penalty rate. The TAF auctions started at amounts of $20 billion, but as the crisis worsened, the Fed raised the amounts dramatically, with a total outstanding of over $400 billion. (The European Central Bank conducted similar operations, with one auction in June 2008 of over 400 billion euros.)

[7] As we saw in Chapter 4, interest rates can go very slightly negative at certain times, but this number is so close to zero that for all practical purposes we can take the lower bound for interest rates to be zero.

3. **New Lending Programs:** The Fed broadened its provision of liquidity to the financial system well beyond its traditional lending to banking institutions. These actions included lending to investment banks, as well as lending to promote purchases of commercial paper, mortgage backed-securities, and other asset-backed securities. In addition, the Fed engaged in lending to J.P. Morgan to assist in its purchase of Bear Stearns and to AIG to prevent its failure. The enlargement of the Fed's lending programs during the 2007–2009 financial crisis was indeed remarkable, expanding the Fed's balance sheet by over $1 trillion by the end of 2008, with the balance-sheet expansion continuing after. The number of new programs over the course of the crisis spawned a whole new set of abbreviations, including the TAF, TSLF, PDCF, AMLF, MMIFF, CPFF, and TALF. These facilities are described in more detail in the Inside the Fed box, "Fed Lending Facilities During the Global Financial Crisis."

Asset Purchases

The Fed's open market operations normally involve only purchase of government securities, particularly those that are short-term. However, during the crisis the Fed started two new asset purchase programs to lower interest rates for particular types of credit.

1. In November 2008, the Fed set up a Government Sponsored Entities Purchase Program in which the Fed eventually purchased $1.25 trillion of mortgage-backed securities (MBS) guaranteed by Fannie Mae and Freddie Mac. Through these purchases, the Fed hoped to prop up the MBS market and to lower interest rates on residential mortgages to stimulate the housing market.
2. In November 2010, the Fed announced that it would purchase $600 billion of long-term Treasury securities at a rate of about $75 billion per month. This purchase program, which became known as *QE2* (which stands for Quantitative Easing 2, not the Cunard cruise ship) was intended to lower long-term interest rates. Although *short-term* interest rates on Treasury securities hit a floor of zero during the global financial crisis, *long-term* interest rates did not. Since investment projects have a long life, long-term interest rate are more relevant than short-term ones to investment decisions. The Fed's purchase of long-term Treasuries to lower long-term interest rates could therefore help stimulate investment spending and the economy.

Quantitative Easing Versus Credit Easing

The result of these programs of liquidity provision and asset purchases resulted in an unprecedented expansion of the Federal Reserve's balance sheet. From before the financial crisis began in September 2007 to when the crisis was over at the end of 2009, the amount of Federal Reserve assets rose from about $800 billion to over $2 trillion. This expansion of the balance sheet is referred to as **quantitative easing**, because as shown in Chapter 17, it leads to a huge increase in the monetary base. Because this increase in the monetary base, also known as high-powered money, would usually result in an expansion of the money supply, it could be a powerful force to stimulate the economy in the near term and possibly produce inflation down the road.

There are reasons to be very skeptical. First, as we saw in the final application in Chapter 17, the huge expansion in the Fed's balance sheet and the monetary base did

Inside the Fed — Fed Lending Facilities During the Global Financial Crisis

During the global financial crisis, the Federal Reserve became very creative in assembling a host of new lending facilities to help restore liquidity to different parts of the financial system. The new facilities, the dates they were created, and their functions are listed in the table below.

Lending Facility	Date of Creation	Function
Term Auction Facility (TAF)	December 12, 2007	To make borrowing from the Fed more widely used, extends loans of fixed amounts to banks at interest rates that are determined by competitive auction rather than being set by the Fed, as with normal discount lending
Term Securities Lending Facility (TSLF)	March 11, 2008	To provide sufficient Treasury securities to act as collateral in credit markets, lends Treasury securities to primary dealers for terms longer than overnight against a broad range of collateral
Swap Lines	March 11, 2008	Lends dollars to foreign central banks in exchange for foreign currencies so that these central banks can in turn make dollar loans to their domestic banks
Loans to J.P. Morgan to buy Bear Stearns	March 14, 2008	Buys $30 billion of Bear Stearns assets through nonrecourse loans to J.P. Morgan to facilitate its purchase of Bear Stearns
Primary Dealer Credit Facility (PDCF)	March 16, 2008	Lends to primary dealers (including investment banks) so that they can borrow on similar terms to banks using the traditional discount window facility
Loans to AIG	September 16, 2008	Loans $85 billion to AIG
Asset-Backed Commercial Paper Money Market Mutual Fund Liquidity Facility (AMLF)	September 19, 2008	Lends to primary dealers so that they can purchase asset-backed commercial paper from money market mutual funds so that these funds can sell this paper to meet redemptions from their investors
Commercial Paper Funding Facility (CPFF)	October 7, 2008	Finances purchase of commercial paper from issuers
Money Market Investor Funding Facility (MMIFF)	October 21, 2008	Lends to special-purpose vehicles that can buy a wider range of money market mutual fund assets
Term Asset-Backed Securities Loan Facility (TALF)	November 25, 2008	Lends to issuers of asset-backed securities against these securities as collateral to improve functioning of this market

not result in a large increase in the money supply because most of it just flowed into holdings of excess reserves. Second, because the federal funds rate had already fallen to the zero-lower-bound, the expansion of the balance sheet and the monetary base could not lower short-term interest rates any further and thereby stimulate the economy. Third, increase in the monetary base does not mean that banks will increase lending because they can just add to their holdings of excess reserves instead of making loans. Indeed, this appears to be exactly what happened during the global financial crisis, when the huge increase in the monetary base led primarily to a massive rise in excess reserves and bank lending did not increase. A similar phenomenon seems to have occurred when the Bank of Japan engaged in quantitative easing after the bubble burst in the stock and real estate markets; yet not only did the economy not recover, but also inflation even turned negative.

Does skepticism about quantitative easing mean that the Fed's nonconventional monetary policy actions would be ineffective at stimulating the economy? Chairman Bernanke has argued that the answer is no because the Fed's policies were directed not at expanding the Fed's balance sheet but rather at **credit easing**—that is, altering the composition of the Fed's balance sheet in order to improve the functioning of particular segments of the credit markets. Indeed, Chairman Bernanke has been adamant that the Fed's policies should not be characterized as quantitative easing.

Altering the composition of the Fed's balance sheet can stimulate the economy in several ways. First, when the Fed provides liquidity to a particular segment of the credit markets that has seized up, it can help unfreeze the market and thereby enable it to allocate capital to productive uses and consequently stimulate the economy. Second, when the Fed purchases particular securities, it increases the demand for those securities, and as we saw in Chapter 6, it can lower the interest rates on those securities relative to other securities. Thus, even if short-term interest rates have hit a floor of zero, asset purchases can lower interest rates for borrowers in particular credit markets and thereby stimulate spending. For example, purchases of GSE mortgage-backed securities appear to have lowered the interest rates on these securities and led to a substantial decline in residential mortgage rates. Purchase of long-term government securities could also lower their interest rates relative to short-term interest rates, and because long-term interest rates are likely to be more relevant to investment decisions, these asset market purchases could boost investment spending. Recent research appears to support this viewpoint, with estimates of the decline in long-term interest rates from the Fed's asset purchase programs on the order of 100 basis points (one percentage point).[8]

Commitment to Future Policy Actions

Although short-term interest rates could not be driven below zero in the aftermath of the global financial crisis, the Federal Reserve could take another route to lower long-term interest rates, which, as we have mentioned above, would stimulate the economy. This route involved a commitment by the Fed to keep the federal funds rate at zero for a long period of time. To see how this would work, recall the discussion of the expectations theory of the term structure of interest rates in Chapter 6. There we saw that long-term interest rates will equal an average of the short-term interest rates that

[8]See, for example, Joseph Gagnon, Mathew Raskin, Julie Remache, and Brian Sack, "Large Scale Asset Purchases by the Federal Reserve: Did They Work?" *Federal Reserve Bank of New York Economic Policy Review*, Volume 17, Number 1 (May 2011), pp. 41–59.

markets expect to occur over the life of the long-term bond. By committing to the future policy action of keeping the federal funds rate at zero for an extended period, the Fed could lower the market's expectations of future short-term interest rates, thereby causing the long-term interest rate to fall. Michael Woodford of Columbia University has referred to such a strategy as **management of expectations**.

The Fed pursued this strategy when it announced after its FOMC meeting on December 16, 2008, that not only would it lower the federal funds rate target to between zero and ¼%, but also that "the Committee anticipates that weak economic conditions are likely to warrant exceptionally low levels of the federal funds rate for some time." The Fed then continued to use this language in its FOMC statements for several years afterward, even committing to an actual date of mid-2013 at its FOMC meeting in August of 2011. Although long-term interest rates on Treasury securities did subsequently fall, it is not clear how much of this decline was due to the Fed's attempt to manage expectations versus weakness in the economy.

There are two types of commitments to future policy actions: conditional and unconditional. The commitment to keep the federal funds rate at zero for an extended period starting in 2008 was *conditional* because it mentioned that the decision was predicated on a weak economy going forward. If economic circumstances changed, the FOMC was indicating that it might abandon the commitment. Alternatively, the Fed could have made an *unconditional* commitment by just stating that it would keep the federal funds rate at zero for an extended period without indicating that this decision was based on the state of the economy. An unconditional commitment has the advantage of being stronger than a conditional commitment because it does not suggest that the commitment will be abandoned and so is likely to have a larger effect on long-term interest rates. Unfortunately, it has the disadvantage that even if circumstances change in such a way that it would be better to abandon the commitment, the Fed may feel it cannot go back on its word and do so.

The problem of an unconditional commitment is illustrated by the Fed's experience in the 2003–2006 period. In 2003, the Fed became worried that inflation was too low and that the probability of a deflation was significant. At the August 12, 2003, FOMC meeting, the FOMC stated, "In these circumstances, the Committee believes that policy accommodation can be maintained for a considerable period." Then when the Fed started to tighten policy at its June 30, 2004, FOMC meeting, it changed its statement to "policy accommodation can be removed at a pace that is likely to be measured." Then for the next ten FOMC meetings through June 2006, the Fed raised the federal funds rate target by exactly ¼ percentage point at every single meeting. The market interpreted the FOMC's statements as indicating an unconditional commitment, and this is why the Fed may have been constrained not to deviate from ¼ percentage point moves at every FOMC meeting. In retrospect, this commitment led to monetary policy that was too easy for too long, with inflation subsequently rising to well above desirable levels, and, as discussed in Chapter 9, it may have helped promote the housing bubble whose bursting led to such devastating consequences for the economy.

MONETARY POLICY TOOLS OF THE EUROPEAN CENTRAL BANK

Like the Federal Reserve, the European System of Central Banks (which is usually referred to as the European Central Bank) signals the stance of its monetary policy by setting a **target financing rate**, which in turn sets a target for the **overnight cash rate**.

Like the federal funds rate, the overnight cash rate is the interest rate for very short-term interbank loans. The monetary policy tools used by the European Central Bank are similar to those used by the Federal Reserve and involve open market operations, lending to banks, and reserve requirements.

Open Market Operations

Like the Federal Reserve, the European Central Bank uses open market operations as its primary tool for conducting monetary policy and setting the overnight cash rate at the target financing rate. **Main refinancing operations** are the predominant form of open market operations and are similar to the Fed's repo transactions. They involve weekly **reverse transactions** (purchase or sale of eligible assets under repurchase or credit operations against eligible assets as collateral) that are reversed within two weeks. Credit institutions submit bids, and the European Central Bank decides which bids to accept. Like the Federal Reserve, the European Central Bank accepts the most attractively priced bids and makes purchases or sales to the point where the desired amount of reserves are supplied. In contrast to the Federal Reserve, which conducts open market operations in one location at the Federal Reserve Bank of New York, the European Central Bank decentralizes its open market operations by having them be conducted by the individual national central banks.

A second category of open market operations is the **longer-term refinancing operations**, which are a much smaller source of liquidity for the euro-area banking system and are similar to the Fed's outright purchases or sales of securities. These operations are carried out monthly and typically involve purchases or sales of securities with a maturity of three months. They are not used for signaling the monetary policy stance, but instead are aimed at providing euro-area banks access to longer-term funds.

Lending to Banks

As for the Fed, the next most important tool of monetary policy for the European Central Bank involves lending to banking institutions, which is carried out by the national central banks, just as discount lending is performed by the individual Federal Reserve Banks. This lending takes place through a standing lending facility called the **marginal lending facility**. There, banks can borrow (against eligible collateral) overnight loans from the national central banks at the **marginal lending rate**, which is set at 100 basis points above the target financing rate. The marginal lending rate provides a ceiling for the overnight market interest rate in the European Monetary Union, just as the discount rate does in the United States. As in the systems in the United States, Canada, Australia, and New Zealand, the Eurosystem has another standing facility, the **deposit facility**, in which banks are paid a fixed interest rate that is 100 basis points below the target financing rate. The prespecified interest rate on the deposit facility provides a floor for the overnight market interest rate, while the marginal lending rate sets a ceiling. This creates a channel/corridor, but with a much wider range of 100 basis points on either side.

Reserve Requirements

Like the Federal Reserve, the European Central Bank imposes reserve requirements such that all deposit-taking institutions are required to hold 2% of the total amount of checking deposits and other short-term deposits in reserve accounts with national central banks. All institutions that are subject to minimum reserve requirements have access to the European Central Bank's standing lending facilities and participate in open market operations. Like the Federal Reserve, the European Central Bank pays interest on reserves. Consequently, the banks' cost of complying with reserve requirements is low.

Summary

1. A supply and demand analysis of the market for reserves yields the following results: When the Fed makes an open market purchase or lowers reserve requirements, the federal funds rate declines. When the Fed makes an open market sale or raises reserve requirements, the federal funds rate rises. Changes in the discount rate and the interest rate paid on reserves may also affect the federal funds rate.
2. Conventional monetary policy tools include open market operations, discount policy, reserve requirements, and interest on reserves. Open market operations are the primary tool used by the Fed to implement monetary policy in normal times because they occur at the initiative of the Fed, are flexible, are easily reversed, and can be implemented quickly. Discount policy has the advantage of enabling the Fed to perform its role of lender of last resort, while raising interest rates on reserves to increase the federal funds rate avoids the need to conduct massive open market operations to reduce reserves when banks have accumulated large amounts of excess reserves.
3. Conventional monetary policy tools no longer are effective when the zero-lower-bound problem occurs, in which the central bank is unable to lower short-term interest rates because they have hit a floor of zero. In this situation, central banks use nonconventional monetary policy tools, which involve liquidity provision, asset purchases, and commitment to future policy actions. Liquidity provision and asset purchases lead to an expansion of the central bank balance sheet, which is referred to as *quantitative easing*. Expansion of the central bank balance sheet by itself is unlikely to have a large impact on the economy, but changing the composition of the balance sheet, which is what liquidity provision and asset purchases accomplished and is referred to as *credit easing*, can have a large impact by improving the functioning of credit markets.
4. The monetary policy tools used by the European Central Bank are similar to those used by the Federal Reserve System and involve open market operations, lending to banks, and reserve requirements. Main financing operations—open market operations in repos that are typically reversed within two weeks—are the primary tool to set the overnight cash rate at the target financing rate. The European Central Bank also operates standing lending facilities, which ensure that the overnight cash rate remains within 100 basis points of the target financing rate.

Key Terms

conventional monetary policy tools, p. 434

credit easing, p. 444

defensive open market operations, p. 434

deposit facility, p. 446

discount window, p. 436

dynamic open market operations, p. 434

federal funds rate, p. 425

lender of last resort, p. 437

longer-term refinancing operations, p. 446

main refinancing operations, p. 446

management of expectations, p. 445

marginal lending facility, p. 446

marginal lending rate, p. 446

matched sale–purchase transaction (reverse repo), p. 436

nonconventional monetary policy tools, p. 441
overnight cash rate, p. 445
primary dealers, p. 434
quantitative easing, p. 442
repurchase agreement (repo), p. 434
reverse transactions, p. 446
standing lending facility, p. 436
target financing rate, p. 445
zero-lower-bound problem, p. 441

Questions

All questions are available in **MyEconLab** *at* www.myeconlab.com.

1. If the manager of the open market desk hears that a snowstorm is about to strike New York City, making it difficult to present checks for payment there and so raising the float, what defensive open market operations will the manager undertake?
2. During the holiday season, when the public's holdings of currency increase, what defensive open market operations typically occur? Why?
3. If the Treasury has just paid a large bill to defense contractors and as a result its deposits with the Fed fall, what defensive open market operations will the manager of the open market desk undertake?
4. If float decreases below its normal level, why might the manager of domestic operations consider it more desirable to use repurchase agreements to affect the monetary base than an outright purchase of bonds?
5. "The only way that the Fed can affect the level of borrowed reserves is by adjusting the discount rate." Is this statement true, false, or uncertain? Explain your answer.
6. "The federal funds rate can never be above the discount rate." Is this statement true, false, or uncertain? Explain your answer.
7. "The federal funds rate can never be below the interest rate paid on reserves." Is this statement true, false, or uncertain? Explain your answer.
8. Why is paying interest on reserves an important tool for the Federal Reserve to manage crises?
9. Why are repurchase agreements used to conduct most short-term monetary policy operations, rather than simply buying and selling securities outright?
10. Most open market operations are typically repurchase agreements. What does this tell us about the likely volume of defensive open market operations relative to dynamic open market operations?
11. Following the global financial crisis in 2008, assets on the Federal Reserve's balance sheet increased dramatically, from approximately $800 billion at the end of 2007 to $3 trillion in 2011. Many of the assets held are longer-term securities acquired through various loan programs instituted as a result of the crisis. In this situation, how could reverse repos (matched sale–purchase transactions) help the Fed reduce its assets held in an orderly fashion, while reducing potential inflationary problems in the future?
12. "Discount loans are no longer needed because the presence of the FDIC eliminates the possibility of bank panics." Is this statement true, false, or uncertain?
13. What are the disadvantages of using loans to financial institutions to prevent bank panics?
14. You often read in the newspaper that the Fed has just lowered the discount rate. Does this signal that the Fed is moving to a more expansionary monetary policy? Why or why not?
15. How can the procyclical movement of interest rates (rising during business cycle expansions and falling during business cycle contractions) lead to a procyclical movement in the money supply as a result of Fed discount loans? Why might this movement of the money supply be undesirable?
16. "If reserve requirements were eliminated, it would be harder to control interest rates." Is this statement true, false, or uncertain?
17. "Considering that raising reserve requirements to 100% makes complete control of the money supply possible, Congress should authorize the Fed to raise reserve requirements to this level." Discuss.
18. Compare the use of open market operations, loans to financial institutions, and changes in reserve requirements to control the money supply on the basis of the following criteria: flexibility, reversibility, effectiveness, and speed of implementation.

19. Why was the Term Auction Facility more widely used by financial institutions than the discount window during the global financial crisis?

20. What are the advantages and disadvantages of *quantitative easing* as an alternative to conventional monetary policy when short-term interest rates are at the zero lower-bound?

21. Why is the composition of the Fed's balance sheet a potentially important aspect of monetary policy during a crisis?

22. What is the main advantage and disadvantage of an unconditional policy commitment?

Applied Problems

All applied problems are available in MyEconLab *at* www.myeconlab.com.

23. If a switch occurs from deposits into currency, what happens to the federal funds rate? Use the supply and demand analysis of the market for reserves to explain your answer.

24. Why is it that a decrease in the discount rate does not normally lead to an increase in borrowed reserves? Use the supply and demand analysis of the market for reserves to explain.

25. Using the supply and demand analysis of the market for reserves, indicate what happens to the federal funds rate, borrowed reserves, and nonborrowed reserves, holding everything else constant, under the following situations.

a. The economy is surprisingly strong, leading to an increase in the amount of checkable deposits.

b. Banks expect an unusually large increase in withdrawals from checking deposit accounts in the future.

c. The Fed raises the target federal funds rate.

d. The Fed raises the interest rate on reserves above the current equilibrium federal funds rate.

e. The Fed reduces reserve requirements.

f. The Fed reduces reserve requirements, and sterilizes this by conducting an open market sale of securities.

Web Exercises

1. Go to www.federalreserve.gov/fomc/. This site reports activity by the FOMC. Scroll down to Calendar and click on the statement released after the last meeting. Summarize this statement in one paragraph. Be sure to note whether the committee has decided to increase or decrease the federal funds rate target. Now review the statements of the past two meetings. Has the stance of the committee changed?

2. Go to www.federalreserve.gov/releases/h15/update/. What is the current federal funds rate? What is the current Federal Reserve discount rate (define this rate as well)? Have short-term rates increased or declined since the end of 2008?

Web References

www.federalreserve.gov/fomc/fundsrate.htm

This site lists historical federal funds rates and discusses Federal Reserve targets.

www.frbdiscountwindow.org/

Information on the operation of the discount window and data on current and historical interest rates.

www.federalreserve.gov/monetarypolicy/reservereq.htm

Historical data and discussion about reserve requirements.

www.federalreserve.gov/fomc

A discussion about the Federal Open Market Committee, list of current members, meeting dates, and other current information.

19 The Conduct of Monetary Policy: Strategy and Tactics

Preview

Getting monetary policy right is crucial to the health of the economy. Overly expansionary monetary policy leads to high inflation, which decreases the efficiency of the economy and hampers economic growth. Monetary policy that is too tight can produce serious recessions in which output falls and unemployment rises. It can also lead to deflation, a fall in the price level, such as occurred in the United States during the Great Depression and in Japan more recently. As we saw in Chapter 9, deflation can be especially damaging to an economy, because it promotes financial instability and can worsen financial crises.

Now that we understand the tools that central banks such as the Federal Reserve use to conduct monetary policy, we can consider how central banks *should* conduct monetary policy. To explore this subject, we start by looking at the goals for monetary policy and then examine one of the most important strategies for the conduct of monetary policy, inflation targeting. We then discuss tactics, that is, the choice and setting of the monetary policy instrument. After examining the strategies and tactics, we can evaluate the Fed's conduct of monetary policy in the past, with the hope that it will indicate where monetary policy may head in the future.

THE PRICE STABILITY GOAL AND THE NOMINAL ANCHOR

Over the past few decades, policymakers throughout the world have become increasingly aware of the social and economic costs of inflation and more concerned with maintaining a stable price level as a goal of economic policy. Indeed, **price stability**, which central bankers define as low and stable inflation, is increasingly viewed as the most important goal of monetary policy. Price stability is desirable because a rising price level (inflation) creates uncertainty in the economy, and that uncertainty might hamper economic growth. For example, when the overall level of prices is changing, the information conveyed by the prices of goods and services is harder to interpret, which complicates decision making for consumers, businesses, and government, thereby leading to a less efficient financial system.

Not only do public opinion surveys indicate that the public is hostile to inflation, but a growing body of evidence also suggests that inflation leads to lower economic growth. The most extreme example of unstable prices is *hyperinflation*, such as Argentina, Brazil, Russia, and Zimbabwe have experienced in the recent past. Hyperinflation has proved to be very damaging to the workings of the economy.

Inflation also makes it difficult to plan for the future. For example, it is more difficult to decide how much to put aside to provide for a child's college education in an inflationary environment. Furthermore, inflation can strain a country's social fabric: Conflict might result, because each group in the society may compete with other groups to make sure that its income keeps up with the rising level of prices.

The Role of a Nominal Anchor

Because price stability is so crucial to the long-run health of an economy, a central element in successful monetary policy is the use of a **nominal anchor**, a nominal variable such as the inflation rate or the money supply, which ties down the price level to achieve price stability. Adherence to a nominal anchor that keeps the nominal variable within a narrow range promotes price stability by directly promoting low and stable inflation expectations. A more subtle reason for a nominal anchor's importance is that it can limit the **time-inconsistency problem**, in which monetary policy conducted on a discretionary, day-by-day basis leads to poor long-run outcomes.

The Time-Inconsistency Problem

The time-inconsistency problem is something we deal with continually in everyday life. We often have a plan that we know will produce a good outcome in the long run, but when tomorrow comes, we just can't help ourselves and we renege on our plan because doing so has short-run gains. For example, we make a New Year's resolution to go on a diet, but soon thereafter we can't resist having one more bite of that rocky road ice cream—and then another bite, and then another bite—and the weight begins to pile back on. In other words, we find ourselves unable to *consistently* follow a good plan over *time;* the good plan is said to be *time-inconsistent* and will soon be abandoned.

Monetary policymakers also face the time-inconsistency problem. They are always tempted to pursue a discretionary monetary policy that is more expansionary than firms or people expect because such a policy would boost economic output (or lower unemployment) in the short run. The best policy, however, is *not* to pursue expansionary policy, because decisions about wages and prices reflect workers' and firms' expectations about policy; when they see a central bank pursuing expansionary policy, workers and firms will raise their expectations about inflation, driving wages and prices up. The rise in wages and prices will lead to higher inflation, but will not result in higher output on average. (We examine this issue more formally in Web Chapter 3.)

A central bank will have better inflation performance in the long run if it does not try to surprise people with an unexpectedly expansionary policy, but instead keeps inflation under control. However, even if a central bank recognizes that discretionary policy will lead to a poor outcome (high inflation with no gains in output), it still may not be able to pursue the better policy of inflation control, because politicians are likely to apply pressure on the central bank to try to boost output with overly expansionary monetary policy.

A clue to how we should deal with the time-inconsistency problem comes from how-to books on parenting. Parents know that giving in to a child to keep him from acting up will produce a very spoiled child. Nevertheless, when a child throws a tantrum, many parents give him what he wants just to shut him up. Because parents don't stick to their "do not give in" plan, the child expects that he will get what he wants if he behaves badly, so he will throw tantrums over and over again. Parenting books suggest a solution to the time-inconsistency problem (although they don't call it that): Parents should set behavior rules for their children and stick to them.

A nominal anchor is like a behavior rule. Just as rules help to prevent the time-inconsistency problem in parenting by helping adults resist pursuing the discretionary policy of giving in, a nominal anchor can help prevent the time-inconsistency problem in monetary policy by providing an expected constraint on discretionary policy.

OTHER GOALS OF MONETARY POLICY

Although price stability is the primary goal of most central banks, five other goals are continually mentioned by central bank officials when they discuss the objectives of monetary policy: (1) high employment and output stability, (2) economic growth, (3) stability of financial markets, (4) interest-rate stability, and (5) stability in foreign exchange markets.

High Employment and Output Stability

High employment is a worthy goal for two main reasons: (1) the alternative situation—high unemployment—causes much human misery; and (2) when unemployment is high, the economy has both idle workers and idle resources (closed factories and unused equipment), resulting in a loss of output (lower GDP).

Although it is clear that high employment is desirable, how high should it be? At what point can we say that the economy is at full employment? At first, it might seem that full employment is the point at which no worker is out of a job—that is, when unemployment is zero. But this definition ignores the fact that some unemployment, called *frictional unemployment*, which involves searches by workers and firms to find suitable matchups, is beneficial to the economy. For example, a worker who decides to look for a better job might be unemployed for a while during the job search. Workers often decide to leave work temporarily to pursue other activities (raising a family, travel, returning to school), and when they decide to reenter the job market, it may take some time for them to find the right job.

Another reason that unemployment is not zero when the economy is at full employment is *structural unemployment*, a mismatch between job requirements and the skills or availability of local workers. Clearly, this kind of unemployment is undesirable. Nonetheless, it is something that monetary policy can do little about.

This goal for high employment is not an unemployment level of zero but a level above zero consistent with full employment at which the demand for labor equals the supply of labor. This level is called the **natural rate of unemployment**.

Although this definition sounds neat and authoritative, it leaves a troublesome question unanswered: What unemployment rate is consistent with full employment? In some cases, it is obvious that the unemployment rate is too high. The unemployment rate in excess of 20% during the Great Depression, for example, was clearly far too high. In the early 1960s, on the other hand, policymakers thought that a reasonable goal was 4%, a level that was probably too low, because it led to accelerating inflation. Current estimates of the natural rate of unemployment place it between $4\frac{1}{2}$ and 6%, but even this estimate is subject to much uncertainty and disagreement. It is possible, for example, that appropriate government policy, such as the provision of better information about job vacancies or job training programs, might decrease the natural rate of unemployment.

The high employment goal can be thought of in another way. Because the level of unemployment is tied to the level of economic activity in the economy, a particular level of output is produced at the natural rate of unemployment, which naturally enough is referred to as the **natural rate of output** but is more often referred to as **potential output**.

Trying to achieve the goal of high employment thus means that central banks should try to move the level of output toward the natural rate of output. In other words, they should try to stabilize the level of output around its natural rate.

Economic Growth

The goal of steady economic growth is closely related to the high-employment goal because businesses are more likely to invest in capital equipment to increase productivity and economic growth when unemployment is low. Conversely, if unemployment is high and factories are idle, it does not pay for a firm to invest in additional plants and equipment. Although the two goals are closely related, policies can be specifically aimed at promoting economic growth by directly encouraging firms to invest or by encouraging people to save, which provides more funds for firms to invest. In fact, this approach is the stated purpose of *supply-side economics* policies, which are intended to spur economic growth by providing tax incentives for businesses to invest in facilities and equipment and for taxpayers to save more. Active debate continues over what role monetary policy can play in boosting growth.

Stability of Financial Markets

As our analysis in Chapter 9 showed, financial crises can interfere with the ability of financial markets to channel funds to people with productive investment opportunities and lead to a sharp contraction in economic activity. The promotion of a more stable financial system in which financial crises are avoided is thus an important goal for a central bank. Indeed, as we saw in Chapter 16, the Federal Reserve System was created in response to the bank panic of 1907 to promote financial stability.

Interest-Rate Stability

Interest-rate stability is desirable because fluctuations in interest rates can create uncertainty in the economy and make it harder to plan for the future. Fluctuations in interest rates that affect consumers' willingness to buy houses, for example, make it more difficult for consumers to decide when to purchase a house and for construction firms to plan how many houses to build. A central bank may also want to reduce upward movements in interest rates for the reasons we discussed in Chapter 16: Upward movements in interest rates generate hostility toward central banks and lead to demands that their power be curtailed.

The stability of financial markets is also fostered by interest-rate stability, because fluctuations in interest rates create great uncertainty for financial institutions. An increase in interest rates produces large capital losses on long-term bonds and mortgages, losses that can cause the failure of the financial institutions holding them. In recent years, more pronounced interest-rate fluctuations have been a particularly severe problem for savings and loan associations and mutual savings banks, many of which got into serious financial trouble in the 1980s and early 1990s.

Stability in Foreign Exchange Markets

With the increasing importance of international trade to the U.S. economy, the value of the dollar relative to other currencies has become a major consideration for the Fed.

A rise in the value of the dollar makes American industries less competitive with those abroad, and declines in the value of the dollar stimulate inflation in the United States. In addition, preventing large changes in the value of the dollar makes it easier for firms and individuals purchasing or selling goods abroad to plan ahead. Stabilizing extreme movements in the value of the dollar in foreign exchange markets is thus an important goal of monetary policy. In other countries, which are even more dependent on foreign trade, stability in foreign exchange markets takes on even greater importance.

SHOULD PRICE STABILITY BE THE PRIMARY GOAL OF MONETARY POLICY?

In the long run, no inconsistency exists between the price stability goal and the other goals mentioned earlier. The natural rate of unemployment is not lowered by high inflation, so higher inflation cannot produce lower unemployment or more employment in the long run. In other words, there is no long-run trade-off between inflation and employment. In the long run, price stability promotes economic growth as well as financial and interest-rate stability. Although price stability is consistent with the other goals in the long run, in the short run price stability often conflicts with the goals of output stability and interest-rate stability. For example, when the economy is expanding and unemployment is falling, the economy may become overheated, leading to a rise in inflation. To pursue the price stability goal, a central bank would prevent this overheating by raising interest rates, an action that would initially cause output to fall and increase interest-rate instability. How should a central bank resolve this conflict among goals?

Hierarchical Versus Dual Mandates

Because price stability is crucial to the long-run health of the economy, many countries have decided that price stability should be the primary, long-run goal for central banks. For example, the Maastricht Treaty, which created the European Central Bank, states, "The primary objective of the European System of Central Banks [ESCB] shall be to maintain price stability. Without prejudice to the objective of price stability, the ESCB shall support the general economic policies in the Community," which include objectives such as "a high level of employment" and "sustainable and non-inflationary growth." Mandates of this type, which put the goal of price stability first, and then say that as long as it is achieved other goals can be pursued, are known as **hierarchical mandates**. They are the directives governing the behavior of such central banks as the Bank of England, the Bank of Canada, and the Reserve Bank of New Zealand, as well as the European Central Bank.

In contrast, the legislation defining the mission of the Federal Reserve states, "The Board of Governors of the Federal Reserve System and the Federal Open Market Committee shall maintain long-run growth of the monetary and credit aggregates commensurate with the economy's long-run potential to increase production, so as to promote effectively the goals of maximum employment, stable prices, and moderate long-term interest rates." Because, as we learned in Chapter 5, long-term interest rates will be very high if inflation is high, this statement in practice is a **dual mandate** to achieve two coequal objectives: price stability and maximum employment (output stability).

Is it better for an economy to operate under a hierarchical mandate or a dual mandate?

Price Stability as the Primary, Long-Run Goal of Monetary Policy

Because no inconsistency exists between achieving price stability in the long run and the natural rate of unemployment, these two types of mandates are not very different *if* maximum employment is defined as the natural rate of employment. In practice, however, a substantial difference between these two mandates could exist, because the public and politicians may believe that a hierarchical mandate puts too much emphasis on inflation control and not enough on stabilizing output.

Because low and stable inflation rates promote economic growth, central bankers have come to realize that price stability should be the primary, long-run goal of monetary policy. Nevertheless, because output fluctuations should also be a concern of monetary policy, the goal of price stability should be seen as primary only in the long run. Attempts to keep inflation at the same level in the short run, no matter what, would likely lead to excessive output fluctuations.

As long as price stability is a long-run, but not short-run, goal, central banks can focus on reducing output fluctuations by allowing inflation to deviate from the long-run goal for short periods and, therefore, can operate under a dual mandate. However, if a dual mandate leads a central bank to pursue short-run expansionary policies that increase output and employment without worrying about the long-run consequences for inflation, the time-inconsistency problem may recur. Concerns that a dual mandate might lead to overly expansionary policy is a key reason why central bankers often favor hierarchical mandates in which the pursuit of price stability takes precedence. Hierarchical mandates can also be a problem if they lead to a central bank behaving as what the Governor of the Bank of England, Mervyn King, has referred to as an "inflation nutter"—that is, a central bank that focuses solely on inflation control, even in the short run, and so undertakes policies that lead to large output fluctuations. The choice of which type of mandate is better for a central bank ultimately depends on the subtleties of how it will work in practice. Either type of mandate is acceptable as long as it operates to make price stability the primary goal in the long run, but not the short run.

INFLATION TARGETING

The recognition that price stability should be the primary long-run goal of monetary policy and the value of having a nominal anchor to achieve this goal has led to a monetary policy strategy known as inflation targeting. **Inflation targeting** involves several elements: (1) public announcement of medium-term numerical objectives (targets) for inflation; (2) an institutional commitment to price stability as the primary, long-run goal of monetary policy and a commitment to achieve the inflation goal; (3) an information-inclusive approach in which many variables (not just monetary aggregates) are used in making decisions about monetary policy; (4) increased transparency of the monetary policy strategy through communication with the public and the markets about the plans and objectives of monetary policymakers; and (5) increased accountability of the central bank for attaining its inflation objectives. New Zealand was the first country to formally adopt inflation targeting in 1990, followed by Canada in 1991, the United Kingdom in 1992, Sweden and Finland in 1993, and Australia and Spain in

1994. Israel, Chile, and Brazil, among others, have also adopted a form of inflation targeting.[1]

Inflation Targeting in New Zealand, Canada, and the United Kingdom

We begin our look at inflation targeting with New Zealand, because it was the first country to adopt it. We then go on to examine the experiences in Canada and the United Kingdom, which were next to adopt this strategy.[2]

New Zealand As part of a general reform of the government's role in the economy, the New Zealand parliament passed a new Reserve Bank of New Zealand Act in 1989, which became effective on February 1, 1990. Besides increasing the independence of the central bank, moving it from being one of the least independent to one of the most independent among developed countries, the act committed the Reserve Bank to a sole objective of price stability. The act stipulated that the minister of finance and the governor of the Reserve Bank should negotiate and make public a Policy Targets Agreement, a statement that sets out the targets by which monetary policy performance will be evaluated, specifying numerical target ranges for inflation and the dates by which they are to be reached. An unusual feature of the New Zealand legislation is that the governor of the Reserve Bank is held highly accountable for the success of monetary policy. If the goals set forth in the Policy Targets Agreement are not satisfied, the governor is subject to dismissal.

The first Policy Targets Agreement, signed by the minister of finance and the governor of the Reserve Bank on March 2, 1990, directed the Reserve Bank to achieve an annual inflation rate within a 3–5% range. Subsequent agreements lowered the range to 0–2% until the end of 1996, when the range was changed to 0–3% and later to 1–3% in 2002. As a result of tight monetary policy, the inflation rate was brought down from above 5% to below 2% by the end of 1992 (see Figure 1, panel a), but at the cost of a deep recession and a sharp rise in unemployment. Since then, inflation has typically remained within the targeted range, with the exception of brief periods in 1995, 2000, and 2008, when it exceeded the range by a small amount. (Under the Reserve Bank Act, the governor could have been dismissed, but after parliamentary debates he retained his job.) Since 1992, New Zealand's growth rate has generally been high, with some years exceeding 5%, and unemployment has come down significantly.

Canada On February 26, 1991, a joint announcement by the minister of finance and the governor of the Bank of Canada established formal inflation targets. The target ranges were 2–4% by the end of 1992, 1.5–3.5% by June 1994, and 1–3% by December 1996. After the new government took office in late 1993, the target range was set at 1–3% from December 1995 until December 1998 and has been kept at this level. Canadian inflation has also fallen dramatically since the adoption of inflation targets, from above 5% in 1991, to a 0% rate in 1995, and to around 2% subsequently (see Figure 1, panel b). As was the case in New Zealand, however, this decline was not without cost: Unemployment soared to above 10% from 1991 until 1994, but then declined substantially.

[1]A precursor to the inflation-targeting strategy is monetary targeting. It is discussed in an appendix to this chapter that is on the Companion Website at www.pearsonhighered.com/mishkin.

[2]If you are interested in a more detailed discussion of experiences with inflation targeting in these and other countries see Ben S. Bernanke, Thomas Laubach, Frederic S. Mishkin, and Adam S. Posen, *Inflation Targeting: Lessons from the International Experience* (Princeton: Princeton University Press, 1999).

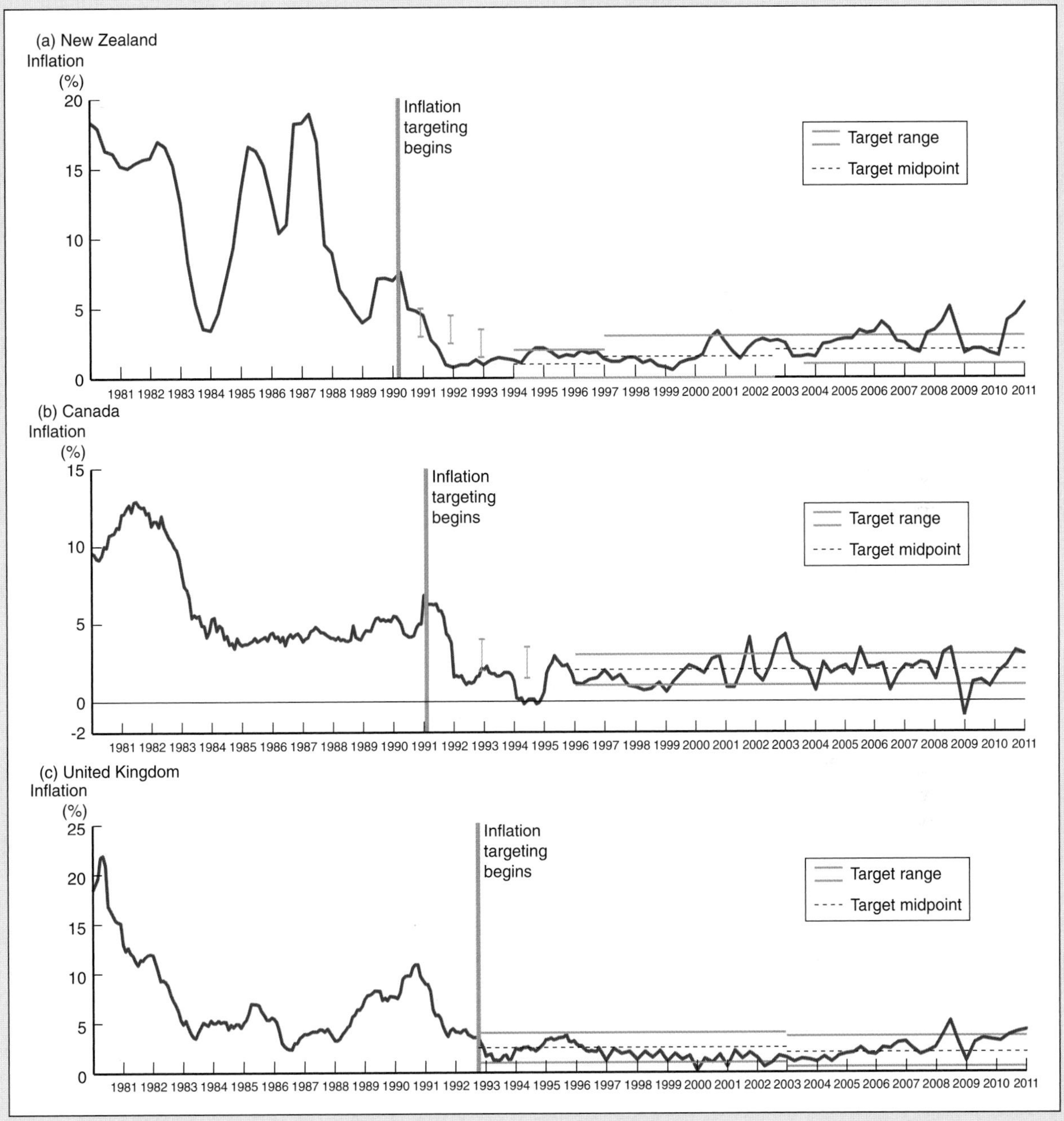

FIGURE 1 Inflation Rates and Inflation Targets for New Zealand, Canada, and the United Kingdom, 1980–2011

Inflation-targeting countries have significantly reduced the rate of inflation and eventually have achieved their inflation targets.

Source: Ben S. Bernanke, Thomas Laubach, Frederic S. Mishkin, and Adam S. Poson, *Inflation Targeting: Lessons from the International Experience* (Princeton: Princeton University Press, 1999), updates from the same sources, and www.rbnz.govt.nz/statistics/econind/a3/ha3.xls.

United Kingdom In October 1992, the United Kingdom adopted an inflation target as its nominal anchor, and the Bank of England began to produce an *Inflation Report*, a quarterly report on the progress being made in achieving that target. The inflation target range was initially set at 1–4% until the next election (spring 1997 at the latest), with the intent that the inflation rate should settle down to the lower half of the range (below 2.5%). In May 1997, the inflation target was set at 2.5% and the Bank of England was given the power to set interest rates henceforth, granting it a more independent role in monetary policy.

Before the adoption of inflation targets, inflation had already been falling in the United Kingdom, with a peak of 9% at the beginning of 1991 and a rate of 4% at the time of adoption (see Figure 1, panel c). By the third quarter of 1994, it was at 2.2%, within the intended range. Subsequently, inflation rose, climbing slightly above the 2.5% level by the end of 1995, but then fell and has remained close to the target since then, except for the period from 2008 to 2011. In December 2003, the target was changed to 2.0% for a slightly different measure of inflation. Meanwhile, growth of the U.K. economy was strong until 2008, causing a substantial reduction in the unemployment rate.

Advantages of Inflation Targeting

Because an explicit numerical inflation target increases the accountability of the central bank, inflation targeting has the potential to reduce the likelihood that the central bank will fall into the time-inconsistency trap of trying to expand output and employment in the short run by pursuing overly expansionary monetary policy. A key advantage of inflation targeting is that it can help focus the political debate on what a central bank can do in the long run—that is, control inflation—rather than what it cannot do, permanently increase economic growth and the number of jobs through expansionary monetary policy. Thus inflation targeting has the potential to reduce political pressures on the central bank to pursue inflationary monetary policy and thereby to reduce the likelihood of the time-inconsistency problem.

Inflation targeting has the advantage that it is readily understood by the public and is thus highly transparent. Indeed, inflation-targeting regimes put great stress on making policy transparent and on regular communication with the public. Inflation-targeting central banks have frequent communications with the government, some mandated by law and some in response to informal inquiries, and their officials take every opportunity to make public speeches on their monetary policy strategy. Although these techniques are also commonly used in countries that have not adopted inflation targeting, inflation-targeting central banks have taken public outreach a step further: Not only do they engage in extended public information campaigns, including the distribution of glossy brochures, but they also publish documents like the Bank of England's *Inflation Report*. The publication of these documents is particularly noteworthy, because they depart from the usual dull-looking, formal reports of central banks and use fancy graphics, boxes, and other eye-catching design elements to engage the public's interest.

The above channels of communication are used by central banks in inflation-targeting countries to explain the following concepts to the general public, financial market participants, and politicians: (1) the goals and limitations of monetary policy, including the rationale for inflation targets; (2) the numerical values of the inflation targets and how they were determined; (3) how the inflation targets are to be achieved, given current economic conditions; and (4) reasons for any deviations from targets. These communications have improved private sector planning by reducing uncertainty about monetary policy, interest rates, and inflation; they have promoted public debate of monetary policy, in part by educating the public about what a central bank can and cannot achieve; and they have helped clarify the responsibilities of the central bank and of politicians in the conduct of monetary policy.

Another key feature of inflation-targeting regimes is the tendency toward increased accountability of the central bank. Indeed, transparency and communication go hand in hand with increased accountability. The strongest case of accountability of a central bank in an inflation-targeting regime is in New Zealand, where the government has the right to dismiss the Reserve Bank's governor if the inflation targets are breached, even for one quarter. In other inflation-targeting countries, the central bank's accountability is less formalized. Nevertheless, the transparency of policy associated with inflation targeting has tended to make the central bank highly accountable to the public and the government. Sustained success in the conduct of monetary policy as measured against a preannounced and well-defined inflation target can be instrumental in building public support for a central bank's independence and for its policies. This building of public support and accountability occurs even in the absence of a rigidly defined and legalistic standard of performance evaluation and punishment.

The performance of inflation-targeting regimes has been quite good. Inflation-targeting countries seem to have significantly reduced both the rate of inflation and inflation expectations beyond what would likely have occurred in the absence of inflation targets. Furthermore, once down, inflation in these countries has stayed down; following disinflations, the inflation rate in targeting countries has not bounced back up during subsequent cyclical expansions of the economy.

Disadvantages of Inflation Targeting

Critics of inflation targeting cite four disadvantages of this monetary policy strategy: delayed signaling, too much rigidity, the potential for increased output fluctuations, and low economic growth. We look at each in turn and examine the validity of these criticisms.

Delayed Signaling Inflation is not easily controlled by the monetary authorities. Furthermore, because of the long lags in the effects of monetary policy, inflation outcomes are revealed only after a substantial lag. Thus an inflation target is unable to send immediate signals to both the public and markets about the stance of monetary policy.

Too Much Rigidity Some economists have criticized inflation targeting because they believe it imposes a rigid rule on monetary policymakers and limits their ability to respond to unforeseen circumstances. However, useful policy strategies exist that are "rule-like" in that they involve forward-looking behavior that limits policymakers from systematically engaging in policies with undesirable long-run consequences. Such policies avoid the time-inconsistency problem and would best be described as "constrained discretion."

Indeed, inflation targeting can be described exactly in this way. Inflation targeting, as actually practiced, is far from rigid and is better described as "flexible inflation targeting." First, inflation targeting does not prescribe simple and mechanical instructions on how the central bank should conduct monetary policy. Rather, it requires the central bank to use all available information to determine which policy actions are appropriate to achieve the inflation target. Unlike simple policy rules, inflation targeting never requires the central bank to focus solely on one key variable. Second, inflation targeting, as practiced, contains a substantial degree of policy discretion. Inflation targets have been modified depending on economic circumstances, as we have seen. Moreover, central banks under inflation-targeting regimes have left themselves considerable scope to respond to output growth and fluctuations through several devices.

Potential for Increased Output Fluctuations An important criticism of inflation targeting is that a sole focus on inflation may lead to monetary policy that is too tight when inflation is above target and thus may result in larger output fluctuations. Inflation targeting does not, however, require a sole focus on inflation—in fact, experience has shown that inflation targeters display substantial concern about output fluctuations. All the inflation targeters have set their inflation targets above zero.[3] For example, currently, New Zealand, Canada, the United Kingdom, and Sweden set the midpoint of their inflation target at 2%, while Australia has its midpoints at 2.5%.

The decision by inflation targeters to choose inflation targets above zero reflects the concern of monetary policymakers that particularly low inflation can have substantial negative effects on real economic activity. Deflation (negative inflation in which the price level actually falls) is especially to be feared because of the possibility that it may promote financial instability and precipitate a severe economic contraction (as discussed in Chapter 9). The deflation in Japan in recent years has been an important factor in the weakening of the Japanese financial system and economy. Targeting inflation rates of above zero makes periods of deflation less likely. This is one reason why some economists both within and outside Japan have been calling on the Bank of Japan to adopt an inflation target at levels of 2% or higher.

Inflation targeting also does not ignore traditional stabilization goals. Central bankers in inflation-targeting countries continue to express their concern about fluctuations in output and employment, and the ability to accommodate short-run stabilization goals to some degree is built into all inflation-targeting regimes. All inflation-targeting countries have been willing to minimize output declines by gradually lowering medium-term inflation targets toward the long-run goal.

Low Economic Growth Another common concern about inflation targeting is that it will lead to low growth in output and employment. Although inflation reduction has been associated with below-normal output during disinflationary phases in inflation-targeting regimes, once low inflation levels were achieved, output and employment returned to levels at least as high as they were before. A conservative conclusion is that once low inflation is achieved, inflation targeting is not harmful to the real economy. Given the strong economic growth after disinflation in many countries (such as New Zealand) that have adopted inflation targets, a case can be made that inflation targeting promotes real economic growth, in addition to controlling inflation.

[3]Consumer price indexes have been found to have an upward bias in the measurement of true inflation, so it is not surprising that inflation targets would be chosen to exceed zero. However, the actual targets have been set to exceed the estimates of this measurement bias, indicating that inflation targeters have decided on targets for inflation that exceed zero even after measurement bias is accounted for.

THE FEDERAL RESERVE'S MONETARY POLICY STRATEGY

The United States has achieved excellent macroeconomic performance (including low and stable inflation) until the onset of the global financial crisis without using an explicit nominal anchor such as an inflation target. Although the Federal Reserve has not articulated an explicit strategy, a coherent strategy for the conduct of monetary policy exists nonetheless. This strategy involves an implicit, but not an explicit, nominal anchor in the form of an overriding concern by the Federal Reserve to control inflation in the long run. In addition, it involves forward-looking behavior that includes careful monitoring for signs of future inflation, using a wide range of information, coupled with periodic "preemptive strikes" by monetary policy against the threat of inflation.

As emphasized by Milton Friedman, monetary policy effects have long lags. In industrialized countries with a history of low inflation, the inflation process seems to have tremendous inertia: Estimates from large macroeconometric models of the U.S. economy, for example, suggest that monetary policy takes over a year to affect output and over two years to have a significant impact on inflation. For countries that have experienced highly variable inflation, and therefore have more flexible prices, the lags may be shorter.

The presence of long lags means that monetary policy cannot wait to respond until inflation has begun. If the central bank waits until overt signs of inflation appear, it will already be too late to maintain stable prices, at least not without a severe tightening of policy: Inflation expectations will already be embedded in the wage- and price-setting process, creating an inflation momentum that will be hard to halt. Inflation becomes much harder to control once it has been allowed to gather momentum, because higher inflation expectations become ingrained in various types of long-term contracts and pricing agreements.

To prevent inflation from getting started, therefore, monetary policy needs to be forward-looking and preemptive. That is, depending on the lags from monetary policy to inflation, monetary policy needs to act long before inflationary pressures appear in the economy. For example, suppose it takes roughly two years for monetary policy to have a significant impact on inflation. In this case, even if inflation is currently low but policymakers believe inflation will rise over the next two years with an unchanged stance of monetary policy, they must tighten monetary policy *now* to prevent the inflationary surge.

Under Alan Greenspan and Ben Bernanke, the Federal Reserve has been successful in pursuing a preemptive monetary policy. For example, as discussed in the appendix to this chapter, the Fed raised interest rates from 1994 to 1995 before a rise in inflation got a toehold. As a result, inflation not only did not rise, but fell slightly. As discussed in the appendix, the Fed also conducted preemptive strikes against economic downturns. For example, the Fed started easing monetary policy in September 2007 at the onset of the global financial crisis, even though the economy was growing strongly at the time and inflation was rising. (However, in this case, the Fed's preemptive policy was not sufficient to overcome the massive negative shock to the economy from the disruption to financial markets.) This preemptive, forward-looking monetary policy strategy is clearly also a feature of inflation-targeting regimes, because monetary policy instruments are adjusted to take account of the long lags in their effects in an effort to hit future inflation targets. However, the Fed's policy regime might best be described as a "just do it" policy, and differs from inflation targeting in that it does not officially have a nominal anchor and is much less transparent in its monetary policy strategy.

Advantages of the Fed's "Just Do It" Approach

The Fed's "just do it" approach, which has some key elements of inflation targeting, has many of the same advantages. As with inflation targeting, the central bank uses many sources of information to determine the best settings for monetary policy. The Fed's forward-looking behavior and stress on price stability also help to discourage overly expansionary monetary policy, thereby ameliorating the time-inconsistency problem.

Another key argument for the Fed's "just do it" strategy is its demonstrated success. The Federal Reserve reduced inflation in the United States from double-digit levels in 1980 to an average rate close to 3% over the last 30, which is arguably consistent with the price stability goal. At the same time, economic growth has been good, averaging around 3% over the same period, with relatively steady growth up until the global financial crisis hit the economy hard. Indeed, up until recently, the performance of the U.S. economy was the envy of the industrialized world.

Disadvantages of the Fed's "Just Do It" Approach

Given the success of the Fed's "just do it" strategy in the United States, why should the United States consider other monetary policy strategies? (If it ain't broke, why fix it?) The answer is that the "just do it" strategy has some disadvantages that may cause it to work less well in the future.

One disadvantage of the strategy is its lack of transparency. The Fed's close-mouthed approach about its intentions gives rise to a constant guessing game about what it is going to do. This high level of uncertainty leads to unnecessary volatility in financial markets and creates doubt among producers and the general public about the future course of inflation and output. Furthermore, the opacity of its policy making makes it hard to hold the Federal Reserve accountable to Congress and the general public: The Fed can't be held accountable if there are no predetermined criteria for judging its performance. Low accountability may make the central bank more susceptible to the time-inconsistency problem, whereby it may pursue short-term objectives at the expense of long-term ones.

Probably the most serious problem with the Fed's "just do it" approach is its strong dependence on the preferences, skills, and trustworthiness of the individuals in charge of the central bank. In recent years in the United States, Federal Reserve chairmen Alan Greenspan and Ben Bernanke and other Federal Reserve officials have emphasized forward-looking policies and inflation control, with great success. The Fed's prestige and credibility with the public has risen accordingly. But the Fed's leadership will periodically change, and there is no guarantee that future leaders will be committed to the same approach. Nor is there any guarantee that the relatively good working relationship that has existed between the Fed and the executive and legislative branches will always continue. In a different economic or political environment, the Fed might face strong pressure to engage in overly expansionary policies, raising the possibility that time inconsistency may become a more serious problem. In the past, after a successful period of low inflation, the Federal Reserve has reverted to inflationary monetary policy—the 1970s are one example—and without an explicit nominal anchor, this could certainly happen again.

Another disadvantage of the "just do it" approach is that it has some inconsistencies with democratic principles. As described in Chapter 16, there are good reasons—notably, insulation from short-term political pressures—for the central bank to have some degree of independence, as the Federal Reserve currently does, and the evidence does generally support central bank independence. Yet the practical economic arguments for central bank independence coexist uneasily with the presumption that government policies should be made democratically, rather than by an elite group.

In contrast, inflation targeting can make the institutional framework for the conduct of monetary policy more consistent with democratic principles and avoid some of the above problems. The inflation-targeting framework promotes the accountability of the central bank to elected officials, who are given some responsibility for setting the goals for monetary policy and then monitoring the economic outcomes. However, under inflation targeting as it has generally been practiced, the central bank has complete control over operational decisions, so that it can be held accountable for achieving its assigned objectives.

The Fed's monetary policy strategy may move more toward inflation targeting in the future, particularly since Chairman Ben Bernanke has been an advocate of inflation targeting (see the Inside the Fed box, "Chairman Bernanke and Inflation Targeting").

LESSONS FOR MONETARY POLICY STRATEGY FROM THE GLOBAL FINANCIAL CRISIS

Our discussion of the events during the global financial crisis in previous chapters suggests four basic lessons for economists and policymakers about how the economy works.[4]

1. *Developments in the financial sector have a far greater impact on economic activity than was earlier realized.* Although before the crisis, economists and policymakers generally recognized that financial frictions could play an important role in business cycle fluctuations, as we saw in Chapter 9, the global financial crisis made it abundantly clear that the adverse effects of financial disruptions on economic activity could be far worse than originally anticipated.
2. *The zero-lower-bound on interest rates can be a serious problem.* As we saw in Chapter 18, the zero-lower-bound on interest rates has forced the Federal Reserve to use nonconventional monetary policy tools, not only during the crisis but also during the 2003–2006 period. Although we have seen that these nonconventional tools can help stimulate the economy, they are more complicated to use than conventional tools and their impact on the economy is more uncertain, so they may be harder to use effectively.
3. *The cost of cleaning up after a financial crisis is very high.* As we saw in Chapter 9, financial crises are followed by deep recessions. But in addition, recoveries from financial crises are very slow. Carmen Reinhart of the Petersen Institute for International Economics and Vincent Reinhart of the American Enterprise Institute have documented that economic growth is significantly lower during the decade following financial crises and unemployment rates stay persistently higher for a decade after crisis episodes. In addition, in the aftermath of financial crises government

[4]For a more detailed discussion of the lessons of the global financial crisis for monetary policy strategy, see Frederic S. Mishkin, "Monetary Policy Strategy: Lessons from the Crisis," in Marek Jarocinski, Frank Smets, and Christian Thimann, eds., *Monetary Policy Revisited: Lessons from the Crisis*, Sixth ECB Central Banking Conference (Frankfurt, European Central Bank, 2011), pp. 67–118.

Inside the Fed Chairman Bernanke and Inflation Targeting

Ben Bernanke, a former professor at Princeton University, became the Federal Reserve chairman in February 2006, after serving as a member of the Board of Governors from 2002 to 2005 and then as chairman of the Council of Economic Advisors. Bernanke is a world-renowned expert on monetary policy and, while an academic, wrote extensively on inflation targeting, including articles and a book written with the author of this text.*

Bernanke's writings suggest that he is a strong proponent of inflation targeting and increased transparency in central banks. In an important speech given at a conference at the Federal Reserve Bank of St. Louis in 2004, he described how the Federal Reserve might approach a movement toward inflation targeting: The Fed should announce a numerical value for its long-run inflation goal.† Bernanke emphasized that announcing such an objective for inflation would be completely consistent with the Fed's dual mandate of achieving price stability and maximum employment, and therefore might be called a ***mandate-consistent inflation objective***, because it would be set above zero to avoid deflations, which have harmful effects on employment. In addition, it would not be intended to be a short-run target that might lead to excessively tight control of inflation at the expense of overly high employment fluctuations.

Since becoming Fed chairman, Bernanke has made it clear that any movement toward inflation targeting must result from a consensus within the FOMC. After Chairman Bernanke set up a subcommittee to discuss Federal Reserve communication, which included discussions about announcing a specific numerical inflation objective, the FOMC made a partial step in the direction of inflation targeting in November 2007, when it announced a new communication strategy that lengthened the horizon for FOMC participants' inflation projections to three years. In many cases, the three-year horizon would be sufficiently long so that the projection for inflation under "appropriate policy" would reflect each participant's inflation objective because at that horizon inflation should converge to the long-run objective.

A couple of relatively minor modifications suggested by the author of this book when he was a governor of the Federal Reserve could move the Fed even further toward inflation targeting.** The first modification requires lengthening the horizon for the inflation projection. The goal would be to set a time sufficiently far off so that inflation would almost surely converge to its long-run value by then. Second, the FOMC participants would need to be willing to reach a consensus on a single value for the mandate-consistent inflation objective. With these two modifications, the longer-run inflation projections would in effect be an announcement of a specific numerical objective for the inflation rate and so serve as a flexible version of inflation targeting. In October 2010, Chairman Bernanke gave a speech advocating exactly this approach. However, he was unable to convince his colleagues on the FOMC to adopt it.†† Whether the Federal Reserve will move in this direction in the future is still highly uncertain.

*Ben S. Bernanke and Frederic S. Mishkin, "Inflation Targeting: A New Framework for Monetary Policy," *Journal of Economic Perspectives*, vol. 11, no. 2 (1997); Ben S. Bernanke, Frederic S. Mishkin, and Adam S. Posen, "Inflation Targeting: Fed Policy After Greenspan," *Milken Institute Review* (Fourth Quarter, 1999): 48–56; Ben S. Bernanke, Frederic S. Mishkin, and Adam S. Posen, "What Happens When Greenspan Is Gone," *Wall Street Journal*, January 5, 2000, p. A22; and Ben S. Bernanke, Thomas Laubach, Frederic S. Mishkin, and Adam S. Posen, *Inflation Targeting: Lessons from the International Experience* (Princeton, NJ: Princeton University Press, 1999).

†Ben S. Bernanke, "Inflation Targeting," Federal Reserve Bank of St. Louis, *Review*, vol. 86, no. 4 (July/August 2004): 165–168.

**See Frederic S. Mishkin, "Whither Federal Reserve Communications," speech given at the Petersen Institute for International Economics, Washington, DC, July 28, 2008, http://www.federalreserve.gov/newsevents/speech/mishkin20080.

††Ben S. Bernanke, "Monetary Policy Objectives and Tools in a Low-Inflation Environment," speech given at the Federal Reserve Bank of Boston's conference, Revisiting Monetary Policy in a Low-Inflation Environment, October 15, 2010, http://www.federalreserve.gov/newsevents/speech/bernanke20101015a.htm.

indebtedness almost always sharply increases and can lead to defaults on government debt, which has become a major concern in Europe in the aftermath of the crisis.[5]

4. *Price and output stability do not ensure financial stability.* Before the recent financial crisis, the common view both in academia and in central banks was that achieving price and output stability would promote financial stability. However, the success of central banks in stabilizing inflation and the decreased volatility of business cycle fluctuations before 2007, which became known as the Great Moderation, did not protect the economy from financial instability. Indeed, it may have promoted it. The low volatility of both inflation and output fluctuations may have lulled market participants into thinking less risk was present in the economic system than was really the case, leading them to take excessive risks, which helped promote the global financial crisis.

What implications do these lessons have for monetary policy strategy? We first look at how these lessons might affect our thinking about inflation targeting and then on how central banks should respond to asset-price bubbles.

Implications for Inflation Targeting

Earlier in the chapter, we outlined the arguments for inflation targeting, and none of the above lessons contradict these arguments. Although support for the inflation-targeting strategy is not weakened by the lessons from the financial crisis, they do suggest that inflation targeting may need to be more flexible and modified on several dimensions. First, we look at what these lessons might mean for the level of the inflation target.

Level of the Inflation Target As our discussion earlier in the chapter indicates, central banks typically have an inflation target around the 2% level. The seriousness of the zero-lower-bound problem raises the question of whether this target level is too low. A controversial paper written by researchers at the IMF, including its chief economist, has suggested that the inflation target might be raised from the 2% to the 4% level.[6] It argues that with expectations of inflation anchored to this target, by lowering the nominal interest rate to zero, the real interest rate, $i_r = i - \pi^e$, could be decreased to as low as -4% ($= 0 - 4\%$), rather than -2% ($= 0 - 2\%$), with the 2% inflation target. Conventional monetary policy, which involves manipulating the nominal policy rate, would then be able to become more expansionary when interest rates fell to a floor of zero than it could with the lower inflation target. Another way of stating this is to say that the zero-lower-bound on the policy rate would be less binding with a higher inflation target.

Although this argument is theoretically sound and raising the inflation target has benefits, we also have to look at its costs. The benefits of a higher inflation target accrue only when the zero-lower-bound problem occurs. Although this was a major problem during the global financial crisis, such episodes have not been very frequent. If the zero-lower-bound problem is rare, then the benefits of a higher inflation target are not very

[5]See Carmen M. Reinhart and Vincent R. Reinhart, "After the Fall," *Macroeconomic Challenges: The Decade Ahead*, Federal Reserve Bank of Kansas City Economic Symposium, 2010, manuscript available at http://www.kansascityfed.org; and Carmen M. Reinhart and Kenneth S. Rogoff, *This Time Is Different: Eight Centuries of Financial Folly* (Princeton, NJ: Princeton University Press, 2009).

[6]Olivier Blanchard, Giovanni Dell'Ariccia, and Paolo Mauro, "Rethinking Monetary Policy," *Journal of Money, Credit and Banking*, vol. 42, Issue Supplement S1 (September 2010): 199–217.

large because they are only available infrequently. However, the costs of higher inflation in terms of the distortions it produces in the economy, mentioned early in the chapter, are ongoing. Thus, although these costs may not be that large in any given year, they add up and may outweigh the intermittent benefits of a higher inflation target when the zero-lower-bound occurs.

Another problem with a higher inflation target is that the history of inflation suggests that it is more difficult to stabilize the inflation rate at a 4% level than at a 2% level. Once inflation starts to rise above this level, the public is likely to believe that price stability is no longer a credible goal of the central bank, and then the question arises, if a 4% level of inflation is OK, then why not 6%, or 8%, and so on? Indeed, this is what seems to have happened in the 1960s, when economists such as Paul Samuelson and Robert Solow of MIT, both eventual recipients of the Nobel Prize, argued that policymakers should be willing to tolerate higher inflation rates in the 4–5% range. But when inflation rose to that level, the policy authorities could not contain it at that level and it kept on rising to double digit levels by the early 1980s. Getting inflation back down again during the Volcker era was very costly. No central banker wants to go through that cycle again, and this is why central bankers have been so hostile to the IMF researchers' suggestion.

Flexibility of Inflation Targeting We have seen that inflation targeting as actually practiced would be better described as "flexible inflation targeting." However, before the global financial crisis, this flexibility involved allowing some short-run deviations of inflation from the inflation target in order to promote output stability as well as price stability. Two lessons from the crisis—that financial instability can have devastating effects on the economy and that achieving price and output stability does not ensure financial stability—have led to a recognition that central banks need to pay more attention to financial stability not only in designing inflation-targeting regimes, but also in any monetary policy framework, such as the "just do it" approach of the Federal Reserve. Particularly important in this regard is the issue of how central banks should respond to asset-price bubbles, which we discuss immediately below.

How Should Central Banks Respond to Asset-Price Bubbles?

Over the centuries, economies have been periodically subject to **asset-price bubbles**, pronounced increases in asset prices that depart from fundamental values, which eventually burst resoundingly. The story of the global financial crisis, discussed in Chapter 9, indicates how costly these bubbles can be. The bursting of the asset-price bubble in the housing market brought down the financial system, leading to an economic downturn, a rise in unemployment, disrupted communities, and direct hardship for families forced to leave their homes after foreclosures. The high cost of asset-price bubbles raises the following question: What should central banks do about them? Because asset prices are a central element in how monetary policy affects the economy (the transmission mechanisms of monetary policy discussed in Chapter 25), monetary policy certainly needs to respond to asset prices in order to obtain good outcomes in terms of inflation and output. Hence, the issue of how monetary policy might respond to asset-price movements is not whether it should respond at all, but whether it should respond at a level over and above that called for in terms of the objectives of stabilizing inflation and employment. Another way of defining the issue is whether monetary policy should try to pop, or slow, the growth of potential asset-price bubbles to minimize damage to the economy when these bubbles burst. Alternatively, rather than responding directly to possible asset-price bubbles, should the monetary authorities respond only to the asset-price declines that occur after a bubble bursts, to stabilize both output and inflation? These opposing positions have been characterized as *leaning* against asset-price bubbles versus *cleaning up* after the bubble bursts, and so the debate over what to do about asset-price bubbles has been labeled the "lean versus clean" debate.

The "Greenspan Doctrine": Why Central Banks Should Not Try to Prick Asset-Price Bubbles But Should Just Clean Up After They Burst Under Alan Greenspan, the Federal Reserve took the position that central banks should not try to prick bubbles, and this became known as the "Greenspan doctrine." His doctrine was based on the following five arguments:

1. Asset-price bubbles are nearly impossible to identify. If central banks or government officials knew that a bubble was in progress, why wouldn't market participants know as well? If so, then a bubble would be unlikely to develop, because market participants would know that prices were getting out of line with fundamentals. Unless central bank or government officials are smarter than market participants, an unlikely situation given the savvy of especially talented (and high earning) market participants, they will be unlikely to identify when bubbles of this type are occurring. A strong argument, then, exists for not responding to suspected bubbles.
2. Although some economic analysis suggests that raising interest rates can diminish asset price increases, raising interest rates may be very ineffective in restraining bubbles, because market participants expect such high rates of return from buying bubble-driven assets. Furthermore, raising interest rates has often been found to cause a bubble to burst more severely, thereby increasing damage to the economy. Another way of saying this is that bubbles are departures from normal behavior, and it is unrealistic to expect that the usual tools of monetary policy will be effective in abnormal conditions.
3. Many different asset prices exist, and at any one time a bubble may be present in only a fraction of asset markets. Monetary policy actions are a very blunt instrument in such a case, as such actions would be likely to affect asset prices in general, rather than the specific assets that are experiencing a bubble.
4. Monetary policy actions to prick bubbles can have harmful effects on the aggregate economy. If interest rates are raised significantly to curtail a bubble, the economy will slow, people will lose jobs, and inflation can fall below its desirable level. Indeed, as arguments 2 and 3 suggest, the rise in interest rates necessary to prick a bubble may be so high that it can be done only at great cost to workers and the economy. This is not to say that monetary policy should not respond to asset prices per se. The level of asset prices does affect aggregate demand (discussed in Chapter 25) and thus the evolution of the economy. Monetary policy should react to fluctuations in asset prices to the extent that they affect inflation and economic activity.
5. As long as policymakers respond in a timely fashion, by easing monetary policy aggressively after an asset bubble bursts, the harmful effects of a bursting bubble can be kept at a manageable level. Indeed, the Greenspan Fed acted exactly in this way after the stock market crash of 1987 and the bursting of the tech bubble in the stock market in 2000. Aggressive easing after the stock market bubbles burst in 1987 and 2000 was highly successful. The economy did not enter a recession after the stock market crash of 1987, whereas the recession was very mild after the tech bubble burst in 2000.

Two Types of Asset-Price Bubbles To understand the response to the Greenspan doctrine, we first need to ask whether there are different kinds of bubbles that require different types of responses. Asset-price bubbles are of two types: one that is driven by credit and a second that is driven purely by overly optimistic expectations (which Alan Greenspan referred to as "irrational exuberance").

Credit-Driven Bubbles When a credit boom begins, it can spill over into an asset-price bubble. Easier credit can be used to purchase particular assets and thereby raise their prices. The rise in asset values, in turn, encourages further lending for these assets, either because it increases the value of collateral, making it easier to borrow, or because it raises the value of capital at financial institutions, which gives them more capacity to lend. The lending for these assets can then further increase demand for them and hence raise their prices even more. This feedback loop—in which a credit boom drives up asset prices, which in turn fuels the credit boom, which drives asset prices even higher, and so on—can generate a bubble in which asset prices rise well above their fundamental values.

Credit-driven bubbles are particularly dangerous, as the recent global financial crisis has demonstrated. When asset prices come back down to earth and the bubble bursts, the collapse in asset prices then leads to a reversal of the feedback loop in which loans go sour, lenders cut back on credit supply, the demand for assets declines further, and prices drop even more. These were exactly the dynamics in housing markets during the global financial crisis. Driven by a credit boom in subprime lending, housing prices rose way above fundamental values; but when housing prices crashed, credit shriveled up and housing prices plummeted.

The resulting losses on subprime loans and securities eroded the balance sheets of financial institutions, causing a decline in credit (deleveraging) and a sharp fall in business and household spending, and therefore in economic activity. As we saw during the global financial crisis, the interaction between housing prices and the health of financial institutions following the collapse of the housing price bubble endangered the operation of the financial system as a whole and had dire consequences for the economy.

Bubbles Driven Solely by Irrational Exuberance Bubbles that are driven solely by overly optimistic expectations, but that are not associated with a credit boom, pose much less risk to the financial system. For example, the bubble in technology stocks in the late 1990s described in Chapter 7 was not fueled by credit, and the bursting of the tech-stock bubble was not followed by a marked deterioration in financial institutions' balance sheets. The bursting of the tech-stock bubble thus did not have a very severe impact on the economy, and the recession that followed was quite mild. Bubbles driven solely by irrational exuberance are therefore far less dangerous than those driven by credit booms.

The Case for Leaning Versus Cleaning The recent crisis has clearly demonstrated that the bursting of credit-driven bubbles not only can be extremely costly but also are very hard to clean up. Furthermore, credit-driven bubbles can occur even if price and output stability exists in the period leading up to them. Indeed, as we have seen, price and output stability might actually encourage credit-driven bubbles because it leads market participants to underestimate the amount of risk in the economy. The global financial crisis has therefore provided a much stronger case for leaning against potential bubbles rather than cleaning up afterward.

However, the distinction between the two types of bubbles, one of which (credit-driven) is much more costly than the other, suggests that the lean versus clean debate may have been miscast. Rather than leaning against potential asset-price bubbles, which would include both credit-driven and irrational exuberance-type bubbles, the case is much stronger for leaning against credit booms, which would involve leaning against credit-driven asset-price bubbles, but not asset-price bubbles driven by irrational exuberance. In addition, it is much easier to identify credit booms than asset-price bubbles. When asset-price bubbles are rising rapidly at the same time that credit is booming, the likelihood is greater that asset prices are deviating from fundamentals, because laxer credit standards are driving asset prices upward. In this case, central bank or government officials have a greater likelihood of identifying that a booms is in progress; this was indeed the case during the housing market bubble in the United States because these officials did have information that lenders had weakened lending standards and that credit extension in the mortgage markets was rising at abnormally high rates.

The case for leaning against credit-driven bubbles seems strong, but what policies will be most effective in restraining them?

Macroprudential Policies First, it is important to recognize that the key principle to consider in designing effective policies to lean against credit booms is to curb excessive risk taking. Only when this risk taking is excessive are credit booms likely to develop, and so it is natural to look to prudential regulatory measures to constrain credit booms. Regulatory policy to affect what is happening in credit markets in the aggregate is referred to as **macroprudential regulation**, and it does seem to be the right tool for reigning in credit-driven bubbles.

Financial regulation and supervision, either by central banks or by other government entities, with the usual elements of a well-functioning prudential regulatory and supervisory system, as described in Chapter 11, can prevent excessive risk taking that can trigger a credit boom, which in turn leads to an asset-price bubble. These elements include adequate disclosure and capital requirements, prompt corrective action, close monitoring of financial institutions' risk management procedures, and close supervision to enforce compliance with regulations. More generally, regulation should focus on preventing leverage cycles. As the global financial crisis demonstrated, the rise in asset prices that accompanied the credit boom resulted in higher capital buffers at financial institutions, supporting further lending in the context of unchanging capital requirements, which led to higher asset prices, and so on; in the bust, the value of the capital dropped precipitously, leading to a cut in lending. Capital requirements that are countercyclical, that is, adjusted upward during a boom and downward during a bust, might help eliminate the pernicious feedback loops that promote credit-driven bubbles.

A rapid rise in asset prices accompanied by a credit boom provides a signal that market failures or poor financial regulation and supervision might be causing a bubble to form. Central banks and other government regulators could then consider implementing policies to rein in credit growth directly or implement measures to make sure credit standards are sufficiently high.

Monetary Policy The fact that the low interest rate policies of the Federal Reserve from 2002 to 2005 were followed by excessive risk taking suggests to many that overly easy monetary policy might promote financial instability, as was discussed in Chapter 9. Although it is far from clear that the Federal Reserve is primarily to blame for the housing bubble, research does suggest that low interest rates can encourage excessive risk taking in what has been called the "risk-taking channel of monetary policy." Low interest rates may increase the incentives for asset managers in financial institutions to search for higher yields and hence increase risk taking. Low interest rates may also increase the demand for assets, raising their prices and leading to increased valuation of collateral, which in turn encourages lenders to lend to riskier borrowers.

The risk-taking channel of monetary policy suggests that monetary policy should be used to lean against credit booms. However, many of the objections to using monetary policy to prick booms behind the Greenspan doctrine are still valid, so wouldn't it be better to use macroprudential supervision to constrain credit booms, leaving monetary policy to focus on price and output stability?

This argument would be quite strong if macroprudential policies were able to do the job. However, there are doubts on this score. Prudential supervision is subject to more political pressure than monetary policy because it affects the bottom line of financial institutions more directly. Thus they have greater incentives to lobby politicians to discourage macroprudential policies that would rein in credit booms, particularly during a credit boom when they are making the most money. In addition, financial institutions are often very good at finding loopholes to avoid regulation, as we discovered in Chapter 12, and so macroprudential supervision may not be effective. The possibility that macroprudential policies may not be implemented sufficiently well to constrain credit booms suggests that monetary policy may have to be used instead.

An important lesson from the global financial crisis is that central banks and other regulators should not have a laissez-faire attitude and let credit-driven bubbles proceed without any reaction. How to do this well, however, is indeed a daunting task.

TACTICS: CHOOSING THE POLICY INSTRUMENT

Now that we are familiar with the alternative strategies for monetary policy, let's look at how monetary policy is conducted on a day-to-day basis. Central banks directly control the tools of monetary policy—open market operations, reserve requirements, the discount rate, and the interest rate on reserves—but knowing the tools and the strategies for implementing a monetary policy does not tell us whether policy is easy or tight. For that, we can observe the **policy instrument** (also called an **operating instrument**), a variable that responds to the central bank's tools and indicates the stance (easy or tight) of monetary policy. A central bank like the Fed has at its disposal two basic types of policy instruments: reserve aggregates (total reserves, nonborrowed reserves, the monetary base, and the nonborrowed base) and interest rates (federal funds rate and other short-term interest rates). (Central banks in small countries can choose another policy instrument, the exchange rate, but we leave this topic to Chapter 21.) The policy instrument might be linked to an **intermediate target**, such as a monetary aggregate like M2 or a long-term interest rate. Intermediate targets stand between the policy instrument and the goals of monetary policy (e.g., price stability, output growth); they are not as directly affected by the tools of monetary policy, but might be more closely linked to the goals of monetary policy. As a study aid, Figure 2 shows a schematic of the linkages between the tools of monetary policy, policy instruments, intermediate targets, and the goals of monetary policy.

As an example, suppose the central bank's employment and inflation goals are consistent with a nominal GDP growth rate of 5%. The central bank might believe that the 5% nominal GDP growth rate will be achieved by a 4% growth rate for M2 (an intermediate target), which will in turn be achieved by a growth rate of 3% for nonborrowed

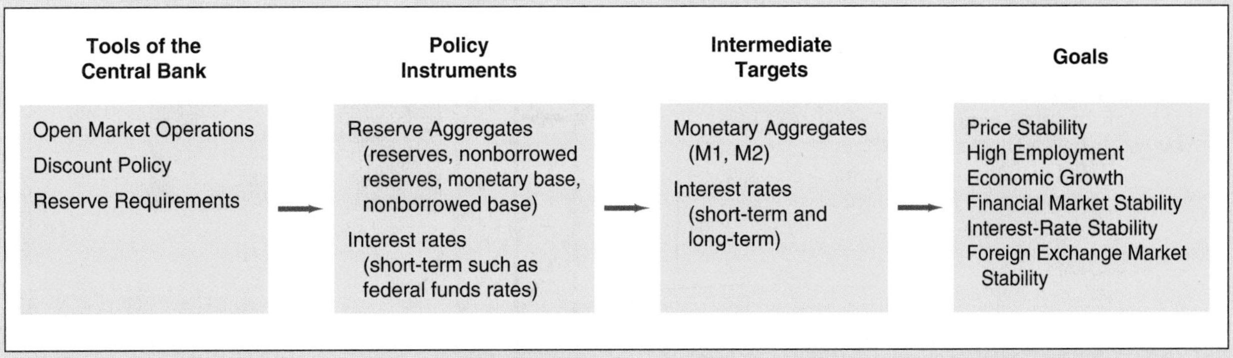

FIGURE 2 Linkages Between Central Bank Tools, Policy Instruments, Intermediate Targets, and Goals of Monetary Policy

The tools of the central bank are used to change the policy instruments to achieve the intermediate target and then the goals of monetary policy.

reserves (the policy instrument). Alternatively, the central bank might believe that the best way to achieve its objectives would be to set the federal funds rate (a policy instrument) at, say, 4%. Can the central bank choose to target both the nonborrowed reserves and the federal-funds-rate policy instruments at the same time? The answer is no. The application of supply and demand analysis to the market for reserves we developed in Chapter 18 explains why a central bank must choose one or the other.

Let's first see why choosing an aggregate target involves losing control of the interest rate. Figure 3 contains a supply and demand diagram for the market for reserves. Although the central bank expects the demand curve for reserves to be at R^{d^*}, it fluctuates between $R^{d'}$ and $R^{d''}$ because of unexpected fluctuations in deposits (and hence

FIGURE 3

Result of Targeting on Nonborrowed Reserves

Targeting on nonborrowed reserves of NBR^* will lead to fluctuations in the federal funds rate between i'_{ff} and i''_{ff} because of fluctuations in the demand for reserves between $R^{d'}$ and $R^{d''}$.

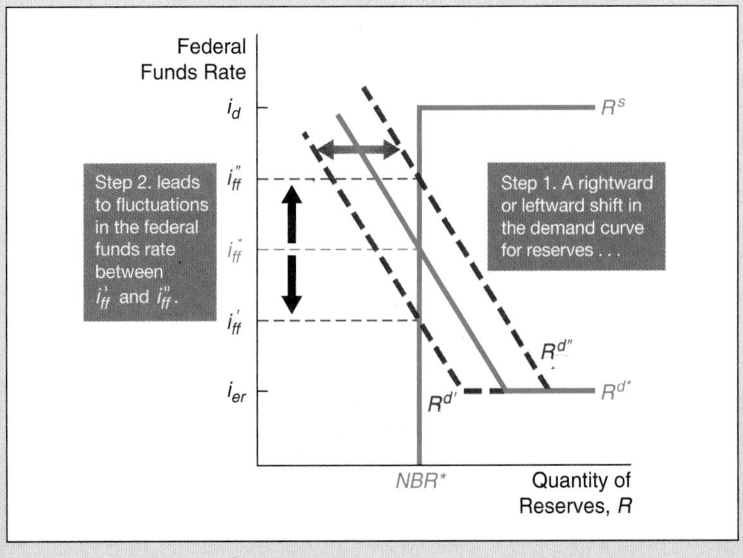

FIGURE 4

Result of Targeting on the Federal Funds Rate

Targeting on the interest rate i_{ff}^* will lead to fluctuations in nonborrowed reserves between NBR′ and NBR″ because of fluctuations in the demand for reserves between $R^{d'}$ and $R^{d''}$.

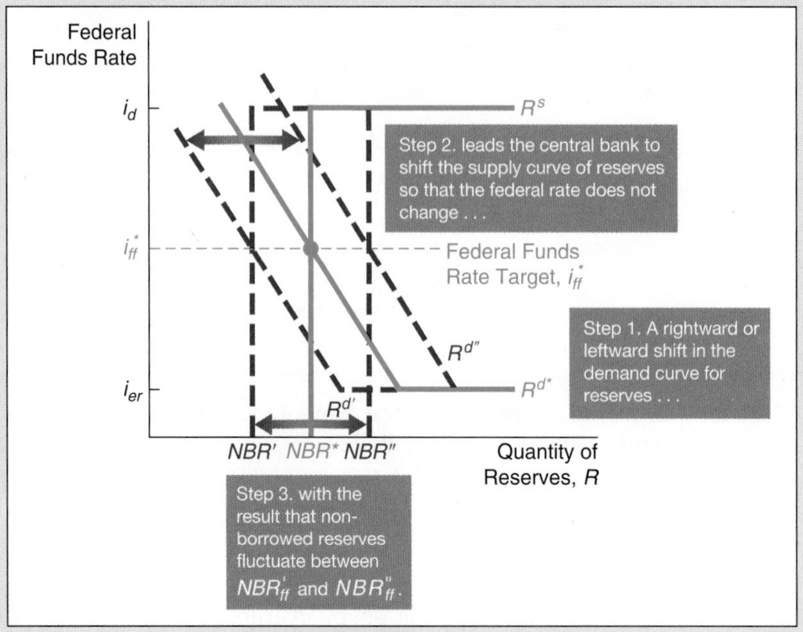
Federal Funds Rate
i_d
R^s
Step 2. leads the central bank to shift the supply curve of reserves so that the federal rate does not change . . .
i_{ff}^*
Federal Funds Rate Target, i_{ff}^*
Step 1. A rightward or leftward shift in the demand curve for reserves . . .
$R^{d''}$
i_{er}
$R^{d'}$
R^{d*}
NBR′ NBR* NBR″
Quantity of Reserves, R
Step 3. with the result that non-borrowed reserves fluctuate between NBR'_{ff} and NBR''_{ff}.

required reserves) and changes in banks' desire to hold excess reserves. If the central bank has a nonborrowed reserves target of NBR^* (say, because it has a target growth rate of the money supply of 4%), it expects that the federal funds rate will be i_{ff}^*. However, as the figure indicates, the fluctuations in the reserves demand curve between $R^{d'}$ and $R^{d''}$ will result in a fluctuation in the federal funds rate between i'_{ff} and i''_{ff}. Pursuing an aggregate target implies that interest rates will fluctuate.

The supply and demand diagram in Figure 4 shows the consequences of an interest-rate target set at i_{ff}^*. Again the central bank expects the reserves demand curve to be at R^{d*}, but it fluctuates between $R^{d'}$ and $R^{d''}$ due to unexpected changes in deposits or banks' desire to hold excess reserves. If the demand curve rises to $R^{d''}$ the federal funds rate will begin to rise above i_{ff}^* and the central bank will engage in open market purchases of bonds until it raises the supply of nonborrowed reserves to NBR'' at which point the equilibrium federal funds rate is again at i_{ff}^*. Conversely, if the demand curve falls to $R^{d'}$ and lowers the federal funds rate, the central bank would keep making open market sales until nonborrowed reserves fall to NBR'' and the federal funds rate returns to i_{ff}^*. The central bank's adherence to the interest-rate target thus leads to a fluctuating quantity of nonborrowed reserves and the money supply.

The conclusion from the supply and demand analysis is that interest-rate and reserve (monetary) aggregate targets are incompatible. A central bank can hit one or the other, but not both. Because a choice between them has to be made, we need to examine what criteria should be used to select a policy instrument.

Criteria for Choosing the Policy Instrument

Three criteria apply when choosing a policy instrument: The instrument must be observable and measurable, it must be controllable by the central bank, and it must have a predictable effect on the goals.

Observability and Measurability Quick observability and accurate measurement of a policy instrument are necessary because it will be useful only if it signals the policy stance rapidly. Reserve aggregates like nonborrowed reserves are straightforward to measure, but some lag in reporting of reserve aggregates (a delay of two weeks) exists. Short-term interest rates, like the federal funds rate, by contrast, not only are easy to measure but also are observable immediately. Thus, it seems that interest rates are more observable and measurable than are reserves and, therefore, are a better policy instrument.

However, as we learned in Chapter 4, the interest rate that is easiest to measure and observe is the nominal interest rate. It is typically a poor measure of the real cost of borrowing, which indicates with more certainty what will happen to the real GDP. This real cost of borrowing is more accurately measured by the real interest rate—that is, the nominal interest rate adjusted for expected inflation ($i_r = i - \pi^e$). Unfortunately, real interest rates are extremely difficult to measure, because we do not have a direct way to measure expected inflation. Given that both interest rates and aggregates have observability and measurability problems, it is not clear whether one should be preferred to the other as a policy instrument.

Controllability A central bank must be able to exercise effective control over a variable if it is to function as a useful policy instrument. If the central bank cannot control the policy instrument, knowing that it is off track does little good, because the central bank has no way of getting it back on track.

Because of shifts in and out of currency, even reserve aggregates, such as nonborrowed reserves, are not completely controllable. Conversely, the Fed can control short-term interest rates, such as the federal funds rate, very tightly. It might appear, therefore, that short-term interest rates would dominate reserve aggregates on the controllability criterion. However, a central bank cannot set short-term real interest rates because it does not have control over expectations of inflation. Once again, a clear-cut case cannot be made that short-term interest rates are preferable to reserve aggregates as a policy instrument, or vice versa.

Predictable Effect on Goals The most important characteristic of a policy instrument is that it must have a predictable effect on a goal. If a central bank can accurately and quickly measure the price of tea in China and can completely control its price, what good will that do? The central bank cannot use the price of tea in China to affect unemployment or the price level in its country. Because the ability to affect goals is so critical to the usefulness of any policy instrument, the tightness of the link from reserve or monetary aggregates to goals (output, employment, and inflation) or, alternatively, from interest rates to these goals, has been the subject of much research and debate. In recent years, most central banks have concluded that the link between interest rates and goals such as inflation is tighter than the link between aggregates and inflation. For this reason, central banks throughout the world now generally use short-term interest rates as their policy instrument.

TACTICS: THE TAYLOR RULE

As we have seen, the Federal Reserve and most other central banks currently conduct monetary policy by setting a target for short-term interest rates like the federal funds rate. But how should this target be chosen?

John Taylor of Stanford University has come up with an answer, called the **Taylor rule**. The Taylor rule indicates that the federal (fed) funds rate should be set equal to the inflation rate plus an "equilibrium" real fed funds rate (the real fed funds rate that is consistent with full employment in the long run) plus a weighted average of two gaps: (1) an inflation gap, current inflation minus a target rate; and (2) an output gap, the percentage deviation of real GDP from an estimate of its potential (natural rate) level.[7] This rule can be written as follows:

$$\text{Federal funds rate target} = \text{inflation rate} + \text{equilibrium real fed funds rate} + \frac{1}{2}(\text{inflation gap}) + \frac{1}{2}(\text{output gap})$$

Taylor has assumed that the equilibrium real fed funds rate is 2% and that an appropriate target for inflation would also be 2%, with equal weights of $\frac{1}{2}$ on the inflation and output gaps. For an example of the Taylor rule in practice, suppose that the inflation rate were at 3%, leading to a positive inflation gap of 1% (= 3% − 2%), and real GDP was 1% above its potential, resulting in a positive output gap of 1%. Then the Taylor rule suggests that the federal funds rate should be set at 6% [= 3% inflation + 2% equilibrium real fed funds rate + $\frac{1}{2}$ (1% inflation gap) + $\frac{1}{2}$ (1% output gap)].

An important feature of the Taylor rule is that the coefficient on the inflation gap, 1/2, is positive. If the inflation rate rises by 1 percentage point, then the federal funds target is raised by 1.5 percentage points, and so by more than one-to-one. In other words, a rise in inflation by 1 percentage point leads to a real federal funds rate increase of $\frac{1}{2}$ percentage point. The principle that the monetary authorities should raise nominal interest rates by more than the increase in the inflation rate has been named the **Taylor principle**, and it is critical to the success of monetary policy. Suppose the Taylor principle is not followed and nominal rates rise by *less* than the rise in the inflation rate, so that real interest rates *fall* when inflation rises. Serious instability then results because a rise in inflation leads to an effective easing of monetary policy, which then leads to even higher inflation in the future. Indeed, this was a feature of monetary policy in the 1970s that led to a loss of the nominal anchor and the era of the so-called "Great Inflation," when inflation rates climbed to double-digit levels. Fortunately, since 1979, the Taylor principle has become a feature of monetary policy, with much happier outcomes on both the inflation and the aggregate output fronts.

The presence of an output gap in the Taylor rule might indicate that the Fed should care not only about keeping inflation under control but also about minimizing business cycle fluctuations of output around its potential level. Caring about both inflation and output fluctuations is consistent with the Fed's dual mandate and with many statements by Federal Reserve officials that controlling inflation and stabilizing real output are important concerns of the Fed.

An alternative interpretation of the presence of the output gap in the Taylor rule is that the output gap is an indicator of future inflation, as stipulated in **Phillips curve theory**. Phillips curve theory indicates that changes in inflation are influenced by the state of the economy relative to its productive capacity, as well as by other factors.

[7]The original formulation of the Taylor rule can be found in John B. Taylor, "Discretion Versus Policy Rules in Practice," *Carnegie-Rochester Conference Series on Public Policy* 39 (1993): 195–214. However, a more intuitive discussion with a historical perspective can be found in John B. Taylor, "A Historical Analysis of Monetary Policy Rules," in *Monetary Policy Rules*, ed., John B. Taylor (Chicago: University of Chicago Press, 1999), pp. 319–341.

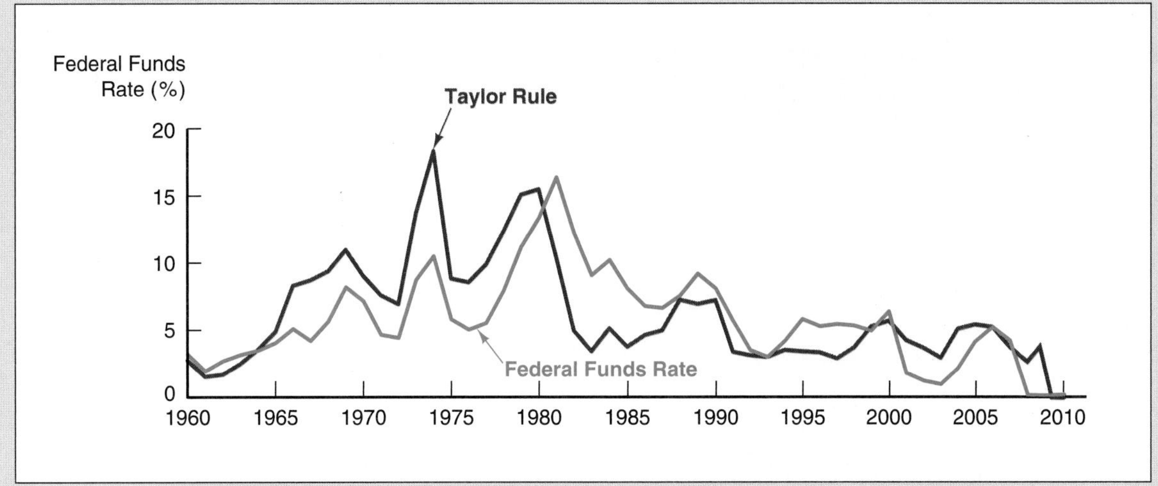

FIGURE 5 The Taylor Rule for the Federal Funds Rate, 1960–2011
The Taylor rule does a pretty good job of describing the Fed's setting of the federal funds rate under chairmen Greenspan and Bernanke, but it did not work very well in the 1970s.

Source: Federal Reserve; www.federalreserve.gov/releases and author's calculations.

This productive capacity can be measured by potential GDP, which is a function of the natural rate of unemployment, the rate of unemployment consistent with full employment. A related concept is the **NAIRU**, the **nonaccelerating inflation rate of unemployment**, the rate of unemployment at which there is no tendency for inflation to change. Simply put, the theory states that when the unemployment rate is above NAIRU with output below potential, inflation will come down, but if it is below NAIRU with output above potential, inflation will rise. Prior to 1995, the NAIRU was thought to reside around 6%. However, with the decline in unemployment to around the 4% level in the late 1990s, with no increase (and even a slight decrease) in inflation, some critics have questioned the value of Phillips curve theory. Either they claim that it just doesn't work any more or, alternatively, they believe that great uncertainty exists about the value of NAIRU, which may have fallen to below 5% for reasons that are not absolutely clear. Phillips curve theory is now highly controversial, and critics question whether it should be used as a guide for the conduct of monetary policy.

As Figure 5 shows, the Taylor rule does a pretty good, but not perfect, job of describing the Fed's setting of the federal funds rate under chairmen Greenspan and Bernanke. (It did not work very well in the 1970s, which reflects that the Taylor principle was not being followed, explaining why monetary policy outcomes were so poor.) Does this mean that the Fed should fire all its economists and put a computer in charge that simply has to compute the Taylor rule setting for the federal funds rate? This would certainly save the taxpayers a lot of money. Although the Fed does not do this, it does make use of the Taylor rule in thinking about how to conduct monetary policy (see the Inside the Fed box, "The Fed's Use of the Taylor Rule"). Given the above reasons, it is no surprise that the Taylor rule does not explain all the movements in the federal funds rate in Figure 5. For this reason, financial institutions hire Fed watchers, as described in the second Inside the Fed box.

Inside the Fed The Fed's Use of the Taylor Rule

Why hasn't the Fed put the federal funds rate on Taylor rule autopilot, guided by a computer? There are several reasons why the Fed hasn't taken this drastic action. First and foremost, no perfect model of the economy exists, so even the best and brightest economists do not know the current inflation rate and output gap with certainty at any given moment. Since the economy is changing all the time, the Taylor rule coefficients are unlikely to stay constant in any event.

Even if we could determine these rates with certainty, monetary policy is by necessity a forward-looking activity because it takes a long time for monetary policy to affect the economy. Good monetary policy requires that the Fed forecast where inflation and economic activity are going to be in the future, and then adjust the policy instrument accordingly. The Fed will therefore look at a much wider range of information than just the current inflation rate and output gap in setting policy, as is done in the Taylor rule. In other words, the conduct of monetary policy is as much an art as it is a science, requiring both careful analytics and human judgment. The Taylor rule leaves out all the art, and so is unlikely to produce the best monetary policy outcomes. For example, financial crises, such as that which occurred from 2007 to 2009, require complex monetary policy actions because changes in credit spreads (the difference between interest rates on securities with credit risk and those without) may alter how the federal funds rate affects investment decisions, and therefore economic activity.

The bottom line is that putting monetary policy on autopilot with a Taylor rule with fixed coefficients would be a bad idea. The Taylor rule is, however, useful as a guide to monetary policy. If the setting of the policy instrument is very different from what the Taylor rule suggests, policymakers should ask whether they have a good reason for deviating from this rule. If they don't, as during the Chairman Burns era in the 1970s, then they might be making a mistake. Indeed, the FOMC makes use of Taylor rule estimates in exactly this way by referring to these estimates to inform their decisions about the federal funds rate target.*

*For an in-depth discussion of the FOMC's actual use of the Taylor rule in its policy deliberations, see Pier Francesco Asso, George A. Kahn, and Robert Leeson, "The Taylor Rule and the Practice of Central Banking," Federal Reserve Bank of Kansas City Working Paper RWP 10-05 (February 2010).

Inside the Fed Fed Watchers

As we have seen, the most important player in the determination of U.S. interest rates is the Federal Reserve. When the Fed wants to inject reserves into the system, it conducts open market purchases of bonds, which cause bond prices to increase and their interest rates to fall, at least in the short term. If the Fed withdraws reserves from the system, it sells bonds, thereby depressing their price and raising their interest rates. Knowing what actions the Fed might be taking can thus help investors and financial institutions to predict the future course of interest rates with greater accuracy. Because, as we have seen, changes in interest rates have a major impact on investors and financial institutions' profits, they are particularly interested in scrutinizing the Fed's behavior. To assist in this task, financial institutions hire *Fed watchers*, experts on Federal Reserve behavior who may have worked in the Federal Reserve System and so have an insider's view of Federal Reserve operations. A Fed watcher who can accurately predict the course of monetary policy is a very valuable commodity, and successful Fed watchers therefore often earn very high salaries, well into the six-figure range and sometimes even higher.

Summary

1. The six basic goals of monetary policy are price stability (the primary goal), high employment (output stability), economic growth, stability of financial markets, interest-rate stability, and stability in foreign exchange markets.

2. Having a strong nominal anchor is a key element in successful monetary policy. It helps promote price stability by tying down inflation expectations and limiting the time-inconsistency problem, in which monetary policymakers conduct monetary policy in a discretionary way that focuses on short-run objectives but produces poor long-run outcomes.

3. Inflation targeting has several advantages: (1) It enables monetary policy to focus on domestic considerations; (2) it is readily understood by the public and is highly transparent; (3) it increases accountability of the central bank; and (4) it appears to ameliorate the effects of inflationary shocks. It does have some disadvantages, however: (1) Inflation is not easily controlled by the monetary authorities, so that an inflation target is unable to send immediate signals to both the public and markets; (2) it might impose a rigid rule on policymakers, although this has not been the case in practice; and (3) a sole focus on inflation may lead to larger output fluctuations, although this has also not been the case in practice.

4. In recent years, the Federal Reserve has had a strategy of having an implicit, not an explicit, nominal anchor. This strategy has the following advantages: (1) It enables monetary policy to focus on domestic considerations; (2) it does not rely on a stable money–inflation relationship; and (3) it has had a demonstrated success, producing low inflation with the longest business cycle expansion in U.S. history. However, it does have some disadvantages: (1) It has a lack of transparency; (2) it is strongly dependent on the preferences, skills, and trustworthiness of individuals in the central bank and the government; and (3) it has some inconsistencies with democratic principles, because the central bank is not highly accountable.

5. Four lessons can be learned from the global financial crisis: (1) Developments in the financial sector have a far greater impact on economic activity than was earlier realized; (2) the zero-lower-bound on interest rates can be a serious problem; (3) the cost of cleaning up after a financial crisis is very high; and (4) price and output stability do not ensure financial stability.

6. The lessons from the financial crisis provide an argument for more flexible inflation targeting, possibly with a higher inflation target. The lessons also suggest that there is a case for monetary policy to lean against credit booms, but not asset-price bubbles.

7. Because interest-rate and aggregate policy instruments are incompatible, a central bank must choose between them on the basis of three criteria: measurability, controllability, and the ability to affect goal variables predictably. Central banks now typically use short-term interest rates as their policy instrument.

8. The Taylor rule indicates that the federal funds rate should be set equal to the inflation rate plus an "equilibrium" real fed funds rate plus a weighted average of two gaps: (1) an inflation gap, current inflation minus a target rate; and (2) an output gap, the percentage deviation of real GDP from an estimate of its potential (natural rate) level. The output gap in the Taylor rule could represent an indicator of future inflation, as stipulated in Phillips curve theory. However, this theory is controversial, because high output relative to potential as measured by low unemployment has not seemed to produce higher inflation in recent years.

Key Terms

Questions

All questions are available in MyEconLab *at* www.myeconlab.com.

1. What are the benefits of using a nominal anchor for the conduct of monetary policy?
2. What incentives arise for a central bank to fall into the time-inconsistency trap of pursuing overly expansionary monetary policy?
3. Why would it be problematic for a central bank to have a primary goal of maximizing economic growth?
4. "Since financial crises can impart severe damage to the economy, a central bank's primary goal should be to ensure stability in financial markets." Is this statement true, false, or uncertain? Explain.
5. "A central bank with a dual mandate will achieve lower unemployment in the long run than a central bank with a hierarchical mandate in which price stability takes precedence." Is this statement true, false, or uncertain? Explain.
6. Why is a public announcement of numerical inflation rate objectives important to the success of an inflation-targeting central bank?
7. How does inflation targeting help reduce the time-inconsistency of discretionary policy?
8. What methods have inflation-targeting central banks used to increase communication with the public and increase the transparency of monetary policy making?
9. Why might inflation targeting increase support for the independence of the central bank to conduct monetary policy?
10. "Because inflation targeting focuses on achieving the inflation target, it will lead to excessive output fluctuations." Is this statement true, false, or uncertain? Explain.
11. What are the key advantages and disadvantages of the monetary strategy used at the Federal Reserve under Alan Greenspan and Ben Bernanke in which the nominal anchor is only implicit?
12. "The zero-lower-bound on short-term interest rates is not a problem, since the central bank can just use quantitative easing to lower intermediate and longer-term interest rates instead." Is this statement true, false, or uncertain? Explain.
13. If higher inflation is bad, then why might it be advantageous to have a higher inflation target, rather than a lower target closer to zero?
14. Why aren't most central banks more proactive at trying to use monetary policy to eliminate asset-price bubbles?
15. Why would it be better to *lean* against credit-driven bubbles and *clean* after other types of asset bubbles crash?
16. According to the Greenspan Doctrine, under what conditions might a central bank respond to a perceived stock market bubble?
17. Classify each of the following as either a policy instrument or an intermediate target, and explain why.
    a. The ten-year Treasury bond rate
    b. The monetary base
    c. M1
    d. The fed funds rate
18. "If the demand for reserves did not fluctuate, the Fed could pursue both a reserves target and an interest-rate target at the same time." Is this statement true, false, or uncertain? Explain.
19. What procedures can the Fed use to control the federal funds rate? Why does control of this interest rate imply that the Fed will lose control of nonborrowed reserves?
20. Compare the monetary base to M1 on the grounds of controllability and measurability. Which do you prefer as an intermediate target? Why?
21. "Interest rates can be measured more accurately and quickly than reserve aggregates; hence an interest rate is preferred to the reserve aggregates as a policy instrument." Do you agree or disagree? Explain your answer.
22. How can bank behavior and the Fed's behavior cause money supply growth to be procyclical (rising in booms and falling in recessions)?
23. What does the Taylor rule imply that policymakers should do to the fed funds rate under the following scenarios?
    a. Unemployment rises due to a recession.
    b. An oil price shock causes the inflation rate to rise by 1% and output to fall by 1%.
    c. The economy experiences prolonged increases in productivity growth while actual output growth is unchanged.
    d. Potential output declines while actual output remains unchanged.
    e. The Fed revises its (implicit) inflation target down.

Applied Problems

All applied problems are available in MyEconLab *at* www.myeconlab.com.

24. If the Fed has an interest-rate target, why will an increase in the demand for reserves lead to a rise in the money supply? Use a graph of the market for reserves to explain.

25. Since monetary policy changes through the fed funds rate occur with a lag, policymakers are usually more concerned with adjusting policy according to changes in the forecasted or expected inflation rate, rather than the current inflation rate. In light of this, suppose that monetary policymakers employ the Taylor rule to set the fed funds rate, where the inflation gap is defined as the difference between expected inflation and the target inflation rate. Assume that the weights on both the inflation and the output gaps are ½, the equilibrium real fed funds rate is 2%, the inflation rate target is 2%, and the output gap is 1%.

a. If the expected inflation rate is 4%, then at what should the fed funds rate be set according to the Taylor rule?

b. Suppose half of Fed economists forecast inflation to be 3%, and half of Fed economists forecast inflation to be 5%. If the Fed uses the average of these two forecasts as its measure of expected inflation, then what should the fed funds rate be according to the Taylor rule?

c. Now suppose half of Fed economists forecast inflation to be 0%, and half forecast inflation to be 8%. If the Fed uses the average of these two forecasts as its measure of expected inflation, then what should the fed funds rate be according to the Taylor rule?

d. Given your answers to (a) – (c) above, do you think it is a good idea for monetary policymakers to use a strict interpretation of the Taylor rule as a basis for setting policy? Why or why not?

Web Exercises

1. The Federal Open Market Committee (FOMC) meets about every six weeks to assess the state of the economy and to decide what actions the central bank should take. The minutes of this meeting are released three weeks after the meeting; however, a brief press release is made available immediately. Find the schedule of minutes and press releases at www.federalreserve.gov/fomc/.

a. When was the last scheduled meeting of the FOMC? When is the next meeting?

b. Review the press release from the last meeting. What did the committee decide to do about short-term interest rates?

c. Review the most recently published meeting minutes. What areas of the economy seemed to be of most concern to the committee members?

2. It is possible to access other central bank websites to learn about their structure. One example is the European Central bank. Go to www.ecb.int/index.html. On the ECB home page, find information about the ECB's strategy for monetary policy.

3. Many countries have central banks that are responsible for their nation's monetary policy. Go to www.bis.org/cbanks.htm and select one of the central banks (for example, Norway). Review that bank's website to determine its policies regarding application of monetary policy. How does this bank's policies compare to those of the U.S. central bank?

Web References

www.federalreserve.gov/pf/pf.htm

Review what the Federal Reserve reports as its primary purposes and functions.

www.economagic.com/

A comprehensive listing of sites that offer a wide variety of economic summary data and graphs.

www.federalreserve.gov/releases/H3

Historic and current data on the aggregate reserves of depository institutions and the monetary base.

www.federalreserve.gov/aboutthefed/relatedWebSites.htm

The Federal Reserve provides links to other central bank Web pages.

Web Appendix

Please visit the Companion Website at www.pearsonhighered.com/mishkin to read the Web appendix to Chapter 19:

Appendix: **Monetary Targeting**

APPENDIX TO CHAPTER 19

Fed Policy Procedures: Historical Perspective

The well-known adage "The road to hell is paved with good intentions" applies as much to the Federal Reserve as it does to human beings. Understanding a central bank's goals and the strategies it can use to pursue them cannot tell us how monetary policy is actually conducted. To understand the practical results of the theoretical underpinnings, we have to look at how the Fed has actually conducted policy in the past. This historical perspective not only will show us how our central bank carries out its duties but will also help us interpret the Fed's activities and see where U.S. monetary policy may be heading in the future.

THE EARLY YEARS: DISCOUNT POLICY AS THE PRIMARY TOOL

When the Fed was created, changing the discount rate was the primary tool of monetary policy; the Fed had not yet discovered that open market operations were a more powerful tool for influencing the money supply, and the Federal Reserve Act made no provisions for changes in reserve requirements. The guiding principle for the conduct of monetary policy was that as long as loans were being made for "productive" purposes—that is, to support the production of goods and services—providing reserves to the banking system to make these loans would not be inflationary. This theory, now thoroughly discredited, became known as the **real bills doctrine**. In practice, it meant that the Fed would make loans to member commercial banks when they showed up at the discount window with *eligible paper*, loans to facilitate the production and sale of goods and services. (Since the 1920s, the Fed has not conducted discount operations in this way.) The Fed's act of making loans to member banks was initially called *rediscounting*, because the original bank loans to businesses were made by discounting (loaning less than) the face value of the loan, and the Fed would be discounting them again. (Over time, when the Fed's emphasis on eligible paper diminished, the Fed's loans to banks became known as *discounts*, and the interest rate on these loans, the *discount rate*, which is the terminology we use today.)

By the end of World War I, the Fed's policy of rediscounting eligible paper and keeping interest rates low to help the Treasury finance the war had led to a raging inflation; in 1919 and 1920, the inflation rate averaged 14%. The Fed decided that it could no longer follow the passive policy prescribed by the real bills doctrine because it was inconsistent with the goal of price stability, and for the first time the Fed accepted the responsibility of playing an active role in influencing the economy. In January 1920, the Fed raised the discount rate from $4\frac{3}{4}\%$ to 6%, the largest jump in its history, and eventually raised it further, to 7% in June 1920, where it remained for nearly a year. The result of this policy was a sharp decline in the money supply and an especially sharp recession in 1920–1921. Although the blame for this severe recession can clearly be laid at the Fed's doorstep, in one sense the Fed's policy was very successful: After an initial decline in the price level, the inflation rate went to zero, paving the way for the prosperous Roaring Twenties.

DISCOVERY OF OPEN MARKET OPERATIONS

In the early 1920s, a particularly important event occurred: The Fed accidentally discovered open market operations. When the Fed was created, its revenue came exclusively from the interest it received on the discount loans it made to member banks. After the 1920–1921 recession, the volume of discount loans shrank dramatically, and the Fed was pressed for income. It solved this problem by purchasing income-earning securities. In doing so, the Fed noticed that reserves in the banking system grew and there was a multiple expansion of bank loans and deposits. This result is obvious to us now (we studied the multiple deposit creation process in Chapter 14), but to the Fed at that time it was a revelation. A new monetary policy tool was born, and by the end of the 1920s, it was the most important weapon in the Fed's arsenal.

THE GREAT DEPRESSION

The stock market boom in 1928 and 1929 created a dilemma for the Fed. It wanted to temper the boom by raising the discount rate, but it was reluctant to do so, because that would mean raising interest rates to businesses and individuals who had legitimate needs for credit. Finally, in August 1929, the Fed raised the discount rate, but by then it was too late; the speculative excesses of the market boom had already occurred, and the Fed's action merely hastened the stock market crash and pushed the economy into recession.

The weakness of the economy, particularly in the agricultural sector, led to what Milton Friedman and Anna Schwartz labeled a "contagion of fear" that triggered substantial withdrawals from banks, building to a full-fledged panic in November and December 1930. For the next two years, the Fed sat idly by while one bank panic after another occurred, culminating in the final panic in March 1933, at which point the new president, Franklin Delano Roosevelt, declared a bank holiday. (Why the Fed failed to engage in its lender-of-last-resort role during this period is discussed in the Inside the Fed box on bank panics.) The spate of bank panics from 1930 to 1933 were the most severe in U.S. history, and Roosevelt aptly summed up the problem in his statement, "The only thing we have to fear is fear itself." By the time the panics were over in March 1933, more than one-third of the commercial banks in the United States had failed.

In Chapter 17, we examined how the bank panics of this period led to a decline in the money supply of more than 25%. The resulting unprecedented decline in the money supply during this period is thought by many economists, particularly monetarists, to have been the major contributing factor to the severity of the depression, never equaled before or since.

Inside the Fed **Bank Panics of 1930–1933: Why Did the Fed Let Them Happen?**

The Federal Reserve System was totally passive during the bank panics of the Great Depression period and did not perform its intended role of lender of last resort to prevent them. In retrospect, the Fed's behavior seems quite extraordinary, but hindsight is always clearer than foresight.

The primary reason for the Fed's inaction was that Federal Reserve officials did not understand the negative impact that bank failures could have on the money supply and on economic activity. Friedman and Schwartz report that the Federal Reserve officials "tended to regard bank failures as regrettable consequences of bank management or bad banking practices, or as inevitable reactions to prior speculative excesses, or as a consequence but hardly a cause of the financial and economic collapse in process." In addition, bank failures in the early stages of the bank panics "were concentrated among smaller banks and, since the most influential figures in the system were big-city bankers who deplored the existence of smaller banks, their disappearance may have been viewed with complacency."[*]

Friedman and Schwartz also point out that political infighting may have played an important role in the passivity of the Fed during this period. The Federal Reserve Bank of New York, which until 1928 was the dominant force in the Federal Reserve System, strongly advocated an active program of open market purchases to provide reserves to the banking system during the bank panics. However, other powerful figures in the Federal Reserve System opposed the New York bank's position, and the bank was outvoted. (Friedman and Schwartz's discussion of the politics of the Federal Reserve System during this period makes for fascinating reading, and you might enjoy their highly readable book.)

[*]Milton Friedman and Anna Jacobson Schwartz, *A Monetary History of the United States, 1867–1960* (Princeton, NJ: Princeton University Press, 1963), p. 358.

RESERVE REQUIREMENTS AS A POLICY TOOL

The Thomas Amendment to the Agricultural Adjustment Act of 1933 provided the Federal Reserve's Board of Governors with emergency power to alter reserve requirements with the approval of the president of the United States. In the Banking Act of 1935, this emergency power was expanded to allow the Fed to alter reserve requirements without the president's approval.

The first use of reserve requirements as a tool of monetary control proved that the Federal Reserve was capable of adding to the blunders that it had made during the bank panics of the early 1930s. By the end of 1935, banks had increased their holdings of excess reserves to unprecedented levels, a sensible strategy, considering their discovery during the 1930–1933 period that the Fed would not always perform its intended role as lender of last resort. Bankers now understood that they would have to protect themselves against a bank run by holding substantial amounts of excess reserves. The Fed viewed these excess reserves as a nuisance that made it harder to exercise monetary control. Specifically, the Fed worried that these excess reserves might be lent out and would produce "an uncontrollable expansion of credit in the future."[1]

To improve monetary control, the Fed raised reserve requirements in three steps: August 1936, January 1937, and May 1937. The result of this action was, as we would

[1]Milton Friedman and Anna Jacobson Schwartz, *A Monetary History of the United States, 1867–1960* (Princeton, NJ: Princeton University Press, 1963), p. 524.

expect from our money supply model, a slowdown of money growth toward the end of 1936 and an actual decline in 1937. The recession of 1937–1938, which commenced in May 1937, was a severe one and was especially upsetting to the American public because even at its outset unemployment was intolerably high. So not only does it appear that the Fed was at fault for the severity of the Great Depression contraction in 1929–1933, but, to add insult to injury, it was responsible for aborting the subsequent recovery. The Fed's disastrous experience with varying its reserve requirements made it far more cautious in the use of this policy tool in the future.

WAR FINANCE AND THE PEGGING OF INTEREST RATES: 1942–1951

With the entrance of the United States into World War II in late 1941, government spending skyrocketed, and to finance it the Treasury issued huge amounts of bonds. The Fed agreed to help the Treasury finance the war cheaply by pegging interest rates at the low levels that had prevailed before the war: $\frac{3}{8}$% on Treasury bills and $2\frac{1}{2}$% on long-term Treasury bonds. Whenever interest rates rose above these levels and the price of bonds began to fall, the Fed would make open market purchases, thereby bidding up bond prices and driving interest rates down again. The result was a rapid growth in the monetary base and the money supply. The Fed had thus in effect relinquished its control of monetary policy to meet the financing needs of the government.

When the war ended, the Fed continued to peg interest rates, and because there was little pressure on them to rise, this policy did not result in an explosive growth in the money supply. When the Korean War broke out in 1950, however, interest rates began to climb, and the Fed found that it was again forced to expand the monetary base at a rapid rate. Because inflation began to heat up (the consumer price index rose 8% between 1950 and 1951), the Fed decided that it was time to reassert its control over monetary policy by abandoning the interest-rate peg. An often bitter debate ensued between the Fed and the Treasury, which wanted to keep its interest costs down and so favored a continued pegging of interest rates at low levels. In March 1951, the Fed and the Treasury came to an agreement known as the Accord, in which pegging was abandoned but the Fed promised that it would not allow interest rates to rise precipitously. After Eisenhower's election as president in 1952, the Fed was given complete freedom to pursue its monetary policy objectives.

TARGETING MONEY MARKET CONDITIONS: THE 1950s AND 1960s

With its freedom restored, the Federal Reserve, then under the chairmanship of William McChesney Martin, Jr., took the view that monetary policy should be grounded in intuitive judgment based on a feel for the money market. The policy procedure that resulted can be described as one in which the Fed targeted on money market conditions, and particularly on interest rates.

An important characteristic of this policy procedure was that it led to more rapid growth in the money supply when the economy was expanding and a slowing of money growth when the economy was in recession. The *procyclical monetary policy* (a positive association of money supply growth with the business cycle) is explained by the following step-by-step reasoning. As we learned in Chapter 5, a rise in national income ($Y\uparrow$) leads to a rise in market interest rates ($i\uparrow$). With the rise in interest rates, the Fed would purchase bonds to bid their price up and lower interest rates to their target level. The resulting increase in the monetary base caused the money supply to rise and the business cycle expansion to be accompanied by a faster rate of money growth. In summary:

$$Y\uparrow \Rightarrow i\uparrow \Rightarrow MB\uparrow \Rightarrow M\uparrow$$

In a recession, the opposite sequence of events would occur, and the decline in income would be accompanied by a slower rate of growth in the money supply ($Y\downarrow \Rightarrow M\downarrow$).

A further problem with using interest rates as the primary operating instrument is that they may encourage an inflationary spiral to get out of control. As we saw in Chapter 5, when inflation and hence expected inflation rises, nominal interest rates rise via the Fisher effect. If the Fed attempted to prevent this increase by purchasing bonds, this would also lead to a rise in the monetary base and the money supply:

$$\pi\uparrow \Rightarrow \pi^e\uparrow \Rightarrow i\uparrow \Rightarrow MB\uparrow \Rightarrow M\uparrow$$

Higher inflation could thus lead to an increase in the money supply, which would increase inflationary pressures further.

By the late 1960s, the rising chorus of criticism of procyclical monetary policy by prominent monetarist economists such as Milton Friedman, Karl Brunner, and Allan Meltzer and concerns about inflation finally led the Fed to abandon its focus on money market conditions.

TARGETING MONETARY AGGREGATES: THE 1970s

In 1970, after Arthur Burns was appointed chairman of the Board of Governors, the Fed committed itself to the use of monetary aggregates as intermediate targets. Did monetary policy cease to be procyclical? A glance at Figure 4 in Chapter 1 indicates that monetary policy was as procyclical in the 1970s as in the 1950s and 1960s. What went wrong? Why did the conduct of monetary policy not improve? The answers to these questions lie in the Fed's operating procedures during the period, which suggest that its commitment to targeting monetary aggregates was not very strong.

Every six weeks, the Federal Open Market Committee would set target ranges for the growth rates of various monetary aggregates and would determine what federal funds rate (the interest rate on funds loaned overnight between banks) it thought consistent with these aims. The target ranges for the growth in monetary aggregates were fairly broad—a typical range for M1 growth might be 3% to 6%; for M2, 4% to 7%—while the range for the federal funds rate was a narrow band, say, from $7\frac{1}{2}\%$ to $8\frac{1}{4}\%$. The trading desk at the Federal Reserve Bank of New York was then instructed to meet both sets of targets, but as we saw earlier, interest-rate targets and monetary aggregate targets might not be compatible. If the two targets were incompatible—say, the federal funds rate began to climb higher than the top of its target band when M1 was growing too rapidly—the trading desk was instructed to give precedence to the federal funds rate target. In the situation just described, this would mean that although M1 growth was too high, the trading desk would make open market purchases to keep the federal funds rate within its target range.

The Fed was actually using the federal funds rate as its operating instrument. During the six-week period between FOMC meetings, an unexpected rise in output (which would cause the federal funds rate to hit the top of its target band) would then induce open market purchases and a too-rapid growth of the money supply. When the FOMC met again, it would try to get money supply growth back on track by raising the target range on the federal funds rate. However, if income continued to rise unexpectedly, money growth would overshoot again. This is exactly what occurred from June 1972 to June 1973, when the economy boomed unexpectedly: M1 growth greatly exceeded its target, increasing at approximately an 8% rate, while the federal funds rate climbed from $4\frac{1}{2}\%$ to $8\frac{1}{2}\%$. The economy soon became overheated, and inflationary pressures began to mount.

The opposite chain of events occurred at the end of 1974, when the economic contraction was far more severe than anyone had predicted. The federal funds rate fell dramatically, from over 12% to 5%, and persistently bumped against the bottom of its target range. The trading desk conducted open market sales to keep the federal funds rate from falling, and money growth dropped precipitously, actually turning negative by the beginning of 1975. Clearly, this sharp drop in money growth when the United States was experiencing one of the worst economic contractions of the postwar era was a serious mistake.

Using the federal funds rate as an operating instrument promoted a procyclical monetary policy despite the Fed's lip service to monetary aggregate targets. If the Federal Reserve really intended to pursue monetary aggregate targets, it seems peculiar that it would have chosen an interest rate for an operating instrument rather than a reserve aggregate. The explanation for the Fed's choice of an interest rate as an operating instrument is that it was still very concerned with achieving interest-rate stability and was reluctant to relinquish control over interest-rate movements. The incompatibility of the Fed's policy procedure with its stated intent of targeting on the monetary aggregates had become very clear by October 1979, when the Fed's policy procedures underwent drastic revision.

NEW FED OPERATING PROCEDURES: OCTOBER 1979–OCTOBER 1982

In October 1979, two months after Paul Volcker became chairman of the Board of Governors, the Fed finally de-emphasized the federal funds rate as an operating instrument by widening its target range more than fivefold: A typical range might be from 10% to 15%. The primary operating instrument became nonborrowed reserves, which the Fed would set after estimating the volume of discount loans the banks would borrow. Not surprisingly, the federal funds rate underwent much greater fluctuations after it was de-emphasized as an operating instrument. What is surprising, however, is that the deemphasis of the federal funds target did not result in improved monetary control. After October 1979, the fluctuations in the rate of money supply growth *increased* rather than decreased, as would have been expected. In addition, the Fed missed its M1 growth target ranges in all three years of the 1979–1982 period.

The likely reason for the target misses was that Volcker was not serious about controlling monetary aggregates, but rather wanted to avoid being blamed for the high interest rates that would be necessary to bring inflation down. Interest-rate movements during this period support this interpretation of Fed strategy. After the October 1979 announcement, short-term interest rates were driven up by nearly 5%, until in March 1980 they exceeded 15%. With the imposition of credit controls in March 1980 and the rapid decline in real GDP in the second quarter of 1980, the Fed eased up on its policy and allowed interest rates to decline sharply. When recovery began in July 1980, inflation remained persistent, still exceeding 10%. Because the inflation fight was not yet won, the Fed tightened the screws again, sending short-term rates above the 15% level for a second time. The 1981–1982 recession and its large decline in output and high unemployment began to bring inflation down. With inflationary psychology apparently broken, interest rates were allowed to fall.

The Fed's anti-inflation strategy during the October 1979–October 1982 period was neither intended nor likely to produce smooth growth in the monetary aggregates. Indeed, the large fluctuations in interest rates and the business cycle, along with financial innovation, helped generate volatile money growth.

DE-EMPHASIS OF MONETARY AGGREGATES: OCTOBER 1982–EARLY 1990s

In October 1982, with inflation in check, the Fed returned, in effect, to a policy of smoothing interest rates. It did this by placing less emphasis on monetary aggregate targets and shifting to borrowed reserves (discount loan borrowings) as an operating instrument. To see how a borrowed reserves target produces interest-rate smoothing, let's consider what happens when the economy expands ($Y\uparrow$) so that interest rates are driven up. The rise in interest rates ($i\uparrow$) increases the incentives for banks to borrow more from the Fed, so borrowed reserves rise ($DL\uparrow$). To prevent the resulting rise in borrowed reserves from exceeding the target level, the Fed must lower interest rates by bidding up the price of bonds through open market purchases. The outcome of targeting on borrowed reserves, then, is that the Fed prevents a rise in interest rates. In doing so, however, the Fed's open market purchases increase the monetary base ($MB\uparrow$) and lead to a rise in the money supply ($M\uparrow$), which produces a positive association of money and national income ($Y\uparrow \Rightarrow M\uparrow$). Schematically,

$$Y\uparrow \Rightarrow i\uparrow \Rightarrow DL\uparrow \Rightarrow MB\uparrow \Rightarrow M\uparrow$$

A recession causes the opposite chain of events: The borrowed reserves target prevents interest rates from falling and results in a drop in the monetary base, leading to a fall in the money supply ($Y\downarrow \Rightarrow M\downarrow$).

The de-emphasis on monetary aggregates and the change to a borrowed reserves target led to much smaller fluctuations in the federal funds rate after October 1982 but continued to have large fluctuations in money supply growth. Finally, in February 1987, the Fed announced that it would no longer even set M1 targets. The abandonment of M1 targets was defended on two grounds. The first was that the rapid pace of financial innovation and deregulation had made the definition and measurement of money very difficult. The second is that a breakdown in the stable relationship between M1 and economic activity had occurred. These two arguments suggested that a monetary aggregate such as M1 might no longer be a reliable guide for monetary policy. As a result, the Fed switched its focus to the broader monetary aggregate M2, which it felt had a more stable relationship with economic activity. However, in the early 1990s, this relationship also broke down, and in July 1993, Board of Governors chairman Alan

Greenspan testified in Congress that the Fed would no longer use any monetary targets, including M2, as a guide for conducting monetary policy. Finally, legislation in 2000 amending the Federal Reserve Act dropped the requirement that the Fed report target ranges for monetary aggregates to Congress.

FEDERAL FUNDS TARGETING AGAIN: EARLY 1990s AND BEYOND

Having abandoned monetary aggregates as a guide for monetary policy, the Federal Reserve returned to using a federal funds target in the early 1990s. In February 1994, the Fed adopted a new policy procedure. Instead of keeping the federal funds target secret, as it had done previously, the Fed now announced any federal funds rate target change. As mentioned in Chapter 13, around 2:15 p.m., after every FOMC meeting, the Fed now announces whether the federal funds rate target has been raised, lowered, or kept the same. As a result of these announcements, the outcome of the FOMC meeting is now big news, and the media devote much more attention to FOMC meetings, because announced changes in the federal funds rate feed into changes in other interest rates that affect consumers and businesses.

PREEMPTIVE STRIKES AGAINST INFLATION

The recognition that monetary policy needs to be more forward-looking has prompted the Fed to be more preemptive. Starting in February 1994, after the economy returned to rapid growth, but the unemployment rate was still high—well above 6%—the Fed began a preemptive strike to head off future inflationary pressures that ultimately raised the federal funds rate from 3% to 6% by February 1995. This preemptive strike against inflation was highly successful because inflation actually fell from around the 3% to the 2% level.

With strong growth of the economy in 1999 and heightened concerns about inflation, the Fed began to raise the federal funds rate from $4\frac{3}{4}\%$ in June 1999 to $6\frac{1}{2}\%$ in May 2000. In this case, the Fed was a little too late in its preemptive strike, and inflation rose from around 2% to over 3% by 2000.

After the economy's return to steady growth following the 2001 recession, the Fed again started raising interest rates at a "measured pace" of 25 basis points (0.25 percentage point) at every single FOMC meeting, starting from an extremely low level of 1% in June 2004 to $5\frac{1}{4}\%$ by June 2006. Although the Fed did begin to act when unemployment was high, well above 5%, the measured pace of the federal funds rate increases put the Fed a little behind the curve: Inflation crept up from around the 2% to the 3% level, and then jumped dramatically in 2008 to the 5% level with the surge in energy and other commodity prices.

By the standards of the 1970s and 1980s, the Fed's preemptive strikes worked quite well in keeping inflation within a fairly narrow range. Nonetheless, sometimes the preemptive strikes against inflation were not quite preemptive enough.

PREEMPTIVE STRIKES AGAINST ECONOMIC DOWNTURNS AND FINANCIAL DISRUPTIONS: LTCM, ENRON, AND THE GLOBAL FINANCIAL CRISIS

The Fed has also acted preemptively against negative shocks to aggregate demand and especially to those associated with financial disruptions. It lowered the federal funds rate in early 1996 to deal with a possible slowing of the economy and then took the dramatic step in late September and mid-October of 1998 of reducing the federal funds rate target by $\frac{3}{4}$ of a percentage point when the collapse of Long Term Capital Management led to concerns about the health of the financial system. The financial markets soon calmed down, and the economy kept on expanding.

With the weakening of the economy in January 2001 (just before the start of the recession in March 2001), the Fed began to ease monetary policy aggressively, taking the federal funds rate down by 1 percentage point even before the recession began, from 6% to 5%. The Federal Reserve then lowered the federal funds rate down to 1% by June 2003. The result was a very mild recession in which the unemployment rate did not go much above 6%.

With the onset of the global financial crisis in August 2007, the Fed began to ease policy even in the face of a strong economy, with growth above 3% in the third quarter of 2007, unemployment below 5%, and inflation rising because of the increase in energy prices. The potential for the financial disruption to weaken the economy and to produce an adverse feedback loop—in which credit markets worsened, which would weaken economic activity and, in turn, weaken credit markets further—encouraged the Fed to take preemptive action, cutting the federal funds rate by $\frac{1}{2}$ percentage point in September. At the same time, the Fed implemented large liquidity injections into the credit markets to try to get them working again (discussed in the previous chapter). By October 2008, unfortunately, the global financial crisis reached a particularly vicious stage, with an appreciable weakening of the economy. Subsequent easing of monetary policy lowered the federal funds rate to zero in December 2008, and the Fed then engaged in the nonconventional monetary policy described in Chapter 15.

These preemptive attacks against negative shocks to aggregate demand were particularly successful during the Greenspan era in keeping economic fluctuations very mild. The economic expansion from 1991 to 2001 was the longest in U.S. history, and the subsequent recession in 2001 was quite mild. The magnitude of the financial disruption during the global financial crisis, however, was so great that the preemptive actions by the Federal Reserve were not enough to contain the crisis, and the economy suffered accordingly.

INTERNATIONAL CONSIDERATIONS

The increasing importance of international trade to the American economy has also brought international considerations to the forefront of Federal Reserve policy making in recent years. By 1985, the strength of the dollar had contributed to a deterioration in American competitiveness with foreign businesses. In public pronouncements, Chairman Volcker and other Fed officials made it clear that the dollar was at too high a value and needed to come down. Because, as we will see in Chapter 17, expansionary monetary policy is one way to lower the value of the dollar, it is no surprise that the Fed engineered an acceleration in the growth rates of the monetary aggregates in 1985 and 1986 and that the value of the dollar declined. By 1987, policymakers at the Fed agreed that the dollar had fallen sufficiently, and sure enough, monetary growth in the United States slowed. These monetary policy actions by the Fed were encouraged by the process of **international policy coordination,** in which countries agreed to enact policies cooperatively.

International considerations also played a role in the Fed's decision to lower the federal funds rate by $\frac{3}{4}$ of a percentage point in the fall of 1998. Concerns about the potential for a worldwide financial crisis in the wake of the collapse of the Russian financial system at that time and weakness in economies abroad, particularly in Asia, stimulated the Fed to take a dramatic step to calm down markets. International considerations, although not the primary focus of the Federal Reserve, are likely to be a major factor in the conduct of U.S. monetary policy in the future.

Part 5

International Finance and Monetary Policy

Crisis and Response: Foreign Exchange Market Turmoil and the IMF

From 2002 until 2008, the U.S. dollar steadily declined in value relative to other currencies. Indeed, a major concern of policymakers was that the dollar might crash, with adverse effects on both economic activity and inflation. With the credit markets seizing up in September and October 2008, after the failure of Lehman Brothers, an amazing thing happened. Instead of continuing its decline, the dollar appreciated sharply. The same "flight to quality" that led investors to step up their purchases of U.S. Treasury securities also led them to want to hold more U.S. dollars, thereby bidding up the dollar's value.

The dollar's higher value made imported goods—ranging from flat-screen televisions to wines—cheaper to purchase and traveling abroad more affordable. But this good news for the U.S. dollar was often bad news for other currencies. Many countries in Latin America and Eastern Europe now found their currencies in free fall. The International Monetary Fund (IMF) stepped in and set up a new lending facility to make loans to distressed countries with fewer strings attached than was true for the IMF's previous lending programs. The IMF started making loans to the tune of billions of dollars. The IMF, which had looked as though it was on the sidelines as the global financial crisis spread worldwide, now was moving to front and center.

The global financial crisis has demonstrated that events that started in the United States have worldwide ramifications and that international financial institutions like the IMF have an important role in responding to make sure that the international financial system continues to work well. Chapter 20 outlines how the foreign exchange market functions and how exchange rates between different countries' currencies are determined. In Chapter 21, we examine how the international financial system operates and how it affects monetary policy.

20 The Foreign Exchange Market

Preview

In the mid-1980s, American businesses became less competitive with their foreign counterparts; subsequently, in the 1990s and 2000s, their competitiveness increased. Did this swing in competitiveness occur primarily because American management fell down on the job in the 1980s and then got its act together afterwards? Not really. American business became less competitive in the 1980s because American dollars became worth more in terms of foreign currencies, making American goods more expensive relative to foreign goods. By the 1990s and 2000s, the value of the U.S. dollar had fallen appreciably from its highs in the mid-1980s, making American goods cheaper and American businesses more competitive.

The price of one currency in terms of another is called the **exchange rate**. As you can see in Figure 1, exchange rates are highly volatile. The exchange rate affects the economy and our daily lives, because when the U.S. dollar becomes more valuable relative to foreign currencies, foreign goods become cheaper for Americans and American goods become more expensive for foreigners. When the U.S. dollar falls in value, foreign goods become more expensive for Americans and American goods become cheaper for foreigners.

Fluctuations in the exchange rate also affect both inflation and output, and are an important concern to monetary policymakers. When the U.S. dollar falls in value, the higher prices of imported goods feed directly into a higher price level and inflation. At the same time, a declining U.S. dollar, which makes U.S. goods cheaper for foreigners, increases the demand for U.S. goods and leads to higher production and output.

We begin our study of international finance by examining the **foreign exchange market**, the financial market where exchange rates are determined.

FOREIGN EXCHANGE MARKET

Most countries of the world have their own currencies: The United States has its dollar; the European Monetary Union, its euro; Brazil, its real; and China, its yuan. Trade between countries involves the mutual exchange of different currencies (or, more usually, bank deposits denominated in different currencies). When an American firm buys foreign goods, services, or financial assets, for example, U.S. dollars (typically, bank deposits denominated in U.S. dollars) must be exchanged for foreign currency (bank deposits denominated in the foreign currency).

The trading of currencies and bank deposits denominated in particular currencies takes place in the foreign exchange market. Transactions conducted in the foreign

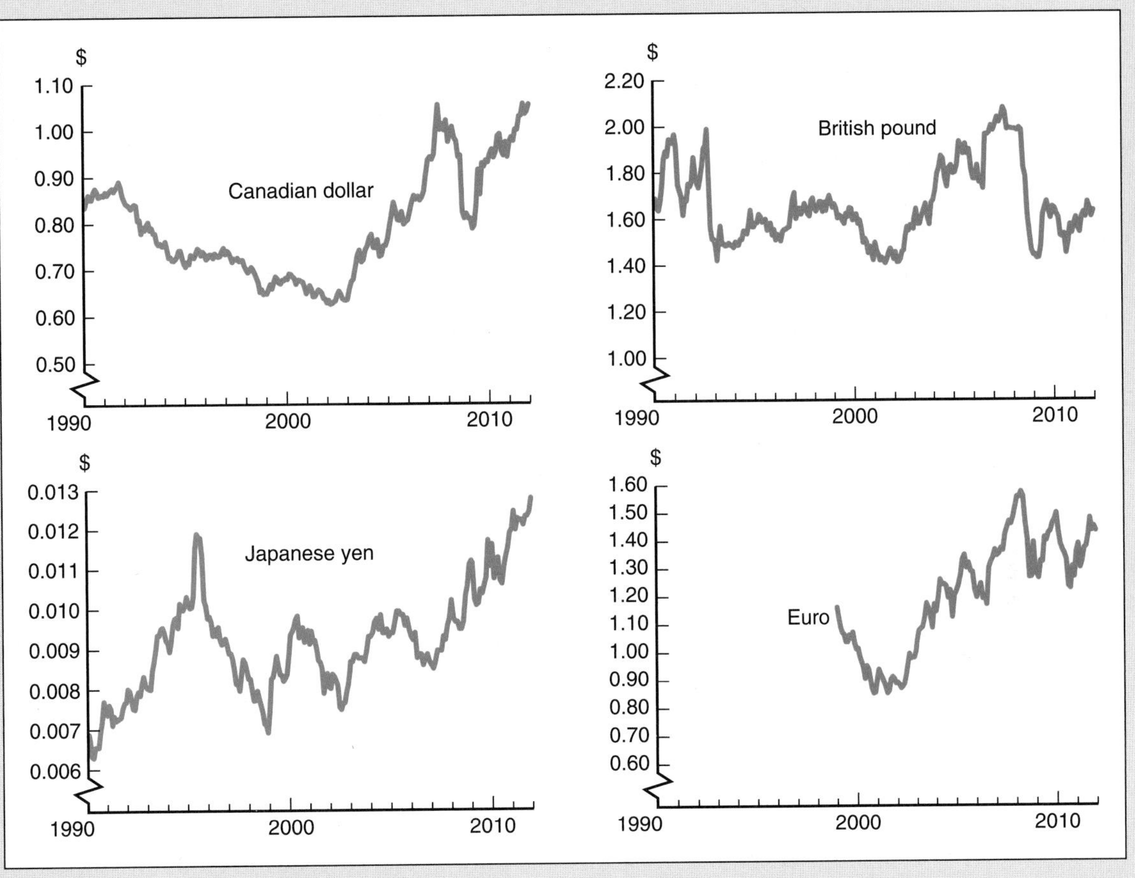

FIGURE 1 Exchange Rates, 1990–2011
Exchange rates are highly volatile. Note that exchange rates are quoted as $ per unit of foreign currency, so that a rise in these plots indicates a strengthening of the currency (weakening of the dollar).
Source: Federal Reserve; www.federalreserve.gov/releases/h10/hist.

exchange market determine the rates at which currencies are exchanged, which in turn determine the cost of purchasing foreign goods and financial assets.

What Are Foreign Exchange Rates?

There are two kinds of exchange rate transactions. The predominant ones, called **spot transactions**, involve the immediate (two-day) exchange of bank deposits. **Forward transactions** involve the exchange of bank deposits at some specified future date. The **spot exchange rate** is the exchange rate for the spot transaction, and the **forward exchange rate** is the exchange rate for the forward transaction.

When a currency increases in value, it experiences **appreciation**; when it falls in value and is worth fewer U.S. dollars, it undergoes **depreciation**. At the beginning of 1999, for example, the euro was valued at 1.18 dollars; as indicated in the Following

Following the Financial News Foreign Exchange Rates

Foreign exchange rates are published daily in newspapers and Internet sites such as www.finance.yahoo.com. Exchange rates for a currency such as the euro are quoted in two ways: U.S. dollars per unit of domestic currency or domestic currency per U.S. dollar. For example, on August 9, 2011, the euro exchange rate was quoted as $1.42 per euro and 0.70 euro per dollar. Americans generally would regard the exchange rate with the euro as $1.42 per euro, while Europeans think of it as 0.70 euro per dollar.

Exchange rates typically are quoted for the spot transaction (the spot exchange rate) and for forward transactions (the forward exchange rates) that will take place one month, three months, and six months in the future.

the Financial News box, "Foreign Exchange Rates," on August 9, 2011, it was valued at $1.42 dollars. The euro *appreciated* by 20%: $(1.42 - 1.18/1.18) = 0.20 = 20\%$. Equivalently, we could say that the U.S. dollar, which went from a value of 0.85 euro per dollar at the beginning of 1999 to a value of 0.70 euro per dollar on August 9, 2011, *depreciated* by 17%: $(0.70 - 0.85)/0.85 = -0.17 = 17\%$.

Why Are Exchange Rates Important?

Exchange rates are important because they affect the relative price of domestic and foreign goods. The dollar price of French goods to an American is determined by the interaction of two factors: the price of French goods in euros and the euro/dollar exchange rate.

Suppose that Wanda the Winetaster, an American, decides to buy a bottle of 1961 (a very good year) Château Lafite Rothschild to complete her wine cellar. If the price of the wine in France is 1,000 euros and the exchange rate is $1.42 to the euro, the wine will cost Wanda $1,420 (= 1,000 euros × $1.42/euro). Now suppose that Wanda delays her purchase by two months, at which time the euro has appreciated to $1.70 per euro. If the domestic price of the bottle of Lafite Rothschild remains 1,000 euros, its dollar cost will have risen from $1,420 to $1,700.

The same currency appreciation, however, makes the price of foreign goods in that country less expensive. At an exchange rate of $1.42 per euro, a Dell computer priced at $2,000 costs Pierre the Programmer 1,408 euros; if the exchange rate increases to $1.70 per euro, the computer will cost only 1,176 euros.

A depreciation of the euro lowers the cost of French goods in America but raises the cost of American goods in France. If the euro drops in value to $1.00, Wanda's bottle of Lafite Rothschild will cost her only $1,000 instead of $1,420, and the Dell computer will cost Pierre 2,000 euros rather than $1,408.

Such reasoning leads to the following conclusion: ***When a country's currency appreciates (rises in value relative to other currencies), the country's goods abroad become more expensive and foreign goods in that country become cheaper (holding domestic prices constant in the two countries). Conversely, when a country's currency depreciates, its goods abroad become cheaper and foreign goods in that country become more expensive.***

Depreciation of a currency makes it easier for domestic manufacturers to sell their goods abroad and makes foreign goods less competitive in domestic markets. From 2002 to 2011, the depreciated dollar helped U.S. industries sell more goods, but it hurt American consumers because foreign goods were more expensive. The prices of French wine and cheese and the cost of vacationing abroad all rose as a result of the weak dollar.

How Is Foreign Exchange Traded?

You cannot go to a centralized location to watch exchange rates being determined; currencies are not traded on exchanges such as the New York Stock Exchange. Instead, the foreign exchange market is organized as an over-the-counter market in which several hundred dealers (mostly banks) stand ready to buy and sell deposits denominated in foreign currencies. Because these dealers are in constant telephone and computer contact, the market is very competitive; in effect, it functions no differently from a centralized market.

An important point to note is that although banks, companies, and governments talk about buying and selling currencies in foreign exchange markets, they do not take a fistful of dollar bills and sell them for British pound notes. Rather, most trades involve the buying and selling of bank deposits denominated in different currencies. So when we say that a bank is buying dollars in the foreign exchange market, what we actually mean is that the bank is buying *deposits denominated in dollars*. The volume in this market is colossal, exceeding $4 trillion per day.

Trades in the foreign exchange market consist of transactions in excess of $1 million. The market that determines the exchange rates given in the Following the Financial News box is not where one would buy foreign currency for a trip abroad. Instead, we buy foreign currency in the retail market from dealers such as American Express or from banks. Because retail prices are higher than wholesale, when we buy foreign exchange, we obtain fewer units of foreign currency per dollar—that is, we pay a higher price for foreign currency—than the exchange rates in the Following the Financial News box indicate.

EXCHANGE RATES IN THE LONG RUN

Like the price of any good or asset in a free market, exchange rates are determined by the interaction of supply and demand. To simplify our analysis of exchange rates in a free market, we divide it into two parts. First, we examine how exchange rates are determined in the long run; then we use our knowledge of the long-run determinants of the exchange rates to help us understand how they are determined in the short run.

Law of One Price

The starting point for understanding how exchange rates are determined is a simple idea called the **law of one price**: If two countries produce an identical good, and transportation costs and trade barriers are very low, the price of the good should be the same throughout the world no matter which country produces it. Suppose that American steel costs $100 per ton and identical Japanese steel costs 10,000 yen per ton. For the law of one price to hold, the exchange rate between the yen and the dollar must be 100 yen per dollar ($0.01 per yen), so that one ton of American steel sells for 10,000 yen in Japan (the price of Japanese steel) and one ton of Japanese steel sells for $100 in the United States (the price of U.S. steel). If the exchange rate were 200 yen to the dollar, Japanese steel would sell for $50 per ton in the United States or half the price of American steel, and American steel would sell for 20,000 yen per ton in Japan, twice the price of Japanese steel. Because American steel would be more expensive than Japanese steel in both countries and is identical to Japanese steel, the demand for American steel would go to zero. Given a fixed dollar price for American steel, the resulting excess supply of American steel will be eliminated only if the exchange rate falls to 100 yen per dollar, making the price of American steel and Japanese steel the same in both countries.

Theory of Purchasing Power Parity

One of the most prominent theories of how exchange rates are determined is the **theory of purchasing power parity (PPP)**. It states that exchange rates between any two currencies will adjust to reflect changes in the price levels of the two countries. The theory of PPP is simply an application of the law of one price to national price levels rather than to individual prices. Suppose that the yen price of Japanese steel rises 10% (to 11,000 yen) relative to the dollar price of American steel (unchanged at $100). For the law of one price to hold, the exchange rate must rise to 110 yen to the dollar, a 10% appreciation of the dollar. Applying the law of one price to the price levels in the two countries produces the theory of purchasing power parity, which maintains that if the Japanese price level rises 10% relative to the U.S. price level, the dollar will appreciate by 10%.

Another way of thinking about purchasing power parity is through a concept called the **real exchange rate**, the rate at which domestic goods can be exchanged for foreign goods. In effect, it is the price of domestic goods relative to the price of foreign goods denominated in the domestic currency. For example, if a basket of goods in New York costs $50, while the cost of the same basket of goods in Tokyo costs $75 because it costs 7500 yen while the exchange rate is at 100 yen per dollar, then the real exchange rate is 0.66 (= $50/$75). The real exchange rate is below 1.0, indicating that it is cheaper to buy the basket of goods in the United States than in Japan. The real exchange rate for the U.S. dollar is currently low against many other currencies, and this is why we are seeing New York overwhelmed by so many foreign tourists going on shopping sprees. The real exchange rate indicates whether a currency is relatively cheap or not. Another way of describing the theory of PPP is to say that it predicts that the real exchange rate is always equal to 1.0, so that the purchasing power of the dollar is the same as that of other currencies, such as the yen or the euro.

As our U.S./Japanese example demonstrates, the theory of PPP suggests that if one country's price level rises relative to another's, its currency should depreciate (the other country's currency should appreciate). As you can see in Figure 2, this prediction is borne out in the long run. From 1973 to 2011, the British price level rose 94% relative to the U.S. price level, and as the theory of PPP predicts, the dollar appreciated against the pound—although by 53%, an amount smaller than the 94% increase predicted by PPP.

Yet, as the same figure indicates, PPP theory often has little predictive power in the short run. From early 1985 to the end of 1987, for example, the British price level rose relative to that of the United States. Instead of appreciating, as PPP theory predicts, the U.S. dollar actually depreciated by 40% against the pound. So even though PPP theory provides some

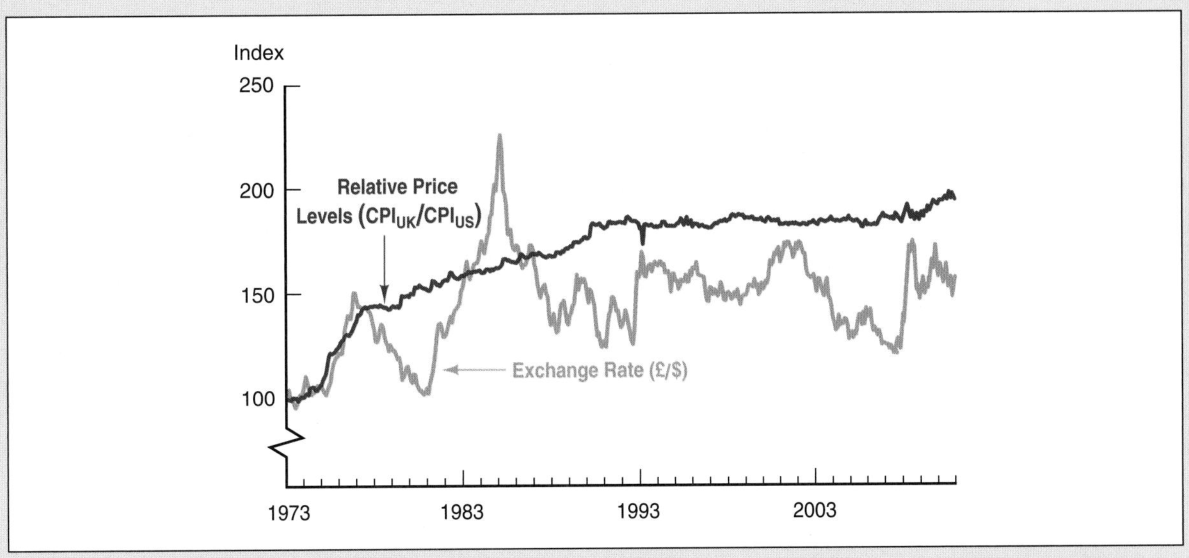

FIGURE 2 Purchasing Power Parity, United States/United Kingdom, 1973–2011 (Index: March 1973 = 100.)

Over the whole period, the rise in the British price level relative to the U.S. price level is associated with a rise in the value of the dollar, as PPP predicts. However, the PPP relationship does not hold over shorter periods.

Source: ftp.bls.gov/pub/special/requests/cpi/cpiai.txt.

guidance to the long-run movement of exchange rates, it is not perfect and in the short run is a particularly poor predictor. What explains PPP theory's failure to predict well?

Why the Theory of Purchasing Power Parity Cannot Fully Explain Exchange Rates

The PPP conclusion that exchange rates are determined solely by changes in relative price levels rests on the assumption that all goods are identical in both countries and that transportation costs and trade barriers are very low. When this assumption is true, the law of one price states that the relative prices of all these goods (that is, the relative price level between the two countries) will determine the exchange rate. The assumption that goods are identical may not be too unreasonable for American and Japanese steel, but is it a reasonable assumption for American and Japanese cars? Is a Toyota the equivalent of a Chevrolet?

Because Toyotas and Chevys are obviously not identical, their prices do not have to be equal. Toyotas can be more expensive relative to Chevys, and both Americans and Japanese will still purchase Toyotas. Because the law of one price does not hold for all goods, a rise in the price of Toyotas relative to Chevys will not necessarily mean that the yen must depreciate by the amount of the relative price increase of Toyotas over Chevys.

Furthermore, PPP theory does not take into account that many goods and services (whose prices are included in a measure of a country's price level) are not traded across borders. Housing, land, and services such as restaurant meals, haircuts, and golf lessons are not traded goods. So even though the prices of these items might rise and lead to a higher price level relative to another country's, the exchange rate would experience little direct effect.

Factors That Affect Exchange Rates in the Long Run

In the long run, four major factors affect the exchange rate: relative price levels, trade barriers, preferences for domestic versus foreign goods, and productivity. We examine how each of these factors affects the exchange rate while holding the others constant.

The basic reasoning proceeds along the following lines: Anything that increases the demand for domestically produced goods that are traded relative to foreign traded goods tends to appreciate the domestic currency because domestic goods will continue to sell well even when the value of the domestic currency is higher. Similarly, anything that increases the demand for foreign goods relative to domestic goods tends to depreciate the domestic currency because domestic goods will continue to sell well only if the value of the domestic currency is lower. In other words, ***if a factor increases the demand for domestic goods relative to foreign goods, the domestic currency will appreciate; if a factor decreases the relative demand for domestic goods, the domestic currency will depreciate***.

Relative Price Levels In line with PPP theory, when prices of American goods rise (holding prices of foreign goods constant), the demand for American goods falls and the dollar tends to depreciate so that American goods can still sell well. By contrast, if prices of Japanese goods rise so that the relative prices of American goods fall, the demand for American goods increases, and the dollar tends to appreciate, because American goods will continue to sell well even with a higher value of the domestic currency. ***In the long run, a rise in a country's price level (relative to the foreign price level) causes its currency to depreciate, and a fall in the country's relative price level causes its currency to appreciate.***

Trade Barriers Barriers to free trade such as **tariffs** (taxes on imported goods) and **quotas** (restrictions on the quantity of foreign goods that can be imported) can affect the exchange rate. Suppose that the United States increases its tariff or puts a lower quota on Japanese steel. These increases in trade barriers increase the demand for American steel, and the dollar tends to appreciate because American steel will still sell well even with a higher value of the dollar. ***Increasing trade barriers causes a country's currency to appreciate in the long run.***

Preferences for Domestic Versus Foreign Goods If the Japanese develop an appetite for American goods—say, for Florida oranges and American movies—the increased demand for American goods (exports) tends to appreciate the dollar, because the American goods will continue to sell well even at a higher value for the dollar. Likewise, if Americans decide that they prefer Japanese cars to American cars, the increased demand for Japanese goods (imports) tends to depreciate the dollar. ***Increased demand for a country's exports causes its currency to appreciate in the long run; conversely, increased demand for imports causes the domestic currency to depreciate.***

Productivity When productivity in a country rises, it tends to rise in domestic sectors that produce traded goods rather than nontraded goods. Higher productivity, therefore, is associated with a decline in the price of domestically produced traded goods relative to foreign traded goods. As a result, the demand for domestic traded goods rises,

SUMMARY TABLE 1

Factors That Affect Exchange Rates in the Long Run

Factor	Change in Factor	Response of the Exchange Rate, E^*
Domestic price level†	↑	↓
Trade barriers†	↑	↑
Import demand	↑	↓
Export demand	↑	↑
Productivity†	↑	↑

*Units of foreign currency per dollar: ↑ indicates domestic currency appreciation; ↓ , depreciation.
†Relative to other countries.
Note: Only increases (↑) in the factors are shown; the effects of decreases in the variables on the exchange rate are the opposite of those indicated in the "Response" column.

and the domestic currency tends to appreciate. If, however, a country's productivity lags behind that of other countries, its traded goods become relatively more expensive, and the currency tends to depreciate. ***In the long run, as a country becomes more productive relative to other countries, its currency appreciates.***[1]

Our long-run theory of exchange rate behavior is summarized in Table 1. We use the convention that the exchange rate E is quoted so that an appreciation of the domestic currency corresponds to a rise in the exchange rate. In the case of the United States, this means that we are quoting the exchange rate as units of foreign currency, say, euros, per dollar.[2]

EXCHANGE RATES IN THE SHORT RUN: A SUPPLY AND DEMAND ANALYSIS

We have developed a theory of the long-run behavior of exchange rates. However, because factors driving long-run changes in exchange rates move slowly over time, if we are to understand why exchange rates exhibit such large changes (sometimes several percent) from day to day, we must develop a supply and demand analysis of how current exchange rates (spot exchange rates) are determined in the short run.

The key to understanding the short-run behavior of exchange rates is to recognize that an exchange rate is the price of domestic assets (bank deposits, bonds, equities, and so on, denominated in the domestic currency) in terms of foreign

[1]A country might be so small that a change in productivity or the preferences for domestic or foreign goods would have no effect on prices of these goods relative to foreign goods. In this case, changes in productivity or changes in preferences for domestic or foreign goods affect the country's income but will not necessarily affect the value of the currency. In our analysis, we are assuming that these factors can affect relative prices and consequently the exchange rate.

[2]Exchange rates can be quoted either as units of foreign currency per domestic currency or as units of domestic currency per foreign currency. In professional writing, many economists quote exchange rates as units of domestic currency per foreign currency so that an appreciation of the domestic currency is portrayed as a fall in the exchange rate. The opposite convention is used in the text here, because it is more intuitive to think of an appreciation of the domestic currency as a rise in the exchange rate.

assets (similar assets denominated in the foreign currency). Because the exchange rate is the price of one asset in terms of another, the natural way to investigate the short-run determination of exchange rates is with a supply and demand analysis that uses an asset market approach, which relies heavily on the theory of portfolio choice developed in Chapter 5. As you will see, however, the long-run determinants of the exchange rate we have just outlined also play an important part in the short-run asset market approach.

In the past, supply and demand approaches to exchange rate determination emphasized the role of import and export demand. The more modern asset market approach used here emphasizes stocks of assets rather than the flows of exports and imports over short periods, because export and import transactions are small relative to the amount of domestic and foreign assets at any given time. For example, foreign exchange transactions in the United States each year are well over 25 times greater than the amount of U.S. exports and imports. Thus, over short periods, decisions to hold domestic or foreign assets have a much greater role in exchange rate determination than the demand for exports and imports does.

Supply Curve for Domestic Assets

We start by discussing the supply curve. In this analysis we treat the United States as the home country, so domestic assets are denominated in dollars. For simplicity, we use euros to stand for any foreign country's currency, so foreign assets are denominated in euros.

The quantity of dollar assets supplied is primarily the quantity of bank deposits, bonds, and equities in the United States, and for all practical purposes we can take this amount as fixed with respect to the exchange rate. The quantity supplied at any exchange rate is the same, so the supply curve, *S*, is vertical, as shown in Figure 3.

Demand Curve for Domestic Assets

The demand curve traces out the quantity demanded at each current exchange rate by holding everything else constant, particularly the expected future value of the exchange rate. We write the current exchange rate (the spot exchange rate) as E_t, and the expected exchange rate for the next period as E^e_{t+1}. As the theory of portfolio choice suggests, the most important determinant of the quantity of domestic (dollar) assets demanded is the relative expected return of domestic assets. Let's see what happens as the current exchange rate E_t falls.

Suppose we start at point *A* in Figure 3, where the current exchange rate is at E_A. With the future expected value of the exchange rate held constant at E^e_{t+1}, a lower value of the exchange rate—say at E^*—implies that the dollar is more likely to rise in value, that is, appreciate. The greater the expected rise (appreciation) of the dollar, the higher is the relative expected return on dollar (domestic) assets. The theory of portfolio choice then tells us that because dollar assets are now more desirable to hold, the quantity of dollar assets demanded will rise, as is shown by point *B* in Figure 3. If the current exchange rate falls even further to E_C, there is an even higher expected appreciation of the dollar, a higher expected return, and therefore an even greater quantity of dollar assets demanded. This effect is shown at point *C* at Figure 3. The resulting demand curve, *D*, which connects these points, is downward-sloping, indicating that at lower current values of the dollar (everything else being equal), the quantity demanded of dollar assets is higher.

FIGURE 3
Equilibrium in the Foreign Exchange Market
Equilibrium in the foreign exchange market occurs at point *B*, the intersection of the demand curve *D* and the supply curve *S* at an exchange rate of E^*.

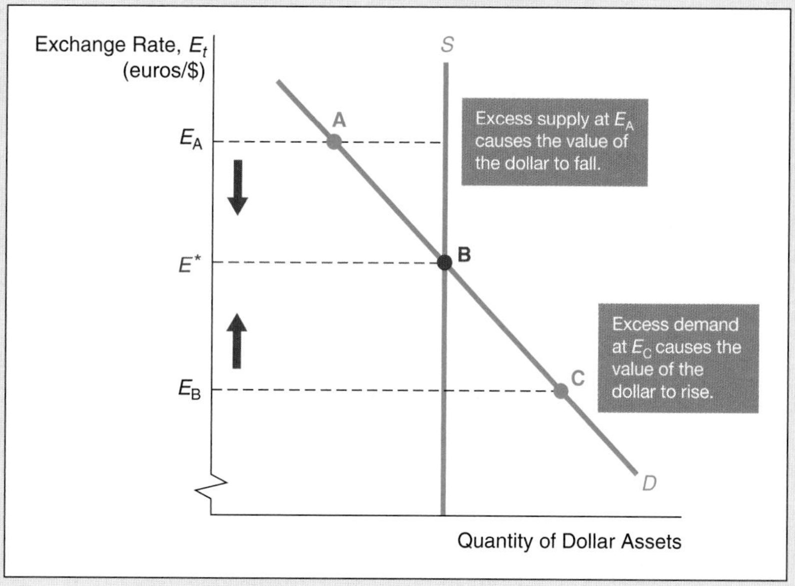

Equilibrium in the Foreign Exchange Market

As in the usual supply and demand analysis, the market is in equilibrium when the quantity of dollar assets demanded equals the quantity supplied. In Figure 3, equilibrium occurs at point *B*, the intersection of the demand and supply curves. At point *B*, the exchange rate is E^*.

Suppose that the exchange rate is at E_A, which is higher than the equilibrium exchange rate of E^*. As we can see in Figure 3, the quantity of dollar assets supplied is then greater than the quantity demanded, a condition of excess supply. Given that more people want to sell dollar assets than want to buy them, the value of the dollar will fall. As long as the exchange rate remains above the equilibrium exchange rate, an excess supply of dollar assets will continue to be available, and the dollar will fall in value until it reaches the equilibrium exchange rate of E^*.

Similarly, if the exchange rate is less than the equilibrium exchange rate at E_C, the quantity of dollar assets demanded will exceed the quantity supplied, a condition of excess demand. Given that more people want to buy dollar assets than want to sell them, the value of the dollar will rise until the excess demand disappears and the value of the dollar is again at the equilibrium exchange rate of E^*.

EXPLAINING CHANGES IN EXCHANGE RATES

The supply and demand analysis of the foreign exchange market illustrates how and why exchange rates change.[3] We have simplified this analysis by assuming the amount

[3]An alternative way to understand how and why exchange rates change is with the *interest parity condition*, an important concept in international finance that shows the relationship between domestic interest rates, foreign interest rates, and the expected appreciation of domestic currency. The interest parity condition and how it explains the determination of exchange rates is discussed in an appendix to this chapter.

of dollar assets is fixed: The supply curve is vertical at a given quantity and does not shift. Under this assumption, we need to look at only those factors that shift the demand curve for dollar assets to explain how exchange rates change over time.

Shifts in the Demand for Domestic Assets

As we have seen, the quantity of domestic (dollar) assets demanded depends on the relative expected return of dollar assets. To see how the demand curve shifts, we need to determine how the quantity demanded changes, holding the current exchange rate, E_t, constant, when other factors change.

For insight into which direction the demand curve shifts, suppose you are an investor who is considering putting funds into domestic (dollar) assets. When a factor changes, decide whether at a given level of the current exchange rate, holding all other variables constant, you would earn a higher or lower expected return on dollar assets versus foreign assets. This decision tells you whether you want to hold more or fewer dollar assets and thus whether the quantity demanded increases or decreases at each level of the exchange rate. Knowing the direction of the change in the quantity demanded at each exchange rate indicates which way the demand curve shifts. In other words, if the relative expected return of dollar assets rises, holding the current exchange rate constant, the demand curve shifts to the right. If the relative expected return falls, the demand curve shifts to the left.

Domestic Interest Rate, i^D Suppose that dollar assets pay an interest rate of i^D. When the domestic interest rate on dollar assets i^D rises, holding the current exchange rate E_t and everything else constant, the return on dollar assets increases relative to foreign assets, so people will want to hold more dollar assets. The quantity of dollar assets demanded increases at every value of the exchange rate, as shown by the rightward shift of the demand curve from D_1 to D_2, in Figure 4. The new equilibrium is reached at point 2, the intersection of D_2 and S, and the equilibrium exchange rate rises from E_1 to E_2. ***An increase in the domestic interest rate i^D shifts the demand curve for domestic assets, D, to the right and causes the domestic currency to appreciate*** ($E\uparrow$).

FIGURE 4
Response to an Increase in the Domestic Interest Rate, i^D

When the domestic interest rate i^D increases, the relative expected return on domestic (dollar) assets increases and the demand curve shifts to the right. The equilibrium exchange rate rises from E_1 to E_2.

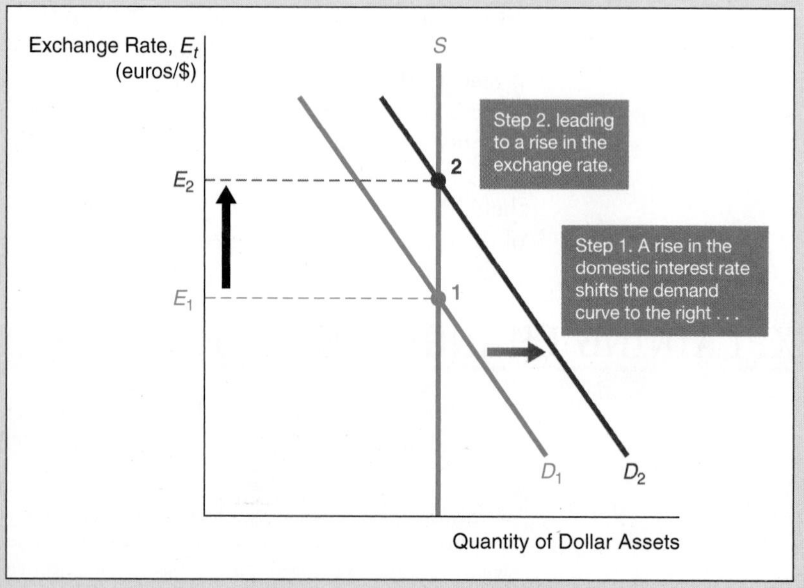
Exchange Rate, E_t (euros/\$)
S
Step 2. leading to a rise in the exchange rate.
2
E_2
Step 1. A rise in the domestic interest rate shifts the demand curve to the right . . .
1
E_1
D_1
D_2
Quantity of Dollar Assets

FIGURE 5
Response to an Increase in the Foreign Interest Rate, i^F
When the foreign interest rate i^F increases, the relative expected return on domestic (dollar) assets falls and the demand curve shifts to the left. The equilibrium exchange rate falls from E_1 to E_2.

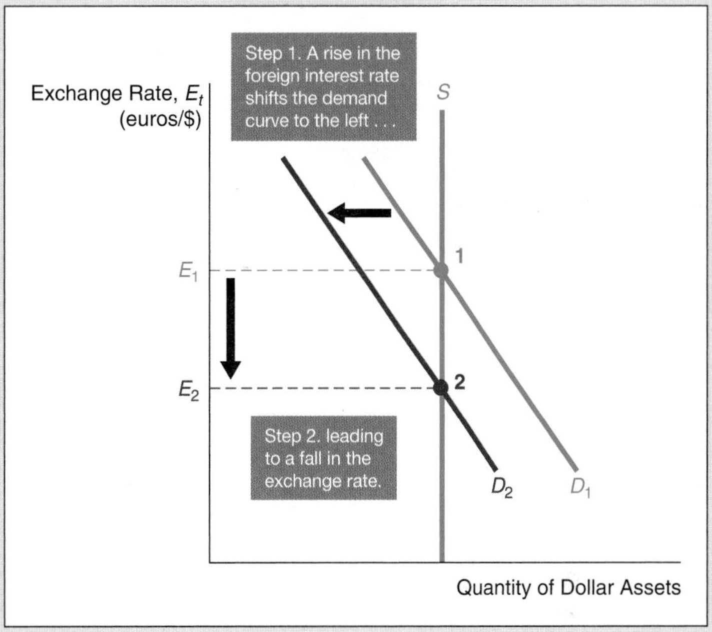
Exchange Rate, E_t
(euros/$)
Step 1. A rise in the foreign interest rate shifts the demand curve to the left . . .
S
1
2
E_1
E_2
Step 2. leading to a fall in the exchange rate.
D_2
D_1
Quantity of Dollar Assets

Conversely, if i^D falls, the relative expected return on dollar assets falls, the demand curve shifts to the left, and the exchange rate falls. ***A decrease in the domestic interest rate i^D shifts the demand curve for domestic assets, D, to the left and causes the domestic currency to depreciate ($E\downarrow$).***

Foreign Interest Rate, i^F Suppose that the foreign asset pays an interest rate of i^F. When the foreign interest rate i^F rises, holding the current exchange rate and everything else constant, the return on foreign assets rises relative to dollar assets. Thus the relative expected return on dollar assets falls. Now people want to hold fewer dollar assets, and the quantity demanded decreases at every value of the exchange rate. This scenario is shown by the leftward shift of the demand curve from D_1 to D_2, in Figure 5. The new equilibrium is reached at point 2, when the value of the dollar has fallen. Conversely, a decrease in i^F raises the relative expected return on dollar assets, shifts the demand curve to the right, and raises the exchange rate. To summarize, ***an increase in the foreign interest rate i^F shifts the demand curve D to the left and causes the domestic currency to depreciate; a fall in the foreign interest rate i^F shifts the demand curve D to the right and causes the domestic currency to appreciate.***

Changes in the Expected Future Exchange Rate, E^e_{t+1} Expectations about the future value of the exchange rate play an important role in shifting the current demand curve, because the demand for domestic assets, like that for any durable good, depends on the future resale price. Any factor that causes the expected future exchange rate, E^e_{t+1}, to rise increases the expected appreciation of the dollar. The result is a higher relative expected return on dollar assets, which increases the demand for dollar assets at every exchange rate, thereby shifting the demand curve to the right from D_1 to D_2, in Figure 6. The equilibrium exchange rate rises to point 2 at the intersection of the D_2 and S curves. ***A rise in the expected future exchange rate, E^e_{t+1},***

FIGURE 6
Response to an Increase in the Expected Future Exchange Rate, E^e_{t+1}
When the expected future exchange rate increases, the relative expected return on domestic (dollar) assets rises and the demand curve shifts to the right. The equilibrium exchange rate rises from E_1 to E_2.

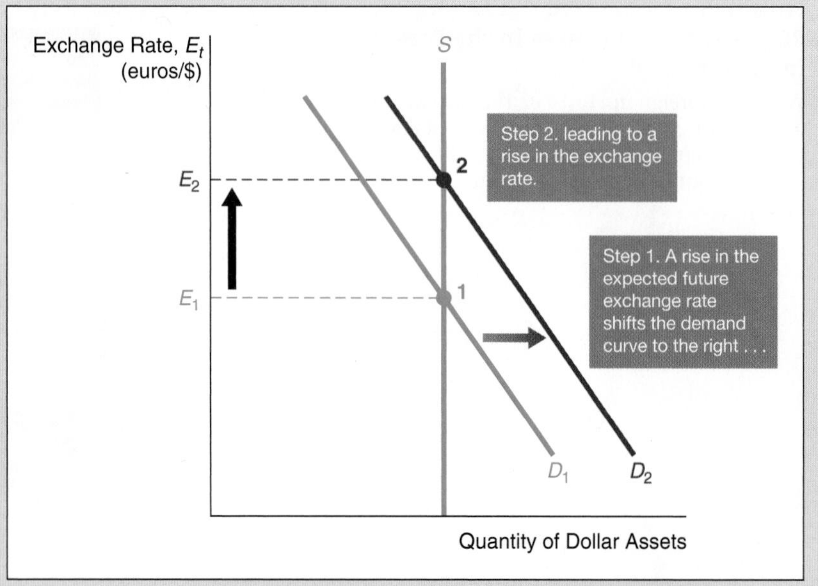

Exchange Rate, E_t
(euros/$)
S
E_2
E_1
2
1
Step 2. leading to a rise in the exchange rate.
Step 1. A rise in the expected future exchange rate shifts the demand curve to the right . . .
D_1
D_2
Quantity of Dollar Assets

shifts the demand curve to the right and causes an appreciation of the domestic currency. According to the same reasoning, ***a fall in the expected future exchange rate,*** E^e_{t+1}, ***shifts the demand curve to the left and causes a depreciation of the currency***.

Earlier in the chapter we discussed the determinants of the exchange rate in the long run: the relative price level, relative trade barriers, import and export demand, and relative productivity (refer to Summary Table 1). These four factors influence the expected future exchange rate. The theory of purchasing power parity suggests that if a higher American price level relative to the foreign price level is expected to persist, the dollar will depreciate in the long run. A higher expected relative American price level should thus have a tendency to lower E^e_{t+1}, lower the relative expected return on dollar assets, shift the demand curve to the left, and then lower the current exchange rate.

Similarly, the other long-run determinants of the exchange rate can influence the relative expected return on dollar assets and the current exchange rate. Briefly, the following changes, all of which increase the demand for domestic goods relative to foreign goods, will raise E^e_{t+1}: (1) expectations of a fall in the American price level relative to the foreign price level; (2) expectations of higher American trade barriers relative to foreign trade barriers; (3) expectations of lower American import demand; (4) expectations of higher foreign demand for American exports; and (5) expectations of higher American productivity relative to foreign productivity. By increasing E^e_{t+1}, all of these changes increase the relative expected return on dollar assets, shift the demand curve to the right, and cause an appreciation of the domestic currency, the dollar.

Recap: Factors That Change the Exchange Rate

Summary Table 2 outlines all the factors that shift the demand curve for domestic assets and thereby cause the exchange rate to change. Shifts in the demand curve occur when one factor changes, holding everything else constant, including the current exchange rate. Again, the theory of portfolio choice tells us that changes in the relative expected return on dollar assets are the source of shifts in the demand curve.

SUMMARY TABLE 2

Factors That Shift the Demand Curve for Domestic Assets and Affect the Exchange Rate

Factor	Change in Factor	Change in Quantity Demanded of Domestic Assets at Each Exchange Rate	Response of Exchange Rate, E_t	
Domestic interest rate, i^D	↑	↑	↑	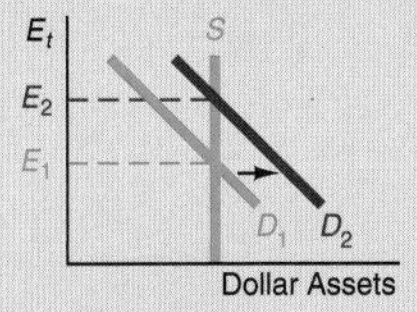
Foreign interest rate, i^F	↑	↓	↓	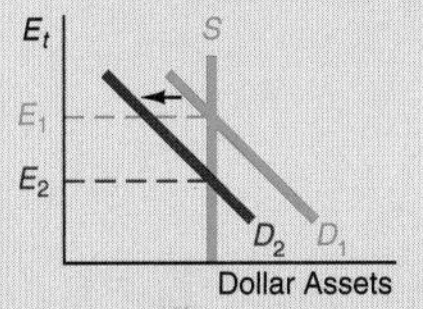
Expected domestic price level*	↑	↓	↓	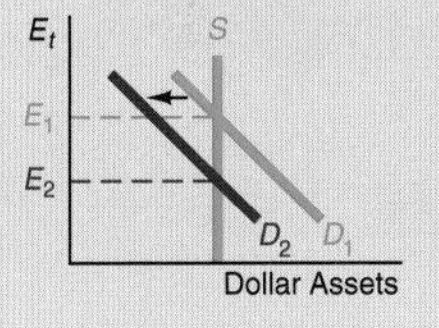
Expected trade barriers*	↑	↑	↑	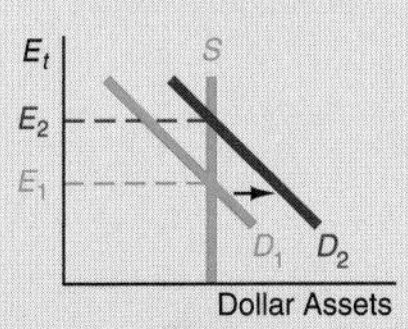
Expected import demand	↑	↓	↓	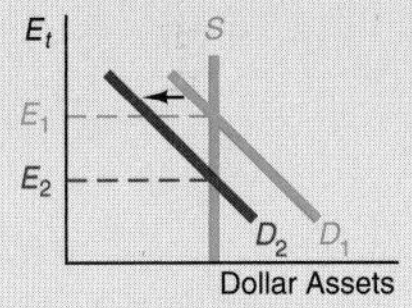
Expected export demand	↑	↑	↑	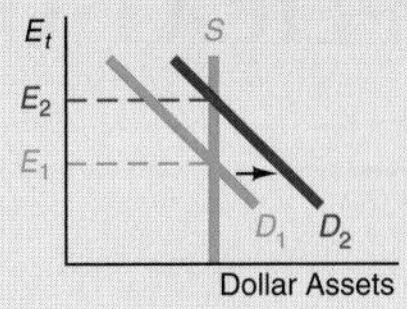
Expected productivity*	↑	↑	↑	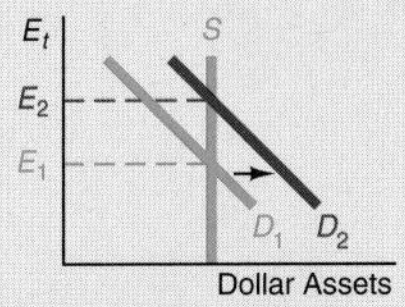

*Relative to other countries.

Note: Only increases (↑) in the factors are shown; the effects of decreases in the variables on the exchange rate are the opposite of those indicated in the "Response" column.

Let's review what happens when each of the seven factors in Table 2 changes. Remember that to understand which direction the demand curve shifts, consider what happens to the relative expected return on dollar assets when the factor changes. If the relative expected return rises, holding the current exchange rate constant, the demand curve shifts to the right. If the relative expected return falls, the demand curve shifts to the left.

1. When the interest rates on domestic assets i^D rise, the expected return on dollar assets rises at each exchange rate and so the quantity demanded increases. The demand curve therefore shifts to the right, and the equilibrium exchange rate rises, as is shown in the first row of Table 2.

2. When the foreign interest rate i^F rises, the return on foreign assets rises, so the relative expected return on dollar assets falls. The quantity demanded of dollar assets then falls, the demand curve shifts to the left, and the exchange rate declines, as in the second row of Table 2.

3. When the expected price level is higher, our analysis of the long-run determinants of the exchange rate indicates that the value of the dollar will fall in the future. The expected return on dollar assets thus falls, the quantity demanded declines, the demand curve shifts to the left, and the exchange rate falls, as in the third row of Table 2.

4. With higher expected trade barriers, the value of the dollar is higher in the long run and the expected return on dollar assets is higher. The quantity demanded of dollar assets thus rises, the demand curve shifts to the right, and the exchange rate rises, as in the fourth row of Table 2.

5. When expected import demand rises, we expect the exchange rate to depreciate in the long run, so the expected return on dollar assets falls. The quantity demanded of dollar assets at each value of the current exchange rate therefore falls, the demand curve shifts to the left, and the exchange rate declines, as in the fifth row of Table 2.

6. When expected export demand rises, the opposite occurs because the exchange rate is expected to appreciate in the long run. The expected return on dollar assets rises, the demand curve shifts to the right, and the exchange rate rises, as in the sixth row of Table 2.

7. With higher expected domestic productivity, the exchange rate is expected to appreciate in the long run, so the expected return on domestic assets rises. The quantity demanded at each exchange rate therefore rises, the demand curve shifts to the right, and the exchange rate rises, as in the seventh row of Table 2.

APPLICATION ◆ Effects of Changes in Interest Rates on the Equilibrium Exchange Rate

Our analysis has revealed the factors that affect the value of the equilibrium exchange rate. Now we use this analysis to take a closer look at the response of the exchange rate to changes in interest rates and money growth.

Changes in domestic interest rates i^D are often cited as a major factor affecting exchange rates. For example, we see headlines in the financial press like this one: "Dollar Recovers as Interest Rates Edge Upward." But is the view presented in this headline always correct?

Not necessarily, because to analyze the effects of interest rate changes, we must carefully distinguish the sources of the changes. The Fisher equation (Chapter 4) states that a nominal interest rate such as i^D equals the real interest rate plus expected inflation: $i = i_r + \pi^e$. The Fisher equation thus indicates that the interest rate i^D can change for two reasons: Either the real interest rate i_r changes or the expected inflation rate π^e changes. The effect on the exchange rate is quite different, depending on which of these two factors is the source of the change in the nominal interest rate.

FIGURE 7
Effect of a Rise in the Domestic Interest Rate as a Result of an Increase in Expected Inflation

Because a rise in domestic expected inflation leads to a decline in expected dollar appreciation that is larger than the increase in the domestic interest rate, the relative expected return on domestic (dollar) assets falls. The demand curve shifts to the left, and the equilibrium exchange rate falls from E_1 to E_2.

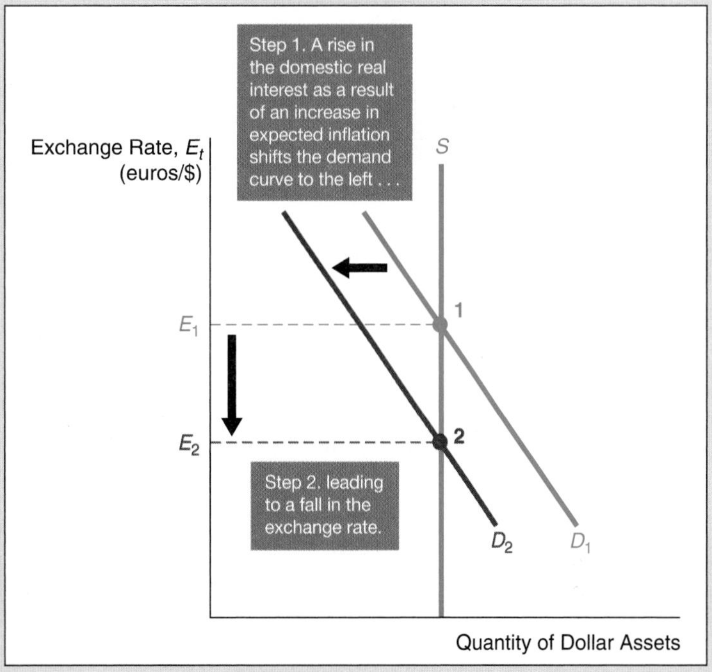
Step 1. A rise in the domestic real interest as a result of an increase in expected inflation shifts the demand curve to the left . . .
Exchange Rate, E_t (euros/$)
S
1
2
E_1
E_2
Step 2. leading to a fall in the exchange rate.
D_2
D_1
Quantity of Dollar Assets

Suppose that the domestic real interest rate increases, so that the nominal interest rate i^D rises while expected inflation remains unchanged. In this case, it is reasonable to assume that the expected appreciation of the dollar will be unchanged because expected inflation is unchanged. In this case, the increase in i^D increases the relative expected return on dollar assets, raises the quantity of dollar assets demanded at each level of the exchange rate, and shifts the demand curve to the right. We end up with the situation depicted in Figure 4, which analyzes an increase in i^D, holding everything else constant. Our model of the foreign exchange market produces the following result: ***When domestic real interest rates rise, the domestic currency appreciates.***

When the nominal interest rate rises because of an increase in expected inflation, we get a different result from the one shown in Figure 4. The rise in expected domestic inflation leads to a decline in the expected appreciation of the dollar, which is typically thought to be larger than the increase in the domestic interest rate i^D. As a result, at any given exchange rate, the relative expected return on domestic (dollar) assets falls, the demand curve shifts to the left, and the exchange rate falls from E_1 to E_2, as shown in Figure 7. Our analysis leads to this conclusion: ***When domestic interest rates rise due to an expected increase in inflation, the domestic currency depreciates.***

Because this conclusion is completely different from the one reached when the rise in the domestic interest rate is associated with a higher real interest rate, we must always distinguish between real and nominal measures when analyzing the effects of interest rates on exchange rates.

APPLICATION ◆ Why Are Exchange Rates So Volatile?

The high volatility of foreign exchange rates surprises many people. Thirty or so years ago, economists generally believed that allowing exchange rates to be determined in the free market would not lead to large fluctuations in their values. Recent experience has proved them wrong. If we return to Figure 1, we see that exchange rates over the 1990–2011 period have been very volatile.

The asset market approach to exchange rate determination that we have outlined in this chapter gives a straightforward explanation of volatile exchange rates. Because expected appreciation of the domestic currency affects the expected return on domestic assets, expectations about the price level, inflation, trade barriers, productivity, import demand, export demand, and the money supply play important roles in determining the exchange rate. When expectations about any of these variables change, as they do—and often, at that—our model indicates that the expected return on domestic assets, and therefore the exchange rate, will be immediately affected. Because expectations on all these variables change with just about every bit of news that appears, it is not surprising that the exchange rate is volatile. Because earlier models of exchange rate behavior focused on goods markets rather than asset markets, they did not emphasize changing expectations as a source of exchange rate movements, and so these earlier models could not predict substantial fluctuations in exchange rates. The failure of earlier models to explain volatility is one reason why they are no longer so popular. The more modern approach developed here emphasizes that the foreign exchange market is like any other asset market in which expectations of the future matter. The foreign exchange market, like other asset markets such as the stock market, displays substantial price volatility, and foreign exchange rates are notoriously hard to forecast.

APPLICATION ◆ The Dollar and Interest Rates

In the chapter preview, we mentioned that the dollar was weak in the late 1970s, rose substantially from 1980 to 1985, and declined thereafter. We can use our analysis of the foreign exchange market to understand exchange rate movements and help explain the dollar's rise in the early 1980s and fall thereafter.

Some important information for tracing the dollar's changing value is presented in Figure 8, which plots measures of real and nominal interest rates and the value of the dollar in terms of a basket of foreign currencies (called an **effective exchange rate index**). We can see that the value of the dollar and the measure of real interest rates tend to rise and fall together. In the late 1970s, real interest rates were at low levels, and so was the value of the dollar. Beginning in 1980, however, real interest rates in the United States began to climb sharply, and at the same time so did the dollar. After 1984, the real interest rate declined substantially, as did the dollar.

Our model of exchange rate determination helps explain the rise in the dollar in the early 1980s and its fall thereafter. As Figure 4 indicates, a rise in the U.S. real interest rate raises the relative expected return on dollar assets, which leads to purchases of dollar assets that raise the exchange rate. This is exactly what happened in the 1980–1984 period. The subsequent fall in U.S. real interest rates then reduced the relative expected return on dollar assets, which lowered the demand for them and thus lowered the exchange rate.

The plot of *nominal* interest rates in Figure 8 also demonstrates that the correspondence between nominal interest rates and exchange rate movements is not nearly as close as that between real interest rates and exchange rate movements. This is also exactly what our analysis predicts. The rise in nominal interest rates in the late 1970s was not reflected in a corresponding rise in the value of the dollar; indeed, the dollar actually fell in the late 1970s. Figure 8 explains why the rise in nominal rates in the late 1970s did not produce a rise in the dollar. As a comparison of the real and nominal interest rates in the late 1970s indicates, the rise in nominal interest rates reflected an increase in expected inflation, not an increase in real interest rates. As our analysis in Figure 7

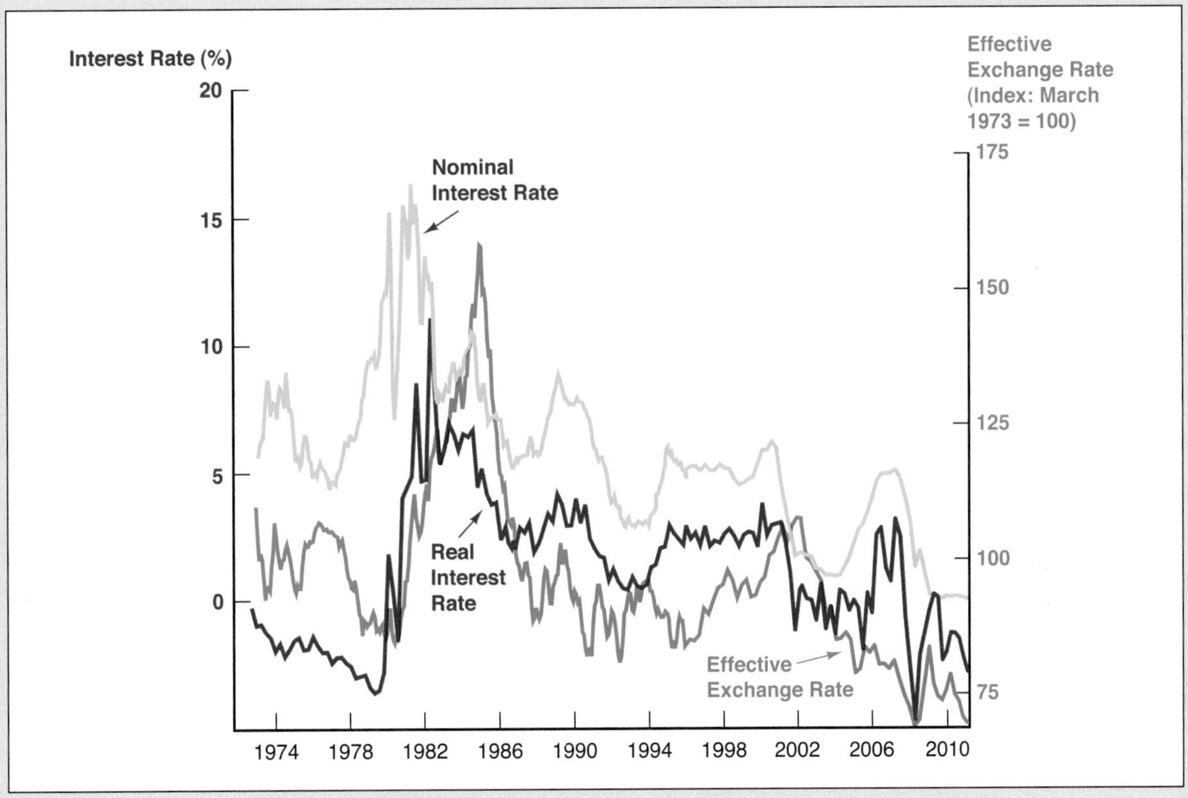

FIGURE 8 Value of the Dollar and Interest Rates, 1973–2010

The correspondence between nominal interest rates and exchange rate movements is not nearly as close as that between real interest rates and exchange rate movements.

Sources: Federal Reserve; www.federalreserve.gov/releases/h10/summary/indexn_m.txt; real interest rate from Figure 1 in Chapter 4.

demonstrates, the rise in nominal interest rates stemming from a rise in expected inflation should lead to a decline in the dollar, and that is exactly what happened.

If the story has a moral, it is that a failure to distinguish between real and nominal interest rates can lead to poor predictions of exchange rate movements. The weakness of the dollar in the late 1970s and the strength of the dollar in the early 1980s can be explained by movements in real interest rates, but not by movements in nominal interest rates.

APPLICATION ◆ The Global Financial Crisis and the Dollar

With the start of the global financial crisis in August 2007, the dollar began an accelerated decline in value, falling by 9% against the euro until mid-July of 2008, and 6% against a wider basket of currencies. After hitting an all-time low against the euro on July 11, the dollar suddenly shot upward, by over 20% against the euro by the end of October and 15% against a wider basket of currencies. What is the relationship between the global financial crisis and these large swings in the value of the dollar?

During 2007, the negative effects of the financial crisis on economic activity were mostly confined to the United States. The Federal Reserve acted aggressively to lower interest rates to counter the contractionary effects, decreasing the federal funds rate target by 325 basis points from September 2007 to April 2008. In contrast, other central banks like the ECB did not see the need to lower interest rates, particularly because high energy prices had led to a surge in inflation. The relative expected return on dollar assets thus declined, shifting the demand curve for dollar assets to the left, as in Figure 5, leading to a decline in the equilibrium exchange rate. Our analysis of the foreign exchange market thus explains why the early phase of the global financial crisis led to a decline in the value of the dollar.

We now turn to the rise in the value of the dollar. Starting in the summer of 2008, the effects of the global financial crisis on economic activity began to spread more widely throughout the world. Foreign central banks started to cut interest rates, with the expectation that further rate cuts would follow, as indeed did occur. The expected decline in foreign interest rates then increased the relative expected return of dollar assets, leading to a rightward shift in the demand curve and a rise in the value of the dollar, as shown in Figure 4. Another factor driving the dollar upward was the "flight to quality" when the global financial crisis reached a particularly virulent stage in September and October. Both Americans and foreigners now wanted to put their money in the safest assets possible: U.S. Treasury securities. The resulting increase in the demand for dollar assets provided an additional reason for the demand curve for dollar assets to shift out to the right, thereby helping to produce a sharp appreciation of the dollar ◆.

Summary

1. Foreign exchange rates (the price of one country's currency in terms of another's) are important because they affect the price of domestically produced goods sold abroad and the cost of foreign goods bought domestically.
2. The theory of purchasing power parity suggests that long-run changes in the exchange rate between the currencies of two countries are determined by changes in the relative price levels in the two countries. Other factors that affect exchange rates in the long run are tariffs and quotas, import demand, export demand, and productivity.
3. In the short run, exchange rates are determined by changes in the relative expected return on domestic assets, which cause the demand curve to shift. Any factor that changes the relative expected return on domestic assets will lead to changes in the exchange rate. Such factors include changes in the interest rates on domestic and foreign assets, as well as changes in any of the factors that affect the long-run exchange rate and hence the expected future exchange rate.
4. The asset market approach to exchange rate determination can explain the volatility of exchange rates, the rise of the dollar in the 1980–1984 period and its subsequent fall, and changes in the value of the dollar during the global financial crisis.

Key Terms

Questions

All questions are available in MyEconLab *at* www.myeconlab.com.

1. When the euro appreciates, are you more likely to drink California or French wine?
2. "A country is always worse off when its currency is weak (falls in value)." Is this statement true, false, or uncertain? Explain your answer.
3. When the U.S. dollar depreciates, what happens to exports and imports in the United States?
4. If the Japanese price level rises by 5% relative to the price level in the United States, what does the theory of purchasing power parity predict will happen to the value of the Japanese yen in terms of dollars?
5. If the demand for a country's exports falls at the same time that tariffs on imports are raised, will the country's currency tend to appreciate or depreciate in the long run?
6. When the Federal Reserve conducts an expansionary monetary policy, what happens to the money supply? How does this affect the supply of dollar assets? .
7. From 2009 to 2011, the economies of Australia and Switzerland suffered relatively mild effects from the global financial crisis. At the same time, many countries in the euro area were hit hard with high unemployment and burdened with unsustainably high government debts. How should this affect the euro/Swiss franc and euro/Australian dollar exchange rates?
8. In the mid- to late 1970s, the yen appreciated relative to the dollar, even though Japan's inflation rate was higher than America's. How can this be explained by an improvement in the productivity of Japanese industry relative to American industry?
9. Suppose the president of the United States announces a new set of reforms that includes a new anti-inflation program. Assuming the announcement is believed by the public, what will happen to the exchange rate for the U.S. dollar?
10. If the British central bank lowers interest rates to reduce unemployment, what will happen to the value of the pound in the short run and the long run?
11. If the Indian government unexpectedly announces that it will be imposing higher tariffs on foreign goods one year from now, what will happen to the value of the Indian rupee today?
12. If nominal interest rates in America rise but real interest rates fall, predict what will happen to the U.S. exchange rate.
13. If American auto companies make a breakthrough in automobile technology and are able to produce a car that gets 200 miles to the gallon, what will happen to the U.S. exchange rate?
14. If Mexicans go on a spending spree and buy twice as much French perfume, Japanese TVs, English sweaters, Swiss watches, and Italian wine, what will happen to the value of the Mexican peso?
15. Through the summer and fall of 2008, as the global financial crisis began to take hold, international financial institutions and sovereign wealth funds significantly increased their purchases of U.S. Treasury securities as a safe haven investment. How should this affect U.S. dollar exchange rates?
16. In March 2009, the Federal Reserve announced a *quantitative easing* program designed to lower intermediate and longer-term interest rates. What effect should this have on the dollar/euro exchange rate?

Applied Problems

All applied problems are available in MyEconLab *at* www.myeconlab.com.

17. A German sports car is selling for 70,000 euros. What is the dollar price in the United States for the German car if the exchange rate is 0.90 euro per dollar?
18. If the Canadian dollar to U.S. dollar exchange rate is 1.28 and the British pound to U.S. dollar exchange rate is 0.62, what must be the Canadian dollar to British pound exchange rate?
19. The New Zealand dollar to U.S. dollar exchange rate is 1.36, and the British pound to U.S. dollar exchange rate is 0.62. If you find that the British pound to New Zealand dollar were trading at 0.49, what would you do to earn a riskless profit?

20. In 1999, the euro was trading at $0.90 per euro. If the euro is now trading at $1.16 per euro, what is the percentage change in the euro's value? Is this an appreciation or depreciation?

21. The Mexican peso is trading at 10 pesos per dollar. If the expected U.S. inflation rate is 2% while the expected Mexican inflation rate is 23% over the next year, given PPP, what is the expected exchange rate in one year?

22. If the price level recently increased by 20% in England while falling by 5% in the United States, how much must the exchange rate change if PPP holds? Assume that the current exchange rate is 0.55 pound per dollar.

For Problems 23–25, use a graph of the foreign exchange market for dollars to illustrate the effects in each problem.

23. If expected inflation drops in Europe, so that interest rates fall there, what will happen to the exchange rate for the U.S. dollar?

24. If the European central bank decides to pursue a contractionary monetary policy to fight inflation, what will happen to the value of the U.S. dollar?

25. If a strike takes place in France, making it harder to buy French goods, what will happen to the value of the U.S. dollar?

Web Exercises

1. The Federal Reserve maintains a website that lists the exchange rates between the U.S. dollar and many other currencies. Go to www.newyorkfed.org/markets/foreignex.html. Go to the historical data from 1999 and later and find the euro.
   a. What has been the percentage change in the euro–dollar exchange rate between the euro's introduction and now?
   b. What has been the annual percentage change in the euro–dollar exchange rate for each year since the euro's introduction?

2. International travelers and business people frequently need to accurately convert from one currency to another. It is often easy to find the rate needed to convert the U.S. dollar into another currency. It can be more difficult to find exchange rates between two non-U.S. currencies. Go to www.xe.com/ucc/full/. This site lets you convert from any currency into any other currency. How many Lithuanian litas can you currently buy with one Chilean peso?

Web References

www.newyorkfed.org/markets/foreignex.html

Get detailed information about the foreign exchange market in the United States.

http://quotes.ino.com/chart/

Go to this website and click on Exchange List to get market rates and time charts for the exchange rate of the U.S. dollar to major world currencies.

http://www.oecd.org/department/0,3355,en_2649_34357_1_1_1_1_1,00.html

The purchasing power parities home page includes the PPP program overview, statistics, research, publications, and OECD meetings on PPP.

www.federalreserve.gov/releases/

The Federal Reserve reports current and historical exchange rates for many countries.

http://fx.sauder.ubc.ca

The Pacific Exchange Rate Service at the University of British Columbia's Sauder School of Business provides information on how market conditions are affecting exchange rates and allows easy plotting of exchange rate data.

APPENDIX TO CHAPTER 20

The Interest Parity Condition

All the results in the text can be derived with a concept that is widely used in international finance. The *interest parity condition* shows the relationship between domestic interest rates, foreign interest rates, and the expected appreciation of the domestic currency. To derive this condition, we examine how expected returns on domestic and foreign assets are compared.

COMPARING EXPECTED RETURNS ON DOMESTIC AND FOREIGN ASSETS

As in the chapter, we treat the United States as the home country, so domestic assets are denominated in dollars. For simplicity, we use euros to stand for any foreign country's currency, so foreign assets are denominated in euros. To illustrate further, suppose that dollar assets pay an interest rate of i^D and do not have any possible capital gains, so that they have an expected return payable in dollars of i^D. Similarly, foreign assets have an interest rate of i^F and an expected return payable in the foreign currency, euros, of i^F. To compare the expected returns on dollar assets and foreign assets, investors must convert the returns into the currency unit they use.

First, let us examine how François the Foreigner compares the returns on dollar assets and foreign assets denominated in his currency, the euro. When he considers the expected return on dollar assets in terms of euros, he recognizes that it does not equal i^D; instead, the expected return must be adjusted for any expected appreciation or depreciation of the dollar. If François expects the dollar to appreciate by 3%, for example, the expected return on dollar assets in terms of euros would be 3% higher than i^D because the dollar is expected to become worth 3% more in terms of euros. Thus, if the interest rate on dollar assets is 4%, with an expected 3% appreciation of the dollar, the expected return on dollar assets in terms of euros is 7%: the 4% interest rate plus the 3% expected appreciation of the dollar. Conversely, if the dollar were expected to depreciate by 3% over the year, the expected return on dollar assets in terms of euros would be only 1%: the 4% interest rate minus the 3% expected depreciation of the dollar.

Writing the current exchange rate (the spot exchange rate) as E_t and the expected exchange rate for the next period as E^e_{t+1}, the expected rate of appreciation of the dollar is $(E^e_{t+1} - E_t)/E_t$. Our reasoning indicates that the expected return on dollar assets R^D in terms of foreign currency can be written as the sum of the interest rate on dollar assets plus the expected appreciation of the dollar.[1]

$$R^D \text{ in terms of euros} = i^D + \frac{E^e_{t+1} - E_t}{E_t}$$

However, François's expected return on foreign assets R^F in terms of euros is just i^F. Thus, in terms of euros, the relative expected return on dollar assets (that is, the difference between the expected return on dollar assets and euro assets) is calculated by subtracting i^F from the expression above to yield

$$\text{Relative } R^D = i^D - i^F + \frac{E^e_{t+1} - E_t}{E_t} \tag{1}$$

As the relative expected return on dollar assets increases, foreigners will want to hold more dollar assets and fewer foreign assets.

Next let us look at the decision to hold dollar assets versus euro assets from Al the American's point of view. Following the same reasoning we used to evaluate the decision for François, we know that the expected return on foreign assets R^F in terms of dollars is the interest rate on foreign assets i^F plus the expected appreciation of the foreign currency, equal to minus the expected appreciation of the dollar, $(E^e_{t+1} - E_t)/E_t$:

$$R^F \text{ in terms of dollars} = i^F - \frac{E^e_{t+1} - E_t}{E_t}$$

If the interest rate on euro assets is 5%, for example, and the dollar is expected to appreciate by 3%, then the expected return on euro assets in terms of dollars is 2%. Al earns the 5% interest rate, but he expects to lose 3% because he expects the euro to be worth 3% less in terms of dollars as a result of the dollar's appreciation.

Al's expected return on the dollar assets R^D in terms of dollars is just i^D. Hence, in terms of dollars, the relative expected return on dollar assets is calculated by subtracting the expression just given from i^D to obtain

$$\text{Relative } R^D = i^D - \left(i^F - \frac{E^e_{t+1} - E_t}{E_t}\right) = i^D - i^F + \frac{E^e_{t+1} - E_t}{E_t}$$

This equation is the same as Equation 1 describing François's relative expected return on dollar assets (calculated in terms of euros). The key point here is that the relative expected return on dollar assets is the same—whether it is calculated by François

[1]This expression is actually an approximation of the expected return in terms of euros, which can be more precisely calculated by thinking how a foreigner invests in dollar assets. Suppose that François decides to put one euro into dollar assets. First he buys $1/E_t$ of U.S. dollar assets (recall that E_t, the exchange rate between dollar and euro assets, is quoted in euros per dollar), and at the end of the period he is paid $(1 + i^D)(1/E_t)$ in dollars. To convert this amount into the number of euros he expects to receive at the end of the period, he multiplies this quantity by E^e_{t+1}. François's expected return on his initial investment of one euro can thus be written as $(1 + i^D)(E^e_{t+1}/E_t)$ minus his initial investment of one euro:

$$(1 + i^D)\left(\frac{E^e_{t+1}}{E_t}\right) - 1$$

This expression can be rewritten as

$$i^D\left(\frac{E^e_{t+1}}{E_t}\right) + \frac{E^e_{t+1} - E_t}{E_t}$$

which is approximately equal to the expression in the text because, E^e_{t+1}/E_t is typically close to 1. To see this, consider the example in the text in which $i^D = 0.04$; $(E^e_{t+1} - E_t)/E_t = 0.03$, so $E^e_{t+1}/E_t = 1.03$. Then François's expected return on dollar assets is $(0.04 \times 1.03) + 0.03 = 0.0712 = 7.12\%$, rather than the 7% reported in the text.

in terms of euros or by Al in terms of dollars. Thus, as the relative expected return on dollar assets increases, both foreigners and domestic residents respond in exactly the same way—both will want to hold more dollar assets and fewer foreign assets.

INTEREST PARITY CONDITION

We currently live in a world in which **capital mobility** exists: Foreigners can easily purchase American assets, and Americans can easily purchase foreign assets. If few impediments to capital mobility are present and we are looking at assets that have similar risk and liquidity—say, foreign and American bank deposits—then it is reasonable to assume that the assets are perfect substitutes (that is, equally desirable). When capital is mobile and when assets are perfect substitutes, if the expected return on dollar assets is above that on foreign assets, both foreigners and Americans will want to hold only dollar assets and will be unwilling to hold foreign assets. Conversely, if the expected return on foreign assets is higher than on dollar assets, both foreigners and Americans will not want to hold any dollar assets and will want to hold only foreign assets. For existing supplies of both dollar assets and foreign assets to be held, it must therefore be true that no difference exists in their expected returns; that is, the relative expected return in Equation 1 must equal zero. This condition can be rewritten as

$$i^D = i^F - \frac{E^e_{t+1} - E_t}{E_t} \qquad (2)$$

This equation, which is called the **interest parity condition**, states that the domestic interest rate equals the foreign interest rate minus the expected appreciation of the domestic currency. Equivalently, this condition can be stated in a more intuitive way: The domestic interest rate equals the foreign interest rate plus the expected appreciation of the foreign currency. If the domestic interest rate is higher than the foreign interest rate, there is a positive expected appreciation of the foreign currency, which compensates for the lower foreign interest rate. A domestic interest rate of 5% versus a foreign interest rate of 3% means that the expected appreciation of the foreign currency must be 2% (or, equivalently, that the expected depreciation of the dollar must be 2%).

The interest parity condition can be looked at in several ways. First, recognize that interest parity means simply that the expected returns are the same on both dollar assets and foreign assets. To see this, note that the left side of the interest parity condition (Equation 2) is the expected return on dollar assets, while the right side is the expected return on foreign assets, both calculated in terms of a single currency, the U.S. dollar. Given our assumption that domestic and foreign assets are perfect substitutes (equally desirable), the interest parity condition is an equilibrium condition for the foreign exchange market. Only when the exchange rate is such that expected returns on domestic and foreign assets are equal—that is, when interest parity holds—will investors be willing to hold both domestic and foreign assets.

With some algebraic manipulation, we can rewrite the interest parity condition in Equation 2 as

$$E_t = \frac{E^e_{t+1}}{i^F - i^D + 1}$$

This equation produces exactly the same results that we find in the supply and demand analysis in the text: If i^D rises, the denominator falls and so E_t rises. If i^F rises, the denominator rises and so E_t falls. If E^e_{t+1} rises, the numerator rises and so E_t rises.

21 The International Financial System

Preview

As the U.S. economy and the economies of the rest of the world grow more interdependent, a country's monetary policy can no longer be conducted without taking international considerations into account. In this chapter, we examine how international financial transactions and the structure of the international financial system affect monetary policy. We also examine the evolution of the international financial system during the past half century and consider where it may be heading in the future.

INTERVENTION IN THE FOREIGN EXCHANGE MARKET

In Chapter 20, we analyzed the foreign exchange market as if it were a completely free market that responds to all market pressures. Like many other markets, however, the foreign exchange market is not free of government intervention; central banks regularly engage in international financial transactions called **foreign exchange interventions** to influence exchange rates. In our current international environment, exchange rates fluctuate from day to day, but central banks attempt to influence their countries' exchange rates by buying and selling currencies. We can use the exchange rate analysis we developed in Chapter 20 to explain the impact of central bank intervention on the foreign exchange market.

Foreign Exchange Intervention and the Money Supply

The first step in understanding how central bank intervention in the foreign exchange market affects exchange rates is to see the impact on the monetary base from a central bank sale in the foreign exchange market of some of its holdings of assets denominated in a foreign currency (called **international reserves**). Suppose that the Fed decides to sell $1 billion of its foreign assets in exchange for $1 billion of U.S. currency. (This transaction is conducted at the foreign exchange desk at the Federal Reserve Bank of New York—see the Inside the Fed box.) The Fed's purchase of dollars has two effects. First, it reduces the Fed's holding of international reserves by $1 billion. Second, because the Fed's purchase of currency removes it from the hands of the public, currency in circulation falls by $1 billion. We can see this in the following T-account for the Federal Reserve:

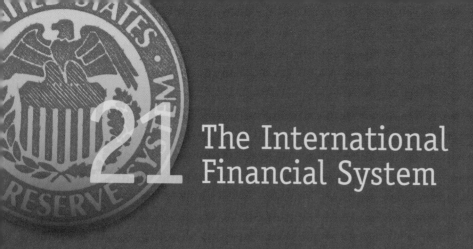

Inside the Fed — A Day at the Federal Reserve Bank of New York's Foreign Exchange Desk

Although the U.S. Treasury is primarily responsible for foreign exchange policy, decisions to intervene in the foreign exchange market are made jointly by the U.S. Treasury and the Federal Reserve's FOMC (Federal Open Market Committee). The actual conduct of foreign exchange intervention is the responsibility of the foreign exchange desk at the Federal Reserve Bank of New York, which is right next to the open market desk.

The manager of foreign exchange operations at the New York Fed supervises the traders and analysts, who follow developments in the foreign exchange market. Every morning at 7:30, a trader on staff who has arrived at the New York Fed in the predawn hours speaks on the telephone with counterparts at the U.S. Treasury and provides an update on overnight activity in overseas financial and foreign exchange markets. Later in the morning, at 9:30, the manager and his or her staff hold a conference call with senior staff at the Board of Governors of the Federal Reserve in Washington. In the afternoon, at 2:30, they have a second conference call, which is a joint briefing of officials at the board and the Treasury. Although by statute the Treasury has the lead role in setting foreign exchange policy, it strives to reach a consensus among all three parties—the Treasury, the Board of Governors, and the Federal Reserve Bank of New York. If they decide that a foreign exchange intervention is necessary that day—an unusual occurrence, as a year may go by without a U.S. foreign exchange intervention—the manager instructs his traders to carry out the agreed-on purchase or sale of foreign currencies. Because funds for exchange rate intervention are held separately by the Treasury (in its Exchange Stabilization Fund) and the Federal Reserve, the manager and his or her staff are not trading the funds of the Federal Reserve Bank of New York; rather, they act as an agent for the Treasury and the FOMC in conducting these transactions.

As part of their duties, before every FOMC meeting, the staff help prepare a lengthy document full of data for the FOMC members, other Reserve Bank presidents, and Treasury officials. It describes developments in the domestic and foreign markets over the previous five or six weeks, a task that keeps them especially busy right before the FOMC meeting.

Federal Reserve System

Assets		Liabilities	
Foreign assets (international reserves)	−\$1 billion	Currency in circulation	−\$1 billion

Because the monetary base is made up of currency in circulation plus reserves, this decline in currency implies that the monetary base has fallen by \$1 billion.

If, as is more likely, the persons buying the foreign assets pay for them by checks written on accounts at domestic banks rather than with currency, then the Fed deducts the \$1 billion from the reserve deposits it holds for these banks. The result is that deposits with the Fed (reserves) decline by \$1 billion, as shown in the following T-account:

Federal Reserve System			
Assets		**Liabilities**	
Foreign assets (international reserves)	−\$1 billion	Deposits with the Fed (reserves)	−\$1 billion

In this case, the outcome of the Fed sale of foreign assets and the purchase of dollar deposits is a \$1 billion decline in reserves and, as before, a \$1 billion decline in the monetary base because reserves are also a component of the monetary base.

We now see that the outcome for the monetary base is exactly the same when a central bank sells foreign assets to purchase domestic bank deposits or domestic currency. This is why when we say that a central bank has purchased its domestic currency, we do not have to distinguish whether it actually purchased currency or bank deposits denominated in the domestic currency. We have thus reached an important conclusion: ***A central bank's purchase of domestic currency and corresponding sale of foreign assets in the foreign exchange market leads to an equal decline in its international reserves and the monetary base.***

We could have reached the same conclusion by a more direct route. A central bank sale of a foreign asset is no different from an open market sale of a government bond. We learned in our exploration of the money supply process that an open market sale leads to an equal decline in the monetary base; therefore, a sale of foreign assets also leads to an equal decline in the monetary base. By similar reasoning, a central bank purchase of foreign assets paid for by selling domestic currency, like an open market purchase, leads to an equal rise in the monetary base. Thus we reach the following conclusion: ***A central bank's sale of domestic currency to purchase foreign assets in the foreign exchange market results in an equal rise in its international reserves and the monetary base.***

The intervention we have just described, in which a central bank allows the purchase or sale of domestic currency to have an effect on the monetary base, is called an **unsterilized foreign exchange intervention**. But what if the central bank does not want the purchase or sale of domestic currency to affect the monetary base? All it has to do is to counter the effect of the foreign exchange intervention by conducting an offsetting open market operation in the government bond market. For example, in the case of a \$1 billion purchase of dollars by the Fed and a corresponding \$1 billion sale of foreign assets, which, as we have seen, would decrease the monetary base by \$1 billion, the Fed can conduct an open market purchase of \$1 billion of government bonds, which would increase the monetary base by \$1 billion. The resulting T-account for the foreign exchange intervention and the offsetting open market operation leaves the monetary base unchanged:

Federal Reserve System			
Assets		**Liabilities**	
Foreign assets (international reserves)	−\$1 billion	Monetary base	0
Government bonds	+\$1 billion		

FIGURE 1
Effect of an Unsterilized Purchase of Dollars and Sale of Foreign Assets
A purchase of dollars and the consequent open market sale of foreign assets decreases the monetary base and the money supply. The resulting fall in the money supply leads to a rise in domestic interest rates, which raises the relative expected return on dollar assets. The demand curve shifts to the right from D_1 to D_2, and the equilibrium exchange rate rises from E_1 to E_2.

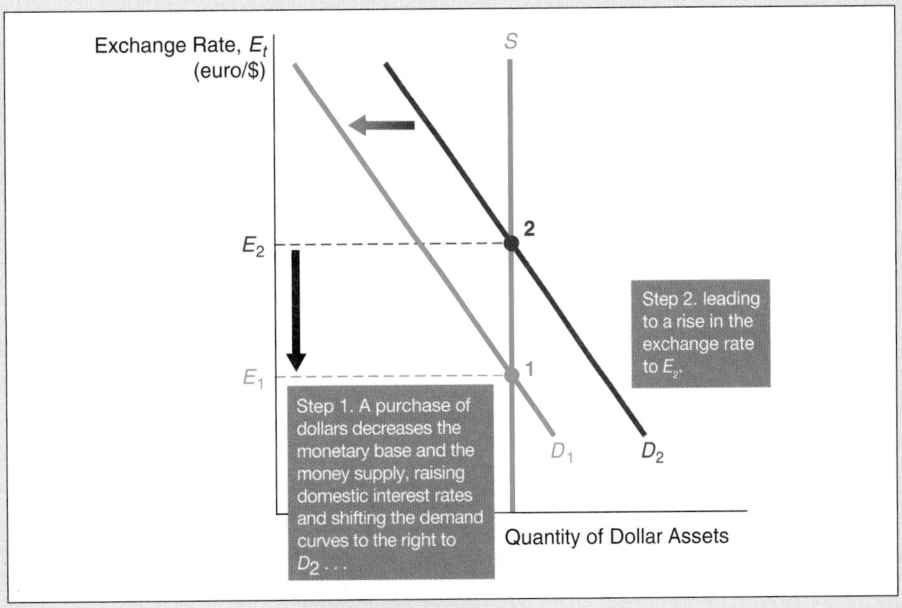
Exchange Rate, E_t (euro/$)
S
E_2
E_1
2
1
Step 2. leading to a rise in the exchange rate to E_2.
Step 1. A purchase of dollars decreases the monetary base and the money supply, raising domestic interest rates and shifting the demand curves to the right to D_2 . . .
D_1
D_2
Quantity of Dollar Assets

A foreign exchange intervention with an offsetting open market operation that leaves the monetary base unchanged is called a **sterilized foreign exchange intervention**.

Now that we understand that there are two types of foreign exchange interventions—unsterilized and sterilized—let's look at how each affects the exchange rate.

Unsterilized Intervention

Intuition might lead you to suspect that if a central bank wants to raise the value of the domestic currency, it should buy its currency in the foreign exchange market and sell foreign assets. Indeed, this intuition is correct for the case of an unsterilized intervention.

Recall that in an unsterilized intervention, if the Federal Reserve decides to buy dollars and therefore sells foreign assets in exchange for dollar assets, this works just like an open market sale of bonds to decrease the monetary base. Hence the purchase of dollars leads to a decrease in the money supply, which raises the domestic interest rate and increases the relative expected return on dollar assets. The result is that the demand curve shifts to the right from D_1 to D_2 in Figure 1, and the exchange rate rises to E_2.[1]

Our analysis leads us to the following conclusion about unsterilized interventions in the foreign exchange market: ***An unsterilized intervention in which domestic currency is bought and foreign assets are sold leads to a fall in international reserves, a fall in the money supply, and an appreciation of the domestic currency.***

[1]An unsterilized intervention in which the Fed sells dollars increases the amount of dollar assets slightly because it leads to an increase in the monetary base while leaving the amount of government bonds in the hands of the public unchanged. The curve depicting the supply of dollar assets would thus shift to the right slightly, which also works toward lowering the exchange rate, yielding the same conclusion derived from Figure 1. Because the resulting increase in the monetary base would be only a minuscule fraction of the total amount of dollar assets outstanding, the supply curve would shift by an imperceptible amount. This is why Figure 1 is drawn with the supply curve unchanged.

The reverse result is found for an unsterilized intervention in which domestic currency is sold and foreign assets are purchased. The sale of domestic currency and purchase of foreign assets (increasing international reserves) works like an open market purchase to increase the monetary base and the money supply. The increase in the money supply lowers the interest rate on dollar assets. The resulting decrease in the relative expected return on dollar assets means that people will buy less dollar assets, so the demand curve shifts to the left and the exchange rate falls. ***An unsterilized intervention in which domestic currency is sold and foreign assets are purchased leads to a rise in international reserves, a rise in the money supply, and a depreciation of the domestic currency.***

Sterilized Intervention

The key point to remember about a sterilized intervention is that the central bank engages in offsetting open market operations, so that there is no impact on the monetary base and the money supply. In the context of the model of exchange rate determination we have developed here, it is straightforward to show that a sterilized intervention has almost *no effect* on the exchange rate. A sterilized intervention leaves the money supply unchanged and thus has no direct way of affecting interest rates.[2] Because the relative expected return on dollar assets is unaffected, the demand curve would remain at D_1 in Figure 1, and the exchange rate would remain unchanged at E_1.

At first it might seem puzzling that a central bank purchase or sale of domestic currency that is sterilized does not lead to a change in the exchange rate. A central bank–sterilized purchase of domestic currency cannot raise the exchange rate, because with no effect on the domestic money supply or interest rates, any resulting rise in the exchange rate would mean that an excess supply of dollar assets would arise. With more people willing to sell dollar assets than to buy them, the exchange rate would have to fall back to its initial equilibrium level, where the demand and supply curves intersect.

BALANCE OF PAYMENTS

Because international financial transactions, such as foreign exchange interventions, have considerable effects on monetary policy, it is worth knowing how these transactions are measured. The **balance of payments** is a bookkeeping system for recording all receipts and payments (private sector and government) that have a direct bearing on the movement of funds between a nation and foreign countries. Here we examine the key items in the balance of payments that you often hear about in the media.

[2]A sterilized intervention changes the amount of foreign securities relative to domestic securities in the hands of the public, called a portfolio balance effect. Through this effect, the central bank might be able to Influence the interest differential between domestic and foreign assets, which in turn affects the relative expected return of domestic assets. Empirical evidence has not revealed this portfolio balance effect to be significant. However, a sterilized intervention could indicate what central banks want to happen to the future exchange rate and so might provide a signal about the course of future monetary policy. In this way a sterilized intervention could lead to shifts in the demand curve for domestic assets and ultimately affect the exchange rate. However, the future change in monetary policy—not the sterilized intervention—is the source of the exchange rate effect. For a further discussion of the signaling and portfolio balance effects and the possible differential effects of sterilized versus unsterilized intervention, see Paul Krugman, Maurice Obstfeld, and Mark Melitz, *International Economics: Theory and Policy*, 9th ed. (Boston: Addison-Wesley, 2012).

Global Why the Large U.S. Current Account Deficit Worries Economists

The massive U.S. current account deficit in recent years, which in 2010 was 11% of GDP, worries economists for several reasons. First, it indicates that at current exchange rate values, foreigners' demand for U.S. exports is far less than Americans' demand for imports. As we saw in the previous chapter, low demand for U.S. exports and high U.S. demand for imports may lead to a future decline in the value of the U.S. dollar. Some economists estimate that this decline could be very large, with the U.S. dollar depreciating by as much as 50%.

Second, the current account deficit means that foreigners' claims on U.S. assets are growing, and these claims will have to be paid back at some point. Americans are mortgaging their future to foreigners; when the bill comes due, Americans will be poorer. Furthermore, if Americans have a greater preference for dollar assets than foreigners do, the movement of American wealth to foreigners could decrease the demand for dollar assets over time, also causing the dollar to depreciate.

The hope is that the eventual decline in the dollar resulting from the large U.S. current account deficit will be a gradual one, occurring over a period of several years. If the decline is precipitous, however, it could potentially disrupt financial markets and hurt the U.S. economy.

The **current account** shows international transactions that involve currently produced goods and services. The difference between merchandise exports and imports, the net receipts from trade, is called the **trade balance**. When merchandise imports are greater than exports (by $118.7 billion in 2010), we have a trade deficit; if exports are greater than imports, we have a trade surplus.

Additional items included in the current account are the net receipts (cash flows received from abroad minus cash flows sent abroad) from three categories: investment income, service transactions, and unilateral transfers (gifts, pensions, and foreign aid). In 2010, for example, net investment income was $170.9 billion for the United States because Americans received more investment income from abroad than they paid out. Americans bought less in services from foreigners than foreigners bought from Americans, so net services generated $142.1 billion in receipts. Because Americans made more unilateral transfers to foreign countries (especially foreign aid) than foreigners made to the United States, net unilateral transfers were −$33.4 billion. The sum of the previous three items plus the trade balance is the current account balance, which in 2010 showed a deficit of $160.9 billion (−$118.7 + $170.9 + $142.1 − $33.4 = −$160.9).

Another important item in the balance of payments is the **capital account**, the net receipts from capital transactions (e.g., purchases of stocks and bonds, bank loans, etc.). In 2010 the capital account was close to zero, indicating that capital flowing out of the United States and capital coming in were balanced.[3] The sum of the current account and the capital account equals the **official reserve transactions balance** (net change in government international reserves), which was −$160.9 billion in 2010 (−$160.9 + 0 = −$160.9 billion). When economists refer to a surplus or deficit in the balance of payments, they actually mean a surplus or deficit in the official reserve transactions balance.

[3]The capital account balance number reported here includes a statistical discrepancy item that represents errors due to unrecorded transactions involving smuggling and other capital flows (−$39 billion in 2004). Many experts believe that the statistical discrepancy item, which keeps the balance of payments in balance, is primarily the result of large hidden capital flows, and this is why it is included in the capital account balance.

Because the balance of payments must balance, the official reserve transactions balance, which equals the current account plus the capital account, tells us the net amount of international reserves that must move between governments (as represented by their central banks) to finance international transactions; that is,

$$\text{Current account} + \text{capital account} = \text{net change in government international reserves}$$

This equation shows us why the current account receives so much attention from economists and the media. The current account balance tells us whether the United States (private sector and government combined) is increasing or decreasing its claims on foreign wealth. A surplus indicates that America is increasing its claims on foreign wealth and thus is increasing its holdings of foreign assets (both good things for Americans); a deficit (as in 2010) indicates that the United States is reducing its holdings of foreign assets and foreign countries are increasing their claims on the United States.[4] The large U.S. current account deficit in recent years, which in 2010 was over $150 billion, has raised serious concerns that these large deficits may have negative consequences for the U.S. economy (see the Global box, "Why the Large U.S. Current Account Deficit Worries Economists").

EXCHANGE RATE REGIMES IN THE INTERNATIONAL FINANCIAL SYSTEM

Exchange rate regimes in the international financial system are classified into two basic types: fixed and floating. In a **fixed exchange rate regime**, the value of a currency is pegged relative to the value of another currency (called the **anchor currency**) so that the exchange rate is fixed in terms of the anchor currency. In a **floating exchange rate regime**, the value of a currency is allowed to fluctuate against all other currencies. When countries intervene in foreign exchange markets in an attempt to influence their exchange rates by buying and selling foreign assets, the regime is referred to as a **managed float regime** (or a dirty float).

In examining past exchange rate regimes, we start with the gold standard of the late nineteenth and early twentieth centuries.

Gold Standard

Before World War I, the world economy operated under the **gold standard**, a fixed exchange rate regime in which the currency of most countries was convertible directly into gold at fixed rates, so exchange rates between currencies were also fixed. American dollar bills, for example, could be turned in to the U.S. Treasury and exchanged for approximately $\frac{1}{20}$ ounce of gold. Likewise, the British Treasury would exchange $\frac{1}{4}$ ounce of gold for £1 sterling. Because an American could convert $20 into 1 ounce of gold, which could be used to buy £4, the exchange rate between the pound and the

[4]The current account balance can also be viewed as showing the amount by which total saving exceeds private sector and government investment in the United States. Total U.S. saving equals the increase in total wealth held by the U.S. private sector and government. Total investment equals the increase in the U.S. capital stock (wealth physically in the United States). The difference between them is the increase in U.S. claims on foreign wealth.

dollar was effectively fixed at $5 to the pound. The fixed exchange rates under the gold standard had the important advantage of encouraging world trade by eliminating the uncertainty that occurs when exchange rates fluctuate.

As long as countries abided by the rules under the gold standard and kept their currencies backed by and convertible into gold, exchange rates remained fixed. However, adherence to the gold standard meant that a country had no control over its monetary policy, because its money supply was determined by gold flows between countries. Furthermore, monetary policy throughout the world was greatly influenced by the production of gold and gold discoveries. When gold production was low in the 1870s and 1880s, the money supply throughout the world grew slowly and did not keep pace with the growth of the world economy. The result was deflation (falling price levels). Gold discoveries in Alaska and South Africa in the 1890s greatly expanded gold production, causing money supplies to increase rapidly and price levels to rise (inflation) until World War I.

The Bretton Woods System

After World War II, the victors set up a fixed exchange rate system that became known as the **Bretton Woods system**, after the New Hampshire town in which the agreement was negotiated in 1944. The Bretton Woods system remained in effect until 1971.

The Bretton Woods agreement created the **International Monetary Fund (IMF)**, headquartered in Washington, DC, which had 30 original member countries in 1945 and currently has over 180. The IMF was given the task of promoting the growth of world trade by setting rules for the maintenance of fixed exchange rates and by making loans to countries that were experiencing balance-of-payments difficulties. As part of its role of monitoring the compliance of member countries with its rules, the IMF also took on the job of collecting and standardizing international economic data.

The Bretton Woods agreement also set up the International Bank for Reconstruction and Development, commonly referred to as the **World Bank**. Headquartered in Washington, DC, it provides long-term loans to help developing countries build dams, roads, and other physical capital that would contribute to their economic development. The funds for these loans are obtained primarily by issuing World Bank bonds, which are sold in the capital markets of the developed countries. In addition, the General Agreement on Tariffs and Trade (GATT), headquartered in Geneva, Switzerland, was set up to monitor rules for the conduct of trade between countries (tariffs and quotas). The GATT has since evolved into the **World Trade Organization (WTO)**.

Because the United States emerged from World War II as the world's largest economic power, with over half of the world's manufacturing capacity and the greater part of the world's gold, the Bretton Woods system of fixed exchange rates was based on the convertibility of U.S. dollars into gold (for foreign governments and central banks only) at $35 per ounce. The fixed exchange rates were to be maintained by intervention in the foreign exchange market by central banks in countries besides the United States that bought and sold dollar assets, which they held as international reserves. The U.S. dollar, which was used by other countries to denominate the assets that they held as international reserves, was called the **reserve currency**. Thus an important feature of the Bretton Woods system was the establishment of the United States as the reserve currency country.

The Bretton Woods system was abandoned in 1971, but the fixed exchange rate was only abandoned in 1973. From 1979 to 1990, however, the European Union instituted among its members its own fixed exchange rate system, the European Monetary

Global The Euro's Challenge to the Dollar

With the creation of the European Monetary System and the euro in 1999, the U.S. dollar is facing a challenge to its position as the key reserve currency in international financial transactions. Adoption of the euro increases integration of Europe's financial markets, which could help them rival those in the United States. The resulting increase in the use of euros in financial markets will make it more likely that international transactions are carried out in the euro. The economic clout of the European Union rivals that of the United States: Both have a similar share of world GDP (around 20%) and world exports (around 15%). If the European Central Bank can make sure that inflation remains low so that the euro becomes a sound currency, this should bode well for the euro.

However, for the euro to eat into the dollar's position as a reserve currency, the European Union must function as a cohesive political entity that can exert its influence on the world stage. There are serious doubts on this score, however, particularly with the "no" votes on the European constitution by France and the Netherlands in 2005 and the recent fiscal problems in Greece and elsewhere in the European Union.

Most analysts think it will be a long time before the euro beats out the dollar in international financial transactions.

System (EMS). In the *exchange rate mechanism* (ERM) in this system, the exchange rate between any pair of currencies of the participating countries was not supposed to fluctuate outside narrow limits, called the "snake." In practice, all of the countries in the EMS pegged their currencies to the German mark.

Even after the breakup of the Bretton Woods system, the U.S. dollar has kept its position as the reserve currency in which most international financial transactions are conducted. However, with the creation of the euro in 1999, the supremacy of the U.S. dollar may be subject to a serious challenge (see the Global box).

How a Fixed Exchange Rate Regime Works

Figure 2 shows how a fixed exchange rate regime works in practice by using the supply and demand analysis of the foreign exchange market we learned in the previous chapter. Panel (a) describes a situation in which the domestic currency is fixed relative to an anchor currency at E_{par}, while the demand curve has shifted left to D_1, perhaps because foreign interest rates have risen, thereby lowering the relative expected return of domestic assets. At E_{par}, the exchange rate is now *overvalued:* The demand curve D_1 intersects the supply curve at an exchange rate E_1, which is lower than the fixed (par) value of the exchange rate E_{par}. To keep the exchange rate at E_{par}, the central bank must intervene in the foreign exchange market to purchase domestic currency by selling foreign assets. This action, like an open market sale, means that both the monetary base and the money supply decline, driving up the interest rate on domestic assets, i^D.[5] This increase in the domestic interest rate raises the relative expected return on domestic assets, shifting the demand curve to the right. The central bank will continue purchasing

[5]Because the exchange rate will continue to be fixed at E_{par}, the expected future exchange rate remains unchanged and so does not need to be addressed in the analysis.

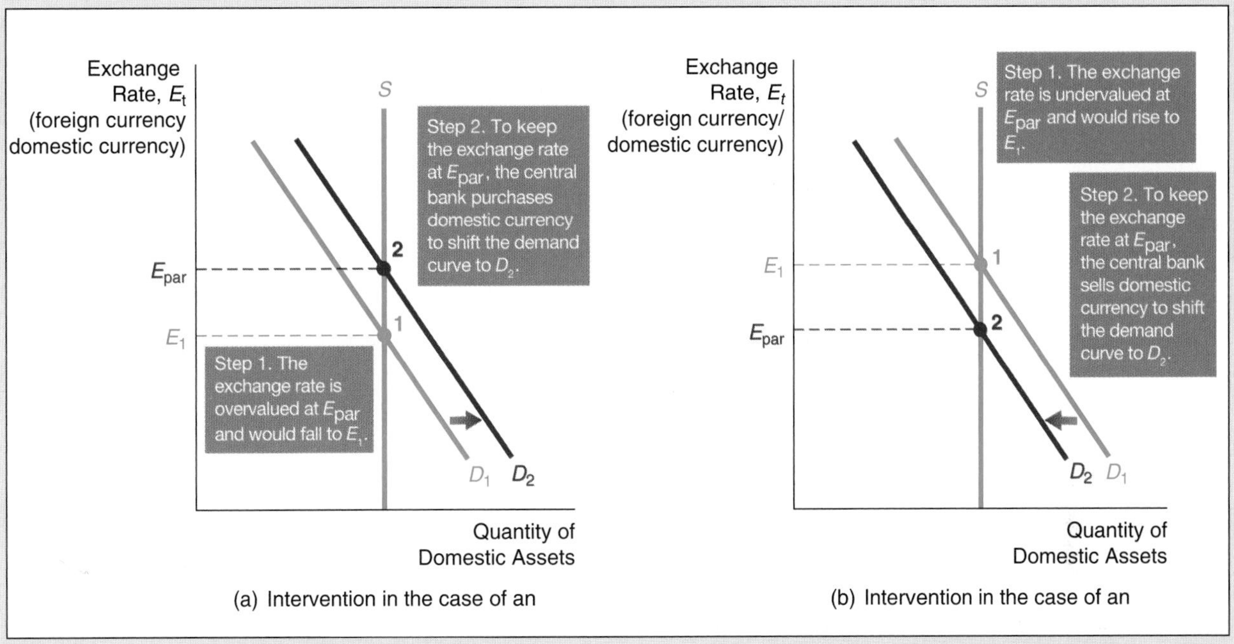

FIGURE 2 Intervention in the Foreign Exchange Market Under a Fixed Exchange Rate Regime
In panel (a), the exchange rate at E_{par} is overvalued. To keep the exchange rate at E_{par} (point 2), the central bank must purchase domestic currency to shift the demand curve to D_2. In panel (b), the exchange rate at E_{par} is undervalued, so the central bank must sell domestic currency to shift the demand curve to D_2 and keep the exchange rate at E_{par} (point 2).

domestic currency until the demand curve reaches D_2 and the equilibrium exchange rate is at E_{par} at point 2 in panel (a).

We have thus come to the conclusion that ***when the domestic currency is overvalued, the central bank must purchase domestic currency to keep the exchange rate fixed, but as a result it loses international reserves.***

Panel (b) in Figure 2 describes the situation in which the demand curve has shifted to the right to D_1 because the relative expected return on domestic assets has risen and hence the exchange rate at E_{par} is undervalued: The initial demand curve D_1 intersects the supply curve at exchange rate E_1, which is above E_{par}. In this situation, the central bank must sell domestic currency and purchase foreign assets. This action works like an open market purchase to increase the money supply and lower the interest rate on domestic assets i^D. The central bank keeps selling domestic currency and lowering i^D until the demand curve shifts all the way to D_2, where the equilibrium exchange rate is at E_{par}—point 2 in panel (b). Our analysis thus leads us to the following result: ***When the domestic currency is undervalued, the central bank must sell domestic currency to keep the exchange rate fixed, but as a result, it gains international reserves.***

Devaluation and Revaluation As we have seen, if a country's currency is overvalued, its central bank's attempts to keep the currency from depreciating will result in a loss of international reserves. If the country's central bank eventually runs out of international reserves, it cannot keep its currency from depreciating, and a **devaluation** must occur, in which the par exchange rate is reset at a lower level.

If, by contrast, a country's currency is undervalued, its central bank's intervention to keep the currency from appreciating leads to a gain of international reserves. As we will see shortly, the central bank might not want to acquire these international reserves, and so it might want to reset the par value of its exchange rate at a higher level (a **revaluation**).

Perfect Capital Mobility If perfect capital mobility exists—that is, if there are no barriers to domestic residents purchasing foreign assets or foreigners purchasing domestic assets—then a sterilized exchange rate intervention cannot keep the exchange rate at E_{par} because, as we saw earlier in the chapter, the relative expected return of domestic assets is unaffected. For example, if the exchange rate is overvalued, a sterilized purchase of domestic currency will leave the relative expected return and the demand curve unchanged, so pressure for a depreciation of the domestic currency is not removed. If the central bank keeps purchasing its domestic currency but continues to sterilize, it will just keep losing international reserves until it finally runs out of them and is forced to let the value of the currency seek a lower level.

The Policy Trilemma One important implication of the foregoing analysis is that a country that ties its exchange rate to an anchor currency of a larger country loses control of its monetary policy. If the larger country pursues a more contractionary monetary policy and decreases its money supply, this would lead to lower expected inflation in the larger country, thus causing an appreciation of the larger country's currency and a depreciation of the smaller country's currency. The smaller country, having locked in its exchange rate to the anchor currency, will now find its currency overvalued and will therefore have to sell the anchor currency and buy its own to keep its currency from depreciating. The result of this foreign exchange intervention will then be a decline in the smaller country's international reserves, a contraction of its monetary base, and thus a decline in its money supply. Sterilization of this foreign exchange intervention is not an option because this would just lead to a continuing loss of international reserves until the smaller country was forced to devalue its currency. The smaller country no longer controls its monetary policy, because movements in its money supply are completely determined by movements in the larger country's money supply.

Our analysis therefore indicates that a country (or monetary union like the Eurozone) can't pursue the following three policies at the same time: (1) free capital mobility, (2) a fixed exchange rate, and (3) an independent monetary policy. Economists call this result the **policy trilemma** (or, more graphically, the **impossible trinity**). Figure 3 illustrates the policy trilemma. A country can choose only two of the three options, which are denoted by each side of the triangle. In option 1, a country (or monetary union) chooses to have capital mobility and an independent monetary policy, but not a fixed exchange rate. The Eurozone and the United States have made this choice. Hong Kong and Belize have chosen option 2, in which there is free capital mobility and the exchange rate is fixed, so the country does not have an independent monetary policy. Other countries, like China, have chosen option 3, in which they have a fixed exchange rate and pursue an independent monetary policy, but do not have free capital mobility because they have **capital controls**, restrictions on the free movement of capital across the borders.

The policy trilemma thus leaves countries with a difficult choice. Do they accept exchange rate volatility (option 1), give up an independent monetary policy (option 2), or restrict capital flows (option 3)?

FIGURE 3
The Policy Trilemma
A country (or monetary union) cannot pursue the following three policies at the same time: (1) free capital mobility, (2) a fixed exchange rate, and (3) an independent monetary policy. Instead, it must choose two of the three policies on each side of the triangle.

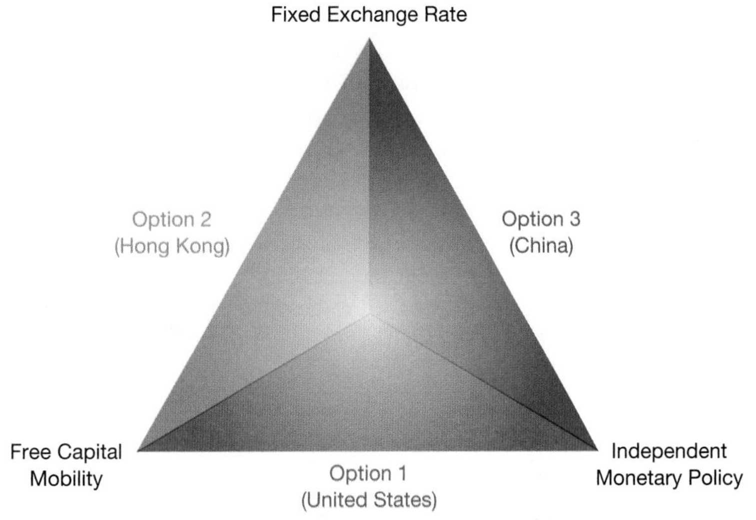

APPLICATION ◆ How Did China Accumulate over $3 Trillion of International Reserves?

By 2011, China had accumulated over $3 trillion of international reserves. How did the Chinese get their hands on this vast amount of foreign assets? After all, China is not yet a rich country.

The answer is that China pegged its exchange rate to the U.S. dollar at a fixed rate of 12 cents to the yuan (also called renminbi) in 1994. Because of China's rapidly growing productivity and an inflation rate that is lower than that in the United States, the long-run value of the yuan has increased, leading to a higher relative expected return for yuan assets and a rightward shift of the demand for yuan assets. As a result, the Chinese found themselves in the situation depicted in panel (b) of Figure 2, in which the yuan is undervalued. To keep the yuan from appreciating above E_{par} to E_1 in the figure, the Chinese central bank has been engaging in massive purchases of U.S. dollar assets. Today the Chinese government is one of the largest holders of U.S. government bonds in the world.

The pegging of the yuan to the U.S. dollar has created several problems for Chinese authorities. First, the Chinese now own a lot of U.S. assets, particularly U.S. Treasury securities, which have very low returns. Second, the undervaluation of the yuan has meant that Chinese goods are so cheap abroad that many countries have threatened to erect trade barriers against these goods if the Chinese government does not allow an upward revaluation of the yuan. Third, as we learned earlier in the chapter, the Chinese purchase of dollar assets has resulted in a substantial increase in the Chinese monetary base and money supply, which has the potential to produce high inflation in the future. Because the Chinese authorities have created substantial roadblocks to capital mobility, they have been able to sterilize most of their exchange rate interventions while maintaining the exchange rate peg. Nevertheless, they still worry about inflationary pressures. In July 2005, China finally made its peg somewhat more flexible by letting the value of the yuan rise 2.1% and subsequently allowed it to appreciate at a gradual pace. The central bank also indicated that it would no longer fix the yuan to the U.S. dollar, but would instead maintain its value relative to a basket of currencies. However, in 2008 during the global financial crisis, China reimposed the peg, but then dropped it in June 2010.

Why did the Chinese authorities maintain this exchange rate peg for so long, despite the problems? One answer is that they wanted to keep their export sector humming by keeping the prices of their export goods low. A second answer might be that they wanted to accumulate a large amount of international reserves as a "war chest" that could be sold to buy yuan in the event of a speculative attack against the currency at some future date. Given the pressure on the Chinese government to further revalue its currency from government officials in the United States and Europe, further adjustments in China's exchange rate policy in the future are likely. ◆

How the Bretton Woods System Worked Under the Bretton Woods system, exchange rates were supposed to change only when a country was experiencing a "fundamental disequilibrium"—that is, large persistent deficits or surpluses in its balance of payments. To maintain fixed exchange rates when countries had balance-of-payments deficits and were losing international reserves, the IMF would loan deficit countries international reserves contributed by other members. As a result of its power to dictate loan terms to borrowing countries, the IMF could encourage deficit countries to pursue contractionary monetary policies that would strengthen their currency or eliminate their balance-of-payments deficits. If the IMF loans were not sufficient to prevent depreciation of a currency, the country was allowed to devalue its currency by setting a new, lower exchange rate.

A notable weakness of the Bretton Woods system was that although deficit countries losing international reserves could be pressured into devaluing their currencies or pursuing contractionary policies, the IMF had no way to force surplus countries to revise their exchange rates upward or pursue more expansionary policies. Particularly troublesome in this regard was the fact that the reserve currency country, the United States, could not devalue its currency under the Bretton Woods system even if the dollar was overvalued. When the United States attempted to reduce domestic unemployment in the 1960s by pursuing an inflationary monetary policy, a fundamental disequilibrium of an overvalued dollar developed. Because surplus countries were not willing to revise their exchange rates upward, adjustment in the Bretton Woods system did not take place, and the system collapsed in 1971. Attempts to patch up the Bretton Woods system with the Smithsonian Agreement in December 1971 proved unsuccessful, and by 1973, America and its trading partners had agreed to allow exchange rates to float.

Managed Float

Although most exchange rates are currently allowed to change daily in response to market forces, central banks have not been willing to give up their option of intervening in the foreign exchange market. Preventing large changes in exchange rates makes it easier for firms and individuals purchasing or selling goods abroad to plan into the future.

Furthermore, countries with surpluses in their balance of payments frequently do not want to see their currencies appreciate, because it makes their goods more expensive abroad and foreign goods cheaper in their country. Because an appreciation might hurt sales for domestic businesses and increase unemployment, surplus countries have often sold their currency in the foreign exchange market and acquired international reserves.

Countries with balance-of-payments deficits do not want to see their currency lose value, because it makes foreign goods more expensive for domestic consumers and can stimulate inflation. To keep the value of the domestic currency high, deficit countries have often bought their own currency in the foreign exchange market and given up international reserves.

The current international financial system is a hybrid of a fixed and a flexible exchange rate system. Rates fluctuate in response to market forces but are not determined solely by them. Furthermore, many countries continue to keep the value of their currency fixed against other currencies, as was the case in the European Monetary System before the introduction of the euro (to be described shortly).

Another important feature of the current system is the continuing de-emphasis of gold in international financial transactions. Not only has the United States suspended convertibility of dollars into gold for foreign central banks, but since 1970 the IMF has been issuing a paper substitute for gold, called **special drawing rights (SDRs)**. Like gold in the Bretton Woods system, SDRs function as international reserves. Unlike gold, whose quantity is determined by gold discoveries and the rate of production, SDRs can be created by the IMF whenever it decides that a need arises for additional international reserves to promote world trade and economic growth.

The use of gold in international transactions was further de-emphasized by the IMF's elimination of the official gold price in 1975 and by the sale of gold by the U.S. Treasury and the IMF to private investors in an effort to demonetize it. Currently, the price of gold is determined in a free market. Investors who want to speculate in it are able to purchase and sell gold at will, as are jewelers and dentists who use gold in their businesses.

European Monetary System (EMS)

In March 1979, eight members of the European Economic Community (Germany, France, Italy, the Netherlands, Belgium, Luxembourg, Denmark, and Ireland) set up the European Monetary System (EMS), in which they agreed to fix their exchange rates vis-à-vis one another and to float jointly against the U.S. dollar. Spain joined the EMS in June 1989, the United Kingdom in October 1990, and Portugal in April 1992. The EMS created a new monetary unit, the *European currency unit* (ECU), whose value was tied to a basket of specified amounts of European currencies.

The exchange rate mechanism (ERM) of the European Monetary System worked as follows. The exchange rate between every pair of currencies of the participating countries was not allowed to fluctuate outside narrow limits around a fixed exchange rate. (The limits were typically $\pm$ 2.25% but were raised to $\pm$ 15% in August 1993.) When the exchange rate between two countries' currencies moved outside these limits, the central banks of both countries were supposed to intervene in the foreign exchange market. If, for example, the French franc depreciated below its lower limit against the German mark, the Bank of France was required to buy francs and sell marks, thereby giving up international reserves. Similarly, the German central bank was required to intervene to sell marks and buy francs and consequently increase its international reserves. The EMS thus required that intervention be symmetric when a currency fell outside the limits, with the central bank having the weak currency giving up international reserves and the one having the strong currency gaining them. Central bank intervention was also very common even when the exchange rate was within the limits, but in this case, if one central bank intervened, no others were required to intervene as well.

A serious shortcoming of fixed exchange rate systems, such as the Bretton Woods system or the European Monetary System, is that they can lead to foreign exchange crises involving a "speculative attack" on a currency—massive sales of a weak currency or purchases of a strong currency that cause a sharp change in the exchange rate. In the following application, we use our model of exchange rate determination to understand how the September 1992 exchange rate crisis that rocked the European Monetary System came about.

APPLICATION ◆ The Foreign Exchange Crisis of September 1992

In the aftermath of German reunification in October 1990, the German central bank, the Bundesbank, faced rising inflationary pressures, with inflation having accelerated from below 3% in 1990 to near 5% by 1992. To get monetary growth under control and to dampen inflation, the Bundesbank raised German interest rates to near double-digit levels. Figure 4 shows the consequences of these actions by the Bundesbank in the foreign exchange market for British pounds. Note that in the diagram, the pound is the domestic

FIGURE 4 Foreign Exchange Market for British Pounds in 1992

The realization by speculators that the United Kingdom would soon devalue the pound decreased the relative expected return on British pound assets, resulting in a leftward shift of the demand curve from D_2 to D_3. The result was the need for a much greater purchase of pounds by the British central bank to raise the interest rate so that the demand curve would shift back to D_1 and keep the exchange rate E_{par} at 2.778 German marks per pound.

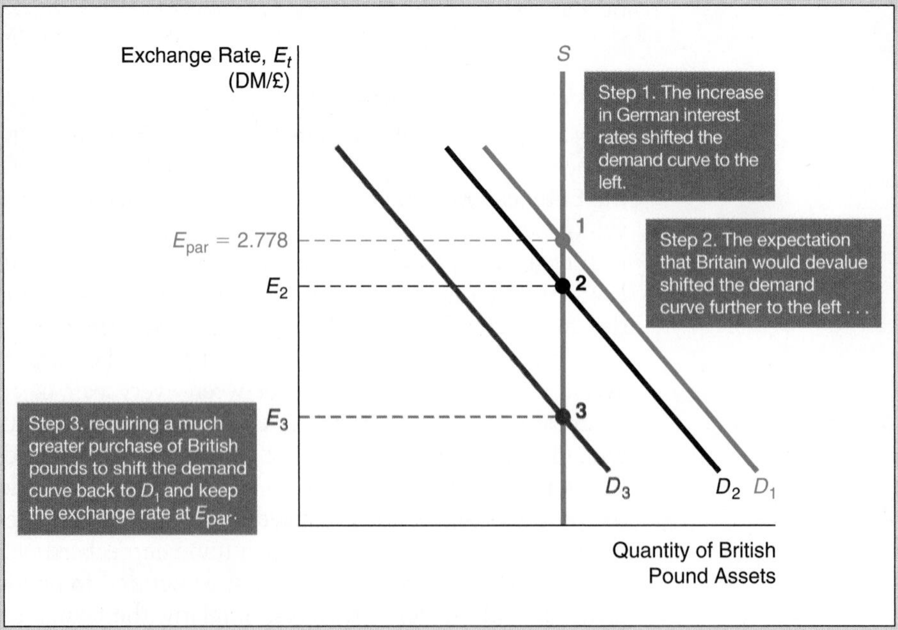
Exchange Rate, E_t (DM/£)
S
Step 1. The increase in German interest rates shifted the demand curve to the left.
E_{par} = 2.778
E_2
1
2
Step 2. The expectation that Britain would devalue shifted the demand curve further to the left . . .
E_3
3
Step 3. requiring a much greater purchase of British pounds to shift the demand curve back to D_1 and keep the exchange rate at E_{par}.
D_3
D_2 D_1
Quantity of British Pound Assets

currency and the German mark (deutsche mark, DM, Germany's currency before the advent of the euro in 1999) is the foreign currency.

The increase in German interest rates i^F lowered the relative expected return of British pound assets and shifted the demand curve to D_2 in Figure 4. The intersection of the supply and demand curves at point 2 was now below the lower exchange rate limit at that time (2.778 marks per pound, denoted E_{par}). To increase the value of the pound relative to the mark and to restore the mark/pound exchange rate to within the exchange rate mechanism limits, one of two things had to happen. The Bank of England would have to pursue a contractionary monetary policy, thereby raising British interest rates sufficiently to shift the demand curve back to D_1 so that the equilibrium would remain at point 1, where the exchange rate would remain at E_{par}. Alternatively, the Bundesbank would have to pursue an expansionary monetary policy, thereby lowering German interest rates. Lower German interest rates would raise the relative expected return on British assets and shift the demand curve back to D_1 so that the exchange rate would be at E_{par}.

The catch was that the Bundesbank, whose primary goal was fighting inflation, was unwilling to pursue an expansionary monetary policy, and the British, who were facing their worst recession in the postwar period, were unwilling to pursue a contractionary monetary policy to prop up the pound. This impasse became clear when in response to great pressure from other members of the EMS, the Bundesbank was willing to lower its lending rates by only a token amount on September 14 after a speculative attack was mounted on the currencies of the Scandinavian countries. So at some point in the near future, the value of the pound would have to decline to point 2. Speculators now knew that depreciation of the pound was imminent. As a result, the relative expected return of the pound fell sharply, shifting the demand curve left to D_3 in Figure 4.

As a result of the large leftward shift of the demand curve, a huge excess supply of pound assets now existed at the par exchange rate E_{par}, which caused a massive sell-off of pounds (and purchases of marks) by speculators. The need for the British central bank to intervene to raise the value of the pound now became much greater and required a huge rise in British interest rates. After a major intervention effort on the part of the Bank of England, which included a rise in its lending rate from 10% to 15%, which still wasn't enough, the British were finally forced to give up on September 16: They pulled out of the ERM indefinitely and allowed the pound to depreciate by 10% against the mark.

Speculative attacks on other currencies forced devaluation of the Spanish peseta by 5% and the Italian lira by 15%. To defend its currency, the Swedish central bank was forced to raise its daily lending rate to the astronomical level of 500%! By the time the crisis was over, the British, French, Italian, Spanish, and Swedish central banks had intervened to the tune of \$100 billion; the Bundesbank alone had laid out \$50 billion for foreign exchange intervention. Because foreign exchange crises lead to large changes in central banks' holdings of international reserves and thus significantly affect the official reserve asset items in the balance of payments, these crises are also referred to as **balance-of-payments crises**.

The attempt to prop up the European Monetary System was not cheap for these central banks. It is estimated that they lost \$4 to \$6 billion as a result of exchange rate intervention during the crisis. What the central banks lost, the speculators gained. A speculative fund run by George Soros ran up \$1 billion of profits during the crisis, and Citibank traders reportedly made \$200 million. When an exchange rate crisis comes, life can certainly be sweet for exchange rate speculators.

APPLICATION ◆ Recent Foreign Exchange Crises in Emerging Market Countries: Mexico 1994, East Asia 1997, Brazil 1999, and Argentina 2002

Major currency crises in emerging market countries have been a common occurrence in recent years. We can use Figure 4 to understand the sequence of events during the currency crises in Mexico in 1994, East Asia in 1997, Brazil in 1999, and Argentina in 2002. To do so, we just need to recognize that dollars are the foreign currency, whereas the domestic currency was either pesos, baht, or reals. (Note that the exchange rate label on the vertical axis would be in terms of dollars/domestic currency and that the label on the horizontal axis would be the quantity of domestic currency (say, pesos) assets.

In March 1994, political instability in Mexico (the assassination of the ruling party's presidential candidate) sparked investors' concerns that the peso might be devalued. The result was that the relative expected return on domestic assets fell, thus moving the demand curve from D_1 to D_2 in Figure 4. In the case of Thailand in May 1997, the large current account deficit and the weakness of the Thai financial system raised similar concerns about the devaluation of the domestic currency, with the same effect on the demand curve. In Brazil in late 1998 and Argentina in 2001, concerns about fiscal situations that could lead to the printing of money to finance the deficit, and thereby raise inflation, also meant that a devaluation was more likely to occur. The concerns thus lowered the relative expected return on domestic assets and shifted the demand curve from D_1 to D_2. In all of these cases, the result was that the intersection of the supply and demand curves was below the pegged value of the domestic currency at E_{par}.

To keep their domestic currencies from falling below E_{par}, these countries' central banks needed to buy the domestic currency and sell dollars to raise interest rates and shift the demand curve to the right, losing international reserves in the process. At first, the central banks were successful in containing the speculative attacks. However, when more bad news broke, speculators became even more confident that these countries could not defend their currencies. (The bad news was everywhere: In Mexico, an uprising took place in Chiappas amid revelations about problems in the banking system; Thailand experienced the failure of a major financial institution; Brazil had a worsening fiscal situation, along with the threat by a governor to default on his state's debt; and in Argentina, a full-scale bank panic and an actual default on the government debt occurred.) As a result, the relative expected returns on domestic assets fell further, and the demand curve moved much farther to the left to D_3, and the central banks lost even more international reserves. Given the stress on the economy from rising interest rates and the loss of reserves, eventually the monetary authorities could no longer continue to defend the currency and were forced to give up and let their currencies depreciate. This scenario happened in Mexico in December 1994, in Thailand in July 1997, in Brazil in January 1999, and in Argentina in January 2002.

Concerns about similar problems in other countries then triggered speculative attacks against them as well. This contagion occurred in the aftermath of the Mexican crisis (jauntily referred to as the "Tequila effect") with speculative attacks on other Latin American currencies, but no further currency collapses took place. In the East Asian crisis, however, fears of devaluation spread throughout the region, leading to a scenario akin to that depicted in Figure 4. Consequently, one by one, Indonesia, Malaysia, South Korea, and the Philippines were forced to devalue sharply. Even Hong Kong, Singapore, and Taiwan were subjected to speculative attacks, but because these countries had healthy financial systems, the attacks were successfully averted.

As we saw in Chapter 9, the sharp depreciations in Mexico, East Asia, and Argentina led to full-scale financial crises that severely damaged these countries' economies. The foreign exchange crisis that shocked the European Monetary System in September 1992 cost central banks a lot of money, but the public in European countries were not seriously affected. By contrast, the public in Mexico, Argentina, and the crisis countries of East Asia were not so lucky: The collapse of these currencies triggered by speculative attacks led to the financial crises described in Chapter 9, producing severe depressions that caused hardship and political unrest. ◆

CAPITAL CONTROLS

Because capital flows were an important element in the currency crises in Mexico and East Asia, politicians and some economists have advocated that emerging market countries avoid financial instability by restricting capital mobility. Are capital controls a good idea?

Controls on Capital Outflows

Capital outflows can promote financial instability in emerging market countries, because when domestic residents and foreigners pull their capital out of a country, the resulting capital outflow forces a country to devalue its currency. This risk is why some politicians in emerging market countries have recently found capital controls particularly attractive. For example, Prime Minister Mahathir of Malaysia instituted capital controls in 1998 to restrict outflows in the aftermath of the East Asian crisis.

Although these controls sound like a good idea, they suffer from several disadvantages. First, empirical evidence indicates that controls on capital outflows are seldom effective during a crisis because the private sector finds ingenious ways to evade them and has little difficulty moving funds out of the country. Second, the evidence suggests that capital flight may even increase after controls are put into place, because confidence in the government is weakened. Third, controls on capital outflows often lead to corruption, as government officials get paid off to look the other way when domestic residents are trying to move funds abroad. Fourth, controls on capital outflows may lull governments into thinking they do not have to take the steps to reform their financial systems to deal with the crisis, with the result that opportunities to improve the functioning of the economy are lost.

Controls on Capital Inflows

Although most economists find the arguments against controls on capital outflows persuasive, controls on capital inflows receive more support. Supporters reason that if speculative capital cannot come in, then it cannot go out suddenly and create a crisis. Our analysis of the financial crises in East Asia in Chapter 9 provides support for this view by suggesting that capital inflows can lead to a lending boom and excessive risk taking on the part of banks, which then helps trigger a financial crisis.

However, controls on capital inflows have the undesirable feature that they may block from entering a country those funds that would be used for productive investment opportunities. Although such controls may limit the fuel supplied to lending booms through capital flows, over time they produce substantial distortions and misallocation of resources as households and businesses try to get around them. Indeed, as with controls on capital outflows, controls on capital inflows can lead to corruption. Serious doubts arise over whether capital controls can be effective in today's environment, in which trade is open and where many financial instruments make it easier to get around these controls.

On the other hand, a strong case can be made for improving bank regulation and supervision so that capital inflows are less likely to produce a lending boom and encourage excessive risk taking by banking institutions. For example, restricting banks in how fast their borrowing can grow might substantially limit capital inflows. Supervisory controls that focus on the sources of financial fragility, rather than the symptoms, can enhance the efficiency of the financial system, rather than hampering it.

THE ROLE OF THE IMF

The International Monetary Fund was originally set up under the Bretton Woods system to help countries deal with balance-of-payments problems and stay with the fixed exchange rates by lending to deficit countries. When the Bretton Woods system of fixed exchange rates collapsed in 1971, the IMF took on new roles.

The IMF continues to function as a data collector and provide technical assistance to its member countries. Although the IMF no longer attempts to encourage fixed exchange rates, its role as an international lender has become more important recently. This role first came to the fore in the 1980s during the Third World debt crisis, in which the IMF assisted developing countries in repaying their loans. The financial crises in Mexico in 1994–1995 and in East Asia in 1997–1998 led to huge loans by the IMF to these and other affected countries to help them recover from their financial crises and to prevent the spread of these crises to other countries. Then, starting in 2010, the IMF made large loans to Greece, Ireland, and Portugal to help them avoid a default on their government debt. This role, in which the IMF acts like an international lender of last resort to cope with financial instability, is indeed highly controversial.

Should the IMF Be an International Lender of Last Resort?

As we saw in Chapter 18, in large industrialized countries when a financial crisis occurs and the financial system threatens to seize up, domestic central banks can address matters with a lender-of-last-resort operation to limit the degree of instability in the banking system. In emerging market countries, however, where the credibility of the central bank as an inflation fighter may be in doubt and debt contracts are typically short-term and denominated in foreign currencies, a lender-of-last-resort operation becomes a double-edged sword—as likely to exacerbate the financial crisis as to alleviate it. For example, when the U.S. Federal Reserve engaged in a lender-of-last-resort operation during the 1987 stock market crash, after the 2001 terrorist destruction of the World Trade Center, and during the global financial crisis (Chapter 18) there was almost no sentiment in the markets that substantially higher inflation would result. However, for a central bank with less inflation-fighting credibility than the Fed, central bank lending to the financial system in the wake of a financial crisis—even under the lender-of-last-resort rhetoric—may well arouse fears of inflation spiraling out of control, causing an even greater currency depreciation and still greater deterioration of balance sheets. The resulting increase in moral hazard and adverse selection problems in financial markets, along the lines discussed in Chapter 9, would only worsen the financial crisis.

Central banks in emerging market countries, therefore, have only a very limited ability to successfully engage in a lender-of-last-resort operation. However, liquidity provided by an international lender of last resort does not have these undesirable consequences, and in helping to stabilize the value of the domestic currency, it strengthens domestic balance sheets. Moreover, an international lender of last resort may be able to prevent contagion, the situation in which a successful speculative attack on one emerging market currency leads to attacks on other emerging market currencies, spreading financial and economic disruption as it goes. Because a lender of last resort for emerging market countries is needed at times, and because it cannot be provided domestically, a strong rationale exists for an international institution to fill this role. Indeed, since Mexico's financial crisis in 1994, the International Monetary Fund and other international agencies have stepped into the lender-of-last-resort role and provided emergency lending to countries threatened by financial instability.

However, support from an international lender of last resort brings risks of its own, especially the risk that the perception it is standing ready to bail out irresponsible financial institutions may lead to excessive risk taking of the sort that makes financial crises more likely. In the Mexican, East Asian, and Irish crises, governments in the crisis countries used IMF support to protect depositors and other creditors of banking institutions from losses. This safety net creates a well-known moral hazard problem because the depositors and other creditors have less incentive to monitor these banking institutions and withdraw their deposits if the institutions are taking on too much risk. The result is that these institutions are encouraged to take on excessive risks. An international lender of last resort must find ways to limit this moral hazard problem, or it can actually make the situation worse. The international lender of last resort can make it clear that it will extend liquidity only to governments that put the proper measures in place to prevent excessive risk taking. In addition, it can reduce the incentives for risk taking by restricting the ability of governments to bail out stockholders and large uninsured creditors of domestic financial institutions. Some critics of the IMF believe that the IMF has not put enough pressure on the governments to which it lends to contain the moral hazard problem.

One problem that arises for international organizations like the IMF engaged in lender-of-last-resort operations is that they know if they don't come to the rescue, the country will suffer extreme hardship and possible political instability. Politicians in the crisis country may exploit these concerns and engage in a game of chicken with the international lender of last resort: They resist necessary reforms, hoping that the IMF will cave in. Elements of this game were present in the Mexican crisis of 1994 and were also a particularly important feature of the negotiations between the IMF and Indonesia during the East Asian crisis.

How Should the IMF Operate?

The IMF would produce better outcomes if it made clear that it will not play this game. Just as giving in to ill-behaved children may be the easy way out in the short run, but supports a pattern of poor behavior in the long run, some critics worry that the IMF may not be tough enough when confronted by short-run humanitarian concerns.

For example, these critics have been particularly critical of the IMF's lending to the Russian government, which resisted adopting appropriate reforms to stabilize its financial system.

The IMF has also been criticized for imposing on the East Asian countries so-called austerity programs that focused on tight macroeconomic policies rather than on microeconomic policies to fix the crisis-causing problems in the financial sector. Such programs are likely to increase resistance to IMF recommendations, particularly in emerging market countries. Austerity programs allow politicians in these countries to label institutions such as the IMF as being antigrowth, rhetoric that helps politicians mobilize the public against the IMF and avoid doing what they really need to do to reform the financial system in their country. IMF programs focused instead on reforms of the financial sector would increase the likelihood that the IMF will be seen as a helping hand in the creation of a more efficient financial system.

An important historical feature of successful lender-of-last-resort operations is that the faster the lending is done, the lower the amount that actually has to be lent. An excellent example involving the Federal Reserve occurred in the aftermath of the stock market crash on October 19, 1987 (Chapter 18). At the end of that day, to service their customers' accounts, securities firms needed to borrow several billion dollars to maintain orderly trading. However, given the unprecedented developments, banks were nervous about extending further loans to these firms. Upon learning this, the Federal Reserve engaged in an immediate lender-of-last-resort operation, making it clear that it would provide liquidity to banks making loans to the securities industry. What is striking about this episode is that the extremely quick intervention of the Fed not only resulted in a negligible impact of the stock market crash on the economy, but also meant that the amount of liquidity that the Fed needed to supply to the economy was not very large.

The ability of the Fed to engage in a lender-of-last-resort operation within a day of a substantial shock to the financial system stands in sharp contrast to the amount of time it has taken the IMF to supply liquidity during the recent crises. Because IMF lending facilities were originally designed to provide funds after a country was experiencing a balance-of-payments crisis, and because the conditions for the loan had to be negotiated, it takes several months before the IMF can make funds available. By this time, the crisis can get much worse—and much larger sums of funds are then needed to cope with the crisis, often stretching the resources of the IMF. One reason central banks can lend so much more quickly than the IMF is that they have set up procedures in advance to provide loans, with the terms and conditions for this lending agreed upon beforehand. The need for quick provision of liquidity, to keep the loan amount manageable, argues for similar credit facilities at the international lender of last resort, so that funds can be provided quickly, as long as the borrower meets conditions such as properly supervising its banks or keeping budget deficits low.

The flaws in IMF lending programs discussed above led to the avoidance of borrowing from the IMF by emerging market countries. Countries did not want to be subjected to harsh austerity programs and also were unhappy with IMF delays in disbursing funds during a crisis. As an alternative to the IMF, countries built up substantial cushions of international reserves to deal with balance-of-payments problems on their own. IMF lending therefore shrank to very low levels, even creating a shortfall of revenue for its operations because it was no longer earning income by making loans. The IMF was at risk of becoming irrelevant—until the global financial crisis. With the global financial crisis, the IMF's role as an international lender of last resort returned, as can be seen in the Global box, "The Global Financial Crisis and the IMF."

Global The Global Financial Crisis and the IMF

Because financial institutions in emerging market countries had limited exposure to subprime mortgages, the early stages of the subprime financial crisis had little impact on their economies. However, when the global financial crisis became more virulent in October 2008, a number of emerging market countries, as well as Iceland and former communist countries, found that foreigners were pulling funds out of their financial systems, not only putting domestic banks under stress but also causing a sharp depreciation of their currencies.

The role of the IMF as an international lender of last resort now came to the fore. Toward the end of October, the IMF extended $25 billion in loans to Hungary, $16.5 billion to the Ukraine, and $2 billion to Iceland. These loans stipulated that the countries would have to undergo belt tightening to get their fiscal houses in order.

The IMF recognized, however, that, as the Managing Director of the IMF, Dominique Strauss-Kahn phrased it, "exceptional times call for an exceptional response," and that a new type of lending program was needed to overcome the reluctance of countries to borrow from it during the crisis at hand. The IMF created a new lending program at the end of October 2008, called the Short-Term Liquidity Facility, with $100 billion of funds. It provides three-month loans to countries whose economies are judged by the IMF to be basically sound, but under stress. These condition-free loans could be disbursed very quickly. In addition, these loans would not have austerity programs attached to them, making them far more attractive to potential borrowing countries.

In 1999, the IMF tried to implement a similar facility called the Contingent Credit Line, but it was unsuccessful because it required preapproval from the IMF, and countries were reluctant to apply for it because doing so might suggest that they were likely to get into trouble. The Short-Term Liquidity Facility and later lending facilities do not require countries to apply for it. The IMF can just determine that a country has access and give it a loan if needed. It is too soon to determine whether these new lending facilities will overcome some of the criticisms leveled against previous IMF lending programs, but they do appear to be a step in the right direction.

The debate on whether the world would be better off with the IMF operating as an international lender of last resort is currently a hot one. Much attention is being focused on making the IMF more effective in performing this role, and redesign of the IMF is at the center of proposals for a new international financial architecture to help reduce international financial instability.

INTERNATIONAL CONSIDERATIONS AND MONETARY POLICY

Our analysis in this chapter so far has suggested several ways in which monetary policy can be affected by international matters. Awareness of these effects can have significant implications for the way monetary policy is conducted.

Direct Effects of the Foreign Exchange Market on Monetary Policy

When central banks intervene in the foreign exchange market, they acquire or sell off international reserves, and their monetary base is affected. When a central bank intervenes in the foreign exchange market, it gives up some control of its monetary policy.

For example, in the early 1970s, the German central bank faced a dilemma. In attempting to keep the German mark from appreciating too much against the U.S. dollar, the Germans acquired huge quantities of international reserves, leading to a rate of money growth that the German central bank considered inflationary.

The Bundesbank could have tried to halt the growth of the money supply by stopping its intervention in the foreign exchange market and reasserting control over its own monetary policy. Such a strategy has a major drawback when the central bank is under pressure not to allow its currency to appreciate: The lower price of imports and higher price of exports as a result of an appreciation in its currency will hurt domestic producers and increase unemployment.

Because the U.S. dollar has been a reserve currency, the U.S. monetary base and money supply have been less affected by developments in the foreign exchange market. As long as foreign central banks, rather than the Fed, intervene to keep the value of the dollar from changing, American holdings of international reserves are unaffected. The ability to conduct monetary policy is typically easier when a country's currency is a reserve currency.[6]

Balance-of-Payments Considerations

Under the Bretton Woods system, balance-of-payments considerations were more important than they are under the current managed float regime. When a nonreserve currency country is running balance-of-payments deficits, it necessarily gives up international reserves. To keep from running out of these reserves, under the Bretton Woods system it had to implement contractionary monetary policy to strengthen its currency—exactly what occurred in the United Kingdom before its devaluation of the pound in 1967. When policy became expansionary, the balance of payments deteriorated, and the British were forced to "slam on the brakes" by implementing a contractionary policy. Once the balance of payments improved, policy became more expansionary until the deteriorating balance of payments again forced the British to pursue a contractionary policy. Such on-again, off-again actions became known as a "stop-go" policy, and the domestic instability it created was criticized severely.

Because the United States is a major reserve currency country, it can run large balance-of-payments deficits without losing huge amounts of international reserves. This does not mean, however, that the Federal Reserve is never influenced by developments in the U.S. balance of payments. Current account deficits in the United States suggest that American businesses may be losing some of their ability to compete because the value of the dollar is too high. In addition, large U.S. balance-of-payments deficits lead to balance-of-payments surpluses in other countries, which can in turn lead to large increases in their holdings of international reserves (this was especially true under the Bretton Woods system). Because such increases put a strain on the international financial system and may stimulate world inflation, the Fed worries about U.S. balance-of-payments and current account deficits. To help shrink these deficits, the Fed might pursue a more contractionary monetary policy.

Exchange Rate Considerations

Unlike balance-of-payments considerations, which have become less important under the current managed float system, exchange rate considerations now play a greater role

[6]However, the central bank of a reserve currency country must worry about a shift away from the use of its currency for international reserves.

in the conduct of monetary policy. If a central bank does not want to see its currency fall in value, it may pursue a more contractionary monetary policy to raise the domestic interest rate, thereby strengthening its currency. Similarly, if a country experiences an appreciation in its currency, its domestic industry may suffer from increased foreign competition and may pressure the central bank to ease monetary policy in order to lower the exchange rate.

The pressure to manipulate exchange rates seems to be greater for central banks in countries other than the United States, but even the Federal Reserve is not completely immune. The growing tide of protectionism stemming from the inability of American firms to compete with foreign firms because of the strengthening dollar from 1980 to early 1985 stimulated congressional critics of the Fed to call for a more expansionary monetary policy to lower the value of the dollar. As we saw in Chapter 19, the Fed let money growth surge. A policy to bring the dollar down was confirmed in the Plaza Agreement of September 1985, in which the finance ministers from the five most important industrial nations in the free world (the United States, Japan, West Germany, the United Kingdom, and France) agreed to intervene in foreign exchange markets to achieve a decline in the dollar. The dollar continued to fall rapidly after the Plaza Agreement, and the Fed played an important role in this decline by continuing to expand the money supply at a rapid rate.

TO PEG OR NOT TO PEG: EXCHANGE-RATE TARGETING AS AN ALTERNATIVE MONETARY POLICY STRATEGY

In Chapter 19, we discussed two monetary policy strategies that could be followed to promote price stability: inflation targeting and the Federal Reserve's "just do it" strategy. One other strategy also uses a strong nominal anchor to promote price stability: **exchange-rate targeting** (sometimes referred to as an **exchange rate peg**).

Targeting the exchange rate is a monetary policy strategy with a long history. It can take the form of fixing the value of the domestic currency to a commodity such as gold, the key feature of the gold standard described earlier in the chapter. More recently, fixed exchange rate regimes have involved fixing the value of the domestic currency to that of a large, low-inflation country like the United States (the *anchor country*). Another alternative is to adopt a *crawling target* or *peg*, in which a currency is allowed to depreciate at a steady rate so that the inflation rate in the pegging country can be higher than that of the anchor country.

Advantages of Exchange-Rate Targeting

Exchange-rate targeting has several advantages. First, the nominal anchor of an exchange-rate target directly contributes to keeping inflation under control by tying the inflation rate for internationally traded goods to that found in the anchor country. It does this because the foreign price of internationally traded goods is set by the world market, whereas the domestic price of these goods is fixed by the exchange-rate target. For example, until 2002 in Argentina the exchange rate for the Argentine peso was exactly one to the dollar, so that a bushel of wheat traded internationally at five dollars had its price set at five pesos. If the exchange-rate target is credible (i.e., expected to be adhered to), the exchange-rate target has the added benefit of anchoring inflation expectations to the inflation rate in the anchor country.

Second, an exchange-rate target provides an automatic rule for the conduct of monetary policy that helps mitigate the time-inconsistency problem described in Chapter 19. As we saw earlier in the chapter, an exchange-rate target forces a tightening of monetary policy when there is a tendency for the domestic currency to depreciate or a loosening of policy when there is a tendency for the domestic currency to appreciate, so that discretionary monetary policy is less of an option. The central bank will therefore be constrained from falling into the time-inconsistency trap of trying to expand output and employment in the short-run by pursuing overly expansionary monetary policy.

Third, an exchange-rate target has the advantage of simplicity and clarity, which makes it easily understood by the public. A "sound currency" is an easy-to-understand rallying cry for monetary policy. In the past, for example, this aspect was important in France, where an appeal to the "franc fort" (strong franc) was often used to justify tight monetary policy.

Given its advantages, it is not surprising that exchange-rate targeting has been used successfully to control inflation in industrialized countries. Both France and the United Kingdom, for example, successfully used exchange-rate targeting to lower inflation by tying the values of their currencies to the German mark. In 1987, when France first pegged its exchange rate to the mark, its inflation rate was 3%, two percentage points above the German inflation rate. By 1992, its inflation rate had fallen to 2%, a level that can be argued is consistent with price stability, and was even below that in Germany. By 1996, the French and German inflation rates had converged, to a number slightly below 2%. Similarly, after pegging to the German mark in 1990, the United Kingdom was able to lower its inflation rate from 10% to 3% by 1992, when it was forced to abandon the exchange rate mechanism (ERM).

Exchange-rate targeting has also been an effective means of reducing inflation quickly in emerging market countries. For example, before the devaluation in Mexico in 1994, its exchange-rate target enabled it to bring inflation down from levels above 100% in 1988 to below 10% in 1994.

Disadvantages of Exchange-Rate Targeting

Despite the inherent advantages of exchange-rate targeting, several serious criticisms of this strategy can be made. The problem (as we saw earlier in the chapter) is that with capital mobility the targeting country can no longer pursue its own independent monetary policy and use it to respond to domestic shocks that are independent of those hitting the anchor country. Furthermore, an exchange-rate target means that shocks to the anchor country are directly transmitted to the targeting country, because changes in interest rates in the anchor country lead to a corresponding change in interest rates in the targeting country.

A striking example of these problems occurred when Germany was reunified in 1990. In response to concerns about inflationary pressures arising from reunification and the massive fiscal expansion required to rebuild East Germany, long-term German interest rates rose until February 1991 and short-term rates rose until December 1991. This shock to the anchor country in the exchange rate mechanism (ERM) was transmitted directly to the other countries in the ERM whose currencies were pegged to the mark, and their interest rates rose in tandem with those in Germany. Continuing adherence to the exchange-rate target slowed economic growth and increased unemployment in countries such as France that remained in the ERM and adhered to the exchange rate peg.

A second problem with exchange-rate targets is that they leave countries open to speculative attacks on their currencies. Indeed, one aftermath of German reunification was the foreign exchange crisis of September 1992. As we saw earlier, the tight monetary policy in Germany following reunification meant that the countries in the ERM were subjected to a negative demand shock that led to a decline in economic growth and a rise in unemployment. It was certainly feasible for the governments of these countries to keep their exchange rates fixed relative to the mark in these circumstances, but speculators began to question whether these countries' commitment to the exchange rate peg would weaken. Speculators reasoned that these countries would not tolerate the rise in unemployment that resulted from keeping interest rates high enough to fend off attacks on their currencies.

At this stage, speculators were, in effect, presented with a one-way bet, because the currencies of countries like France, Spain, Sweden, Italy, and the United Kingdom could go in only one direction and depreciate against the mark. Selling these currencies before the likely depreciation occurred gave speculators an attractive profit opportunity with potentially high expected returns. The result was the speculative attack in September 1992. Only in France was the commitment to the fixed exchange rate strong enough that France did not devalue. The governments in the other countries were unwilling to defend their currencies at all costs and eventually allowed their currencies to fall in value.

The different responses of France and the United Kingdom after the September 1992 exchange rate crisis illustrate the potential cost of an exchange-rate target. France, which continued to peg its currency to the mark and was thus unable to use monetary policy to respond to domestic conditions, found that economic growth remained slow after 1992 and unemployment increased. The United Kingdom, on the other hand, which dropped out of the ERM exchange rate peg and adopted inflation targeting, had much better economic performance: Economic growth was higher, the unemployment rate fell, and yet its inflation was not much worse than France's.

In contrast to industrialized countries, emerging market countries (including the transition countries of Eastern Europe) may not lose much by giving up an independent monetary policy when they target exchange rates. Because many emerging market countries have not developed the political or monetary institutions that allow the successful use of discretionary monetary policy, they may have little to gain from an independent monetary policy, but a lot to lose. Thus they would be better off by, in effect, adopting the monetary policy of a country like the United States through targeting exchange rates than by pursuing their own independent policy. This is one of the reasons that so many emerging market countries have adopted exchange-rate targeting.

Nonetheless, exchange-rate targeting is highly dangerous for these countries, because it leaves them open to speculative attacks that can have far more serious consequences for their economies than for those of industrialized countries. Indeed, the successful speculative attacks in Mexico in 1994, East Asia in 1997, and Argentina in 2002 plunged their economies into full-scale financial crises that devastated their economies.

An additional disadvantage of an exchange-rate target is that it can weaken the accountability of policymakers, particularly in emerging market countries. Because exchange-rate targeting fixes the exchange rate, it eliminates an important signal that can help constrain monetary policy from becoming too expansionary and thereby limit the time-inconsistency problem. In industrialized countries, particularly in the United States, the bond market provides an important signal about the stance of monetary policy. Overly expansionary monetary policy or strong political pressure to engage in overly expansionary monetary policy produces an inflation scare in which inflation expectations surge, interest rates rise because of the Fisher effect (described in Chapter 5), and long-term bond prices sharply decline. Because both central banks and politicians want to avoid this kind of scenario, overly expansionary monetary policy will be less likely.

In many countries, particularly emerging market countries, the long-term bond market is essentially nonexistent. Under a floating exchange rate regime, however, if monetary policy is too expansionary, the exchange rate will depreciate. In these countries the daily fluctuations of the exchange rate can, like the bond market in the United States, provide an early warning signal that monetary policy is too expansionary. Just as the fear of a visible inflation scare in the bond market constrains central bankers from pursuing overly expansionary monetary policy and constrains politicians from putting pressure on the central bank to engage in overly expansionary monetary policy, fear of exchange rate depreciations can make overly expansionary monetary policy, and the time-inconsistency problem, less likely.

The need for signals from the foreign exchange market may be even more acute for emerging market countries, because the balance sheets and actions of their central banks are not as transparent as in industrialized countries. Targeting the exchange rate can make it even harder to ascertain the central bank's policy actions. The public is less able to keep a watch on the central bank and the politicians pressuring it, which makes it easier for monetary policy to become too expansionary.

When Is Exchange-Rate Targeting Desirable for Industrialized Countries?

Given the above disadvantages with exchange-rate targeting, when might it make sense? In industrialized countries, the biggest cost to exchange-rate targeting is the loss of an independent monetary policy to deal with domestic considerations. If an independent, domestic monetary policy can be conducted responsibly, this can be a serious cost indeed, as the comparison between the post-1992 experiences of France and the United Kingdom indicates. However, not all industrialized countries have found that they are capable of conducting their own monetary policy successfully, either because the central bank is not independent or because political pressures on the central bank lead to an inflationary bias in monetary policy. In these cases, giving up independent control of domestic monetary policy may not be a great loss, while the gain of having monetary policy determined by a better-performing central bank in the anchor country can be substantial.

Italy provides an example: It was not a coincidence that the Italian public had the most favorable attitude of all those in Europe toward the European Monetary Union. The past record of Italian monetary policy was not good, and the Italian public recognized that having monetary policy controlled by more responsible outsiders had benefits that far outweighed the costs of losing the ability to focus monetary policy on domestic considerations.

A second reason why industrialized countries might find targeting exchange rates useful is that it encourages integration of the domestic economy with its neighbors. Clearly, this was the rationale for long-standing pegging of the exchange rate to the deutsche mark by countries such as Austria and the Netherlands, and the more recent exchange rate pegs that preceded the European Monetary Union.

To sum, exchange-rate targeting for industrialized countries is probably not the best monetary policy strategy to control the overall economy unless (1) domestic monetary and political institutions are not conducive to good monetary policy making or (2) an exchange-rate target has other important benefits that have nothing to do with monetary policy.

When Is Exchange-Rate Targeting Desirable for Emerging Market Countries?

In countries whose political and monetary institutions are particularly weak and who therefore have been experiencing continued bouts of hyperinflation, a characterization that applies to many emerging market (including transition) countries, exchange-rate targeting may be the only way to break inflationary psychology and stabilize the economy. In this situation, exchange-rate targeting is the stabilization policy of last resort. However, if the exchange-rate targeting regimes in emerging market countries are not always transparent, they are more likely to break down, often resulting in disastrous financial crises.

Are there exchange rate strategies that make it less likely that the exchange rate regime will break down in emerging market countries? Two such strategies that have received increasing attention in recent years are currency boards and dollarization.

Currency Boards

One solution to the problem of lack of transparency and commitment to the exchange-rate target is the adoption of a **currency board**, in which the domestic currency is backed 100% by a foreign currency (say, dollars) and in which the note-issuing authority, whether the central bank or the government, establishes a fixed exchange rate to this foreign currency and stands ready to exchange domestic currency for the foreign currency at this rate whenever the public requests it. A currency board is just a variant of a fixed exchange-rate target in which the commitment to the fixed exchange rate is especially strong because the conduct of monetary policy is, in effect, put on autopilot, and taken completely out of the hands of the central bank and the government. In contrast, the typical fixed or pegged exchange rate regime does allow the monetary authorities some discretion in their conduct of monetary policy because they can still adjust interest rates or print money.

A currency board arrangement thus has important advantages over a monetary policy strategy that just uses an exchange-rate target. First, the money supply can expand only when foreign currency is exchanged for domestic currency at the central bank. Therefore, the increased amount of domestic currency is matched by an equal increase in foreign exchange reserves. The central bank no longer has the ability to print money and thereby cause inflation. Second, the currency board involves a stronger commitment by the central bank to the fixed exchange rate and may therefore be effective in bringing down inflation quickly and in decreasing the likelihood of a successful speculative attack against the currency.

Although they solve the transparency and commitment problems inherent in an exchange-rate target regime, currency boards suffer from some of the same shortcomings: the loss of an independent monetary policy and increased exposure of the economy to shocks from the anchor country, and the loss of the central bank's ability to create money and act as a lender of last resort. Other means must therefore be used to cope with potential banking crises. In addition, if a speculative attack on a currency board occurs, the exchange of the domestic currency for foreign currency leads to a sharp contraction of the money supply, which can be highly damaging to the economy.

Global Argentina's Currency Board

Argentina has had a long history of monetary instability, with inflation rates fluctuating dramatically and sometimes surging to beyond 1,000% per year. To end this cycle of inflationary surges, Argentina decided to adopt a currency board in April 1991. The Argentine currency board worked as follows. Under Argentina's convertibility law, the peso/dollar exchange rate was fixed at one to one, and a member of the public could go to the Argentine central bank and exchange a peso for a dollar, or vice versa, at any time.

The early years of Argentina's currency board looked stunningly successful. Inflation, which had been running at an 800% annual rate in 1990, fell to less than 5% by the end of 1994, and economic growth was rapid, averaging almost 8% per year from 1991 to 1994. In the aftermath of the Mexican peso crisis, however, concern about the health of the Argentine economy resulted in the public's pulling money out of the banks (deposits fell by 18%) and exchanging pesos for dollars, thus causing a contraction of the Argentine money supply. The result was a sharp drop in Argentine economic activity, with real GDP shrinking by more than 5% in 1995 and the unemployment rate jumping above 15%. Only in 1996 did the economy begin to recover.

Because the central bank of Argentina had no control over monetary policy under the currency board system, it was relatively helpless to counteract the contractionary monetary policy stemming from the public's behavior. Furthermore, because the currency board did not allow the central bank to create pesos and lend them to the banks, it had very little capability to act as a lender of last resort. With help from international agencies, such as the IMF, the World Bank, and the Inter-American Development Bank, which lent Argentina more than $5 billion in 1995 to help shore up its banking system, the currency board survived.

However, in 1998 Argentina entered another recession, which was both severe and very long lasting. By the end of 2001, unemployment reached nearly 20%, a level comparable to that experienced in the United States during the Great Depression of the 1930s. The result was civil unrest and the fall of the elected government, as well as a major banking crisis and a default on nearly $150 billion of government debt. Because the Central Bank of Argentina had no control over monetary policy under the currency board system, it was unable to use monetary policy to expand the economy and get out of its recession. Furthermore, because the currency board did not allow the central bank to create pesos and lend them to banks, it had very little capability to act as a lender of last resort. In January 2002, the currency board finally collapsed and the peso depreciated by more than 70%. The result was the full-scale financial crisis described in Chapter 9, with inflation shooting up and an extremely severe depression. Clearly, the Argentine public is not as enamored of its currency board as it once was.

Currency boards have been established in the territory of Hong Kong (1983) and countries such as Argentina (1991), Estonia (1992), Lithuania (1994), Bulgaria (1997), and Bosnia (1998). Argentina's currency board, which operated from 1991 to 2002 and required the central bank to exchange U.S. dollars for new pesos at a fixed exchange rate of 1 to 1, is one of the most interesting. For more on this subject, see the Global box, "Argentina's Currency Board."

Dollarization

Another solution to the problems created by a lack of transparency and commitment to the exchange-rate target is **dollarization**, the adoption of a sound currency, like the U.S. dollar, as a country's money. Indeed, dollarization is just another variant of a fixed exchange-rate target with an even stronger commitment mechanism than a currency board provides. A currency board can be abandoned, allowing a change in the value of the currency, but a change of value is impossible with dollarization: A dollar bill is always worth one dollar, whether it is held in the United States or outside it.

Dollarization has been advocated as a monetary policy strategy for emerging market countries: It was discussed actively by Argentine officials in the aftermath of the devaluation of the Brazilian real in January 1999 and was adopted by Ecuador in March 2000. Dollarization's key advantage is that it completely avoids the possibility of a speculative attack on the domestic currency (because there is none). (Such an attack is still a danger even under a currency board arrangement.)

Dollarization is subject to the usual disadvantages of an exchange-rate target (the loss of an independent monetary policy, increased exposure of the economy to shocks from the anchor country, and the inability of the central bank to create money and act as a lender of last resort). Dollarization has one additional disadvantage not characteristic of currency boards or other exchange-rate target regimes. Because a country adopting dollarization no longer has its own currency, it loses the revenue that a government receives by issuing money, which is called **seignorage**. Because governments (or their central banks) do not have to pay interest on their currency, they earn revenue (seignorage) by using this currency to purchase income-earning assets such as bonds. In the case of the Federal Reserve in the United States, this revenue is usually in excess of $30 billion per year. If an emerging market country dollarizes and gives up its currency, it needs to make up this loss of revenue somewhere, which is not always easy for a poor country.

Summary

1. An unsterilized central bank intervention in which the domestic currency is sold to purchase foreign assets leads to a gain in international reserves, an increase in the money supply, and a depreciation of the domestic currency. Available evidence suggests, however, that sterilized central bank interventions have little long-term effect on the exchange rate.
2. The balance of payments is a bookkeeping system for recording all payments between a country and foreign countries that have a direct bearing on the movement of funds between them. The official reserve transactions balance is the sum of the current account balance plus the items in the capital account. It indicates the amount of international reserves that must be moved between countries to finance international transactions.
3. Before World War I, the gold standard was predominant. Currencies were convertible into gold, thus fixing exchange rates between them. After World War II, the Bretton Woods system and the IMF were established to promote a fixed exchange rate system in which the U.S. dollar, the reserve currency, was convertible into gold. The Bretton Woods system collapsed in 1971. We now have an international financial system that has elements of a managed float and a fixed exchange rate system. Some exchange rates fluctuate from day to day, although central banks intervene in the foreign exchange market, while other exchange rates are fixed.
4. Controls on capital outflows receive support because they may prevent domestic residents and foreigners from pulling capital out of a country during a crisis and make devaluation less likely. Controls on capital inflows make sense under the theory that if speculative capital cannot flow in, then it cannot go out suddenly and create a crisis. However, capital controls suffer from several disadvantages: They are seldom effective, they lead to corruption, and they may allow governments to avoid taking the steps needed to reform their financial systems to deal with the crisis.
5. The IMF has recently taken on the role of an international lender of last resort. Because central banks in emerging market countries are unlikely to be able to perform a lender-of-last-resort operation successfully, an international lender of last resort like the IMF is needed to prevent financial instability. However, the

IMF's role as an international lender of last resort creates a serious moral hazard problem that can encourage excessive risk taking and make a financial crisis more likely, but refusing to lend may be politically hard to do. In addition, it needs to be able to provide liquidity quickly during a crisis to keep manageable the amount of funds lent.

6. Three international considerations affect the conduct of monetary policy: direct effects of the foreign exchange market on monetary policy, balance-of-payments considerations, and exchange rate considerations. Inasmuch as the United States has been a reserve currency country in the post–World War II period, U.S. monetary policy has been less affected by developments in the foreign exchange market and its balance of payments than is true for other countries. However, in recent years, exchange rate considerations have been playing a more prominent role in influencing U.S. monetary policy.

7. Exchange-rate targeting has the following advantages as a monetary policy strategy: (1) It directly keeps inflation under control by tying the inflation rate for internationally traded goods to that found in the anchor country to whom its currency is pegged; (2) it provides an automatic rule for the conduct of monetary policy that helps mitigate the time-inconsistency problem; and (3) it is simple and clear. Exchange-rate targeting also has serious disadvantages: (1) It results in a loss of independent monetary policy; (2) it leaves the country open to speculative attacks; and (3) it can weaken the accountability of policymakers because the exchange rate signal is lost. Two strategies that make it less likely that the exchange rate regime will break down are currency boards, in which the central bank stands ready to automatically exchange domestic for foreign currency at a fixed rate, and dollarization, in which a sound currency like the U.S. dollar is adopted as the country's money.

Key Terms

anchor currency, p. 522
balance of payments, p. 520
balance-of-payments crisis, p. 531
Bretton Woods system, p. 523
capital account, p. 521
capital controls, p. 543
currency board, p. 543
current account, p. 521
devaluation, p. 525
dollarization, p. 544
exchange rate peg, p. 539
exchange-rate targeting, p. 539
fixed exchange rate regime, p. 522
floating exchange rate regime, p. 522
foreign exchange interventions, p. 516
gold standard, p. 522
impossible trinity, p. 526
International Monetary Fund (IMF), p. 523
international reserves, p. 516
managed float regime (dirty float), p. 522
official reserve transactions balance, p. 521
policy trilemma, p. 526
reserve currency, p. 523
revaluation, p. 526
seignorage, p. 545
special drawing rights (SDRs), p. 529
sterilized foreign exchange intervention, p. 518
trade balance, p. 521
unsterilized foreign exchange intervention, p. 518
World Bank, p. 523
World Trade Organization (WTO), p. 523

Questions

All questions are available in MyEconLab at www.myeconlab.com.

1. If the Federal Reserve buys dollars in the foreign exchange market but conducts an offsetting open market operation to sterilize the intervention, what will be the impact on international reserves, the money supply, and the exchange rate?

2. If the Federal Reserve buys dollars in the foreign exchange market but does not sterilize the intervention, what will be the impact on international reserves, the money supply, and the exchange rate?

3. For each of the following, identify in which part of the balance-of-payments account it appears (current

account, capital account, or net change in international reserves) and whether it is a receipt or a payment.

a. A British subject's purchase of a share of Johnson & Johnson stock
b. An American's purchase of an airline ticket from Air France
c. The Swiss government's purchase of U.S. Treasury bills
d. A Japanese's purchase of California oranges
e. $50 million of foreign aid to Honduras
f. A loan by an American bank to Mexico
g. An American bank's borrowing of Eurodollars

4. Why does a balance-of-payments deficit for the United States have a different effect on its international reserves than a balance-of-payments deficit for the Netherlands?

5. How can a large balance-of-payments surplus contribute to a country's inflation rate?

6. Why can balance-of-payments deficits force some countries to implement a contractionary monetary policy?

7. Under the gold standard, if Britain became more productive relative to the United States, what would happen to the money supply in the two countries? Why would the changes in the money supply help preserve a fixed exchange rate between the United States and Britain?

8. What is the exchange rate between dollars and Swiss francs if one dollar is convertible into $\frac{1}{20}$ ounce of gold and one Swiss franc is convertible into $\frac{1}{40}$ ounce of gold?

9. "Inflation is not possible under the gold standard." Is this statement true, false, or uncertain? Explain your answer.

10. What are some of the disadvantages of China's pegging the yuan to the dollar?

11. If a country's par exchange rate was undervalued during the Bretton Woods fixed exchange rate regime, what kind of intervention would that country's central bank be forced to undertake, and what effect would it have on its international reserves and the money supply?

12. "The abandonment of fixed exchange rates after 1973 has meant that countries have pursued more independent monetary policies." Is this statement true, false, or uncertain? Explain your answer.

13. "If a country wants to keep its exchange rate from changing, it must give up some control over its money supply." Is this statement true, false, or uncertain? Explain your answer.

14. Why is it that in a pure flexible exchange rate system, the foreign exchange market has no direct effects on the money supply? Does this mean that the foreign exchange market has no effect on monetary policy?

15. Why did the exchange rate peg lead to difficulties for the countries in the ERM when German reunification occurred?

16. How can exchange-rate targets lead to a speculative attack on a currency?

17. What are the advantages and disadvantages of having the IMF as an international lender of last resort?

18. How can the long-term bond market help reduce the time-inconsistency problem for monetary policy? Can the foreign exchange market also perform this role?

19. "Balance-of-payments deficits always cause a country to lose international reserves." Is this statement true, false, or uncertain? Explain your answer.

20. How can persistent U.S. balance-of-payments deficits stimulate world inflation?

21. What are the key advantages of exchange-rate targeting as a monetary policy strategy?

22. When is exchange-rate targeting likely to be a sensible strategy for industrialized countries? When is exchange-rate targeting likely to be a sensible strategy for emerging market countries?

23. What are the advantages and disadvantages of currency boards and dollarization over a monetary policy that uses only an exchange-rate target?

Applied Problems

All applied problems are available in MyEconLab *at* www.myeconlab.com.

24. Suppose the Federal Reserve purchases $1,000,000 worth of foreign assets.

a. If the Federal Reserve purchases the foreign assets with $1,000,000 in currency, show the effect of this open market operation, using T-accounts. What happens to the monetary base?

b. If the Federal Reserve purchases the foreign assets by selling $1,000,000 in T-bills, show the effect of this open market operation, using T-accounts. What happens to the monetary base?

25. Suppose the Mexican central bank chose to peg the peso to the U.S. dollar and commit to a fixed peso/dollar exchange rate. Use a graph of the market for peso assets (foreign exchange) to show and explain how the peg must be maintained if a shock in the U.S. economy forces the Fed to pursue contractionary monetary policy. What does this say about the ability of central banks to address domestic economic problems while maintaining a pegged exchange rate?

Web Exercises

1. The Federal Reserve publishes information online that explains the workings of the foreign exchange market. One such publication can be found at www.ny.frb.org/education/addpub/usfxm. Review the table of contents and open Chapter 10, the evolution of the international monetary system. Read this chapter and write a one-page summary that discusses why each monetary standard was dropped in favor of the succeeding one.

2. The International Monetary Fund stands ready to help nations facing monetary crises. Go to www.imf.org. Click on the tab labeled About the IMF. What is the stated purpose of the IMF? How many nations participate and when was it established?

Web References

http://research.stlouisfed.org/fred2

This website contains exchange rates, balance of payments, and trade data.

www.imf.org/external/np/exr/facts/sdr.htm

Find information about special drawing rights, allocation, valuation, and SDR users' guide.

http://users.erols.com/kurrency/intro.htm

A detailed discussion of the history, purpose, and function of currency boards.

Part 6

Monetary Theory

Crisis and Response: The Perfect Storm of 2007–2009

In 2007 and 2008, the U.S. economy was hit by a perfect storm of formidable shocks. By the end of 2007, oil prices had risen from $60 per barrel at the beginning of the year to $100 and reached a peak of over $140 in July 2008. The oil price shock was both contractionary and inflationary, and as a result led to both higher inflation and unemployment—and many unhappy drivers at gas pumps.

If this supply shock were not bad enough, the global financial crisis hit the economy starting in August 2007 and caused a contraction in both household and business spending. This shock led to a further rise in unemployment, with some weakening of inflationary pressure further down the road.

The result of this perfect storm of adverse shocks was the most severe economic contraction since the Great Depression, with unemployment rising from the 4.6% level in 2006 and 2007 to the 10% level by the end of 2009. Inflation also accelerated from 2.5% in 2006 to over 5% by the middle of 2008, but with the increase in the unemployment rate and the decline of oil and other commodity prices by the fall of 2008, inflation rapidly came back down again.

Although the Fed's aggressive monetary policy aimed to address the contractionary forces in the economy, lawmakers wanted additional action. In February 2008 and then again in February 2009, the U.S. Congress passed stimulus packages, first of $150 billion and then of $787 billion. However, although both stimulus packages helped boost GDP, they were overwhelmed by the continuing worsening of the financial crisis, and the economy went into a tailspin.

The impact of the perfect storm of adverse shocks highlights the need to understand how monetary and other government policies affect inflation and economic activity. Chapter 22 discusses how the quantity theory of money explains inflation in the long run and presents how theories of the demand for money have evolved. Aggregate supply and demand analysis, the basic framework that will enable us to study the effect of monetary policy on output and inflation, is then developed in Chapters 23. In Chapter 24, we expand on aggregate supply and demand analysis in order to understand how monetary policy can be used to stabilize the economy and inflation. Chapter 25 outlines the transmission mechanisms through which monetary policy affects the aggregate economy.

22 Quantity Theory, Inflation, and the Demand for Money

Preview

In earlier chapters, we spent a lot of time and effort learning what the money supply is, how it is determined, and what part the Federal Reserve System plays in it. Now we are ready to explore the role of the money supply and monetary policy in determining inflation and total production of goods and services (aggregate output) in the economy. The study of the effect of money and monetary policy on the economy is called **monetary theory**, and we examine this branch of economics in the chapters of Part 6.

When economists mention *supply*, the word *demand* is sure to follow, and the discussion of money is no exception. The supply of money is an essential building block in understanding how monetary policy affects the economy, because it suggests the factors that influence the quantity of money in the economy. Not surprisingly, another essential part of monetary theory is the demand for money.

After discussing the quantity theory and its link to the demand for money, we delve more deeply into what determines the demand for money. A central question in monetary theory is whether or to what extent the quantity of money demanded is affected by changes in interest rates. Because this issue is crucial to how we view money's effects on aggregate economic activity, we focus on the role of interest rates in the demand for money.

QUANTITY THEORY OF MONEY

Developed by the classical economists in the nineteenth and early twentieth centuries, the quantity theory of money is a theory of how the nominal value of aggregate income is determined. Because it also tells us how much money is held for a given amount of aggregate income, it is a theory of the demand for money. The most important feature of this theory is that it suggests that interest rates have no effect on the demand for money.

Velocity of Money and Equation of Exchange

The clearest exposition of the classical quantity theory approach is found in the work of the American economist Irving Fisher, in his influential book *The Purchasing Power of Money*, published in 1911. Fisher wanted to examine the link between the total quantity of money M (the money supply) and the total amount of spending on final goods and services produced in the economy $P \times Y$, where P is the price level and Y is aggregate output (income). (Total spending $P \times Y$ is also thought of as aggregate nominal income for the economy or as nominal GDP.) The concept that provides the link between M and $P \times Y$ is called the **velocity of money** (often reduced to *velocity*), the average number of times per year (turnover) that a dollar is spent in buying the total amount of goods and services produced in the economy. Velocity V is defined more precisely as total spending $P \times Y$ divided by the quantity of money M:

$$V = \frac{P \times Y}{M} \tag{1}$$

If, for example, nominal GDP ($P \times Y$) in a year is \$10 trillion and the quantity of money (M) is \$2 trillion, we can calculate velocity to be as follows:

$$V = \frac{\$10 \text{ trillion}}{\$2 \text{ trillion}} = 5$$

The value of 5 for velocity means that the average dollar bill is spent five times in purchasing final goods and services in the economy.

By multiplying both sides of this definition by M, we obtain the **equation of exchange**, which relates nominal income to the quantity of money and velocity:

$$M \times V = P \times Y \tag{2}$$

The equation of exchange thus states that the quantity of money multiplied by the number of times that this money is spent in a given year must equal nominal income (the total nominal amount spent on goods and services in that year).[1]

As it stands, Equation 2 is nothing more than an identity—a relationship that is true by definition. It does not tell us, for instance, that when the money supply M changes, nominal income ($P \times Y$) changes in the same direction; a rise in M, for example, could be offset by a fall in V that leaves $M \times V$ (and therefore $P \times Y$) unchanged. To convert the equation of exchange (an *identity*) into a *theory* of how nominal income is determined requires an understanding of the factors that determine velocity.

Determinants of Velocity Irving Fisher reasoned that velocity is determined by the institutions in an economy that affect the way individuals conduct transactions. If people use charge accounts and credit cards to conduct their transactions, as they can today, and consequently use money less often when making purchases, less money is

[1]Fisher actually first formulated the equation of exchange in terms of the nominal value of transactions in the economy PT:

$$MV_T = PT$$

where P = average price per transaction
T = number of transactions conducted in a year
$V_T = PT/M$ = transactions velocity of money

Because the nominal value of transactions T is difficult to measure, the quantity theory has been formulated in terms of aggregate output Y as follows: T is assumed to be proportional to Y so that $T = vY$, where v is a constant of proportionality. Substituting vY for T in Fisher's equation of exchange yields $MV_T = vPY$, which can be written as Equation 2 in the text, in which $V = V_T/v$.

required to conduct the transactions generated by nominal income (M falls relative to $P \times Y$), and velocity $(P \times Y)/M$ will increase. Conversely, if it is more convenient for purchases to be paid for with cash, checks, or debit cards (all of which are money), more money is used to conduct the transactions generated by the same level of nominal income, and velocity will fall. Fisher took the view that the institutional and technological features of the economy would affect velocity only slowly over time, so velocity would normally be reasonably constant in the short run.

Demand for Money Another way of interpreting Fisher's quantity theory is in terms of the **demand for money**, the quantity of money that people want to hold.

Because the quantity theory of money tells us how much money is held for a given amount of nominal spending, it is, in fact, a theory of the demand for money. To illustrate, let's first divide both sides of the equation of exchange by V to yield the following:

$$M = \frac{1}{V} \times PY$$

When the money market is in equilibrium, money supply equals money demand, so we can replace M in the equation by M^d. In addition, since in the quantity theory of money velocity is assumed to be constant, we can be replace $1/V$ with a constant k. Substituting k for $1/V$ and M^d for M, we can rewrite the equation as

$$M^d = k \times PY \tag{3}$$

Equation 3 tells us that because k is constant, the level of transactions generated by a fixed level of nominal income PY determines the quantity of money M^d that people demand. Therefore Fisher's theory suggests that the demand for money is purely a function of income, and interest rates have no effect on the demand for money.[2]

From the Equation of Exchange to the Quantity Theory of Money

Fisher's view that velocity is fairly constant in the short run, so that $V = \overline{V}$, transforms the equation of exchange into the **quantity theory of money**, which states that nominal income (spending) is determined solely by movements in the quantity of money M.

$$P \times Y = M \times \overline{V} \tag{4}$$

The quantity theory equation above indicates that when the quantity of money M doubles, $M \times \overline{V}$ doubles and so must $P \times Y$, the value of nominal income. To illustrate, let's assume that velocity is 5, nominal income (GDP) is initially \$10 trillion, and the money supply is \$2 trillion. If the money supply doubles to \$4 trillion, the quantity theory of money tells us that nominal income will double to \$20 trillion (= 5 × \$4 trillion)

[2]While Fisher was developing his quantity theory approach to the demand for money, a group of classical economists in Cambridge, England led by Alfred Marshall and A. C. Pigou, came to similar conclusions, although with slightly different reasoning. They derived Equation 3 by recognizing that two properties of money motivate people to hold it: its utility as a medium of exchange and as a store of wealth.

Quantity Theory and the Price Level

Because the classical economists (including Fisher) thought that wages and prices were completely flexible, they believed that the level of aggregate output Y produced in the economy during normal times would remain at the full-employment level. Hence Y in the equation of exchange could also be treated as reasonably constant in the short run and thus assigned a fixed value of $\bar{Y}$ in Equation 4. Dividing both sides of Equation 4 by $\bar{Y}$, we can then write the price level as follows:

$$P = \frac{M \times \bar{V}}{\bar{Y}} \tag{5}$$

The quantity theory of money theory, as represented by Equation 5 implies that if M doubles, P must also double in the short run because $\bar{V}$ and $\bar{Y}$ are constant. In our example, if aggregate output is \$10 trillion, velocity is 5, and the money supply is \$2 trillion, then the price level equals 1.0.

$$P = 1.0 = \frac{\$2 \text{ trillion} \times 5}{\$10 \text{ trillion}} = \frac{\$10 \text{ trillion}}{\$10 \text{ trillion}}$$

When the money supply doubles to \$4 trillion, the price level must also double to 2.0 because

$$P = 2.0 = \frac{\$4 \text{ trillion} \times 5}{\$10 \text{ trillion}} = \frac{\$20 \text{ trillion}}{\$10 \text{ trillion}}$$

Classical economists relied on the quantity theory of money to explain movements in the price level. In their view, ***changes in the quantity of money lead to proportional changes in the price level***.

Quantity Theory and Inflation

We now transform the quantity theory of money into a theory of inflation. You might recall from high school math the mathematical fact that the percentage change ($\%\Delta$) of a product of two variables is approximately equal to the sum of the percentage changes of each of these variables. In other words,

$$\text{Percentage Change in } (x \times y) = (\text{Percentage Change in } x) + (\text{Percentage Change in } y)$$

Using this mathematical fact, we can rewrite the equation of exchange as follows:

$$\%\Delta M + \%\Delta V = \%\Delta P + \%\Delta Y$$

Subtracting $\%\Delta Y$ from both sides of the preceding equation, and recognizing that the inflation rate, π, is the growth rate of the price level, that is, $\%\Delta P$,

$$\pi = \%\Delta P = \%\Delta M + \%\Delta V - \%\Delta Y$$

Since we assume velocity is constant, its growth rate is zero, so the quantity theory of money is also a theory of inflation:

$$\pi = \%\Delta M - \%\Delta Y \tag{6}$$

Because the percentage change in a variable at an annual rate is the same as the growth rate in that variable, this equation can also be stated in words: ***the quantity theory of inflation indicates that the inflation rate equals the growth rate of the money supply minus the growth rate of aggregate output***. For example, if the aggregate output is growing at 3% per year and the growth rate of money is 5%, then inflation is 2% (= 5% − 3%). If the Federal Reserve increases the money growth rate to 10%, then the quantity theory of inflation in Equation 6 indicates that the inflation rate will rise to 7%(= 10% − 3%).

APPLICATION ◆ Testing the Quantity Theory of Money

Now that we have fully outlined the quantity theory of money, let's put it to the test with actual data over the long and short runs.

The Quantity Theory of Money in the Long Run The quantity theory of money provides a long-run theory of inflation because it is based on the assumption that wages and prices are flexible. Panel (a) plots ten-year averages of U.S. inflation rates against the ten-year average rate of U.S. money growth (M2) from 1870 through 2000. Because the growth rate of aggregate output Y over ten-year periods does not vary very much, Equation 6 indicates that the ten-year inflation rate should be the ten-year money growth rate minus a constant (the rate of aggregate output growth). Thus a strong positive relationship should exist between inflation and money growth rates—and this relationship is borne out in panel (a) of Figure 1. Decades with higher growth rates of the U.S. money supply typically see higher average inflation rates.

Does the quantity theory also explain differing long-run inflation rates across countries? It certainly does. Panel (b) of Figure 1 plots the average inflation rate over the ten-year period from 2000 to 2010 against the ten-year money growth rate for several countries. Note that countries with high money growth, such as Turkey, Ukraine, and Zambia, tend to have higher inflation.

The Quantity Theory of Money in the Short Run Does the quantity theory of money provide a good explanation of short-run inflation fluctuations as well? Figure 2 provides evidence on the link between money growth and inflation in the short run by plotting the annual U.S. inflation rate from 1965 to 2010 against the annual money (M2) growth rate. (The money supply lags by two years to allow for the time it takes for changes in money growth to affect inflation.) The relationship between inflation and money growth on an annual basis is not strong at all. There are many years—such as 1963–1967, 1983–1985, 2003–2005, 2008–2009—where money growth is high, but inflation is low. Indeed, it is hard to see a positive correlation at all between money growth and inflation in Figure 2.

The conclusion from this evidence is that ***the quantity theory of money is a good theory of inflation in the long run, but not in the short run.*** Another way of stating this conclusion is that Milton Friedman's statement that "inflation is always and everywhere a monetary phenomenon" (mentioned in Chapter 1) is accurate in the long run, but is not supported by the data for the short run. This insight tells us that the classical assumption that wages and prices are completely flexible may not be a good assumption for short-run fluctuations in inflation and aggregate output. For this reason, we relax this assumption in the following chapters of the book when we develop models of short-run inflation and output fluctuations. ◆

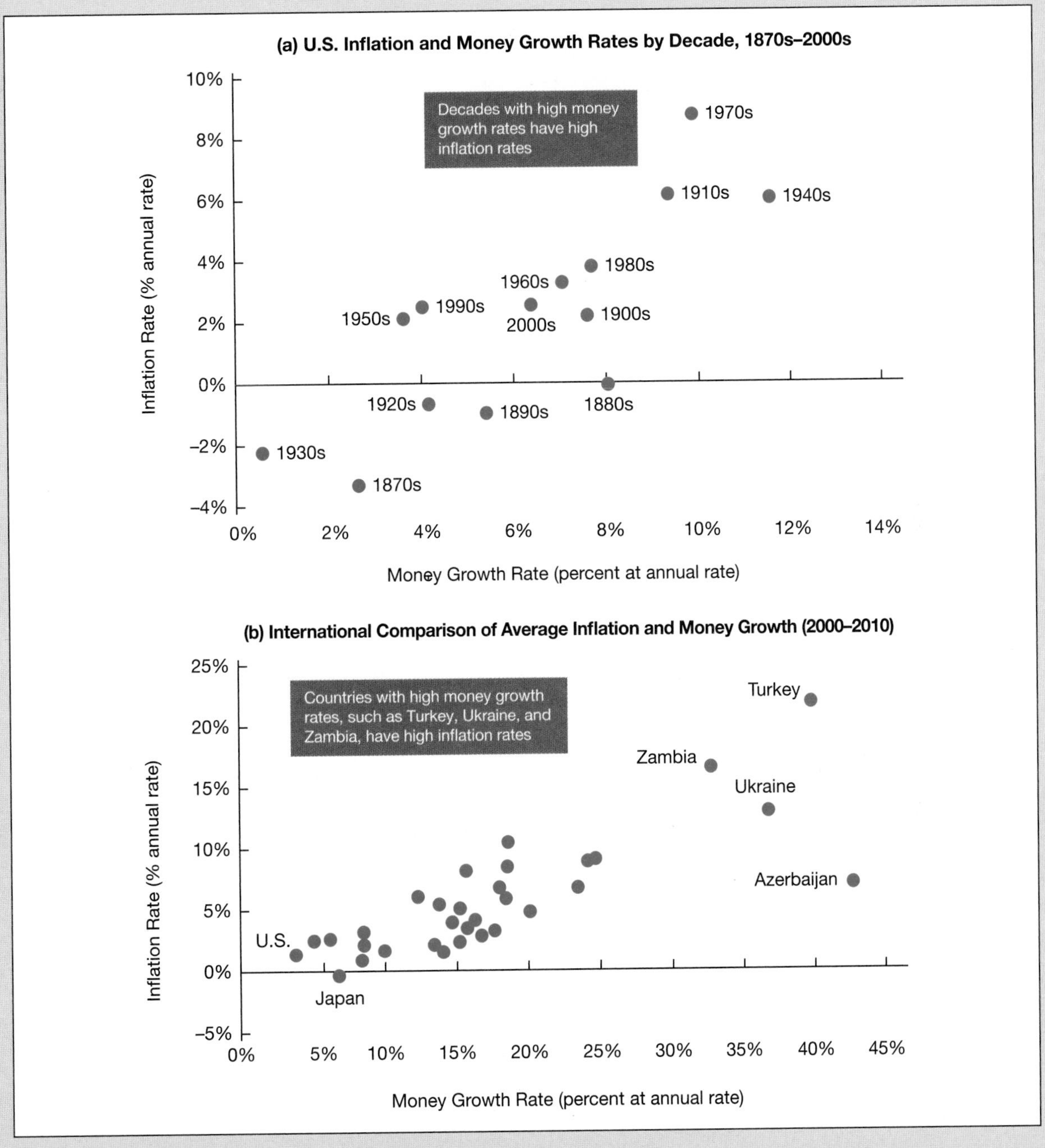

FIGURE 1 Relationship Between Inflation and Money Growth

In panel (a), decades with higher money growth rates (the 1910s, the 1940s, and the 1970s) typically have a higher average inflation rate. This relationship also holds in panel (b), where we examine the ten-year inflation and money growth rates from 2000–2010 for various countries.

Sources: For panel (a), Milton Friedman and Anna Schwartz, *Monetary trends in the United States and the United Kingdom: Their Relation to Income, Prices, and Interest Rates, 1867–1975,* Federal Reserve Economic Database (FRED), Federal Reserve Bank of St. Louis, http://research.stlouisfed.org/fred2/categories/25 and Bureau of Labor Statistics at http://data.bls.gov/cgi-bin/surveymost?cu. For panel (b), International Financial Statistics. International Monetary Fund, www.imfstatistics.org/imf/.

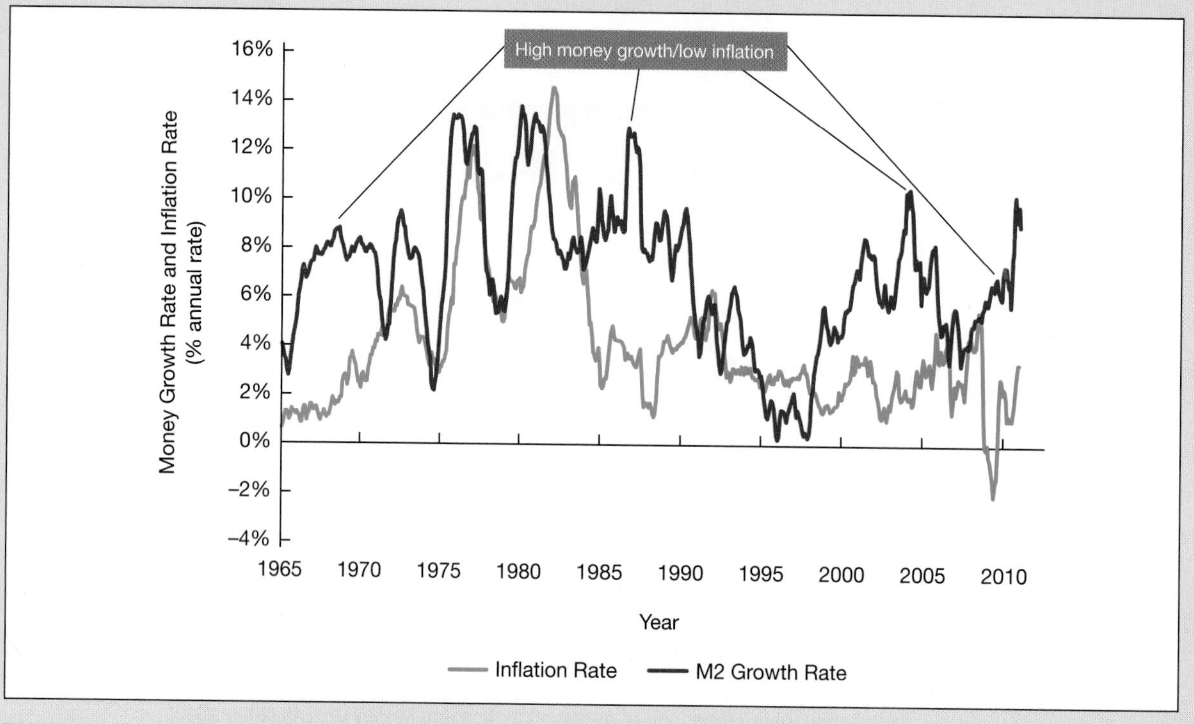

FIGURE 2 Annual U.S. Inflation and Money Growth Rates, 1965–2010

Plots of the annual U.S. inflation rate against the annual money (M2) growth rate from two years earlier (to allow for lagged effects from money growth to inflation) do not support a short-run link between inflation and money growth. There are many years (1963–1967, 1983–1985, and 2003–2005) in which money growth is high, yet inflation is low.

Sources: FRED, Federal Reserve Economic Data, Federal Reserve Bank of St. Louis; Bureau of Labor Statistics, http://research.stlouisfed.org/fred2/categories/25; accessed September 30, 2010.

BUDGET DEFICITS AND INFLATION

Budget deficits can be an important source of inflationary monetary policy. To see how this could be the case, we need to look at how a government finances its budget deficits.

Government Budget Constraint

Because the government has to pay its bills just as we do, it has a budget constraint. We can pay for our spending in two ways: raise revenue (by working) or borrow. The government also enjoys these two options: raise revenue by levying taxes or go into debt by issuing government bonds. Unlike us, however, it has a third option: The government can create money and use it to pay for the goods and services it buys.

Methods of financing government spending are described by an expression called the **government budget constraint**, which states the following: The government budget deficit *DEF*, which equals the excess of government spending *G* over tax revenue *T*, must equal the sum of the change in the monetary base ΔMB and the change in government bonds held by the public ΔB. Algebraically, this expression can be written as follows:

$$DEF = G - T = \Delta MB + \Delta B \tag{7}$$

To see what the government budget constraint means in practice, let's look at the case in which the only government purchase is a $100 million supercomputer. If the government convinces the electorate that such a computer is worth paying for, it will probably be able to raise the $100 million in taxes to pay for it, and the budget deficit will equal zero. The government budget constraint then tells us that no issue of money or bonds is needed to pay for the computer, because the budget is balanced. If taxpayers think that the supercomputer is too expensive and refuse to pay taxes for it, the budget constraint indicates that the government must pay for it by selling $100 million of new bonds to the public or by, in effect, printing $100 million of currency to pay for the computer. In either case, the budget constraint is satisfied. The $100 million deficit is balanced by the change in the stock of government bonds held by the public ($\Delta B = \$100$ million) or by the change in the monetary base ($\Delta MB = \$100$ million).

The government budget constraint thus reveals two important facts: ***If the government deficit is financed by an increase in bond holdings by the public, there is no effect on the monetary base and hence on the money supply. But if the deficit is not financed by increased bond holdings by the public, the monetary base and the money supply increase.***

There are several ways to understand why a deficit leads to an increase in the monetary base when the public's bond holdings do not increase. The simplest case is when a government's treasury has the legal right to issue currency to finance its deficit. Financing the deficit is then very straightforward: The government just pays for the spending that is in excess of its tax revenues with new currency. Because this increase in currency adds directly to the monetary base, the monetary base rises and the money supply with it through the process of multiple deposit creation described in Chapter 17.

In the United States, however, and in many other countries, the government does not have the right to issue currency to pay for its bills. In this case, the government must finance its deficit by first issuing bonds to the public to acquire the extra funds to pay its bills. Yet if these bonds do not end up in the hands of the public, the only alternative is that they are purchased by the central bank. For the government bonds not to end up in the hands of the public, the central bank must conduct an open market purchase, which, as we saw in Chapter 17, leads to an increase in the monetary base and in the money supply. This method of financing government spending is called **monetizing the debt** because, as indicated by the two-step process described, government debt issued to finance government spending has been removed from the hands of the public and has been replaced by high-powered money. This method of financing, or the more direct method when a government just issues the currency directly, is also, somewhat inaccurately, referred to as **printing money** because high-powered money (the monetary base) is created in the process. The use of the word *printing* is misleading because what is essential to this method of financing government spending is that the monetary base increases when the central bank conducts open market purchases, just as it would if more currency were put in circulation.

We thus see that a budget deficit can lead to an increase in the money supply if it is financed by the creation of high-powered money. However, because the quantity theory of money explains inflation only in the long run, to produce inflation, the budget deficit must be persistent, that is, last for a substantial period of time. This leads to the following conclusion: ***Financing a persistent deficit by money creation will lead to a sustained inflation.***

Hyperinflation

The analysis here can be used to explain **hyperinflations**, periods of extremely high inflation of more than 50% per month. Many economies—both poor and developed—have experienced hyperinflation over the past century, but the United States has been spared such turmoil. One of the most extreme examples of hyperinflation throughout world history occurred recently in Zimbabwe in the 2000s, and it is discussed in the application that follows.

APPLICATION ◆ The Zimbabwean Hyperinflation

We now use our analysis to explain the Zimbabwean hyperinflation that started in the early 2000s.

After the expropriation of farms, which were redistributed to supporters of Robert Mugabe, the president of the country, agricultural output plummeted, and, along with it, tax revenue. The result was that the government's expenditures now massively exceeded revenues. The government could have obtained revenues to cover its expenditures by raising taxes, but given the depressed state of the economy, generating revenue in this way was both hard to do and would have been politically unpopular. Alternatively, the government could have tried to finance its expenditure by borrowing from the public, but given the distrust of the government, this was not an option. There was only one route left: the printing press. The government could pay for its expenditures simply by printing more currency (increasing the money supply) and using it to make payments to individuals and businesses. This is exactly what the Zimbabwean government did and the money supply began to increase rapidly.

As predicted by the quantity theory, the surge in the money supply led to a rapidly rising price level. In February 2007, the Reserve Bank of Zimbabwe, the central bank, outlawed price increases on many commodities. Although this tactic has been tried before by governments in countries experiencing hyperinflations, it has never worked: Criminalizing inflation cannot stop inflation when the central bank keeps on printing money. In March 2007, the inflation rate hit a record of over 1,500%. By 2008, Zimbabwe's official inflation rate was over 2 million percent (but unofficially over 10 million percent). In July 2008, the Zimbabwean central bank issued a new \$100 billion bank note and shortly later issued a \$100 trillion dollar bill, the highest denomination dollar note on record. That's a lot of zeros, but don't be too impressed. Although holding one of these bills made you a trillionaire, it could not even buy a bottle of beer. Zimbabwean currency became worth less than toilet paper.

In 2009, the Zimbabwean government allowed the use of foreign currencies like the dollar for all transactions, but the damage had already been done. The hyperinflation wreaked havoc on the economy, and an extremely poor country became even poorer. ◆

KEYNESIAN THEORIES OF MONEY DEMAND

In his famous 1936 book *The General Theory of Employment, Interest and Money*, John Maynard Keynes abandoned the quantity theory view that velocity was a constant and developed a theory of money demand that emphasized the importance of interest rates.

In his theory of the demand for money, which he called the **liquidity preference theory**, Keynes presented three motives behind the demand for money: the transactions motive, the precautionary motive, and the speculative motive.

Transactions Motive

In the quantity theory approach, individuals are assumed to hold money because it is a medium of exchange that can be used to carry out everyday transactions. Keynes initially accepted the quantity theory view that the transactions component is proportional to income. Later, he and other economists recognized that new methods for payment, referred to as **payment technology**, could also affect the demand for money. For example, credit cards enable consumers to make even very small purchases without needing to hold money. Electronic payments that can be made from investors' brokerage accounts can also reduce money demand. As payment technology advances, the demand for money would be likely to decline relative to income.

Precautionary Motive

Keynes also recognized that people hold money as a cushion against unexpected wants. Suppose that you have been thinking about buying a new Wii entertainment system and now see that it is on sale at 25% off. If you are holding money as a precaution for just such an occurrence, you can immediately buy it. Keynes argued that the precautionary money balances people want to hold would also be proportional to income.

Speculative Motive

Keynes also believed people choose to hold money as a store of wealth, which he called the *speculative motive*. Because the definition of money in Keynes's analysis includes currency (which earns no interest) and checking account deposits (which typically earn little interest), he assumed that money earns no interest and hence its opportunity cost relative to holding other assets, such as bonds, is the nominal interest rate on bonds, i. As the interest rate i rises, the opportunity cost of money rises (it is more costly to hold money relative to bonds) and the quantity of money demanded falls.

Putting the Three Motives Together

In putting the three motives for holding money balances together into a demand for money equation, Keynes was careful to distinguish between nominal quantities and real quantities. Money is valued in terms of what it can buy. If, for example, all prices in the economy double (the price level doubles), the same nominal quantity of money will only be able to buy half as many goods. Keynes thus reasoned that people want to hold a certain amount of **real money balances** (the quantity of money in real terms). Combining the three motives for holding money balances into a demand for real money balances led to what Keynes called the liquidity preference function, which is written as follows:

$$\frac{M^d}{P} = L(\underset{-}{i}, \underset{+}{Y}) \tag{8}$$

Equation 8 says that the demand for real money balances is negatively related to the nominal interest rate and is positively related to real income.

Later Keynesian economists, such as Nobel Prize winner James Tobin, expanded the analysis and showed that interest rates play a more important role in money demand than even Keynes supposed. They demonstrated that even the transactions and precautionary demand for money would also be negatively related to the interest rate.[3]

An important implication of Keynesian theories of money demand is that velocity is not a constant but will fluctuate with changes in interest rates. To illustrate, we write the liquidity preference function as follows:

$$\frac{P}{M^d} = \frac{1}{L(i,Y)}$$

Multiplying both sides of this equation by Y and recognizing that we can replace M^d by M because they must be equal in money market equilibrium, we solve for velocity:

$$V = \frac{PY}{M} = \frac{Y}{L(i,Y)} \tag{9}$$

We know that the demand for money is negatively related to interest rates; when i goes up, $L(i,Y)$ declines, and therefore velocity rises. Because interest rates have substantial fluctuations, Keynesian theories of the demand for money indicate that velocity has substantial fluctuations as well. Thus Keynesian theories cast doubt on the classical quantity theory view that nominal income is determined primarily by movements in the quantity of money.

PORTFOLIO THEORIES OF MONEY DEMAND

Related to Keynes's analysis of the demand for money are so-called portfolio theories of money demand, in which people decide how much of an asset such as money they want to hold as part of their overall portfolio of assets.[4]

Theory of Portfolio Choice and Keynesian Liquidity Preference

In Chapter 5, we developed the theory of portfolio choice, which stated that the demand for an asset is positively related to wealth, expected return relative to other assets, and relative liquidity, whereas it is negatively related to its risk relative to other assets. This theory of portfolio choice can justify the conclusion from the Keynesian liquidity preference function that the demand for real money balances is positively related to income and negatively related to the nominal interest rate.

[3]Three famous papers that elaborated on Keynes's approach to the demand for money are as follows: William J. Baumol, "The Transactions Demand for Cash: An Inventory Theoretic Approach," *Quarterly Journal of Economics* 66 (1952): 545–556; James Tobin, "The Interest Elasticity of the Transactions Demand for Cash," *Review of Economics and Statistics* 38 (1956): 241–247; and James Tobin, "Liquidity Preference as Behavior Towards Risk," *Review of Economic Studies* 25 (1958): 65–86. For further discussion of the models in these papers, see the first appendix to this chapter, which can be found on the Companion Website, www.pearsonhighered.com/mishkin.

[4]This is the approach taken by Milton Friedman in his famous paper, "The Quantity Theory of Money: A Restatement," in *Studies in the Quantity Theory of Money*, ed. Milton Friedman (Chicago: University of Chicago Press, 1956), 3–21.

Because income and wealth tend to move together, when income is higher, wealth is likely to be as well. Hence, higher income means that wealth is higher, and the theory of portfolio choice then indicates that the demand for the money asset will rise and the demand for real money balances will be higher.

As interest rates rise, the expected return for money does not change. However, the return for bonds, an alternative asset, goes up. Thus, although the expected *absolute* return of money did not change, money's expected return *relative* to bonds went down. In other words, as the theory of portfolio choice indicates, higher interest rates make money less desirable, and the demand for real money balances falls.

Other Factors That Affect the Demand for Money

The theory of portfolio choice indicates that other factors besides income and the nominal interest rate can affect the demand for money. We look at each of these in turn.

Wealth. The theory of portfolio choice posits that as wealth increases, investors have more resources to purchase assets, increasing the demand for money. However, when income is held constant, greater wealth has only a small effect on the demand for money. In general, investors will hold only a small amount of money in their investment portfolio, preferring interest-bearing assets with similar risk and liquidity profiles, such as money market mutual funds, that are not included in measures of money such as M1. Currency and checkable deposits are sometimes said to be **dominated assets**, because investors can hold other assets that pay higher returns and yet are perceived to be just as safe.

Risk. It's hard to imagine an asset less risky than money. Currency will always be accepted, unless there's a revolution and the new government does not accept the old government's currency. And bank deposits are safe as long as deposit insurance exists. In the theory of portfolio choice, however, risk is always measured relative to another asset. Thus, if the stock market becomes more volatile, money can become less risky relative to stocks and demand for it will increase. In addition, although money is extremely safe on a nominal basis, its real return (the nominal return minus expected inflation) can become highly variable when inflation becomes very variable. Higher variability in the real return of money lowers demand for money, as people shift into alternative assets known as **inflation hedges**, whose real returns are less affected than that of money when inflation varies. Popular inflation hedges include TIPS (Treasury Inflation Protected Securities), gold, and real estate.

Liquidity of Other Assets. In recent years, financial innovation has led to the development of new liquid assets, such as money market mutual funds or home equity lines of credit, that allow households to write checks that are backed by their homes. As these alternative assets become more liquid, the relative liquidity of money falls and so the demand for money would fall as well.

Summary

Our analysis of the demand for money using Keynesian and portfolio theories indicates that seven factors affect the demand for money: interest rates, income, payment technology, wealth, riskiness of other assets, inflation risk, and liquidity of other assets. As a study aid, Summary Table 1 indicates the response of money demand to changes in each of these factors and gives a brief synopsis of the reasoning behind each response.

SUMMARY TABLE 1

Factors That Determine the Demand for Money

Variable	Change in Variable	Money Demand Response	Reason
Interest rates	↑	↓	Opportunity cost of money rises
Income	↑	↑	Higher transactions
Payment technology	↑	↓	Less need for money in transactions
Wealth	↑	↑	More resources to put into money
Risk of other assets	↑	↑	Money relatively less risky and so more desirable
Inflation risk	↑	↓	Money relatively more risky and so less desirable
Liquidity of other assets	↑	↓	Money relatively less liquid and so less desirable

EMPIRICAL EVIDENCE FOR THE DEMAND FOR MONEY

Here we examine the empirical evidence for the two key issues that distinguish different theories of money demand and affect their conclusions about whether the quantity of money is the primary determinant of aggregate spending: Is the demand for money sensitive to changes in interest rates and is the demand for money function stable over time?[5]

Interest Rates and Money Demand

We have established that if interest rates do not affect the demand for money, velocity is more likely to be constant—or at least predictable—so that the quantity theory view that aggregate spending is determined by the quantity of money is more likely to be true. However, the more sensitive to interest rates the demand for money is, the more unpredictable velocity will be, and the less clear the link between the money supply and aggregate spending will be. Indeed, there is an extreme case of ultrasensitivity of the demand for money to interest rates, called the **liquidity trap**, in which conventional monetary policy has no direct effect on aggregate spending, because a change in the money supply has no effect on interest rates.[6]

The evidence for the interest sensitivity of the demand for money is remarkably consistent. Neither extreme case is supported by the data: In situations in which

[5]If you are interested in a more detailed discussion of the empirical research on the demand for money, you can find it in a second appendix for this chapter on the Companion Website, www.pearsonhighered.com/mishkin.

[6]If the demand for money is ultrasensitive to interest rates, a tiny change in interest rates produces a very large change in the quantity of money demanded. Hence, in this case, the demand for money is completely flat in the supply and demand diagrams of Chapter 5. Therefore, a change in the money supply that shifts the money supply curve to the right or left results in it intersecting the flat money demand curve at the same unchanged interest rate.

nominal interest rates have not hit a floor of zero, the demand for money is sensitive to interest rates, and little evidence is present that a liquidity trap has ever existed. However, when nominal interest rates fall to zero, they can go no lower. In this situation, a liquidity trap has occurred because the demand for money is now completely flat. Indeed, exactly this situation has occurred in the United States in recent years, which is why the Federal Reserve has had to resort to nonconventional monetary policy.

Stability of Money Demand

If the money demand function, like the one in Equation 8, is unstable and undergoes substantial, unpredictable shifts, as Keynes believed, then velocity is unpredictable, and the quantity of money may not be tightly linked to aggregate spending, as it is in the quantity theory. The stability of the money demand function is also crucial to whether the Federal Reserve should target interest rates or the money supply. If the money demand function is unstable and so the money supply is not closely linked to aggregate spending, then the level of interest rates the Fed sets will provide more information about the stance of monetary policy than will the money supply.

Until the early 1970s, evidence strongly supported the stability of the money demand function. However, after 1973, the rapid pace of financial innovation, which changed the items that could be used for money, led to substantial instability in estimated money demand functions. The instability of the money demand function calls into question whether our theories and empirical analyses are adequate. It also has important implications for the conduct of monetary policy, because it casts doubt on the usefulness of the money demand function as a tool to provide guidance to policy makers. In particular, because the money demand function has become unstable, velocity is now harder to predict. Monetary policy makers have found that the money supply does not provide reliable information on the future course of the economy, leading them to think of monetary policy in terms of the setting of interest rates. The instability of money demand has thus led to a downgrading of the focus on money supply in the conduct of monetary policy.

Summary

1. The quantity theory of money as expressed by the equation of exchange, $M \times V = P \times Y$, indicates that nominal spending is determined solely by movements in the quantity of money. The quantity theory indicates that (1) changes in the quantity of money lead to proportional changes in the price level, because $P = (M \times \bar{V})/\bar{Y}$, and (2) the inflation rate is the growth rate of the money supply minus the growth rate of aggregate output—that is, $\pi = \%\Delta M - \%\Delta Y$. These implications of the quantity theory are borne out in the data in the long run, but not the short run.
2. The government budget constraint indicates that a deficit must be financed by either money creation or the issuing of government bonds. That is, $DEF = G - T = \Delta MB + \Delta B$. Combining this fact with the quantity theory indicates that financing a persistent deficit by money creation will lead to a sustained inflation. This analysis helps explain hyperinflations, in which inflation and money growth go to extremely high levels because of massive budget deficits.
3. John Maynard Keynes suggested three motives for holding money: the transactions motive, the precautionary motive, and the speculative motive. His resulting liquidity preference theory views the transactions and precautionary components of money demand as proportional to income. However, the speculative component of money demand is viewed as sensitive to interest rates as well as to expectations about the future movements of interest rates. This theory, then, implies that velocity is unstable and cannot be treated as a constant.

4. Portfolio theories of money demand indicate that the demand for money is determined not only by interest rates, income, and payment technology, as in the Keynesian analysis, but also by wealth, riskiness of other assets, inflation risk, and liquidity of other assets.
5. Two main conclusions can be reached from the research on the demand for money: The demand for money is sensitive to interest rates, but little evidence exists that it is or has been ultrasensitive (liquidity trap). Since 1973, money demand has been found to be unstable, with the most likely source of the instability being the rapid pace of financial innovation. Because the money demand function is found to be both unstable and sensitive to interest rates, velocity cannot be viewed as constant and is not easily predictable. This situation has led to a downgrading of the focus on money supply and a greater emphasis on interest rates in the conduct of monetary policy.

Key Terms

demand for money, p. 552
dominated assets, p. 561
equation of exchange, p. 551
government budget constraint, p. 556
hyperinflations, p. 558
inflation hedges, p. 561
liquidity trap, p. 562
liquidity preference theory, p. 559
monetizing the debt, p. 557
monetary theory, p. 550
payment technology, p. 559
printing money, p. 557
quantity theory of money, p. 552
real money balances, p. 559
velocity of money, p. 551

Questions

All questions are available in MyEconLab *at* www.myeconlab.com.

1. How would you expect velocity to typically behave over the business cycle?
2. If velocity and aggregate output are reasonably constant (as the classical economists believed), what happens to the price level when the money supply increases from \$1 trillion to \$4 trillion?
3. If credit cards were made illegal by congressional legislation, what would happen to velocity? Explain your answer.
4. "If nominal GDP rises, velocity must rise." Is this statement true, false, or uncertain? Explain your answer.
5. Why would a central bank be concerned about persistent, long-term budget deficits?
6. "Persistent budget deficits always lead to higher inflation." Is this statement true, false, or uncertain? Explain your answer.
7. Suppose a new "payment technology" allows individuals to make payments using U.S. Treasury bonds (i.e., U.S. Treasury bonds are immediately cashed when needed to make a payment and that balance is transferred to the payee). How do you think this payment technology would affect the transaction components of the demand for money?
8. The use of some payment technologies requires some infrastructure (e.g., merchants need to have access to credit card swiping machines). In most developing countries, this infrastructure is either nonexistent or very costly. Everything else being the same, would you expect the transaction component of the demand for money to be greater or smaller in a developing country than in a rich country?
9. What three motives for holding money did Keynes consider in his liquidity preference theory of the demand for real money balances? On the basis of these motives, what variables did he think determined the demand for money?
10. In many countries, people hold money as a cushion against unexpected needs arising from a variety of potential scenarios (e.g., banking crises, natural disasters, health problems, unemployment, etc.) that are not usually covered by insurance markets. Explain the

effect of such behavior on the precautionary component of the demand for money.

11. In Keynes's analysis of the speculative demand for money, what will happen to money demand if people suddenly decide that the normal level of the interest rate has declined? Why?

12. Why is Keynes's analysis of the speculative demand for money important to his view that velocity will undergo substantial fluctuations and thus cannot be treated as constant?

13. According to the portfolio theories of money demand, what are the four factors that determine money demand? What changes in these can increase the demand for money?

14. Explain how the following events will affect the demand for money according to the portfolio theories of money demand:
   a. The economy experiences a business cycle contraction.
   b. Brokerage fees decline, making bond transactions cheaper.
   c. The stock market crashes (*Hint:* Consider both the increase in stock price volatility following a market crash and the decrease in wealth of stockholders).

15. Suppose a given country experienced low and stable inflation rates for quite some time, but then inflation picked up and over the past decade has been relatively high and quite unpredictable. Explain how this new inflationary environment would affect the demand for money according to portfolio theories of money demand. What would happen if the government decides to issue inflation-protected securities?

16. Consider the portfolio choice theory of money demand. How do you think the demand for money will be affected during a hyperinflation (i.e., monthly inflation rates in excess of 50%)?

17. Both the portfolio choice and Keynes's theories of the demand for money suggest that as the relative expected return on money falls, demand for it will fall. Why would the portfolio choice approach predict that money demand is unaffected by changes in interest rates? Why did Keynes think that money demand is affected by changes in interest rates?

18. Why does the Keynesian view of the demand for money suggest that velocity is unpredictable?

19. What evidence is used to assess the stability of the money demand function? What does the evidence suggest about the stability of money demand and how has this affected monetary policy making?

20. Suppose that a plot of the values of M2 and nominal GDP for a given country over 40 years shows that these two variables are very closely related. In particular, a plot of their ratio (nominal GDP/M2) yields very stable and easy-to-predict values. On the basis of this evidence, would you recommend the monetary authorities of this country to conduct monetary policy by focusing mostly on the money supply rather than on setting interest rates? Explain why.

Applied Problems

All applied problems are available in MyEconLab *at* www.myeconlab.com.

21. Suppose the money supply *M* has been growing at 10% per year, and nominal GDP, *PY*, has been growing at 20% per year. The data are as follows (in billions of dollars):

	2010	2011	2012
M	100	110	121
PY	1,000	1,200	1,440

Calculate the velocity in each year. At what rate is velocity growing?

22. Calculate what happens to nominal GDP if velocity remains constant at 5 and the money supply increases from $200 billion to $300 billion.

23. What happens to nominal GDP if the money supply grows by 20% but velocity declines by 30%?

24. If velocity and aggregate output remain constant at $5 and $1,000 billion, respectively, what happens to the price level if the money supply declines from $400 billion to $300 billion?

25. Suppose the liquidity preference function is given by

$$L(i,Y) = \frac{Y}{8} - 1{,}000i$$

Calculate velocity for each period, using the money demand equation, along with the following table of values

	Period 1	Period 2	Period 3	Period 4	Period 5	Period 6	Period 7
Y (in billions)	12,000	12,500	12,250	12,500	12,800	13,000	13,200
Interest rate	0.05	0.07	0.03	0.05	0.07	0.04	0.06

Web Exercises

1. The formula for computing the velocity of money is GDP/M1. Go to www.research.stlouisfed.org/fred2 and look up the GDP. Next go to www.federalreserve.gov/Releases/h6/Current/ and find M1. Compute the most recent year's velocity of money and compare it to its level in 2002. Has it risen or fallen? Suggest reasons for its change since that time.
2. John Maynard Keynes is among the most well-known economic theorists. Go to http://www.newschool.edu/nssr/het/profiles/keynes.htm and write a one-page summary of his life and contributions.

Web References

www.usagold.com/gildedopinion/puplava/20020614.html

A summary of how various factors affect the velocity of money.

http://www.newschool.edu/nssr/het/profiles/keynes.htm

A brief history of John Maynard Keynes.

Web Appendices

Please visit the Companion Website at www.pearsonhighered.com/mishkin to read the Web appendices to Chapter 22.

Appendix 1: **The Baumol-Tobin and the Tobin Mean-Variance Models of the Demand for Money**

Appendix 2: **Empirical Evidence on the Demand for Money**

23 Aggregate Demand and Supply Analysis

Preview

In earlier chapters, we focused considerable attention on monetary policy, because it touches our everyday lives by affecting the prices of the goods we buy and the quantity of available jobs. In this chapter, we develop a basic tool, aggregate demand and supply analysis, that will enable us to study the effects of monetary policy on output and prices. *Aggregate demand* is the total amount of output demanded at different inflation rates. *Aggregate supply* is the total amount of output that firms in the economy want to sell at different inflation rates. As with the supply and demand analysis from your earlier economics courses, equilibrium occurs at the intersection of the aggregate demand and aggregate supply curves.

Aggregate demand and supply analysis will enable us to explore how aggregate output and inflation are determined. (The Following the Financial News box indicates where and how often data on aggregate output and the inflation rate are published.) Not only will the analysis help us interpret the past, but also recent episodes in the business cycle, such as the recent severe recession in 2007–2009.

AGGREGATE DEMAND

The first building block of aggregate supply and demand analysis is the **aggregate demand curve**, which describes the relationship between the quantity of aggregate output demanded and the inflation rate when all other variables are held constant.

Aggregate demand is made up of four component parts: **consumption expenditure**, the total demand for consumer goods and services; **planned investment spending**,[1] the total planned spending by business firms on new machines, factories, and other capital goods, plus planned spending on new homes; **government purchases**, spending by all levels of government (federal, state, and local) on goods and services (paper clips, computers, computer programming, missiles, government workers, and so on); and **net exports**, the net foreign spending on domestic goods and services, equal to exports minus imports. Using the symbols C for consumption expenditure, I for planned investment spending, G for government spending, and NX for net exports, we can write the following expression for aggregate demand Y^{ad}:

$$Y^{ad} = C + I + G + NX$$

[1]Recall that economists restrict use of the word *investment* to the purchase of new physical capital, such as a new machine or a new house, that adds to spending on newly produced goods or services. This differs from every day use of the term by noneconomists who use the word investment to describe purchases of common stocks or bonds, purchases that do not necessarily involve newly produced goods and services. But when economists speak of investment spending, they are referring to the purchase of new physical assets such as new machines or new houses—purchases that add to aggregate demand.

Following the Financial News — Aggregate Output, Unemployment, and Inflation

Newspapers and Internet sites periodically report data that provide information on the level of aggregate output, unemployment, and the price level. Here is a list of the relevant data series, their frequency, and when they are published.

Aggregate Output and Unemployment

Real GDP: Quarterly (January–March, April–June, July–September, October–December); published three to four weeks after the end of a quarter.

Industrial production: Monthly. Industrial production is not as comprehensive a measure of aggregate output as real GDP, because it measures only manufacturing output; the estimate for the previous month is reported in the middle of the following month.

Unemployment rate: Monthly; previous month's figure is usually published on the Friday of the first week of the following month.

Inflation Rate

There are several different measures of the inflation rate that are calculated from different measures of the price level.

GDP deflator: Quarterly. This comprehensive measure of the price level (described in the appendix to Chapter 1) is published at the same time as the real GDP data.

Consumer price index (CPI): Monthly. The CPI is a measure of the price level for consumers (also described in the appendix to Chapter 1); the value for the previous month is published in the third or fourth week of the following month.

PCE deflator: Quarterly. This is another measure of the price level for consumers. It is calculated in a similar way to the GDP deflator, but applies only to the items that are in the personal consumption expenditure category of GDP. It is published at the same time as the real GDP data.

Producer price index (PPI): Monthly. The PPI is a measure of the average level of wholesale prices charged by producers and is published at the same time as industrial production data.

Deriving the Aggregate Demand Curve

The first step to deriving the aggregate demand curve is to recognize that when the inflation rate rises ($\pi\uparrow$), the monetary authorities will raise the real interest rate ($r\uparrow$) in order to keep inflation from spiraling out of control. Next we can examine the effects of higher real interest rates on the individual components of aggregate demand. The resulting higher cost of financing purchases of new physical capital makes investment less profitable and causes planned investment spending to decline ($I\downarrow$). Because, as shown in Equation 1, planned investment spending is included in aggregate demand, the decline in planned investment spending causes aggregate demand to fall ($Y^{ad}\downarrow$). A higher inflation rate therefore leads to a lower level of the quantity of aggregate output demanded ($\pi\uparrow \Rightarrow Y^{ad}\downarrow$), and so the aggregate demand curve slopes down as in Figure 1. Schematically, we can write the mechanism just described as follows:[2]

$$\pi\uparrow \Rightarrow r\uparrow \Rightarrow I\downarrow \Rightarrow Y^{ad}\downarrow$$

[2]Note that an additional mechanism for a downward sloping aggregate demand curve operates through net exports, and is discussed in Web Chapters 1 and 2.

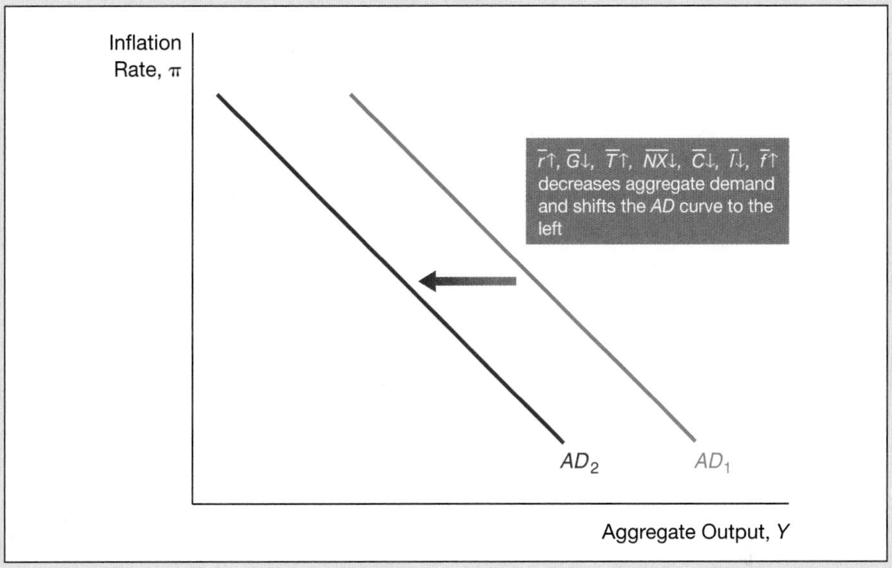
Inflation Rate, π
$\bar{r}\uparrow$, $\bar{G}\downarrow$, $\bar{T}\uparrow$, $\overline{NX}\downarrow$, $\bar{C}\downarrow$, $\bar{I}\downarrow$, $\bar{f}\uparrow$ decreases aggregate demand and shifts the *AD* curve to the left
AD_2
AD_1
Aggregate Output, *Y*

FIGURE 1

Leftward Shift in the Aggregate Demand Curve

The aggregate demand curve shifts to the left from AD_1 to AD_2 when there is an autonomous tightening of monetary policy ($\bar{r}\uparrow$), a decrease in government purchases ($\bar{G}\downarrow$), an increase in taxes ($\bar{T}\uparrow$), a decrease in net exports ($\overline{NX}\downarrow$), a decrease in autonomous consumption expenditure ($\bar{C}\downarrow$), a decrease in autonomous investment ($\bar{I}\downarrow$), or an increase in financial frictions ($\bar{f}\uparrow$).

Factors That Shift the Aggregate Demand Curve

Seven basic factors (often referred to as **demand shocks**) can shift the aggregate demand curve to a new position: (1) autonomous monetary policy, (2) government purchases, (3) taxes, (4) autonomous net exports, (5) autonomous consumption expenditure, (6) autonomous investment, and (7) financial frictions. As we examine each case, we ask what happens when each of these factors changes holding the inflation rate constant. As a study aid, Summary Table 1 summarizes the shifts in the aggregate demand curve from each of these seven factors.

1. *Autonomous monetary policy*. We have already noted that when current inflation rises, the central bank will raise the real interest rate to keep inflation from spiraling out of control. However, there are central-bank movements in the real interest rate that are autonomous, denoted by $\bar{r}$, which are movements unrelated to the variables in the model, such as the current level of the inflation rate. When the Federal Reserve decides to increase this autonomous component of the real interest rate, $\bar{r}$, the higher real interest rate at any given inflation rate leads to a higher cost of financing investment projects, which leads to a decline in investment spending and the quantity of aggregate demand, as the following schematic demonstrates.

$$\bar{r}\uparrow \Rightarrow I\downarrow \Rightarrow Y^{ad}\downarrow$$

   Therefore aggregate demand falls at any given inflation rate and the aggregate demand curve shifts to the left as in Figure 1.
2. *Government purchases*. An increase in government purchases at any given inflation rate adds directly to aggregate demand expenditure, and hence aggregate demand rises:

$$\bar{G}\uparrow \Rightarrow Y^{ad}\uparrow$$

   Aggregate demand, therefore, rises at any given inflation rate and the aggregate demand curve shifts to the right as in Figure 2.

SUMMARY TABLE 1

Factors That Shift the Aggregate Demand Curve

Factor	Change	Shift in Aggregate Demand Curve
Autonomous monetary policy, $\bar{r}$	↑	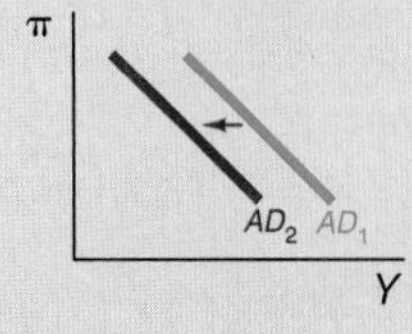
Government purchases, $\bar{G}$	↑	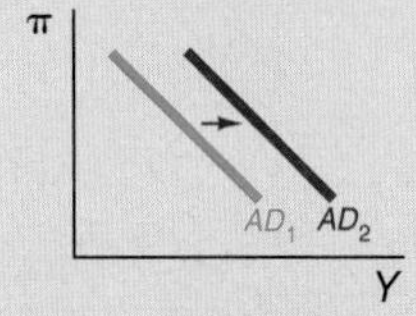
Taxes, $\bar{T}$	↑	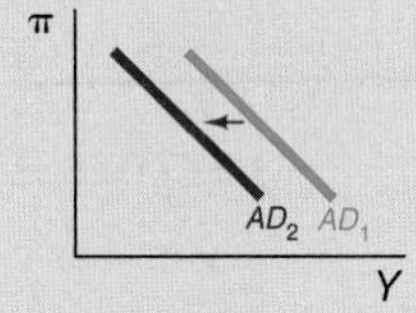
Autonomous net exports, $\overline{NX}$	↑	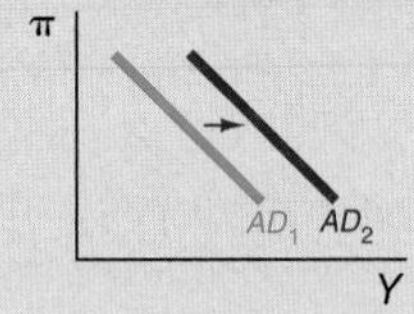
Autonomous consumption expenditure, $\bar{C}$	↑	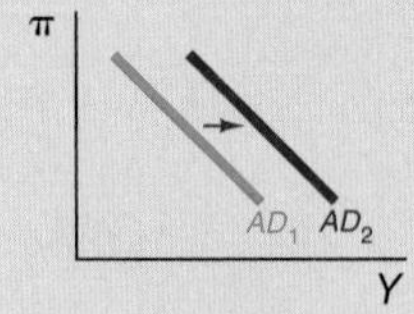
Autonomous investment, $\bar{I}$	↑	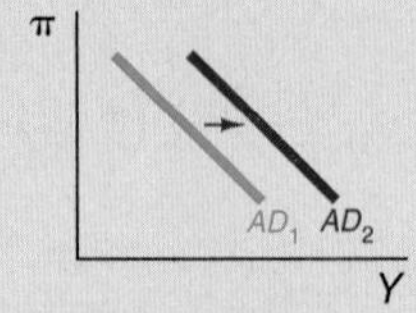
Financial frictions, $\bar{f}$	↑	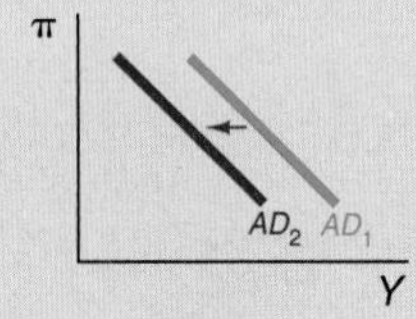

Note: Only increases (↑) in the factors are shown. The effect of decreases in the factors would be the opposite of those indicated in the "Shift" column.

FIGURE 2

Rightward Shift in the Aggregate Demand Curve

The aggregate demand curve shifts to the right from AD_1 to AD_2 when there is an autonomous easing of monetary policy ($\bar{r}\downarrow$), an increase in government purchases ($\bar{G}\uparrow$), a decrease in taxes ($\bar{T}\downarrow$), an increase in net exports ($\overline{NX}\uparrow$), an increase in autonomous consumption expenditure ($\bar{C}\uparrow$), an increase in autonomous investment ($\bar{I}\uparrow$), or a decrease in financial frictions ($\bar{f}\downarrow$).

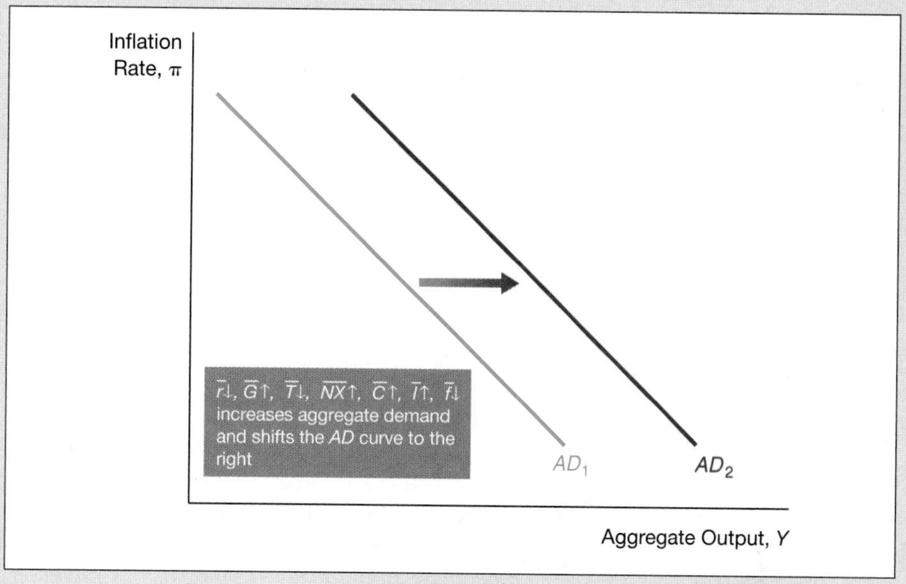

3. *Taxes.* At any given inflation rate, an increase in taxes lowers disposable income, which will lead to lower consumption expenditure and aggregate demand, so that aggregate demand falls:

$$\bar{T}\uparrow \Rightarrow C\downarrow \Rightarrow Y^{ad}\downarrow$$

Aggregate demand falls at any given inflation rate and the aggregate demand curve shifts to the left as in Figure 1.

4. *Autonomous net exports.* An autonomous increase in net exports at any given inflation rate adds directly to aggregate demand and so raises aggregate demand:

$$\overline{NX}\uparrow \Rightarrow Y^{ad}\uparrow$$

Aggregate demand rises at any given inflation rate and the aggregate demand curve shifts to the right as in Figure 2.

5. *Autonomous consumption expenditure.* When consumers become more optimistic, autonomous consumption expenditure rises and so they spend more at any given inflation rate. Aggregate demand therefore rises:

$$\bar{C}\uparrow \Rightarrow Y^{ad}\uparrow$$

Aggregate demand rises at any given inflation rate, and the aggregate demand curve shifts to the right as in Figure 2.

6. *Autonomous investment.* When businesses become more optimistic, autonomous investment rises and they spend more at any given inflation rate. Planned investment increases, and aggregate demand rises.

$$\bar{I}\uparrow \Rightarrow Y^{ad}\uparrow$$

Aggregate demand rises at any given inflation rate, and the aggregate demand curve shifts to the right as in Figure 2.

7. *Financial frictions.* The real cost of borrowing reflects not only the real interest rate on default-free debt instruments, r, but also financial frictions, denoted by $\bar{f}$, which are additions to the real cost of borrowing because of asymmetric information problems in financial markets that were described in Chapter 8. When financial frictions increase, the real cost of borrowing increases, so that planned investment spending falls at any given inflation rate and aggregate demand falls.

$$\bar{f}\uparrow \Rightarrow Y^{ad}\downarrow$$

Aggregate demand falls at any given inflation rate, and the aggregate demand curve shifts to the left as in Figure 1.

The conclusion from this analysis is as follows: ***Aggregate demand increases at any given inflation rate, and the aggregate demand curve shifts to the right when there is: (1) an autonomous easing of monetary policy ($\bar{r}\downarrow$), (2) an increase in government purchases ($\bar{G}\uparrow$), (3) a decrease in taxes ($\bar{T}\downarrow$), (4) an increase in net exports ($\overline{NX}\uparrow$), (5) an increase in autonomous consumption expenditure ($\bar{C}\uparrow$), (6) an increase in autonomous investment $\bar{I}\uparrow$, or (7) a decrease in financial frictions ($\bar{f}\downarrow$). Conversely, the aggregate demand curve shifts to the left when any of these factors change in the opposite direction.***

AGGREGATE SUPPLY

To complete our analysis we need to derive an **aggregate supply curve**, the relationship between the quantity of output supplied and the price level. In the typical supply and demand analysis, we have only one supply curve, but because prices and wages take time to adjust to their long-run level, the aggregate supply curve differs in the short and long runs. First, we examine the long-run aggregate supply curve. We then derive the short-run aggregate supply curve. Then we look at how both these curves shift over time and how the economy moves from the short run to the long run.

Long-Run Aggregate Supply Curve

The amount of output that can be produced in the economy in the long run is determined by the amount of capital in the economy, the amount of labor supplied at full employment, and the available technology. As discussed in Chapter 19, some unemployment cannot be helped because it is either frictional or structural. Thus at full employment, unemployment is not at zero, but is rather at a level above zero at which the demand for labor equals the supply of labor. This **natural rate of unemployment** is where the economy gravitates to in the long run. Many economists believe that the natural rate of unemployment is currently around 5%.

The level of aggregate output produced at the natural rate of unemployment is called the **natural rate of output** but is more often referred to as **potential output**: It is where the economy settles in the long run for any inflation rate. Hence the long-run

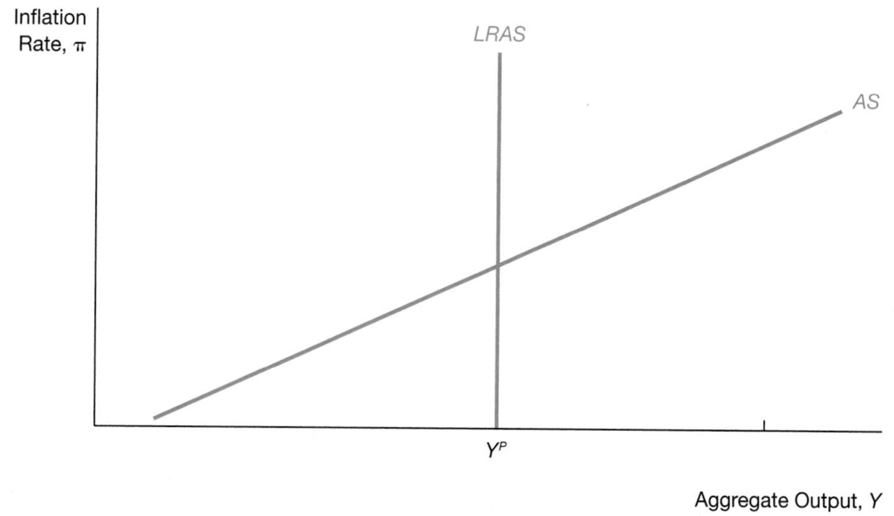

FIGURE 3 Long- and Short-Run Aggregate Supply Curves
The amount of aggregate output supplied at any given inflation rate is at potential output in the long run, so that the long-run aggregate supply curve *LRAS* is a vertical line at Y^P. The short-run aggregate supply curve, *AS*, is upward-sloping because as Y rises relative to Y^P, labor markets get tighter and inflation rises.

aggregate supply curve (*LRAS*) is vertical at potential output, denoted by Y^P, as drawn in Figure 3.

Short-Run Aggregate Supply Curve

The short-run aggregate supply curve is based on the intuition that three factors drive inflation: (1) expectations of inflation, (2) output gap and (3) price (supply) shocks.

Expected Inflation, π^e Workers and firms care about wages in real terms—that is, in terms of the goods and services that wages can buy. When workers expect the price level to be rising, they will adjust nominal wages upward one-for-one with the rise in expected inflation, so that the real wage rate does not decrease. Because wages are the most important cost of producing goods and services, overall inflation will also rise one-for-one with increases in expected inflation.

Output Gap The **output gap** is defined as the difference between aggregate output and potential output, $Y - Y^P$. When output exceeds its potential level and the output gap is high, there is very little slack in the economy and workers will demand higher wages and firms will take the opportunity to raise prices. The result will be higher inflation. Conversely, when the output gap is negative, there will be a lot of slack in the economy and workers will accept smaller increases in wages and firms will need to lower prices to sell their goods, resulting in lower inflation. The short-run aggregate supply curve will therefore be upward-sloping, as is depicted in Figure 3, because the higher is aggregate output, the greater is the output gap, the less slack there is in the economy, and inflation will be higher.

Price (Supply) Shocks **Supply shocks** occur when there are shocks to the supply of goods and services produced in the economy that translate into **price shocks**, that is, shifts in inflation that are independent of the amount of slack in the economy or expected inflation. For example, when supply of oil is restricted, as has occurred several times when wars have taken place in the Middle East, the resulting rise in the price of oil led firms to raise prices to reflect increased costs of production, thus driving up inflation. Energy price shocks can also occur when demand increases from developing countries like China, as occurred in 2007–2008 and again in 2011, again driving up inflation. Price shocks could also come from a rise in import prices or from **cost-push shocks**, in which workers push for wages higher than productivity gains, thereby driving up costs and inflation.

Short-Run Aggregate Supply Curve Putting all the analysis together results in a short-run aggregate supply curve that can be written as follows:[3]

$$\begin{array}{ccccccc} \pi & = & \pi^e & + & \gamma(Y - Y^P) & + & \rho \\ \text{Inflation} & = & \text{Expected Inflation} & + & \gamma \times \text{Output Gap} & + & \text{Price Shock} \end{array} \qquad (2)$$

where

$$\begin{aligned} \pi &= \text{inflation,} \\ \pi^e &= \text{expected inflation,} \\ Y - Y^P &= \text{output gap,} \\ \gamma &= \text{the sensitivity of inflation to the output gap,} \\ \rho &= \text{price shock.} \end{aligned}$$

The short-run aggregate supply curve in Equation 2 tells us that inflation is driven by three factors: (1) expectations of inflation, (2) output gaps, and (3) price shocks. Equation 2 also shows that the short-run aggregate supply curve is upward-sloping, as is shown in Figure 3, because a higher level of output Y means that the output gap, $Y - Y^P$, is higher, and this produces a higher level of inflation.

Price Stickiness and the Short-Run Aggregate Supply Curve The short-run aggregate supply curve in Equation 2 implies that wages and prices are sticky, meaning that the aggregate price level adjusts slowly over time. The more flexible wages and prices are, the more they, and inflation, respond to deviations of output from potential output; That is, more flexible wages and prices imply that the absolute value of γ is higher, which implies that the short-run aggregate supply curve is steeper. If wages and prices are completely flexible, then γ becomes so large that the short-run aggregate supply curve is vertical, and it would be identical to the long-run aggregate supply.

[3]A more detailed derivation of the short-run aggregate supply curve based on the Phillips curve, the relationship between unemployment and inflation, can be found in the appendix to this chapter.

SHIFTS IN AGGREGATE SUPPLY CURVES

Now that we have examined the long-run and short-run aggregate supply curves, we can look at why each of these curves shift.

Shifts in the Long-Run Aggregate Supply Curve

The quantity of output supplied in the long run is determined by the three factors that cause potential output to change and thus shift the long-run aggregate supply curve: (1) the total amount of capital in the economy, (2) the total amount of labor supplied in the economy, and (3) the available technology that puts labor and capital together to produce goods and services. When any of these three factors increases, potential output rises, say, from Y_1^P to Y_2^P, and the long-run aggregate supply curve shifts to the right from $LRAS_1$ to $LRAS_2$, as in Figure 4.

Because all three of these factors typically grow fairly steadily over time, Y^P and the long-run aggregate supply curve will keep on shifting to the right at a steady pace. To keep things simple in diagrams later in this and following chapters, when Y^P is growing at a steady rate, we represent Y^P and the long-run aggregate supply curve as fixed.

Another source of shifts in the long-run aggregate supply curve is changes in the natural rate of unemployment. If the natural rate of unemployment declines, labor is being more heavily utilized, and so potential output will increase. A decline in the natural rate of unemployment thus shifts the long-run aggregate supply curve to the

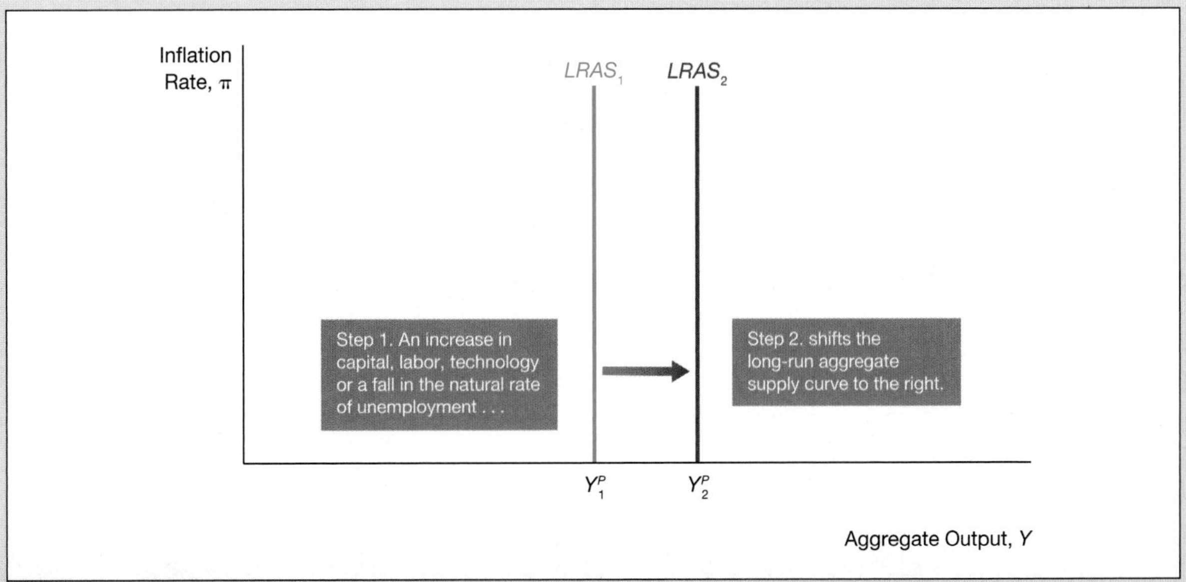

FIGURE 4 Shift in the Long-Run Aggregate Supply Curve
The long-run aggregate supply curve shifts to the right from $LRAS_1$ to $LRAS_2$ when there is (1) an increase in the total amount of capital in the economy, (2) an increase in the total amount of labor supplied in the economy, (3) an increase in the available technology, or (4) a decline in the natural rate of unemployment. An opposite movement in these variables shifts the *LRAS* curve to the left.

right from $LRAS_1$ to $LRAS_2$, as in Figure 4. A rise in the natural rate of unemployment would have the opposite effect, shifting the long-run aggregate supply curve to the left.

The conclusion from this analysis is as follows: ***The long-run aggregate supply curve shifts to the right when there is (1) an increase in the total amount of capital in the economy, (2) an increase in the total amount of labor supplied in the economy, (3) an increase in the available technology, or (4) a decline in the natural rate of unemployment. An opposite movement in these variables shifts the*** **LRAS** ***curve to the left.***

Shifts in the Short-Run Aggregate Supply Curve

The three terms on the right-hand side of Equation 2 for the short-run aggregate supply curve suggest that three factors can shift the short-run aggregate supply curve: (1) expected inflation, (2) price shocks, and (3) a persistent output gap. As a study aid, Summary Table 2 summarizes the shifts in the short-run aggregate supply curve from each of these three factors.

Expected Inflation What if a newly appointed chairman of the Federal Reserve does not think that inflation is costly and so is willing to tolerate an inflation rate that is two percentage points higher? Households and firms will then expect that the Fed will pursue policies that will let inflation rise, say, by two percentage points, in the future

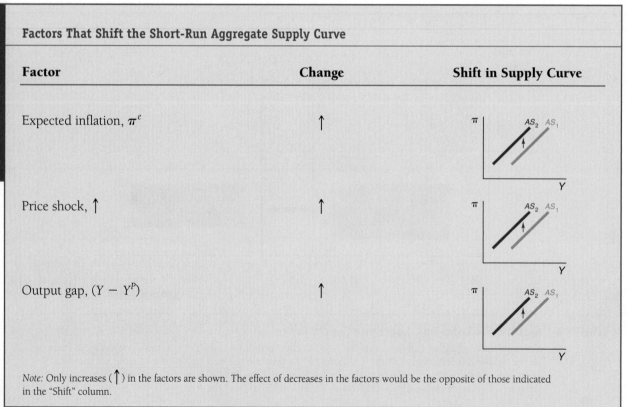

SUMMARY TABLE 2

Factors That Shift the Short-Run Aggregate Supply Curve

Factor	Change	Shift in Supply Curve
Expected inflation, π^e	↑	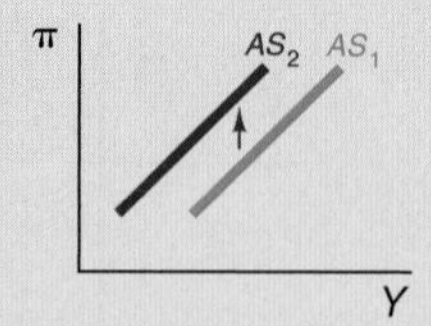
Price shock, ↑	↑	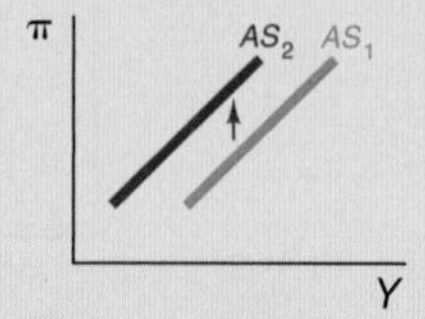
Output gap, $(Y - Y^P)$	↑	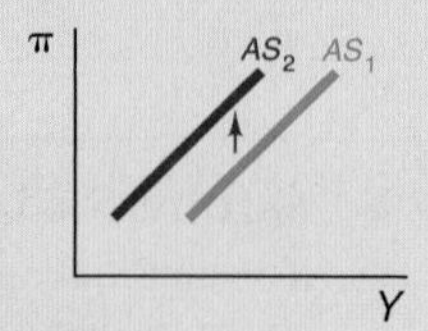

Note: Only increases (↑) in the factors are shown. The effect of decreases in the factors would be the opposite of those indicated in the "Shift" column.

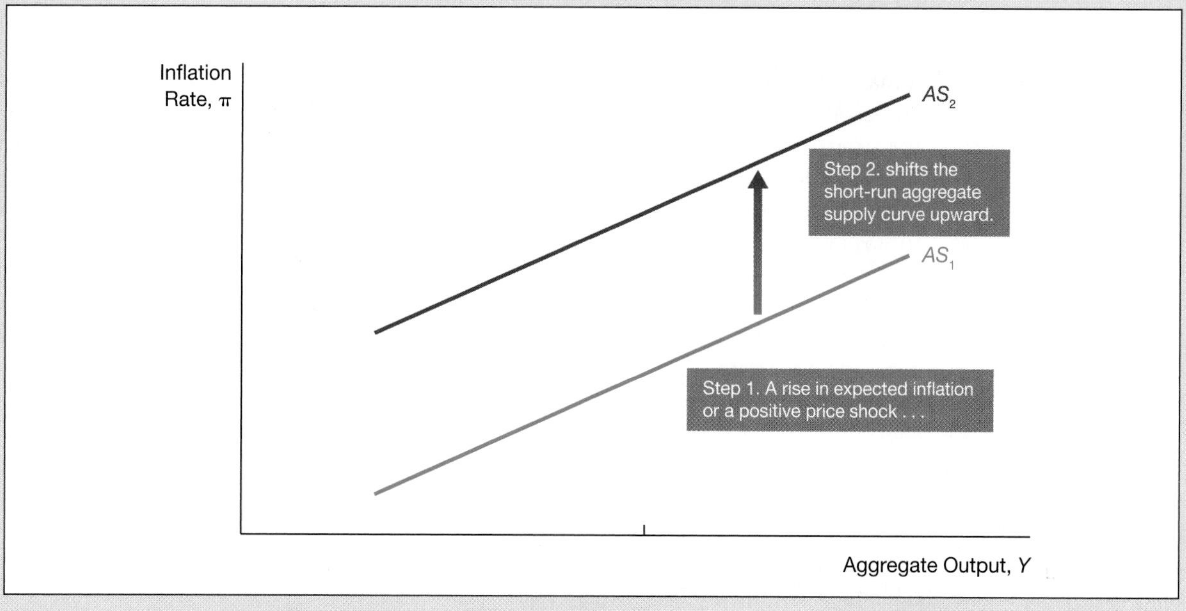

FIGURE 5 Shift in the Short-Run Aggregate Supply Curve from Changes in Expected Inflation and Price Shocks

A rise in expected inflation or a positive price shock shifts the short-run aggregate supply curve upward from AS_1 to AS_2. (A decrease in expected inflation or a negative price shock would lead to a downward shift of the *AS* curve.)

and will want to raise wages and prices by this amount. In such a situation, expected inflation will jump by two percentage points, and the short-run aggregate supply curve will shift upward and to the left from AS_1 to AS_2, as in Figure 5. ***A rise in expected inflation causes the short-run aggregate supply curve to shift upward and to the left. Conversely, a decline in expected inflation causes the short-run aggregate supply curve to shift down and to the right. The larger is the change in expected inflation, the larger is the shift.***

Price Shock Suppose that energy prices suddenly shoot up because terrorists destroy a number of oil fields. This supply restriction (an unfavorable supply shock) causes the price shock term in Equation 2 to jump up, and so the short-run aggregate supply curve will shift up and to the left from AS_1 to AS_2, as in Figure 5. A favorable supply shock which drives down prices, will have the opposite effect and cause the short-run aggregate supply curve to shift down and to the right. ***Unfavorable supply shocks that drive up prices cause the short-run aggregate supply curve to shift up and to the left, while favorable supply shocks that lower prices cause the short-run aggregate supply curve to shift down and to the right.***

Persistent Output Gap We have already seen that a higher output gap leads to higher inflation, causing a movement along the short-run aggregate supply curve. We represent this movement from point 1 to point 2 on the initial short-run aggregate supply curve AS_1 in Figure 6. A persistent output gap, however, will cause the short-run aggregate supply curve to shift by affecting expected inflation. To see this, consider what happens if the aggregate output stays above potential output, $Y^2 > Y^P$, so the output gap remains persistently positive, say, at point 2 on the initial short-run aggregate supply curve, AS_1. Because inflation rises to π_2, expected inflation will rise next period and so the short-run aggregate supply curve next period, AS_2, will then shift upward. If output remains above potential output at point 3, then then inflation will rise further to π_3. As the vertical arrow indicates, the short-run aggregate supply curve will then shift upward to AS_3 next period.

When will the short-run aggregate supply curve stop rising? It will stop only when output returns to its potential level and the output gap disappears. Suppose this happens when inflation is at π_4 and aggregate output $Y = Y^P$. Because the output gap is zero, the aggregate supply curve drawn through point 4, AS_4, has no further reason to shift because inflation and expected inflation will stop rising.

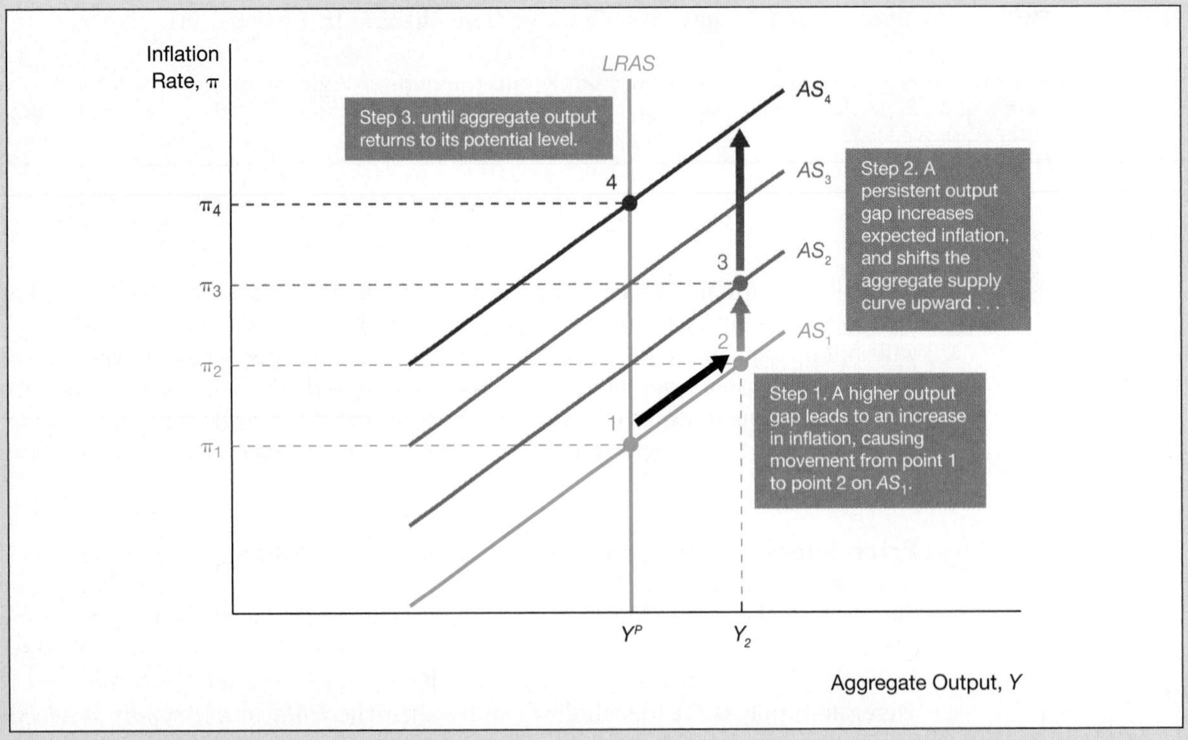

FIGURE 6 Shift in the Short-Run Aggregate Supply Curve from a Persistent Positive Output Gap
When output is above potential, the economy moves along the AS_1 curve from point 1 to point 2, and inflation rises to π_2. If output continues to remain above potential output, where the output gap is positive, the short-run aggregate supply curve shifts up to AS_2 and then to AS_3. The short-run aggregate supply curve stops shifting up when the economy reaches point 4 on the short-run aggregate supply curve, AS_4, where the output gap is zero.

The same reasoning indicates that if aggregate output is kept below potential for a period of time, $Y < Y^P$, then the short-run aggregate supply curve will shift downward and to the right. This downward shift of the aggregate supply curve will only stop when output returns to its potential level and the economy is back on the long-run aggregate supply curve.

Our analysis yields the following conclusion: ***When aggregate output is above potential output, so that a persistent positive output gap exists, the short-run aggregate supply curve shifts up and to the left. Conversely, when aggregate output falls below potential output, the short-run aggregate supply curve shifts down and to the right. Only when aggregate output returns to potential output does the short-run aggregate supply curve stop shifting.***

EQUILIBRIUM IN AGGREGATE DEMAND AND SUPPLY ANALYSIS

We can now put the aggregate demand and supply curves together to describe **general equilibrium** in the economy, when all markets are simultaneously in equilibrium at the point where the quantity of aggregate output demanded equals the quantity of aggregate output supplied. We represent general equilibrium graphically as the point where the aggregate demand curve intersects the aggregate supply curve. However, recall that we have two aggregate supply curves: one for the short run and one for the long run. Consequently, in the context of aggregate supply and demand analysis, there are short-run and long-run equilibriums. In this section, we illustrate equilibrium in the short and long runs. In following sections we examine aggregate demand and aggregate supply shocks that lead to changes in equilibrium.

Short-Run Equilibrium

Figure 7 illustrates a short-run equilibrium in which the quantity of aggregate output demanded equals the quantity of output supplied. In Figure 7, the short-run aggregate demand curve *AD* and the short-run aggregate supply curve *AS* intersect at point *E* with an equilibrium level of aggregate output at Y^* and an equilibrium inflation rate at π^*.

How the Short-Run Equilibrium Moves to the Long-Run Equilibrium over Time

Usually in supply and demand analysis, once we find the equilibrium at which the quantity demanded equals the quantity supplied, typically additional analysis is not needed. In *aggregate* supply and demand analysis, however, that is not the case. Even when the quantity of aggregate output demanded equals the quantity supplied at the intersection of the aggregate demand curve and the short-run aggregate supply curve, if output differs from its potential level ($Y^* \neq Y^P$), the short-run equilibrium will move over time. To understand why, recall that if the current level of inflation changes from its initial level, the short-run aggregate supply curve will shift as wages and prices adjust to a new expected rate of inflation.

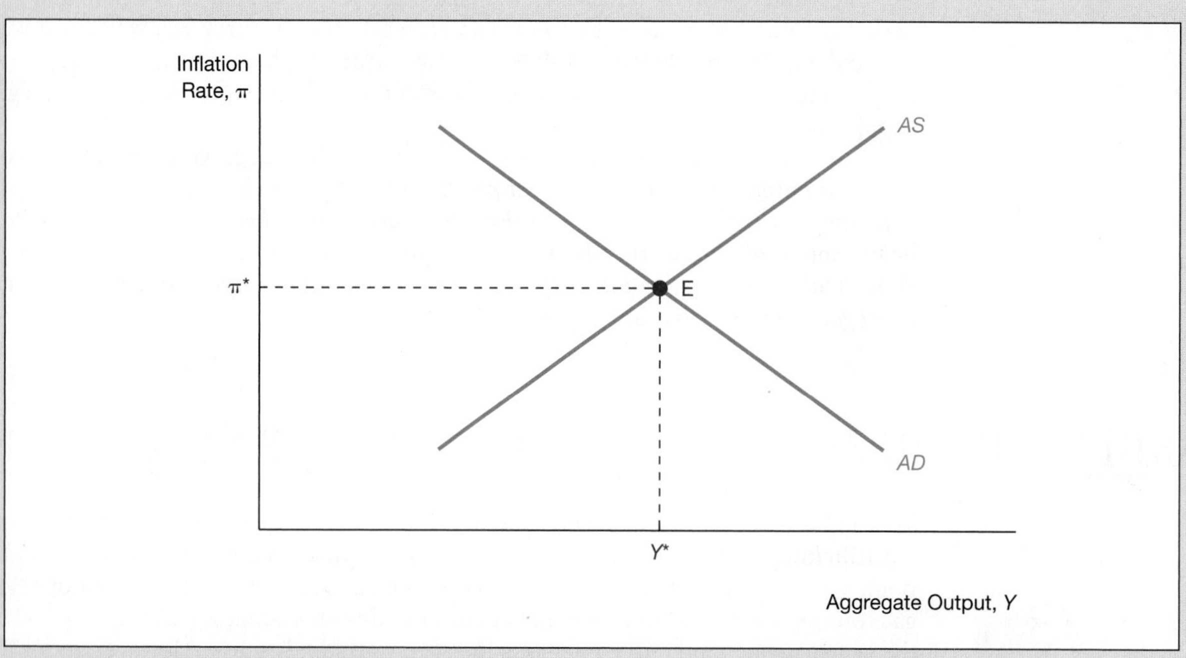

FIGURE 7 Short-Run Equilibrium
Short-run equilibrium occurs at point *E* at the intersection of the aggregate demand curve *AD* and the short-run aggregate supply curve *AS*.

We look at how the short-run equilibrium changes over time in response to two situations: when short-run equilibrium output is initially above potential output (the natural rate of output) and when it is initially below potential output.

In panel (a) of Figure 8, the initial equilibrium occurs at point 1, the intersection of the aggregate demand curve *AD* and the initial short-run aggregate supply curve AS_1. The level of equilibrium output, Y_1, is greater than potential output Y^P, and there is excessive tightness in the labor market. Hence, the positive output gap at Y_1 drives wages up and causes firms to raise their prices at a more rapid rate. Inflation will then rise above the initial inflation rate, π_1. Hence, next period, firms and households adjust their expectations and expected inflation is higher. Wages and prices will then rise more rapidly, and the aggregate supply curve shifts up and to the left from AS_1 to AS_2.

The new short-run equilibrium at point 2 is a movement up the aggregate demand curve and output falls to Y_2. However, because aggregate output Y_2 is still above potential output Y^P, wages and prices increase at an even higher rate, so inflation again rises above its value last period. Expected inflation rises further, eventually shifting the aggregate supply curve up and to the left to AS_3. The economy reaches long-run equilibrium at point 3 on the vertical long-run aggregate supply curve (*LRAS*) at Y^P. Because output is at potential, there is no further pressure on inflation to rise and thus no further tendency for the aggregate supply curve to shift.

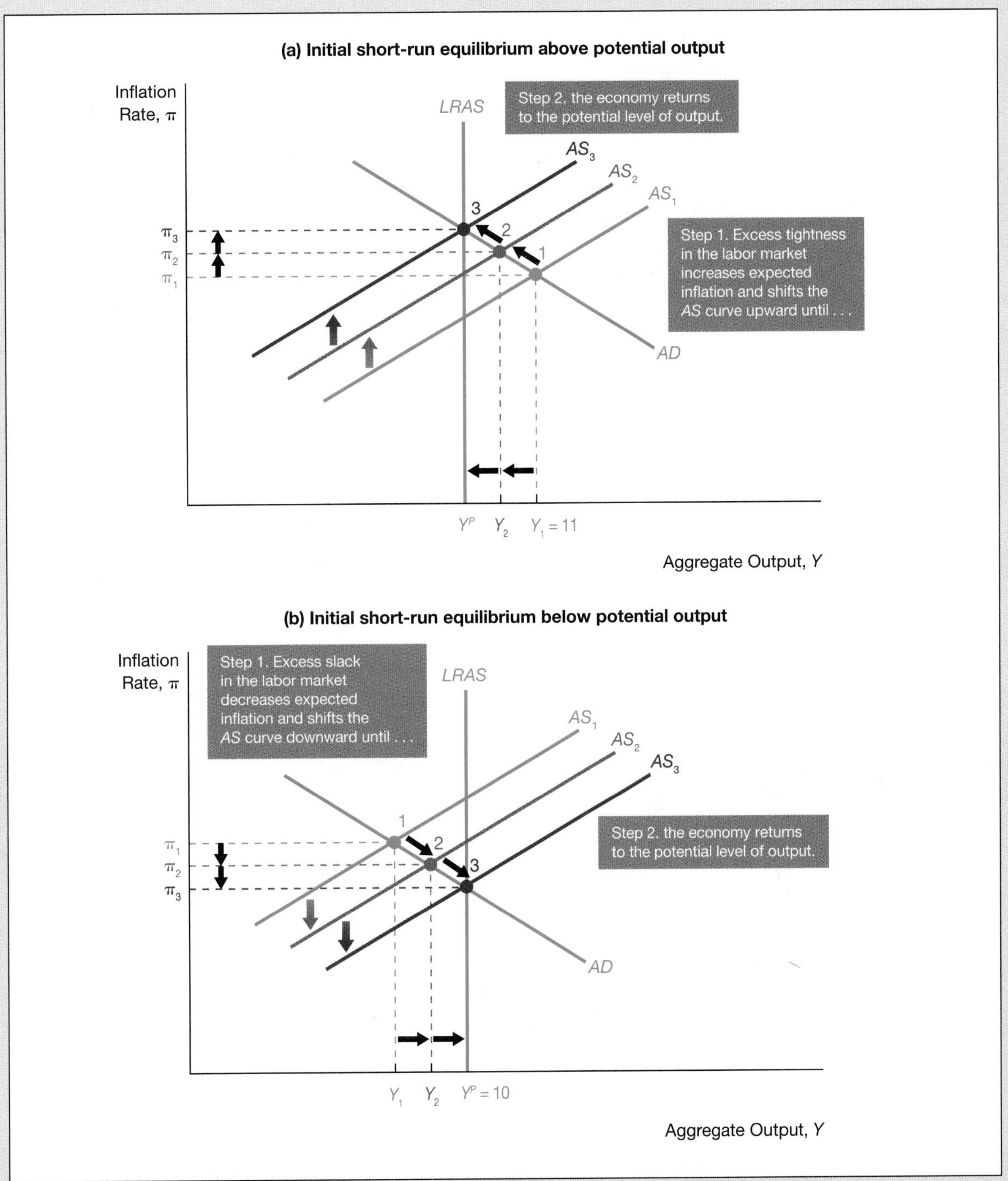

FIGURE 8 Adjustment to Long-Run Equilibrium in Aggregate Supply and Demand Analysis

In both panels, the initial short-run equilibrium is at point 1 at the intersection of *AD* and AS_1. In panel (a), initial short-run equilibrium is above potential output, the long-run equilibrium, so the short-run aggregate supply curve shifts upward until it reaches AS_3, where output returns to Y^P. In panel (b), initial short-run equilibrium is below potential output, so the short-run aggregate supply curve shifts down until output returns to Y^P. In both panels, the economy's self-correcting mechanism returns it to the level of potential output.

The movements in panel (a) indicate that the economy will not remain at a level of output higher than potential output over time. Specifically, the short-run aggregate supply curve will shift to the left, raise the inflation rate, and cause the economy (equilibrium) to move upward along the aggregate demand curve until it comes to rest at a point on the long-run aggregate supply curve (*LRAS*) at potential output Y^P.

In panel (b), at the initial equilibrium at point 1, output Y_1 is below the level of potential output. Because unemployment is now above its natural rate, there is excess slack in the labor markets. This slack at Y_1 decreases inflation, which decreases expected inflation and shifts the short-run aggregate supply curve in the next period down and to the right to AS_2.

The equilibrium will now move to point 2 and output rises to Y_2. However, because aggregate output Y_2 is still below potential, Y^P, inflation again declines from its value last period, shifting the aggregate supply curve down until it comes to rest at AS_3. The economy (equilibrium) moves downward along the aggregate demand curve until it reaches the long-run equilibrium point 3, the intersection of the aggregate demand curve (*AD*) and the long-run aggregate supply curve (*LRAS*) at Y^P. Here, as in panel (a), the economy comes to rest when output has again returned to its potential level.

Self-Correcting Mechanism

Notice that in both panels of Figure 9, regardless of where output is initially, it returns eventually to potential output, a feature we call the **self-correcting mechanism**. The self-correcting mechanism occurs because the short-run aggregate supply curve shifts up or down to restore the economy to the long-run equilibrium at full employment (aggregate output at potential) over time.

CHANGES IN EQUILIBRIUM: AGGREGATE DEMAND SHOCKS

With an understanding of the distinction between the short-run and long-run equilibria, you are now ready to analyze what happens when there are **demand shocks**, shocks that cause the aggregate demand curve to shift. Figure 9 depicts the effect of a rightward shift in the aggregate demand curve due to positive demand shocks caused by the following:

- An autonomous easing of monetary policy ($\bar{r}\downarrow$, a lowering of the real interest rate at any given inflation rate)
- An increase in government purchases ($\bar{G}\uparrow$)
- A decrease in taxes ($\bar{T}\downarrow$)
- An increase in net exports ($\overline{NX}\uparrow$)
- An increase in autonomous consumption expenditure ($\bar{C}\uparrow$)
- An increase in autonomous investment ($\bar{I}\uparrow$)
- A decrease in financial frictions ($\bar{f}\downarrow$)

Figure 9 shows the economy initially in long-run equilibrium at point 1, where the initial aggregate demand curve AD_1 intersects the short-run aggregate supply AS_1 curve at Y^P and the inflation rate at π_1. Suppose that consumers and businesses become more optimistic and the resulting increases in autonomous consumption and investment create a positive demand shock that shifts the aggregate demand curve to the right to AD_2. The economy moves up the short-run aggregate supply curve AS_1 to point 2, and both output and inflation rise to Y^2 and π_2, respectively. However, the

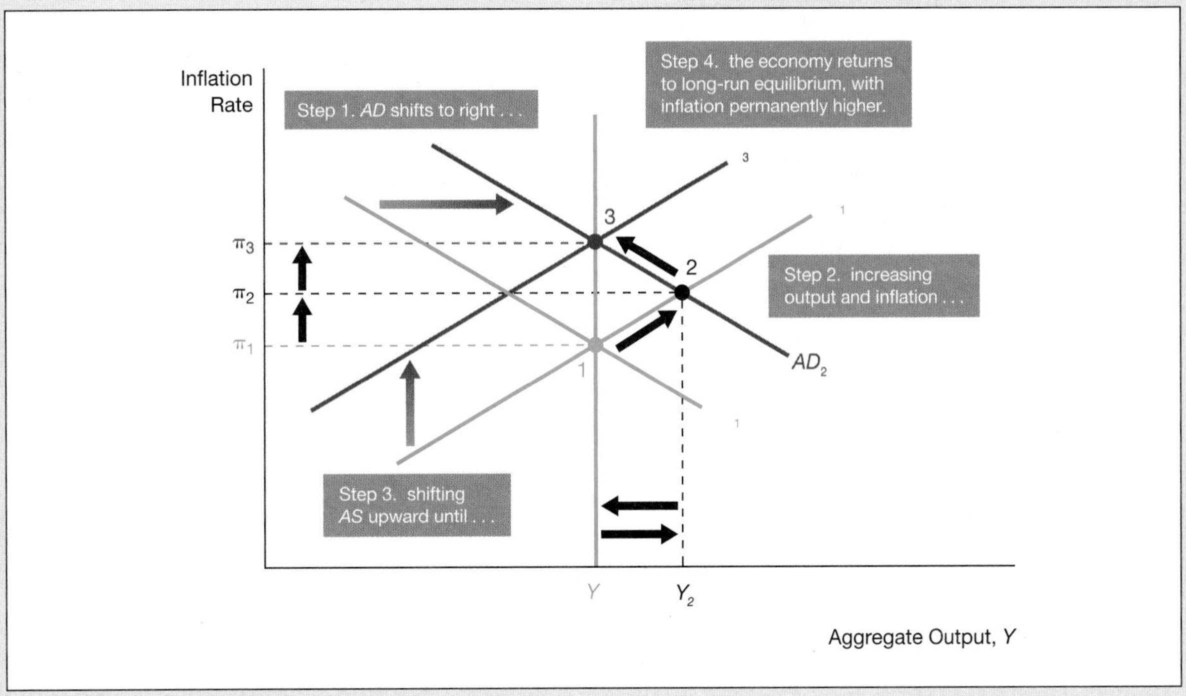

FIGURE 9 Positive Demand Shock

A positive demand shock shifts the aggregate demand curve upward from AD_1 to AD_2 and moves the economy from point 1 to point 2, resulting in higher inflation at π_2 and higher output of Y_2. Because output is greater than potential output and expected inflation increases, the short-run aggregate supply curve begins to shift up, eventually reaching AS_3. At point 3, the economy returns to long-run equilibrium, with output at Y^P and the inflation level rising to π_3.

economy will not remain at point 2 in the long run, because output at Y_2 is above potential output. Expected inflation will rise, and the short-run aggregate supply curve will eventually shift upward to AS_3. The economy (equilibrium) thus moves up the AD_2 curve from point 2 to point 3, which is the point of long-run equilibrium where inflation equals π_3 and output returns to Y^P. ***Although the initial short-run effect of the rightward shift in the aggregate demand curve is a rise in both inflation and output, the ultimate long-run effect is only a rise in inflation because output returns to its initial level at*** Y^P.[4]

We now turn to applying the aggregate demand and supply model to demand shocks, as a payoff for our hard work constructing the model. Throughout the remainder of this chapter, we will apply aggregate supply and demand analysis to a number

[4]Note the analysis here assumes that each of these positive demand shocks occurs holding everything else constant, the usual ceteris paribus assumption that is standard in supply and demand analysis. Specifically this means that the central bank is assumed to not be responding to demand shocks. In the next chapter, we relax this assumption and allow monetary policymakers to respond to these shocks. As we will see, if monetary policymakers want to keep inflation from rising as a result of a positive demand shock, they will respond by autonomously tightening monetary policy.

of business cycle episodes, both in the United States and in foreign countries, over the past 40 years. To simplify our analysis, we always assume in all examples that aggregate output is initially at the level of potential output.

APPLICATION ◆ The Volcker Disinflation, 1980–1986

When Paul Volcker became the chairman of the Federal Reserve in August 1979, inflation had spun out of control and the inflation rate exceeded 10%. Volcker was determined to get inflation down. By early 1981, the Federal Reserve had raised the federal funds rate to over 20%, which led to a sharp increase in real interest rates. Volcker was indeed successful in bringing inflation down, as panel (b) of Figure 10 indicates, with the inflation rate falling from 13.5% in 1980 to 1.9% in 1986. The decline in inflation came at a high cost: The economy experienced the worst recession since World War II, with the unemployment rate averaging 9.7% in 1982.

This outcome is exactly what our aggregate demand and supply analysis predicts. The autonomous tightening of monetary policy decreased aggregate demand and shifted the aggregate demand curve to the left from AD_1 to AD_2, as we show in panel (a) of Figure 10. The economy moved to point 2, indicating that unemployment would rise and inflation would fall. With unemployment above the natural rate and output below potential, the short-run aggregate supply curve shifted downward and to the right to AS_3. The economy moved toward long-run equilibrium at point 3, with inflation continuing to fall, output rising back to potential output, and the unemployment rate moving toward its natural rate level. Figure 10 panel (b) shows that by 1986 the unemployment rate had fallen to 7% and the inflation rate was 1.9%, just as our aggregate demand and supply analysis predicts.

The next period we will examine, 2001–2004, again illustrates negative demand shocks—this time, three at once.

APPLICATION ◆ Negative Demand Shocks, 2001–2004

In 2000, the U.S. economy was expanding when it was hit by a series of negative shocks to aggregate demand.

1. The "tech bubble" burst in March 2000, and the stock market fell sharply.
2. The September 11, 2001, terrorist attacks weakened both consumer and business confidence.
3. The Enron bankruptcy in late 2001 and other corporate accounting scandals in 2002 revealed that corporate financial data were not to be trusted. Interest rates on corporate bonds rose as a result, making it more expensive for corporations to finance their investments.

All these negative demand shocks led to a decline in household and business spending, decreasing aggregate demand and shifting the aggregate demand curve to the left from AD_1 to AD_2 in panel (a) of Figure 11. At point 2, as our aggregate demand and supply analysis predicts, unemployment rose and inflation fell. Panel (b) of Figure 11 shows that the unemployment rate, which had been at 4% in 2000, rose to 6% in 2003, while the annual rate of inflation fell from 3.4% in 2000 to 1.6% in 2002. With unemployment

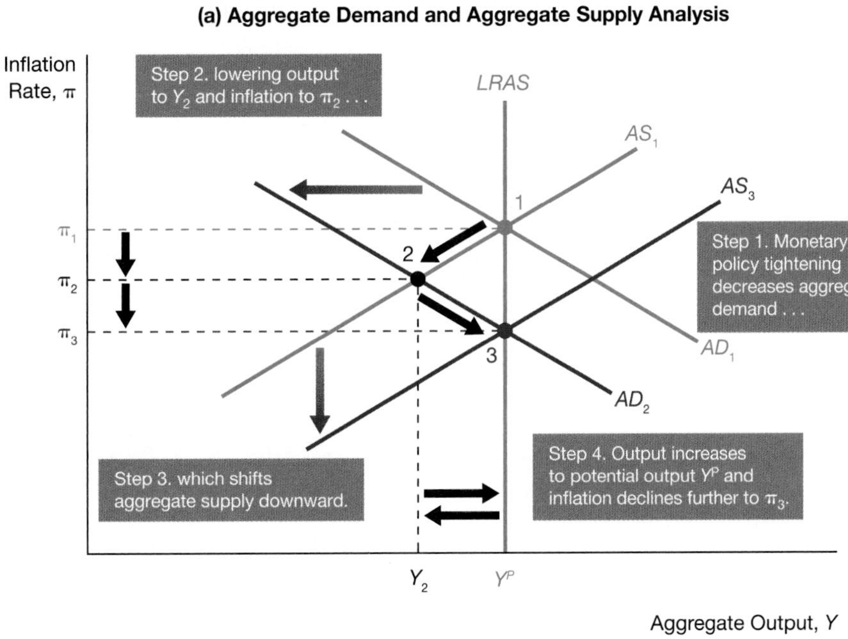
(a) Aggregate Demand and Aggregate Supply Analysis
Inflation Rate, π
Step 2. lowering output to Y_2 and inflation to π_2 . . .
LRAS
AS_1
AS_3
1
Step 1. Monetary policy tightening decreases aggregate demand . . .
π_1
π_2
π_3
2
3
AD_1
AD_2
Step 3. which shifts aggregate supply downward.
Step 4. Output increases to potential output Y^P and inflation declines further to π_3.
Y_2
Y^P
Aggregate Output, Y

(b) Unemployment and Inflation, 1980–1986

Year	Unemployment Rate (%)	Inflation (Year to Year) (%)
1980	7.1	13.5
1981	7.6	10.3
1982	9.7	6.2
1983	9.6	3.2
1984	7.5	4.3
1985	7.2	3.6
1986	7.0	1.9

FIGURE 10 The Volcker Disinflation

Panel (a) shows that Fed Chairman Volcker's actions to decrease inflation were successful but costly: The autonomous monetary policy tightening caused a negative demand shock that decreased aggregate demand and in turn inflation, resulting in soaring unemployment rates. The data in panel (b) support this analysis: Note the decline in the inflation rate from 13.5% in 1980 to 1.9% in 1986, while the unemployment rate increased as high as 9.7% in 1982.

Source: Economic Report of the President.

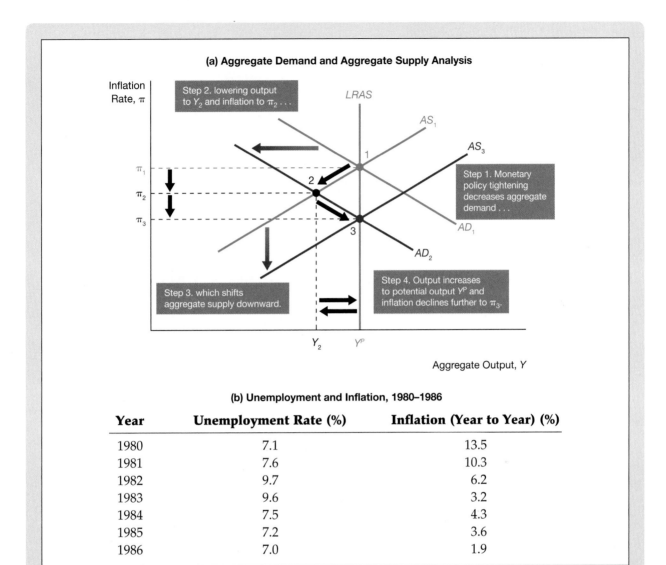

above the natural rate (estimated to be around 5%) and output below potential, the short-run aggregate supply curve shifted downward to AS_3, as we show in panel (a) of Figure 11. The economy moved to point 3, with inflation falling, output rising back to potential output, and the unemployment rate returning to its natural rate level. By 2004, the self-correcting mechanism feature of aggregate demand and supply analysis began to come into play, with the unemployment rate dropping back to 5.5% (see Figure 11 panel (b)).

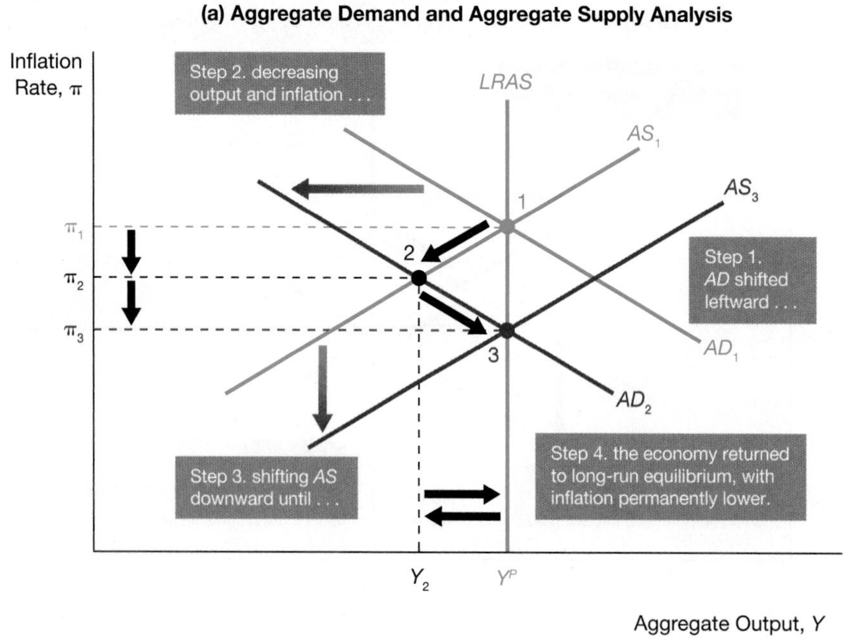
(a) Aggregate Demand and Aggregate Supply Analysis
Inflation Rate, π
Step 2. decreasing output and inflation . . .
LRAS
AS1
AS3
1
2
3
π1
π2
π3
Step 1. AD shifted leftward . . .
AD1
AD2
Step 3. shifting AS downward until . . .
Step 4. the economy returned to long-run equilibrium, with inflation permanently lower.
Y2
YP
Aggregate Output, Y

(b) Unemployment and Inflation, 2000–2004

Year	Unemployment Rate (%)	Inflation (Year to Year) (%)
2000	4.0	3.4
2001	4.7	2.8
2002	5.8	1.6
2003	6.0	2.3
2004	5.5	2.7

FIGURE 11 Negative Demand Shocks, 2001–2004

Panel (a) shows that the negative demand shocks from 2001–2004 decreased consumption expenditure and investment, shifting the aggregate demand curve to the left from AD_1 to AD_2. The economy moved to point 2, where output fell, unemployment rose, and inflation declined. The large negative output gap when output was less than potential caused the short-run aggregate supply curve to begin falling to AS_3. The economy moved toward point 3, where output would return to potential: Inflation declined further to π_3, and unemployment fell back again to its natural rate level of around 5%. The data in panel (b) support this analysis, with inflation declining to around 2% and the unemployment rate dropping back to 5.5% by 2004.

Source: Economic Report of the President.

CHANGES IN EQUILIBRIUM: AGGREGATE SUPPLY (PRICE) SHOCKS

The aggregate supply curve can shift from temporary supply (price) shocks in which the long-run aggregate supply curve does not shift, or from permanent supply shocks in which the long-run aggregate supply curve does shift. We look at these two types of supply shocks in turn.

Temporary Supply Shocks

In our discussion of the short-run aggregate supply curve earlier in the chapter, we showed that inflation will rise independently of tightness in the labor markets or of increases in expected inflation when there is a temporary supply shock, such as a change in the supply of oil that causes prices to rise. When the temporary shock involves a restriction in supply, we refer to this type of supply shock as a *negative (or unfavorable) supply shock*, and it results in a rise in commodity prices. Examples of temporary negative supply shocks are a disruption in oil supplies, a rise in import prices when a currency declines in value, or a cost-push shock from workers pushing for higher wages that outpace productivity growth, driving up costs and inflation. When the supply shock involves an increase in supply, it is called a *positive (or favorable) supply shock*. Temporary positive supply shocks can come from a particularly good harvest or a fall in import prices.

To see how a temporary supply shock affects the economy using our aggregate supply and demand analysis, we start by assuming that the economy has output at its potential level of Y^P and inflation at π_1 at point 1 in Figure 12. Suppose that a temporary negative supply shock occurs because of a war in the Middle East. When the negative supply shock hits the economy and oil prices rise, the price shock term ρ causes inflation to rise above π_1, and the short-run aggregate supply curve shifts up and to the left from AS_1 to AS_2.

The economy will move up the aggregate demand curve from point 1 to point 2, where inflation rises above π_1 but aggregate output *falls* below Y^P. We call a situation of rising inflation but a falling level of aggregate output, as pictured in Figure 12, **stagflation** (a combination of the words *stagnation* and *inflation*). Because the supply shock is temporary, productive capacity in the economy does not change, and so Y^P and the long-run aggregate supply curve *LRAS* remains stationary. At point 2, output is therefore below its potential level at Y_2, so inflation falls and shifts the short-run aggregate supply curve back down to where it was initially at AS_1. The economy (equilibrium) slides down the aggregate demand curve AD_1 (assuming that the aggregate demand curve remains in the same position) and returns to the long-run equilibrium at point 1 where output is again at Y^P and inflation is at π_1.

Although a temporary negative supply shock leads to an upward and leftward shift in the short-run aggregate supply curve, which raises inflation and lowers output initially, the ultimate long-run effect is that output and inflation are unchanged.

A favorable (positive) supply shock—say, an excellent harvest of wheat in the Midwest—moves all the curves in Figure 12 in the opposite direction and so has the opposite effects. ***A temporary positive supply shock shifts the short-run aggregate supply curve downward and to the right, leading initially to a fall in inflation and a rise in output. In the long run, however, output and inflation will be unchanged (holding the aggregate demand curve constant).***

We now will once again apply the aggregate demand and supply model, this time to temporary supply shocks. We begin with negative supply shocks in 1973–1975 and 1978–1980. (Recall that we assume that aggregate output is initially at its potential level.)

APPLICATION ◆ Negative Supply Shocks, 1973–1975 and 1978–1980

In 1973, the U.S. economy was hit by a series of negative supply shocks:

1. As a result of the oil embargo stemming from the Arab–Israeli war of 1973, the Organization of Petroleum Exporting Countries (OPEC) engineered a quadrupling of oil prices by restricting oil production.

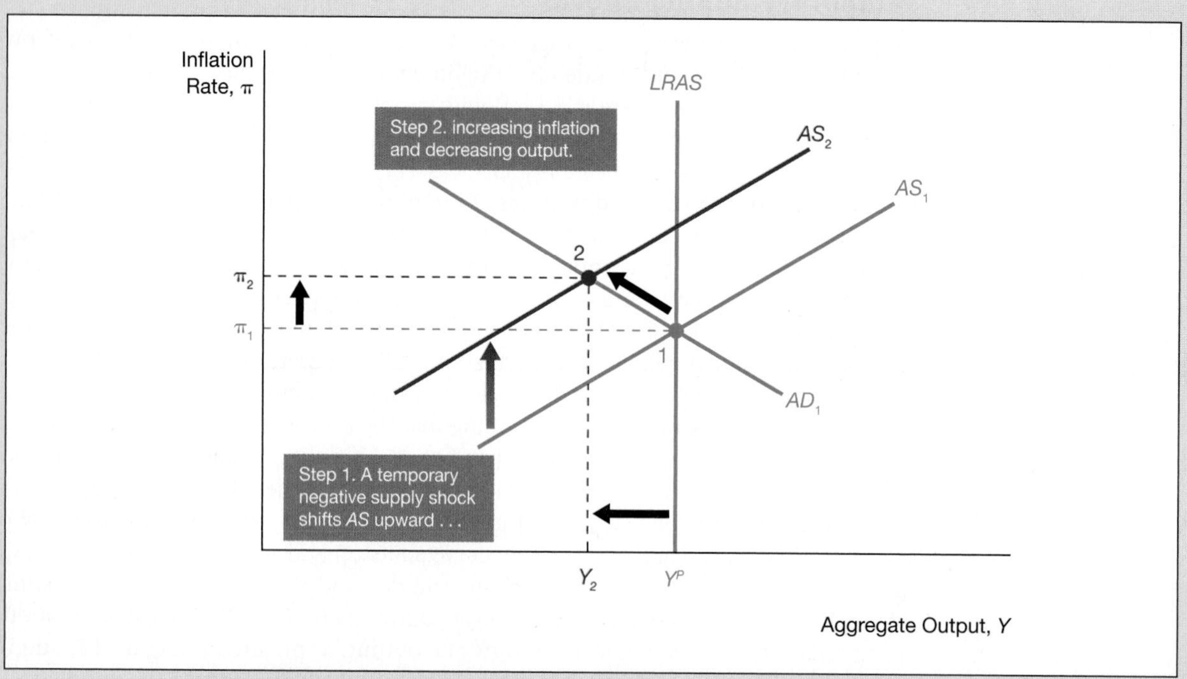

FIGURE 12 Temporary Negative Supply Shock
A temporary negative supply shock shifts the short-run aggregate supply curve from AS_1 to AS_2 and the economy moves from point 1 to point 2, where inflation increases to π_2 and output declines to Y_2. Because output is less than potential, the negative output gap lowers inflation and the short-run aggregate supply curve begins to shift back down, eventually returning to AS_1, where the economy is again at the initial long-run equilibrium at point 1.

2. A series of crop failures throughout the world led to a sharp increase in food prices.
3. The termination of U.S. wage and price controls in 1973 and 1974 led to a push by workers to obtain wage increases that had been prevented by the controls.

The triple thrust of these events shifted the short-run aggregate supply curve sharply upward and to the left from AS_1 to AS_2 in panel (a) of Figure 13, and the economy moved to point 2. As the aggregate demand and supply diagram in Figure 13 predicts, both inflation and unemployment rose (inflation by 3 percentage points and unemployment by 3.5 percentage points, as per panel (b) of Figure 13).

The 1978–1980 period was almost an exact replay of the 1973–1975 period. By 1978, the economy had just about fully recovered from the 1973–1975 supply shocks, when poor harvests and a doubling of oil prices (as a result of the overthrow of the Shah of Iran) again led to another sharp upward and leftward shift of the short-run aggregate supply curve in 1979. The pattern predicted by Figure 13 played itself out again—inflation and unemployment both shot upward.

Permanent Supply Shocks and Real Business Cycle Theory

But what if the supply shock is not temporary? A permanent negative supply shock—such as an increase in ill-advised regulations that causes the economy to be less efficient, thereby reducing supply—would decrease potential output from, say, Y_1^P to Y_2^P and shift the long-run aggregate supply curve to the left from $LRAS_1$ to $LRAS_2$ in Figure 14.

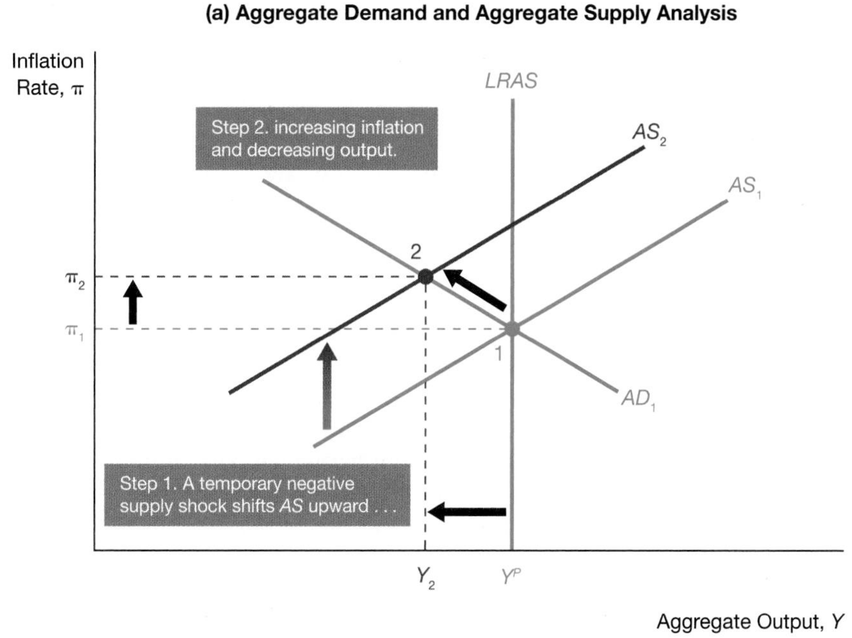

(b) Unemployment and Inflation, 1973–1975 and 1978–1980

Year	Unemployment Rate (%)	Inflation (Year to Year) (%)
1973	4.8	6.2
1974	5.5	11.0
1975	8.3	9.1
1978	6.0	7.6
1979	5.8	11.3
1980	7.1	13.5

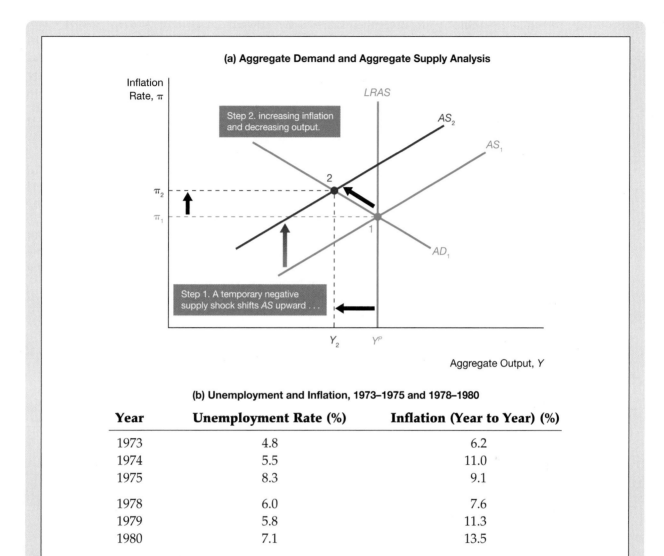

FIGURE 13 Negative Supply Shocks, 1973–1975 and 1978–1980

Panel (a) shows that the temporary negative supply shocks in 1973 and 1979 led to an upward shift in the short-run aggregate supply curve from AS_1 to AS_2. The economy moved to point 2, where output fell, and both unemployment and inflation rose. The data in panel (b) support this analysis: Note the increase in the inflation rate from 6.2% in 1973 to 9.1% in 1975 and the increase in the unemployment rate from 4.8% in 1973 to 8.3% in 1975. In the 1978–1980 shock, inflation increased from 7.6% in 1978 to 13.5% in 1980, while the unemployment rate increased from 6.0% in 1978 to 7.1% in 1980.

Source: Economic Report of the President.

Because the permanent supply shock will result in higher prices, there will be an immediate rise in inflation, and so the short-run aggregate supply curve will shift up and to the left from AS_1 to AS_2. Although output at point 2 has fallen to Y_2, it is still above Y_2^P: The positive output gap means that the aggregate supply curve will shift up and to the left. It continues to do so until it reaches AS_3 at the intersection with the aggregate demand curve AD and the long-run aggregate supply curve $LRAS_2$. Now because output is at Y_2^P at point 3, the output gap is zero and at an inflation rate of π_3 no further upward pressure on inflation occurs.

One group of economists, led by Edward Prescott of Arizona State University, believe that business cycle fluctuations result from permanent supply shocks alone, and their theory of aggregate economic fluctuations is called **real business cycle theory**. This theory views shocks to tastes (workers' willingness to work, for example) and technology (productivity) as the major driving forces behind short-run fluctuations in the business cycle, because these shocks lead to substantial short-run fluctuations in Y^P. Shifts in the aggregate demand curve, perhaps as a result of changes in monetary policy, by contrast, are not viewed as being particularly important to aggregate output fluctuations. Because real business cycle theory views most business cycle fluctuations as resulting from fluctuations in the level of potential of output, it does not see much need for policies to eliminate high unemployment. Real business cycle theory is highly controversial and is the subject of intensive research.

Figure 14 generates the following result when we hold the aggregate demand curve constant: ***A permanent negative supply shock leads initially to both a decline in output and a rise in inflation. However, in contrast to a temporary supply shock, in the long run the negative supply shock, which results in a fall in potential output, leads to a permanent decline in output and a permanent rise in inflation.***[5]

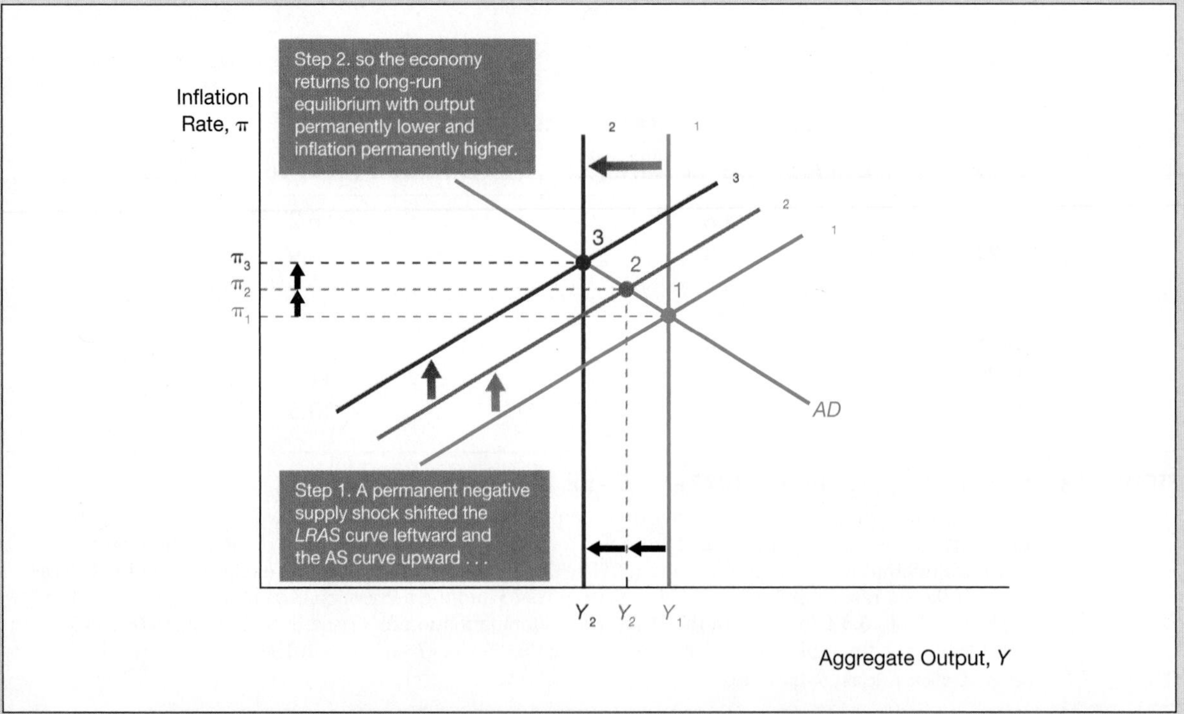

FIGURE 14 Permanent Negative Supply Shock

A permanent negative supply shock leads initially to a decline in output and a rise in inflation. In the long run, it leads to a permanent decline in output and a permanent rise in inflation, as indicated by point 3, where inflation has risen to π_3 and output has fallen to Y^P_2.

[5]The results on the effect of permanent supply shocks assume that monetary policy is not changing, so that the aggregate demand curve remains unchanged. Monetary policymakers, however, might want to shift the aggregate demand curve to keep inflation at the same level. For example, see the following chapter.

The opposite conclusion follows from a positive supply shock, say, because of the development of new technology that raises productivity. ***A permanent positive supply shock lowers inflation and raises output both in the short run and in the long run.***

To this point, we have assumed that potential output Y^P and hence the long-run aggregate supply curve are given. However, over time, the potential level of output increases as a result of economic growth. If the productive capacity of the economy is growing at a steady rate of 3% per year, for example, every year Y^P will grow by 3% and the long-run aggregate supply curve at Y^P will shift to the right by 3%. To simplify the analysis, when Y^P grows at a steady rate, we represent Y^P and the long-run aggregate supply curve as fixed in the aggregate demand and supply diagrams. Keep in mind, however, that the level of aggregate output pictured in these diagrams is actually best thought of as the level of aggregate output relative to its normal rate of growth (trend).

The 1995–1999 period serves as an illustration of permanent positive supply shocks, as the following application indicates.

APPLICATION ◆ Positive Supply Shocks, 1995–1999

In February 1994, the Federal Reserve began to raise interest rates. It believed the economy would be reaching potential output and the natural rate of unemployment in 1995, and it might become overheated thereafter, with output climbing above potential and inflation rising. As we can see in panel (b) of Figure 15, however, the economy continued to grow rapidly, with the unemployment rate falling to below 5% in 1997. Yet inflation continued to fall, declining to around 1.6% in 1998.

Can aggregate demand and supply analysis explain what happened? Two permanent positive supply shocks hit the economy in the late 1990s.

1. Changes in the health care industry, such as the emergence of health maintenance organizations (HMOs), reduced medical care costs substantially relative to other goods and services.
2. The computer revolution finally began to impact productivity favorably, raising the potential growth rate of the economy (which journalists dubbed the "new economy").

In addition, demographic factors, such as an increase in the relative number of older workers who are less likely to be unemployed, led to a fall in the natural rate of unemployment. These factors led to a rightward shift in the long-run aggregate supply curve to $LRAS_2$ and a downward and rightward shift in the short-run aggregate supply curve from AS_1 to AS_2, as shown in panel (a) of Figure 15. Aggregate output rose, and unemployment fell, while inflation also declined.

Conclusions

Aggregate demand and supply analysis yields the following conclusions.[6]

1. A shift in the aggregate demand curve—caused by changes in autonomous monetary policy (changes in the real interest rate at any given inflation rate), government

[6]The aggregate demand and supply analysis can also be used to understand the effects of macroeconomic shocks on asset prices. This analysis can be found in the second web Appendix for this chapter that is on the Companion Website at www.pearsonhighered.com/mishkin.

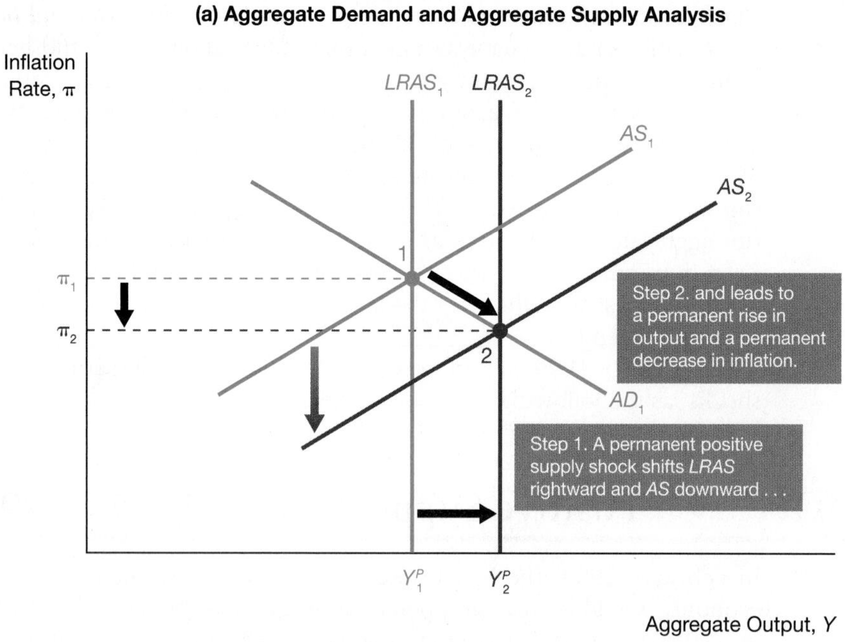
(a) Aggregate Demand and Aggregate Supply Analysis
Inflation Rate, π
LRAS1
LRAS2
AS1
AS2
1
π1
π2
2
Step 2. and leads to a permanent rise in output and a permanent decrease in inflation.
AD1
Step 1. A permanent positive supply shock shifts LRAS rightward and AS downward . . .
Y^P_1
Y^P_2
Aggregate Output, Y

(b) Unemployment and Inflation, 1995–1999

Year	Unemployment Rate (%)	Inflation (Year to Year) (%)
1995	5.6	2.8
1996	5.4	3.0
1997	4.9	2.3
1998	4.5	1.6
1999	4.2	2.2

FIGURE 15 Positive Supply Shocks, 1995–1999

Panel (a) shows that the positive supply shocks from lower health care costs and the rise in productivity from the computer revolution led to a rightward shift in the long-run aggregate supply curve from $LRAS_1$ to $LRAS_2$ and a downward shift in the short-run aggregate supply curve from AS_1 to AS_2. The economy moved to point 2, where aggregate output rose, and unemployment and inflation fell. The data in panel (b) support this analysis: Note that the unemployment rate fell from 5.6% in 1995 to 4.2% in 1999, while the inflation rate fell from 2.8% in 1995 to 2.2% in 1999.

Source: Economic Report of the President.

purchases, taxes, autonomous net exports, autonomous consumption expenditure, autonomous investment or financial frictions—affects output only in the short run and has no effect in the long run. Furthermore, the initial change in inflation is lower than the long-run change in inflation when the short-run aggregate supply curve has fully adjusted.

2. A temporary supply shock affects output and inflation only in the short run and has no effect in the long run (holding the aggregate demand curve constant).

3. A permanent supply shock affects output and inflation both in the short and in the long run.
4. The economy has a self-correcting mechanism that returns it to potential output and the natural rate of unemployment over time.

Now let's look at an application—this time with both supply and demand shocks at play—featuring the 2007–2009 financial crisis.

APPLICATION ◆ Negative Supply and Demand Shocks and the 2007–2009 Financial Crisis

At the beginning of 2007, higher demand for oil from rapidly growing developing countries like China and India and slowing of production in places like Mexico, Russia, and Nigeria drove up oil prices sharply from around the $60 per barrel level. By the end of 2007, oil prices had risen to $100 per barrel and reached a peak of over $140 in July 2008. The run-up of oil prices, along with increases in other commodity prices, led to a negative supply shock that shifted the short-run aggregate supply curve in panel (a) of Figure 16 sharply upward from AS_1 to AS_2. To make matters worse, a financial crisis hit the economy starting in August 2007, causing a sharp increase in financial frictions, which led to contraction in both household and business spending (discussed in Chapter 9). This negative demand shock shifted the aggregate demand curve to the left from AD_1 to AD_2 in panel (a) of Figure 16 and moved the economy to point 2. These shocks led to a rise in the unemployment rate, a rise in the inflation rate, and a decline in output, as point 2 indicates. As our aggregate demand and supply analysis predicts, this perfect storm of negative shocks led to a recession starting in December 2007, with the unemployment rate rising from the 4.6% level in 2006 and 2007 to 5.5% by June 2008, and with the inflation rate rising from 2.5% in 2006 to 5% in June 2008 (see panel (b) of Figure 16).

After July 2008, oil prices fell sharply, shifting short-run aggregate supply back downward to AS_1. However, in the fall of 2008, the financial crisis entered a particularly virulent phase following the bankruptcy of Lehman Brothers, decreasing aggregate demand sharply to AD_3. As a result, the economy moved to point 3, with the unemployment rate rising to 10% by the end of 2009, while the inflation rate fell to 2.8% (see panel (b) of Figure 16).

AD/AS ANALYSIS OF FOREIGN BUSINESS CYCLE EPISODES

Our aggregate demand and supply analysis also can help us understand business cycle episodes in foreign countries. Here we look at two: the business cycle experience of the United Kingdom during the 2007–2009 financial crisis and the quite different experience of China during the same period.

(a) Aggregate Demand and Aggregate Supply Analysis

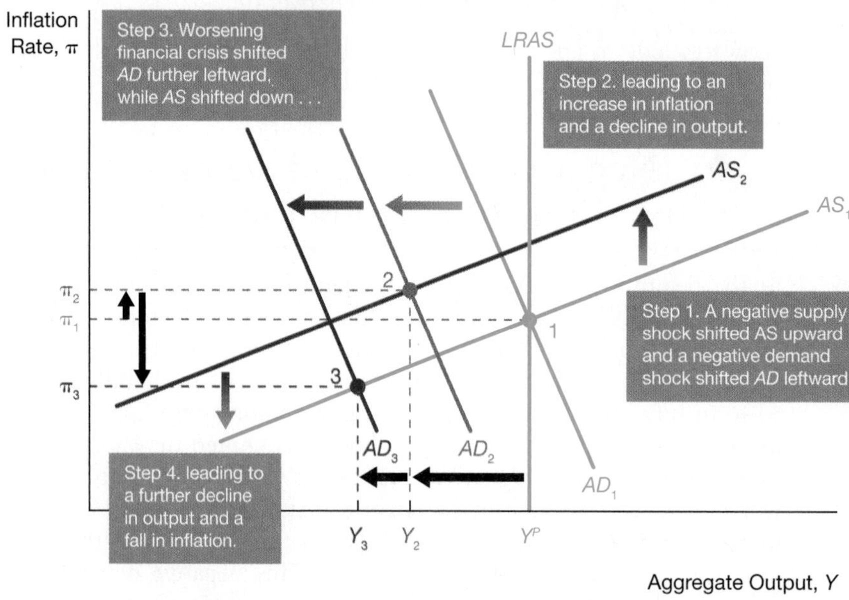
Inflation Rate, π
Step 3. Worsening financial crisis shifted AD further leftward, while AS shifted down . . .
LRAS
Step 2. leading to an increase in inflation and a decline in output.
AS2
AS1
π2
π1
π3
2
1
3
Step 1. A negative supply shock shifted AS upward and a negative demand shock shifted AD leftward . . .
AD3
AD2
AD1
Step 4. leading to a further decline in output and a fall in inflation.
Y3
Y2
YP
Aggregate Output, Y

(b) Unemployment and Inflation During the Perfect Storm of 2007–2009

Year	Unemployment Rate (%)	Inflation (Year to Year) (%)
2006	4.6	2.5
2007	4.6	4.1
2008, June	5.5	5.0
2008, Dec.	7.2	0.1
2009, June	9.5	–1.2
2009, Dec.	10.0	2.8

FIGURE 16 Negative Supply and Demand Shocks and the 2007–2009 Crisis

Panel (a) shows that the negative price shock from the rise in the price of oil shifted the short-run aggregate supply curve up from AS_1 to AS_2, while a negative demand shock from the financial crisis led to a sharp contraction in spending, resulting in the aggregate demand curve moving from AD_1 to AD_2. The economy thus moved to point 2, where a sharp contraction occurred in aggregate output, which fell to Y_2, and a rise in unemployment, while inflation rose to π_2. The fall in oil prices shifted the short-run aggregate supply curve back down to AS_1, while the deepening financial crisis shifted the aggregate demand curve to AD_3. As a result, the economy moved to point 3, where inflation fell to π_3 and output to Y_3. The data in panel (b) support this analysis: Note that unemployment rose from 4.6% in 2006 to 5.5% in June 2008, while inflation rose from 2.5% to 5.0%. Then in the aftermath of the financial crisis and the decline of oil prices, by the end of 2009 the unemployment rate rose to 10%, while inflation fell to 2.8%.

Source: Economic Report of the President.

APPLICATION ◆ The United Kingdom and the 2007–2009 Financial Crisis

As in the United States, the rise in the price of oil in 2007 led to a negative supply shock. In Figure 17 panel (a), the short-run aggregate supply curve shifted up from AS_1 to AS_2 in the United Kingdom. The financial crisis did not at first have a large impact on spending,

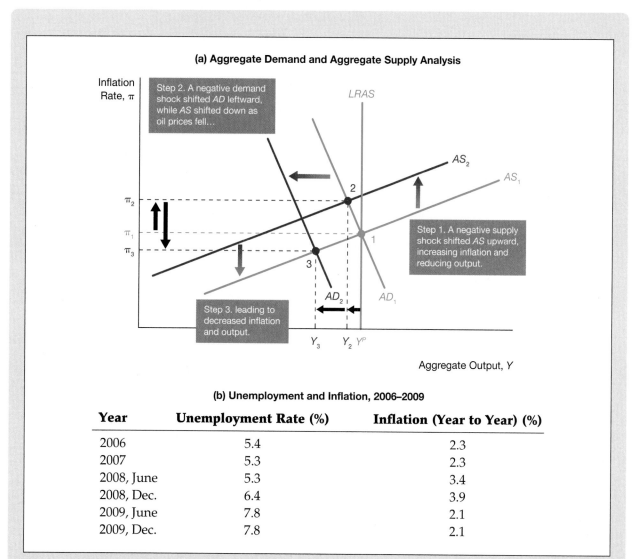

(a) Aggregate Demand and Aggregate Supply Analysis

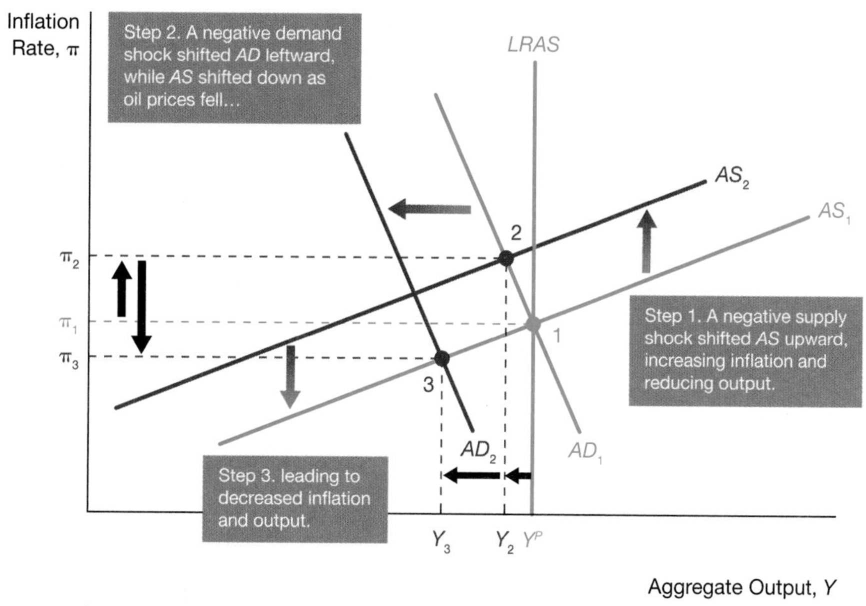
Inflation Rate, π
Step 2. A negative demand shock shifted AD leftward, while AS shifted down as oil prices fell...
LRAS
AS2
AS1
2
π2
π1
π3
1
3
Step 1. A negative supply shock shifted AS upward, increasing inflation and reducing output.
AD2
AD1
Step 3. leading to decreased inflation and output.
Y3
Y2
YP
Aggregate Output, Y

(b) Unemployment and Inflation, 2006–2009

Year	Unemployment Rate (%)	Inflation (Year to Year) (%)
2006	5.4	2.3
2007	5.3	2.3
2008, June	5.3	3.4
2008, Dec.	6.4	3.9
2009, June	7.8	2.1
2009, Dec.	7.8	2.1

FIGURE 17 U.K. Financial Crisis, 2007–2009

Panel (a) shows that a supply shock in 2007 from rising oil prices shifted the short-run aggregate supply curve up and to the left from AS_1 to AS_2 in the United Kingdom. The economy moved to point 2. With output below potential and oil prices falling after July 2008, the short-run aggregate supply curve began to shift down to AS_1. A negative demand shock following the escalating financial crisis after the Lehman Brothers bankruptcy shifted the aggregate demand curve to the left to AD_2. The economy now moved to point 3, where output fell to Y_3, unemployment rose, and inflation decreased to π_3. The data in panel (b) support this analysis: Note that the unemployment rate increased from 5.4% in 2006 to 7.8% in December 2009, while the inflation rate rose from 2.3% to 3.9% and then fell to 2.1% over this same time period.

Source: Office of National Statistics, UK. www.statistics.gov.uk/statbase/tsdtimezone.asp.

so the aggregate demand curve did not shift and equilibrium instead moved from point 1 to point 2 on AD_1. The aggregate demand and supply framework indicates that inflation would rise, which is what occurred (see the increase in the inflation rate from 2.3% in 2007 to 3.9% in December 2008 in Figure 17 panel (b)). With output below potential and oil prices falling after July 2008, the short-run aggregate supply curve shifted down to AS_1. At the same time, the financial crisis after the Lehman Brothers bankruptcy impacted spending worldwide, causing a negative demand shock that shifted the aggregate demand curve to the left to AD_2. The economy now moved to point 3, with a further fall in output, a rise in unemployment, and a fall in inflation. As the aggregate demand and supply analysis predicts, the U.K. unemployment rate rose to 7.8% by the end of 2009, with the inflation rate falling to 2.1%.

APPLICATION ◆ China and the 2007–2009 Financial Crisis

The financial crisis that began in August 2007 at first had very little impact on China.[7] When the financial crisis escalated in the United States in the fall of 2008 with the collapse of Lehman Brothers, all this changed. China's economy had been driven by extremely strong export growth, which up until September of 2008 had been growing at over a 20% annual rate. Starting in October 2008, Chinese exports collapsed, falling at around a 20% annual rate through August 2009.

The negative demand shock from the collapse of exports led to a decline in aggregate demand, shifting the aggregate demand curve to AD_2 and moving the economy from point 1 to point 2 in Figure 18 panel (a). As aggregate demand and supply analysis indicates, China's economic growth slowed from over 11% in the first half of 2008 to under 5% in the second half, while inflation declined from 7.9% to 4.4%, and then became negative thereafter (see Figure 18 panel (b)).

Instead of relying solely on the economy's self-correcting mechanism, the Chinese government proposed a massive fiscal stimulus package of $580 billion in 2008, which at 12.5% of GDP was three times larger than the U.S. fiscal stimulus package relative to GDP. In addition, the People's Bank of China, the central bank, began taking measures to autonomously ease monetary policy. These decisive actions shifted the aggregate demand curve back to AD_1 and the Chinese economy very quickly moved back to point 1. The Chinese economy thus weathered the financial crisis remarkably well, with output growth rising rapidly in 2009 and inflation becoming positive thereafter. ◆

[7] Note that just as in the rest of the world, China experienced an increase in energy prices that initially shifted up the short-run aggregate supply curve. Hence, as in the U.K., in 2007 the Chinese economy experienced a rise in inflation and a slight slowing of growth. This is not depicted in Figure 18 as it was in Figure 17 because doing so would have made Figure 18 too complex.

Summary

1. The aggregate demand curve indicates the quantity of aggregate output demanded at each inflation rate, and it is downward sloping. The primary sources of shifts in the aggregate demand curve are (1) autonomous monetary policy, (2) government purchases, (3) taxes, (4) net exports, (5) autonomous consumption expenditure, (6) autonomous investment, and (7) financial frictions.
2. The long-run aggregate supply curve is vertical at potential output. The long-run aggregate supply curve shifts when technology changes, when there are long-run changes to the amount of labor or capital, or when the natural rate of unemployment changes. The short-run aggregate supply curve slopes upward because inflation rises as output rises relative to potential

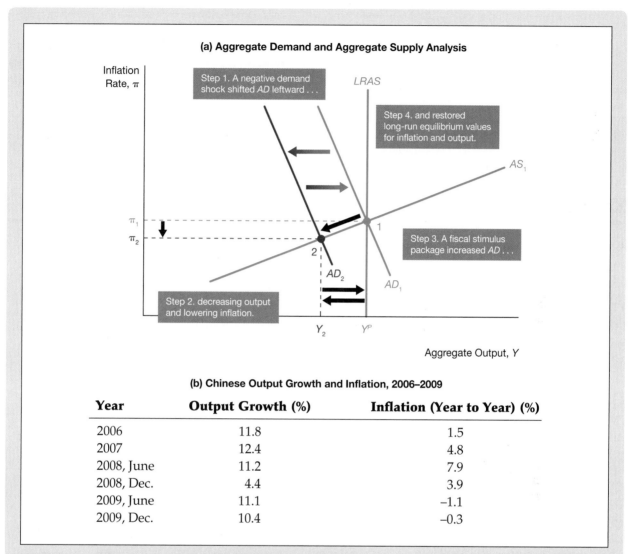

(a) Aggregate Demand and Aggregate Supply Analysis

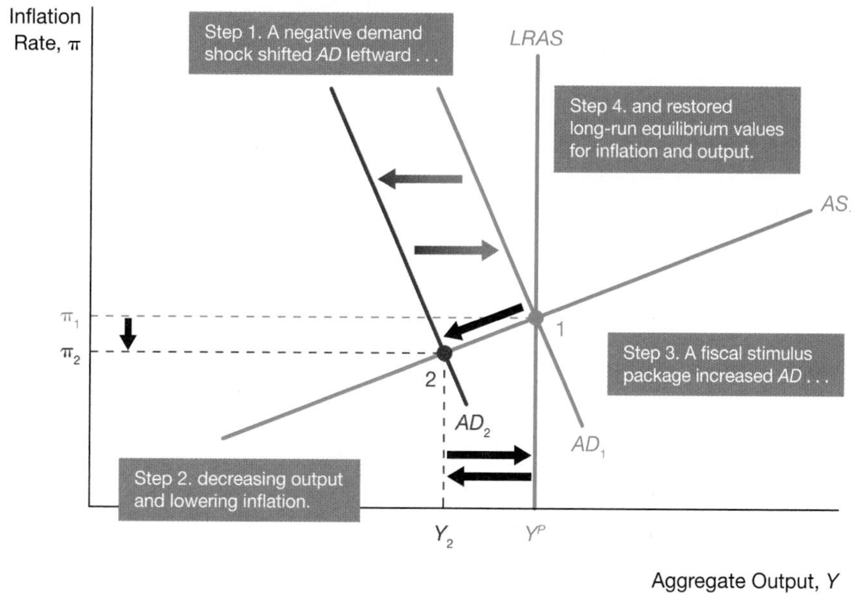
Inflation Rate, π
Step 1. A negative demand shock shifted AD leftward . . .
LRAS
Step 4. and restored long-run equilibrium values for inflation and output.
AS1
π1
π2
1
2
Step 3. A fiscal stimulus package increased AD . . .
AD2
AD1
Step 2. decreasing output and lowering inflation.
Y2
YP
Aggregate Output, Y

(b) Chinese Output Growth and Inflation, 2006–2009

Year	Output Growth (%)	Inflation (Year to Year) (%)
2006	11.8	1.5
2007	12.4	4.8
2008, June	11.2	7.9
2008, Dec.	4.4	3.9
2009, June	11.1	–1.1
2009, Dec.	10.4	–0.3

FIGURE 18 China and the Financial Crisis, 2007–2009

Panel (a) shows that the collapse of Chinese exports starting in 2008 led to a negative demand shock that shifted the aggregate demand curve to AD_2, moving the economy to point 2, where output growth fell below potential and inflation declined. A massive fiscal stimulus package and autonomous easing of monetary policy shifted the aggregate demand curve back to AD_1, and the economy very quickly moved back to long-run equilibrium at point 1. The data in panel (b) support this analysis: Note that output growth slowed but then bounced back again, and inflation began to fall at a less rapid rate.

Source: International Monetary Fund. 2010. International Financial Statistics. Country Tables, February. http://www.imfstatistics.org/IMF/imfbrowser.aspx?docList=pdfs&path=ct%2f20100201%2fct_pdf%2f20100121_CHN.pdf.

output. The short-run supply curve shifts when there are price shocks, changes in expected inflation, or persistent output gaps.

3. Equilibrium in the short run occurs at the point where the aggregate demand curve intersects the short-run aggregate supply curve. Although this is where the economy heads temporarily, the self-correcting mechanism leads the economy to settle permanently at the long-run equilibrium where aggregate output is at its potential. Shifts in either the aggregate demand curve

or the short-run aggregate supply curve can produce changes in aggregate output and inflation.

4. A positive demand shock shifts the aggregate demand curve to the right and initially leads to a rise in both inflation and output. However, in the long run it leads only to a rise in inflation, because output returns to its initial level at Y^P.

5. A temporary positive supply shock leads to a downward and rightward shift in the short-run aggregate supply curve, which lowers inflation and raises output initially. However, in the long-run output and inflation are unchanged. A permanent positive supply shock leads initially to both a rise in output and a decline in inflation. However, in contrast to a temporary supply shock, in the long run the permanent positive supply shock, which results in a rise in potential output, leads to a permanent rise in output and a permanent decline in inflation.

6. Aggregate supply and demand analysis is also just as useful for analyzing foreign business cycle episodes as it is for domestic business cycle episodes.

Key Terms

aggregate demand curve, p. 567
aggregate supply curve, p. 572
cost-push shocks, p. 574
consumption expenditure, p. 567
demand shocks, p. 569
government purchases, p. 567
equilibrium, p. 579
natural rate of output, p. 572
natural rate of unemployment, p. 572
net exports, p. 567
output gap, p. 573
planned investment spending, p. 567
potential output, p. 572
price shocks, p. 574
real business cycle theory, p. 590
self-correcting mechanism, p. 582
stagflation, p. 587
supply shocks, p. 574

Questions

All questions are available in MyEconLab *at* www.myeconlab.com.

1. Explain why the aggregate demand curve slopes downward and the short-run aggregate supply curve slopes upward.
2. Identify changes in three factors that will shift the aggregate demand curve to the right and changes in three different factors that will shift the aggregate demand curve to the left.
3. "The depreciation of the dollar from December 2008 to December 2009 had a positive effect on aggregate demand in the U.S." Is this statement true, false, or uncertain? Explain your answer.
4. What determines the unemployment rate when output is at potential?
5. As the labor force becomes more productive over time, how does that affect the long-run aggregate supply curve?
6. Why are central banks so concerned about inflation expectations?
7. If prices and wages are perfectly flexible, then $\gamma = 0$ and changes in aggregate demand have a smaller effect on output." Is this statement true, false, or uncertain? Explain your answer.
8. What factors shift the short-run aggregate supply curve? Do any of these factors shift the long-run aggregate supply curve? Why?
9. If large budget deficits cause the public to think that there will be higher inflation in the future, what is likely to happen to the short-run aggregate supply curve when budget deficits rise?
10. Internet sites that allow people to post their resumes reduce the cost of a job search. How do you think the Internet has affected the natural rate of unemployment?
11. When aggregate output is below the natural rate of output, what will happen to the inflation rate over time if the aggregate demand curve remains unchanged? Why?
12. Suppose that the public believes that a newly announced anti-inflation program will work and so lowers its expectations of future inflation. What will happen to aggregate output and the inflation rate in the short run?

13. If the unemployment rate is above the natural rate of unemployment, holding other factors constant, what will happen to inflation and output?
14. What happens to inflation and output in the short run and the long run when government spending increases?
15. What factors led to a decrease in both the unemployment rate and the inflation rate in the 1990s?
16. Are there any "good" supply shocks?
17. Why did the Federal Reserve pursue inherently recessionary policies in the early 1980s?
18. In what ways is the Volcker disinflation considered a success? What are the negative aspects of it?
19. Why did China fare much better than the United States and the United Kingdom during the 2007–2009 financial crisis?

Applied Problems

All applied problems are available in MyEconLab *at* www.myeconlab.com.

20. Using an aggregate demand and supply graph, show and describe the effects in both the short run and the long run of the following:
    a. A temporary negative supply shock.
    b. A permanent negative supply shock.
21. Many of the resources devoted to the January 2009 U.S. stimulus package encouraged investment in research and development of new technologies (e.g., more fuel-efficient cars, wind and solar power) and infrastructure investment (roads, bridges, and transportation networks). Assuming this policy results in a positive productivity change for the U.S. economy, what does aggregate demand and supply analysis predict in terms of inflation and output? Use a graph to demonstrate.
22. Proposals have come before Congress that advocate the implementation of a national sales tax. Predict the effect of such a tax on both the aggregate supply and demand curves, showing the effects on output and inflation. Use a graph of aggregate supply and demand to demonstrate.
23. Suppose the inflation rate remains relatively constant, and output decreases and the unemployment rate increases. Using an aggregate demand and supply graph, show how this is possible.
24. Classify each of the following as a supply or demand shock. Use a graph to show the effects on inflation and output in the short run and the long run.
    a. Financial frictions increase.
    b. Households and firms become more optimistic about the economy.
    c. Favorable weather produces a record crop of wheat and corn in the Midwest.
    d. Steel workers go on strike for 4 weeks.
25. During the first half of 2010, Fed officials discussed the possibility of increasing interest rates as a way of fighting potential increases in expected inflation. If the public came to expect higher inflation rates in the future, what would be the effect on the short-run aggregate supply curve? Show your answer, using an aggregate demand and supply graph.

Web Exercises

1. The financial crisis from 2007–2009 sent the United States into the worst recession since the end of World War II, with the unemployment rate rising to above 10%. Go to research.stlouisfed.org/fred2/categories/12 and click on the Series ID link "UNRATE" (Civilian Unemployment Rate). What has happened to the unemployment rate since the last reported figure in Figure 16?
2. In the beginning of 2009, the Federal Open Market Committee warned in their statement dated January 28, 2009, that "... the Committee sees some risk that inflation could persist for a time below rates that best foster economic growth and price stability in the longer term." Go to research.stlouisfed.org/fred2/categories/9 and click on the Series ID link "CPIAUCSL" (Consumer Price Index for All Urban Consumers: All Items-SA). Then click on the link "% Chg. From Yr. Ago." What has happened to the inflation rate since the last reported figure in Table 16?

Web References

www.bls.gov

The home page of the Bureau of Labor Statistics lists information on unemployment and price levels.

www.census.gov/compendia/statab

Statistics on the U.S. economy in an easy-to-understand format.

www.research.stlouisfed.org/fred2/

A database of U.S. economic data hosted by the Federal Reserve Bank of St. Louis.

Web Appendices

Please visit the Companion Website at www.pearsonhighered.com/mishkin to read the Web appendices to Chapter 23:

Appendix 1: Effects of Macroeconomic Shocks on Asset Prices

Appendix 2: Aggregate Demand and Supply: A Numerical Example

Appendix 3: The Algebra of the Aggregate Demand and Supply Model

Appendix 4: The Taylor Principle and Inflation Stability

APPENDIX TO CHAPTER 23

The Phillips Curve and the Short-Run Aggregate Supply Curve

This appendix discusses the *Phillips curve*, which describes the relationship of unemployment and inflation, and shows how it can be used to derive the short-run aggregate supply curve in the chapter.

THE PHILLIPS CURVE

In 1958, New Zealand economist A.W. Phillips published a famous empirical paper that examined the relationship between unemployment and wage growth in the United Kingdom.[1] For the years 1861 to 1957, he found that periods of low unemployment were associated with rapid rises in wages, while periods of high unemployment had low growth in wages. Other economists soon extended his work to many other countries. Because inflation is more central to macroeconomic issues than wage growth, they estimated the relationship of unemployment with inflation. The negative relationship between unemployment and inflation they found for many countries became known, naturally enough, as the *Phillips curve*.

The idea behind the Phillips curve is quite intuitive. When labor markets are *tight*—that is, the unemployment rate is low—firms may have difficulty hiring qualified workers and may even have a hard time keeping their present employees. Because of the shortage of workers in the labor market, firms will raise wages to attract needed workers and raise their prices at a more rapid rate.

Phillips Curve Analysis in the 1960s

Because wage inflation feeds directly into overall inflation, in the 1960s the Phillips curve became extremely popular as an explanation for inflation fluctuations because it seemed to fit the data so well. As shown by panel (a) of Figure 1's plot of the U.S. inflation rate against the unemployment rate from 1950 to 1969, a very clear negative relationship exists between unemployment and inflation. The Phillips curve in that period seemed to imply that there is a long-run trade-off between unemployment and inflation—that is, policymakers can choose policies that lead to a higher rate of inflation and end up with a lower unemployment rate on a sustained basis. This apparent trade-off was very influential in policy circles in the 1960s, as we can see in the FYI box, "The Phillips Curve Tradeoff and Macroeconomic Policy in the 1960s."

[1]A.W. Phillips, "The Relationship Between Unemployment and the Rate of Change of Money Wages in the United Kingdom, 1861–1957," *Economica* 25 (November 1958): 283–299.

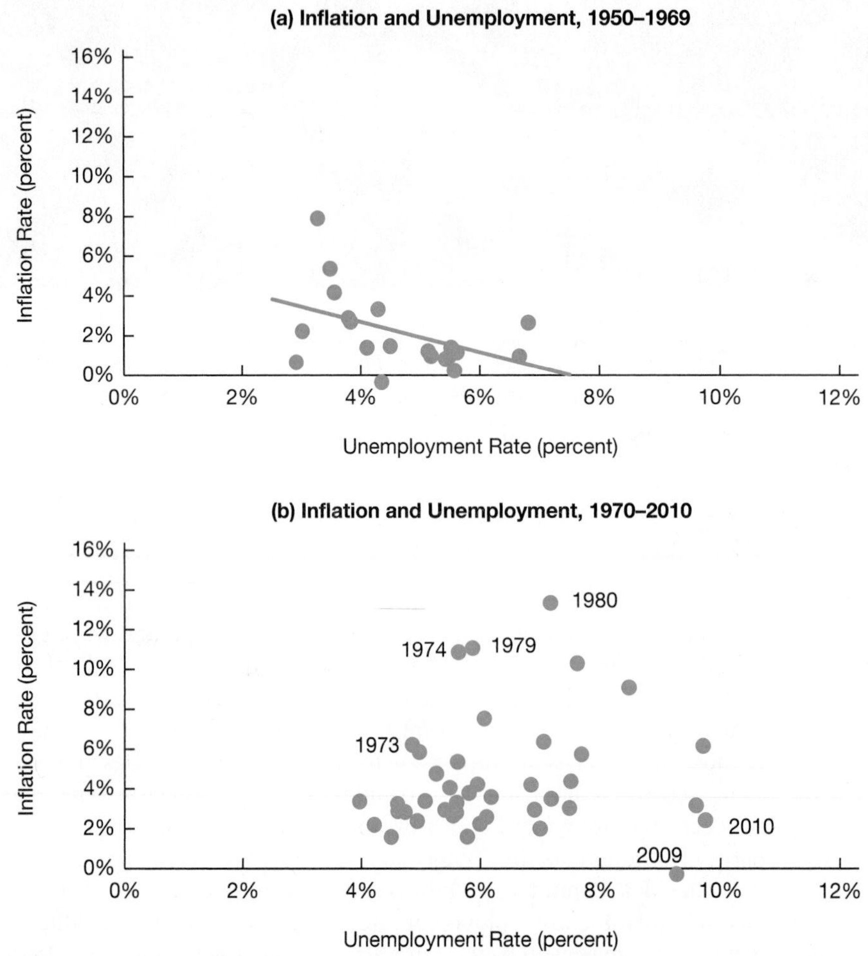

FIGURE 1 Inflation and Unemployment in the United States, 1950–1969 and 1970–2010

The plot of inflation against unemployment over the 1950–1969 period in panel (a) shows that a higher inflation rate was generally associated with a lower rate of unemployment. Panel (b) shows that after 1970, the negative relationship between inflation and unemployment disappeared.

Source: Economic Report of the President. www.gpoaccess.gov/eop/.

The Friedman-Phelps Phillips Curve Analysis

In 1967 and 1968, Milton Friedman and Edmund Phelps pointed out a severe theoretical flaw in the Phillips curve analysis.[3] It was inconsistent with the view that workers and firms care about *real* wages, the amount of real goods and services that wages can purchase, not *nominal* wages. Thus when workers and firms expect the price level to be rising, they will adjust nominal wages upward so that the real wage rate does not decrease. In other words, wage and overall inflation will rise one-for-one with increases in expected inflation, as well as respond to tightness in the labor market. In addition, the Friedman-Phelps analysis suggested that in the long run the economy would reach the level of unemployment that would occur if all wages and prices were flexible, which

FYI The Phillips Curve Tradeoff and Macroeconomic Policy in the 1960s

In 1960, Paul Samuelson and Robert Solow published a paper outlining how policymakers could exploit the Phillips curve tradeoff. The policymaker could choose between two competing goals—inflation and unemployment—and decide how high an inflation rate he or she would be willing to accept to attain a lower unemployment rate.[2] Indeed, Samuelson and Solow even said that policymakers could achieve a "nonperfectionist" goal of a 3% unemployment rate at what they considered to be a tolerable inflation rate of 4–5% per year. This thinking was influential in the Kennedy and then Johnson administrations, and contributed to the adoption of policies in the mid-1960s to stimulate the economy and bring the unemployment rate down to low levels. At first these policies seemed to be successful because the subsequent higher inflation rates were accompanied by a fall in the unemployment rate. However, the good times were not to last: From the late 1960s through the 1970s, inflation accelerated, yet the unemployment rate remained stubbornly high.

they called the *natural rate of unemployment*.[4] The natural rate of unemployment is the full-employment level of unemployment, because some unemployment will still exist even when wages and prices are flexible.

The Friedman-Phelps reasoning suggested a Phillips curve that we can write as follows:

$$\pi = \pi^e - \omega(U - U_n) \quad (1)$$

where π represents inflation, π^e expected inflation, U the unemployment rate, U_n the natural rate of unemployment, and ω the sensitivity of inflation to $U - U_n$. The presence of the π^e term explains why Equation 1 is also referred to as the *expectations-augmented Phillips curve*: It indicates that inflation is negatively related to the difference between the unemployment rate and the natural rate of unemployment ($U - U_n$), a measure of tightness in the labor markets called the *unemployment gap*.

The expectations-augmented Phillips curve implies that long-run unemployment will be at the natural rate level, as Friedman and Phelps theorized. Recognize that in the long run, expected inflation must gravitate to actual inflation, and Equation 1 therefore indicates that U must be equal to U_n.

The Friedman-Phelps expectations-augmented version of the Phillips curve displays no long-run tradeoff between unemployment and inflation. To show this, Figure 2 presents the expectations-augmented Phillips curve, marked as PC_1, for a given expected inflation rate of 2% and a natural rate of unemployment of 5%. (PC_1 goes through point 1 because Equation 1 indicates that when $\pi = \pi^e = 2\%$, $U = U_n = 5\%$, and its slope

[2]Paul A. Samuelson and Robert M. Solow, "Analytical Aspects of Anti-Inflation Policy," *American Economic Review* 50 (May 1960, Papers and Proceedings): 177–194.

[3]Milton Friedman outlined his criticism of the Phillips curve in his 1967 presidential address to the American Economic Association: Milton Friedman, "The Role of Monetary Policy," *American Economic Review* 58 (1968): 1–17. Phelps's reformulation of the Phillips curve analysis was in Edmund Phelps, "Money-Wage Dynamics and Labor-Market Equilibrium," *Journal of Political Economy* 76 (July/August 1968, Part 2): 687–711.

[4]As we discussed in Chapter 13, there will always be some unemployment that is either *frictional unemployment*, unemployment that occurs because workers are searching for jobs, or *structural unemployment*, unemployment that arises from a mismatch of skills with available jobs and is a structural feature of the labor markets. Thus even when wages and prices are fully flexible, the natural rate of unemployment is at a level above zero.

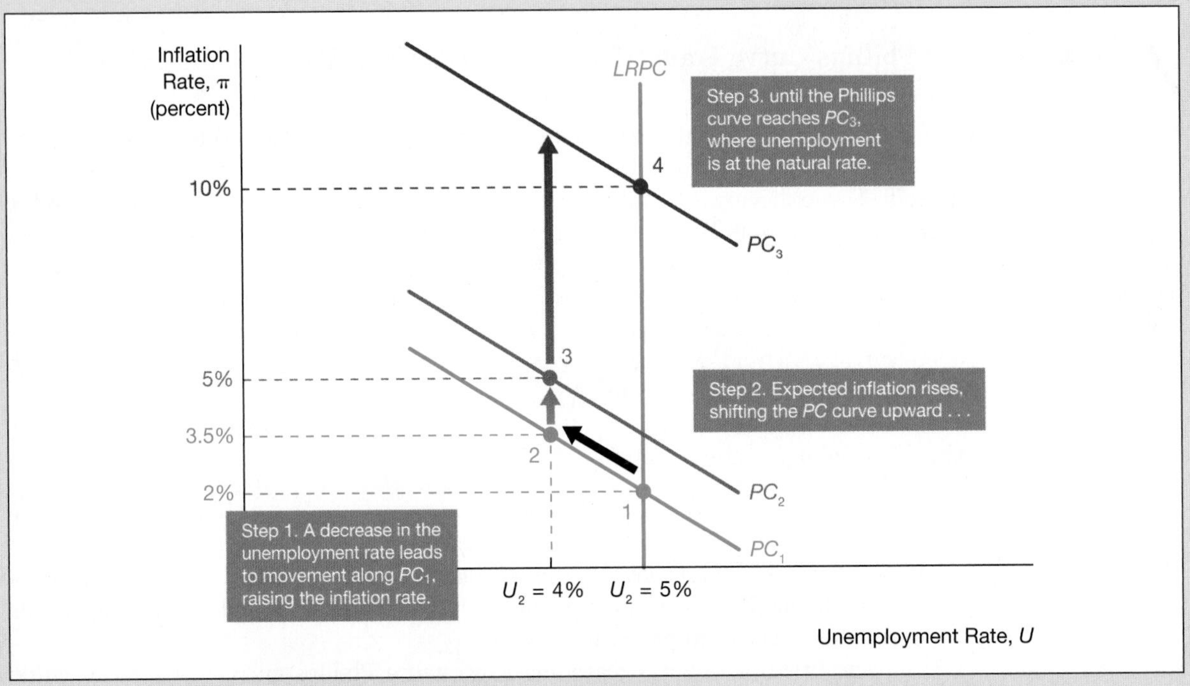

FIGURE 2 The Short- and Long-Run Phillips Curve

The expectations-augmented Phillips curve is downward-sloping because a lower unemployment rate results in a higher inflation rate for any given level of expected inflation. If the economy moves due to a decline in the unemployment rate from point 1 to point 2 on PC_1, the inflation rate rises. If unemployment remains at 4%, inflation rises further, shifting the short-run expectations-augmented Phillips curve upward to PC_2 and to point 3. Eventually, when the economy reaches point 4, when $\pi^e = \pi = 10\%$, the expectations-augmented Phillips curve, PC_3, will stop shifting because unemployment is at the natural rate of unemployment. The line connecting points 1 and 4 is the long-run Phillips curve, *LRPC*, and shows that long-run unemployment is at the natural rate of unemployment for any inflation rate.

is $-\omega$.) Suppose the economy is initially at point 1, where the unemployment rate is at the natural rate level of 5%, but then government policies to stimulate the economy cause the unemployment rate to fall to 4%, a level below the natural rate level. The economy then moves along PC_1 to point 2, with inflation rising above 2%, say, to 3.5%. Expected inflation will then rise as well, so the expectations-augmented Phillips curve will shift upward from PC_1 to PC_2. Continued efforts to stimulate the economy and keep the unemployment rate at 4%, below the natural rate level, will cause further increases in the actual and expected inflation rates, causing the expectations-augmented Phillips curve to continue shifting upward.

When will the expectations-augmented Phillips curve stop rising? It will stop only when unemployment is back at the natural rate level, that is, when $U = U_n = 5\%$. Suppose that this happens when inflation is at 10%; then expected inflation will also be at 10% because inflation has settled down to that level, with the expectations-augmented Phillips curve at PC_3 in Figure 2. The economy will now move to point 4, where $\pi = \pi^e = 10\%$, and unemployment is at the natural rate $U = U_n = 5\%$. We thus see that in the long run, when the expectations-augmented Phillips curve is no longer shifting, the economy will be on points like 1 and 4. The line connecting these points is thus the *long-run Phillips curve*, which we mark as *LRPC* in Figure 2.

Figure 2 leads us to three important conclusions:

1. ***There is no long-run trade-off between unemployment and inflation*** because, as the vertical long-run Phillips curve shows, a higher long-run inflation rate is not associated with a lower level of unemployment.
2. ***There is a short-run trade-off between unemployment and inflation*** because with a given expected inflation rate, policymakers can attain a lower unemployment rate at the expense of a somewhat higher inflation rate, as at point 2 in Figure 2.
3. ***There are two types of Phillips curves, long run and short run***. The expectations-augmented Phillips curves—PC_1, PC_2, and PC_3—are actually short-run Phillips curves: They are drawn for given values of expected inflation and will shift if deviations of unemployment from the natural rate cause inflation and expected inflation to change.

The Phillips Curve After the 1960s

As Figure 2 indicates, the expectations-augmented Phillips curve shows that the negative relationship between unemployment and inflation breaks down when the unemployment rate remains below the natural rate of unemployment for any extended period of time. This prediction of the Friedman and Phelps analysis turned out to be exactly right. Starting in the 1970s, after a period of very low unemployment rates, the negative relationship between unemployment and inflation, which was so visible in the 1950s and 1960s, disappeared, as we can see in panel (b) of Figure 1. Not surprisingly, given the brilliance of Friedman's and Phelps's work, they were both awarded Nobel Prizes.

The Modern Phillips Curve

With the sharp rise in oil prices in 1973 and 1979, inflation jumped up sharply (see panel (b) of Figure 1), and Phillips-curve theorists realized that they had to add one more feature to the expectations-augmented Phillips curve. *Supply shocks* are shocks to supply that change the output an economy can produce from the same amount of capital and labor. These supply shocks translate into *price shocks*, that is, shifts in inflation that are independent of the tightness in the labor markets or of expected inflation. For example, when the supply of oil is restricted, as it was following the war between the Arab states and Israel in 1973, the price of oil more than quadrupled, and firms had to raise prices to reflect their increased costs of production, thus driving up inflation. Adding price shocks (ρ) to the expectations-augmented Phillips curve leads to the modern form of the short-run Phillips curve:

$$\pi = \pi^e - \omega(U - U_n) + \rho \qquad (2)$$

The modern, short-run Phillips curve implies that wages and prices are sticky. The more flexible wages and prices are, the more they, and inflation, respond to deviations of unemployment from the natural rate; that is, more flexible wages and prices imply that the absolute value of ω is higher, which implies that the short-run Phillips curve is steeper. If wages and prices are completely flexible, then ω becomes so large that the short-run Phillips curve is vertical, and it would be identical to the long-run Phillips curve. In this case, there is no long-run or short-run trade-off between unemployment and inflation.

The Modern Phillips Curve with Adaptive (Backward-Looking) Expectations

To complete our analysis of the Phillips curve, we need to understand how firms and households form expectations about inflation. One simple way of thinking about how firms and households form their expectations about inflation is that they do so by looking at past inflation:

$$\pi^e = \pi_{-1}$$

where π_{-1} is the inflation rate in the previous period. This form of expectations is known as *adaptive expectations* or *backward-looking expectations* because expectations are formed by looking at the past and therefore change only slowly over time.[5] Substituting π_{-1} in for π^e in Equation 2 yields the following short-run Phillips curve:

$$\begin{array}{ccccccc} \pi & = & \pi_{-1} & - & \omega(U - U_n) & + & \rho \\ \text{Inflation} & = & \text{Expected Inflation} & - & \omega \times \text{Unemployment Gap} & + & \text{Price Shock} \end{array} \quad (3)$$

This form of the Phillips curve has two advantages over the more general formulation in Equation 2. First, it takes a very simple mathematical form that is convenient to use. Second, it provides two additional realistic reasons why inflation might be sticky. One reason comes from the view that inflation expectations adjust only slowly as past inflation changes. Inflation expectations are therefore sticky, which results in some inflation stickiness. Another reason is that the presence of past inflation in the Phillips curve formulation can reflect the fact that some wage and price contracts might be backward looking, that is, tied to past inflation, and so inflation might not fully adjust to changes in inflation expectations in the short run.

There is, however, one important disadvantage of the adaptive-expectations form of the Phillips curve in Equation 3: It takes a very mechanical view of how inflation expectations are formed. More sophisticated analysis of expectations formation has important implications for the conduct of macroeconomic policy and is discussed in Chapter 25. For the time being, we will make use of the simple form of the Phillips curve with adaptive expectations, keeping in mind that the π_{-1} term represents expected inflation.

There is another convenient way to look at the adaptive-expectations form of the Phillips curve. By subtracting π_{-1} from both sides of Equation 3, we can rewrite it as follows:

$$\Delta\pi = \pi - \pi_{-1} = -\omega(U - U_n) + \rho \quad (4)$$

Written in this form, the Phillips curve indicates that a negative unemployment gap (tight labor market) causes the inflation rate to rise, that is, accelerate. This relationship is why the Equation 4 version of the Phillips curve is often referred to as an ***accelerationist Phillips curve***. With this formulation, the term U_n has another interpretation. Since inflation stops accelerating (changing) when the unemployment rate is at U_n, we also refer to this term as the *nonaccelerating inflation rate of unemployment* or more commonly as *NAIRU*.

THE SHORT-RUN AGGREGATE SUPPLY CURVE

To complete our aggregate demand and supply model, we need to use our analysis of the Phillips curve to derive a *short-run aggregate supply curve,* which represents the relationship between the total quantity of output that firms are willing to produce and the inflation rate.

[5]An alternative, modern form of expectations makes use of the concept *rational expectations*, where expectations are formed using all available information, and so may react more quickly to new information. We discuss rational expectations and their role in macroeconomic analysis in Chapter 25.

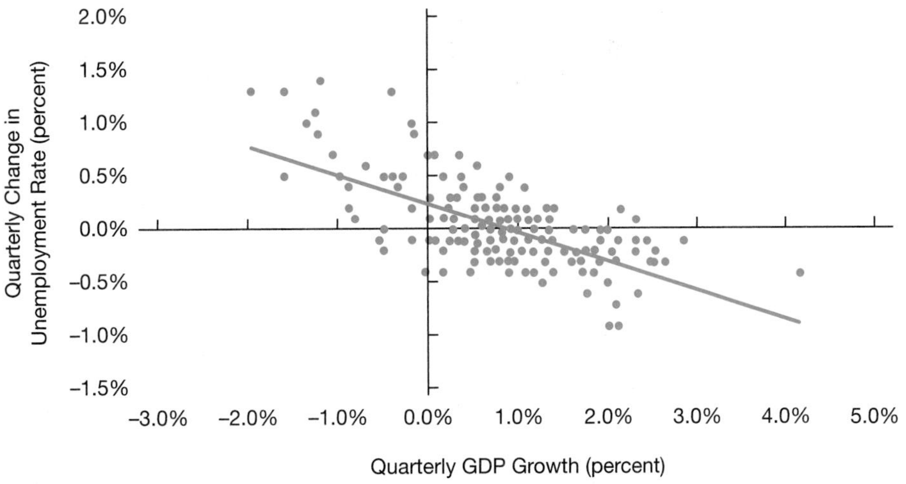

FIGURE 3 Okun's Law, 1960–2010

The plot of the unemployment gap and the output gap reveals a linear relationship, represented by the solid line with a slope of $-\frac{1}{2}$.

Source: Unemployment, quarterly, 1960–2010 and real GDP growth, quarterly, 1960–2010. Bureau of Labor Statistics and Bureau of Economic Analysis.

We can translate the modern Phillips curve into a short-run aggregate supply curve by replacing the unemployment gap $(U - U_n)$ with the *output gap*, the difference between output and potential output $(Y - Y^P)$. To do this, we need to make use of a relationship between unemployment and aggregate output that was discovered by the economist Arthur Okun, once the chairman of the Council of Economic Advisors and later an economist with the Brookings Institution.[6] **Okun's law** describes the negative relationship between the unemployment gap and the output gap.

Okun's Law We show Okun's law in Figure 3, which plots the unemployment gap against the output gap. A tight negative relationship exists between the two variables. When output is above potential, so that the output gap is positive, the unemployment rate is below the natural rate of unemployment; that is, the unemployment gap is negative. The line through the data points in Figure 3 describes this negative relationship, which algebraically is as follows [7]

$$U - U_n = -0.5 \times (Y - Y^P) \tag{5}$$

[6]Arthur M. Okun, "Potential GNP: Its Measurement and Significance," in *Proceeding of the Business and Economics Section: American Statistical Association* (Washington, D.C.: American Statistical Association, 1962), pp. 98–103; reprinted in Arthur M. Okun, *The Political Economy of Prosperity* (Washington, D.C.: Brookings Institution, 1970), pp. 132–145.

[7]The output gap, $Y - Y^P$, in Okun's law is most accurately expressed in percentage terms, so the units of Y and Y^P would be in logs. However, to keep the algebra simple in this and later chapters, we will treat Y and Y^P as in levels and not in logs both in the Okun's law equation and in the short-run aggregate supply curve developed here.

Okun's law thus states that for each percentage point that output is above potential, the unemployment rate is one-half of a percentage point below the natural rate of unemployment. Alternatively, for every percentage point that unemployment is above its natural rate, output is two percentage points below potential output.

Another way of thinking about Okun's law is that a one percentage point increase in output leads to a one-half percentage point decline in unemployment.[8] Why is the unemployment rate decline only half that of the increase in output? When output rises, firms do not increase employment commensurately with the increase, a phenomenon that is known as *labor hoarding*. Rather, they work employees harder, increasing their hours. Furthermore, when the economy is expanding, more people enter the labor force because job prospects are better and so the unemployment rate does not fall by as much as employment increases.

Deriving the Short-Run Aggregate Supply Curve Using the Okun's law Equation 5 to substitute for $U - U_n$ in the short-run Phillips curve Equation 2 yields the following:

$$\pi = \pi^e + 0.5\omega(Y - Y^P) + \rho$$

Replacing 0.5ω by γ, which describes the sensitivity of inflation to the output gap, produces the short-run aggregate supply curve that we already saw as Equation 2 in this chapter:

$$\pi = \pi^e + \gamma(Y - Y^P) + \rho$$

$$\text{Inflation} = \text{Expected Inflation} + \gamma \times \text{Output Gap} + \text{Price Shock}$$

[8]To see this algebraically, take the differences of Equation 5 and assume that U_n remains constant (a reasonable assumption because the natural rate of unemployment only changes very slowly over time). Then,

$$\%\Delta U = -0.5 \times (\%\Delta Y - \%\Delta Y^P)$$

where $\%\Delta$ indicates a percentage point change. Since potential output grows at a fairly steady rate of around three percent a year, $\%\Delta Y^P = 3\%$, we can also write Okun's law as follows:

$$\%\Delta U = -0.5 \times (\%\Delta Y - 3)$$

or

$$\%\Delta Y = 3 - 2.0 \times \%\Delta U$$

Hence we can state Okun's law in the following way: for every percentage point rise in output (real GDP), unemployment falls by one-half of a percentage point. Alternatively, for every percentage point rise in unemployment, real GDP falls by two percentage points.

24 Monetary Policy Theory

Preview

Between September 2007 and December 2008, the Federal Reserve lowered the target for its policy interest rate, the federal funds rate, from $5\frac{1}{4}\%$ all the way down to zero and continued to keep it there for years afterward. Why did the Fed lower interest rates this aggressively and continue to keep them so low?

Could this monetary policy easing spark undesirable inflation? Many commentators in the media thought so. Starting in the early 1960s, when the inflation rate hovered between 1% and 2%, the economy has suffered from higher and more variable rates of inflation. By the late 1960s, the inflation rate had climbed beyond 5%, and by 1974, it reached the double-digit level. After moderating somewhat during the 1975–1978 period, it shot above 10% in 1979 and 1980, slowed to around 5% from 1982 to 1990, declined further to around 2% in the late 1990s, and then climbed above the 5% level in 2008. Inflation has become a major concern of politicians and the public, and how to control it frequently dominates the discussion of economic policy.

In this chapter, we use the aggregate demand–aggregate supply (*AD*/*AS*) framework developed in Chapter 23 to develop a theory of monetary policy. Specifically, we will examine the role of monetary policy in creating inflation and stabilizing the economy. We apply the theory to three big questions: What are the roots of inflation? Does stabilizing inflation stabilize output? Should policy be *activist*—by responding aggressively to fluctuations in economic activity—or passive and *nonactivist*?

RESPONSE OF MONETARY POLICY TO SHOCKS

As we saw in Chapter 19, the central goal of central banks is price stability: that is, they try to maintain inflation, π, close to a target level (π^T), referred to as an **inflation target**, that is slightly above zero. Most central banks set π^T between 1% and 3%. An alternative way to think about how the central bank pursues price stability is that monetary policy should try to minimize the difference between inflation and the inflation target ($\pi - \pi^T$), which we refer to as the **inflation gap**.

In Chapter 19, we learned that central banks also care about stabilizing economic activity. Because economic activity can be sustained only at potential output, this objective of monetary policy can be described as saying that monetary policymakers want to have aggregate output close to its potential level, Y^P. Another way of saying this is that central banks want to minimize the difference between aggregate output and potential output ($Y - Y^P$), i.e., the output gap. In our analysis of aggregate demand and supply in Chapter 23, we examined three categories of economic shocks—demand shocks, temporary supply shocks, and permanent supply shocks—and the consequences of each on inflation and output. In this section, we describe a central bank's policy responses, given its objectives, to each of these shocks. In the case of both demand shocks and permanent supply shocks, policymakers can simultaneously pursue price stability and stability in economic activity. Following a temporary supply shock, however, policymakers can achieve either price stability or economic activity stability, but not both. This tradeoff poses a thorny dilemma for central banks with dual mandates.

Response to an Aggregate Demand Shock

We begin by considering the effects of an aggregate demand shock, such as the disruption to financial markets starting in August 2007 that increased financial frictions and caused both consumer and business spending to fall. The economy is initially at point 1, where output is at Y^P and inflation is at π^T. The negative demand shock decreases aggregate demand, shifting AD_1 in Figure 1 to the left to AD_2. Policymakers can respond to this shock in two possible ways.

No Policy Response Because the central bank does not respond by changing the autonomous component of monetary policy, the aggregate demand curve remains at AD_2 and so the economy goes to the intersection of AS_1 and AD_2. Here, aggregate output falls to Y_2, below potential output Y^P, and inflation falls to π_2, below the inflation target of π^T. With output below potential, slack begins to develop in the labor and product

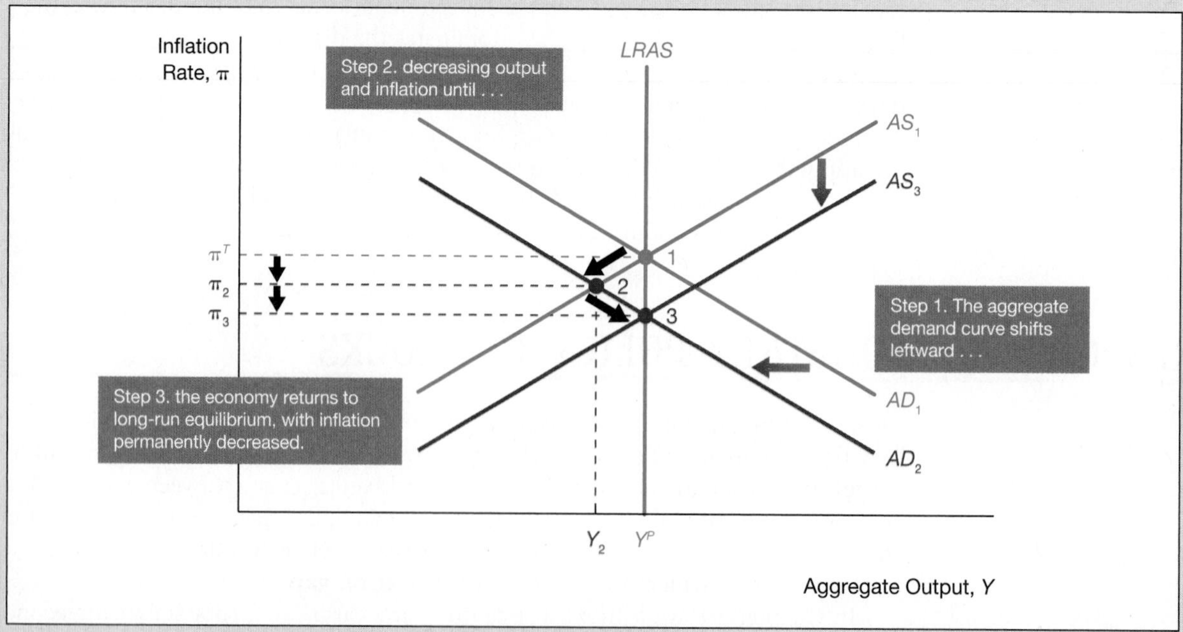

Inflation Rate, π
LRAS
Step 2. decreasing output and inflation until . . .
AS1
AS3
πT
π2
π3
1
2
3
Step 1. The aggregate demand curve shifts leftward . . .
Step 3. the economy returns to long-run equilibrium, with inflation permanently decreased.
AD1
AD2
Y2
YP
Aggregate Output, Y

FIGURE 1 Aggregate Demand Shock: No Policy Response
An aggregate demand shock shifts the aggregate demand curve leftward from AD_1 to AD_2 and moves the economy from point 1 to point 2, where aggregate output falls to Y_2 while inflation falls to π_2. With output below potential, the short-run aggregate supply curve shifts down to AS_3, and the economy moves to point 3, where output is back at Y^P, but inflation has fallen to π_3.

markets, lowering inflation. The short-run aggregate supply curve will shift down and to the right to AS_3, and the economy will move to point 3. Output will again be back at its potential level, while inflation will fall to a lower level of π_3. At first glance, this outcome looks favorable—inflation is lower and output is back at its potential. But aggregate output will remain below potential for some time, and if inflation was initially at its target level, the fall in inflation is undesirable for reasons outlined in both Chapter 9 and Chapter 19.

Policy Stabilizes Economic Activity and Inflation in the Short Run

Policymakers can eliminate both the output gap and the inflation gap in the short run by pursuing policies to increase aggregate demand to its initial level and return the economy to its preshock state. The central bank does this by autonomously easing monetary policy by cutting the real interest rate at any given inflation rate. This action stimulates investment spending and increases the quantity of aggregate output demanded at any given inflation rate, thereby shifting the *AD* curve to the right. As a result, the aggregate demand curve shifts from AD_2 back to AD_1 in Figure 2, and the economy returns to point 1. (The Federal Reserve took exactly these steps by lowering the federal funds rate from 5% to $\frac{1}{4}$% to zero over fifteen months starting in September 2007.)

Our analysis of this monetary policy response shows that ***in the case of aggregate demand shocks, there is no tradeoff between the pursuit of price stability and economic activity stability***. A focus on stabilizing inflation leads to exactly the right monetary policy response to stabilize economic activity. No conflict exists between the dual objectives of

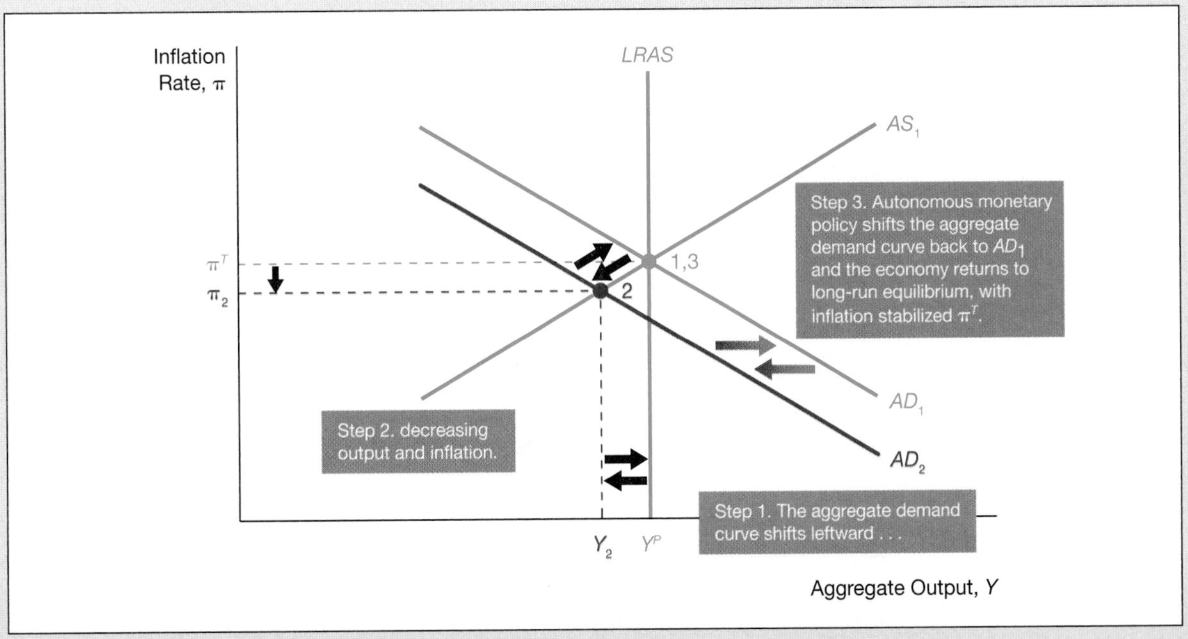

FIGURE 2 Aggregate Demand Shock: Policy Stabilizes Output and Inflation in the Short Run
An aggregate demand shock shifts the aggregate demand curve leftward from AD_1 to AD_2 and moves the economy from point 1 to point 2, where aggregate output falls to Y_2 while inflation falls to π_2. An autonomous easing of monetary policy lowers the real interest rate at any given inflation rate and shifts the *AD* curve back to AD_1. Aggregate output returns to potential at point 1 and inflation returns to its target level.

stabilizing inflation and economic activity, which Olivier Blanchard (formerly of MIT, but now at the International Monetary Fund) referred to as the **divine coincidence**.

APPLICATION ◆ Quantitative (Credit) Easing in Response to the Global Financial Crisis

We have seen that monetary policymakers can counter aggregate demand shocks and stabilize output and inflation by lowering the real interest rate. However, sometimes the negative aggregate demand shock is so large that at some point the central bank cannot lower the real interest rate further because the nominal interest rate hits a floor of zero, as occurred after the Lehman Brothers bankruptcy in late 2008. In this situation when the zero-lower-bound problem arises, the central bank must turn to nonconventional monetary policy of the type that has been discussed in Chapter 18. Although these nonconventional monetary policy measures involve liquidity provision and asset purchases, which result in an expansion of the central bank balance sheet and so are typically referred to as *quantitative easing*, we have seen that they are more accurately characterized as *credit easing*. How did quantitative (credit) easing work to stabilize output and inflation during the global financial crisis?

As we saw in Chapter 9, after the Lehman Brothers collapse, the real cost of borrowing to both households and businesses shot up because financial frictions rose dramatically ($\bar{f}\uparrow$). The higher real cost of borrowing led to a decline in consumption expenditure and planned investment spending, thereby causing a sharp contraction in aggregate demand and a leftward shift of the aggregate demand curve to AD_2, as in Figure 2. Although the Federal Reserve autonomously lowered the federal funds rate to the zero-lower bound, this was insufficient to shift the aggregate demand curve back to AD_1. By engaging in asset purchases and liquidity provision, the Fed was able to reduce financial frictions ($\bar{f}\downarrow$) and lower the real cost of borrowing to households and businesses. The result was that the aggregate demand curve did shift out to the right as shown in Figure 2, thereby avoiding deflation and boosting economic activity so that the economy did not enter a depression, as in the 1930s. However, the negative aggregate demand shock to the economy from the global financial crisis was so great that the Fed's quantitative (credit) easing was insufficient to overcome it, and the Fed was unable to shift the aggregate demand curve all the way back to AD_1. Hence, despite the Federal Reserve's efforts, the economy still suffered a severe recession, with inflation falling below the 2% level.

Response to a Permanent Supply Shock

We illustrate a permanent supply shock in Figure 3. Again the economy starts out at point 1, where aggregate output is at the natural rate Y_1^P and inflation is at π^T. Suppose the economy suffers a permanent negative supply shock because an increase in regulations permanently reduces the level of potential output. Potential output falls from Y_1^P to Y_3^P, and the long-run aggregate supply curve shifts leftward from $LRAS_1$ to $LRAS_3$. The permanent supply shock triggers a price shock that shifts the short-run aggregate supply curve upward from AS_1 to AS_2. Two possible policy responses to this permanent supply shock are possible.

No Policy Response If policymakers leave autonomous monetary policy unchanged, the economy will move to point 2, with inflation rising to π_2 and output

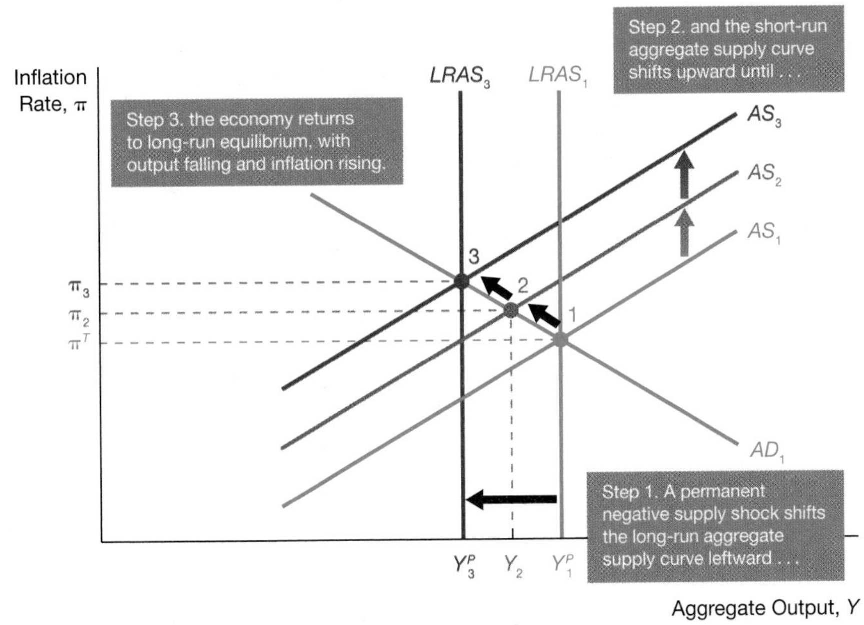

FIGURE 3 Permanent Supply Shock: No Policy Response

A permanent negative supply shock decreases potential output from Y_1^P to Y_3^P, and the long-run aggregate supply curve shifts to the left from $LRAS_1$ to $LRAS_3$, while the short-run aggregate supply curve shifts upward from AS_1 to AS_2. The economy moves to point 2, with inflation rising to π_2 and output falling to Y_2. Because aggregate output is still above potential, the short-run aggregate supply curve would keep on shifting until the output gap is zero when it reached AS_3. The economy moves to point 3, where inflation rises to π_3 while output falls to Y_3^P.

falling to Y_2. Because this level of output is still higher than potential output, Y_3^P, the short-run aggregate supply curve keeps shifting up and to the left until it reaches AS_3, where it intersects AD_1 on $LRAS_3$. The economy moves to point 3, eliminating the output gap but leaving inflation higher at π_3 and output lower at Y_3^P.

Policy Stabilizes Inflation According to Figure 4, monetary authorities can keep inflation at the target inflation rate and stabilize inflation by decreasing aggregate demand. The goal is to shift the aggregate demand curve leftward to AD_3, where it intersects the long-run aggregate supply curve $LRAS_3$ at the target inflation rate of π^T. To shift the aggregate demand to AD_3, the monetary authorities would autonomously tighten monetary policy by increasing the real interest rate at any given inflation rate, thus causing investment spending to fall and lowering aggregate demand at any given inflation rate. The economy thus goes to point 3, where the output gap is zero and inflation is at the target level of π^T.

Here again, keeping the inflation gap at zero leads to a zero output gap, so stabilizing inflation has stabilized economic activity. ***The divine coincidence still remains true when a permanent supply shock occurs: There is no tradeoff between the dual objectives of stabilizing inflation and economic activity.***

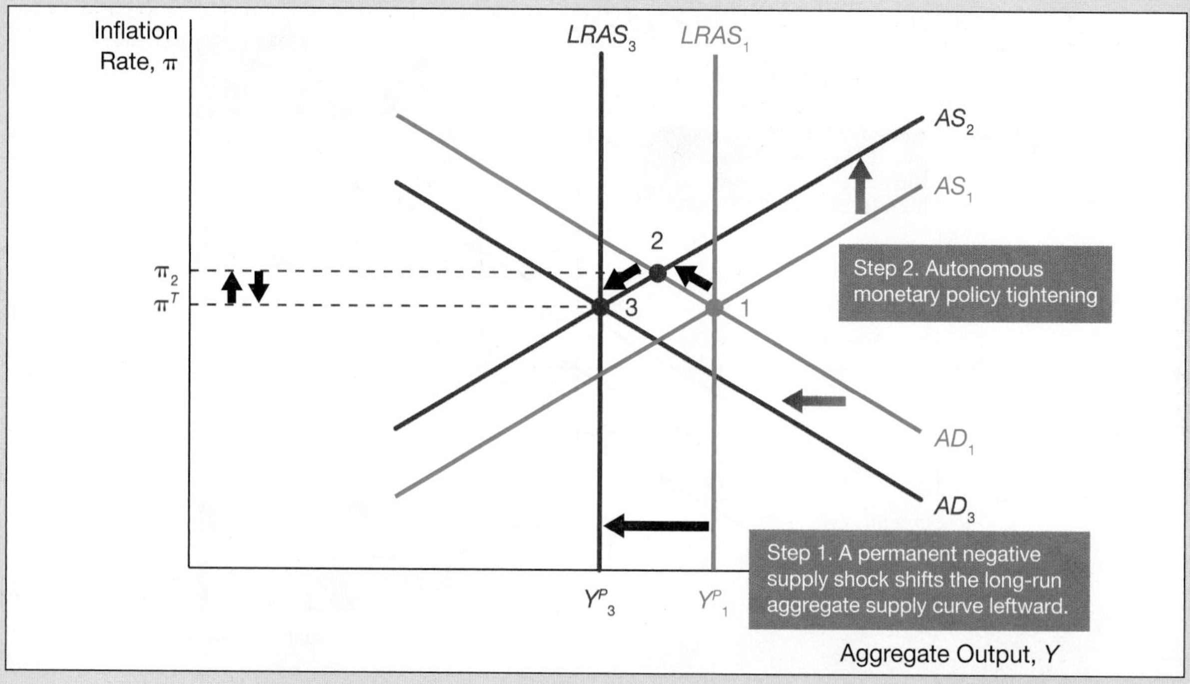

FIGURE 4 Permanent Supply Shock: Policy Stabilizes Inflation
A permanent negative supply shock decreases potential output from Y_1^P to Y_3^P, and the long-run aggregate supply curve shifts to the left from $LRAS_1$ to $LRAS_3$, while the short-run aggregate supply curve shifts upward from AS_1 to AS_2. An autonomous tightening of monetary policy shifts the aggregate demand curve to the left to AD_3, thereby keeping the inflation rate at π^T at point 3.

Response to a Temporary Supply Shock

When a supply shock is temporary, such as when the price of oil surges because of political unrest in the Middle East or because of an act of god, such as a devastating hurricane in Florida, the divine coincidence does not always hold. Policymakers face a short-run tradeoff between stabilizing inflation and economic activity. To illustrate, we start the economy at point 1 in Figure 5, where aggregate output is at the natural rate Y^P and inflation is at π^T. The negative supply shock, say, a rise in the price of oil, shifts the short-run aggregate supply curve up and to the left from AS_1 to AS_2 but leaves the long-run aggregate supply curve unchanged because the shock is temporary. The economy moves to point 2, with inflation rising to π_2 and output falling to Y_2. Policymakers can respond to the temporary supply shock in three possible ways.

No Policy Response One policy choice is not to make an autonomous change in monetary policy, so the aggregate demand curve does not shift. Since aggregate output is less than potential output Y^P, eventually the short-run aggregate supply curve will shift back down to the right, returning to AS_1. The economy will return to point 1 in Figure 5 and close both the output and inflation gaps, as output and inflation return to the initial levels of Y^P and π^T. Both inflation and economic activity stabilize over time. ***In the long run, there is no tradeoff between the two objectives, and the divine coincidence holds.*** While we wait for the long run, however, the economy will undergo a painful period of

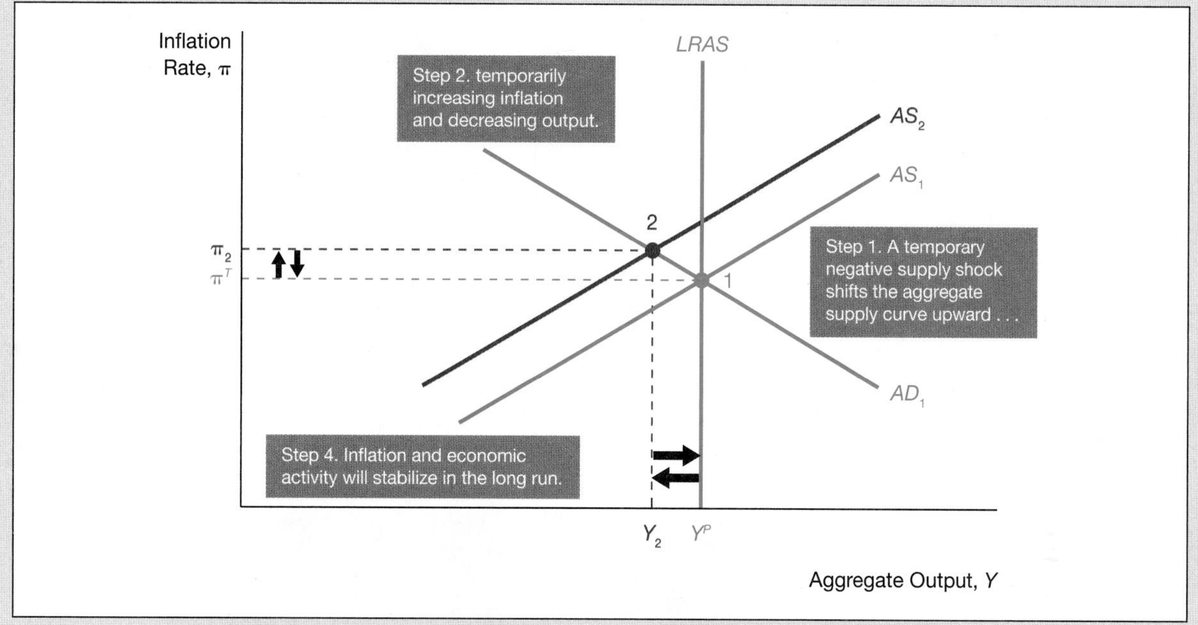

FIGURE 5 Response to a Temporary Aggregate Supply Shock: No Policy Response
A temporary negative supply shock shifts the short-run aggregate supply curve upward from AS_1 to AS_2, moving the economy to point 2, with inflation rising to π_2 and output falling to Y_2. If the autonomous monetary policy remains unchanged, the short-run aggregate supply curve will shift back down and to the right in the long run, eventually returning to AS_1, and the economy moves back to point 1.

reduced output and higher inflation rates. This opens the door to monetary policy to try to stabilize economic activity or inflation in the short run.

Policy Stabilizes Inflation in the Short Run A second policy choice for monetary authorities is to keep inflation at the target level of π^T in the short run by autonomously tightening monetary policy and raising the real interest rate at any given inflation rate. Doing so would cause investment spending and aggregate demand to fall at each inflation rate, shifting the aggregate demand curve to the left to AD_3 in Figure 6. The economy now moves to point 3, where the aggregate demand curve, AD_3, intersects the short-run aggregate supply curve AS_2 at an inflation rate of π^T. Because output is below potential at point 3, the slack in the economy shifts the short-run aggregate supply curve back down to AS_1. To keep the inflation rate at π^T, the monetary authorities will need to move the short-run aggregate demand curve back to AD_1 by reversing the autonomous tightening and eventually, the economy will return to point 1.

As Figure 6 illustrates, stabilizing inflation reduces aggregate output to Y_3 in the short run, and only over time will output return to potential output at Y^P. ***Stabilizing inflation in response to a temporary supply shock has led to a larger deviation of aggregate output from potential, so this action has not stabilized economic activity.***

Policy Stabilizes Economic Activity in the Short Run A third policy is for monetary policymakers to stabilize economic activity rather than inflation in the short run by increasing aggregate demand. According to Figure 7, now they would shift the aggregate demand curve to the right to AD_3, where it intersects the short-run aggregate

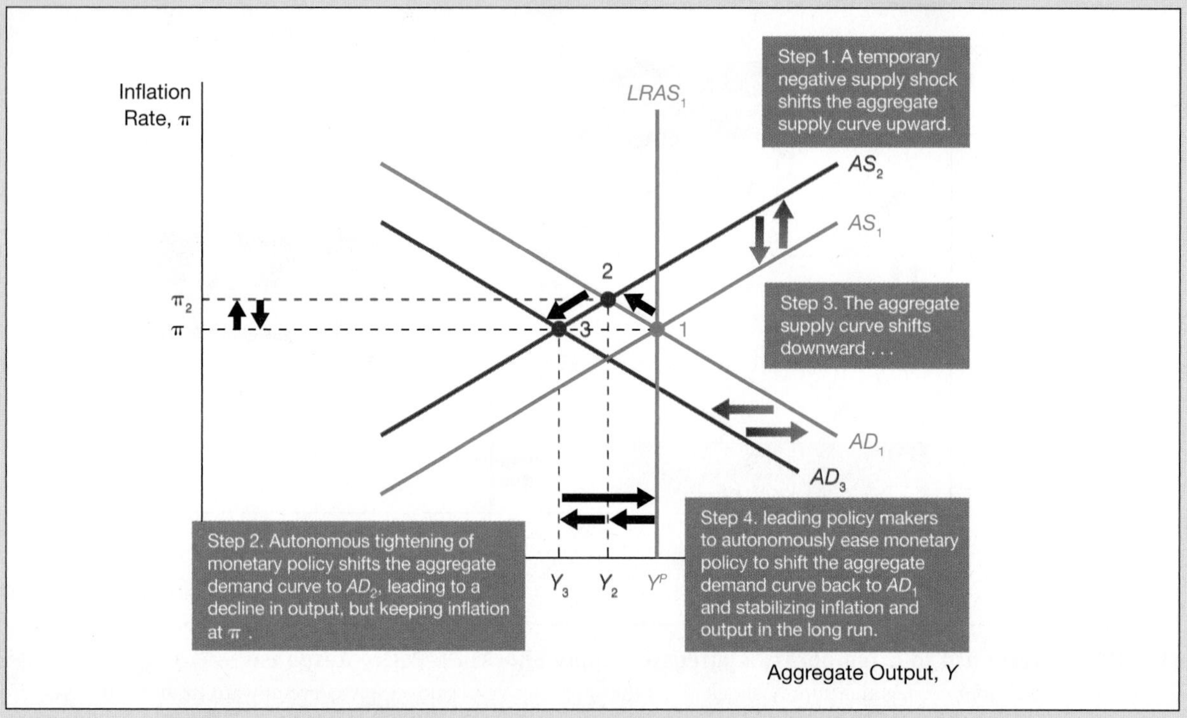

FIGURE 6 Response to a Temporary Aggregate Supply Shock: Short-Run Inflation Stabilization

A temporary negative supply shock shifts the short-run aggregate supply curve from AS_1 to AS_2, moving the economy to point 2, with inflation rising to π_2 and output falling to Y_2. Autonomous tightening of monetary policy shifts the aggregate demand curve to the left to AD_3, and the economy moves to point 3, where inflation is at π^T. With output below potential at point 3, the short-run aggregate supply curve shifts back to AS_1, and to keep the inflation rate at π^T, the autonomous tightening of monetary policy is reversed, shifting the aggregate demand curve back to AD_1 and the economy back to point 1.

supply curve AS_2 and the long-run aggregate supply at point 3. To do this, they would have to autonomously ease monetary policy by lowering the real interest rate at any given inflation rate. At point 3, the output gap returns to zero, so monetary policy has stabilized economic activity. However, inflation has risen to π_3, which is greater than π^T, so inflation has not been stabilized. ***Stabilizing economic activity in response to a temporary supply shock results in a rise in inflation, so inflation has not been stabilized.***

The Bottom Line: The Relationship Between Stabilizing Inflation and Stabilizing Economic Activity

We can draw the following conclusions from this analysis:

1. ***If most shocks to the economy are aggregate demand shocks or permanent aggregate supply shocks, then policy that stabilizes inflation will also stabilize economic activity, even in the short run.***
2. ***If temporary supply shocks are more common, then a central bank must choose between the two stabilization objectives in the short run.***
3. ***In the long run there is no conflict between stabilizing inflation and economic activity in response to shocks.***

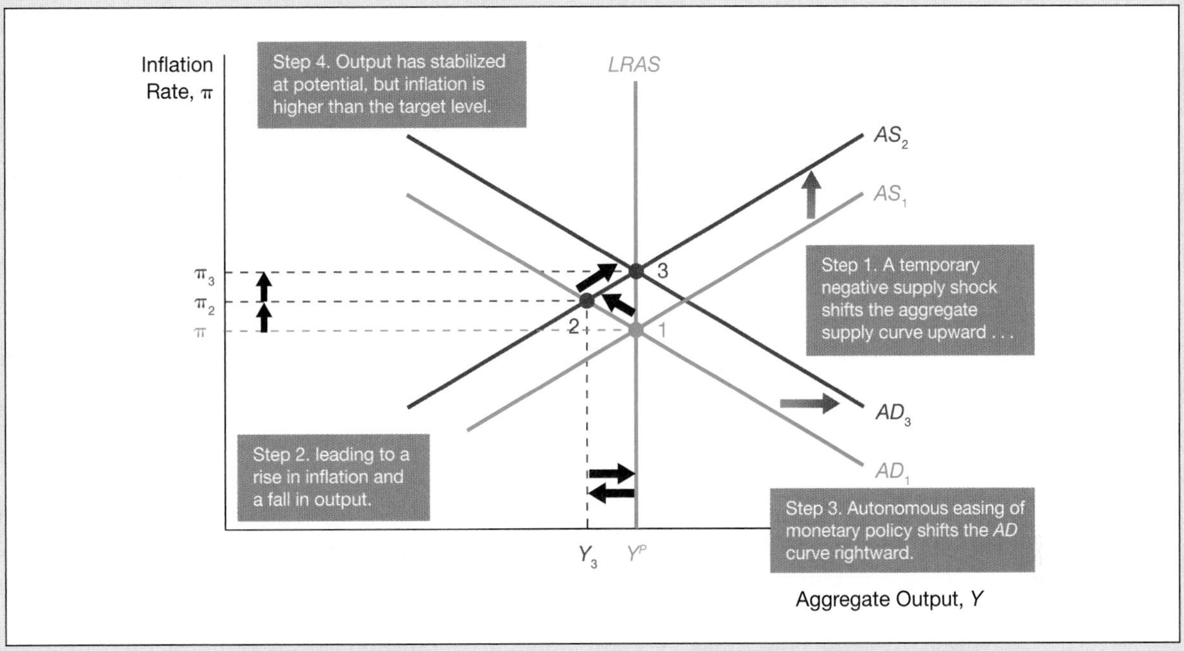

FIGURE 7 Response to a Temporary Aggregate Supply Shock: Short-Run Output Stabilization
A temporary negative supply shock shifts the short-run aggregate supply curve from AS_1 to AS_2, moving the economy to point 2, with inflation rising to π_2 and output falling to Y_2. To stabilize output, autonomous monetary policy easing shifts the aggregate demand curve rightward to AD_3. At point 3, the monetary policy action has stabilized economic activity, but at π_3 inflation is greater than π^T.

HOW ACTIVELY SHOULD POLICYMAKERS TRY TO STABILIZE ECONOMIC ACTIVITY?

All economists have similar policy goals (to promote high employment and price stability), yet they often disagree on the best approach to achieve those goals. Suppose policymakers confront an economy that has high unemployment resulting from a negative demand or supply shock that has reduced aggregate output. **Nonactivists** believe wages and prices are very flexible, so the self-correcting mechanism is very rapid. They argue that the short-run aggregate supply curve will shift down, returning the economy to full employment very quickly. They thus believe government action is unnecessary to eliminate unemployment. **Activists**, many of whom are followers of Keynes and are thus referred to as **Keynesians**, regard the self-correcting mechanism through wage and price adjustment as very slow because wages and prices are sticky. As a result, they believe it takes a very long time to reach the long run, agreeing with Keynes's famous adage that "In the long-run, we are all dead." They therefore see the need for the government to pursue active policy to eliminate high unemployment when it develops.

Lags and Policy Implementation

If policymakers could shift the aggregate demand curve instantaneously, activist policies could be used to immediately move the economy to the full-employment level, as we have seen in the previous section. However, several types of lags prevent this immediate shift from occurring, and there are differences in the length of these lags for monetary versus fiscal policy.

1. The **data lag** is the time it takes for policymakers to obtain data indicating what is happening in the economy. Accurate data on GDP, for example, are not available until several months after a given quarter is over.
2. The **recognition lag** is the time it takes for policymakers to be sure of what the data are signaling about the future course of the economy. For example, to minimize errors, the National Bureau of Economic Research (the private organization that officially dates business cycles) will not declare the economy to be in recession until at least six months after it has determined that one has begun.
3. The **legislative lag** represents the time it takes to pass legislation to implement a particular policy. The legislative lag does not exist for most monetary policy actions, such as lowering interest rates. It is, however, important for the implementation of fiscal policy, when it can sometimes take six months to a year to pass legislation to change taxes or government purchases.
4. The **implementation lag** is the time it takes for policymakers to change policy instruments once they have decided on the new policy. Again, this lag is less important for the conduct of monetary policy than fiscal policy because the Federal Reserve can immediately change its policy interest rate. Actually implementing fiscal policy may take substantial time, however; for example, getting government agencies to change their spending habits takes time, as does changing tax tables.
5. The **effectiveness lag** is the time it takes for the policy actually to have an impact on the economy. The effectiveness lag is both long (often a year or longer) and variable (that is, there is substantial uncertainty about how long this lag is).

The existence of all these lags makes the policymakers' job far more difficult and therefore weakens the case for activism. When unemployment is high, activist policy to shift the aggregate demand curve rightward to restore the economy to full employment may not produce desirable outcomes. Indeed, if the policy lags described above are very long, then by the time the aggregate demand curve shifts to the right, the self-correcting mechanism may have already returned the economy to full employment, so when the activist policy kicks in it may cause output to rise above potential, leading to a rise in inflation. In the situation where policy lags are longer than the time it takes the self-correcting mechanism to work, a policy of nonactivism may produce better outcomes.

The activist/nonactivist debate came to the fore when the Obama administration advocated a fiscal stimulus package early in its administration in 2009 (see the FYI box, "The Activist/Nonactivist Debate over the Obama Fiscal Stimulus Package").

INFLATION: ALWAYS AND EVERYWHERE A MONETARY PHENOMENON

Milton Friedman is famous for his adage that in the long run "Inflation is always and everywhere a monetary phenomenon." Here we will see that this adage is supported by our aggregate demand and supply analysis because it shows that monetary policymakers can target any inflation rate in the long run by shifting the aggregate demand curve

FYI The Activist/Nonactivist Debate over the Obama Fiscal Stimulus Package

When President Obama entered office in January 2009, he faced a very serious recession, with unemployment over 7% and rising rapidly. Although policymakers had been using monetary policy aggressively to stabilize the economy (see Chapters 9 and 18), many activists argued that the government needed to do more by implementing a massive fiscal stimulus package. They argued that monetary policy, which had already lowered the federal funds rate to close to zero and so could not lower nominal interest rates further, would be unable to increase aggregate demand to the full-employment level. On the other hand, nonactivists opposed the fiscal stimulus package, arguing that fiscal stimulus would take too long to work because of long implementation lags. They cautioned that if the fiscal stimulus kicked in after the economy had already recovered, it could lead to increased volatility in inflation and economic activity.

The economics profession split over the desirability of fiscal stimulus. Approximately 200 economists who supported fiscal stimulus signed a petition published in the *Wall Street Journal* and the *New York Times* on January 28, 2009. An opposing petition, also signed by about 200 economists, appeared on February 8. The Obama administration came down squarely on the side of the activists and proposed the American Recovery and Reinvestment Act of 2009, a $787 billion fiscal stimulus package that Congress passed on February 13, 2009. In the House the vote was 246 to 183, with 176 Republicans and 7 Democrats opposing the bill, whereas in the Senate the vote was 60 to 38, with all Democrats supporting the bill, along with 3 Republicans. Even after the fact, the desirability of the 2009 stimulus package is hotly debated, with some indicating it helped stabilize the economy while others believe it was not effective.

with autonomous monetary policy. To illustrate, look at Figure 8, where the economy is at point 1, with aggregate output at potential output Y^P and inflation at an initial inflation target of π_1^T.

Suppose the central bank believes this inflation target is too low and chooses to raise it to π_3^T. It eases monetary policy autonomously by lowering the real interest rate at any given inflation rate, thereby increasing investment spending and aggregate demand. In Figure 8, the aggregate demand curve shifts to AD_3. The economy would then move to point 2 at the intersection of AD_3 and AS_1, with inflation rising to π_2. Because aggregate output is above potential output $Y_2 > Y^P$, the short-run aggregate supply curve would shift up and to the left, eventually stopping at AS_3, with the economy moving to point 3, where inflation is at the higher target level of π_3^T and the output gap is back at zero.

The analysis in Figure 8 demonstrates the following key points:

1. ***The monetary authorities can target any inflation rate in the long run with autonomous monetary policy adjustments.***
2. ***Potential output—and therefore the quantity of aggregate output produced in the long run—is independent of monetary policy.***

CAUSES OF INFLATIONARY MONETARY POLICY

If everyone agrees that high inflation is bad for an economy, why do we see so much of it? Do governments pursue inflationary monetary policies intentionally? We have seen that monetary authorities can set the inflation rate in the long run, so it must be that in

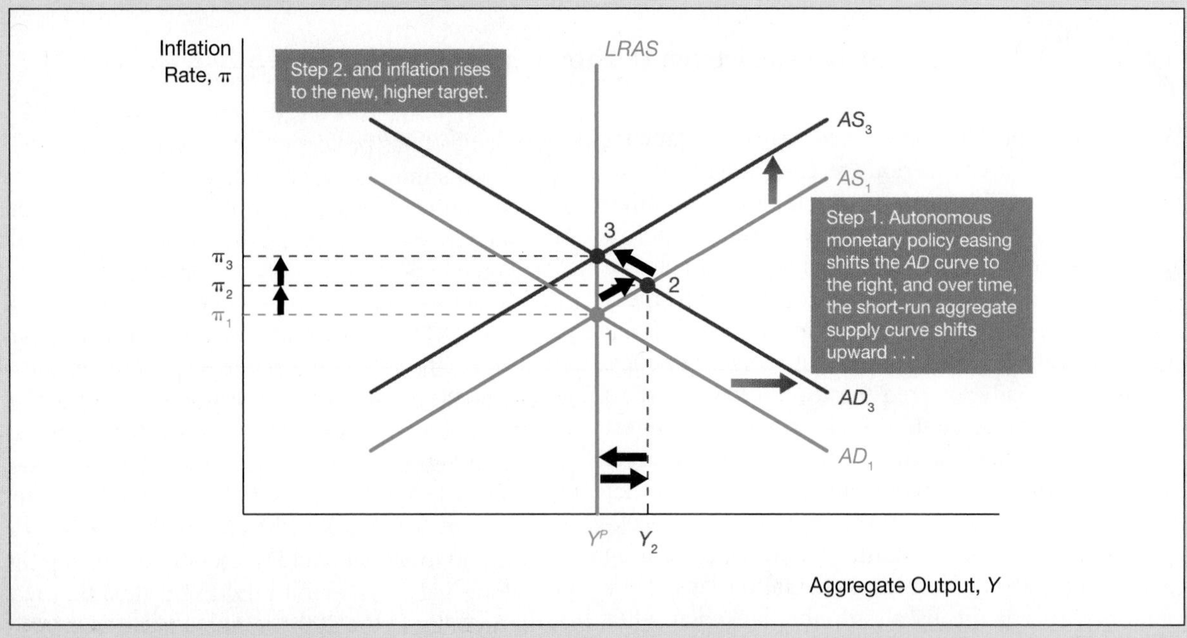

FIGURE 8 A Rise in the Inflation Target
To raise the inflation target to π_3^T, the central bank undertakes an autonomous monetary policy easing, of lowering the real interest rate at any given inflation rate, thereby shifting the aggregate demand curve rightward to AD_3. The economy would then move to point 2 and the short-run aggregate supply curve would shift up and to the left, eventually stopping at AS_3, moving the economy to point 3, with the output gap at zero and inflation at π_3^T.

trying to achieve other goals, governments end up with overly expansionary monetary policy and high inflation. In this section, we will examine the government policies that are the most common sources of inflation.

High Employment Targets and Inflation

The primary goal of most governments is high employment, and the pursuit of this goal can bring high inflation. The U.S. government is committed by law (the Employment Act of 1946 and the Humphrey-Hawkins Act of 1978) to engage in activist policy to promote high employment. Both laws require a commitment to a high level of employment consistent with stable inflation—yet in practice the U.S. government and the Federal Reserve have often pursued a high employment target with little concern about the inflationary consequences of policies. This tendency was true especially in the mid-1960s and 1970s, when the government and the Fed began to take an active role in attempting to stabilize unemployment.

Two types of inflation can result from an activist stabilization policy to promote high employment:

1. **Cost-push inflation** results either from a temporary negative supply shock or a push by workers for wage hikes beyond what productivity gains can justify.
2. **Demand-pull inflation** results from policymakers pursuing policies that increase aggregate demand.

We will now use aggregate demand and supply analysis to examine the effect of a high employment target on both types of inflation.

Cost-Push Inflation Consider the economy Figure 9, which is initially at point 1, the intersection of the aggregate demand curve AD_1 and the short-run aggregate supply curve AS_1. Suppose workers succeed in pushing for higher wages, either because they want to increase their real wages (wages in terms of the goods and services they can buy) above what is justified by productivity gains, or because they expect inflation to be high and wish their wages to keep up with it. This cost-push shock, which acts like a temporary negative supply shock, raises the inflation rate and shifts the short-run aggregate supply curve up and to the left to AS_2. If the central bank takes no action to change the equilibrium interest rate and the monetary policy curve remains unchanged, the economy would move to point 2′ at the intersection of the new short-run aggregate supply curve AS_2 and the aggregate demand curve AD_1. Output would decline to Y' below potential output and the inflation rate would rise to $\pi_{2'}$, leading to an increase in unemployment.

In contrast, activist policymakers with a high employment target would implement policies, such as a cut in taxes, an increase in government purchases, or an autonomous easing of monetary policy, to increase aggregate demand. These policies would shift the aggregate demand curve in Figure 9 to $AD_{2'}$ quickly returning the economy to potential

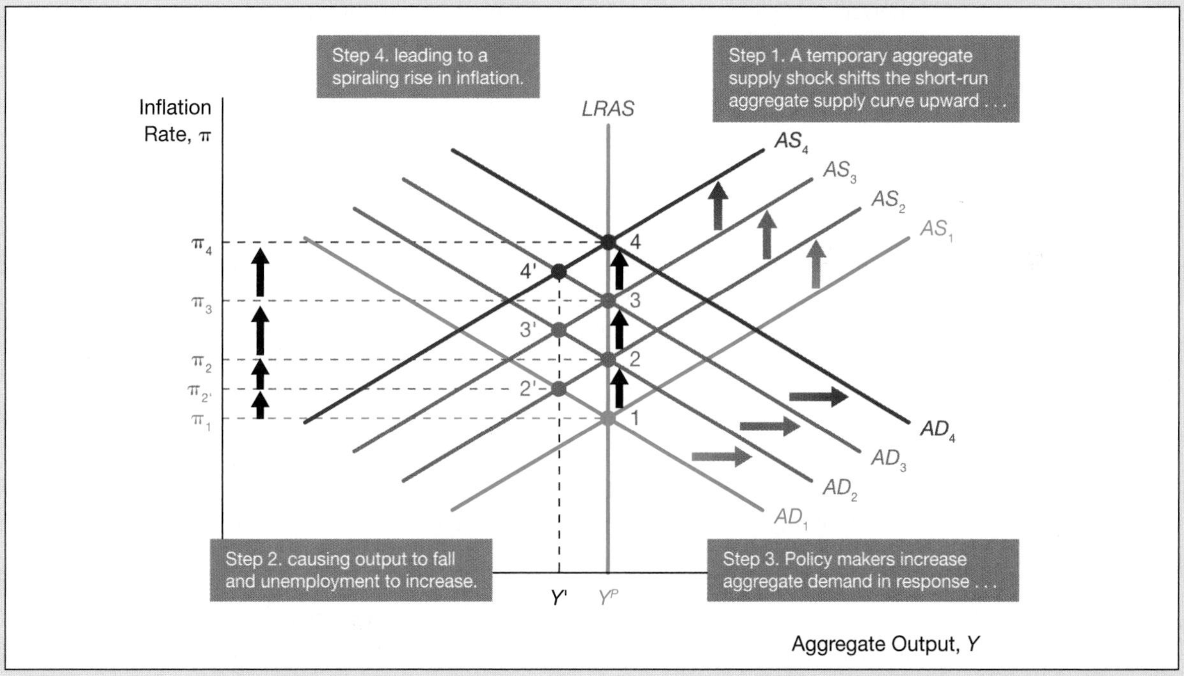

FIGURE 9 Cost-Push Inflation

A cost-push shock (which acts like a temporary negative supply shock) shifts the short-run aggregate supply curve up and to the left to AS_2, and the economy moves to point 2′. To keep aggregate output at Y^P and lower the unemployment rate, policymakers shift the aggregate demand curve to AD_2 so that the economy will return quickly to potential output at point 2 and an inflation rate of π_2. Further upward and leftward shifts of the short-run aggregate supply curve to AS_3 and so on cause the policymakers to keep on increasing aggregate demand, leading to a continuing increase in inflation—a cost-push inflation.

output at point 2 and increasing the inflation rate to π_2. The workers fare quite well, earning both higher wages and government protection against excessive unemployment.

The workers' success might encourage them to seek even higher wages. In addition, other workers might now realize that their wages have fallen relative to their fellow workers, leading them to seek wage increases. As a result, another temporary negative supply shock would occur that would cause the short-run aggregate supply curve in Figure 9 to shift up and to the left again, to AS_3. Unemployment develops again when we move to point 3′, prompting activist policies once again to shift the aggregate demand curve rightward to AD_3 and return the economy to full employment at a higher inflation rate of π_3. If this process continues, the result will be a continuing increase in inflation—a cost-push inflation.

Demand-Pull Inflation The goal of high employment can lead to inflationary fiscal and monetary policy in another way. Even at full employment (the natural rate of unemployment), some unemployment is always present because of frictions in the labor market that complicate the matching of unemployed workers with employers. Consequently, the unemployment rate when employment is full will be greater than zero. When policymakers mistakenly underestimate the natural rate of unemployment and so set a target for unemployment that is too low (i.e., less than the natural rate of unemployment), they set the stage for expansionary monetary policy that produces inflation.

Figure 10 shows how this scenario can unfold, using an aggregate supply and demand analysis. If policymakers have set a 4% unemployment target that is below the 5% natural rate of unemployment, they will be trying to achieve an output target greater than potential output. We mark this target level of output in Figure 10 as Y^T. Suppose that we are initially at point 1: The economy is at potential output but below the target level of output Y^T. To hit the unemployment target of 4%, policymakers must enact policies such as expansionary fiscal policy or an autonomous easing of monetary policy to increase aggregate demand. The aggregate demand curve in Figure 10 shifts to the right until it reaches AD_2 and the economy moves to point 2′, where output is at Y^T and policymakers have achieved the 4% unemployment rate goal—but there is more to the story. At Y^T, the 4% unemployment rate is below the natural rate level, and output is above potential, causing wages to rise. The short-run aggregate supply curve will shift up and to the left, eventually to AS_2, moving the economy from point 2′ to point 2, where it is back at potential output but at a higher inflation rate of π_2. We could stop there, but because unemployment is again higher than the target level, policymakers would once more shift the aggregate demand curve rightward to AD_3 to hit the output target at point 3′—and the whole process would continue to drive the economy to point 3 and beyond. The overall result is a steadily rising inflation rate.

Pursuing too low an unemployment rate target or, equivalently, too high an output target, thus leads to inflationary monetary or fiscal policy. Policymakers fail on two counts: They have not achieved their unemployment target and have caused higher inflation. If, however, the target rate of unemployment is below the natural rate, the process we see in Figure 10 will be well under way before they realize their mistake.

Cost-Push Versus Demand-Pull Inflation. When inflation occurs, how do we know whether it is demand-pull inflation or cost-push inflation? We would normally expect to see demand-pull inflation when unemployment is below the natural rate level, and cost-push inflation when unemployment is above the natural rate level. Unfortunately, economists and policymakers still struggle with measuring the natural rate of unemployment. Complicating matters further, a cost-push inflation can be initiated by a demand-pull inflation, blurring the distinction. When a demand-pull inflation

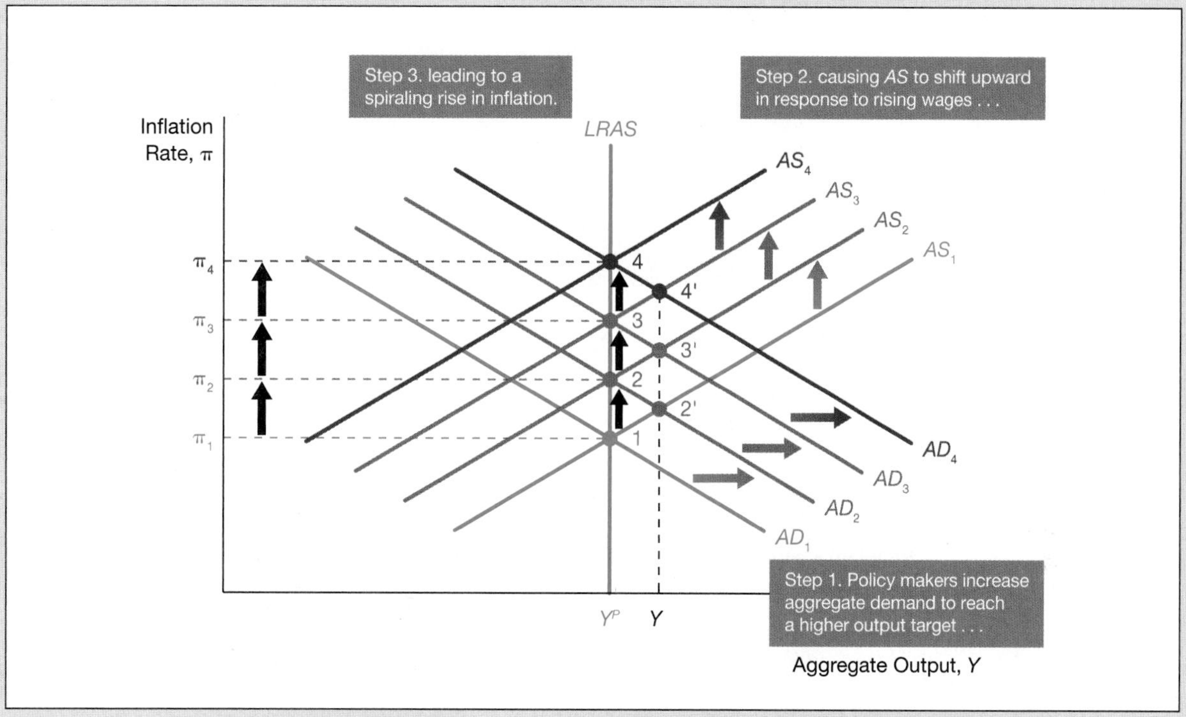

FIGURE 10 Demand-Pull Inflation

Too low an unemployment target (too high an output target of Y^T) causes the government to increase aggregate demand, shifting the *AD* curve rightward from AD_1 to AD_2 to AD_3 and so on. Because the unemployment rate is below the natural rate level, wages will rise and the short-run aggregate supply curve will shift up and leftward from AS_1 to AS_2 to AS_3 and so on. The result is a continuing rise in inflation known as a demand-pull inflation.

produces higher inflation rates, expected inflation will eventually rise and cause workers to demand higher wages (cost-push inflation) so that their real wages do not fall. Finally, expansionary monetary and fiscal policies produce both kinds of inflation, so we cannot distinguish between them on this basis.

In the United States, as we will see in the following application, the primary reason for inflationary policy has been policymakers' adherence to a high employment target. As we saw in Chapter 22, high inflation can also occur because of persistent government budget deficits.

APPLICATION ◆ The Great Inflation

Now that we have examined the roots of inflationary monetary policy, we can investigate the causes of the rise in U.S. inflation from 1965 to 1982, a period dubbed the "Great Inflation."

Panel (a) of Figure 11 documents the rise in inflation during those years. Just before the Great Inflation started, the inflation rate was below 2% at an annual rate; by the late 1970s, it averaged around 8% and peaked at nearly 14% in 1980 after the oil price shock in 1979. Panel (b) of Figure 11 compares the actual unemployment rate to

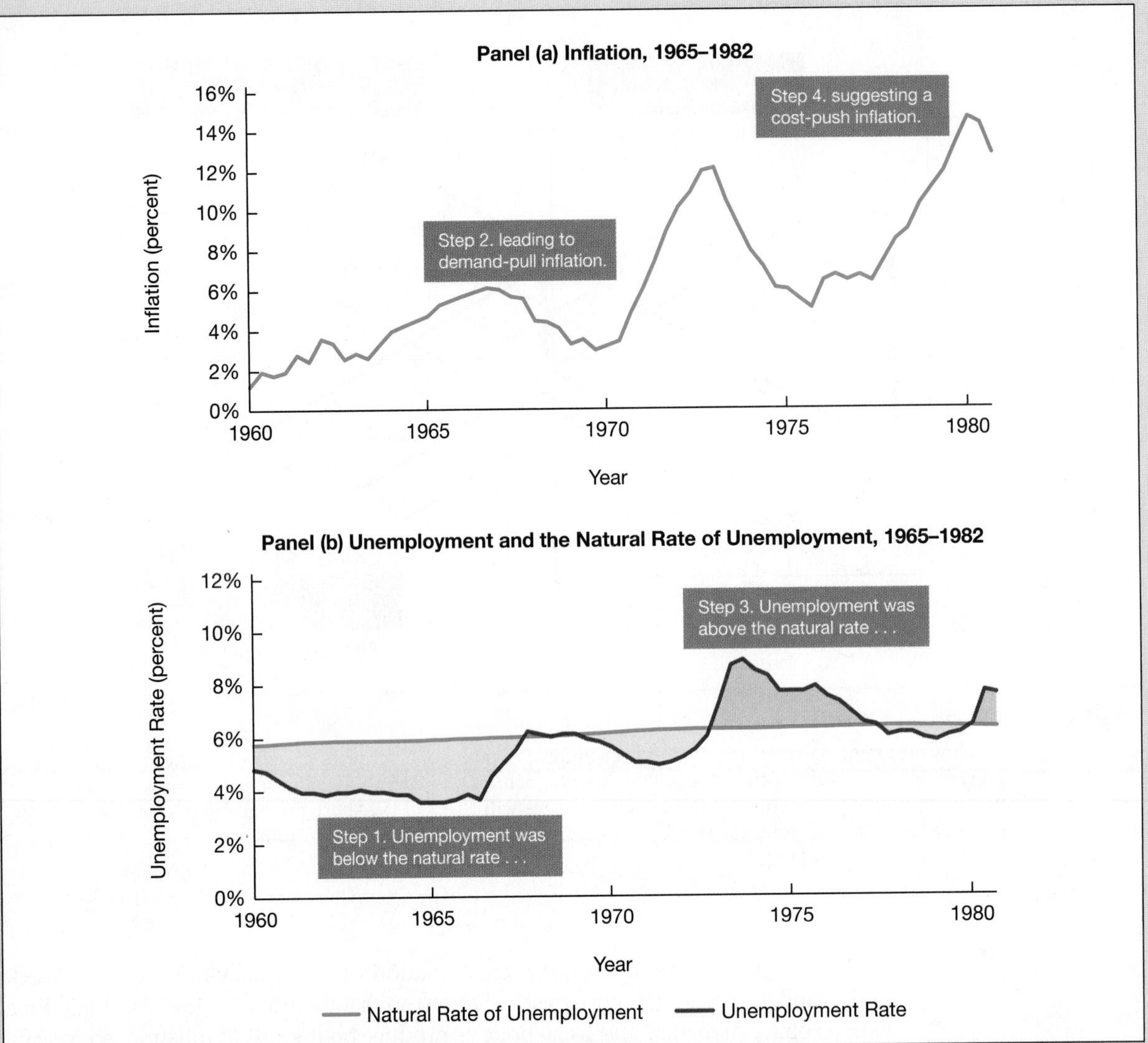

FIGURE 11 Inflation and Unemployment, 1965–1982

As shown in panel (a), the CPI inflation rate was below 2% at an annual rate in the early 1960s, but by the late 1970s, it was averaging around 8% and peaked at over 14% in 1980 after the oil price shock in 1979. As shown in panel (b), the economy experienced unemployment below the natural rate in all but one year between 1960 and 1973, suggesting a demand-pull inflation described in Figure 10. After 1975, the unemployment rate was regularly above the natural rate of unemployment, suggesting a cost-push inflation as delineated in Figure 9.

Source: Economic Report of the President.

estimates of the natural rate of unemployment. Notice that the economy experienced unemployment below the natural rate in all but one year between 1960 and 1973, as represented by the shaded areas. This insight suggests that in 1965–1973, the U.S. economy experienced the demand-pull inflation we described in Figure 10. That is, policymakers pursued a policy of autonomous monetary policy easing that shifted the aggregate demand curve to the right in trying to achieve an output target that was too high, thus increasing inflation. Policymakers, economists, and politicians were committed in the mid-1960s to a target unemployment rate of 4%, a level of unemployment they believed to be consistent with price stability. In hindsight, most economists today agree that the natural rate of unemployment was substantially higher in the 1960s and 1970s, between 5% and 6%, as shown in panel (b) of Figure 11. The inappropriate 4% unemployment target initiated the most sustained inflationary episode in U.S. history.

After 1975, panel (b) of Figure 11 shows that the unemployment rate lingered above the natural rate of unemployment (see shaded area), yet inflation continued, as per panel (a), indicating the phenomenon of a cost-push inflation we described in Figure 9 (the impetus for which was the earlier demand-pull inflation). The public's knowledge that government policy was aimed squarely at high employment explains the persistence of inflation. The higher rate of expected inflation from the demand-pull inflation shifted the short-run aggregate supply curve in Figure 9 upward and to the left, causing a rise in unemployment that policymakers tried to eliminate by autonomously easing monetary policy, shifting the aggregate demand curve to the right. The result was a continuing rise in inflation.

Only when the Federal Reserve committed to an anti-inflationary monetary policy under Chairman Paul Volcker, which involved hiking the federal funds rate to the 20% level, did inflation come down, ending the Great Inflation. ◆

Summary

1. For aggregate demand shocks and permanent supply shocks the price stability and economic activity stability objectives are consistent: Stabilizing inflation stabilizes economic activity even in the short run. For temporary supply shocks, however, there is a tradeoff between stabilizing inflation and stabilizing economic activity in the short run. In the long run, however, no conflict arises between stabilizing inflation and economic activity.
2. Activists regard the self-correcting mechanism through wage and price adjustment as very slow and hence see the need for the government to pursue active, accommodating policy to address high unemployment when it develops. Nonactivists, by contrast, believe that the self-correcting mechanism is fast and therefore advocate that the government avoid active policy to eliminate unemployment.
3. Milton Friedman's view that in the long-run inflation is always and everywhere a monetary phenomenon is borne out by aggregate demand and supply analysis: It shows that monetary policymakers can target any inflation rate in the long run they want through autonomous monetary policy, which adjusts the equilibrium real interest rate using the federal funds rate policy tool to change the level of aggregate demand.
4. Two types of inflation can result from an activist stabilization policy to promote high employment: cost-push inflation, which occurs because of negative supply shocks or a push by workers to get higher wages than is justified by productivity gains; and demand-pull inflation, which results when policymakers pursue high output and employment targets through policies that increase aggregate demand. Both demand-pull and cost-push inflation led to the Great Inflation from 1965 to 1982.

Key Terms

activists, p. 617	data lag, p. 618	divine coincidence, p. 612
cost-push inflation, p. 620	demand-pull inflation, p. 620	effectiveness lag, p. 618

implementation lag, p. 618
inflation gap, p. 609
inflation target, p. 609
Keynesians, p. 617
legislative lag, p. 618
nonactivists, p. 617
recognition lag, p. 618

Questions

All questions are available in MyEconLab *at* www.myeconlab.com.

1. What does it mean for the inflation gap to be negative?
2. "If autonomous spending falls, the central bank should lower its inflation target in order to stabilize inflation." Is this statement true, false, or uncertain? Explain your answer.
3. For each of the following shocks, describe how monetary policymakers would respond (if at all) to stabilize economic activity. Assume the economy starts at a long-run equilibrium.
   a. Consumers reduce autonomous consumption.
   b. Financial frictions decrease.
   c. Government spending increases.
   d. Taxes increase.
   e. The domestic currency appreciates.
4. During the global financial crisis, how was the Fed able to help offset the sharp increase in financial frictions, without the ability to lower interest rates further? Did it work?
5. Why does the divine coincidence simplify the job of policy making?
6. Why do negative supply shocks pose a dilemma for policymakers?
7. In what way is a permanent negative supply shock worse than a temporary negative supply shock?
8. Suppose three economies are hit with the same negative supply shock. In country A, inflation initially rises and output falls; then inflation rises more and output increases. In country B, inflation initially rises and output falls; then both inflation and output fall. In country C, inflation initially rises and output falls; then inflation falls and output eventually increases. What type of stabilization approach did each country take?
9. "Policymakers would never respond by stabilizing a temporary positive supply shock." Is this statement true, false, or uncertain? Explain your answer.
10. The fact that it takes a long time for firms to bring new plant and equipment on line is an illustration of the concept related to what policy problem?
11. If someone told you, "Congress and the Senate couldn't vote themselves out of a phone booth," what type of policy lag are they referring to?
12. Is stabilization policy more likely to be conducted with monetary policy or fiscal policy? Why?
13. "If the data and recognition lags could be reduced, activist policy would more likely be beneficial to the economy." Is this statement true, false, or uncertain? Explain your answer.
14. Why do activists believe the economy's self-correcting mechanism is slow?
15. If the economy's self-correcting mechanism works slowly, should the government necessarily pursue discretionary policy to eliminate unemployment? Why or why not?
16. Suppose one could measure the welfare gains derived from eliminating output (and unemployment) fluctuations in the economy. Assuming these gains are relatively small for the average individual, how do you think this conclusion would affect the activist/nonactivist debate?
17. Given a relatively steep and a relatively flat short-run aggregate supply curve, which one supports the case for nonactivist policy? Why?
18. "Because government policymakers do not consider inflation desirable, their policies cannot be the source of inflation." Is this statement true, false, or uncertain? Explain your answer.
19. How can monetary authorities target any inflation rate they want to?
20. What will happen if policymakers erroneously believe that the natural rate of unemployment is 7%, when it is actually 5%, and pursue stabilization policy?
21. How can demand-pull inflation lead to cost-push inflation?

Applied Problems

All applied problems are available in MyEconLab *at* www.myeconlab.com.

22. Suppose the current administration decides to decrease government expenditures as a means to cut the existing government budget deficit.
    a. Using a graph of aggregate demand and supply, show what the effect would be in the short run. Describe the effects on inflation and output.
    b. What would be the effect on the real interest rate, inflation rate, and output level if the Federal Reserve decides to stabilize the inflation rate?
23. Use a graph of aggregate demand and supply to demonstrate how lags in the policy process can result in undesirable fluctuations in output and inflation.
24. As monetary policymakers care more about inflation stabilization, the slope of the aggregate demand curve becomes flatter. How does the resulting change in the slope of the aggregate demand curve help stabilize inflation when the economy is hit with a temporary negative supply shock? How does this affect output? Use a graph of aggregate demand and supply to demonstrate.
25. Many developing countries suffer from graft and endemic corruption. How does this help explain why these economies have typically high inflation and economic stagnation? Use a graph of aggregate demand and supply to demonstrate.

Web Exercises

1. This chapter discusses the Great Inflation from 1965 to 1982. Go to ftp://ftp.bls.gov/pub/special.requests/cpi/cpiai.txt. Move data into Excel, using the method described at the end of Chapter 1. Delete all but the first and last column (date and annual CPI). Graph these data and compare them to the inflation data in Figure 11.
    a. Has inflation increased or decreased since 1982?
    b. When was inflation at its highest?
    c. When was inflation at its lowest?
    d. Have we ever had a period of deflation? If so, when?
    e. Have we ever had a period of hyperinflation? If so, when?
2. It can be an interesting exercise to compare the purchasing power of the dollar over different periods in history. Go to www.bls.gov/cpi/ and scroll down to the link to the inflation calculator. Use this calculator to compute the following:
    a. If a new home cost $125,000 in 2011, what would it have cost in 1950?
    b. The average household income in 2011 was about $40,000. How much would this have been in 1945?
    c. An average new car cost about $20,000 in 2011. What would this have cost in 1945?
    d. Using the results you found in Exercises b and c, does a car consume more or less of average household income in 2011 than in 1945?

Web References

www.bls.gov/cpi/

The home page of the Bureau of Labor Statistics, which reports inflation numbers.

ftp://ftp.bls.gov/pub/special.requests/cpi/cpiai.txt

Download historical inflation statistics going back to 1913. These data can easily be moved into Microsoft Excel, using the procedure discussed at the end of Chapter 1.

http://www.gpoaccess.gov/eop

The *Economic Report of the President* reports debt levels and gross domestic product, along with many other economic statistics.

25 Transmission Mechanisms of Monetary Policy

Preview

Since 1980, the U.S. economy has been on a roller coaster, with output, unemployment, and inflation undergoing drastic fluctuations. At the start of the 1980s, inflation was running at double-digit levels, and the recession of 1980 was followed by one of the shortest economic expansions on record. After a year, the economy plunged into the 1981–1982 recession, with the unemployment rate climbing to over 10%, and only then did the inflation rate begin to come down to below the 5% level. The 1981–1982 recession was then followed by a long economic expansion that reduced the unemployment rate to below 6% in the 1987–1990 period. With Iraq's invasion of Kuwait and a rise in oil prices in the second half of 1990, the economy again plunged into recession. Subsequent growth in the economy was sluggish at first but eventually sped up, lowering the unemployment rate to below 5% in the late 1990s. In March 2001, the economy slipped into recession, with the unemployment rate climbing to around 6%. By 2007, a recovery brought the unemployment rate below 5%, but with the onset of the global financial crisis, the economy entered a recession in December 2007, with the unemployment rate rising to 10%. Only in July of 2009 did the economy start to recover, making the recession of 2007–2009 the longest recession since World War II. In light of large fluctuations in aggregate output (reflected in the unemployment rate) and inflation, and the economic instability that accompanies them, policymakers face the following dilemma: What policy or policies, if any, should be implemented to reduce fluctuations in output and inflation in the future?

To answer this question, monetary policymakers must have an accurate assessment of the timing and effect of their policies on the economy. To make this assessment, they need to understand the mechanisms through which monetary policy affects the economy. In this chapter, we examine the transmission mechanisms of monetary policy and evaluate the empirical evidence on them to better understand the role that monetary policy plays in the economy. We will see that these monetary transmission mechanisms emphasize the link between the financial system (which we studied in the first three parts of this book) and monetary theory, the subject of this part.

TRANSMISSION MECHANISMS OF MONETARY POLICY

In this section we examine the ways in which monetary policy affects aggregate demand and the economy, which are referred to as **transmission mechanisms of monetary policy**. We start with interest-rate channels, because they are the key monetary transmission mechanism in the *AD/AS* model developed in Chapters 20, 21, and 22 and applied to monetary policy in Chapters 23 and 24.

Traditional Interest-Rate Channels

The traditional view of the monetary transmission mechanism can be characterized by the following schematic, which shows the effect of an easing of monetary policy by lowering the real interest rate:

$$r\downarrow \Rightarrow I\uparrow \Rightarrow Y^{ad}\uparrow \tag{1}$$

where an easing of monetary policy leads to a fall in real interest rates ($r\downarrow$), which in turn lowers the real cost of borrowing, causing a rise in investment spending ($I\uparrow$), thereby leading to an increase in aggregate demand ($Y^{ad}\uparrow$).

Although Keynes originally emphasized this channel as operating through businesses' decisions about investment spending, the search for new monetary transmission mechanisms recognized that consumers' decisions about housing and **consumer dura-** ...ing by consumers on durable items such as automobiles and ...estment decisions. Thus the interest-rate channel of monetary ... Equation 1 applies equally to consumer spending, in which I ...al housing and consumer durable expenditure.

...re of the interest-rate transmission mechanism is its emphasis ... the nominal) interest rate as the rate that affects consumer and ...ddition, it is often the real *long-term* interest rate (not the real ... that is viewed as having the major impact on spending. How is ...ort-term nominal interest rate induced by a central bank result ...nge in the real interest rate on both short- and long-term bonds? ...hat the key is the phenomenon of *sticky prices,* the fact that the ...djusts slowly over time, so that expansionary monetary policy, ...-term nominal interest rate, also lowers the short-term real inter... ns hypothesis of the term structure described in Chapter 6, which ...m interest rate is an average of expected future short-term interest rates, sugge... ...ower real short-term interest rate, as long as it persists, leads to a fall in the real long-term interest rate. These lower real interest rates then lead to rises in business fixed investment, residential housing investment, inventory investment, and consumer durable expenditure, all of which produce the rise in aggregate demand.

That the real interest rate rather than the nominal rate affects spending provides an important mechanism for how monetary policy can stimulate the economy, even if nominal interest rates hit a floor of zero during a deflationary episode. With nominal interest rates at a floor of zero, a commitment to future expansionary monetary policy can raise expected inflation ($\pi^e\uparrow$), thereby lowering the real interest rate, ($r = i - \pi^e\downarrow$) even when the nominal interest rate is fixed at zero, and stimulating spending through the interest-rate channel:

$$\pi^e\uparrow \Rightarrow r\downarrow \Rightarrow I \Rightarrow Y^{ad}\uparrow \tag{2}$$

This mechanism thus indicates that monetary policy can still be effective even when nominal interest rates have already been driven down to zero by the monetary authorities. Indeed, this mechanism explains why the Federal Reserve resorted to the nonconventional monetary policy in December 2008 of committing to keep the federal funds rate at zero for an extended period of time. By so doing, the Fed was trying to keep inflation expectations from falling in order to make sure that real interest rates remained low to stimulate the economy. In addition, the commitment to keep interest rates low for an extended period of time would help lower long-term interest rates, which would also induce greater spending.

Some economists, such as John Taylor of Stanford University, take the position that strong empirical evidence exists for substantial interest-rate effects on consumer and investment spending through the real cost of borrowing, making the interest-rate monetary transmission mechanism a strong one. His position is highly controversial, and many researchers, including Ben Bernanke, now the chairman of the Fed, and Mark Gertler of New York University, believe that the empirical evidence does not support strong interest-rate effects operating through the real cost of borrowing.[1] Indeed, these researchers see the empirical failure of traditional interest-rate monetary transmission mechanisms as having provided the stimulus for the search for other transmission mechanisms of monetary policy.

These other transmission mechanisms fall into two basic categories: those operating through asset prices other than interest rates and those operating through asymmetric information effects on credit markets (the **credit view**). (These mechanisms are summarized in the schematic diagram in Figure 1.)

Other Asset Price Channels

One drawback of the aggregate demand analysis in previous chapters is that it focuses on only one asset price, the interest rate, rather than on many asset prices. In addition to bond prices, two other asset prices receive substantial attention as channels for monetary policy effects: foreign exchange rates and the prices of equities (stocks).

Exchange Rate Effects on Net Exports With the growing internationalization of economies throughout the world and the advent of flexible exchange rates, more attention has been paid to how monetary policy affects exchange rates, which in turn affect net exports and aggregate demand.

This channel also involves interest-rate effects, because, as we saw in Chapter 20, when domestic real interest rates fall, domestic dollar assets become less attractive relative to assets denominated in foreign currencies. As a result, the value of dollar assets relative to other currency assets falls, and the dollar depreciates (denoted by $E\downarrow$). The lower value of the domestic currency makes domestic goods cheaper than foreign goods, thereby causing a rise in net exports ($NX\uparrow$) and hence in aggregate demand($Y^{ad}\uparrow$). The schematic for the monetary transmission mechanism that operates through the exchange rate is

$$r\downarrow \Rightarrow E\downarrow \Rightarrow NX\uparrow \Rightarrow Y^{ad}\uparrow \qquad (3)$$

Tobin's *q* Theory Nobel Prize winner James Tobin developed a theory, referred to as *Tobin's q theory*, that explains how monetary policy can affect the economy through its effects on the valuation of equities (stock). Tobin defines q as the market value of firms divided by the replacement cost of capital. If q is high, the market price of firms is high relative to the replacement cost of capital, and new plant and equipment capital is cheap relative to the market value of firms. Companies can then issue stock and get a high price for it relative to the cost of the facilities and equipment they are buying.

[1]See John Taylor, "The Monetary Transmission Mechanism: An Empirical Framework," *Journal of Economic Perspectives* 9 (Fall 1995): 11–26, and Ben Bernanke and Mark Gertler, "Inside the Black Box: The Credit Channel of Monetary Policy Transmission," *Journal of Economic Perspectives* 9 (Fall 1995): 27–48.

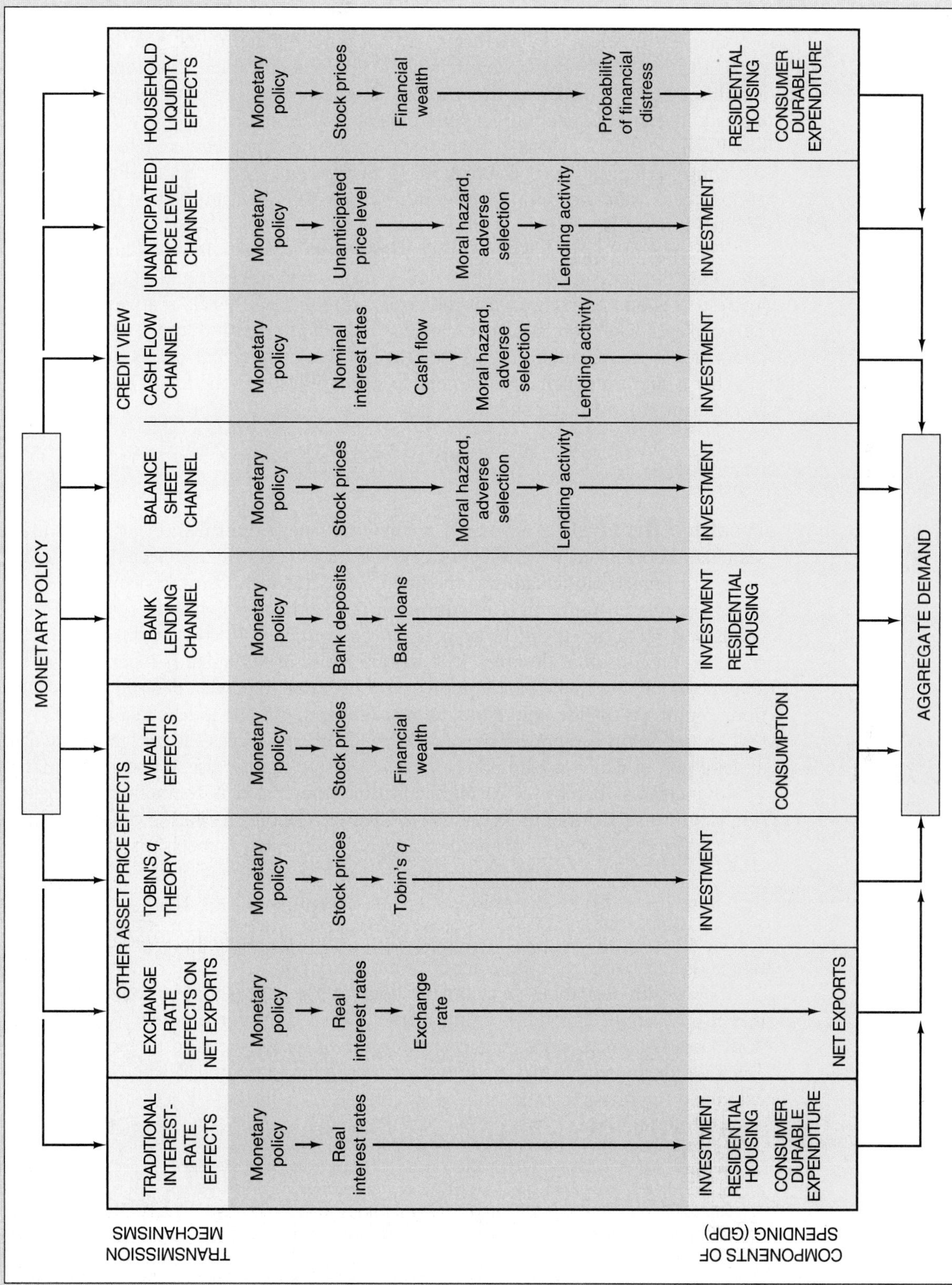

FIGURE 1 The Link Between Monetary Policy and Aggregate Demand: Monetary Transmission Mechanisms

This figure shows the different channels through which monetary policy affects aggregate demand.

Investment spending will rise, because firms can buy a lot of new investment goods with only a small issue of stock.

Conversely, when q is low, firms will not purchase *new* investment goods because the market value of firms is low relative to the cost of capital. If companies want to acquire capital when q is low, they can buy another firm cheaply and acquire old capital instead. Investment spending, the purchase of new investment goods, will then be very low. Tobin's q theory gives a good explanation for the extremely low rate of investment spending during the Great Depression. In that period, stock prices collapsed, and by 1933, stocks were worth only one-tenth of their value in late 1929; q fell to unprecedented low levels.

The crux of this discussion is that a link exists between Tobin's q and investment spending. But how might monetary policy affect stock prices? Quite simply, lower real interest rates on bonds mean that the expected return on this alternative to stocks fall. This makes stocks more attractive relative to bonds, so demand for them increases and raises their price.[2] Combining this with the fact that higher stock prices (P_s) will lead to a higher q, and thus higher investment spending I, leads to the following transmission mechanism of monetary policy:

$$r\downarrow \Rightarrow P_s\uparrow \Rightarrow q\uparrow \Rightarrow I\uparrow \Rightarrow Y^{ad}\uparrow \tag{4}$$

Wealth Effects In their search for new monetary transmission mechanisms, researchers also looked at how consumers' balance sheets might affect their spending decisions. Franco Modigliani was the first to take this tack, using his famous life cycle hypothesis of consumption. **Consumption** is spending by consumers on nondurable goods and services.[3] It differs from *consumer expenditure* in that it does not include spending on consumer durables. The basic premise of Modigliani's theory is that consumers smooth out their consumption over time. Therefore, what determines consumption spending is the lifetime resources of consumers, not just today's income.

An important component of consumers' lifetime resources is their financial wealth, a major part of which is common stocks. When stock prices rise, the value of financial wealth increases, thereby increasing the lifetime resources of consumers, and consumption should rise. Considering that, as we have seen, monetary easing can lead to a rise in stock prices, we now have another monetary transmission mechanism:

$$r\downarrow \Rightarrow P_s\uparrow \Rightarrow \text{wealth}\uparrow \Rightarrow \text{consumption}\uparrow \Rightarrow Y^{ad}\uparrow \tag{5}$$

Modigliani's research found this relationship to be an extremely powerful mechanism that adds substantially to the potency of monetary policy.

The wealth and Tobin's q channels allow for a general definition of equity, so they can also be applied to the housing market, where housing is equity. An increase in house prices, which raises their prices relative to replacement cost, leads to a rise in Tobin's q for housing, thereby stimulating its production. Similarly, housing prices are extremely important components of wealth, so rises in these prices increase wealth,

[2]An alternative way of looking at this transmission mechanism is to use the model discussed in Chapter 7 in which a decrease in the real interest rate lowers the required return on investments in stocks and so increases stock prices. Then the lower yield on stocks reduces the cost of financing investment spending through issuing equity. This way of looking at the link between stock prices and investment spending is formally equivalent to Tobin's q theory.

[3]Consumption also includes another small component, the services that a consumer receives from the ownership of housing and consumer durables.

thereby raising consumption. Monetary expansion, which raises housing prices through the Tobin's q and wealth mechanisms described here, thus leads to a rise in aggregate demand.

Credit View

Dissatisfaction with the conventional stories that interest-rate effects explain the impact of monetary policy on expenditures on durable assets has led to a new explanation based on the problem of asymmetric information in financial markets that leads to financial frictions (see Chapter 8). This explanation, referred to as the *credit view*, proposes that two types of monetary transmission channels arise as a result of financial frictions in credit markets: those that operate through effects on bank lending and those that operate through effects on firms' and households' balance sheets.

Bank Lending Channel The bank lending channel is based on the analysis in Chapter 8, which demonstrated that banks play a special role in the financial system because they are especially well suited to solve asymmetric information problems in credit markets. Because of banks' special role, certain borrowers will not have access to the credit markets unless they borrow from banks. As long as there is no perfect substitutability of retail bank deposits with other sources of funds, the bank lending channel of monetary transmission operates as follows: Expansionary monetary policy, which increases bank reserves and bank deposits, raises the quantity of bank loans available. Because many borrowers are dependent on bank loans to finance their activities, this increase in loans will cause investment (and possibly consumer) spending to rise. Schematically, the monetary policy effect is

$$\text{Bank reserves} \uparrow \Rightarrow \text{bank deposits} \uparrow \Rightarrow \text{bank loans} \uparrow \Rightarrow I \uparrow \Rightarrow Y^{ad} \uparrow \qquad (6)$$

An important implication of the credit view is that monetary policy will have a greater effect on expenditure by smaller firms, which are more dependent on bank loans, than it will on large firms, who can get funds directly through stock and bond markets (and not only through banks).

Although this result has been confirmed by researchers, doubts about the bank lending channel have been raised in the literature, and there are reasons to suspect that the bank lending channel in the United States may not be as powerful as it once was. The first reason this channel is not as powerful is that current U.S. regulations no longer impose restrictions on banks that hinder their ability to raise funds (see Chapter 12). Prior to the mid-1980s, certificates of deposit (CDs) were subjected to reserve requirements and Regulation Q deposit rate ceilings, which made it hard for banks to replace deposits that flowed out of the banking system during a monetary contraction. With these regulatory restrictions abolished, banks can more easily respond to a decline in bank reserves and a loss of retail deposits by issuing CDs at market interest rates that do not have to be backed up by required reserves. Second, the worldwide decline of the traditional bank lending business (also discussed in Chapter 12) has rendered the bank lending channel less potent. Nonetheless, many economists believe that the bank lending channel played an important role in the slow recovery in the United States during the 2007–2009 recession.

Balance Sheet Channel Even though the bank lending channel may be declining in importance, it is by no means clear that this is the case for the other credit channel, the balance sheet channel. Like the bank lending channel, the balance sheet channel arises from the presence of financial frictions in credit markets. In Chapter 8, we saw that the lower the net worth of business firms, the more severe the adverse selection and moral hazard problems in lending to these firms. Lower net worth means that lenders in effect have less collateral for their loans, so their potential losses from adverse selection are higher. A decline in net worth, which raises the adverse selection problem, thus leads to decreased lending to finance investment spending. The lower net worth of businesses also increases the moral hazard problem because it means that owners have a lower equity stake in their firms, giving them more incentive to engage in risky investment projects. Because taking on riskier investment projects makes it more likely that lenders will not be paid back, a decrease in businesses' net worth leads to a reduction in lending and hence in investment spending.

Monetary policy can affect firms' balance sheets in several ways. Easing of monetary policy, which causes a rise in stock prices ($P_s\uparrow$) along the lines described earlier, raises the net worth of firms and so leads to higher investment spending ($I\uparrow$) and aggregate demand ($Y^{ad}\uparrow$) because of the decrease in adverse selection and moral hazard problems. This leads to the following schematic for one balance sheet channel of monetary transmission:

$$\begin{aligned} r\downarrow \Rightarrow P_s\uparrow \Rightarrow \text{firms' net worth}\uparrow \Rightarrow \text{adverse selection}\downarrow,\\ \text{moral hazard}\downarrow \Rightarrow \text{lending}\uparrow \Rightarrow I\uparrow \Rightarrow Y^{ad}\uparrow \end{aligned} \tag{7}$$

Cash Flow Channel Another balance sheet channel operates by affecting cash flow, the difference between firms' cash receipts and cash expenditures. An easing of monetary policy, which lowers nominal interest rates, also causes an improvement in firms' balance sheets because it raises cash flow. The rise in cash flow increases the liquidity of the firm (or household) and thus makes it easier for lenders to know whether the firm (or household) will be able to pay its bills. The result is that adverse selection and moral hazard problems become less severe, leading to an increase in lending and economic activity. The following schematic describes this additional balance sheet channel:

$$\begin{aligned} i\downarrow \Rightarrow \text{firms' cash flow}\uparrow \Rightarrow \text{adverse selection}\downarrow,\\ \text{moral hazard}\downarrow \Rightarrow \text{lending}\uparrow \Rightarrow I\uparrow \Rightarrow Y^{ad}\uparrow \end{aligned} \tag{8}$$

An important feature of this transmission mechanism is that *nominal* interest rates affect firms' cash flow. Thus this interest-rate mechanism differs from the traditional interest-rate mechanism discussed earlier, in which the real interest rate affects investment. Furthermore, the short-term interest rate plays a special role in this transmission mechanism, because interest payments on short-term (rather than long-term) debt typically have the greatest impact on the cash flow of households and firms.

A related mechanism involving adverse selection through which expansionary monetary policy that lowers interest rates can stimulate aggregate demand involves the credit-rationing phenomenon. As discussed in Chapter 10, credit rationing occurs in cases where borrowers are denied loans even when they are willing to pay a higher interest rate. This happens because individuals and firms with the riskiest investment projects are exactly the ones who are willing to pay the highest interest rates, for if the high-risk investment succeeds, they will be the primary beneficiaries. Thus higher interest rates increase the adverse selection problem, and lower interest rates reduce it. When expansionary monetary policy lowers interest rates, risk-prone borrowers make up a lower fraction of those demanding loans, so lenders are more willing to lend, raising both investment and aggregate demand, along the lines of parts of the schematic in Equation 8.

Unanticipated Price Level Channel A third balance sheet channel operates through monetary policy effects on the general price level. Because in industrialized countries debt payments are contractually fixed in nominal terms, an unanticipated rise in the price level lowers the value of firms' liabilities in real terms (decreases the burden of the debt) but should not lower the real value of the firms' assets. An easing of monetary policy, which raises inflation and hence leads to an unanticipated rise in the price level ($P\uparrow$) therefore raises real net worth, which lowers adverse selection and moral hazard problems, thereby leading to a rise in investment spending and aggregate demand, as in the following schematic:

$$\begin{aligned} r\downarrow \Rightarrow \pi\uparrow \Rightarrow \text{unanticipated } P\uparrow \Rightarrow \text{firms' real net worth}\uparrow \\ \Rightarrow \text{adverse selection}\downarrow, \text{moral hazard}\downarrow \Rightarrow \text{lending}\uparrow \Rightarrow I\uparrow \Rightarrow Y^{ad}\uparrow \end{aligned} \tag{9}$$

The view that unanticipated movements in the price level affect aggregate demand has a long tradition in economics: It is the key feature in the debt-deflation view of the Great Depression outlined in Chapter 9.

Household Liquidity Effects Although most literature on the credit channel focuses on spending by businesses, the credit view should apply equally well to consumer spending, particularly on consumer durables and housing. Declines in bank lending induced by a monetary contraction should cause a decline in durables and housing purchases by consumers who do not have access to other sources of credit. Similarly, increases in interest rates cause a deterioration in household balance sheets, because consumers' cash flow is adversely affected.

Another way of looking at how the balance sheet channel may operate through consumers is to consider liquidity effects on consumer durable and housing expenditures, which were found to be important factors during the Great Depression (see the FYI box, "Consumers' Balance Sheets and the Great Depression"). In the liquidity effects view, balance sheet effects work through their impact on consumers' desire to spend rather than on lenders' desire to lend. Because of asymmetric information about their quality, consumer durables and housing are very illiquid assets. If, as a result of a bad income shock, consumers needed to sell their consumer durables or housing to raise money, they would expect a big loss because they could not get the full value of these assets in a distress sale. (This is just a manifestation of the lemons problem described in Chapter 8.) In contrast, if consumers held financial assets (such as money in the bank, stocks, or bonds), they could easily sell them quickly for their full market value and raise the cash. Hence, if consumers expect a higher likelihood of finding themselves in financial distress, they would rather hold fewer illiquid consumer durable or housing assets and more liquid financial assets.

A consumer's balance sheet should be an important influence on his or her estimate of the likelihood of suffering financial distress. Specifically, when consumers have a large amount of financial assets relative to their debts, their estimate of the probability of financial distress is low, and they will be more willing to purchase consumer durables or housing. When stock prices rise, the value of financial assets increases as well; consumer durable expenditure will also rise because consumers have a more secure financial position and a lower estimate of the likelihood of suffering financial distress. This

FYI Consumers' Balance Sheets and the Great Depression

The years between 1929 and 1933 witnessed the worst deterioration in consumers' balance sheets ever seen in the United States. The stock market crash in 1929, which caused a slump that lasted until 1933, reduced the value of consumers' wealth by $737 billion (in 2000 dollars), and as expected, consumption dropped sharply (by over $100 billion). Because of the decline in the price level in that period, the level of real debt consumers owed also increased sharply (by over 20%). Consequently, the value of financial assets relative to the amount of debt declined sharply, increasing the likelihood of financial distress. Not surprisingly, spending on consumer durables and housing fell precipitously: From 1929 to 1933, consumer durable expenditure declined by over 50%, while expenditure on housing declined by 80%.*

*For further discussion of the effect of consumers' balance sheets on spending during the Great Depression, see Frederic S. Mishkin, "The Household Balance Sheet and the Great Depression," *Journal of Economic History* 38 (1978): 918–937.

leads to another transmission mechanism for monetary policy, operating through the link between money and stock prices:

$$\begin{aligned} r\downarrow \Rightarrow P_s\uparrow \Rightarrow \text{value of households' financial assets}\uparrow \\ \Rightarrow \text{likelihood of financial distress}\downarrow \\ \Rightarrow \text{consumer durable and housing expenditure}\uparrow \Rightarrow Y^{ad}\uparrow \end{aligned} \tag{10}$$

The illiquidity of consumer durable and housing assets provides another reason why a monetary easing, which lowers interest rates and thereby raises cash flow to consumers, leads to a rise in spending on consumer durables and housing. A rise in consumer cash flow decreases the likelihood of financial distress, which increases the desire of consumers to hold durable goods or housing, thus increasing spending on them and hence aggregate demand. The only difference between this view of cash flow effects and that outlined in Equation 8 is that it is not the willingness of lenders to lend to consumers that causes expenditure to rise, but the willingness of consumers to spend.

Why Are Credit Channels Likely to Be Important?

There are three reasons to believe that credit channels are important monetary transmission mechanisms. First, a large body of evidence on the behavior of individual firms supports the view that financial frictions of the type crucial to the operation of credit channels do affect firms' employment and spending decisions. Second, evidence shows that small firms (which are more likely to be credit-constrained) are hurt more by tight monetary policy than large firms, which are unlikely to be credit-constrained. Third, and maybe most compelling, the asymmetric information view of financial frictions at the core of the credit channel analysis is a theoretical construct that has proved useful in explaining many other important phenomena, such as why many of our financial institutions exist, why our financial system has the structure that it has, and why financial crises are so damaging to the economy (topics discussed in Chapters 8 and 9). The best support for a theory is its demonstrated usefulness in a wide range of applications.

By this standard, the asymmetric information theory supporting the existence of credit channels as an important monetary transmission mechanism has much to recommend it.

APPLICATION ◆ The Great Recession

With the advent of the financial crisis in the summer of 2007, the Fed began a very aggressive easing of monetary policy. The Fed dropped the target federal funds rate from $5\frac{1}{4}\%$ to $\frac{1}{4}\%$ to 0% over a fifteen-month period from September 2007 to December 2008. At first, it appeared that the Fed's actions would keep the growth slowdown mild and prevent a recession. However, the economy proved to be weaker than the Fed or private forecasters expected, with the most severe recession in the post-World War II period beginning in December 2007. Why did the economy become so weak despite this unusually rapid reduction in the Fed's policy instrument?

The subprime meltdown led to negative effects on the economy from many of the channels we have outlined above. The rising level of subprime mortgage defaults, which led to a decline in the value of mortgage-backed securities and CDOs, resulted in large losses on the balance sheets of financial institutions. With weaker balance sheets, these financial institutions began to deleverage and cut back on their lending. With no one else to collect information and make loans, adverse selection and moral hazard problems, and hence financial frictions, increased in credit markets, leading to a slowdown of the economy. Credit spreads also went through the roof, with the increase in uncertainty from failures of so many financial markets. The decline in the stock market and housing prices also weakened the economy, because it lowered household wealth. The decrease in household wealth led to restrained consumer spending and weaker investment, because of the resulting drop in Tobin's q.

With all these channels operating, it is no surprise that despite the Fed's aggressive lowering of the federal funds rate, the economy still took a bit hit. ◆

LESSONS FOR MONETARY POLICY

What useful implications for central banks' conduct of monetary policy can we draw from the analysis in this chapter? Four basic lessons can be learned.

1. ***It is dangerous always to associate the easing or the tightening of monetary policy with a fall or a rise in short-term nominal interest rates***. Because most central banks use short-term nominal interest rates—typically, the interbank rate—as the key operating instrument for monetary policy, the danger exists that central banks and the public will focus too much on short-term nominal interest rates as an indicator of the stance of monetary policy. Indeed, it is quite common to see statements that always associate monetary tightenings with a rise in the interbank rate and monetary easings with a decline in the rate. We do not make this mistake in the analysis in this book because we have been careful to associate monetary easing or tightening with changes in *real* and not *nominal* interest rates.

2. ***Other asset prices besides those on short-term debt instruments contain important information about the stance of monetary policy because they are important***

elements in various monetary policy transmission mechanisms. As we have seen in this chapter, economists have come a long way in understanding that other asset prices besides interest rates have major effects on aggregate demand. As we saw in Figure 1, other asset prices, such as stock prices, foreign exchange rates, and housing prices, play an important role in monetary transmission mechanisms. Furthermore, the discussion of such additional channels as those operating through the exchange rate, Tobin's *q*, and wealth effects provides additional reasons why other asset prices play such an important role in monetary transmission mechanisms. Although economists strongly disagree among themselves about which channels of monetary transmission are the most important—not surprising, given that economists, particularly those in academia, always like to disagree—they do concur that other asset prices play an important role in the way monetary policy affects the economy.

The view that other asset prices besides short-term interest rates matter has important implications for monetary policy. When we try to assess the stance of policy, it is critical that we look at other asset prices in addition to short-term interest rates. For example, if short-term interest rates are low or even zero and yet stock prices are low, housing prices are low, and the value of the domestic currency is high, monetary policy is clearly tight, not easy.

3. ***Monetary policy can be effective in reviving a weak economy even if short-term interest rates are already near zero.*** We have recently entered a world where inflation is not always the norm. Japan, for example, recently experienced a period of deflation when the price level was actually falling. In the United States, the federal funds rate hit a floor of zero by the end of 2008. One common view is that when a central bank has driven down short-term nominal interest rates to nearly zero, the monetary policy can do nothing more to stimulate the economy. The transmission mechanisms of monetary policy described here indicate that this view is false. As our discussion of the factors that affect the monetary base in Chapter 17 indicated, expansionary monetary policy to increase liquidity in the economy can be conducted with open market purchases, which do not have to be solely in short-term government securities. For example, purchases of private securities, as the Federal Reserve did in 2009, can reduce financial frictions by lowering credit spreads and stimulating investment spending. In addition, a commitment to future expansionary monetary policy helps revive the economy by raising general price-level expectations and by reflating other asset prices, which then stimulate aggregate demand through the channels outlined here. Policies of this type are the nonconventional monetary policies we discussed in Chapter 18. Nonconventional monetary policy can be a potent force for reviving economies that are undergoing deflation and have short-term interest rates near zero. Indeed, as we saw in Chapter 9, aggressive nonconventional monetary policy during the recent financial crisis helped prevent the Great Recession from turning into a Great Depression and also helped the economy avoid a deflationary episode as occurred during the Great Depression era.

4. ***Avoiding unanticipated fluctuations in the price level is an important objective of monetary policy, thus providing a rationale for price stability as the primary long-run goal for monetary policy.*** As we saw in Chapter 19, central banks in recent years have been placing greater emphasis on price stability as the primary long-run goal for monetary policy. Several rationales have been proposed for this goal, including the undesirable effects of uncertainty about the future price level on business decisions and hence on productivity, distortions associated with the interaction of nominal contracts and the tax system with inflation, and increased social conflict stemming from inflation. The discussion here of monetary

transmission mechanisms provides an additional reason why price stability is so important. As we have seen, unanticipated movements in the price level can cause unanticipated fluctuations in output, an undesirable outcome. Particularly important in this regard is the knowledge that, as we saw in Chapter 9, price deflation can be an important factor leading to a prolonged financial crisis, as occurred during the Great Depression. An understanding of the monetary transmission mechanisms thus makes it clear that the goal of price stability is desirable, because it reduces uncertainty about the future price level. Thus the price stability goal implies that a negative inflation rate is at least as undesirable as too high an inflation rate. Indeed, because of the threat of financial crises, central banks must work very hard to prevent price deflation.

APPLICATION ◆ Applying the Monetary Policy Lessons to Japan

Until 1990, it looked as if Japan might overtake the United States in per capita income. Since then, the Japanese economy has been stagnating, with deflation and low growth. As a result, Japanese living standards have been falling further and further behind those in the United States. Many economists take the view that Japanese monetary policy is in part to blame for the poor performance of the Japanese economy. Could applying the four lessons outlined in the previous section have helped Japanese monetary policy perform better?

The first lesson suggests that it is dangerous to think that declines in interest rates always mean that monetary policy has been easing. In the mid-1990s, when short-term interest rates began to decline, falling to nearly zero in the late 1990s and early 2000s, the monetary authorities in Japan took the view that monetary policy was sufficiently expansionary. Now it is widely recognized that this view was incorrect, because the falling and eventually negative inflation rates in Japan meant that real interest rates were actually quite high and that monetary policy was tight, not easy. If the monetary authorities in Japan had followed the advice of the first lesson, they might have pursued a more expansionary monetary policy, which would have helped boost the economy.

The second lesson suggests that monetary policymakers should pay attention to other asset prices in assessing the stance of monetary policy. At the same time interest rates were falling in Japan, stock and real estate prices were collapsing, thus providing another indication that Japanese monetary policy was not easy. Recognizing the second lesson might have led Japanese monetary policymakers to recognize sooner that they needed a more expansionary monetary policy.

The third lesson indicates that monetary policy can still be effective even if short-term interest rates are near zero. Officials at the Bank of Japan have frequently claimed that they have been helpless in stimulating the economy, because short-term interest rates had fallen to nearly zero. Recognizing that monetary policy can still be effective even when interest rates are near zero, as the third lesson suggests, would have helped them to take monetary policy actions that would have stimulated aggregate demand by raising other asset prices and inflationary expectations.

The fourth lesson indicates that unanticipated fluctuations in the price level should be avoided. If the Japanese monetary authorities had adhered to this lesson, they might have recognized that allowing deflation to occur could be very damaging to the economy and would be inconsistent with the goal of price stability. Indeed, critics of the Bank of Japan have suggested that the bank should announce an inflation target to promote the price stability objective, but the bank has resisted this suggestion.

Heeding the advice from the four lessons in the previous section might have led to a far more successful conduct of monetary policy in Japan in recent years. ◆

Summary

1. The transmission mechanisms of monetary policy include traditional interest-rate channels that operate through the real cost of borrowing and affect investment; other asset price channels such as exchange rate effects, Tobin's q theory, and wealth effects; and the credit view channels—the bank lending channel, the balance sheet channel, the cash flow channel, the unanticipated price level channel, and household liquidity effects.
2. Four lessons for monetary policy can be drawn from this chapter: (a) It is dangerous always to associate monetary policy easing or tightening with a fall or a rise in short-term nominal interest rates; (b) other asset prices besides those on short-term debt instruments contain important information about the stance of monetary policy because they are important elements in the monetary policy transmission mechanisms; (c) monetary policy can be effective in reviving a weak economy even if short-term interest rates are already near zero; and (d) avoiding unanticipated fluctuations in the price level is an important objective of monetary policy, thus providing a rationale for price stability as the primary long-run goal for monetary policy.

Key Terms

consumer durable expenditure, p. 629

consumption, p. 632

credit view, p. 630

transmission mechanisms of monetary policy, p. 628

Questions

All questions are available in MyEconLab *at* www.myeconlab.com.

1. In 2009, in the wake of the global financial crisis when interest rates were at their lowest, the U.S. government instituted a "cash for clunkers" program and later a "cash for appliances" program. Both rebate programs were designed in part to stimulate new spending on automobiles and major appliances. What does this say about views of the health of the interest rate channel during that time?
2. "Considering that consumption is nearly 2/3 of total GDP, this means that the interest rate, wealth, and household liquidity channels are the most important monetary policy channels in the U.S." Is this statement true, false, or uncertain? Explain your answer.
3. How can the interest rate channel still function when short term nominal interest rates are at the zero lower bound?
4. Lars Svensson, a deputy governor of the Swedish central bank, proclaimed that when an economy is at risk of falling into deflation, central bankers should be "responsibly irresponsible" with monetary expansion. What does this mean, and how does it relate to the monetary transmission mechanism?
5. Describe an advantage and a disadvantage to monetary policy of having so many different channels through which monetary policy can operate.
6. "If countries fix their exchange rate, the exchange rate channel of monetary policy does not exist." Is this statement true, false, or uncertain? Explain your answer.

7. In the 2007–2009 recession, the value of common stocks in real terms fell by 50%. How might this decline in the stock market have affected aggregate demand and thus contributed to the severity of this recession? Be specific about the mechanisms through which the stock market decline affected the economy.
8. "The costs of financing investment are related only to interest rates; therefore, the only way that monetary policy can affect investment spending is through its effects on interest rates." Is this statement true, false, or uncertain? Explain your answer.
9. Predict what will happen to stock prices after a monetary easing. Explain your prediction.
10. From mid-2008 to early 2009, the Dow Jones Industrial Average declined by approximately 50%, while real interest rates were low or were falling. What does this suggest would have happened to investment?
11. Economist Franco Modigliani found that the most important transmission mechanisms of monetary policy involve consumer expenditure. Describe how at least two of these mechanisms work.
12. In the late 1990s, the stock market was rising rapidly, the economy was growing, and the Federal Reserve kept interest rates relatively low. Comment on how this policy stance would affect the economy as it relates to the Tobin q transmission mechanisms.
13. During and after the global financial crisis, the Fed reduced the fed funds rate to nearly zero. At the same time, the stock market fell dramatically and housing market values declined sharply. Comment on the effectiveness of monetary policy in this period through the wealth channel.
14. During and after the global financial crisis, the Fed provided banks with large amounts of liquidity. Banks' excess reserves increased sharply, while credit extended to households and firms decreased sharply. Comment on the effectiveness of the bank lending channel during this time.
15. Why does the credit view imply that monetary policy has a greater effect on small businesses rather than large firms?
16. Why might the bank lending channel be less effective than it once was?
17. One of the classic features of the global financial crisis is the failure of high-profile investment banks and financial firms, such as Lehman Brothers, Bear Stearns, and AIG. These firms experienced sharp contractions in the value of their balance sheets due to risky asset holdings. Comment on how this would affect the economy, as it relates to the balance sheet channel.
18. If adverse selection and moral hazard increase, how does this affect the ability of monetary policy to address economic downturns?
19. How does the Great Depression demonstrate the unanticipated price level channel?
20. How are the wealth effect and household liquidity effect similar? How are they different?
21. Following the global financial crisis, mortgage rates reached record low levels in 2011.
    a. What effect should this have, according to the household liquidity effect channel?
    b. During the same time, most banks raised their credit standards significantly, making it much more difficult to qualify for home loans and refinance existing loans. How does this alter your answer to part (a)?
22. What evidence exists to support the credit view of monetary policy?
23. "A decrease in short-term nominal interest rates necessarily implies a stance of monetary easing." Is this statement true, false, or uncertain? Explain your answer.
24. How does the case of Japan support the "four lessons for monetary policy"?

Applied Problems

All applied problems are available in MyEconLab *at* www.myeconlab.com.

25. Suppose the economy is in recession, and monetary policymakers lower interest rates to stabilize the economy. Use an aggregate supply and demand diagram to demonstrate the effects of a monetary easing when the transmission mechanisms are functioning normally, and when the transmission mechanisms are weak, such as during a deep downturn or when significant financial frictions are present.

Web Exercises

1. Figure 1 shows the relationship between estimated real interest rates and nominal interest rates. Go to www.martincapital.com/ and click on "U.S. Financial Data" and then "U.S. Financial Charts," then on "nominal versus real market rates" to find data showing real interest rates and nominal interest rates. When do the nominal and real interest rates give a very different picture about the tightness of monetary policy? How might this have led monetary policymakers to make mistakes if they focused entirely on nominal interest rates?
2. Go to www.econlib.org/library/Enc1/Recessions.html and review the material reported on recessions.
   a. What is the formal definition of a recession?
   b. What are the problems with the definition?
   c. What are the three D's used by the National Bureau of Economic Research (NBER) to define a recession?
   d. Review Chart 1. What trend is apparent about the length of recessions?

Web References

www.martincapital.com/

Click on "U.S. Financial Data," then on "U.S. Financial Charts" and then on "nominal versus real market rates" to find up-to-the-minute data showing the spread between real rates and nominal rates.

www.conference-board.org/economics/bci

A site with extensive data on the factors that define business cycles.

Web Appendix

Please visit the Companion Website at www.pearsonhighered.com/mishkin to read the Web appendix to Chapter 25:

Appendix : **Evaluating Empirical Evidence: The Debate Over the Importance of Money to Economic Fluctuations**

Glossary

activists Economists who regard the self-correcting mechanism through wage and price adjustment as very slow because wages and prices are sticky and so see the need to pursue active policy to eliminate high unemployment when it develops. **617**

adaptive expectations Expectations of a variable based on an average of past values of the variable. **147**

adverse selection The problem created by asymmetric information before a transaction occurs: The people who are the most undesirable from the other party's point of view are the ones who are most likely to want to engage in the financial transaction. **39**

agency theory The analysis of how asymmetric information problems affect economic behavior. **167**

aggregate demand curve A relationship between the price level and the quantity of aggregate output demanded when the goods and money markets are in equilibrium. **567**

aggregate income The total income of factors of production (land, labor, capital) in the economy. **22**

aggregate output The total production of final goods and services in the economy. **7**

aggregate price level The average price of goods and services in an economy. **8**

aggregate supply curve The relationship between the quantity of output supplied and the price level. **572**

anchor currency A currency to which other countries' currencies are pegged. **522**

annuities Financial contracts under which a customer pays an annual premium in exchange for a future stream of annual payments beginning at a set age, say 65, and ending when the person dies. **302**

appreciation Increase in a currency's value. **493**

arbitrage Elimination of a riskless profit opportunity in a market. **151, 330**

asset A financial claim or piece of property that is a store of value. **2**

asset management The acquisition of assets that have a low rate of default and diversification of asset holdings to increase profits. **220**

asset market approach An approach to determine asset prices using stocks of assets rather than flows. **94**

asset price bubbles Increases in asset prices in the stock and real estate markets that are driven well above their fundamental economic values by investor psychology. **188**

asset transformation The process of turning risky assets into safer assets for investors by creating and selling assets with risk characteristics that people are comfortable with and then using the funds acquired by selling these assets to purchase other assets that may have far more risk. **39**

asymmetric information The unequal knowledge that each party to a transaction has about the other party. **39**

automated banking machine (ABM) One location that provides an automated teller machine (ATM), an Internet connection to the bank's Web site, and a telephone link to customer service. **275**

automated teller machine (ATM) An electronic machine that provides banking services 24-hours a day. **275**

balance of payments A bookkeeping system for recording all payments that have a direct bearing on the movement of funds between a country and foreign countries. **520**

balance-of-payments crisis A foreign exchange crisis stemming from problems in a country's balance of payments. **531**

balance sheet A list of the assets and liabilities of a bank (or firm) that balances: Total assets equal total liabilities plus capital. **213**

bank failure A situation in which a bank cannot satisfy its obligations to pay its depositors and other creditors and so goes out of business. **242**

bank holding companies Companies that own one or more banks. **272**

bank panic The simultaneous failure of many banks, as during a financial crisis. **188**

banks Financial institutions that accept money deposits and make loans (such as commercial banks, savings and loan associations, and credit unions). **6**

Basel Accord An agreement that required that banks hold as capital at least 8% of their risk-weighted assets. **248**

Basel Committee on Banking Supervision An international committee of bank supervisors that meets under the auspices of the Bank for International Settlements in Basel, Switzerland. **247**

behavioral finance A subfield of finance that applies concepts from other social sciences such as anthropology, sociology, and, particularly, psychology to understand the behavior of securities prices. **156**

Board of Governors of the Federal Reserve System A board with seven governors (including the chairman) that plays an essential role in decision making within the Federal Reserve System. **374**

bond A debt security that promises to make payments periodically for a specified period of time. **2**

borrowed reserves A bank's borrowings from the Fed. **403**

branches Additional offices of banks that conduct banking operations. **284**

Bretton Woods system The international monetary system in use from 1945 to 1971 in which exchange rates were fixed and the U.S. dollar was freely convertible into gold (by foreign governments and central banks only). **523**

brokerage firms Firms that participate in securities markets as brokers, dealers, and investment bankers. **315**

brokers Agents for investors; they match buyers with sellers. **28**

bubble A situation in which the price of an asset differs from its fundamental market value. **155**

budget deficit The excess of government expenditure over tax revenues. **11**

budget surplus The excess of tax revenues over government expenditures. **11**

business cycles The upward and downward movement of aggregate output produced in the economy. **7**

call option An option contract that provides the right to buy a security at a specified price. **338**

capital Wealth, either financial or physical, that is employed to produce more wealth. **27**

capital account An account that describes the flow of capital between a country and other countries. **521**

capital adequacy management A bank's decision about the amount of capital it should maintain and then acquisition of the needed capital. **220**

capital buyout funds A private equity fund that makes investments in established businesses. **320**

capital controls Restrictions on the free movement of capital across borders. **526**

capital market A financial market in which longer-term debt (generally with original maturity of greater than one year) and equity instruments are traded. **29**

capital mobility A situation in which foreigners can easily purchase a country's assets and the country's residents can easily purchase foreign assets. **515**

carried interest A share of the profit paid to a private equity fund. **321**

cash flow The difference between cash receipts and cash expenditures. **204**

cash flows Cash payments to the holder of a security. **66, 141**

central bank The government agency that oversees the banking system and is responsible for the amount of money and credit supplied in the economy; in the United States, the Federal Reserve System. **10, 269**

closed-end fund A mutual fund in which a fixed number of nonredeemable shares are sold at an initial offering, then traded in the over-the-counter market like common stock. **317**

coinsurance A situation in which only a portion of losses are covered by insurance, so that the insured suffers a percentage of the losses along with the insurance agency. **308**

collateral Property that is pledged to the lender to guarantee payment in the event that the borrower is unable to make debt payments. **164**

commodity money Money made up of precious metals or another valuable commodity. **56**

common stock A security that is a claim on the earnings and assets of a company. **4**

community banks Small banks with local roots. **289**

compensating balance A required minimum amount of funds that a firm receiving a loan must keep in a checking account at the lending bank. **232**

conflicts of interest A manifestation of the moral hazard problem, particularly when a financial institution provides multiple services and the potentially competing interests of those services may lead to a concealment of information or dissemination of misleading information. **41, 353**

consol A perpetual bond with no maturity date and no repayment of principal that periodically makes fixed coupon payments. **74**

consumer durable expenditure Spending by consumers on durable items such as automobiles and household appliances. **631**

consumption Spending by consumers on nondurable goods and services (including services related to the ownership of homes and consumer durables). **632**

consumption expenditure The total demand for consumer goods and services. **567**

conventional monetary policy tools The usual tools of monetary policy that the Federal Reserve uses to control the money supply and interest rates: open market operations, discount lending, and reserve requirements **434**

cost-push inflation Inflation that occurs because of the push by workers to obtain higher wages. **620**

cost-push shocks Price shocks in which workers push for wages higher than productivity gains, thereby driving up costs and inflation. **574**

costly state verification Monitoring a firm's activities, an expensive process in both time and money. **174**

coupon bond A credit market instrument that pays the owner a fixed interest payment every year until the maturity date, when a specified final amount is repaid. **69**

coupon rate The dollar amount of the yearly coupon payment expressed as a percentage of the face value of a coupon bond. **69**

credit boom A lending spree when financial institutions expand their lending at a rapid pace. **186**

credit default swaps Financial insurance contracts that provide payments to holders of bonds if they default. **194, 304, 347**

credit derivatives Derivatives that have payoffs to previously issued securities, but ones that bear credit risk. **346**

credit easing Altering the composition of the Fed's balance sheet in order to improve the functioning of particular segments of the credit markets. **444**

credit options Options in which for a fee, the purchaser has the right to get profits that are tied either to the price of an underlying risky security or to an interest rate. **347**

credit rationing A lender's refusal to make loans even though borrowers are willing to pay the stated interest rate or even a higher rate or restriction of the size of loans made to less than the full amount sought. **232**

credit risk The risk arising from the possibility that the borrower will default. **220**

credit spread The difference between the interest rate on loans to households and businesses and the interest rate on completely safe assets that are sure to be paid off, such as U.S. Treasury securities. **191**

credit swap A transaction in which risky payments on loans are swapped for each other. **347**

credit view Monetary transmission mechanisms operating through asymmetric information effects on credit markets. **629**

credit-linked note A type of credit derivative that combines a bond and a credit option. **348**

credit-rating agencies Investment advisory firms that rate the quality of corporate and municipal bonds in terms of the probability of default. **120**

currency Paper money (such as dollar bills) and coins. **31**, **52**

currency board A monetary regime in which the domestic currency is backed 100% by a foreign currency (say, dollars) and in which the note-issuing authority, whether the central bank or the government, establishes a fixed exchange rate to this foreign currency and stands ready to exchange domestic currency at this rate whenever the public requests it. **543**

currency mismatch When emerging market economies denominate many debt contracts in foreign currency, while their assets are denominated in domestic currency. **205**

currency swap The exchange of a set of payments in one currency for a set of payments in another currency. **344**

current account An account that shows international transactions involving currently produced goods and services. **521**

current yield An approximation of the yield to maturity that equals the yearly coupon payment divided by the price of a coupon bond. **76**

data lag The time it takes for policymakers to obtain data indicating what is happening to the economy. **618**

dealers People who link buyers with sellers by buying and selling securities at stated prices. **28**

debt deflation A situation in which a substantial decline in the price level sets in, leading to a further deterioration in firms' net worth because of the increased burden of indebtedness. **189**

default A situation in which the party issuing a debt instrument is unable to make interest payments or pay off the amount owed when the instrument matures. **31**, **118**

default-free bonds Bonds with no default risk, such as U.S. government bonds. **119**

defensive open market operations Open market operations intended to offset movements in other factors that affect the monetary base (such as changes in Treasury deposits with the Fed or changes in float). **434**

defined-benefit plan A pension plan in which benefits are set in advance. **310**

defined-contribution plan A pension plan in which benefits are determined by the contributions into the plan and their earnings. **310**

deleveraging When financial institutions cut back on their lending because they have less capital. **186**

demand curve A curve depicting the relationship between quantity demanded and price when all other economic variables are held constant. **91**

demand for money The quantity of money that people want to hold. **552**

demand shocks Shocks that can shift the aggregate demand curve, including changes in the money supply, changes in government expenditure and taxes, changes in net exports, changes in consumer and business spending, and financial frictions. **569**

demand-pull inflation Inflation that results when policymakers pursue policies that shift the aggregate demand curve. **620**

deposit facility The European Central Bank's standing facility in which banks are paid a fixed interest rate 100 basis points below the target financing rate. **446**

deposit outflows Losses of deposits when depositors make withdrawals or demand payment. **220**

deposit rate ceiling Restriction on the maximum interest rate payable on deposits. **278**

depreciation Decrease in a currency's value. **493**

devaluation Resetting of the fixed value of a currency at a lower level. **525**

discount bond A credit market instrument that is bought at a price below its face value and whose face value is repaid at the maturity date; it does not make any interest payments. Also called a zero-coupon bond. **69**

discount loans A bank's borrowings from the Federal Reserve System; also known as advances. **215**

discount rate The interest rate that the Federal Reserve charges banks on discount loans. **222**, **397**

discount window The Federal Reserve facility at which discount loans are made to banks. **436**

disintermediation A reduction in the flow of funds into the banking system that causes the amount of financial intermediation to decline. **278**

diversification Investing in a collection (portfolio) of assets whose returns do not always move together, with the result that overall risk is lower than for individual assets. **39**

dividends Periodic payments made by equities to shareholders. **28**, **141**

divine coincidence Phrase coined by Olivier Blanchard, referring to the situation in which a policy to stabilize inflation is also the right policy to stabilize economic activity—with no conflict between them. **612**

dollarization The adoption of a sound currency, like the U.S. dollar, as a country's money. **544**

dominated assets Assets such as currency and checkable assets which earn lower returns than other assets which are just as safe. **561**

dual banking system The system in the United States in which banks supervised by the federal government and banks supervised by the states operate side by side. **271**

dual mandate A central bank mandate that features two co-equal objectives: price stability and maximum employment. **454**

duration analysis A measurement of the sensitivity of the market value of a bank's assets and liabilities to changes in interest rates. **234**

dynamic open market operations Open market operations that are intended to change the level of reserves and the monetary base. **434**

e-cash Electronic money that is used on the Internet to purchase goods or services. **58**

e-finance A new means of delivering financial services electronically. **6**

easing of monetary policy Lowering of the federal funds rate. **380**

economies of scale The reduction in transaction costs per dollar of transaction as the size (scale) of transactions increases. **38**

economies of scope The ability to use one resource to provide many different products and services. **41, 287, 354**

Edge Act corporation A special subsidiary of a U.S. bank that is engaged primarily in international banking. **296**

effective exchange rate index An index reflecting the value of a basket of representative foreign currencies. **508**

effectiveness lag The time it takes for a policy to actually have an impact on the economy. **618**

efficient market hypothesis The application of the theory of rational expectations to financial markets. **149**

electronic money (e-money) Money that exists only in electronic form and substitutes for cash as well. **57**

emerging market economics Economies in an earlier stage of market development that have recently opened up to the flow of goods, services, and capital from the rest of the world. **201**

equation of exchange The equation MV = PY, which relates nominal income to the quantity of money. **551**

equities Claims to share in the net income and assets of a corporation (such as common stock). **28**

equity capital See net worth. **172**

equity multiplier (EM) The amount of assets per dollar of equity capital. **226**

Eurobonds Bonds denominated in a currency other than that of the country in which they are sold. **36**

Eurocurrencies A variant of the Eurobond; foreign currencies deposited in banks outside the home country. **36**

Eurodollars U.S. dollars that are deposited in foreign banks outside the United States or in foreign branches of U.S. banks. **36**

European option An option that can be exercised only at the expiration date of the contract. **337**

excess demand A situation in which quantity demanded is greater than quantity supplied. **93**

excess reserves Reserves in excess of required reserves. **216, 397**

excess supply A situation in which quantity supplied is greater than quantity demanded. **93**

exchange rate The price of one currency stated in terms of another currency. **492**

exchange-rate peg Fixing the value of the domestic currency to the value of another currency, so the exchange rate is fixed. **539**

exchange-rate targeting See exchange-rate peg. **539**

exchanges Secondary markets in which buyers and sellers of securities (or their agents or brokers) meet in one central location to conduct trades. **29**

exercise price (strike price) The price at which the purchaser of an option has the right to buy or sell the underlying financial instrument. Also known as the strike price. **337**

expectations theory The proposition that the interest rate on a long-term bond will equal the average of the short-term interest rates that people expect to occur over the life of the long-term bond. **128**

expected return The return on an asset expected over the next period. **88**

face value A specified final amount paid to the owner of a coupon bond at the maturity date. Also called par value. **69**

fair-value accounting See mark-to-market accounting. **252**

federal funds rate The interest rate on overnight loans of deposits at the Federal Reserve. **32, 378, 425**

Federal Open Market Committee (FOMC) The committee that makes decisions regarding the conduct of open market operations; composed of the seven members of the Board of Governors of the Federal Reserve System, the president of the Federal Reserve Bank of New York, and the presidents of four other Federal Reserve banks on a rotating basis. **374**

Federal Reserve banks The 12 district banks in the Federal Reserve System. **373**

Federal Reserve System (the Fed) The central banking authority responsible for monetary policy in the United States. **10**

fiat money Paper currency decreed by a government as legal tender but not convertible into coins or precious metal. **56**

financial crisis A major disruption in financial markets that is characterized by sharp declines in asset prices and the failures of many financial and nonfinancial firms. 6, **185**

financial derivatives Instruments that have payoffs that are linked to previously issued securities, used as risk reduction tools. **274, 327**

financial engineering The process of researching and developing new financial products and services that would meet customer needs and prove profitable. **192, 272**

financial frictions Asymmetric information problems that act as a barrier to efficient allocation of capital. **185**

financial futures contract A futures contract in which the standardized commodity is a particular type of financial instrument. **329**

financial futures option (futures option) An option in which the underlying instrument is a futures contract. Also called a futures option. **337**

financial globalization The process of economies opening up to flows of capital and financial firms from other nations. **201**

financial innovation When an economy introduces new types of financial products. **186**

financial intermediaries Institutions (such as banks, insurance companies, mutual funds, pension funds, and finance companies) that borrow funds from people who have saved and then make loans to others. **5**

financial intermediation The process of indirect finance whereby financial intermediaries link lender-savers and borrower-spenders. **37**

financial liberalization The elimination or restrictions on financial markets. **186**

financial markets Markets in which funds are transferred from people who have a surplus of available funds to people who have a shortage of available funds. **2**

financial panic The widespread collapse of financial markets and intermediaries in an economy. **45**

financial supervision (prudential supervision) Overseeing who operates financial institutions and how they are operated. **250**

fire sales Forced, rapid sales of assets to raise needed funds. **188**

fiscal policy Policy that involves decisions about government spending and taxation. **11**

Fisher effect The outcome that when expected inflation occurs, interest rates will rise; named after economist Irving Fisher. **101**

fixed exchange rate regime A regime in which central banks buy and sell their own currencies to keep their exchange rates fixed at a certain level. **522**

fixed-payment loan A credit market instrument that provides a borrower with an amount of money that is repaid by making a fixed payment periodically (usually monthly) for a set number of years. **69**

float Cash items in process of collection at the Fed minus deferred-availability cash items. **403**

floating exchange rate regime An exchange rate regime in which the values of currencies are allowed to fluctuate against one another. **522**

foreign bonds Bonds sold in a foreign country and denominated in that country's currency. **35**

foreign exchange intervention An international financial transaction in which a central bank buys or sells currency to influence foreign exchange rates. **516**

foreign exchange market The market in which exchange rates are determined. **12, 492**

foreign exchange rate See exchange rate. **12**

forward contract An agreement by two parties to engage in a financial transaction at a future (forward) point in time. **328**

forward exchange rate The exchange rate for a forward transaction. **493**

forward transaction A transaction that involves the exchange of bank deposits denominated in different currencies at some specified future date. **493**

free-rider problem The problem that occurs when people who do not pay for information take advantage of the information that other people have paid for. **169**

fully funded Describing a pension plan in which the contributions to the plan and their earnings over the years are sufficient to pay out the defined benefits when they come due. **310**

fundamental economic values Values of assets based on realistic expectations of their future income streams. **188**

futures contract A contract in which the seller agrees to provide a certain standardized commodity to the buyer on a specific future date at an agreed-on price. **273**

futures options See financial futures option. **337**

gap analysis A measurement of the sensitivity of bank profits to changes in interest rates, calculated by subtracting the amount of rate-sensitive liabilities from the amount of rate-sensitive assets. **233**

general equilibrium When all markets are simultaneously in equilibrium at the point where the quantity of aggregate output demanded equals the quantity of aggregate output supplied. **579**

generalized dividend model Calculates that the price of stock is determined only by the present value of the dividends. **143**

goal independence The ability of the central bank to set the goals of monetary policy. **382**

gold standard A fixed exchange rate regime under which a currency is directly convertible into gold. **522**

Gordon growth model A simplified model to compute the value of a stock by assuming constant dividend growth. **143**

government budget constraint The requirement that the government budget deficit equal the sum of the change in the monetary base and the change in government bonds held by the public. **557**

government purchases Spending by all levels of government (federal, state, and local) on goods and services. **567**

government-sponsored enterprises (GSEs) Federally sponsored agencies that function as private corporations with close ties to the government. **321**

gross domestic product (GDP) The value of all final goods and services produced in the economy during the course of a year. **11**

haircuts The excess amount of collateral above the amount of the loan. **196**

hedge To protect oneself against risk. **273, 327**

hedge funds A special type of mutual fund that engages in "market-neutral strategies" **318**

hierarchical mandate A mandate for the central bank that puts the goal of price stability first, but as long as it is achieved other goals can be pursued. **454**

high-powered money The monetary base. **397**

hyperinflation An extreme inflation in which the inflation rate exceeds 50% per month. **55, 558**

implementation lag The time it takes for policymakers to change policy instruments once they have decided on a new policy. **618**

impossible trinity Another term for the policy trilemma, in which a country cannot pursue the following three policies at the same time: free capital mobility, a fixed exchange rate, and an independent monetary policy. **526**

incentive-compatible Having the incentives of both parties to a contract in alignment. **176**

income The flow of earnings. **53**

indexed bond A bond whose interest and principal payments are adjusted for changes in the price level, and whose interest rate thus provides a direct measure of a real interest rate. **84**

inflation The condition of a continually rising price level. **8**

inflation gap The difference between inflation and the inflation target. **609**

inflation hedges Alternative assets whose real returns are less affected than that of money when inflation varies. **491**

inflation rate The rate of change of the price level, usually measured as a percentage change per year. **8**

inflation target A central bank target for the inflation rate. **609**

inflation targeting A monetary policy strategy that involves public announcement of a medium-term numerical target for inflation. **455**

initial public offering (IPO) Shares of newly issued stock. **314, 355**

instrument independence The ability of the central bank to set monetary policy instruments. **382**

interest parity condition The observation that the domestic interest rate equals the foreign interest rate plus the expected appreciation in the foreign currency. **515**

interest rate The cost of borrowing or the price paid for the rental of funds (usually expressed as a percentage per year). **3**

interest-rate forward contracts A forward contract that is linked to a debt instrument. **328**

interest-rate risk The possible reduction in returns associated with changes in interest rates. **80, 220**

interest-rate swap A financial contract that allows one party to exchange (swap) a set of interest payments for another set of interest payments owned by another party. **344**

intermediate target Any of a number of variables, such as monetary aggregates or interest rates, that have a direct effect on employment and the price level and that the Fed seeks to influence. **470**

intermediate-term With reference to a debt instrument, having a maturity of between one and ten years. **28**

international banking facilities (IBFs) Banking establishments in the United States that can accept time deposits from foreigners but are not subject to either reserve requirements or restrictions on interest payments. **296**

International Monetary Fund (IMF) The international organization created by the Bretton Woods agreement whose objective is to promote the growth of world trade by making loans to countries experiencing balance-of-payments difficulties. **523**

international policy coordination Agreements among countries to enact policies cooperatively. **490**

international reserves Central bank holdings of assets denominated in foreign currencies. **516**

inverted yield curve A yield curve that is downward-sloping. **126**

investment banks Firms that assist in the initial sale of securities in the primary market. **28**

junk bonds Bonds with ratings below Baa (or BBB) that have a high default risk. **121**

Keynesian A follower of John Maynard Keynes who believes that movements in the price level and aggregate output are driven by changes not only in the money supply but also in government spending and fiscal policy and who does not regard the economy as inherently stable. **617**

large, complex banking organizations (LCBOs) Large companies that provide banking as well as many other financial services. **287**

law of one price The principle that if two countries produce an identical good, the price of this good should be the same throughout the world no matter which country produces it. **495**

legislative lag The time it takes to pass legislation to implement a particular policy. **618**

lender of last resort Provider of reserves to financial institutions when no one else would provide them to prevent a financial crisis. **437**

leverage cycle A feedback loop from a boom in issuing credit, leading to higher asset prices, resulting in higher capital buffers at financial institutions, which supports further lending, which raises prices further, etc.; in the bust, asset prices fall, leading to a cut in lending, a decline in asset prices, and so on. **256**

leverage ratio A bank's capital divided by its assets. **247**

leveraged buyout (LBO) A purchase of a publicly-traded firm by buying all of its shares, while financing the purchase by increasing the leverage (debt) of the firm. **320**

liabilities IOUs or debts. **26**

liability management The acquisition of funds at low cost to increase profits. **220**

liquid Easily converted into cash. **29**

liquidity The relative ease and speed with which an asset can be converted into cash. **55, 89**

liquidity management The decisions made by a bank to maintain sufficient liquid assets to meet the bank's obligations to depositors. **220**

liquidity preference framework A model developed by John Maynard Keynes that predicts the equilibrium interest rate on the basis of the supply of and demand for money. **104**

liquidity preference theory John Maynard Keynes's theory of the demand for money. **559**

liquidity premium theory The theory that the interest rate on a long-term bond will equal an average of short-term interest rates expected to occur over the life of the long-term bond plus a positive term (liquidity) premium. **132**

liquidity services Services financial intermediaries provide to their customers to make it easier for them to conduct their transactions. **38**

liquidity trap A case of ultrasensitivity of the demand for money to interest rates in which conventional monetary policy has no direct effect on aggregate spending because a change in the money supply has no effect on the interest rate. **562**

load funds Open-end mutual funds sold by salespeople who receive a commission that is paid at the time of purchase and is immediately subtracted from the redemption value of the shares. **318**

loan commitment A bank's commitment (for a specified future period of time) to provide a firm with loans up to a given amount at an interest rate that is tied to some market interest rate. **231**

loan sale The sale under a contract (also called a secondary loan participation) of all or part of the cash stream from a specific loan, thereby removing the loan from the bank's balance sheet. **235**

long position A contractual obligation to take delivery of an underlying financial instrument. **327**

long-term With reference to a debt instrument, having a maturity of ten years or more. **28**

longer-term refinancing operations A category of open market operations by the European Central Bank that are similar to the Fed's outright purchases or sales of securities. **446**

M1 A measure of money that includes currency, traveler's checks, and checkable deposits. **59**

M2 A measure of money that adds to M1: money market deposit accounts, money market mutual fund shares, small-denomination time deposits, savings deposits, overnight repurchase agreements, and overnight Eurodollars. **60**

macro hedge A hedge of interest-rate risk for a financial institution's entire portfolio. **332**

macroeconomic models Models to forecast the effects of policy on economic activity that use collections of equations that describe statistical relationships among many economic variables. **593**

macroprudential supervision Supervision that focuses on the safety and soundness of the financial system in the aggregate. **256**

main refinancing operations Weekly reverse transactions (purchase or sale of eligible assets under repurchase agreements or credit operations against eligible assets as collateral) that are reversed within two weeks and are the primary monetary policy tool of the European Central Bank. **446**

managed float regime An exchange rate regime in which countries attempt to influence their exchange rates by buying and selling currencies (also called a dirty float). **522**

management advisory services When an accounting firm provides its client with auditing services and nonaudit consulting services creating a potential conflict of interest problem. **356**

management of expectations Term coined by Michael Woodford that refers to the commitment of the Fed to keeping the federal funds rate at zero for an extended period in order to cause the long-term interest rate to fall. **445**

margin requirement A sum of money that must be kept in an account (the margin account) at a brokerage firm. **335**

marginal lending facility The European Central Bank's standing lending facility in which banks can borrow (against eligible collateral) overnight loans from the national central bank at a rate 100 basis points above the target financing rate. **446**

marginal lending rate The interest rate charged by the European Central Bank for borrowing at its marginal lending facility. **446**

mark-to-market accounting An accounting method in which assets are valued in the balance sheets at what they would sell for in the market. **252, 335**

market equilibrium A situation occurring when the quantity that people are willing to buy (demand) equals the quantity that people are willing to sell (supply). **93**

market fundamentals Items that have a direct impact on future income streams of a security. **155**

matched sale–purchase transaction An arrangement whereby the Fed sells securities and the buyer agrees to sell them back to the Fed in the near future; sometimes called a reverse repo. **436**

maturity Time to the expiration date (maturity date) of a debt instrument. **28**

medium of exchange Anything that is used to pay for goods and services. **53**

micro hedge A hedge for a specific asset. **332**

microprudential supervision Supervision that focuses on the safety and soundness of individual financial institutions. **256**

monetary aggregates The measures of the money supply used by the Federal Reserve System (M1 and M2). **59**

monetary base The sum of the Fed's monetary liabilities (currency in circulation and reserves) and the U.S. Treasury's monetary liabilities (Treasury currency in circulation, primarily coins). **396**

monetary policy The management of the money supply and interest rates. **10**

monetary theory The theory that relates changes in the quantity of money to changes in economic activity. **7, 550**

monetizing the debt A method of financing government spending whereby the government debt issued to finance government spending is removed from the hands of the public and is replaced by high-powered money instead. Also called printing money. **557**

money (money supply) Anything that is generally accepted in payment for goods or services or in the repayment of debts. **7**

money center banks Large banks in key financial centers (New York, Chicago, San Francisco). **224**

money market A financial market in which only short-term debt instruments (generally those with original maturity of less than one year) are traded. **29**

money multiplier A ratio that relates the change in the money supply to a given change in the monetary base. **412**

money supply The quantity of money. **7**

monoline insurance companies Insurance companies that specialize in credit insurance alone. **305**

moral hazard The risk that one party to a transaction will engage in behavior that is undesirable from the other party's point of view. **40**

mortgage-backed securities Securities that cheaply bundle and quantify the default risk of the underlying high-risk mortgages. **33, 192**

mortgages Loans to households or firms to purchase housing, land, or other real structures, in which the structure or land itself serves as collateral for the loans. **33**

multiple deposit creation The process whereby, when the Fed supplies the banking system with $1 of additional reserves, deposits increase by a multiple of this amount. **404**

national banks Federally chartered banks. **271**

natural rate level of output The level of aggregate output produced at the natural rate of unemployment at which there is no tendency for wages or prices to change. **453, 573**

natural rate of unemployment The rate of unemployment consistent with full employment at which the demand for labor equals the supply of labor. **452, 572**

net exports Net foreign spending on domestic goods and services, equal to exports minus imports. **498, 567**

net worth The difference between a firm's assets (what it owns or is owed) and its liabilities (what it owes). Also called equity capital. **172**

no-load funds Mutual funds sold directly to the public on which no sales commissions are charged. **318**

nominal anchor A nominal variable such as the inflation rate, an exchange rate, or the money supply that monetary policymakers use to tie down the price level. **451**

nominal interest rate An interest rate that does not take inflation into account. **81**

nonaccelerating inflation rate of unemployment (NAIRU) The rate of unemployment when demand for labor equals supply, consequently eliminating the tendency for the inflation rate to change. **475**

nonactivists Economists who believe wages and prices are very flexible, so the self-correcting mechanism is very rapid; they thus do not see the need to pursue policies to return the economy to full employment. **617**

nonborrowed monetary base The monetary base minus discount loans (borrowed reserves). **403**

nonconventional monetary policy tools Non-interest rate tools central banks use to stimulate the economy: liquidity provision, asset purchases, and commitment to future monetary policy actions. **441**

notional principal The amount on which interest is being paid in a swap arrangement. **344**

off-balance-sheet activities Bank activities that involve trading financial instruments and the generation of income from fees and loan sales, all of which affect bank profits but are not visible on bank balance sheets. **235, 247**

official reserve transactions balance The current account balance plus items in the capital account. **521**

open interest The number of contracts outstanding. **333**

open market operations The Fed's buying or selling of bonds in the open market. **376, 398**

open market purchase A purchase of bonds by the Fed. **398**

open market sale A sale of bonds by the Fed. **398**

open-end fund A mutual fund in which shares can be redeemed at any time at a price that is tied to the asset value of the fund. **317**

operating instrument A variable that is very responsive to the central bank's tools and indicates the stance of monetary policy (also called a policy instrument). **470**

opportunity cost The amount of interest (expected return) sacrificed by not holding an alternative asset. **105**

optimal forecast The best guess of the future using all available information. **147**

option A contract that gives the purchaser the option (right) to buy or sell the underlying financial instrument at a specified price, called the exercise price or strike price, within a specific period of time (the term to expiration) **337**

originate-to-distribute model A business model in which the mortgage is originated by a separate party, typically a mortgage broker, and then distributed to an investor as an underlying asset in a security. **193**

output gap The difference between aggregate output and potential output. **573**

over-the-counter (OTC) market A secondary market in which dealers at different locations who have an inventory of securities stand ready to buy and sell securities "over the counter" to anyone who comes to them and is willing to accept their prices. **29**

overnight cash rate The interest rate for very-short-term interbank loans in the euro area. **446**

par value See face value. **69**

payment technology Methods of payment that include credit cards and electronic payments. **559**

payments system The method of conducting transactions in the economy. **56**

perpetuity See consol. **74**

Phillips curve theory A theory suggesting that changes in inflation are influenced by the state of the economy relative to its production capacity, as well as to other factors. **474**

planned investment spending Total planned spending by businesses on new physical capital (e.g., machines, computers, apartment buildings) plus planned spending on new homes. **567**

policy instrument A variable that is very responsive to the central bank's tools and indicates the stance of monetary policy (also called an operating instrument). **470**

policy trilemma Situation in which a country cannot pursue the following three policies at the same time: free capital mobility, a fixed exchange rate, and an independent monetary policy. **526**

political business cycle A business cycle caused by expansionary policies before an election. **385**

portfolio A collection or group of assets. **39**

potential output The level of aggregate output produced at the natural rate of unemployment (also called *natural rate of output*). **453, 573**

preferred habitat theory A theory that is closely related to liquidity premium theory, in which the interest rate on a long-term bond equals an average of short-term interest rates expected to occur over the life of the long-term bond plus a positive term premium. **132**

premium The amount paid for an option contract. **337**

present discounted value See present value. **66**

present value Today's value of a payment to be received in the future when the interest rate is i. Also called present discounted value. **66**

price shocks Shifts in inflation that are independent of the amount of slack in the economy or expected inflation. **574**

price stability Low and stable inflation. **450**

primary dealers Government securities dealers, operating out of private firms or commercial banks, with whom the Fed's open market desk trades. **434**

primary market A financial market in which new issues of a security are sold to initial buyers. **28**

principal–agent problem A moral hazard problem that occurs when the managers in control (the agents) act in their own interest rather than in the interest of the owners (the principals) due to different sets of incentives. **173, 193**

printing money See monetizing the debt. **557**

private equity fund A fund that makes long term investments in companies that are not traded in public markets. **320**

prudential supervision See financial supervision. **250**

put option An option contract that provides the right to sell a security at a specified price. **338**

quantitative easing An expansion of the Federal Reserve's balance sheet. **444**

quantity theory of money The theory that nominal income is determined solely by movements in the quantity of money. **552**

quotas Restrictions on the quantity of foreign goods that can be imported. **498**

rate of capital gain The change in a security's price relative to the initial purchase price. **78**

rate of return See return. **77**

rational expectations Expectations that reflect optimal forecasts (the best guess of the future) using all available information. **147**

real bills doctrine A guiding principle (now discredited) for the conduct of monetary policy that states that as long as loans are made to support the production of goods and services, providing reserves to the banking system to make these loans will not be inflationary. **481**

real business cycle theory A theory that views real shocks to tastes and technology as the major driving force behind short-run business cycle fluctuations. **590**

real exchange rate The rate at which domestic goods can be exchanged for foreign goods; i.e., the price of domestic relative to foreign goods denominated in domestic currency. **496**

real interest rate The interest rate adjusted for expected changes in the price level (inflation) so that it more accurately reflects the true cost of borrowing. **81**

real money balances The quantity of money in real terms. **552**

real terms Terms reflecting actual goods and services one can buy. **82**

recession A period when aggregate output is declining. **7**

recognition lag The time it takes for policymakers to be sure of what the data are signaling about the future course of the economy. **618**

regulatory arbitrage A process in which banks keep on their books assets that have the same risk-based capital requirement but are relatively risky, such as a loan to a company with a very low credit rating, while taking off their books low-risk assets, such as a loan to a company with a very high credit rating. **248**

reinsurance An allocation of a portion of the insurance risk to another company in exchange for a portion of the insurance premium. **304**

repurchase agreement (repo) An arrangement whereby the Fed, or another party, purchases securities with the understanding that the seller will repurchase them in a short period of time, usually less than a week. **196, 434**

reputational rents Profits that a firm earns because it is trusted by the marketplace. **361**

required reserve ratio The fraction of deposits that the Fed requires be kept as reserves. **216, 397**

required reserves Reserves that are held to meet the Fed's requirement that for every dollar of deposits at a bank, a certain fraction must be kept as reserves. **216, 397**

reserve currency A currency, such as the U.S. dollar, that is used by other countries to denominate the assets they hold as international reserves. **523**

reserve requirements Regulation making it obligatory for depository institutions to keep a certain fraction of their deposits in accounts with the Fed. **216**

reserves Banks' holding of deposits in accounts with the Fed plus currency that is physically held by banks (vault cash). **216, 397**

residual claimant The right as a stockholder to receive whatever remains after all other claims against the firm's assets have been satisfied. **141**

restrictive covenants Provisions that restrict and specify certain activities that a borrower can engage in. **165**

return The payments to the owner of a security plus the change in the security's value, expressed as a fraction of its purchase price. More precisely called the rate of return. **77**

return on assets (ROA) Net profit after taxes per dollar of assets. **226**

return on equity (ROE) Net profit after taxes per dollar of equity capital. **226**

revaluation Resetting of the fixed value of a currency at a higher level. **526**

reverse transactions Purchase or sale of eligible assets by the European Central Bank under repurchase agreements or credit operations against eligible assets as collateral that are reversed within two weeks. **446**

risk The degree of uncertainty associated with the return on an asset. **38, 89**

risk premium The spread between the interest rate on bonds with default risk and the interest rate on default-free bonds. **119**

risk sharing The process of creating and selling assets with risk characteristics that people are comfortable with and then using the funds acquired by selling these assets to purchase other assets that may have far more risk. **39**

risk structure of interest rates The relationship among the interest rates on various bonds with the same term to maturity. **118**

seasoned issue A stock issued for sale for which prior issues currently sell in the market. **314**

secondary market A financial market in which securities that have previously been issued (and are thus secondhand) can be resold. **28**

secondary reserves Short-term U.S. government and agency securities held by banks. **216**

secured debt Debt guaranteed by collateral. **164**

securitization The process of transforming illiquid financial assets into marketable capital market instruments. **192, 277**

security A claim on the borrower's future income that is sold by the borrower to the lender. Also called a financial instrument. **2**

segmented markets theory A theory of term structure that sees markets for different-maturity bonds as completely separated and segmented such that the interest rate for bonds of a given maturity is determined solely by supply of and demand for bonds of that maturity. **131**

seignorage The revenue a government receives by issuing money. **545**

self-correcting mechanism A characteristic of the economy that causes output to return eventually to the natural rate level regardless of where it is initially. **582**

shadow banking system A system in which bank lending is replaced by lending via the securities market. **195, 272**

short position A contractual obligation to deliver an underlying financial instrument. **327**

short sales Borrowing stock from brokers and then selling the stock in the market, with the hope that a profit will be earned by buying the stock back again ("covering the short") after it has fallen in price. **157**

short-term With reference to a debt instrument, having a maturity of one year or less. **28**

simple deposit multiplier The multiple increase in deposits generated from an increase in the banking system's reserves in a simple model in which the behavior of depositors and banks plays no role. **407**

simple loan A credit market instrument providing the borrower with an amount of funds that must be repaid to the lender at the maturity date along with an additional payment (interest). **67**

smart card A stored-value card that contains a computer chip that lets it be loaded with digital cash from the owner's bank account whenever needed. **57**

sovereign wealth funds A state-owned investment fund that invests in foreign assets. **317**

special drawing rights (SDRs) An IMF-issued paper substitute for gold that functions as international reserves. **529**

specialist A dealer-broker operating in an exchange who maintains orderly trading of the securities for which he or she is responsible. **316**

speculative attack A situation in which speculators engage in massive sales of a currency. **204**

spinning When an investment bank allocates shares of hot, but underpriced initial public offerings to executives of other companies in return for their companies' future business with the investment bank. **355**

spot exchange rate The exchange rate for a spot transaction. **493**

spot transaction The predominant type of exchange rate transaction, involving the immediate exchange of bank deposits denominated in different currencies. **493**

stagflation A situation of rising inflation but a falling level of aggregate output. **588**

standing lending facility A lending facility in which healthy banks are allowed to borrow all they want from a central bank. **436**

state banks State-chartered banks. **271**

state-owned banks Banks that are owned by governments. **180**

sterilized foreign exchange intervention A foreign exchange intervention with an offsetting open market operation that leaves the monetary base unchanged. **519**

stock A security that is a claim on the earnings and assets of a company. **4**

stock option An option on an individual stock. **337**

store of value A repository of purchasing power over time. **55**

stress tests Tests of financial institutions that calculate losses and the need for more capital under dire scenarios. **252**

structured credit products Securities that are derived from cash flows of underlying assets and are tailored to have particular risk characteristics that appeal to investors with different preferences. **192**

subprime mortgages Mortgages for borrowers with less than stellar credit records. **192**

superregional banks Bank holding companies similar in size to money center banks, but whose headquarters are not based in one of the money center cities (New York, Chicago, San Francisco). **287**

supply curve A curve depicting the relationship between quantity supplied and price when all other economic variables are held constant. **92**

supply shock Any change in technology or the supply of raw materials that can shift the aggregate supply curve. **574**

swap A financial contract that obligates one party to exchange (swap) a set of payments it owns for a set of payments owned by another party. **343**

sweep account An arrangement in which any balances above a certain amount in a corporation's checking account at the end of a business day are "swept out" of the account and invested in overnight repos that pay the corporation interest. **279**

systemically important financial institutions (SIFIs) Firms designated by the Financial Stability Oversight Council as systemically important that are subject to additional oversight and regulation by the Federal Reserve. **264**

T-account A simplified balance sheet with lines in the form of a T that lists only the changes that occur in balance sheet items starting from some initial balance sheet position. **217**

target financing rate The European Central Bank's target for the overnight cash rate, the interest rate for very-short-term interbank loans in the euro area. **446**

tariffs Taxes on imported goods. **498**

Taylor principle The principle that the monetary authorities should raise nominal interest rates by more than the increase in the inflation rate. **474**

Taylor rule Economist John Taylor's monetary policy rule that explains how the federal funds rate target is set. **474**

term structure of interest rates The relationship among interest rates on bonds with different terms to maturity. **118**

theory of efficient capital markets See efficient market hypothesis. **149**

theory of portfolio choice A theory of how much of an asset people want to hold in their portfolio, with the amounts determined by wealth, expected returns, risk, and liquidity. **90**

theory of purchasing power parity (PPP) The theory that exchange rates between any two currencies will adjust to reflect changes in the price levels of the two countries. **496**

thrift institutions (thrifts) Savings and loan associations, mutual savings banks, and credit unions. **41**

tightening of monetary policy A rise in the federal funds rate. **380**

time-inconsistency problem The problem that occurs when monetary policymakers conduct monetary policy in a discretionary way and pursue expansionary policies that are attractive in the short run but lead to bad long-run outcomes. **451**

trade balance The difference between merchandise exports and imports. **521**

transaction costs The time and money spent trying to exchange financial assets, goods, or services. **37**

transmission mechanisms of monetary policy The channels through which the money supply affects economic activity. **628**

Troubled Asset Relief Plan (TARP) Provision of the Bush administration's Economic Recovery Act of 2008 that authorized the Treasury to spend $700 billion to purchase subprime mortgage assets from troubled financial institutions or to inject capital into these institutions. **200**

underfunded Describing a pension plan in which the contributions and their earnings are not sufficient to pay out the defined benefits when they come due. **310**

underwrite Purchase securities from a corporation at a predetermined price and then resell them in the market. **28**, **45**

underwriters Investment banks that guarantee prices on securities to corporations and then sell the securities to the public. **314**

unemployment rate The percentage of the labor force not working. **7**

unexploited profit opportunity A situation in which an investor can earn a higher than normal return. **151**

unit of account Anything used to measure value in an economy. **54**

unsecured debt Debt not guaranteed by collateral. **164**

unsterilized foreign exchange intervention A foreign exchange intervention in which a central bank allows the purchase or sale of domestic currency to affect the monetary base. **518**

value at risk (VaR) Calculations that measure the size of the loss on a trading portfolio that might happen 1% of the time over a short period—say 2 weeks. **252**

vault cash Currency that is physically held by banks and stored in vaults overnight. **216**

velocity of money The rate of turnover of money; the average number of times per year that a dollar is spent in buying the total amount of final goods and services produced in the economy. **551**

venture capital firm A financial intermediary that pools the resources of its partners and uses the funds to help entrepreneurs start up new businesses. **174, 320**

virtual bank A bank that has no building but rather exists only in cyberspace. **275**

wealth All resources owned by an individual, including all assets. **53, 88**

World Bank The International Bank for Reconstruction and Development, an international organization that provides long-term loans to assist developing countries in building dams, roads, and other physical capital that would contribute to their economic development. **523**

World Trade Organization (WTO) An organization headquartered in Geneva, Switzerland, that monitors rules for the conduct of trade between countries (tariffs and quotas). **523**

yield curve A plot of the interest rates for particular types of bonds with different terms to maturity. **126**

yield to maturity The interest rate that equates the present value of payments received from a credit market instrument with its value today. **70**

zero-coupon bond See discount bond. **69**

Credits

DESIGN IMAGES

Chapter opener Federal Reserve Seal: Nomad_Soul/Shutterstock

Following the Financial News box: newspaper stock report icon: Brian Hagiwara/Brand X Pictures/Getty Images

Global box model of earth icon: Alex Staroseltsev/Shutterstock

FYI box magnifying glass icon: Vitaly Korovin/Shutterstock

Inside the Fed box: U.S. Supreme Court building exterior icon: Fstock/Shutterstock

TEXT CREDITS

Page 3 Federal Reserve Bulletin; www.federalreserve.gov/releases/H15/data.htm.

Page 5 Based on Dow Jones Indexes: http://nance.yahoo.com/?u.

Page 8 Based on Federal Reserve Bulletin, p. A4, Table 1.10; www.federalreserve.gov/releases/h6/hist/h6hist1.txt.

Page 9 Based on www.stls.frb.org/fred/data/gdp/gdpdef; www.federalreserve.gov/releases/h6/hist/h6hist10.txt.

Page 10 Based on International Financial Statistics. www.imf-statistics.org/imf.

Page 11 Based on Federal Reserve Bulletin, p. A4, Table 1.10; www.federalreserve.gov/releases/h6/hist/h6hist1.txt.

Page 12 www.gpoaccess.gov/usbudget/fy06/sheets/hist01z2.xls.

Page 13 Federal Reserve: www.federalreserve.gov/releases/H10/summary/indexbc_m.txt/.

Page 32 Based on Federal Reserve Flow of Funds Accounts; Federal Reserve Bulletin. 2008, 3rd Quarter.

Page 43 Federal Reserve Flow of Funds Accounts: www.federalreserve.gov/releases/Z1/.

Page 59 www.federalreserve.gov/releases/h6/hist.

Page 61 Federal Reserve Economic Database (FRED), Federal Reserve Bank of Saint Louis, http://research.stlouisfed.org/fred2/categories/25.

Page 83 Nominal rates from www.federalreserve.gov/releases/H15. The real rate is constructed using the procedure outlined in Frederic S. Mishkin, "The Real Interest Rate: An Empirical Investigation," *Carnegie-Rochester Conference Series on Public Policy 15* (1981): 151–200. This procedure involves estimating expected inflation as a function of past interest rates, inflation, and time trends and then subtracting the expected inflation measure from the nominal interest rate.

Page 101 Expected inflation calculated using procedures outlined in Frederic S. Mishkin, "The Real Interest Rate: An Empirical Investigation," *Carnegie-Rochester Conference Series on Public Policy 15* (1981): 151–200. These procedures involve estimating expected inflation as a function of past interest rates, inflation, and time trends.

Page 103 Federal Reserve: www.federalreserve.gov/releases/H15/data.htm.

Page 114 Federal Reserve: www.federalreserve.gov/releases/h6/hist/h6hist1.txt.

Page 119 Board of Governors of the Federal Reserve System, Banking and Monetary Statistics, 1941–1970; Federal Reserve: www.federalreserve.gov/releases/h15/data.htm.

Page 127 Federal Reserve: www.federalreserve.gov/releases/h15/data.htm.

Page 137 Federal Reserve Bank of St. Louis; U.S. Financial Data, various issues; Wall Street Journal, various dates.

Page 163 Andreas Hackethal and Reinhard H. Schmidt, "Financing Patterns: Measurement Concepts and Empirical Results," *Johann Wolfgang Goethe-Universitat Working Paper No. 125*, January 2004. The data are from 1970–2000 and are gross flows as percentage of the total, not including trade and other credit data, which are not available.

Page 187 Figure 15.1: "Sequence of Events in Financial Crises in Advanced Economies" from *Macroeconomics: Policy and Practice*, 1st Edition by Frederic S. Mishkin. Copyright © 2011 by Frederic S. Mishkin. Printed and Electronically reproduced by permission of Pearson Education, Inc., Upper Saddle River, New Jersey.

Page 190 Fig. 15.2 "Stock Price Data During the Great Depression Period" from *Macroeconomics: Policy and Practice*, 1st Edition by Frederic S. Mishkin. Copyright © 2011 by Frederic S. Mishkin. Printed and Electronically reproduced by permission of Pearson Education, Inc., Upper Saddle River, New Jersey.

Page 191 Fig. 15.4 "Credit Spreads During the Great Depression" from *Macroeconomics: Policy and Practice*, 1st Edition by Frederic S. Mishkin. Copyright © 2011 by Frederic S. Mishkin. Printed and Electronically reproduced by permission of Pearson Education, Inc., Upper Saddle River, New Jersey.

Page 194 Fig. 15.5 "Housing Prices and the Financial Crisis of 2007–2009" from *Macroeconomics: Policy and Practice*, 1st Edition by Frederic S. Mishkin. Copyright © 2011 by Frederic S. Mishkin. Printed and Electronically reproduced by permission of Pearson Education, Inc., Upper Saddle River, New Jersey.

Page 197 Fig. 15.6 "Stock Prices and the Financial Crisis of 2007–2009" from *Macroeconomics: Policy and Practice*, 1st Edition by Frederic S. Mishkin. Copyright © 2011 by Frederic S. Mishkin. Printed and Electronically reproduced by permission of Pearson Education, Inc., Upper Saddle River, New Jersey.

Page 199 Fig. 15.8 "Credit Spreads and the 2007–2009 Financial Crisis" from *Macroeconomics: Policy and Practice*, 1st Edition by Frederic S. Mishkin. Copyright © 2011 by Frederic S. Mishkin. Printed and Electronically reproduced by permission of Pearson Education, Inc., Upper Saddle River, New Jersey.

Page 201 Fig. W.1 "Sequence of Events in Emerging Market Financial Crisis" from *Macroeconomics: Policy and Practice*, 1st Edition by Frederic S. Mishkin. Copyright © 2011 by Frederic S. Mishkin. Printed and Electronically reproduced by permission of Pearson Education, Inc., Upper Saddle River, New Jersey.

Page 214 www.federalreserve.gov/releases/h8/current/.

Page 260 www.fdic.gov/bank/historical/bank/index.html.

Page 262 Data from Gerard Caprio and Daniela Klingebiel, "Episodes of Systemic and Borderline Financial Crises" mimeo., World Bank, October 1999; Luc Laeven and Fabian Valencia, "Resolution of Banking Crises: The Good, the Bad and the Ugly," *IMF Working Paper No. WP/10/46* (June 2010) and Luc Laeven, Banking Crisis Database at http://www.luclaeven.com/Data.htm.

Page 263 Luc Laeven and Fabian Valencia, "Resolution of Banking Crises: The Good, the Bad and the Ugly," *IMF Working Paper No. WP/10/46* (June 2010) and Luc Laeven, Banking Crisis Database at http://www.luclaeven.com/Data.htm.

Page 281 Federal Reserve Flow of Funds Accounts; Federal Reserve Bulletin.

Page 284 www2.fdic.gov/qbp/2008sep/cb4.html.

Page 284 www.federalreserve.gov/releases/h8/20081229.

Page 286 www2.fdic.gov/qbp/qbpSelect.asp?menuitem=STAT.

Page 297 http://topforeignstocks.com/2008/07/25/the-top-10-banks-in-the-world-2008/.

Page 375 Federal Reserve Bulletin.

Page 417 Milton Friedman and Anna Jacobson Schwartz, *A Monetary History of the United States, 1867–1960* (Princeton, NJ: Princeton University Press, 1963), p. 309.

Page 418 Federal Reserve Bulletin; Milton Friedman and Anna Jacobson Schwartz, *A Monetary History of the United States, 1867–1960* (Princeton, NJ: Princeton University Press, 1963), p. 333.

Page 419 Milton Friedman and Anna Jacobson Schwartz, *A Monetary History of the United States, 1867–1960* (Princeton, NJ: Princeton University Press, 1963), p. 333.

Ch 17 Web Appendix 1 Table 1 Federal Reserve: www.federalreserve.gov/releases and author's calculations.

Ch 17 Web Appendix 1 Summary Table 2 Federal Reserve Bulletin.

Ch 17 Web Appendix 3 Figure 1 Federal Reserve Bulletin and Banking and Monetary Statistics. www.federalreserve.gov/releases/h6/hist/h6hist1.txt

Page 457 Ben S. Bernanke, Thomas Laubach, Frederic S. Mishkin, and Adam S. Poson, *Inflation Targeting: Lessons from the International Experience* (Princeton: Princeton University Press, 1999), updates from the same sources, and www.rbnz.govt.nz/statistics/econind/a3/ha3.xls.

Page 475 Federal Reserve: www.federalreserve.gov/releases and author's calculations.

Page 423 Federal Reserve: www.federalreserve.gov/releases/h10/hist.

Page 497 ftp.bls.gov/pub/special/requests/cpi/cpiai.txt.

Page 509 Federal Reserve: www.federalreserve.gov/releases/h10/summary/indexn_m.txt; real interest rate from Figure 1 in Chapter 4.

Page 573 Fig. 11.3 "Long-Run and Short-Run Aggregate Supply Curve" from *Macroeconomics: Policy and Practice*, 1st Edition by Frederic S. Mishkin. Copyright © 2011 by Frederic S. Mishkin. Printed and Electronically reproduced by permission of Pearson Education, Inc., Upper Saddle River, New Jersey.

Page 575 Fig. 11.5 "Shift in the Long-Run Aggregate Supply Curve" from *Macroeconomics: Policy and Practice*, 1st Edition by Frederic S. Mishkin. Copyright © 2011 by Frederic S. Mishkin. Printed and Electronically reproduced by permission of Pearson Education, Inc., Upper Saddle River, New Jersey.

Page 577 Fig. 11.6 "Shift in the Short-Run Aggregate Supply Curve from Changes in Expected Inflation and Price Shocks" from *Macroeconomics: Policy and Practice*, 1st Edition by Frederic S. Mishkin. Copyright © 2011 by Frederic S. Mishkin. Printed and Electronically reproduced by permission of Pearson Education, Inc., Upper Saddle River, New Jersey.

Page 578 Fig. 11.7 "Shift in the Short-Run Aggregate Supply Curve from a Persistent Positive Output Gap" from *Macroeconomics: Policy and Practice*, 1st Edition by Frederic S. Mishkin. Copyright © 2011 by Frederic S. Mishkin. Printed and Electronically reproduced by permission of Pearson Education, Inc., Upper Saddle River, New Jersey.

Page 580 Fig. 12.1 "7 Short-Run Equilibrium" from *Macroeconomics: Policy and Practice*, 1st Edition by Frederic S. Mishkin. Copyright © 2011 by Frederic S. Mishkin. Printed and Electronically reproduced by permission of Pearson Education, Inc., Upper Saddle River, New Jersey.

Page 581 Fig. 12.2 "Adjustment to Long-Run Equilibrium in Aggregate Supply and Demand Analysis" from *Macroeconomics: Policy and Practice*, 1st Edition by Frederic S. Mishkin. Copyright © 2011 by Frederic S. Mishkin. Printed and Electronically reproduced by permission of Pearson Education, Inc., Upper Saddle River, New Jersey.

Page 583 Fig. 12.3 "Positive Demand Shock" from *Macroeconomics: Policy and Practice*, 1st Edition by Frederic S. Mishkin. Copyright © 2011 by Frederic S. Mishkin. Printed and Electronically reproduced by permission of Pearson Education, Inc., Upper Saddle River, New Jersey.

Page 585 Fig. 12.4 "The Volcker Disinflation" from *Macroeconomics: Policy and Practice*, 1st Edition by Frederic S. Mishkin. Copyright © 2011 by Frederic S. Mishkin. Printed and Electronically reproduced by permission of Pearson Education, Inc., Upper Saddle River, New Jersey.

Page 586 Fig. 12.5 "Negative Demand Shocks, 2001–2004" from *Macroeconomics: Policy and Practice*, 1st Edition by Frederic S. Mishkin. Copyright © 2011 by Frederic S. Mishkin. Printed and Electronically reproduced by permission of Pearson Education, Inc., Upper Saddle River, New Jersey.

Page 588 Fig. 12.6 "Temporary Negative Supply Shocks" from *Macroeconomics: Policy and Practice*, 1st Edition by Frederic S. Mishkin. Copyright © 2011 by Frederic S. Mishkin. Printed and Electronically reproduced by permission of Pearson Education, Inc., Upper Saddle River, New Jersey.

Page 589 Fig. 12.7 "Figure 13 Negative Supply Shocks, 1973–1975 and 1978-1980" from *Macroeconomics: Policy and Practice*, 1st Edition by Frederic S. Mishkin. Copyright © 2011 by Frederic S. Mishkin. Printed and Electronically reproduced by permission of Pearson Education, Inc., Upper Saddle River, New Jersey.

Page 590 Fig. 12.8 "Permanent Negative Supply Shock" from *Macroeconomics: Policy and Practice*, 1st Edition by Frederic S. Mishkin. Copyright © 2011 by Frederic S. Mishkin. Printed and Electronically reproduced by permission of Pearson Education, Inc., Upper Saddle River, New Jersey.

Page 592 Fig. 12.9 "Positive Supply Shocks, 1995–1999" from *Macroeconomics: Policy and Practice*, 1st Edition by Frederic S. Mishkin. Copyright © 2011 by Frederic S. Mishkin. Printed and Electronically reproduced by permission of Pearson Education, Inc., Upper Saddle River, New Jersey.

Page 594 Fig. 12.10 "Negative Supply and Demand Shocks and the 2007-2009 Crisis" from *Macroeconomics: Policy and Practice*, 1st Edition by Frederic S. Mishkin. Copyright © 2011 by Frederic S. Mishkin. Printed and Electronically reproduced by permission of Pearson Education, Inc., Upper Saddle River, New Jersey.

Page 595 Fig. 12.11 "UK Financial Crisis, 2007–2009" from *Macroeconomics: Policy and Practice*, 1st Edition by Frederic S. Mishkin. Copyright © 2011 by Frederic S. Mishkin. Printed and Electronically reproduced by permission of Pearson Education, Inc., Upper Saddle River, New Jersey.

Page 597 Fig. 12.12 "China and the Financial Crisis 2007–2009" from *Macroeconomics: Policy and Practice*, 1st Edition by Frederic S. Mishkin. Copyright © 2011 by Frederic S. Mishkin. Printed and Electronically reproduced by permission of Pearson Education, Inc., Upper Saddle River, New Jersey.

Page 602 Fig. 11.1 "Inflation and Unemployment in the United States, 1950–1969 and 1970–2009" from *Macroeconomics: Policy and Practice*, 1st Edition by Frederic S. Mishkin. Copyright © 2011 by Frederic S. Mishkin. Printed and Electronically reproduced by permission of Pearson Education, Inc., Upper Saddle River, New Jersey.

Page 604 Fig. 11.2 "The Short and Long-Run Phillips Curve" from *Macroeconomics: Policy and Practice*, 1st Edition by Frederic S. Mishkin. Copyright © 2011 by Frederic S. Mishkin. Printed and Electronically reproduced by permission of Pearson Education, Inc., Upper Saddle River, New Jersey.

Page 607 Fig. 11.4 "Okun's Law," from *Macroeconomics: Policy and Practice*, 1st Edition by Frederic S. Mishkin. Copyright © 2011 by Frederic S. Mishkin. Printed and Electronically reproduced by permission of Pearson Education, Inc., Upper Saddle River, New Jersey.

Ch 23 Web Appendix 1 Fig. 12.3 "Positive Demand Shock" from *Macroeconomics: Policy and Practice*, 1st Edition by Frederic S. Mishkin. Copyright © 2011 by Frederic S. Mishkin. Printed and Electronically reproduced by permission of Pearson Education, Inc., Upper Saddle River, New Jersey.

Ch 23 Web Appendix 1 Fig. 12A2.1 "Response to an Autonomous Monetary Easing" from *Macroeconomics: Policy and Practice*, 1st Edition by Frederic S. Mishkin. Copyright © 2011 by Frederic S. Mishkin. Printed and Electronically reproduced by permission of Pearson Education, Inc., Upper Saddle River, New Jersey.

Ch 23 Web Appendix 1 Fig. 12A2.2 "Response to a Positive Spending Shock" from *Macroeconomics: Policy and Practice*, 1st Edition by Frederic S. Mishkin. Copyright © 2011 by Frederic S. Mishkin. Printed and Electronically reproduced by permission of Pearson Education, Inc., Upper Saddle River, New Jersey.

Ch 23 Web Appendix 1 Fig. 12A2.3 "Response to a Negative Supply Shock" from *Macroeconomics: Policy and Practice*, 1st Edition by Frederic S. Mishkin. Copyright © 2011 by Frederic S. Mishkin. Printed and Electronically reproduced by permission of Pearson Education, Inc., Upper Saddle River, New Jersey.

Ch 23 Web Appendix 1 Fig. 12A2.4 "Response to a Permanent Negative Supply Shock" from *Macroeconomics: Policy and Practice*, 1st Edition by Frederic S. Mishkin. Copyright © 2011 by Frederic S. Mishkin. Printed and Electronically reproduced by permission of Pearson Education, Inc., Upper Saddle River, New Jersey.

Ch 23 Web Appendix 2 Fig. 12.3 "Response to a Shift in Aggregate Demand" from *Macroeconomics: Policy and Practice*, 1st Edition by Frederic S. Mishkin. Copyright © 2011 by Frederic S. Mishkin. Printed and Electronically reproduced by permission of Pearson Education, Inc., Upper Saddle River, New Jersey.

Ch 23 Web Appendix 4 Fig. 12A1.1 "Not Following the Taylor Principle Leads to Unstable Inflation" from *Macroeconomics: Policy and Practice*, 1st Edition by Frederic S. Mishkin. Copyright © 2011 by Frederic S. Mishkin. Printed and Electronically reproduced by permission of Pearson Education, Inc., Upper Saddle River, New Jersey.

Page 610 Fig. 13.2 "Aggregate Demand Shock: No Policy Response" from *Macroeconomics: Policy and Practice*, 1st Edition by Frederic S. Mishkin. Copyright © 2011 by Frederic S. Mishkin. Printed and Electronically reproduced by permission of Pearson Education, Inc., Upper Saddle River, New Jersey.

Page 611 Fig. 13.3 "Aggregate Demand Shock: Policy Stabilizes Output and Inflation in the Short Run" from *Macroeconomics: Policy and Practice*, 1st Edition by Frederic S. Mishkin. Copyright © 2011 by Frederic S. Mishkin. Printed and Electronically reproduced by permission of Pearson Education, Inc., Upper Saddle River, New Jersey.

Page 613 Fig. 13.4 "Permanent Supply Shock: No Policy Response" from *Macroeconomics: Policy and Practice*, 1st Edition by Frederic S. Mishkin. Copyright © 2011 by Frederic S. Mishkin. Printed and Electronically reproduced by permission of Pearson Education, Inc., Upper Saddle River, New Jersey.

Page 614 Fig. 13.5 "Permanent Supply Shock: Policy Stabilizes Inflation" from *Macroeconomics: Policy and Practice*, 1st Edition by Frederic S. Mishkin. Copyright © 2011 by Frederic S. Mishkin. Printed and Electronically reproduced by permission of Pearson Education, Inc., Upper Saddle River, New Jersey.

Page 615 Fig. 13.6 "Response to a Temporary Aggregate Supply Shock: No Policy Response" from *Macroeconomics: Policy and Practice*, 1st Edition by Frederic S. Mishkin. Copyright © 2011 by Frederic S. Mishkin. Printed and Electronically reproduced by permission of Pearson Education, Inc., Upper Saddle River, New Jersey.

Page 616 Fig. 13.7 "Response to a Temporary Aggregate Supply Shock: Short-Run Inflation Stabilization" from *Macroeconomics: Policy and Practice*, 1st Edition by Frederic S. Mishkin. Copyright © 2011 by Frederic S. Mishkin. Printed and Electronically reproduced by permission of Pearson Education, Inc., Upper Saddle River, New Jersey.

Page 617 Fig. 13.8 "Response to a Temporary Aggregate Supply Shock: Short-Run Output Stabilization" from *Macroeconomics: Policy and Practice*, 1st Edition by Frederic S. Mishkin. Copyright © 2011 by Frederic S. Mishkin. Printed and Electronically reproduced by permission of Pearson Education, Inc., Upper Saddle River, New Jersey.

Page 620 Fig. 13.10 "A Rise in the Inflation Target" from *Macroeconomics: Policy and Practice*, 1st Edition by Frederic S. Mishkin. Copyright © 2011 by Frederic S. Mishkin. Printed and Electronically reproduced by permission of Pearson Education, Inc., Upper Saddle River, New Jersey.

Page 621 Fig. 13.11 "Cost-Push Inflation" from *Macroeconomics: Policy and Practice*, 1st Edition by Frederic S. Mishkin. Copyright © 2011 by Frederic S. Mishkin. Printed and Electronically reproduced by permission of Pearson Education, Inc., Upper Saddle River, New Jersey.

Page 623 Fig. 13.12 "Demand-Pull Inflation" from *Macroeconomics: Policy and Practice*, 1st Edition by Frederic S. Mishkin. Copyright © 2011 by Frederic S. Mishkin. Printed and Electronically reproduced by permission of Pearson Education, Inc., Upper Saddle River, New Jersey.

Page 624 Fig. 13.13 "Inflation and Unemployment" from *Macroeconomics: Policy and Practice*, 1st Edition by Frederic S. Mishkin. Copyright © 2011 by Frederic S. Mishkin. Printed and Electronically reproduced by permission of Pearson Education, Inc., Upper Saddle River, New Jersey.

Ch 25 Web Appendix 1 Nominal rates from www.federalreserve.gov/releases/h15/update/. The real rate is constructed using the procedure outlined in Frederic S. Mishkin, "The Real Interest Rate: An Empirical Investigation," *Carnegie-Rochester Conference Series on Public Policy 15* (1981): 151–200.

Index

Guide to Commonly Used Symbols

Symbol	Term
Δ	change in a variable
π	inflation rate
π^e	expected inflation
π^T	inflation target
AD	aggregate demand curve
AS	aggregate supply curve
B^d	demand for bonds
B^s	supply of bonds
BR	borrowed reserves
c	currency ratio
C	yearly coupon payment
C	currency
C	consumption expenditure
D	demand curve
D	checkable deposits
DL	discount loans
e	excess reserves ratio
E_t	exchange (spot) rate
E_{par}	par (fixed) exchange rate
$(E^e_{t+1} - E_t)/E_t$	expected appreciation of domestic currency
EM	equity multiplier
ER	excess reserves
$\bar{f}$	for financial frictions
G	government purchases
i	interest rate (yield to maturity)
i_d	discount rate
i^D	interest rate on domestic assets
i^F	interest rate on foreign assets
i_{or}	interest rate paid on reserves
I	planned investment spending
IS	IS curve
m	money multiplier
M	money supply